DANIEL BOONE, Frontispiece.

BIOGRAPHICAL CYCLOPEDIA

OF THE

COMMONWEALTH

OF

KENTUCKY

EMBRACING BIOGRAPHIES OF MANY OF THE PROMINENT MEN AND FAMILIES
OF THE STATE

COMPILED AND PUBLISHED BY THE

JOHN M. GRESHAM COMPANY

CHICAGO—PHILADELPHIA

1896

This volume was reproduced from
An 1896 edition located in the
John E Ladson's private Library
Vidalia, Georgia

All rights reserved. No part of this publication may be reproduced,
stored in a retrieval system, transmitted in any form, posted
on to the web in any form or by any means without
the prior written permission of the publisher.

Please direct all correspondence and orders to:

www.southernhistoricalpress.com
or
**SOUTHERN HISTORICAL PRESS, Inc.
PO Box 1267
375 West Broad Street
Greenville, SC   29601**
southernhistoricalpress@gmail.com

Originally published: Chicago, IL, 1896
New Material Copyright 1980
By: The Rev. Silas Emmett Lucas, Jr.
ISBN #0-89308-192-2
All rights Reserved.
Printed in the United States of America

PREFACE.

THE greatest of English historians, Macaulay, and one of America's ablest and most brilliant writers of the Nineteenth Century, have said: The history of a country is best told in a record of the lives of its people. In conformity with this idea, the Biographical Cyclopedia of the Commonwealth of Kentucky has been prepared. Instead of going to musty records and taking from there dry statistical matter that would be appreciated but by few, our corps of writers have gone to the people, the men and women who have, by their force of character, brought the state to a rank, in many respects, second to none among those comprising this great and noble country; and from their lips we have the story of their life struggles. No more interesting or instructive matter could be presented to an intelligent public. In this volume will be found complete sketches of many whose lives are worthy of imitation of generations yet to come. It tells how many with limited advantages and whose environments were of the simplest kind have become great men and women, and whose influence extends throughout the land. It tells of men who have risen from the lower walks of life to eminence as statesmen, and whose names have become renowned. It tells of those in every walk of life who have striven to succeed, and records how success has usually crowned their efforts. It also tells of many who, not seeking the applause of the world, have pursued "the even tenor of their way," content to have it said of them, as Christ said of the woman performing a deed of mercy—"they have done what they could." It tells of how that many, in the pride of strength of young manhood, left the plow and the anvil, the lawyer's office and the counting room, left every trade and profession, and at their country's call went forth valiantly "to do or die" for the land which gave them birth and, which next to their God, their highest homage was due.

Generations yet unborn will greatly appreciate this book and preserve it as a sacred treasure, and a precious souvenir of those who gave the best years of their lives in the interest of civilization and progress. Great care has been taken in the compilation of this volume, and every opportunity possible given those who are represented to insure correctness in what has been written, and the publisher is giving to his patrons a work of few errors of consequence.

The sketches of many will be missed in this book. For this the publisher is not to blame. Not having a proper conception of the work, some refused to give the information necessary to compile a biography, while others were indifferent. Occasionally some member of the family would oppose the enterprise, and on account of such opposition the support of the interested one would be withheld. In some instances men could never be found, though repeated calls were made at their places of business. For many sketches of the pioneers of the State and men of prominence we are indebted to Collins' carefully prepared and very excellent history of Kentucky, and for which we give full credit.

JOHN M. GRESHAM, Publisher.

Chicago, May 18, 1896.

BIOGRAPHICAL CYCLOPEDIA

OF

KENTUCKY.

THOMAS W. BULLITT, one of the leading attorneys of Louisville, was born at Oxmoor, Jefferson County, eight miles from Louisville, May 17, 1838. His father, William Christian Bullitt, was born at the same place in 1793, and died at the residence of his daughter, Mrs. Henry Chenowith, near Oxmoor, August 28, 1877, at the age of eighty-four years. He spent his whole life on the farm, except a short time when he was engaged in the practice of law in Louisville, an occupation for which he was well equipped, but which he abandoned on account of ill health. He was a Whig in early life, but voted for President Franklin Pierce, and from that time until his death he was a pronounced Democrat. He was a member of the Constitutional Convention of 1849-50, but was never an office seeker, although he was always earnest and active in the interest of his party. He was a man of great strength of character, with decided firmness and excellent judgment. His hospitality was proverbial, and in this kindness he heartily seconded his excellent wife, who loved all young people and loved to have her house well filled. They really kept "open house" at all times, entertaining friend and stranger in such a manner that through them and others like them the State of Kentucky became noted for its hospitality.

Alexander Scott Bullitt (grandfather) was a native of Prince William County, Virginia, who came to Kentucky in 1783, when about 21 years of age, and purchased a tract of one thousand acres of land lying on what is now the Louisville and Shelbyville turnpike, and called it Oxmoor. This valuable property has been in possession of the Bullitt family over one hundred years, no part of it having been sold.

A. S. Bullitt was president of the convention which framed the constitution of Kentucky in 1799, and was the first lieutenant governor under that constitution. In 1785 he married the daughter of Col. William Christian, whose wife was a sister of Patrick Henry of Virginia. Col. Christian came to Jefferson County in 1785 and was killed by the Indians in 1786. He was buried at Oxmoor, the oldest burying ground in Kentucky, where all the descendants of the families who have since died have been "'gathered to their fathers." The burying ground is on what was Col. Christian's home, adjoining Oxmoor, and is scrupulously cared for by the family, a permanent fund having been provided for the purpose, and is in the form of a trust in the hands of the Fidelity Trust Co. Governor Bullitt died in 1816.

Cuthbert Bullitt (great-grandfather) was a Virginia lawyer of renown, and was one of the Judges of the Supreme Court of Virginia at the time of his death.

Benjamin Bullitt (great-great-grandfather) was a Virginia farmer whose father, Joseph Bullitt, a

French Huguenot, came from the province of France and settled at Port Tobacco, Maryland, on the Chesapeake Bay, in 1685.

Mildred Ann Fry Bullitt (mother) was a native of Albemarle County, Virginia. She survived her husband about two years and died in 1879 in her eighty-second year. She was a faithful Christian and a member of the Presbyterian Church. Her father, Joshua Fry (grandfather), removed from Virginia when she was three years old and settled in Danville. His wife was the daughter of Dr. Thomas Walker of Albemarle County, Virginia, whose farm was, and is now, known as Castle Hill.

Thomas W. Bullitt received his early training at home and in the common schools near Oxmoor and at Centre College, graduating in 1858. He then went to Philadelphia and read law with his brother, John C. Bullitt, finishing his law course in the law department of the University of Pennsylvania, and was admitted to the Philadelphia bar in 1861, where he commenced the practice of law with his brother. He remained only until the spring of 1862, when he returned to Kentucky and joined the Confederate army under Gen. John Morgan; and later accompanied that dashing officer with seventy-five comrades in a raid upon the Ohio Penitentiary. He did not escape with Morgan and the others, but remained in the prison at Columbus about eight months, when he was transferred to Fort Delaware, and there he remained until about a month prior to the close of the war, when he was paroled for exchange and sent to Richmond.

After the war, Col. Bullitt returned to Louisville and commenced the practice of law, in which he has been vastly more successful than he was as a Confederate soldier. He has distinguished himself by his remarkable industry, his good judgment and his careful study of legal subjects bearing especially upon corporations. In addition to his lucrative law business, he has been and is connected with a number of large corporations, banks, railroads and other enterprises in which he is a director as well as attorney.

He inaugurated the Fidelity Trust Company of Louisville, the first trust company organized west of the Alleghany mountains, and later organized the Kentucky Title Insurance Company, in which he is a director.

He has been a Democrat ever since he became a voter, but has not aspired to office.

He is a member of the Presbyterian Church (South) and a liberal supporter of the church and its work.

Col. Bullitt was married in 1871 to Anna Priscilla, daughter of Hon. Caleb Logan of the Louisville Chancery Court. Her mother was the daughter of Dr. Louis Marshall, who was a brother of Chief Justice John Marshall. They have six children living: William Marshall, James B., Agatha M., Alexander S., Keith L. and Myra L.

CHARLES BALDWIN POYNTZ, distiller of Maysville, late railroad commissioner, and an influential citizen, son of Samuel B. and Mary (Dewees) Poyntz, was born in Maysville, July 17, 1853. He was educated, principally, in Cincinnati, Ohio, to which city his father removed in 1865; and was employed in the accounting department of the Indianapolis and St. Louis Railroad for several years, and was made assistant paymaster of that company when he was twenty-five years of age. He was located in Indianapolis for eight years of the time that he was in the service of the railroad company.

In 1881 he resigned and came to Maysville to engage in the distillery and jobbing business with his father and brother, Benjamin B. Poyntz, and was a member of the firm of Samuel B. Poyntz & Sons until the death of the senior member of the firm in 1890, when he and his brother took charge of the business, since which time the well known house has sustained its reputation as one of the most reliable and substantial establishments in the state.

In 1886 Mr. Poyntz was elected to the Maysville City Council and was made president of that body in 1887. In 1888 he was a delegate to the National Democratic Convention which gave President Cleveland his second nomination; in 1889 he was elected to the Kentucky Senate from Mason and Lewis Counties and was recognized as one of the ablest men in that body, being chairman of the Finance Committee; was chairman of the Ninth Congressional District Democratic

Committee for eight years; and at the same time chairman of the Appellate Court District Committee, and was appointed Railroad Commissioner for the Third (Eastern) District in 1892, which office he held until December, 1895. His record as a business man and as an official is one in which his friends indulge a pardonable pride. It is without spot, scratch or blemish.

Mr. Poyntz was married December 24, 1878, to Alice Craig of Crawfordsville, Indiana, an accomplished and charming woman.

Samuel B. Poyntz, father of Charles B. Poyntz, was born in Mason County in 1819; died August, 1890. He was for some years engaged in the wholesale grocery business in Cincinnati, and for many years before his death he was similarly engaged—in connection with distilling—in Maysville. He was a gentleman of high character and standing, and one of the most successful business men in northern Kentucky.

Mary Dewees Poyntz (mother) was the eldest daughter of John Coburn Dewees, one of five sisters, all of whom were remarkable for their personal attractions.

William Poyntz (paternal grandfather) was a native of Pennsylvania and one of the early settlers of Kentucky. His wife was a Miss Baldwin of Washington, Mason County.

John Coburn Dewees (maternal grandfather), a native of Lexington, Kentucky, was for many years a leading citizen of Mason County. His wife, Maria Bayless, was connected by marriage and blood with many of the principal families of this state, and was a sister of the late Dr. Benjamin Bayless, an eminent surgeon of Louisville.

LUCIEN CLAY DALLAM, a retired merchant and banker of Henderson, son of Nathan Smith and Sarah (Hicks) Dallam, was born in Princeton, Kentucky, May 17, 1829. He went to school only a few years and in 1842, when only thirteen years of age, went to work in the County Clerk's office in Livingston County, and served one year as deputy, and returned to Princeton and served four years there in a similar capacity. He then began his mercantile career in partnership with his brother, William J. Dallam, and remained in Princeton until 1854, when they removed to Henderson. The two brothers were in partnership in the dry goods business in Princeton and Henderson about eight years. The firm dissolved in 1856 and Lucien C. Dallam continued the business alone until 1859, when his brother-in-law, Thomas Soaper, who had been clerking for him, was admitted into partnership. This business relation continued under the most favorable auspices until 1876, when Mr. Soaper purchased the interest of Mr. Dallam and the latter retired from mercantile pursuits.

He was one of the chief organizers of the Henderson National Bank in 1865, which was opened for business in January, 1866, and Mr. Dallam was elected president of that bank, a position which he held continuously until February, 1892, when he resigned. He is, however, still interested in the bank, in which he is a leading stockholder. This bank had an original capital of $100,000, which has been increased several times until it has been doubled, and has accumulated a surplus of $100,000. Its average annual dividends have been from ten to twelve per cent, and the bank examiners have pronounced it one of the best managed institutions of the kind in the state. It has never charged borrowers of small sums a larger per cent than it charged its patrons of larger means. Mr. Dallam was the leading spirit in this bank for more than twenty-six years, and its success was largely due to his excellent judgment and ability as a financier.

He was the first President of the Henderson Bridge Company; served many years as chairman of the Board of Sinking Fund Commissioners of the City of Henderson and also served in the City Council. He is president of the Henderson Humane Society, and was Senior Warden of St. Paul's Episcopal Church for many years. In all of his business, official and church relations he has been governed by a wise and conservative policy and has endeared himself to the people of Henderson.

Mr. Dallam was married in 1855 to Elizabeth Soaper, daughter of William Soaper and sister of Thomas and R. H. Soaper, sketches of both of whom will be found in this work.

The children of Lucien C. and Elizabeth (Soaper) Dallam are: Susan Henderson, wife of

Henry Burnett of Paducah; Clarence, born April 14, 1863, a graduate of the University of Virginia, class of 1886, now practicing law in Paducah, married Cantey McDowell Venable of Charlottesville, Virginia; Charles Edward, born in 1865, graduate of the University of Virginia, class of 1885, now assistant cashier of the Henderson National Bank; Elizabeth Soaper, wife of George Wadsworth Cobb of Chicago, and Sarah Hicks, wife of Muscoe Burnett of Paducah.

Nathan Smith Dallam (father) was born in Harford County, Maryland, December 19, 1782; married Sarah Hicks in 1807 at Winchester, Clark County, Kentucky, at which place he was located for a time after leaving Maryland. He soon removed to Hopkinsville, where he was clerk of the County and Circuit Courts for many years, and also represented his county in the legislature a number of terms; was a Whig and a personal friend of Henry Clay; left Hopkinsville about 1825 and went to Princeton, then the "Athens of the West," and held various official positions of honor and trust until the time of his death, June 1, 1837.

He had ten children, whose names were James Lawrence, Mary Frances, Maria, Frances Henry, Jane Marian, Charles B., William J., Edward Winston, Lucien Clay and Virginia Josephine, all of whom are deceased except Lucien C. and Mrs. Mary Frances Duncan, a widow now eighty years of age.

Sara Hicks (mother) was born in Richmond, Virginia, in 1792. Her parents died, leaving her an orphan at a tender age and she came with her guardian to Winchester, Clark County, Kentucky, where she was married to Nathan Smith Dallam in 1807.

The original pioneer and ancestor of the Dallam family, Richard Dallam (great-great-grandfather), came from Wales, England, in 1680, and married Elizabeth Martin in Maryland, who was known in the colonial times as "Pretty Bettie Martin." Many interesting reminiscences of this remarkable woman are still cherished by her descendants. She lived to the advanced age of 114 years. William Dallam, son of Richard Dallam and "Pretty Betty Martin" Dallam, was the great-grandfather. Francis Matthews Dallam, who came to Kentucky from Maryland and married Martha Cassandra Smith, was the grandfather, and Nathan Smith Dallam, who married Sara Hicks, was the father of the subject of this sketch, Lucien Clay Dallam of Henderson, Kentucky.

MILTON JAMISON DURHAM, cashier of the Central Bank of Lexington, ex-Judge of the Circuit Court, ex-member of Congress, ex-Comptroller of the United States Treasury, etc., son of Benjamin and Margaret (Robinson) Durham, was born in Boyle (then a part of Mercer) County, Kentucky, May 16, 1824. He was brought up on his father's farm, and at the age of nineteen entered Asbury University, Greencastle, Indiana, from which institution he graduated in 1844, when Bishop Simpson was its president. He taught school at Perryville a short time and read law with the late Joshua F. Bell of Danville; attended the Louisville Law School and was graduated in March, 1850; located the same year in Danville, which was the principal scene of his labors and of a remarkably successful career until his removal to Lexington in 1890.

In 1861 and the year following he was Circuit Judge of his district by appointment of Governor Magoffin; in 1872 he was elected to Congress by the Democratic party; was re-elected in 1874 and again in 1876, representing the Eighth Congressional District. While in Congress he served on many important committees, including Banking and Currency, Coinage, Weights and Measures, Expenditures in the Department of Justice; Chairman of the Committee on Revision of Law, and the Committee on Appropriations. In 1885 he was appointed First Comptroller of the United States Treasury by President Cleveland, and held that office until April, 1889.

In 1890, Judge Durham's health being greatly impaired by a serious attack of La Grippe, his physician advised him to abandon his law practice, and following this advice, he sought another field and assisted in organizing the Central Bank of Lexington, with a capital of 200,000, and was elected Cashier of the bank, in which position he has demonstrated his ability as a financier. He is also treasurer of the Blue Grass Building and Loan Association, one of the strongest organizations of the kind in the State.

HON. M. J. DURHAM.

From 1872 to 1876 he was Grand Sire of the Grand Lodge, I. O. O. F., of the United States.

Judge Durham is widely known throughout the state and country as an active, energetic business man, and for many years as a distinguished member of the Democratic party, while in his present sphere of action, he is universally recognized as a zealous friend of every effort for the elevation of the masses, especially the laboring community, and a willing helper in every good work; an honest and upright business man, and, what is more rare, an honest politician; has always taken an active and prominent part in politics, and in every relation in life, public and private, he has been noted for his uniform kindness and consideration for others. Few men have more stanch friends or enthusiastic admirers than Judge Durham.

His history is an example of the possibilities, under the operation of our free institutions, that are offered to rising young men, who, with native talent, honorable purpose and industry, may surmount all difficulties and attain success and honor without the patronage of the influential or the arts of the demagogue. He is strictly a temperance man, having never taken a dram of spirituous liquors in his life, and never treated any person to liquor in any of his canvasses or at any other time.

Judge Durham was married in 1850 to Martha J. Mitchell, daughter of Judge James P. Mitchell of Boyle County. She died in 1879, leaving four sons and one daughter: Louis H., deceased; Benjamin J., James Wesley, Robert M. and Ora B., who married Albert Morris of Louisville.

He was again married in 1886 to Mrs. Margaret Letcher Carter, daughter of the late Dr. Samuel M. Letcher of Lexington.

Judge Durham is a member of the Methodist Episcopal Church (South), as were all of his forefathers since their settlement in this country.

Benjamin Durham (father) was a native of the patriotic County of Mechlenburg, Va., which, in the days of the great struggle for American independence, furnished six hundred men to serve in the siege and capture of Lord Cornwallis at Yorktown, October 19, 1781. He removed to Kentucky with his father when four years of age, and settled in what is now Boyle County in 1782, and made his home there until the day of his death, in 1847, at the age of sixty-nine years. He was a blacksmith and a farmer, and was highly esteemed by his neighbors. He was a class leader in the Methodist Church, and was known as a man of correct business principles, whose daily life was the best evidence of the sincerity of his religious profession. His aim in life was to do all the good in his power for his friends and neighbors. He had no ambition to be great and the simplicity of his life was the source of his strength and true greatness. He was a believer in and a faithful advocate of the Jeffersonian democracy, but was not an office-seeker.

John Durham (grandfather), who removed from Mechlenburg County, Virginia, to Kentucky in 1782, organized the first Methodist Church west of the Alleghany Mountains, which was located seven miles from Danville. Humility was the distinguishing trait of his character; and if at any time he brought himself into prominence it was by an attempt to accomplish some good work. He was through life an honest and upright man. He was a farmer and a most excellent neighbor, who left his impress upon the community in which he lived. He died at the age of seventy-six years.

The Durham family was originally from England, and settled in Virginia about the close of the Seventeenth Century.

Margaret Robinson Durham (mother) was born in Virginia in 1776, and died in Boyle County, Kentucky, in 1854. She was a true and consistent member of the Methodist Church.

Jacob Robinson (maternal grandfather) was also a native of Virginia, most of whose useful and exemplary life was spent in Boyle County, where he died. The Robinsons are of English and Scotch descent, and were noted for their energy and thrift.

LEE H. BROOKS, Vice-President of the "Cincinnati Leaf Tobacco Warehouse Co.," and Manager of the Globe Warehouse, the largest establishment of the kind in the world, and recently President of the Chamber of Commerce of Cincinnati, but for eighteen years a resident of

Covington, was born in Bristol, Addison County, Vermont, May 18, 1840.

In this great country, abounding in opportunities and rich resources, where so many men have risen from obscurity to eminence, a man's abilities are measured by the successes he has achieved. He is the architect of his own fortune. Most men who start in life without capital —save their inherent talents, energy and enterprise—and succeed, do so by force of their native endowments, and are not indebted to assistance from friends, capital or circumstances except as they have created them in making their way to position, wealth and honor. The subject of this sketch is an example of what a young man may do if he has the natural sagacity to discover opportunities and the ability and energy to improve them.

Mr. Brooks received his early education principally in the High School of Shelby, New York, and began his remarkably successful career as a clerk in a grocery, when he was sixteen years of age. Not satisfied with the education he had received, he worked industriously during the day and studied at night, saving his earnings so that at the end of one year he had the means—which his father could not provide—to defray his expenses for two years in the Albion Academy in Orleans County, New York, and there completed his studies.

He went to Portsmouth, Ohio, where he taught school for four years, but this occupation was too confining for him, and rather tame for a man of his active temperament, and he took a position as clerk on an Ohio River passenger steamer, and was on the river for about five years, occupying every position on the steamer, from clerk to captain, and had a license as pilot from the Government, a document which he still prizes as a reminiscence of his younger days.

There came a time when he must seek a broader and more promising field where his energies and natural talents would be more likely to bring deserved reward, and in 1868 he gave up his pleasant life on the river to accept a position in Cincinnati as Secretary and Treasurer of the Planters Tobacco Warehouse Company, where he soon gave evidence of his superior ability as a business man. By his energy, business tact and sound judgment he began to accomplish great things for his employers. The value of his services was recognized by them, and at the end of one year he became a partner in the concern. He remained with the Planters until 1872, when he disposed of his interest and determined to establish a new house, and formed a partnership with William Waterfield and opened the "Globe Tobacco Warehouse." In this Mr. Brooks showed his ability in the conduct of commercial affairs to such an extent that in 1883 the business had increased so immensely that they were compelled to enlarge their warerooms. They accordingly purchased the adjoining building and erected the largest tobacco warehouse in the world. At this time also the firm was reorganized under the name of "The Brooks, Waterfield Company," Mr. Brooks becoming President of the concern with the result of an ever increasing and successful business. Mr. Waterfield died in 1888, but his share in the business was retained as a good investment by his estate.

In 1892 all of the tobacco warehouses of Cincinnati were consolidated and Mr. Brooks was elected Vice-President of the Company and Manager of the Globe Warehouse. In this responsible position he has helped to conduct the combined business of seven large warehouses in a manner that has been highly satisfactory to the members of the colossal enterprise, and in this has achieved the crowning success of a remarkable business career, now at its zenith.

His early experience on the river was exceedingly pleasant and fascinating, and in leaving the active pursuits of the steamboatman he retained his love for the charming life upon the water, and still holds stock in the various steamboat companies. He is the friend of the river men, and they are great admirers of their former associate, as is evinced by the fact that one of the finest passenger steamers bears the name of "Lee H. Brooks."

He is President of the company which owns Coney Island, the famous resort for Cincinnati people; is director in the Ohio Valley National Bank; President of the Pettibone Manufacturing Company, the large establishment in which all kinds of paraphernalia for lodges, societies, schools, etc., are manufactured, and in which four hundred and fifty people are constantly employed; President of the Smith-Kasson Company, the largest retail shoe house in Cincinnati; and besides these, holds leading positions in other business enterprises.

Although a resident of Covington, Mr. Brooks is fully identified with the interests of Cincinnati, which is abundantly proven by the fact of his having been President of the Cincinnati Chamber of Commerce, the most influential commercial body in the city. Such an election is regarded as the greatest honor that can be bestowed upon any one in the commercial world, an honor which is due only to the most able and influential business man. He filled this position with perfect satisfaction to all until October, 1890.

Mr. Brooks, with his varied career, his indomitable will and energy, surmounting any and all difficulties and rising to his present high position in the business world, is a perfect type of the American citizen, an example which may serve many an ambitious youth, showing what may be done even with limited resources and few opportunities. Solely by his own efforts and native talents, beginning without aid or influence, he has steadily risen until he is among the most honored business men of Cincinnati, and in his special line holds the most influential and leading position in the world.

He also occupies a noteworthy position in the social world and in the highest benevolent orders, of which he is a valued and helpful member. He first entered a Masonic lodge in 1864 and has taken all of the degrees of the York and Scottish Rites and takes a great pride in being called a "Shiner." He is perhaps more devoted to Masonry than the Elks or Knights of Pythias, of which he is an honored member.

Politics have no attractions for Mr. Brooks, and he would hardly accept an office if it were tendered him without the usual bitter strife which office-seekers have to pass through on the way to victory or defeat.

Mr. Brooks owns many residences in Cincinnati and Covington, including his elegant home in Covington, in which he has lived for eighteen years. He was married in 1866 to Laura A. Tone of Locust Corner, Clermont County, Ohio, and is blessed with an interesting family of four children: Charles G., George A., Ada and Rosella. His eldest daughter, a graduate of Wesleyan College, is the wife of Henry Kasson of the Smith-Kasson (shoe) Company. Mr. Brooks is a great lover of his family, which is surrounded by the comforts and luxuries of an ideal home; enjoys meeting his friends, entertains them royally; is fond of music and choice literature; has a fine library; and is well informed, not only in the affairs of the active business life which he leads, but also in the current events. It is in the social aspect of his nature that he appears to the best advantage in the estimation of those who enjoy his genial and intellectual companionship.

Mr. Brooks' father, Cyrus S. Brooks, was born in Vermont in 1812. He was a farmer there for many years, and in 1848 he removed to Orleans County, New York, and engaged in the shoe business at Shelby Centre, where he was recognized as a prominent citizen. He afterwards removed to Wheelersburg, Scioto County, Ohio, but, preferring his former home, returned to Shelby, New York, in about two years, and there resumed his former occupation. His death, in 1860, resulted from a kick from a horse. His wife was Sophia Hazleton, who was born in Vermont in 1816, and is now living with her son, the subject of this sketch, in Covington.

Mr. Brooks comes of an old New England family, his ancestor, John Brooks, having immigrated to this country from England about one hundred and fifty years ago. He settled in the State of New York, where his three sons were born. It was one of these brothers who settled in Vermont one hundred and twenty-five years ago and surveyed a large tract of land in Addison County, reclaiming it from a wilderness and living there all his life. This has been handed down from father to son and is still in the possession of the family.

One of the sons of this early pioneer was Mr. Brooks' grandfather, so he is purely American by birth and descent. On his mother's side he is related to the noted Colonel Hawkins, who was an officer on General Washington's staff during the whole time of the Revolutionary war.

CYRUS B. GRAHAM, M. D., an industrious and capable young physician of Henderson, is a descendant of an old Scotch Covenanter family whose history is traced back nearly two hundred years.

In the early part of the Eighteenth Century, in what is now Sterlingshire, Scotland, in Clan Grahame, 'neath the shadows of Ben Leith and near the shores of beautiful Loch Katrine, was born Hugh Methven Grahame. He was closely related to the Grahames of Glasgow and was a man of "plodding industry and sober worth." He was one of the Scotch Covenanters, with all of the sturdy independence of that class. Regardless of the persecution of the minions of Charles II, he would meet those of his religious belief among the hills, "In some deep dell by rocks o'er canopied," and worship God according to the dictates of their own conscience, unawed by the fear of Church or State. Hoping to enjoy greater freedom of thought, Hugh Graham with his family emigrated to near Belfast, Ireland, where his bones lie buried. Here, in 1772, Richard Graham (grandfather) was born. The family then emigrated to America, settling in South Carolina. Richard Graham married Hannah Bishop of North Carolina, and with several other families started on the long journey through the wilderness to Kentucky. Many interesting stories of that journey have been told by an old slave woman, "Aunt Sylvia," who was a litle girl at that time, and accompanied the party. The men of the company walked along beside their wagons, which were drawn by slow-moving oxen, the wagons containing women, children and household goods. It was a land of sunshine and shadow—the shadow of the many inroads of the savage tribes still hung over it, while the sunshine of the future in the homes to be built was with them. Richard Graham was in that day considered a man of some means, and old Aunt Sylvia often recounted with pride the fact that "Marse Dick had three slaves, his wagon and oxen, one cow and a fine mare."

Richard Graham located in what is now Hopkins County, and acquired a large body of land, and was principally engaged in agricultural pursuits and also operated a tannery, the only one in that section. He had a brother who was a soldier in the war of 1812, and who was wounded in the battle of New Orleans.

Richard Graham had three sons and six daughters; his eldest son, Harvey, served in the Mexican war and also in the Union army in the war of the rebellion. The other sons, LeRoy and Cyrus (twins), were born in 1814 on the Graham plantation in Hopkins County. LeRoy was tall and straight as an arrow, with deep blue eyes and black curly hair; quick to take offense, yet ever ready to forgive; fond of his dog and gun, and more devoted still to the deep, majestic forest, where he would spend days and nights with no companion save his faithful dog and trusty weapon. He was known as a dead shot with the rifle and kept that community supplied with game. Passionately fond of music, on returning from his hunting expeditions, it would not be long until he would have his violin, fife or clarionet in his hand and repair to the "quarters," where he would get the darkies together for a dance. At the corn-huskings and other frolics he was a welcome guest and an active participant. He was also very fond of horses, and took pride in owning the fastest horses in the neighborhood. In fact, his staid Presbyterian kinsfolk were shocked and often shook their heads at LeRoy's sporting proclivities.

With all his love for fun, which he inherited from his Irish mother, he had enough of the canny Scot blood of his father to make him a close trader, and in the matter of business he was shrewd and successful. He bought produce with which he loaded a flat-boat in Tradewater River and floated it into the Ohio, thence down the Father of Waters to New Orleans, where he disposed of his boat and cargo at a profit, and, as was the custom then, he returned through the country on foot.

LeRoy Graham was married three times. His first wife was Alice Parker; his second a Miss Slaton and his third a Miss King. He was married to Alice Parker in 1852. She was a daughter of Benjamin and Mary Howard Jennings Parker of Hopkins County, who were married January 5, 1826. Benjamin Parker was a Virginian and a son of Sir Peter Parker, a British Admiral, who bombarded Charleston, S. C., in the Revolutionary war, and a man of considerable wealth. Mary Howard Jennings Parker was a daughter of Colonel William Jennings and Marian Smith Jennings. Colonel Jennings was Deputy Governor of Virginia and also Superintendent of Indian Affairs in Colonial Virginia. He was the youngest son of Thomas Jennings, who was the second son of William Jennings, Bart., England.

After his marriage LeRoy Graham located in Nebo, Hopkins County, and engaged in dealing in tobacco and in general merchandising and was for years postmaster of the place. He was in business there for probably thirty-five years, and was widely known by his uprightness and honorable dealing. He became a staid and quiet citizen and an exemplary member of the Methodist Church. During the war he was a Union man. He belonged to neither of the great political parties, but was independent in his political views.

The result of his union with Alice Parker was three daughters and two sons: Jennie Graham, Frances Graham, Olive Graham, Cyrus B. Graham (subject of this sketch), and Edwin R. Graham, who died in 1888.

Cyrus B. Graham, whose long lines of ancestry are thus briefly sketched, was born in Nebo, Hopkins County, Kentucky, in 1862. His mother, Alice (Parker) Graham, died when he was a babe. As soon as he learned to read he became an omnivorous reader of history and stories of travel, these being the principal literature at hand. At the age of fourteen he had read Rollins' Ancient History, Gibbon's Rome and several works on Anatomy and Physiology and Gudlow on Medical Examination. He spent a greater portion of his time at his grandmother Parker's home, where he found an excellent library, and while there read everything he could get his hands on. His aunts used to say, "Thank the Lord, Cyrus has something to read, because when he is reading we are all safe; when he is not he is sure to be in mischief."

At the age of fourteen his father sent him to the farm to bring the horses. When he arrived at the farm, two miles from town, the sun was just peeping over the treetops. He hung the bridles on the fence corner and kept on down the road until he reached his grandmother's, eight miles away. He was received with open arms, but with some misgivings as to the future of the runaway boy. He returned to Nebo the next fall and worked in a tobacco factory and store until spring, reading at night until late hours. The next two years were spent in the factory, store or on the farm. He rented land, helped to clear it, sold the timber and the rails which he made, and in this way obtained money with which to buy books; drove a team, plowed or did any kind of work for a little pay; he helped to dig a well one winter when he could find nothing else to do, receiving twenty-five cents a day. The next three years he spent in traveling in the west and south, and what money he made he spent for books, which he would read and then give away. His valise generally contained more books than clothing. He worked at the carpenter trade for two years and would often work till near midnight to make extra money with which to buy books, and having access to good libraries he lost no time in getting all he could out of them.

He borrowed money and attended the Green River Academy at Madisonville for five months, and at the end of the term received a certificate, and taught school for six months. He then went to Cumberland University, Lebanon, Tennessee; was "elected" with three others to wash dishes, and for this was allowed a small reduction in his board bill. He remained in college three years, teaching school occasionally and selling books during vacation to procure money to defray his expenses. He traveled extensively over the south, visiting the colleges as a general agent, and did some newspaper work.

He took a short course in the Mobile College of Medicine; studied and practiced under Dr. James P. Bone of Arlington, Tennessee; entered the medical department of Vanderbilt University at Nashville, Tennessee, and was graduated in the class of 1891. He traveled for a wholesale drug house during vacations and thus made money to pay his way through school.

After receiving his license as a physician he located first at St. Charles, Kentucky, and practiced for two years; removed thence to near

Nashville, Tennessee; and a few months later, October 4, 1893, was married to Frances Duncan, daughter of Marion and Juliet (Mullins) Duncan of Henderson, Kentucky, and located in that city.

Dr. Graham is a popular young physician; a member of the Henderson County Medical Association and a member of the Board of Health. He has every promise of the bright future which a man of his energy and industry deserves.

PETER B. MUIR, one of the senior members of the Louisville bar, having been prominent as judge and attorney for half a century, was born in Nelson County, Kentucky, October 19, 1822, and at the age of about ten years was left an orphan, his father having died in 1830 and his mother in 1833. His father, Jasper Muir, was a native of Maryland, who came to Nelson County with his parents when a child about the beginning of the present century. After attaining his majority he married Isabella Brown, daughter of Peter Brown, and engaged in farming in Nelson County, but died at an early age in 1830.

Dr. William Muir (grandfather) was a native of Scotland and a graduate of Edinborough College, who came to America and located in Maryland, where he resided a few years before removing to Nelson County, Kentucky, where he continued the practice of medicine until the time of his death in 1838, having reached the good old age of eighty-four years. He was a fine scholar and a very successful and popular physician.

Judge Muir's mother, Isabella Brown, was a native of Maryland, as was her father, Peter Brown, who came with his family to Nelson County very early in the century, where he was engaged in farming on quite a large scale. He died at the age of eighty-four years. His daughter, Isabella Muir, died in 1833, when still a young woman.

Left an orphan without fortune when a mere child, the outlook for the lad was not encouraging. But he secured a good education, chiefly in the country schools, under the direction of his learned grandfather, and at Hanover College, where he spent two years before commencing the study of law. He was licensed to practice law in 1845, some months after his marriage to Sophronia Rizer, a lady of great beauty and loveliness. His success was assured from the time he opened his office in Bardstown in January, 1846. He was elected County Attorney and served three years, when he formed a partnership with Honorable Thomas W. Riley, and this firm did a leading practice. In January, 1852, they removed their office to Louisville, where they were equally successful.

Mr. Muir, while yet a comparative stranger, was elected a member of the City Council, and served for a term of two years, and in 1856, four years after coming to Louisville, was elected to the legislature. In 1857 he was elected Judge of the Circuit Court for the unexpired term of Judge Bullock, and the partnership of Riley & Muir was dissolved. He was again elected for a full term without opposition, but resigned about the middle of the term and became the first Judge of the Jefferson Court of Common Pleas. That office he held for four years, when he resigned and returned to the bar in partnership with the late Martin Bijur. The firm of Muir & Bijur continued about three years, during which time they were among the leading practitioners of the Louisville bar. George M. Davie was then admitted to the firm, which for several years was known throughout the state as one of the leading law firms in Kentucky. In 1877 that firm was dissolved and Judge Muir continued his work without a partner until he was joined by D. I. Heyman. The firm of Muir & Heyman continued for several years with marked success. In 1890 his son, Upton W. Muir, was admitted to the firm, which was known as Muir, Heyman & Muir. After a successful practice of four and a half years that firm was dissolved, Mr. Heyman retiring and the business continued by father and son under the present firm name of P. B. & Upton W. Muir. The Judge and his son are hard workers and no law firm in Kentucky stands higher. In the meantime Judge Muir has from time to time occupied an important chair in the law department of the University of Louisville, in which capacity he has rendered valuable service in the training of hundreds of young men, who remember him as the able teacher and the friend of the young men of the bar.

In the capacity of Judge he was regarded as one of the best judges on the bench, and was greatly endeared to the hearts of the people. His relation to the bar was of an intimate and almost affectionate nature, and the practitioners in his court had the highest regard for him personally while they acknowledged his superiority in legal attainments. His resignation was purely voluntary on his part, for he could have retained his place on the bench indefinitely; but the work was severe and the compensation was inadequate to satisfy the ambition of a man of his scholarly and legal attainments, besides he preferred the position of advocate to that of the judge, and so he gave up the ermine for the greater liberty of the practitioner.

As a lawyer Judge Muir has always commanded the profound respect of his brethren at the bar. His indomitable energy, his accurate and complete knowledge of the Civil Code and Statute laws, his fair and strictly legitimate manner of conducting his cases, his effort to secure sound and honest legal action, thoroughly equipped in every way for his high calling, courteous and deferential toward his opponent, faithful and persevering in behalf of his client, he commands the respect and confidence of judge and jury, and whatever may be the issue, he leaves no doubt in the mind of his client as to the wise and careful management of his case. His ripe experience, sound judgment and elegant, scholarly bearing entitle him to the honored position which he holds as the Nestor of the Louisville bar.

He is a member of the Presbyterian Church, and his religious convictions govern every principle of action in professional life as well as in his daily walk and conversation.

His son and associate in business is forging ahead, and is well up in the front ranks of the legal profession, for which he possesses the natural qualifications and has been prepared by a thorough course of study, as well as by several years of practical experience as a practicing attorney. He graduated from the University of Virginia in the class of 1886, taking the degree of Master of Arts and the debater's prize, a fifty dollar gold medal. He afterwards entered the law department of the same institution, and there graduated in 1887. During the past eight years he has been associated with his venerable father, taking an active interest in all the cases which come to the firm. He represents the younger element in the profession; and with a clear legal mind, a thorough knowledge of law, industrious, persevering and attentive to the interests of his clients he is an able assistant, to whom his father gives a liberal share of credit for his success.

Judge Muir's wife died in 1885, leaving seven children: Belle, wife of Harry Weisinger, the tobacco manufacturer of Louisville; Thomas R., Sydney S., Upton W., Lilian, wife of A. L. Semple of Louisville; Nellie, wife of A. H. Smith of Springfield, Illinois, and Sophronia.

Upton W. Muir was married in 1888 to Miss Hebe Harrison, daughter of Julian Harrison of the famous Virginia family of that name.

JOHN HARDIN McHENRY, deceased, late postmaster of Owensboro, son of John Hardin and Hannah (Davis) McHenry, was born in Hartford, Ohio County, Kentucky, February 21, 1832. His father was born in Washington County, October 13, 1797, and died in Owensboro, November 1, 1871. He received his education, principally, from his father, and studied law under his uncle Martin D. Hardin, a distinguished lawyer of Frankfort, and was admitted to the bar in 1819. He began the practice of law at Leitchfield, where he was postmaster; and November 22, 1820, Governor Adair appointed him Major of the Eighty-seventh Regiment State Militia; and in 1821 Commonwealth attorney for the new judicial district, embracing Daviess, Henderson, Breckenridge, Ohio and Muhlenberg Counties. He removed to Hartford and entered upon the duties of this office, which he held until 1839, when he resigned. In 1840 he was elected to the legislature; January 26, 1843, was appointed by Governor Robert P. Letcher—on the advice of the Senate—a member of the Board of Overseers of Transylvania University. In 1845 he was elected to Congress from the Second District by the Whig party, to which he belonged. In 1849 he was a member of the State Constitutional Convention, representing Ohio and Hancock Counties.

He removed to Owensboro in 1853, where he continued the practice of law until the time of his death. He was a most able lawyer, a hard worker and enjoyed the confidence and esteem of all who knew him; and there were few men in the state who were more widely known or more universally beloved.

Hannah Davis McHenry, mother of John Hardin McHenry, was born November 4, 1800, in Virginia; was married in Muhlenberg County, Kentucky, November 11, 1823; and died in Owensboro, July 23, 1862. She was a daughter of Henry and Frances (Randall) Davis. Frances Randall and a brother were left orphans at an early age. He was afterward in the United States Navy, and was drowned while trying to ford the Potomac River.

The children of Hannah Davis and John Hardin McHenry were as follows: Martin D. McHenry, Henry D. McHenry, William H. McHenry, Barnabas McHenry, John H. McHenry, Mrs. (Dr.) Hale, Mrs. Robert Craig, L. S. McHenry and W. E. McHenry.

A number of the Davis men, relatives of Mrs. McHenry's father, were in the Revolutionary war; others served in the war of 1812; and those who came to Kentucky as pioneers endured great hardship and suffered much from the depredations of the Indians.

Barnabas McHenry (grandfather) was a native of Maryland, who came to Kentucky soon after the Revolutionary war and was a distinguished pioneer preacher who organized many of the Methodist Churches in Kentucky and the west. He was a very able man and was consecrated to his work. He died of cholera, June 15, 1833. His wife, Sarah Hardin, daughter of John and Jane Davis Hardin, died of cholera the next day after her husband's death, June 16, 1833, and they were buried in one grave.

John Hardin (great-grandfather) was born October 1, 1753, and was killed by the Indians in 1792. When the first call for troops was made by the Continental Congress he recruited a company of soldiers and joined General David Morgan's Rifle Corps; was in the march from Boston to Canada, and in every engagement of that Corps until 1780. At the battle of Saratoga he performed a distinguished service, for which he received publicly the thanks of General Gates. In 1792 he was sent by special order of General Washington on a mission of peace to the Indians in Northern Ohio (then territory) and was murdered by them. He was a son of Martin and Mary (Waters) Hardin.

Martin Hardin (great-great-grandfather) was a son of Martin Hardin, the French Huguenot. King George, through Lord Fairfax, granted a tract of land in Fauquier County, Virginia, to Martin Hardin, junior, in 1748, who made a will in 1799 and died in 1800, at his home in Fauquier County.

John Hardin McHenry was educated in Hanover College, Indiana; at Center College, Danville, Kentucky, and was three years at West Point. Returning to Kentucky, he studied law and was graduated from the law department of the University of Louisville in 1857. He began the practice of his profession with his father and later was in partnership with Judge W. T. Owen. Mr. McHenry was one of the ten captains selected by lot by Governor Morehead, April 9, 1859, to go to Utah; but the trouble was settled by A. S. Johnson and R. E. Lee before he was called upon to perform his duty on that mission.

In 1861 he recruited the Seventeenth Kentucky Infantry for the Union army; and on the first day of October, 1861, was in the first engagement on Kentucky soil. His regiment was with General Grant at Fort Donelson and at Shiloh, and was afterward consolidated with the Twenty-fifth Kentucky Infantry, and the new regiment was placed under his command. When President Lincoln issued his first proclamation on the subject of emancipation in 1862, Colonel McHenry took issue with the Government, for which he was dismissed. He was greatly loved by his men, who regretted his departure from the service.

He returned to his home in Owensboro, and in 1863 was a candidate for Congress, but was defeated by George H. Yeaman. He made a contest for the seat, but it was given to Mr. Yeaman.

In 1881 and 1882 he took exceptions to the preference shown to ex-confederate soldiers by the state government in the matter of appointments; and he inaugurated the campaign known as the Union Democratic Movement, in which ex-Lieutenant-Governor R. T. Jacob received 75,000 votes for Governor. He was a Democrat until the nomination of James G. Blaine for President, when he became a Republican.

Mr. C. C. Watkins, having been appointed Postmaster of Owensboro by President Harrison, resigned his office, and Colonel McHenry was appointed Postmaster March 26, 1891; was confirmed by the Senate December 16, 1891, and died during his term of office, July 7, 1893.

For two years he was Grand Master, and at the time of his death was Past Grand Master Workman of the A. O. U. W. of Kentucky, a Mason and a member of the G. A. R.

Colonel McHenry was one of the best lawyers in Kentucky, a fine speaker and eloquent pleader, keen and alert in the management of his cases and a successful practitioner at the bar. He was an obliging and competent official, an ideal soldier and an honorable, upright citizen who won the respect and esteem of the entire community. He was universally popular throughout the state, in which he was a prominent figure during the greater part of his busy and useful life.

Colonel John H. McHenry was married December 30, 1868, to Josephine Phillips, daughter of Joseph Francis and Elizabeth Sue (Simpson) Phillips, whose ancestry is traced back to one of the earliest settlements in the United States.

Joseph Francis Phillips, father of Mrs. McHenry, was born in 1809. His father's name was William Phillips, who married a Miss Graham of Virginia, whose mother's maiden name was Robinson. But to go back to the progenitor of the Phillips family in America: Rev. Joseph Phillips of Boxford, England, and his wife, Elizabeth, came to this country with Governor Winthrop and settled in Watertown, Massachusetts, in the early years of the seventeenth century, about 1630. Their children were Elizabeth, Abigail and Samuel, the last named of whom was a minister at Rowley, Massachusetts. His son, Theophilus, appears in 1686 as one of the guarantees of the Charter of Newton, Long Island, by Governor Dongan of New York. Philip Phillips, son of Theophilus, was born December 27, 1648, and removed to New Jersey, locating at Lawrenceville, about six miles from Trenton, and had three sons: Theophilus, born May 15, 1673; William, born January 27, 1676, and Philip, born December 27, 1678. The last named son was captain in a Hunterdon County regiment and was promoted to major in 1727, serving in the regiment commanded by Colonel John Reading, who was afterward Governor of New Jersey. Major Phillips died in 1740. His wife's name was Elizabeth, and they had six children, Philip, Abner, Samuel, John, Esther and Ruth. Samuel (third son of Major Phillips) was the father of five children, Jonathan, Elias, John, Samuel and Asher. Jonathan, the eldest of these children, was a captain in the Second Regiment of New Jersey in the Continental army. He married Elizabeth Houston, sister of Honorable William Churchill Houston. Elias, the second son of Samuel Phillips, was adjutant of the First Regiment of Hunterdon Militia in the Revolutionary war. He married Elizabeth Phillips, his cousin, daughter of Colonel Joseph Phillips. John, the third son of Samuel Phillips, married a sister of Elizabeth, wife of Elias. Colonel Joseph Phillips (son of William and father-in-law of Elias and John) an officer in the Revolutionary war, was born 1708; died 1778. His children were: Abigail, wife of Captain Edward Yard; Mary, above mentioned; Frances, Elizabeth, above mentioned; William, and Dr. Joseph Phillips, who was a surgeon in the United States army and served with Generals St. Claire, Wayne and Wilkinson, and who died in Lawrenceville, N. J.

Previous to the Revolutionary war Colonel Joseph Phillips was captain of a company in the old French and Indian war, having left New Jersey in the party commanded by Major Trent.

William, his grandson, came from New Jersey; married in Virginia, and later settled at Frankfort, Kentucky, where he died in 1864. Under General William Henry Harrison fought at the battle of Tippecanoe November 7, 1811.

Elizabeth Sue Simpson Phillips (mother of Mrs. McHenry) was a daughter of Benjamin and Pauline (Ballard) Simpson. Pauline Ballard was a sister of Andrew Jackson Ballard and Judge Bland Ballard, late of Louisville; and was a daughter of James and Susan Cox Ballard, who was a daughter of Sallie Piety Cox. Sallie Piety was a daughter of Lord Piety of Ireland. Mrs. McHenry's mother often told of hearing her great-great-grandmother, Lady Piety, say to her daughter, all of the generations being present: "Arise, daughter, and go to thy daughter, for thy daughter's daughter hath a daughter."

James Ballard, great-grandfather of Mrs. McHenry, was a brother of Bland Ballard, the celebrated Indian fighter, and their father's name was Bland Ballard, a Colonel in the Revolutionary war; and prior to the war was an inspector of tobacco in Virginia, by appointment of the Crown of England.

EDWARD L. HUTCHINSON, an accomplished lawyer and president of the City Council of Lexington, was born in Summerville, South Carolina, July 31st, 1858; graduated from the Porter Academy, Charleston, in 1875, and attended Union College at Schenectady, New York, four years, from which he graduated in 1879, with the degree of Bachelor of Arts. Returning to Charleston, he taught in Porter Academy for one year; went to Lexington in 1880 as tutor in the family of Alexander Jeffrey, and remained in that position for three years, during which time he studied law with the firm of Beck & Thornton, the senior member of which was Senator James B. Beck; was admitted to the bar in 1883; went to New York City and clerked in the law office of Henry Daily, Jr., and in the early part of 1884 returned to Lexington and located permanently in the practice of his profession.

Two years later he was elected City Attorney; was re-elected in April, 1888; was elected by the people as a member of the Board of Aldermen in 1892, and served two years; in 1894 was appointed by Mayor Duncan to fill a vacancy in the Board of Councilmen, and upon the retirement of Mr. Kaufman was elected president of the Board; was returned by the people at the next election in 1895, and was again elected president of the Board.

Mr. Hutchinson is president of the Union Club, of which many of the most prominent men in the state are, or have been, members, including James B. Beck, John G. Carlisle, J. C. S. Blackburn, and others of national reputation.

Mr. Hutchinson is also president of the Country Club, one of the most popular institutions in the Blue Grass country; secretary of the Union Building & Loan Association; is a member of the Odd Fellows Fraternity and of the Knights of Pythias; is fond of hunting and other out-door sports; is a typical club man and a leader in Lexington society.

With all of these interests, public and private, and with the highest social reputation, Mr. Hutchinson is devoted to his profession and is one of the busiest and most industrious lawyers at the Lexington bar, upon the roll of which are names of some of the most illustrious members of the legal profession in the world, and among the active spirits of the present day there is no name that is more worthy of honor than that of Edward L. Hutchinson, who commands the esteem of the bench, of the members of the profession and of the populace.

His father, M. E. Hutchinson, was a distinguished lawyer of Charleston, South Carolina, who died in September, 1884.

Edward L. Hutchinson (grandfather) was born on the old Hutchinson plantation known as "Travelers' Rest," located near the old Dorchester Fort and church, between Summerville and Charleston, South Carolina.

Louisa (Bonneau) Hutchinson, mother of the subject of this sketch, was a member of a distinguished family of French Huguenot descent, who trace their ancestry back to the time of the landing of some of their members in South Carolina during Cromwell's day.

CHARLES RUSSELL GARR, M. D., an able physician and surgeon of Flemingsburg, Kentucky, son of Benjamin Lewis and Kizia (Russell) Garr, was born in Jefferson County, Kentucky, November 5, 1858; was educated in Jefferson College; studied medicine in the Hospital College of Medicine, Louisville, graduating February 26, 1880; located in Hillsboro, Fleming County, and practiced medicine in that vicinity until February 24, 1889, when he removed to Flemingsburg and formed a partnership with Dr. Lucien McDowell, with whom he was associated for two years, when Dr. C. W. Aitkin (see sketch of Dr. Aitkin in this volume) became a member of the firm, which is known as McDowell, Garr & Aitkin, one of the strongest combinations in the medical profession in Kentucky.

Dr. Garr is a most active, industrious and accomplished physician, who is held in the highest esteem by the people of the county in which he has been practicing medicine and surgery for more than fifteen years; is a strong advocate of temperance; a faithful member of the Presbyterian Church and a worthy descendent of an ancestry noted for piety and good citizenship.

Dr. Garr married Sallie Rebecca Crain, daughter of James W. Crain of Hillsboro, October 9, 1883. She was born January 1, 1862; was educated at Millersburg, graduating in 1879, and was a pupil of Professor A. G. Murphy, who is now president of Bethel College at Russellville, and whose sketch will be found in this volume.

Dr. and Mrs. Garr have two children: Charles Crain Garr, born October 12, 1884, and Clyde Lewis Garr, born May 3, 1887.

Benjamin Lewis Garr (father) was born in Culpeper County, Virginia, August 27, 1820. He was educated in the common schools of Jefferson County, Kentucky, having removed from Virginia with his parents in 1827. He was engaged in farming when the California gold fever was at its height, and he followed the crowd and became interested in mining in California. Three years later he entered the Mexican army as a private under General Prescott, and served two years; was in many of the noted engagements of the war, including the battle of Buena Vista.

Returning from the war he resumed the occupation of a farmer in Jefferson County, where he remained until 1885, when he removed to Shelby County, and died there October 27, 1887.

He was married June 3, 1856, to Kizia Russell, who was born in Shelby County, January 17, 1837, and died December 24, 1894. They had four children: Elizabeth Virginia, Charles Russell, Mary Margaret and Nathaniel L. Garr.

Jacob Garr (grandfather) was born in Madison County, Va., March 20, 1782. He moved to Kentucky and was a farmer in Jefferson County, where he died. He married Susan Garr, his cousin, who was born in Culpeper County, Virginia, February 3, 1774, and died in Jefferson County, July 7, 1864.

Andrew Garr (grandfather) was born in Culpeper County, Virginia, in 1750, and died there March 4, 1819. He married Christina Wilhoite, who was born October, 1750, and died October 4, 1837.

Lorenz Garr (great-great-grandfather) was born in Dinkelsbuehl, Germany, November 29, 1716; died in 1753. He emigrated to America with a colony from his native place when sixteen years of age, and afterwards married Dorothea Blankenbaker, who came over from Germany in the same ship. He spelled the name Gaar.

Andreas Gar (great-great-great-grandfather), who spelled his name still differently, was born in Germany, June 14, 1685; married Eva Seidelmann in Bavaria, February 23, 1711. He was a master weaver, which indicates that he possessed skill of no ordinary kind. In the Lutheran Church at Illenschwang are paintings of the twelve apostles and on the back of one of these is written the name of Andreas Gar, donor. In the church book a record is made that Andreas Gar had "left three florins to have a clean wooden cross made in memory of him, should he not be heard from and should he be deemed as lost on the voyage to America." He also applied to the burgomaster and City Council for a letter of character and the seal of the ancient city of Dinkelsbuehl attests that "Andreas Gar has been a good citizen and is worthy of all confidence and esteem." He also secured a letter from his pastor, showing his religious standing.

John (or Hans) Gar (great-great-great-great-grandfather), a native of Franconia—one of the divisions of Bavaria of the German Empire—was a lineal descendent of the Gars who were honored with a crest by the great Emperor Charles V. in 1519. This family was mentioned as an "old and very good family." John Gar was a Lutheran and the probability is that the Gars espoused the cause of the great Reformer at a very early date in the reformation. "He lived in the village of

Frankenhofen and engaged in the peaceful occupation of weaving, loved and honored by his neighbors, living a peaceful and industrious life, he reared his family in the fear of the Lord and engrafted into his posterity those traits of character that have distinguished them for generations. A great trial came to the good man in his declining years; his oldest son (Andreas Gar, the progenitor of the family in America) had heard of the new colony of Pennsylvania, founded by the great William Penn, to whose domains were invited the persecuted of the world, with the assurance of religious liberty. A company of emigrants was formed and Andreas Gar was a leader among them. Perhaps nothing but old age kept the father from going; he could not survive the long and perilous voyage. With what anxious solicitude the patriarch must have waited for news from his long absent loved ones; and what joy must have filled his soul to learn that they had arrived safely and were established in peace and full religious liberty."

The facts concerning John Gar and Andreas Gar are taken from a history of the Garr family, compiled by John C. Garr of Kokomo, Indiana, which states that the names of the descendants of Andreas Garr number sixteen thousand.

ROBERT ANDERSON FIELD, Superintendent of Schools of Boyd County and a resident of Catlettsburg, son of James M. and Mary Ann (Eatham) Field, was born in Carter County, Kentucky, August 1, 1862.

His father was born in Nashville, Tennessee, March 10, 1820, and has been a stock trader and farmer, living in Boyd County since 1879. He enjoys the peace and quietude of domestic life, taking no active part in political matters, but votes the Democratic ticket—straight. He is a member of the Methodist Episcopal Church and a good citizen and neighborly neighbor.

Anderson Field (grandfather) was born in Pennsylvania, October, 1789, and removed to Tennessee in 1804 and was engaged in farming near Nashville. He came to Carter County, Kentucky, in 1858, where he died in 1878. His wife was Elizabeth Morris, a native of Pennsylvania. She died in Carter County in 1868. They were members of the Methodist Church. Mr. Field voted the Democratic ticket for seventy years.

Robert A. Field's mother, Mary Ann (Eatham) Field, was born in Boyd County, August 12, 1823; was married to James M. Field in May, 1853, and is now living with her venerable husband in Boyd County.

Hartwell Eatham (grandfather), a native of Virginia, was a farmer in Boyd County, where he died in 1850. His wife's name was Iby McGuire. Both branches of the Field family were of English extraction.

Robert A. Field was educated in the schools of Grayson and Catlettsburg and finished his education at Lebanon, Ohio. He taught school in Cannonsburg and Sandy City for five years; and in 1890, he was elected Superintendent of Public Schools, and re-elected 1893 without opposition, in which position he has materially advanced the cause of education in Boyd County. He is thoroughly qualified for his work, having been a teacher and having a great interest in the work of improving the school system.

He is a member of a number of benevolent and social societies, including the Knights of the Golden Eagle and the Mutual Protection Association.

He was married to Rebecca Ann Moore, daughter of Enoch Moore, June 12, 1889. She was born in Lawrence County, Ohio, March 31, 1861; and was educated at Ironton and Ada, Ohio. They have four children: Marie, born July 17, 1890; Robert Arnold, born December 9, 1891; Vernon C., born December 11, 1892, and Esther, born November 4, 1894.

JOHN GOODMAN, M. D., of Louisville, was born in Frankfort, Kentucky, July 22, 1837; son of John and Jane M. (Winter) Goodman.

His father was a native of Hersfeldt, Germany, who came to America in 1795, locating in Savannah, Georgia. On account of yellow fever there at times, he removed to Kentucky at the solicitation of the Clays, who were particular friends of Mr. Goodman. He domiciled with Henry Clay for a time, and remained in Lexington and vicinity three or four years before taking up his residence in Frankfort, where he lived until the time of his death in 1849, at the age of seventy years. Mr. Goodman was a Whig and a truly loyal citizen, although of foreign birth. He was a member of the Presbyterian Church. He was a lover of music, and devoted much of his time to teaching others musical accomplishments. He also taught drawing, an art in which he was thoroughly skilled. He engraved the plates for the first bank notes printed in Kentucky and made the press on which, with his own hands, he printed the notes. He also engraved and printed a map of Louisville in 1806. He was an enthusiastic mineralogist and took much interest in the coal fields at the head of the Kentucky River. His wife, Jane M. Winter, was a native of Maryland; a member of the Presbyterian Church; died in Frankfort in 1844, aged fifty-two years.

Dr. Goodman received a careful and thorough education in the schools of Frankfort and Woodford County, spending three years under the tutelage of the noted Professor Sayre of Frankfort, which enabled him to finish his collegiate course at Georgetown in two years, whence he graduated in 1856.

He read medicine with Dr. Lewis Rogers of Louisville and attended the lectures for two years at the Medical Department of the University of Louisville. He graduated from Tulane University, New Orleans, in 1859. Thus equipped for the battle of life, he returned to Louisville and began a most successful career as a general practitioner of medicine, giving especial attention to the treatment of the diseases of women and children and to obstetrics.

Dr. Goodman has been closely identified with the medical colleges of Louisville as Demonstrator of Anatomy in the Kentucky School of Medicine, at the same time instructing a private class; as adjunct Professor of Diseases of Women in the University of Louisville; as Professor of Obstetrics in the Louisville Medical College; and at the same time Professor of Obstetrics and Diseases of Women and Children in the Kentucky School of Medicine. He was the originator of the ordinance establishing the Louisville Board of Health in 1867 or 1868, the city having had no Board of Health prior to that time, while at the present time, under the able direction of the efficient Health Officer, Dr. W. P. White, it is one of the best organizations of that character in the United States.

Dr. Goodman was a member of the Board of School Trustees of Louisville for three years; member of the Board of Charity Commissioners for five years and physician in the Industrial School of Reform (House of Refuge) for twenty-five years. He has held membership in the American Gynecological Society; in the Kentucky State Medical Society; in the Louisville Medical Society and of the College of Physicians of Louisville.

Dr. Goodman has been twice married. He first married Carrie D., daughter of Dr. Henry Miller, a celebrated physician of Louisville. Mrs. Goodman died in 1883, leaving one son, Henry M. Goodman, now a practicing physician associated with his father, and Professor of Chemistry in the University of Louisville.

Dr. Goodman was again married in 1885 to Mrs. Rosetta S. (Jones) Kalfus, daughter of R. R. Jones of Louisville.

WYATT H. INGRAM, JR., Secretary and Treasurer of the Henderson Trust Company, son of Wyatt H. and Kate (Milton) Ingram, was born in Henderson County, Kentucky, September 21, 1869. He was educated, principally, in the Kentucky State Agricultural and Mechanic College of Lexington, Kentucky. Returning home he was offered and accepted the important and responsible position of Secretary and Treasurer of the Henderson Trust Company, which had been organized by Mr. J. A. Priest in 1889, with a paid-up capital of $75,000. The company does a general banking, trust and savings business, acts as administrator, executor, assignee, trustee, attorney, for non-residents, etc., and a large share of the labor and responsibility of the concern with its multifarious duties devolves upon Mr. Ingram, whose industry and sound business judgment qualify him in an eminent degree for the position he has occupied since he was twenty-one years of age. The building occupied by the Trust Company was recently remodeled and is one of the finest in the state, embodying all modern improvements and conveniences, with safety vaults of the highest order, providing security against burglary, fire or accident.

Mr. Ingram gives his whole time and undivided attention to the business of the Trust Company, and is not interested in politics. He is a member of the Knights of Pythias and of the Knights of the Ancient Essenic Order, and enjoys a high social position in the best families of Henderson.

Wyatt H. Ingram (father) was born in Henderson in 1832 and is a prosperous farmer and one of the most respected and substantial citizens of the county. He married Kate Milton, who was born in Lexington in 1832, and they had three sons and four daughters: Loulou, wife of J. A. Priest, President of the Henderson Trust Company, and a prominent business man of Henderson; J. Milton, an architect in Palo Alto, California, who assisted in the design and construction of the great Stanford University buildings; Annie, wife of Dr. C. B. Watts of Chicago; Marie L., Wyatt H., Matie F. and Bushrod T. Ingram.

Wyatt Ingram (grandfather) was born in Orange County, Virginia, in 1783, and came to Kentucky with his father and to Henderson County in 1803. His father, William Ingram, died in 1806, when Wyatt Ingram was twenty-three years of age, and the estate being insolvent, the burden of the support of a large family fell upon the son. He paid his father's debts, divided the property equally between the children and paid the expense of educating his brothers and sisters out of his own pocket. He was married December 8, 1813, to Jane McGready, daughter of Reverend Joseph McGready, the great Presbyterian revivalist of 1800.

Wyatt Ingram shipped produce to New Orleans, building his own flat-boats on Green River, floating them to Henderson, and after loading them would float them to New Orleans, sell his stock and boat and return home on foot. He walked from New Orleans to Henderson as many as thirteen times, having the proceeds of his cargo securely belted about him. The tedious journey with its hardships and dangers in those early times required courage of a high order.

His reputation for integrity and square dealing, for his kindness and helpfulness to others was known far and wide. He was one of the most influential men of his day, a leader in all public enterprises, and gave liberally of his means for the public good. He left a large and valuable estate, consisting mostly of farm lands in the county and realty in the city. He died December 15, 1850, and a plain slab marks his resting place in Fernwood Cemetery. He said: "If I have done any good it will be found out; no need to emblazon it at my grave."

There were seven children born to Wyatt Ingram and Jane McGready: Frank, Emily, Louisa, William, Wyatt (father), James and Jane. Of these Frank died when young; Emily married Robert D. Letcher and died several years later; Louisa married Honorable John W. Crockett, and died, leaving one son, Wyatt Ingram; William is bookkeeper in the City of Louisville; Wyatt is a farmer in Henderson County; James organized and commanded a company in the Confederate army during the war, and died since; Jane is the wife of Dr. Ben Letcher.

HENRY BASCOM ASBURY of Augusta, prohibition candidate for State Treasurer in 1895, was born in Bracken County, February 28, 1834. He received a good common school education and after leaving school he settled down to the quiet life of a Bracken County farmer, which occupation he continued until 1890, when he removed to Augusta and became interested with F. A. Neider in the wholesale manufacture of carriage hardware, in which business he has continued until the present time.

In the Prohibition State Convention held in Louisville, June, 1895, he was nominated for election to the office of State Treasurer. This honor was conferred by his party, not only as a recognition of his valuable services in the party, but on account of his unquestioned integrity and other qualifications for a position requiring the services of a strictly honest man. Mr. Asbury has taken quite an active and aggressive part in the battle for prohibition, and is a recognized leader in the affairs and counsels of his party; and unlike most politicians, he very consistently combines his politics with his religion, having been a member of the Methodist Episcopal Church since he was fifteen years of age.

Mr. Asbury has been twice married. His first wife was Tolitha B. Hitch, daughter of Maria (Cramer) and Archie Hitch. She was born October 22, 1839, died November 8, 1885. His present wife, whom he married February 26, 1892, was Minnie Hollis, daughter of B. O. Hollis, a resident of Bracken County, near Brookville. By his first marriage there were three children born: Taylor Asbury, born December 20, 1860, now a farmer in Bracken County, near Germantown, married Estella Byar; Nina Mai, born May 22, 1866, studied medicine under Dr. J. M. Patterson of Augusta, graduated from the Cleveland Medical College of Homoeopathy in 1892, married E. Sherman Stevens of Ohio, with whom she was sent as a Missionary to Japan by the Christian Church; and Jessie J., born March 16, 1877. Henry Bryan, born October 2, 1893, is the only child of the second marriage.

JUSTUS J. HETSCH, postmaster of Newport, and publisher of the Kentucky Journal, one of the best known and most popular men in his city, was born in Newport, Kentucky, September 2, 1851. He enjoyed all of the advantages of the excellent city schools, graduating from the Newport High School and then taking a classical course of five years in Baldwin University and German Wallace College of Berea, Ohio, graduating with distinction in 1869.

He was inclined to a professional career and began the battle of life as a teacher in the public schools of Newport and was thus employed for three years, when he resigned to engage in the newspaper and printing business; was made president of the Newport Printing and Newspaper Company which was organized in 1872, and has been its president until the present time.

In 1876, during the memorable Tilden campaign, his company established the Kentucky Journal, a vigorous Democratic newspaper, which at once became popular throughout Kentucky on account of the aggressive and progressive position it assumed in national and state politics. During the nineteen years of its healthy existence, the Journal has lost none of its popularity and has maintained a circulation and patronage that few papers in the state have ever enjoyed.

Mr. Hetsch has been and is a Democrat "in season and out of season," and the valuable services which he has rendered his party, personally as well as through the medium of the Journal, have been recognized not only in local affairs but throughout the state. In recognition of his services and of his ability as a party leader, his friends secured his appointment by President Cleveland as Postmaster of Newport, and he took charge of the postoffice July 6, 1893. He has greatly improved and facilitated the business of the office to the entire satisfaction of the public, and is one of the most accommodating and efficient postmasters Newport has had since it became a city.

Mr. Hetsch served his county for six years as Courthouse Commissioner. He has held other public positions of trust, and is a member of a number of benevolent orders, including Masons and Knights Templar, in each of which he is enthusiastic and popular.

He was married November 30, 1892, to Anna S. Reichel, a most estimable lady of Newport.

OTWAY W. RASH, a former druggist and a well-known business man and farmer of Henderson, son of Benjamin L. and Agnes J. (Nisbet) Rash, was born in Hopkins County, Kentucky, January 30, 1850. His father was also born in that county in 1819, where he still resides and is now retired, having been a farmer nearly all his life. He is an elder in the Christian Church, in which he has been an active and influential officebearer for many years. His father was Stephen Rash, who was a well-known resident of Hopkins County for many years.

Agnes J. Nisbet Rash (mother) was born in Hopkins County, where she resided during her whole life, and died January 1, 1877. Her father, James Nisbet, was a Virginian by birth, who came to Hopkins County when he was a child in company with his father, James Nisbet, Sr., who was a native of Virginia and a soldier in the Revolutionary war. They were both well-to-do farmers in Hopkins County, where they lived and died and were buried.

Otway W. Rash was favored with an excellent common school education, remaining on his father's farm until he was seventeen years of age.

He then engaged as a clerk in the drugstore of N. M. Holeman, then in Madisonville, now proprietor of Dawson Springs. Two years later, in 1869, he was employed in the drugstore of J. B. Johnston in Henderson, and after one year's service with him, was similarly employed with George Lyne for four years; and, on the first of August, 1874, he embarked in the drug business on his own account. He continued in this until 1889, when he sold out and has for the past three years been engaged in the tobacco business, putting up strips for the English market, and is interested in several business enterprises of considerable magnitude. He is a director of the Planters Bank and is a member of the Henderson Board of Education. He steadily adheres to the faith of his father and mother, and is a member of the Christian Church.

Mr. Rash was married December 14, 1871, to Sallie E. Robertson, daughter of Alexander Robertson of Henderson County; and they have three sons living: James R., Otway W. and Benjamin Campbell Rash, who will no doubt follow the splendid example of their father and will become useful and highly respected citizens.

GUSTAVUS HOLZHAUER, deceased, a popular druggist and highly educated gentleman of Newport, was born in Wurtemberg, Germany, August 2, 1847. He was educated in the city of Stuttgart, where he studied the Latin, French and English languages. After leaving school he served an apprenticeship of three and a half years in a drug store and was employed as a clerk in the store for six months.

In July, 1866, when nineteen years of age, he came to America, locating at Madison, Indiana, where he was employed as a drug clerk for two years, when he removed to Newport and was similarly engaged until 1870, when he embarked in the drug business on his own account, and continued in that business for more than twenty-five years until his death, November 22, 1895, since which time the business has been conducted by his son, Louis P. Holzhauer.

Besides having the leading establishment of the kind in the city, Mr. Holzhauer was financially interested in a number of other enterprises. He was a stockholder and director in the Newport National Bank, of which he was one of the organizers; a director in the Covington Mutual Fire Insurance Company; a member of the Board of School Trustees, representing the Fifth Ward; president of the Lincoln League Club; and was quite prominent in local Republican politics.

He was frequently urged by influential citizens, without regard to party politics, to become a candidate for office, particularly for the Mayoralty of Newport; but he had no personal ambition for office, being interested in politics from a conviction of duty and with a view to securing the best men for offices of trust. There was none of the selfish nature in his political work which characterizes the latter day politician.

Mr. Holzhauer was a member of St. Paul's Lutheran Church, and a member of the Newport Lodge and Newport Commandery of Free and Accepted Masons, in both of which he was a useful and influential worker and a liberal helper of others.

Mr. Holzhauer was married in 1872 to Amelia Kauther of Cincinnati, Ohio. He had one son and three daughters: Louis P. Holzhauer, who, until his father's death, was in charge of Ingram & Company's Chemical Laboratory, Detroit, Michigan. The daughters are Edna, Irma and Clara.

Mr. Holzhauer's father was a flour miller in Germany, and was in comfortable circumstances. He and his wife died in Wurtemberg.

E. E. ABBETT, Deputy Internal Revenue Collector, Covington, son of Henry J. and Mary J. F. (Gill) Abbett, was born in Warsaw, August 20, 1855. Henry J. Abbett was born January 27, 1811, in Philadelphia, Pennsylvania. He served an apprenticeship with a cabinet maker and received his education at night schools; removed to Carrollton, Kentucky, where he subsequently read law with Judge Winslow. He removed from Carrollton to Warsaw, where he practiced law successfully for many years; represented Gallatin County in the State Legislature in 1845; was afterward County Attorney and served for two terms as County Judge. He continued his practice until 1880, when, on account of ill health, he retired and lived quietly until his death in 1889. He was president of the Warsaw Deposit Bank from its organization to the time of his death, a period of about fifteen years. During the war he sympathized with the South and adhered to the principles of the Democratic party; was a prominent Odd Fellow and a charter member of Kentucky Lodge No. 39. He was quiet in manner and a man of sterling character. His father, Jonathan Abbett, was born in Pennsylvania, August 11, 1775, and died August 21, 1821. His wife was Eliza H. McDowell. William Abbett (great-grandfather), wedded Catherine Cunnard.

Mary J. F. Gill Abbett (mother) was the daughter of William Gill, and was a native of Virginia; born in 1825; removed to Fleming County, from thence to Gallatin County, where she and Henry J. Abbett were married, April 27, 1841. She now resides in Warsaw, and is in the seventy-first year of her age. Her father was also a native of Virginia, a miller by trade, and a major in the War of 1812. Her maternal grandfather, Samuel Roundtree, was a major in the Revolutionary War.

E. E. Abbett was one of five children of Henry J. and Mary J. F. Abbett. His primary education was received partly in private schools, and in 1873 he attended the Kentucky Military Institute in Franklin County. In 1874 he studied in the Ohio Medical College, preparing for the medical profession, which idea he relinquished and came to Covington as division deputy under Collector George H. Davison, which position he filled for two years, when he was promoted to the chief deputyship and held this important position until July, 1889. In 1893 Mr. Abbett became chief deputy collector of internal revenue of the Sixth district under Collector Davezac, and at present occupies this position. Previous to his accepting his present place, Mr. Abbett held the office of County Superintendent of Public Schools in Gallatin County, which office he resigned to accept the deputyship under President Cleveland's first administration. On December 10, 1878, Mr. Abbett was united in marriage to Nannie Chambers, a daughter of Dr. A. B. Chambers of Gallatin County, and they have four children: Anna G., born January 25, 1880; Harry, born August 29, 1884; Edward B., born October 20, 1888; Leon G., born November 4, 1891.

CHARLES BARRINGTON SIMRALL, a distinguished corporation lawyer, son of John W. G. and Mary Barton Simrall, was born in Madison, Indiana, February 18, 1843. The Simrall family came originally from Scotland in the early part of the eighteenth century and settled in Pennsylvania, from whence they moved to Virginia, and were later among the earliest settlers in Kentucky, as early as 1776.

On his mother's side Mr. Simrall is descended from the French Huguenots, who fled from France on the revocation of the Edict of Nantes. They came to America about 1687, and settled in South Carolina and Georgia.

Mr. Simrall was for several years a student at Miami University, Oxford, Ohio, and completed his general education in Tubingen, Germany. On his return from Europe he entered the Cincinnati Law School, from which he was graduated in 1867, and at once began the practice of his chosen profession in Cincinnati.

He is attorney for the following railroad companies: The Cincinnati Southern, for which he has been the general attorney for Kentucky since 1869; the Chesapeake & Ohio Railway Company, the Cincinnati, New Orleans & Texas Pacific Railroad Company, and the South Covington & Cincinnati Street Railway Company, besides various banks and manufacturing companies. He is the vice-president of the German National Bank of Covington, and is connected as director in various other corporate enterprises. He has made corporate law a specialty, and devotes his time almost exclusively to that branch of the practice.

Mr. Simrall is a Democrat in politics, but has never participated actively therein.

He is a member of the Masonic Fraternity, and belongs to the First Presbyterian Church of Covington.

In 1868 Mr. Simrall was married to Isabella Downing Price, daughter of John and Josephine Downing Price of Covington.

Mrs. Simrall was educated at Daughter's College, Harrodsburg, Ky. They have six daughters.

Though Mr. Simrall's practice is for the most part in Cincinnati, he has resided in Covington for over forty years, of which place he is a prominent citizen, having been much interested in municipal affairs and the bettering of the condition of the city.

REV. JAMES OSGOOD ANDREW VAUGHT, pastor of the Methodist Episcopal Church, South, Versailles, is the son of William P. and Ann L. (Gragg) Vaught. His father was a native of Wythe County, Virginia, and came with his parents when a child to Kentucky and located near Somerset. In 1865 he removed to Harrodsburg, where he now resides. He was a farmer and a local preacher in the Methodist Church, but is now retired, being seventy-three years of age.

Andrew Vaught (grandfather) was a native of Wythe County, Virginia. After removing to Kentucky he resided in or near Somerset until he died at the age of ninety-five. The Vaughts came to this country about the year 1780, and they have been prominent in the Methodist Church for over one hundred years. Rev. S. K. Vaught (uncle), who died a few years ago, was one of the most distinguished ministers in the Methodist Church in West Virginia.

Ann L. Gragg Vaught (mother) is a native of Pulaski County and is now in her sixty-sixth year, and a mother in the Methodist Church.

Elisha P. Gragg (grandfather) was a native of Pulaski County, where he resided until the time of his death in his seventieth year. His father was a native of Virginia, but removed to Kentucky about 1790.

The Graggs are of English descent, and, like the Vaughts, have been Methodists for over one hundred years.

Rev. James O. A. Vaught was born in Somerset, February 9, 1847. He received the best education the schools of Somerset could afford and then went to Harmonia College, Russellville, Indiana, and graduated in 1870. In the following year he entered the ministry of the Methodist Episcopal Church, South. Among the principal places where he has had charge are Clarksburg and Point Pleasant, West Virginia; Ashland, Catlettsburg, Paris, Newport, Millersburg, Richmond, Harrodsburg and Versailles, Kentucky, to which last named place he came in 1895. This is one of the leading churches in the state. Bishop Kavanaugh was married in Versailles and spent thirty years of his life there.

Mr. Vaught and Annie E., daughter of C. S. Ulen of Catlettsburg, were married in 1873. They have one son and four daughters living: Anna Louise, Kate H., Stephen K., Sarah H., Mattie M. Miss Kate H. Vaught, second daughter, is Professor of Sciences in Millersburg Female College.

GEORGE LEE WILLIS, editor of the Frankfort Capital, is the son of Rev. Jackson S. and Mary J. (Long) Willis. His father was a native of Madison County and moved to Shelby County when a young man, where he resided until the time of his death in 1883. He was a minister in the Christian Church and a preacher in Shelby County for forty years. During the war his sympathies were decidedly with the Southern people, and he narrowly escaped arrest on account of his fearless expression of opinion.

Henry Willis (grandfather) was a native of Virginia, who removed to Kentucky with other members of his family and located in Madison County about the beginning of the present century. He was a farmer on an extensive scale. He belonged to an old Virginia family of English descent.

Mary J. Long Willis was a native of Shelby County. She died in 1870, aged forty-eight years.

Alexander Long (grandfather) was a farmer in Woodford and Shelby Counties, and died in Shelby County at the age of seventy years.

George L. Willis was born in Shelby County August 4, 1862. He received a good education, and in 1886 went to Louisville, where for five years he was engaged in the different newspaper offices as reporter, city editor, telegraph editor, etc., and in December, 1889, he was sent to Frankfort as legislative correspondent for the Courier-Journal and the Evening Times. He

JUDGE W. E. ARTHUR.

filled this position acceptably until January, 1894, when the Weekly Capital was converted into a daily newspaper, and he was chosen editor. The Capital is the successor of the old "Kentucky Yeoman," which was established in 1840. It is a local newspaper, the state official paper, and, like its editor, Democratic in politics.

Mr. Willis was married in December, 1892, to Ruth Stanton, daughter of Major Henry T. Stanton, Kentucky's poet laureate.

MALCOLM YEAMAN, a successful lawyer and respected citizen of Henderson, was born in Hardin County, Kentucky, March 9, 1841. His father, Stephen Minor Yeaman, was born in Meade County in 1799. He removed to Hardin County, where he was engaged in farming until his death in 1854.

Malcolm Yeaman's mother, Lucretia Helm, was born in 1809. She survived her husband until 1886, retaining the full vigor of a bright intellect to the last. She was a life-time member of the Methodist Episcopal Church, and was a beloved and exemplary Christian woman. The education of the younger members of her large family devolved upon her after her husband's death, and she devoted herself to this work with a result that was exceedingly gratifying to her in her declining years. Her eldest son, John H. Yeaman, was a minister in the Baptist Church, who died soon after entering the ministry. George H. Yeaman, an eminent lawyer, served two terms in Congress from the Second Kentuck District, and was for six years United States Minister Plenipotentiary to Copenhagen, subsequently locating in New York in the practice of law, where he now resides. William Pope Yeaman is one of the leading Baptist ministers in Missouri. Harvey Yeaman was a brilliant lawyer in Henderson, who removed to Louisville, and subsequently to Colorado, where he died. Malcolm Yeaman was the fifth son. Caldwell Yeaman, who studied law with his brother Malcolm, went to Colorado and soon took rank among the leading lawyers of that state; established a number of successful business enterprises and for several years filled the office of Circuit Judge, and now resides in Denver. Mary Lucretia Yeaman, the only daughter and the youngest child, died when she was just blooming into young womanhood.

Malcolm Yeaman read law with his brother, George H. Yeaman, in Owensboro, and was admitted to the bar in 1861, and since 1863 has devoted his whole time to the practice of his profession in Henderson. He has adhered to his purpose to resist the temptations to gain wealth or fame by any other than the legitimate pursuit of his chosen profession.

Although a democrat, he has not sought political preferment; and being a man of business ability might have made money in many of the avenues that are always open to men of judgment and moderate capital, but the allurements of wealth and the honors of office have not been permitted to turn him aside from the higher purpose to be a successful lawyer, faithful to those who entrust their cause to his keeping and upholding the high standard of his honorable calling. With such a purpose kept steadily in view, Mr. Yeaman has attained success in an eminent degree, and has won the confidence and esteem of the intelligent people in the enlightened community in which he lives. He is an elder in the Presbyterian Church, and a citizen in whom all who know him have the utmost confidence.

Mr. Yeaman was married in 1861 to Julia Van Pradells Moore, daughter of Dr. John R. Moore, for many years a leading physician in Louisville, who removed to Pettis County, Missouri, a short time before the Civil war. They have still living four sons and two daughters: Rev. Marion V. P. Yeaman, a minister in the Presbyterian Church; Lelia, wife of W. J. Marshall, Jr., of Henderson; Dr. Malcolm H. Yeaman, a physician just entering the practice; Harvey Yeaman and James M. Yeaman, who are studying law, and Julia, now in school. Their oldest son, John Rochester, was, with several companions, drowned in Puget Sound in May, 1893.

WILLIAM E. ARTHUR. The paternal grandfather of Mr. Arthur was the Reverend William Arthur, who was graduated at the University of Glasgow, Scotland, and was consecrated to the service of God as a clergyman of the Presbyterian Church. He was united in marriage with Agnes Gammel of Scotland and subsequently in the course of his ministry came to the United States in 1793, and was located at intervals in Maryland, New York, Pennsylvania and finally in Ohio, where he died many years since at Zanesville. He left seven children: Michael, William, John, Gammel, Jane, Margaret and Nancy.

William Arthur (father) was born in the County of Lancaster, Pennsylvania, in 1798, and was educated by his parents. He was prepared for the bar, but became a merchant. He was married to Eliza Parsons of Maryland, who was the second daughter of William and Sarah Parsons of Harford County, Maryland.

William E. Arthur is a native of Cincinnati, Ohio, and was born March 3, 1825. In 1832 his parents with their children were permanently settled at Covington, Kentucky, and in 1834 his father died. Judge Arthur was educated at private schools and by private tutors in Covington and in Harford County, Maryland. He was prepared for the bar in the office of the Honorable John W. Stevenson and Honorable James T. Morehead, who were his law preceptors. In 1850 he was admitted to the bar by Honorable William F. Bullock, then of the Sixth Judicial District, and the Honorable James Prior, then of the Eighth Judicial District of Kentucky, and immediately thereafter entered upon the practice of his profession. In 1856 he was elected by the Democratic party attorney for the Commonwealth of Kentucky in the Ninth Judicial District, and served for a term of six years. In the Presidential campaign of 1860 he was the Democratic elector for the Tenth Congressional District on the ticket of Breckenridge and Lane. In 1866 he was elected by the same party Judge of the Criminal Court for the Ninth Judicial District for a term of six years. He served two years, resigning in 1868. In 1870 he was elected to the Forty-second Congress from the Sixth Congressional District; was re-elected to the Forty-third Congress in 1872, and served through both terms on Committee on Elections and on a Committee on Railways and Canals.

Among Judge Arthur's speeches of any length in the House were those on the following subjects: Executive Despotism and Congressional Usurpation, the House having under consideration the bill (H. R. No. 320) to enforce the provisions of the fourteenth amendment to the Constitution of the United States and for other purposes. (March 31, 1871.)

Texas Election. The House having under consideration the following resolution (January 10, 1872):

Resolved, That W. T. Clark has a prima facie right to a seat as Representative from the Third Congressional District of the State of Texas and is entitled to take the oath of office as a Member of this House, without prejudice to the right of any person claiming to have been elected thereto, to contest his right to said seat upon the merits.

The Decline of Local Self-Government and Advance of Centralism, the House having met for debate in Committee of the Whole on the State of the Union (March 2, 1872).

Election Contest—Gooding versus Wilson. The House having under consideration the report of the Committee on Elections upon the contested electon case of Gooding versus Wilson from the Fourth District of Indiana. (April 22, 1872.)

Profusion of the Union and Profligacy of the Administration. The House having met for debate in Committee of the Whole on the state of the Union. (May 4, 1872.)

Free Trade—Inter-State Commerce. The House having under consideration the bill (H. R. No. 1385) to regulate commerce. (March 3 and 4, 1874.)

In August, 1886, he was elected by his party Judge of the Circuit Court for the Twelfth Judicial District and served out his term, ending January 1, 1893, when he resumed the practice of law.

In 1855 Judge Arthur was united in marriage with Addie Southgate, daughter of the late Honorable W. W. Southgate, and after her decease in 1858, in December, 1860, he wedded Etha Southgate, a younger sister of his first wife. By the last marriage Judge Arthur has two children surviving, Sidney and May. Sidney Arthur is a graduate of Dartmouth College of the class of 1887 and of the Law School of the Cincinnati College of the class of 1890, and has entered on the practice of his profession with his father. May Arthur was educated at the Bartholomew English and Classical School of Cincinnati, and at Madame Fredin's French and English School, Eden Park, Walnut Hills, of the same city.

REV. DANIEL STEVENSON, D. D., President of Union College, Barbourville, was born in Versailles, Woodford County, Kentucky, November 12th, 1823. His father, Daniel Stevenson, born in Mason County, moved to Versailles when a young man, and soon afterward married Miss Elizabeth West of Scott County. Thomas Stevenson, the paternal grandfather, a native of Frederick County, Maryland, married Miss Sarah Evans, daughter of Job Evans, of the same state and county, and one of the seven or eight persons composing the first class of Methodists that was formed in America. In 1786 Thomas Stevenson, with his wife and children, moved to Kentucky, then a part of Virginia, descending the Ohio River in a flatboat, and landing at what is now Maysville, but soon took up his residence at Kenton Station, near Washington, in Mason County. The maternal grandfather, Thomas West, was born in Virginia, where he married Miss Atha Fant. They came to Kentucky at a little later period than the Stevensons, and settled in Scott County.

Dr. Stevenson's rudimentary education was received at schools in and near Versailles. For a time he was a clerk in a store; entered Transylvania University at Lexington in 1843, and graduated there in 1847, taking one of the honors of his class. The following winter he spent in Mississippi, teaching and studying law, and the winter next after that in Clark County, Kentucky, teaching. He was then elected to a professorship in Whitewater Female College, Centerville, Indiana. In 1849 he married, in Kentucky, Miss Sarah Ann Corwine, daughter of Rev. Richard and Mrs. Sarah Corwine, the father being of the Corwine family of Salem, Massachusetts, and the mother, of the Hitt family of Virginia.

In 1850 Dr. Stevenson resigned his position in Whitewater College and returned, with his wife and their infant child, to Kentucky, and opened a girls' school in Versailles. In the autumn of 1851, having previously begun to preach, he became a member of the Kentucky Conference of the Methodist Episcopal Church, South, and was stationed, successively, at Orangeburg, Taylorsville, Danville, Newport, Carrollton Millersburg, Shelbyville, Frankfort.

During the Civil war he was decidedly in favor of the preservation of the Union, and in the Union Convention held in 1863 for the nomination of candidates for the state offices he was nominated for the office of Superintendent of Public Instruction, and, with the other nominees on the ticket, was elected. Up to this time the clerical work of this office had been done in the Auditor's office. There was no separate room and no separate clerkship for the Department of Education. Dr. Stevenson secured provision for both from the Legislature, and the system and order which he introduced into the work of the office soon began to have their effect in the schools throughout the state. In addition to this he did a great deal of visiting in different parts of the state in promotion of the cause of common school education. At the expiration of his term of office in 1867 he was renominated for the position by the Republican Convention, but the entire ticket was defeated.

At the close of the war in 1865, he, with seventeen other members of the Kentucky Conference of the Methodist Episcopal Church, South, withdrew therefrom in consequence of the bitter opposition which was made by the majority of the members of the Conference to their advocacy of the idea of the reunion of the dissevered parts of Episcopal Methodism, and united with the Methodist Episcopal Church.

On going out of office in 1867 he preached for a time at Parkersburg, West Virginia, and then at Lexington, Kentucky. Under his pastorate at this place the beautiful Methodist Church on Broadway was built. He was next in the Presiding Eldership, then pastor of Trinity Church, Louisville, after which he went to New England, where he spent four years and a half as a member of the New Hampshire Conference.

Returning to Kentucky in 1879, he opened the Augusta Collegiate Institute in the Old Augusta College building, Augusta. He resigned his position at this place in 1886, and soon thereafter became president of Union College at Barbourville, in which capacity he is now acting.

Dr. Stevenson has always taken a deep interest in the cause of education in his own church. He was one of the founders of the Wesleyan College, originally at Millersburg, but now at Winchester. He is an earnest advocate of higher education among the ministers of his church, and has done much to raise the standard of ministerial education in his own Conference. His special work in his present position is the training of young men for the ministry. He is deeply interested, moreover, in the history of the Methodist Church in Kentucky, and also in the history of the state. He is a member of the Filson Club of Louisville.

Dr. Stevenson is recognized as one of the leading Methodist ministers in Kentucky, and has been twice elected to represent his Conference in the General Conference. He is a contributor to the church papers, and has published two or three books. He received the title of A. M. in cursu, from his Alma Mater, and that of Doctor of Divinity from the Ohio Wesleyan University.

Dr. Stevenson was the only one of the state officers elected with him in 1863 who voted for Mr. Lincoln for re-election as President in 1864. He has for some time been voting with the Prohibition party. In 1887 he was nominated by that party for the office of Superintendent of Public Instruction, in his absence from the nominating convention. He is clear in his political views, but is in no sense a politician.

Dr. and Mrs. Stevenson have had seven children, three of whom are dead. Of the four living, one is a member of the North Ohio Conference, and Professor of History in the Ohio Wesleyan University; another is the wife of Rev. J. W. Sutherland, pastor of the Congregational Church at Webster Groves, Mo.; another the wife of Mr. J. E. Dunbar, a merchant of Augusta, Kentucky, and the other a lawyer in Des Moines, Iowa.

PATRICK McDONALD, of Frankfort, is a son of John and Margaret (Purcell) McDonald; was born in Schuylkill County, Pennsylvania, November 14, 1847. His father was born in Ireland, and came to the United States at an early age, and after remaining in Kentucky a short while removed to Pennsylvania, and then back to Kentucky, locating at Frankfort. There he remained until his death, in May, 1866. He was an industrious man, and was popular with everyone. He was a member of the Catholic Church, in which faith he died. He was twice married, his last wife being Miss Bridget Donoghue, who preceded him to the grave in 1864.

Patrick McDonald is well known throughout the state. When his parents located in Frankfort he was but two years old. His mother died when he was too young to realize the great loss, and this was followed by his father's death before he arrived at an age to be able to care for an infant half-brother and sister, who were left on his hands for support. At the age of twelve years he entered the old Yeoman office, then owned by Col. S. I. M. Major, where he learned the printer's trade, serving as foreman, job printer and manager, holding the last position until the paper suspended in 1886.

Mr. McDonald started the "Western Argus" the same year. It is a weekly twenty-eight column Democratic paper, with a rapidly increasing circulation, which he still owns and edits, his son Patrick, Jr., aiding as assistant editor. He is open in his opinions on any subject, and upon all public matters expresses himself freely. He was justice of the peace of Frankfort for over twenty years, his last term expiring January 1, 1895. He has been prominent in Frankfort's history for more than twenty years. He originated and constructed an electric street car line five miles in length and was a warm advocate of all public improvements.

He was second assistant clerk of the House of Representatives of Kentucky during the sessions of 1885-86, and was enrolling clerk of the Senate of Kentucky from 1887 to 1891. He was president of the Board of Trade of Frankfort for one term, and for five years was treasurer of the Sinking Fund Commissioners of Franklin County. During his term as justice of the peace he was the leader in public improvements in the county, and during his term of office more than one hundred miles of turnpike were constructed in the county; while the bridge system was improved by the erection of iron bridges in place of the old wooden structures, the last being the destruction of the old wooden bridge connecting North and South Frankfort, which has been replaced by a beautiful steel structure at a cost of sixty-five thousand dollars.

He was the delegate to the World's Columbian Catholic Congress from the Frankfort diocese at the World's Fair.

Mr. McDonald has always taken an active part in political affairs, no one ever questioning his Democracy, which is of the Andrew Jackson type.

He was married in September, 1866, to Ann Flynn of Frankfort. They have one son, Patrick, and one daughter, Jennie.

McCAULEY C. SWINFORD of Cynthiana, son of John P. and Sallie (Terry) Swinford, was born in Pendleton County, March 24, 1857.

His father, John Patterson Swinford, was born in Harrison County, April 8, 1828; and for the past fifteen years has been a resident farmer of Fleming County.

William Swinford (grandfather) was a native of Harrison County, where he owned a farm which has belonged to the Swinford family for five generations and which now belongs to McCauley C. Swinford.

The great-grandfather Swinford was a native of North Carolina and was one of the very early settlers of Harrison County. His ancestors were from England.

Sallie Terry Swinford (mother) died in 1859, when McCauley was two years old. She was a native of Harrison County. Her father, William Terry, was born in Spottsylvania County, Virginia; moved to Harrison County, where he lived to an advanced age.

McCauley C. Swinford, after leaving school and quitting the farm, began the study of law in the office of Judge John Q. Ward, then a prominent attorney in Cynthiana, and also with Louis M. Morlin, and was admitted to the bar October 9, 1879. Having been a faithful student at home and in the law offices, he was well equipped for the lucrative practice which he has enjoyed since entering the profession.

In November, 1889, he formed a law partnership with D. L. Evans under the firm name of Swinford & Evans; and success has followed this relationship up to the present time.

In October, 1882, he was elected County School Commissioner, and in 1884 he was elected for two years again, the name of the office being changed to Superintendent of Public Schools. In August, 1886, he was elected County Attorney for a term of four years, and in August, 1890, he was reelected and held the office of County Attorney until January, 1895. At no time did he have any opposition, either for the nomination or for the election.

In the County Democratic Convention, held May 11, 1895, he received the nomination for representative in the State Legislature, and was elected in November, 1895, over John W. Mattox, the Republican candidate, by 501 majority.

Mr. Swinford and Mrs. Nannie T. Smith, daughter of James C. King of Harrison County, were married March 2, 1880. They have three sons and one daughter: Virgil C., Urban M., Charles L. and Annie.

JAMES S. WITHERS, cashier of the National Bank of Cynthiana, was born in Cynthiana, September 4, 1830. His father, William A. Withers, was born in Stafford County, Virginia, in 1798, and came to Kentucky in 1812. He lived for a short time in Mason County, but removed to Harrison County, where he had his residence until the time of his unfortunate death in 1864. He was killed at the siege of Jackson, Mississippi, while moving some furniture belonging to his son, Col. William T. Withers of the Confederate artillery. He was a drygoods merchant in Cynthiana and was visiting his son when he was killed. He was not in the service himself.

Benjamin Withers (grandfather) was a native of Stafford County, Virginia, and, after removing to Kentucky in 1812, was a farmer in Harrison County. His ancestors were English and were related to the celebrated poet, Robert Withers, of Witheral. He was a Lieutenant in the war of the Revolution and was present at the surrender of Yorktown.

Eliza Perrin Withers (mother) was a native of Harrison County. She was born in 1806 and died in 1848. Her father, Archibald Perrin, was a Kentuckian, of French descent. He died in 1863.

James S. Withers, after attending the best schools in the county, attended the University of Missouri, graduating in 1853. He succeeded his father in the drygoods business in Cynthiana until 1857, when he became cashier of the Deposit Bank of Cynthiana, which was merged into the Commercial Bank of Kentucky in 1862. In 1871 it was nationalized, since which time it has been known as the National Bank of Cynthiana. It is one of the most substantial banking houses in the interior of the state, having a capital of one hundred and fifty thousand dollars and a surplus of ninety thousand dollars. Mr. Withers has been cashier of this bank since its organization in 1857, and has probably served as a bank cashier longer than any one in Kentucky. He is one of the most careful bankers in the state and enjoys the confidence of his associates in business and of the entire community.

Mr. Withers was married in May, 1856, to Kittie Remington, daughter of Greenup Remington of Harrison County. They have one son and two daughters living: Eliza, wife of Joseph W. Davis of Paris; Elizabeth, wife of Bailey D. Berry of Cynthiana, and Rodney S. Withers.

Mr. Withers belongs to the Christian Church, of which his father and mother and his grandfather were devoted members.

JOHN A. WILLIAMSON, a retired steamboat captain and a man well and favorably known on the river between Cincinnati and New Orleans, and for many years a resident of Newport, was born in Portsmouth, Ohio, June 9, 1826. He is the son of Samuel Williamson, a native of Norfolk, Virginia, who moved to Charleston, West Virginia, where he married Mary Slack in 1808, and made his home there until 1825. He was one of the first men who discovered salt on the Kanawha in 1809 or 1810. He taught school for awhile, having received a good education. In 1825 he concluded to move west with his family and started down the river in a flatboat and when he reached Portsmouth, Ohio, he stopped near the mouth of the Scioto and remained there for four or five months. During that time his son, John A., the subject of this sketch, was born. Then he moved across the river to a farm in Kentucky and followed farming until the spring of 1833, when he removed to Newport. This occurred, unfortunately, during the cholera plague, which was fatal to so many in 1833, and of which disease he died soon after his arrival at Newport, being forty-eight years of age. His wife was a native of Pennsylvania and died in Newport in 1879, aged eighty-nine years.

Capt. John A. Williamson has lived in Newport since 1833, and his education was limited to a few months in private schools. At the age of fifteen years he went to work on a steamboat that ran from Cincinnati to New Orleans, and became a pilot before he was eighteen years of age. In 1852 he attended as a delegate the Louisville convention that drafted the law known as steamboat inspection law, which required every pilot and engineer to have a license. He soon acquired an interest in a line of boats and continued on the river until 1870, and held a large interest in this line until 1882. From 1870 to 1876 Captain Williamson operated a full line of boats between Cincinnati and St. Louis, and at the same time owned and managed a boat store.

In 1871 he bought the street railway at Newport and operated it successfully until 1891, when he sold out. He owned the Newport ferry from 1866 to 1874. In 1884 he conceived the idea of building the Central railroad bridge across the Ohio river between Newport and Cincinnati, and organized a company to build and operate the bridge, which was completed August 29, 1891. It was incorporated under the name of the Central Railway and Bridge Company, of which he has been the president since its inception. It was chartered by Kentucky as the Central Railway and Bridge Company, and by the state of Ohio as the Central Bridge Company.

For fourteen years Captain Williamson was president of the Newport Light Company, and has been for many years identified with the business interests and material growth of Newport, and he is one of her best and most enterprising citizens.

In 1848 he was married to Elizabeth Kirby in Cincinnati and they have one son living, Lawrence Williamson.

The house in which Captain Williamson lives has been his home since February 22, 1850.

HON. ANDREW HARRISON WARD, attorney-at-law of Cynthiana, was born in Harrison County, January 3, 1815. His parents were Andrew and Elizabeth (Headington) Ward. His father was a native of Culpeper County, Virginia, who became one of the pioneers of Harrison County, where he died in 1842 at the age of seventy-two years. He was a soldier in the war of 1812, and in the subsequent Indian wars under Gen. Harrison, for whom his son was named. He was a favored nephew of Gen. William Ward, a Revolutionary soldier, a brother of Artemus Ward, who was voted for, for commander of the Colonial army. Gen. William Ward gave Andrew Ward a section of land in Champaign County, Ohio, several town lots in Urbana, and six acres of land on Mud River for a tannery, on condition that Andrew, who was a tanner, would teach William Ward's son the trade. Accordingly he took up his residence in Ohio and was the first white man who lived in Urbana. The Indians drove him away shortly before he entered the war of 1812. His father's name was Andrew Ward, a native of Virginia, who with six brothers fought in the Revolutionary war. The Wards are of Irish extraction, but resided in England several years before coming to America.

Elizabeth Headington Ward was born in Baltimore County, Maryland, in 1773. She came to Kentucky when only twelve years of age, while the Indians were hostile and when schools were out of the question. She died in Harrison County in 1840. Her father, Zebulon Headington, was a Virginian. He married in Maryland and came to Kentucky in 1785 and settled in Harrison County, where he spent the remainder of his days. He died in 1839, when within a few months of one hundred years of age. He too was a Revolutionary soldier, serving in the commissary department, and was on his way to Yorktown and so near that he could hear the heavy guns firing when he learned that Cornwallis had surrendered.

Andrew Harrison Ward when a boy divided his time between the ordinary farm labors and the winter schools. After reaching the limit of the county school teacher's resources he went to Transylvania University. In 1842 he began the study of law and was admitted to the bar in 1844, beginning his professional career in Cynthiana at once, where he has enjoyed a lucrative practice in both civil and criminal law ever since. The old lawyers of his acquaintance agree that he has been engaged in more cases of capital offense than any other living lawyer in the state. He defended the first and only case of treason ever tried in Kentucky. In 1884 he was employed to go to North Dakota to defend twenty-four indictments, two each against twelve persons charged with murder. He never defended a client who was hung, and no one of them ever got more than ten years in the penitentiary.

In his earlier years he was a whig and since the extinction of that party he has been a democrat, but he has never regretted his early political education. In 1863 he was elected to the Legislature, in which he served with distinction until 1865. In 1866 he was elected to Congress, and at the expiration of the XXXIX. Congress he retired from public life, steadily refusing office, but still retaining an active interest in politics. He never asked for, or sought any office. His nomination and election to Congress was without his seeking. He has voted fifteen times for President and has been an active presidential campaigner since 1840.

He was not a soldier in the Civil war, but he helped to defend his town and was one of the three hundred and thirty citizens of Cynthiana who gave Gen. Morgan his first fight when he undertook to raid the town. He was opposed to the rebellion. Mr. Ward has been married three times. First to Ellen V. Moore of Harrison County, September, 1846. She died in 1848, leaving one daughter, Mollie M., now the wife of George T. Gaddy of Woodford County. His first wife's grandmother was a cousin of Gen.

William Henry Harrison, for whom Mr. Ward cast his first presidential vote, and his last one against Benjamin Harrison, his grandson. His second marriage was to Elizabeth Ware of Cynthiana, December 31, 1857. She died in 1865, and on the 28th of April, 1868, he married Helen H. Lair of Cynthiana, and by this union he has three sons and two daughters: Bertie M., wife of Judge W. T. Lafferty of Cynthiana; Harry R., Catherine, Paul S., and Ashley F. Ward.

Although he is now past four score years, Mr. Ward is still actively engaged in the practice of his profession, and has lost none of his reputation as one of the leading lawyers of the state. He is a prominent member of the Christian Church, and is Superintendent of the Sunday School, and teacher of its Bible class.

He enjoys the confidence and respect of the profession with which he has been prominently identified for over fifty years; of the community in which he has lived all his life, and of the church in which he has been a leading spirit, and in the Sunday School in which he holds the position usually surrendered to younger men. His years have apparently had no effect upon his vitality, and his arduous labors only serve to keep him young.

CHAPEZE WATHEN, a descendant of an old and honored family of Kentucky and a distinguished lawyer and popular citizen of Owensboro, was born in Breckinridge County, Kentucky, February 10, 1858. His father, Benedict Wathen, was born in Baltimore, Maryland, August 15, 1801, and came to Kentucky with his parents when he was quite young. He received his primary education in Washington County; graduated from the Medical Department of Transylvania University and located at Hardinsburg, Breckinridge County, where he was a leading practicing physician for many years. Later he bought a farm, on which he spent the closing years of a useful life. This farm was known as Mount Merino, and upon it Dr. Wathen and his brother Richard, who was also a physician, established a high grade literary school, which they conducted, greatly to the advantage of the community. The matrimonial alliances of these two brothers were of a very unusual nature, in that they married four sisters. Benedict married Elizabeth Chapeze, and after her death married her sister, Eulalie Fleget Chapeze (mother); while Dr. Richard Wathen first married Susan Chapeze, a sister of Benedict's two wives, who died, and then he married Mary Chapeze, another sister; and thus four sisters were the wives of two brothers. The Wathens are descendants of English parentage.

Eulalie Chapeze (mother of Chapeze Wathen) is a native of Bardstown, Kentucky; was educated principally at St. Catherine Academy in Washington County and is now living in Breckinridge County in the seventy-first year of her age.

Benjamin Chapeze (grandfather) was born in Trenton, New Jersey, and received his education in the Catholic schools. When he came to Kentucky he followed farming for a while, studying law in the meantime. His pursuit of legal knowledge was made under difficulties, taking his books and notes to the field with him and studying at odd times. He was duly admitted to the bar in 1815 and located in Shepherdsville, where he practiced for two years; then went to Elizabethtown and was there two years. In 1820 he removed to Bardstown and practiced in Nelson, Meade, Hardin, Bullitt, Breckinridge, Spencer, Washington and Marion Counties, where he had a large clientele and was exceedingly popular on account of his splendid ability, unquestioned integrity and great force of character. He was known as "the Honest Lawyer," a very rare compliment in those days. He was very much of a gentleman—neat in dress, courteous and genial in manner and of fine personal attractions. He cared little for politics, but was twice an "Old Court" representative of Nelson County in the Legislature and a colleague of Ben Hardin. He afterward affiliated with the Jackson Republicans, who were called Democrats, and who, in Kentucky, had been for the most part, "New Court" men. In 1828 he was a presidential elector on the Jackson ticket, and was more or less prominent in state and national politics during the remainder of his brilliant career. In September, 1839, he defended a man charged with murder in Elizabethtown and, after speaking for two hours, he was overcome by exhaustion. The doctors were called and advised bleeding, and the little strength he had left was thus taken from him and he died nine days later, September 26, 1839. He died in the full confidence of the Catholic religion. Benjamin Chapeze was married May 7, 1812, to Elizabeth Shepherd, daughter of Adam Shepherd, an early settler, who was the first man who ventured to live outside of a fort in Bullitt County. The town of Shepherdsville, on Salt River, was named in his honor.

Dr. Henry Chapeze (great-grandfather) was a native of France, who came to America during the Revolution, and held the post of surgeon in the patriot army and after the war he married Sarah Kenny, a lady of Irish birth, and located in Bardstown, where he died in 1810.

Chapeze Wathen, a worthy descendant of a noble ancestry, was educated at St. Joseph College, Bardstown, and in the law department of the University of Louisville, from which latter institution he was graduated in March, 1881. He located in Brandenburg, and, after practicing alone for four years, was then associated with J. M. Richardson for eight years. He was Commonwealth Attorney of the then Sixth now Ninth Judicial District, from August, 1886, until 1893, this long term having been made possible by the new Constitution, and his excellent service for the state called forth the highest praise from the people.

In the spring of 1893 Mr. Wathen removed to Owensboro, a city in which he was by no means a stranger, his reputation as a dignified and capable lawyer and an elegant, courteous gentleman having preceded him. He found many friends, and has made many new ones in his new home, and has also found a field of labor quite congenial to his taste.

Mr. Wathen was married January 15, 1891, to Mary Fairleigh, daughter of James Fairleigh of Brandenburg. They have two daughters, Jane Murray and Eulalie. Mr. Wathen is a member of the Catholic Church and Mrs. Wathen is a Presbyterian.

ELIJAH DUDLEY WALKER, the leading lawyer of Hartford, son of Richard Logan and Mahala (Harris) Walker, and a descendant of one of the families whose names embellish the early history of the state, was born in Hartford, Kentucky, January 29, 1827. He received his literary training in the private schools of his native town, and began the study of law with Robert J. Smart in Independence, Missouri, when he was sixteen years of age, remaining there about twenty months. He was admitted to the practice of law in Missouri at the age of eighteen, but returned to Kentucky and read law with John H. McHenry (see biographical sketch) and was admitted to the Kentucky bar in 1846, when nineteen years of age. He began his brilliant career as a lawyer in Hartford 1849, and will soon have completed a half century of professional work, having made a name and fame that extends beyond the borders of his state.

He was elected to the State Senate in August, 1857, and was the youngest member of that body. After serving one term of four years he declined a re-election, preferring to devote himself exclusively to his profession. He has, however, given much of his time to the furtherance of the interests of the Democratic party, his most recent service in that capacity being on the platform committee in the convention of 1895, which nominated P. Wat. Hardin for Governor.

While Judge Walker's professional career has been marked by signal success, having been prominent in hundreds of cases, many of which have been of historic interest, and, while a record of his experiences as lawyer, judge, legislator and citizen would serve as an object lesson for ambitious young men, and would be of deep interest to the legal profession in Kentucky, it is the purpose of this sketch to place on record a brief history of the families of which he and his wife are worthy and honored descendants. It has cost him an effort to keep out of politics, his name having been mentioned for Governor and United States Senator under circumstances which would have fired the ambition of almost any other man who would have grasped the opportunity, and, with only a little effort, reached fame and national distinction.

Judge Walker was married August 17, 1857, to Elvira English, whose interesting ancestry is given herewith. They have five children: Mahala Logan, Lizzie Crutcher, Lulu Dix, Lida and Robert Dudley. Of these Mahala Logan married J. Edwin Rowe, Commonwealth Attorney of Owensboro, and they have three children: Ella Walker, Bessie R. and Lula E.

Lida Walker married A. J. Casey of Owensboro, April 17, 1894, and has one child, named Walker.

Robert Dudley Walker is studying law with his father. The other children are at home.

Lizzie Walker has attracted attention as a writer of verse, whose songs are adding so much to the literary treasure of the south. Following literature for the love of it, she has become an inspiration, not only to her own circle of friends and the people of her locality, but also to a wide circle of admiring readers. She inherits her literary talent directly from her mother, who is accomplished, brilliant and versatile, and whose literary ambition is merged with all the mother's pride in her daughter. Her ancestors were people of culture, some of whom possessed marked talent in literature. Her talent shone forth brightly even in early girlhood, and in school she was first and brightest, and she won the medal of honor in the Latin class in one of the best colleges in the south. Returning to her home in the freshness and enthusiasm of young womanhood she took to song as the form of literary expression best suited to her genius. Her poems at once rose to public notice and favor and were much admired. In every line of her work there is a delicacy and refinement and a sort of natural classicism that appeals strongly to the sympathy and admiration of the reader. The following lines are selected at random as an illustration of her work, in which the reflective element enters rather more than would be expected of one so young and joyous:

"'Tis well that life hath much of gladness,
 Knoweth something, too, of sadness,
 Bringeth hope for each to-morrow,
 Sendeth comfort, oft, for sorrow;
 Giveth while it taketh pleasure,
 Teacheth man his soul to treasure;
 Showeth as the days go by
 How to live, how to die.
   'Tis well—'tis well."

Miss Walker is a beautiful young lady of medium stature, an open eye and a spiritual face, large blue eyes as clear as the lake or the sky above it; dark hair, easy address, with perfect self-possession and a dignity of carriage that impresses her friends with the sense of

"A soul at ease and beautiful."

The Walker home at Hartford, which has long been in the possession of the family, is the ideal and type of that "Southern home where social and domestic virtues have so grown, flourished and blossomed as to make the name redolent with all the memories and musings which cluster around the word home in its best and most elegant estate." The above quotation is from the pen of the distinguished historian, Dr. John Clark Ridpath, in his review of Miss Walker's poems.

JUDGE WALKER'S ANTECEDENTS—THE WALKERS.

Richard Logan Walker (father) was a native of Washington County, Kentucky, and was educated in the schools of that county. He removed to Hartford about the year 1820 and engaged in merchandising and farming, shipping the product of his farm and that of others to the Ohio River in wagons and thence by flatboat to the New Orleans market. He was a soldier in the war of 1812, and was sheriff of Ohio County from 1820 to 1827, and for one term subsequently. The date of his marriage to Mahala Harris is not given. He died in 1857, and she survived him until 1860 and died, and is buried by his side at Hartford. They had five children: Nathan Harris, Richard Logan, Sallie Ann, Elijah Dudley and William L. D.

William Walker (grandfather) was a native of Fairfax County, Virginia, and was a soldier in the Revolutionary war. He married Polly Logan, a member of a distinguished family of Virginia.

MRS. ELVIRA ENGLISH WALKER'S ANCESTRY— THE HYNES FAMILY.

William Hynes came from Coleraine, Ireland, Londonderry County. When he came to America he worked in the printing office with Dr. Benjamin Franklin in Philadelphia in 1745.

Thomas Hynes, son of William, came from

Maryland to Kentucky in 1779. A younger brother, Colonel Andrew Hynes, came with him. Thomas Hynes' wife's name was Abigail. They came down the Ohio River, and landed where Louisville now stands. There was only one house there, the fort built by General George Rogers Clark in the spring of 1779, after he had captured a number of British forts in the summer of 1778 and spring of 1779. Clark had but one hundred and seventy-five men, and for seventeen days they were up to their waists and chins in water at Vincennes in February, 1779.

Thomas Hynes and his wife, Abigail, and five children passed in a short time from the fort to the falls of the Ohio to a fort on the north bank of Salt River, about three-fourths of a mile above Shepherdsville. They had nine children: Hannah, Andrew, William R., Sally, Polly, Nancy, Thomas, Rachel and Elizabeth. Thomas Hynes, the father of the above named children, fought in the Revolutionary war, and was a captain under General George Washington.

After Thomas Hynes moved into the fort on Salt River he bought, in 1785, of Jacob Myers the upper half of said Myers' four hundred acre pre-emption on Salt River, including the site of the fort. The deed from Myers to Thomas Hynes is recorded in deed book No. 1 in the clerk's office of Jefferson County. In 1788 he moved to Nelson County, on Lick Creek, about four miles from Boston. Thomas Hynes died in 1796 in the thirty-fifth year of his age at the above mentioned place. Abigail Hynes died in Nelson County December 4, 1821, in the seventy-fifth year of her age.

The children of Thomas and Abigail Hynes married as follows:

William R. married twice; his first wife was a Miss Lawrence, by whom he had seven children; his second wife was a Miss Chenault, by whom he had twelve children, and among the number was Rev. Thomas W. Hynes of Bond County, Illinois.

Sally Hynes, Mrs. Walker's grandmother, married William Crutcher, and had six children.

Polly Hynes married R. C. Slaughter.

Colonel Andrew Hynes, Jr., died in Nashville, Tennessee, January 21, 1849. Mrs. Mary J. McReary of St. Louis and Mrs. Lavinia Gay are among his children.

Colonel Andrew Hynes was one of the trustees appointed by an act of the Virginia Legislature in 1780 to lay off the town of Louisville; and in deed book No. 1, in the Jefferson County Court, will be found many deeds made by him. He was one of the delegates from Nelson County to the constitutional convention in 1792. He laid off Elizabethtown, and it was named for his wife Elizabeth.

Elizabeth Crutcher, youngest child of Sally and William Crutcher, married Robert English of Hardin County, Kentucky. She had three children, Elvira, Horace and Emma.

Many of the above facts are taken from papers written by Judge William R. Thompson, son of Polly Hynes, who married Volen Thompson. These facts were written by Judge Thompson only a short time before his death, which occurred in 1893. He was a member of the third constitutional convention of Kentucky. The original from which these extracts are taken is in the hands of Mr. Robert Duvall, Nolin, Hardin County.

CHARLES KENNEDY WHEELER, attorney at law, Paducah, Kentucky, son of James and Elizabeth (Watkins) Wheeler, was born in Christian County, near Hopkinsville, Kentucky, April 18, 1863.

His father was born in London, Middlesex County, England, April 11, 1811, and was educated at Oxford College. He came to America when about seventeen years of age, and was first employed as clerk to Judge Black of the South Carolina Supreme Court. He subsequently studied medicine and attended Transylvania University at Lexington and was a graduate of the medical department of that institution. After practicing for one year in Paris, Kentucky, he removed to Talladega, Alabama, where he followed his profession until 1840, when he removed to Christian County, Kentucky, purchased a farm and retired from the active practive of medicine.

Dr. Wheeler was twice married; first in Paris to Miss Metcalfe, a relative of Governor Metcalfe;

and second to Elizabeth Watkins of Appomattox County, Virginia.

He was one of the most scholarly men of his day and his hospitable home was the resort of many of the most influential men of the south. He was a Whig during the life of that party, and afterward was welcomed to the councils of the Democracy. He was a Mason of high degree, and a member of the Episcopal Church, in which faith he died March 17, 1886.

James Wheeler (grandfather) was born in London, England, and was a man of means, who had no special occupation, and would have been known as a capitalist had he lived in this country nearly a hundred years later. His wife's name was Susan Kennedy, in whose remembrance the middle name of the subject of this sketch was given.

Elizabeth Watkins Wheeler (mother) was born in 1821, in Appomattox County, Virginia, four miles from the place where General Lee surrendered to General Grant in 1865. She was educated in private schools in Richmond and was a lady of fine accomplishments, in every way a suitable companion for her intelligent and scholarly husband. She is now living in Christian County, Kentucky, in the home which was noted for hospitality in the time of Dr. Wheeler's great popularity.

Joel Watkins (grandfather) was born in Appomattox County, Virginia, on the day of the birth of the Republic, July 4, 1776. He received a fine education in the University of Virginia. His wife's maiden name was Dolly Jones, a native of the same county. He was a wealthy Virginia planter, and owned a great many slaves, and was one of the most influential men of his day. The day of his death is not remembered, nor is that of his wife's, but she survived him some twenty years and died at the old homestead.

Samuel Watkins (great-grandfather) was a captain in the Revolutionary war.

The Watkins family is one of three families in the United States who received the title to their land from King George, it having descended from the oldest son in each family. They originally came from England.

Charles K. Wheeler received an academic education at Stewart College, Clarksville, Tennessee, graduating when seventeen years of age. He then entered the law department of the Cumberland University, Lebanon, Tennessee, and was graduated in 1880. He began the practice of law very soon thereafter, and, with the exception of a period of five years when he was in partnership with Judge Campbell, has been alone in the practice of his profession ever since, and has enjoyed a very liberal share of the business of the Paducah bar. He is devoted to his work and seldom turns aside to indulge in politics. He is one of the most brilliant men in the profession; and being one of the finest speakers on the platform as well as on the forum, his services are in demand by his party in all important political campaigns, and he wields great power through the medium of his splendid oratory.

He was assistant elector in the Presidential campaigns of 1884 and 1888, on the Democratic ticket. He is a member of the Democratic State Executive Committee from the First Congressional District, and takes a leading part in the councils of his party, but is not an office seeker. He was elected, however, to the office of Corporate Counsel of Paducah in 1892, the duties of which position are strictly in the line of his profession.

Mr. Wheeler was married October 10, 1888, to Mary K. Gutherie, daughter of J. J. Gutherie, of Paducah. Mrs. Wheeler was born in Paducah February —, 1870, and was educated in the best schools of the city, subsequently taking a musical course in the Cincinnati College of Music, and in addition to other accomplishments is a musician of rare talent. They have two children, James and Mary, and the happy family is domiciled in one of the loveliest homes in Paducah.

JOHN A. STRATTON, the well-known and highly successful real estate dealer of Louisville, was born in Henry County, Kentucky, February 24, 1854.

His father, Elisha B. Stratton, was born near Richmond, Virginia, and came to Kentucky about the year 1820. He first located in Trimble County and subsequently removed to Henry County, where he was a farmer and stock raiser. During the war he was a speculator, and after his removal to Louisville in 1863 he was for a while engaged in a brokerage business, and became interested in the large trunk manufacturing establishment, which is now known as the Chilton-Guthrie Company. He was a leading member of the Baptist Church, and being a man of fine intelligence and of pure mind and upright character, he was frequently called upon to preach the gospel. He died in 1878 at the age of sixty-eight years.

William Stratton (grandfather) was a native of Virginia, where he lived and died. The family, of English descent, came to America during the seventeenth century, one branch settling in Massachusetts and another in Virginia.

Mary Antle Stratton (mother) was a native of Henry County, and died there when John A. Stratton was only six years of age. Her father, John Antle, a native of Virginia, was one of the pioneers of Kentucky and took part in the Indian fights which occurred in the early part of the century. He was a long-time resident of Henry County, and died there in 1858.

John A. Stratton was about nine years of age when he removed to Louisville with his father. He attended a private school taught by Honorable Albert S. Willis in the county and subsequently attended the Louisville public schools. At the age of sixteen he became a partner with his father in the firm of Stratton & Snodgrass in the manufacture of trunks, but sold out a year later and returned to school. He abandoned his studies a year later on account of failing health, and engaged in the manufacture of hemp brushes in partnership with Smith & Rammers. For two years he was traveling salesman for the firm, at the end of which time he bought out his partners, and for a short time conducted the business alone; but he was compelled to abandon the work on account of its injurious effect upon his lungs.

He traveled extensively for a year recuperating his health, and as out-door exercise seemed to be essential to life, his physician employed him as collector. He undertook other collections, including house rents, and his business grew until he found himself one of the leading real estate agents of the city. In this his success was phenomenal. He carefully studied and familiarized himself with the values of real property, studied the laws relating to the same, and by his unerring judgment, business sagacity and industry soon established a reputation as a safe man to handle the property of others.

In the time he has been in this business he has made more sales and negotiated larger deals than any other agent in the city. His fee in a single transaction at the usual percentage to agents amounted to $20,000. He has been employed to divide, adjust and settle some of the largest estates in Louisville, and in almost every important suit at law involving the value of realty he is called as an expert and eminently fair witness.

He foresaw the advance in Louisville property some years ago and made many valuable deals for his clients and for himself. He is a fine real estate lawyer, and can give his attorney points in matters pertaining to his particular line of business. A man of means and large liberality, he is prominent in all matters in which public-spirited citizens seek to promote the growth and prosperity of the city, and exerts all of his energies to that end. He is a large stockholder in a number of enterprises in the city.

Mr. Stratton was married in 1874 to Mamie Varble, daughter of Captain Pink Varble, deceased, of Louisville; and they have one son, Frank L. Stratton. Captain Varble was one of the best known pilots and steamboatmen on the Ohio River, an exceedingly popular and worthy citizen, who died in 1892.

WILBUR FITZALAN STIRMAN, M. D., one of the most popular and distinguished surgeons and physicians of Owensboro, son of Dr. William Doswell and Rachel (Wall) Stirman, was born in Owensboro, Kentucky, June 2, 1856. His father was also an eminent physician of Owensboro for more than thirty years. He was born in Washington County, Kentucky, December 12, 1820, and was educated in the schools of that county and, after reading medicine with Dr. Linton in St. Louis, was graduated from the medical department of the St. Louis University, February 29, 1844. He was elected Demonstrator of Anatomy in that institution the following year, and held that position for two years. In 1849 he resigned the professorship in the university and returned to Kentucky, and located in Rumsey, McLean County, remaining there but a short time, when he removed to Owensboro, where he continued to reside until his death, May 8, 1893.

In 1858 he was called to the chair of Professor of Anatomy in the Kentucky School of Medicine at Louisville, and spent the winter months in that city until 1861, when he resigned on account of the interruption of the school's business upon the outbreak of the war. After this his whole time was given to the practice of his profession.

He was a dignified, scholarly gentleman, warm hearted, sympathetic and gentle; and his genial manner in the sickroom made him a favorite, but his great worth was as the true physician, in whom his patients trusted implicitly.

He was no less prominent as a citizen, for he was greatly interested in the progress and welfare of the community and was ever ready to help a good cause by word or deed. During the later years of his useful life he was regarded by his many friends and acquaintances as the "Grand Old Man" of Owensboro, while in medical circles he was acknowledged the mentor of the profession. He belonged to several local, state and national medical associations, and helped them along. He was not a politician, but as a good citizen he exercised the right of suffrage and voted the Democratic ticket. He was a true and faithful Christian in connection with the Methodist Episcopal Church; and in all spheres of life in which he was called to act, he was the same dignified scholar, the kind physician, the respected citizen and the beloved Christian gentleman.

He married Rachel Anne Wall, November 29, 1849. She was born in McLean County, Kentucky, April 29, 1829; and was educated at Mrs. Tevis' Science Hill Academy, Shelbyville. She survives her husband, and is now living in Owensboro, greatly loved for her personal worth and lovely Christian character. She is the mother of five sons and one daughter: William Wall Stirman, deceased; Fannie Conway, wife of Joseph L. Lee of Owensboro; Dr. Wilbur F. Stirman, the subject of this sketch; Middleton Goldsmith Stirman, married Sarah D. Perkins; Joseph Scobee Stirman, married Martha Lumpkin, and Frederick Victor, married Susan Gilmour.

James H. Stirman (grandfather) was a native of Roanoke County, Virginia, where he was a merchant and planter for many years. He was a captain in the War of 1812, and received three gunshot wounds at the battle of Thames and fell within twenty-six feet of the spot where Tecumseh fell. He recovered from his wounds and subsequently removed to Memphis, Tennessee, where he died in 1820. His wife was Elizabeth L. Doswell, daughter of Thomas Doswell of Hanover County, Virginia, who removed to Washington County, Kentucky, where their marriage took place. The Doswells belonged to an old Virginia family, whose ancestors came to that state from England.

Bannister Wall (maternal grandfather), a tobacconist, was born in Pearson County, North Carolina, and married Sarah Tate Thompson, who was born in Nelson County, Kentucky, but at the time of their marriage were living in McLean County.

Boyd Wall (great-grandfather) married Elizabeth Wade, and they were residents of North Carolina.

Sarah Tate Thompson (grandmother), wife of Bannister Wall, was a daughter of Anthony Thompson, native of Pennsylvania, and Rachel Handley of Virginia.

Anthony Thompson (great-grandfather) was a son of James Thompson and Sarah Finley, both of Pennsylvania.

Dr. Wilbur F. Stirman received a good literary education in the Owensboro schools; at Hanover College, Indiana, in which he took the Sophomore and Junior courses; and then went to Vanderbilt University, Nashville, Tennessee, from which he was graduated in the class of 1877. In the following autumn he went to the St. Louis Medical College, from which he graduated in medicine in 1879. He spent the three years following in hospital work in St. Louis, thereby gaining a valuable experience.

In 1881 he joined his father in Owensboro, under the firm name of Stirman & Stirman, and this partnership relation continued until the death

of the senior member, May 8, 1893. After entering upon the duties of the profession with his father, Dr. Stirman took several post-graduate courses in the Polyclinic Institute, New York City. He succeeded to the large practice of his father and has taken his place in the hearts of the people, who have the same confidence in the son that they had so implicitly placed in the father.

Dr. Stirman is especially distinguished as a surgeon, and is acknowledged by the profession as the ablest surgeon in the county. His services are in demand in all cases in which important surgical skill is required, and other physicians rarely undertake serious work of that character without his assistance or consultation with him. Aside from this branch of work, for which he has especially prepared himself, he enjoys a very extensive general practice, for which he is naturally adapted, being kind, considerate and gentle in the sickroom, and having acquired a knowledge of medicine which few men of his age in the state have attained. He has inherited and cultivated many of the fine traits of character of his distinguished father and is quite as popular as a citizen as he is as a physician and surgeon.

In recognition of his ability as a surgeon, he is employed in that capacity by the Louisville & Nashville Railroad Company; the Louisville, St. Louis & Texas Railroad Company; the Chesapeake & Ohio Railroad Company, and the Electric Street Railway Company of Owensboro.

He is a member of the McDowell Medical Society, and of the American Medical Association. Dr. Stirman is faithful to the principles of the Democratic party, and his vote helps to swell the comfortable majority of the Democracy in his city and county.

Socially Dr. Stirman is a great favorite, being a companionable, genial and courteous gentleman of scholarly attainments, whose becoming dignity is lost sight of in the company of his friends and associates.

HON. JOHN W. BARR of Louisville, Judge of the United States District Court, was born in Versailles, December 17, 1826. His early instruction was received in private schools in his native county, and his legal education at Transylvania University, Lexington, whence he was graduated when twenty years of age.

His father, William Barr, was also a native Kentuckian, born in Fayette County, near Lexington, in 1796. He received a good education in the best private schools; was engaged for many years in the mercantile business in Versailles and Louisville, continuing in the former place until 1840, when he disposed of his interests there and removed to Mississippi, where he engaged in cotton planting. He devoted his best energies to business, enjoying a quiet life and caring but little for politics, although he was a Whig of very strong convictions. He died in Washington County, Mississippi, in 1844.

Judge Barr's paternal grandfather was a native of Pennsylvania, and a farmer, removing to Fayette County in 1787, where he spent the remainder of his days, farming near Lexington.

Dr. John Watson (maternal grandfather) was a native of Maryland; married Nancy Howe, daughter of Major Howe of Virginia; came to Woodford County when a young man and engaged in the practice of medicine, where he continued his professional work during the remainder of his life. His daughter, Ann Watson (mother), was born in Virginia in 1808. She received a liberal education in Woodford County; was married to William Barr in 1825, and died in Versailles in 1829, at the early age of twenty-one years. She was a devout member of the Presbyterian Church.

After completing his legal studies at Lexington, Judge Barr returned to Versailles, remaining there but a short time when he removed to Louisville and engaged in the practice of his profession in partnership with the late Joseph B. Kinkead. This partnership continued for eight years, when it was dissolved by mutual consent, the parties thereto remaining steadfast friends until the death of Mr. Kinkead.

Judge Barr continued to practice in the higher courts alone until 1864, when he entered into partnership with Hon. John Kemp Goodloe. In 1868 Judge Alexander P. Humphrey came into the firm, which continued without change until 1880, when Mr. Barr was appointed United States

District Judge, in the place of Judge Bland Ballard, deceased.

Although a stanch Whig in his early days and an ardent Republican ever since the organization of that party, Judge Barr has never been active in party affairs and has never sought political preferment. But he has held many offices of trust and honor in Louisville. From 1868 to 1871 he was President of the Louisville Sinking Fund Commissioners; for twenty years he was a director of the Bank of Kentucky; he served a number of terms as representative of his ward in the City Council. In all of his relations in public life he has enjoyed the respect and confidence of his fellow citizens.

In November, 1859, he married Susan Rogers, daughter of Col. Jason Rogers of Louisville. Mrs. Barr was a highly educated and cultured lady, receiving the best instruction that the schools of Louisville and a private school in New York could afford. She was a member of the Presbyterian Church, a devout Christian. She died in 1871, leaving seven children, two sons and five daughters: John W. Barr, Jr., Anna W., Caroline H., Susan R., Josephine P., Elise R. and Jason Rogers Barr.

Judge Barr and his family attend the College Street Presbyterian Church.

M. K. SCOTT, a leading wholesale hardware merchant of Paducah, son of John and Martha (Broaddus) Scott, was born in Louisville, Kentucky, August 17, 1832. His father was born in Chillicothe, Ohio, in 1794, and was educated there, removing to Louisville when he was a young man, where he was engaged in blacksmithing on a very extensive scale. He was a soldier and an Indian fighter in the troublous times of the early years of the present century; was wounded in the battle of Tippecanoe, and was in a number of serious engagements with the Indians. He was in business in Louisville for fifty years, retiring in 1865, when he went to Paducah to live with his son, and died there in 1868. He was strictly a man of business and cared nothing for politics, personally; but, during the life of the Whig party, he voted with it and wished it success. He was a strong Union man during the war of the '60's, but he was advanced in years and, having served his country faithfully in his younger days, he took no active part in the struggle between the sections. He was a good citizen, and a pious member of the Presbyterian Church. His ancestors were from Ireland.

Martha Broaddus Scott (mother) was a native of Culpeper County, Virginia, who came to Louisville after receiving her education in her native county, and was married there to John Scott. The Broaddus family was one of the first to settle in Virginia and were distinguished for their intelligence and fine traits of character. M. K. Scott, after attending the public schools of Louisville, learned the tinner's trade, in which he was employed in Louisville and New Orleans.

On the first day of August, 1851, he took steamer from the latter city for Cuba, having tendered his services as a private soldier in the cause of Cuba against Spain. There were four hundred and fifty men in the party and they were nine days on the water, finally running on a reef a mile from land, so that the men were forced to go ashore in boats. They were discovered and fired on by the inhabitants, but without great loss. General Lopez, a native born Cuban, but opposed to the Spanish Government, was in command. After landing Lopez took three hundred and fifty men and started for the interior of the island, leaving one hundred men under General W. L. Crittenden (nephew of John J. Crittenden, United States Senator from Kentucky), with instructions to bring ammunition, baggage and supplies. Crittenden was attacked by Spanish troops and fifty of his one hundred men were slain on the spot. With the remaining fifty men he attempted to escape in a schooner, expecting to be picked up by an American vessel, but they were captured by a Spanish man-of-war and taken to Havana, where Crittenden and all of his men were shot. The Spaniards commanded the soldiers to turn their backs to the squad of executioners and kneel; and all of them did so except Crittenden, who faced his slayers and said, "A Kentuckian kneels to none but God." This sentiment has been commemorated in a poem by

Mary E. (Wilson) Betts: "He Never Turned His Back on the Enemy."

Fortunately, Mr. Scott was with Lopez, whose forces had a successful fight with the enemy the next (Sunday) morning. After the battle, Lopez went to the mountains to escape from a superior force. The next Sunday after the first battle they had another battle at General Lopez' plantation, and again resorted to the mountains and again, on the following Sunday, they defeated the enemy in another battle. Four weeks after landing they were defeated again, their ammunition having given out. The command then broke up into small parties and sought refuge in the mountains; and, after waiting some time, they resolved to risk going to the seacoast, where they hoped to be picked up by a friendly vessel. In attempting this Mr. Scott, with a party of five, was captured. One of the party, named Mahon, from Maysville, Kentucky, had been chosen by lot to go into the valley to secure provisions. He was successful in his mission, but on his way back he ate all of the provisions he had received. While the party was cussing and discussing the situation, they saw that they were pursued by Spanish soldiers, accompanied by bloodhounds and, after a lively chase, all were captured. Mr. Scott was forced by the hounds to climb a tree. When the soldiers came up they advised him to come down and as he obeyed a bayonet was thrust into his back. He was bound and taken to a town called St. Christopher and, with others of his party, put in stocks. Mahon was not captured for a few days. They were kept in the stocks for four or five hours, when they were released and given the privilege of the town. A few days later they were sent to Havana and placed in Potter prison, their heads were shaved and they were dressed in prison clothes and placed in irons. They were in this sorry plight about three weeks, when they were placed on board a vessel bound for the quicksilver mines in Africa. They were one hundred and five days going from Havana to Vigo, Spain; and, while in quarantine at the latter place, owing to the intercession of the American consul, they were pardoned by the queen. The Germans and Hungarians did not claim citizenship in the United States and their respective governments would not recognize them, so they were sent to Africa. The American consul took charge of the party and furnished them with provisions for six weeks while waiting for passage.

Mr. Scott landed safely in New York, March 10, 1852, entirely satisfied with his war experience. He at once returned to his home in Louisville, and for three years was employed by Bridgeford & Company, when he went to Paducah, where he was engaged by E. R. Hart for seven years. In 1863 he embarked in the tinning and hardware business in Paducah on his own account, and has continued with the most satisfactory results until the present time.

As to politics, Mr. Scott is a Democrat without political aspirations. He is faithful in business, devoted to his family and can be depended upon for a good turn in behalf of his friends and neighbors.

Mr. Scott was married in July, 1857, to Elizabeth Applegate; and they have eight children living: Frank, William, Elizabeth, Anna, Belle, Ruebie, Etta, Richard and Irene. Two of their children, Harry and Walter, are deceased.

DR. SAMUEL C. SMITH, formerly of Henderson, now a resident and practicing physician of Audubon, Henderson County, was born in Lunenburg County, Virginia, July 12, 1831. He completed his education at Hampden-Sidney College, Virginia, and graduated in medicine at the National Medical College, Washington, D. C. (the medical department of Columbian University), in 1861. In 1862 he entered the service of the Confederate States of America in the capacity of surgeon, and was assigned to duty at Chimborazo Hospital, in the city of Richmond, Virginia; was transferred to Farmville, Virginia, in 1863, where he served until the close of the war. He removed from Virginia to Henderson in September, 1870, and was a practicing physician in that city until 1892, when he removed to Audubon (a suburb of Henderson), his present place of residence and the center of his field of operations, practicing in the city of Henderson, where his office is located, and in the surrounding counties in Kentucky and Indiana.

Dr. Smith is a member of the Kentucky State Medical Society, the McDowell Medical Society and other organizations for the promotion of medical science. He has been a member of the Presbyterian Church since 1863.

He married Susan J. Street, daughter of Peter W. Street of Lunenburg County, Virginia, in 1854. They had ten children, five of whom died in infancy and five are now living, viz.: Jessie S., wife of Dr. J. K. Hayes, now of Hanson's Station; Lillian, wife of G. Rives Williams, grocer of Henderson; Annie M., wife of William M. Carr of Morganfield, and Walter S. and William A. Smith, both of whom are unmarried and living in Henderson.

Dr. Anthony W. Smith (father) was also a native of Lunenburg County, Virginia, and was a celebrated physician and surgeon, having served in a professional capacity during the war with Great Britain in 1812. He was a ruling elder in the Presbyterian Church for many years; contributed his quota to the medical and surgical literature of his day, and at the time of his death in 1858, was the oldest Mason in his native county. He graduated in medicine from the University of Pennsylvania in 1818, and located in the city of Baltimore, where he married Miss Margaret E. B. Wheeler of Easton, Maryland; and, after her death, he returned to his native county and state with an only son, O. M. Smith, now deceased. He married Ann M. McRobert of Prince Edward County, Virginia, in 1826, and there were five children by this union, viz.: John Henry, Emily Montford, Camilla, Samuel C. and Henrietta A. Emily Montford died in infancy. Camilla, married James Hayes, Jr., and settled in Mecklenburg County, Virginia; died from effects of fall from a buggy. Jno. Henry died in his sixty-ninth year from apoplexy, unmarried. Henrietta married James Hayes after the death of her sister Camilla and is still living—being a widow.

Dr. S. C. Smith, the subject of this sketch, is now in his sixty-fourth year and is still engaged in active practice of all the branches of his profession. Office and address is 100 1-2 Main street, Henderson.

FRANK O. YOUNG, M. D., a well-known and popular physician of Lexington, son of Richard B. and Jane (O'Neal) Young, was born in Lexington, Kentucky, November 13, 1854.

Richard B. Young was a native of Fayette County and when quite young became a resident of Lexington, where he was a leather merchant for many years and where he died, January 26, 1873, in the sixty-sixth year of his age. He was a consistent Christian in connection with the Baptist Church. In politics he was an enthusiastic follower of Henry Clay, and after the disruption of the old Whig party, he voted the Democratic ticket.

Ambrose Young (grandfather) was also a native of Fayette County and was an enterprising and industrious farmer until the time of his death, which occurred in 1849, when he had reached an advanced age.

Richard Young (great-grandfather) was of Scotch-Irish descent, and was born in Virginia. He came to Kentucky and was a Fayette County farmer and a highly respected citizen of the county until the day of his death.

Jane O'Neal Young (mother) was a native of Harper's Ferry, Virginia. Her parents died when she was a child and she then came to Kentucky, where she found a home with relatives in Woodford County. She is now living and is a devoted member of the Christian Church. Her father, Frank O'Neal, was a native of Ireland who came to America in the first decade of the present century, and died in Virginia, when he was in the prime of life.

Frank O. Young was educated in Lexington, attending the primary schools and Transylvania University for a time and was graduated from Beech Grove College in 1870. He read medicine with Dr. Hawkins Brown of Hustonville, Kentucky, graduated in medicine from Medical Department of the University of Louisville, Kentucky, and in March, 1874, before he was twenty years of age, he located at Liberty, Casey County, where he practiced medicine for six years. He then removed to Lancaster, where he practiced for two years, after which he returned to Lexington, his native city, and located permanently and was soon recognized as one of the most successful physicians in Fayette County. He is a member of the Kentucky State Medical Society, Medical Society of Lexington and Fayette County and of the Medical Society of Central Kentucky; president of the Board of Aldermen and acting Mayor of Lexington; president of the Lexington Board of Health and of the Saturday Night Building and Loan Association. He is a Knight Templar, an Odd Fellow, a Knight of Pythias, an Elk and a member of the Christian Church.

Dr. Young was married June 15, 1881, to Addie Barkley, daughter of William L. Barkley of Fayette County. She died December 18, 1892.

Dr. Young is a self-made man, as it is owing to his own exertions that he has won his way to the front both as a citizen and as a physician. He is one of the most popular men in his profession, and there are few men in Lexington who have been more zealous for the upbuilding and material progress of that beautiful city.

REV. WILLIAM CARSON TAYLOR, D. D., pastor of the Baptist Church at Frankfort and one of the most eloquent pulpit orators in Kentucky, was born in Taylorsburg, Henry County, Virginia, February 7, 1858. He is a son of Rev. James I. Taylor, who was a minister in the Baptist Church, but is now retired from active work in the ministry and is engaged in farming in Oregon, to which state he removed from Virginia in 1874. He was born in 1831 in Taylorsburg, a town which takes its name from the Taylor family.

Reuben Taylor (grandfather) was born in Taylorsburg in 1790, and was engaged in agricultural pursuits in Henry County, where he died in 1864. He was quite prosperous in his occupation, and was one of the leading citizens in his county and a prominent member of the Baptist Church. Three of his brothers were soldiers in the war of 1812.

George Taylor (great-grandfather), a native of Wales, came to America in 1772; and in 1779 took a large tract of land in Henry County, receiving his title from the government when General Washington was President of the United States and Thomas Jefferson was Governor of Virginia. He died in Henry County in 1823.

Ruth Taylor (mother) is a native of North Carolina, and is now residing in Oregon, and is well advanced in years.

William C. Taylor remained on the farm in his native county until he was sixteen years of age, when he removed with his parents to the state of Oregon. Soon after arriving there he entered the State University of Oregon, in which institution he received his classical education; and subsequently attended the New York Theological Seminary at Rochester and, after three years' preparation for the work of the ministry, was graduated from that institution in 1887.

He accepted a pastorate in the city of Buffalo and was ordained in July, 1887. He labored there with gratifying success for four years and, as one of the results of his work, founded the Fillmore Avenue Baptist Church of Buffalo.

On the second day of January, 1891, he accepted a call from the Baptist congregation of Frankfort, and at once assumed the duties of pastor of that church. Under his ministration this congregation has steadily increased in numbers, strength and usefulness and was never before in as prosperous a condition as it is to-day.

Mr. Taylor is an eloquent speaker, an able minister, excellent pastor and enjoys the confidence of his people. Interesting and pleasing in conversation, warm and sincere in his friendships, he commands the respect and good will of the community, in which he has been the instrument of accomplishing great good.

He was married May 15, 1889, to Ida Meyer, daughter of C. C. Meyer of Rochester, New York; and they have two daughters, Ruth and Esther.

Dr. Taylor was honored with the title of Doctor of Divinity by the Georgetown College, Georgetown, Kentucky, at its annual commencement of 1895. During the latter part of that summer and the following autumn he made a tour of Palestine, Egypt and several European countries with a view to special study of Biblical and historical literature.

EUGENE M. TERRY, Master Lock Manager of the Louisville & Portland Canal, son of John and Mary Moss Terry, was born in Glasgow, Kentucky, August 13, 1838. His father was born in Louisa, Virginia, and came to Kentucky with his father, William M. Terry, when he was nine years of age. They first settled in Todd County and when John Terry reached his manhood, he went to Glasgow and lived there until 1848, when he removed to Louisville and engaged in the wholesale grocery business. He was a member of and officer in the First Christian Church, an upright citizen and successful business man. He died in 1873, aged sixty-three years.

William M. Terry (grandfather) was a native of Virginia, who removed to Todd County in 1819, or about that time, and was a farmer and highly esteemed citizen of that county until the day of his death in 1858. He was at one time sheriff of Todd County.

Mary Moss Terry (mother) was born in Barren County, near Glasgow, in 1819 and died in Louisville in 1894. She was a lifetime member of the Christian Church and was greatly loved by the congregation with which she was connected in Louisville.

Josiah Moss (grandfather) was a native of Virginia; was a popular hotel keeper in Glasgow, and at the same time owned and operated a farm in Barren County. He died in Glasgow at the age of seventy years.

Eugene M. Terry came to Louisville with his father's family in 1848 and continued his schooling in that city. After leaving school he was a clerk in his father's grocery until the breaking out of the war, when he entered the government service in the commissary department in Louisville, in which he served for three years; but just before the close of the war he gave up this position and was engaged in the leaf tobacco trade for two years. He was then in the railroad contracting business for two years, after which he served in the city engineer's department of the city as superintendent of public works for a term of five years, afterwards being variously engaged in contracting, etc., until October, 1893, when he was appointed Master Lock Manager of the Louisville & Portland Canal by the Secretary of War.

Mr. Terry was married in 1863 to Bettie M. Spalding, daughter of the late Daniel Spalding of Louisville; and they have three sons and four daughters: Hattie, Florence, Eugenia, John, Daniel, Bessie and Charles. Hattie is the wife of W. P. Kennedy, a farmer of Jefferson County; and Eugenia is the wife of E. B. Casler of Louisville.

ANDREW JACKSON WORSHAM, Mayor of the City of Henderson, is a son of the late Elijah W. Worsham and Mariam (Graham) Worsham, and was born in Henderson County, Kentucky, May 17, 1850.

His father, by honest effort, faithful application and fine judgment, had gained a competency which enabled him to give his children the best educational advantages, and Andrew was sent to private schools in Henderson, to Smith's Military Institute at Eminence and to a commercial college at Poughkeepsie, New York.

He applied himself to his studies diligently and acquitted himself with credit to himself and to his father, who had been so mindful of his son's welfare.

In the month of August, 1873, his father removed with his family to California and settled near San Francisco on the San Joaquin river. A. J. Worsham there engaged in ranching for the period of two years.

On the 10th of November, 1873, he had the most thrilling experience of his life. In company with a friend named Duncan Cargill, he undertook to cross the river. The high winds had made the river, which was one and a half miles wide at that point, very rough; and when they started a perfect wind storm set in at dark and the waves were rolling and white caps flying house-top high. They struggled manfully, but progressed very slowly until they reached the middle of the stream, when the boat was capsized, the two men were thrown into the cold waves, and Cargill was drowned. The situation was very appalling, and, exhausted from his exertions and chilled by the water, Worsham still clung to the up-turned boat. It was about 10 o'clock when they left the shore, it was near midnight when the boat capsized. Near daylight he had drifted near the shore and had almost lost consciousness, when a Mr. Sutherland came to his rescue, lifting him from the water, carried him on his shoulder to his home, where restoratives were administered and his life saved.

On the 7th of June, 1876, not quite three years after his experience as related above, Mr. Worsham was united in marriage to Florence Rhorer at her home in San Francisco, California. As a result of this union they have seven living children: John C., Mariam J., Milton R., Ludson, Arch. D., George A., and Virginia Rhorer Worsham.

Soon after marriage he was elected Superintendent of the Calcutta Gold and Silver Mining Company, and removed to Gold Hill, Nevada, where he engaged in mining, until the spring of 1877, when he removed to Banning, where he engaged in merchandising. Mr. Worsham was also postmaster of Banning during his residence there. He returned to Henderson in 1881; and with his father engaged in the wholesale liquor and distilling business under the firm name of E. W. Worsham & Company, which partnership continued until the death of his father, December 31, 1891. In November following, the distillery was incorporated in the name of the Worsham Distilling Company, with D. C. Worsham, President; A. J. Worsham, Vice President, and R. D. Reynols, Secretary and Treasurer.

On the 5th of November, 1895, Mr. Worsham was elected Mayor of Henderson, a position for which he is qualified in an eminent degree, having served in the City Council, and being a man of unusual business capacity. Mayor Worsham is a republican in politics, and his election in a democratic city was due in a large measure to his popularity and to the generally conceded fact that he was the man for the place. He is a member of several leading benevolent orders, including the Odd Fellows, Elks, Knights of Pythias and A. O. U. W.

He is a very industrious man, attending diligently to his business, and is always ready to assist in the promotion of a good cause. In the brief time which he has been chief executive for his city, he has applied his well known business methods in the management of the affairs of the city, and has inaugurated a policy of reform which promises to distinguish his administration as one of the most progressive the city has ever enjoyed.

Elijah W. Worsham (father) was born near Henderson, February 12, 1823. His father, Ludson Worsham (grandfather) removed from Indiana to Kentucky in 1820 and purchased a farm about half a mile above Evansville on the Ohio river. In 1832, Ludson Worsham, having a contract for carrying mail between Henderson and Evansville, Elijah Worsham, then nine years of age, was required to make the weekly trip between these two points on horseback. He performed this duty manfully for three years and was frequently frightened out of his wits as he passed through the wilderness. His early education was fragmentary, the schools of those days not being the best, and his opportunities of attending even these were limited to such times as he could be spared from the work on the farm.

In 1844, when twenty-one years of age, he married Mariam J. Graham, a lady of great beauty. In 1847 he purchased a farm near Bloomington, where he lived for three years, and in 1850 he removed to his father's old place. He was an active politician, and in 1855 he was elected to the legislature by the American, or Know-Nothing party. In 1859, he purchased a farm within two miles of Henderson on the Owensboro road. In 1863, he built the Overton tobacco factory, and began tobacco stemming on an extensive scale. In 1867 he removed from his farm to Henderson.

In 1870 he formed a partnership with A. S. Winstead, and, under the firm name of E. W. Worsham & Company, bought and sold liquors at wholesale and manufactured bitters and malarial medicines. In 1873, in company with others, he purchased a large tract of Tule lands in California and moved to that state. His experience in wheat raising on these lands for two years was satisfactory, but he sold out and went to San Francisco, remained one year, and thence to Los Angeles, where he engaged in raising sheep and other successful ventures. In 1881 he returned to Henderson, and, under the firm name of E. W. Worsham & Company, built a large sour mash distillery, now known as the Worsham Distillery.

Thus he had many ups and downs, yet by his superior judgment, keen foresight and careful management, he held his own and amassed a splendid fortune. He willingly served the public in any way in his power; was a member of the school board and the city council and was twice elected President of the Henderson Fair Company. He joined the Odd Fellows' order in 1844, and was a useful and active member, at one time serving as Deputy District Grand Master. He united with the Baptist Church in 1846, and was an influential member until 1870, when he withdrew. He died December 31, 1891, in the sixty-ninth year of his age.

THOMAS RODMAN, president of the Farmers' Bank of Kentucky, Frankfort, is a worthy member of one of the most prominent families in the state. He has had a most successful business career, and is to-day one of the leading citizens of Frankfort. He is a son of John and Patsy (Foree) Rodman, who were descended, respectively, from Irish and Huguenot ancestry.

John Rodman was born in Pennsylvania in 1787, and in 1790 came to Kentucky and located near the present site of Louisville, where he remained one year with his father, and then removed to Shelby County and subsequently to Henry County, where he died in 1833. He was a man of influence and prominence in his county, having served one term in the Legislature and being a member of the State Senate at the time of his death. He was a leading and exemplary member of the Methodist Episcopal Church. His father, Hugh Rodman, was born in Pennsylvania, and was one of the early settlers in Jefferson County, subsequently removing to Shelby County, and later to Henry County, Kentucky.

Patsy Foree Rodman (mother) was a native of Virginia, and died in Frankfort in 1883 at the age of eighty-seven years. Her father, William Foree, a Huguenot, came to this country upon the revocation of the Edict of Nantes and located, first, in South Carolina, where he lived a short time, and then removed to Virginia, where he married Magdalene Loe, and spent the remainder of his days in that state.

Thomas Rodman was born in New Castle, Henry County, Kentucky, August 10, 1823. His education was limited and at the age of fourteen he was apprenticed to a dry goods firm for a term of four years. His compensation during the first year of his service was fifteen cents a day. His employers soon realized, however, that young Rodman possessed a talent for business far above the mediocre; and, after a few years of faithful service, he was given an interest in the establishment and was admitted as a partner. He continued in that business and prospered until 1863, when he removed to Frankfort and engaged in the dry goods business in that city, where he was quickly recognized as one of the leading and most successful merchants in central Kentucky. After being in the dry goods business in Frankfort for nearly a quarter of a century, he sold out in 1887 and retired from mercantile pursuits.

It was largely due to his ability and excellent judgment in financial matters that, soon after his retirement, he was elected president of the Farmers' Bank, one of the oldest and most favorably known banking houses in the South. This position he has filled to the entire satisfaction of all who are in any way identified with the bank.

For thirty years he has been one of the trustees of the Georgetown Baptist College and for the same number of years he has been a member of and a deacon in the Baptist Church, and is a member of the Executive Board of the Baptist Association. As a stanch democrat he has been frequently urged to become a candidate for the legislature and other offices, but has steadily declined all such honors. Among his friends in and around Frankfort, he is known as the "general peace-maker," a title which he has earned on account of his having arbitrated many misunderstandings, preventing unwise and unnecessary litigation, and in some cases personal conflict, among his friends and neighbors.

Mr. Rodman is a self-made man in the truest sense of that term, having risen from an apprentice boy to the presidency of one of the most substantial banking institutions in the country. His ability as a financier is recognized by the leading business men of the community, while his career as a merchant and business man has been marked by all of the characteristics of an honest and upright man.

He is a member of a family who have attained

prominence and success in their callings. His brother, Dr. James Rodman (see sketch), is an eminent physician of Hopkinsville, who was for twenty-eight years superintendent of the Western Kentucky Asylum for the Insane at that place; his brother, John Rodman, deceased, was Attorney General of Kentucky for eight years and his brother, J. L. Rodman, is a prominent dry goods merchant in Frankfort.

Mr. Rodman has been twice married; first in 1844 to Sarah E. Thomasson, daughter of Captain Joseph M. Thomasson of Henry County. She died in 1857, leaving three children, two of whom are now living. His second marriage was in 1858 to Julia Willoughby of New York, who died in 1886, leaving four children.

REV. JOHN STEELE SWEENEY, generally known as Elder Sweeney, the able pastor of the First Christian Church, Paris, was born in Liberty, Casey County, Kentucky, September 4, 1834, and belongs to a family of distinguished ministers who have been and are among the brightest lights in the Christian and Baptist Churches. He is a son of Rev. Guirn E. and Talitha (Campbell) Sweeney, both of whom are natives of Kentucky. His father, born in Lincoln County in 1807, was for many years a minister in the Baptist Church, but in the early days of Alexander Campbell and his able and distinguished confrere, Barton W. Stone, he left the Baptist denomination and accepted the doctrines of the founder of the Christian Church. He has been preaching the gospel for sixty-five years, and while having no charge at present, still preaches occasionally when opportunity is offered. He is remarkably well preserved for a man over eighty-eight years of age. His faculties are clear and he preaches with wonderful power and irresistible logic. He is now living with his son in Paris.

His wife, Talitha Campbell, was a daughter of John Campbell, of Scotch descent, and a relative of Rev. Alexander Campbell. They had a family of eight sons and daughters, all of whom reached maturity, and four sons and two daughters are now living. All of the sons are ministers of the gospel: Rev. W. G. Sweeney, who is at present Collector of Customs at Dubuque, Iowa, and a Christian minister; Elder John S. Sweeney of Paris; Rev. George W. Sweeney of Chicago; and Rev. Zachariah T. Sweeney, minister and lecturer, of Columbus, Indiana, who was Consul General to Turkey during President Harrison's administration. He is one of the ablest ministers and most popular lecturers in the country. The daughters of Rev. G. E. Sweeney are married and are active members of the Christian Church.

Rev. Job Sweeney (grandfather) was a native of Belfast, Ireland, who came to the United States with his father, Moses Sweeney, when he was three years of age. He was for many years one of the leading Baptist ministers in Lincoln and adjoining counties. It was not customary to pay the preachers large salaries, and, like many other ministers, he devoted a part of his time to the cultivation of his farm in order to support his family.

Moses Sweeney (great-grandfather) was one of the pioneers of Lincoln County, and was contemporary with Daniel Boone. Soon after his arrival in Kentucky, one of his children was killed by the Indians.

Elder John S. Sweeney was brought up on the farm, attending the irregular sessions of the district school. At the age of nineteen years, he went to the Oakland Institute at Columbia, Kentucky, taught by an old Englishman by the name of Saunders, a prominent educator of his day, at that time a Unitarian, but who subsequently joined the Christian Church. He was in this academy for two years and he then took up the study of law at Columbia and, after a careful preparation, was admitted to the bar.

He removed to Jacksonville, Illinois, where for a short time he was engaged in the practice of law; but, finding that this profession was not congenial to his tastes, he abandoned it and accepted the editorial management of the Bible Advocate, the state organ of the Christian Church of Illinois. He remained in this capacity for two years, when the personnel of the paper was changed and he then turned his attention to religious work of another character. This paper, after having gone through several evolutions and changes, is now the Christian Evangelist, published at St. Louis, and is one of the very ablest religious journals published by the Christian Church. During his residence in Jacksonville, Mr. Sweeney devoted his entire time to his paper and to ministerial work in the Christian Church. When he relinquished his connection with the paper, he engaged in evangelical work throughout Illinois and other Western cities, making his home in Winchester, Illinois. During his evangelical labors, he preached on an average of one sermon a day.

His first regular charge where he confined himself to pastoral work exclusively was in Chicago, to which place he removed in 1864. Three years later he resigned, but was afterwards recalled and for two years was pastor of the Wabash Avenue Christian Church. During his last stay, some of the very best people of Chicago became members of this church, including Mr. Potter Palmer and wife and the wife of the Honorable Fred Grant, and many other wealthy and distinguished citizens of Chicago.

In 1871 Elder Sweeney removed to Paris, where he has labored most successfully for over a quarter of a century, and where he presides over one of the largest congregations in Kentucky, the membership of which is made up of the most prominent people in Bourbon County. When he came to this church in 1871, the membership was only three hundred, but under his ministration it is now nearly twelve hundred.

In the meantime Elder Sweeney has done a great work in organizing and building up other churches. For many years he was one of the leading controversialists in his church, and his reputation in this regard extends throughout the country. He has been engaged in over one hundred debates, held in nearly every state in the Union and in Canada, and has discussed religious questions with Methodists, Presbyterians, Baptists and infidels. He is a stanch believer in the religious doctrine of his church and is well able to defend his denomination against the most intelligent adversaries.

During the war, Rev. Sweeney was nominated for Congress by his party, but declined to become a candidate for a political office.

He is generally known throughout the country as an able minister and platform speaker. He is a public spirited citizen and takes a deep interest in all that pertains to the welfare of the community and religious work at large.

In 1858 he married Mary E. Coons of Winchester, Illinois, who died in 1873. He was again married, in 1876, to Alice Monin of Hardin County, by whom he has five children, four boys and one girl.

A. WILKES SMITH, of Richmond, one of the most learned members of the medical and dental profession in the state, a practicing physician-dentist in Richmond, was born in Champaign County, Ohio, September 12, 1844.

His father, James Smith, was a native of New York who came to Kentucky with his parents when he was a child, in 1817. He lived in Georgetown until he was twenty years of age, when he went to Champaign County, Ohio, and lived there until 1869. He then removed to Trenton, Indiana, where he died in 1883, aged sixty-eight years. He was a man of fine scholarly attainments, and of excellent traits of character, which distinguished him as a man of unusual intelligence and ability. During the earlier years of his business career, he was employed as a civil engineer, but the greater part of his life was spent in merchandising.

John Smith (grandfather) was a native of England, who came to the United States in 1812, or about that time, and after stopping a short time in New York city, came to Georgetown, Kentucky, where he spent the remainder of a long and useful life, reaching the unusual age of nearly one hundred years. He was a general merchant in Georgetown and was known as a man of sterling integrity and honesty. Being an elder in the Baptist Church, he was probably more widely known and respected as Elder Smith. He conducted the services at more funerals than any other minister in Scott County, and few men were as well known in the county. He married Margaret Britton of New Jersey, a sister of Colonel Britton, who formed a colony in the early settlement of Oregon. She was a lady of great beauty and intelligence, and was quite active as a co-laborer with her husband in religious work. She died of cholera in the epidemic of 1839.

Mary Lang Smith (mother) was born in Martinsburg, Virginia, in 1817, and is still living with Dr. Smith in Richmond. Thomas Lang (grandfather) was a native of Virginia and was for many years a resident of Martinsburg, Virginia. He was a prosperous planter, and served his country as an officer in the war of 1812. He married Elizabeth Elliott of Virginia, daughter of Colonel William Elliott of Revolutionary fame. The Langs are of English extraction, whose ancestors were among the most illustrious families of Virginia and Maryland. His sword, used in the Revolutionary war, is still in the possession of his family.

Dr. A. Wilkes Smith enjoyed fair advantages in the common schools of Champaign County, Ohio, while his scholarly father encouraged and aided him in making rapid advancement. After this elementary work, he studied the classics and sciences under able private tutors. He was thrown upon his own resources at an early age, on account of reverses in his father's business, and this probably was one of the most useful experiences of his youth. While studying medicine he taught school and earned the money to pay his way.

At the age of nineteen he went to Philadelphia, where he continued the study of medicine for several years with a view to entering the United States navy as a surgeon; but before reaching the goal of his ambition he learned that South America was a promising field for dentistry and he accordingly took up that branch of the medical profession and graduated from the Pennsylvania College of Dentistry in March, 1871. At this time his father's health failed and he was called home and afterwards was sent to Kentucky to look after his grandfather's estate, which was in litigation, and he eventually abandoned his purpose to go to South America.

Of Southern parentage, his affections were naturally with the people and institutions of the South, and he decided to make his home in Kentucky. He accordingly selected the garden of the Blue Grass State and located in Richmond in June, 1871. Believing that medicine and dentistry should go together, that the dentist should be a physician and surgeon, he has made a special feature of Oral Surgery, and has made a reputation in his county and state and throughout the United States as a dental surgeon who has few equals in the profession and no superior in the country.

From 1875 to 1879 he was lecturer on Oral Surgery in the Ohio College of Dentistry at Cincinnati, and during that period was President of the Kentucky State Dental Association. In 1881 he was elected Professor of Physiology in the Central University at Richmond, which position he holds at the present time. In 1882 the Hospital College of Medicine of Louisville conferred upon him the degree of M. D. and elected him lecturer on Oral Dental Surgery, which office he held for several years.

He was editor of the dental department of the medical journal, "Progress," which was published for several years in Louisville. In 1887 he founded the Louisville College of Dentistry, as the dental department of Central University is known, and served two years as dean of the faculty and six years as president of the college. The increasing labors and responsibilities of these positions, together with the imperative duties of a growing practice, caused a temporary impairment of his health, and he was on that account compelled to resign the office of president of the Dental College, accepting the honorary appointment of Emeritus Professor of Oral and Dental Surgery, in which relation to the College he stands at present. During his active work in that institution in Louisville he conducted an oral surgical clinic semi-weekly, in which many operations were performed and a number of new appliances were used which were original with Dr. Smith.

In 1891 he was elected president of the Richmond Board of Health, and in 1895 was elected Health Officer of that city, a position which he is filling with great acceptance to the public.

Dr. Smith is a member of the Kentucky State Dental Association, of which he served a term as president; a member of the American Dental Association; a member of the Kentucky State Medical Society; of the American Medical Association; of the Northeast Kentucky Medical Association; Censor of the Medico-Chirurgical College of Philadelphia, and a member of the Practitioners' Club of Richmond. He is a valued contributor to the pages of the leading dental journals of the country. With all of his duties, professional and official, Dr. Smith is a prominent figure in social life; is Past Commander of Richmond Commandery No. 19, Free and Accepted Masons, and was the first Captain-General of the Commandery; is a leading member of the Presbyterian congregation of Richmond; was also one of the originators of the Century Club, and was its president for three years; and in all movements for the advancement of his city and the enlightenment of his fellow men, he is usually found in the front ranks, an industrious worker, a willing helper and a leader in whom his neighbors place the highest confidence.

Dr. Smith and Bertha O'Donnell Cecil Miller, daughter of James C. and Mary (Poe) Miller, of Louisville, were united in marriage November 8, 1881. Mrs. Smith is a lineal descendant of John O'Donnell, who was quartermaster-general in the Revolutionary war, also a descendant of the distinguished Poe and Byrd families of Virginia, and is regent of the Richmond Chapter of the Daughters of the Revolution. She is a woman of superior intelligence, fine literary attainments and rare personal beauty and amiability. She presides over their home with tact, and the doctor ascribes much of his success in later years to her helpfulness and popularity. Doctor and Mrs. Smith have two children living: Elliott Poe and Bertha Evelyn Byrd. Another son, named A. Wilkes Smith, died in infancy.

"Westover Terrace," the beautiful home of Dr. Smith, situated in the outskirts of the city, is so called for the ancestral home of the Byrds of Virginia. It is a model of convenience and architectural beauty, and was designed and constructed by Dr. Smith, whose versatility of genius, industry, energy and faithfulness to every duty would have insured him success in any calling.

THOMAS EDWARD MOSS, ex-attorney general of Kentucky, was born in Greensburg, Green County, Kentucky, March 14, 1839.

His parents were Thomas S. T. and Judith Campbell Bullock Moss. His father was a native of North Carolina and was a resident of Greensburg from 1808 until his death in 1851. His grandfather was a soldier in the war of 1812. The Moss family is of Scotch origin, and the progenitor of the family in the United States located in Massachusetts, where, tradition says, there were seven brothers, six of whom spelled the name "Morse," and one spelled it "Moss."

Judith Campbell Bullock Moss (mother) was born in Perryville, Kentucky. Her father was a native of Virginia.

Thomas E. Moss was about fourteen years of age when he removed with his widowed mother from Greensburg to a farm in Hickman County, near Columbus, Kentucky. His father left a small estate and a large family and his mother needed his assistance on the farm, so that he received but a meager education, but after remaining on the farm for two years, he attended the Columbia College in Adair County one year. He then attended school and studied under private teachers until 1858, and in 1859 entered the law department of the University of Louisville, from which he was graduated in March, 1860, receiving a diploma to practice law.

The night after President Lincoln issued his proclamation calling for troops, Mr. Moss left his home and joined the Second Regiment Kentucky Infantry, C. S. A., as a private soldier, mustered in at Camp Boon, notwithstanding he had recruited most of a company of which he should have been captain. He was made sergeant major and later adjutant of the regiment. His commission stated that his promotion was for gallant conduct on the field. Mr. Moss denies that there was any occasion for such recognition, but since he received more wounds than any other man in his regiment, it is probable that his superiors were justified in securing his promotion for meritorious services. The surrender at Hartsville was made to him, the commander of the opposing forces delivering his sword to Mr. Moss.

He was wounded, left on the field and captured at the battle of Murfreesboro; was sent to Fort Norfolk and there sentenced to be hung in retaliation for the deeds of others; was placed on board the steamer "Maple Leaf" and ordered to Fort Delaware, and during the voyage he got up a mutiny and overpowered the commander and guards; landed the boat and escaped with his fellow prisoners. He rejoined the army and continued in the service until the close of the war.

Returning to Hickman County, he found all of his mother's lands in possession of squatters from Tennessee. He soon left there and went to Paducah, where he began the practice of law in partnership with Judge Bigger. The firm of Bigger & Moss continued without interruption until the election of Mr. Moss as attorney general in 1875. He served his state in that capacity for four years—during the administration of Governor McCreary—after which he served two or three terms in the legislature, in which he distinguished himself by his superior knowledge of public affairs and by his active work in behalf of his constituents.

Mr. Moss was married February 28, 1871, in Covington, Kentucky, to Margaret Bright, daughter of the distinguished Senator Jesse D. Bright of Indiana. They have three children: Mrs. Mary Wheat, Jesse Bright and Thomas E. Moss, Jr.

SAMUEL ALEXANDER PIPER, President of the First National Bank of Maysville, son of Samuel Calvin and Eliza A. (Smith) Piper, was born in Nicholas County, Kentucky, December 8, 1828. His father, Samuel C. Piper, was born in Nicholas County in September, 1807, and was educated in the common schools of his county and became a farmer in connection with trading in which he operated extensively. He was one of the most popular men in the county, being scrupulously honest and square in all his dealings. He was in the prime of life in the best days of the old Whig party, and was steadfast in his adherence to the principles of that political party. He was a faithful member of the Presbyterian Church and his life was consistent with his profession. He died in 1873 and is buried at Carlisle, Kentucky. His father, Samuel Piper, was a native of Pennsylvania, who moved to Kentucky in the early history of the state.

Eliza A. Piper (mother) was born in Bourbon County, August 20, 1809; was married in September, 1827; died April 12, 1870, and is buried at Carlisle.

Alexander Smith (grandfather) was one of the most progressive and influential farmers of Bourbon County. He was a Captain in the War of 1812.

Samuel A. Piper enjoyed the usual training in the common schools in connection with his duties on the farm, and for some years after reaching his majority he was a farmer, and was quite successful in that vocation, giving considerable attention to financial matters; and when the Wells & Mitchell Bank was organized in Maysville in 1873 he was prominent among the five men who were interested in the enterprise. In 1880 this bank was reorganized and the name changed to First National Bank, and Mr. Piper was made one of the directors. In 1890 he was elected president of the bank, a position which he has filled with great credit alike to himself and the institution over which he presides. Prior to his election to the presidency of the bank he had been engaged for a short time in dealing in grain in Maysville, which has been his residence since May, 1893.

Mr. Piper was married September 6, 1855, to Ellen Fitzgerald, daughter of David Fitzgerald. She was born in Mason County in 1832, where she was given a fine education. Her father was a soldier in the War of 1812, and afterward moved to Mason County and was an extensive farmer and land owner.

Two daughters were born to S. A. and Ellen A. Piper: Annie E. was born October 27, 1862, married January 20, 1881, to S. A. Shanklin, and has had three children; James Alexander, born March 14, 1883, died May 12, 1887; Ellen F., born March 7, 1889, and Agnes Virginia, born April 15, 1892. The second daughter of Mr. and Mrs. Piper, Mollie Ryan, was born January 26, 1865; married Peter P. Parker November 8, 1888; has two children: Preston Piper, born November 21, 1889, and Samuel Alexander, born August 8, 1891.

Mr. Piper is an elder in the Central Presbyterian Church of Maysville, and before removing to that city had been an elder for twenty years. His ancestors as far back as he can trace them were of the Presbyterian faith.

JOHN D. WALKER, Vice President and Secretary of the Blue Grass Tobacco Company of Lexington, and one of the most enterprising and successful business men of the Blue Grass capital, was born in Brookville, September 13, 1850, where he enjoyed the ordinary advantages in the way of schooling. He was employed with his father for a few years, and learned the carpenter's trade and was engaged in building and painting for three or four years, and then abandoned this work to engage in the manufacture of wooden stirrups, and in the two years that he was thus occupied he built up a good trade, which he disposed of and embarked in the drug business, which he continued until 1876. Being an active, wide-awake citizen, he involuntarily drifted into local politics and served in various city offices until 1882, when he was elected sheriff of Bracken County, serving two years, and was then marshal of the county for two years, having by special act of the legislature the same jurisdiction as that of sheriff. During this term of office, he began buying and shipping tobacco, and this led him to Cincinnati, where he was engaged in tobacco brokerage for two years.

In 1885 he took the road for P. J. Sorg of Middletown, Ohio, one of the largest manufacturers of plug tobacco in the country. In 1886-7 he traveled for Overby Wells Tobacco Company, manufacturers of chewing and smoking tobacco (now of Lexington, formerly W. T. Overby & Co. of Paris, Kentucky), and in 1888 he was one of the organizers of the Blue Grass Tobacco Company and was elected Vice President and Secretary of the company, a position in which he has rendered efficient service, building up an extensive trade in twist and plug tobacco of high grade.

Mr. Walker was very active and successful as a Democratic politician in his native county, but has devoted his whole time to his business in the Blue Grass Tobacco Company since he became a citizen of Lexington.

He was married in 1880 to Jennie Freeze, daughter of G. P. Freeze of Brookville. He is a steward in the Hill Street Methodist Church, and a member of the Knights of the Ancient Essenic Order, Independent Order of Odd Fellows and Improved Order of Redmen.

His father, Jacob Walker, was a native of Lexington, who removed to Bracken County and made his home in Brookville until the time of his death in 1868. He was a merchant and acted as Postmaster of Brookville for many years prior to the war under Democratic administrations. He was a member of the Methodist Episcopal Church and a man of very decided opinions and great force of character who was highly respected and admired by his fellow-citizens.

John Walker (grandfather) was a native of Virginia and a distinguished minister in the Christian Church, who died of cholera in Bracken County in 1844. He was of German and Scotch-Irish origin.

Melissa Hamilton Walker (mother) is a native of Bracken County and is still a resident of Brookville. Her mother, Elizabeth Hamilton, was a native of Bracken County and died in the seventy-fifth year of her age.

LORENZO D. PEARSON, the oldest and deservedly the most highly respected undertaker of Louisville, was born in Shelby County, Kentucky, January 27, 1810; and is still engaged in business with his sons, giving them his counsel and support and the benefit of his long experience, a business which has certainly made him friends in thousands of households in Jefferson County. Few men have chosen an occupation to which they were better suited than has Mr. Pearson. Always kind, affable, gentle in his manner and sweetly sympathetic in his disposition, he has often come as a loving friend into the house of mourning and performed the kindly offices of the undertaker in such a manner and with such delicacy as to lessen the sorrow of those who have been bereft of their friends and loved ones. In the half century or more in which Mr. Pearson has served the community he has entombed enough bodies to people a great city, were they alive. He has witnessed the sorrow of thousands of mourners, and in all of his experience in the performance of his sacred duty, no man can say that he ever failed to appreciate and respect the grief of those whom he served. This slight tribute by one who has known him intimately for a third of a century is given from a sense of justice in behalf of a man who has performed a difficult duty for his fellow man as faithfully and as sacredly as the minister who is expected to console the bereaved in the presence of death.

Lorenzo D. Pearson came to Louisville when he was about twenty-one years of age. He had learned the trade of the cabinet-maker in Shelbyville, but his schooling had been limited, so he took up his studies for a few months before settling down to his work in the shop. But he did not have the means to continue this and he worked at his trade for two years, and then found employment with J. V. W. Smith, the leading undertaker in Louisville at that time, and after remaining with him for fifteen years Mr. Pearson began business on his own account in 1848. In the intervening years he has been one of the most active and successful business men in the city, to which he came without means when it was little more than a village and has risen steadily until he has acquired a competency, and by his energy, ability and uprightness has become one of its most honored and useful citizens.

Mr. Pearson was married in 1842 to Mary Ann Duhurst, daughter of John Duhurst, formerly of Philadelphia, but at that time a resident of Louisville. He has six children now living, three sons and three daughters: Emma L., wife of Nathan Steinberg; Edward C., Lorenzo D., Jr., Kate, Leila A., wife of R. F. Pelouze, and George E., all of whom reside in Louisville. His sons are in business with him and are carefully sustaining the reputation of their esteemed father.

Mr. Pearson is a son of Peter and Susan (Crow) Pearson. His father was a native of South Carolina, and removed to Shelby County, Kentucky, when a young man and engaged in farming. While assisting in the building of a log house in 1813 he was accidentally killed by a log rolling over him. His father was a native of England, who came to America about one hundred years ago and lived and died in South Carolina.

Susan Crow Pearson (mother) was a native of Garrard County, Kentucky, and died in Louisville, in 1872, in the eighty-fifth year of her age. She was almost a life-time member of the Methodist Episcopal Church, and her son has not departed from the faith in which he was brought up.

John Crow (grandfather) was a native of Ireland, who came to America and was a soldier in the Revolutionary war, after which he was a farmer in Garrard and Jessamine Counties, Kentucky, and died in Shelby County when over one hundred years old.

REV. CHARLES BOOTH PARSONS, D. D., was born in Enfield, Connecticut, July 23, 1805. His father died in 1820, and Charles being the eldest of four children, he left home at a tender age and found employment as an errand boy in a New York store. He was induced to join an amateur dramatic company and soon took a leading place in their amusements. On one occasion he played the part of Sir Edward Mortimer in the "Iron Chest," and one of the city papers compared the young actor to the elder Kean, who was one of the leading actors of that time. This stimulated Mr. Parsons' ambition, and he shortly afterward accepted an offer to join a theatrical company in Charleston, South Carolina. His success was immediate and almost unparalleled, and in the fifteen years of his life upon the stage he was one of its most brilliant stars of the time. His success was at its height, and his prospects for the future most promising, when a change came over him which turned his talents into another channel. The following extract from his autobiography, "Pulpit and Stage," gives a thrilling account of his conversion:

"There was to be a communion in the Presbyterian Church which I had been attending in the afternoon of the Sabbath, to which the preacher invited all to attend who felt interested in that ordinance, whether they were professors or not. They might show by their presence that they desired to honor the feast, though they might not be entitled to participate in it at the present time. It was a stormy afternoon, but I determined to attend. When I arrived at the church I took a seat back, and, by accident, on the left hand. It might have been providential. It so happened, too, that I was the only person present who was not entitled to partake of the sacred elements. The preacher very touchingly alluded to the circumstance in his prayer, the full force of which fell upon my heart—

the isolated stranger who was on the left of the fold, who had come through the storm to be a spectator to the feast. He prayed that this stranger might be converted and be admitted to the fellowship of the righteous through the Spirit of God. My heart said 'Amen,' while a flood of tears I could not restrain attested, to myself at least, the sincerity of my feelings. I retired to the hotel after service, and locking myself in my room knelt down by my bedside overwhelmed with agony of mind and almost the victim of despair. The prayer of the poor publican was uppermost in my mind, and I exclaimed aloud, 'Lord, be merciful.' What was that? A voice close to me seemed to say: 'Believe on the Lord Jesus Christ and thou hast eternal life.' I raised my head and gazed around the room, but saw no one. I then looked under the bed, thinking some one of my friends perhaps in order to play me a trick had concealed himself there. But all was vacant and silent. Again I addressed myself to my prayer, and again seemingly the same response was made. 'Surely,' thought I, 'this is the Lord and so I will receive it.' My heart beat heavily and seemed to labor to keep life within me. My tongue faltered, but faith helped me to ejaculate: 'Lord, I do believe; help thou my unbelief.' A flood of light flashed through the room; I sank down in rapture upon the floor, my heart grew joyous and I was a converted man."

Previous to his conversion he had made professional engagements for nearly a year in advance, which, after anxious thought and earnest prayer, he concluded it was his duty to fulfill, and he did so, knowing it would subject him to uncharitable criticism. At length he bade farewell to the stage forever; and being filled with a new purpose and inspired by high aims, he devoted himself to the study of the Scriptures with great earnestness. He soon became a local preacher in the Methodist Episcopal Church, and after the usual probation period was admitted to the traveling connection September 15, 1841.

He preached with most happy effect for two years in the Jefferson circuit and in 1843 was ordained a deacon by Bishop Morris. He then preached at Frankfort two years. On the 14th of September, 1845, he was ordained elder by Bishop J. Soule and was clothed with the full power of a minister. He was sent to St. Louis in charge of the Fourth Street Church, and while there the degree of Doctor of Divinity was conferred upon him by the Board of Curators of St. Charles (Missouri) College. Having returned to Kentucky, he was invited to preach the dedication sermon of a large church in St. Louis, and in 1855 he was called to the pastorate of that church. He found a small membership, but his two years of earnest labor resulted in an increase in the membership of over five hundred. In 1857-8 he was presiding elder of the East Louisville district and was subsequently appointed pastor of the Walnut Street Methodist Church, which was erected under his pastorate. He was assigned to that congregation a number of times. He was again called to St. Louis, serving a third term in that city.

In the celebrated disagreement among the Methodists Dr. Parsons was appointed one of the peace commissioners, and after the division between the North and the South, he cast his lot with the South branch of the church, remaining until the troubles culminated in war between the sections, when, true to his convictions, he returned to the Mother Church, where his views were in harmony with those with whom he was associated. The latter years of his life were spent in the ministry of the Methodist Church (not South), of which the membership in Louisville was quite small. His preaching, however, always attracted large audiences and his unflinching loyalty to his country made him a tower of strength in the church that was composed of a handful of loyal people.

In 1868 he went to Pittsburgh to dedicate a church, and on reaching the wharf on his return to Louisville his lower limbs were stricken with paralysis. During his protracted illness which followed every available means was used to restore him to health, but the disease was of a progressive character and terminated in his death December 8, 1871.

All through life Dr. Parsons maintained an exalted character. Even when engaged as an actor it was impossible to know him without being impressed with the marked propriety and dignity of his conduct. As a minister he was one of the most able and eloquent in the pulpit. He possessed in an eminent degree all of the requisites of a true orator—great emotions and passions, genius, fancy, imagination, gesture, attitude, intonations and facial expression—all were employed to accomplish the mighty purpose of a heart that was burdened with the responsibility of saving souls. His words well chosen and his thoughts inspired by a holy purpose and clothed in purest diction, commanded the attention and admiration of every hearer. He was a true and loyal citizen, a devoted husband and an affectionate father, who faithfully discharged his whole duty in every relation in life.

Dr. Parsons was married to Emily C. Oldham, who survives him, and is still a resident of the City of Louisville. She was born in Jefferson County in 1813. Her parents, William and Elizabeth (Field) Oldham, were natives of Jefferson County. Her maternal grandfather, Reuben Field, a native of Culpeper County, Virginia, came to Kentucky before the close of the last century. He was a prominent pioneer in the early settlement of the state, and served in the war for American independence.

Dr. and Mrs. Parsons were the parents of five children. Their son, Honorable Edward Y. Parsons, was elected to Congress in 1875 and died in Washington in 1876.

Frank Parsons, Commonwealth Attorney, one of the most brilliant and eloquent lawyers of Louisville, is a son of the late Rev. Dr. Charles Booth Parsons, an eminent divine, whose biography is given above.

Emily (Oldham) Parsons (mother) is a native of Jefferson County and a resident of Louisville, well advanced in years, a devout Christian and a "mother in Israel."

Frank Parsons was born in Louisville, Kentucky, January 2, 1850. He received a liberal education, attending the City High School, from which he graduated, and then took a course in the Indiana State University at Bloomington. He studied law with Jackson & Parsons, and was admitted to practice at the Louisville bar in March, 1874. He was engaged in a general practice until August, 1887, when he was elected Commonwealth Attorney by a majority of seven thousand votes over General Alpheus Baker, who was at that time one of the most capable lawyers in Louisville. He was re-elected for a second term, and has discharged the arduous duties of that office with fidelity to the public and with a high regard for the majesty of the law. He is a man of quiet, even temperament, courteous and polite to his witnesses, of dignified, scholarly bearing and has made one of the best prosecutors who has ever managed the cases of the Commonwealth in the Criminal Court of Louisville.

With a fine knowledge of the law, a keen sense of the responsibilities of his position, he has the moral courage to defend the rights of the people against evil doers of high or low degree. He is equally at home in preparing and conducting his cases, but he is particularly noted for the eloquence of his pleadings, being one of the most finished speakers at the Louisville bar.

He enjoys the respect and confidence of the legal fraternity, and being candid and careful in his pleadings, his arguments have tremendous weight with judge and jury. Without any attempt at pyrotechnic display of oratory for the purpose of winning applause, he is easily the most pleasing and attractive speaker in the Criminal Division where oratory is of more avail than in the Civil Courts. In this, and in many other respects, he resembles his father, who was one of the most brilliant orators of his day. At the last election for the office he now holds he had no opposition, being a strong Democrat, but the Republicans brought out nobody to oppose him, presumably because of his rare fitness for the office.

Frank Parsons was married in 1873 to Minnie Dent, daughter of the late Colonel Henry Dent, one of the most distinguished citizens of Louisville.

JAMES KENNEDY PATTERSON, Ph. D., LL.D., F. R. Hist. S., F. S. A. Scot., President of the State College of Kentucky, and of which under its reorganization he may justly be regarded as the founder, is a son of Andrew and Janet (Kennedy) Patterson, and was born in the City of Glasgow, Scotland, March 26, 1833. In 1842 he, with his father, came to this country and settled in Bartholomew County, Indiana.

His father subsequently removed to Hancock County, Indiana, where he lived until his death in 1862, in the sixty-second year of his age. His occupation in Scotland had been that of a calico printer, but after his arrival in this country he lived on a farm until his death. In religion he was a Presbyterian; in politics a Whig. His wife, Janet Kennedy, who still survives, lives with her son James. She, too, is a Presbyterian, with which faith her ancestors for generations had been identified.

The Pattersons from whom Dr. Patterson is descended were allied as a collateral branch with the Pattersons of whom William Patterson, founder of the Bank of England, in the latter part of the seventeenth century, was the most conspicuous representative.

For some years after coming to America Dr. Patterson's educational advantages were meager. In 1849-50 he attended a school in Madison, Indiana, taught by Robert French, where he finished the elementary branches and laid a foundation for classics and mathematics. During the next year he taught and in May, 1851, entered Hanover College, Indiana, where he graduated at the head of his class in 1856. From 1856 to 1859 he had charge of the Presbyterian Academy, Greenville, Kentucky. In the latter year he was elected Principal of the Preparatory Department of Stewart College (now Southwestern University), Clarksville, Tennessee. The following year he became Professor of Latin and Greek in the same college. In 1861 he was elected Principal of Transylvania in Lexington, and when that institution was consolidated with and merged into the Kentucky University he became Professor of Latin in the latter. In 1866 he became Professor of History and Metaphysics in the Agricultural and Mechanical College of Kentucky, and in 1869 its president. On the reorganization of the college in 1880 he was re-elected President of the State College of Kentucky (Agricultural and Mechanical College), which office he still holds.

When the college was reorganized and placed on a broader basis a tax of one-half of one per cent. on each $100 of taxable property in the Commonwealth was levied for its benefit. This tax he was largely instrumental in securing. Two years later the denominational colleges of Kentucky united in a movement to procure its repeal. For three months it was the principal question before the Legislature. Dr. Patterson fought and defeated the combination—one of the most powerful ever formed in Kentucky—single handed and alone. When the question of the constitutionality of the tax was brought forward he argued the defense in reply to Judge Lindsay before the Legislature. In the Court of Appeals, whither the case was carried, Judge Holt affirmed several years later the constitutionality of the tax on the lines of the argument laid down by Dr. Patterson. The college which in 1880 had an income of only $10,000 per annum, now has a yearly income from federal and state aid of over $80,000. It has the best equipped departments of Chemistry, Botany, Zoology, Geology, Civil Engineering and Mechanical Engineering in the South; and its Alumni take equal rank with the best who enter Johns Hopkins University for the prosecution of post-graduate courses of study. It has seven courses of study and twenty-seven professors.

In 1875 Dr. Patterson was appointed by Governor Leslie delegate from Kentucky to the International Congress of Geographical Sciences, which met in Paris, France. On his return he made a report to the Legislature, ten thousand copies of which were printed by the state. In 1890 he was appointed by Governor Buckner delegate from Kentucky to the British Association for the Advancement of Science. On this occasion leave of absence was granted him for one year. With his wife and son he sailed for Europe in June, 1890, and returned in August, 1891, during which time they traveled in England, Scotland, Belgium, France, Italy, Austria, Germany and Switzerland.

In 1875 he received from Hanover College the degree of doctor of philosophy; in 1880 he was elected a fellow of the Royal Historical Society of Great Britain; in 1880 a fellow of the Society of Antiquarians of Scotland; and in 1896 received the degree of doctor of laws from Lafayette College Pennsylvania.

During the years 1871-72-73-74 he contributed most of the editorial matter on foreign politics which appeared in the Courier-Journal of Louisville, and the first articles which appeared in that paper on the tariff question were from his pen. He contributed about the same time a series of papers on Comparative Philology to Home and School, edited by Major Davis of Louisville, which were well received by prominent men throughout the South. To the local press he has also been a frequent contributor.

During the sixties and early seventies Dr. Patterson was an indefatigable student of languages, and in addition to Latin, Greek and Hebrew, acquired a good knowledge of Sanskrit, Gothic, Anglo-Saxon, German and French. Latterly he has devoted more time to history, metaphysics and political science, in which subjects he is regarded as an authority by his contemporaries.

In 1859 Dr. Patterson married Miss Lucelia W. Wing, youngest daughter of Captain Charles F. Wing of Greenville, Kentucky. Two children were born of this marriage: Jeannie, who died in infancy, and William A. Patterson, who died June 3, 1895, in the twenty-eighth year of his age. He was a young man of fine natural endowments and excellent education. His knowledge of French, logic, metaphysics and history was equalled by none of his age in Kentucky. His command of English, in the compass of his vocabulary and in exuberance and delicacy of expression, was a marvel for one of his years. He was the idol of his parents and had been the constant companion of his father from his childhood. Dr. Patterson has obtained a site on the college grounds on which to erect and endow a library building to commemorate and perpetuate the name of his only son, William Andrew Patterson, whose name it will bear. William A. Patterson had for some time prior to his decease been assistant professor of history and of the English language and literature in the State College.

Lucelia W. Wing is descended on her father's side from the Wings of New Bedford, Massachussets, and on her mother's side from the Russells and Campbells of Virginia. She is a lady of extensive reading and rare cultivation and refinement. Hon. Edward Rumsey, who married her eldest sister, represented his district in Congress and was one of the most gifted men of his day. His uncle, James Rumsey, was the inventor of the steamboat, as shown by the resolution of Congress in 1839 awarding a gold medal to his son. Her nephew, Edward Rumsey Wing, was United States Minister to Ecuador, where he died in 1874.

Of the immediate family of Dr. Patterson but few survive: William Kennedy Patterson, professor of Greek in Transylvania, died in 1862; Andrew McFarland Patterson, professor of Latin in the same institution, died in 1863; Alexander L. Patterson, died in 1865. Besides the subject of this sketch Walter K. Patterson, of a family of five sons, alone survives. He was born in 1844, and is now and for sixteen years has been principal of the Academy of the State College, of which his older brother has for nearly thirty years been president.

HARRISON D. TAYLOR was born March 31st, 1802, in Frederick County, Virginia, and died April 8th, 1889, after a successful and useful life, at the advanced age of eighty-seven years. His parents were of Welsh and English origin and derived the name of Harrison from an intermarriage into the Harrison family of Virginia. His grandfather, also named Harrison Taylor, emigrated to Ohio County, Kentucky, the latter part of the last century, his father having died without a will, and under the feudal laws of that time the eldest son inherited the property and left Harrison shareless, who, declining to be a pensioner on his brother's charity, boldly struck out for the frontier. It was not long until he married Miss Jane Curlette and settled far back in the woods, and as the county improved he built a mill on a stream in Frederick County by which the main road passed, leading from the east across the Alleghany Mountains to the then great unexplored West. He raised a large family and bore the reputation of an honest miller, which in after years gained him the title of "Honest Old Taylor at the mill." Who should wish to trace their origin to a higher source? as "there is no legacy so rich as honesty." The subject of this sketch was the son of Rev. Thomas Taylor, a pioneer Methodist minister in Ohio County. Although through life a large contributor to the support of his church he never asked nor received a cent for his services as preacher of the gospel.

While in the vigor of his manhood it was his practice to work at hard labor through the week and ride many miles away on Sunday to fill some appointment, frequently going to Muhlenberg, Grayson, Breckinridge and even Hardin Counties to preach. Of him it may be truly said his heart was always right, his failings were but virtue in excess. He had five sons: Nicholas, Wesley, Harrison D., Milton and Thomas, and one daughter, Frances. The third son, Harrison, was a man who lived without fear and died without reproach. His boyhood days were spent on his father's farm where he had but small chance of obtaining an education, but such was his burning ambition for knowledge that whilst he followed the plow he carried his grammar in his pocket and conjugated his verbs as he went along, and at night by means of a bright wood fire he pursued his studies. At last upon attaining his majority he decided upon law as a profession, and moved to Hartford, the county seat, where he studied with Judge Henry Pirtle, one of the most distinguished lawyers of the state. His mother, one of the illustrious women of her day, a model of all the duties of social, religious and domestic life, had instilled in him the principle to do right whatever else might happen. And the following story will illustrate his strong characteristics in that direction. His father having arranged for his board he packed up and went to town dressed in homespun from head to foot quite ignorant of the customs and manners of town life. At the tavern where he stopped there was a bar, of course, which was frequented constantly by the most brilliant young men of the place; in the little room to which he had been assigned he noticed old packs of cards laying around, and saw that it had been a resort for gamblers. He had not more than arrived at this conclusion when he heard the voices of three gentlemen in the bar below. Then the proprietor remarked in a bland voice: "O, yes, just walk up;

you will find a good fire; a young Mr. Taylor is up there, but he will have no objection." But before they had ascended the steps he had argued the question pro and con in his mind. First he thought, "I am here a lone boy, noticed by no one; how pleasant it would be to become intimate with such distinguished gentlemen—the leading doctor, lawyer and most accomplished young gentlemen of leisure and fortune in the community. How will it look for so uncouth a chap as I," glancing at his homespun, "to refuse such a favor;" but by the time they had entered the room and asked his permission to play he had decided. "Gentlemen," he said, " I am here for the purpose of study, and although I would like to accommodate you, I think it best to decline." The old doctor wheeled around, audibly muttering curses as he retired, but the other two politely bowed themselves out, and that young man, distinguished for his wealth, family connections and mental endowments, was ever after that his warmest friend.

It is needless to say that none of the attractions of town life allured him, so firm was his determination to do right and his ambition to learn. He was admitted to the bar in 1825. As a practicing lawyer he was a model of industry and fidelity to his clients, of which he had a large share. He had the confidence of the people as an honest, fair dealing, truthful, noble-spirited man. His practice at the bar was restricted by his own choice and taste to chancery causes and for many years after his retirement from active practice his opinions on the vexed questions which so frequently arise in equity, was sought after and esteemed by the Hartford bar. His habits of close study, formed in early life, clung to him in old age. His mind was broad and liberal and he had a most extensive knowledge of all subjects. In the domain of history, the sciences, literature, politics and religion he possessed a vast and varied store of accurate information. He made the first authentic survey of Rough and Green Rivers by directions of the Government, which resulted in establishing permanent navigation of Green River. His excellent knowledge of land titles and of surveying enabled him to acquire a vast amount of real estate in Ohio County. It has been said of him that by his leniency and indulgence he afforded many struggling young farmers the opportunity to retain their homes. His influence was on the side of every good enterprise and every broad charity. His house was the home of the friendless and especially was he interested in those struggling to acquire an education. He wrote a valuable history of Ohio County and many other interesting papers; and was a member of the Filson Club, the principal historical society of the state. He never aspired to political honors and never held office but once (county attorney), and was elected to that without being a candidate. He was in early times a Whig and great admirer and personal friend of Henry Clay, but after the retirement of the great commoner he affiliated with the Democratic party.

His first marriage was to Miss Mary Daviess in 1828, by whom he had several children: Henry Pirtle, Fannie, Randall, Thomas and Margaret, all of whom are dead but Thomas, who is a farmer near Hartford. His second marriage was to Mrs. Kittie Trible, of Owensboro, who survived him. His eldest son, Dr. Henry Pirtle Taylor, married Miss Sallie May of Daviess County. Two of their children are living, Harrison P. Taylor and Mary Taylor. The former married Miss Mary Pendleton, daughter of Dr. John E. Pendleton of Hartford, Kentucky, and to them were born two children, Sallie and John Pendleton.

FERDINAND ADAM NEIDER of Augusta, son of Adam and Barbara (Quill) Neider, was born in Wheeling, West Virginia, March 2, 1851.

His father was born in Prussia in 1805. He came to America when about twenty-five years of age and settled in Wheeling, West Virginia, where he was engaged in the manufacture of gas until 1855, when he retired, five years before his death.

Barbara Quill, his wife, was also a native of Prussia. They were married in Wheeling in 1831. She was born in 1814 and died in 1877.

Ferdinand A. Neider was educated in the public and Catholic schools of Wheeling. At the age of seventeen years he left home and school and began the battle of life for himself. He was stationed at different times in Columbus and Cincinnati, Ohio, and Madison, Indiana. In Cincinnati he learned the carriage-making trade; and in 1870, when nineteen years of age, he located in Augusta and engaged in carriage making. In 1883 he began the manufacture of carriage trimmings, and has now one of the most successful and popular establishments of the kind, of which there are only seven in the United States.

Mr. Neider is a mechanical genius, having patented some thirty different inventions in the line of his business, and from the profits in these inventions and in the manufacture of trimmings and novelties and the sale of carriage hardware he has accumulated a handsome fortune.

Being public-spirited, hospitable and liberal with his means for the public good and for the pleasure of his friends, he is naturally one of the most popular and useful citizens of Augusta.

He is considered an all-round man in politics as well as in affairs pertaining to the prosperity of his adopted city. He votes the Democratic ticket in national elections; but is neutral in local politics, always voting the ticket, or for the man, he considers the most likely to serve the public faithfully.

Mr. Neider is a member of the Catholic Church, as were his father and mother.

January 29, 1873, he married Maggie Sherwood of Augusta. They have three children: Bertha Estelle, Maggie and Bonnie May.

DR. RICHARD PRETLOW, deceased, was born in Southampton County, Virginia, November 27, 1811. His parents were Edna (Bailey) and Samuel Pretlow, who removed from Virginia to Springboro, Ohio, when the son was seventeen years of age. Dr. Pretlow, having secured a liberal education in the best schools of the day, went to Cincinnati when twenty-one years of age and attended the Ohio Medical College, graduating in 1835. He began his professional career in Richmond, Indiana, and gained a wide reputation as a physician in the course of several years of practice. In 1843 he removed to Covington, where he was engaged in the practice of medicine for over half a century. His death February 20, 1894, was mourned by the entire community in which he had lived so long, and in which he was universally known and respected.

Many expressions of sorrow and tributes to his memory were published in the newspapers of the city, among which was the following, written by Hon. John Sanford, one of his many devoted friends:

"Another link has been broken which binds the present with the earlier history of Covington. There are not many of them left, and in the death of Dr. Richard Pretlow we have lost one to which many will cling with loving remembrance. For fifty years he practiced medicine in our city. A calling that required him to move along the private pathways of life, that lead within the home circle, and is associated with family affliction.

"There are no memories so tender as those which cling around the name of one who brings comfort to us at such a time. The announcement of the death of Dr. Pretlow on yesterday moved across our city like a shadow, and tears came everywhere in eyes that were unused to the melting mood. The kindly face that had so often beamed beside the bed of pain—the tender hand that had so often brought comfort, and the voice that had so often encouraged hope, were all gathered on the silent shore.

"He was a modest, unassuming man, who walked along the sequestered vale of life with no ambition save that of good for his fellows. In all his surroundings, whether as citizen, physician, friend, husband or father, he might have been taken as a model, and humanity would have been elevated by the pattern. He had accumulated a very handsome estate, but not one dollar of it was ever wrung from the suffering poor.

"If they were able to pay him for his services it was all right; if they were not, they received his attention all the same. The world was made better in his life, and in his death it has lost one of its endearing charms. May he rest in peace."

Dr. Pretlow was not only devoted to his profession, but endeared himself to all classes by his kindly disposition and his never-failing interest in the general welfare of the community. He was a man of superior judgment in matters of business and was identified with the Farmers' Bank of Kentucky of Covington, and was its president for many years.

He attended the Presbyterian Church, of which he was a trustee, and Mrs. Pretlow put a beautiful and artistic memorial window in the church, representing "Christ, the Great Physician," in memory of her devoted husband.

Dr. Pretlow built a beautiful home on the corner of Fourth and Greenup streets, Covington, in which he lived for fifty years.

He was in no sense a politician, but took great interest as a Republican in political questions.

In 1837 Dr. Pretlow married Elizabeth A. Lynch of Lynchburg, Virginia. She lived with him for thirty years; died in 1867, and was buried in Highland Cemetery. By this marriage there are two children living: Mrs. Frank Prague of Covington, and Samuel D. Pretlow. He married again, June 1, 1869, Cassie Prague, daughter of Edward and Sarah A. Prague of Springdale, Ohio.

Dr. Pretlow's ancestors were English, and they brought the brick with them to build their house in Virginia.

JAMES ALLEN McCANE, clerk of the Bracken County Court, son of Thomas and Nancy D. (Anderson) McCane, was born in Bracken County, March 3, 1854. His father is also a native of Bracken County. He was born May 18, 1820, and since his school days, which were spent in the county schools, he has devoted himself to farming near Augusta. He was married November 29, 1849, to Nancy D. Anderson.

DR. JAMES T. REDDICK of Paducah was born in Sumner County, Tennessee, Feb. 15, 1859. His father, James W. Reddick, was born in the same county in 1836, and was a prominent farmer and trader there who became a Primitive Baptist minister in middle life and preached successfully in Sumner and adjoining counties for twenty-five years. He was a forcible speaker, a man of strong convictions and exerted a great influence for good in his community. Outside of the ministry he was a citizen of prominence and influence.

John A. Reddick (grandfather) was also a native of Sumner County; a farmer and a man of most excellent character; honest, industrious, a leading member of the Primitive Baptist Church, a good citizen and neighbor and a Democratic voter.

John Parish (maternal grandfather) was a native of Tennessee and a farmer all of his life.

Dr. James T. Reddick divided his time between the farm and the schoolroom when he was a boy, giving the most of his time to farm work. But he was studious and by studying at home succeeded in obtaining a fair primary education. He read medicine at night after working on the farm during the day. His preceptor was Dr. W. H. Neal, a prominent physician of Sumner County. At the age of nineteen he entered the medical department of the University of Tennessee at Nashville and was graduated from that institution at the age of twenty-one years, receiving the honors of his class. He first settled in Hopkins County, Kentucky, where he practiced for ten years and then removed to Paducah in 1890, where he has gained a large practice and secured an excellent standing among the ablest physicians in the city.

He is a prominent and influential member of a number of benevolent orders, a Mason and Odd Fellow in all the branches of those orders and a member of the Elks. He is a member of the Board of Trustees of the public schools, ex-president of the Paducah Medical and Surgical Society, vice-president of the Southwestern Kentucky Medical Association, member of the State Medical Association and of the American Medical Association.

Dr. Reddick married Miss Willie Coleman in 1881, and they have three children: Beulah, Clifford and Willie. The doctor and his family are members of the Baptist Church.

THOMAS D. RYAN, leading merchant and a highly honored citizen of Augusta, son of David and Martha (Bufford) Ryan, was born in Mercer County, Kentucky, May 2, 1828, and was educated in the common schools and at the Augusta College. Very soon after leaving school he embarked in the mercantile business, first in 1844 as a clerk for his brother, James B. Ryan, and soon became a partner in the house. They went to Peoria, Illinois, and there engaged in a dry goods venture. Six months later James B. Ryan sold his interest to Thomas D. Ryan and returned to Augusta. After one year's experience in Peoria Thomas D. Ryan also returned to Augusta and opened a dry goods store on his own account.

In 1862 he enlisted in the Seventh Regiment, Kentucky Cavalry, United States Army, under Colonel Metcalfe, and later under Colonel John K. Faulkner of Garrard County, in General Green Clay Smith's brigade. He was sergeant for a time, and after the battle of Richmond was acting commissary until his discharge. Among the important engagements he was in were the cavalry fight at Big Hill, the battles of Richmond and Stone River and numerous battles around Franklin and in Central Tennessee. He received a desperate wound in his head at the battle of Richmond, Kentucky, which wound threatened his life, and was honorably discharged, the papers bearing the signature of General W. S. Rosecrans.

In 1864 he was appointed United States assessor and deputy collector of internal revenue for Bracken County, which office he held for three years.

In 1867 he went to Cincinnati and was employed as salesman in the wholesale dry goods house of Steadman, Shaw & Company, afterward Steadman & Wilcox. The latter firm consolidated with Shaw, Barbour & Company, under the style of Barbour, Steadman & Herrod. Mr. Ryan followed each of these changes, receiving a handsome salary; but in 1873 he left that house for a similar position with Chambers, Stevens & Company, wholesale dry goods dealers, and was with them for four years.

In 1877 he returned to Augusta and opened a retail dry goods store, and has continued in that business until the present time without interruption. His honesty, integrity and other excellent traits of character have made him a host of friends in the county, in which he is well and favorably known.

Mr. Ryan is an ardent and unflinching Republican and a man of influence in his party. It is his boast that he has never scratched a ticket. He is a member of the Presbyterian Church, and his daily "walk and conversation" are in keeping with his profession. As a citizen of Augusta he is public spirited and enterprising, popular and influential.

Mr. Ryan was married in 1850 to Laura Angeline McCormick, daughter of John E. McCormick. Mrs. Ryan died in 1878, and he was married a second time, December 24, 1880, to Rosa R. Crawford of Steubenville, Ohio, daughter of Thomas Crawford of that city. He has one adopted daughter, Helen Morrison Ryan, daughter of R. J. Morrison of Steubenville, Ohio.

David Ryan (father) was a native of Westmoreland County, Virginia, who came to Harrod's Station, Mercer County, with his mother, who was a widow, when he was ten years of age. They remained in the station for one year before they were able to make a settlement on the land which his mother had bought on account of the depredations of the Indians. He obtained an ordinary education and became a successful farmer in Mercer County, where he died in 1854. He was a soldier in the war of 1812, and was in Shelby's Light Horse Brigade, and was highly honored by being detailed as one of the guards in charge of Perry's prisoners taken on the lakes. After he was an old man he received a land warrant for one hundred and sixty acres for his military services. He was a Democrat in politics, a man of strong convictions with the courage to stand up for what he believed to be right and to denounce the wrong. His chief characteristics were his love of home and of the Methodist Church, of which he was a member for many years.

He had three brothers and two sisters who came with their mother from Virginia. Solomon and John took part in the battle of Blue Lick, the last of the great battles with the Indians, who were driven from the state. He married a Miss Runion and raised a large family on a fine farm in Mercer County, Kentucky.

One of his sisters married Edward Sutterfield and lived in Mercer County. The other sister married Samuel Jones, who owned one of the finest farms in Mercer County.

Thomas D. Ryan's grandfather was a native of Ireland, who came to America and located in Westmoreland County, Virginia, where he died a short time before his widow removed to Kentucky.

Martha Bufford Ryan (mother) was a native of Virginia, and was of Scotch descent.

REV. JOHN M. RICHMOND, D. D., President of Princeton (Kentucky) College, was born in Ayr, Ontario, Canada, May 13, 1848. He is a son of William and Ann (Dickey) Richmond, natives of Ayrshire, Scotland, who removed to Canada in 1838. They were members of the Presbyterian Church, in which Mr. Richmond was an elder for thirty years. He was a farmer and citizen of Ayr until 1879, when he died, in the seventieth year of his age.

Matthew Richmond (grandfather) was a native of Scotland and was associated with Robert Burns on Mossgiel farm, being with the bard when he wrote some of his celebrated poems.

Dr. Richmond's mother, Ann Dickey Richmond, was a Presbyterian of the strictest sect and a devout Christian woman. She lived to the extreme age of eighty-five years and died in Ayr, Canada, in 1892.

Dr. Richmond's early schooling was obtained in the town of Ayr, after which he attended the Collegiate Institute at Galt, and completed his literary studies in Toronto University with the class of 1868. He then attended the Princeton Theological Seminary in New Jersey, completing his course in 1871. The degree of doctor of divinity was conferred upon him by Parsons College (Iowa) in 1887.

His first charge after entering the ministry was the Hoge Presbyterian Church, Columbus, Ohio, where he remained five years. He was then pastor of the First Presbyterian Church at Ypsilanti, Michigan, for five years; then pastor of the Shady Side Presbyterian Church, Pittsburgh, Pennsylvania, for seven years; and was then pastor of the Central Presbyterian Church, Louisville, for six years, resigning his pastorate in 1894 to accept the presidency of the Collegiate Institute at Princeton, Kentucky. This institution, which is conducted under the auspices of the Presbyterian Church, was established in 1881, with the especial object in view of preparing young men for the ministry; and it has never been in as prosperous a condition as it is now under Dr. Richmond's able management.

Dr. Richmond is a thoroughly orthodox Presbyterian, a man of natural talent, well equipped for the work of minister or teacher, a pleasing, forcible speaker, an excellent teacher, and has developed fine executive ability in the short time he has had charge of the college at Princeton. The trustees of the institution realized the importance of placing a man of ability at the head of affairs and in selecting Dr. Richmond for the responsible position they removed one of the best ministers from Louisville, where Dr. Richmond was held in the highest esteem by his congregation and members of sister churches.

He has been twice married: first in 1871 to Juliette Eyre Phillips, daughter of Louis W. R. Phillips of Princeton, New Jersey. She died in 1882, leaving one son, William Dickey Richmond, and one daughter, Margaret Craig Richmond. His second marriage was in November, 1884, to Annie M. Gordon, daughter of Chief Justice Isaac G. Gordon of Pennsylvania.

WILLIAM M. SMITH, United States Attorney for the district of Kentucky, was born in Christian County, Kentucky, January 3, 1853. He is the son of Samuel R. and Mary J. (Pattillo) Smith. His father was born in Granville County, North Carolina, in 1826, where, after attaining his majority, he engaged in the business of a planter. He removed to Christian County, Kentucky, in the early fifties, and followed farming on a large scale, owning a large number of slaves; but after the slaves were given their freedom he engaged in the cotton business, continuing in that about eight years, when he removed to Graves County, Kentucky, where he died in 1892. He was an ardent Democrat and sympathized with the South in the late war; traveled extensively and enjoyed life, but never cared for political honors. His father (W. M. Smith's grandfather) was also a native of North Carolina, who fought in the Revolutionary War, and was tendered a commission as lieutenant, but declined on account of his health and was compelled to return to his home, and died there. His ancestors were English people.

Mr. W. M. Smith's maternal grandfather, William Pattillo, was a native of Corsica, who came to America when he was quite young and engaged in general merchandise. He married Miss Ann Mayfield of Warren County, who was quite wealthy. Mr. Pattillo was a man of fine education and was still engaged in his studies when he died at the age of thirty-two. His daughter, Mary J. (Pattillo) Smith, received a college education and was a lady of fine literary attainments, a member of the Episcopal Church, and died in Graves County in 1875.

William M. Smith is the sixth of eleven children. After attending the country schools he graduated at Mayfield College and then attended the Law Department of the University of Louisville, finishing his legal course in 1872. He at once commenced the practice of law with Mr. A. B. Stublefield in Mayfield, a partnership which was terminated after two years by the death of the senior member of the firm. Mr. Smith continued the business alone for two years and then he was for a time associated with Judge W. M. Miller, and later with Judge W. W. Tice. This relation was dissolved by mutual consent and the firm of Robertson, Smith & Robbins was formed and continued until Mr. Smith's appointment as United States district attorney in February, 1894.

Mr. Smith was county attorney for four years, was a member of the Kentucky Legislature for two years, 1889-90, was a presidential elector in 1888, and held other positions of responsibility which were conferred upon him by the people of his county.

Mr. Smith married Miss Augusta N. Anderson, daughter of Hon. Lucien Anderson of Mayfield, September 26, 1874. Mrs. Smith died in 1879, leaving three sons, Harry A., Terry Pattillo, and Lucien R. In 1884 he married Miss Dellah M. Sherrill, daughter of Col. Lee Sherrill of Ballard County, and there are three children as a result of this marriage.

Mr. Smith is a Democrat of the Cleveland type, and while he has held a number of positions, elective and appointive, he is not a politician. His delight is in the law, and he gives his time wholly to his official and professional duties. He is a member of the Christian Church.

GEORGE WASHINGTON MERRITT, a highly popular young attorney of Russellville, was born in Christian County, Kentucky, August 11, 1857.

His father, Washington Merritt, was born in Todd County, Kentucky, July 5, 1835, and removed in 1856 to Christian County, where he engaged in farming. He lost all of his property during the civil war, and in 1865 he removed to Robertson County, Tennessee, where he died January 10, 1878. He was married October 29, 1854, to Lucy A. Waller, who was born in Pottsylvania County, Virginia, November 20, 1834. She was educated in the common and private schools of Todd County. She was the mother of four children: Leonard Ross, born August 22, 1855, died July 31, 1885; George Washington; Louisa Alice, born June 14, 1860, married Stephen Plaster, who died in October, 1891, and married Miss Knight of Butler County, Alabama; Rosa Lee, born September 3, 1868, wife of Edward Collier of Fort Deposit, Alabama.

Daniel Ross Merritt (paternal grandfather) was born in Williamson County, Tennessee, January 10, 1800, was educated at Franklin College; was a graduate in medicine; removed to Todd County, Kentucky, in 1821, where he practiced medicine until 1838, when he abandoned his profession in order to give his attention to a very large landed estate. He was married three times: first to a widow Fort, whose children were William J., Eliza and one who died in infancy. His second wife was a widow Vance, whose children were Cordilia, Allie, Daniel and Washington (father). His third wife was Penelope Hannum, who was the mother of Richard, Henry Clay, Fisher Harrison, Rosabella, Montgomery, an eminent lawyer of Henderson, Philander and Charlotte, a total of fourteen sons and daughters. Mr. Merritt died in July, 1883. Five of the sons were in the Confederate army.

Benjamin Leonard Waller (maternal grandfather) was born in Pottsylvania County, Virginia, January 12, 1810, and died October 18, 1866. He was a fine Greek and Latin scholar, was for fourteen years a prominent teacher and educator, in connection with his farming interests. He removed to Todd County, Kentucky, in 1838, when Lucy A. Waller Merritt (mother) was three years of age, and taught school for twelve years, at the same time looking after the business of his farm. He married Dorothy Wilson, a native of Virginia, and they had nine children: Lucy A. (mother), Eliza, Benjamin, Nannie, George, Zachary Taylor, Sallie, Wilson and Cora. Two of the sons were in the Confederate army. They were members of the Christian Church.

George W. Merritt attended the common schools in Robertson County, Tennessee, and graduated from Southwestern Presbyterian University, Clarksville, in the class of 1880. He entered the law department of Cumberland University, at Lebanon, Tennessee, February 1, 1882, and was graduated in June, 1884. He taught school at intervals while attending college, and for one year following his graduation from the law school at Fort Deposit, Alabama.

He was admitted to the bar in January, 1886, and began the practice of his profession in Russellville, in which he has met with gratifying success. He has made his way to prominence in his profession and to success in business through his own industry and perseverance, and commands the respect and confidence of the community in which he is universally known.

Mr. Merritt was married August 31, 1832, to Etta Sory, daughter of Thomas W. Sory. She was born in Robertson County, Tennessee, August 29, 1857. They have three children living: Vernon Washington, born October 18, 1883; Minnie Ross, born August 9, 1886, and Benjamin Leonard, born February 11, 1888, died in infancy; Sory, born December 11, 1894.

FRANK F. WALLER of Lawrenceburg was born in Burlington, Boone County, August 29, 1858. His father, William H. Waller, was born in Virginia in 1823 and came to Kentucky when a young man and engaged in buying and selling horses, cattle and sheep in Boone and Kenton Counties; removed to Mt. Sterling in 1868, where he was engaged with S. Wolverton & Co., proprietors of a number of stage lines, and remained with them until the railroads destroyed their business. He has been principally engaged in farming for some years past.

Mary E. Sherrill Waller (mother) was born in Kentucky in 1835. She was the daughter of B. W. Sherrill, a merchant of Burlington, Boone County.

Frank F. Waller's early education was somewhat neglected, as he went to work as a clerk in a hardware store at Mt. Sterling when only twelve years of age. In that way, however, he obtained a knowledge of business which has served him well in a successful business career. Before he was fifteen, he was appointed messenger of the Adams Express Co. on the L. C. & L. Railway, and filled that position for nine years, picking up further information and acquiring a knowledge of human nature of which few men of his age could boast. After leaving the road, he was appointed the company's agent at Eminence and was there for one year, when he resigned to accept a government appointment in the revenue service. He resigned after two years' service and returned to Eminence and began business in partnership with J. S. McKendrick, dealing in lumber and coal. This partnership continued for three years, when they sold out and went to Lexington and opened a coal and lumber office there. On account of sickness in his family, Mr. Waller remained there only six months and then went to New Castle and formed a partnership with Mr. Monroe and engaged in the lumber and coal business under the firm name of Monroe and Waller, while at the same time they owned a transfer and stage line running from Eminence to New Castle, carrying passengers and freight, which proved a very successful and prosperous venture. He continued in these enterprises until 1893, when he removed to Lawrenceburg and engaged again in dealing in coal and lumber in connection with other kinds of building materials. In this venture he has enjoyed continued success.

Mr. Waller married Marie L. Sacra of Shelby County, August 22, 1876. They have four sons and one daughter: Harold M., Ben. F., Otis S., Joseph K. and Lucille.

Mr. and Mrs. Waller are active members of the Baptist Church, and are highly respected by a host of friends and acquaintances,

MARMADUKE BECKWITH MORTON, Clerk of the Logan County Court,, Russellville, was born in Logan County, Kentucky, August 16, 1840.

His father, William I. Morton, was born in Louisa County, Virginia, September 9, 1786, and was educated in the common schools of that county. He came to Russellville in 1810, and after taking a course of legal studies practiced law for a great many years. He was a very public-spirited man, progressive in his ideas, and was a leader in the old Whig party. He was postmaster of Russellville for several terms; was elected county attorney of Logan County in 1836, and held that office many years; served his district in the Legislature at one time; in 1854 was appointed judge of the Logan County Court; was deeply interested in religion, and frequently preached the gospel in the Baptist Church in Russellville, also at the Liberty and Friendship Churches in Logan County and in Tennessee. He was three times married, first December 4, 1805, to Rebecca Haden of Fluvanna County, Virginia, daughter of Colonel Joseph Haden. Mrs. Morton died, leaving five children: Eleanor Beckwith, Amanda Pocohontas, Mary Virginia, Joseph William and George Richard.

His second wife was Louisa McCormick, who died, and left one child, Peter Henry Morton. His third wife was Mrs. Clarissa McCleland, whose maiden name was Clarissa Harlow McCormack. She was born in Lincoln County, November 16, 1802. She married John McCleland May 5, 1822, who died, and she then married W. I. Morton in 1832, November 13. The children of this union were: Clarissa M. Morton, Joseph W. Morton, Marmaduke B. Morton and Martha L. Morton.

William Jordan Morton (grandfather) was born in Northern Virginia November 15, 1754. He was known as a "gentleman," having inherited large wealth and owning a great many slaves. His chief characteristic was his loyalty and his intense hatred of the "Tories." He was married March 16, 1779, to Martha Prior, daughter of William and Sarah Prior. She was born April 6, 1761, and died March, 1800. They were the parents of twelve children: Peter, born December 16, 1779; Sarah, born November 10, 1781; Rebecca, born May 21, 1783; Francis, born March 9, 1785; William I. (father), born September 9, 1786; Mary, born March 31, 1788; Joseph, born February 28, 1790; John, born January 21, 1792; Elizabeth born September 12, 1794; Marmaduke B., born September 13, 1796; Henry Prior, born September 3, 1798; Martha, born March 15, 1800.

Marmaduke B. Morton, the tenth child named above, held the same office for twenty years that is now held by his nephew, whose name heads this sketch.

Joseph Morton (great-grandfather) was a native of Virginia. Special history unknown.

John McCormick (maternal grandfather) was a farmer of Lincoln County, Kentucky. He married Leanna Masterson, daughter of Edward and Eleanor (Coleman) Masterson. They removed from Lincoln County to North Carolina. They had five children: James, Caleb, Mary, Leanna and Leah.

Daniel McCormick (maternal great-grandfather) was a native of Ireland, who came to the United States when he was about nineteen years of age, and located in Philadelphia; married Sarah Hollingsworth, and had nine children: John, Joseph, William, Daniel, Sarah, Nancy, Hannah and Martha.

Marmaduke B. Morton received his education in private schools and in Bethel College, Russellville, attending the latter institution the first year of its existence. At the age of fourteen he left school and entered the office of the clerk of the County Court as deputy and served in that capacity for about five years. During the Civil war he looked after his aged mother and her property. After the close of the war he engaged in merchandising at Auburn for four or five years, and was subsequently engaged in farming, but abandoned that occupation and traveled fifteen years for a wholesale hardware establishment in Louisville; from 1890 to 1894 he served as deputy sheriff of Logan County; in November, 1894, he was elected clerk of the Logan County Court.

Mr. Morton has been a member of the Baptist Church since 1860; is a Master Mason and a highly esteemed and popular citizen.

He was married December 7, 1869, to his cousin, Virginia Morton, daughter of Joseph Morton. She was born in Logan County, February 13, 1844, and was educated in the best schools of Logan County. They have had eight children, six of whom are living:

Henry Prior, born December 25, 1870.

Overton Harris, born October 1, 1871; died November 10, 1885.

Joseph Jordan, born April 21, 1878; died June 25, 1891.

Francis Alexander, born March 4, 1875.

Clarissa Louisa, born June 23, 1876.

William I., born April 6, 1878.

James Hanna, born December 1, 1879.

Virginia, born June 11, 1882.

PROFESSOR ABNER GOFF MURPHY, President of the Logan Female College, Russellville, was born in Knox County, Ohio, October 18, 1831. He is a son of William and Sarah Ann (McKinney) Murphy.

His father was born in Maryland, April 17, 1804, and was educated in log school houses in Belmont and Knox Counties, Ohio. He was a farmer and tanner by occupation, and a very worthy and highly esteemed citizen of Knox County, Ohio, until the day of his death, January 2, 1885. He was a steward in the Methodist Church, very liberal in the support of his own congregation, and there were few churches in the county to which he did not contribute. He was elected colonel of the Ohio State Militia and served in that capacity for five years. He was a Whig in the days of that political party, and a Republican after its dissolution. He was married December 27, 1830, to Sarah Ann McKinney, and they had three children, only one of whom, Prof. A. G. Murphy, is living. Elizabeth died in 1843, and Lydia died in 1837.

Sarah Ann McKinney Murphy (mother) was born in Loudoun County, Virginia, December 27, 1809, and was educated in excellent private schools in Leesburg, Loudoun County, Virginia, and was a woman of rare intellectual endowments and attainments.

Abner Murphy (grandfather) was a native of Maryland, who went to Ohio, where he was en-

gaged in farming and tanning. He was an orthodox Quaker and a man of many noble traits of character. He married Sarah Gattan, who was born in Dundee, Scotland, in 1775, and died in Knox County, Ohio, in 1853. Her parents immigrated to America when she was a child. Abner and Sarah Murphy had ten children: Hiram, Robert, William (father), Jane, Mary, Basil, Rachel, Eleanor, Sallie and Elias.

Abner Murphy's father was a native of the north of Ireland, an Irish Quaker, who settled in Maryland in 1773.

George J. McKinney (maternal grandfather) was born in Loudoun County, Virginia, in 1787, and removed to Knox County, Ohio, where he was a farmer. He married Elizabeth Thomas, daughter of Leonard Taylor Thomas, who was born in Buoys Island, in the Potomac, son of Captain Thomas, who belonged to the English army and served in the French and Indian war. After the close of the war he resigned his commission in the regular army and married the widow of Colonel Leonard Taylor. All of the Taylor family were members of the Episcopal Church.

James Johnston, who was George McKinney's maternal grandfather and the great-great-grandfather of Prof. A. G. Murphy, was a soldier in the Revolutionary war, whose residence was near Philadelphia. After the war he went to Loudoun County, Virginia, and bought a large tract of land, upon which he lived until he was ninety years old, and died in 1830.

Prof. Abner G. Murphy was educated in the Ohio Wesleyan University at Delaware. He entered the preparatory department in 1845, remaining one year. In 1849 he entered again, taking the full course in the University proper, and was graduated in the class of 1855.

He went to Millersburg, Kentucky, soon afterwards and held the chair of Latin and Greek in the Millersburg Male and Female Collegiate Institute until 1859, when he was placed in charge of the Kentucky Wesleyan College, of which he was the principal organizer. He remained there until 1881, when he went to Shelbyville and taught Latin and Greek for some time; but returned to Millersburg and was connected with the Female College until 1886, when he was elected president of the Logan Female College at Russellville.

Prof. Murphy has instructed hundreds of young men who have risen to eminence in almost every profession and calling in life, who owe much to his wise and helpful advice. Few men can look back over a useful and well spent life with greater satisfaction. But Prof. Murphy is by no means on the retired list, as his usefulness has not been impaired by long service in the field of education and his advancing years and ripe scholarship and untarnished Christian character have given him a hold upon the confidence and respect of the people of Russellville, and qualify him in an eminent degree for the splendid work in which he is engaged in their midst.

Prof. Murphy's first wife was Emily Savage, daughter of Pleasant M. Savage. She was born in Mason County, in 1829; and was educated in Lexington, Kentucky, and Clarksville, Tennessee, completing a very thorough course at the latter place under the instruction of Dr. Irvine, a distinguished educator of his day. There were six children by this marriage: George William, born November 3, 1859, died March 12, 1864; Elizabeth R., born December 3, 1860; Clara M., born February 22, 1863; Mary B., born March 18, 1864; Harriet, born March 18, 1864, died in infancy; Irwine S., born April 27, 1867. Mrs. Emily S. Murphy died July 5, 1867.

Prof. Murphy's second wife, to whom he was married May 28, 1889, was Mary G. Williams, who was born in Parkersburg (now West), Virginia, and was educated in Dr. Prettyman's Female College, Louisville, Kentucky.

EPHRAIM D. SAYRE, President of the Security Trust and Safety Vault Company of Lexington, was born in Elizabeth, New Jersey, September 25, 1820. His father, James C. Sayre, was born in the same city, November 11, 1781, and was driven from his home to Madison by the army in the Revolutionary war. He was married May 16, 1867, to Elizabeth P. Hamilton of Elizabeth, New Jersey, who was related to Alexander Hamilton. In 1825 Mr. J. C. Sayre came to Louisville, leaving his family in Elizabeth, who followed him in 1827. He purchased a farm near the city which is now that part of Louisville bounded by Main, Jefferson, Twenty-first and Twenty-sixth streets. He was a coach trimmer by trade and, before coming to Kentucky, had been in the Merchant Service, commanding a vessel which ran between New York and New Orleans from 1804 to 1825. He lived on his farm after coming to Kentucky and died October 6, 1847, when sixty-six years of age. His brother, David A. Sayre, was born in Madison, New Jersey, in 1793; came to Lexington in 1811; founded the Sayre Bank in 1820 and the Sayre Female Institute in 1853. His death in 1870 was greatly lamented by his city and state, for he was one of the greatest public benefactors that ever lived in Kentucky.

Ephraim D. Sayre lived on the farm mentioned and attended school in Louisville, receiving an education which prepared him for the successful business career which he began in 1839, when nineteen years of age, in the Alsop Mills, corner of Eighth and Jefferson streets (then in the suburbs of Louisville), and afterwards was with Glover, McDougall & Co. in the Union Foundry. February, 1848, he went to Lexington and entered the banking house of his uncle, David A. Sayre, whom he succeeded in the business at a later day, maintaining the high credit and standing of the bank by his excellent management of its affairs.

During his long residence in Lexington he has occupied many positions of trust, and the confidence placed in him by his fellow citizens has never been regretted. He was treasurer of the Agricultural and Mechanical Association for thirty-nine years—from 1850 to 1889; and has been the secretary and treasurer of the Lexington Cemetery Company since 1850, a very responsible position, which he has filled to the entire satisfaction of the directors and lot owners, which may be inferred by the fact that he carries securities for the cemetery of over eighty-two thousand dollars.

He organized the Security Trust and Safety Vault Company of Lexington, one of the most solid financial institutions in central Kentucky, and has been its president after the first year since its origin; and as long as he may be able to give it the benefit of his superior judgment and ability as a financier and manager of trusts, it is not probable that he will have a competitor for this responsible position.

Mr. Sayre and Mary E..Woodruff were married in 1850 and they have five children who have reached maturity. Mr. Sayre is a man of vigorous constitution, careful in his habits, and although a little past seventy-five years of age, is in good health and is in the full enjoyment of all of his faculties, and has had the benefit of extensive travel, having returned, in March, 1896, from a trip to the West Indies, South America and Cuba, which was one of the most delightful of the many excursions he has made.

JOHN G. SIMRALL, a leading lawyer and distinguished jurist of Louisville, son of Rev. John G. and Sarah (Bullock) Simrall, was born in Fayette County, Kentucky, March 18, 1840. His father was a noted Presbyterian minister and his mother was a daughter of Waller Bullock, a native of Virginia, but for a long time a prominent farmer of Fayette County, Kentucky, and a near neighbor and intimate friend of Henry Clay. He was a violent Democrat, but in all other matters he was an enthusiastic admirer of the great commoner. His eldest son, Rev. Dr. Joseph J. Bullock, who died about two years ago, married a sister of General John C. Breckenridge, and was at one time chaplain of the United States Senate.

Judge Simrall's paternal grandfather, James Simrall, was a native of Virginia who came to Kentucky when he was a boy and was one of the earliest settlers of Shelby County. He recruited a regiment and commanded it during the war of 1812. He was a gallant soldier, a brave and daring officer and was conspicuous in many engagements. He survived the dangers and hardships of army life, but died a few years later from the effects of exposure while in the service of his country.

John G. Simrall received his primary education in the Fayette County schools, under the immediate guidance and assistance of his scholarly father; and, at the age of fourteen, was sufficiently advanced to enter Centre College at

Danville, from which he was graduated as salutatorian of his class in 1857. There were forty-seven graduates in the class, including Senator J. C. S. Blackburn, ex-Governor James B. McCreary, Judges Dulaney, Hunt, McKay and others who have figured prominently in the history of Kentucky during the last quarter of the century.

Mr. Simrall was employed as a teacher in the family of Junius Ward of Mississippi for one year following his graduation, and then began the study of law in the office of Judge Robertson of Lexington. After two years of careful instruction by his distinguished preceptor, he was well prepared for the senior class in the law department of the University of Louisville, from which he graduated with high honors in March, 1861.

He began the practice of law in Louisville in partnership with Judge William S. Bodley, with whom he was pleasantly associated until the death of Judge Bodley in 1878. A partnership was then entered into between Mr. Simrall and Temple Bodley, a son of his former partner, and this relation was dissolved in 1882 when Governor L. P. Blackburn appointed Mr. Simrall vice chancellor of the Louisville Chancery Court, in the place of Honorable Alfred T. Pope, who had resigned. After serving this unexpired term, Judge Simrall was elected judge of the Law and Equity Court, which superseded the Vice Chancellor's Court. This election occurred in 1884 and was for a term of six years, a deserved compliment to a faithful officer and a splendid recognition of his ability and probity as judge of one of the highest courts in the city. This endorsement was especially marked, as he had no opposition in the Democratic convention in which he was nominated, or by the opposing party in the general election which took place in August, 1884. In this exalted position he more than met the expectation of his most sanguine friends, and his resignation two years later was regretted by members of the bar and by the public, who had great confidence in him as an able and upright jurist.

He resumed the practice of law, which offered larger compensation, and in which he has been most successful, having no superior in the profession at the Louisville bar. Notwithstanding his purpose to devote himself exclusively to his large practice in the higher courts, his friends persuaded him to become a candidate for the vacancy in the Court of Appeals in 1895. He was an independent Democratic candidate; but it was not a Democratic year, and he could not stoop to modern electioneering methods. Believing that a high judicial office should not be trailed in the dust or gained by political intrigue, he cheerfully submitted to honorable defeat. It was an instance in which politics triumphed over the better judgment of the people. The acceptance of the office would have required great personal sacrifice on the part of Judge Simrall, and he could not have enjoyed the honors of the position if they had been dissipated by any question as to the manner of his election.

Judge Simrall was married in 1863 to Cornelia Smith, daughter of Thomas P. Smith of Louisville, a lady of unusual literary attainments and culture and endowed with superior intellectual and social faculties. They are members of the Second Presbyterian Church.

They have one daughter, Nellie, who married Lindley M. Kneasbey, now professor of the science of government at Bryn Mawr, Pennsylvania. The marriage a few years ago was one of the most brilliant social events that has ever taken place in the city.

DAVID A. SAYRE, banker, was born March 12, 1793, in Madison, New Jersey. His parents were in humble circumstances, but were industrious and honest, and, above all, were Christians. In 1811 he came to Kentucky and settled at Lexington, where he resided continuously until his death. At the time of his arrival in Lexington, he was without money and without friends. He had acquired a knowledge of silver-plating, and to that devoted himself until 1823, and for the next six years connected with his trade a broker's office. In 1829, he turned his attention wholly to the banking business, in which he amassed a large fortune, and for half a century was one of the most valuable citizens Lexington ever had. He had a rare combination of gifts; although greatly devoted to the acquisition of wealth, was at the same time a cheerful giver, and never displayed the traits of the miser or spendthrift; trusted to his head in trading, and to his heart in giving, and rarely found either to fail him. Without a very liberal education, he belonged to that class of men who despise alike help or hindrance in making their way in the world. He brought unbounded cheerfulness everywhere into his presence, and, while being innately modest, detested rowdyism and profanity. He possessed peculiarities and eccentricities, but they rather served to bring him into general favor. He was a man of strong and subtle intellect, which gave him great promptitude in action, and his conclusions hardly ever failed in bringing about the highest good. He was always ready to co-operate in any public enterprise by which the city in which he resided, or the state of his adoption, might receive benefit, ever contributing with a liberal hand to the accomplishment of that end. His influence and power were not felt alone among business men. His office was the resort of the most distinguished men of Central Kentucky, numbering among his associates Clay, Crittenden, Wickliffe and Morehead, and by them his advice was considered wise and good. The manner in which he used his wealth, probably more than anything else, is worthy of regard; avarice never took possession of him, and bitter thoughts never poisoned the milk of human kindness in his heart. As he grew rich, he commenced distributing; and, as he advanced in age, he became more gentle and loving. He was an earnest Presbyterian of the Calvanistic school, and yet was without narrowness or bigotry in his views and charities. He recognized his dependence on his Creator, and therefore felt his obligations to man. It was this, no doubt, to a great extent, which led him to bestow his bounties, and to extend his hand for the good of those around him. He looked well after the interests of his family, then to the interests of his neighbors, and, finally, to the general public; and, having no children of his own to be educated, he devoted his means and heart largely to the education of others. In 1854, he donated to the trustees, in perpetuity, for female education, the costly buildings and grounds now occupied by the institution known as the Sayre Female Institute. To that magnificent gift he added largely during his life, until the institution which bears his name, in the completeness of its appointments for educational purposes, ranks as one of the first in the valley of the Mississippi. In 1825, Mr. Sayre married Abby V. Hammond, of Norfolk, Virginia, who was his faithful counselor and encouraged him in his good works. She still survives him. He died in Lexington, September 10, 1870, and his death was accompanied by every demonstration of sorrow and respect, from the citizens at large, the officers of Sayre Institute, of which he was the founder and benefactor, and from the Northern Bank of Kentucky, with which he had been from time to time connected. The fountain of his moral life and actions was Christianity, and, abiding firmly in the fulfillment of the great faith in which he had lived, he sank peacefully into the arms of death. His place may not be filled in a generation.

JOHN M'CANN, Justice of the Peace, Louisville, Kentucky, has fought his way from the obscurity in which he served an apprenticeship in a machine shop to a position of honor and trust, in which he commands the respect of the community, and is now one of the best known and most popular citizens of Louisville. He was born in that city June 27, 1848, and was educated in the Catholic and public schools, and, when he left school, he thought he would like to be a machinist and he worked at that trade with commendable industry for two years. Believing that his employer was not pushing him along as fast as he should, after two years of drudgery, he abandoned the trade and went on the river as a barkeeper, a more attractive life and a more profitable business. After three years of this, he thought it too easy for a man of his physical ability and mental capacity and he quit the river and was employed as a molder in the foundry of Grainger & Company for two and a half years, when, in 1871, he was elected constable, which office he filled so industriously and efficiently for four years that his friends told him he might as well be the magistrate, and to this office he was duly elected in 1875 and has served in the same capacity continuously for more than twenty years,

In 1887 his friends concluded that he should go up a little higher and they elected him state senator, in which relation he served four years with distinction and was re-elected in 1890 and served until July, 1893, when he resigned. Under the old constitution he had held the offices of senator and magistrate, but as he could not hold both under the new constitution, he resigned his seat in the senate and completed his term as magistrate, to which he was again re-elected in 1894.

Squire McCann has always taken a lively interest and an active part in politics, and is so popular that he could easily have any office to which he might aspire, simply for the asking. He has made the duties of the magistrate a careful study, has familiarized himself with the law bearing upon such cases as come under his jurisdiction, with the result that he has secured a more liberal share of business than any other magistrate in the city. Coming up from the machine shop, he has acquired a knowledge of human nature, and, as a justice of the peace, a fund of general information and a knowledge of law which would qualify him for a much higher station in the legal profession; but he is ambitious only to do his duty, and this he believes may be done in an humble sphere as well as in a more exalted station.

Mr. McCann was married in October, 1871, to Mary E. Parker, daughter of Charles Parker of Louisville, but formerly of LaRue County. They have one daughter living, whose name is Ada.

Mr. McCann's father, James McCann, was a native of Ireland, who married Mary Condon before leaving the old country, and came to the United States in 1839. They at once located in Louisville, where Mr. McCann was engaged in the grocery business until 1868, when he died. Mrs. McCann survived him until 1886, when she died, aged sixty-three years.

CAPT. JOHN H. M'BRAYER of Lawrenceburg, whose fame has become world-wide on account of the superior whiskey which bears his name, was born in Lawrenceburg, June 17, 1826. On his next birthday he will be three score and ten years of age, and yet he is an active, vigorous man, attentive to business, full of energy and as wide awake as any of the younger men around him.

His father, Alexander McBrayer, was a Kentuckian who was well educated and one of the most intelligent and successful business men of his generation. He began life, as many others did at that time, as a trader; but became a merchant tailor in Lawrenceburg, in which business he continued until his death, which occurred at an early age in 1828. His father, William McBrayer, was a native of North Carolina.

Susan Wright McBrayer (mother) was born in Augusta County, Virginia, April 29, 1797, and died at the country home of her son, James A. McBrayer, March 19, 1887, being ninety years of age. Her father, John Wright, was a Virginian by birth, who came to Kentucky when he was quite young and lived for a time in Cumberland County. He afterwards removed to Greene County, Ohio, and while clearing out a farm was killed by the falling of a tree.

Capt. McBrayer received a good common school education in Lawrenceburg and vicinity. At the age of nineteen he enlisted for one year's service in the Mexican war. He commanded a company known as the "Salt River Tigers." It was by his order that the memorable charge on Santa Anna's men was made that won the day at Buena Vista and which settled the differences between the United States and Mexico. Thus, before he was twenty years of age, he had made a reputation for a strength of character which he has maintained through half a century. His reminiscences of the lively times he experienced in Mexico are always of the deepest interest to his friends and would make a thrilling chapter in history.

After his return from Mexico, he was in the mercantile business in Lawrenceburg for ten years, during which time, in 1848, he established the distillery which has produced the best whiskey ever made in Kentucky and which is known throughout the world by his name. He is largely interested in the product of a distillery now conducted by J. R. Walker, the reputation of which he guards with jealous care.

Capt. McBrayer has never cared for office, but served two years as sheriff of his (Anderson)

County in 1861-2 by appointment of the County Court. He is an Odd Fellow and a Mason, through which orders he has done much for the aid of others.

Capt. McBrayer has been quite successful in his business enterprises and takes great interest in public affairs, and is particularly well posted in matters of finance. He has theories of his own respecting the national currency, and is able to express them in clear and vigorous language. He does not pose as an orator or a public speaker, but he can interest any audience and can express his ideas in clear, good English. He favors the blending of silver and gold, making a coin that is neither gold nor silver and is both. He would make the present silver half dollar a dollar by adding eleven and two-thirds grains of gold, and so with the silver dollar, add twenty-two grains of gold and make it a two-dollar piece. He says: "This is the shortest method to make a parity in the two metals, and secure domestic quiet in finance."

HON. JAMES MADISON M'ARTHUR of Dayton, Kentucky, now in the eighty-fifth year of his age, has been prominent in public affairs for over fifty years, and has done much for the public improvement of Newport and Dayton. The latter place was laid out by him and largely built up through his individual enterprise.

Mr. McArthur was born near Georgetown, Kentucky, January 3, 1810, and in 1815 his parents removed to Newport, where he was educated in the best private schools; and at the age of fifteen years he entered Center College at Danville and studied for one year. He had no predilection for professional life, preferring a business career, which he planned and carried out with unusual success. He began by investing and trading in real estate in Campbell County, and stuck to his purpose, until, at one time or another, he had actually owned more than one-third of the land in Campbell County. He then turned his attention to the improvement of Newport; opened the first street in that city; invested his capital in the building of houses for residences and business; helped others by selling land on ten years' time and building houses for those who did not have the money to pay for their houses, adopting a plan very similar to the present plan of building and loan associations.

While in Newport he was president of the City Council for ten consecutive years. He established the Newport Safety Fund Bank, of which he was president from 1852 to 1856; and it was his generous spirit which led the bank to make too many loans, resulting in the failure of the banking institution. This crippled Mr. McArthur financially, but it did not dampen his ardor in the work of improvement to which he had devoted his life.

Having removed from Newport to Dayton in 1848, he was for many years actively engaged in building up the new town, which he had laid out with the assistance of James T. Berry and Henry Walker. He was president of the Dayton Council for eight years; built the street railway between Newport and Dayton in 1870 and sold it in 1879.

Mr. McArthur was twice elected to the legislature, in 1846 and in 1873. He introduced and secured the passage of what is known as the "Cemetery Act;" was the originator of an act levying tax on real estate to assist in establishing public schools; and also secured the passage of the "Mechanics Lien Law;" and was instrumental in securing the enactment of various other laws for the public good.

Mr. McArthur married Mary J. Stricker, daughter of Charles Stricker of Philadelphia. She was born January 18, 1819; died April 6, 1893, and is buried in Evergreen Cemetery, Newport. They had seven children: Peter, born May 23, 1838; Mary, born April 10, 1840, died June 1, 1865; Alice, born March 4, 1842; Annie, born September 30, 1844; Charles, born June 8, 1847; Ida, born June 1, 1850, died March 17, 1894; and William H., born October 23, 1858.

Mr. and Mrs. McArthur lived happily together for fifty-six years. He is a remarkably well preserved man; has never worn glasses, his eyesight never having failed, and now, at the age of eighty-five, he can read the finest print in ordinary use.

His father, Peter McArthur, was born in Argyleshire, Scotland, in 1764. He came to America in 1784 and located near Georgetown. He was employed as surveyor in central Kentucky and southern Ohio, and was for a long time engaged in locating land warrants for soldiers of the Revolution. In 1815 he removed to Newport and kept a hotel. He died in July, 1828, and is buried in Evergreen Cemetery, Newport. He was a cousin of General Duncan McArthur, who was governor of Ohio.

Mary Michie McArthur (mother) was born in Louisa County, Virginia, in 1769. She was first married to William Tompkins, who lived but a short time after their marriage. She was married to Peter McArthur, December 26, 1800; died September 15, 1853, and is buried in Evergreen Cemetery, Newport. She was of Irish descent.

M. V. MONARCH of Owensboro, king of the whiskey trade in Kentucky, known throughout the world as the manufacturer of the famous "Monarch" brand of whiskey, respected and loved by his neighbors and fellow-citizens, charitable toward those who need a helping hand, phenomenally successful in business and possessing a magnificent fortune, is a native of the county of which he has been a resident all his life. He is a son of Thomas and Susan (Daviess) Monarch and was born March 10, 1842. His father was born in Maryland, March 25, 1801. He was educated in Washington County, Kentucky and, on reaching manhood, engaged in farming in that county, subsequently removing to Marion County, where he lived until 1832, when he removed to Daviess County and became one of the most popular citizens, and was a prominent farmer until the day of his death, November 13, 1881. In the earlier years of his life, he was a Whig of pronounced convictions, but he did not follow his party until its dissolution. He foresaw the inevitable, and believing the principles of the Democratic party were more in accord with his views, he was welcomed to the ranks of that party in 1852 and was ever after that a prominent figure in the councils of the local Democracy. He was proverbially kind, generous and honest; a member of the Catholic Church and an excellent citizen. His father was a native of France who came to America soon after the Declaration of Independence and was a farmer in Maryland, where he died in 1842.

Susan Daviess Monarch (mother) was born in Washington County, Kentucky, April 13, 1801. She was a lady of great intelligence and decision of character; dignified, yet kind and respectful, and stood by her convictions unflinchingly and impressed those who knew her as a woman who would have filled any station in high life with credit to her sex. She left her impress upon the community in which she lived and died, having done her duty. She survived her husband until May 14, 1889, rounding out a useful and noble life of a little more than eighty-eight years.

Mrs. Monarch's family (Daviess) was a branch of the original English family from which Jefferson Davis was descended, although the name was spelled differently, and her people were among the pioneers of Daviess County, which received their name.

M. V. Monarch inherited many of the fine traits of character for which his mother and her ancestors were distinguished. Under the immediate direction of his mother, his receptive mind was well trained. He was kept in school until twenty years of age, finishing in Cecilian College in Hardin County in 1865. He began his business career in the same year, buying and selling tobacco, in which he made a good start. He soon abandoned this, however, and engaged in distilling, operating alone until 1870, when he entered into partnership with E. P. Payne. The business of the concern grew into magnificent proportions and the concern was subsequently incorporated as the M. V. Monarch Mercantile Company, with Mr. Monarch as president, a position which he has held continuously until the present time. Messrs. Monarch and Payne were the principal stockholders and owners until the death of Mr. Payne, September 9, 1895, a calamity which did not disturb the business of the corporation to the extent that would have resulted under a partnership arrangement.

In this establishment the famous Monarch whiskey, known all over the world, is manufactured under Mr. Monarch's personal supervision; but he is also a large shareholder and owner in two other distillery companies, of which he is president, The John Hanning Distillery Company and the famous Sour Mash Distillery Company. He is a large stockholder in the Owensboro National Bank and has other investments in business enterprises in Owensboro, besides his elegant home and other real estate. He is receiver of the Owensboro, Falls of Rough & Green River Railroad Company, by appointment of Court.

Mr. Monarch is one of the most public spirited men in Owensboro and is identified with all public measures looking to the improvement of the city and the advancement of society. It is known, moreover, among his neighbors, although he has sacredly guarded the fact as a secret, that he and his estimable wife are most generous in their donations to the cause of charity, while their liberality to the worthy poor, in the way of private charity, approaches extravagance. Mr. Monarch's home is an ideal one, and his devotion to his family is one of his most beautiful traits. He is known far and wide for his unstinted liberality and his hospitable entertainment of friends and strangers. Handsome in his personal appearance, gentle in manner, of kind and pleasing address, easy of approach, ready to respond to every appeal, or to lend a helping hand in any good work, he is unquestionably one of the best and most popular citizens of Owensboro.

Mr. Monarch was married September 20, 1869, to Elizabeth Ann O'Bryan, who was born December 23, 1844, and was educated in St. Francis Academy in Owensboro. She is a daughter of William O'Bryan and is in hearty accord and sympathy with her companion, being a devoted wife and ideal mother. They have a happy family of five children, who are somewhat scattered at present. Jessie, their first child, died in infancy; Henry Lamar, born May 11, 1872, is now in the law department of the Catholic University, Washington, D. C., being the first student enrolled on the books after the inauguration of that department in this famous institution; Daniel D., born August 14, 1874, is contracting agent for the C. & O. Railroad; Erminie, born June 11, 1876, now a pupil in St. Mary College, near Notre Dame, Indiana; M. V. Monarch, Jr., born September 14, 1878, is a student in Notre Dame College, Indiana; Benita, born May 23, 1881, is at home. It is the purpose of the parents of these young people, whose prospects for a happy future are now so bright, to give them the advantages of a complete and thorough education, so that they may be prepared for whatever may befall them in after life.

Mr. and Mrs. Monarch are members of the Catholic Church. Mr. Monarch voted the Democratic ticket until the nomination of James G. Blaine for President, at which time he voted the Republican ticket, and has affiliated with the latter party since that date.

JAMES A. M'CANE received his education principally in the Augusta College, and when nineteen years of age he began to teach school, continuing until 1875, when he was appointed deputy clerk of the County Court and served until February, 1882, when he resigned to become a candidate for the clerkship, to which he was elected in August, 1882; again in 1886; again in 1890, and for the fourth time in 1894.

His great popularity and success are due, not only to his efficiency in the transaction of the business of the office, but to his accommodating disposition and pleasing address.

March 18, 1880, he was married to Lizzie B., daughter of P. H. Clayton of Bracken County. She was born April 9, 1860. They have two children: Harvey Clayton McCane, born April 29, 1882, and Lewie Allen McCane, born March 22, 1891.

Samuel McCane (grandfather) was born January 30, 1791, in Pennsylvania; came to Kentucky early in life and resided in Bracken County to time of his death on February 5, 1864; followed farming and trading; made several trips with horses and farming products to New Orleans. Married in Bracken County, September 3, 1818, to Nancy Heaverin. She was born September 6, 1795, and died April 8, 1857.

Nancy D. Anderson McCane (mother) was born in Bracken County, September 2, 1827, and is still living with her husband in her native county.

James J. Anderson (maternal grandfather) was born in Virginia, April 10, 1788; came to Mason

County, this state, while a young man, where he married Nancy D. Allen, April 10, 1815, and soon afterward came to Bracken County, where he died, October 31, 1831. His occupation was farming. His wife, Nancy D. Allen, was born August 17, 1795, and died in Bracken County, February 21, 1866.

Mr. McCane's ancestors for several generations were members of the Methodist Episcopal Church; and in the matter of politics the connection is solidly Democratic.

HARVEY MYERS, son of Aurelia Bridgman and Aaron Myers, was born in Chenango County, New York, February 10, 1828. When but a boy Mr. Myers left his home and located in the west. By hard work he managed to educate himself, and about the year 1852 located in Trimble County, where he taught school and read law. He was admitted to the bar of that county, and, after a few years practice, removed to Covington, where his ability and fidelity were at once recognized. He very soon formed a law partnership with Hon. John W. Stevenson, just then elected Governor of Kentucky, and afterwards United States Senator. Though the practice of this firm was great, and the burden of it fell upon Mr. Myers, he found time to prepare and publish the first Code of Practice of Kentucky, known as Myers' Code, which is held in the highest esteem by the bar of the state. In 1867 he compiled and published a supplement to the General Statutes of Kentucky, known as Myers' Supplement.

In politics he was a Republican; and in 1865 was nominated by the Union party for the legislature and elected; but it having been charged that bayonets were used at the polls in his behalf, and investigation satisfying him of the truth of the charges, he declined the office. In declining the office, Mr. Myers said:

"On the day of the election bodies of armed soldiers were placed before and around each voting place in the county, and there remained throughout the entire day. Early in the day, numbers of citizens, while approaching the polls in an orderly and peaceful manner for the purpose of tendering their votes, were arrested by the soldiers and marched away under guard to a prison, and there held in close confinement until the next day, when they were discharged without any charge being preferred against them. In some instances, persons, on coming in sight of the polls, were met by a military officer, told that they would not be allowed to vote, and ordered to depart; and, while obeying the order and departing from the polls, squads of soldiers were sent in pursuit, by whom they were arrested and marched through the streets to prison and confined as stated above. I could not lend my sanction or approval to such a proceeding, as I must have done by accepting this election." This was at that time probably the only instance of declination of office in Kentucky.

He was shot down in his office by a disappointed litigant whom Mr. Myers had opposed in the courts, March 28, 1874. At a meeting of the bar of Kenton and Campbell Counties, on the occasion of his death, the following resolutions were adopted:

Your Committe directed to report resolutions to this meeting of the Bar of Kenton in respect to a deceased member, our brother, Harvey Myers, offer these resolutions:

Resolved, That we mourn the loss of Harvey Myers, whose death occurred last Saturday, as one of the saddest events of our times, and we are not able to employ language equal to the expression of the feelings of sadness experienced by his brethren and associates upon this occasion.

2. Harvey Myers had been for twenty years among us, a man in the full vigor of life, of robust manhood and vigorous mind; he had reached the front rank of his profession at the age of forty-six years, and in a large sense of the expression, he was a law abiding and an honest man.

3. Harvey Myers will be remembered among his acquaintances and friends for his virtues in his profession, as a citizen, and as a husband and a father—in all these relations he has left no better man, but an example for imitation and emulation.

4. We ask the president of this meeting to send copies of these resolutions to the courts of this county to be recorded, and a copy to the family of our deceased brother.

5. That we will attend the funeral of the de-

ceased as a body, and that we will wear the usual badge of mourning for thirty days.

6. That an invitation is extended to the Bar of Campbell and adjoining counties to unite with us to attend the funeral.

7. That a Committee of Arrangements for the funeral be appointed, consisting of five, to be selected from the Bar of Kenton and Campbell Counties.

SIMPSON S. MEDDIS, real estate dealer and agent, of Louisville, Kentucky, was born on his father's farm in Jefferson County, so near the city that it is now in one of the most beautiful suburbs of Louisville. His father, Matthew Meddis, was a native farmer of Jefferson County, Kentucky, where he spent his whole life. He was born in 1804 and died in 1881.

Godfrey Meddis (grandfather) was a long-time resident of Jefferson County, and was a soldier in the war of 1812. He was with General Jackson in the battle of New Orleans, and died in that city from a fever which he contracted while in the service. His ancestors were from Germany.

Apphia Seaton Meddis (mother) was born in Jefferson County, Kentucky, in 1817, and is still living in her native county. Her father, George Seaton (grandfather) was a native farmer of the same county, where he died in 1835, aged sixty years. His ancestors were from England.

Simpson S. Meddis left his father's farm when he was sixteen years of age, and was appointed deputy sheriff of Jefferson County, an office which he held under different sheriffs for fifteen years, and from which he retired to engage in the carpet business with his father-in-law, George W. Small. A year and a half later he accepted the position of teller in the banking house of Odor, Taylor & Company, and was with the bank for four years, until it went into liquidation. Mr. Meddis then engaged in the real estate and auctioneering business, to which he has devoted his entire time ever since.

In 1875 he formed a co-partnership with Charles Southwick, under the firm name of Meddis & Southwick, a very fortunate business relation, which has continued without interruption for over twenty years, in which time they have bought and sold real estate of the value of many millions of dollars. They have been in all this time, and are now, the leading men in their business in the city of Louisville. Their long experience, together with their familiarity with property and its value, and their unswerving integrity and strictly honorable methods of business, have won for them the confidence of the people, while their judgment is sought in nearly all real estate transactions of importance.

Mr. Meddis' services as auctioneer are in demand, not only in his own city and county, but in other parts of the state, and frequently in other states; and not only in sales of realty, but in fine stock sales and other occasions when large interests are involved. His sales are attended with unqualified success on account of his superior knowledge and excellent judgment. His reputation as an auctioneer in large sales is not merely local, but national.

Mr. Meddis married Eliza H. Small, daughter of George W. Small, of Louisville, in 1861, and they have two sons: George S. and Victor N. Meddis.

HON. HARVEY MYERS, Jr., attorney at law, Covington, was born December 24, 1859. His father, as stated in the foregoing sketch, was a native of Chenango County, New York, a self-made man and a lawyer of great ability and a man of the highest integrity, whose untimely taking off is mentioned elsewhere.

Young Myers did not experience the difficulties which his father met with in obtaining an education. The excellent public schools of Covington were open to him, and his father was ambitious in his behalf. He made good use of his opportunities, and after leaving school he studied law in the office of the Honorable Theo. F. Hallam, and was admitted to the bar in 1881, and was a partner of Mr. Hallam for thirteen years.

In 1886 Mr. Myers was elected to the legislature on the Democratic ticket, and was three times re-elected, and in 1889 was elected Speaker of the House of Representatives, and was one of the most popular presiding officers that has ever served in that body.

Although his father was a Republican, Mr. Myers has been for years one of the acknowledged leaders of the Democratic party in Covington and vicinity; and is exceedingly popular with men in all parties, being faithful to the best interests of his city and state. He is one of the most prominent attorneys in Covington and has an extensive practice. He is a prominent Mason, and is Exalted Ruler of the Covington Lodge of Elks.

Mr. Myers was married November 9, 1888, to Carrie Wells, daughter of H. B. Wells, of Memphis, Tennessee. They have four children.

WILLIAM M. IRVINE, late of Richmond, Kentucky, a successful business man and prominent banker, was a native of the city in which he spent a useful and honorable life. He was a son of Adam and Minerva (Stone) Irvine, and was born June 1, 1825. He was educated at Cambridge University, and was especially prepared for the legal profession, but on account of failing health at the close of his collegiate course, necessitating employment in the open air, he became a tiller of the soil; was especially interested in fine stock and owned some of the best horses and cattle in the state.

After a few years of life on the farm, his health was improved, and he engaged in the banking business in Richmond, and was for a long time cashier of the Farmers' National Bank. Then president of the Second National. He was then elected vice-president of the First (now Richmond) National Bank, which position he held until his death, which occurred February 23, 1891.

He owned a fancy farm of two hundred and ten acres near the city, and for ten years prior to his death was engaged in culling and training fine horses, in which he took a deep interest for the pleasure and recreation that the occupation afforded, as well as for the handsome profits which he derived from his sales.

The suburban home, "Irvinton," in which his wife resides, is one of the most attractive places in the vicinity of Richmond; and there he surrounded himself and family with every comfort and convenience, providing everything to indicate the sweetness and pleasures of life; and these evidences of his thoughtfulness remain in their beauty and freshness, a constant reminder of the tender and loving husband and father. The premises embrace sixteen acres of ground, upon which there are shrubbery, plants and flowers in their season, and greenhouses in which the choicest flowers are propagated for the beautifying of the home in winter, all of which, with the elegance of the surroundings and the interior of the home, tell of the generous and gentle character of a man whose business never occupied his mind to the exclusion of his home and family.

Mr. Irvine was a model business man, highly esteemed for his unquestioned integrity and sound judgment. He was a member of the Presbyterian Church and a liberal supporter of the gospel, and his deportment in business and in all of the affairs of a busy life was in harmony with his religious profession.

He never sought office or public recognition, and would not even accept an office, although frequently importuned to become a candidate for positions of trust and honor.

He was married November 3d, 1846, to his cousin, Elizabeth S. Irvine, daughter of Colonel David and Susanah Hart (McDowell) Irvine. Their home was blessed by the birth of five children, one of whom, Bessie D. Irvine, died of typhoid fever October 22, 1883, while attending school in New York. The loss of this lovely and promising child was the greatest sorrow the parents were ever called upon to bear. Beautiful and lovely in person, she was a child of unusual brightness and intelligence, and gave promise of developing into that charming womanhood for which her illustrious ancestors were so distinguished. She was sent to one of the best schools in the east in order to give her every opportunity for improving those talents and virtues with which she was so richly endowed.

Adam Irvine (father) was a native of Madison County, a graduate of Old Transylvania University, and a man of fine scholarly attainments, a highly honored and universally respected citizen of his county. He married Minerva Stone, a native of Madison County, in 1824, and died about a year later, three months before his son, William M., was born.

Colonel William Irvine (grandfather) was a gallant soldier and colonel in the Revolutionary war, and in the Indian wars of later years, and was carried off the battlefield at Boonesboro with a severe gunshot wound, which might not have proven fatal, but he was thrown across a horse and in that way his injury was aggravated so as to cause his death a few years later.

Christopher Irvine, a son of Colonel William and uncle of William M. Irvine, was a noted Indian fighter in Kentucky, and followed them into Indiana and Ohio, and was killed by them in the latter state.

Elizabeth S. (Irvine) Irvine, who survives her husband, the late William M. Irvine, is a daughter of David Irvine, granddaughter of Colonel William Irvine of Revolutionary fame, who was also her husband's grandfather. She is a granddaughter of Dr. Ephraim McDowell and a great-granddaughter of Governor Isaac Shelby; and is a lady of elegant refinement and superior intelligence, an honored and worthy descendant of the illustrious people who fought for American independence and figured conspicuously in the early settlement of the "dark and bloody ground."

She has no children living, having buried five; still occupies the lovely home in which her lamented husband took so much pleasure and comfort, her brother, David W. Irvine, living with her.

David Irvine, Sr., father of Mrs. Elizabeth S. Irvine, at the age of nineteen, joined the militia and engaged in the Indian wars and skirmishes of those perilous times. When his father, Colonel William Irvine, Sr., died, David took his place as Circuit Clerk, and this office was held by father and son for a period of forty years. David resigned eventually, having other business of greater importance. He married Susanah Hart McDowell, daughter of the celebrated physician, Dr. Ephraim McDowell.

William M. Irvine's mother, Minerva Stone, was a native of Madison County and a daughter of Colonel William Stone, who was a gallant soldier in the Revolutionary war, and an antagonist whom the Indians greatly feared in the early settlement of the Blue Grass State.

For more extended history of the McDowells and Shelbys, see biographies of H. C. McDowell and Wallace McDowell Shelby in this volume.

JOHN Y. OLDHAM, M. D., a distinguished physician of Lexington, son of Dr. William B. and Laura A. (Mathews) Oldham, was born in New Castle, Henry County, Kentucky, March 19, 1866. His father was born in Jefferson County, near Louisville, and graduated from the Kentucky School of Medicine in 1856, carrying off the highest honors of his class. He was a physician at the Marine Hospital in Louisville for a number of years, and subsequently removed to New Castle, Henry County, where he was engaged in the practice of his profession until the time of his death, August 18, 1877.

Presley B. Oldham (grandfather) was born in Jefferson County, Kentucky, June 15, 1808, and died in his native county in 1861. He owned large tracts of land and was very successful as a business man. His ancestors were English people of the highest respectability. He married Margaret Keller, who was born July 29, 1813, and died at the old home place June 2, 1877.

Laura A. Mathews Oldham (mother) was born in New Castle in 1841; died March 24, 1896.

Caleb M. Mathews (grandfather) was born near Staunton, Virginia, October 29, 1810, and was raised on a farm in Woodford County, Kentucky. He studied law under George H. Robertson of Lexington, and graduated from Transylvania, law department, in 1837; married Mrs. Frances S. Beazley, nee Edwards; located in New Castle and cultivated a small farm and garden in connection with his legal work. He spent his money and devoted much time to the education of his large and now influential family. He was largely instrumental in establishing Henry College, of which he was a trustee for twenty-five years. He was prominently connected with the best movements for the advancement of educational interests in the county, and was conspicuous in all good work. He died in New Castle June 8, 1891.

John Mathews (great-grandfather) belonged to an influential Virginia family. He came to Kentucky in 1811, and settled in Woodford County, and died in 1813, leaving a widow and three sons. His wife, Sarah McDowell (great-grandmother), was a daughter of Major General Joseph McDowell, an officer in the Revolutionary war; sister of General Joseph McDowell of Ohio; sister-in-law of Governor Allen Trimble of Ohio; cousin of Governor James McDowell of Virginia; aunt of Governor John P. Gaines of Oregon; sister-in-law of Colonel L. Ford of the United States Army; and a relative of Dr. Ephraim McDowell of Danville, Kentucky.

Dr. John Y. Oldham enjoyed excellent educational advantages, attending the public schools in New Castle until he was thirteen years of age, when he took a three years' course in the State College at Lexington, and was one year in Central University, in Richmond, after which he read medicine with his uncle, Joseph McDowell Mathews of Louisville, and graduated from the Kentucky School of Medicine in 1885. His first work in the line of his profession was as an assistant to Dr. Dudley S. Reynolds in his office practice, and in the Hospital College of Medicine, in which capacity he was employed for two years. In September, 1887, he opened his office in Lexington, making a specialty of the treatment of diseases of the eye, ear, nose and throat, in which he was at once successful, and soon established an enviable reputation.

Dr. Oldham is a member of the Kentucky State Medical Society; the Mississippi Valley Medical Association, and the Lexington and Fayette County Medical Society, and is an occasional contributor to medical periodicals on the subjects pertaining to his special line of practice. He is a member of Merrick Lodge No. 31, I. O. O. F.; of the Ancient Essenic Order, Lodge No. 262; and of the Benevolent Protective Order of Elks, in which he holds the office of Esteemed Lecturing Knight. He is also a member of the First Presbyterian Church of Lexington.

Dr. Oldham was married March 29, 1887, to Mary S. Flood, daughter of Major John H. Flood of Lynchburg, Virginia, and has two sons: J. Harry Oldham and William B. Oldham.

ADAM SMYRL of Bellevue, a member of the firm of Smyrl & Hughes, No. 59 West Fourth. street, Cincinnati, Ohio, was born in County Tyrone, Ireland, March 8, 1843. He was particularly fortunate in his school days, and embraced the opportunities which his parents gave him in the common schools and best academies in the county.

He came to America in 1869, stopping near Worcester, Massachusetts. He found employment in one of the large woolen mills there, and stuck to it until he mastered the business, which he followed in the New England States until 1876. His mother, having arrived in this country, was living in Bellevue, and when he came to visit her in 1876 she persuaded him to remain with her.

He accepted a position in the house of C. H. Bishop & Co., flour merchants, and continued with them until 1883, when he formed a partnership with W. C. McClanahan and embarked in the flour, grain and commission business in Cincinnati. The firm of Smyrl & McClanahan continued until 1888, when Mr. McClanahan withdrew, and a new firm under the style of Smyrl, Armstrong & Hughes was formed, in which name the business was continued until 1894, when Mr. Armstrong retired and the name was changed to Smyrl & Hughes. The extensive business of this house is the best evidence of Mr. Smyrl's ability and integrity as a business man. Although his principal place of business is in Cincinnati, he is greatly interested in the town in which he has his residence, and is one of the most enterprising citizens of Bellevue.

He is president of the Bellevue and Dayton Land Company; also president of the South Bellevue Development Company, and is interested in other enterprises pertaining to the advancement of the community in which he lives. He has been a director of the Cincinnati Chamber of Commerce; was a member of the Bellevue City Council for eight years; is president of the Jamestown Magisterial District of Bellevue; was chairman of the Bellevue School Board, and is president of the L. J. Crawford Republican Club of Bellevue. While he is not in any sense a politician, he is deeply interested in the success of the Republican party.

He is a member and trustee of the Presbyterian Church; superintendent of the Sabbath school, and is a good citizen, honored and respected by all who know him.

Mr. Smyrl was married May 3, 1882, to Mary L. Milligan, daughter of Samuel Milligan of Cincinnati. She is also a member of and active worker in the Presbyterian Church.

Mr. Smyrl's parents, Gabriel and Sarah Ann (Bell) Smyrl, were natives of County Tyrone, Ireland. His father died in his native country at the age of forty-six years, in 1856. He was a man of fine intelligence and a devoted Christian in connection with the Presbyterian Church; had many friends in his country. He had visited America, and seen considerable for a man in the humble position of a farmer. After his death Mrs. Smyrl came to this country, where some of her relatives had preceded her, and finally made her home in Bellevue, where she reached the good old age of four score years, and died in November, 1893.

Mr. Smyrl has several brothers, who are respected citizens of Bellevue.

DR. JOSEPHUS MARTIN of Cynthiana, son of Dr. William H. and Mary F. (Whitehead) Martin, was born at Robinson Station, Harrison County, August 14, 1861. His father was also born in Harrison County, of which he has been a resident all his life; has practiced medicine in the county fifty-one years, and is supposed to be the first physician who performed laperotomy in the United States. This was in 1852. He is a graduate of the Jefferson Medical College of Philadelphia; also attended the old Transylvania College at Lexington, Kentucky. He had a very large practice not only in the immediate vicinity of his home at Robinson, but throughout the county. He was a member of the late Constitutional Convention, and has always been noted for great moral courage. His mother was a daughter of Josephus Perrin, who represented Harrison County in the legislature a number of times.

William Martin (grandfather) was born in Harrison County, January 4, 1790, and was a farmer in that county until his death in 1831, aged forty-one years. He was a soldier in the war of 1812; married Katherine Clopton Perrin, whose grandfather, Josephus Perrin, came to Virginia from England with three brothers, who fought in the war of the Revolution.

Mary F. Whitehead Martin (mother) was a native of Claysville, Harrison County, and a devout member of the Christian Church. She died in 1863. Her father, Nimrod Whitehead, was a native of Harrison County, and was a son of Capt. John Whitehead, of Virginia.

Dr. Josephus Martin was educated in the public schools of Cynthiana and at Georgetown College. He read medicine with his father and attended the Ohio Medical College at Cincinnati, graduating in 1885. He at once entered upon the practice of his profession in the county, and in 1892 removed to Cynthiana, where he has been remarkably successful.

Dr. Martin is a member of the Kentucky State Medical Society. He was married in 1886 to A. Stella Garnett, daughter of William T. and Dorcas (Ewalt) Garnett of Harrison County. They are members of the Baptist Church.

THOMAS SAMUEL VENABLE, banker and wholesale merchant, of the firm of Venable & McJohnson, of Owensboro, was born in Prince Edward County, Virginia, June 17, 1840. He came with his father to Owensboro November 21, 1860, having been educated in his native county, and for many years has been a member of the above mentioned firm, wholesale and retail dealers in grain and seeds, and president of the Owensboro Savings Bank. He was elected elder in the Presbyterian Church in 1870, and is greatly devoted to his church and its good work. In politics, he is for the prohibition of the liquor traffic. The members of the Venable family have been staunch Presbyterians as far back as their history can be traced.

Mr. Venable was married August 2, 1864, to Sallie Quicksall Anderson, daughter of James B. and Mary (Robertson) Anderson. She was born at "Wood Lawn," her father's home, near Owensboro, November 13, 1844. Their children's names are: Virginia Woodson, born July 4, 1865; graduated from the Owensboro High School June, 1880; also graduated from the High School of Detroit, Michigan, in 1882; married James Truman Shaw of Detroit, May 14, 1889, and resides in Detroit, where her husband is in business.

James Anderson Venable, born March 9, 1868;

graduated from the Owensboro High School in 1885; immediately entered the Owensboro Savings Bank as clerk; remained in the bank until January, 1889, when his uncle, T. S. Anderson, who had been owner of the bank, having gone to Detroit and engaged in the same business, James accepted a position in that institution, and in 1892, without his solicitation, was elected Cashier of the Michigan Car Company; afterwards engaged with his brother-in-law, James T. Shaw, in the grain business in Detroit, under the firm name of J. S. Lapham & Company.

Mary Ann Venable, born October 27, 1875; died May 8, 1880.

Matilda Tyler Venable, born December 4, 1876.

Elizabeth Thompkins Venable, born September 21, 1882.

Samuel Lewis Venable (father) was born in Prince Edward County, Virginia, January 8, 1803. He received a very fine education, and was a distinguished Latin and Greek scholar. On reaching his majority, his father gave him a farm and a number of slaves, having given all of his sons the same start in life. He was an elder in the Presbyterian Church and a man of most excellent character. He was married October 3, 1833, to Virginia Woodson Bransford, daughter of Benjamin Bransford of Cumberland County, Virginia. She was born October 16, 1813, and died September 21, 1895. She was descended on her mother's side from the noted family of Woodsons, who intermarried with the Venables. There were three sons and one daughter in this family: Goodridge Wilson, born August 16, 1836; Nathaniel Benjamin, born August 29, 1838; Thomas Samuel, born June 17, 1840, and Elizabeth Mary, born November 29, 1844.

Nathaniel Venable (grandfather) was born in Virginia, March 28, 1768, and died in 1837. He married his first cousin, Martha Venable, generally called Madam Pattie Venable, February 28, 1799. He was a very wealthy planter of Virginia, owning large tracts of land and several hundred slaves.

Abraham Venable (great-grandfather) was born in Virginia in January, 1725, and died in 1778. He married Elizabeth Micheaux, who was born June 18, 1731.

Abraham Venable (great-great-grandfather) was born March 22, 1700, and died March 16, 1768. He married Martha Davis, who was born in 1703, and died in 1765.

The earliest ancestor of the Venable family of whom anything is known came from New Rouen, in Normandy, France, where there is a town called Venables, so named from this family. He accompanied William the Conqueror, and took part in the battle of Hastings. He settled in the County Palatinate of Chester, and was one of the Palatine barons of the County. About the close of the Seventeenth Century two of the younger brothers of the family, Abraham and Joseph Venable, emigrated to America. Joseph went to the Colony of Lord Baltimore and settled at Snow Hill (now West) Virginia. A license was obtained for the erection of a Presbyterian house of worship on Joseph Venable's land, and now, after a lapse of more than a century and a half, the Presbyterian Church which was then organized still prospers at Snow Hill.

The other brother, Abraham, journeyed up the James River and settled in Hanover, now Fluvanna County, Virginia, and there married a widow, whose maiden name was Mildred Lewis, and these two were the great-great-great-grandparents of Thomas S. Venable.

Mr. Venable's grandmother—who was a granddaughter of Nannie Micheaux and her husband, Richard Woodson—distinctly remembered hearing her grandmother relate the early history of the family.

In the reign of Louis XIV, during the religious persecution consequent upon the revocation of the Edict of Nantes, there lived a man named Roche in the city of Sedan, who was Madam Pattie Venable's great-great-grandfather. He had three daughters, the eldest about eighteen, who, as was the custom, had been examined by the priests or government officials; and her father, fearing she would be taken from him and placed in a Catholic school, sent her and his married niece, who had an infant child, to a seaport, that they might embark for Holland. They were escorted by men dressed in women's clothes. The guards were attracted by the crying of the child, and "nine lusty men captured and carried them to prison."

The father was permitted to ransom his daughter and take her home, but his niece was retained in prison and was required to walk the streets every morning, exposed to the ridicule and scoffs of the Catholics, as a penalty for her attempt to escape. Her husband had gone to Holland previously under the guise of a ship carpenter.

Mr. Roche, after paying a certain amount of tribute annually for the privilege of living in peace, determined again to send his daughters to Holland. On the journey Susanna Roche, the younger daughter (who was mother Venable's great-grandmother), was taken very sick and was taken to a public house. While there they were suspected of being Huguenots, and narrowly escaped the vigilance of the soldiers. They went thence to Amsterdam, where their father visited them and provided them with comforts, for he said that the more he had been persecuted the more the Lord had prospered him. Their mother also went to see them, carrying money in her hair.

The elder of the two sisters married and went to the West Indies. The younger, Susanna Roche, married Abram Michaux. She was a lacemaker while in Holland, and her husband was a gauze weaver. They remained in Holland until they had five or six children, when they came to America and located first in Stafford County, Virginia, and later, when they proposed to go to Manikin, the previous settlers there objected, saying they were not entitled to their portion of the land granted by King William to the Huguenots, as they had not come in time, but the king thought differently and decided in their favor. However, they declined settling there, and took up land on the James River at the place now known as Michaux Ferry.

Susanna (Roche) Michaux was the mother of twelve children, seven daughters and five sons. The daughters were: Jane, who married Le Grande; Susanna, married Quinn; Judith, married Morgan; Elizabeth, married Lanbourn Woodson; Nannie, married Richard Woodson; Esther, married Alexander Cunningham, and there was one daughter who did not marry. The sons were: Jacob, who married Judith Woodson; John, James and Paul, who remained out of wedlock.

PINCKNEY THOMPSON, M. D., one of the oldest and most distinguished physicians of Henderson, was born in an humble sphere of life, in Livingston County, Kentucky, April 15, 1828. His father, William Thompson, was a native of North Carolina, whose family settled in Livingston County before Kentucky was admitted to the Union. He was apprenticed or bound to Colonel Ramsey, a farmer, until twenty-one years of age, and on reaching his majority volunteered in Captain Barbour's company, which assembled at Henderson and marched overland to join Gen. Samuel Hopkins' army, then stationed at Vincennes, Indiana. The company arrived too late for the battle of Tippecanoe and returned to Henderson. William Thompson made several trading trips to New Orleans, and while there was pressed into the service by General Jackson. After a short service he was honorably discharged and returned to Livingston County on foot, a very usual means of transportation in those days; settled down to hard work on the farm and was thus engaged for sixty years. He died in 1871 at the residence of his son in Henderson. His wife, Jane (Thompson) Thompson, a native of Livingston County, whose father, William Thompson, came to that county from North Carolina in 1796, and with whom he lived happily for fifty-eight years, survived him about four months and died in January, 1872. They are buried in the beautiful cemetery at Henderson.

Pinckney Thompson received his first lessons in Livingston County when the backwoods log cabin schoolroom was the only avenue to education. But he improved every hour and by the light of the traditional log fire, after a hard day's work on the farm he assiduously prepared himself for the profession to which he was naturally inclined. In 1849 he began the study of medicine under Dr. D. B. Saunders of Smithland, a very distinguished physician of that time, continuing with him until 1851, when he went to Louisville and studied under the preceptorship of Dr. T. G. Richardson, demonstrator of anatomy in the medical department of the University of Louisville, who subsequently became professor of surgery in the Louisiana University. At the same time Dr. Thompson attended the University of

Louisville for two years and was graduated March 4, 1853, having served previous to his graduation in the Louisville City Hospital, in which capacity he gained much practical knowledge.

After visiting his old home he located in Henderson, arriving April 15, 1853; and, without any money, and with only three acquaintances in the city, began the practice of his profession. He was not long in securing a lucrative business, and in the forty-two years of professional life he has enjoyed the reputation of being one of the most successful physicians in the community. He has operated in tracheotomy three times, twice successfully; in lithotomy three times, successfully, and has performed two successful operations for cancer in the breast; besides a large number of minor, yet difficult, operations.

Dr. Thompson is a member of the Henderson Medical Club, of the McDowell Medical Society, of the Kentucky State Medical Society, of the American Medical Association, and of the American Public Health Association; has been president of the Henderson Medical Club, of the State Medical Society, of the McDowell Medical Society, and was for sixteen years president of the State Board of Health; and is prominent and aggressive in all matters pertaining to the public health and the advancement of the medical profession.

He is also quite active and prominent in church work, and in 1869 he conceived the idea of establishing a Mission Sunday school for the benefit of children who were not attending other schools. He carried out this idea, eventually donating a lot and erecting a building for the purpose, and for a number of years supporting the school, mostly at his own expense. He has been superintendent of this school for twenty-seven years. From this humble beginning the Second Presbyterian Church of Henderson was founded. There is nothing in which he prides himself more or in which he takes a greater interest than his large family of Sunday school children. For the past twenty years Dr. Thompson has been president of the Henderson County Auxiliary Bible Society of the American Society, and has been an elder in the Presbyterian Church since 1862. He is also a Master and Royal Arch Mason.

In the line of his profession Dr. Thompson has always been found in the front ranks. As president of the State Board of Health he visited Hickman during the yellow fever epidemic and made an able report to the board; was present at the meeting of the Sanitary Council of the Mississippi Valley at Memphis in 1879, and was elected vice-president. He has always taken great interest in sanitary matters and probably did more than any other man to secure the enactment incorporating the State Board of Health and established it upon a sound and practical basis. At one time when the state appropriation was inadequate for the purposes of the board, he visited Washington and secured from the National Board sufficient help to guarantee a successful fight against epidemics; and in many other ways he has done efficient work for the advancement of medical science. He has been identified in every movement for the improvement of Henderson, taking an active interest in its educational institutions and contributing his quota to the material building up of the city. He was one of the first and most active trustees of the public school and was the first president of that board and author of the law creating the colored school of Henderson.

Dr. Thompson was married November 26, 1857, to Nannie S. Holloway, daughter of William S. Holloway, and has two sons who are young men of great promise, Starling H. and Dr. William Irving Thompson.

HON. JOHN WILLIAM CALDWELL, of Russellville, Kentucky, son of Austin and Louisa Harrison Caldwell, was born in that place January 15, 1838. The early traditions of his father's family induce the belief that they were of Danish or Norman origin with a strong Celtic cross. They emigrated from Ireland to America in early times and settled in Virginia. From that state five of the sons of his great-grandfather, Oliver Caldwell, moved to Kentucky. John, the eldest, and a half-brother to the other four, married a Miss Akers and located in Hardin County. In 1834 his son, Austin, moved to Logan County, where he subsequently married the young widow of his half uncle, David Caldwell.

Mrs. Louisa Harrison Caldwell was born in Virginia, October 20, 1805, and was educated in Richmond. Her father, Peyton Harrison, moved about 1809 from Virginia to Logan County, Kentucky. Her mother, Eliza Mary Barclay, who was educated in Paris, France, was the daughter of Thomas J. Barclay, who came to America from Straban, Ireland, and was in the consular and diplomatic service of this government in the days of the Confederation. The crest of the family was a naked arm wielding a broken javelin. Mrs. Caldwell's father, Peyton Harrison, was born at "Clifton," the country seat of his father, Carter Harrison, and was educated at "Hampden Sidney College," in Prince Edward County, Virginia. His mother, Susanna Randolph, was the youngest daughter of Isham Randolph of "Dungeness," Goochland County, Virginia. Carter Henry Harrison was the son of Benjamin Harrison of "Berkley," and Anne Carter, daughter of Robin Carter of "Curratoman," who is known in Virginia history as "King Carter," on account of his large landed estates. Benjamin Harrison was also the father of Benjamin Harrison, the signer of the Declaration of Independence, and of General Charles Harrison of the Revolutionary war; and was the grandfather of President William Henry Harrison.

In 1843 Austin Caldwell, the father of John W. Caldwell, died in Russellville, Kentucky, under twenty-nine years of age, leaving him, his only living child, with an estate so much embarrassed that he had no opportunity to receive a collegiate education. All his school training was received in the common schools of Russellville and Christian County before he had reached the age of fourteen, about which time he, in care of his maternal uncle, Dr. Robert Peyton Harrison, went overland to what was then practically the frontier of Texas. He remained in that state four or five years, working on a farm, clerking, carrying a surveyor's chain and hunting. During his life in Texas he had many perilous adventures and hair-breadth escapes in swimming swollen rivers and fighting bears, Mexican lions and other wild beasts. He was fond of reading and spent all of his leisure time over the pages of poetry, romance, history and such scientific works as came within his reach. He returned to Kentucky in his nineteenth year—a perfect athlete, inured to hardship, a dead shot with a rifle, a good horseman, and with a wide knowledge of men gleaned on the frontier.

A few months afterward he began the study of law in Russellville with his kinsman, William Morton, Esq., then a prominent lawyer of the Logan County bar. He attended one course of lectures in the law department of the Louisville University in the winter of 1856-7, winning the honors of the junior class. In the fall of 1857 he commenced the practice of his profession in Logan County, and soon established himself as a lawyer, giving early evidence of forensic ability.

When quite young he married Miss Sallie J. Barclay, daughter of Hugh Barclay, she having shortly before graduated with the honors of her class at the celebrated school, Science Hill, at Shelbyville, Kentucky, which was then conducted by the well known educator, Mrs. Julia A. Tevis. One son and two daughters were the result of this marriage.

When the Civil war broke out, though he had opposed the secession of his state from the Union, guided by his sympathy with the South, he volunteered as a private, and was immediately elected captain of the "Logan Grays," a company then being recruited in Logan County for the Confederate service. On the entrance of the Confederates into Kentucky under General S. B. Buckner Captain Caldwell reported his company to him at Bowling Green, and it was assigned as Company A, Ninth Kentucky Brigade, which was commanded by General John C. Breckenridge. On the retreat of General Albert Sidney Johnston south from Bowling Green Captain Caldwell had command of the Ninth Kentucky Regiment until he was relieved by the return of Colonel Thomas H. Hunt from New Orleans. He participated in the battle of Shiloh, where he received three or four contused wounds on his body and had his left arm badly broken, losing sixty-five per cent. of his company, killed and wounded. He was at once promoted to the rank of major of the Ninth Kentucky, and six weeks later, on the reorganization of the regiment, he was unanimously elected lieutenant-colonel. Early in the spring of 1863, on the resignation of Thomas H. Hunt, he was made colonel. Until the close of the war he continued in command of his regiment when not commanding the First Kentucky, better known as the "Orphans' Brigade," and is said to have been in command of this famous military organization longer than any of its regular brigadier-generals (Breckenridge, Hanson or Helm), except General Joseph H. Lewis. Colonel Caldwell was again badly wounded at Chickamauga, his left arm being broken through the elbow and a slight wound received in his left side. The Board of Army Surgeons, on account of his injuries, offered to retire him from the service, but he declined; and after a two months' absence returned, with his arm in a sling, to the army at Dalton, Georgia, taking command of his regiment before the opening of the celebrated campaign between Johnston and Sherman. During that campaign the march of Sherman through Georgia and the subsequent fighting in South Carolina, when not in command of his regiment, he was in command of the "Orphans' Brigade." After the close of hostilities he surrendered with the brigade at Washington, Georgia, and was paroled a prisoner of war May 6, 1865. He immediately returned to his home in Kentucky, and in the fall of that year he resumed his practice as a lawyer at the Russellville bar.

In August, 1866, he was elected judge of the Logan County Court, held that office for eight years, and did a large and lucrative practice in the criminal, circuit and higher courts of the commonwealth, establishing a reputation as a lawyer of ability and one of the most successful jury advocates that ever practiced at the Russellville bar. Two years after his retirement from the office of county judge he was, in 1876, elected as a Democrat to represent the Third District of Kentucky in the Forty-fifth Congress, and was re-elected to the Forty-sixth and Forty-seventh. On account of ill-health and the necessity of looking after his private affairs, over the protest of his constituents, he declined a renomination to the Forty-eighth Congress, though he had no opposition, and the Republicans conceded that it was impossible to defeat him in the district.

His congressional career, while not a brilliant one, was honest and conservative. Several of his speeches in the House of Representatives were given a wide publication through a part of the daily and country press, and the New York Sun said of him: "He is a Democrat with an honest record; always at his post, and invariably opposed to corrupt and extravagant legislation." He was the stern and unflinching advocate of home rule, tariff reform, hard money and economy in public expenditures. On his retirement from Congress he did not resume the practice of law, but became the president of Logan County Bank, which position he now holds.

JAMES A. CURRY, the senior member of the firm of Curry, Tunis & Norwood, a leading wholesale grocery establishment of Lexington, is a son of James and Katherine (Stagg) Curry, and was born in Harrodsburg, Kentucky, June 23, 1829. His father was born in Mercer County, March 25, 1796. He was a contractor and builder and a man of many admirable traits of character, honored and highly respected by all of his neighbors; a deacon in the Presbyterian Church for many years; a member of the Sons of Temperance, a strong and reputable organization of his time, and was a soldier in the War of 1812, serving in Colonel Slaughter's regiment, which participated in the battle of New Orleans under the immediate command of Major-General John Adair. He was a Henry Clay Whig, strong in his convictions and influential in his party. His home was in Harrodsburg, where he died in 1878.

William Curry (grandfather) was born near Staunton, Virginia, and came to Mercer County, Kentucky, in 1790. He married Anna Hill, a relative of General A. P. Hill; was a successful farmer in Mercer County, a member of the Presbyterian Church, a model Christian gentleman and was prominently identified with the old Whig party.

Katherine Stagg Curry (mother) was born in Gettysburgh, Pennsylvania. She came to Kentucky with her father's family when she was a young lady. Her father, Daniel Stagg, located on a fine tract of land about three miles west of Harrodsburg and there established the old Stagg homestead. He married Mary Conover of Hackensack, New Jersey.

James Stagg (great-grandfather) was a soldier in a company of militia from Morris County, New Jersey, in the Revolutionary war. His wife was Leah Brewer of New Jersey.

James Stagg (great-great-grandfather) was one of the Covenanters of Scotland who fled to Holland to escape persecution on account of their religious belief. He first went to Holland, with many others, and subsequently came to the United States, locating in Hackensack, New Jersey. His wife's maiden name was Anna Christie.

James A. Curry, whose ancestry is partially given above, was educated in Harrodsburg, and at the age of fifteen, during the brilliant Presidential campaign in which Clay and Frelinghuysen were the Whig candidates, he was employed as a clerk in the Harrodsburg postoffice. After one year's service in that office he was apprenticed to a tailor and served his full term of four years in learning his trade. When about twenty years of age he began the business of merchant tailoring in Harrodsburg, which he continued until 1856, when he engaged in the drug and book business, continuing there until 1878, when he removed to Danville, where he was in the same business until 1883. In that year he disposed of his store in Danville, removed to Lexington and became the senior member of the wholesale grocery firm of Curry, Howard & Murray. Mr. Murray died in 1885 and J. T. Tunis became a member of the firm, the style of which was changed to Curry, Howard & Co. In 1890 Mr. Norwood took the place of Mr. Howard, who withdrew, and the present firm of Curry, Tunis & Norwood was established.

The citizens of Lexington and the grocery dealers throughout the state will testify to the high standing and unswerving integrity of the company over which Mr. Curry has presided with commendable watchfulness throughout its successful career. As a citizen his character has always been in keeping with the high moral and religious convictions which he inherited from his Scotch Covenanter ancestors and which were inculcated by the careful training of his Christian parents. In politics his affiliations are with the Republican party, the rightful descendant of the old Whig party, in which he was brought up.

He voted for Bell and Everett in the final struggle of that party to recover its supremacy, and failing in this he fell in with the new party which adopted the principles of the old.

Mr. Curry is closely identified with and deeply interested in the work of the Presbyterian Church, in which he has been an elder for twenty-five years, serving in Harrodsburg, Danville and in the Second Presbyterian Church of Lexington. In 1886 and again in 1893 he was a commissioner to the General Assembly, and in the Assembly of 1893 was one of the committee of fifteen who found a verdict in the famous trial of Dr. Briggs for heresy; he is a member of the executive committee in charge of the missionary work of the Presbyterian Church in Kentucky; chairman of the Committee on Systematic Benevolence in Ebenezer Presbytery; president of the Young Men's Christian Association of Lexington, in which he takes a deep interest and which is largely indebted to his wise counsel for its usefulness, popularity and excellent standing, and has been a member of the Board of Trustees of Center College for twelve years past. He is president of the Lexington and Vicinity Bible Society, a life member of the American Sunday School Union, life member of the American Tract Society and life member of the American Bible Society.

Mr. Curry's chief characteristic, aside from his proverbial honesty and integrity in business matters, is his faithful devotion to the church and its work; and in this there is no show of ostentation or personal pride, but on the contrary a seeming unconsciousness of the superiority which others accord to him.

Mr. Curry was married September 21, 1852, to Elizabeth Porter Lewis, daughter of Thomas P. Lewis of Harrodsburg. Mrs. Curry was born in Harrodsburg January 4, 1833. They have four children, whose names and the names of the persons whom they married and the names of their children are as follows:

(1) Kate: educated at Daughters' College, Harodsburg, and at College Hill, near Cincinnati, Ohio; now the wife of Major C. H. Tebbetts, superintendent and commandant of Culver Military Academy at Culver, Indiana, situated on Lake Maxinkuckee; their children are: James

Curry, Mary Winlock, Jonas M., Elizabeth Porter and Marian.

(2) Thomas Porter Curry: graduated from Center College, receiving the highest honors in the class of 1875; is the patentee of the Curry railway signal; a resident of Danville; married Anna Roach, daughter of Edwin Roach, and has two children, Edwin Porter and Kate.

(3) Mary: educated at Danville; wife of J. T. Tunis, who is a graduate of Center College, class of 1881; a resident of Lexington and a member of the firm of Curry, Tunis & Norwood; they have two children, James Curry Tunis and John Theodore Tunis, Jr.

(4) James Howard Curry: educated in Danville and at the Kentucky University, Lexington; now in business with his father; married Elizabeth Norton Sage, daughter of Osmer Sage of Lexington, and has one son, James A. Curry, Jr.

GEORGE COX, a son of a salesman of respectable standing, was born in the city of London on the first day of March, 1791, and according to a good old English custom was christened at the Church of St. Mary Magdalen, Bermondsey, on the 1st of April following.

His father was John Cox, third son of Henry Cox, born at Ross, Herfordshire, May 13, 1756; and his mother was Mary Cowell, born October 26, 1756. They were married at the Parish Church of St. James, Clerkenwell, London, May 2, 1784. The result of this union, which was a most happy one, was eight children: Edward and Henry, dying in childhood; John, born September 24, 1789, and supposed to have been killed in Spain or Portugal while serving his country in the Peninsular war, under the command of the Duke of Wellington; George, the subject of this sketch; Ann Maria, born January 11, 1793, died December 12, 1867; Frances, mother of the late James Wormald of Maysville; Margaret, died in infancy, and Esther became the wife of George Herbst, May 8, 1834, dying in 1840.

There are authentic records which trace Mr. Cox's ancestry back for more than three hundred years, but the purpose of this article is to treat of the individual whose lifework affords a shining example.

His father was employed in the hosiery shop of a man named Marsh, and into this shop the son was taken at the early age of nine years, and from that period to the day of his death he devoted his energies to well directed industry. His mother died February 20, 1811, and was laid to rest in the burial ground of St. Mary, Newington, Surrey, July 16, 1814. His father married again, his second wife being Elizabeth Caroline Rose.

In 1817, at the age of twenty-six, and after a service of seventeen years in the shop of Mr. March, Mr. Cox determined to seek a home in the "Western World," and he succeeded in getting his father, stepmother, his sisters and a number of his cousins to come with him. They landed at Baltimore and came from that point overland as far as Pittsburgh, where they took a flat-boat down the Ohio for Maysville, their destination being Lexington, Kentucky, then the foremost city of the west. Here the party located, and for several months George Cox sought in vain for employment. During these months he made the acquaintance of Ann Hopkinson, an English girl, born in Nottingham, July.15, 1796. From Lexington he went to Cincinnati, where he found employment for a short time, and on April 10, 1819, he returned to Lexington and made Miss Hopkinson his wife.

With her he came to Maysville to engage in business, his only capital being $300 in money, a strong frame, good health, industry, and, above all, honesty. He opened a small store in a frame house on Front street, above Market, one-half of the house being occupied by his cousin and brother-in-law, Edward Cox, as a book store and bindery. Both families lived in the second story of the building.

Mr. Cox was a methodical merchant from the very start. He kept a record of every transaction. The first item of goods sold by the merchant is set down thus: "1819, May 5, Quills, 6 1-4 cents." His simple system of keeping accounts enabled him to know what he was doing at all times. He paid for articles as he bought them, and when they were gone, if he had money to replace them, it was evident that he was neither losing money nor getting in debt. At the end of each week he footed up his sales, the first entry of that kind in his account book for the week from May 31 to June 6, 1819, $23.37 1-2. From this modest beginning George Cox's business grew until his name was as familiar to the merchants of the east as that of any man in the Union, and it carried with it a prestige that might well be envied.

It was not many years before increasing business obliged Mr. Cox to secure larger quarters, and he moved into the building now occupied by St. Charles on Front street. Here he remained until 1840, when he bought the property immediately across the alley, and this he occupied as store and dwelling until 1850, when the site now occupied on Second street was purchased. William H., Mr. Cox's eldest son, was at about that time admitted to a partnership in the house under the firm name of George Cox & Son. Their business grew until it was perhaps the largest retail dry goods trade in Northern Kentucky. Mr. Cox was among the few Englishmen who became Americanized.

In 1851 he paid a visit to London, but found little pleasure in the trip. Nearly all his relatives had died or removed to other lands, and upon his return to Maysville he told his family: "I am an American now; I am no longer an Englishman."

He was an unflinching friend of the government during the dark days of the rebellion and loaned largely of his means to aid in carrying on the war, taking in return government bonds, despite the protests of many of his friends that the bonds would be worthless. He reasoned that if the government was lost everything was lost, and he would rather sacrifice his fortune in the effort to save his government.

Mr. Cox was a liberal contributor to every public enterprise and every worthy object. He was opposed to taxing the public for railroads and other internal improvements, believing that they should be built by public enterprise. His death, September 21, 1881, removed from Maysville her stanchest merchant. Although possessed of a large fortune, consisting of real and personal property, he made no will, expressing that the law would make an equitable and satisfactory division among his heirs, a confidence that was not misplaced.

ZACK PHELPS, one of the most brilliant all-round lawyers of the Louisville bar, son of James S. Phelps, the prominent tobacco warehouseman, was born in Christian County, Kentucky, July 7, 1857. He came to Louisville with his parents when he was six years of age and attended the public schools, graduating from the Male High School in 1877. He was made class historian and carried off the second honor of his class. At the close of his school life, his health being impaired, he went to Salt Lake City, Utah, and while recuperating there began the study of law in the office of Judge J. C. Hemingray. After a careful course of study he passed a highly creditable examination before Mr. Justice Schaffer of the United States Supreme Court, who gave him a certificate authorizing him to practice law.

He returned to Louisville in 1880 and began a most successful career as an attorney. He soon formed a partnership with the late W. L. Jackson, Jr., who was later elected judge of the Circuit Court to succeed his father. A few years later J. T. O'Neal became a member of the young firm, and the three continued in partnership for six years, until the elevation of Mr. Jackson to the bench. The dissolution of the firm followed, and Mr. Phelps became associated with W. W. Thum, under the firm name of Phelps & Thum, which is one of the most popular and widely known law firms in the city at the present time.

In 1890 Mr. Phelps took a prominent part in the movement to secure a new constitution of the state and made a number of speeches throughout the state favoring a constitutional convention. He was elected by the people of Louisville as a member of the convention which framed the present constitution of Kentucky in 1890-91. His labors in that body were of a character requiring an intimate and varied knowledge of law and he distinguished himself as one of the most active and influential workers for the public good.

Mr. Phelps has devoted a great deal of his valuable time to public life in the interests of others and for the advancement of his city and state, but has had no aspiration for office, preferring to devote his best efforts to the legal profession, in which he has gained an enviable reputation as an all-round lawyer of versatile ability of

KENTUCKY BIOGRAPHIES. 87

the highest order, and especially as an expert cross-examiner of witnesses.

In October, 1893, Mr. Phelps was selected by Honorable Charles D. Jacob, ex-mayor of Louisville, to meet Colonel Bennett H. Young in debate upon municipal affairs, the main issue being a comparison between the administrations of ex-Mayor Jacob and (then) Mayor Henry S. Tyler. In this sort of contest Mr. Phelps was easily the superior of his able opponent, being loaded with facts, and having an aptitude for debate and controversy which is rarely excelled. He carried off the honors for Mr. Jacob, and his enthusiastic audience carried their champion out of the hall on their shoulders. This is only one of the numerous victories on the stump and in the court room, in which he has exerted the power of the ready speaker and won the victory over men of acknowledged ability, or convinced a jury by his fine logic and practical eloquence.

On the first day of January, 1881, Mr. Phelps was married to Amy Kaye, daughter of John and Amanda Kaye of Louisville, and the family group in their beautiful home on New Broadway, in the Highlands, consists of the father and mother and four children, John, Zack, Mary Glass and Amy.

Mr. Phelps' father, James S. Phelps, was born in Hopkinsville, Christian County, Kentucky, March 8, 1830. He was educated mainly under the instruction of James D. Rumsey of Hopkinsville and in a school taught by a venerable Baptist minister near that place. He served for some time as deputy in the office of the clerk of the court, and studied law in the office of Henry J. Stites. He was admitted to the bar and opened an office, but shortly afterward engaged in the mercantile business in partnership with Joseph K. Grant, a venture which proved quite successful. In 1856 he sold his interest in the store to his partner and in 1862 removed to Louisville and engaged in the tobacco warehouse business under the firm name of Phelps, Caldwell & Company. This house was sold in 1867 to Ray & Company. The Planters splendid warehouse was erected in 1875 by Mr. Phelps and the firm of J. S. Phelps & Company was formed, John C. Durrett being Mr. Phelps' partner. The present company, of which Mr. Phelps is president, was incorporated in 1881 with a capital stock of $150,000, which is owned by himself and four sons.

He is one of the founders and is a liberal supporter of the Highland Baptist Church; has been prominently connected with the Odd Fellows, and served several years as grand deputy of the state; a Democrat, but not a politician; a business man of sterling integrity; an honored and highly respected citizen.

James S. Phelps and Mary Jane Glass, daughter of Zachariah and Mary Jane Glass of Hopkinsville, were married July 25, 1849.

John H. Phelps (grandfather) was born in Virginia in July, 1790. He came to Kentucky with his brother and married Caroline Shipp, a member of a well known and highly respected family of Christian County. Caroline Shipp Phelps died in 1830, and John H. Phelps was married again to a sister of Governor James T. Morehead.

The Phelps family is probably of English descent, but the progenitor of the family in Virginia left no record of his ancestry.

Zachariah Glass (maternal grandfather) was a native of Christian County and a merchant in Hopkinsville for many years, and was subsequently elected, and oftentimes re-elected clerk of the County Court, and at the time of his death, in 1855, was one of the wealthiest men in Christian County.

THORNTON M. DORA, son of William and Elizabeth (Morris) Dora, was born in Bracken County, May 3, 1833. His father, also a native of Bracken County, was born September 6, 1802, and was educated in the country schools. He engaged in farming for some years, and in 1849 embarked in the mercantile business in Brooksville, in which he was very energetic and highly successful. He was a Whig, but was never active in political matters. He was a member of the Methodist Episcopal Church, going with the Southern wing of that body after the division, in which he was a faithful member and an office bearer until the time of his death, October 28, 1855. He was buried in Mount Zion Cemetery, near Brooksville.

Ferdinand Dora (grandfather) was born in Maryland, May 13, 1758, and came to Kentucky during the early settlement of the state, located in Bracken County and was the founder and builder of the first country church in Bracken County. It was built of logs and was known as "Dora Church." A brick building known as Mount Zion Church now occupies the site. He died January 24, 1830, and his wife, Nancy Beauchamp, died January 10, 1840. Both were members of the M. E. Church.

John Dora (great-grandfather) was born near London, England, where the name was spelled Dore. After coming to America, the name was changed to Dora. On his arrival in this country he located in Somerset County, Maryland, near Baltimore. He had five sons who served in the Revolutionary War, two of whom, Jesse and Benjamin, have not been heard from since. His first wife was a Miss Tillman of Maryland.

John Dora, or Dore, was the only child of his father and mother, who belonged to a very wealthy family in England.

Elizabeth Morris Dora (mother) was born in Bracken County, February 13, 1808, and was educated in Augusta. She and William Dora were married November 17, 1825. She was the mother of eight children, three sons and five daughters. She was a devoted member of the Methodist Church and died in the faith February 2, 1882. Her father, Dickison Morris, was a native of Virginia, and was one of the pioneers of Bracken County. Being one of the first civil engineers in the county, he surveyed a great many tracts of land in Bracken and adjoining counties. He married Fannie Buckner, daughter of Philip and Tabitha Buckner. The Morris family was of Scotch extraction.

Thornton M. Dora on reaching manhood taught school for two years and while thus engaged, in 1853, commenced the study of law, reading under the instruction of John H. Bonde of Brooksville. In 1854 he went to Chicago, Ill., and studied with his uncle, B. S. Morris, for one year. In 1855 his father died and he returned to take charge of the estate, and by this event his plan of life was changed and he became a merchant, taking up his father's business, which he has successfully followed since with the exception of about two years which he spent on the farm.

He was elected police judge in 1865 and served for many years, being frequently re-elected. He has also been a magistrate and notary public since 1864, and was for many years a deputy county clerk. Since March, 1863, Mr. Dora has resided at Germantown.

During the war his sympathies were with the South and he was quite liberal in his support of the "cause."

He was married March 16, 1858, to Matilda Frances, daughter of John and Elizabeth Reed, who was born August 17, 1837. She graduated from Science Hill Academy, Shelbyville, in 1856. They have had two children: Samantha Bell, born December 16, 1858, died January 3, 1860, and Neppie Eugenia, born February 24, 1861, married May 26, 1880, to W. D. Reneker, who died in November, 1885; to them was born a daughter (Dora Reneker), November 25, 1882. In December, 1888, she became the wife of Stephen Douglas Rigdon, now living in Toledo, Ohio, and to them two sons have been born—Thornton and Thurman.

EDWARD LESLIE WORTHINGTON, one of the leading members of the Mason County bar and a member of one of the prominent pioneer families of Kentucky, was born in Mason County October 20, 1851. He is a son of Madison Worthington, who was also a native of Mason County, and a grandson of Thomas T. Worthington, a native of Maryland. Thomas T. Worthington emigrated from his native state and settled in Mason County at a very early day and was one of the first sheriffs of the county. He located about nine miles west of Maysville in the Fern Leaf neighborhood. Samuel Worthington (great-grandfather) came to this country from England about the year 1660, and became a resident of Maryland, where he lived and died.

Madison Worthington (father) wedded Elizabeth Bledsoe, daughter of Benjamin Bledsoe, one of the pioneers of Mason County.

E. L. Worthington grew to manhood on his father's farm and in 1869 entered Kentucky University (formerly Transylvania), where he remained a student during 1869 and 1870. In 1872 he entered the Cincinnati Law School and was graduated from that institution in the spring of 1874. He was subsequently admitted to the bar, but remained on the farm until 1880, when he located in Maysville, and at once took rank as one of the most successful practitioners in the county. In 1885 he was elected by the Democratic party to the state senate from the district composed of the counties of Mason and Lewis. During a term of four years in that body he took an active and leading part in its deliberations and was a member of the judiciary committee.

Mr. Worthington's law practice is not confined to the local courts in Maysville, but has a great many cases before the Court of Appeals and a large clientele in the counties adjoining Mason. He is industrious and zealous in the prosecution of his work and any cause entrusted to his hands is sure of careful attention, and, if just, is almost sure of a verdict. He is assiduous in the preparation of all the business he brings into court, relying more upon this and the weight of evidence than upon a display of oratory before the jury, but when a strong plea is needed he has few superiors as an advocate. Mr. Worthington is a thorough lawyer, a popular and influential citizen, an honored member of one of the first families and a representative Kentucky gentleman.

EMMETT FIELD, Judge of the Common Pleas Division of the Jefferson Circuit Court of Louisville, son of William H. and Mary (Young) Field, was born in Louisville, Kentucky, October 28, 1841. His father was born in Culpeper County, Virginia, in 1816, and was educated and studied law in that state. When he was twenty-two years of age he came to Kentucky and practiced law in Westport, Oldham County, for some years and then removed to Louisville and formed a law partnership with Preston S. Loughborough, with whom he was associated for a long time. Several years before the Civil war he removed to Pettis County, Missouri, and purchased a farm upon which he lived until June 5, 1861, when he was killed at his home by Union soldiers. He was in sympathy with the south, but was a non-participant in the war.

Henry Field (grandfather) was a farmer in Culpeper County, Virginia, and a member of an old and distinguished family whose people were closely associated with the early development of the state.

Dr. Henry Young (maternal grandfather) was a physician of repute who lived near Bedford and practiced his profession in Trimble County, Kentucky.

Judge Field, now one of the most distinguished jurists on the Louisville bench, received his collegiate education at Westminster College, Fulton, Missouri, and before he was twenty years of age he stepped out of the schoolroom and into the ranks of the Confederate army. He enlisted in the Second Regiment Missouri Cavalry, commanded by Colonel Alexander, later by Colonel McGoffin, and still later by Colonel Robert McCullough, with whom he remained a greater part of the time that he was in the service. Returning to Louisville he entered the law department of the University of Louisville, from which he graduated.

The first two years of his professional career were spent in Springfield, Washington County, after which he joined his brother, Richard Field, in Louisville and was associated with him in the practice of law. This partnership was dissolved on account of the failing health of his brother, who removed to Minnesota, and Judge Field was alone in business until his elevation to the bench, with the exception of about one year, when he was associated with Buford Twyman.

In 1886 Mr. Field was elected judge of the Court of Common Pleas, now known as the Jefferson Circuit Court, Common Pleas Division, and has served in that high judicial position for nearly ten years. He is a skilled lawyer and an able judge, and is highly esteemed for the wisdom and impartiality of his decisions. His frequent re-election, in opposition to strong political forces, is probably the highest testimonial of his worth and of the esteem in which he is held by the bar and the people of Louisville.

He is a most genial, polished gentleman, a Democrat, but not a politician, and is unbiased by party prejudice in the discharge of his duties on the bench.

Judge Field has been a professor in the law department of the University of Louisville during the past ten years, and while his duties in this relation require much time and research, he enjoys its labors as a relief from the exacting requirements of the judge, and is deeply interested in the success and progress of his Alma Mater, in which so many distinguished attorneys in the city and state have acquired a knowledge of the legal profession.

Judge Field was married in 1869 to Sue McElroy, daughter of Anthony McElroy of Springfield, Kentucky. She was educated in Professor Sloan's school in Danville. They are members of the Presbyterian Church, and enjoy a high social position in Louisville society. They reside in the beautiful suburb of Crescent Hill.

GEORGE W. FRANTZ, proprietor of one of the largest tanneries in the United States, a man of large fortune made by his own honest industry, a broad-minded, liberal politician and public-spirited citizen, formerly chief of the fire department, and recently elected park commissioner of Louisville, was born in Cincinnati, Ohio, September 6, 1844.

His father, David Frantz, was born in Alsace, Germany, August 30, 1810, and came to the United States in 1829, stopping first in Baltimore, where he was employed as a journeyman tanner for two years, and then walked from Baltimore to Cincinnati, where he was superintendent of the tannery of the old firm of A. M. Taylor & Company until 1847, when he came to Louisville as a partner of A. M. Taylor and established the tannery now owned by his son, George W. Frantz, situated at the corner of Franklin and Buchanan streets. They began in a small way and continued to work together until 1856, when A. M. Taylor withdrew and H. W. Taylor took his place in the firm. This partnership continued until January 1, 1864, when Mr. Taylor withdrew and David Frantz, Jr., and George W. Frantz were admitted to the firm under the style of D. Frantz & Sons. On the first day of January, 1886, the senior member of the firm retired and the business was continued by the sons under the firm name.

David Frantz was one of the best and most industrious citizens of Louisville and was successful through his industry, honesty and square dealing. He was a member of the German Lutheran Church, and a man of great moral courage and strength of character. He died in 1891, aged eighty-one years.

Christina Staebler Frantz (mother) was born in Wurtemberg, Germany, in 1805, and was married to Mr. Frantz in Cincinnati. She was a faithful member of the German Lutheran Church, and a noble Christian woman. Her father, Jonathan Staebler, was a native of Germany, but came to this country some years before his death.

George W. Frantz was educated in the Louisville public schools and spent two years in the Lutheran College at St. Charles, Missouri. At the age of eighteen years he was well qualified for the prominent part he has taken in the management of large business interests and in public affairs, to which he has given much attention.

On the fourth day of March, 1862, he began work in his father's tannery and, as above stated, became a partner in the concern on the first day of January, 1864; and on the first day of February, 1895, on the retirement of his brother, he became the sole proprietor of the oldest and largest tannery in Louisville. He made many improvements and increased the capacity of the plant a hundred-fold. The yard covers an area of four acres of ground and the establishment employs one hundred men, who, with the recent improvements in machinery and the increased facilities, can accomplish as much as twice that number of men could do under the old regime.

Mr. Frantz has always been a Democrat and has taken a lively interest in politics from the business man's standpoint, being opposed to the drawing of party lines in city politics. In 1878 he was elected by the City Council chief engineer of the fire department, but the constant diligence required of him in the department conflicted with his business interests, and after two years of efficient service he retired from that office, having placed the department upon a better footing and upon a higher standard of excellence than it had ever reached before.

In 1895 he was nominated by the Republican party, without his wish or consent, for the important office of park commissioner—a nomination which was a high compliment to his business ability—and although a Democrat, he accepted the nomination and was elected by a large majority, receiving almost as many Democratic as Republican votes. While he is very much gratified by his election under such circumstances, he realizes his responsibility to the general public, and has given much thought and labor to the development of the extensive park system of the city. His ability as a financier, together with his high regard for the judicious expenditure of public funds, has made him one of the most useful and popular of the six park commissioners.

Being a self-made man, whose fortune has been acquired by great industry, close personal attention to business and honesty of purpose, he knows the value of a dollar, and applies the rules of private business in the disposition of the public funds more rigidly than he does in conducting the affairs of his own establishment. He will see that the money entrusted to the park commissioners is judiciously expended. At the same time he is broad and liberal in his views of the public needs, and is neither penurious nor lavish in the use of money for needed improvements.

A man of ample fortune, noted for his generous public spirit and deeply interested in the progress of the city, Mr. Frantz enjoys the confidence and good will of men of all parties. Besides being a large property holder in the city, and having extensive business interests in which he has a vast amount of capital invested, Mr. Frantz owns one hundred and sixty thousand acres of land in Crosby County, Texas, worth an average of five dollars per acre, and which is increasing in value. This land, the finest in the state, was purchased some years ago by a syndicate of Louisville capitalists for ranching purposes and a company was organized and known as the Kentucky Cattle Raising Company. They owned forty thousand head of cattle at one time, but the business failed through mismanagement, and Mr. Frantz became the purchaser of the land in order to save himself and his friends from loss, and it has proven a good investment.

Mr. Frantz is a Knight Templar, an Odd Fellow, a member of the Knights of Honor and a member of the Methodist Church, South.

He was married April 5, 1866, to Mary M. Enderlin of Louisville, and has five sons and one daughter: George W. Frantz, Jr., Emma E., wife of John W. Klein of Louisville; Walter L., David W., Edwin A. and Harold W. Frantz.

REVEREND WILLIAM H. FELIX, pastor of the Baptist Church, Lexington, son of Josiah and Jane Ann (Shouse) Felix, was born in Mortinsville, Woodford County, Kentucky, October 6, 1838.

His father was a native Kentuckian, and when a young man he settled in Woodford County, where he married and lived up to the time of his death in 1867, aged fifty-nine years. He was a member of the Baptist Church, and a follower of the political teachings of Henry Clay, but after the dissolution of the old Whig party he acted with the State Rights party of Mr. Jefferson.

Josiah Felix was long a justice of the peace under the Constitution of 1799. He was an industrious farmer and also was largely engaged in the manufacture of bagging and rope. These articles were carried on steamboats to New Orleans and other cities of the Southern states. He was an energetic and successful business man, and employed on an average of one hundred operatives in his hemp factory, and managed a large farm. He was strictly honest and never forgot the smallest item of expense in his business operations. He was of German descent.

Jane Ann Shouse (mother) was a native of Woodford County. She died in 1893, in her eighty-fourth year. She was a well preserved lady, and a faithful and worthy member of the Baptist Church.

William H. Felix remained on his father's farm until he was sixteen years of age. In 1855 he entered Georgetown College, and was graduated from that institution in June, 1860. He then took charge of a Baptist Church at New Castle in Henry County, Kentucky. He was ordained by Doctor Duncan R. Campbell, president of Georgetown College, who preached the ordination sermon.

At this time the Civil war between the states was inaugurated, and he, still pursuing the ministry, read law; was admitted to the bar in 1862, and practiced law one year at Shelbyville.

In September, 1863, Mr. Felix was called home to take charge of the First Baptist Church, Lexington, Kentucky, and served this church until 1869, when he received a call from the Pilgrim Baptist Church of New York City, and was pastor of that church for one year. In 1870 he accepted a call to the First Baptist Church of Covington, where he remained as pastor for fourteen years and resigned in 1884. For two years thereafter he served country churches in order to regain his health. In 1887 he was called to the church at Lexington, his present charge.

When he came to Lexington in 1887, the church had four hundred and twenty-five members; after his eight years of labor there are now eight hundred and forty-five, a gain of four hundred and twenty-five, having himself received six hundred into the church.

Rev. William H. Felix is a Baptist minister of high character and renown, and wherever he is known he is greatly loved and respected. As a minister he is energetic and faithful. In his spirits he is seldom greatly elevated or depressed, a uniform dignity marking his deportment in daily life. His conversation is entertaining, and his sermons abound in rich thought, plain expression and solemn appeals to the conscience. There are few men whose labors in the ministry have produced a greater portion of good.

Mr. Felix was married in 1861 to Mattie Haydon, daughter of Thomas Haydon of Louisville, Kentucky. She died in 1871, leaving four children: Mary, wife of Hamilton Wright of Hartwell, Ohio; Jennie, now Mrs. Caldwell of Visalia, Kentucky; Josie, wife of Richard Cummings of Covington, and Mattie, wife of William Bain of Lexington.

Rev. Felix was married the second time in 1875 to Camilla Hemmingray, and by this union one son and one daughter have been born: William H., Jr., and Annie Bradford Felix.

TIMOTHY ALEXANDER FIELD, wholesale grocer of Ashland, son of James L. and Mary (Hicks) Field, was born in Kanawha County, West Virginia, July 30, 1863. His father, James L. Field, was born in Bedford County, Virginia, November 13, 1837, and was educated in the common schools of Kanawha County, West Virginia. He was a merchant of Charleston, West Virginia, and at one time served as superintendent of schools in Kanawha County, West Virginia. He was a deacon in the Baptist Church and was active in all good work. He married Mary Matilda Hicks January 9, 1862. She was born October 4, 1844 in Kanawha County, West Virginia. They had twelve children, of whom Timothy Alexander, the subject of this sketch, was the eldest.

John Field (grandfather) was born in Fairfax County, Virginia, and was a manager of salt furnaces. He married Elizabeth Thurman, a cousin to Senator Allen G. Thurman of Ohio. He died December 4, 1880.

Timothy A. Field received his education in Kanawha County, West Virginia; in 1885 engaged in the mercantile and lumber business in Carter County, Kentucky, and in 1888 he removed to Ashland and embarked in the wholesale grocery business with Thomas J. Crump, the firm name being Crump & Field, a house which is well known throughout Northeastern Kentucky.

Mr. Field is a member of the City Council of Ashland, having been elected by the Republicans, to which party he belongs. He is a Knight Templar, a popular citizen and a successful business man. He was married June 10, 1887, to Hattie Crump, daughter of Thomas J. Crump. They have two children living, James Thomas and Dorothea Crump.

DR. LAMME STEELE GIVENS of Cynthiana was born in that city January 14, 1866. His father, David A. Givens, was born in Cynthiana in 1831. He was engaged in the mercantile business for many years. He was also largely engaged in raising cattle and brought the first imported Jersey cattle to this county. For many years he was very successful, making large sales of Jerseys in New York City and other places. He served as justice of the peace, but never held any other office. He was an elder in the Presbyterian Church, and a highly respected citizen of his native town, and died July 26, 1895. His father, Col. Alexander Givens, was born in Cynthiana in 1792. He was a farmer and stock raiser, and was a colonel in the state militia. He died in 1840, at the age of forty-eight years. His father, George Givens, was a native of Virginia, a soldier in the Revolutionary war, and was one of the earliest settlers of Harrison County. He was of Scotch-Irish descent.

Margaret Keller Givens (mother) was born in Cynthiana in 1838. She was a faithful member of the Presbyterian Church, and died in 1882. Her father, Abraham Keller, was born in Cynthiana in 1808 and died there in 1868, aged sixty years. He was the distiller of the renowned brand of "A. Keller Whisky." This distillery is still in operation and is owned by Ashbrook Bros.

Dr. L. S. Givens, after leaving the public schools of Cynthiana, attended Central University and graduated from the Ohio Medical College, Cincinnati, in 1887. He spent the next year abroad in the hospitals of Berlin and London, and in 1889 he began the general practice of medicine in Cynthiana, giving especial attention to diseases of the nose, throat and ear. He is a member of the Kentucky Medical Society and a contributor to the medical journals. He is coroner of the county, having been elected to that office on the Democratic ticket in 1894.

Dr. Givens and Nettie Martin, daughter of Reed M. Martin of Cynthiana, were married, November 18, 1891. They are members of the Presbyterian Church and are prominent in society.

REV. BERNARD GREIFENKAMP, rector of St. Augustine's Church, Augusta, was born in Cincinnati, November 20, 1858. The days of his boyhood were spent in Newport, where his parents made their home; and, after receiving his primary schooling, he went to St. Xavier College in Cincinnati, where he took the degree of A. M. in 1879. He then went to St. Francis Seminary, Milwaukee, Wisconsin, and finished his studies with distinction in 1882. He was ordained to the priesthood in the same year at Covington by Rt. Rev. A. M. Toebbe. He at once began the work of the ministry as assistant rector of St. Aloysius Church, Covington, and labored in that capacity for four and a half years. He then was placed in charge of the St. Augustine's Church at Augusta, and in the nine years of his ministry in that place he has enjoyed the love and confidence of his parishioners and the respect of the entire community. He is a modest, unassuming gentleman, a fine scholar and, withal, a diligent student, an eloquent speaker and a wise counsellor. His work has been fraught with good results in his parish and in the community, and his worth is appreciated by all classes of citizens, and by Christians of all denominations.

Father Greifenkamp's ancestors were from Germany and were among the earliest settlers of Cincinnati, where his parents lived at the time of his birth.

WILLIAM ALVIS GUTHRIE, M. D., of Franklin, Kentucky, son of Francis M. and Nancy (Marcum) Guthrie, was born in Clinton County, Kentucky, August 31, 1864. His father is a native of the same county, where he has been a farmer and a lumber merchant since reaching his manhood. He is a good citizen, an excellent neighbor and a member of the Methodist Church.

Anderson Guthrie (grandfather) was also a native of Kentucky, and a farmer of Clinton County, and died there in 1893 at the age of seventy-eight years. His father was a native of Virginia, who came to Kentucky very early in the present century, and his father (great-great-grandfather) was born in Ireland and came to America and settled in Virginia, but in what year the records of the family do not show.

Nancy Marcum Guthrie (mother) is a native of Cumberland County, Kentucky, a daughter of Basil Marcum, a well-known citizen of that county.

William A. Guthrie attended school in his native county and spent some time in the Alexander College at Burksville, and three years at a high school in Cumberland County. He then read medicine with Dr. W. G. Hunter of Burksville, and subsequently went to the University of Tennessee at Nashville, from the medical department of which he was graduated in 1889. He first settled in Summer Shade, Metcalfe County; and, after practicing there for three years, he went to New York and took a course in diseases of women and in surgery in the Post-graduate

Medical College of that city. In 1891 he returned to Kentucky and located in Franklin, his present residence. In 1893-94 he built his large brick sanitarium, which he designed for a home or hospital for the treatment of the diseases of women, a specialty in which he has had marvelous success. This enterprise has been rewarded with a very large patronage; and is one of the most noted and flourishing institutions of the kind in southern Kentucky. Dr. Guthrie has an extensive general practice also, but gives special attention to the treatment of the diseases of women and surgery. He is a member of the American Medical Association, the Kentucky State Medical Society and the Southern Kentucky Medical Association, and is a contributor to the medical journals.

He married Emma L. Keen, daughter of William Keen of Cumberland County, and has one son, Samuel Richard Guthrie.

Dr. William A. Guthrie left home when he was thirteen years of age to attend school and since that time he has made his own way in the world, and has laid the foundation for a splendid fortune and fame in his profession. Beginning without means of his own and continuing without help, he has met with marvelous success and is destined to become one of the most eminent physicians of the state.

COL. JOHN T. GATHRIGHT of Louisville, son of Owen Gathright, was born in Shelby County, August 11, 1841. His father was a native of Shelby County, residing in Shelby and Oldham Counties until 1858, when he removed to Louisville and was for a while actively engaged in business pursuits, but retired many years before his death, which occurred in 1892, in the seventy-seventh year of his age. He was a member of the Christian Church and a man of the highest integrity. He was a Whig until 1856, and a Republican after the organization of that party.

John Gathright (grandfather) was a native of Richmond, Virginia; came to Oldham County about the year 1800, and afterwards moved to Shelby County and located on a farm which has belonged to his family ever since. He died in 1858, at the age of seventy-eight years.

Eliza Austin Gathright (mother), who survives her husband, is also a native of Oldham County. Her father, James Austin, was also a native of Oldham County, a farmer and a soldier in the War of 1812. He took part in the battle of New Orleans, which point he reached by flat boat and, after the war was over, returned to his home on foot. He reached the good old age of eighty-eight years.

John Austin (maternal great-grandfather) was a Virginian of Scotch-Irish descent; a soldier in the Revolutionary war; fought in the battle of Bunker Hill; came to Kentucky soon after peace was declared, and followed farming in Oldham County. He lived to the extreme age of one hundred and nine years.

John T. Gathright came to Louisville when fifteen years of age and completed his education in the high school. After a brief business experience in his father's store, during which he was a lieutenant of militia, he enlisted in the Federal army in 1861 as a private in Company A, Twenty-second Regiment, K. V. I. At the organization of his regiment he declined the office of major in favor of a friend who had given much of his time and money towards the organization of the regiment. He was made quartermaster sergeant, however, and was promoted to first lieutenant May 18, and to captain of his company, July 1, 1862.

Captain Gathright was with his regiment in all of its engagements under General Garfield and took part in the several campaigns in Southeastern Kentucky, East Tennessee and West Virginia. In the autumn of 1862 he was ordered with his regiment to Vicksburg, and engaged in the first assault upon that city in what was known as the battle of Walnut Hills or Chickasaw Bayou. He was detailed with the left wing of his regiment to lead the assault on the Confederate works, and out of the two hundred and sixty-six men in his command, over two hundred were killed, wounded or captured; and he was twice wounded, but not seriously. He afterward assisted in the attack upon Arkansas Post, which resulted in the capture of the post with its commander, General Churchill, and six thousand prisoners. He returned to Vicksburg about the time General Grant assumed command of the army of the Mississippi, where he saw active service in the front, and was offered promotion to the rank of colonel on the staff of General Grant by the general in person, but was not able to accept the promotion as his physicians at that time had despaired of his life.

Returning to his home in Louisville, he was made senior colonel in charge of the militia, which was by no means an empty honor at that time.

Col. Gathright was one of the original members of the firm of Harbison & Gathright, the large wholesale house which is still in existence; but sold his interest to Mr. Harbison and engaged in the manufacture of saddlery, making many valuable inventions which have proven quite profitable.

He has always affiliated with the Democratic party, which he helped to reorganize after the war, in 1865, being at that time a member of the Democratic City Executive Committee.

In 1879 he was elected State senator from his district, receiving a highly complimentary majority over four competitors. He introduced a number of important measures in the legislature, all of which were for the advancement of the best interests of his city and State, among which were: A bill to abolish the fee system in county offices; a charter for the first trust company organized in Louisville; amendment to the charter of the Louisville & Nashville R. R., by which that company was enabled to perfect its great system of roads in the south to the great advantage of Louisville merchants; assisted in securing a charter for the Louisville Southern R. R.; secured the State endowment of the Kentucky Agricultural and Mechanical College when it was detached from the Kentucky University, etc.

He was one of the promoters of the Louisville, St. Louis & Texas R. R., and has been active and successful in aiding many other public enterprises from which he has gained nothing personally.

In 1885 Col. Gathright was appointed surveyor of customs of the Port of Louisville by President Cleveland, an appointment that was made entirely on account of business qualifications and not through political influence. The wisdom of this appointment was verified by the fact that the business of the surveyor's office was increased about four hundred per cent under his administration.

Col. Gathright was married in 1864 to Sallie Dunlap, daughter of T. G. Dunlap, of Shelby County. He has been a member of the Presbyterian Church since 1866 and an elder since 1869. He is a member of the Louisville Commandery, F. and A. M.

JOHN W. GALVIN, M. D., a popular physician of Louisville, son of Dennis and Catherine (Cowley) Galvin, was born in Cadyville, Clinton County, New York, January 1, 1861. His father is a native of Ireland, who came to America with his parents when he was one year of age and located in Troy, New York, and removed to Cadyville, his present home, forty-five years ago. He is a farmer and an industrious and intelligent citizen, and is highly respected in the community in which he has spent the greater portion of his life. His father was a native of Athlone and died a short time after coming to this country.

Catherine Cowley Galvin (mother) was born in Troy, New York, in 1836, and died in 1869, when the subject of this sketch was eight years of age. She and her husband were members of the Catholic Church. Her father, John Cowley, was a native of Edinburgh, Scotland, and was a resident of Troy, New York, for many years, and died there in 1873.

Dr. John W. Galvin was educated in the High School of Plattsburg, New York, and after completing his schooling went to St. Louis and engaged in the manufacture of picture frames, molding and fancy furniture, which he followed industriously until 1889, when he came to Louisville and matriculated in the medical department of the University of Louisville, from which he was graduated in 1893. He at once commenced the practice of medicine in Louisville and in the short time in which he has been engaged in the healing art has built up a large general practice.

Dr. Galvin deserves great credit for his ambition and for the manner in which he has carried out his purpose to prepare himself for the responsible duties of the physician. He is unquestionably a self-made man, and he will make his mark in his profession if industry and careful study is any guarantee of success. His practice is already large and he has won the confidence of his patients and their friends by his genial manner and obliging, kindly disposition and the professional skill with which he treats the cases which are intrusted to his care.

Dr. Galvin was married in 1885 to Sallis Toucray, daughter of Alexander and Eleanor Toucray, of St. Louis. They have one son, Wallace Galvin.

LYNCH GRAY, President of the Farmers' & Traders' Bank of Owensboro, was born in Nelson County, Kentucky, May 28, 1828. His father, Patrick L. Gray, was born in Baltimore, Maryland, in 1800. After obtaining a good education in the schools of Baltimore he removed, in 1820, to Nelson County, Kentucky, and became interested in farming, an occupation in which there was a wholesome rivalry among the early settlers of Nelson County. He removed to Hardin County in 1841 and followed agricultural pursuits until 1854, when he died. He lived in the exciting political times of Henry Clay and was a Whig to the last. His religious faith was strong and he was an honored member of the United Baptist Church.

James L. Gray (grandfather), a native of Baltimore and a captain at sea, was killed in the War of 1812, when defending his city at the time the British soldiers landed at Chesapeake Bay. The Grays were of English and Irish extraction.

Mary Howlett Gray, mother of Lynch Gray, was born in Baltimore in 1798. She received a fine education in that city before coming to Kentucky. She died in 1861.

John Howlett, a native of Baltimore, accompanied a colony of people who made the journey to Nelson County in wagons, bringing their teams, servants, furniture and other equipments for life in the new country. He married Drusilla Johnson. The Howlett family originally came from England.

Lynch Gray was educated in Nelson County and, having removed to Hardin County, he learned the trade of a wagon and buggy maker, in which business he was engaged at West Point from 1847 to 1851, when he removed to Daviess County and continued in the same line of business for three years. From 1855 to 1860 he was engaged in farming and stock trading and, retiring from this in 1860, he removed to Owensboro. He took no part in the Civil war, but was in strong sympathy with the south.

He was interested in various enterprises in the city and county until 1876, when, with the co-operation of others, he organized the Farmers' & Traders' Bank. Dr. Alfred Dodd Hill was elected president and on his death December 23, 1878, Mr. Gray was elected president, a position which he has held and ably filled for twenty years. The capital stock of this bank is $100,000, and it is one of the most substantial banking houses in the Ohio valley. Mr. Gray is ably assisted in the management of the affairs of the bank by his cashier, G. A. Williams.

Mr. Gray is also interested in a number of other enterprises; is a stockholder and director in the City Savings Bank; director in the Gravel Road Company of Daviess County; and, among other helpful enterprises, is a stockholder in the Female College. He is not in politics, but votes the Democratic ticket and wishes his party success. He is a leading member of the Baptist Church and a member of the Masonic Fraternity.

Mr. Gray was married October 24, 1854, to Louisa Shoemaker, daughter of Price Shoemaker of Daviess County. She was a native of that county and was born in March, 1830, and died October 22, 1870. She was the mother of two daughters: Mary Sephrona Gray, born July 4, 1855; married A. J. Mitchell of Owensboro, February, 1878, and they are the parents of two children, Louis A. Mitchell and A. J. Mitchell, Jr. The second daughter, Cynthia Gray, born January 6, 1857, married James M. Haynes, a dry goods merchant of Owensboro, February, 1879, and they have one child, Gray Haynes.

Mr. Gray was married a second time to Mary Frances Haynes, daughter of Frank Haynes of Daviess County, February 24, 1877,

He has risen by his own efforts from a position in the wagon shop of his employer to the presidency of a bank which owes its existence to his enterprise, and its excellent standing among the financial institutions of the country to his wise counsel and ability as a financier. There are few self-made men of to-day who have succeeded by honest means in accomplishing as much as Mr. Gray has done.

CHARLES E. GRAHAM of Paducah, clerk of the McCracken County Court, son of Z. C. and Rachel (Ratliff) Graham, was born in Grahamville (named for his father), McCracken County, Kentucky, February 4, 1872. His father was born in Bloomington, Indiana, February 6, 1847, and removed with his father to Paducah, April 3, 1858. He was engaged in farming in McCracken County for some time, and in 1877 he began merchandising in Grahamville, where he is still in business. Mr. Graham's sympathies were with the south during the late war, but he was not an active participant in the struggle. He is a straight-out Democrat, interested in the success of his party, but has never sought political preferment.

William Graham (grandfather) was born in Monroe County, near Bloomington, Indiana, May 30, 1822, and died in McCracken County, March 5, 1872. He was a merchant in Bloomington during the greater part of his life. He married Margaret Purdy, a native of Wheeling, West Virginia, who is now a resident of McCracken County. She is a daughter of M. A. Purdy, who was born in Providence in the West Indies, of Scotch and French parentage. His wife was a native of Charleston, South Carolina, whose name and antecedents are not now recalled.

Rachel Ratliff Graham (mother) was born in McCracken County, Kentucky, April 18, 1852, and was married April 2, 1871. Her father, Alexander Ratliff, was born in Virginia in 1820 and died in 1878. His wife was a native of Kentucky, whose maiden name was Hines. All of these were members of the Baptist Church, and were people of the highest standing in the community in which they lived.

Charles E. Graham attended the common schools of McCracken County until sufficiently advanced to enter a classical school, when he went to Clinton College, Clinton, Kentucky, and from there to the Smith Commercial College, where he graduated in five weeks. He then engaged in merchandising and in the tobacco business with his father in Grahamville until 1894, when he was elected clerk of the McCracken County Court. His election to this responsible position, when he was only twenty-two years of age, is perhaps the best evidence of his popularity and the highest testimonial of his good character. He has had charge of the office since January, 1895, and has demonstrated his ability to discharge its duties in a manner that is highly commended by the court and the members of the bar. He is the youngest county clerk in the state, and the office is one of the highest importance, requiring the assistance of two deputies.

Mr. Graham is a Democrat, and even at this early age is something of a politician, having rendered valuable services for his party and obtained his reward.

RICHARD HENDERSON SOAPER, tobacconist of Henderson, was born in Henderson County, Kentucky, February 7, 1836, and is the eldest son of William and Susan Fannie (Henderson) Soaper. He was educated in the private schools of Henderson; Shelbyville College and Kenyon College, Ohio. No means were spared to give him a thorough collegiate education. Upon his return from college he was given a position in his father's tobacco stemmery and in a very short time he mastered the science of handling the weed, and subsequently acquired an interest in the business. He remained with his father until 1867, when he established a house of his own. His father joined him in this enterprise a little later and they continued together until his father's death in 1881, since which time he has continued the business in Henderson in partnership with his brother. In 1868 Mr. Soaper established a branch house in Uniontown, with a capacity of five hundred hogsheads per annum; and this, with his Henderson house, he has operated most successfully, buying and shipping about one thousand hogsheads annually, for which the principal markets are Liverpool and London. In addition to his large tobacco interests in this country and Europe, Mr. Soaper owns two valuable farms in the river bottom, one of five hundred and twenty-eight acres and the other of four hundred and twenty-six acres. These lands are noted for their productiveness of either corn or tobacco. His annual crops are very large, and so well systematized are his farming operations that nothing but an overflow or an unprecedented drouth can prevent him from reaping a handsome income from this source every year.

His plant in Henderson was destroyed by fire February 10, 1894, but it was immediately rebuilt on even a larger scale than before. The present building is 160x75 feet, four stories high, two stories of brick and two of frame, with an L 80x65 feet. An average force of sixty-five or seventy hands are employed in this establishment.

His father, William Soaper, left a large and varied estate and Richard H. was made executor of his will. The property consisted of lands, houses and lots, moneys, bonds, stocks and other possessions, which were to be apportioned among nine devisees. It was a difficult undertaking, but Mr. Soaper settled this great estate without a complaint from anyone, another evidence that he is one of the ablest business men of the times.

He has acquired a wide knowledge of men and of the world, together with much valuable experience, by his extensive travels at home and abroad. His career has been characterized by great energy, prudent care, superior judgment and undoubted integrity. He is devoted to his friends, is warm hearted and enjoys social life to the highest degree, but has never married. He is as regular as a clock in his habits, always prompt in keeping engagements and punctual to the minute in his attendance at his office; and with these characteristics it is not strange that he is pointed out by his neighbors as a model business man.

Mr. Soaper was raised a Whig, but he had not reached his twenty-first year, when that party was disbanded and he has never identified himself with any particular party or organization. He has no desire for office and would not accept one if tendered him by the unanimous vote of the people. In politics, church and charity he is free to exercise his own will. He gives with a liberal hand, keeping his own counsel and obeying the dictates of his noble, generous heart.

His father, William Soaper, was born in Loudoun County, Virginia, April 28, 1795, and was educated in the ordinary schools of that state and in Maryland. He came to Henderson in 1820, and with very limited means engaged in the saddlery business, frequently traveling through the country, but subsequently engaged in purchasing and stemming tobacco in partnership with Judge Thomas Fowles. This partnership was dissolved by mutual consent after some years and he continued in the same line of business, with most remarkable success, accumulating a very large fortune. He was married November 2, 1830, to Susan Fannie Henderson, whose natal day was May 9, 1813. Her father, Richard Henderson, was a nephew of Richard Henderson for whom the city and county of Henderson were named. Mrs. Soaper's father was married in North Carolina, March 6, 1807, to Annie Alves and came to Henderson in 1812.

THOMAS SOAPER, one of the oldest and leading merchants of Henderson, second son of William and Susan Frances (Henderson) Soaper, was born in Henderson, Kentucky, January 20, 1838. A sketch of his elder brother, Richard Henderson Soaper, with a brief history of the family, is given in this volume.

Thomas Soaper was reared in his native city, attending a private school taught by Professor McCulloch; and in 1856 went to Kenyon College at Gambier, Ohio, for one year, and then entered Hanover College, where he pursued his studies for another year.

Returning to Henderson in 1857, he was employed as a clerk or salesman in the dry goods house of L. C. Dallam, and in 1859 purchased an interest in the establishment and was associated with Mr. Dallam, his brother-in-law, for sixteen years in the well-known house of Dallam & Soaper. In January, 1876, he purchased Mr. Dallam's interest, since which time the business has been conducted in the name of Thomas

Soaper. In 1892 he succeeded Mr. Dallam as president of the Henderson County Bank.

Mr. Soaper is one of the most successful merchants of Henderson, a fact which is due to his remarkable ability as a business man, as well as to the reputation he has gained for honesty and sincerity. He is a man of strong convictions, warm in his friendships, but not ostentatious or demonstrative, a genial companion and a tender and devoted husband and father.

He is a faithful and devout member of the Episcopal Church, in which he was confirmed in 1860. For more than thirty years he has been a member of the church vestry, of which he was treasurer for many years, and has been senior warden since 1876; has represented his church a number of times in the diocesan conventions, and has been one of the foremost men in all matters of interest to the parish; was superintendent of the Sunday school for many years; is a member of the Masonic fraternity; and is a Democratic voter.

In addition to valuable real property in Henderson, including his elegant residence, he owns a farm of one hundred and ninety acres of rich bottom land in the county; another one of five hundred acres in the county and one of two hundred and five acres in Union County, which farms he cultivates through employes, under the direction of a competent superintendent, the products of which afford a handsome income.

Mr. Soaper was married October 12, 1862, to Cora Cook, daughter of Dr. John B. Cook, formerly of Huntsville, Alabama, and founder of the Henderson & McDowell Medical Societies. Mr. and Mrs. Soaper have two charming daughters: Bettie Cook and Susan Henderson.

COL. LORENZO D. HUSBANDS, a leading attorney of Paducah, was born in Christian County, in December, 1823. His father, Harmon Husbands, son of Robert Husbands, was born in Rowan County, North Carolina, in August, 1776. He received the best education that the schools of his time could afford. He removed to Christian County in 1805 and was a pioneer farmer and surveyor. He removed to Ballard County in 1845 and died there in 1856. He was a Democrat until 1840 when he became a Henry Clay Whig. His wife was Sarah Renshaw, daughter of a Mr. Renshaw, a farmer, who lived to a great age and died near Port Royal, Tennessee. They had five daughters and four sons, all of whom are deceased except Mrs. Frances O. Lovelace, of Texas, and Col. L. D. Husbands, the subject of this sketch.

The progenitors of the family in this country were William and John Husband, who came from England and settled in Pennsylvania. The descendants went to North Carolina, where Robert (father) was born. The name was originally Husband, and was changed to Husbands by Col. L. D. Husbands.

Col. L. D. Husbands was educated in private schools, great care being taken in his early training, and commenced reading law in 1845 with James B. Husbands, in Paducah, and was admitted to the bar in that city in 1849, and has been a practitioner uninterruptedly for forty-seven years. He was in partnership with Col. G. H. Morrow from 1850 to 1852; with A. Boyd from 1854 until 1861; with William Husbands from 1873 to 1883, and with his nephew, James G. Husbands, since 1886.

In 1851 he was elected county attorney of McCracken County and served until 1855, when he was elected commonwealth attorney to fill out the unexpired term of Hon. Oscar Turner, and held that office for one year; was elected to the legislature from McCracken and Ballard Counties, in 1859, and was present at all of the regular and called sessions during Governor Magoffin's administration, preceding the Civil War, since which time he has not been a candidate for any political or judicial office. He was a member of the City Council of Paducah and of the Board of School Trustees in the early '50's.

Col. Husbands was married the first time in 1851 to Hannah Singleton, who was born in Hines County, Mississippi, in 1834, and died in 1856. She was the mother of one son, Gip, born January 24, 1856, who is a farmer near Paducah. He was again married in 1859 to Mrs. Mary E. Bullock, widow of John M. Bullock, a lawyer, of Hickman. Her maiden name was Mary E. Cook, daughter of John W. Cook, a farmer of Christian County. She was born in Princeton, and was educated principally in Bethel Female College, Hopkinsville. They have three children: Cook Husbands is a bookkeeper in the American-German Bank of Paducah, married Mintie Fowler, daughter of Capt. J. Fowler, February, 1884; while the other children, Dow and Sallie, are unmarried. The children were educated in the best private schools and are graduates. Cook Husbands attended the University of Virginia, where he studied law and was admitted to the bar and was for a short time associated with his father; was deputy postmaster for four years, under President Cleveland's first administration, and was appointed postmaster by President Harrison to fill a vacancy for a few months, on account of his efficiency and familiarity with the office, although he was a Democrat.

WALKER C. HALL, attorney-at-law, Covington, son of Mary J. McCloud and John Arnold Hall, was born in Covington, June 14, 1863. His father was born in Kenton County in 1813 and was educated in the country schools; was a farmer and stock trader, and was assessor of Kenton County from 1864 to 1872. During the Civil War his sympathies were with the Union, and after the war he voted the Democratic ticket. He died May 14, 1890, and is buried at Independence, in Kenton County.

Thomas Hall (grandfather) was born in North Ireland; came to Virginia when a young man, and taught school for a number of years. His father came to America from Ireland and was a soldier in the War of the Revolution.

Mary J. McCloud Hall (mother) was born and educated in Kenton County and was married to John A. Hall in 1859. She is now living in Covington.

Walker C. Hall enjoyed superior advantages in the public schools of Covington, and afterwards took a course in the Central Normal College, Danville, Indiana. In 1885, when twenty-two years of age, he was elected principal of the West Covington public schools, and served in that capacity for two years, when, in 1887, he was elected principal of the First District public schools, in Covington. He held this position four years, the latter part of which time he spent in studying law.

He then attended the Cincinnati Law School, graduating in 1890. He began the practice of law in September of the same year in partnership with James P. Tarvin, under the style of Tarvin & Hall, which partnership was dissolved on the first of March, 1895, since which time Mr. Hall has conducted a large practice without an associate.

He is interested in a number of land syndicates and other business enterprises.

Mr. Hall was married August 10, 1887, to Minnie Belle Britting, daughter of Louis K. Britting, manufacturer of the well-known Britting pianos, of Cincinnati. Mrs. Hall was educated in the schools of Ludlow and in the Cincinnati High School, and is a lady of unusual intelligence and refinement. They have one child, Leslie Virgil, born April 18, 1892.

WILLIAM M. HANNA, M. D., a distinguished member of the medical profession and a highly respected citizen of Henderson, son of John S. and Jane (King) Hanna, was born in Shelby County, Kentucky, September 25, 1837.

His father, John S. Hanna, was born in Harrodsburg in 1798, and was educated there. He was an excellent farmer and a prominent citizen of his county; was married in 1825 to Jane King, daughter of Thomas and Anna (McAfee) King, and they had seven children: Margaret, Thomas, James, Samuel, William M., John S. and Eliza Hanna. Mr. Hanna and his wife were members of the Presbyterian Church, and he was an elder for many years. He was a member of the Old State Militia, and was every ready to do his duty, as soldier or citizen. He died in 1878, and is buried in Shelbyville.

Thomas Hanna (grandfather) was born in Virginia and came to Kentucky about the time of the war for independence; married Margaret Smith, daughter of Colonel Smith, of North Carolina; died in Shelby County, Kentucky.

James and Martha Hanna (great-grandparents) were natives of the north of Ireland, where they were married. They came to America and settled in Berkeley County (now West), Virginia. Four of their twelve children were born in Ireland, and eight in Virginia. After living in Berkeley County some years they emigrated to Kentucky, about the time of the Revolutionary War, and located in Mercer County with the early settlers.

Thomas King (maternal grandfather), a Virginia farmer, came to Shelby County, Kentucky, and married Annie McAfee, then living in Harrodsburg. They had six children, including Jane, who married John S. Hanna. Mr. King and his family were members of the Presbyterian Church, and were among the best people of Shelby County, where they lived, died and are buried.

Margaret Smith Hanna (grandmother) was a daughter of Colonel John Smith and Margaret Dobbins Smith, natives of North Carolina. Colonel Smith won his military title in the Revolutionary War, and after peace was declared he removed to Kentucky and made his home in Shelby County.

Dr. William M. Hanna was graduated from Centre College, Danville, in the class of 1858, receiving the degree of A. B. In 1859 he began the study of medicine in Shelbyville with Dr. A. S. Frederick; matriculated in the University of Louisville, in 1862, and after graduating in medicine from that institution, he spent one year in the United States Marine Hospital at Louisville, in which service he gained valuable practical experience.

In 1862 he enlisted as a private soldier in the Confederate army, under General Morgan, and was with him in his famous raids in Indiana and Ohio. In 1863 he was assigned as assistant surgeon of the Second Kentucky Cavalry, in which capacity he served until the close of the war. His service in the army was equivalent to as many years of schooling, being of the most practical nature.

After the close of the war, Dr. Hanna located at Henderson and has remained there, engaged in the line of his profession, without interruption, for over thirty years. He soon took his place among the leading physicians of the city, where he is held in the highest esteem and enjoys the confidence of the entire community. He is a man of fine personal appearance and pleasing address, of kind disposition and sympathetic nature; a constant and a diligent student, keeping pace with the advancement in medical science; is a member of the Henderson County Medical Society, the Kentucky State Medical Society, and of the American Academy of Medicine and American Medical Association. He is an elder in the Presbyterian Church, as was his father before him, both branches of his family having belonged to that church for several generations. In the matter of politics he is simply an independent Democratic voter.

Dr. Hanna was married in 1865 to Mary Matthews, daughter of Rev. William C. Matthews, D. D. They have three children living: Mary, John and Jane.

Dr. William C. Matthews, father of Mrs. Hanna, was one of the most learned and distinguished ministers in the Presbyterian Church (North). He began preaching at Martinsburg (now West), Virginia; was pastor of the Presbyterian Church at Shelbyville for twenty-five years, and of a church in Louisville for five years. His death, in 1880, was mourned by a wide circle of friends and acquaintances throughout the State.

CHARLES LEONARD HARRISON, city clerk of Bellevue, son of William H. and Sarah A. (Winwood) Harrison, was born in Cincinnati, Ohio, July 26, 1856. His father, Rev. William H. Harrison, was born in Frederick, Maryland, in 1818; and was pastor of the First English Lutheran Church, Cincinnati, for twenty-five years, and at the same time was a member of the Board of Education, in Cincinnati, and also a member of the Union Board of High Schools, and held these offices for over twenty years. He died in Cincinnati, of cholera, in 1866.

Zephaniah Harrison (grandfather) was a brother of President William Henry Harrison, and was a resident of Frederick, Maryland.

Sarah A. Winwood Harrison (mother) was born in Springfield, Ohio, in 1828; and is now living at Linwood, Ohio.

Dr. Benjamin Winwood (grandfather) was a practicing physician of Springfield, Ohio, and was a surgeon in the Union army and died in the service in 1864 in Memphis, Tennessee. His father came from England.

Charles L. Harrison grew to manhood in Cincinnati; and, after leaving school, in which he had enjoyed excellent advantages, he became a civil engineer, and in connection with his brother, William H. Harrison, built the Cincinnati & Eastern Narrow Gauge Railroad.

He became a resident of Bellevue, Kentucky, October 31, 1883; and in 1888 he was elected city clerk, and was re-elected in 1890 and again in 1892, and in November, 1893, he was re-elected for a term of four years, under the new city charter. His personal popularity and his efficiency in the discharge of his official duties are fully attested by his frequent election to this office.

In July, 1895, he published the first weekly issue of the Newport Republican, of which he is editor and proprietor, and which is already an important factor in local politics. As indicated by its name it is a Republican journal; and it is a vigorous mouth-piece for the party in whose interests its weekly visits are made. Mr. Harrison personally is regarded as a leader in the Republican ranks; and, with the aid of his paper, he wields an influence in local politics that is hard for the opposing party to overcome. He enjoys the honor of having been a delegate to the convention at Louisville which nominated W. O. Bradley for governor, and he deserves much credit for the active part he took in securing the election of Mr. Bradley.

Mr. Harrison is a highly respected citizen of Bellevue, a member of the Dayton Presbyterian Church, and a member of the Blue Lodge of Masons.

He was married in 1888 to R. Ella, daughter of Piersol Shaner, deceased, of Vanceburg, Kentucky.

JAMES MADISON HUGHES, a prominent citizen of Paris, and the president of the Citizen's Bank of that city, was born in Nicholas County, Kentucky, April 20, 1825. For many years he has been a citizen of Bourbon County, closely identified with her business interests.

He is a son of Jesse Hughes, a native of Bourbon County, and a grandson of David W. Hughes, who was a major in the war of the Revolution, and a native of Virginia, who removed to Kentucky in 1784 and pre-empted one thousand acres of land in the neighborhood of Paris, and also a tract of land in Clark County. He remained in Kentucky for a while and then returned to Virginia and brought his wife and children and resided on this tract of one thousand acres for a few years. He afterwards removed to a tract on Flat Creek, where he remained until his death. His wife was Margaret Frame, daughter of an immigrant from north of Ireland. His father was a native of Wales.

Jesse Hughes (father) wedded Priscilla Parker, a daughter of Thomas Parker of Maryland. Thomas Parker removed to Kentucky and settled on Cane Ridge, four miles from Paris. Jesse Hughes was prominent in the business affairs of Bourbon County for many years. He died at Carlisle in 1854. He had eight children, three of whom are now living, two sons in Texas and one son in Bourbon County.

James M. Hughes' early years were spent on a farm in Nicholas County; and in 1854, the year of his father's death, he was elected clerk of the Nicholas County Circuit Court, and served in that office for four years. At the expiration of that time, in 1859, he removed to Millersburg, Bourbon County, and formed a partnership with his nephew, John G. Smedley, in the dry goods trade, and remained actively engaged in that business until 1866, when he took charge of the County Court's office, retaining his interest in the dry goods store. Mr. Hughes was four times re-elected to this office and held it for twenty consecutive years, at the end of which time he refused further election on account of impaired health. For many years he has been one of the leading directors of the Citizens' Bank, and for the past six or eight years has served as its president. The capital stock of this bank is $100,000, with a surplus of $20,000 and average deposits of nearly $100,000. In 1861 Mr. Hughes was married to Mrs. Sally Holliday Kenney of Millersburg. She died in 1865; and he subsequently married Rebecca A. Roseberry, sister of Hiram M. Roseberry, president of the Agricultural Bank of Paris. They have one daughter, Jessie.

In addition to his large city interests, Mr. Hughes owns a farm of one hundred acres within a mile of Paris, which he superintends, and in which he takes a good deal of pride.

JOSIAH HARRIS, a prominent member of the Paducah bar, was born in Columbia, Adair County, Kentucky, November 14, 1840. His father, Josiah Harris, was born in Maryland, April 26, 1810, and removed to Kentucky with his father when he was a young man, and located at Elizabethtown. He subsequently removed to Adair County, where he owned considerable land and was a merchant. A few years later he went to Louisville, where he was engaged in the same business at the beginning of the Civil war. His sympathies were with the Union, but he took no active part in the war and cared but little for politics. He was a member of the Christian Church and was greatly interested in its work; conscientious in business, and was devoted to his home. He died in Louisville, August 6, 1865, and is buried in Cave Hill Cemetery.

Josiah Harris (grandfather) was a native of Maryland who came to Kentucky as before indicated. His father Josiah (great-grandfather) was a captain in the Revolutionary war and was mortally wounded at the battle of Cowpens. Realizing that he must die, he sent a small breast-pin plate to his wife as a token of his affection and as a souvenir of the battle. This little pin has been held by the family as a great treasure, and was given to the subject of this sketch by his father. The Harris family originally came from England.

Sallie Wiles King Harris (mother) was born in Cumberland County, November 20, 1820, and was educated at Danville, Kentucky. She married Josiah Harris January 16, 1839, and died January 16, 1878. She was a devout member of the Christian Church.

Milton King (grandfather) was born in Albemarle County, Virginia, May 30, 1801, and came to Kentucky with his parents when a youth. He was circuit clerk of Cumberland County for fifty years to a day. He afterwards removed to Paducah and lived a retired life until October 4, 1884, when he died. His wife was Sallie Wiles, daughter of General Wiles of Virginia. She died in 1840.

Samuel King (great-grandfather) was a Virginian of Welsh extraction.

Josiah Harris, lawyer of Paducah, who bears, and has honored the name of his father, grandfather and great-grandfather, was educated in Columbia, Kentucky, in that excellent school of which John L. McKee was president. He finished his work in the school room at the age of nineteen and entered the law office of King & King of Paducah and attended the law department of the University of Louisville, graduating from that institution when he was twenty years of age, having taken the full two years' course in one year. He passed a rigid examination conducted by Judge Zack Wheat, Governor Thomas E. Bramlette and Judge George W. Kavanaugh and was granted license to practice law when twenty years of age.

In his first work he was associated with Judge Wintersmith of Louisville, but when the Civil war commenced, he went to New Orleans as paymaster in the shipyards where the Confederate Government was engaged in building gunboats. He remained there until the approach of the fleet under General Ben F. Butler, when he left New Orleans and returned to Paducah.

When the war was over he resumed the practice of his profession, locating in Paducah. He took a lively interest in politics and became an enthusiastic Prohibitionist; was a candidate for representative in the legislature in 1872 and was defeated; was candidate for state senator in 1876 and was again defeated; was elected to the legislature for the term of 1883-4; was defeated for re-election in 1885 on account of the anti-whiskey legislation, which he had favored; was a candidate for attorney general on the Prohibition ticket in 1887; was twice a candidate for Congress, in 1889 and 1891, and was nominated for governor of Kentucky by the Prohibition party in 1892. He was chairman of the executive committee of his party from 1888 until 1892 and was prominent in all the councils of his party. Mr. Harris is not in politics for revenue or for office, but from principle; and an occasional defeat does not deter him from trying again, if he may thereby advance the cause which he has so much at heart.

Mr. Harris was twice married and is now a widower. His first marriage occurred June 5, 1864, to Cora Endera, daughter of Henry Endera, an early settler of Paducah and one of the first merchants of that city. She was born December

19, 1842, and died January 9, 1879. His second marriage was to Mattie Dunn of Livingston County, Kentucky, June 4, 1882. She was a daughter of Captain George Dunn of Smithland. She was born March 28, 1859, and died August 10, 1894. He has one daughter, Hallie, the child of his first wife. She was born April 1, 1868; married Charles L. Wurtham of Louisville, January 1, 1889, and is the mother of three children, Cora, Josiah Harris and Summers Wurtham.

Mr. Harris is a member of the Presbyterian Church and is a highly respected citizen of the city in which he has made his home for nearly a third of a century.

JOHN P. HOBSON, a leading attorney at law of Elizabethtown, son of Willis W. and Arabella (Bolling) Hobson, was born in Powhattan County, Virginia, September 3, 1850.

His father was a native of the same county, where he is still engaged in farming, and is one of the best citizens of the county. He was a soldier in General Wickham's brigade in the Confederate army.

Joseph Hobson (grandfather) and Caleb Hobson (great-grandfather) were born in Powhattan County, Virginia, where they lived and died. Atwood Hobson (great-great-grandfather) was a native of England, who came to the United States in 1744 and settled in Powhattan County. All of these men were excellent citizens, quiet and unostentatious, "diligent in business, fervent spirit, serving the Lord," and no name is more highly honored in the community in which the Hobsons have lived for six or seven generations.

Arabella Bolling Hobson (mother) was a native of Petersburg, Virginia, a devout member of the Presbyterian Church, in which her husband, Willis W. Hobson, has been an elder for forty-five years, and a lady of exceptional intelligence and purity of character. She died at the age of fifty-five years, May 20, 1882.

John P. Bolling (maternal grandfather) was born in Amelia County, Virginia, of which he was sheriff at one time. He died in Petersburg, April, 1861.

John P. Hobson was brought up in Powhattan County, attending the district and private schools until he was prepared for college, when he went to the Washington and Lee University, from which he received his diploma signed by Robert E. Lee, in June, 1870. He then came to Kentucky and taught school in Lynnland Institute in Hardin County for three years, after which he began the study of law with A. M. Brown of Elizabethtown, and was admitted to the bar in 1873. He at once began the practice of his chosen profession in Elizabethtown, and met with almost immediate success, soon taking rank among the leading lawyers of his section. He has never actively engaged in politics or any outside business ventures that would prevent him from entire devotion to his legal work.

Mr. Hobson was married February 25, 1885, to Ella Nourse, daughter of Charles E. Nourse of Elizabethtown; and they have four sons and one daughter: Charles N., Peyton, Mary B., Willis E. and Robert P. Hobson. Mr. and Mrs. Hobson are active members of the Presbyterian Church.

CHARLES E. HOGE, Cashier of the State National Bank of Frankfort, and a member of the large contracting firm of Mason, Hoge & Company, was born in Albemarle County, Virginia, May 5, 1845.

His father, Rev. Peter C. Hoge, was a native of Augusta County, Virginia, and a graduate of a Virginia college. For ten or twelve years he was a Presbyterian minister, but left that denomination and was for many years a distinguished preacher in the Baptist Church, in which he labored successfully. He was a man of high character and a preacher of more than ordinary power and was well known and highly esteemed throughout his state. He removed from Augusta to Albemarle County in 1844 and made his home there until his death in 1876, at the age of sixty-six years.

Captain James Hoge (grandfather) was a native of Scotland who came to the United States when he was qutie young and served as a captain in the war of the Revolution, following which he located on a farm in Augusta County, Virginia, near Staunton, where he died in 1812. A brother of Charles E. Hoge has in his possession a number of letters written by General Washington to Captain Hoge (grandfather), from which it is seen that he was a man of worth, a soldier and a patriot who was held in the highest esteem by General Washington. The Hoge family in Scotland trace their ancestry back for several centuries.

Sarah Keer Hoge (mother) was a native of Augusta County, Virginia, and a faithful member of the Baptist Church. She died in Albemarle County, Virginia, in 1872, four years prior to the death of her husband.

Charles E. Hoge remained in his native county until he was twenty-three years of age, receiving his education principally in the high school for boys in Scottsville, Virginia, taught by Professor David Pinckney Powers, an eminent educator of his day. It was Mr. Hoge's intention to prepare for the medical profession, but this purpose was interfered with by the Civil war, and in 1863 he enlisted as a private in Braxton's battalion of artillery. Soon after his enlistment he was detailed for duty as quartermaster's clerk, in which capacity he served until the final surrender at Appomattox Court House, April 9, 1865.

Returning to his home, he formed a co-partnership with General James C. Hill, of Confederate fame, and J. I. Lewis, a capitalist, and engaged in a general mercantile business in Scottsville. In connection with this business the firm operated a line of canal boats between Lynchburg and Richmond. The business of the firm prospered beyond their expectations, but Mr. Hoge withdrew from the firm in July, 1868, and went to Augusta County, Virginia, where most of his relatives lived, and embarked in the wholesale grocery business in Staunton, Virginia, in which he is still the senior partner of the firm of Hoge & Hutchinson.

In 1870 he became a partner of Captain C. R. Mason of Virginia, one of the largest railroad contractors in the south, under the firm name of Mason & Hoge. Their first contract in which Mr. Hoge was interested was for the building of the "Big Fill" at Jerry's Run on the Chesapeake & Ohio Railroad, seven miles east of White Sulphur Springs. This is probably the largest fill in the world, containing over one million cubic yards. They also built the Lewis Tunnel on that road, which is four thousand four hundred feet in length.

In 1872 H. P. and S. B. Mason, sons of the senior member of the firm, were admitted to partnership in the company and the name was changed to Mason, Hoge & Company. On the death of Captain Mason in 1885, the business was continued by his sons and Mr. Hoge without change in the style of the firm. To give an idea of the magnitude of the business of this enterprising company, mention is made of a few of their larger contracts: They built the Elizabeth, Lexington & Big Sandy Railroad; the extension of the Kentucky Central from Paris to Livingston, Kentucky, a distance of thirty-three miles; the Maysville and Big Sandy Railroad from Ashland to Cincinnati, including the (now C. & O.) bridge over the Ohio river between Covington and Cincinnati; the Corbin extension of the Louisville & Nashville Railroad through Pineville and Middlesboro, including the Cumberland Gap tunnel, also eighteen miles of road between that tunnel and Big Stone Gap for the same company; the Ohio & Atlantic from Bristol, Tennessee, to Big Stone Gap; the Louisville Southern Railroad from Louisville to Harrodsburg; the Kentucky Midland from Frankfort to Paris, a distance of forty miles; a section of twenty-six miles of the Norfolk & Western Railroad between Bluefield, Virginia, and Kenova, West Virginia, including one or two sections on the Ohio side of the river; they had a large contract with William H. Vanderbilt on the South Pennsylvania Railroad, and after doing work to the amount of over half a million dollars the contract was terminated by the sale of the road to the Pennsylvania Central Railroad Company. Their present contract, one of the largest they have ever undertaken, is for the building of six miles of the Chicago Drainage Canal, the work upon which will approximate five million dollars.

In August, 1889, the State National Bank of Frankfort, Kentucky, was organized, with a capital of $150,000, the stock of which was taken by subscription in twenty-four hours. General Fayette Hewett, then auditor of state, was elected president, and Mr. Charles E. Hoge, the subject of this sketch, was made cashier. H. P. Mason, of the same firm, was elected vice president. The bank has flourished ever since its organization and there has been no change in its officers.

Mr. Hoge is also a stockholder and director in the Safety Vault & Trust Company of Frankfort, and a stockholder in the Kentucky Building & Loan Association of Frankfort. His interest in the wholesale grocery house of Hoge & Hutchinson at Staunton, Virginia, is looked after by the resident partner. He has made his home in Frankfort since 1882 and is identified with the material, social, political and religious interests of the city. He is a member and generous supporter of the Presbyterian Church, and a willing, cheerful helper in every good cause.

Mr. Hoge was married October 14, 1868, to Anne B. French, daughter of Stephen French of Prince William County, Virginia; and they have two sons and three daughters: Stephen F., Evelyne B., Hildred Merrill, Mary Kerr and Percy Echols. The eldest son, Stephen F. Hoge, graduated third in his class from the Virginia Military Institute, with the degree of Civil Engineer, in 1891, and is now a member of the firm of Mason, Hoge & Company, in charge of a branch of the work on the Chicago Drainage Canal.

DOCTOR J. OLIVER JENKINS, of Newport, Kentucky, one of the leading and most successful members of the medical profession of that city, is a native of Cincinnati, Ohio. Born August 8, 1851; son of William and Lemarian (Mann) Jenkins. William Jenkins was born in Bristol, England, and came here with his parents to the United States in 1820. In 1846 William Jenkins removed to Cincinnati, which has been his home ever since. William Jenkins is now seventy-nine years of age, has always been a member of the Methodist Episcopal Church, and a Republican in politics. In his early manhood he learned the trade of tanning, which he carried on, in connection with his father and brothers, for a number of years.

John Jenkins (grandfather) was also a native of England, who, after his arrival in this country in 1820, located with his family at Newark, N. J., whence he removed in 1824 to Northern Pennsylvania, where he remained until the time of his death, which occurred in 1858. William Jenkins wedded Lemarian Mann, a native of Cincinnati, in 1850.

Dr. James O. Jenkins spent his youth in his native city and was educated in the public schools. After leaving school in 1869 he commenced to learn the trade of electro-plating, but gave it up soon on account of ill-health. After recovering his health he was employed as assistant librarian for a number of years in the "Public Library of Cincinnati," and during that time he occupied his spare moments in the study of medicine. In the fall of 1873 he entered the Ohio Medical College. In 1880 he again returned to the Ohio Medical College, and after two years of study was graduated with honors from that well-known institution, in the class of 1882. He immediately located in Newport, Kentucky, where he has since practiced and earned a reputation as one of the most successful general practitioners in Northern Kentucky. Dr. Jenkins is a member of the State Medical Society and of the Mississippi Valley Medical Association, and is a contributor to some of the leading medical journals of the country.

He was married in 1883 to Mary A. Clark, daughter of John Clark, of Cincinnati, Ohio, and they have one son and two daughters: Robert C., Ruth L., and Grace, one daughter, Helen, having died of pneumonia October 4, 1886.

Dr. Jenkins is Democratic in politics, and after the organization of the Board of Health of Newport, in 1892, he was one of its first members. He has always taken an active and conspicuous part in the cause of education, and in 1893 was elected president of the Board of Education of the City of Newport for a term of two years, ending December 31, 1895.

MAJOR J. PAUL JONES, a prominent farmer of Boyd County, near Ashland, and a distinguished and influential citizen of the county, was born in Uniontown, Fayette County, Pennsylvania, September 30, 1823.

His father, Edward Jones, was a native of Merthyr-Tydvil, Glamorganshire, South Wales, who came to America and settled in Uniontown, Pennsylvania, where he lived for a period of twenty-five years, when he started to return to his old home on a visit, but was lost in the "President," a ship which went down in mid-ocean. His father was a native of Wales.

Sarah Howell Jones (mother), a native of the same neighborhood in Wales, removed to Madison, Wisconsin, after her husband's death, and made her home there until her death. She and her husband were members of the Baptist Church.

J. Paul Jones received a good education in college in Uniontown, Pennsylvania, completing his literary studies in 1842. He then began the study of medicine, but through the influence of a friend, he was induced to accept a position as manager of a furnace for William Lindsay Pogue, at Amanda, which position he held for two or three years. In 1840 he resumed the study of medicine. Returning to Amanda, and having married a daughter of his former employer, he engaged in business with his father-in-law, and took an active part in the management of the business for several years. He then went to farming in Greenup (now Boyd) County.

In 1861 he entered the Union army as captain of cavalry, but was transferred to the position of regimental quartermaster, in which capacity he served for several months, and then returned to his home and recruited a battalion of six companies for the Twenty-second Regiment of Kentucky State troops. He was made major and was in command of the battalion until the close of the war. The principal work of his command was skirmishing and fighting guerrillas, one of the most difficult and annoying duties a soldier is called upon to perform. In this case it was very necessary, and the work of Colonel Jones' command was of the highest importance.

After the close of the war Major Jones returned to his farm, which had in the meantime been under the capable management of his estimable wife, and has given it his undivided attention until the present time. Unlike many soldiers of distinction and men of education and marked ability, Major Jones has never aspired to political preferment. Intensely a Union man in his sentiments during the war, he has affiliated with the Democratic party during the past thirty years, and could have had almost any favor in the gift of the people merely by indicating his willingness to accept. He is a prominent member of the Grand Army of the Republic, and takes a deep interest in the affairs of veteran soldiers.

Major Jones was married February 2, 1846, to Anna Amanda Pogue, daughter of William L. Pogue. She was born May 24, 1829, and received a superior education in a seminary at Steubenville, Ohio, and was a lady of rare accomplishments. She was, among other things which distinguished her as a lady of great strength of character, an accomplished equestrienne, and could ride any horse she ever saw. During her husband's absence in the army, she conducted the business of the farm with excellent business tact, without neglecting her household or social duties. She died on the 16th day of September following Major Jones' return from the war. Her father, William L. Pogue, was one of the first white men born in Harrodsburg, Kentucky. He died in Ashland, March 31, 1881. His wife, Ann McCormick, was a native of Richmond, Virginia.

The children of Major and Anna Amanda Pogue Jones were: Anna Amanda, deceased; Sallie Flournoy, Robert William, Fannie Wells, Harriet Milton, Mary Louisa, Lottie Culver, and Lindsay, who died in infancy.

WASHINGTON FITHIAN, M. D., physician and surgeon, was born January 8, 1825, in Salem County, New Jersey. His parents were Joel and Sarah Dick (Sinickson) Fithian. His father, Dr. Joel Fithian, was a native of New Jersey; in 1831, moved to Oxford, Ohio, and followed the medical profession through life. His mother was the daughter of Andrew Sinickson, of New Jersey; and members of both families were officers or soldiers in the War of the Revolution, and were among the early settlers in New Jersey. The subject of this sketch received a liberal education, mainly at Miami University, at Oxford, Ohio, where he graduated in 1845. In that year he began the study of medicine; prepared for his profession under his father, at Oxford; attended lectures regularly, and graduated in the Ohio College of Medicine, at Cincinnati, in 1848. In the same year he located at North Middletown, Kentucky, and entered upon the practice of his profession. He established a valuable and successful practice at North Middletown, and remained there fifteen years. He spent a part of the year 1863 in Shelbyville, and in 1864 removed to Paris, where he has given his time and best energies to his profession, to which he is greatly attached, and in which he occupies an enviable position. He is a member of the Licking Valley Medical Society; has contributed with his pen to the medical literature of the day; and, by his practice, writings and example, has been an advocate of the most elevated standard for the noble profession. In politics he is an independent voter. His first presidential vote was for General Taylor, and he voted with the Whig party during its existence. At the election preceding the war he voted for Bell and Everett. During the Rebellion he was an earnest Union man, and was several months a surgeon in the Federal army. He is associated with the Methodist Church, and has been distinguished for his great integrity of character through life and his exceptional personal, social and professional habits. He was married in September, 1850, to Lucinda, daughter of Reubin Hutchcraft, of Bourbon County.

FAYETTE HEWITT, president of the State National Bank of Frankfort, is descended from an old French Huguenot family of that name who settled on the James River, in Virginia, in 1689. His mother, Eliza Chastain, was also a descendant of French Protestant refugees who were driven from France during the bloody reign of Louis XIV., when, by his order, the Edict of Nantes was revoked in 1685, forty thousand of the Huguenots left their native country and settled in the American provinces. This country has never had better citizens than those sturdy Huguenots and their descendants. Many thousands of them are among the most prominent people—in the pulpit, at the bar, and in the halls of legislature, and there is no record to show that any one of them has ever disgraced himself, his ancestors or his country.

General Fayette Hewitt's father, Robert Hewitt, was a native of Bedford County, Virginia, who came to Kentucky in 1829. He was for many years principal of an academy at Elizabethtown, Hardin County, and was a man of fine scholarly attainments, who enjoyed a high reputation as an educator. He devoted his life to teaching, but died at the early age of thirty-nine years, in 1850.

John Hewitt (grandfather) was a native and farmer of Bedford County, Virginia. He was a highly respected citizen, and in the War of 1812 he served his country well at the head of his regiment. He died in his native county, in 1841.

Eliza Chastain Hewitt (mother) was a native of Frederick County, Virginia; daughter of Rev. Louis Chastain, one of the early ministers in the Methodist Episcopal Church, in Virginia, who was sent to Kentucky for the purpose of organizing and building up churches. Mrs. Hewitt survived her husband, residing in Elizabethtown until the day of her death, in 1876.

General Hewitt was born in Hardin (now Larue) County, Kentucky, near the birthplace of Abraham Lincoln, October 15, 1831. He received his early education under the careful instruction of his father, who died when Fayette was eighteen years of age. He at once succeeded his father as principal of the school and continued the academy for ten years, fully sustaining the high standard of the school, and making for himself a reputation as one of the most competent educators in the State. He was compelled to resign in 1859, on account of failing health, and went south for the purpose of recuperating.

In 1860 he received an appointment in the Postoffice Department at Washington, under President Buchanan. This he resigned in March, 1861, and soon afterwards was appointed adjutant-general under President Davis of the Confederacy. He served in this capacity in the trans-Mississippi department and with General Breckenridge as adjutant-general of a brigade, enduring all manner of hardships and sufferings in behalf of the cause that was lost. He had three horses killed under him, in different battles, and several bullets pierced his clothing, but he escaped unhurt. He participated in many bloody battles throughout the war, and distinguished himself as a daring, gallant and fearless soldier.

When he returned home it had been his intention to practice law, but the Kentucky legislature had passed a law that no one who had been a soldier in the Confederate army should practice law in the State, and he resumed the profession of teacher, taking charge of a select female school at Elizabethtown. When the law prohibiting him from practicing was repealed, a year later, he was at once admitted to the bar of Hardin County, and made a successful beginning in the legal profession; but in 1867 Governor Stevenson appointed him quartermaster general, which office he held until 1876, when he resigned and returned to Elizabethtown with the intention of practicing law; but on account of the death of his brother, in Louisville, he removed to that city to settle the estate.

In August, 1879, he was elected State auditor, and assumed the duties of that office January 1, 1880. He was twice re-elected State auditor, and held that office until November, 1889, when he resigned to accept the presidency of the State National Bank of Frankfort, since which time he has given his attention to the affairs of that bank and to other financial matters, having been president of the Frankfort Safety Vault & Trust Company since its organization, and being general manager of the Kentucky Investment & Building Association.

Virgil Hewitt, brother of the general, was adjutant of the Sixth Regiment Kentucky Infantry, C. S. A., in the brigade of General Joseph H. Lewis; and was severely wounded a number of times in the hard-fought battles of Tennessee and Georgia. He was county clerk of Hardin County and deputy clerk of the Court of Appeals, and assistant auditor of State until January, 1896. Another brother, Fox Hewitt, participated in some of the battles around Richmond, and after the war was clerk of the County Court of Hardin County.

JOSEPH FITHIAN, a member of the medical firm of W. and J. Fithian, and an honored and substantial citizen of Paris, was born in Philadelphia, Pennsylvania, November 18, 1830. He removed to Oxford, Ohio, with his father's family when he was quite young and was educated in the Miami University, at that place, which, at that time, was one of the leading educational institutions in the country.

He read medicine with his father, who was one of the most noted physicians of Oxford, and attended Jefferson Medical College, at Philadelphia, from which he was graduated in 1854.

In the same year he located in North Middletown, Bourbon County, and began the practice of medicine and continued there with excellent success until 1861, when he went to Missouri, remaining there but a short time.

He served in the Union army for three and a half years as surgeon of the Eighteenth Regiment Kentucky Infantry, and during that time was frequently detailed as brigade and division surgeon.

Following the close of the war he resumed his professional work in North Middletown and practiced with marked success in that vicinity until 1871, when he removed to Paris. Here he soon took a leading position among the most eminent physicians of the city and county, a position which he has maintained without a question as to his professional ability or his high social standing.

A scholarly and highly cultured gentleman, he is deeply interested in the cause of education, and has been a member of the Board of Education ever since its organization in 1874, and is now its president.

He is an elder in the Presbyterian Church, and was elected to represent Ebenezer Presbytery in the General Assembly, which met in Saratoga, in 1883.

Dr. Fithian was married December 23, 1856, to Emma K. Owen, daughter of G. W. Owen, of Bourbon County; and they have three children: Dr. Frank Fithian, a successful young physician, of Paris, and two daughters, Nellie and Georgia.

Dr. Joseph Fithian's father, Joel Fithian, M. D., was a native of Cumberland County, New Jersey, and a graduate of Pennsylvania University. His principal work as a physician was performed at Oxford, Ohio, in which place he located in 1831, and where he spent the remainder of a useful life.

Amos Fithian (grandfather) was a soldier in the Revolutionary War; and his brother, Philip Victor Fithian, a Presbyterian minister, was a chaplain in the patriot army.

According to tradition, the Fithian family came from Kent County, England, where some of the members lived as long ago as 1648. In 1683 William Fithian, the progenitor of the family in the United States, located at Easthampton, Long Island, where his will is recorded. Whether he was the grandfather or great-grandfather of Amos Fithian, who was Dr. Joseph Fithian's grandfather, is not definitely known.

Sarah Dick Sinickson Fithian (mother) was a daughter of Thomas Sinickson, of New Jersey, who was a captain in the Revolutionary War, and was in the battle of Princeton. Her uncle, Colonel Sinickson, of the patriot army, made himself so conspicuous and so obnoxious to the opposing authorities that Lord Howe offered a reward of one hundred pounds for his apprehension, dead or alive. Colonel Sinickson and another uncle of Mrs. Fithian were members of the Constitutional Congress.

Andrew Sinickson, the original founder of the distinguished family in America, came to this country with a Swedish colony under Peter Minuet, which settled near Chester, Pennsylvania. Andrew Sinickson afterwards removed to Salem County, in that State, and entered a tract of land the title to which remains in the family to this day.

W. HOWARD McCORKLE, the junior member of the well-known dry goods firm of McMichael & McCorkle, of Lexington, was born in Lexington, Virginia, May 9, 1861. He received his education in the country schools of Rockbridge County and in the classical schools of Lexington, Virginia, conducted by Jacob Fuller and Henry B. Jones, captain of Liberty Hall Volunteers, and at Washington and Lee University. Leaving there in 1879 he located in New York City, where he was engaged in the cotton commission business until 1883, when he came to Lexington, Kentucky. Here he engaged in stock raising until 1887, when, in the fall of that year, he became a member of the above-mentioned firm, wholesale and retail dealers in dry goods. Mr. McCorkle is a Democrat in politics and a member of the Board of Aldermen. He was first elected to that body in 1893, and was made chairman of the Joint Ways and Means Committee. He is also a member of the Board of School Trustees.

In November, 1887, he was united in marriage to Sarah B. McMichael, a native of Lexington, and a graduate of Hamilton College. She is a daughter of Robert McMichael, one of the oldest and most highly respected business men of Lexington.

Alexander McCorkle, the founder of the McCorkle family in Rockbridge County, was a native of Ulster Province, Ireland. He settled in the Colony of Virginia in 1760, and wedded Mary Steels. His son, Samuel McCorkle, was an active participant in the War of the Revolution. His wife was Margaret McCullum. John McCorkle, a brother of Samuel, was an ensign in Capt. James Gilmore's company of militia from Rockbridge County that marched to meet Tarleton's raiders in South Carolina. In the battle of the Cowpens, which followed, he received a wound in the wrist, which, owing to the fearfully cold weather, resulted in lock-jaw and death. He is said to have been buried near McCowan's Ford, in North Carolina.

The following notice of the death of W. Howard McCorkle's father, a sketch of his family, appeared in the Rockbridge County (Virginia) News:

"William H. McCorkle, an old and highly respected citizen of Rockbridge, died at his home, three miles southeast of Lexington, Tuesday morning, at eight o'clock. He had been in quite infirm health for some time, but his death, at this time, was not anticipated. He was born in November, 1819, and was a son of William McCorkle, who lived upon and owned the farm on which William H. McCorkle lived and died. This place has belonged to the family for several generations, and is the very first deed that appeared on the records of the county after it was founded in 1778.

"His grandfather was Samuel McCorkle, one of the first grand jurors of this county, who, with his two brothers, John and William, and their father, were pioneer settlers in the hill country, southeast of Lexington, and there, since 1760,

W. H. McCORKLE.

their descendants have lived. His mother was Nancy Welch, of Fancy Hill neighborhood. Mr. McCorkle married Virginia Wilson, daughter of the late James Wilson, Sr., of Buffalo, who survives him with five sons and one daughter: Charles E., who resides at the old home; Walter E., a lawyer of New York City; Reverend Dr. E. W., of Clifton Forge; and W. Howard, of Lexington, Kentucky. Mrs. John T. Dunlop, of Rockbridge, and Henry, the youngest son, are also at home. Mr. McCorkle was a thrifty and industrious farmer, a good citizen, exemplary Christian, and a man of exceptionally fine common sense. He gave his children the best opportunities, and lived to be paid for his exertions in their behalf, by the success and by the honorable position he saw them attain."

W. Howard McCorkle, since his residence in Lexington, Kentucky, has identified himself with the business interests of the city, and by his uniform suave and genial manners, his courtesy and manly bearing towards all, has won for himself a host of friends and an enviable position among the leading citizens of Lexington.

Mr. McCorkle's father was connected with the Civil Service of the Confederate States, and, though past the required age, marched at different times with the Home Guards to meet the enemy. His kinsmen in both lines, as officers and privates, served as soldiers under Lee, Stonewall Jackson and J. E. B. Stuart, many of them were killed, wounded and imprisoned.

JAMES R. W. SMITH, a prominent attorney and acting judge of the Louisville City Court, was born in New Albany, Indiana, August 28, 1842. His father, Major Isaac P. Smith, was a native of Springfield, New Jersey, who removed to New Albany in 1835. He was an architect and builder and was appointed architect and superintendent of the State Prison at Jeffersonville. He built the county jail and the city hall in New Albany and was architect and builder of many of the finest buildings in that city. During the Civil war he was quartermaster of the Twenty-third Indiana regiment until the organization of the Seventeenth Army Corps, when he was detailed by General James B. McPherson as acting assistant quartermaster general of transportation on General McPherson's staff, and served in that position until the death of General McPherson at Atlanta. After the war he held an important position in the quartermaster's department in Jeffersonville until within a short time before his death, which occurred January 7, 1887, when he was eighty years of age. Major Smith was a member of the Second Presbyterian Church of New Albany for many years and a resident of the city for over fifty years before his death.

Abby H. Campbell Smith (mother) was a native of Newark, New Jersey, and is now a resident of New Albany, greatly advanced in years; a member of the Second Presbyterian Church and a lady of education and refinement, beloved by a large circle of devoted friends, and noted for her deeds of charity.

Judge James R. W. Smith spent his boyhood in New Albany attending the public schools and finishing his preparatory education in a celebrated academy, of which Professor O. V. Tousley was principal.

He then began the study of law in the office of Judge David W. La Follette, and after reading with him for two years, went to the Cincinnati Law College and was graduated with the first honor of his class, April 19th, 1865. Since May 1st, of the same year, he has been a practitioner of the Louisville bar.

He has represented the Eleventh Ward in the Louisville School Board a number of terms beginning in 1876. In 1883 he was elected state senator for a term of four years from the Thirty-eighth senatorial district, comprising the Eighth and Twelfth Wards inclusive. In this capacity Judge Smith distinguished himself as a man of ability and of the highest integrity, taking a very active part in all measures of importance, and not caring for a law committee, was made chairman of the railroad committee. He was state senator during the memorable senatorial contest for a caucus nomination for United States senator between Hon. John S. Williams and Hon. J. C. S. Blackburn, and made a reputation as a man of firmness and individual opinion by refusing to change his vote from "Old Cerro Gordo Williams" to Blackburn, though petitioned to do so by his constituents in an immense petition.

When the new city charter for Louisville was adopted, providing the judge of the Police Court should have a vacation during the months of July and August each year, and authorizing the mayor to appoint a judge to preside during the absence of the judge of the Court, Mayor Tyler appointed Judge Smith to this important position, which he filled with signal ability during the months of July and August, 1894 and 1895, and many times in the absence of the regular judge. He demonstrated his fitness for the office by just and fearless rulings, and by an adminstration of the law without fear or favor for the protection of the people against crime, criminals and deeds of violence. The criminal was punished and crime suppressed, while justice was tempered with mercy to the youthful offender or those guilty of a first offense or deserving mercy. The criminal and habitual law breakers were very shy of the Police Court when Judge Smith was on the bench; and he made for himself a reputation as a criminal judge that is not confined to Louisville, but known and recognized throughout the country. The celebrated detective, William Pinkerton, when in Louisville, visited the Police Court and expressed the opinion that "Judge Smith was one of the best men for such a position he knew and that no thieves would come to the city with him on the bench."

Judge Smith was married October 21, 1869, to Anna E. Baldwin of Cincinnati, Ohio. Mrs. Smith is a graduate of Glendale Female College of Glendale, Ohio, and a lady of considerable literary ability. She is a member and president of Ladies' Missionary Society of Covenant Presbyterian Church of Louisville, and member of Ladies' Board of Managers of Presbyterian Orphan Asylum, and also corresponding secretary of the Synodical Missionary Society of Kentucky.

Judge Smith is in politics a Democrat, though of conservative tendencies, and has taken a prominent part in nearly every state and national contest since he came to Kentucky, his services being in demand in political campaigns. As a public speaker he has been a logician or argumentative speaker, or dealer in facts and figures, instead of a rhetorician. He prefers the law to politics, and declined public positions in the consular service or that would take him away from Louisville.

Judge Smith was raised in the Presbyterian Church, both of his parents having been members of that church over fifty years. He is a member of no secret-orders except the Louisville Lodge of Elks and Cherokee Tribe, Improved Order of Red Men, of Louisville. He has always resided in one locality in the Eleventh Ward in Louisville and been popular with the people, though fearless, outspoken and frank in his opinions.

STEPHEN GIRARD KINNER, Circuit Judge of the Twentieth Judicial District, residing in Catlettsburg, was born in Lawrence County, Kentucky, July 20, 1848.

His father, H. H. Kinner, was also born in that county, February 12, 1825, and was a merchant and lumber dealer in the Sandy Valley. During the war he took no active part, but he openly expressed his sympathy with the Confederacy. He was an old line Whig as long as that party was in existence and he then became a Democrat, taking great interest in political matters, but seeking no office. He was a member of the Methodist Episcopal Church, South; a Mason and one of the best citizens; died, January 3, 1893.

David Kinner (grandfather) was born in the southwestern part of Virginia, October 18, 1800, and came to Lawrence County, where he followed farming; married Mary Stewart of Virginia; died July 29, 1851. His ancestors came from England.

Mehaha Curnutte Kinner (mother) was born February 6, 1830; married David Kinner, December 2, 1846, and is now living in Boyd County, near Catlettsburg. Her father, Reuben Curnutte, was born in Virginia, January 18, 1793; came to Lawrence County and was one of the leading farmers and stock raisers of that county. He belonged to the old Whig party; was a member of the Methodist Episcopal Church and was a prominent and influential citizen. The Curnuttes belonged to an old Virginia family of Welsh extraction.

Judge S. G. Kinner was educated in the common schools of Boyd County; at South Bend,

Indiana, in 1866; Center College, Danville, in 1867, and in the Ohio Wesleyan University at Delaware, Ohio, in 1868-9; entered the law office of Ireland & Hampton, Catlettsburg, Kentucky, in 1870, and was admitted to the bar in 1872; began the practice of law without an associate; formed a partnership with Hon. K. F. Pritchard, one of the most eminent jurists of the state, and was associated with him from 1878 to 1880. In 1874 he was elected county attorney, in which capacity he served four years in connection with a growing practice; in 1880 was elected commonwealth attorney of the Sixteenth Judicial District; re-elected in 1886, and, at the expiration of his second term in 1892, was elected circuit judge of the district for a term of five years. In his second race for commonwealth attorney, he was accorded the nomination without opposition in his own party; nor did the Republican party nominate a candidate against him. He received the unanimous nomination for circuit judge and was elected without opposition. He is a fine lawyer, an able jurist and a highly honored and respected citizen; a prominent Mason and Odd Fellow, and a member of the Methodist Church, South.

On the 14th of September, 1870, he married Ceres Wellman, daughter of Zerelda (Bowen) and Jeremiah Wellman of Wayne County, West Virginia. She was born in that county, July 24, 1847, and was educated in the best schools of the county. They have four children: Mary, born November 14, 1871; Lute Belle, born January 24, 1877; Ceres, born August 22, 1881, and Sallie, born March 27, 1885.

HENRY L. KREMER, wharfmaster, Louisville, Kentucky, was born in that city, September 3, 1858, and is a son of Annie (Hendricks) and the late Charles Kremer, who was wharfmaster in Louisville for twenty-seven years prior to his death, December 6, 1893.

Charles Kremer was born in Louisville in 1830, on the present site of the Louisville Hotel. His parents were well-to-do Germans of the Catholic religion. He was educated in the parochial schools and accepted the religion of his father, to which he adhered faithfully during all of his life. He learned the trade of coppersmith, but was ambitious and energetic and did not long confine himself to the narrow limits of the shop, but soon became a leader in local politics. He was a man of fine intellect, good judgment and wide influence; and he naturally drifted into political life, not merely for revenue, but because of the interest he manifested in the progress of the city. His popularity was attested by his election and often repeated re-election to the office of wharfmaster, a position of trust and responsibility in which he faithfully served the public until the day of his death. He was devoted to his family and was kind and indulgent to his children and a true and stanch friend and neighbor.

Henry Kremer (grandfather) was a native of Germany, who came to the United States, landing in Baltimore when he was a boy and subsequently coming to Louisville, where he married Mary Markley, a native of Williamsport, Pennsylvania, who came to Louisville on a flat boat in 1820. He was a dealer in feed and grain and a man of influence, particularly with the German element of society.

Annie Hendricks Kremer (mother) is a native of Louisville, daughter of James Hendricks, who was born in Ireland and came to Louisville in the '20's. He was a fine machinist and iron worker, and was for a long time connected with the Coleman rolling mill until it suspended operation. He is still a resident of Louisville and very active for a man of eighty-six years of age.

Henry L. Kremer was educated in the Louisville public schools, which he left at the age of fourteen years to accept the position of bookkeeper in the foundry of John G. Baxter. He held that position for seven years, and was then for a time bill-clerk in the Louisville & Nashville Railroad office. On the first day of January, 1880, he was appointed assistant city assessor and held that office until 1885, when he resigned and was elected to represent the Eighth and Ninth wards in the state legislature, receiving a large majority over the Republican candidate. He was re-elected for three consecutive terms, serving throughout eight years with distinction. During his last term he was chairman of the railroad committee, whose duty it was to prepare the laws governing railroads under the new constitution. He also took an active part in forming the new city charter, and was otherwise diligent in securing legislation for the benefit of the city. During this time, while not engaged at Frankfort, he was interested in contracting and street building. When his father died, in 1893, he was elected to fill the vacancy and has been wharfmaster for two years.

Mr. Kremer was married February 22, 1882, to Etta Belle Krack, daughter of Dr. J. A. Krack, who was for many years city assessor.

HON. WILLIAM W. KIMBROUGH of Cynthiana, judge of the Circuit Court, son of John M. and Susan (Jones) Kimbrough, was born in Harrison County, May 19, 1843.

His father was also a native of Harrison County and a very successful and popular farmer and an active member of the Methodist Episcopal Church. He died in 1868, at the age of sixty-three.

William Kimbrough (grandfather) was a Virginian, a bricklayer by trade, but after coming to Kentucky he located near Cynthiana and followed farming. . He was of Scotch-Irish descent.

Susan Jones Kimbrough (mother) was born in Nicholas County. She and her husband were consistent members of the Methodist Episcopal Church. She died in 1880, aged seventy years. Her father, Moses Jones, was a Kentuckian and an extensive farmer in Nicholas County. ·

Judge Kimbrough attended the county schools and completed his education in Miami University at Oxford, Ohio, at that time one of the leading educational institutions in the country. After leaving school he was deputy circuit clerk of Harrison County for fifteen months. He then read law with W. W. Trimble of Cynthiana and was admitted to the bar in 1867. He moved to Bates County, Missouri, in September, 1871, and returned to Kentucky in March, 1875, when he located in Mount Olivet, Robertson County, and practiced law there for thirteen years. He was county attorney of Robertson County from 1878 to 1882. In June, 1888, he returned to Cynthiana and resumed the practice of law in his old home. In September, 1892, he was nominated by the Democratic party for the office of judge of the Circuit Court of the Eighteenth Judicial District and was elected easily for a term of five years. He assumed the duties of his office January 1, 1893.

Judge Kimbrough was married in 1869 to Johanah C. Ridgely of Jessamine County. His son, Daniel R. Kimbrough, is deputy circuit clerk of Harrison County.

JASPER BUSTOW KARN, County Judge of Daviess County, son of Christopher and Ann (Bustow) Karn, was born in the same county, Kentucky, March 7, 1848. His father was a native of the same county, where he spent his life in farming, and died in 1878. His father, also named Christopher, was a native of Pennsylvania, who came to Kentucky early in the century and married Leah Boone, a native Kentuckian and a relative of Daniel Boone, and was a farmer in Daviess County, where he died, in 1847. The ancestors of the Karn family were from Germany.

Ann Bustow Karn (mother) was born in Daviess County, in 1828, and died in 1882. Her father, Jasper Bustow, for whom Judge Karn was named, was a Baptist preacher in Daviess County, where he died in 1847. His wife was Rachel Barnhill, whose ancestors were of Irish extraction.

Jasper B. Karn, after obtaining his education in the Daviess County schools, was a teacher in the county for three years, reading law at the same time under the instruction of Sweeney & Stewart, of Owensboro, and was admitted to the bar in 1870; but did not begin the practice of law until 1872, when he gave up the business of the pedagogue. He quietly pursued his chosen profession, steadily gaining a profitable practice and making his way to the front.

He served two terms as city judge, prior to his election as county judge, in 1890. He was re-elected in 1894 and is now serving his sixth year in that important office. He is a gentleman of quiet demeanor and a dignity becoming the office which he has faithfully filled so long.

He is a member of the Masonic Order, Knights of Pythias, and Knights of Honor.

Judge Karn has been twice married. His first

wife was Sallie Fuqua, daughter of Perry Fuqua, of Daviess County. She died December 13, 1881, leaving two children: Virgia, who died in 1892, and Eva, who was born November 15, 1878. His second marriage occurred October 12, 1884, to Rose Roberts, daughter of Dr. Henry Roberts, of Owensboro. By this union there are three children: Robert, Fredrick and Rose.

FRED KAMLEITER, a prominent and successful merchant of Paducah, was born in Shillingsfurst, Bavaria, November 4, 1840. He was educated in Germany, leaving school when fourteen years of age, and two years later, in 1856, came to America and located in Cairo, Illinois, where he found employment as a laborer. He remained there until the call for troops, in 1861, when he enlisted with the sharpshooters, Company M, Fourth Missouri Infantry, under Captain Harvey.

During a service of three months this regiment was commanded by Dr. Hammer, and was a part of the command of General Sigel, with whom Mr. Kamleiter was well acquainted. He was in the battles of Wilson's Creek; at Carthage, Missouri; Fort Donelson; Pittsburg Landing, and Corinth, Mississippi. After serving the term for which he had enlisted, he joined Battery C, Second Illinois Artillery, under Captain Flood; and in this he served until the close of the war. He was with General Rosecrans all through the war, from the latter part of 1861 till 1865.

Returning home, he found employment for a short time in Mound City, Illinois; and in 1866 arrived in Paducah, where he was engaged as a salesman for a year or two, and in 1869 established the retail grocery which is now one of the leading mercantile concerns in that city. He soon became identified with the best interests of the city and is known as one of the most enterprising and liberal public-spirited citizens.

He was the representative of the Fourth Ward in the City Council from 1883 to 1893, being elected on the Republican ticket; is a stockholder in the German National Bank, and in the Citizens' Bank, in which he has been a director; a stockholder in the Paducah Trust Company, in the Citizens' Street Railway Company and in the Paducah Fair Association; is largely interested in real estate, owning some fifteen buildings; and is comparatively a rich man, especially considering that he began to hew out his own fortune as a day laborer. He is quite popular among the benevolent orders, and is a member of the Odd Fellows, Masons, Knight Templars, Knights of Honor, A. O. U. W., and is Commandant of Grant Post No. 59, G. A. R. He is also a member of the Lutheran Church and a liberal supporter of the cause of religion.

Mr. Kamleiter was married November 28, 1868, to Margaret Beyer, daughter of Tobias Beyer. She was born in Bavaria, Germany, December 6, 1841, and came to America with her parents when she was three years of age. They have three children, two of whom are married and have families: Katie, born December 26, 1869; married March 24, 1892, to E. W. Brockman; has one child, Fredrick, born September 19, 1894. Louisa, born March 5, 1870; married March 27, 1893, to Charles Scholz, of Evansville, Indiana; has one child, Norman Fredrick. Henry Kamleiter, born December 15, 1872; is now in business in Paducah.

Mr. Kamleiter's father, John Fredrick Kamleiter, was a mechanic in his native town in Bavaria, Germany.

HENRY TIMBERLAKE DUNCAN of Lexington was born in Paris, Bourbon County, Kentucky, August 31, 1836; and is a son of the late Henry T. and Eliza (Pike) Duncan, natives of Bourbon County, Kentucky.

His grandfather, Daniel Duncan, was a native of Pennsylvania, who left that state and settled in Kentucky in the year 1798, and was a merchant in Paris for thirty-six years—1798 to 1834.

The Duncans came from the highlands and lowlands of Scotland. A branch of this Scotch family came from Dumfreeshire and settled in Virginia in 1694, and another branch settled in New York and Pennsylvania in 1735. In the history of Western Pennsylvania, the Rev. Joseph Duncan is spoken of as a Presbyterian minister, preaching in a log church in 1739. Whether this Scotch pioneer preacher was related to Henry T. Duncan or not, is not known. Tradition states, however, that the Rev. Joseph Duncan settled in Kentucky about the year 1789, leaving several sons, and one of his grandsons was at one time governor of the territory of Illinois. This grandson was a cousin of the subject of this sketch.

Henry T. Duncan (father) was for many years a leading lawyer and manufacturer in Paris. He died in Lexington in 1881, at the age of 81.

Samuel Pike (maternal grandfather) was a native of England, who erected the first cotton mills west of the Allegheny Mountains, and whose death occurred in 1838, leaving a fortune of some four hundred thousand dollars, which in that day was considered a very large amount of money for one man to control.

Henry T. Duncan was prepared for college by private instructors and at the age of seventeen years, entered Harvard College and was graduated from that institution in the class of 1859. After leaving college he became a student of jurisprudence under the late Chief Justice, George Robertson; and was admitted to practice in the courts after four months' study.

In a short time after this he took editorial charge of the "Observer and Reporter," a political paper, famous in the days of Mike Wickliffe. This was just before the close of the Civil war, and the paper was soon seized and held by the Federal authorities for a time, but was returned to its proprietors. At this time it was edited by T. J. Bush and the late William A. Dudley.' Mr. Duncan remained with them for seven or eight months, when he returned to the practice of law. He subsequently formed a partnership with Hart Gibson and J. J. Miller, and in 1870 founded the Lexington "Daily Press," which Mr. Duncan owned and edited until November, 1893, when he assumed the duties of mayor of Lexington. He was nominated to this office by the Democratic party and was elected without opposition. His administration of Lexington's municipal affairs was one of the most noteworthy and sensational in the city's history. He instituted a searching investigation of the city's affairs for preceding years and unearthed a condition of municipal rottenness which startled and amazed the public. He discovered large shortages in the department of city collector, running back over many years and through several administrations. His administration was characterized by reform methods, strict business principles and great economy in public expenditures. Perhaps the most worthy and lasting feature however of his administration was the splendid improvements inaugurated and perfected by him in the public schools, both white and colored. Under his progressive and intelligent directorship they were rescued from the old fogy methods in which they had been conducted for a quarter of a century, and brought to a degree of efficiency that will now compare favorably with the public schools of any city of equal size in the south or west. In his race for re-nomination, however, he was defeated. His exposures of official rottenness stirred up an active host of enemies who encompassed his defeat by making a coalition with the A. P. A. vote, which was very large. Two primaries were necessary to decide the contest. The first was declared a tie and the second resulted in Mr. Duncan's defeat by only eleven votes, nearly 2,500 votes being cast. His successful opponent was Joseph B. Simrall, whom he had defeated for the nomination two years prior.

Soon after his election in 1893 the "Daily Press" was consolidated with the "Daily Transcript," and the two journals were succeeded by the "Press-Transcript," which was for one year edited by Mr. Duncan's son, Henry T. Duncan, Jr. The paper was then purchased by S. G. Boyle, half owner of the "Press-Transcript," and Mr. Duncan's son took up the profession of law.

After Mr. Duncan's first experience in the newspaper business he resumed the practice of law with the late Judge W. B. Kinkead, and was in partnership with him for four or five years.

In 1862 Mr. Duncan was a member of the State Guards, serving as adjutant on the staff of General James S. Jackson, who was killed at the battle of Perryville in October, 1862.

Henry T. Duncan was united in marriage in 1860 to Lillie, daughter of George W. Brand of Lexington; and they had ten children, nine of whom still survive. His eldest son, George Brand Duncan, was graduated from West Point in 1886, and is now adjutant of the Fourth United

States Infantry, stationed at Fort Sherman, Idaho. The second son, Edward, is now engaged in the revenue service; Henry T., Jr., has adopted the profession of law; Daniel graduated from West Point in the class of 1895. The daughters are: Eliza, wife of John R. Allen, county attorney of Fayette County; Nanny; Lilly, wife of George Otis Draper, son of Congressman Draper, and a wealthy cotton machine manufacturer of Hopedale, Mass; Margaret and Fanny.

CHARLES L. KING, a leading merchant of Corydon, president of the Deposit Bank and president of the Anchor Rolling Mills Company, of Corydon, was born in Henderson County, Kentucky, March 12, 1838.

His father, James H. King, was a native of Virginia, who removed to Union County, Kentucky, about the year 1829, and engaged in farming. About the year 1832 he removed to Henderson County and was a farmer there for a few years, but soon engaged in the milling business; sold out his mill in 1856 and went to Hickman and engaged in the dry goods business.

He was married in 1828 to Caroline Brinkley, and had ten children: John M., George W., James T., Charles L., Alexander, Edward S., Harbut A., Mary A., Martha C., and Sarah I. Mr. and Mrs. King died in Hickman in 1864, and they are buried at Hickman, Kentucky.

C. L. King (grandfather) was a native of Virginia, and his father was a native of Ireland, who came to Virginia in very early times.

Charles Brinkley (maternal grandfather) was a native of Virginia, whose antecedents are not known.

Charles L. King was educated in the schools of Hickman, and at the age of twenty-one years became a partner in his father's store, under the firm name of J. H. King & Son. They were fairly successful merchants, and after three years they closed out their business and Charles L. established another store with S. C. Wilson as his partner, the firm name being King & Wilson. They closed out at Hickman in 1866.

In 1866 Mr. King moved to Corydon and engaged in the same business there, in which he has continued in connection with other enterprises until the present time. From 1874 until 1878 his brother, Edward S. King, was in partnership with him, and the firm was King & Bro. C. L. and H. A. King succeeded Edward S., under the firm name, and the establishment is still known by that firm name.

Mr. King is largely interested in other business enterprises, being president of the Anchor Rolling Mills; president of the Corydon Deposit Bank; director in the Henderson National Bank; director in the Henderson Woolen Mills Company, etc. He has been an extensive dealer in real estate during the past fifteen years, and is the owner of valuable property in Corydon and vicinity.

He is a man of the highest integrity, esteemed by all who know him for his generous spirit and upright character. Being a man of sound business judgment, successful in all of his undertakings, he wields a strong influence in the community, and is recognized as a leading citizen of Henderson County.

Mr. King was married in 1864 to Mrs. Sallie (Powell) Sheffer, daughter of Harrison A. Powell, a sketch of whose life will be found in this volume. They have four children: Anna, Addie, Maude and Harbut.

JOHN FRANCIS LOCKETT, a prominent lawyer and politician of Henderson, was born in Henderson County, Kentucky, December 5, 1856. He is the eldest son of Rev. Paschal H. and Elmira (Eakins) Lockett. His father was born in Henderson County, June 21, 1832. He studied law when quite young and upon his being admitted to the bar, was regarded by his friends as among the most brilliant lawyers of his day. He was a Whig in politics and followed the changes of that party while it existed and after the beginning of the Civil war became a Democrat. In the exciting times just prior to the war he took an active interest and on more than one occasion met upon the rostrum speakers of the opposing party, holding his own among the best of them. He was elected judge of the Henderson County Court in 1866 and held that office for three consecutive terms, until 1882. During the latter year of his official life he devoted much of his time to the study of theology, and frequently preached the gospel. Upon his defeat for re-election in 1882 he began preaching, and it was not long until he was called to the pastorate of the Baptist Church at Trenton, Kentucky, where he was greatly beloved by all Christian people.

Captain Francis Lockett (grandfather) was a native of Mecklenburg County, Virginia, and was the author of a popular treatise on the cultivation of tobacco. He came to Henderson when it was scarcely more than a wilderness, and at once became a leader of men, whose advice and counsel were sought by his neighbors. He was a captain of the militia in Virginia and a leader in social and business life in Kentucky. He was a member of the legislature, 1815-17; was then elected State Senator and served until 1819, and was succeeded by the late Governor Archibald Dixon. The Locketts were English people, known as "Roundheads," who came to this country in the time of Charles II.

Elmira Eakins Lockett (mother) was born in Henderson County, Kentucky, May 5, 1843. Her father, John Eakins, was one of the early settlers of Henderson County.

William Hickman (father's maternal grandfather) was a Baptist minister, and was the first to proclaim the gospel in Kentucky. He commenced preaching at Harrodsburg in 1776, when on a tour of observation, merely, and after several months returned to Virginia and remained there several years. He then located in Kentucky and was an earnest laborer in his chosen field for over fifty years, and was familiarly known as "Father Hickman." Paschal Hickman was a soldier at the battle of River Raisin, the terrible massacre in which hundreds of his comrades were slain. Hickman County takes its name from him.

William Hickman (grandfather) was a native of Franklin County, and was also a preacher of considerable distinction.

John Francis Lockett was a pupil in the Henderson ward and high schools, during the superintendency of that finished scholar and disciplinarian, Professor Maurice Kirby, who is now principal of the Louisville male high school. He gained an education worthy of his teacher, and few young men have started upon the voyage of life more thoroughly equipped. At an early age he chose the legal profession, and applied himself assiduously to the acquirement of a knowledge of law, reading in his father's office; and in 1879 he was admitted to the bar. Like his father, he proved a graceful, pleasing speaker and an able lawyer. For three years, up to and including August, 1886, he was prosecuting attorney and was county judge from August, 1886, to January, 1895, proving himself a most efficient officer and accomplished jurist.

He was married April 14, 1881, to Minnie, only daughter of Alvan L. Jones of Henderson, and they have four children: Alvan, Hickman, Sarah and Marie.

Mrs. Lockett's maternal great-grandfather, Augustine Eastin, was a Baptist preacher, who came from Virginia to Kentucky at the time Boonesborough and Bryant's Station were established by the very early pioneers. At one time he was arrested and confined in the jail at Richmond, Virginia, for preaching to the British soldiers; and, for persisting in his purpose to continue to do so, was threatened to be shot. His son, General Zachariah Eastin, was born in Virginia, January 11, 1777. He was a colonel in the War of 1812, and fought at Tippecanoe and River Raisin and, in fact, was throughout the campaign with Generals Shelby, Metcalfe and Desha and Colonel Richard M. Johnson of Tecumseh fame. While engaged in this campaign, Colonel Eastin was promoted to the rank of brigadier-general, which commission he held until 1824, when he resigned on account of some misunderstanding between himself and General Desha. General Eastin came to Henderson in 1843, where he died some years later.

STEPHEN M. LOOMIS, County Attorney, Falmouth, son of John W. and Harriet K. Loomis, was born in Pendleton County, February 3, 1864. His father is also a native of Pendleton County, in which he has spent his life as a farmer.

Rev. Thomas J. Loomis (grandfather), a native of Dayton, Kentucky, was a prominent Baptist minister, who was well known in the northern part of the state. He resided in Kenton County for many years, where he died in 1880 in the seventy-fifth year of his age.

Harriet K. Loomis (mother) was born in Pendleton County in 1828 and is still a resident of that county.

Stephen M. Loomis received a good education in the county schools and in Nelson Business College, Cincinnati. Being an expert penman he taught penmanship for some time and in 1883, at the age of nineteen, he became a partner in the music publishing house of Allen Bros., Arcade, Cincinnati. He continued in this for about two years, when he disposed of his interest and accepted the position of bookkeeper in the store of J. Glasscock in Williamstown, where he remained until 1889, when he returned to his home, located in Falmouth, and engaged in the real estate business. He soon began the study of law under Judge L. P. Fryer at that place and was admitted to the bar in 1892, and has since then combined the practice of law with his real estate business. In November, 1894, he was elected county attorney on the Republican ticket by a handsome majority, defeating his preceptor, who was the opposing candidate. He took charge of the office in January, 1895, and has made a reputation as a faithful and efficient attorney. As an attorney he was associated with Col. Weden O'Neal of Cincinnati in the trial of the Rachford-Finn assassination case and also in the Downard-Vogelsong assassination case, both of which tragedies were enacted in Falmouth and created widespread interest.

Mr. Loomis is a great friend of the newspaper men and he has since early in his 'teens been connected with the press, both as correspondent and editor. He is a fearless, entertaining and forcible writer and would make a very successful newspaper man. He has always taken an active interest in politics and it is during a heated campaign that his trenchant pen is called mostly into use in educating and swaying public sentiment.

His parents being unable to give him the education they wished him to have, encouraged him in his studies at home and his early personal efforts to acquire a good business education, he having taught public schools in Grant and Pendleton Counties, before entering business college.

He was married in 1891 to Miss Mayme Hall, daughter of J. B. Hall, and granddaughter of Col. H. Bullock of Falmouth, has built him a nice home in West Falmouth, where he expects to make his future home. He is building up a good law practice and enjoys the highest esteem and confidence of his constituents.

HON. GEORGE W. LAIL, Judge of Harrison County Court, son of Charles and Louisa (Ingels) Lail, was born near Colemansville, Harrison County, October 23, 1838. His father was born in Harrison County, September 15, 1807. He followed farming all his life and was justice of the peace for twelve years. He died May 20, 1861.

John Lail (grandfather) was a native of Bucks County, Pennsylvania, who came to Kentucky when an infant with his parents. When only three years of age he was captured by the Indians at Fort Hinkson, Bourbon County, now known as Ruddles Mills. His mother afterward recovered him by trading some blankets for him. An older brother was captured at the same time, who was never restored to his family; but when twenty-four years of age he paid his brother, John Lail, a visit, coming from Missouri, where he had located. John Lail was a farmer. He died at the age of seventy-seven years. The Lails were of German descent, and belonged to an old Pennsylvania family.

Louisa Ingels Lail (mother) was a native of Harrison County. She was born April 18, 1814, and died February 20, 1880. Her father, Joseph Ingels, was a native of North Carolina, who came to the northern part of Harrison County and farmed all his life. Her mother, Mary Bryan Ingels, was a niece of Daniel Boone and daughter of William Bryan, who settled what is now known as Bryan Station, and who was killed by the Indians.

Judge Lail was educated in the common schools and was engaged in farming until the beginning of the Civil war. He enlisted in the Confederate army, April 22, 1861, joining Company C, First Kentucky Infantry, in which he served for twelve months, and was wounded in the first fight at Drainsville, Loudoun County, Virginia.

He recovered from his wound sufficiently to re-enlist in October, 1862; this time joining Company B, Second Battalion Mounted Infantry; which was commanded by Col. Thomas Johnson of Mt. Sterling. He entered this service as a private, but was soon elected second lieutenant and served in that capacity until the close of the war. He was in Camp Chase when the war ended, having been captured February 1, 1865, while at home on a furlough.

Returning to his old home, he settled down to the quiet life of a farmer. He was justice of the peace from 1882 to 1895. In November, 1894, he was elected county judge on the Democratic ticket, and assumed the duties of that office in January, 1895.

Judge Lail was married June 15, 1871, to Florence Day, daughter of N. C. Day of Harrison County. They have eight children living, four sons and four daughters: Maud, Jennie, Wade Hampton, Louisa, Ina, Charles E., Rodney F., and George Shirley.

D. D. BELL, deceased, formerly a beloved and exemplary citizen of Lexington, Kentucky, was born in that city June 6, 1849, and died at his home in Lexington June 26, 1892. He was a son of the lamented Henry Bell, a brief sketch of whose noble life is given in connection herewith. Like his father, D. D. Bell's chief characteristic was his unstinted generosity and kindly regard for the poor and needy and the hospitality which he lavished upon his friends and acquaintances, who always found a hearty welcome in his palatial home. He welcomed the stranger to Lexington and to his house and gave his city a good name by his personal kindness and the magnificent entertainment which he provided for visitors. He appreciated good fellowship and was never so happy as when entertaining those who enjoyed his generous hospitality.

He was a loyal friend and he had no enemy. He was a public-spirited citizen, who was always ready to aid with his means or by personal effort any enterprise which he thought would be helpful to the city; a public benefactor, and a philanthropist who sought to cover up his deeds of charity, but the instances of his generosity were so numerous that he was constantly being found out. It was said of him that he gave car loads of coal to the poor and none but the recipient was aware of it, while others gave a cart-load and the fact was published in all the papers. Truly, he was a noble, generous man, who gave to others as the Lord had given to him.

He was a man of marked ability in business affairs whose surroundings and opportunities were favorable, it is true, but he grasped opportunities and improved them, and made great advancement through good business management; nevertheless, his chief object in life was to do good to his fellowmen, and he was never so much absorbed in business or so fascinated with his success in money making that he forgot to be thoughtful of others. His home was a veritable palace, where he surrounded himself and his family with comfort and luxury. But he was, withal, a plain man, without ostentation, unassuming in his everyday life, and no one would suppose from his demeanor that he was the wealthiest man in Lexington.

D. D. Bell took the place of his father, Henry Bell, as director in the Northern Bank, and upon his death the surviving directors, as they had done on his father's death, adopted resolutions of respect, expressing their sincere sorrow, regretting that they would no more enjoy his genial companionship and wise counsel, and testifying to their high regard for his many good and honorable qualities of mind and heart, their sincere affection for his person in life and their grief in his death.

To his intimate friends alone he revealed the many sterling qualities which stamped him as a man with a full realization of the responsibilities of life, and they alone saw the cheerful courage with which he assumed and discharged every obligation that these responsibilities imposed. The sunny side of his nature was always presented to the world, and to those whom he met casually he rarely disclosed his remarkable knowledge of human nature or his accurate and methodical business acquirements. His whole life was guided by the golden rule, and the world that knew him was made brighter and happier for his having been in it. His acquaintance extended throughout the whole country, and there was

mourning in nearly every state and city when the telegraph flashed the unwelcome tidings of his death throughout the land.

His bright and useful life was suddenly cut off in the midst of his usefulness. He was stricken with paralysis on Wednesday and died on the following Sunday, June 26, 1892. He was mourned in the city as if each individual acquaintance had met with a personal loss; women and children and even stout-hearted men wept in the streets.

Mr. Bell was happily married April 5, 1880, to Sydney S. Sayre, daughter of the distinguished banker and financier, E. D. Sayre, a sketch of whose life is given in this work; and this union of two families who were life-long friends, strengthened the ties between the members of these households and made them as one. He left his companion and an only daughter, Clara D. D. Bell, but the circle of relatives and friends who were bereaved by his untimely end embraced a city full of mourners, who have never found another to take the place of D. D. Bell in their affections.

JAMES CAMPBELL, Lawyer and ex-Circuit Court Judge of Paducah, was born in that city April 9, 1843. After the usual preliminary schooling he went to Stewart College, Clarksville, Tennessee, for two years and then spent two years in European schools, and after returning home he matriculated in the McGill College and University, Montreal, Canada, where he studied for one year, and was licensed to practice law at Paducah. He was admitted to McCracken County bar in 1866, and has made Paducah his home and the practice of law his profession for thirty years.

He was a member of the City Council for two years, and in 1881 he was elected to succeed Honorable Edward Crossland as Circuit Court judge of the First Judicial District of Kentucky, embracing the seven "Purchase" counties of McCracken, Ballard, Hickman, Fulton, Calloway, Marshall and Graves, and also Livingston County, beyond the Tennessee River. He served until the expiration of his term, but was not a candidate for re-election. At the close of his administration the unusual compliment of commendatory resolutions, endorsing his course as a man and a judge, were passed by the bar and the officers of the court and the people in each county in his judicial district. This endorsement was more gratifying to him than a re-election would have been had he sought to retain the office.

Judge Campbell was married in 1868 to Mary K. Wheeler, daughter of Dr. James Wheeler of Christian County. They have four children: Wheeler, born in 1869 and admitted to the bar of Paducah in 1890; Bessie, Jeanette and James Campbell, Jr.

James Campbell (father) was born in Petersburg, Virginia, in 1798, and came to this state early in the present century, and was one of the most prominent lawyers in Western Kentucky. He was for some time judge of the Circuit Court. He died in Paducah in 1880, in the eighty-second year of his age. His father was a Scotchman, born in Argyleshire, and was the only member of his family who came to America. He was a citizen of Petersburg, Virginia, and an officer in the Revolutionary war. His wife (grandmother) was Mademoiselle Victoire de la Porte, a royalist, who fled from France with her family and her uncle, Baron du Boeuf, during the French Revolution of 1789. She was in the palace of the Tuileries, a member of the household, and witnessed the famous massacre of the Swiss Guards. She met and married Mr. Campbell in Virginia.

Dixon Given (maternal grandfather) was a prominent citizen of Livingston County, who for many years represented his district in the Kentucky Senate.

WILLIAM J. DAVIS, Secretary and Treasurer of the Louisville School Board, is a son of William Kincaid and Sarah M. (Zimmerman) Davis of Darlington C. H., South Carolina. His father was born in South Carolina in 1809 and was a cotton planter in Fairfield District, South Carolina, until his removal to Charleston in 1848, where he was a successful cotton factor and where his death occurred in 1872.

Jonathan Davis (grandfather) of Fairfield, South Carolina, was a large cotton planter and a Baptist minister, as, indeed, were nearly all of his male ancestors in this country.

James Davis (great-grandfather) was an officer

in General Sumter's Brigade in Northern South Carolina during the Revolutionary war—one of seven brothers, sons of John Davis, planter, Fairfield, S. C.—who entered the patriot army in one company of cavalry, but two of whom survived.

The family is of Welsh extraction, the first ancestor in this country, David Davis, purchasing thirty thousand acres of land from William Penn and settling his congregation, whom he brought over at his own expense from Pembroke County, Wales, in 1710. The church which he built is still standing about thirty miles from Philadelphia. Benedict gives an account of this religious movement in his history of the Baptists; and the Rev. John Davis, whilom pastor of the Second Baptist Church of Boston, published a history of the "Welsh Tract" Baptists, giving many interesting facts concerning that colony.

William J. Davis was born in Fairfield County, South Carolina, March 23, 1839. He was eight years of age when his father removed to Charleston, and he was educated in that city, graduating with the highest honors at the "Citadel," the State Military Academy.

Soon after the beginning of the late Civil war, January 19, 1861, he was commissioned first lieutenant and shortly after captain in the First South Carolina Infantry, P. A. C. S., and was with that regiment until January, 1863, when his service was commuted to Morgan's Cavalry. He served as commander of scouts and as adjutant-general in General Duke's Brigade of that division until the close of the conflict, except when confined as a prisoner of war. When the war closed he returned to South Carolina, but removed to Louisville in May, 1866. He was connected with the house of John P. Morton & Company for some time, having charge of their educational publications, and did excellent work as palaeontologist in connection with the State Geological Survey, devoting several years to that branch of public service.

In 1877 he was elected secretary and treasurer of the Louisville School Board, to which position he has been re-elected annually for nineteen years without opposition.

Major Davis has been an industrious student and writer, having contributed many articles to newspapers and magazines on various topics and has published in pamphlet form numerous articles and monographs on geological subjects, physical geography and natural history, among which may be mentioned especially "The Fossil Corals of Kentucky," which was published by the state in 1880.

Major Davis has devoted his leisure hours and much of his valuable time to the advancement of science in the line which he marked out in early life. His work has already proved of incalculable benefit to his state, and will be greatly appreciated by future generations. His lectures on geology, fossils of Kentucky, natural history, etc., have attracted attention among scholars and students and are exceedingly instructive and interesting even to those who make no pretentions to scientific knowledge.

Major Davis was married in December, 1866, to Frances Cunningham, daughter of Cleland T. Cunningham of Springfield, Kentucky, and they have eight children, six sons and two daughters: William J., Cleland, Francis, Edith, Edwin, Ethel Churchill, Basil Duke and Warren Offutt. The eldest son, William J. Davis, Jr., is first assistant electrical and mechanical engineer in the testing department of the General Electric Company at Schenectady, New York. The second son, Cleland Davis, is ensign in the United States Navy, now stationed at Washington, D. C. The third son, Francis Davis, is a civil engineer, employed on a railroad in process of construction between La Follette, Tennessee, and Middlesborough, Kentucky. The fourth son, Edwin Davis, graduated with the honors of his class from the High School of Louisville and is studying medicine. The other children are at home, and are capable of taking important places in the work of the coming generation.

HENRY BELL, father of D. D. Bell, was born in Georgetown, Delaware, March 28, 1808. He married Clarissa Davis, daughter of Daniel Davis of Salisbury, Maryland, and came to Kentucky when he was a young man, and made his mark, not as the popular politician and statesman, but as a merchant and financier, who was honored for his integrity and universally loved for his goodness of heart and many deeds of charity. A man of strong intellect, well informed on all topics of the day, he was still a most companionable man.

He was an associate and confidential friend of such men of his time as the Wickliffs, Johnsons, Paynes, Wards, Prentice, Wooley, Brand, Morgan, Hunt and others whose names are found in the history of the "mellow, happy" ante-bellum days; and he wielded an influence among men and in politics which made others conspicuous while he modestly remained in the background. He accumulated a princely fortune, and his hand was ever ready to respond to the promptings of a noble and generous heart in behalf of the poor and distressed.

While phenomenally successful in business, attracting attention to his wonderful ability as a merchant and financier, he was even more conspicuous for his broad charity and generous gifts to the poor of the city. He could not wait for those in need to come to him, but sought opportunities of helping others and alleviating distress, just as other men seek opportunities for investment.

When his health failed and he was advised to go to Florida he consented, but thinking of those who would miss his benefactions he left $500 to be distributed to the poor of his city during his absence. He was then in his seventy-fifth year, and his advanced years and failing health made the trip to the South of no avail, and he died in Jacksonville, Florida, April 7, 1883.

The following tender tribute to his memory was written by Jennie C. Morton and printed in the Frankfort "Yeoman":

A NAME IN WHITE.

Tho' dead, he leaves his life to speak—
　The best, his meed of praise;
He needs no tributes that we make,
　Nor poet's glowing lays.
No, no; this noble man has said:
　"If I have lived in vain,
No gilded words above me spread
　Can blot out any stain.

"'Tis what we do, what we have been,
　That's good and wise and true,
Must stand the test at last all men
　Here are submitted to."

To live the life approved the best—
　For life in death goes on—
We live in hearts and lives we've blest,
　Not words, when we are gone.

A kindly man, with genial smile,
　And gentle, tender heart,
One in whose Scottish blood no guile
　Had ever smallest part.
There was no waver in his course,
　His life-way pointed straight;
And by its own unswerving force
　He won his goodly fate.

Now dead, he speaketh thro' his deeds:
　The test death makes and leaves;
Found his life all sown with seeds
　Up-bearing golden sheaves.
From North to South, from East to West,
　The plaudit is the same,
They whose hearts and lives he blest
　Now rise to bless his name.
　　　　　　JENNIE C. MORTON.

WILLIAM ANDREW BYRON, Attorney at Law, Brooksville, was born in Mason County, March 23, 1860; son of Andrew and Ellen (Ryan) Byron. His father was born in County Limerick, Ireland, January, 1818, and came to America in 1849. He located in Mason County, where he engaged in farming. He had received a collegiate education in the old country and was one of the most intelligent citizens of the county. He was a Democrat in politics and a member of the Catholic Church. He died May 11, 1887, and is buried in the Catholic Cemetery at Brooksville. His wife was also a native of County Limerick; born in 1826; came to America in 1849; located in Maysville and was married to Mr. Byron in 1851. She is a member of the Catholic Church and is now living near Brooksville. They had five children, one daughter and four sons, of whom William A. Byron is the youngest.

He was reared on his father's farm, remaining until fourteen years of age, when he entered Augusta College and continued his studies there until 1878, when, for the want of means, he withdrew, having reached a high grade of proficiency in his studies. He taught school for several years in Bracken County and in the spring of 1884 commenced the study of law in the office of Hon. R.

K. Smith, and in the fall of the same year entered the senior class in the Cincinnati Law School, graduating in 1885. He returned to the schoolhouse, however, after completing his law course, and for seven years was engaged in teaching before commencing the practice of law in Brooksville, in the spring of 1892.

Mr. Byron is a versatile writer and an eloquent speaker.

CHARLES M. COWLES of Falmouth, junior member of the distillery firm of O. W. Cowles & Son, and Clerk of the Pendleton County Court, was born in Butler, Pendleton County, January 24, 1866.

His father, Ovid W. Cowles, is a native of Litchfield County, Connecticut, who came to Kentucky in 1856 and located at Butler, where he still resides.

Maria Ducker Cowles (mother) was born in Butler in 1840.

Charles Cowles has been identified in business with his father since he was eighteen years of age. He takes especial interest in their large grazing farm, which is devoted principally to the breeding of Southdown sheep.

In November, 1894, he was elected clerk of the Pendleton County Court, being the first Republican elected to any office in the county for thirty years. He is an active politician and the success of the ticket was largely due to his efforts. He is a most efficient officer.

Mr. Cowles was married in 1889 to Marguerite Jeffries, daughter of R. B. McDonald of Falmouth.

HON. JOHN BLADES CLARKE of Brookville, Bracken County, was born April 14, 1833.

His father, John Clarke, was born in Bracken County in November, 1804, and was educated in the county schools. He was one of the most intelligent and progressive farmers of his day. He was an exceptionally honest man, a devout Christian, a great lover of his home and a good citizen. He died October 21, 1875, and was buried in Mount Zion Cemetery, near Augusta.

Abner Clarke (grandfather) was born in Yorkshire, England, March 16, 1775; and when quite young came to the United States and settled in the Shenandoah Valley, Virginia. In 1797 he came to Bracken County, near Augusta, where he died September 14, 1850. He married Rachel Howard, daughter of John Howard of Bracken County. She was born in 1774 and died March 20, 1835. Abner Clarke was the fourth and youngest son of Stephen Clarke (great-grandfather), who was born in Yorkshire, England, February 14, 1741.

Hon. J. B. Clarke's mother, Mary (Blades) Clarke, was a native of Jessamine County; was married to John Clarke May 15, 1829. She was a devout member of the Presbyterian Church. Her father, Samuel Blades, was a native of Maryland, who came to Kentucky, first settling in Jessamine, and afterward in Bracken County, where he died. He was a pillar in the Presbyterian Church and a consistent Christian. The Blades were of Scotch descent.

Hon. John Blades Clarke received a good education in the Augusta schools and under the tutelage of Harvey King. After leaving school in 1851, he returned to his father's farm, and in the winter of 1851-2 taught school in the county, after which he read law for three years with Judge Joseph Doniphan in Augusta. He passed a critical examination by the late Julge Alvin Duval and William Moore and received his certificate April 20, 1854. In January, 1855, he went to Rockport, Indiana, where he commenced the practice of law, but on account of his wife's ill-health returned to Bracken County in the following September, and located in Brookville December 10, 1855, where he has continued to reside until the present time.

He was elected county attorney in 1857, and was elected on the Democratic ticket as state senator in 1867, serving four years. In 1874 he was elected to Congress from the then Ninth Congressional District, and was re-elected in 1876, serving until 1879.

He married Cordelia A., daughter of Christopher and Elizabeth (Bradford) Robertson, who was born September 4, 1835; died December 26, 1884. There were six children: Bion, born June 23, 1858, died November 2, 1885; William R., born October 22, 1861; John B., born February 19, 1864; Cordelia, born September 1, 1867, died August 10, 1868; Harry, born July 18, 1869, and Clarence, born June 23, 1873.

John B. Clarke, Jr. (son) married Alice Dudley of Falmouth, May 1, 1887. They have three children: Katharine, Bion and Robert.

HON. ASHER GRAHAM CARUTH of Louisville, Kentucky, is the son of Henry Clay Caruth, who was born July 10, 1814, in Tennessee; educated in Allen County, Kentucky, and was for many years a merchant and banker in Louisville, but retired several years ago. He was a member of the Board of Aldermen a number of years. He is still a resident of Louisville. His father, Captain Walter Caruth, served in the Revolutionary war, in which he gained his military title. He came to Kentucky over one hundred years ago, before the state was admitted to the Union.

Asher G. Caruth's mother was a daughter of George Washington Mansfield. She was born in Allen County, Kentucky, where she received her education. Her father was a member of the Kentucky Legislature for several years, and was also a member of the convention which framed the constitution of the state in 1850. He died in Allen County in 1851.

A. G. Caruth was born in Scottville, Allen County, Kentucky, February 7, 1844. He attended school in Philadelphia and graduated at the High School of Louisville in June, 1864. He finished his law course in the law department of the University of Louisville in 1866, and has practiced his profession ever since.

He was a presidential elector in 1876, and was attorney of the Board of Trustees of the Louisville Public Schools by annual election from 1873 to 1880, when he was elected commonwealth attorney for the Ninth Judicial District of Kentucky for a term of six years and was re-elected without opposition in 1886.

He resigned this office in March, 1887, to take his seat as a member of the Fiftieth Congress, to which he had been elected in November, 1886. He was three times re-elected, and served in the Fiftieth, Fifty-first, Fifty-second and Fifty-third Congresses as a Democrat.

Since retiring from the public service he has resumed the practice of law, which he did not relinquish entirely during his eight years in Congress.

Mr. Caruth was married February 23, 1871, to Miss Ella Terry, daughter of John Terry, for many years a wholesale grocery merchant in Louisville. She received her education in Louisville, and is a lady of many attainments, and entirely worthy of the many honors which she has shared with her very popular husband.

WALLACE McDOWELL SHELBY, Collector of Internal Revenue at Lexington, is descended from Revolutionary ancestry. His great-great-grandfather, Isaac Shelby, first governor of Kentucky, was a brave and patriotic soldier from the beginning to the close of the War of the Revolution. He was born December 11, 1750, in the vicinity of Hagerstown, in the colony of Maryland, whence his father, General Evan Shelby, and grandfather settled after their arrival in the colonies from Wales. Governor Shelby was a lieutenant in his father's company in the great battle with the Indians at Point Pleasant October 10, 1774, at the mouth of the Kanawha, at the close of which battle Evan Shelby was the commanding officer, Colonels Lewis Fleming and Field being killed or disabled. The result of this battle gave peace to Northwestern Virginia at the critical period of the colony. Coming so close upon the eventful contest of the Revolution it deterred the Indians from uniting with the British until 1776. Isaac Shelby was the true hero of the battle of King's Mountain. His great victory here over Colonel Ferguson October 7, 1780, occurred at the gloomiest period of the Revolution and was the first link in the great chain of events in the South which established the independence of the United States. History has heretofore, though improperly, ascribed demerit to the battle of Cowpens in 1781, but it belongs justly to the victory on King's Mountain, which turned the tide of war in the South as the victory under Washington at Trenton and of Bennington under Starke did to the North. Isaac Shelby was the first man to organize the expedition that terminated in the victory of King's Mountain, and after the close of the war settled in Kentucky, and upon the admission of Kentucky into the Union in 1792 he became her first governor. In 1812 he was the second time elected governor and entered the field in person in the War of 1812, and was in the battle of the Thames October 5, 1813. No greater patriot nor braver man ever lived than Isaac Shelby. His zeal and love for his country knew no bounds. His death occurred July 18, 1826, at the age of seventy-six years.

Wallace McDowell Shelby is a native of Fayette County, Kentucky. He was born July 17, 1860, and is the son of Thomas Hart and Florence (McDowell) Shelby. His father, the son of Thomas Shelby, was also a native of Fayette County, where he resided on a farm until 1893, when he removed to Lexington, where he was appointed revenue collector of the Seventh District by President Cleveland. He took charge of this office October 1, 1893, and died February 19, 1895, aged sixty-six years. He was a man of lofty character and unswerving integrity. He was a prominent member of the Walnut Hill Presbyterian Church. He was reared on the farm and became an extensive farmer and cattle breeder. His farm was one of the finest tracts of land in the "Blue Grass," embracing seven hundred acres.

Thomas Shelby (grandfather) was born in Lincoln County, Kentucky, and was with his father and brother James in the second war for independence. At the age of twenty years Thomas Shelby removed to Fayette County, where he took charge of three thousand acres of land that had been given him by his father, Governor Isaac Shelby. His death occurred February 14, 1869, in the eighty-second year of his age. At his death he deeded his children each seven hundred acres of land.

Florence McDowell Shelby (mother) is also a native of Lincoln County, and is a member of the Presbyterian Church. Her father, William Wallace McDowell (see sketches of McDowells on another page), was a nephew of Thomas Shelby, who was born in Lincoln County, Kentucky, and emigrated to Marion County, Missouri, where he resided many years and died.

Wallace M. Shelby was reared on his father's farm in Fayette County and received his education at Central University, Richmond, Kentucky. After leaving college he went to Missouri and accepted a position as chief clerk under his uncle, Shelby McDowell, who was superintendent of the Pacific Railway Company. In 1885 Mr. Shelby returned to Kentucky and received the appointment of United States gauger under General James F. Robinson, who was collector of internal revenue under President Cleveland's first administration. He held this position until February, 1889, when he resigned. He was then engaged in mercantile business in Lexington until his father's appointment as collector, when he was appointed chief deputy, and at his father's death he received the appointment of collector. In 1886 Mr. Shelby married Margaret Bryan, daughter of Joseph H. Bryan of Fayette County, and has two children, Florence McDowell and Joseph Bryan. The Harts, McDowells, Bryans and Wallaces are all families of prominence and many of them were Revolutionary soldiers.

REV. WARNER T. BOLLING, D. D., pastor of Hill Street Methodist Church, Lexington, one of the most eloquent pulpit orators of Kentucky, was born in Greene County, Alabama, May 25, 1846, and is a son of Warner T. Bolling and Harriet Smith, his wife. He is descended from a distinguished family who settled in the colony of Virginia with the Randolphs, Madisons, Meades and Taylors in 1685. The Bollings are of English ancestry, and intermarried with the Bland and Randolph families.

Warner T. Bolling (father) was a native of Petersburg, Virginia, and when quite a young man emigrated to Alabama, where he resided some years, afterward removing to Nashville and thence to Knoxville, Tennessee, where he died in 1856, in the fifty-sixth year of his age. He was a planter in Alabama, but retired from active business some years before his death. He was an aristocratic, scholarly gentleman, and a consistent member of the Episcopal Church.

Harriet Smith Bolling (mother) was born in the vicinity of Richmond, Virginia, and died in Knoxville, Tennessee, in the same year that her husband died, when she was fifty-four years of age. She was a devout member of the Methodist Episcopal Church, and a woman of many rare accomplishments and personal attractions.

Warner T. Bolling was reared in Knoxville and in Memphis, Tennessee, removing to the latter place some time after the death of his parents. He was a student in Emory and Henry College in 1861; and in that year, at the age of fifteen, he enlisted in Company C, Second Regiment Tennessee Infantry, in which he served four years in the Confederate army. He received a severe wound, breaking his right arm, in the battle of Chickamauga, and also received a flesh wound in the battle of Lookout Mountain. His regiment belonged to the division commanded by General Cleburne, who was killed in the battle of Franklin in 1864.

Mr. Bolling left college to join the army at such an age that his education was by no means complete and after the war the South was left in such a state that he was unable to resume his studies in college. But by wonderful energy, great perseverance and close application, he pursued his studies alone and acquired a well grounded and thorough education, and in the truest sense may be styled a self-made man. His fine scholarship was recognized by the faculty of St. Charles College, who conferred upon him the degree of doctor of divinity in 1886.

After four years of study Mr. Bolling entered the ministry of the Methodist Episcopal Church in 1869, since which time he has preached the gospel in Tennessee, West Virginia, Missouri, Colorado and Kentucky. For three years he was pastor of one of the leading churches in Denver and for six years in Missouri, and came to Kentucky in the early part of 1890 and had charges in Covington and Winchester, and in 1894 was sent to Lexington and placed in charge of Hill Street Methodist Church. Under the itinerant system of the Methodist Episcopal Church Dr. Bolling has several times been transferred by order of the bishops to do special work in the states of Colorado, Missouri and West Virginia,

He is universally esteemed and appreciated as a minister and as a citizen by the people of Lexington, regardless of sect or class, being an eloquent speaker, a profound scholar and a man of sound judgment and acknowledged ability.

Rev. Dr. Bolling has been twice married. His first wife, to whom he was married in 1870, was Mary Coley, by whom he had three children, two of whom are living: Robert E. Bolling, who is engaged in business in Cincinnati, and Margaret E. Bolling. His present wife, to whom he was married in 1882, was Willie R. Jeter of Virginia, a woman of rare judgment and Christian character. By this union there have been five children: Louise, Warner, Arthur, Mary Randolph and Helen Meade. Of these Warner and Arthur are deceased.

Dr. Bolling is president of the Board of Education, of the Kentucky Conference, of the M. E. Church, South, and takes an active interest in the educational movements of the day.

VERY REVEREND FERDINAND BROSSART, B. G., is a native of Buchelberg, Rhenish Bavaria, and was born October 19, 1849, and since 1888 has been the popular and able rector of St. Mary's Cathedral at Covington. He was the sixth child born to Ferdinand Brossart and his wife, Catherine Diesel, who were both natives of Buchelberg, Rhenish Bavaria. His parents, like many others of Germany, had conceived a great distaste and horror of militaryism and longed to take their five sons and one daughter to a country free of those feudalistic environments, and soon emigrated to the United States and located at Cincinnati in 1851. The father returned to his native country and there sold his property and then returned to this country and bought an extensive farm in Kentucky, upon which he resided until his death in 1883. Father Brossart commenced his clerical and preparatory studies for the priesthood at St. Francis' College at Cincinnati and at Mount St. Mary's of the West. His philosophical studies were taken at the Petit Seminary of St. Nicholas, in the diocese of Ghent, in Belgium, and his theological studies were taken in the University of Louvain, Belgium, where he finished his course in 1872, and returned to the diocese of Covington. In October of the same year he was appointed by the Right Reverend Bishop Toebbe to the pastorate of St. Edward's Church at Cynthiana. In 1876 Father Brossart was transferred to St. Pius' Church in Scott County, where he remained for sixteen months. He was next appointed pastor of the Church of Annunciation at Paris, where he attended to the spiritual wants of that church until November, 1878, when he succeeded the late Father Bekkers as pastor of St. Paul's Church at Lexington. Father Brossart remained as its pastor until July, 1888, when he was selected by the Right Reverend Bishop C. P. Maes, D. D., vicar-general of the Covington diocese, as rector of St. Mary's Cathedral, where he is at present stationed. He is also the editor and manager of the "Cathedral Chimes," which is published at Covington.

JOSEPH BRYAN, M. D., one of the leaders in the medical profession in Lexington and Fayette County and a descendant of a noble ancestry, was born in Fayette County, Kentucky, December 24, 1849, and is a son of Daniel Bryan and Sarah (Pettit) Bryan.

Dr. Bryan was educated in the Kentucky University at Lexington and studied medicine in the Bellevue Hospital Medical College, New York, one of the leading medical colleges in the United States, and after graduating in 1873, he spent two years as house surgeon of the first surgical division in Bellevue Hospital. After passing a competitive examination by the examining board he was given his choice of six positions and chose the first surgical division. There was no pay attached to this position, the appointment being purely honorary, but it was a high compliment to his faithfulness as a student and to his ability as a surgeon. After holding this position his allotted time, and gaining much valuable experience in surgery, Dr. Bryan returned to Lexington in 1875 and began the practice of medicine and surgery, to which he has given his whole time and attention for a period of over twenty years.

Few men in professional life have enjoyed greater success or personal popularity. A man of education, culture and refinement, genial in his manner and of kindly disposition, he is respected by all who know him and revered by those who have enjoyed an intimate acquaintance with him. An able physician and a scholarly gentleman, he is accorded a leading position among the members of the medical fraternity.

As a citizen he is public spirited and enterprising and is always ready to assist in furthering any good cause. His only office is that of a member of the Board of Health, in which he serves the city without a monetary consideration.

Dr. Bryan and Mrs. Jessie M. Brown, widowed daughter of Thomas McGrath, were married in 1884.

An interesting history of the Bryan family and its connections is given in an old newspaper which is in possession of a member of the family, the essential points of which are as follows:

Morgan Bryan, the first of the name of which there is any authentic account, was born in Denmark and was the only son of William Bryan. He was a Dane by birth, but not by origin, as the Bryans were Irish, and Morgan Bryan removed to Ireland and lived there a while before coming to America. He located in Pennsylvania and there married Martha Stood, a Dutch girl who had lived in France, but fled from that country on account of religious persecution. Her father and mother died on the voyage to America, and she was adopted by strangers, and after reaching womanhood married Morgan Bryan. They removed from Pennsylvania to Virginia and lived near Winchester until two of their sons were grown, married and settled. They then removed to the Valley of the Yadkin River in North Carolina, where they owned lands, as the records show. Morgan Bryan and Martha Stood had seven sons and three daughters: Joseph, Elenor, Rebecca, Mary, Samuel, Morgan, John, William, James and Thomas. Of these William married Mary Boone and Rebecca married Daniel Boone, the noted pioneer of Kentucky.

Many years after the Bryans had settled in North Carolina there was a great exodus from that state on account of political persecution and illegal taxation, and the Boones and Bryans, being united by the intermarriage of their families, became possessed of the idea of living in a country where they would be untrammeled by unjust and obnoxious laws and regulations; and, being attracted by the accounts of the fertile fields, beautiful rivers and fine forests of Kentucky, they left their homes and took up the tedious journey to the land in which they afterward became distinguished citizens.

William Bryan (great-great-grandfather), son of Morgan Bryan, was the first settler at Bryan Station. That he came to the station many years prior to the date given in history is evident from the records at Salisbury, North Carolina, which show that he disposed of his lands there prior to that date. It was in 1779 that he, with his family and three of his brothers, Joseph, James and Morgan, arrived at the fort. William Bryan (great-great-grandfather) headed a hunting expedition in company with eleven others and in a skirmish with Indians he was wounded and died in the station a few days later, greatly lamented by his companions and family. He was born March 7, 1733, and died in 1780. His wife, Mary Boone, was born November 10, 1736, and died July, 1819. Their children were: Samuel, Daniel (great-grandfather), William, Phoebe, Hannah, John, Sarah, Abner, Elizabeth and Mary. Daniel, the second son, was born February 10, 1758, and died February 27, 1845. He married Elizabeth Turner and their children were: William, Louis, Samuel, Joseph and Mary.

Joseph Bryan (grandfather) was born in 1799 and died in 1887. He married Mary Cartmell, who was born February 9, 1804. Her father, Elijah Cartmell, was born February 25, 1763. Joseph Bryan and Mary Cartmell's children were: Elijah, Daniel, Joseph and Mary.

Daniel Bryan, second son, is Dr. Joseph Bryan's father. He was born May 5, 1825, and was graduated from Bethany College in the class of 1848. He was a distinguished mathematician and a good scholar, but chose no profession, preferring the life of a farmer. He lived in Fayette County for many years and in 1880 removed to Houstonia, Pettis County, Missouri, which is his present place of residence.

Sarah Pettit Bryan (mother) was born in 1829 and was educated in Mr. Broadus' school in Lexington. Her marriage to Daniel Bryan was celebrated January 25, 1849. She died in 1882. Her grandfather, Harry Pettit, was a native of Fayette County, and a farmer. He married Julia Atchison, daughter of Hamilton Atchison and sister of Dr. Thomas Atchison, professor of theory and practice in Vanderbilt University, Nashville, Tennessee. Harry Pettit died in 1874. The Atchisons were of Irish extraction. Mrs. Bryan's grandfather, Pettit, was a native of France.

HON. GEORGE W. MORRIS, president of the Louisville Gas Company, is the son of John and Elizabeth (Jones) Morris. He was born in Gloucestershire, England, January 27, 1823. His father and mother were natives of England, who came to the United States in 1827, locating in New York City, and afterward, in 1831, removing to Troy, New York, where they continued to reside until the time of their death. They gave careful attention to the education and religious training of their children. Mr. Morris was a ruling elder in the Presbyterian Church for fifty years. He was for many years a manufacturer of carriages, but retired long before his death, which occurred in 1881, when he was in his eighty-eighth year. Prior to the late war he was a Democrat, but after the beginning of the war he became a Republican, but took no active part in political affairs.

Elizabeth Morris (mother) was born in England in 1795. She was a woman of great Christian virtue and a beloved member of the Presbyterian Church. She died in 1860.

George W. Morris received a good English education in Troy, leaving school, however, when only fourteen years of age to clerk in a mercantile establishment, in which he remained until he was twenty-three years of age, in the meantime teaching school in the vicinity of Troy. When he came to Louisville he had the usual experience of the young man among strangers, and it was some time before he found employment. He was glad to accept a position as bookkeeper in the tobacco house of E. Holbrook at two hundred dollars a year. He was afterward bookkeeper in the wholesale dry goods house of Emory, Low & Co. for three years before embarking in the wholesale grocery business as a member of the firm of Fonda, Moore & Co. (See George H. Moore.) He continued in this for twenty years, conducting the business alone after the withdrawal of his partners, and was notably one of the most successful merchants of Louisville.

In 1867 he disposed of his grocery interests and for seventeen years was a member of the firm of George S. Moore & Co., large iron dealers, controlling the product of twenty-five blast furnaces. He withdrew from this firm in 1885 when elected to his present position, president of the Louisville Gas Company, to which for ten years past he has given his best attention.

Few men have done more for the public good, without hope of reward or fear of criticism; and if one were to ask one hundred citizens to write the names of ten of the most worthy and popular citizens of Louisville, the name of George W. Morris would be near the top, if not first in every such list. His career has been characterized by great energy, prudence and liberality, controlled by a superior judgment and marked throughout by unquestioned integrity. Notwithstanding his devotion to business pursuits, he has given much attention to letters, acquiring an education, limited in his youth, which places him in rank with the learned men of his day and generation. As an evidence of this, the degree of A. M. was conferred upon him in 1865. His interest in public affairs has been as unselfish as it has been energetic and unremitting. In 1851 he advocated, before the people and through the press, the necessity for a new city charter; was one of the earliest advocates for loaning the credit of the city to aid in building railroads; was elected a member of the first board of trustees of the university and public schools of Louisville, under the charter of 1851; contributed largely to the present admirable public school system of the city, being a member of the school board for twelve years and its president for five years, being elected and re-elected without opposition; and as presiding officer of that and other bodies he gained unusual distinction as a parliamentarian. For several years he was a director in the Kentucky Mechanics' Institute, and delivered the fifth annual address before that association in 1857. In 1860 he was elected president of the Board of Trade, serving two years; in 1864 he was a member of the City Council, and in 1866 he was the Democratic nominee for mayor of the city (an office in which it was difficult at that time to place a man of Mr. Morris' standing). In 1870 he represented his ward in the City Charter Convention, and was president of that body. In 1873, on solicitation of the best citizens without reference to party, he became a candidate and was elected by a unanimous vote to the state legislature, but was compelled, on account of pressing business engagements, to resign before entering upon the duties of the office.

Mr. Morris was a director in the Bank of Louisville for ten years, and for twenty-two years has been and is a director in the Bank of Kentucky, which is acknowledged the most substantial banking institution in the state. He was one of the incorporators of the Mutual Life Insurance Company of Kentucky in 1868, and has remained in its directory until the present time; was a director in the Franklin Insurance Company of Louisville for thirty-five years and was its president for eight years, and has been a director and president of the Indiana Cotton Mills Company—whose office is in Louisville—for twelve years. He has been grand treasurer of the Grand Lodge of Kentucky, and of the Grand Encampment of Kentucky, Independent Order of Odd Fellows, for thirty-seven years—an order of which he has been a zealous member for many years, frequently serving the order in its various offices and otherwise aiding it in its benevolent work. He is, and has been, interested in many other institutions and enterprises too numerous to mention, and even now at his advanced age he is a very active, busy man.

Notwithstanding his many business interests and his labors for the advancement of the city's welfare, he has always been active and zealous in church affairs, being an elder in the Second Presbyterian Church (formerly Dr. Stuart Robinson's); he has frequently represented the church in its higher courts. He was for many years superintendent of the Sabbath school, and his attention to details in all the affairs of the church, his ability and willingness to perform any duty, with gentleness of spirit and exemplary Christian demeanor, have won the hearts of the people of the congregation and the children of the Sabbath school in a measure that is exceedingly gratifying to him as he approaches the close of a busy and useful life.

Mr. Morris was married in 1848 to Caroline, daughter of James and Abigail Wallace of New York State. Mrs. Morris was a lady of superior intelligence and of fine personal attractions. She died in 1894, leaving three children: Carrie, widow of Rowan Boone, a direct descendant of the pioneer, Daniel Boone; John S. Morris and Wallace W. Morris, all of Louisville.

JOHN C. WILLIS, educator and lecturer, now residing in Mitchell, Indiana, was born in Anderson County, near Lawrenceburg, Kentucky, November 1, 1862, and is a son of James Emmons Willis and Mary Ellen Gordon Willis.

His father, James E. Willis, was also a native of Anderson County. He was a merchant of Lawrenceburg at the outbreak of the war, and was also interested in farming. He enlisted in the Union army and served with distinction throughout the Civil war. He took great interest in politics, being an ardent Republican, and on two occasions was the candidate of his party for the legislature. He was a faithful member and supporter of the Christian Church. He died in 1888, at the age of forty-eight years, greatly lamented by his family and by the entire community in which he had lived.

John Gordon (maternal grandfather) was also a native and resident of Anderson County, a prominent and useful citizen, and died in 1862.

John C. Willis' early education was received in the public schools of his native county. He attended college in Danville, Indiana, and Lexington, Kentucky. He took his post-graduate course at the University of Wooster (Ohio), and received from this institution the degree of Ph. D.

He began his life-work as an educator in the common schools in Woodford County, and in a short time became principal of an academy at Orr, Anderson County, which position he filled acceptably for two years, in that time building up the largest school ever conducted in that place.

He then was called to the chair of mathematics and civil engineering in Mountain City College, Tennessee; and, while holding this position, he conducted several surveys for railroads around Chattanooga and Lookout Mountain. He was compelled to resign his professorship in this college on account of ill health. One year later he returned to Lawrenceburg and there organized the Kentucky Normal College, an institution which attained remarkable success during the three years of his administration.

He then accepted the presidency of Ashland College, at Shelbyville, which position he held for three years, leaving it in 1894 to accept the presidency of the Indiana Normal College at Mitchell, Indiana, an institution which has flourished under his able management and has grown to be one of the great normal schools of the country; hundreds of students are there enrolled each year.

Mr. Willis has taken high rank as a civil engineer, having taught many classes and surveyed many railroads. His executive ability is fully attested by the fact that every institution over which he has presided has had marvelous growth and success. As a teacher he ranks with the best educators in this country, having taught thousands of students, coming from all parts of the United States.

For several years he has been a successful institute instructor and lecturer, and during the past two years has lectured before more institutes in Kentucky than any other instructor. Few men have accomplished more for the cause of education in the state then Professor Willis.

He was married July 10, 1889, to Liccie Milton of Shelbyville, Kentucky. He is a Royal Arch Mason, and an elder in the Christian Church.

OLIVER FRANCIS LEE BECKETTE, a member of the firm of R. H. Vansant & Company, lumber dealers, of Ashland, was born in Cabell County, West Virginia, October 1, 1861. He received his education in his native county and at Marshall College, Huntington, West Virginia, graduating from that institution in the class of 1886. He went to Mount Savage in March, 1887, and took charge of the books of the Lexington & Carter County Mining Company, remaining there for five years. He was then employed as bookkeeper for the Leon Lumber Company at Leon, Carter County, for a period of two years. On the first of April, 1894, he became a member of the well-known lumber establishment of R. H. Vansant & Company, at Ashland. He is a man of fine business qualifications, upright in his dealings; one of the most popular young business men of Ashland; a Republican voter; a member of the Masonic Order; a Knight Templar, and a steward in the Methodist Episcopal Church, of which he became a member January 26, 1896.

Mr. Beckette was married June 1, 1892, to Samantha Prichard, daughter of Wiley Prichard of Mt. Savage, Kentucky. She was born January 27, 1866, and educated in the best schools of Mt. Sterling, Kentucky.

Andrew L. Beckette (father) was born in Cabell County, now West Virginia, July 25, 1824, where he has been engaged for the greater part of his life in farming. During the recent war he was commissioned captain by Governor Wise, and served three years in the One Hundred and Twentieth Regiment of Virginia Militia. He is postmaster at Fudges' Creek, Cabell County, a position which he has held continuously since 1870, being one of the few Republicans who have not been disturbed by Democratic administrations. He is greatly devoted to his home and does not care for political or social distinction.

James Beckette (grandfather) was born in Montgomery County, Virginia, September 18, 1774; served in the infantry arm of the militia in the War of 1812; was engaged in farming in Cabell County before the State of Virginia was divided; married Hannah Lee, who was a first cousin of General Robert E. Lee. His father's name was Richard Beckette, whose ancestors were from England, with a mixture of German blood in their veins.

Hannah Lee Beckette (grandmother) was born in Patrick County, Virginia, September 20, 1788, and died December 16, 1862. She was a daughter of William Lee.

Emily S. (Hatfield) Beckette, mother of Oliver F. L. Beckette, was born in Cabell County, West Virginia, September 22, 1824. She married Andrew L. Beckette in 1848, and died January 3, 1883. She was well educated and highly cultured, a member of the Methodist Episcopal Church (Northern branch), and a lady of most exemplary Christian character.

Adam Hatfield (grandfather) was born in Tazewell County, Virginia, October 19, 1774. He was a farmer by occupation; a soldier in the War of 1812, and in General Wayne's war with the Indians. He died June 18, 1855. He married Mary Williams, who was born in Tazewell County, Virginia, February 12, 1782, and died November 15, 1847. Adam Hatfield's father's name was Andrew Hatfield, whose ancestors were Germans, if he was not a native of Germany himself.

HENRY ORENDORF, M. D., of Louisville, was born in Breckinridge County, Kentucky, October 6, 1841, and is a member of a very old family whose names are found in the early annals of this country, and who were driven from Germany nearly two hundred years ago by Louis XIV. on account of their religious opinions. They fled to England and eventually made their way to the United States, some time prior to the Revolutionary war. Some of the members settled in Virginia, some in Pennsylvania and others in Maryland, and, as the tradition goes, a number of the men became good soldiers in the cause of liberty. One of the Orendorfs, of Frederick County, Virginia, "raised" twenty-four children—eighteen sons and six daughters; seven sons served in the same company in the War of 1812, and four of them afterward owned adjoining farms in Virginia and reared eleven children each.

A reunion of the family was held at Bloomington, Illinois, in October, 1886, when the fact was developed that there were representatives of the family in thirty-two states and territories. Many interesting legends and reminiscences of the family were brought to light at this reunion, and the rather peculiar fact was commented upon that notwithstanding they were driven from the "Faderland" on account of their religion, not one had been found in the vast number of descendants who was a minister of the gospel, and not one of the female members of the family had married a

HENRY ORENDORF, M. D.

minister. They are, however, moral and religious people, the majority of them being church members, and they represent nearly all other professions and occupations.

Henry Orendorf is the son of Mexico Orendorf, a native of Fincastle, Virginia, who came to Kentucky over sixty years ago and located in Breckinridge County, where he engaged in farming and trading in live stock until he was forty-two years of age, and died in 1854.

Jesse Orendorf (grandfather) was born in Frederick County, Virginia, near Winchester, and removed to Fincastle, Virginia, and subsequently to Breckinridge County, Kentucky, with his son, Mexico, and was a farmer in that county, where he lived to be eighty years of age.

Christian Orendorf (great-grandfather) was born in Germany in 1726, and was probably one of those who fled from the Lower Palatinate in the time of Louis XIV. The Orendorfs were descended from noble ancestry. One of the Orendorfs left England and went to Canada with General Wolfe and later settled in the Mohawk Valley.

Mary Kane Orendorf (mother) was born in Salem, Virginia, in 1818, and is now a resident of Louisville. Her father, Thomas Kane, was a native of Virginia and a farmer, who came to Breckinridge County about sixty years ago, where he died of cholera in 1849. The Kanes were of English extraction.

Henry Orendorf grew to manhood in his native county, receiving his education in private schools and in Franklin (Indiana) College, which he attended for two years and completed his collegiate course at the Cecilian College in Hardin County. He then attended the Kentucky School of Medicine in Louisville, from which he was graduated in 1871. He then was employed as interne in the City Hospital for eighteen months, after which he entered the office of Dr. J. M. Holloway in Louisville and was associated with him for four years, being in the meantime visiting physician at the City Hospital.

In 1876 he went to Savannah, Georgia, as acting assistant surgeon, U. S. A., at that post. He remained there three months, and on account of yellow fever was transferred to Blackville, South Carolina, and two months later was again transferred to Charleston in the same capacity. He returned to Louisville in 1877, since which time he has been engaged in the practice of his profession in that city.

In 1879 he was elected to the chair of materia medica and therapeutics in the Kentucky School of Medicine, a position which he still occupies. He is also clinical lecturer on Genito-Urinary and Diseases of the Skin, in the same institution.

Dr. Orendorf has been a member of all the medical societies as they have come and gone, and at present holds his membership in the principal national, state and city medical societies and associations.

He was united in marriage May 12, 1876, to Mattie Ormsby, youngest daughter of the late Colonel Stephen Ormsby, of Louisville, who commanded the famous Louisville Legion in the Mexican war. She is a granddaughter of Judge Stephen Ormsby, who was the first Federal judge of Kentucky. Dr. and Mrs. Orendorf have two daughters and one son: Louisa Ormsby, Marie Ormsby and Stephen Ormsby Orendorf.

One of the legends of the Orendorf family, which has been published in many newspapers, is worth repeating here:

Mary Madaline Orendorf, a beautiful young lady of seventeen summers, was present at an entertainment given a number of patriot officers in Baltimore during the Revolutionary war. General Horatio Gates, a war-worn veteran, the hero of many battles and the conqueror of Burgoyne, was present, and upon meeting Miss Orendorf surrendered for the first time in his life; and, through her father, made a formal proposal of marriage. General Gates was an accomplished and popular officer and was flushed with the honors conferred upon him for his many conquests. He was possessed of great wealth, and offered to lay at her feet his heart, hand and fortune; but she refused his proposal because he was old enough to be her father. She afterward married a son of Jonathan Hager, founder of historical old Hagerstown. Her husband died in a few years, leaving a handsome young widow with one child and a large estate. Luther Martin, one of the most prominent lawyers of Maryland, fell desperately in love with her, and after a brief courtship, during which he indited numerous letters (some of which are handed down to posterity as model declarations of love) he was accepted. But the engagement was broken off in a way that the following letter will explain:

"Baltimore, July 26, 1800.
"My Very Dear, Amiable Mrs. Hager:
"I have been told since you left town that on last Sunday week I was at your lodgings." (She was visiting friends in Baltimore.) "Of this I have no recollection. I doubt not I made a foolish figure, but I think it impossible that I should have behaved with rudeness or impropriety. Was that the reason, my dear Mrs. Hager, of the coldness and reserve you appeared to me with on Monday morning when I called on you before I went to Annapolis? If so, I will not blame you; but be assured you shall never see me again in a situation that I know not what I do, unless it should proceed from the intoxication of love. In the heat of summer my health requires that I should drink in abundance to supply the amazing waste from perspiration. But having found that I was so unexpectedly affected, as I was, by soda water and brandy, I have determined to mix my waters with less dangerous liquors. Nay, I am not only confining myself to mead, cider, beer, hock, mixed with soda water, but I am accustoming myself to drink water alone. Thus, if we live to see each other again you will find me most completely reformed and one of the soberest of the sober."

After writing this letter he was in Richmond, Virginia, arguing a law case. When he returned he found awaiting him a letter which drew out an answer from him, in which he said: "I returned much fatigued, but in good health, but, alas! alas! what is health to a poor wretch, who, before you hear from him again will most probably be tucked up, swinging from the limb of some convenient tree........resemblant of the human shape which some prudent farmers hang up in their corn fields to scare the birds away. Yes, my dearest madam, be not alarmed should you hear that your swain, in a fit of despair, has, in the French style, given you the slip by sticking his neck in the noose." But he did not destroy his life, and was employed in a legal capacity by Mrs. Hager, who subsequently married Colonel Lawrence of Virginia.

WILBUR FISK BROWDER, one of the most distinguished lawyers in the state, and a prominent citizen of Russellville, was born in Clarksville, Tennessee, December 12, 1848. His father, David Browder, was born in Dinwiddie County, Virginia, near Petersburg, November 11, 1818, and came to Logan County, Kentucky, with his parents in 1819. He was educated in what was known as Russellville Academy, in a building which is still standing and now used as a public school. When he had reached his majority he became largely interested in buying tobacco and preparing it for the foreign markets. In 1842, having married a second time, he removed to Clarksville, Tennessee, where he continued in the tobacco business in connection with merchandising. He had extensive business interests in the city and was one of the leading and most enterprising citizens of Clarksville. He subsequently removed to Montgomery, Alabama, where he was engaged in merchandising and cotton planting until his death, January 6, 1871.

David Browder was married April 16, 1838, to Mary Evans, who was born in Logan County in July, 1819. She belonged to one of the oldest and most respectable families in the state. She died in October, 1839, leaving no children. Mr. Browder was married again November 8, 1842, to Elizabeth E. Irvine, daughter of Caleb Irvine, a native of Tennessee. She was born in Robertson County, Tennessee, May 18, 1823, and was educated in the Russellville Female Academy, which is now known as Logan College. She survived her husband about three years, and died in Russellville, July 28, 1874. There were ten children by this marriage: Bettie G., born September 28, 1843, died June 7, 1845; James Thomas, born January 9, 1845, died April 14, 1845; Robert Irvine, born August 30, 1846, died July 19, 1893; Wilbur F., born December 12, 1848; Helen May, born February 21, 1851, died August 5, 1851; David, born September 12, 1852, died November

24, 1856; Caleb Ewing, born April 22, 1854, died April 25, 1871; Richard D., born June 15, 1856; Edward M., born September 11, 1859; Fannie Irvine, born July 11, 1863.

Richard Browder (grandfather) was born in Dinwiddie County, Virginia, April 1, 1789. He came to Logan County, Kentucky, with his brothers, William C. and Robert, in 1819; these three brothers purchased three farms of five hundred acres each, upon which they lived and prospered. Richard Browder was married in Dinwiddie County, Virginia, February 24, 1813, to Elizabeth Anderson, who died in Logan County, June 2, 1858.

David Browder (great-grandfather), a native of Virginia, married Sallie Pegram, also a Virginian, and they lived and died in their native county.

Richard Browder (great-great-grandfather), a Virginian by birth and lifetime resident, had two sons, Charles and John, who were killed in the Revolutionary war.

Caleb Irvine (maternal grandfather) was drowned while attempting to cross Mayfield Creek in Graves County, Kentucky, when he was twenty-four years of age. He married Elizabeth Ewing Mitchell of Robertson County, Tennessee, who lived to be eighty years of age, and died in 1867. They had three children: Elizabeth E. (mother) and two sons, Robert Green Irvine, who became a distinguished Methodist minister, was a member of the Tennessee Conference when he was twenty-one years of age. He became widely known throughout the state as one of the leading preachers in the Methodist Church. The second son, Caleb Ewing Irvine, enlisted for the Mexican war in 1847, and was engaged with General Winfield Scott in all of his engagements in the war with Mexico and was present at the final surrender of the Mexican army. He was captain of a company and was only twenty-two years of age at the close of the war. He wrote his sister (Wilbur F. Browder's mother) that he did not intend to return to the States, but told her that as long as she received the "Oregonian" newspaper through the mail she would know that he was alive, and when that paper ceased to make its visits she would know that he was dead. The paper came to her for seven years, and then, coming no longer, his friends supposed he was dead. For twenty years they heard nothing of him, but in 1885 the family learned that he was a circuit judge in Montana, residing at Deer Lodge. They learned, further, that the district which he served on the bench was strongly Republican in politics, but he had been frequently elected as a Democrat. After the close of the Mexican war he had been appointed captain in the United States army, but did not accept the commission. This promotion was offered him on account of his bravery and gallantry in battle. He died in 1889, having given no reason for thus isolating himself from his family.

Wilbur F. Browder received the best education that the wealth and fondest ambition of his parents could afford. His private tutor in Montgomery, Alabama, was Dr. Moses, now the honored rabbi of the Jewish Temple, Louisville, Kentucky, who prepared him for college. In 1865 he entered the University of Virginia at Charlottesville, remaining three years and graduating in the class of 1868, in which were many students who have since that time become men of national distinction, including Senators Daniel and Faulkner, John S. Wise, a distinguished lawyer of New York; George P. Raney, chief justice of Florida; Rev. Dr. Whitsett, president of the Louisville Baptist Theological Seminary; Judge Alexander P. Humphrey; Judge William O. Harris of Louisville; Hon. Ben T. Perkins of Elkton, Todd County, and quite a number of gentlemen who have acquitted themselves with honor and credit in the National House of Representatives.

In September, 1868, Mr. Browder began the study of law in the State University at Lexington, Kentucky, and graduated from that institution in June, 1869, before he was twenty-one years of age. His instructors in law were Madison C. Johnson, who was dean of the faculty, John B. Huston and William Cassius Goodloe.

In November, 1869, he was admitted to the bar in Russellville and at once began the practice of his profession in that city, with the result that he is to-day not only a leading member of the bar of Russellville, but one of the best known and most successful lawyers of the state. He has never been a candidate for any political office, although it has been difficult for a man of his ability and popularity to keep out of office. As a means of diversion from the exacting duties of his extensive practice and to help his friends, he has indulged to some extent in politics, but has steadily set his face against all temptations to run for, or to accept, any political office, even in the line of his profession.

In 1874 he was appointed register in bankruptcy for the Third Congressional District by the chief justice of the Supreme Court of the United States, upon the recommendation of Judge Bland Ballard of the United States Circuit Court of Kentucky; and he accepted and held that office until the repeal of the bankrupt law in 1878. He was appointed master commissioner of Logan County in 1880, but resigned that office in the same year. He was local attorney for the Louisville & Nashville Railroad Company from 1882 to 1889, when his territory was extended and he was made district attorney for that company. He was one of the organizers of the Logan County Bank, in which he has been a director and stockholder since it was opened for business.

Mr. Browder was married January 18, 1872, to Bettie B. Wills, who was born in Logan County, March 11, 1849. She was educated principally in St. Mary's College, St. Louis, Missouri, from which institution she is a graduate. She is a lady of rare accomplishments, being a fine Latin and French scholar. Her father, John M. Wills, was born in Logan County, July 26, 1821; married Eliza H. Bibb, who was born in Russellville, February 27, 1827. She was a niece of George M. Bibb of Russellville, who was the first chancellor of the old Louisville Chancery Court; was judge of the Kentucky Court of Appeals; United States senator from Kentucky, and secretary of the treasury under President Pierce.

Mr. and Mrs. Browder have five sons: Wilbur F., Jr., born November 24, 1872; educated at Bethel College, Russellville, and at the University of the South at Suwanee, Tennessee, where he was a member of the class of 1890; is now engaged in manufacturing leather in Russellville.

Marion Castner, born June 6, 1874; graduated from Bethel College, June 18, 1892; from the University of Virginia in the class of 1894; and from the University of Berlin, Germany, in September, 1895; has chosen journalism for his profession.

John Caldwell, born March 27, 1876; graduated from Bethel College in June, 1895; now a student at the University of Virginia.

Lucien McClure, born February 6, 1878; now a student in Bethel College.

Eugene Irvine, born July 4, 1882; in school in Russellville.

W. F. Browder, Jr., was married November 23, 1893, to Harriet Morton Frazer. She was born in Russellville, July 30, 1871, and is a daughter of Thomas A. Frazer, deceased, who was a very prominent citizen of Russellville and cashier of the Bank of Russellville at the time of his death. Wilbur F. Browder, Jr., is the father of Wilbur F. Browder the third, who was born February 19, 1895.

ARCHIBALD DIXON, M. D., physician and surgeon, of Henderson, son of Governor Archibald Dixon and Elizabeth Robertson Cabell Dixon, was born in Henderson, Kentucky, March 4, 1844. After attending the local schools he was sent to the Sayre Institute, Frankfort; and afterwards to the University of Toronto, Canada. Returning from school, he followed the business of farming on his place near Henderson until 1876, spending much of his leisure time in reading medical works, and was thus prepared for the study of medicine in the Louisville Medical College, from which he graduated in 1877, dividing the honors with four of the brightest men in the class. In that year he lost his property and began life anew, as a physician in Henderson, depending upon his profession for the support of his family.

He encountered the usual difficulties of a young physician in a field entirely occupied by older men of excellent reputation, who held their patrons against all comers, and he had to take his chances among them. It was a hard struggle for a time, but these circumstances did not dampen his professional zeal. He devoted himself to the work before him with an energy and an application to his studies seldom equaled. His success was soon assured; and, while others were predicting his failure, he was even then enjoying some of the fruits of his labors. He made a manly fight against poverty and obscurity, and by his faithfulness to his calling, his genial manner and marked ability, he won the battle against unequal odds; and, among the many distinguished physicians of Henderson, he was soon known as one of the first in his profession.

Dr. Dixon is a member of the Mississippi Valley Medical Association, the second largest association of the kind in the United States. In 1885 the distinguished honor of president was conferred upon him by this society, and he served with a dignity and intelligence that made him a host of friends. He is also a member of the Kentucky State Medical Society, of which he was president in 1893; member of other societies and clubs in the medical profession, and is a frequent contributor to the leading medical journals. He is a member of the Episcopal Church, and is a Knight Templar and a Knight of Pythias.

Dr. Dixon was married in December, 1864, to Maggie Herndon of Frankfort, a most intelligent and accomplished lady; and they have two sons and two daughters: Wynn, Archibald, Maggie and Julia.

Dr. Dixon is a son of Governor Archibald Dixon, who was born in Caswell County, North Carolina, April 2, 1802, and came to Henderson with his father's family in 1805. He enjoyed but limited advantages in the way of an early education, as the settlement was new and the country a wilderness. He studied law and soon took a commanding position at the bar. In 1830 he was elected by the Whig party to represent his county in the legislature, and in 1836 was elected state senator. In 1844 he was elected lieutenant governor on the Whig ticket with Governor Owsley; was a candidate for governor in the next election (1848), but was defeated by Mr. Crittenden; was a member of the Constitutional Convention in 1849 and was the Whig candidate for chairman of that body, but his Democratic opponent, Mr. Guthrie of Louisville, was elected by a majority of two votes; was the candidate of the Whig party for governor in 1850, but, owing to dissensions in the party at that time, was defeated; was elected to the United States Senate in 1852 to fill the unexpired term of Henry Clay, who resigned on account of impaired health, and served until 1855. In the campaign of 1860 Governor Dixon espoused the cause of Douglas. In that year and in 1861 he devoted himself unceasingly in the effort to stay the tide of disunion, and made speeches of extraordinary power and eloquence in behalf of the Union. When the war came on he suffered heavily in loss of property, but was true to the Union. He took an active part in the days of reconstruction, but did not again enter the political arena. He died April 26, 1876.

Governor Dixon was twice married; first in March, 1834, to Elizabeth Robertson Cabell, who died in 1851, leaving six children. His second marriage occurred in October, 1853, to Sue Bullitt of Jefferson County, by whom he had three children. Five of the six children of his first marriage reached maturity: Rebecca Hart, wife of Governor John Young Brown; Susan Bell, deceased, who was twice married—first to Cuthbert Powell, second to Major John J. Reeve; Dr. Archibald Dixon, Honorable Henry C. Dixon and Joseph C. Dixon.

Dr. William Cabell, a native of England and a graduate of Royal College of Surgeons in London, immigrated to Goochland, now Nelson County, Virginia, in 1723 or 1724. He had four sons: William; Joseph, also a physician; John and Nicholas. Dr. Joseph Cabell married Mary Hopkins, aunt of General Samuel Hopkins, and the children of that marriage were: Joseph, Mary, who married John Breckinridge; Ann, who married Benjamin Harrison; and Elizabeth. The second time he married Ann E. Bolling, daughter of Archibald Bolling of Red Oak, Buckingham County, Virginia, whose wife was Jane Randolph. Archibald Bolling was lineally descended from Colonel Robert Bolling of Petersburg, Virginia, whose wife was a granddaughter of the Indian princess Pocahontas.

Captain Wynn Dixon (grandfather) was a native of North Carolina, who joined the army when sixteen years of age and served throughout the Revolution. He moved from North Carolina to Henderson in 1804. His father, Colonel Henry

Dixon, commanded a regiment in the Revolutionary war and was killed at the battle of Eutaw Springs. Light Horse Harry Lee, in his memoirs of the Revolution, pays Colonel Henry Dixon a high compliment for his gallantry and bravery at the battle of Camden.

Rebecca Hart Dixon, Governor Dixon's mother, was a daughter of David Hart of North Carolina, who, with his brothers, Nathaniel and Thomas, were three of nine members of the Henderson Grant Company, who, in 1775, through their agent, Daniel Boone, purchased from the Indians all of the land lying between the Kentucky and Cumberland rivers; and established at Booneville the first government in Kentucky, called Transylvania.

Dr. Dixon's reputation, especially away from home, is in surgery, in which he is regarded as one of the most skillful in the state.

He was also appointed by Governor Brown as a member of the State Board of Health in 1894.

JOHN HULL DAVIDSON, ex-Mayor, and one of the most enterprising citizens of Lexington, was born in that city, August 23, 1855.

His father, James T. Davidson, was for a period of twenty-nine years an official in the Northern Bank of Kentucky. He came to this state from the District of Columbia in 1839. His father was James Davidson, who was the first cashier of the Bank of United States at Washington. The mother of J. Hull Davidson, Mrs. Catherine M. Davidson, was a daughter of Jacob Hull, a farmer and large land owner of Fayette County.

Hull Davidson, as he is familiarly known, received his education at the old Transylvania University and, after leaving college, like his father and grandfather, he became a bank officer, serving as individual bookkeeper in the First National Bank of Lexington for eight years. Having engaged in the plumbing and gas fixture business as a silent partner while in the bank, Mr. Davidson found his business growing to such a rapid extent that he resigned his position in the bank and devoted himself to his new business. After several years of successful business with his partner, R. D. Williams, he bought the old Lanckart foundry on Short street, by which means they were enabled to increase their facilities. Mr. Davidson soon afterward organized the present Lexington Plumbing Company.

In 1884, in company with Charles Seelbach and J. A. Simonds, he leased the Phoenix Hotel, of which he was proprietor until 1891, when he bought the entire property and formed the present Phoenix Hotel Company, in which he is the largest stockholder.

The Lexington Chamber of Commerce owes its organization to Mr. Davidson, who was elected president during its second year.

In the reform movement in politics in 1886, Mr. Davidson was elected as a member of the first Board of Aldermen; and later, in 1888, was elected City Collector by an overwhelming vote, and was re-elected without opposition in 1890. Mr. Davidson thought he would retire from politics in 1891, but a demand was made on him to become a candidate for the mayoralty, which he declined to consider until after he had addressed a personal circular letter to the voters, asking if it were their wish to have him run for that office. This novel procedure resulted in such a deluge of endorsements that he made the race and was elected by an overwhelming majority. At the close of his term he declined a re-election, as the duties of the office interfered too seriously with his business pursuits. During his short term of seventeen months he got together the neglected records of the four years which preceded his term, and had them properly copied and restored. The public schools were thoroughly reorganized and enlarged, and the police force increased. When he took charge of the office the city was burdened with an immense bank indebtedness; and he floated, for the first time, Lexington bonds at 4 1-2 per cent, and after paying off the indebtedness, much of which was bearing 7 or 8 per cent interest, with money borrowed at 4 1-2 per cent, he also refunded all the 6 per cent bonds which could be called in at the new rate. This was considered a great feat in financiering, and has resulted in great profit to the city since he has been out of office, by the low rate of interest established. Besides starting a sinking fund, the expenses of the city were greatly reduced, although the number of miles of brick streets were doubled. Mr. Davidson left the office with $65,000 in the treasury, and Lexington had a credit second to no other city in Kentucky.

Mr. Davidson has been out of politics since November, 1893, and is now engaged in several large business enterprises. He has found time to aid in many new business ventures, in a number of which he has served as director.

He is one of the busiest men in Lexington, and is always willing to lend a hand or to lead the way in behalf of any public or private enterprise which may redound to the interests of the city of which he is one of the most public spirited and enterprising citizens. He has acted as host in entertaining many large delegations of guests who have visited Lexington during the past ten years, and has thereby made an extensive acquaintance, including prominent men and capitalists throughout the country.

In 1876 Mr. Davidson married Magdalen Lancaster, daughter of the late M. P. Lancaster, one of the oldest and best known citizens of Lexington; and they have two children, a son and a daughter.

After the death of Mr. Lancaster Mr. Davidson became a member of the firm of M. P. Lancaster & Co., and with his brother-in-law, A. B. Lancaster, is now conducting one of the most successful business houses in Lexington, Kentucky. Mr. Davidson was one of the two delegates from Kentucky who attended the convention at St. Louis of the Nicaragua Canal project. Governor Brown also appointed Mr. Davidson a commissioner of the Eastern Kentucky Lunatic Asylum, a post of duty which he is now filling.

WILLIAM FITZHUGH DANDRIDGE, member of the firm of Mason, Hoge & Company, of Frankfort, Kentucky, was born in Shepherdstown, Jefferson County, (now West) Virginia, November 18, 1849.

His father, Philip Pendleton Dandridge, was a native of the same county, where he carried on extensive farming operations. He also gave considerable time to civil engineering, and, prior to the war, aided in the development of mining in the Kanawha Valley, where he had large interests in coal and timber lands. In 1858 he removed to Winchester, Virginia; and at the commencement of the war between the states, entered the Confederate service in the State Department at Richmond, remaining until the close of the war. His first wife was Caroline Goldsborough, daughter of ex-Governor Goldsborough of Maryland. She died in 1854, about five years after the birth of the subject of this sketch. Mr. Dandridge's second wife, by whom he had no children, was a daughter of President Zachary Taylor, and widow of General William W. S. Bliss, who was General Taylor's famous adjutant general in the Mexican war.

Mr. W. F. Dandridge's grandfather, Adam Stephen Dandridge, was a native farmer of Jefferson County, (now West) Virginia, his birthplace, which he inherited when very young, being the fine estate known as "The Bower," to which his father, Captain Alexander Spottswood Dandridge, had retired at the close of the Revolution. Captain Dandridge's earlier home was in what was then New Kent County. His father, Nathaniel West Dandridge, was one of the three sons of Captain William Dandridge, royal navy, and his wife, Unity West, a descendant of John West, governor of Virginia 1635; another of these three sons, John, was the father of Martha Dandridge, wife of General Washington. Nathaniel West Dandridge was but a lad, when, as one of the "Knights of the Horseshoe," he followed Governor Spottswood into the beautiful valley of Virginia, where, more than half a century later, his son (whose mother was Dorothea, daughter of Governor Spottswood) established the home which still remains in possession of his descendants of the same name.

The Honorable Charles Goldsborough (maternal grandfather) was a member of Congress from 1805 to 1817; and was governor of Maryland from 1818 to 1819. He was fifth in descent from Nicholas Goldsborough of Dorsetshire, England, who settled in 1670 upon the eastern shore of Maryland, founding there the large family connection (Goldsboroughs, Lloyds, Tilghmans, etc.) which has furnished to the state, in each generation, able and useful men.

After the death of his mother, in 1854, William

F. Dandridge, then five years of age, was taken care of by his mother's relatives in Cambridge, Maryland, until he was ten years of age, when he returned to his father at Winchester, Virginia. He enjoyed excellent advantages under his father's care in the way of education, and became especially interested in civil engineering. Soon after leaving school he entered the service of the Baltimore & Ohio Railroad Company as civil engineer. He was employed by that company until 1875, when he undertook a contract in the construction of the Cincinnati Southern Railroad in Grant County, Kentucky. After completing this work, he went to Cincinnati and took the contract for building the Cincinnati, Lebanon & Northwestern Railroad. In 1877 he returned to the service of the Baltimore & Ohio Railroad Company as general agent of the express department, with headquarters in Cincinnati. He held this position until October, 1881, when he removed to Winchester, Kentucky, and became a member of the firm of Mason, Hoge & Company, one of the most extensive contracting companies in the United States. In 1886 he removed to Covington in order to superintend the work of his company in the construction of the Chesapeake & Ohio Railroad bridge at that point. After completing that structure, in 1888, Mr. Dandridge removed to Frankfort, his present home.

Mr. Dandridge was married in December, 1888, to Mary B. Winn, daughter of Colonel Robert Winn of Winchester, Kentucky; and has one child, Elise Winn Dandridge.

Mr. Dandridge is a direct descendant of Governor Alexander Spottswood of Virginia, whose daughter, Dorothea, married Nathaniel West Dandridge, formerly of the British navy, whose daughter Dorothea married Patrick Henry, October 9, 1777.

Another daughter of Governor Spottswood married Bernard Moore of King Williams County, Virginia, whose son Augustine married Sarah Rind, and their daughter married Carter Braxton, one of the signers of the Declaration of Independence.

Alexander Spottswood, son of Governor Spottswood, was a brigadier general in the Revolutionary war, whose wife was a daughter of William Augustine Washington and a niece of General George Washington.

One of the descendants of Governor Spottswood, Ann Hill Carter, was the second wife of General Henry Lee, and the mother of General Robert E. Lee. The large connection in Virginia embraced the names of many of the most distinguished men of the country for many generations; Spottswood, Dandridge, Washington, Lee, Braxton, Carter, Fitzhugh and many others.

JUDGE SAMUEL M'DOWELL was the son of Captain John McDowell, who was killed by the Indians December 25, 1742, in what is now Rockbridge County, Virginia, and what was then the frontier. He was born in the colony of Pennsylvania in 1735, and moved to Virginia in 1737, where his grandfather, Ephraim McDowell, was settling a colony of Scotch-Irish.

As a youth he saw frequent service against the Indians and was a soldier in Samuel Lewis' company at Braddock's defeat. In Dunmore's war (1774) he was a captain of a company from Augusta County, Virginia, and was conspicuous at the battle of Point Pleasant. In the Revolution he was colonel of a regiment from Augusta, participated in General Greene's campaign in North Carolina, the turning point of the war, and was in the pursuit which drove Cornwallis to Wilmington. For several years before the Revolution he represented Augusta in the House of Burgesses. In all the meetings and movements in Colonial Virginia which led to the struggle for independence he had an active part; of every deliberative body which assumed progressively advancing ground against monarchical and parliamentary encroachments upon popular and individual rights, he was a prominent member; notably, the Williamsburg conventions, the latter of which (1776) instructed the Virginia delegates to the Continental Congress to "declare the united colonies free and independent states." When the Virginia state government was driven by the British from its capital, he was selected as one of the State Council, a most important and responsible position in that trying time. In 1783 he, with Col. Thomas Marshall, was appointed surveyor of public lands in Fayette County, then comprising one-third of the district of Kentucky. During the same year he presided as one of the judges of the first District Court ever held in Kentucky (March, 1783), John Floyd and George Winter being his associate judges. In 1784 he removed his family from Virginia to what is now Mercer County, Kentucky, and in 1786 he was one of the presiding judges at the first County Court held in Kentucky. Over the convention which met in Danville in 1785, and over all the subsequent conventions which assembled for the consideration of the separation of Kentucky from Virginia and the formation of a state constitution, he presided, "his social position, his solid attainments, his matured convictions, his high character, his judicial temper, his fine presence, his popular manners and his peculiar and varied experience of public life combining to admirably qualify him for the position, and to center upon him the attention, confidence and respect of the able men who were associated with him in those early throes of inchoate state." "It was by the moderation and patient discretion of the presiding officer, and the calm patriotism of others like him, as well as by the keen vigilance of Colonel Thomas Marshall, and far more than by the fierce and direct assaults of others, which savored of personal and partisan animosities, that the 'sagacious policy of calculated procrastination' was adopted, the schemes of conspirators who plotted to tear Kentucky from her connection with Virginia and even from her moorings to the general government and to achieve in lieu through a political and commercial alliance with cruel and treacherous Spain, were thwarted; a solution of the difficulties of a separation from Virginia legally and peacefully reached, and all the commercial advantages of the free and unobstructed navigation of the Mississippi were finally obtained." "In the troublesome and unsettled times in Kentucky, he was the 'central figure of an historic group, conspicuous, like himself, for courage, intelligence, fortitude, dignity of character and mental poise.' All were representative men—types of a cultivated class and of a vigorous, aggressive and enduring race." "After having presided over the nine conventions which considered the question of a separation from Virginia, Judge Samuel McDowell was also president of the convention which, in 1792, framed the first state constitution for Kentucky. He was one of the first circuit court judges and one of the first district judges of the new state—appointed by old 'King Mountain' Shelby, by whose side he had fought at Point Pleasant, as well as the first United States judge—appointed by Washington, under whose eye he had served in the campaign on the Monongahela, in 1755, and who well knew his worth. In these positions, as in all others, he acquitted himself with credit and honor. He was a Federalist of the school of Washington. He lived to the good old age of eighty-two years, and died honored of all at the residence of his son, Colonel Joseph McDowell, near Danville, September 25, 1817."—Green's Historic Families of Kentucky.

THOMAS S. PETTIT, a prominent business man and politician of Owensboro, and one of the best known and personally popular men in the state, was born in Frankfort, Kentucky, December 21, 1843, and is a son of Duane and Elizabeth (Zook) Pettit. After his primary schooling in Frankfort, he attended Georgetown College and then learned the printing trade, for which he had a fancy and a remarkable aptitude. He became an adept in all of the mechanical work of the printing office while he was yet in his teens, but he was too ambitious to stick to the cases, and in 1864 he went to Owensboro, and purchased the "Monitor" newspaper from a Mr. Woodruff, and began at once to attract attention by publishing a lively local paper and advocating the principles of the Democratic party. Unlike his predecessor, he freely criticised the Republican party and its war policy, and his articles on such topics brought down the wrath of the United States authorities upon his head; and, as a result, on the 17th of November, 1864, he was arrested by order of General Stephen G. Burbridge, imprisoned and "banished to the Southern Confederacy," under the general charge of being "notoriously disloyal;" and was sent under escort to Memphis and there transferred across the lines. He spent the following months until May, 1865, traveling within the Confederate lines, and then, the war being over, he returned to Owensboro and resumed the publication of the Monitor, in which he published in several consecutive numbers a detailed and interesting account of his trip through Dixie, giving his experiences and impressions and relating the hardships and privations which he necessarily suffered during his enforced vacation. These articles attracted much attention and had a very wide circulation, bringing the young editor into prominent notice. The Monitor was one of the brightest papers in the state, and Mr. Pettit soon became widely known as one of the most enterprising newspaper men of Kentucky.

He was the first man to establish a successful newspaper in Owensboro—and he did this before he was twenty years of age—and brought the first Gordon and power presses to that section of Kentucky.

In 1868 he was elected assistant clerk of the House of Representatives, which position he held for six years, when he was appointed private secretary of Governor James B. McCreary, which he resigned to accept the position of reading clerk in the national House of Representatives at Washington. During his service in the Legislature and in Congress, he had the distinction of being known as the best reader in the United States. His strong voice and clear and distinct enunciation enabled him to read, not only so as to be heard from all parts of the house, but he had a ready conception and a quick understanding and could read intelligently documents which he had never seen before. His services in the house were cut short by the Republicans gaining the ascendancy.

To go back to the '60's again: On the death of John S. McFarland in 1869, through the influence and personal popularity of Senator Thomas C. McCreery, President Johnson appointed Mr. Pettit assessor of internal revenue for the Second District, the duties of which he performed with ability and fidelity until the close of Mr. Johnson's administration.

In the fall of 1882 Mr. Pettit was a candidate for Congress against J. B. Clay of Henderson and was defeated, after an exciting race, by less than one hundred and fifty votes. In that contest Union was the pivotal county, and the friends of Clay looked after it in such a way as to secure the majority for their candidate. Mr. Pettit has attended more State Conventions than any man in Kentucky and has been elected secretary of all of them, and in this capacity has rendered the Democratic party valuable services, which have been appreciated and highly complimented. He was one of the secretaries in the Democratic National Convention which nominated and elected Cleveland, and was called to serve in the same position four years thereafter and selected as one of the notification committee to inform Cleveland and Thurman of their selection for President and Vice-President.

Mr. Pettit's political views have not been strictly in harmony with the Democratic party for some years and he has been one of the ablest leaders of the People's party, having been a candidate of that party for governor in 1895.

He served with ability and distinction as a delegate to the last Constitutional Convention of Kentucky, and advocated such reforms as the secret official ballot, the taxing of corporations like individuals and the two-thirds verdict of juries in civil cases. He was afterwards chosen by a large majority as one of the representatives of Daviess County in the General Assembly, so as to put into practical operation the provisions of the new constitution, and his election in this instance followed one of the bitterest contests ever known in the state.

He is still actively interested in politics, not for revenue or for honor, but from principle. Having strong convictions upon topics of national import, he has the courage to stand up for them and does not wait to count the noses of those who are ready to stand by him before expressing his sentiments.

He has for many years been engaged in industrial or manufacturing enterprises in Owensboro —too numerous to mention in this brief sketch— and his success, which has been uniformly good, has brought him a fair share of this world's goods. Popular with all classes, industrious, enterprising, generous and philanthropic, he is easily one of the best citizens of Owensboro. He has always been ready to participate in public enterprises, and, in questions of public interest, has always been found on the right side and in the front.

He is Past Grand Master of the Masonic Fraternity, and deservedly holds a high social position.

Mr. Pettit was married in December, 1870, to Margaret Blair, daughter of J. H. Blair, who was a prominent merchant of Owensboro in his day. They have one son, Harvey Blair Pettit.

EPHRAIM M'DOWELL, surgeon, son of Judge Samuel McDowell and Mary McClung, was born in Rockbridge County, Virginia, in 1771, and died in Danville, Kentucky, in 1830.

"He attended classical schools in Georgetown and Bardstown, Kentucky, and studied medicine in Staunton, Virginia, completing his medical education in Edinburgh in 1793 and 1794. He began to practice in Danville, Kentucky, in 1785, and for years was the foremost practitioner in the southwest. In 1817 he was made a member of the Medical Society of Philadelphia. He received the degree of M. D. from the University of Maryland in 1825. In 1809 he successfully performed the operation for extirpation of the ovary, the first on record, and acquired in consequence European celebrity. A description of this with other cases he published in the Philadelphia Eclectic Repertory and Analytic Review in 1817. He also acquired fame as a lithotomist. Dr. McDowell's account of his operations on the ovaries were received with incredulity in many places, especially abroad, but at this time his title to the name of 'the father of ovariotomy' is generally recognized. He was a man of culture and liberal views, and had he lived in a less primitive community might have obtained wealth and world-wide celebrity in his life-time. In person he was stout, nearly six feet in height, with a florid complexion and black eyes. He was one of the founders and an original trustee of Centre College, Danville, and a few months before his final illness began to build a large mansion near that town. On the 14th of May, 1879, a granite monument with a medallion of Dr. McDowell was erected to his memory, the memorial address being made by Dr. Samuel D. Gross of Philadelphia, before the Kentucky Medical Society. This is located near the center of Danville, in a public square known as 'McDowell Park.'"—Appleton's Cyclopedia of American Biography.

Dr. McDowell was thirty years old when he married Sarah, a daughter of Governor Shelby. Their only son, Wallace McDowell, is the father of Mrs. Florence Shelby, widow of the late Thomas H. Shelby, late collector of the Seventh District of Kentucky. One of his daughters married Major David C. Irvine of Madison County, Kentucky. The other members of his family married and moved from the state.

CYRUS MENANDER BROWN of Hopkinsville, ex-Sheriff and ex-Circuit Court Clerk of Christian County, and a prominent Republican politician, was born in Christian County February 26, 1850.

His father, Enoch A. Brown, was born in Georgia in 1805, came to Kentucky with his father in 1812 and settled on a farm twelve miles north of Hopkinsville. He was married in 1830 to Sallie Basher, who was born in South Carolina in 1809, and they lived together fifty-two years. He joined the Christian Church in 1831 under the preaching of Alexander Campbell, the founder of that denomination, and became a prominent local preacher. He distinguished himself particularly as the officiating minister at most of the marriages that occurred in the northern part of the county. He married one man twenty years after he had married his son, and twenty years later he married the son's son. It was a common saying that a wedding party was not complete without his presence. He was a man of very decided convictions and took an interest in politics, being a prominent Democrat prior to the war, a Union man during the war and then drifted into the Republican party. He was elected to the Legislature in 1863 and served with distinction until 1865. He died in 1882 and his wife died in 1884. They had ten children, five of whom survived their parents: Omar S. Brown, a farmer in the northern part of Christian County; Dr. M. D. Brown, a man of great ability and the only Democrat in the family, now residing in Anson, Jones County, Texas; Mrs. Onie J. Clark, wife of V. C.

Clark of Crofton, Christian County; Cyrus M. Brown, the subject of this sketch, and Mrs. Medoria S. Linn, of Emporia, Lyon County, Kansas, whose husband, now deceased, was a lawyer of eminence, a graduate of the Boston Law School; a soldier in the Twenty-fifth Kentucky Regiment commanded by General Shackelford; was a law partner with the late Senator Plumb of Kansas and had a brilliant prospect, but died at the early age of forty years. Albert E. Brown (brother) was in the Union army as second lieutenant, Company A, Twenty-fifth Kentucky V. I., and was killed at Shiloh, April 6, 1862.

Cyrus M. Brown was reared on his father's plantation and received a partial education prior to the war, which interfered with his schooling; but he pursued his studies with diligence although with difficulty, and at the age of eighteen he began teaching school and for ten years he taught and studied, at the same time attending to his duties on the farm. In 1880 he was elected sheriff of Christian County by the Republican party, receiving a majority of eight hundred and ten votes over his Democratic opponent; was re-elected in 1882, and in 1886, after an acrimonious contest, was elected clerk of the Circuit Court. He held that office for six years and four months and could have been re-elected, but declined to be a candidate; remained in his successor's office as deputy for one year, and was elected to the Legislature in November, 1895, having no opposition except the candidate of the Populists, Mr. R. C. Crushew, whom he beat 3,005 votes.

Mr. Brown has been a liberal contributor to the newspapers; is a fluent and forcible writer, an eloquent speaker and a man of great personal magnetism; has been a Mason since he was twenty-one years of age, frequently holding office in L. M. Cox Lodge, 527; has been a delegate to a number of Republican conventions, and is a wide-awake, enthusiastic politician and leader in his party.

DR. ROMULUS CULVER BIGGS of Ashland, son of William Biggs and Lucy Davis Biggs, was born in Greenup County, Kentucky, August 27, 1843. His father, William Biggs, was born in Montgomery County, October 19, 1800, and although ninety-five years of age, is now hale and hearty and in the possession of all his faculties. He removed to Greenup County when thirteen years of age, and at fourteen he was mail carrier from Greenupburg to Little Sandy Salt Works. When sixteen he was deputy sheriff of Greenup County. At that time the county embraced a very large area so that it was necessary for him to travel thousands of miles, mostly through an unsettled country, in the discharge of his duties, and this was accomplished on horseback. When eighteen he left home and went to boating on the Kanawha and Ohio Rivers, and for two years steered a keel boat on the river between Charleston and Louisville. He also worked in the salt works on the Kanawha and for a time traded in iron. He made his last trip to New Orleans, where he traded in flatboats in 1827 and quit the river. He returned to Greenup County and engaged in general merchandising, stock trading and farming. In everything in which he engaged he was successful, and he has accumulated a very large fortune. He owns the homestead in Greenup County, consisting of a tract of one thousand acres of land; the Waring farm of nine hundred acres in Greenup County, Kentucky; a blue grass farm of five hundred and seventy-five acres in Greenbrier County, West Virginia; two thousand acres of farm and timber lands in Arkansas; the Biggs House in Portsmouth, Ohio, and is a large stockholder in the Lexington and Big Sandy Railroad Company. When the Biggs House was opened in Portsmouth, Ohio, in 1872, the citizens of that city gave Mr. Biggs a handsome ovation and presented him with a gold-headed cane as an evidence of their appreciation of his enterprise.

At the advanced age of ninety-five years he attends personally to the transaction of all of his business; is well preserved mentally and physically and wears his years as lightly as most men of sixty. He spends most of his time with his son, G. N. Biggs, and his daughter, Mrs. Beardsley of Huntington, West Virginia, but continues to claim his residence in Greenup County, which is his voting place, and he never fails to go there to vote the Democratic ticket in all important elections. He was married to Lucy Davis, daughter of George W. Davis, October 12, 1837, and is the father of twelve children.

Romulus Culver Biggs was educated in the Greenup County schools, in Wesleyan College at Delaware, Ohio, and at Danville, Kentucky; attended the Medical College of Ohio at Cincinnati, and the Bellevue Hospital Medical College, New York, graduating in 1868. He began the practice of medicine at Coalton, Kentucky; was for some time in Greenup and Anderson Counties and located in Ashland in August, 1889, and is now one of the leading physicians of that place. He is a member of the Northeastern Kentucky Medical Association; is a Democratic voter, a highly respected citizen and a member of the Methodist Church.

He was united in marriage July 11, 1889, to Emma Frances Brown.

WILLIAM ADAIR M'DOWELL, son of Colonel Samuel McDowell and Anne Irvine, born on Shawnee river, in Mercer County, Kentucky, in 1795, died in Evansville, Indiana, in 1853. "He was educated at Washington College, Virginia, which he left to serve in the war of 1812. He studied medicine with his uncle, Ephraim McDowell, with whom he practiced after receiving his degree from the medical department of the University of Pennsylvania in 1818. He devoted much time to the study of pulmonary consumption, and the result of his chemical observations was published in a monograph entitled, 'A Demonstration of the Curability of Pulmonary Consumption' (Louisville, 1843)."—Appleton's Cyclopedia of American Biography.

MORRIS BALDAUF, a successful merchant of Henderson, was born in Bavaria, Germany, in 1836. He came to the United States, arriving in New York September 13, 1853. He came direct to Louisville and was a peddler of merchandise for three years, making his headquarters in the last named city. In 1856 he went to Hardinsburg, Breckinridge County, and formed a partnership with Louis Ichenhouser and engaged in general merchandising. He sold his interests there in 1860 and went to Cloverport and was a clerk in a store there until 1864, when he went to New Albany and joined his brother in the clothing business. They quit New Albany in 1866 and returned to Cloverport, where he and his brother opened a general store, which they successfully operated until 1878, when they removed to Henderson, and were partners until January 1, 1895, when his brother retired from the firm, leaving Morris Baldauf sole proprietor. He is a director in the Planters State Bank, and was a member of the City Council for one year, but resigned.

He was married in 1864 to Lena Kahn, and has four children: Julius, Minnie, Levi and Cora. His eldest son, Julius, is a graduate in pharmacy and chemistry, and is proprietor of the leading wholesale and retail drug store in Henderson. Levi, his second son, is a student in the Philadelphia College of Pharmacy.

Morris Baldauf is a son of Leopold and Ella Kahn Baldauf, natives of Bavaria. His father spent a good part of his life as a farmer, but was a merchant later in life, and was in moderate circumstances. Nathan H. Baldauf (grandfather) was a native of the same country, and a poor man, but honest and highly respected. Grandfather Kahn was an honest dairyman in Bavaria.

COLONEL SAMUEL M'DOWELL, son of Judge Samuel McDowell and Mary McClung, was born in Rockbridge, Virginia, in 1764. His tender years prevented him from going in the patriot army at the beginning of the Revolution. Before its close, however, he disappeared from home at the age of seventeen years, joined Lafayette as a private soldier in the final campaign against Cornwallis, remained with that command to the end of the struggle, which he witnessed at Yorktown, in the siege and fighting at which place he took a lively hand. He removed with his father's family to Mercer County, Kentucky, in 1784, there located and there continued to reside during the remainder of his honored life. In the defense of the district he saw frequent additional service as a soldier under General Charles Scott and General Hopkins. Washington gave another evidence of his confidence in and regard for the family by appointing him the first United States marshal for Kentucky when the state was organized in 1792. He was an ardent lover of his country, and his attachment to the Union, probably enhanced by the efforts of the Spanish clique to dissever Kentucky from the general government, was so inculcated in his family, that at the breaking out of the Civil war, of his eleven grandsons then living, nine were officers in the Union army, one being too infirm and the others too young to bear arms. This is the more remarkable where in Kentucky families were so divided.

JOHN LAWSON, familiarly known in Kentucky and along the western rivers as Captain Jack Lawson, an honored citizen of Paducah, now in his ninety-first year, has had a career as full of adventure, excitement and interest as it has been full of years. He made the first locomotive in England and ran it from Liverpool to Manchester, and after building a locomotive in the shops of the Stephenson Manufacturing Company in Liverpool for the first railroad built in America, he brought it to this country and attracted world-wide attention at that time. His career since that time has been one of unusual interest, a full account of which would necessarily embody much of the history of the United States.

Captain Lawson was born in Liverpool, England, August 18, 1805, and is a son of James and Sarah (Travis) Lawson, natives of that city. After obtaining a fairly good education in the schools of Liverpool he learned the trade of machinist, and while employed in that capacity built the first steam locomotive that was ever run in the world; and was employed as its engineer, running between Liverpool and Manchester.

After this he built an engine in the shops of the Stephenson Manufacturing Company in Liverpool for the little railroad from Baltimore to Green Springs, and was sent to this country by the manufacturers in charge of the engine, which he set up and engineered until his successor had learned how to run it. Three separate delegations were sent by the managers of the World's Fair to induce Captain Lawson to go to Chicago as their guest, but he declined the honor.

He was twenty-one years of age when he brought his locomotive to Baltimore; and was in that city about three years, when he went to Philadelphia and assisted in constructing the first locomotive built in the now celebrated Baldwin Locomotive Works, and rode it on its first trip to Germantown. After this he went to Petersburg, Virginia, and was for a time employed as engineer on the Petersburg & Roanoke River Railroad. His next stop was in Alabama, where he lived for three years, and was married to Emily Speed.

He became interested in the great avenues of commerce on the western rivers and embarked in the business of steamboating, and for over fifty years he traveled the waters of the Mississippi from New Orleans to the head of navigation, as well as all of the great tributaries of the "Father of Waters." He began his career on the river as an engineer, but he soon left the boiler deck to take command of the vessel, and afterward built and owned many of the finest boats on the river.

When the first railroad was built connecting Paducah with the outside world Captain Jack's experience was again called into requisition, and for a time he was an engineer on the new road. He returned to the river, however, as that means of transportation had not then been superseded by the railroad.

When the war came on he was the owner of a number of fine boats which he tendered to the authorities for the use of the Confederacy. Seven of his boats, lying in the Yazoo River, before the siege of Vicksburg, were in danger of being captured by the Union soldiers, and he burned them to prevent their falling into the hands of the enemy. He also built and fitted out the gunboat "General Polk," which met a similar fate. He then enlisted in the Third Kentucky Regiment and served as a private soldier in the Confederate army until the close of the war. He returned to steamboating after the war, and his operations were principally confined to the Cumberland River. He recuperated his fortune to some extent, but he never fully recovered his heavy losses incident to the war.

During President Cleveland's first term Captain Jack was appointed engineer of the government building in Paducah, the only office he ever held or sought, and is still holding this position,

CAPT. JOHN LAWSON.

He has been a citizen of Paducah for fifty-six years and of the United States for nearly seventy years, in which time he has seen many changes and has witnessed and assisted in the introduction of many improvements which have made a new world of the "new world" to which he came in his young manhood. He remembers with pride his first Presidential vote, which was for Andrew Jackson, and his adherence to the principles of "Old Hickory" has never been questioned. He is just as steadfast in his religious faith, being an honored member of the Presbyterian Church, and has been a Knight Templar.

He has entered the tenth decade of a most eventful and useful life, solitary and alone, his companion for sixty years having died October 16, 1891, and his three children having "gone before" in years long past. But aside from the tender family ties thus broken no man has more friends who wish him well, and these are ever ready to minister to his comfort.

Captain Lawson's parents were natives of England, who also lived in Liverpool. His mother died soon after he came to America, and his father lived to a great age and died about ten years ago. His grandfather, Robert Lawson, was also a native of England, and a highly respected citizen of Liverpool.

CHARLES LOUIS LOOS, President of the Kentucky University, Lexington, was born in Woerth, Department of the Lower Rhine (Alsace), France, December 22, 1823. His father, Jacques G. Loos, was born in the same place in 1795, and came to America in 1832 and located in Stark County, Ohio. In 1834 he sent for his family, who arrived in time to be with him only a few weeks before his death. His wife, Catherine Kull, was born in Bavaria in 1800. She survived him until 1868 and died in Allegheny, Pennsylvania.

Charles L. Loos remained in Stark County, Ohio, for seven years after his father's death, attending the public school, himself teaching at sixteen. He was reared in the Lutheran Church, but united with the Christian Church in 1838, and began to preach when only seventeen years of age. In 1842 he entered Bethany College in Virginia, an institution that was founded by Alexander Campbell, and graduated in the class of 1846. After finishing his studies he taught in the primary department of his alma mater for three years. He then went to Wellsburg, in the same county, and was preacher of the Christian Church at that place for one year.

His next charge was at Somerset, Pennsylvania, where he preached for five years, and during the last two years of his ministry there conducted a collegiate academy on his own responsibility, a school that was flourishing under his able management. He also edited for two years a religious monthly called The Disciple. In January, 1856, he was called to the First Christian, now the Central, Church on Ninth street, Cincinnati, Ohio. During his stay of one year in that city he was co-editor of the Christian Age, a weekly newspaper published by his denomination.

In January, 1857, he accepted the presidency of the college at Eureka, Illinois, where he remained nearly two years, serving as president of the college and as preacher of the Eureka congregation at the same time.

In the latter part of 1858 he returned to Bethany College as professor of ancient languages. For twelve years of this time he was preacher of the church at Bethany; for seven years co-editor of The Millennial Harbinger. He continued his labors there until June, 1880, when he accepted the presidency of the Kentucky University. This responsible position has enabled him to exercise his remarkable ability as an executive and to carry into practical utility his excellent theories in educational matters, and he has abundant compensation for his arduous labors in watching the steady growth of the university, not only in the increased attendance, but also in the high educational standard which it has gained and is maintaining under his able management.

Mr. Loos has been president of the Foreign Christian Missionary Society for a number of years, and has been a lifetime contributor to the leading journals of his denomination; is always ready, willing and able to preach the gospel; is a true and loyal citizen and independent voter;

and is above all devoted to the education of the youth and the elevation of society.

He was married in July, 1848, to Rosetta E. Kerr, daughter of Rev. John Kerr of Newry, Ireland. They were the parents of eleven children. Mrs. Loos died January 30, 1893, seven of her children surviving her: Charles, a teacher in the High School at Dayton, Ohio; William J., editor of the Christian Guide, published in Louisville, and a minister of the gospel; Oberline T., a farmer in the northwestern part of the State of Washington; Louisa L., wife of John M. L. Campbell of Detroit, Michigan; Emily K., wife of Dr. A. S. Dabney of Lexington, Kentucky; Frederic V., minister of the Christian Church at Liberty, Missouri, and Wilhelmina, who is at home with her father. Four children died before the mother, three in childhood, and Carrie D., wife of E. T. Williams, missionary in Nankin, China.

JOHN W. SCHNEIDER, a well known and successful promoter and business man of Newport, Kentucky, was born in that city December 31, 1851; and is a son of Adam and Catherine (Goller) Schneider.

Adam Schneider was a native of Gahans, Saxony, Germany, and emigrated from his native land to the United States in 1847, locating in Newport the same year. He followed the occupation of a stonemason in early life, but later was engaged in distilling and milling, and was a prominent and useful citizen, being for a time a member of the City Council. He was a member of the German Lutheran Church, and a faithful attendant until his death in 1885.

Catherine Goller Schneider was born in Bayreuth, Bavaria, in 1826, and is living in Newport at the present time.

John W. Schneider after leaving the public schools entered Nelson's Commercial College at Cincinnati at the age of thirteen years. He kept his father's books in the whiskey and flour business until he was seventeen years of age, and was next employed in the carpenter trade, at which he worked for one year; but he did not like that trade and gave it up to become a laborer for the Little Miami Railroad. This was a little too difficult for him and he went to St. Louis in the early part of 1870, where he was employed as bookkeeper in a hotel and grocery establishment. He remained there for four years, returning to Newport in 1875, where he accepted a position as car sealer for the Little Miami Railroad Company at Cincinnati. He was next employed as a solicitor for the Clay Fire & Marine Company. He was subsequently elected secretary of the Newport Stock Provision Mart; and July 1, 1875, accepted the position of bookkeeper in the First National Bank at Newport, which was opened for business on that day. While Mr. Schneider was still engaged in the bank he was elected treasurer of the Campbell County Building & Loan Association of Newport, and secretary of the Licking Valley Building Association; and February 1, 1878, was elected secretary of the German Mutual Fire Insurance Company of Covington; January 1, 1879, was elected member of the School Board; September 1, 1879, he was elected secretary of the Newport & Lick Turnpike Company; June 10, 1880, was elected secretary of the Newport Mutual Fire Insurance Company; Jan. 1, 1881, was elected treasurer of the Board of Education, and served until January, 1885; August 1, 1881, was elected treasurer of the Citizens' Building Association, and served until 1886, when the National was organized with Mr. Schneider as treasurer; August 10, 1882, was elected secretary of the Red Men's Hall Association; September 1, 1882, was elected secretary of the old State Road Company; in 1883, he received the charter for the Protestant Children's Home, and acted as secretary pro tem. in its organization, having been the organizer, but refused to act as permanent secretary or accept any position in the home.

He also organized the syndicate known as the Bellevue Improvement Company, with G. R. Harms as president and himself as secretary; the Orlando Land Company, with T. A. Widrig president; the Clifton Suburban Home & Building Company, with J. E. McCracken president; the South Covington Land Company, with M. T. Shine as president; organized the East Bellevue Lot Association in 1886, with B. H. Kroger president and C. W. Nagel secretary; organized the Glen Park Land Company in 1888, of which he was a director, and resigned January 1, 1891; organized the South Bellevue Land & Development Company in 1892; organized the Fort Thomas Land Company in 1893, with eight hundred and twenty-seven acres in the Highlands. In this latter enterprise George B. Kerper of Cincinnati acted as president.

It is needless to add that as a promoter and organizer Mr. Schneider stands without a rival, and no man could have accomplished what he has done if he had not enjoyed the confidence of the business community in the highest degree.

John W. Schneider and Bertha Hanke Utz were married August 26, 1875.

JOHN TRIMBLE, one of the most eminent and distinguished lawyers and jurists of his day, was born in Paris, Kentucky, December 4, 1783. He was liberally educated by an uncle who resided in the family, and at the age of nineteen he became private secretary to Robert Evans, then territorial governor of Indiana. Young Trimble remained in this capacity at Vincennes, at that time capital of the Territory of Indiana, when he returned to Kentucky and became a student at law in the office of Colonel George Nicholas, who at that time was one of the greatest jurists in the country. Judge Trimble practiced law from 1807 to 1862; was then appointed circuit judge and removed to Cynthiana; resigned that office and was immediately appointed by Governor Desha, on January 15, 1825, third judge of the New Court of Appeals, which he held for a short time and resigned. In May, 1826, he was tendered the United States judgeship for the District of Kentucky by President J. Q. Adams, but ill-health prevented his acceptance. He was a representative in the Kentucky Legislature in 1826-33-35; was a strong advocate of the proposed railroad from Charleston to Cincinnati, which excited the opposition of his party, and was never a candidate again. His death occurred July 9, 1852, at Cynthiana. He was an able lawyer and few could cope with him in arguing an abstract question of law depending on principle. He was as noble as a citizen and as true as a friend as he was able as a lawyer. Few knew the general variety of his knowledge and the scope of his critical judgment.

His father was William Trimble, who emigrated to Kentucky and settled in Clark County in 1780, not far from Boonsboro.

Robert Trimble, a brother of John—and for whom Trimble County was named—was born in Berkeley County, Virginia, in 1777; read law under George Nicholas until the death of Nicholas, when he finished his studies in the office of James Brown; was licensed to practice before the Court of Appeals in 1803, and in the same year was elected to the Legislature from Bourbon County. He cared little for politics and later in life refused to become a candidate for the United States Senate, preferring to devote his time to his profession. In 1808 he was commissioned second judge of the Court of Appeals; in 1810 was appointed chief justice of Kentucky, but on account of limited means he declined to accept the first judicial position of the Commonwealth. After retiring from the bench he again took up the practice of law, and in 1813 was appointed United States district attorney for the state. In 1816 he was appointed by President Madison United States judge for the District of Kentucky and filled this office until 1826, when he was promoted by President J. Q. Adams to the Supreme bench of the United States. He died August 25, 1828. Judge Trimble studied law as a principle and comprehended it as a science. In 1818 the sole professorship of law in Transylvania University, which was tendered him by the board and his acceptance urged by Mr. Clay, but he declined. Chief Justice Marshall and Judge Storey pronounced him to be not only of the first lawyers, but one of the most profound men they had ever known. His private virtues and his simple, noble nature were above all that which were derived from great intellect and lofty station.

William W. Trimble was a son of John and Eliza (Porter) Trimble and was born in Cynthiana, Kentucky, December 31, 1821, and was educated at Danville and under the private instruction of his father, who took a great interest in his education. His uncle, Robert Macmillan, was a professor in a college in Edinburgh, Scotland, who came to America, and studied with him, along with his brothers Robert, John and James, who became probably the best educated men in the state. William W. Trimble commenced the practice of law at Cynthiana, where he remained for about twenty years, when in 1873 he removed to Covington. He attended solely to the practice of his profession and was one of the best informed men in law and the general literature of his day. He was an ardent Republican, a Mason and an Episcopalian. He married Mary Barlow, daughter of Martin Barlow and Frances (Cantrell) Barlow. Her parents died when she was young, and was reared in the family of Colonel Joseph Cantrell of Bourbon. Six children were born to Martin Barlow and Frances Cantrell: Fannie, wife of George Fackler, of New York City; Kate, wife of Edward J. Woolsey of the same city; Helen, wife of Arthur Highton of London, England; William Pitt, who was educated at Frankfort-on-the-Main, where he graduated, and at the Cincinnati Law School, and is now practicing law at Seattle, Washington; Robert, who was educated at Harvard and Kenyon College, Ohio, and Lawrence, who died in early youth.

James Barlow, a cousin of Mrs. W. W. Trimble's father, was one of the greatest inventors in the state. He invented the planitarium, the most useful and complete astronomical apparatus in the world.

Judge William W. Trimble was the author of Trimble's Kentucky Digest, which is now used in the Cincinnati Law School as a text book. The judge died August 31, 1886, and is buried at Cynthiana.

HENRY CLAY M'DOWELL, son of William Adair McDowell and Maria Hawkins Harvey, born in Fincastle, Virginia, in 1832, coming to Kentucky in 1839, when his father returned to his native state. He graduated at the Louisville Law School and won his way to a successful practice in the profession, being for some years a partner of his brother-in-law, Judge Bland Ballard. He was among the earliest in Kentucky to take up arms for the Union on the breaking out of the Civil war, and was commissioned by Mr. Lincoln as assistant adjutant general and served on the staff of General Rosecrans and General Boyle. He was afterwards commissioned by Mr. Lincoln as United States marshal for Kentucky, being the same office, for the same state, held by his grandfather, Colonel Samuel McDowell, under commission of General Washington. He married Anne Clay, daughter of Lieutenant Colonel Henry Clay, who was killed at the battle of Buena Vista, and having purchased the farm of "Ashland," the home of her grandfather, Henry Clay, he there resides, devoting himself to agricultural pursuits, and giving some attention to the Lexington & Eastern Railway Co., of which he is president. In politics he was first a Whig and then a Republican.

SAMUEL B. CALDWELL, one of the most prominent, enterprising and really public-spirited citizens of Paducah, was born in Henry County, Tennessee, November 2, 1824. He was only three months old when his parents removed to Galloway County, Kentucky. His father was an industrious farmer, and the doctor shared the labors of the farm, when he would have preferred the privileges of the schoolroom. He was virtually educated between the plow handles; but he was not inclined to follow agricultural pursuits, and prepared himself for professional life by reading and studying on Sundays and rainy days. He found this a difficult and narrow way; but by persistent effort and close application to his studies, he acquired a good primary education. He was blind for three years on account of ophthalmia and went to St. Louis, Missouri, to have his eyes treated by Dr. Van Sant, and while under his care began the study of medicine with a view of becoming an oculist; but with the restoration of his sight he went to the University of Missouri and took one course in the medical department of that institution in 1854-5. From that time until 1870 he was a very successful practitioner, after which, becoming interested in numerous enterprises, he gradually gave up his profession, giving more attention to real estate and its improvement.

He has been the land purchasing agent and investor for the Norton Brothers for a number of years, making for them many valuable investments in the "Purchase" and in other parts of the state and in other states, and is now interested in large tracts of farm, timber, iron, lead and coal lands in Hopkins County. Besides numerous other enterprises, Dr. Caldwell is largely interested in and prominently connected with several leading local ventures and investments, among which is the West End Improvement Company, of which he is president. This company was organized in 1891 and owns one hundred and sixteen acres, adjacent to the City of Paducah and lying on both sides of the Broadway extension, containing some attractive residences, his own among the rest. This tract of ground is platted into about four hundred lots, and is valued at $50,000.

He is a large stockholder in and president of the General Electric Light & Power Company and a director in the Paducah Electric Street Railway Company, whose lines run through the property of the West End Improvement Company to La Belle Park; was the promoter of and is a stockholder in the Paducah Fair and Exposition Association; is director and stockholder in the Paducah and Lovelaceville Gravel Road Company; a large stockholder in the Palmer House, in the Paducah Furnace Company, in the Paducah Wheel Stock Company, in the Paducah Peanut Company, the Paducah Building & Loan Association, the Kentucky Building & Loan Association, together with other enterprises and industries, all of which are for the promotion of the general good of the city. Although past three score and ten, Dr. Caldwell is one of the most active, energetic and enterprising men in the community in which he lives.

A man of high moral and religious character, beloved and highly respected by all who know him, and stands pre-eminently one of the first citizens of Paducah. He has been liberal in his support of the cause of religion, and there is not an evangelical denomination in Paducah that has not been benefited by his subscriptions. By these and kindred actions he has endeared himself to the people of Paducah and made for himself a name which will survive him many years, and his work and exemplary life will be held up as an example to future generations.

Dr. Caldwell was married in 1856 to Elizabeth Napier of Boyle County, Kentucky. They had four children, two of whom are living: Mary E. Caldwell and S. B. Caldwell, Jr., born June 1, 1860; educated in Paducah and at Hustonville College; admitted to the bar in 1883, and is a practicing attorney at the Paducah bar.

Dr. Caldwell's father, John L. Caldwell, was born in South Carolina in 1800. He came to Kentucky with his parents in 1806, and lived in Warren County until 1820, when he married Myra Morgan, a native of North Carolina, and in 1823, removed to Henry County, Tennessee. He remained there two years, and in 1825 removed to Callaway County and to McCracken County in 1834, subsequently going to Illinois in 1843, where he died in 1863. His father, Matthew Caldwell, was related to John C. Calhoun.

Myra Morgan Caldwell's father was a native of North Carolina, who removed to Kentucky in 1806. He was of Scotch-Irish extraction. Her maternal grandfather, Charles Richardson, a native of North Ireland, was a soldier in the Revolutionary War.

CHARLES JACOB BRONSTON, at present State Senator from the county of Fayette, was born in Richmond, Madison County, Kentucky, July 29, 1848. He is the only child of Thomas S. and Sallie A. (Bronston) Bronston. His father was a native of Fayette County, but spent most of his life in Madison County, where, equipped with a common school education, tireless energy and sterling honesty, he became a leader both in public as a politician, and in private as a citizen; also becoming one of the three founders of the Christian Church in that county. Thomas S. Bronston was a son and namesake of Thomas S. Bronston, a native of Chambersburg, Pennsylvania, who was a brother of Jacob Bronston (maternal grandfather), who was a Madison County farmer and trader and one of the pioneer preachers in the Christian Church in that county. Sallie A. Bronston (mother), was also a native of Madison County. Thomas S. Bronston (father) was assistant secretary of state during the term, 1875-9, that Governor James B. McCreary was the chief executive of Kentucky, and was collector of internal revenue for the Eighth district during Grover Cleveland's first administration. He died December 17, 1890, at the age of seventy-four years.

Charles J. Bronston obtained his early education at a public school in his native county, and completed it at Kentucky University, Lexington, Kentucky, graduating in 1869 with the highest honors of his class, of which he was valedictorian. One year later he took a special course in the study of law at the University of Virginia, having as preceptor that prince of law teachers, John B. Minor, who died within the last two years. Soon after obtaining a license to practice, he became a law partner of Hon. James B. McCreary, afterwards governor of Kentucky, and who for ten years has been and is now congressman from the Eighth district. At the age of twenty-six Mr. Bronston married Susie Wallace Hughes, daughter of William T. Hughes, of Fayette County. His wife died May 14, 1891, leaving six children, three girls and three boys. In 1879 he was elected commonwealth's attorney for the district composed of Madison, Fayette, Clark, Bourbon, Scott, Woodford and Jessamine, soon after his election removing to Lexington, where he has since resided. He held this position until Fayette County became a separate district, the Twenty-second Judicial, when he was again elected without opposition to the same office, holding it altogether for fifteen years, when he resigned to accept a seat in the state senate as the representative from the county of Fayette.

As a prosecutor, he was extremely vigorous, regardless of the social standing, race or color of the defendant. He has been employed to assist in prosecuting in criminal cases of great aggravation in various parts of the state.

When the constitutional convention met in September, 1890, Mr. Bronston sat in the convention as the representative from the city of Lexington. Though one of the youngest members of that body, he at once took rank with the leaders, men skilled in common, parliamentary and constitutional law, and possibly had more to do with the present condition of the organic law of the state than any other member of the convention. He is now a member of the state senate and his achievements as a leader of the Democratic party in that most memorable senatorial contest are too well known to require any further mention. He has always been an ardent supporter of the principles of Democracy, firmly believing that the future welfare and happiness of the great mass of the common people depends on the ultimate triumph of the tenets promulgated by the great leaders of Democracy. All of the political offices that have fallen to Mr. Bronston's lot, virtually won without opposition, have been filled with honor to his state and with credit to himself. One of his enthusiastic friends says of him: "As a lawyer, statesman and orator, he has won a national reputation, and as a man of general ability stands second to none of Kentucky's great sons. In his opposition to an avowed enemy he is relentless, for a tried and true friend he knows no sacrifice too great."

BENJAMIN F. PROCTER, Attorney-at-Law of Bowling Green, son of Thomas L. S and Agnes H. (Carson) Procter, was born in Logan County, Kentucky, near South Union, November 26, 1849. His father was born near Winchester, Kentucky, and when nine years of age removed with his father's family to Logan County, where he subsequently became a farmer and mill-owner and a highly-respected citizen and a prominent member of the Baptist Church. He died at the age of seventy-three years in 1881.

Benjamin Procter (grandfather) was a Virginian, who came to Kentucky when he was a young man, settled near Winchester, and thence moved to Logan County, where he became a farmer. He was a captain of militia, a prominent citizen of the county, and died in Logan County in 1853, aged seventy years. His ancestors were of English descent, and were a race of lawyers.

Agnes H. Carson Procter (mother) was a native of Butler County, Kentucky; died in Logan County in 1870 at the age of fifty-six years.

Thomas Carson (grandfather) was a native of Virginia, who came to Kentucky in the early part of the century and settled near Morgantown, where he led the life of a farmer. He married a Miss Dinwiddie of Virginia.

Benjamin F. Procter was educated in the common schools of Logan County and at Bethel College, and after leaving school read law and was admitted to the bar in 1873. In the same year he located in Bowling Green, and in 1874 was elected corporation counsel for the city; was re-elected for two consecutive terms, and from 1884 to 1887 served as Warren Circuit Court Commissioner. He has never held any other public office, and has not asked any other favor of the public or of his party, preferring to give his undivided attention to his profession, which requires all of his time, and in which he has been highly successful. During the past several years he has given especial attention to corporation law, in which branch he has as large a practice as any lawyer in Southern Kentucky. He has accumulated considerable property, including valuable real estate in Bowling Green. His father was at one time quite wealthy, but lost his fortune during the Civil War, so that Mr. Procter had to look out for himself at an early age. He is one of the most courteous men, and a typical Kentucky gentleman.

He was married in 1876 to Lila Pendleton, daughter of Rev. Dr. J. M. Pendleton, of Upland, Pennsylvania. They are members of the Baptist Church, and have a high social standing in Bowling Green.

DR. ROBERT STUART, a prominent physician of Henderson, was born in Shelby County, Kentucky, December 1, 1837; son of Olivia (Hall) and Rev. David Todd Stuart. His father, David T. Stuart, was born in the parsonage attached to Walnut Hill Church (near Lexington) July 27, 1812; took the degree of A. B. in Transylvania University at the age of twenty years. In 1832 he entered Princeton, N. J., and studied the regular course of theology. At the request of Rev. William L. Breckinridge he passed the summer of 1836 in preaching at the Fourth Presbyterian Church, Louisville, Kentucky, where he formed the acquaintance of Miss Olivia W. Hall, whom he subsequently married.

He preached for fifteen years to the churches of Shiloh and Olivet in Shelby County. In June, 1851, he removed to Shelbyville and took charge of the Shelbyville Female College, where he continued until his death, September 26, 1868. Eleven children were born to him, viz.: Robert, Winchester, John, Theodore, David T., Isabella, Amelia, Mary Lou, Maggie, Florence and Annie.

Rev. Robert Stuart (grandfather) was of Irish-Scotch parentage, and was born in Virginia; received a collegiate and theological training at Hampden Sidney, and came to Kentucky before the beginning of the nineteenth century. In 1798 he was elected one of the first three professors of Transylvania University, and held the position of professor of languages for a number of years.

For more than half a century he filled the pulpit of the Walnut Hill Church, Fayette County, Kentucky. The degree of D. D. conferred upon him was merited by his learning and long service. He died at the age of eighty-four years in Nicholasville, Kentucky. His wife, Hannah Todd, a member of one of the best families of Lexington, died in 1832. They had eight children.

Dr. Robert Stuart attended his junior year in Center College in 1855. In 1857 he graduated from Jefferson College, Cannonsburg, Pennsylvania. He attended one course of lectures in the Kentucky School of Medicine, Louisville, Kentucky, and graduated from the Jefferson School of Medicine, Philadelphia, Pa., in the spring of 1860.

He first practiced his profession in Yelvington, Daviess County, Kentucky, where he made the acquaintance of Miss Susan E. Read of Owensboro, Kentucky, a most beautiful and accomplished woman, to whom he was united in marriage May 8, 1861. In February, 1862, he accepted the position of assistant surgeon in the Second Kentucky Cavalry, and served in that capacity until the summer of 1863, when he was compelled to resign on account of impaired health. He was present at the battle of Shiloh, being detailed to accompany the Louisville Legion on the field and attend to their wounded. He was also present at the battles of Stone River and Perryville, Kentucky, and accompanied his regiment in the march of Buell's legions in the pursuit of Bragg's army to Louisville and back again to Tennessee.

After returning from the war he settled in Henderson County, Kentucky, and practiced his profession for more than twenty years at Zion, a quiet village six miles from the city of Henderson.

On December 19, 1891, he had the misfortune to lose his faithful wife after a long and painful illness—one of earth's purest and brightest jewels. In 1893 he removed to Henderson, where he is at present located; is a member of a number of medical societies; elder in the First Presbyterian Church and a citizen of high standing. He is the father of six children: Robert, Benjamin, Annie, Alice W., Mary and Susan Elizabeth.

THOMAS HUNT STUCKY, M. D., a prominent physician of Louisville, son of Harry Stucky and Sallie (Sweeney) Stucky, was born in Louisville March 21, 1860. His father, one of the best known citizens of Louisville, was born in Jefferson County, Kentucky, September 19, 1827. He was brought up on his father's farm and received a good common school education. In 1846 he went to Louisville and entered the office of the clerk of the County Court and served as first deputy clerk for eight years. In 1861 he was elected city auditor and in 1862 was elected clerk of the Louisville Chancery Court, and after serving one term of six years, declined a re-election. In 1869 he was elected secretary and treasurer of the board of directors of the sinking fund. He held that office eight years and resigned, since which time he has been acting as commissioner and general trustee and assignee in the settlement of estates, a business in which his services are much in demand. In 1878 he was elected alderman from the sixth ward and served the city in that capacity for sixteen years, consecutively, being re-elected every two years, and generally without opposition. He declined another election, although he could have held that office indefinitely, as he was one of the few men in the general council who were above reproach and concerning whom no suspicion of unfair dealing ever entered the minds of his constituents.

He was married in December, 1856, to Sallie K. Sweeney, daughter of Rev. Joseph A. Sweeney, of Virginia. They are the parents of Dr. Joseph A. Stucky, of Lexington, whose biography is given briefly herewith; Dr. Thomas Hunt Stucky, the subject of this sketch, and Virginia Stucky, who is much younger than her brothers and is at home with her parents.

Frederick Stucky (grandfather) was born in Jefferson County, Kentucky, in 1801, and was a resident and farmer of his native county nearly all of his life, but died in Owen County, Indiana, in 1893, where he had been living for some time with a son. Although he reached the advanced age of ninety-two years, he retained all of his faculties until the last day of his life. His wife, Louisa Myers, was born in Jefferson County, Kentucky, in 1815, and died in 1882. His father, who was the great-grandfather of the Doctors Stucky, was a native of Maryland, who came to Kentucky, and was one of the earliest pioneers of Jefferson County. The Stucky family is of Swiss origin.

Dr. Thomas Hunt Stucky completed his studies in the Louisville high school at a very early age and in 1876 he went to Bethany College, West Virginia, an institution that was founded by Alexander Campbell; returned to Louisville in 1878 and read medicine with Dr. David Cummins, one of the ablest and most distinguished physicians of Louisville, at the same time attending the Hospital College of Medicine, from which he graduated in 1880, when twenty years of age. He then took post graduate courses in Bellevue Medical College, New York, and at Strausberg and Leipsic, Germany, making special studies in the latter two schools in pathology and surgery.

In 1882 he returned to Louisville and settled down to the practice of his profession. He gave especial attention to diseases of the digestive organs, but attended to a general practice, in which he soon became one of the leading physicians among a city full of doctors, some of whom enjoyed a national reputation. While others have been passing away, Dr. Stucky has steadily grown in popular favor and has to-day no superior in the medical profession.

During the past ten years he has been connected with the Hospital College of Medicine and occupies at present the chair of theory and practice and clinical medicine in that college. He is a member of the principal medical associations, including the American Medical Association, the Mississippi Valley Medical Association, the Kentucky State Medical Society, the Tri-State Medical Association, the Mitchell (Indiana) Medical Society, the Medical Chirurgical Association of Louisville and the Jefferson County Medical Association. He is also a member of several benevolent orders, including the Chosen Friends, the Royal Arcanum and is a thirty-second degree Mason. He is a baseball enthusiast and is president of the Louisville club, and in spite of the ups and downs of that storm-tossed aggregation, he has managed to steer it clear of the breakers.

Dr. Stucky's grandparents and their parents were members of the Methodist Church, but he and his father's family belong to the Christian Church.

Dr. Stucky was married in 1883 to Laura Prewitt, daughter of Levi Prewitt, of Fayette County, and his excellent wife is one of the most charming ladies in Louisville society.

JOSEPH ADDISON STUCKY, M. D., one of the most successful physicians of Lexington, son of Harry and Sallie Kemp (Sweeney) Stucky, was born in Jefferson County, Kentucky, September 6, 1858. His ancestry is given in the foregoing sketches of his father, Harry Stucky, and his brother, Dr. Thomas Hunt Stucky.

Dr. J. A. Stucky was educated in the Louisville high school; studied medicine with Dr. J. M. Bodine, of Louisville, and Dr. W. O. Sweeney, of Lexington; attended the medical department of the University of Louisville, from which he graduated in 1878; located in Lexington, and began the practice of his profession, in which he was eminent as a general practitioner until 1885, when he began to confine his practice to the treatment of diseases of the ear, nose and throat, to which specialty he has given his attention with remarkable success. There are few more skillful physicians and surgeons in the country and in the line to which he has given his special attention he has few equals and no superiors.

Dr. Stucky is a member of the International Medical Congress; ex-president of the American Rhinological Society; member of the Kentucky State Medical Society; of the Lexington and Fayette County Medical Society; of the American Medical Association and fellow of the American Laryngological, Rhinological and Otological Society. He was for five years surgeon for the Chesapeake & Ohio Railroad Company; lectures before the training schools in the Protestant Infirmary and St. Joseph's Hospital; takes a very active interest in the Young Men's Christian Association, being a member of the state executive committee and ex-president of the State Association; is an influential and industrious member of the Christian Church, and keeps his politics in line with his religious profession by voting the Prohibition ticket. He is a man of strong convictions, and has the moral courage to stand up for what he believes to be right and to oppose what he conceives to be wrong. His sincerity and his exemplary life and gentlemanly deportment have distinguished Dr. Stucky as a man of influence for whom the people in the community have the highest regard.

Dr. Stucky was married in 1881 to Nellie McGarvey, daughter of Professor J. W. McGarvey, of Lexington. They have three sons and two daughters living: John McGarvey, William Sweeney, Lillie E., Harry Clarke and Nellie McGarvey.

SAMUEL P. HAGER, of Ashland, son of Daniel and Violet (Porter) Hager, was born in Floyd County, May 22, 1834. He has a very interesting record of the history of his father's family going back nearly one hundred and fifty years. John Hager, the elder, was born in Hesse Cassel, Germany, December 28, 1759, and came to America under peculiar circumstances. He was one of the drafted soldiers sent from Germany to aid the English in the Revolutionary War; but on his arrival upon the scene of conflict, he deserted and entered the Federal army and served under Gen. Sumter until the close of the war. He settled in Lynchburg, Virginia, and afterwards moved to Amherst County, Virginia. There he married Mary Schrader, a native of Virginia, in 1785; removed to Kentucky in 1806 and settled at the mouth of Beaver Creek, Floyd County; removed to the mouth of John's Creek, where he died in February, 1819. His wife died in 1847. They had seven children: John, George, William, Elizabeth, Henry, James M. and Daniel.

Daniel Hager (father) was born in Amherst County, Virginia, November 15, 1801; came to Floyd County with his father's family in 1806.

They settled near the mouth of Beaver Creek on the Big Sandy and later at the mouth of John's Creek, where he received his schooling and was engaged in farming until 1840; in 1843 he purchased the Hayden farm on Sandy River, in Johnson County, and in 1845 removed his family to that place; in 1852 he removed to Paintsville, where he was engaged in merchandising and in the hotel business until 1858, when he removed to his farm, where he resided until 1871, when he again removed to Paintsville, where he died July 5, 1887, aged eighty-six years, having been for many years a member of the Methodist Church. He was the first sheriff of Johnson County (1844); was a member of the legislature in 1845-6; for a number of years before the Civil War, he held a commission as brigadier-general and commander-in-chief of all the militia in eastern Kentucky, a district comprising fifteen counties; was a southern sympathizer and spent nearly all of his time in Virginia during the Civil War. He was a man of great strength of character and a good citizen. He was a lifelong Democrat, having voted for General Jackson in 1824.

Violet Porter Hager (mother) was born in Russell County, Virginia, February 4, 1804; married Daniel Hager, January 31, 1822; died in Paintsville, February 22, 1879, aged seventy-three years. She was of Scotch-Irish descent. They were the parents of twelve children, six sons and six daughters: John Jackson, Henry George, William James, Mary Jane, Martha Ann, Amanda Burns, Samuel Patton, Emily Elizabeth, Daniel Marion, Louisa, Benjamin Franklin and Violet Vertrees.

Samuel P. Hager received such education as was afforded at that time in country schools. Having left school in 1852 he entered his father's store at Paintsville and worked for him until 1856, when he began business in a small way for himself. In 1857 his brother-in-law, William Stafford, was admitted as a partner, the style of the firm being Hager & Stafford. In the fall of that year they sold out the store and Mr. Hager went to Tinney's Grove in Ray County, Missouri, where he engaged in the business of merchandising, continuing until April, 1859, when he returned to Paintsville. During the war he owned a steamboat in partnership with his brother Henry and others, which they operated on the Big Sandy and Ohio rivers. In 1865 he sold his interest in the steamboat and resumed the mercantile business in Paintsville at a time when prices were falling as rapidly as they had risen from 1862 to 1864, and when a majority of beginners in business failed. But by hard labor and close attention to business he soon became the leading merchant and one of the most successful business men of the place.

In 1881 he sold a half interest in his store to his brother, Daniel M., and removed to Ashland, Kentucky, where he now resides.

He has been in the insurance business since 1886. Is senior member of the firm of Hager & Hager at Ashland City, and also of the firm of S. P. Hager & Bro. at Paintsville, Kentucky. He is a stockholder in a number of enterprises in Ashland, of which city he is one of the most enterprising citizens.

He is vice-president of the Merchants' National Bank; director in the Ashland & Catlettsburg Street Railroad Company and was one of the originators of the enterprise, and is a prominent Mason, having filled the chairs in his lodge, chapter and commandery, and is at present Eminent Commander of Ashland Commandery No. 28.

During the war Mr. Hager was a Union man, and in this respect differed from his father's sentiments. He is a Democrat in politics, but takes no active part in the affairs of his party, never having offered himself as a candidate for office, though frequently solicited to do so. He is a member in the highest standing of the Methodist Episcopal Church, South.

Mr. Hager was married November 21, 1860, to Angie R. Brown, daughter of Judge Thomas S. Brown, of Johnson County. She was born in Johnson County April 4, 1844; and they have four children living: William C., born August 31, 1861; Harry H., born March 19, 1864; Edgar, born December 7, 1861; John S., born January 14, 1871. Two children are deceased: Frederick, born April 9, 1866, died September 9, 1870; Paul V., born August 11, 1873, died November 2, 1875.

William C. is a member of the firm of Hager & Hager; married Ida Lady, daughter of Daniel Lady, May 15, 1884, and they have three chil-

JUDGE JOSEPH H. LEWIS.

dren, named Adah, Hazel and Mary Elizabeth. Harry H. is cashier of the Oxley Stave Company, Chattanooga, Tennessee; married Lizzie Hampton, daughter of Charles Hampton, of Catlettsburg, March 18, 1889; his wife died within two years after marriage and her only child died about a year later. Edgar received a collegiate education in the Kentucky Wesleyan College, Millersburg, graduating in 1888; studied law in the law department of Boston University, graduating in June, 1892; was admitted to the bar in August, 1892, and is now a practitioner at the Ashland bar. John S. is a graduate of the Kentucky Wesleyan College, Millersburg, and is assistant cashier of the Merchants' National Bank of Ashland.

HONORABLE JOSEPH H. LEWIS, one of the most distinguished judges of the Kentucky Court of Appeals, who was commander of the famous Orphans' Brigade in the Civil war, was born in the southern part of Barren County, Kentucky, October 29, 1824.

His father, John Lewis, was a native of Mercer County, Kentucky, and after reaching manhood removed to Barren County, where he engaged in farming. He was a volunteer in the War of 1812, and fought under General Jackson in the battle of New Orleans. He belonged to a family noted for longevity and was eighty-four years of age at the time of his death in 1876. Before the war he was considered a wealthy man, but the ravages of war left him without property and he left no estate.

Joseph Lewis (grandfather) was a Virginian by birth, who removed to Mercer County before Kentucky was admitted to the Union of states, and was prominently identified with the early development of the state. The Lewis family is of French origin. The ancestors, leaving France, first went to Wales and thence to the United States, settling in Virginia.

Judge Lewis' mother, Eliza Martz Reed Lewis, was a daughter of Lewis Reed, who was a native of New Jersey. He removed to Philadelphia, and subsequently became a resident of Henderson County, Kentucky, where he died.

Joseph H. Lewis went to Centre College, Danville, from which institution he was graduated in 1843, at the age of nineteen years. He read law in the office of Judge C. C. Tompkins, and was duly admitted to the bar in Glasgow in 1845, and at once entered upon the practice of his profession in that city. In 1850 he was elected to the legislature on the Whig ticket; was re-elected in 1851 and 1853, and took an active part in the important work of the sessions. He remained in the Whig party until the "Know-Nothing" craze, when he identified himself with the Democratic party.

In September, 1861, he volunteered his services in the Confederate army and was commissioned colonel of the Sixth Regiment of Kentucky Infantry, and remained in command of that regiment until after the battle of Chickamauga, when he was promoted to the rank of general for meritorious conduct upon the battlefield. He then took command of the famous Orphans' Brigade, and was conspicuous in the later battles until the close of the war. He was a brave and fearless soldier and inspired his men with the courage and daring which made his brigade so famous. He was in the thickest of the fight at Shiloh, Jackson and Vicksburg, and in all of the hard-fought engagements from Dalton to Atlanta, and in the siege of Savannah. After the surrender he returned to his home in Glasgow and resumed the practice of law; was re-elected to the legislature in 1868, and was made chairman of the committee on education.

In 1870 he was elected to Congress from the then Third district to fill a vacancy for one year, and at the next general election he was returned for a full term, so that he served three years in the United States House of Representatives.

In 1880 General Lewis was elected Circuit Judge of his district, but soon resigned this office to become a candidate for judge of the Court of Appeals, and was elected to fill an unexpired term, caused by the death of Judge M. H. Coper, since which time he has been twice re-elected and has served on the appellate bench continuously for over thirteen years.

Judge Lewis has been twice married. His first wife was Sarah Rogers, daughter of Dr. George Rogers of Glasgow. She died in 1858, leaving two children: John Lewis, who is in business in

Glasgow; and Eliza, wife of S. H. Burnham, now residing in Lincoln, Nebraska.

He was married the second time in 1883 to Cassandra F., widow of I. P. Johnson, daughter of General Thompson B. Flournoy of Arkansas.

SCYON AMBLER BASS, a leading Attorney-at-Law of Russellville, son of Scyon M. and Mary (Chick) Bass, was born in Butler County, Kentucky, March 15, 1855.

His father was born in Nelson County, Tennessee, August 28, 1827; was educated in the common schools and became a farmer in his native county, where he remained until 1867, when he removed to Butler County, Kentucky, and engaged in the same business. A few years ago he removed to Auburn, Logan County, where he is now living. He has always been a stock trader, making a specialty of fine horses, and is still interested in this branch of his business. He has been a prominent Democrat, but never an office-seeker; is a high Mason and a member of the Methodist Episcopal Church, South. He was married in 1846 to Mary Chick, who was born in Virginia, March 15, 1823. She removed with her parents to Tennessee when she was quite young and was educated in the latter state. The children of Scyon M. and Mary (Chick) Bass were:

Thadeus, born December 10, 1847, now a farmer in Logan County; married a Miss Stanley.

Corilla, born in 1849; married John C. Phaland, and is now residing at Auburn.

Perlina, born in 1853; was the wife of Virgil Gray, who was a member of General John H. Morgan's cavalry in the late war. They both died in 1872.

Scyon Ambler, born March 15, 1855, subject of this sketch.

Mary Frances, born in 1857, now the wife of Joseph S. Ray, residing at Auburn.

Scyon Bass (grandfather) was a native of North Carolina; removed to Silver Springs, Tennessee, where he was a merchant for more than fifty years. His home was within a few miles of that of President Jackson. He was a Whig of decided convictions; a member of the Baptist Church, and a highly esteemed citizen of his county. He married Mary Ragland, and was the father of six children: Solomon; Harmon, born in 1814, and died at the age of eighty years; Cader, whose home is Tennessee; Scyon M. (father); Julia and Polly.

Scyon Bass (great-grandfather) was born August 1, 1781, and died August 28, 1847. He was married three times—first to Miss Brantley, a native of Halifax Court House, Virginia, who was the mother of one son, Bennett Bass. After the death of his first wife he married her sister, who was the mother of Solomon Bass. His third wife was Mary Perry, who was born in Virginia, July 3, 1789, and died May 18, 1857. Her children were Harmon, who died at the age of eighty-four years; Hetty, who married Kemp, and Harrison died at the age of eighteen years; Cader, born in 1818; Julia, born in 1822; Scyon M., born August 8, 1825; Harriet and Almeta died when young; Turner and Lucretia.

Solomon Bass (great-great-grandfather) was a native of France, who emigrated to America and settled in Virginia, and was the father of six children: Scyon, Jones, Cader, Oren, Nancy, Hearta. The sons of Solomon Bass were born in Virginia and all of them removed to Tennessee, where they died.

Ambler Chick (maternal grandfather) was born in Virginia in 1795. He removed to Tennessee as early as 1820, where he owned a plantation and was largely engaged in the cultivation of cotton, owning a large number of negroes. In 1852 he removed to Logan County, Kentucky, and raised large crops of tobacco and wheat. He married Mary Ragland (also the name of the wife of grandfather, Scyon Bass, but probably not related), who was born and educated in Virginia. Their children were Burril, Judeth, John, Pettis, Davis, William, Virginia and Perlina.

William Chick (maternal great-grandfather) and Mary Ragland (still another of the same name) were natives of Wales, who emigrated to America and settled in Virginia, but the date of their coming has not been recorded.

Scyon Ambler Bass, lawyer, of Russellville, was educated at Auburn, Logan County, Kentucky, and began the study of law at Bowling Green in the office of that triumvirate of Kentucky jurists, Judge W. L. Dulaney (see sketch), John

M. Porter and Thomas H. Hines. After reading in this office for one year he went to Cumberland University, his preceptors being Judge Nathan Green and Robert L. Carothers, and was graduated and admitted to the Tennessee bar in 1877.

In the following year he was admitted to the bar in Kentucky and began the practice of law in Russellville, where he has since distinguished himself as a lawyer of ability and excellent judgment.

In March, 1890, he was appointed master commissioner of the Logan Circuit Court for a term expiring in 1897.

During the whole time in which he has practiced law in Russellville, he has been extensively interested in stock raising on his farm in the county; is a silent partner in the firm of W. C. Seward & Company, and from 1880 to 1885 was a member of the firm of Clay & Bass, but took no active part in the management of the business; in 1893 was elected president of the Russellville Tanning & Harness Company, and is interested in a cattle ranch in Presidio County, Texas. But with all of these interests and investments he is devoted to his profession and gives his law business his best attention.

Mr. Bass was married November 18, 1879, to Mrs. Anneta Seward, whose maiden name was Carter. She was born July 7, 1853, and was educated in the Louisville high school and at Mrs. Tevis' Science Hill Academy in Shelbyville. Her first husband was William J. Seward, of Franklin, deceased.

The children of Scyon A. and Anneta Carter Bass are: Edwin Lucas, born January 16, 1881; Mary Ellen, born August 5, 1882; Russell Martin, born May 6, 1884, and Minnie Louise, born November 29, 1889.

REV. JOSEPH RENNIE, Pastor of Stuart Robinson Memorial Presbyterian Church, Louisville, was born in Richmond, Virginia, July 15, 1860. His father, Rev. Joseph R. Rennie, is also a native of Richmond, now residing in Amelia Court House, Virginia, and is pastor of the Presbyterian Church in that place. He was a farmer until he was forty-eight years of age, when he entered the ministry from a conviction of duty.

He has been remarkably successful, and is exceedingly popular with his congregation, one of the most intelligent in the state. He served throughout the war; was with Stonewall Jackson in his Valley campaign, and with the Richmond Howitzers as driver of a caisson, a very dangerous and much exposed position. He was a good soldier, a highly respected citizen, and is a very influential preacher.

Joseph Rennie (grandfather) was a native of Kelso, Scotland, who came to New York with James Thorburn, the celebrated seed man. He removed to Virginia about the year 1835, and died in Richmond in 1865, aged sixty-five years. He was an elder in the First Presbyterian Church of Richmond. He was the first landscape gardener that came to Richmond.

Mr. Rennie's mother, Ella (Powell) Rennie, was born in Richmond in 1839. She is, of course, a member of the Presbyterian Church at Amelia Court House, of which her husband is pastor.

After his primary education, Mr. Rennie spent two years in Richmond College and then entered Hampton-Sidney College, whence he graduated in 1885. He then attended the Union Theological Seminary in Prince Edward County, Virginia, graduating in the spring of 1888. In 1887 he was licensed to preach by the East Hanover Presbytery, which he had supplied a year previous while pursuing his theological studies. Immediately after graduation, he was called to the pastorate of the Chase City (Virginia) Presbyterian Church, of which he had charge for three years. In October, 1890, he went to Oxford, North Carolina, and supplied the church at that place until 1892, when he came to Louisville and took charge of the Stuart Robinson Memorial Presbyterian Church, located in St. James Court, in which he has met with gratifying success, the membership of the congregation having been more than doubled under his preaching and numbering at the present writing about one hundred and fifty members.

Mr. Rennie was very popular in his college days, and usually represented his college society on public occasions, carrying off the honors. He graduated with high honors, and has sustained the reputation he made then as a profound thinker and eloquent speaker,

During his residence in Richmond he was a member of the Second Presbyterian Church, of which the Rev. M. D. Hoge was the pastor.

Mr. Rennie was married in October, 1888, to Ellen Eugenia, daughter of Dr. Charles Parke Goodall of Richmond, Virginia. She is related to the large Christian family of Virginia.

JOSHUA T. GRIFFITH, Clerk of the Daviess County Court, Owensboro, son of Daniel M. and Virginia Shelby (Todd) Griffith, was born in Owensboro, April 1, 1861, and received his education in the schools of that city. During President Cleveland's first administration he was deputy collector of Internal Revnue under Hunter Wood, collector of the Second district. He was elected clerk of the Daviess County Court, and is now serving his second term in that office, in which his faithful attention to business and gentlemanly demeanor have won for him a popularity which few men in the county enjoy. He was married June 11, 1891, to Jettie Rothchild, and has one child, Virginia Griffith, born January 29, 1895.

Mr. Griffith is a descendant of a long line of ancestry on both sides of the family, who figured conspicuously in the early history of the Republic, state and county; and he reveres the names and deeds of his noble ancestry, whose lives were unblemished by word or act, while he cherishes the laudable ambition to emulate their good works and to preserve their name unspotted before the world, as becomes the scion of a noble ancestry.

William Griffith, the first of the name to come to America, arrived from London, England, in June, 1675, and settled on the Severn River in Anne Arundel County, Maryland.

He was married to Sarah Maccubbin, daughter of John and Elinor Maccubbin, and had the following children, viz.: Orlando, born October 17, 1688; Sophia, born April 27, 1691; Charles, born January 20, 1693; William, born April 15, 1697.

William Griffith died 1699, leaving a will, proved at Annapolis, Maryland, October 23, 1699.

Sarah Griffith, his widow, married Thomas Reynolds, sheriff of Anne Arundel County, Maryland, and died April 22, 1716.

Orlando Griffith, born October 17, 1688, eldest son of William and Sarah, married June 6, 1717, at Annapolis, Maryland, Katherine Howard, daughter of John and Mrs. Katherine Greenberry Ridgely, and had the following children, viz.: Sarah, born May 13, 1718; Nicholas, died in infancy; Henry, born February 14, 1720; Greenberry, born December 31, 1727; Joshua, born January 25, 1730; Benjamin, born November 22, 1732; Lucretia, born February 5, 1739; Orlando, Jr., born April 27, 1741; Charles Greenberry, born May 17, 1744.

Orlando Griffith died March, 1757, leaving a will dated April 8, 1753; proved April 25, 1757, at Annapolis, Maryland.

His wife, Katherine Howard Griffith, died February, 1783.

Henry Griffith, born February 14, 1720, son of Orlando, married second time—June 4, 1751—Ruth Hammond, daughter of John and Ann Hammond, and had the following children, viz.: Samuel, born May 7, 1752; John H., born April 20, 1754; Philemon, born August 29, 1756; Charles, born December 16, 1758; Ann, born February 24, 1762; Joshua, born March 25, 1764; Eleanor, born March 9, 1766; Elizabeth, born December 16, 1768, and Ruth.

Henry Griffith died September 28, 1794. His will was probated at Rockville, Maryland, October 10, 1794. Ruth, his wife, died January 27, 1782.

Joshua Griffith (great-grandfather) of Maryland, born March 25, 1764, was twice married: first in 1783 to Elizabeth Ridgeley of Anne Arundel County, Maryland. She was born in 1765 and died in 1797. His second wife's name, county and state were the same as that of his first wife. She was born in 1769; married Joshua Griffith in 1798 and died in 1803. By the first marriage there were three children: Lydia, married in 1808 to Warner Crow; Remus, born 1786, married in 1809 to Sallie Handley, died 1845; and Ruth, married Moses Cummins. By the second marriage there was one child: William (grandfather), who was first married to Aria Mosely, in 1822; and again to Martha Hopkins, in 1848, and one child of this union, Carey, died in infancy. His children by his first wife (Aria Mosely) were Ridgely, born in 1823, died in 1841; William Henry, born in 1825, married Margaret Calhoun in 1845, died in 1848; and Daniel M. (father), born February 28, 1826, married Virginia Shelby Todd in October, 1857, died November 3, 1893.

Joshua Griffith (great-grandfather) was one of the most charitable men of his day. The following instance of his love and generosity towards his neighbors is remembered: At a time when there was a great scarcity of provisions in the county, a number of men came to him wanting to buy his large stock of provisions, but he positively declined to sell, saying, if they had money to buy provisions with they would not suffer, and he must care for his neighbors and supply the wants of those who had neither money or meat. He had some knowledge of medicine and, although he was not an educated physician, his medical advice was sought by his neighbors for miles around. He cheerfully rendered what service he could to ameliorate the sufferings of others, but he never charged one cent for such services. He was one of the few men who lived and died in the county without an enemy. His useful life, so helpful to others, was spared until he reached a ripe old age, being eighty-two years old when he died.

William Griffith (grandfather) was born in Maryland, and died in 1845. He was eleven years of age when he came to Kentucky and, owing to the primitive condition of the country, schools were impossible, but he received a fair education in schools at Hartford and at St. Joseph College. He was a soldier in the War of 1812-14; and, upon the organization of Daviess County and the opening of the County Court, he was appointed the first clerk of the court. He was afterward admitted to the bar and practiced law for several years. In 1822 he married Aria Mosely, daughter of Captain Thomas Mosely, an early settler in Kentucky, who came from Virginia. She died in 1828; and, in 1841, he married Martha Hopkins, daughter of General Edmund Hopkins of Henderson County. He became largely interested in real estate, owning at different times many thousands of acres of land. Titles for larger landed possessions passed through his hands than were ever given by any other individual in Daviess County, unless by his son, who succeeded him. He encouraged and secured the settlement of a great number of families in different parts of the county, selling land at low prices and on favorable terms. He was gifted with superior business qualifications and was generous to a fault. He would say to the surveyors of the land which he proposed to sell to throw in five or ten acres rather than make it short by a rood. He was prominent in the development of the county and was a popular leader in every movement for the public weal. He served his county in the legislature for a number of terms and his district in the senate three or four terms, and in this he served his constituents industriously and conscientiously.

The excellent name of his honored father was kept in remembrance by the noble deeds of the son, whose life was full of charitable deeds, generous consideration for others and whose public spirited enthusiasm and enterprise did so much to make his county one of the best in the Ohio Valley.

Daniel M. Griffith (father) was the eldest son of William Griffith. He received a collegiate education at Centre College and at old Transylvania, graduating from the latter in the class of 1847. He studied law and was duly admitted to the bar, but abandoned the active practice of his profession in order to attend to the large landed estate of his father; and became quite as extensively interested in real estate as his father had been. His legal training served him well in this business, as he was especially well versed in the intricate laws relative to titles and conveyances. His personal knowledge of almost every acre of land in the county, together with an unerring judgment as to its value, gave him great advantage in the purchase and sale of property, and he was the owner of or the agent for thousands of acres of land in Daviess and adjacent counties.

Business reverses, such as are liable to all men of large enterprises, came to Mr. Griffith and he virtually had to begin at the bottom again and rebuild his fortune; and, by patient perseverance, business tact and large experience, he fully recovered his losses and owned a larger estate at the time of his death than he had ever owned before. Like his father and his grandfather, he was in his day the most widely known and popular citizen in the county. He was a man of unimpeachable character; few men could have been concerned in as many real estate transactions, large and small, without incurring the displeasure of some of the parties to such transactions. His honesty and integrity were never questioned. He never deceived anyone to gain a personal advantage. Only those who knew him personally and intimately could appreciate the true nobility of his character, his kindness and gentleness toward all, his generosity and liberality to those who needed assistance, his fidelity to his friends, and above all, his sacred devotion to his family. Alway calm and self-possessed, he never deviated from the courtesy which he held was due to every man, whether prince or pauper. There was no harshness in his nature and the humblest menial could approach him with the assurance that he would be kindly received. By his uprightness and straightforwardness he won friends from among all classes. He left the impress of his strong personality upon the community in which he was a prominent figure, and his death was looked upon as a public calamity. Popular as he was and qualified as few men are for public service, he never aspired to office and only once, in 1847, did he yield to the solicitation of friends, who elected him to the legislature. Some few years before his death, which occurred November 3, 1893, he adopted the faith of the Catholic religion, having contemplated that step for many years.

Daniel M. Griffith was married in October, 1857, to Virginia Shelby Todd, daughter of Charles S. Todd and granddaughter of Governor Isaac Shelby. Her father was minister plenipotentiary to Russia under President Harrison's administration. The maternal ancestry of Joshua T. Griffith were prominent in the early history of the state and nation, and their lives and deeds having become a matter of history a repetition is uncalled for in this volume. The names of the children of Daniel M. and Virginia Shelby Todd Griffith were as follows: Letitia, born in 1858,

married H. C. Watkins in 1880, and died in 1894, leaving two children—Virginia, born in 1883, and Shelton, born in 1888; Virginia, born in 1859, died in 1877; Joshua T., born April 1, 1861, married June 11, 1891, to Jettie Rothchild, has one child, Virginia, born January 29, 1895; Florence, born 1863, married H. A. Miller, now living in Asheville, North Carolina, her children are Amelia, born in 1886; Virginia, born in 1888; Griffith, born in 1889, died 1890; Daniel M., born September 19, 1867, married Susan M. Herr, November 7, 1895; Rose, born 1865, married Dr. E. S. Watkins in 1887 and had three children: Sue R. and Rose Yandell (twins), born in 1888, Rose Yandell died 1884; Ruth, born 1870, died 1884; Todd, born 1871, died 1880; Clinton, born 1873; Mary Ridgeley, born 1876.

JOHN S. FRITZ, Chief of Police of Hopkinsville, was born in Christian County, Kentucky, June 21, 1864. His father, John G. Fritz, was a native of the same county, born in August, 1825; was educated in the public schools of the county; at the age of eighteen years began farming on his own account, giving especial attention to the cultivation of tobacco and eventually doing a very extensive tobacco brokerage business. He was a member of the Methodist Church, a Mason and Democratic voter who could always be relied upon by his party.

Solomon Fritz (grandfather), a native of Kentucky, was the inventor and manufacturer of the celebrated Fritz gun.

Jane F. Hord Fritz (mother) was a native of Christian County, daughter of William Hord, a Virginian by birth, who removed to Christian County and was one of the representative farmers until the time of his death in 1880.

John S. Fritz, after receiving his primary schooling in Hopkinsville, went to Cumberland University, Lebanon, Tennessee, and later to a commercial college in Evansville, Indiana, from which he was graduated in 1883. His first employment was as bookkeeper for the tobacco firm of Gant & Gaither, of Hopkinsville, with whom he remained two and a half years. He was then in the livery business with his brother for two years, and was subsequently appointed deputy under Sheriff Boyd. He served one year on the police force in Hopkinsville and was re-appointed, but resigned to accept the position of bookkeeper for Sheriff West and gave up that position in 1891 to accept his appointment as chief of police, in which office he has rendered valuable service to the city and to which he has been re-appointed from year to year until the present time.

John S. Fritz and Mary Rogers, daughter of ex-Sheriff Rogers, of Christian County, were married November 11, 1890, and they have two children: Cora Ruth and Jane.

He is a prominent Knight of Pythias. He takes some interest in politics and always puts his cross under the rooster.

LEW B. BROWN, Lawyer, and Editor of the Spencer Courier, Taylorsville, Kentucky, was born in Madison, Arkansas, June 13, 1861. His father, George Llewellyn Brown, was a native of Paris, Tennessee, who traveled extensively and finally settled in Madison, Arkansas, where he established the Pioneer newspaper before the war. He bitterly opposed the secession in his paper, but when the war began he enlisted in St. Francis County, Arkansas, served as a special messenger and was subsequently promoted to the rank of major in the Confederate army. He returned to Arkansas after the war closed and died in Ozark in 1875, being then the editor of the Ozark Banner. He was a man of fine intelligence and held a high rank in the Masonic Order.

George Young (maternal grandfather) was a native of Kentucky and a tailor by trade. He was engaged in business in Bardstown for a number of years, and subsequently removed to Arkansas, where he died in 1870.

Lew B. Brown attended the common schools in Madison, Forrest City and Ozark, Arkansas, and in Cloverport, Kentucky; and supplemented a meager English education by active work as reporter for the Louisville newspapers, including the Courier-Journal, Evening Times and Sunday Truth, and as accredited correspondent for the New York Morning Journal, Chicago Herald, Pittsburg Leader, New Orleans Times-Democrat and others. After an apprenticeship of fourteen years in this capacity and as a practical printer, he removed to Taylorsville and purchased the Spencer Courier, now owned and edited by him. His first newspaper venture was the Monthly Visitor, which he conducted at Ozark at the age of fourteen.

He read law under Hon. G. G. Gilbert, of Shelbyville, and Hon. Charles A. Wilson, of Louisville, and in June, 1894, was licensed to practice by the Court of Appeals. He is now a full-fledged lawyer-editor and one of the best practitioners at the Taylorsville bar. He won his first case before a jury and made a reputation which he has easily sustained and which has given him a large share of the legal business of his county.

Mr. Brown is an able journalist, a fine lawyer, an enterprising citizen and a popular member of the Odd Fellows Lodge, Knights of Labor, Typographical Union, and is secretary of the Democratic County Committee, and chairman of the Democratic campaign committee. He makes good use of his opportunities in political work, and is an acknowledged leader in his party and an important factor in the advancement of the material interests of his town and county.

He was married February 11, 1885, to Emma J. Struby, of Louisville, who was the mother of three children: Llewellyn Chauncey, Albert Young and Barbara Sunshine. Mrs. Brown died of heart failure December 19, 1895, superinduced by the excitement and grief occasioned by the sudden death of her little son. She was a member of the Baptist Church, in which she and her husband were recognized as among the leading and most earnest and liberal workers in the cause of Christianity. After Mr. Brown's law business had grown so rapidly, Mrs. Brown assisted him as local editor of the "Spencer Courier" and had developed great talent in newspaper work.

SAMUEL HOUSTON of Paducah—a lawyer of prominence and fine ability, of strict integrity and high moral standing in his profession and as a citizen—was born in Paducah, Kentucky, on November 25, 1838.

His ancestors on his father's side were of the hardy Scotch-Irish stock, who immigrated to America in the early part of the eighteenth century, and became soldiers in the colonial and revolutionary wars, and when independence and peace were declared were pioneers and farmers, who aided in reducing the aboriginal west to civilization.

His father, Eli M. Houston, was a native of Miami County, Ohio, a contractor and builder, who removed to Paducah in 1834, and in the following year was married to Sarah Best. In 1842 he removed to Hickman, Kentucky, and in 1846 to Memphis, Tennessee, where he was superintendent of construction in the navy yard. In 1850, when gold was discovered, he went to California, and afterward was one of the discoverers of the Washoe mines in Nevada, where he died and was buried at Gold Hill in 1860. He was a man of fine intellect—handsome, bold, restless and ambitious, who followed the star of empire westward.

David Houston (grandfather) was a native of Mecklenburg County, North Carolina, who in 1785 migrated west with his father's family, and resided in Garrard County, Kentucky, for many years. In 1806 he married Miss McKinney, and in 1808 removed to Miami County, Ohio, where he lived and died on his farm, in 1833. He was a member of the Presbyterian Church.

William Houston (great-grandfather), a native of Belfast, County Antrim, Ireland, came to America about 1735 and settled on a farm in Westmoreland County, Pennsylvania, where he married Mary Montgomery (great-grandmother). He was in the colonial army at Braddock's defeat, and having served through the war, removed to Virginia, thence to Mecklenburg County, North Carolina, where he lived many years. In 1785 he removed to Garrard County, Kentucky, and in 1800 removed to Dickson County, Tennessee. In 1808 he removed to Miami County, Ohio, where he settled on a farm, and died in 1810 at an advanced age.

Sarah Best Houston (mother) was a daughter of Thomas and Margaret Best, who immigrated from England to America in 1800, and first located in Cincinnati, Ohio, and in the following year settled and lived for over a quarter of a century in Lebanon, Ohio. In 1834 Thomas Best and his family removed to Paducah.

Eli M. and Sarah Best Houston (parents) had nine children, four only of whom are now living.

Sam Houston's education was conducted with a view to professional life, and at an early age chose the law as best suited to his inclination. For this he fully prepared himself, and in 1859, when twenty-one years of age, was admitted to the bar and began the practice of his profession in his native city. He was city attorney from May, 1862, to September, 1872, being elected and several times re-elected as a Democrat. He has never permitted himself to become a politician, nor has he held any other office, preferring to devote himself to his law practice, which requires his undivided time and attention. He has always been active in matters looking to the substantial prosperity of the city. He suggested the building of the city hall, and gave his influence toward its construction and completion, and was one of the leaders in the movement of citizens to secure the construction of the United States government building in Paducah. Mr. Houston is a quiet, dignified gentleman, but has always been at the front, where the advancement of the public interest requires ready thought and steady purpose.

STEPHEN K. SNEED. It has been said that the time to commence the training of a child is when its grandmother is an infant. The rule is a good one, and Stephen Kutesoff Sneed owes much to its application. His good training reaches farther back than the limits of this sketch permit us to go.

Mr. Sneed was born October 6, 1841, in Granville County, North Carolina, under the roof of the ancestral mansion, "Montpelier," where his forefathers had lived since 1760. His father was Richard Sneed, a physician, respected by all and beloved by those with whom he was brought into professional contact. His mother was Lucy Henderson. Dr. Sneed and Miss Henderson had married in North Carolina, the native state of them both, and in 1851 removed to Kentucky, settling in the city of Henderson, where they resided until their death—Dr. Sneed in 1861 and Mrs. Sneed in 1868.

His paternal grandfather was Stephen Sneed, a captain under General Daniel Morgan, commander of the famous riflemen, and at Bemis'

Heights and at the Cowpens Captain Sneed dealt lusty blows for our independence.

His maternal grandfather was Leonard Henderson, an eminent lawyer and for many years chief justice of North Carolina, whose learning and ability were largely instrumental in formulating the jurisprudence of that state. Chief Justice Henderson was the son of Colonel Richard Henderson. Few names have more impressed themselves upon the history of Kentucky than that of Colonel Henderson. His ancestors were among the earliest settlers in Virginia, where he was born in 1735. Whilst a youth his parents emigrated to Granville County, North Carolina. He studied law and rose rapidly to wealth and distinction. The fertile wilderness lying between the Cumberland, Kentucky and Ohio rivers attracted his adventurous spirit. By the treaty of Wataga, made by him with the Cherokee nation of Indians, he, in consideration of ten thousand pounds sterling, acquired the whole of that territory, comprising what is now about one-half of the state of Kentucky. He named his empire Transylvania, called to his aid a few associates, organized a form of government, became its president, and convened a parliament at Boonesborough, of which Daniel Boone was a member. But the Legislature of Virginia, which then embraced Kentucky, becoming jealous of Colonel Henderson's growing power, declared void the treaty of Wataga, but by the same legislative act, in consideration of his services to the state, granted to him and his associates a body of over two hundred thousand acres of land, embracing what is now a good part of the county and all of the city that bears his name. The rich county and the beautiful city of Henderson, with its refinement, culture and wealth, her splendid churches and schools, her prosperous manufactories, her broad streets and beautiful parks, are worthy monuments to the memory of their illustrious founder.

Young Sneed, in those early years of his life prior to the removal of his parents to Kentucky, received that instruction, parental and scholastic, always bestowed upon the scions of the best southern families. After establishing their home in Henderson the boy was sent to the academy of W. H. Delano, a successful instructor as well as accomplished linguist and well-equipped lawyer. In his early maturity he read law for two years under the direction of Harvey Yeaman, an association which, notwithstanding the disparity of ages of tutor and pupil, grew into a deep friendship that lasted until Mr. Yeaman's death. Mr. Sneed never applied for admission to the bar, a profession he would have honored, and in which his subsequent career furnishes proof that he would have made his way to the first ranks.

His first actual business experience was in the drug stores, then conducted by Ira Delano and George Lyne, whence he was soon called to the position of bookkeeper, and afterwards teller of the Farmers' Bank. Upon the organization of the Henderson National Bank in 1865, though a young man for such a responsibility, he was made its cashier and for several years was also its vice-president. A biography of Mr. Sneed would be, during the period of its existence, a history of this bank, which very soon after its organization took, and has ever since maintained a position among the most successful financial institutions of the state. Although having a watchful care over every detail of its business, his administration of its affairs has not been confined to mere cent per cent routine. His large and comprehensive knowledge of all that pertains to finance has given the bank a success and history that is rarely attained by those out of metropolitan environments. In the annual councils of the Union, as well as of his own state, he has long been recognized as one of the leaders, often called to serve upon their most important committees, as well as to discuss intricate and grave questions of finance.

But, arduous as Mr. Sneed's duties to his bank have been, it is greatly to his credit, as well as to the advantage of his community, that it has not absorbed all his thought and care. Not only has he found time to indulge a strong love for the best literature, until his extensive and varied reading, added to a genial and courteous disposition, has made him a most interesting and popular member of cultured society; but no useful enterprise or commendable charity of his city has ever appealed to him in vain, but has often met with the most substantial response. And with it all, though never seeking office, he always evinces an active interest in the affairs of the state and Union. During all his mature life, St. Paul's Episcopal Church has felt his helpful hand, and for many years as vestryman, at present junior warden, and not infrequently in the higher ecclesiastical courts his counsel is sought.

On May 10, 1871, at "Benvenue," the old Soaper homestead near Henderson, where the bride had been reared amid ideal home surroundings, Mr. Sneed married Marianna, second daughter of William and Susan Henderson Soaper. The kindest providence has smiled upon the union, but its chiefest blessing is the unbroken family circle—father, mother and six children: Susan Henderson, Lucy Henderson, Kate Soaper, Marianna Soaper, William Soaper and Stephen Kutesoff.

In 1881 the five sons and five daughters and many grandchildren of the father of Mrs. Sneed gathered around his couch. He died full of years and of that respect of neighbors and affection of kindred that constitutes the highest earthly honor. One among the largest fortunes ever accumulated in Kentucky by fair dealing was the result of his business life. The mother of Mrs. Sneed (who was a mother in Israel as well) did not long survive him, having died in 1890.

CAPTAIN PHILLIP BURTON THOMPSON, one of Kentucky's most able and distinguished lawyers, of Harrodsburg, son of John B. and Nancy Porter (Robards) Thompson, was born in Harrodsburg, Kentucky, January 8, 1821.

Captain Thompson's descent is traceable on the mother's side to the Huguenot refugees (Porter and Dutois) from the troubles of St. Bartholomew, who came to America and settled, and a solitary pair of Welsh emigrants, George and Sally Hill, who about the same time came to this country.

Anne Porter (Captain Thompson's great-grandmother) married Archibald Sampson, and of this marriage Archibald Sampson and Elizabeth Barbara Sampson were born. Their mother was left a young and handsome as well as a very wealthy widow. Her children had all the advantages of wealth given them in their education—Elizabeth in this country and Archibald in Cambridge, England. The latter died within a few weeks after his return to this country, and his large estate was distributed equally between his own sister, Barbara, and the children of his mother and Captain Lewis, her second husband. This Barbara was Captain Thompson's grandmother. She married George Robards, a descendant of George and Sally Hill of Wales, before mentioned on his mother's side of the house, and paternally of William Robards of Virginia, the father of the Robards families of the south and west. This George Robards when very young, scarcely more than a lad, entered the ranks of the revolutionary soldiers. He was in many of the noted battles of those days and came out of the war wearing the title of captain. Of his and Barbara Sampson's marriage were born many children, one of whom, Nancy, was the mother of Captain Thompson.

Captain Thompson's paternal descent was of the Thompsons, a widely known family of English descent. The first notable member was Roger Thompson, said to have been knighted on the battlefield by Charles II. of England. One of his descendants was sent out to Virginia on application of the governor for help to suppress Bacon's rebellion. It is said he espoused the cause of the Americans and resigned his commission. Be that as it may, he settled in this country. Later on one of his descendants of the same name, William Thompson, was a resident of Albemarle County, Virginia. He married a Miss Claiborne and to them were born several children, among them four sons: Roger, George, Leonard and John. Several, if not all of these, served in the Revolutionary war, and after it was over moved to Kentucky and settled upon large tracts of land, which land has been inherited by their children. John, the youngest of the four sons, married Miss Susan Burton, and of this marriage, one of several children, was born John Burton Thompson, the father of Captain Thompson. Both of Captain Thompson's grandfathers being old soldiers of the Revolution, and living on adjoining plantations, they were naturally thrown much together, and it is not surprising that they were eventually connected by marriage, as before stated. Col. John Thompson's son, John Burton Thompson, marrying Captain George Robards'

KENTUCKY BIOGRAPHIES.

daughter, Nancy Porter. Of this marriage eleven children were born, four sons and seven daughters: Hon. John B. Thompson, one of Kentucky's most eminent statesmen, who served his party in places of trust, once as lieutenant-governor, later for many years in both houses of Congress; Judge Henry Thompson, who married Miss Eliza Jane, daughter of Governor Allan Trimble of Ohio, and one of the ablest lawyers of that, the state of his adoption; Charles Thompson, a planter of Mississippi, later of Kentucky, a man of high standing and integrity. Of the daughters, Sallie, the eldest, married Joseph Johnson of Louisiana, who was at the time of his death president of the state senate; Patsey, who died in infancy; Maria, who married William Daveiss, a farmer of Mercer County, who for a while in politics served his party in the state senate; Elizabeth Barbara, who married Colonel Henry Phillips, politician and planter of the South; Anne Porter, wife of Dr. Carey A. Trimble, who at the time of his marriage was connected with the Cincinnati Medical College, afterward a member of Congress; Susan Burton, wife of Henry Massie of Chillicothe, Ohio, son of General Massie, a successful lawyer and financier, and Katharine, wife of Walter A. Dun, a farmer of Madison County, Ohio.

Captain Phil B. Thompson, the youngest of the four brothers, was born January 8, 1821. He was educated at Centre College, Danville, Kentucky, and Jefferson College, Cannonsburg, Pennsylvania. He acquired his profession—that of law—with and became the partner of his brother, John B. Thompson, being admitted to the bar in 1840. Before reaching his majority he married Miss Martha Montgomery of Mississippi, daughter of Davis Montgomery and Elizabeth (Harper) Davis Montgomery; was a kinsman of the eminent preacher, Samuel Davis, and belonged to the Montgomery of military distinction.

Miss Montgomery was born August 22, 1823, and was not twenty years of age when she married Captain Thompson, and rarely, if ever, has a family received into its connection a bride of such rare patrician beauty as was hers—beauty that she wore to her death, with the regal grace befitting such a heritage. But far beyond her beauty of face was that of character, so eminently hers. A faithful wife, devoted mother, extending this care to her children of the third generation, a sincere friend, of quick and tender sympathy, a loyal Christian, esteemed, beloved and honored. She was a member of the Christian Church for fifty years, and died April 15, 1895.

When Governor Owsley called for two regiments of soldiers to enter the ranks in the invasion of Mexico, Captain Thompson raised a company, of which he was chosen the chief officer. This company was incorporated with Colonel William R. McKee's command and proceeded to join General Taylor's army of occupation at Point Isabel.

After the war with Mexico was over, Captain Thompson returned to Harrodsburg, where he continued the practice of law until the Civil war, when he again enlisted, this time taking with him his sons, all three of whom were under eighteen years of age—Davis Montgomery, now Dr. Thompson; John and Phil Burton (twins). John is now one of the ablest lawyers in Kentucky, and Phil an ex-Congressman, now a practitioner of law in Washington City. John Thompson married Miss Martha Anderson, daughter of Rev. Henry T. Anderson of Virginia, a minister of the Christian Church, and a distinguished linguist and translator. One child is the fruit of this marriage, Philip Burton, a young lawyer, educated at Harvard University.

Philip B., Jr., married Miss Mary Garnett. Their children are Garnett and Mattie. Garnett married Miss Lizzie Young of Jessamine County, of which marriage there are two children, a daughter, Mattie, and a son, Philip. Phil B. Thompson's daughter, Mattie, a celebrated belle and beauty, married William Leonard Davis, to whom has been born one son, Worthington Davis.

Captain Thompson has rarely shown any political aspirations, and only once served his party in the legislative hall. He has for many years been eminent in his profession, and ranks among the first, if indeed he is not the first criminal lawyer of the state. His first case was the celebrated Wilkinson-Redding case; he also defended James Arnold, who killed Robert Little, in which case he was associated with Governor W. O. Bradley and Senator Dan W. Voorhees. Another celebrated case was that of Thomas Buford, who killed Judge Elliott of the Court of Appeals, in which he was associated with Evan E. Settle of Owenton, and Major W. R. Kinney of Louisville; and these are only a few of the many noted cases in which he has won a national reputation as one of the finest criminal lawyers in the country.

HENRY CHARLES KEHOE, M. D., the popular homeopathic physician and druggist of Flemingsburg, son of James and Nora (Conroy) Kehoe, was born in Lewis County, Kentucky, August 6, 1857.

His father, James Kehoe, a native of Dublin, Ireland, came to America in the early 40's. He received a good education in Dublin, and was qualified for almost any profession he might have chosen, but he preferred the peaceful and independent life of a farmer. On his arrival in this country he first located in New York. Soon afterwards he removed to Lewis County, Kentucky, where he was engaged in farming until during the Civil War, when he enlisted in the Union army.

Nora Conroy Kehoe (mother) was born in Dublin, Queen's County, Ireland, November 26, 1819, and was married June 29, 1846. Her family was very prominent in the Irish rebellion of 1812, and her grandfather, who was a general, was asked to go into the "inclosure," and not knowing the penalty, he refused to do so, and they were fired upon by the soldiers and he and his entire command were killed. Mrs. Kehoe was a relative of Reverend John O'Hanlon, who has written the best history of Ireland, and a second cousin of the poet, Thomas Moore, with whom she was intimately acquainted. She was a woman of education and culture; endowed with strong will power and great force of character. Being left a widow at the close of the war, with the family treasury—like the government vaults at that time—somewhat depleted, she took courage, and, with Christian resignation and hopeful assurance, undertook the task of raising her children for the various avocations of life. How well she performed her arduous task is best shown by an extract from a letter which she received from one of her sons just prior to her death, which occurred February 6, 1895: "You have been blessed with long years, and have seen your family well raised and, for the most part, prosperous. Your life has been a splendid and noble sacrifice in behalf of those whom you have loved so well and faithfully, and your every example has been one of elevating nobility and beautiful grace, of transcendent Christian devotion and unalloyed integrity that will live among the stars and be forever a charm to those you leave behind. May God bless you and spare you long to enjoy your well-won battle of life."

James Kehoe and Nora Conroy were the parents of eight children, a brief sketch of each of whom follows:

(1.) Mary Kehoe, born in New York in 1847, wife of James J. Harrahan, general manager of the Illinois Central Railroad, with headquarters in Chicago, and one of the best known railroad men in America.

(2.) Thomas Kehoe, born in New York in 1849; is engaged in the monumental business in Knoxville, Tennessee; an expert workman and designer, who designed and executed the monument to which was awarded the first prize at the Centennial Exposition at Philadelphia in 1876, competing with some of the best sculptors in the United States and Canada. He was the youngest enlisted soldier in the Federal army in the late Civil war, having enlisted when he was six months past thirteen years of age; served two and a half years in Bierbower's Company, Forty-sixth Regiment Kentucky Volunteer Infantry; married a Miss Mattox of Owensboro.

(3.) William Kehoe, born in Cincinnati in 1851; educated in Maysville; learned printing and became owner and publisher of the Carlisle "Mercury," and later of the Cynthiana Democrat; disposed of his interest in the latter to accept the position of private secretary to Hon. John G. Carlisle; after serving in that position for eight years was appointed by the speaker chief stenographer of the House of Representatives, at a salary of about $5,000 a year; is a large stockholder in the Mergenthaler type setting machine —now used by the principal daily newspapers throughout the country—and prospective president of the company; married Mattie Webster of Cynthiana.

(4.) J. Dexter Kehoe, born in Lewis County, Kentucky, in 1853; learned the printer's trade; became interested in politics and received the Democratic nomination for representative in Mason County before he was twenty-four years of age, but was defeated by two votes by Robert A. Cochran, now deceased; was again nominated, two years later, and was elected by a majority of seven hundred votes, defeating Honorable A. A. Wadsworth; was again elected to the legislature, being the first man re-elected from Mason County in succession; was a candidate for the Democratic nomination for Congress, and failed by only half a vote, Mr. Powers receiving the nomination; for many years he managed the public printer's office in Frankfort, resigning this to accept the position of chief of the Bureau of Printing, Engraving Department, in Washington, and is pronounced by "Round's Printer's Cabinet" the best printer in the United States; has filled other positions of honor and trust, and at this writing is being strongly urged to make the race for Congress in the Ninth Kentucky District.

(5.) Mark F. Kehoe, born in Lewis County, Kentucky, in 1855, is a cigarmaker by trade; has served in the Maysville City Council for many years, and is a canvasser for the Cigarmakers' International Union—a position requiring fine business tact and ability—with headquarters in Chicago.

(6.) Henry Charles Kehoe, M. D., the principal subject of this sketch, was educated in Maysville; learned the printer's trade and was connected with the Carlisle Mercury before attending the Pulte Medical College at Cincinnati, from which he graduated in the class of 1884-5, and then went to Cynthiana and succeeded his brother as editor and publisher of the Democrat; sold the paper in 1887 and began the practice of medicine at Cynthiana, and, in 1892, located at Flemingsburg, where he is now engaged in the practice of homeopathy and is also interested in the drug house of H. C. Kehoe & Company. He has filled offices in the State Homeopathic Society and written largely for medical journals.

Dr. Kehoe was married October 8, 1880, to Genevieve Loudenback, who is closely related to the family of the late Governor Thomas E. Bramlette. Her mother is Martha Bramlette, who was a daughter of Henry Bramlette. Mrs. Kehoe is related on other lines of ancestry to some of the best families in the state. They have two children: Fannie Bruce, born in 1881, and Pannell Bramlette, born in 1883. Dr. Kehoe is a member of the Knights of Pythias, Odd Fellows, a Master Mason and a Knight Templar.

(7.) Jennie Kehoe was born in Maysville in 1859; educated in the Convent at Maysville; married Charles Reed, a farmer of Mason County.

(8.) James N. Kehoe, born in Mason County in 1862; educated in Maysville; read law under Judge Thomas F. Hargis at Louisville; was duly admitted to the bar and is a practicing attorney of Maysville; is master commissioner of Mason County; member of the State Democratic Executive Committee and prominent in local and state politics; married Hannah Kain.

JOSEPH A. HODGE, an eminent physician of Henderson, was born in Livingston County, Kentucky, February 2, 1829, and is the son of Edwin and Nancy S. (Hughes) Hodge. His father was also born in Livingston County in 1805, and was educated in the common schools. He became a representative farmer; married Nancy S. Hughes in 1828, and they had three children: Mary, Lavinia and Joseph A. Livingston County was divided in 1842, and Edwin Hodge lived in that part which is now Crittenden County, and died in 1837.

Robert Hodge (grandfather) was a native of North Carolina, who came to Kentucky about the beginning of the present century. He was three times married, his first wife being Miss Northern; his second wife Miss Armistead, and his third wife, name not known.

Henry Hodge (great-grandfather) was one of three brothers who came from England in colonial days. One of the brothers went to Virginia, one to Maryland and Henry to North Carolina. One of these brothers, Anthony, for whom Dr. Joseph A. Hodge was named, always bore the name of "Hodges," as do his descendants to this day.

After the death of Edwin Hodge, Nancy S. Hughes Hodge (mother) married Dr. J. S. Giliam, a Virginian by birth, but at that time a resident of Livingston (now Crittenden) County. He was in many respects a remarkable man, and proved a most kind and indulgent stepfather, and it was through his assistance and influence that Joseph A. Hodge became a physician.

Joseph Hughes (maternal grandfather) was born in North Carolina, and removed to Livingston County, Kentucky, where he was a farmer; was somewhat inclined to politics, being a "dyed in the wool" Democrat, and was at one time a member of the Kentucky Legislature. His father was a soldier in the Revolutionary War.

Joseph A. Hodge was educated in the best schools of Crittenden County; studied medicine with Dr. J. S. Giliam, of Marion, and attended the Louisville University, graduating in 1850, when twenty-one years of age. He practiced medicine in Marion and vicinity from 1850 to 1863, when he removed to Henderson, arriving April 28, 1863, where he is still actively engaged in his work for the relief of suffering humanity. He is a member of the American Medical Association, the Henderson County Medical Club, the Kentucky State Medical Society, of which he was president in 1875, the McDowell Medical Society, and was for a long time a member of the board of examiners of the Third Judicial District of Kentucky.

He was an old time Whig, but since the war has voted the Democratic ticket. He is a man of the highest moral character, and a member of the Presbyterian Church.

On the fourth day of December, 1851, Joseph A. Hodge and Susan A. Linthicum, daughter of Dr. Rufus Linthicum, of Muhlenberg County, were united in marriage, having become acquainted four years previous to the date of their marriage, when she was a pupil in St. Vincent Academy in Union County. She died May 1, 1891, leaving seven children: Edwin, Mary L., Eliza A., Emma, Antonia M., William A. and Nellie D. Hodge. Of these Edwin married Fannie Ditto, daughter of Thomas Ditto, of Brandenburg, and has two children: Thomas Ditto and Edwin.

Mary L. is the wife of Dr. L. Worsham, of Evansville, Indiana, and has five children: Hodge, Eliza, Edwin, Ludson and Mary Lavinia.

Eliza A. is the wife of Henry Berry, formerly of Memphis, Tenn., now a resident of Washington, D. C., and has three children: Susan Hodge, Henry and Louisa.

Antonia M. is the wife of Henry Soaper, of Henderson, and has two children: William and Mary Lavinia.

Nellie D. is the wife of Charles Hunter Dishman, of Pensacola, Florida, and has three children: Susan Hodges, Charles H. and Dorothy.

The two unmarried children of Dr. Hodge, William Anthony and Emma, are at home with their father.

ROBERT A. WATTS, deceased, late secretary and treasurer of the Louisville Railway Company, son of Philip H. and Elizabeth (McCampbell) Watts, was born in Shelby County, Kentucky, December 18, 1823. His father was a native of Albemarle County, Virginia, who came to Kentucky in 1818 and located in Shelby County, where he lived until 1846, when he went to the territory of Iowa. He remained there only a short time, removing to Indiana, near Terre Haute, where he died at the age of seventy-three years, in 1865. He was one of the prominent educators of his day and most of his life was spent in teaching private schools. He was a soldier in the war of 1812, a loyal citizen and a devout member of the Presbyterian Church.

Charles Watts (grandfather) was a native of Virginia, a soldier in the Revolutionary war and a farmer in Virginia and in Indiana, to which territory he removed before its admission to statehood, and died there in 1846, at the age of ninety-one years.

David Watts (great-grandfather) was a resident of Virginia and was probably born in England, as he was of English descent.

Elizabeth McCampbell, mother of R. A. Watts, was born in Rockbridge County, Virginia, in 1784 and died in Shelby County in 1844. Her father, Robert McCampbell, was born in Pennsylvania and went to Rockbridge County, Virginia, where he was a planter, and died in 1815, aged seventy-one years. He was a patriot soldier in the Revolutionary war. The McCampbells are a distinguished Virginia family of Scotch-Irish extraction.

Robert A. Watts spent his youth in Shelbyville and was carefully educated by his father. He began business early in life as a merchant in Shelbyville; and removed to Danville in 1845, where he lived until 1855. While there, he was secretary and treasurer of the Lexington & Danville Railroad Company, of which General Leslie Combs was president. This contemplated road was the beginning of one of the divisions of the present line of the Cincinnati Southern Railroad. Under the direction of the celebrated engineer, John A. Roebling, who afterwards built the Brooklyn bridge, the towers for the high bridge over the Kentucky river were built by this company. But the company failed while the towers were in process of erection.

In 1856 Mr. Watts went west and spent two years in Minnesota, then a territory, and in Chicago, where he was in the real estate and banking business. Returning to Kentucky in October, 1858, he became a permanent citizen of Louisville, which was his home until the time of his death, with the exception of one year which he spent in Colorado. He was engaged as clerk in a bank for two or three years. When the Southern Telegraph Company was organized by General J. T. Boyle, who was its first president, Mr. Watts was made secretary and treasurer of the company, holding the office two or three years and until the consolidation of the Southern with the Western Union Telegraph Company. This line was constructed between Cincinnati and Memphis and was the means of reducing the rates one-half, and the terms of the consolidation provided that the former exorbitant rates should not be restored. The consolidation took place under the presidency of General E. Kirby Smith, who succeeded General Boyle.

Mr. Watts' next venture, in which he was quite successful, was as agent for the University Publishing Company of New York City, of which General John B. Gordon was president. This company published text books prepared especially for southern schools by the professors in the University of Virginia, which were exceedingly popular in the south after the war. The house is still in existence and from its presses are issued many of the most popular school books of the present day. Mr. Watts was the agent for this publishing house until 1872. After spending a year in Colorado, he became chief clerk in the auditor's office of the Louisville & Lexington Railroad while it was in the hands of a receiver.

In 1878 he was elected secretary and treasurer of the Louisville City Railway Company. In 1891 this company and the Central Passenger Railway Company were consolidated under the name of the Louisville Railway Company, embracing all of the street-car lines in the city and its suburbs. Mr. Watts was elected secretary and treasurer of the new company, which office he held at the time of his death, March 6, 1896.

Mr. Watts was married in 1851 to Margaret Mills Anderson, daughter of Honorable Simeon H. Anderson of Lancaster, Kentucky, who died in 1840 while a member of Congress. Mrs. Watts' maternal grandfather was Governor William Owsley of Kentucky. Mr. Watts left his wife and one son and one daughter: Robert A. Watts, Jr., and Julia B., wife of W. W. Mead, a commander in the United States navy. His daughter, Gretta, wife of Archibald Wilson of Nelson County, died in 1893.

Mr. Watts and his family were Presbyterians, and he had been a member of the church of his father and ancestors since 1837.

MITCHELL CARY ALFORD, Lawyer of Lexington and ex-lieutenant-governor of Kentucky, was born in Fayette County, Kentucky, July 10, 1856. At an early age he entered the Kentucky University at Lexington, and was graduated from that institution in the class of 1877, and in the following year took up the study of law. In 1879, after two years' study in the law department of the Kentucky University, he graduated with high honors.

He immediately commenced the practice of law, forming a partnership with Z. F. Smith, a college mate, under the firm name of Alford & Smith, which partnership existed for some seven or eight years and was terminated by the death of Mr. Smith. Mr. Alford then became associated with Judge Matt Walton, with whom he practiced for five or six years, when this partnership was dissolved, since which time Mr. Alford has been engaged in his profession alone.

About two years after his admission to the bar he was appointed master commissioner of the Fayette Circuit Court and held that office for four years. The next office he held was that of judge of the Recorder's Court of the city of Lexington, to which he was elected and served one full term of two years; was re-elected to the same office, but resigned just prior to the expiration of the term to make the race for State Senator in the Lexington district. He was elected to this office and served the full term of four years, taking an active part in that body, of which he was the youngest member. In the first session of his term, Mr. Alford served as chairman of the committee on appropriations, and in the second session was chairman of the committee on railroads. While a member of the Senate, Governor Alford's popularity became so general throughout the state, that in the gubernatorial convention of 1891 he was nominated without opposition for the office of lieutenant-governor on the ticket with John Young Brown, and was elected. For several years he held the position of chairman of the State Democratic Central Committee, and was only recently succeeded in that place by General John B. Castleman, of Louisville. He is president of the State League of Democratic Clubs, composed of some 400 organizations throughout the state, which is a high honor and is the best evidence that the Democratic party of Kentucky recognizes and appreciates his ability as an organizer and campaigner. Governor Alford is a "sound money" Democrat and was one of the several candidates for the office of governor on the Democratic ticket to succeed Mr. Brown. His defeat in the convention was due to political conditions rather than to the lack of willing supporters. Had he received the nomination he would have been elected by the usual Democratic majority.

Aside from his successful career in politics, he has been identified with various extensive business enterprises. He was one of the promoters and organizers of the First National Bank in Middlesborough, and at the first meeting of its board of directors, was elected president of that corporation. Shortly afterward he sold his entire stock in the bank, for prudential reasons, and resigned the presidency. During the "booming" days of Middlesborough he was president of several important land companies of the "Mountain City." He is also one of the stockholders and the treasurer of the Phoenix Hotel Company of Lexington, and is in possession of other valuable property.

With his fine ability as a lawyer and business man, and with the young Democracy of the state ready and willing to honor him, his success in the future is assured and he can afford to wait for honors that have only been deferred.

JOHN R. GRACE, who was one of the most able judges of the Court of Appeals, having had an experience of nearly forty years upon the bench prior to his induction into his late exalted position, was born in Trigg County, Kentucky, May 27, 1834, and died suddenly in Frankfort, February 20, 1896.

His father, William Grace, and his grandfather, George Grace, were native farmers of Trigg County, their ancestors having settled in the county during the eighteenth century. His mother, Mary (Organ) Grace, was a native of Wilson County, Tennessee.

Judge Grace was educated in the common schools of his neighborhood, and being of a studious turn of mind, acquired a fund of information unusual for a boy of his limited opportunities, and at the age of nineteen years he took up the study of law in the office of Matthew Mays of Cadiz. After a careful course of reading he attended the law department of the University of Louisville, from which institution he graduated in 1855.

In the same year he returned to Cadiz, and being duly admitted to the bar, began the practice of his profession. In a short time he formed a partnership with his former preceptor, under the firm name of Mays & Grace. This business relation continued without interruption until 1865, when the firm was dissolved and Judge Grace became associated with Judge Burnett, whose death occurred in the following year.

In 1858 Judge Grace was elected county judge of Trigg County, and served a term of four years. In 1868 he was elected circuit judge of the then Second Judicial District (embracing the counties of Trigg, Christian, Muhlenberg, Hopkins, Caldwell and Lyon) and was re-elected for a series of terms aggregating twenty-six years, which is sufficient proof of the high esteem in which he was held by the people of his district. But a higher endorsement was given him in his election as judge of the Court of Appeals from the First Appellate District, composed of eighteen counties in the western part of the state. He was inducted into that office January 7, 1895, for a term of eight years, succeeding Judge Caswell Bennett, deceased, but after serving a little more than a year, he died, unattended, in his room at the Capital Hotel in the morning of February 20, 1896. He had been complaining for some days, but had so far recovered that he was able to go to the breakfast table on the morning of his death, and had just returned to his room and was alone when he received the fatal stroke. The funeral services were held in the court house at his old home in Cadiz, no church in the place being large enough to accommodate those who desired to pay a last tribute of respect to the most distinguished citizen. His remains were accompanied to his home by committees from both branches of the legislature and by members of the Court of Appeals.

Judge Grace was married to Emily Terry in 1859 and she died in 1861, so that he enjoyed only about two years of married life.

JAMES HERVEY BARBOUR, M. D., an eminent physician of Falmouth, son of Nathaniel and Hannah (Ashburn) Barbour, was born in New Richmond, Clermont County, Ohio, February 29, 1824.

His father, Nathaniel Barbour, was a native of Hunterdon County, New Jersey, where he was engaged in agricultural pursuits; but removed to Cincinnati, Ohio, in 1808, prior to the war of 1812, in which he participated as a member of Captain Snell's Light Horse Cavalry. After the war he removed to New Richmond (1817), where he was for many years a merchant, removing to his farm in that vicinity in 1832, where he died in 1848. He was seriously wounded by the firing of a swivel, a custom adopted by the steamboat men as a signal for their departure. This accident caused the City Council of Cincinnati to pass an ordinance prohibiting the firing of the swivel in that port.

Nathaniel Barbour (grandfather) followed his son to Cincinnati in 1809 and settled in Clermont County, near Mulford, where he died. The Barbours were among the early settlers of New Jersey, and were conspicuous in the war of the Revolution against England.

Dr. Barbour's mother, Hannah (Ashburn) Barbour, a native of Bolton, England, was a daughter of Thomas Ashburn, an English manufacturer for the American market. The embargo in 1807 brought him to Cincinnati, where he owned fifty acres in the city, afterwards the Litel property, and was quite wealthy. After the war of 1812 he became the owner of one thousand acres of land in Clermont County, Ohio, upon which he laid out one-half of the town of New Richmond. He left a family history showing his direct lineage from 1688 down to the present time.

Dr. J. H. Barbour was raised on a farm in Clermont County, Ohio, and attended the district school during the winter months. At the age of seventeen he entered the Clermont Academy, where he studied for three or four years, and in 1847 and 1848 he took a more thorough course in classics and science in the Miami University at Oxford, Ohio. While acquiring his education, he spent some time in teaching in order to obtain means to defray his expenses.

In 1848 he began to read medicine with Dr. Daniel Barbour of Falmouth, Kentucky, a noted physician of that time. He attended two courses of lectures in the Medical College of Ohio at Cincinnati, and graduated in 1852. He at once began the practice of medicine in Falmouth, and was soon known as one of the leading physicians of the county; and after a professional life of forty-three years in that place he is still an active and busy physician of the highest professional standing.

Dr. Barbour has been a prominent and influential politician ever since he was old enough to exercise the right of suffrage. His first presidential vote was cast for General Taylor. While the Whig party was in existence he was its faithful supporter, and in the presidential election in 1860 he voted for Bell and Everett. In 1864 he voted for Abraham Lincoln for president. During the war of the Rebellion, he was an earnest supporter of the National Government, and since that time has been identified with the Republican party.

He was a delegate to the national Republican convention in Chicago in 1880, and was one of the "big four" Kentuckians in that body who broke the unit rule, the state convention having instructed delegates to vote as a unit, and voted against General Grant, defeating his aspirations for a third term, and in this he voted according to the instructions of his district. The national convention recognized the right of districts to instruct. He has attended nearly all the Republican state conventions held in the state since the war and has been prominent in the councils of his party.

He is a member of a number of medical associations, and keeps step with the advancement in medical science; has written numerous articles for the medical journals and has been an active and useful citizen during all of the years of his residence in Falmouth. He is a member of the Presbyterian Church, and has been an elder for many years. In all of his relations to the community he has maintained an unimpeachable character and enjoys the respect and confidence of all men. Dr. Barbour is related to many prominent people in Clermont and Hamilton Counties, Ohio; the late Judge Ashburn of Milford and that eminent lawyer of Cincinnati, Thomas Barbour Paxton, and others of the same name were his cousins.

Dr. Barbour was married December 27, 1852, to Emaline Houser, daughter of Samuel T. Houser, who was a prominent lawyer of Falmouth. Dr. Barbour has four sons and three daughters living:

Ashburn Kennett Barbour, an attorney at law in Helena, Montana.

Hervey Barbour, a graduate of Centre College, Danville, Kentucky, now private secretary of ex-Governor Houser, Helena, Montana.

Dr. George Houser Barbour, a graduate of Centre College and also of the Ohio Medical College, Cincinnati, a practicing physician in Helena, Montana.

Max Wilson Barbour, a student in the Ohio Medical College, Cincinnati.

Mary, wife of John A. Sutton of Cincinnati, Ohio.

Louise Barbour Spradling, wife of J. H. Spradling, a prominent young lawyer of Louisville, Kentucky; and Miss Sue Barbour.

Mrs. Emiline (Houser) Barbour is a sister of ex-Governor Houser of Montana, who was one of the pioneers of that state. They trace their ancestry back for many generations, and the progenitor of the family in America settled in North Carolina before the Revolutionary war. The family formed a part of the Moravian colony that settled at Bethania, North Carolina, in 1759.

Dr. Barbour's brothers, Daniel, Wilson and Nathaniel J., have been prominent in public and professional life; Daniel, now dead, stood very high as a physician and a man of superior intellect, and Wilson, now a resident of New Richmond, Ohio, and a farmer, was a soldier in the Seventh Regiment Ohio Cavalry, enlisting as a private, and was promoted to a lieutenancy; Nathaniel J., a physician, was assistant surgeon of the Fifty-ninth Regiment Ohio Infantry, and was in many of the most serious engagements of the war, serving until the fall of Atlanta. He was a leading physician of New Richmond, Ohio, where he died in 1885, when forty-seven years of age.

JAMES A. MITCHELL, Attorney-at-Law of Bowling Green, son of. James and Martha (Stockton) Mitchell, was born in (now) Metcalfe County, Kentucky, July 4, 1843. His father was a native of the same county and was born in 1817. He lived in his native county until 1877, when he removed to Glasgow and died there in 1894, when seventy-seven years of age. He was a farmer and dealer in live stock, a highly respected citizen and a faithful member of the Christian Church.

Elzy Mitchell (grandfather) was born in Green

County and was a prosperous farmer. He died in 1856 at the age of sixty-five years.

William Mitchell (great-grandfather) came from West Virginia, near Wheeling, and was one of the early settlers of Green County. The Mitchells originally came from Ireland.

Martha Stockton Mitchell (mother) was born in Edmonton, Barren County, in 1824, and died in the same county (now Metcalfe) in 1845, when twenty-one years of age.

Dr. Joseph B. Stockton (maternal grandfather) was a native of Virginia who removed to Barren County with his parents when he was a mere child and became one of the most prominent physicians and distinguished citizens of his county, serving one term as representative in the legislature, in 1840, and otherwise aiding his people in the capacity of public servant. He died in Barren (now Metcalfe) County in 1870, aged seventy-two years.

Rev. Robert Stockton (maternal grandfather), a native of Virginia and a Kentucky pioneer, was a noted Baptist minister who distinguished himself as such in the Green River country in the early years of the present century. His ancestors were from Scotland.

James A. Mitchell grew to manhood in his native county, attended Columbia Seminary and was in Center College in 1862, when he joined the Confederate army under General Morgan. While on the noted Ohio raid in 1863, he was captured and was a prisoner of war at Camp Chase, Columbus, Ohio, for one month, and at Camp Douglas, Chicago, for eighteen months, when he was exchanged. He then went to Richmond, Virginia, arriving there February 28, 1865. After General Lee's surrender, Mr. Mitchell, with a remnant of General Morgan's command, crossed the mountains to Charlotte, North Carolina, where Jefferson Davis and the members of his cabinet halted in their retreat from Richmond. An escort for the distinguished party was made up under command of Major Theophilis Steel, now a prominent physician in New York, and Mr. Mitchell was made orderly sergeant of the escort. They conducted Mr. Davis and his cabinet as far as Greenville, South Carolina, at which place the escort was given charge of the Confederate treasury; and, loading the coin and paper money in wagons, they crossed the state of South Carolina and halted near Washington, Georgia, at which point the money in the treasury was divided among the soldiers, there being $32 in coin for each man. Here the president and the members of his cabinet dispersed, each one being permitted to look out for himself. The soldiers then organized a private squad under the command of the late W. S. Edwards of Louisville and proceeded as far as Athens, Georgia, where they were paroled May 7, 1865. Mr. Mitchell still has his parole of that date in his possession.

He returned to Kentucky and taught school in his native county for one year. In the autumn of 1866 he entered the law department of Washington College, Virginia, of which General Robert E. Lee was then president. There were twenty-two members in the class of that year and twenty-one of them were ex-Confederate soldiers. He was graduated in the class of 1867, and the diploma which he received at that time bears the signature of General Lee.

Mr. Mitchell began his professional career at Madisonville, Kentucky, in partnership with Polk Lafoon, remaining there until August, 1868, when he removed to Bowling Green and located permanently. He has devoted himself exclusively to the practice of his profession, having no political ambition, asking and accepting no office, except that of member of the school board, which he has held since its organization thirteen years ago, and in which he feels a commendable pride. For eleven years past he has been the trusted attorney of the Louisville & Nashville Railroad Company, representing a district of five counties, and has rendered the company efficient service in a legal capacity. With this responsible position and a large general practice, Mr. Mitchell's time is fully employed and he enjoys a handsome income as a reward for his arduous services.

James A. Mitchell was married in 1869 to Sallie Barclay, daughter of the late Samuel A. Barclay of Bowling Green. She died in 1883, leaving three sons and two daughters: Robert, now regimental clerk of the Sixth Regiment of United States Cavalry, stationed at Fort Meyer, near Washington, D. C.; Martha, wife of George Ellis, merchant of Glasgow; Samuel B., a student in Ogden College; Louise and Julius B., who are living at home. He was again married September 22, 1886, to Carrie Burks, daughter of the late Henry H. Burks, of Barren County, and they have one daughter, Katherine. Miss Burks graduated with the first honor in 1878 from the Louisville Female High School, thereafter spent several years in the Boston School of Oratory, and at the time of her marriage occupied the chair of elocution and physical culture in the Southern Business and Normal College of Bowling Green.

Mr. Mitchell is a member of the First Presbyterian Church and has been an elder for twenty-five years. His wife is a member of the Methodist Church.

ALEXANDER C. TOMPKINS, member of the legislature from Daviess County and an extensive dealer in tobacco of Owensboro, is a native of Virginia and a descendant of a distinguished and honored family of that state. He is a son of William W. and Frances Samuellor (Pendleton) Tompkins, and was born in Charlottesville, Virginia, February 28, 1840.

His father, William W. Tompkins, was born in Bedford County, Virginia, in 1812. After attending excellent private schools in Charlottesville, he was elected county clerk of Albemarle County, which office he held for several years. During the Civil war he served the Confederacy in the commissary department, and died April 5, 1865, a few days before the surrender of General Lee. He married Frances Samuellor Pendleton, daughter of Henry Pendleton, and was the father of five children: Henry Pendleton, Alexander C., John N., Frederick Windon and Joseph B. Tompkins.

Dr. John Tompkins (grandfather) was educated in Bedford County, Virginia, and was a practicing physician in that county. His wife was a Miss Montgomery of Nelson County, Virginia.

Henry Pendleton (maternal grandfather) was a native of Louisa County, Virginia, and owned a large plantation in that county, and was one of the most popular and highly respected citizens.

Alexander C. Tompkins was educated in Charlottesville and in the Albemarle Military Institute, in which he spent two years, finishing his schooling at the age of eighteen years. He gave his attention to farming for a while before coming to Henderson, Kentucky, in 1859, where he was similarly engaged until in the spring of 1862, when he returned to Virginia and enlisted in the Twenty-third Regiment Virginia Infantry, in which he served as a sergeant under General Robert E. Lee and took an active part in all of the engagements in Virginia, including the battles of Kernstown, Cross Keys, Port Republic, seven days' battle around Richmond, the second battle of Manassas, the taking of Harper's Ferry and the battle of Antietam. He was transferred to the Second Regiment Virginia Cavalry, commanded by General Fitzhugh Lee, having been promoted to lieutenant. In this regiment he took part in the engagements at Kelly's Ford, Chancellorsville, Gettysburg, the Wilderness, Cold Harbor, and was in a number of battles in the vicinity of Richmond and Petersburg. At Appomattox Court House his regiment cut its way through the lines of the opposing army, and reaching Lynchburg, disbanded April 10, 1865.

After the war was over, he resumed his former occupation of a farmer in Nelson County, Virginia; and subsequently returned to Henderson, Kentucky, and engaged in farming in that county until March, 1867, when he removed to Daviess County, where he owned a large tract of farming land, which he cultivated mostly in tobacco, and on which he built a large stemmery and prepared tobacco for the European market.

In 1876 he removed to Owensboro and engaged in dealing in tobacco on an extensive scale, which proved a fortunate venture and resulted in the establishment of his present large stemmery, which he has conducted with unvarying success. Mr. Tompkins is one of the most popular business men in Owensboro; of a warm social nature, liberal in his views and charitable towards others; generous and public spirited in all matters concerning the city's advancement; fond of his home; devoted to his church and a hustler in business and politics.

Strictly speaking, he is not a politician, but his personal popularity and his splendid business qualifications have led him into official positions, rather against his inclinations, and certainly to the detriment of his personal business. In 1882-4 he served as a member of the City Council, and he has been a member of the School Board for eight years. In 1893 he was elected to the legislature by the Democratic party; was re-elected in 1895, and is the present able representative from Daviess County.

Mr. Tompkins was married June 12, 1868, to Elizabeth Mary Venable, daughter of Samuel Lewis and Virginia (Bransford) Venable; she was born November 29, 1844, received a superior education, and is one of the most refined and highly cultured ladies in Owensboro society. Mr. and Mrs. Tompkins are members of the Presbyterian Church, and in the work of the church they are no less active than he is in the world of politics and business.

THOMAS H. ARMSTRONG, a merchant of Augusta, son of James Wesley and Eliza Jane (Marshall) Armstrong, was born in Augusta, Kentucky, November 19, 1858. He was educated principally in the old Augusta College, and after leaving school engaged in the mercantile business with his father and has continued in the same line until the present time, taking his father's place not only in the wholesale grocery establishment, but in the affairs of public interest and in the hearts of the people.

Mr. Armstrong was married February 16, 1886, to Tena Reynolds, daughter of ex-Congressman William Reynolds of Bracken County. Mrs. Armstrong was born in 1858, and was educated under the careful teaching of Professor Bluett of Augusta College, and is one of the most accomplished ladies of the city in which she resides. Mr. and Mrs. Armstrong have three children: Amy Lee, James W. and Ada.

James Wesley Armstrong (father) was born in West Union, Ohio, February 14, 1822, and was a graduate of the old Methodist College of Augusta, and subsequently went to Transylvania University and graduated from the law department of that institution, but did not become a practitioner. He returned to Augusta and engaged in the manufacture of carriage hardware, and later in the wholesale grocery business, in which he continued until his death. He had a very extensive trade and sold goods throughout the northeastern and central portions of the state in competition with similar establishments in larger cities. He was deputy county clerk for a long term of years, and served his city in the Board of Councilmen for four years. He was a Democrat in politics, but his popularity was confined to no party organization.

He had more friends and wielded a greater influence and power in his county than any man who ever lived in it. One of his chief characteristics, for which he was loved and honored, was his liberality with his ample means, in bestowing charity and helping any cause which he believed to be for the general good of the community. He dispensed his charity with a lavish hand, and it was said that he literally threw money away, while he considered that he was laying up treasures in heaven. During the late Civil war, his sympathies were with the southern people, and he contributed large sums of money to help the cause of the Confederacy.

As an instance of his integrity and his loyalty to the South, the following incident is related: He was the patentee of a breech-loading gun for which the Remingtons had made him an offer and he went to New York to close the trade. The contract was drawn up by Samuel J. Tilden, and the consideration to be paid Mr. Armstrong was $150,000 and a royalty of fifty cents on each gun manufactured. After consideration he said it must be stipulated in the contract that no guns should be sold to the authorities of the United States government. Remington said he would not agree to this stipulation, as he thought that would be his only chance of making any money, to which Mr. Armstrong replied that he would not sell guns to kill rebels with, and so the sale was declared off. The authorities on the other side could not purchase his invention for lack of money, and thus, for the sake of principle, he refused a handsome fortune.

There was mourning in many households when James Wesley Armstrong died on the 13th of October, 1877, and the high esteem in which he was held was testified by the presence of the largest concourse in attendance at his funeral obsequies that has ever been witnessed in Bracken County.

William Armstrong (grandfather) was born in Rapahilla, Ireland, March 11, 1780, and came to America when fifteen years of age, arriving in New York June 22, 1795. There is no record available concerning his brother Johnson and sisters, whose names were Mary, Jane and Margaret; but his brother John settled in Maysville and James in Augusta.

On the 4th day of August, 1805, William Armstrong was married, near Washington, Kentucky, to Sarah Lee, by Rev. Caleb Jarvis Taylor. Sarah Lee was born in Virginia, August 22, 1787, and was closely related to "Light Horse Harry" Lee and General Robert E. Lee of the Confederate army. There were born to William and Sarah Lee Armstrong eleven children, all of whom were born in West Union, Ohio, except the youngest, who was born in Cincinnati:

Johnson, born May 23, 1806.

Mary Ann, born September 29, 1807; married to C. A. Campbell at Cincinnati, September 11, 1827, by Rev. Dr. Rooter; married the second time to L. Tomlinson at Ripley, in 1843.

Margaret, born August 26, 1809; married to S. S. Shropshire, by Rev. William Page, March 7, 1827, at West Union.

Jane Lee, born August 23, 1811; married to George Colling, September, 1830, at West Union, by Rev. I. Meek.

Sarah Anne, born June 11, 1813; married to William Reynolds, at West Union, by Rev. G. W. Walker; married the second time to C. E. Doddridge at Kanawha.

Matilda G., born August 22, 1815; married to Dr. J. P. Hamilton, at West Union, by Rev. G. W. Walker.

William McKendree, born July 15, 1818; married to Amanda Fitzallen Shaw, at Ripley, Ohio, by Rev. W. M. D. Ryan, August 10, 1843.

Caroline S., born April 11, 1820; married to G. W. Pegman, at Ripley, Ohio, April 5, 1838.

James Wesley (father), born February 14, 1822; married to Eliza J. Marshall, at Augusta, Kentucky, November 18, 1846.

Eliza M., born June 27, 1825; married to Horace Elmaker, October 10, 1843.

Julia O., born February 29, 1828; married E. W. Merriwether, at Augusta, Kentucky, November 28, 1844.

William Armstrong (grandfather) was a dry goods merchant in West Union, Ohio, and amassed a large fortune. He was an exemplary citizen and a pillar in the Methodist Church.

Eliza Jane Marshall Armstrong (mother) was born in Augusta, Kentucky, March 1, 1824, and was a graduate of a college or classical school in Sewickly, Pennsylvania. She was one of the organizers of the Baptist congregation in Augusta, and was always associated with that church. She was the mother of nine children, eight of whom are living. She was past seventy years of age at the time of her death, August 9, 1894.

Martin Marshall (maternal grandfather) was born in Virginia, September 11, 1777, and died in Augusta, September 19, 1853. He was one of the first settlers in Augusta; a lawyer and in every way worthy of the great name of Marshall. He was married March 16, 1803, to Matilda Taliaferro, who was born in Virginia, September 30, 1787, and died in Augusta, March 1, 1843.

JOHN HELM MALLORY, Mayor of Bowling Green, Kentucky, son of Robert T. and Sarah (Barner) Mallory, was born in Bowling Green, July 31, 1844. He was educated in the city schools and at the age of seventeen, in 1861, he was employed in a drug store as a clerk and served in that capacity until 1867, when he engaged in the drug business on his own account. He very soon established a good reputation and a profitable business, in which he has continued without interruption until the present time. In the spring of 1894 he admitted to partnership Mr. J. H. Barclay, who had been his clerk for seven years, under the firm name of Mallory & Barclay, and this house is now, unquestionably, the leading drug store in the Park City.

John H. Mallory is now serving his fifth term as mayor of Bowling Green, having been first elected to that office in 1875; after serving one term was elected for two consecutive terms of two years each, the time of office expiring in 1881. He was again elected mayor in 1893 for a term of two years and was re-elected in 1894 under the new constitution for four years. His administration of the affairs of the city has been commended in the highest degree by all classes of citizens, a fact which is fully attested by his frequent election to the mayoralty. He has been connected with the city government since 1870, having been a member of the City Council and commissioner of the sinking fund when he was not serving in the higher capacity of mayor.

Mr. Mallory is interested in a number of business enterprises and is president of the Standard Construction Company of Bowling Green, and is vice president of the Hopkinsville Water Company.

He has been twice married; first in 1866 to Belle Potter, daughter of P. J. Potter of Bowling Green. She died in 1887, and in 1893 he married his present wife, who was Blanche Lawrence of Grenada, Mississippi.

Robert T. Mallory (father) was a native of Virginia who removed to Bowling Green when he was a young man and married Sarah Barner. Both of them died in 1849, leaving their boy an orphan at the tender age of five years. With the aid of kind friends in his boyhood, he was enabled to secure a good education, and it may be said that he has had to make his own way in the world since he was a mere child. The habit of self reliance formed in youth has served him well in business and in official life, and he is to-day one of the most honored and respected citizens of the city which owes much to him for its growth and prosperity.

ISAAC HERSCHEL GOODNIGHT, attorney at law of Franklin, son of Isaac and Lucinda (Billingsby) Goodnight, born in Allen County, Kentucky, January 31, 1849. His father was born in Lincoln County, Kentucky.

Jacob Goodnight (grandfather), whose wife was a Miss Hoover, was a native of Mecklenburg County, North Carolina.

Michael Goodnight (great-grandfather), a native of Germany, came to America during colonial days, leaving Germany on account of religious proscription. He first located in Virginia and later removed to Mecklenburg County, North Carolina, and was a member of the Mecklenburg convention which adopted, in 1775, the first declaration of independence, much of which is engrafted into the Jeffersonian declaration. He had two sons who were soldiers in the Revolution. He moved to Kentucky in 1780, and settled at Harlan's Station, now in Mercer County. He was killed by Indians on one of his return business trips to North Carolina. He had twenty-four children. His son Isaac was born in the old fort near Harrodsburg, on January 1, 1782, being the first male white child born in Kentucky. This distinction is challenged by the heirs of Judge Logan, who was born at Harrodsburg, December 8, 1786.

Lucinda Billingsby Goodnight (mother) was born in Tennessee and was a daughter of John Billingsby, who came to Kentucky from east Tennessee and located in that part of Warren which is now Simpson County. His wife was Mary Doak, whose family was of Scotch-Irish origin.

Isaac H. Goodnight grew to manhood on the farm in Allen County and in 1870, at the age of twenty-one, removed with his parents to Franklin, where he has lived continually since. He was schooled in literature and law at Cumberland University, Lebanon, Tennessee, graduating from that institution in 1873. Returning to his home in Franklin, he read law while performing the duties of deputy circuit clerk and was admitted to the bar in 1874. He soon took rank among the leading lawyers of his section. His ability was recognized by the people of his county and in 1877 he was chosen to represent them in the legislature. Although one of the youngest members of that body, he was one of the most useful and active and attracted attention throughout the state. In 1888 he was elected to Congress from the Third district and was re-elected in 1890 and in 1892. After serving three terms, he declined a re-election on account of ill health and because his absence from home was detrimental to his legal business, which is now more remunerative than the compensation of a congressman. His service in Congress was marked by ability. His work on the judiciary committee was especially valuable, he being third on the list of that committee at the time of his retirement.

Mr. Goodnight was united in marriage, March

12, 1879, to Ella Hoy, daughter of Thomas J. and Lucy Milliken Hoy, natives of Simpson County. The only child of this union is a son, Hoy Goodnight. The home of this excellent family is one of the finest residences in Franklin, where hospitality, in the old and true meaning of the word, is dispensed in genuine Kentucky style.

Mr. Goodnight has steadily maintained his position at the head of his profession in southern Kentucky. He has thrown aside all political ambition, and his present aim is to devote his life to his profession, for which he is eminently equipped and to which he is thoroughly devoted.

GEORGE MILTON ELAM, a teacher of teachers, a leading institute instructor, founder and principal of the Blaine Normal School at Blaine, Kentucky, was born in Scott County, Virginia, July 11, 1856. His education was commenced in the common schools of Virginia, after which he went to the high school in Nicholasville, in that state. He then attended Hamilton Institute in Washington County, Virginia, and later the National Normal University at Lebanon, Ohio, and still later Central Normal College, Danville, Indiana, taking the teacher's course, in which he graduated in 1893, also a course in pedagogy, graduating in August, 1894. These different courses were not taken one directly following another, and in the meantime he was following the profession of the teacher, and held teachers' institutes in different parts of the state and in adjoining counties in West Virginia, Virginia, Ohio and Tennessee.

He taught six years in Virginia, commencing in the spring of 1872, when he was sixteen years of age; taught one year in Hamilton Institute, and the remaining time in the common schools. He came to Johnson County in 1879 and was a teacher in the public school for two years. He then removed to Blaine, Lawrence County, where he has been employed as teacher for fifteen years, founding, in the meantime, the Blaine Normal School, an institution which by his industry and skill in training teachers for their profession has proven a great success. A large number of teachers in Lawrence County have attended this school, deriving great benefit; and many from other counties in the state and from other states have availed themselves of its advantages. It is conceded to be one of the best institutions for the training and education of teachers, and has done more than similar schools for the advancement and improvement of the educational system in eastern Kentucky.

Mr. Elam is thoroughly devoted to the cause of education. The same energy and ability applied to another profession or to mercantile pursuits would undoubtedly bring greater pecuniary results, but he cares not so much for the monetary compensation he receives as for the good that he may accomplish in the education and enlightenment of the people of his adopted state.

Professor Elam has filled the office of county examiner with ability for eight years, raising the standard of the qualifications of teachers materially and helping them to attain to that high standard. He was superintendent of the county schools at one time, in which capacity he did much valuable work. He has been quite successful in all of his professional work, as a man must be who loves his vocation.

His success in establishing a Normal School where one was so much needed, and in training others, making professional teachers of many who had merely taught school as a makeshift while waiting for something better to turn up, is a source of gratification and justifiable pride to him; and for this work he enjoys the esteem and gratitude of all intelligent and worthy citizens of his county.

He is a member of the Methodist Church, a Mason and Odd Fellow, and in all of these he is an active and helpful worker.

Professor Elam was married August 29, 1879, to Rebecca E. Bond, daughter of William E. Bond. She was born in Wise County, Virginia, June 7, 1857. Her education commenced in Virginia and was continued in Kentucky and completed in the high school at Flat Gap, Kentucky. She taught school for three years in Johnson County, and has been a willing and able helpmeet in her husband's life work. They have five children living, and two died in infancy:

William N., deceased; Charley M., Martha,

George W., deceased; Harry B., Nancy C. and James K. Elam.

William Elam (father) was born in Russell County, Virginia, July 4, 1826; married Nancy Dingus in 1854; was a farmer in Scott County; a member of the Methodist Church and a citizen of excellent repute. He died in February, 1888, and is buried at the old homestead in Scott County, Virginia.

Nimrod Elam (grandfather) was born in Russell County, Virginia, where he lived and died. His wife's name was Nancy Easterling.

Nancy Dingus Elam (mother), daughter of George Dingus, was born December 25, 1836, and died June 20, 1890.

SAMUEL B. MILLS, M. D., one of the oldest and most highly respected physicians of Louisville, son of William P. and Mary E. (Moore) Mills, was born in Jefferson County, Kentucky, March 9, 1828.

His father, William P. Mills, was a native of Worcester County, Maryland, who came to Kentucky in 1815 and located in Jefferson County, about fifteen miles from Louisville, where he resided until about two years before his death, when he removed to Vigo County, Indiana. He belonged to the Maryland militia and did active duty in guarding the coast in the war of 1812, having been called out at the time Washington City was fired by the enemy. He was a patriotic, honorable, and upright citizen, and reached the good old age of four score years and one. His mother was a Miss Porter, sister of Dr. James Porter, who was a student of the celebrated Dr. Rush of Philadelphia and one of the signers of the declaration of independence and also a near relative of Commodore Porter of the United States navy.

William Mills (grandfather), also a native of Maryland, came to Kentucky in 1815, when Louisville was a very small town. He participated in the closing scenes of the Revolutionary war. He was a resident of Jefferson County from the time of his arrival with the early settlers until he was eighty-six years of age, when he died. His ancestors were of English extraction.

Mary E. Mills, mother of Dr. Mills, was a native of Jefferson County and died at the age of twenty-four years, when the subject of this biographical sketch was two years of age.

Thomas Moore (grandfather) was a native of Delaware, who came to Kentucky very early in the present century and purchased land near Louisville, upon which he spent the remainder of his days. He was seventy-six years old at the time of his death.

Samuel B. Mills was educated in the schools of his native county, principally at an academy in Jeffersontown. After completing his literary schooling, he sold dry goods for a Jeffersontown merchant for two years; and in 1850 he began to read medicine in that village under Dr. John S. Seaton, a very able and popular physician, and one of the most cultured gentlemen of that day; and after graduating from the medical department of the University of Louisville in 1852, Dr. Mills joined his distinguished preceptor in the practice of medicine in Jeffersontown and vicinity. This partnership continued for three years, when Dr. Mills bought his partner out and continued the practice in that vicinity until 1865. From 1861 to 1864 inclusive he was teacher of anatomy, physiology and hygiene in a school at Jeffersontown. In 1865 he removed to Louisville, where he was by no means a stranger, and at once secured a lucrative practice among the best people in the city. He has devoted his time strictly to his professional work, and has never undertaken anything that would in the least interfere with his attention to his patients. He was a member of the Board of Health, in which he did faithful and valuable service for many years. For some years he was a member of the College of Physicians and Surgeons, a medical organization for the regulation of the code of practice in the city; but he is not now a member of any medical association. He has for more than forty years been a member of the Christian Church, and for more than twenty years an elder in the church; has for many years been engaged in benevolent enterprises; has been for twelve years one of the physicians of the Christian Church Widows' and Orphans' Home of Kentucky, of which he has been a member of the board from its organization.

Dr. Mills was married in 1854 to Susan Herr,

daughter of Honorable John Herr, who at one time represented Jefferson County in the Kentucky legislature. Mrs. Mills died in 1868, leaving two sons and two daughters: Susan M., wife of J. M. Allan of Louisville; Arthur P. Mills; Worden S. Mills; and Eva, wife of Dr. S. S. Foss of Jefferson County.

Dr. Mills was married again in 1892 to Bettie Embry of Louisville, who is a native of Madison County, Kentucky.

RUFUS HUMPHREY VANSANT, of the lumber firm of R. H. Vansant & Company, and a popular business man of Ashland, was born in Morgan County, Kentucky, September 8, 1852.

His father, William H. Vansant, was born in Russell County, Virginia, October 15, 1819, and was educated in Scott County, Virginia. He came to Kentucky when he was a young man and taught school in Morgan (now Elliott) County for five years, and was subsequently engaged in stock trading in Eastern Kentucky. He was a man of fine literary attainments, very highly respected for his manly character and sound views upon questions of public interest; was a Union Democrat during the war, and wielded a healthful influence among his neighbors. He died in Elliott County, April 29, 1870, and is buried near Martinsburg. His father was one of the early settlers in Pennsylvania, who migrated to Maryland, Virginia and finally to Russell County, Kentucky, where he died.

Louvisa Hunter Vansant (mother) was born in Greenville, Tennessee, and was educated in Morgan County, Kentucky. She was married to William H. Vansant December 24, 1841. She survived her husband twenty-three years, and died July 3, 1893.

Benjamin Franklin Hunter (grandfather) was born in Tennessee, in 1800; came to Morgan County, Kentucky, and was a farmer there until his death, in 1875. His wife's name was Elizabeth Drake, who was born in Tennessee in 1802, and died in Morgan County in February, 1872. The Hunters were descendants of a highly respectable English family.

Rufus H. Vansant of Ashland was educated in Morgan County, under the careful and able training of his father; taught school in Elliott County from 1870 to 1880, inclusive; was deputy clerk of the Elliott Circuit Court from 1880 to 1886, and was elected clerk in 1886, serving until 1892, making twelve years of service in the circuit clerk's office. He was also master commissioner of the Elliott Circuit Court from 1884 to 1895.

During his service in the clerk's office, in 1881, he became interested in the lumber business at Leon, purchasing the lumber taken from the forests along the Little Sandy River. In this way he became an extensive lumber dealer and broker, and in April, 1894, he came to Ashland and established the firm of which he is the senior member and the energetic and capable manager.

He is a Democratic voter; held office through his connection with that party; and takes an active part in the important political campaigns, in which his fine business qualifications and tact make him a leader and a hard man to beat.

He is a Knight Templar and a Shriner, and a member of a lumber association, known as the "Concatenated Order of Hoo-Hoo."

Mr. Vansant was married December 3, 1879, to Anna V. Hannah, daughter of James W. Hannah of Elliott County. She was born in Kanawha County, West Virginia, September 12, 1862. They have two children living: Mexie, born April 17, 1892, and Harold Henderson, born October 5, 1894. One child died in infancy.

JOHN C. SCHROLL, president of the Newport National Bank, was born in Cincinnati, Ohio, August 20, 1845. His parents removed from that city to Newport in 1848, and he received his education in the common schools of the last named city.

After leaving school he was connected with the Monumental & Building Stone Works, and while interested in that enterprise studied law, attending the Cincinnati Law School for two years, graduating from that institution in 1871. He was duly admitted to the practice of law in the Kentucky courts, and was elected clerk of the circuit, chancery and criminal courts, which offices he held for three terms, or eighteen years; and at the end of the third term, declined further election.

In July, 1892, he assisted in the organizing of

the Newport National Bank, and was elected president of the new organization. The capital stock of the bank ($100,000) was subscribed in one day, showing the confidence the business men placed in Mr. Schroll and Mr. Waller Overton, who were to be respectively president and cashier. The new bank passed through the trying times of the panic of 1893 without a stain upon its credit, or a doubt in the public mind as to its ability to weather the storm. It is now one of the strongest and most popular banking houses in the city. Mr. Schroll devotes almost his entire time to the affairs of the bank, and has developed marked ability as a financier.

He has been a leader in the Democratic party, but is now out of politics. He has recently engaged in the practice of law with Aubrey Barbour, a young man of marked ability, the firm name being Schroll & Barbour.

Mr. Schroll was married in 1870 to Martha Band of Newport. They have two sons and three daughters: Henry Clay, Thomas Benton, Esther, Mattie B., and Laura. John Randolph, the oldest son, died in 1886, aged fourteen years. Mrs. Schroll and the children are members of the Episcopal Church.

Mr. Schroll's father, Martin Schroll, is a native of Bavaria, but came to Cincinnati when he was quite young, and was married at that place in 1840 to Dorothea Fleckenstein. They removed to Newport in 1848, and Mrs. Dorothea Schroll died in 1854. Martin Schroll, now seventy-six years of age, has retired from the marble and building stone business, in which he was engaged for many years, and is living in Bellevue.

ALFRED CARTER HAILEY, County Judge of Boyd County, son of Carter and Elizabeth (Drury) Hailey, was born in Greenup County, Kentucky, May 4, 1835.

His father, Carter Hailey, was a native of Virginia, who removed to Scioto County, Ohio, in 1794; was in the War of 1812, serving one year as drum major and supervisor of the musicians; re-enlisted the second year of the war in company with Andis Buford Hailey, who afterward went to Louisiana and became a cotton planter. After Mr. Hailey was mustered out of service he removed to Greenup County, Kentucky, where he was a farmer until his death, December 25, 1838. He was a man of unusual learning for the times in which he lived. His father, John Hailey, was a native of Virginia, who went to Scioto County, Ohio, and was a farmer there until his death.

Elizabeth Drury Hailey (mother) was a native of Scioto County, Ohio, where she received an excellent education. She was a member of the Methodist Church, and was well known and loved for her many good works. She died in Greenup County, February, 1847.

Judge Hailey was the youngest but one of nine children. He was educated in Catlettsburg, and learned the trade of house and sign painting and decorating, which business he followed industriously until his election as county judge in November, 1894.

He was a gallant soldier in the Union army, enlisting September 27, 1862, in Company D, Thirty-ninth Kentucky Mounted Infantry, and did duty in the cavalry arm of the service throughout the war. His regiment was in the command of General Julius White, for a time and later in General Boyle's command, and still later under Generals S. G. Burbridge and Hobson, and finally under General Palmer. He participated in the battles of King's Salt Works in Virginia, Wariman's Shoals, Mount Sterling, Cynthiana and others, his regiment being confined principally to service in Kentucky.

He entered the army as a private; was elected first lieutenant by a vote of his company, and later captain; was post commissary on the staff of Colonel G. W. Gallup, who commanded the brigade for eighteen months; on March 2, 1865, he was detailed to take charge of a flag of truce and escort Miss Fannie Breckenridge, now Mrs. John Steele of Midway, Kentucky, and Mrs. J. Stoddard Johnston, to Richmond, Virginia; Miss Breckenridge to see her father, General John C. Breckenridge, and Mrs. Johnston her husband. It required about two weeks to make the journey, and there were twenty-five soldiers in the detail.

Judge Hailey has been an active member of the Odd Fellows' fraternity for thirty-two years, and was chosen Deputy Grand Master in 1886. He is an enthusiastic member of the Grand Army of the Republic, and has filled a number of positions of honor and trust in his post. He has always been interested in politics, first as a Whig and later as a Republican. Having no legal education or experience, his election to the office of county judge was due to his prominence and popularity in his party and to his sound judgment and proverbial honesty of purpose.

He was married January 25, 1857, to Luvina H. Friend, daughter of Charles Friend of Floyd County. Mrs. Hailey was born September 16, 1837, and was educated in Floyd County. They have four children living: William H., born December 29, 1857; Mollie C., born February 5, 1860, wife of Frank Johnson of Gallipolis, Ohio; Stella, born May 30, 1868, wife of R. N. Braley of Charleston, West Virginia; Andis Buford, born July 30, 1873, and Curtis H., born 1861, died July 11, 1863.

REVEREND FATHER EDMUND A. BURKE, pastor of the Annunciation Catholic Church, Paris, was born in the city of New York, June 4, 1850. His father, John Burke, removed to Harrodsburg, Kentucky, in 1854, and later to Boyle County, near Danville, where he was engaged in agricultural pursuits. His wife's maiden name was Ann Donnelly.

Father Burke, after receiving his primary schooling in Danville, entered St. Joseph's College at Bardstown, and took a classical course of five years. He then prepared for the priesthood at Mount St. Mary's of the West, and was ordained October 18, 1878.

His first charge was at Florence, Kentucky, which he assumed the same year of his ordination, and remained there for ten years, doing a good work for the church and community.

He then went to Ludlow, where he was stationed for five years, in which time he rendered valuable services; purchasing a fine parochial residence; founding the first English speaking Catholic school, which he placed in charge of the Sisters of Nazareth; erected a church edifice in Independence, and accomplished much other important work in the vicinity of his labors in this field. In 1894 he went to Paris to take the place made vacant by the death of Father John Redman, who had been in charge of the church six years. Father Redman was an exceptionally fine man and accomplished a good work in his parish, and died in the prime of life, at the age of forty-six years.

The Annunciation Church has a large connection, embracing one hundred and seventy-five families, and has a parochial school in which pupils are prepared for college. This is one of several schools in the diocese that received special mention at the World's Fair Catholic Exhibit of Educational Progress. Father Burke is deeply interested in this school, which is taught by the Sisters of Nazareth, and has an average attendance of about one hundred pupils. The school room in the rear of the church was inadequate to the demands of the growing parish, and Father Burke completed last September a magnificent new school building costing five thousand dollars. He is especially diligent in matters of education, in which he has already attained most satisfactory results.

Father Burke is a man of fine literary attainments, amiable in disposition, and a fine speaker. He is an enthusiastic member of the Catholic Knights of America and of the Young Men's Institute.

WILLIAM SLAUGHTER FANT, banker, miller, farmer and all-round business man of Flemingsburg, one of the wealthiest men in northern Kentucky, was born in Fleming County, May 21, 1830.

His father, Nelson Fant, was born in Stafford County, Virginia, April 2, 1777; married Mary P. White in 1810; came to Fleming County in 1813, and spent the remainder of his days in that county; was extensively engaged in farming and grain milling; was baptized and received into the Christian Church by Elder John Smith, and was a Whig of decided convictions.

Mary P. White (mother) was born, educated and married in Stafford County, Virginia. She was the mother of four children: Louise, Juliet, James M. and William S.

James Fant (grandfather) was a native and lifetime resident of Stafford County, Virginia; a farmer and member of the Baptist Church, a man of fine intelligence and splendid character.

Rhoda White (maternal grandfather) was also a native of Stafford County, Virginia; a soldier in the Revolutionary war, and a member of the Baptist Church. He married Mary Ficklen of the same county, in which he lived and died.

William Slaughter Fant, the descendant of these patriots of Revolutionary times, was educated in private schools in Fleming County, and began a most successful business career at the age of sixteen, when he embarked in merchandising in Sherburne as a member of the firm of Garfield & Fant. His partner was a cousin of President Garfield and represented the county in the constitutional convention of 1849-50, and was a member of Congress from Washington Territory. He married Juliet Fant, sister of William S., and was a teacher and preacher in Fleming County, and a very able man.

The partnership of Garfield & Fant continued about two years, and in 1850 Mr. Fant undertook the management of his father's milling business at Sherburne, which at that time was not in a promising condition. He placed it on a good footing, extending the facilities and soon developed into a successful manager. He removed to Flemingsburg in 1869, where he has since been living; but his business has expanded beyond the limits of the county and state, and his various interests are so numerous and extensive that when asked to enumerate them, he admitted that he could hardly do so.

He established a mill at Pleasant Valley, Nicholas County, in 1867, now in operation; the roller mills at Flemingsburg in 1869; was owner of a mill in Mt. Sterling for a short time; became interested as a large stockholder in, and vice-president of the banking house of Pearce & Fant, in Flemingsburg in 1876; has acquired many hundreds of acres of farming lands in Kentucky, Indiana and Texas; owning many tracts in Fleming, Bath and Nicholas Counties, all of which are cultivated under his own management. In Kentucky, his principal crops are grain and tobacco; in Texas his business is principally stockraising.

With all of these diversified interests, he keeps them well in hand and unencumbered, so that it will be seen that from a small beginning with his father, whose business affairs were in a bad shape, he has acquired great wealth, which he is unable, and does not care to compute.

Mr. Fant united with the Christian Church at the age of twenty-seven years, and a few days later, in 1858, he was made an elder, in which relation to the church he stands to-day. This fact, together with his well-known business integrity, is a sufficient testimonial of his excellent character.

Politically his affiliations are with the Republican party.

Mr. Fant and Susan E. Saunders were united in marriage April 14, 1853. She is a daughter of Oliver and Maria (Burns) Saunders; was born near Sharpsburg, Bath County, April 4, 1832, and received a good education in the best private schools of her native county.

Of their children only four are living: Lula, widow of William Warford, deceased; Nelson, married Mollie Knight, and is living in Flemingsburg; Olive, daughter, living in Flemingsburg; Edwin L., married Susan McMullen and died at the age of thirty-three years. William Saunders Fant, in his twentieth year, is bookkeeper in Flemingsburg Roller Mills.

Oliver Saunders, Mrs. Fant's father, was a soldier in the War of 1812.

GREEN BERRY SWANGO, Register of the Land Office at Frankfort, one of the best known and most prominent men of Eastern Kentucky, son of Stephen and Caroline (Trimble) Swango, was born in Wolfe County (then Morgan), Kentucky, February 8, 1846. Stephen Swango was a native and a resident of the same county until his death, which occurred in 1877, at the age of fifty-nine years. He was extensively engaged in farming, and was one of the best business men in his section of the state. He was a member and elder of the Christian Church, was kind and liberal to the poor and stood high as a citizen. He was a Democrat of the old school, but not a politician.

Abraham Swango (grandfather) was born in

that part of Bourbon County which is now Powell County; was a farmer by occupation; and died in 1863 at the old Swango homestead in Wolfe County, at the age of seventy-three years. He was a member of the Baptist Church, and was a soldier in the War of 1812, and was with General Jackson in the battle of New Orleans. His wife, Deborah Ogden, was born in Wolfe County, Kentucky.

Samuel Swango (great-grandfather) was born on the farm owned by George Washington, near Mt. Vernon, Virginia, and came to Kentucky in 1785, or about that date, and located on a farm in that part of Fayette County which is now in Powell County, where he continued to reside for about twenty-five years, when he removed to Wolfe County, and died at an advanced age. He married Betsy Banion of Virginia. His father, Abraham Swango (great-great-grandfather), was a native of Germany, who immigrated to this country in the year 1741, when fourteen years of age, with his father, William Swango (great-great-great-grandfather), and located in Virginia, near Mt. Vernon, where his father died soon after his arrival. His mother died during the voyage and was buried at sea. Abraham Swango was a wagon-maker by trade. He married Alsie Pyles, a lady of Irish birth, who resided in the neighborhood of Mt. Vernon. He was a lessee on General Washington's farm; was a soldier in the Revolutionary war, and removed to Kentucky in 1785.

Caroline Trimble Swango (mother) was born in 1817 in the village of Hazel Green, which was then Montgomery County, Kentucky. She now resides at the old homestead, now in Wolfe County. She has been a consistent member of the Christian Church for fifty years.

Green Berry Swango grew to manhood on the farm on which he now resides in Wolfe County and received his education in the common schools, supplemented by a course in Stillwater Seminary in that county, of which institution his uncle was principal. Since leaving school he has always been engaged in farming, and now owns a part of the old homestead, which was originally a tract of fourteen hundred acres. At the early age of fifteen years, in 1861, Judge Swango joined the Fifth Kentucky Volunteer Infantry, known as the "Ragamuffins," under the command of General John S. Williams of Mt. Sterling, H. C. Swango, an uncle, being captain of Company I of this regiment. After a service of twelve months the Fifth Kentucky Regiment was disbanded and he re-enlisted in the Tenth Kentucky Cavalry and served until the close of the war. He was wounded at the battle of Cynthiana in June, 1864, receiving a gunshot wound in the head, and was left on the field for dead. •This was the closest call he had during his long service in the Confederate army. Judge Swango had one uncle and four cousins of the same name who were killed in the service of the Confederacy. During the last several months of the war Judge Swango was corporal and second sergeant, but most of the time he did duty as a private soldier.

In the fall of 1865 he returned to his home in Wolfe County, where he settled down to farming, but has been more or less engaged in mercantile enterprises also. He has always taken an active part in politics, and is one of the most influential and prominent Democrats in Eastern Kentucky. He has filled many positions of trust and responsibility, having served as school commissioner of his county for two years, justice of the peace for four years and master commissioner of the Circuit Court of his county for six years. In the Legislature of 1877-8 he was chosen doorkeeper of the House of Representatives; in 1882 he was elected county judge of Wolfe County; was re-elected in 1886 and held this office for eight consecutive years. In the Constitutional Convention of 1890-1 Judge Swango ably represented the Counties of Montgomery, Menifee, Powell and Wolfe, and took a leading part in its deliberations. Besides the many political and other positions which he has held in his county he was chairman of the Democratic Central Committee for eight years. In 1891 he was elected register of the land office of Kentucky, in which office he served until the expiration of his term, January, 1896.

Judge Swango was married in 1869 to Eliza J. Young, daughter of Hugh Young of Tazewell County, Virginia, and they have three sons: James H., Charles S. and John Morton. James H. represented Center College in the state oratorical contest, and won the first prize. In 1893 he represented the state in the international oratorical contest, and carried off the honors, receiving the votes of five of the six judges. In 1891, when only twenty years of age, he canvassed the Tenth Congressional District, making public speeches for the Democrats, and meeting the representatives of the Populist and Republican parties in the discussion of the political questions of the day.

Judge Swango, with the assistance of two other gentlemen, organized the Hazel Green Academy, and served as chairman of the Board of Trustees for two years. His children were partially educated in this excellent institution.

WILLIAM HOPKINSON COX, Mayor of Maysville and one of the leading business men and capitalists of that city, is a descendant of an old and honored English family and is endowed with many of the sterling qualities and strong traits of character for which his ancestors have been distinguished for generations. He was born in Maysville, Kentucky, October 22, 1856, and is a son of Elizabeth R. (Newman) and William Hopkinson Cox.

George Cox (grandfather) was born in London, England, in 1791. He came to America and after stopping in Cincinnati, Ohio, a short time, removed to Lexington, Kentucky, in 1817, and two years later, after having prospected in Cincinnati, Lexington and Maysville, concluded that Maysville would eventually be the largest place of the three, and accordingly located permanently in that city. In April, 1819, he opened a retail dry goods store within a square of the present site of the store of his grandsons. It was not long until he had built up a flourishing trade, succeeding beyond his greatest expectations. He continued in business until he had amassed a splendid fortune, and was always satisfied with his choice of Maysville as the best city for a business location He died in 1881, in the ninety-first year of his age. The family name was DeCaux, originally, and the ancestors were Normans, tracing back their relationship to William the Conqueror. (See sketch of George Cox in this volume.)

William Hopkinson Cox, son of George Cox, and father of the present mayor of Maysville, was born in Maysville, and at the age of twelve years began to sell goods in his father's store, and was associated with him as long as his father continued in business, succeeding him after his death. He was for many years vice-president of the State National Bank and was one of the most enterprising citizens, being thoroughly identified with the best interests of the city and enthusiastic in all measures for its advancement. He died in 1885, in the sixty-fifth year of his age; and was succeeded in business by his sons, William H. and George Lissant Cox, now the leading merchants of Maysville.

Elizabeth R. Newman Cox (mother) was born in London, England, and was a daughter of Rev. William H. Newman, an English gentleman and a minister of the Church of England, who came to America early in the present century, and died in 1852.

William Hopkinson Cox, the subject of this sketch, was educated in the private and select schools of Maysville, and at the age of fifteen was thrown upon his own resources, and following his father's example, he began his business career as a clerk in the dry goods store. He was thus employed until the death of his father in 1885, when he became a joint owner of the establishment with his brother; and, notwithstanding his large investments in many other enterprises, he retains his interest in the house of his father and his father's father, and feels a commendable pride in sustaining its splendid reputation.

During the last ten years Mr. Cox has been extensively engaged in building houses and has probably done more than any other individual citizen in improving the city. The Cox Block, on the corner of Third and Market streets, one of the finest buildings in the city, is an example of his enterprise, and would be an ornament to any city. In the rear of this magnificent structure he has built a block of thirteen handsome residences equal in construction and appearance to the finest dwelling houses in the city.

He is identified with almost every movement for the advancement of Maysville; has been president of the State National Bank since 1889, succeeding John T. Wilson, deceased; was a director in the Electric Light & Gas Company, and is a third owner of the Electric Street Railway, one of the first lines in that section of the state, an enterprise which was projected and built by him in connection with Robert A. Cochran and Newton Cooper.

Mr. Cox has never had any desire for political preferment, but having the welfare of the city at heart, and desiring to accomplish some changes that were needed in the city government, he yielded to the solicitation of his fellow-citizens and accepted the nomination and was elected mayor in November, 1893. As the chief executive of the city he has taken a great interest in its progress, and has brought into requisition the qualifications of an upright and capable business man, greatly to the advantage of the public whom he serves.

Mr. Cox was tendered the nomination of his party for Congress in 1888, and this would doubtless have been equivalent to an election, but he declined, preferring to remain at home and serve his people in helping to build up his native city.

William Hopkinson Cox and Sue E. Farrow of Mount Sterling, niece of Chief Justice Peters of the Court of Appeals, were united in marriage in 1880.

THOMAS T. FORMAN, of Lexington. The Forman family in the United States are of English origin, being descended from Robert Forman, an Englishman who left England on account of the persecution of Archbishop Land, in the reign of Charles I. and emigrated to Holland. From Holland he removed in 1645 to the Dutch possessions on Long Island, New York, where he was one of the incorporators of the town of Flushing. Robert's grandson, Samuel, removed from Long Island to Monmouth County, New Jersey, and became high sheriff of that county. Thomas Forman, a grandson of Samuel, removed with his wife and children from Monmouth County, New Jersey, to Mason County, Kentucky, in 1789. The Rev. Ezekiel Forman, D. D., is a grandson of Thomas Forman. The subject of this sketch, Thomas T. Forman, second son of Rev. Ezekiel and Ellen (Russel) Forman, was born in Richmond, Kentucky, December 29, 1852. His father was born in Mason County, Kentucky, and is now the pastor of Memorial Presbyterian Church at New Orleans, where he has been in charge since 1890, until which time he spent all his life in Kentucky, and he was the oldest member in the Presbytery of Transylvania (as to seniority in its membership) when he left the state for the South. He is now, June, 1895, in the seventy-seventh year of his age. During his ministry he has presided over many of the church courts and has commanded the respect and esteem of all who know him. His brother, C. W. Forman, D. D., was a missionary in India for forty-five years, and died in 1894, aged seventy-three years. He was the first foreigner whose remains were borne through the streets of Lahore at a public burial. He was known in India as Baba (grandfather) Forman. At the time of his death he was at the head of schools aggregating some sixteen hundred native pupils, and was greatly beloved by them.

Ezekiel Forman (grandfather) was a native of New Jersey, and settled when quite a young man in Mason County, Kentucky, where he married Dolly Wood, who was the second white child born in what is now Mason County. He was a man of great enterprise and activity, was extensively engaged in farming and trading, and ran a line of flatboats from Maysville to New Orleans. He died in Mason County more than a half century ago, at the age of sixty-five years. The mother of Thomas T. Forman was a native of Danville, Kentucky, and died in her fiftieth year; was a devoted member of the Presbyterian Church, and the daughter of David A. Russel, who was born in Belfast, Ireland, and was of Scotch-Irish extraction. For many years he was a leading elder in the Presbyterian Church at Danville, where he was for many years engaged in mercantile pursuits. He was a man highly respected in his community and of unblemished honor. His death occurred in 1860 at the age of sixty-five.

Thomas T. Forman grew up principally in Richmond and Danville, Kentucky, and received his education in the University of Virginia, and in the Kentucky University, and was graduated from several schools of both these institutions. After leaving school he taught one year at Bardstown, and then read law with Honorable John

Quincy Ward of Cynthiana. He was admitted to the bar in 1873, and from May, 1874, to September, 1890, he practiced law in Cynthiana, when he moved to Lexington, where he has since been in the active and successful practice of his profession. Mr. Forman is a Democrat and while at Cynthiana served as attorney for that city; was attorney for one of the national banks, and was local counsel for the Kentucky Central Railroad Company. Since his residence in Lexington he has served—by the choice of his brethren of the bar—repeatedly as special judge of the Fayette Circuit Court.

Mr. Forman has been a member of the Presbyterian Church for nearly thirty years and an elder in the same for about fifteen years. Shortly after his coming to Lexington the First Presbyterian Church requested him to take charge of the Maxwell Street Presbyterian Mission, a new brick church having been built on Maxwell, between Limestone and Upper streets, with parsonage attached, but without any church organization; and in June, 1891, Mr. Forman did the first work there in organizing an afternoon Sunday school. In May following the organization was made a separate church, and is now self-sustaining, having a membership of between two and three hundred. Mr. Forman has been one of the ruling elders of this church since its organization, and those best acquainted with the history of that church attribute its remarkable growth in a large measure to the work of the subject of this sketch.

In 1876 Mr. Forman was married to Miss Lelia Campbell Donohoo of Bardstown, Kentucky, and of this union four children have been born, three sons and one daughter, all of great promise. The first-born, M. Don. Forman, is expected to complete the course of Bachelor of Arts at Kentucky University in 1896.

In 1890 Mr. Forman was commissioner of West Lexington Presbytery to the General Assembly of the Presbyterian Church, South, at Asheville, North Carolina, and has repeatedly represented his church in his Presbytery, and in the Synod of Kentucky.

Considering the few years he has been a resident of Lexington, and the strength of the bar of that city, he has been employed in very many important cases, and has won the respect of the community and the confidence of the bench and bar. He has never been an aspirant for office. He is a zealous Mason and at the time this is written is Master of Lexington lodge, No. 1, the oldest lodge of Free Masons west of the Alleghanies, having been founded four years prior to the erection of Kentucky into a state.

THOMAS H. FRAYSER, who was an honored citizen and well-known business man of Owensboro, was born in Cumberland County, Virginia, February 9, 1837, and died in Owensboro, Kentucky, December 8, 1894. He received his early training and education in Virginia, and came to Kentucky when he was a young man and was associated for a time with his brother William in the tobacco brokerage. He removed to Calhoun, Kentucky, and from that place to Owensboro, where he was engaged in various enterprises until the time of his death. He was a soldier in the Confederate army under General Mahone, Twelfth Virginia Regiment of the Army of Northern Virginia, and was in a number of engagements, including the battles at Manassas and Fredericksburg. During the last year of his service in the army he was detailed for duty in the commissary department.

During his long residence in Owensboro he was for a time engaged in the tobacco business, and for fourteen years was connected with the wholesale grocery establishment of McJohnson & Company. He was president of the Owensboro Board of Education for nine years, an office for which he was highly qualified, being a man of superior intelligence, of fine business capacity and having a deep interest in the cause of education. He was elected to this position upon the ground of his peculiar qualifications and not on account of his political affiliations, and he served his constituents faithfully.

He was for twenty years a member of the board of stewards of Settle chapel, Methodist Episcopal Church, South, and his business transactions were characterized by his fidelity to the principles which he professed. He was for twelve years the beloved and honored superintendent of the Sunday school, and in appreciation of his services and as a testimonial of their love for him, the school, since his death, has had his life-size portrait hung in the Sabbath school room.

He was married in Petersburg, Virginia, in 1863, to Sallie Harris, and they had ten children, two of whom died in infancy. Those of his children who survive him are: Frederick Harris, Judith Bransford, Mary Susan, Thomas Hatcher, Sarah Catherine, Jessamine, Giles Harris, and Martha Bransford.

Thomas H. Frayser's father, William Frayser, was born in Cumberland County, Virginia, in 1807, and died there in 1882. He was a farmer, and a member of the Methodist Church. He married Judith Bransford, a native of the same county, and a daughter of Benjamin Bransford. Their children were: William; Mary, who married Y. N. French; Susan M., who married H. N. Brazey; Virginia, who married William Brozeal; Benjamin, who was killed while serving in the Confederate army; Robert, who married a Miss Allen of Owensboro; and Thomas H., the subject of this sketch.

Benjamin Bransford (maternal grandfather) was a native of Cumberland County, Virginia, and a very wealthy farmer; whose wife was Lucy Hatcher, of the same county.

JOHN P. PROWSE of Hopkinsville, Clerk of the Christian County Court, was born in Muhlenberg County, Kentucky, December 29, 1844. His father, Colonel George O. Prowse, was born in North Carolina in 1804 and came to Kentucky when quite young, locating in Muhlenberg County, where he was a farmer and took a prominent part in military affairs, being a colonel of the militia by virtue of his knowledge of military tactics and his unquestioned bravery. He died at his home in Muhlenberg County, February 24, 1862. His father came from England and became a prominent citizen of North Carolina.

Francis Wells (maternal grandfather) was a native of North Carolina, who came to Muhlenberg County while quite young and was a prosperous farmer.

John P. Prowse was educated in his native county and lived on the farm with his father until he was twenty-six years of age, when he married and bought a farm, which he retained and operated for three years. In 1873 he sold his farm and engaged in mercantile business in connection with his tobacco trade, in which he was interested for a period of fifteen years. In 1889 he was appointed deputy collector under John Feland, collector Second district, Kentucky, and had his headquarters in Hopkinsville, serving for one year, and in 1890 he was elected clerk of the Christian County Court and was re-elected in 1894 for a second term of four years.

He is an ardent Republican and an active and influential leader in his party. His election to his present office was in a large measure due to his personal popularity, as well as his superior qualifications for the performance of the duties of his office.

John P. Prowse and T. J. Atkinson of Christian County were united in marriage January 13, 1873. They have an interesting group of children: Frank, Charles, Nonie and John P. Prowse, Jr., all of whom are members of the Universalist Church at Hopkinsville.

EDWIN FARLEY, ex-postmaster and prominent citizen of Paducah, Kentucky, son of Michael and Mary (Dolan) Farley, was born August 28, 1842, in Walworth County, Wisconsin, before that territory had been admitted to statehood. His father was born in County Meath, Ireland, in 1809; received a good education and was interested with his father in the manufacture of linen there before he came to America in 1830. He first located in New York, remaining there until 1836, when he removed to the territory of Wisconsin, settling in Walworth County, where he purchased a tract of land, which he cultivated until recently, but is now living with his daughter in Iowa, retired from business, having accumulated a handsome fortune. He was one of the pioneers of Wisconsin and found Indians there at the time of his settlement, but they were not as troublesome as they had been to the early settlers of Kentucky.

While living in New York Mr. Farley married

Mary Dolan, who was born in County Cavan, Ireland, in 1815, and died in Wisconsin in 1885. They were members of the Catholic Church, and prior to the war were strong abolitionists, Mr. Farley being quite active in political matters. Since the war he has been an ardent Republican.

His father was a linen manufacturer in Ireland, who succeeded his father (great-grandfather), in the business. The family is of English descent, one of the members having gone to Ireland a great many years ago, where he established the linen manufactory to which several generations have succeeded.

Ed. Farley was educated principally in the Elkhorn Academy and, soon after completing his course, in August, 1861, he joined the Eighth Wisconsin Infantry, which became famous as the "Live Eagle Regiment," and was in the thickest of the fight in many of the vigorous campaigns in Mississippi, including the battles of Farmington, Corinth, Jackson (in two engagements), Vicksburg, Champion Hill, Yazoo City, Woodville and Franklin, Mississippi, and was severely wounded at the latter place. He was taken prisoner at Iuka, Mississippi, in 1862, and was taken to Vicksburg, where he was paroled, returning to his regiment, January 1, 1863. He also took part in the charge upon Vicksburg, May 22, 1863, and was there during the siege. In October, 1863, he was commissioned first lieutenant in the Third Regiment, United States Cavalry, and was in this service until mustered out, January 26, 1866.

One of the most desperate small battles in which he was engaged was that which resulted in the taking and burning of Black River bridge, November 27, 1864, thereby cutting off communication between General Hood and the reinforcements of his army and his supplies, and preventing Nashville from falling into the hands of the Confederates. This was accomplished by the regiment to which Mr. Farley belonged, after many unsuccessful attempts had been made by other commands. It was one of the most daring exploits of the war, and was complimented by the department commander and the war department. Its accomplishment was attended with great advantage to the Union army, and with disaster to the southern forces. It may be said this was the beginning of the end of the fearful strife between the sections.

After leaving the army Mr. Farley was engaged for two years as a cotton planter in Cohoma County, Mississippi; and in February, 1868, he came to Paducah, where he was a merchant for a short time, subsequently engaging in the manufacture of staves for flour barrels, in which he established a flourishing business.

In 1871 he was appointed deputy collector and gauger of the Second collection district of Kentucky, in which capacity he served the revenue department for five years. He resigned this position to engage in the wholesale grocery business in Paducah. This enterprise was successful for four years, when President Arthur appointed him collector of internal revenue for the Second collection district of Kentucky, with headquarters at Owensboro. He held that responsible office until the first election of President Cleveland.

In 1890 he was appointed postmaster of Paducah by President Harrison, without having made application for the office. There was a spirited contest for the office by other candidates, and some of the authorities of Washington wrote him to ask if he would accept the office. After consulting with a friend to whom he had previously given his support for that office, there being no prospect of a selection from other candidates on account of political complications, he accepted the appointment and served until June, 1894.

Captain Farley has been a prominent figure in local, state and national politics during the past twenty-five years. In 1884 he was the Republican candidate for the legislature in his district in opposition to Meyer Weil, and should have been declared elected, for he had a majority of six votes on the first count, but a lost (?) sheet was found the next day which gave his Democratic competitor a majority of twenty-eight votes and the honors and emoluments of the office.

In 1888 he was the Republican candidate for Congress in the First district, and reduced the majority of the opposing party in the "Democratic Gibraltar" of the state 5,566 votes, the city of Paducah going Republican for the first time since the war. He was a candidate for the constitutional convention in 1890, but was defeated by Judge W. J. Bullitt.

Captain Farley has been an honored member of the Republican State Central Committee for many years, and is a trusted leader in his party in the state and in the local affairs which concern the welfare of his party and the people. He is a member of the Grand Army of the Republic, Odd Fellows, Knights of Honor, Masons, Knight Templars and Ancient Order United Workmen, and is always ready to lend a helping hand in the cause of charity, benevolence and Christianity. His friends are not confined to the orders or the party to which he belongs, and he is one of the most universally popular citizens of Paducah.

Captain Farley was married October 3, 1871, to Ella M. Nunn, who was born in Paducah, May, 1852. They have three sons and four daughters: William H., Marie, Edwin Phillip, Maud, Rosela Ilda, Dora and Herbert Warren; and the family circle remains unbroken.

CHARLES F. JARRETT was born in Hopkinsville, Kentucky, in 1843. He is the only child of G. W. and Emily (Gant) Jarrett. His mother was a daughter of Archibald Gant, a native of Rockbridge County, Virginia, who removed to Hopkinsville at an early date. His father, G. W. Jarrett, was born near White Sulphur Springs, Greenbrier County, now West Virginia, in 1807. The old stone house in which he was born still stands as a specimen of the architecture of 1720. At the age of eighteen he left this home for the Rocky Mountains, where for eight years he was a Santa Fe trader, leading a life of hazard and adventure, full of exciting experiences and hair-breadth escapes. During the greater part of this time his guide and companion was the world-renowned Kit Carson. After amassing a large fortune young Jarrett returned to his Virginia home and removed thence to Kentucky, where he married and spent the remainder of a successful and useful life.

James Jarrett (grandfather) was a planter of Greenbrier County, Virginia, a man of integrity and considerable influence.

Charles F. Jarrett received his early instruction in private schools of his native county and finished his education at Center College, Danville, Kentucky. When eighteen years of age, in July, 1861, he joined the Third Kentucky Regiment at Camp Boone under the command of General Breckenridge and Colonel A. P. Thompson. He was with General N. B. Forrest during the last two years of the war, and was in the foremost of the fight in the fierce battle of Shiloh. There was a fine fiber of dash and bravery in the Jarrett blood which he inherited, and his record as a soldier is full of heroic deeds and personal daring. He entered the army at the beginning of the war, and was there at its close, having never missed a day from duty.

In 1867 he went to Paducah and was a dealer in leaf tobacco for a time in that city. He removed to Hopkinsville in 1875 and continued in the same business in the market known as the "Clarksville district," which is the finest dark tobacco market in the world.

Mr. Jarrett was married in 1873 to Sudie, daughter of Jesse and Susan (Jeffries) McComb. They have one of the most desirable homes in Kentucky, which he has christened "Cedar Glade" —a stock farm embracing four hundred and ninety acres under fine improvement—seven miles southwest of Hopkinsville. Here is where the fine thoroughbred horses such as McCurdys, Hambletonian and Glen Gordon have their home, and where Mr. Jarrett raises standard bred horses, shorthorn cattle and other fine stock. He has a large number of standard brood mares and colts.

Among the big-hearted, public-spirited men of Kentucky he stands in the front rank. Mr. Jarrett not only boasts of an illustrious ancestry, but he is a man of ability and wealth and has a heart that is full of charity. He is the last of the Jarrett family, but he has nobly borne the name of his famous ancestors and will leave a record without stain or blemish.

JAMES FREDERICK POWELL, a prominent tobacconist and highly esteemed citizen of Corydon, Henderson County, was born September 21, 1841, and is a son of Thomas W. and Elizabeth (Dorsey) Powell.

His father was born in Virginia, October 4, 1811, and came to Henderson County when he

EX-GOV. JOHN YOUNG BROWN.

was quite young, and subsequently owned a greater portion of the land upon which the town of Corydon is now situated. He married Elizabeth Dorsey, daughter of Noah Dorsey, and was the father of fifteen children: John A., Mary F., Samuel H., William S., Eveline, Maggie, Pattie, Olivia, Ida, Richard, Henry, Allen, Thomas M. and Edwin R. Powell. Thomas W. Powell died April 2, 1892, and his wife, Elizabeth Dorsey, died December 14, 1891.

Harrison Powell (grandfather) was a native of North Carolina, who removed to Kentucky with his parents when he was a child and located in Henderson County, where he was a prosperous farmer. He married Elizabeth McClanahan. (See sketch of H. A. Powell.)

His father, Willoughby Powell, was a native of North Carolina, who lived for many years in Henderson County.

Thomas McClanahan (maternal great-grandfather) was a native of Virginia, who removed to Logan County, Kentucky, where he died. He was appointed captain of a squadron of Tennessee soldiers in the Revolutionary war. His appointment was by General Nathaniel Greene, whose niece was Captain McClanahan's wife.

Thomas McClanahan (great-great-grandfather) was a Baptist minister of Virginia, whose wife was a Miss Marshall.

Noah Dorsey (maternal grandfather) was a native of Maryland, of Irish extraction, and married a Miss Hall of Jefferson County. They removed to Henderson County very early in the present century, and are buried in the cemetery at Corydon.

James F. Powell was reared on his father's farm, attending the neighborhood schools and also an advanced school in Henderson. He entered the Confederate army at the beginning of the war and remained till its close, serving under Generals John H. Morgan and Basil W. Duke.

After the close of the war he was engaged in merchandising in Corydon, in which he continued successfully for nearly twenty years. In January, 1884, he embarked in the tobacco business, buying and selling, and in connection therewith he soon established a large stemmery at Corydon, in which he prepares tobacco for the European market. He is also extensively interested in farming.

Mr. Powell is one of the most highly respected citizens of Corydon, and is greatly admired for his upright Christian character.

He was married November 18, 1866, to Emma Wilson, daughter of James Wilson, and a native of Southern Arkansas. Mrs. Powell is a lady of very engaging manners, active and energetic in good work and of sterling qualities, which have made her very helpful in her worthy husband's successful career. They have nine children, whose names are as follows: James Basil, Olivia Nora, Della, Annie, Ruby, Ozella, John W., Ruth and Fanny May Powell.

JOHN YOUNG BROWN, who recently retired from the gubernatorial chair of Kentucky, is one of the foremost orators and statesmen of his Commonwealth. He is a son of Thomas D. and Mary (Young) Brown, and was born in Hardin County June 28, 1835. His father was for several terms a member of the Legislature from Hardin County, and also represented that county in the convention which framed the state constitution in 1849-50. As a consequence the future governor spent several winters at the state capital, and received his first lessons in oratory from the many famous speakers of that day, who esteemed it an honor to secure an election to the law-making body of the state. Thomas Brown was himself an orator of no mean reputation, and the Youngs, the maternal ancestors of Governor Brown, were long famed in Kentucky for the brilliancy of their intellect.

John Young Brown entered Center College, Danville, when but sixteen years of age, and graduated from that institution three years later in the class which furnished so many of the famous statesmen of Kentucky and other states. Returning to Hardin County, he read law, and at the age of twenty-one commenced practice at the Elizabethtown bar. For the next few years Mr. Brown was in great demand as a campaign orator. The issue of "Know-nothing-ism" being at this time at its height, and Mr. Brown being one of its most formidable opponents, his life was often threatened by the adherents of this un-Democratic party.

In 1859 the Democrats of his district met at Bardstown and nominated him, over his own protest, as their candidate for Congress. He lacked over a year of being the required age for a congressman, but his constituents would not listen to his oft-repeated declinations. Colonel Jewett, the outgoing congressman, opposed him as an independent, but the young orator met him at every appointment and carried the district by storm, beating his opponent by about two thousand votes. Being under age, he was not allowed to take his seat until the short session of the term, nearly two years after his election.

He was chosen as a state elector on the Douglas ticket in 1860, and held a series of joint debates with the Hon. W. C. P. Breckinridge, who had been his classmate, who was an elector on the ticket headed by the brilliant John C. Breckinridge. These debates added much to the reputation of Mr. Brown. About the close of the war Mr. Brown moved to Henderson, in another congressional district, from which he was again elected to Congress. He was refused his seat on account of alleged disloyalty, but his constituents refused to elect another in his stead, and for two years the district remained without a representative. He was elected again in 1873 and again for the fourth term in 1875, after which he refused to allow his name to be presented. He remained in political retirement until 1891, when he was triumphantly elected governor of Kentucky.

It was during 1874 when Mr. Brown made his famous denunciatory speech in Congress against General Butler, which made his name ring around the continent. A resolution of censure was passed against him for this speech, but he was much applauded for it throughout the South, and a subsequent Congress, by a unanimous vote, ordered the whole matter expunged from the record.

The greatest victory of his life was won by Mr. Brown when he secured the Democratic nomination for governor in 1891. He had very formidable opposition for the nomination in the persons of C. M. Clay, Jr., president of the Constitutional Convention of 1890-91; Dr. J. D. Clardy, also a prominent member of that body—now congressman from the Second District—and ex-Attorney General P. W. Hardin. At the election following his majority over his nearest competitor was over twenty-eight thousand.

Coming into the gubernatorial office at the time of the adoption of the new constitution and the consequent entanglement into which the laws had fallen, the first part of Governor Brown's term was characterized by laborious work and by occasional conflicts with the Legislature. His veto messages were masterly state papers, and it is a satisfactory commentary on their worth when it is known that of the many vetoes sent to the two Assemblies that met during his term of office, all were promptly sustained. He retired from office on December 10th, 1895, and is now engaged in the practice of law in Louisville.

Governor Brown's social life has been pre-eminently a happy one. When quite a young man he was married to Rebecca Dixon, the beautiful and highly accomplished daughter of Hon. Archibald Dixon, lieutenant-governor and United States Senator.

Governor Brown is an orator among the giants in Kentucky, the home of oratory. In his younger days he attained a reputation for eloquence that was not confined to his state or the South. Since his return to political life he has shown that he has not lost the fire of youth, and with the added strength that experience has given he can sway the people as few speakers can. While a reticent man, he is not taciturn, and people who have been thrown with him through official relations or by personal contact, bear testimony to his genial manner and warm-hearted friendship and generous hospitality.

JOHN HAWKINS HART, County Clerk of Henderson County, son of John Bradford Hart and Gabriella Hawkins Hart, was born in Henderson County, Kentucky, November 3, 1856. His father, John Bradford Hart, was also born in Henderson County, July 7, 1819. He went with his father's family to Lexington, and from there to Harrodsburg, where he served several years as deputy circuit clerk under Phil T. Allen. In 1845 he returned to Henderson County, where he was for many years engaged in farming, but subsequently removed to Henderson, and is now a merchant in that city.

William Hart (grandfather) was a native of Caswell Court House, North Carolina, who came to Kentucky in 1796 to look after his interests in a large tract of land which he inherited from his father, and which had been purchased from Richard Henderson & Company. He married Danah Allen Bradford, daughter of John Bradford, editor of the Kentucky Gazette and a native of Virginia. Mr. Hart located on his tract of land near the city of Henderson and spent the remainder of his days there. He was the father of three sons and two daughters: Mrs. Mary Sophia Allen; Mrs. Eleanor Cabell, wife of Robert Cabell of Henderson; John Bradford Hart (father), David Hart, a merchant of Henderson, and Dr. Charles F. Hart, who was a physician in the Western Kentucky Insane Asylum at Hopkinsville for many years, a surgeon in the Union army during the Civil war, and died some years later in Colorado.

David Hart (great-grandfather) was a member of the Transylvania Company to which the Legislature granted two hundred thousand acres of land in Kentucky for important services rendered. He accompanied his brother, Nathaniel Hart, on one of his perilous trips to Kentucky, but returned to North Carolina, where, with his wife, Susanna Nunn, he spent the remainder of his life.

The progenitor of the Hart family in this country was Thomas Hart (great-great-great-grandfather), who emigrated from London, England, to Hanover, Virginia, in 1690, or about that date, where he died, leaving one son, Thomas J. Hart (great-great-grandfather), who married Susanna Rice, an aunt of Rev. Daniel Rice of the Presbyterian Church, who came to Kentucky in 1781.

David Hart (great-grandfather) of North Carolina, was (probably) a son of Thomas J. Hart and Susanna Rice Hart.

Gabriella Hawkins Hart (mother) is a native of Henderson County, Kentucky, and a daughter of Strother J. Hawkins, who was a colonel in the War of 1812 and a merchant in Christian County, who subsequently removed to Henderson County, where he enjoyed the peaceful life of a farmer during his declining years.

John Hawkins Hart, descendant of this long list of ancestors who figured so prominently in the early settlement of Kentucky and Henderson County, started in life as a farmer's boy; but after obtaining a good education in the schools of the county and later in the Henderson public schools, gained much practical business experience in the store of his father, who had in the meantime removed to the city.

After reaching maturity he served the city in the capacity of deputy marshal, under S. A. Young, for several years. In 1890 he was elected to the office of county clerk, his present position, having been re-elected in 1894. In this capacity he has rendered good and faithful service, and by his exemplary life and gentlemanly bearing has shown himself worthy of the honored name which he bears.

He is prominent in the local affairs of the Democratic party, and was a delegate to the Democratic state convention held in Louisville in 1895. He was not responsible, however, for the defeat of the ticket which that convention nominated, as he was vigilant and active in his endeavors to secure the success of his party.

He is a prominent and influential member of a number of benevolent orders, including Knights of Pythias, the Ancient Essenic Order and the Ancient Order of United Workmen.

Mr. Hart was married in 1885 to Susan B. Powell of Henderson, a granddaughter of Governor Dixon, a brief sketch of whose life is given in the biography of his son, Dr. Archibald Dixon, in this work.

LA VEGA CLEMENTS, a worthy descendant of a family of patriots, and a distinguished young attorney of Owensboro, is the eldest son of Samuel A. and Laura (Wagoner) Clements, and was born near Philpott, Daviess County, Kentucky, December 25, 1868. His father was born in Daviess County on March 31, 1839, and was educated in the county schools, and after reaching manhood engaged in merchandising at Philpott, but subsequently removed to Owensboro, where he now resides. His mother, Laura (Wagoner) Clements, is of German descent, and a daughter of Harry Wagoner, who in his day was a worthy and prosperous farmer of Spencer County, Indiana. She was born January 8, 1854, and had the misfortune to lose both of her parents in her early childhood. She was married to S. A. Clements in January, 1868.

La Vega Clements spent his early days in the country, receiving such educational advantages as could be had from the Kentucky public schools. To these and the public schools of Salisbury, Missouri, he is indebted for his education, his parents being unable to afford him any better facilities for his early training. But with this he entered the office of Judge Wilfred Carico of Owensboro in March, 1887, as a law student. After diligent study for more than a year he was admitted to the bar in July, 1888, when only nineteen years of age. He remained with his preceptor until December, 1891, when he formed a law partnership with T. F. Birkhead, with whom he is at present associated. The firm enjoys a large practice, and both are prominent as members of the Owensboro bar. Mr. Clements was elected city attorney of Owensboro in November, 1893, for a term of four years, carrying over his opponent every voting precinct in the city, a compliment which was due to his personal popularity and an evidence of the high esteem in which he was held by the community as a lawyer of ability, a man of upright character and a Christian gentleman. He was married November 16, 1890, to Maggie Brown, daughter of Thomas Brown of Knottsville, Kentucky. They have one child, Gerald S., born October 16, 1894.

Mr. Clements' grandfather, Charles O. Clements, was born near Baltimore, Maryland, January 29, 1808, and emigrated to Kentucky at an early day and settled in Nelson County, near Bardstown; he soon afterwards removed to Daviess County, where he resided until his death, December 29, 1879. He was a soldier in the war with Mexico, and had the honor of serving with General Winfield Scott at the siege of Vera Cruz. His wife, Susan Philpott, was also a native of Maryland, and was born January 12, 1811, and died January 11, 1872. She was a daughter of John S. Philpott, who was born in 1780 and died in 1839, and who was a descendant of a family prominent in the early settlements of Maryland.

William Clements, the father of Charles O. Clements, lived and died in Maryland, and was a soldier in the Revolutionary war under General Marion. He and his brother Charles joined the patriot army at the beginning of the War for Independence, one leaving home one day and the other the next. Charles served under Washington, and, strange to say, they never saw each other during the entire struggle for independence, and at the end returned home as they had left, one day apart. William Clements married Winfred Hardy, a daughter of Frederick Hardy, who lived and died near Baltimore. The Clements family have always been Democrats, and are of English descent, the progenitor of the family in this country being one of the party who accompanied Lord Baltimore in settling the first colony in the wilderness of Maryland.

JAMES H. HAZELRIGG, one of the judges of the Court of Appeals and an able lawyer and jurist, is a member of an old and honored Kentucky family. He is the son of George and Elizabeth (Greene) Hazelrigg, and was born in Montgomery County, Kentucky, December 6, 1848. His father was a native of Clark County, and in later years was a prominent and successful farmer in Montgomery, continuing that occupation until his death in February, 1874, at the age of fifty-four years. He was a leading member of the Christian Church, was originally a Whig in politics and then fell in with the Union and afterward with the Republican party. He held the office of magistrate many years in his county.

Dillard Hazelrigg (grandfather) was a native of Bourbon County, Kentucky, who moved to Montgomery County in 1834, where he was engaged in farming until his death in 1871, in the seventy-second year of his age. His wife was Sally Renick, sister of Abram Renick, the most noted and successful shorthorn breeder of America. He was a prominent churchman (Christian) and took some interest in politics, voting the Whig ticket until the war, when he affiliated with the Democratic party. His father, John Hazelrigg, was a native of Virginia, and came to Kentucky in 1787, and was the founder of the family in this state. His wife was Annie Cleveland, whom he married in Virginia. She was a direct descendant of Oliver Cromwell, her father, Charles, being the grandson of Lord Cleveland, who married Cromwell's daughter.

The Hazelriggs were prominent adherents of Cromwell and figured conspicuously in those stirring times, fighting against the "divine right" of kings.

Elizabeth J. Greene Hazelrigg (mother) was a native of Montgomery County, Kentucky, who died in 1849 at the age of twenty-three years. Her father, Thaddeus Greene, was a native of Virginia, who settled in Montgomery County when quite a young man, where he became a large land and slave owner and a prosperous farmer. His second wife (grandmother) was the sister of Harvey Kerr of Bourbon County, Kentucky, a celebrated breeder of fine saddle horses. Thaddeus Greene died in 1860, at the age of sixty-eight years. He was a stanch Democrat and an influential citizen of his community. His religious belief was that of the "Hard Shell" Baptist denomination, and he belonged to the same family as the Honorable Grant Green, whose sketch appears elsewhere in this volume.

Judge Hazelrigg remained on his father's farm in Montgomery County until he was fifteen years of age, and attended the district schools in the winter months. In 1864 he joined the Confederate army as a private in Company D, of Captain Bedford's company, E. E. Clay's battalion, and served in the ranks until the surrender of his regiment under Colonel Giltner at Mt. Sterling, in May, 1865.

In 1867 Judge Hazelrigg became a student in the Kentucky University at Lexington, and graduated from that institution in the class of 1871. He returned to Mt. Sterling and entered the office of Apperson & Reid as a law student, and was admitted to the bar in 1873. In 1874 he was elected city attorney of Mt. Sterling and held that office until 1882, and was then elected county judge, which latter office he held until 1886. In 1892 he was nominated by the Democratic party for the office of judge of the Court of Appeals; and after a spirited contest in opposition to ex-Chief Justice Holt, the nominee of the Republicans, he was elected in November of the same year. Judge Hazelrigg is a stanch Democrat, having always taken an active interest in the success of his party, and having been for many years chairman of the Montgomery County Executive Committee.

In 1872 Judge Hazelrigg wedded Mattie Laudeman, daughter of James H. Laudeman of Lexington, and this union has been blessed with four daughters and one son: May H., wife of Courtland Chenault of Montgomery County; Elizabeth G., Emily D., Dyke L. and Hattie A., the last named dying in infancy.

Judge Hazelrigg is a member of the Christian Church and a gentleman of pleasing and courteous manners. As a judge in the highest court in the state, he is rapidly pushing himself to the front, and by his careful decisions and wise interpretations of the law, has gained the reputation of being one of the most prominent members of the Kentucky Court of Appeals.

WILLIAM T. ELLIS, ex-member of Congress and a leading attorney of Owensboro, was born in Daviess County, July 24, 1845. He received a fine literary education in his native county considering that before he was sixteen years of age he enlisted in the First Regiment Kentucky Cavalry. He was mustered in October 5, 1861, and "followed the varying fortunes of the Confederacy" till the close of the war, as a private and latterly as a non-commissioned officer in command of scouts.

He returned to his home after the surrender, and resumed his studies, working during vacation to obtain means to defray his expenses. For two years he taught school while still pursuing his studies and reading law. He received his license to practice law in the spring of 1869, and after this attended a course of lectures in the Harvard Law School.

Returning to his home in 1870, he was elected county attorney in August of the same year; served four years and was re-elected in 1874; in 1876 he was Democratic elector for his district on the Tilden and Hendricks ticket; in 1888 he was elected a member of the Fifty-first Congress; was re-elected to the Fifty-second and Fifty-third Congresses; declined further service in the National House of Representatives, and returned to the practice of law at the expiration of his third term, March, 1895. At the close of a brilliant career of six years in Congress he was still one of the younger members and had gained a reputation as one of the brightest and ablest members of the Kentucky delegation. His loyalty to the government and his idea of justice to those who fought to preserve the Union was clearly expressed in a speech made in committee of the whole May 5, 1894, from which the following extracts are taken:

"I do not believe, Mr. Chairman, that the matter of pensions is a political question, though the effort in this body since I have been here has constantly been to make it such. If it had been left to the men who fought the battles of the war on both sides, it never would have been a political question. The wonder to me has always been that Democrats have suffered our Republican friends as a political party to masquerade before the country as the only friend of the Union soldier.

"Why, Mr. Chairman, if the Republican party alone had been left to fight the battles of the war Richmond would never have fallen, and Sheridan's cavalry would have halted long before it reached Appomattox.

"Speaking for myself and who as a boy followed the varying fortunes of the Confederacy from the opening to the close of the war, and correctly reflecting as I think the sentiments of every soldier who wore a Confederate uniform and honored it, I am in favor of a liberal pension for every Union soldier who is disabled, whether that disability results from wounds received in battle or from broken down or shattered health consequent upon the exposure and hardship to which he was subjected while engaged in the service of his country.

"I go further, Mr. Chairman, and say I am in favor of pensioning the dependent widows and children of the Union soldiers who fell in battle and whose silent gravestones mark every mile of the way from Shiloh to Gettysburg.

"The Republican party, as such, has no patent or trade mark entitling it to the exclusive confidence, esteem or votes of Federal soldiers, and the time has come when that fact should be thoroughly understood.

"If the Federal soldier owes the scars he wears, his halting step, his rude crutch and his empty coat sleeve to the punishment he received at the hands of his adversaries, he is entitled at least to know that those who fought him so fiercely in war are his friends in peace, and that they stand ready, not only to co-operate with him in defending the integrity of the national flag, but in securing for him a liberal pension for all the injuries they inflicted upon him. The attitude of the ex-Confederate and his section on this subject has been too long misunderstood and his sentiments too often misrepresented.

"Confederates believed when the armies of the South were disbanded that the war was over. Hungry, clad in rags, without money and without price, they followed with unfaltering trust the Confederacy's altering star of hope, until it sank forever behind the bloody fields on which they won their fame. But when they could no longer contend against fearful odds they saluted the stars and stripes, struck hands with the visitors, and greeted them with the genuine salutation, 'Henceforth, let us have one flag and one country.'"

The spirit of fairness and conservatism indicated in this speech is a fair index of Mr. Ellis' public life. Possibly, however, Mr. Ellis' speech in Congress in opposition to what was known as the Carlisle Bill gave him his widest reputation. Although a member of the Committee on Banking and Currency, which reported the Carlisle Bill, he assailed its provisions furiously. In opposing it he took advanced grounds and predicted that its passage would bring financial ruin upon the whole country. Affirming his allegiance to the Democratic party he assailed the Carlisle Bill as undemocratic and as an unwise and unpatriotic measure. In the course of this speech he denounced the financial policy of Mr. Cleveland's administration and questioned the soundness of the chief executive's democracy. The speech was widely quoted throughout the country.

As a lawyer he stands pre-eminently at the front of the Owensboro bar. He has been a close student of the science of law and with a natural aptitude for the discussion of legal questions, pleasing address, a ready flow of language and a graceful delivery he attracts and holds the attention of his hearers. While he manages his civil cases with excellent judgment and marked ability, it is said by his friends that he rather excels in the criminal practice where adroitness in the examination and cross-examination of witnesses and fine rhetoric are essential to success.

During Mr. Ellis' absence in Congress his law business was conducted by his senior and junior law partners, Hon. W. N. Sweeney and J. J. Sweeney, and it was owing to the fact that the business of the firm had increased to such an extent as to require his whole time, that he declined to remain longer in public life.

William T. Ellis and Alice Coffey, daughter of Colonel C. R. Coffey of Owensboro, Kentucky, were married October 20, 1871. His wife died in 1872, and he was married again November 2, 1876, to Mattie B. Miller, daughter of Dr. W. F. Miller, an eminent physician of Louisville.

Mr. Ellis' father, Luther R. Ellis, was born in Shelby County, Kentucky, November 18, 1818. He was married to Mary M. Kellum of Daviess County and died when he was less than thirty-seven years of age. He left two sons: William T. and Dr. J. W. Ellis.

The Ellis family were natives of Culpeper County, Virginia, and came to Kentucky in 1804. The grandfather of Mr. Ellis first located in Shelby County, but subsequently removed to Daviess County, where he was a large and prosperous farmer.

HARBARD A. POWELL, formerly proprietor of the Corydon coal mine, now retired, son of Harrison and Elizabeth (McClanahan) Powell, was born in 1818.

His father, Harrison Powell, was born in North Carolina in 1786, removed to Tennessee in 1821, and later to Kentucky; stopped in Logan County for a short time and then located in Henderson County, where he was a farmer nearly all his life, and died August 30, 1838. He was drafted for the War of 1812 and furnished a substitute. He married Elizabeth McClanahan and had eleven children, one of whom died in infancy: Willoughby, died at the age of twenty years; Anna, Thomas W., Nancy G., Harrison, Harbard A. (subject), Smith, Elizabeth, Lazarus, James and Louisa.

Willoughby Powell (grandfather) lived for a time in Logan County, and subsequently removed to Henderson County, Kentucky, where he died. He married Mary Whitehead, a sister of Lazarus Whitehead, a prominent member of the bar in Europe, who died a bachelor, leaving a large fortune.

Thomas McClanahan (maternal grandfather) was a native of Virginia, who removed to Logan County, Kentucky, where he died at the age of ninety-six years. He was a captain in the Revolutionary war by appointment of General Nathaniel Greene, who after the war was over sent him out on the frontier in command of a squadron of soldiers, and was stationed at a place called Nickajack, now Nashville, Tennessee. He was a brave and fearless man. Few men of his type ever lived, and he stood high in the community in which he lived and died. He married Nancy Greene, a niece of General Greene.

Thomas McClanahan (great-grandfather) was a native of Virginia and a Baptist minister, whose wife was a Miss Marshall of Virginia.

Harbard Alexander Powell was educated in the common schools of Henderson County, and early in life became a farmer. He was for some time employed on the farm of his father-in-law, and in 1840 he purchased land and by great energy and economy became quite prosperous. In 1857 he built a stemmery and began to deal extensively in tobacco, preparing it for the European market.

When the Corydon Coal Mining Company was organized he was elected president of the company, and within a few years he bought in the stock held by others and became sole proprietor of the mine. In 1894 he sold the property to his son, B. M. Powell, and is now retired from active business pursuits.

He was the first constable elected by the people of Henderson County, and in 1859 served as justice of the peace.

Mr. Powell has been twice married, first to Mary Livesay, a native of Virginia, who died in October, 1856. There were four children by this marriage: Elias L., Louisa, Mary and Nancy. His second wife, to whom he was married December 17, 1857, was Melinda E. Gibson, daughter of James Gibson, a prosperous and successful farmer of Henderson County, whose father, Berryman Gibson, was a soldier in the war of the Revolution. The children by this union are Martha Christina, Burnett M., Anna B., Adah Lee, Jessie A., Melinda J. and Thomas Hart Powell.

JAMES E. PEPPER of Lexington, one of the best known distillers of fine whiskies in the world, whose brands have probably been more universally advertised than any other of the Kentucky distilleries, is a son of the late General Oscar and Annette (Edwards) Pepper, and was born in Woodford County, Kentucky, May 18, 1850.

General Oscar Pepper was also a native of Woodford County, where he was for many years a prominent distiller, in addition to which he owned and cultivated a large farm and was engaged in raising fine stock. He was a prominent Democrat and was a general in the Old State Militia. He died in 1865, at the age of fifty-five years. His wife is still living in Woodford County. Her father was a farmer in Fauquier County, Virginia.

Elijah Pepper (grandfather) was a native of Culpeper County, Virginia, who came to Woodford County, Kentucky, in the year 1780. He erected the first distillery in the state and continued to operate it until he was succeeded by his son Oscar. He was also an extensive farmer and land owner in Woodford County. The Pepper family is an old and honored one whose members were prominent in the colonial days of Virginia. The County of Culpeper was named in honor of Sir John Culpeper, the progenitor of the Pepper family in America, but the name was changed by Elijah Culpeper to Pepper after his removal to Kentucky.

Culpeper County, Virginia, was organized in 1748, its territory embracing the present Counties of Culpeper, Madison and Rappahannock; and there was a long controversy involving the title to several millions of acres of land granted by King James to Sir John Culpeper and others whose rights Sir John had purchased. Lord Fairfax married a daughter of Sir John Culpeper and became the owner of the "Northern Neck" of Virginia. The seventh son of Sir John was doubtless the ancestor of the subject of this sketch, who is therefore a descendant of the English nobility.

James E. Pepper was reared in his native county and after leaving the common schools he went to B. B. Sayre's Institute in Frankfort and was prepared for college, but the death of his father made it necessary for him to take charge of the distillery, and the college course was abandoned.

After spending three years at home he went to New York City in the interest of the distillery and remained there for ten years. In 1880 he returned to Kentucky and established his present large distillery at Lexington, and began the production of the original and genuine "James E. Pepper" whiskey, which is so favorably known throughout the country. He is one of the third generation of a family famous for the excellence of the whiskey made by the Peppers, but his present establishment is far more extensive than was that of his father and grandfather. The plant covers about thirty-five acres of ground in the suburbs of Lexington and has a capacity of fifty barrels a day, employing an average of one hundred men. He has been in the business for over twenty-five years, and has spent a mint of money in perfecting his distillery, but has now the finest plant of the kind in the state.

In addition to his whiskey interests Mr. Pepper owns a large and well stocked farm about one mile from the city limits of Lexington, known as "Meadowthorpe," where he makes his home, and is deeply interested in breeding thoroughbred running horses. This is one of the most highly improved and expensive farms of its size in the state. His residence alone, built in the colonial style, cost $40,000, and his stables are perfect horse palaces. The buildings and premises are supplied with electric light, gas, hot and cold water, and every modern convenience that experience could suggest or money could buy. He takes great delight in his horses, among which are some of the most noted runners of the Blue Grass section.

Mr. Pepper was married in 1890 to Ella Offutt, a member of the well known family of that name in Shelby County.

Mr. Pepper, as the representative distiller, was

called upon to prepare an article for that magnificent publication, "One Hundred Years of American Commerce," which is from the house of D. O. Haynes & Co., of New York, and of which Chauncey M. Depew, LL.D., is editor-in-chief. Mr. Pepper's article, entitled, "American Distillers," deals with the development of the distilling industry in a general way, without laudation of any or even the mention of his own product. There are one hundred articles in the work on the history and development of all our great national industries, each one being written by a representative of the branch of trade or industry in which he has had experience, and it is indeed a high honor to have been invited to contribute to its pages.

Among the contributors are Philip D. Armour, who describes the development of the great meat packing industry; Thomas T. Eckert, president of the Western Union Telegraph Company, who writes of telegraphy; Charles H. Cramp, of shipbuilding; Levi P. Morton, of American banking; Ohio C. Barber, of the manufacture of matches; Francis G. du Pont, of the manufacture of powder; Albert A. Pope, of bicycles; William Steinway, of pianos; Charles L. Tiffany, of jewelry; Charles H. Taylor, editor of the Boston Globe, of journalism; Levi C. Weir, president of the Adams Express Company, of the express business; Fred Pabst, of brewing, and so on through one hundred distinguished names.

MORRIS CAMPBELL HUTCHINS, Judge of Mason County, and a well-known Republican politician of Northern Kentucky, was born in Maysville, Kentucky, April 12, 1842, and is descended from Revolutionary patriots. His father, Morris A. Hutchins, was born in Casanovia, New York, October, 1799, and his mother, Eveline (Campbell) Hutchins, was born in Aberdeen, Ohio, in 1807. Her grandfather, Matthew Campbell, was a native of Scotland, who belonged to the clan of the Campbells, whose chieftan was the Duke of Argyle. Matthew Campbell's father, Sir Colin Campbell, was the second son of one of the Dukes of Argyle, and his mother, Mary Montieth, was the daughter of a Scottish nobleman. Matthew Campbell was the pioneer of Aberdeen, Ohio, which village he laid out about the beginning of the Revolution. He located a section of land opposite Maysville, in Ohio, and was one of the twenty-five pioneers who laid out the city of Cincinnati, as is evidenced by the centennial history of that city. He was a cousin of James Campbell, who commanded the Americans at the battle of King's Mountain, in which he defeated the British. James Campbell, brother of Matthew, was a colonel under General Wilkinson, in the War of 1812, as well as in some of the previous Indian wars. The Campbells who settled in Washington County, Pennsylvania, and in the Shenandoah Valley in Virginia, were descended from two brothers of ducal descent; from the one who settled in Pennsylvania Judge Morris C. Hutchins is in direct line.

Evan Campbell (maternal grandfather) was born in Scotland; emigrated with his father, Sir Matthew Campbell, to America; married Amanda Byers, and died at Aberdeen. He was a large landholder and owned several ferry boats on the Ohio River running between Maysville and Aberdeen.

Benjamin Hutchins (grandfather) was born in the state of New York and was a son of Samuel Hutchins, who was a native of Connecticut and a member of the first legislature of that state. He subsequently removed to Western New York and served as major in the war of the Revolution. Benjamin Hutchins married Jerusha Bradley, whose mother, Anne Morris, was a daughter of Amos Morris, a cousin of Gouverneur Morris and Robert Morris, of Revolutionary fame. A sister of Benjamin Hutchins, Marie, became the wife of Rev. Thomas J. Ruger, who was rector of the Episcopal Church at Janesville, Wisconsin. They were the parents of Major General Ruger, now of the United States army, who succeeded General Scofield in command at Chicago.

Morris A. Hutchins (father) settled in Maysville in 1822, and was engaged in the lumber business until the time of his death, May 2, 1873, in the seventy-fourth year of his age. He was a delegate to the national convention which first nominated Abraham Lincoln for the presidency, and for supporting and voting for Abraham Lincoln in 1860 he was hanged in effigy in Maysville. He was a man of wealth and prominence and of eminent worth. He took a leading part in the opposition to slavery and was a member of the Methodist Episcopal Church.

Judge Morris C. Hutchins was educated principally in the Ohio Wesleyan University. At the breaking out of the Civil war he was the first man in Mason County to volunteer in the Union army, and was sworn into service in Woodruff's Second Kentucky Regiment as a private. In November, 1861, upon the recommendation of General Rosecrans, he was promoted to the rank of second lieutenant, and assigned to Company I, Sixteenth Kentucky Infantry. In September, 1862, he was promoted to first lieutenant, and subsequently to captain of his company. He was continuously in active service until August 3, 1865, and participated in twenty-two battles during the war, and was for many months detailed on the staff of the First brigade, Third division, Twenty-third Army Corps. At the battle of Franklin, Tennessee, he was slightly wounded and was specially mentioned by his general for his bravery and his valuable services in that engagement. In 1866 he returned home and entered the office of the Honorable W. H. Wadsworth as a law student, where he remained for two years, and in 1868 was admitted to the bar. In 1872 he was elected mayor of Maysville, and was re-elected. After leaving the mayor's office he was a member of the City Council, and was appointed master commissioner of the Mason Circuit Court, serving in that office for four years. In 1880 Judge Hutchins was a delegate to the Republican national convention, and was one of the immortal "306" who voted thirty-six times in that convention for General Grant. President Arthur appointed him postmaster at Maysville, and he filled that office most acceptably and gave universal satisfaction. In the August election of 1894 he was nominated by the Republicans for the office of County Judge, being pitted against Thomas R. Phister, one of the most popular Democrats of the county. Judge Hutchins was easily elected and bears the distinction of being the first Republican who has ever held an elective office in Mason County. Judge Hutchins was married in 1870 to Lydia Frances Dimmitt of Maysville, daughter of Ezekial Dimmitt, Esq.

They have two children, a son and a daughter: Dimmitt C., a graduate of the Ohio Wesleyan University, class of 1895; and Essie C. Judge Hutchins is a prominent member of the Masonic fraternity, being a Knight Templar, and is also a member of the military order of the Loyal Legion, of which ex-President Benjamin Harrison was the commander in 1894.

WILLIAM D. BRENT, City Attorney of Covington and a prominent young member of the Kenton County bar, is descended from the old and honored Brent family of Central Kentucky. His parents were John D. and Elizabeth Garvin Brent, who lived in Woodsonville, Hart County, at the time of his birth, December 18, 1852. His father, Captain John D. Brent, was born in Hart County, June, 1826. His education was obtained in the common and private schools, and after reaching his majority he was engaged in general merchandising in Hart County until 1856, when he removed to Louisville and became the proprietor of the Ninth street tobacco warehouse. He entered the Union army in 1861 as captain of Company K, Fifth Kentucky Regiment, which was under the command of Colonel Buckley, and was afterward transferred to General Buell's staff. Captain Brent took part in the battles of Shiloh, Perryville, Chickamauga and other important engagements.

Having resigned his commission in the army on account of ill health, he removed to Covington in 1864 and engaged in the wholesale dry goods business in connection with the house of Pearce, Tolle & Holton, with whom he remained until 1887. In 1880 he was elected a member of the City Council of Covington and served two years. He affiliated with the Democratic party but was not active in politics; was a member of the Masonic fraternity and of the Christian Church. He was not engaged in business for some years before his death, which occurred October 21, 1895. His remains were taken to Bowling Green for interment.

Joshua Brent (grandfather), a Virginian, came to Kentucky in 1783, and settled in what is now Hart County. He was a lieutenant in the command of Colonel Richard Johnson and General Shelby. He was a plantation farmer and for many years was postmaster of the village of Monroe, in Hart County. He was a Whig in the best days of that party; was connected with the Christian Church and with the Masonic order. He died in 1863, and is buried on the old Brent homestead. His wife, Rebecca Worley, was born in Fayette County in 1785, and was one of the most intelligent and highly cultured women in Kentucky. She lived to be ninety years old and died in 1875.

Captain John D. Brent married a daughter of Valentine Garvin in 1847. She was born in Hart County, in the month of September, 1829, and is still living. Valentine Garvin (grandfather) was born in Rockingham County, Virginia, in 1794; removed to Hart County when he was a mere boy and became a prominent planter and slave owner, at one time owning about one hundred slaves. He was an extensive tobacco grower and was one of the most prominent politicians of his time, being an enthusiastic Henry Clay Whig, and in later years a Democrat. He was twice elected to the Kentucky legislature in the early history of the state, and also served as a magistrate for many years. His mother, Barbara (Maggard) Garvin, lived in the fort at Harrodsburg in 1780, and her mother, Kitty Baufman, was also in the fort. Mary Brawner (maternal grandmother) was a native of Charles County, Maryland, and was closely related to the Taylor and Maddox families, who were among the most prominent people of that state. She was a daughter of Isaac Brawner and Ann Maddox Taylor, the latter being a daughter of Robin Taylor. General Smallwood, whose arm was shot off in the battle of Brandywine, was also related to the Taylors, and was a distant cousin of the subject of this sketch. Charles Carroll, one of the signers of the Declaration of Independence, was also a relative.

William D. Brent attended the ordinary district schools and was graduated from the Covington high school in 1872. He taught for one year in the same institution and at the expiration of that time went to Lexington, Virginia, and entered the Washington and Lee University, and was graduated from that well-known university in the class of 1875.

After his return to Covington he entered the office of John Fisk as a student at law, with whom he remained seven years, having been admitted to the bar in 1877. He then formed a partnership with Robert B. Fisk, with whom he was associated for three years. He was a member of the City Council from 1879 to 1882, when he was elected city clerk and served in that capacity for two terms. He was next elected magistrate, and before the expiration of his term of office, he was elected city attorney, of which office he is the present incumbent.

Mr. Brent was married September 15, 1883, to Mollie Belle Chandler, daughter of Lewis Chandler of Cincinnati, Ohio, who was born in 1861; educated in Cincinnati and Grand Rapids, Michigan; died March 27, 1889, and is buried at Bowling Green.

JOHN F. KIMBLEY, M. D., Surgeon-General of Kentucky, one of the oldest physicians and most substantial citizens of Owensboro, was born in Muhlenberg County, Kentucky, September 24, 1823.

His father, Frank E. Kimbley, a native of Louisville, went to Muhlenberg County in 1792, and there married Elizabeth Valandingham, a member of a distinguished Virginia family. They had six children, of whom the subject of this brief biography was the youngest.

John Kimbley (grandfather), a Hollander, emigrated to the United States some time prior to the Revolution, in which he did faithful service for his adopted country. His coming to Kentucky was at a very early date, as may be inferred from the fact that he was a resident of Corn Island, below Louisville, and assisted in the cultivation of the first crop of corn ever produced in Kentucky.

Dr. Kimbley was educated in private schools in Muhlenberg County. When twenty years of age he began the study of medicine at his home, and subsequently attended a course of lectures in St. Louis, and practiced medicine for some time before finishing his professional studies in the Jefferson Medical College of Philadelphia, from which he was graduated in 1849. He had established a good practice in Daviess County before taking the course in Philadelphia, which he resumed with increased confidence and success upon his return. He had accumulated considerable property, including a large number of slaves, before the beginning of the Civil war, and lost heavily as a result of that conflict.

He was a strong Union man and volunteered his services to help put down the rebellion. He was appointed surgeon of the Eleventh Kentucky Infantry, and during the three years and four months of active service in the field, he held various positions of rank in the Cumberland and the Ohio and Tennessee divisions and was one of the chief surgical operators on every battlefield in which his command was engaged. He received the highest commendations of his superior officers for faithful and efficient service. He served as medical director of the Cavalry Corps under Brigadier-General Sturgis, whose order relieving him from duty in that command was as follows:

"Headquarters Cavalry Corps,
"Paris, Kentucky, April 9, 1864.

"The Eleventh Regiment Kentucky Volunteer Infantry having been permanently detached from this command and J. F. Kimbley being surgeon of that regiment, he is hereby relieved from duty as medical director of the Cavalry Corps and will report to his regiment commander for duty. The general commanding cannot, however, thus summarily sever his official connection with Surgeon John F. Kimbley without expressing his deep regret for the necessity which compels him to lose from his staff so estimable a gentleman, and one who has administered the medical department with so much energy, zeal, and ability.

"By order of Brigadier-General Sturgis."

His service in the army was a heavy sacrifice personally, and the loss of his slaves by the emancipation proclamation—which showed no partiality for Union men—together with other losses incident to the war, rendered it necessary for him to begin at the bottom to rebuild his fortune. He soon recovered his valuable practice and has held his high position in the profession and in the confidence of the people, and after more than thirty years of peace he can look back over the past without regret for the gallant part he took in the war or for the temporary loss which it entailed. He became a Republican at the outbreak of the war and heartily supported every measure of that party during the struggle and in the disquietude of the days of reconstruction, and although firm, positive and outspoken in his political views, he is highly respected for his fidelity to his convictions and honesty of purpose.

Dr. Kimbley is now well advanced in years, but his interest in and his devotion to his profession have never waned. He is still a diligent student of medical science, and readily adopts the new discoveries which promise relief to the suffering, but is not easily carried away by new and untried doctrines and methods. He is a member of the Kentucky State Medical Society and of the Daviess County Medical Society and is a subscriber to the leading medical periodicals of the day. He is a member of the Filson Club, and a valuable contributor to the history and early reminiscence of Kentucky through that society of honorable citizens of the state. Dr. Kimbley's life has been wholly devoted to his profession, and his remarkable success and the high position which he enjoys are due to his faithfulness to his patrons, his industry, energy and zeal in the arduous labors of the family physician.

His first wife was Emily C. Windsor, a native of Kentucky, who died in 1852. His second wife was a Mrs. Stout, who was his companion for six years and died in 1860. His present wife was Mrs. Sarah Ray Stubbins, a daughter of ex-Governor Ray of Indiana, whose classical education was received in Oxford (Ohio) Female College and in Europe, where she gave particular attention to the study of the German and French languages. She is a lady of unusual literary attainments and has imparted much of the large fund of information of which she is possessed to her sons, who, after careful study in private schools, she accompanied to Europe and assisted them in the study of foreign languages.

Hugh Kimbley, the eldest son of Dr. and Mrs. Kimbley, is studying medicine in the University of Louisville. Frank R. Kimbley, their second and youngest son, is in the class of '97 in Yale College. They are exemplary young men, of more than ordinary intelligence, who attained distinction in their classes. Dr. Kimbley has seen something of the world himself, having traveled extensively in this country and visited Europe several times. He is now surgeon-general of Kentucky, with the rank of colonel, on the personal staff of Governor Bradley.

ROBERT FRANKLIN RIVES, the wheat king of Kentucky, was born December 7, 1837, on the state line between Kentucky and Tennessee. His father, Robert Rives, was born in Warren County, North Carolina, near the Virginia line, December 16, 1803. He was a son of William and Catherine (Turner) Rives, natives of Dinwiddie County, near Petersburg, Virginia. Catherine Turner was a daughter of Stephen and Susan (Hanover) Turner of Amherst County, Virginia. William and Catherine Rives (grandparents) had ten children, whose names were: Stephen; Thomas; Nancy, whose husband's name was Mabry; William; Sallie, whose husband's name was Moss; Polly, who married Watkins; Robert (father); James; Rebecca, who married Southall, and Susan, who married Cunningham.

Robert Rives (father) was married in 1825 to Rebecca Vaughn, daughter of Susan (Vincent) Vaughn, who was a first cousin of Thomas Jefferson. They had four children: William Vincent, the eldest son, reared a large family, all of whom are dead except Ophenia (Crews); Charles Jefferson, second son, married Annie Brockman, a granddaughter of the distinguished John McDougal of Scotland, and had four children: Noyal, Nebraska, Jennie and Robbie, a daughter who married a Mr. Cayce; Susan, the third child and only daughter, married Thomas Adams, and was the mother of four children: Robert, Rebecca, Charles and Thomas. Robert F. Rives, the subject of this sketch, is the youngest child. His father died August 5, 1885, at the venerable age of eighty-three. His life was an honor to his country, and he transmitted to his large posterity that most priceless heritage known to mankind—an unspotted name.

Robert F. Rives began to solve for himself the problem of life at an early age. When nineteen he superintended his father's farm. At the beginning of the Civil war he was among the first to offer his service to the southern cause. In April, 1861, he joined the Fourteenth Tennessee Infantry, Company L; and, after drilling with that regiment for two months, he was taken ill with fever and was disabled for infantry service.

After the fall of Fort Donelson in February, 1862, he enlisted in Company A, First Kentucky Cavalry, near Murfreesboro, Tennessee; and, after serving six months, his company's time expiring, he joined General Morgan's command. He was a good soldier and was in some severe conflicts. He accompanied General Morgan in his raid through Kentucky, Indiana and Ohio; his battalion led the advance all through the raid and fought more or less every day. The closest call he ever had was when the gunboats at Buffington Island interfered with their crossing, and a large body of Federal cavalry swooped down upon them, and he, with two hundred others, swam the Ohio River, and thus made their escape. They marched through West Virginia to Abingdon, Virginia, and reached the army in time to take part in the battle of Chickamauga. He was in many cavalry fights and, although he had his horse shot under him, he escaped wounds or prison. He was with that captain who, when news came of Lee's surrender, said: "Boys, we have fought a good fight, and now it seems to be over. We are going home. Go home and bring up your children to love our South and, though you may have nothing else to leave them, you can leave them the heritage that they are sons of men who were in Lee's army."

In 1874 Mr. Rives bought of Mr. William Wallace, a place of four hundrd acres, seven miles from Hopkinsville. He afterward added two hundred acres to this farm, besides having the management of two other large tracts of land, which he operates in connection with his own. He grows more wheat than any ten of the average growers, his yield often being fifteen to seventeen thousand bushels.

After the war Robert F. Rives was married to Isabella, daughter of William H. and Elizabeth

(Hardgrove) Pollard of Amelia County, Virginia. After eight years of married life she died, leaving four children: Robert Henry, born September 22, 1869; Franklin, born April 6, 1871; Florence Neal, born September 8, 1872; George Pollard, born April 3, 1874. Of these, Robert Henry, a large planter in Texas, married Miss Eubank of that state, and has one son, Raymond. Franklin, at present a member of the Hopkinsville, Kentucky, bar, graduated from the Cumberland University of Lebanon, Tennessee, with distinguished honors and is already in the front rank of the young lawyers of the state.

Mr. Rives was married (second) to Sally A., daughter of Rev. Jordan and Sarah (Viser) Moore of Montgomery County, Tennessee. By this marriage he has four children: Mary Belle, born September 18, 1879; Jordan Moore, born October 5, 1882; Susan Cleveland, born November 11, 1884; John Lewis, born February 19, 1888.

In his religious association Mr. Rives and family are connected with the Methodist Episcopal Church (South).

When it comes to exercising the prerogative of a citizen at the polls, he votes with the time-honored Democracy of his fathers.

ALEXANDER HILL, proprietor of Walnut Hill Stock Farm, near the city of Owensboro, son of Dr. Alfred David Hill, late of Owensboro, was born in Daviess County, near Owensboro, Kentucky, December 25, 1855.

His father was born in Bertie County, North Carolina, near Albemarle Sound, June 11, 1828. He received a good education in his native county and studied medicine in the Ohio Medical College at Cincinnati, from which he graduated in 1852. After completing his medical course he performed hospital duty in Cincinnati for two or three years, and was offered a professorship in the Ohio Medical College, but declined it. He located in Owensboro, where he began the practice of his profession, but becoming dissatisfied with his vocation, he abandoned it and taught school for a time in Daviess County. His inclinations were toward agricultural pursuits, and he soon abandoned professional work for the life of a farmer, in which occupation he was very successful, and by industry and good management he acquired a great deal of valuable land in the county. In 1873 he leased his several farms, removed to Owensboro, and engaged in merchandising, and soon became one of the leading business men of that city. In 1876, associated with others, he incorporated the Farmers' & Traders' Bank of Owensboro, of which he was elected president, a position which he held until his death. He continued his mercantile business in connection with his banking interests and was a busy and successful man, highly respected and honored by all who had dealings with him. He never sought prominence as a politician, but he was well informed in all matters pertaining to local, state and national government, and could have wielded a strong influence, but he simply voted the Democratic ticket and was satisfied with having done his duty. He was more zealous in religious than political work, being a member of the Methodist Church and for many years a member of the board of deacons, in which capacity his fine business qualifications were of inestimable value to the church. He was married in 1853 to Minerva McFarland, and died December 23, 1878.

Benjamin Hill (grandfather) was a native of North Carolina, a farmer by occupation. His wife was Rachel Alexander. Their only child was Dr. Alfred D. Hill.

Robert W. McFarland (maternal grandfather) was a native of South Carolina who came to Daviess County, Kentucky, with his parents when he was a child, and there married a Miss Phebe Glover, who was the mother of four children: Louisa, Minerva, Robert W., Jr., and Beatrice.

Alexander Hill was educated in the common schools of Daviess County, the high school of Owensboro, and the University of Virginia, attending the latter institution in 1874 and 1875. He began his business career as a clerk in his father's store, and became proprietor of that establishment upon the death of his father. He had quite a fancy for farming and for fine stock and soon became the owner of the beautiful place near the city known as the Walnut Hill Farm, and gave much of his time in the improvement of the place and to raising and training fine saddle and harness horses, an occupation that has given him much pleasure and yielded a handsome profit.

He is actively interested in a number of enterprises, and is an earnest promoter of the advancement of the city. He is vice-president and director of the Farmers' & Traders' Bank, and has been president of the Owensboro Female College, having been one of the most active citizens in procuring its organization. He is president of the board of stewards in the Methodist Church, and like his father takes a deeper interest in church matters than in politics.

He is essentially a business man, and has been remarkably successful in all of his undertakings. He is intensely interested in educational matters, and is known in the community as a man of unswerving integrity and of the most upright moral character.

Mr. Hill was married November 6, 1879, to May Sutherland, daughter of William and Susan (May) Sutherland, natives of Nelson County, Kentucky. Mr. and Mrs. Hill have been blessed with a happy family of four children: Alfred David, born January 13, 1882; Mary Lee, born March 6, 1884; Helen Kimbley, born March 16, 1886; and Alexander Hill, Jr., born August 1, 1893.

THOMAS STUART BRADFORD, M. D., a well-known citizen and eminent physician of Augusta, son of Dr. Jonathan Johnson and Maria L. (Stuart) Bradford, was born in Augusta, Kentucky, November 24, 1848. He was educated in the old Augusta College and in the Pennsylvania University at Philadelphia, and was graduated in medicine from Jefferson Medical College, Philadelphia, in 1871; served for one year in the Blockley Hospital, Philadelphia; came to Augusta the following year and began his lifework in the practice of his profession, in which he has been engaged for about twenty-three years.

Inheriting a love and talent for the medical profession from his father, who was one of the most distinguished physicians and scholarly men of Kentucky; prepared by early training and liberal education for the study of medicine; a graduate of the first medical college in the United States, he was recognized at once as a man of the highest qualifications for the sacred office of family physician; and by patient study, undivided attention to the duties imposed upon him and entrusted to him, he has proven himself one of the most skillful and worthy members of the medical profession in Kentucky, and a worthy son of an illustrious sire.

Dr. Bradford has taken the part of a good citizen in all affairs of public interest, in which his counsel is sought and his judgment relied upon by his fellow citizens. He is an enthusiastic Republican, without being in any sense an office-seeker or an offensive partisan. He was a delegate to the Republican National Convention at Chicago in 1884, and voted in that body, and in the following election, for James G. Blaine.

Dr. Bradford was married December 31, 1875, to Margaret Marshall, daughter of William C. Marshall, and a descendant of a Virginia family which took part in establishing the independence of this country and in founding the Commonwealth of Kentucky. Mrs. Bradford was born in 1851, educated in Augusta, her native place, was a devout and beloved member of the Southern Methodist Church, and a lady whose life was characterized by those splendid virtues of her gifted people. She died March 24, 1893, leaving one son and two daughters: Louis Ewing, born February 15, 1878; Eliza Stuart, born August 20, 1879; and Elizabeth, born November 24, 1880.

Jonathan Johnson Bradford, M. D. (father), was born in Bracken County, near Augusta, June 5, 1808, studied medicine with Dr. F. A. W. Davis, graduated in medicine from Transylvania University in 1830, and was a practicing physician of Augusta for fifty-two years. Besides being a most noted and skillful physician, he was prominently identified with all movements looking to the advancement of his neighbors and fellow citizens. He was a persistent advocate of temperance, lecturing and writing in behalf of that cause, and was elected and served five terms as Grand Master Patriarch of the Sons of Temperance, and was Most Worthy Associate and Most Worthy Patriarch of the National Division of Sons of Temperance of North America from 1868 to 1870. He was an able and accomplished writer on medical subjects and was one of the most active and influential citizens of Augusta. In politics he was a Whig, later a Union man, and after the war a Republican, and was well informed in national and state politics, in which his vote and his voice were true to his honest convictions. His long and useful life was devoted to humanity and to the service of the people whom he loved and by whom he was honored and by whom his memory is greatly revered. He was active and vigorous until the end, and he "paid the debt of nature" August 1, 1878, having reached his allotted three score and ten.

He was married (first) July 8, 1830, to Amanda Thome, daughter of Arthur Thome of Augusta. She died after about two years of married life. He was married (second) November 20, 1834, to Maria Stuart (mother), who was a daughter of James Peyton Stuart, a wholesale dry goods merchant of Pittsburg. She received her education in that city and was endowed with a high degree of intelligence, possessing many traits and virtues which distinguished her as a woman of noble character and a fit companion for her illustrious husband.

The grandfather Bradford was a native of the north of Ireland, who came to America with his parents when he was eight years of age. They settled first at Redstone Fort, now Brownsville, Pennsylvania, and he came to Kentucky when a young man, lived for a time in Bourbon County, and was married there in one of the fortifications known as the Irish fort. He afterward removed to Bracken County, where he was engaged in agricultural pursuits until his death in 1830.

Elizabeth Johnson (grandmother) was a daughter of William Johnson, a lieutenant in the Revolutionary war and a personal friend of George Washington.

James Peyton Stuart (maternal grandfather) was reared and educated in Virginia, and was a native of that state. He was a wholesale dry goods merchant in Pittsburg; married Jane Hunter of Brownsville, Pennsylvania; died in Monongahela City in 1861.

Dr. Joshua T. Bradford, one of the most celebrated ovarian surgeons in the United States and Europe, was a brother and pupil of Dr. Jonathan Johnson Bradford. He was the most successful ovariotomist of his time, and rose to great eminence in his profession, especially in the line of surgery. He practiced medicine for many years in Augusta, retiring from the ordinary routine of the family physician and confining himself to important surgical and consultation work for some years before his death. He was born near Augusta and died October 31, 1871. A sketch of his career is given in Collins' History of Kentucky.

HENRY CLAY HOWARD, judge of the Bourbon County Court, and one of the most promising young attorneys of Paris, son of Colonel Henry Howard, was born in Mt. Sterling, Kentucky, November 14, 1860. He is descended from the Lewis, Clay, and Howard families, whose ancestors were distinguished patriots during Revolutionary times.

His father was a member of the distillery firm of Howard, Barnes & Company of Mt. Sterling, and his grandfather, George Howard, was one of the pioneer merchants of that city. His great-great-grandfather, Thomas Howard, was a native of England, who, on coming to this country, first located in Virginia, but came to Woodford County before the admission of Kentucky to the Union.

His maternal grandfather, Douglas P. Lewis, was a resident of Bourbon County, where he married a daughter of "Colonel Henry Clay of Bourbon," so called to distinguish him from his cousin and contemporary, the great commoner.

Thomas Lewis (maternal great-grandfather) came from Virginia and settled in Fayette County; was a colonel in the Revolutionary war; a member of the first Constitutional Convention; a member of the first Senate of Kentucky; and fourth circuit judge of the Lexington circuit.

Judge Henry Clay Howard was thrown upon his own resources at a very early age—his father's firm having failed in 1870—and he soon developed those splendid qualities which have brought him to the front and made him one of the finest young lawyers of Bourbon County.

After picking up a primary education, limited and unsatisfactory to himself, he began the study of law in the office of ex-Chief Justice Holt at Mt. Sterling; was appointed to a position in the

KENTUCKY BIOGRAPHIES.

Treasury Department, and while there he entered a night class in Columbian University, working in the Treasury Department during the day, studying and reciting at night. After an undergraduate course of two years, he was elected president of the graduating class of 1884, and took the degree of bachelor of laws. The following year he took the post-graduate course and received the degree of master of laws. The time spent in this department of the university is counted as part of the study required for admission to the bar, and after examination he was sworn in as a practicing attorney in the Supreme Court of the District of Columbia, July, 1885. He retained his position in the Treasury Department until February, 1887, when he resigned and came to Paris for the practice of law.

He at once became quite popular and took a leading position among the young lawyers of the Bourbon County bar, so distinguishing himself in his profession and as a leading spirit in Republican politics that his party nominated and elected him judge of the Bourbon County Court in November, 1894.

Although quite a young man, he has the qualifications for his position in an eminent degree, and the record he is making will prepare him for other honors and trusts that are sure to come to the faithful. He is modest, refined and courteous, and has clothed his present office with a new dignity, commanding the respect of the bar and the endorsement of the entire community.

ALLEN G. BERRY, M. D., a scholarly and able physician of Ashland, was born in Chapmansville, West Virginia, August 5, 1859. He came to Kentucky when a child and attended school in Ashland, and subsequently the Normal School at Greenup. He taught in the Greenup County public schools several terms, and in 1883 attended a course of lectures at the Louisville Medical College. In June, 1886, he graduated from the Kentucky School of Medicine in Louisville.

He began the practice of his chosen profession at Millersport, Ohio, and continued there until February, 1888, when he located permanently in Ashland, and rapidly advanced to the front among the leaders of the profession in that city. His general practice has grown with his acquaintance and his success as a careful and competent physician has inspired confidence in his skill.

Dr. Berry is a member of the Northeastern Kentucky Medical Society; a member and medical examiner of the American Order of Union Workmen; a member of the Masonic Order, Poage Lodge, No. 325; Apperson Chapter, No. 81, and the Ashland Commandery, No. 28, Myrtle Castle No. 2 Knights of the Golden Eagle; a member of the Methodist Episcopal Church South, and a citizen of excellent repute and high standing.

Dr. Berry and Lucy Powell, daughter of Luke and Sallie Sweetland Powell, were married in Greenup County, August 23, 1887. Mrs. Berry was born January 11, 1865, and was educated in Greenup County and at Oxford, Ohio. They have had two children: Edgar Allen, born June 24, 1889, and Lillian, born July 2, 1891, both of whom died in infancy.

James Madison Berry (father) was born in Lawrence County, Kentucky, June 7, 1835. His father removed to Virginia when James M. was seven years of age, and he was educated in the schools of the Shenandoah Valley. He returned to Lawrence County in 1865, and lived there until 1870, when he removed to Greenup, where he was a cabinet maker, and was also interested in farming. During the war of the rebellion he served in the Confederate army as first lieutenant of Company D, Second Virginia Cavalry, and was known as a brave and gallant soldier.

He was married November 19, 1857, to Barbara Robinson, daughter of James and Celia Robinson. Dr. A. G. Berry was the only child of this union. Mrs. Berry died April 2, 1860, and James M. Berry and Emily Perry were married February 2, 1861. There were six children by this marriage: William A., Alvin F., Mary, Laura, Luella, and Carrie E. Emily Perry is a daughter of Henry and Mary Chambers Perry, natives of Virginia.

Isaac Berry (grandfather) was born in Montgomery County, Virginia, February 20, 1789; was educated there, and served as a captain of militia in the war of 1812. He removed to Lawrence County, Kentucky, in 1809, where, after the war, he followed the business of a general mechanic until 1842, when he returned to Virginia. He was married in 1808 to Nancy Kelly, daughter of William and Amy Jacobs Kelly. They had thirteen children, seven of whom reached maturity.

Isaac Berry (great-grandfather) was a native of Ireland, who came to this country and settled in eastern Virginia.

James Robinson (maternal grandfather) was a native of New Garden, Russell County, Virginia. He followed the occupation of a tanner.

William Kelley, father of James Madison Berry's second wife (stepmother), was a soldier in the Revolutionary war.

WILLIAM CLINTON GOODLOE.—The Goodloe family of the United States are all descended from two brothers who were born in England about 1700 and emigrated to this country and settled in Spottsylvania County, Virginia. Their names were Robert and George. It is George Goodloe with whom we have to do in this sketch. George Goodloe married in Virginia a Miss Minor. They had five children, three girls and two boys. One of the girls married Ben Tompkins; one Roger Quarles, and one Jesse Harper of Harper's Ferry, Virginia. Their son, Robert Goodloe Harper, rose to distinction in Maryland, was United States Senator and the leader of the old Federalist party.

George's son, Robert, married Miss Sarah Short and settled at her home near the big falls of Roanoke Run in North Hampton County, North Carolina. Robert was born in 1741 and died in North Carolina in 1797. He commanded a company of militia during the Revolutionary war, and built the first state house at Raleigh, North Carolina. His wife, Sarah Short, was born in 1745 and died in Madison County, Kentucky, June 2, 1814.

Their son, William Goodloe, was born in 1769 in North Hampton County, North Carolina. He came to Kentucky when he was eighteen years old in 1787 and settled on Otter Creek in Madison County, three miles east of Richmond. In 1796 he married Susan Woods, daughter of Captain Archibald Woods of Revolutionary fame. They had thirteen children. Their sixth child was William Clinton Goodloe. He was born October 10, 1805. He was educated at the Richmond Male Academy and at Transylvania College at Lexington, graduating there in 1824, under the celebrated Dr. Holley. He read law with his maternal uncle, Avey Woods, and was licensed to practice before he was twenty-one. He began his life work in Richmond. On October 26, 1826, he was married to Miss Almira Owsly, daughter of Judge William Owsly of Lancaster, Kentucky. Being a man of fine talents and great energy and very much in love with his profession, he soon attracted attention by his attainments and ability and was appointed by Governor Morehead or Breathitt commonwealth attorney for the judicial district in which he lived. In 1841 he removed to Frankfort, Kentucky, and entered into partnership with his father-in-law, Judge Owsly, in the practice of the law. He took an active, controlling part in the nomination of Judge Owsly for governor in 1844, defeating the wishes and incurring the enmity of Henry Clay thereby, who desired John J. Crittenden nominated. He moved back to Madison County in the fall of 1846 to his farm and continued the practice of the law. In 1847 Governor Owsly appointed him circuit judge. This office he held until August, 1868. In 1849 the changed constitution of the state made the office elective and in 1850, 1856 and 1862 he was elected to the position. In politics Judge Goodloe was a Whig, but upon the dissolution of that party he united with the American party. He warmly and decidedly espoused the cause of the Union in 1861 and became one of the conspicuous leaders of the Union party in Kentucky. He was an Emancipationist and voted for the Emancipation candidate for the Constitutional Convention in 1849. His able and enthusiastic advocacy of the Union cause in 1861 brought him prominently to the front, and in the fall of that year Governor Denison of Ohio visited Kentucky at the request of Mr. Lincoln and advised the president to declare martial law in the state and appoint Judge Goodloe military governor, as was done in Tennessee in the appointment of Andrew Johnson,

In 1864 Judge Goodloe called a conference of the unconditional Union men of the state at his house in Lexington, Kentucky, to which city he had moved in 1863, and from that conference went forth a call for a convention of Union men who were willing to unite with the great Union party of the nation in nominating Abraham Lincoln for a second term. The convention met in May in Louisville. Judge Goodloe was elected presiding officer. This was the act which united the Union party of Kentucky with the Republican party of the nation. Delegates were sent to Baltimore instructed to vote for Mr. Lincoln for renomination.

In January, 1865, another Republican convention was held in Frankfort, Kentucky, and Judge Goodloe was the second time elected presiding officer.

During the impeachment trial of Andrew Johnson, when Senator Wade of Ohio was expected to succeed to the presidency, Mr. Wade had selected Judge Goodloe for a seat in his cabinet, and so informed him by letter. Judge Goodloe was not a candidate for re-election as circuit judge in 1868, but at the expiration of his term resumed the practice of the law. He loved the position of judge and made an eminent one, though at the sacrifice of the emoluments of his profession. In less than two months after his retirement from the bench he received two fees that amounted to almost as much as his salary of circuit judge for three years. He died August 14, 1870, in his sixty-third year and was buried in Richmond, Kentucky. His children were eight girls, and two boys, Captain A. H. Goodloe of the United States army, and Rev. W. O. Goodloe, D. D., of the Presbyterian ministry.

DANIEL WEBSTER STEELE, Jr., a promising young lawyer of Ashland, son of Captain Daniel Webster and Aremetha R. (Ulen) Steele, was born December 19, 1867, in Boyd County, Kentucky.

His parents removed to Star Furnace, Carter County, in 1873, and one year later removed to Ashland, remaining in that city until 1881, when they returned to their farm in Boyd County. He attended the county schools from 1872 until 1874 —the sessions of which were of five months duration each year; the public schools of Ashland from 1874 to 1881; and the Ashland Collegiate Institute from 1887 to 1890, in the meantime teaching school in order to secure means to defray the expenses of his education. When not teaching or attending college, he performed manual labor about the iron furnaces in Ashland, and carried a hod for a plasterer.

With an ardent thirst for knowledge, determined to prepare himself for a professional career, he had the courage and industry to pursue his studies under difficulties, and the trying experiences of his youth were probably as essential in forming habits of industry and diligence as the education which he acquired through his own efforts.

In January, 1891, he began the study of law with John F. Hager of Ashland, and pursued his studies with diligence until December 12, 1891, when he was admitted to the bar. He remained in Mr. Hager's office until March 30, 1892, when he opened a law office without a dollar or a law book, but he had that which is better than gold—a determination to succeed, confidence in his own ability, faith in humanity, a willingness to work and patience to bide his time.

Few young men have realized upon their investments as quickly and surely as Mr. Steele. By close application to business and indefatigable industry, he has built up a remunerative practice and has succeeded in securing an excellent library. If the first five years of his professional career are a fair index of the future, he will make his mark as one of the leading lawyers of the state.

His father, Daniel Webster Steele, was born in Lebanon, Russell County, Virginia, August 4, 1837, and removed to Kentucky with his parents in 1838. He received his education principally in the county schools of Boyd and Greenup Counties, and taught school before the war.

He enlisted September 23, 1861, in Company B, Twenty-second Regiment Kentucky Volunteer Infantry, as a private, and at the organization of the company was elected second sergeant, afterwards first sergeant and was subsequently promoted to second lieutenant, promoted to first lieutenant December 14, 1863, and was afterwards transferred to Company H as captain.

He participated in the capture of Cumberland Gap; the battle of Tazewell, Tennessee; was in the march from Cumberland Gap to the Ohio river under command of General George W. Morgan; then joined the army of West Virginia at Charleston; afterwards transferred to the army of the Tennessee at Memphis; then in the expedition against Vicksburg; was in the battles of Chickasaw Bluffs, Arkansas Post, Grand Gulf, Port Gibson, Raymond, Champion Hills and Big Black River; was in the general assault on Vicksburg, May 22, 1863; participated in the forty-nine days' siege and the capture of the city on the 4th of July, and the battle of Jackson, Mississippi, July 12, 1863.

Captain Steele is a most ardent Republican, and is a member of the Masonic fraternity. He taught school immediately after the war; tilled the soil until 1873, when he became manager of the Star Furnace in Carter County, Kentucky, and was employed there for one year. He was employed by the Ashland Coal & Iron Railway Company from 1874 till 1881, when he removed to Ashland in order to afford his children the benefit and advantages of the educational facilities of that city, from which place he still controls the management of the farm.

He was married March 2, 1865, to Aremetha R. Ulen. They have six sons and two daughters, the subject of this sketch being the eldest child.

Daniel Steele (grandfather) was born in Stokes County, North Carolina, May 9, 1791. He enlisted in the Twenty-first North Carolina Battalion in 1813, and served until the close of the war in 1815. He was elected to the North Carolina legislature in 1818, and served until 1820, when he removed to Washington County, Virginia, where he married Nancy Spears. He was a bricklayer by trade and built the first courthouse at Lebanon, the county seat of Russell County, Virginia. He afterwards studied medicine, and began his work in that profession about 1825, and continued in the practice until his death in 1863.

Aremetha R. Ulen Steele (mother) was born in Boyd County, March 21, 1843. She was educated in the schools of Catlettsburg, Ashland and Greenup, Kentucky.

Benjamin Ulen (maternal grandfather), a physician and farmer, was born in Virginia in 1790; served in the war of 1812; died in Boyd County, Kentucky, in 1861. He was married three times, and Aremetha Steele was a daughter of his third wife, whose mother was the wife of Louis Napoleon Raison, whose father emigrated from France to San Domingo, where he owned extensive coffee plantations and many slaves. The negroes rebelled against their master, and in order to save his life, he emigrated to Kentucky. This loss impoverished him.

Benjamin Ulen (great-grandfather) of Virginia was pursued at one time by Indians, and rather than be captured and tortured by them, he leaped over a cliff, making a miraculous escape by falling into a grape vine in a buckeye tree. The spot was called "Ulen's Leap," now known as "Lovers' Leap," in West Virginia.

JUDGE CHARLES B. THOMAS, for many years judge of the Circuit Court of the Lexington district, was one of the most popular judges of the state in his day. He was a son of Barak G. and Sarah Ann (Howe) Thomas. Barak G. Thomas was a native of Elkton, Maryland, and was descended from Welsh ancestors, and when quite a young man emigrated from his native state and settled in Charleston, South Carolina. He remained there until 1833, when he removed to Lexington with his family, which was his home until his death, which occurred in 1849 in the sixtieth year of his age. He was a master machinist by trade and was one of the first men who ran a high pressure steam engine in this country. This was on a steamboat which plied the Pedee River in South Carolina. He had two sons and two daughters by his marriage to Sarah Ann Howe: Judge Charles B., and Major Barak G. Thomas of Lexington (see his sketch); the daughters were Salina A. and Sarah A., both of whom died young. Judge Thomas distinguished himself as an able advocate and an upright judge. Before his elevation to the bench he practiced law for many years before the Lexington bar

and was a contemporary of some of the most brilliant men the State ever produced, who were members of the same bar; such men as James B. Clay, George Robertson, M. C. Johnson, F. K. Hunt, R. A. and B. F. Buckner, G. B. Kinkead, J. B. Beck, and John B. Payne. When quite young, Judge Thomas served as city judge, and about the year 1860 was elected circuit judge, his circuit being composed of the counties of Fayette, Scott, Jessamine, Woodford, Clark, Madison, and Bourbon. He remained on the bench until his death in December, 1873, in the fifty-fourth year of his age. He served continuously and most acceptably to the people for a period of thirteen years. During the Civil war, Judge Thomas served in the Southern army as judge-advocate, with the rank of colonel. During the whole of the war he was with the Army of Virginia. He was one of nature's noblemen and had a strong hold upon the affections of the people. Suave and courtious in manner, warm-hearted and kind to his friends, but when upon the bench he was dignified and firm, and his decisions were always just and equitable. Like his father, he was trained in the political school of Jefferson and was a stanch Democrat. He was a man of great courage, determination and force of character, and when he once made up his mind that his judgment was correct, he was firm and unchangeable. His literary education was received at the University of Indiana. He read law with Samuel Shy, Esq., and was soon afterward admitted to the bar. A friend, speaking of him, said: "Charles B. Thomas was truly the people's judge, and this universal sentiment was due largely to his natural impartiality and high sense of honor in all matters. No decision of his could be questioned, because the people said whatever he said was right. He was neat in his dress and pleasant in his manner, and was a 'good mixer' with the people, but when on the bench he seemed not to know his most intimate friend. His prompt decision in almost all cases made the juries and the people generally style him a 'judge by nature.' His great moral courage and high sense of honor tended very much to make him a most popular man."

After Major Thomas left the office of Judge Robertson, his preceptor, writing of him in a letter, said: "I can, without hesitation or qualification, vouch for his intelligence, his high honor, his excellent character and exceptional habits. He will deceive nobody. He will not say what he does not believe, and will faithfully do whatever he undertakes."

MAJOR BARAK G. THOMAS, a prominent horse breeder of Lexington, son of Barak G. and Sarah Ann (Howe) Thomas, and brother of Judge Charles B. Thomas, was born in Charleston, South Carolina, June 9, 1826. He was educated in the University of Indiana, Bloomington, remaining there nearly four years, when he returned to Lexington and entered Transylvania University, in which he studied for two years and graduated in 1845. He then attended the law department of that time-honored institution, graduating in 1847; was admitted to the Fayette County bar and began the practice of law. He soon relinquished this, and accepted a position with the Lexington & Frankfort Railroad Company as civil engineer, and after the completion of that road he was made general freight and passenger agent at Lexington. He served in this capacity some twelve or fourteen years, until the beginning of the Civil war, and in 1861 he enlisted in the Southern army, first under the command of General Kirby Smith, but at Knoxville his regiment was assigned to the brigade of General Abe Buford. Here for a short time he served as chief of commissary, when he was transferred to chief of commissary of General Wheeler's Cavalry Corps and served in this line of duty until the time of his discharge, May 3, 1865.

After the close of the war, Major Thomas accepted a clerkship in a grocery, which was only temporary, as he soon became manager of the Lexington Observer and Reporter, and was thus employed for three years. He was then appointed teller in the Farmers' and Traders' Bank of Lexington and held that responsible position for three years. In 1875 he was elected sheriff of Fayette County, and was re-elected to the same office, serving two full terms. He then turned his attention to the breeding and training of thoroughbred horses, in which he has been remarkably successful and has established a most enviable reputation. He now owns Hirailla, one of the most beautiful country seats and stock farms in central Kentucky. It is located about six miles from Lexington on the Huffman Mill pike, where he keeps about eighty horses. Hirailla is run in connection with Timberland, which belongs to Thomas Gardiner. Among others, Major Thomas has bred the following horses, which in their day were among the very best performers in the country: Hertzog Aureola, Himyar, Lelex, Jewel Band, Ban Fox, King Fox, and Domino.

Major Thomas has held many positions of trust in the county of Fayette and the city of Lexington; has been guardian and administrator of many large estates, and from 1870 to 1875 he filled the office of master commissioner of the Fayette Circuit Court. He is a Democrat of the old school, and it can truthfully be said that in every relation of life he has performed his part with the strictest integrity and honesty. He is a true friend and is universally popular.

WILLIAM THOMAS AULL, chief deputy clerk of the County Court, Owensboro, son of James and Charlotte (McDaniel) Aull, was born in Daviess County, Kentucky, March 16, 1840.

His father was born in Nelson County, January 4, 1818, and received a part of his education in that county before removing to Daviess County in 1832, and completed his schooling in the last named county. He has devoted his life during more than a half century to the honorable business of farming in Daviess County, where he is now living in quiet retirement. He is a faithful member of the Catholic Church.

Benjamin Aull (grandfather) was a native of Frederick, Maryland, who came to Nelson County when he was a youth; married a Miss Redman, daughter of Richard Redman; was a farmer in comfortable circumstances; a member of the Catholic Church, and a highly respected citizen of his county. He died in Daviess County, aged eighty-three years. His father, Aquilla Aull (great-grandfather) was a Virginian of German descent.

Charlotte McDaniel Aull (mother) was born in Nelson County in 1818. Her parents removed to Daviess County with the Aull family, and they bought adjoining farms in the Knottsville precinct. She married James Aull May 6, 1839, and they lived happily together for fifty years. She died as she had lived, in the Catholic faith, in 1893, aged seventy-six years.

Abraham McDaniel (grandfather) was a native farmer of Nelson County, whose ancestors were from Ireland.

William Thomas Aull was educated in Daviess County in the public schools; and on the 30th day of September, 1861, he enlisted in Dr. C. T. Noel's company, First Regiment Kentucky Cavalry, which belonged to the famous Orphans' Brigade. Dr. Noel, the captain of Company A, was killed in 1862, and W. J. Taylor, first lieutenant, took command of the company, with whom Mr. Aull served until the close of the war. He was in the battles of Murfreesboro, Perryville, Chickamauga, Mission Ridge, Round Top Mountain, Atlanta, and other engagements in which the army of Tennessee took part. In the battle of King's Salt Works, Virginia, October 4, 1864, he was severely wounded, necessitating the amputation of his right leg. He was left in the hospital at Liberty, Tazewell County, Virginia, until February 19, 1865, when he was taken to Yorkville and a second amputation was performed. He remained there until he was able to travel, July 10, 1865, when he returned to his home in Daviess County.

He resumed his studies at Pleasant Valley Academy, which he attended for two years, and then taught school for four years.

In 1873 he was elected assessor of Daviess County for a term of four years; in 1878 he was elected constable for a term of two years; in 1880 he became proprietor of a hotel in Owensboro, which was burned January 24, 1882, and in the same year he was elected superintendent of city scales; in 1886 he was employed by Collector Hunter Wood, in the Internal Revenue Department, serving until the close of President Cleveland's first administration, since which time he has been chief deputy clerk of the County Court, a position for which he has the highest qualifications and which he has filled with great satisfaction to his employer, the members of the bar and the general public. He is personally very popular, being of a genial disposition, courteous and obliging, and is highly respected for his honesty, candor and loyalty to his friends. He is a fair-minded and honorable politician, an active worker in the Democratic ranks, and enjoys the unbounded confidence of the entire community, regardless of politics. He is the secretary and a leading spirit in the Daviess County Confederate Association, a purely social organization, in which the embers of the camp-fire are kept burning for memory's sake.

Mr. Aull was married August 29, 1869, to Mary E. Bruner, daughter of George W. and Isabella (Head) Bruner. They are members of the Christian Church and are social favorites in the church and in Owensboro society.

They have four children living: James G., born November 19, 1871; Leroy, born December 13, 1873; Maude L., born June 26, 1876, wife of Charles Usher of Owensboro; W. Jessie, born October 28, 1882.

CHARLES W. NAGEL, Mayor of Bellevue and a prominent real estate dealer in that progressive young city, was born in Detroit, Michigan, April 25, 1852, and is a son of William F. and Catherine (Bodemer) Nagel.

His father was a native of Baden, Germany, who came to the United States in 1847, and located in Detroit, where he married. He removed to Newport in October, 1857, where he was engaged in manufacturing rope until the beginning of the Civil war in 1861. He enlisted in the Fourth Ohio Battery, in which he served throughout the war. During his absence in the service of his adopted country, his family lived in Cincinnati. When he returned he removed to Bellevue, where he resumed his business of making rope, in which he continued until the time of his death, January 19, 1890, his death being due to a complication of diseases contracted while he was in the army. He was quite prominent as a Republican politician, and was a Michigan delegate to the convention that nominated John C. Fremont for President in 1856.

Charles W. Nagel's mother, Catherine (Bodemer) Nagel, is a native of Baden, Germany, and came to America in 1845, when she was twelve years of age. She is now living in Bellevue.

During the years of his boyhood, Charles W. Nagel was a resident at different times of Newport, Cincinnati and Bellevue; and received his education principally in the Cincinnati public schools, finishing with a course in a commercial college in that city. After leaving school he learned the printing trade with Jewett & Adams, by whom he was employed for twenty years. He abandoned his trade in 1885 and engaged in the real estate business in Bellevue, in partnership with T. F. Beyland, whose biography will be found in this volume. In 1891 he was elected secretary of the Mutual Fire Insurance Company of Newport, and in connection with L. J. Crawford purchased the Newport abstract office and completed its records up to date.

He has been quite prominent in politics, and during his residence in Bellevue has held a number of offices; he was a member of the City Council for three years; was city clerk for seven years; examiner of teachers for three years; deputy sheriff for four years, and is now serving his second term as mayor of Bellevue, this being a popular endorsement of his administration during his first term. He was also police judge of his city for one term. From all this it may be inferred that Mr. Nagel is a very useful and popular citizen and trusted official.

He began his career without capital and has accumulated considerable property, including valuable real estate in Bellevue and vicinity.

Mr. Nagel was married in 1881 to Julia Sutkamp of Dubuque, Iowa, and has one son and one daughter living: Herbert Lincoln Nagel and Elfrida Nagel.

NEWTON COOPER, a well-known business man and public spirited citizen of Maysville, was born two miles below that city on the hill overlooking the Ohio river in Mason County, Kentucky, May 19, 1820, and is a son of Hugh Cooper and Catherine (Rickerts) Cooper. Hugh Cooper was a native of Spottsylvania County, Virginia, and was born near the boundary line between that state and North Carolina October

1, 1792. He emigrated with his father from his native state to Kentucky in about the year 1794 and settled in the vicinity of Mt. Sterling. He was a soldier under General Harrison in the war of 1812 and was at the siege of Fort Meigs. He came to Mason County and purchased a farm southwest of Maysville, containing sixty acres, in 1808. Here he carried on farming in connection with shoemaking for two years. He learned his trade under G. Vannatta, and followed it for a short time until his marriage with Catherine Rickerts, who was born in Bedford County, Pennsylvania, in 1792. Shortly after his marriage he built a stoneware pottery one mile below Maysville, which he operated until 1829, when he removed to Maysville, continuing in the same business till his death in 1831. His father, John Cooper, was a South Carolinian by birth; removed to Virginia, and there married Patsey McDaniel, a daughter of Henry McDaniel, a native of Scotland, then living in Spottsylvania County, Virginia, where he owned a plantation and a large number of slaves. He removed to Kentucky about 1793, first making his home in Montgomery County and subsequently removed to Morgan County, where he died.

Hugh and Caroline (Rickerts) Cooper had ten children, of whom four are living: Milton, born April 24, 1815; Newton, Lucy and Mrs. Marian Power. The Coopers are of English, the McDaniels of Scotch and the Rickerts of Welsh ancestry. Ruliff Rickerts was a native of Cecil County, Maryland; removed to Pennsylvania and from there to Kentucky in 1797.

Newton Cooper was reared at the old homestead, and received one year's schooling, but his principal education, which is by no means meagre, has been acquired through an active business career. When quite young he was apprenticed to John C. Reed of Maysville, under whom he served for four years, learning the trade of tin plate and sheet iron making. After the expiration of his apprenticeship in 1838, he formed a partnership with Thomas J. Nicholson in the tin business, which relation continued about one year, when Mr. Cooper purchased Nicholson's interest and conducted it alone the greater part of the time until 1883, when he sold out to two of his apprentices, McClanahan and Shea. In the same year he built his present fine grain storage and tobacco warehouse on Front street, which is 60x145 feet and six stories high.

While attending industriously to his many private interests, he is well known as a public spirited citizen and has been identified with the best interests of his city and county. He is a director in the Gas Company and the Electric Light Company, and owns a one-third interest in the Maysville Electric Street Railway. Messrs. Cooper, Cochran and Cox were the promoters and builders of this road, one of the first constructed in the state. Mr. Cooper has had no time or inclination to seek public office, but under President Grant's first term, and without his knowledge, he was appointed revenue collector of the Tenth District, which place he accepted and for four years administered the affairs of that office most acceptably to the administration and the people of the district.

HON. WILLIAM M'DONALD SHAW, City Solicitor of Covington, son of Lafayette and Harriet McDonald Shaw, was born in Covington, September 27, 1857. His father was born in Campbell County, July 3, 1825, and was educated in the public schools of the county and in the law department of Louisville University. After graduating he began the practice of law in Covington, where he has continued successfully until the present time.

He was judge of the Kenton County Court from 1865 to 1869, and was county attorney for four years. He is thoroughly devoted to his profession and cares little for politics other than a desire for the success of the Republican party, with which he has always affiliated. He is a Universalist. His father, Robert Shaw, was born in Pennsylvania, March 13, 1783.

James Shaw, great-grandfather of W. McD. Shaw, was born in Ireland in 1754.

W. McD. Shaw was educated in the public schools of Covington and the High School of Cincinnati and at Princeton College, graduating in 1882. He then entered the Cincinnati Law School and graduated in 1884, taking the oratorical prize of his class.

He at once began the practice of law with his father, and from 1886 to 1890 he was county attorney of Kenton County. July, 1891, he was appointed assistant United States district attorney for Kentucky, in which capacity he served with signal ability until September, 1893, and in the following November was elected city solicitor of Covington, which office he still holds, in connection with a lucrative law practice.

Mr. Shaw is an ardent Republican and a trusted leader in his party, not only in his county, but throughout the state. In 1888 he was Republican elector for the state at large and made a brilliant campaign for General Harrison for President. He is one of the finest stump orators in the political arena, and a man who makes a friend of every one he meets.

Mr. Shaw is an exemplary member of the Presbyterian Church.

His wife, Ruth Evelyn, daughter of N. M. Holliway of Los Angeles, Cal., was born in Kansas City, Missouri, December 21, 1864, and was educated in that city. They were married October 11, 1893.

WILLIAM W. BLACKWELL of Henderson, past supreme chancellor of the Knights of Pythias of the world, was born in Henderson, April 5, 1849, and is the son of Paul A. and Martha S. (Crymes) Blackwell, natives of Lunenburg County, Virginia, who came to Henderson in 1848. Paul A. Blackwell has been a prominent wholesale and retail hardware merchant in Henderson for thirty years. During the war he held the office of police judge, but never sought or held any other public office.

Chapman Blackwell (grandfather) came to Henderson from Lunenburg County, Virginia, in 1832, and was a son of Robert Blackwell, who was a native Virginian. His ancestors are traced to three Blackwell brothers who came from England two hundred years ago, one of whom located in Blackwell's Island, New York, another in Durham, North Carolina, and the other settled in Virginia. Robert Blackwell (great-grandfather) was a magistrate in Virginia under King George III.

Mr. Blackwell's mother, Martha S. Crymes Blackwell, was a daughter of Leonard Crymes, a native of Virginia.

W. W. Blackwell, after making good use of his school days, and while yet a mere boy, entered his father's hardware store and learned the details of the business thoroughly. He soon displayed remarkable business talent and it was not long until he was given an interest in the establishment, and the growth of the business with his valuable assistance soon attested the wisdom of his father in giving him a responsible position in the management of the business. This partnership has continued until the present writing, under the firm name of P. A. Blackwell & Co. The latter was president of the Gas Commission in 1887, a position which he filled with great credit to himself and to the entire satisfaction of the public.

W. W. Blackwell joined the Knights of Pythias in 1873 and from the first evinced great interest in that order. He made a careful study of its laws and aims, and was soon known as one of the best informed members, and his opinion was relied upon in all matters concerning the order. His advancement was rapid; and, after presiding in his own (Ivy) lodge, he was made representative to the Grand Lodge which met in Covington in 1877, and at that meeting he was elected grand master of the exchequer; at Lexington, in 1878, he was made grand vice-chancellor; at Henderson, in 1879, he was, when only thirty years of age, unanimously chosen grand chancellor of the state, being the youngest Knight ever elected to that office in Kentucky; at Louisville in 1880 the honorable rank of past grand chancellor was conferred on him; at Maysville in 1881 he was elected supreme representative for four years, to represent the Grand Lodge of Kentucky in the Supreme Lodge of the world, and his commission was extended, by unanimous vote, two terms thereafter, 1885 and 1889.

He represented Kentucky at the Supreme meeting held in Detroit in August, 1882, and there received the Supreme Lodge rank, the highest ritualistic rank in the order; attended the Supreme meeting in New Orleans in 1884; in Toronto in 1886; in Cincinnati in 1888; in Milwaukee in 1890, at which session he was elected supreme vice-chancellor by acclamation from the floor, a distinction never before accorded to any member of that august body; in Kansas City in 1892, where he was unanimously elected supreme chancellor of the world; in Washington, D. C., in 1894, where he presided over that distinguished fraternal legislative body, the Supreme Lodge, Knights of Pythias, and at the installation of his successor became a past supreme chancellor, an honor of the highest distinction in the order. During his representative service upon the floor, he was a member of the Supreme Lodge finance committee, composed of five members, whose duty it was to audit the books and look after the vast financial affairs, comprising millions of money, the successful management of which brought him within the pale of promotion; was appointed aid-de-camp with the rank of colonel on the staff of Major General James Carnahan, commander-in-chief of the Uniform Rank—the grandest body of disciplined soldiers in the world —and served thereon eight years with satisfaction to his commander. He compiled and revised the constitutions of the Grand and subordinate lodges, a duty assigned to him by the Grand Lodge of Kentucky, a work which was attended by a multitude of difficulties; but, notwithstanding these difficulties, his report was a masterly one, and was accepted by the Grand Lodge practically as written, by a unanimous vote, which was afterward supplemented by a series of complimentary resolutions and a rising vote of thanks.

In every branch of the work in which Mr. Blackwell has been engaged he has served his constituents faithfully and well, as outspoken statements, of which he has many, fully attest.

The following tribute, written by a brother Knight, referring chiefly to his report as supreme chancellor to the Supreme Lodge, is but one of the many complimentary references that have been made to Mr. Blackwell and his work:

"W. W. Blackwell, Past Supreme Chancellor of the Knights of Pythias of the World:

"There have been other supreme chancellors besides W. W. Blackwell that have rendered an administration of loyalty and devotion, but the present incumbent is certainly entitled to the distinction of having worked harder and devoted more actual time and labor than several of his predecessors put together. He has been in office a little less than two years, yet in that time has visited 46 Grand Lodges in regular session and traveled over 65,000 miles to do so. His voice has been heard by thousands of members while he earnestly advocated constancy and devotion to Pythian principles, and above all loyalty to the government under which we live, the enforced use of the English language on this continent, and cheerful obedience to the Supreme Lodge and the mandates of proper authority—in short, one language, one flag, one country, and the greatest fraternity on earth.

"Every supreme chancellor has made himself especially prominent in some particular line: Van Valkenburg as an author; Douglas, the 'little giant,' in securing a universal conformity in the Grand Lodge constitutions, and putting down rebellion; Ward as a peacemaker; Shaw in executive ability and brilliant rhetoric; but with Blackwell it has been a constant labor in the field; making official visits to the Grand Lodges in session; urging the incorporation of valuable measures looking to the order's welfare; and greater than all, the monumental task of harmonizing all jurisdictions in the 'strictly English ritual.' By his persistent labor, wise counsel and diplomacy, he has smoothed the way to a harmonious session of the Supreme Lodge in 1894, by practically settling beforehand what might have developed into conflict long and serious.

"That Mr. Blackwell has the courage of his convictions will never be questioned by those who have met the man, heard him talk, or read his report; and when, as here, ability goes hand in hand with unflinching courage, there is no mistaking the writer's views or misinterpreting between the lines.

"Were we not personally acquainted, to some degree, with the retiring supreme chancellor, we should not, any the more, fail to understand his views on any topic discussed by him in his report, nor would we need any interpreter to make plain his meaning; but when to this is added knowledge, though ever so slight, of the man, any doubt we may have had concerning his words is displaced by certainty, and friendship broadens into admiration.

"The report is a bold, able document, written by one who is fearless of consequences, without any signs of that policy that usually renders the use of strong words by a sycophant imprudent, and is refreshing to the truth-seeker. Comprehensive and clear in his conception of duty, never doubting the righteousness of his stand when once that stand is taken, and mailed in the armor of a conscience that pervades all his writings, he rains down upon the doomed head of wrong, wherever he finds it, giant blows, the force of which is born of unquestioned conviction.

"His words have in them a ring and power that carries conviction and dismay among the dissenting, and imparts courage and heart to the loyal. Thorough, practical, broad; severe, yet kind; exhaustive, yet concise; plain-spoken, yet conservative in due degree, the report is admirable in the vigor and manliness of its wording. Brother Blackwell assaults most mercilessly every battlement of the enemy, tears down their walls, and Samson-like, carries off the gates of their strongholds, leaving them the choice of unconditional capitulation, or a lonely occupation of their desolate and demoralized position.

"Mr. Blackwell while supreme chancellor traveled 65,000 miles in the United States and Canada, and during his administration he did more than any predecessor in the development of the question, 'Americanizing America,' claiming that it was un-American and detrimental to true patriotism to publish and use a ritual in any other language in a country leading in civilization through the English—our mother tongue. He had while in office perhaps more testimonials of regard than any other man holding the same position, many of which were costly and valuable. A P. S. C. jewel, valued at $1,000, was voted him by the Supreme Lodge, besides other tokens of regard and esteem from different Grand Lodges, and in addition to all this he was paid $3,000 more than his salary by the Supreme Lodge as an additional evidence of their appreciation of his efforts."

W. W. Blackwell and Marcia A. Stinson of Evansville, Indiana, were married October 5, 1869, and they have one son, Ernest, who is following in the footsteps of his father and will make his mark in the world.

W. W. Blackwell is not only one of the most enthusiastic and distinguished Knights of Pythias in the world, but is also an Odd Fellow of high rank and a leading member of his lodge.

CHARLES M. F. STRIGER of Covington, son of Mason and Catherine F. (Blume) Striger, was born in Independence, Kenton County, Kentucky, March 10, 1858. His father was born January 23, 1833, in the same place and in the same house, and was a resident of Independence at the time of his death, November 2, 1895. He was a farmer all the years of his active life.

John Striger (grandfather) was a native of Virginia and became one of the earlier settlers of Kentucky. He was a soldier in the war of 1812. While farming was his principal business, he was also a cooper, and worked industriously at that trade when not busy on the farm. He died at Independence about 1840. His ancestors were from Germany.

Catherine F. Blume Striger was born in Kenton County, Kentucky, December 27, 1838. Her father, Isaac Blume, was a native of Virginia, who came to Kentucky in the early settlement of the state; located in Kenton County, where he died in 1864.

Charles M. F. Striger was brought up a farmer boy, receiving a good education in the country schools. He afterwards received his diploma from Nelson's College in 1880. He taught school in his native place for two years and in 1882 was the Republican candidate for county assessor. He then read law in the office of McKee & Finnell in Covington, and was admitted to the bar in February, 1887. He remained in the office of Judge McKee until 1889, since which time he has been successfully engaged in the practice of law without a partner. He is an active Republican politician, and has been a delegate to every Republican district and county convention since 1882; was Republican presidential elector from the Sixth District in 1888, and made the first thorough canvass ever made by a Republican candidate in the district, when General Harrison was elected. He was one of the thirteen men who received the highest Republican vote ever cast in the state up to that time. In 1893 he was a candidate for city judge of Covington, but was defeated. Mr. Striger is interested in politics for the principle of the thing, and has been willing to sacrifice himself for the purpose of keeping the organization together, even when an election was not probable; but he thinks the time has come when a nomination by the Republican party will not be merely an empty honor. It is but justice to a faithful party worker to say that Mr. Striger has done his part in bringing about this change in public sentiment.

He was nominated by one wing of the Republican party for Congress in the Sixth District in 1892, when there was a notable contest between the two factions before the National Convention at Minneapolis as to which set of delegates should be seated. That convention decided against the faction led by Mr. Striger, and he then told his friends that he could not honorably and consistently remain a candidate, and, to the chagrin of many friends at the time, withdrew from the race.

Mr. Striger at present occupies the position of inspector of illuminating oils. His term will expire August 16, 1899. He is unmarried and enjoys the acquaintance and friendship of all the leading Republicans of the state.

GEORGE WASHINGTON WILLIAMS, deceased, late of Owensboro, one of the leading lawyers of his time, was born in Hancock (then a part of Breckinridge) County, Kentucky, November 27, 1814. He was a son of Otho and Mildred (Anderson) Williams.

His father was a native of Louisa County, Virginia, where he married Mildred Anderson, before removing to Kentucky. The date of his coming to Kentucky is not recorded, but he was one of the pioneers, and a man of great strength of character and moral standing, who was able to encourage and help his neighbors at a time when good leadership was so much needed. He cleared away the forests and literally hewed himself a home and farm out of the wilderness. He was an industrious farmer, laboring with untiring energy in the woods and fields during the week, studying the Bible by the light of his winter fire at night, and preaching the gospel on the Sabbath day. Of course, this was possible only in the Methodist Church, in which the true spirit of religion was counted of more importance in the minister of the gospel than a classical education. But Rev. Otho Williams, farmer, not only preached the gospel on Sunday, but lived it during the week, an example of a godly man whose life was an argument in favor of the religion he preached. In naming his son George Washington, he indicated the patriotism and loyalty to his country which was one of his chief characteristics.

George W. Williams was brought up under the wholesome influence of pious parents, in a new and but partially settled country, and his educational opportunities were limited. The hard fortune that beset his youth, however, only made him the more determined to acquire an education, and ere long the doors of learning were unbarred and by persistent industry and study, he was enabled to drink deeply at the fountain of knowledge.

When twenty years of age, by the aid of his brothers, he was permitted to supplement the superficial schooling which he had received by a two years' course in Louisville, where he applied himself most assiduously; and after this he studied medicine, a profession that proved distasteful to him and which he never practiced. In 1837 he went to Helena, Arkansas, and taught school for one year; and, returning to Louisville, he began the study of law in the office of Thomasson & Boone. He was admitted to the bar in 1840 and opened an office in Hawesville, where he practiced law until 1872. In 1858 he purchased a farm near Hawesville, to which he removed with his family, employing an overseer, and continued his professional work in Hawesville; and, in 1866, he again removed his family to Hawesville, where he lived for six years. In 1872 he removed to Owensboro, where he was soon known as one of the leading lawyers of the city and of the Second Congressional district.

During the greater part of his professional career he was alone, but was at one time in partnership with Eli H. Brown, and at another time, with Colonel J. D. Powers. His political career was not remarkably successful, because he was not a politician, a fact which was by no means discreditable. In 1851-52 he was a member of the legislature, representing Hancock and Ohio Counties; in 1856 he was presidential elector for James Buchanan in the Second district; in 1857 he was the Democratic candidate for the state senate, but was defeated by John B. Bruner, the Know Nothing candidate; in 1867 he was elected circuit judge of the district, but resigned that office in 1870; became a candidate for judge of the Appellate Court in the same year, but withdrew before the day of election; in 1882 he was a candidate for judge of the Supreme Court, and was defeated by Judge Bowden of Russellville by a slight majority.

He completed his half century of professional labor, and during all that time he was conspicuously identified with the administration of justice in the courts of the Second district and in the Appellate Courts of Frankfort. He proved himself not only a profound student of legal science, but his reading and investigations in other fields of knowledge were varied and extensive, and he was one of the best informed men of his day.

Upon the announcement of his death, Monday, September 9, 1890, the courts adjourned until Thursday, a very unusual mark of respect. The members of the bar met and paid tribute to his memory. The remarks made by the leading lawyers recalled the facts that Judge Williams was a man of extraordinary talent and spotless character, a lawyer of the highest attainments, a constant and tireless worker, a generous friend, a sympathizer with the poor and oppressed and an unostentatious, true-hearted gentleman. Resolutions of respect were adopted, from which the following extracts are taken:

"In addition to other marks of our affection and reverence for our deceased associate, the late George W. Williams, we, on behalf of the Owensboro bar and the officers of court, offer this further testimonial:

"Realizing that on like occasions formal expressions are ordinarily regarded but the perfunctory observance of customary respect for the dead, it is deemed proper to here protest that his brethren of this bar testify only to his character and conduct as they have witnessed it, and speak the things that they do know.

"Their estimate and appreciation of the life and character of their late associate is not the sudden offspring of sorrow for his death, but is the declaration of matured opinions formed and cherished while he yet walked in and out in his ministrations at the high altar of justice and of law. . . . .

"As he appeared to the general public he was an absorbed man, and sometimes unjustly counted a cold one. He was often misunderstood and sometimes misconstrued, and it was only given to those who associated with him to thoroughly understand and appreciate the strength and manifold graces that supported and adorned his character.

"In his professional career he at all times manifested those solid and exalted virtues that assure success to the profession and honor to his calling. Endowed by nature with a keen perception and a logical mind, which long experience had polished and profound study had stored, to these he superadded the virtues of diligence, accuracy, patience, integrity and trustworthiness. For more than a generation in the forefront of legal conflict, he has ever been a sword and a shield for his clients, the exponent of exalted lawyership, and, withal, the pink of knightly courtesy.

"As a judge on the circuit bench, he brought to the discharge of his high and responsible duties extensive attainments, befitting dignity, absolute impartiality, the capacity for dispatching business and the correct solution and determination of legal problems.

"As a philosophic thinker his mind was ever open to the reception of truth from any and every quarter, and in dealing with all questions—social, scientific or political—he gave them candid, patient and earnest consideration, and whilst respectful to the opinions of others, thought for himself and came to his own conclusions, which were always logical, original and forcible.

"As a citizen he shirked no duty or responsibility, and while rarely concerned in the conduct of public affairs, he took a live interest in all that affected the common welfare. He was a friend alike of his people and his country, equally attached to the rights of one and the glory of the other.

"As a man he was of strong will, industrious, honest, brave, magnanimous and true, faithful and confiding with his friends, unswerving in his attachments, fixed in his principles, a pleasing companion, and devoted and affectionate to those bound to him by natural ties. Simple in tastes, frugal in habits, dignified and decorous in manner, gracious in address, and at all times and in all companies, by his bearing and appearance, showing that 'His tribe was God Almighty's gentlemen.'

"Resolved, That in his death the community, the state, the bar and his kindred have sustained an irreparable loss. (Signed.) W. N. Sweeney, W. T. Owen, G. W. Jolly, Wilfred Carrico, J. H. McHenry, Lucius P. Little, Committee.

"After the adoption of the resolutions, on motion they were ordered to be spread upon the records of the court and published in the city papers and copies sent to the bereaved widow and the Western Kentucky Bar Association."

His mind was so concentrated on his business that he was frequently misjudged and was regarded by some as cold and haughty, and, while he was not a good mixer, no one was ever more kind or sincerely anxious to help all striving young people to get a start in life, or more ready to aid in any good work for the advancement of others. His quiet demeanor and becoming dignity and his absorption in business militated against his popularity as a politician, and for this reason he did not reach positions to which he sometimes aspired, and for which he was so eminently qualified.

He was married November 15, 1841, in Hancock County, to Mary W. Hamilton, daughter of Sarah and Andrew Hamilton of Boone County, General John Davis, a minister, officiating. Mrs. Williams was born March 31, 1815, and is now living with her devoted daughter, wife of Judge W. P. Baker, in Owensboro. Judge Williams reared a large family, consisting of six sons and three daughters, of whom Hamilton W., Theophilus, James Russell, William, George and Mildred are deceased. The surviving son and daughters are: Ione, married to Judge W. P. Baker of Owensboro; Ruth, wife of W. E. Crutcher of Beaver City, Nebraska; and Hugh Anderson, attorney-at-law of Owensboro.

The children entertain the greatest admiration for their father, whose devotion to his family was one of the most beautiful traits of his exalted character.

WILLIAM W. FIELD, Judge of Bracken County and Attorney-at-Law of Brooksville, son of Charles Anderson Field and Nancy (Toleman) Field, was born June 23, 1844. His father was born in or near Germantown, Kentucky, August 8, 1815; was a farmer by occupation, a member of the Methodist Church, and a Democrat in politics after the dissolution of the Whig party in the state; but while he was enthusiastic in party affairs, he never sought office for himself. He died in November, 1880, and is buried at Mt. Zion graveyard near Augusta. Charles Field's father was William Field, a native Virginian, but who moved to Kentucky at an early day to that part of Mason which is now Bracken County. He was for several terms sheriff of his county, then a much more important office than now. He was a large land owner and a prosperous business man.

The Field family, the first of whom was John Field, were among the early settlers of Virginia. A brother of John Field settled in New York, and from this branch Cyrus Field and others of the name in the East are descended.

Nancy Toleman, the mother of William W. Field, was born and educated in Bracken County. Her father was a native of Maryland, but came to Kentucky when a young man, settling in Bracken County. Her mother was Mary Hevern, whose father was a soldier in the Revolutionary war.

William W. Field was educated at Augusta, Millersburg and Coal Springs; studied law under Judge Doniphan, and afterwards at the Louisville Law School, graduating from that institution in 1871. He began the practice of law in partnership with J. B. Clarke in Brooksville in 1872. This partnership continued for ten years and until Mr. Field was elected county judge in 1882. The next office held by Judge Field was that of delegate from his county to the constitutional convention of 1890-91, which framed the present state constitution, and in the deliberations of that body Mr. Field took an active part. In 1894 Mr. Field was again elected county judge, which position he yet holds. His wife was Nannie E. Smarr, a daughter of John H. Smarr of Bracken County. They have four children: Mary Anderson, Lillian T., John Smarr and Millie W. Mr. Field has always been a Democrat in politics; is a member of the Masonic fraternity; while both Mr. and Mrs. Field are consistent members of the Methodist Church.

JOHN PARKER FULTS, JR., County Attorney of Jefferson County, was born in Louisville December 30, 1870.

His father, John P. Fults, was born near Madison, Jefferson County, Indiana, in 1842. He was a soldier in the Eighty-third Illinois Infantry, under Colonel W. W. McChesney, in the early days of the Civil war, but was discharged on account of physical disability. From 1864 to 1872 he was chief clerk and acting freight agent of the Jeffersonville, Madison & Indianapolis Railroad Company at Louisville; was inspector of customs under James P. Luse, and was subsequently freight cashier for the J. M. & I. Railroad Company; was for seven years bookkeeper in the First National Bank of Louisville, which position he resigned in July, 1889, to accept the office of deputy collector and cashier of the Fifth Internal Revenue District of Kentucky, a position which he held under Albert Scott, collector, during President Harrison's administration. He is a Mason, Knight Templar and Scottish Rite, thirty-second degree. His wife's name is Florence (Parker) Fults, a native of Jeffersonville, Indiana.

Benjamin Franklin Fults (grandfather) was a native of Brighton, New Jersey, who was a soldier under General Winfield Scott. The ancestors of the Fults family were banished from Holland and went to England first, and then came to this country at or about the time the Mayflower brought the pilgrims over, and settled at Plymouth. The name was originally spelled "Foltz," which was changed to Fults by the great-grandfather of John P. Fults, Jr. They were generally men who lived to a great age, and were highly educated, representing the legal, medical and other leading professions, and occupying prominent positions in life.

John P. Fults, Jr., was educated in the Louisville public schools and in the A. and M. State College at Lexington, to which institute he was admitted by appointment from Jefferson County, taking a special course of two years in the classics, English and the languages. He then attended the law department of the University of Louisville, and was admitted to the bar in 1890, after which, before beginning to practice, he traveled extensively in the United States and Mexico, a part of the time as a salesman, but generally as a newspaper correspondent, representing some of the leading newspapers in the country. This experience was of great value to him, especially as he was under age and his very youthful appearance did not recommend him as a lawyer. His newspaper work was of a high order, and he could have made his mark in journalism, both as a writer and as an artist, but he had no intention of adopting it as a profession.

He accompanied the militia to the scene of the Eversole-French feud in 1888 as correspondent and sketch artist for the Louisville Commercial and as special correspondent for the New York Sun, a duty for which he volunteered when "war correspondents" were hard to find, owing to the uncertainty of life in that section of the country at that time.

He has been a member of Company E, First Regiment, Kentucky State Guards of Louisville, for ten years, and has been promoted from the ranks through the non-commissioned offices to first lieutenant, and has gone with his company every time it has been called upon for active duty. Of an adventurous spirit, somewhat reckless and daring, he has always been ready for a skirmish and eager for the fray, and had opportunity offered would have distinguished himself as a soldier.

In 1894, when only twenty-four years of age, he was elected county attorney of Jefferson County, and was one of the most active and efficient Republican campaigners during the canvass prior to the election, and the success of his ticket was due in a large measure to his activity. He has conducted the business of his office since January, 1895, in a manner which has surprised his political opponents and the older lawyers who thought a "boy" should not have been elected to a position of so much importance. His work has met with the approval of all who have business in the County Court. His friends say of him that he can take more men by the hand and call them by name than any man but one in Jefferson County.

Mr. Fults is a director in the Colored Industrial School of Louisville, and is connected with other institutions and enterprises in the city.

He is a member of the Masonic Order, of the Junior Order of American Mechanics, of the Red Men, of the Essenic Order, of the Iroquois Wheeling Club, the Commercial Club and the Garfield Club of Louisville.

JOHN M. BURNS, an attorney-at-law of distinction and ability, of Ashland, was born in Boyd County, Kentucky, March 11, 1825. He was educated in the schools of his native county, and studied law under W. H. Burns at West Liberty, and after his admission to the bar in 1851, formed a partnership with his preceptor. W. H. Burns lived in West Liberty and John M. Burns was then a resident of Whitesburg, Letcher County, while their practice covered a large scope of country, embracing Letcher, Perry and Breathitt Counties.

John M. Burns was elected county attorney of Letcher County, which office he held until 1853, when he removed to Prestonburg. There he formed a co-partnership with John M. Elliott, who was killed by Buford at Frankfort, and was associated with him for six years, during which time, in 1857, he was elected representative of his district, Floyd and Johnson Counties, in the legislature. In 1860 he was elected state senator from the Thirty-third District, embracing Pike, Floyd, Johnson and Magoffin Counties; but when it was discovered that an error had been made in the apportionment of representative districts, and that there was one too many senators, Mr. Burns resigned his seat and delivered a very fine speech, which elicited great applause on the floor and in the galleries. He returned to his home and resumed his work in the legal profession.

In 1864 he removed to Catlettsburg; served two terms as school commissioner, and attended to his practice in Boyd and adjacent counties. From 1883 to 1885 he was revenue agent and inspector for the district of Kentucky and Tennessee, by appointment of President Arthur.

In 1886 he was elected circuit judge of the Sixteenth Judicial District, composed of the counties of Boyd, Carter, Lawrence, Martin, Johnson, Floyd and Pike, and served on the bench the full term with distinction.

Judge Burns has always taken a deep interest and an active part in Republican politics, and has been a delegate to the State Conventions for many years. He is one of the most widely known men in northern Kentucky, and is popular with all classes. He has been a Mason for forty years, and is a member of the Missionary Baptist Church.

He was married, April 25, 1843, to Keziah Clay, daughter of William and Rebecca (Cecil) Clay. There were ten children by this marriage, five of whom are living: Catherine, Roland C., Sophia A., Milton and Minnie. The names of the deceased children are Mary, William, Leonidas H., James Trimble and Cora Lee. Judge Burns married again June 11, 1875, to Josephine Christman. By this marriage there were four children, three of whom are living: Cora Lee, Catherine and Bell Vivian, and Maggie (deceased).

Judge Burns' father, Rowland T. Burns, was born in Monroe County, Virginia, in 1790; was educated in his native place and studied law with John McConnell of Greenup County, Kentucky. He represented Lawrence and Morgan Counties in the legislature in 1830. He was a preacher in the Christian Church, and died when comparatively young, August 19, 1833. His wife was Catherine Brinkley Keyser, who was born in 1790 at Warm Springs, Bath County, Virginia. She died December 14, 1857.

Jeremiah Burns (grandfather) was of Scotch ancestry and a native of Maryland. His wife was a Miss Roland, a native of the Shenandoah Valley, whose parents were natives of France.

Rowland T. Burns, a brother of Judge Burns, is

a resident of Louisa; and Lafayette, another brother, is living on the old Burns homestead in Boyd County. The other brothers and sisters of the subject of this sketch are dead, viz.: Harrison G., William H., Jeremiah, James D., Keziah, Nancy, Rowland and Elizabeth, who married A. C. Hanley of West Virginia.

MR. JOHN D. CLARDY of Christian County, Kentucky, member of the LIVth Congress from the Second District and one of the representative farmers of southern Kentucky, was born in Smith County, Tennessee, August 30, 1828. He is the son of John C. and Elizabeth (Cayce) Clardy. His father was a native of North Carolina who removed to Tennessee and thence to Christian County, Kentucky, and was a progressive and highly successful farmer and a prominent man in the county. He died in 1853 at the age of fifty-six years. He had six sons and two daughters: William D., John D., James M., Benjamin F., Dr. Thomas F. and Henry H. Of these sons Benjamin F. died in the Confederate service during the war, and Henry H. was killed while in the service of the Confederate army. Dr. Thomas F. Clardy was surgeon of the Seventh Kentucky Regiment and was promoted to the rank of brigadier surgeon on General Buford's staff in Forest's Cavalry; died in Christian County February, 1886. The daughters, Mrs. Sarah A. Wills and Mrs. Fannie C. Burke, are both living.

Benjamin Clardy (grandfather) was a native of North Carolina and a farmer, whose life was spent in his native state and in Tennessee, where he died about 1839. His ancestors were Huguenots.

Elizabeth Cayce Clardy (mother) was born in Cumberland County, Virginia, in 1804, and is living at present with her son, J. M. Clardy, on the old homestead in Christian County, where the family settled in 1831. Her father, Fleming Cayce, was a native of Virginia, where he lived and died. His widow removed with her family to Smith County, Tennessee, and died there.

John D. Clardy, after reaching the limit of the county schools, went to Georgetown College, Kentucky, and graduated there in 1848, before he was twenty years of age. He taught school one year and then began the study of medicine with Dr. Nicholas Thomas of Tennessee. After taking a course of one year in the medical department of the University of Louisville, he went to the University of Pennsylvania and received his degree in that institution in 1851, when twenty-two years of age.

He began the practice of medicine at Long View, Kentucky, and remained there three years, then removing to Blandville, Kentucky, where he practiced with signal success until the beginning of the Civil war, when he returned to his native heath and located in his present home, known as "Oakland," situated seven miles southwest of Hopkinsville. Since that time he has added to his possessions until the farm on which he lives consists of five hundred and five acres, besides other large tracts of land, nearly all of which are in Christian County. After locating here he spent most of his time during the war in New York City, where he was a member of the firm of Bacon, Clardy & Company, large dealers in and exporters of tobacco. Before the war nearly all Kentucky tobacco was sent to New Orleans, but traffic in this direction being interrupted by the armies, New York became the outlet for shipments to Europe. This venture proved very successful, but preferring his Kentucky home, he returned in 1866, and while practicing medicine irregularly, devoted his time principally to the extension and improvement of his large estate, at present owning various tracts of farm lands amounting in the aggregate to fifteen hundred acres.

John D. Clardy is by no means a politician in the usual acceptation of that term, but by sheer force of character he has taken a leading position in the Democratic party which he is ever ready to serve to the best of his ability. He was elected a member of the Constitutional Convention in 1890 by over three hundred majority, although his county usually gives a Republican majority of 500 to 1,000; was a candidate for governor before the Democratic convention in 1890, but owing to duties in the Constitutional Convention did not make a thorough canvass of the state, and was defeated by John Young Brown. In 1894 he was nominated for Congress in the district convention, defeating Judge Samuel Vance and William Mc-

Clain of Henderson, and was elected to the Fifty-fourth Congress in November by the unusual Democratic majority in that district of three thousand votes. His Republican opponent was Elijah G. Sebree of Henderson County. Dr. Clardy has expressed his opinion on the money question by saying that he is in favor of the free coinage of silver if it can be kept on a parity with gold.

He was married in 1854 to Ann F. Bacon, a native of Trigg County, daughter of Fielding Bacon. Her grandfather, Captain Edmond Bacon, lived with President Thomas Jefferson for twenty years and was his financial secretary and adviser. He surveyed the ground upon which the University of Virginia was built. This institution was founded by Jefferson and was his "pet," and he contributed largely to its support.

Dr. and Mrs. Clardy have three children: John F., who is a farmer, has a wife but no children, and his home is known as "Rockhollow"; Fleming Cayce, also a farmer, who has a wife and two children, and Fannie C., wife of Rev. John W. Prestridge, who is president of Williamsburg College, Whitley County, Kentucky.

Dr. Clardy's father and grandfather were members of the Baptist Church and he is a deacon in the church of his fathers. His mother—a stanch Baptist—still lives, and at the age of ninety-one retains her mental faculties to a remarkable degree; reads any print without glasses, and writes with much of the accuracy and vigor of former years. A Christian with unclouded faith, awaiting with joyous expectation her summons to come up higher.

WILLIAM L. LYONS, senior member of the well and favorably known firm of W. L. Lyons & Company of Louisville, was born in that city June 3, 1857.

His father, Henry J. Lyons, was born in Washington City, District of Columbia, in 1829, and came to Louisville when he was a young man; was elected clerk of the Circuit Court when he was twenty-one years of age; was re-elected and resigned before the expiration of his second term, and then engaged in the banking business as a member of the firm of Quigley & Lyons; removed to New York City in 1862, and was in a similar business there as the senior member of the firm of Henry J. Lyons & Company until his death, April 11, 1867. During his residence in Louisville he was frequently elected a member of the City Council, and was a vestryman in Calvary Episcopal Church. His death occurred in Louisville, where he was taken ill on his return trip from Cuba, where he had gone with the hope of improving his health. He is buried in Cave Hill Cemetery, Louisville.

John Lyons (grandfather) was born in Washington, D. C., and was married to Nancy Hurley, January 19, 1828. She was a daughter of Henry Hurley, who was a prominent citizen of Washington City.

Laura Simmons Lyons (mother) was born in Bullitt County, Kentucky, in 1838, and died in Louisville in 1878, leaving two sons, William and Henry J. Lyons.

William Simmons (maternal grandfather) was a native farmer of Bullitt County, where he died. He married Matilda Ann Lee, who was a member of the Maryland branch of the distinguished family of that name.

William L. Lyons' early education was begun in New York City and continued in Louisville after his father's death. He completed his studies at Highland Military Academy, Worcester, Massachusetts. He was for some time employed in the general freight and passenger department of the Louisville & Nashville Railroad. In 1878 he began the business of broker in stocks, bonds, grain, provisions and cotton, in which he has continued without interruption until the present time. In 1887 his brother, Henry J. Lyons, was admitted to an interest in the firm. The house has a splendid patronage throughout the country, and is favorably known as sound and thoroughly reliable.

Mr. Lyons is interested in quite a number of enterprises, including the Louisville Silvering & Beveling Company, of which he is vice-president. He is an active member of the Board of Trade, and of the Commercial Club; also a member of the Pendennis Club, a member of the Louisville Commandery Knights Templar, and of Calvary Episcopal Church.

He has been quite prominent in city politics in the past, having served as councilman for eight years, during a considerable portion of which time he was chairman of the finance committee of the Board of Councilmen and president of the Council for three terms. He was for several months mayor pro tem., in which capacity he distinguished himself as a man of sound judgment and fine executive ability. He was one of the most popular members of the City Council and one in whom the business men of the city placed implicit confidence.

Mr. Lyons was married in 1881 to Mary Belle Clay, daughter of Samuel Clay of Lexington. They have two sons and two daughters living: Samuel Clay, Laura S., Mary Rogers and William L. Lyons, Jr.

WILLIAM POAGE, a member of one of the oldest families of Northern Kentucky and a member of the Boyd County bar, was born in Greenup County, Kentucky, August 22, 1854.

His father, Hugh Calvin Poage, was born in the same county in 1830; received a fair common school education and was a teacher before engaging in the mercantile business in Ashland in 1854. During the late war his sympathies were with the Southern people, but he took no active part in the conflict. He is a member of the Methodist Episcopal Church, South, and a member of the Masonic order. The lodge of which he is a member—No. 325, Poage Lodge—was named in honor of the family.

Thomas Hoge Poage (grandfather) was a native of "old" Virginia; came to Greenup County, Kentucky, early in the present century, and engaged in the iron and furnace business, and died in Texas.

William Poage, son of Hugh Calvin and Sarah E. (Davenport) Poage, received a limited education in Ashland and at the age of eighteen years accepted a position as "chief engineer" of a hand-pump on the wharfboat in that city, where he also acted in the capacity of freight clerk and collector for the wharfmaster, R. C. Richardson. During the years 1875-76 he was employed at Buena Vista and Princess iron furnaces by Culbertson, Means & Culbertson, then the leading manufacturers of iron in this section; was also employed in the internal revenue service in Central Kentucky from 1883 to 1885, and while thus engaged he pursued his studies for the legal profession; was admitted to the bar in December, 1886, after a rigid examination by Circuit Judge John M. Burns, Colonel Laban T. Moore and Colonel Frank H. Bruning. He at once began the practice of law in Ashland, and in the course of labor in his chosen field has accomplished very satisfactory results.

In 1890 he was elected city attorney on the Republican ticket, and was re-elected to that office in 1893 for a term of four years.

William Poage and Lauretta Shaw, daughter of John W. Shaw, were united in marriage April 1, 1881. Mrs. Poage was born at Gallipolis, Ohio, January 11, 1863, and is a graduate of the Ashland High School. They have two children: January Paul, born January 1, 1882, and Judith Princess, born December 1, 1883.

GEORGE E. PLATTS, M. D., a graduate of Denison University of Granville, Ohio, and of the Miami Medical College of Cincinnati, a druggist and well known business man of Bellevue, was born in the town of Dent, Hamilton County, Ohio, August 6, 1854, and is a son of David G. and Hannah Ann (Wood) Platts, both of whom were natives of Bridgeton, New Jersey. They came to Hamilton County, Ohio, in 1834, where they lived until three or four years prior to Mr. Platts' death in 1892, when they removed to Bellevue, Kentucky, the present home of Mrs. Platts, who is greatly advanced in years. Mr. Platts was a farmer in Ohio for nearly sixty years and was a quiet and unpretentious citizen, a man of intelligence and culture, and an upright Christian gentleman who commanded the respect and confidence of his neighbors. He was a Republican in politics, having decided convictions, and was free to express his sentiments; but he was not an office-seeker, or in any sense a politician. His antecedents were of French-German extraction.

George E. Platts was educated in the common schools of Dent, at the Denison University of Granville, Ohio, from which he graduated in 1876, and prepared for the medical profession in the Miami Medical College in Cincinnati, graduating in 1882.

He practiced medicine for one year at Cheviot, Hamilton County, Ohio; and in 1883 engaged in the drug business in the thriving little city of Bellevue, a business which has grown in proportion to the growth of the population of the place. Thoroughly equipped for the responsible business of the pharmacist, Dr. Platts has commanded the confidence of his patrons. His drug store requiring all of his time he has abandoned the professional work of the practicing physician.

He takes a lively interest in the prosperity of Bellevue and deals to some extent in real estate. He is particularly interested in the public schools and has served as school examiner, an office for which he is qualified in an eminent degree. He is a Republican, but is devoted to his business and has no aspirations for political preferment.

Dr. Platts was married in 1883 to Kate Davis, daughter of Shipley Davis and Harriet Cullom of Hamilton County, Ohio, and they have one son, Charles Gilman Platts. Mrs. Platts is a graduate of the Cincinnati College of Pharmacy and assists her husband in his business, in which capacity she is thoroughly competent.

WILFORD E. SENOUR, M. D., a young physician of Bellevue, where he has been practicing in the best families for five years past, was born in Independence, Kenton County, Kentucky, July 17, 1866.

His great-grandfather, Bryant Senour, was a native of Scotland, who came to America in the latter part of the eighteenth century and made his home in Kenton County, where Dr. Senour's grandfather, Wilford Senour, his father, Tilman W. Senour, and himself were born.

Wilford Senour (grandfather) was a farmer and resident of Kenton County all his life and died there in 1876.

Tilman W. Senour (father), born and raised in Kenton County, is still a resident of Independence in that county, where he is engaged in farming and dealing in tobacco; a prominent citizen and man of superior intelligence, respected by all who know him, and is known by nearly every one in the county. He is a strong Republican in politics, and takes a lively interest in the success of his party throughout the country.

Dr. Senour's mother, Anna E. (Cox) Senour, also a native of Kenton County, is a daughter of Frederick Cox, a well-to-do farmer of the county. She is now living with her husband in Independence.

Dr. Senour was a typical farmer's boy, going to school when there was nothing to do on the farm; but he had an ambition to learn a profession, and by careful study he was prepared for a classical course, and at the age of eighteen years he entered Central Normal College at Danville, Indiana, from which he graduated in 1889.

He taught in a graded school in Independence for seven months, and was a teacher in the Scioto Commercial College at Chillicothe, Ohio, for a short time before commencing to read medicine with his brother, Dr. U. G. Senour, at Pleasant Ridge, Ohio.

He subsequently attended the medical department of the University of Louisville, from which he graduated in 1891; and in the same year began the practice of medicine in Bellevue, where he was by no means a stranger and where he secured a valuable practice in a short time. He is well equipped for the work of the physician, attentive to his patients, kind and obliging in his disposition and popular with all classes.

He is interested to a considerable extent in real estate, and has acquired a valuable estate, which is, perhaps, the most substantial evidence of his popularity and success in his profession.

JAMES HENDERSON McCONNELL, Judge of the Police Court of Catlettsburg, son of Charles and Belle (Henderson) McConnell, was born in Greenupsburg, Greenup County, Kentucky, July 9, 1854. His parents removed to Catlettsburg in 1860, and he received his education in that place; studied law with Colonel Laban T. Moore and was admitted to the bar in 1874 when he was twenty years of age; practiced law in Catlettsburg alone for seven years; was deputy sheriff of Boyd County for four years; went to the mouth of Pond Creek on the Tug River, opposite Williamstown, West Virginia, and was engaged in the mercantile and timber business for four years, following which he was engaged in steamboating on the Ohio and Big Sandy Rivers for four years; returned to Catlettsburg and was elected police judge in November, 1894, an office which he has filled acceptably and with unusual ability.

Judge McConnell is a man of modest demeanor, well versed in law, a wise counselor and an able pleader, and has greatly raised the standard and dignity of the court over which he presides.

He is popular socially, prominent in Democratic councils, a member of the Methodist Episcopal Church, South, and a Mason.

He was married October 15, 1880, to Ida Rice, daughter of John M. Rice of Louisa. (See sketch of J. W. Rice.)

Charles McConnell (father) was born near Greenupsburg October 31, 1825; was educated at Marietta (Ohio) College; studied law in the University of Louisville; was the first county attorney of Greenup after the erection of that county; returned to Catlettsburg and was judge of the police court at one time and the first judge of the Boyd County Court during the war; retired from the practice of law and engaged in mercantile pursuits, and is now living in Catlettsburg. He is highly esteemed and respected as an upright Christian gentleman. He was married September 28, 1853, to Belle Henderson of Zanesville, Ohio, who was educated in Putnam (Ohio) Seminary and in a select school in Coshocton, Ohio. They had two children: James Henderson, the subject of this sketch, and Lucy Bragg, born May 19, 1856, married George F. Miller of Huntington, West Virginia, and died January 8, 1889.

John McCutcheon McConnell (grandfather) was born in Washington County, Pennsylvania, December 25, 1789; was educated at Cannonsburg (Pennsylvania) College; served time as a shoemaker's apprentice, but ran away and was then apprenticed to a tailor, completed his term of service and received as a reward a horse and bridle and saddle, a suit of clothes and $25 in money. He rode to Chillicothe, Ohio, thence into Kentucky, locating at Prestonsburg; taught school and studied law; removed to Greenup and practiced law there for many years; served in both branches of the Legislature, and was in the Senate in 1824, when General Lafayette visited that body.

He died July 5, 1835, in the prime of his splendid manhood and in the height of his prosperity. He had a very large practice and had accumulated considerable property.

He was married December 17, 1817, to Lucy Bragg Lewis, daughter of Charles Nelson Lewis. She died April 10, 1849. The ancestors of the McConnells came from Londonderry, Ireland, and were Protestants.

Charles Nelson Lewis (great-grandfather) was a native of Greenup (now Carter) County; was a member of the Kentucky Senate, and died while there and was buried in Frankfort. He married Elizabeth Bragg, a descendant of the Braggs of North Carolina, and daughter of Ann Blakemore Bragg, a member of the Virginia family of Blakemores.

James Henderson (maternal grandfather) was born in Belleville, Pennsylvania; married Sarah Spangler of Zanesville, Ohio, September 17, 1826; was a member of the Ohio Senate for two terms and a very talented lawyer; died March 19, 1844.

Sarah Spangler Henderson was born in Zanesville, Ohio, January 1, 1804; died May 29, 1883.

Clinton Spangler (maternal great-grandfather) was born May 14, 1772, and was a merchant of Zanesville. Ann, his wife, was born January 8, 1773; died February 27, 1828.

CLIFTON ARNSPARGER, County Attorney of Bourbon County, one of the ablest young lawyers of Paris, son of Stephen and Martha Todd Arnsparger, was born in Scott County, Kentucky, July 17, 1860.

His father was a native of Bourbon County and was a man of superior intelligence and education. His primary instruction was received in the country schools, but this was followed by a course under the private tutorship of Lyman J. Curtis, one of the ablest educators in the county at that time. He continued his studies after he was twenty years of age. His father having only limited means, he was compelled to earn the money to defray his expenses at school, and this he did by working at the shoemaker's trade. For some time he lived at Centerville, Bourbon County, but subsequently removed to Newtown, Scott County, where he followed his trade and opened a general merchandise store. In connection with that he was postmaster of Newtown for a period of nearly twenty years. Having purchased a small farm he attended to that in connection with his store until 1894, when he retired to his farm, upon which he is now living with his family.

He married Martha Todd of Bourbon County in 1857, and they have four children living: Clifton; James D., married Josie Jones; George and Lizzie. Two others, Fanny and Martha, died in infancy.

Stephen Arnsparger and family are members of the Christian Church. Although a Democrat, he was appointed postmaster under a Republican president, and held that office from time to time through the several changes of administration.

Christopher Arnsparger (grandfather) came to Kentucky from Pennsylvania and was of German descent.

James O. Todd (maternal grandfather) was a farmer and raiser of fine stock in Bourbon County, and took great interest in the famous Bertram stock. His wife was Elizabeth Austin, of Scott County, and they were Presbyterians.

Clifton Arnsparger obtained his primary training in the county schools, and in 1877 went to Georgetown College, from whence he was graduated in 1881; was first employed as a bookkeeper in the wholesale and retail grocery of John S. Gaines at Georgetown, Kentucky, for a short time, and then taught school, but soon gave that up and read law with Judge James E. Cantrill, ex-lieutenant governor, now judge of the Circuit Court. He then attended the Cincinnati law school and graduated in law in 1886; was admitted to the bar and began the practice of his profession in Paris in 1886; was city attorney from 1888 to 1892; was public administrator and guardian for several years by appointment; was elected county attorney in the fall of 1893 to fill a vacancy, and at the November election, 1894, was elected to succeed himself in that office, his present term beginning January 1, 1895.

Among the members of the legal profession and the citizens of Paris he bears the name of a good and faithful servant and a lawyer of more than ordinary ability.

He is a member of the Christian Church, and of Bourbon Lodge No. 23, I. O .O. F.

Mr. Arnsparger and Ruby Lowry, daughter of William and Sobrina (Neal) Lowry of Scott County were married October 16, 1889. There were born to them three children: William S., born August 18, 1890; Sobrina, born June 28, 1892, died in infancy; and Lucien Marion, born February 3, 1896.

JAMES WEIR, lawyer, author and banker and pre-eminently one of the first citizens of Owensboro, is a son of James and Anna (Rumsey) Weir, and was born in Greenville, Kentucky, June 16, 1821.

His father, James Weir, was of Scotch-Irish parentage and was born near Charleston, South Carolina. He came to Kentucky about the close of the last century, or one hundred years ago. He was a man of excellent education, and was employed as a surveyor or civil engineer for some time, but eventually engaged quite extensively in mercantile pursuits, his business extending over a vast territory. He owned stores in Shawneetown and Equality in Illinois, Henderson, Morganfield, Madisonville, Greenville, Lewisburg, Hopkinsville and Russellville in Kentucky, and Gallatin, Tennessee. He had a very large and profitable trade with the Spaniards in New Orleans and in Cuba, and this at a time when all freight between New Orleans and Kentucky was carried on flatboats. Mr. Weir's business, being scattered over so much territory, required him to travel extensively, as an instance of which he often told his son that he had made the journey from New Orleans to Philadelphia and return on horseback not less than twenty-five times, with no other companion but Titus, his faithful old negro servant. He was eminently successful in his many business ventures and left a valuable estate.

James Weir's paternal grandfather was a resident of Charleston, South Carolina, and a soldier in the Revolutionary war, serving from the beginning to the end of the war under General

Sumter. The only compensation he received for his faithful and patriotic service was a little negro girl who had been confiscated from the estate of a Tory. His son David, also a soldier, was killed at Sumter's defeat.

Anna Rumsey Weir (mother) was a lineal descendant of Charles Rumsey, who came to the United States from Wales in 1665 and settled in Maryland. Her uncle, James Rumsey, was the inventor of the application of steam to boats and other vessels, whose son, James, upon proof that his father had run the first vessel by steam in the United States, received a gold medal from Congress as an appreciation of his father's valuable invention. The inventor, James Rumsey, dropped dead while delivering a lecture before the Philosophical Society in London.

James Weir received a collegiate education in Centre College, Danville, Kentucky, from which he graduated in the class of 1840. Very few, if any, of his classmates are now as actively engaged in business as is Mr. Weir. He studied law at the Lexington law school when Judges Robinson, Wooley and Marshall were professors in that grand old institution, and graduated in the winter of 1841. In the following year he began the practice of his profession in Owensboro, where he was a leading member of the bar for over forty years. At the time of his coming Owensboro was a village of two hundred and fifty inhabitants. In 1860 he was made president of the Deposit Bank of Owensboro, which position he has held for thirty-five years. In 1869 he was elected president of the Owensboro & Nashville Railroad Company, and held that position for three years.

When the reporters entered the city of Owensboro to obtain information for the compiling of this volume, they called on a number of the best citizens and asked for a list of the prominent men in the city, and every one of the lists thus given was headed with the name of James Weir. It is hardly necessary to add that among his fellow-citizens he stands pre-eminently as the first citizen of Owensboro. A lawyer of the highest rank, a banker whose judgment and ability are recognized in financial and business circles, and a citizen of great purity of character, he is known of all men as a man of generous nature, kindliness of spirit, and of the highest scholarly attainments. Dignified and withal courteous and obliging, unostentatious in his bearing and unconscious of his superiority, he is greatly loved and respected by everyone in the large circle of his acquaintance.

He is, moreover, a man of letters and an author of celebrity, although he has not recently aspired to literary fame. In 1850 he wrote "Lonz Powers," and in 1852-53 "Simon Kenton" and "Winter Lodge," which novels were published by Lippincott of Philadelphia, and gave promise of a brilliant future, but since that time he has been too much engrossed in his profession and other business matters to devote much time to literature, and his work in that direction has been limited to an occasional sketch for the newspapers and magazines.

He has never posed as an active politician, having never sought or held any political office. He was a Whig in his younger days, and has voted with the Democratic party since the war.

Mr. Weir was married March 1, 1842, to Susan C. Green, daughter of Judge John Green of Danville, Kentucky. Her maternal great-grandfather was Joshua Fry, who was a commander of the Virginia troops under General Braddock in his unfortunate campaign, and was taken sick and died before the battle. Joshua Fry, her grandfather, the son of General Joshua Fry, married Peachey Walker, a member of a distinguished Virginia family.

Mr. and Mrs. Weir have six children, three sons and three daughters: John E. Weir; Dr. James Weir; Paul Weir; Anna Belle, wife of Clinton Griffith; Susan, wife of James L. Maxwell, now residing in Knoxville, Tennessee; and Nora, wife of R. S. Triplett, Jr., now a resident of Waco, Texas.

The stories referred to were written before Mr. Weir was thirty years of age. They were published in book form and supplied to the trade by the Philadelphia house of Lippincott, Gambo & Co. The first of these (1850) was "Lonz Powers, or the Regulators"; a romance of Kentucky, based on actual scenes and incidents of the early days of the "Dark and Bloody Ground."

The second novel, "Simon Kenton," was designed to give a sketch of the habits and striking characteristics of the people of Western North Carolina, immediately following the Revolutionary times, and to introduce Simon Kenton, the scout and Indian fighter, and also his opponent and enemy, Simon Girty, the Tory and renegade. In this volume the character which Kenton represented came off victorious.

"Winter Lodge" is a sequel to "Simon Kenton," in which the author introduces many of the most striking characters who were prominent in the early history of Kentucky, with numerous incidents of the times, descriptions of scenery, Mammoth cave; the battles in which Kenton and Girty were engaged and the habits and marked characteristics of the pioneers. The name, Winter Lodge, is derived from a cabin erected by Kenton, for the hero and heroine, which was ornamented with carpets of buffalo hides and lined with furs. Mr. Weir intended in his younger days to write a third volume of this series, coming down to the War of 1812 and the death of Kenton and Girty, but his increasing business prevented him from accomplishing this, and his literary work of late years has been undertaken as a pastime and recreation rather than a matter of business.

CAPTAIN JOHN F. DAVIS of Louisville, deputy collector of internal revenue, was born in Shelby County, Kentucky, January 8, 1832. His father, Theophilus Davis, was born in Virginia in 1797, and removed to Kentucky when a boy, receiving his education in the common schools of Shelby County, where he engaged in farming. He was an active member of the Baptist Church, taking great interest in church work. He was not a politician, but always voted the Whig ticket. He died at his home in Shelby County in 1845, and is buried in Grove Hill cemetery. James Davis, father of Theophilus and grandfather of Captain John F. Davis, was a native of Virginia, where he died in 1831. He was a member of the Baptist Church and a Whig. Captain Davis' mother, Elizabeth (Foster) Davis, was a native of Nelson County, Kentucky, born in 1810; educated in Shelbyville; member of the Baptist Church; died January 22, 1832. She was the daughter of John Foster, a native of Fauquier County, Virginia; a member of the Baptist Church and a Whig; died 1829.

Captain Davis received a good education in the Shelby County schools, finishing in the freshman class of Shelby College in 1849. After leaving college he was a "clerk" in a dry goods store for a year and then, following the example of his ancestors for several generations, he chose farming for his occupation, which he followed successfully until 1861, when he espoused the cause of the Southern Confederacy, enlisting as a private soldier at Bowling Green, September 15, 1861. He was not long a private, however, for he was almost immediately appointed assistant commissary of subsistence, with the rank of captain of cavalry, and assigned to duty with the Sixth Kentucky Regiment of Volunteer Infantry. He remained on duty with that regiment until October, 1862, when he was promoted to acting chief of subsistence of General John C. Breckenridge's division. He was elected a delegate by representatives of his county to the Russellville convention, October, 1861, and voted in the convention for a resolution declaring Kentucky to be one of the Confederate states. He was painfully wounded in the battle of Shiloh, April 6, 1862. In the winter of 1864-65 he organized the Twentieth Alabama Regiment of Cavalry in North Alabama, with headquarters at Gadsden, and joined General B. J. Hill's brigade, remaining on duty in command of his regiment until the close of the war, surrendering at Gunthersville, Tennessee, May 10, 1865. His commission as colonel never reached him.

Returning to his home in Shelby County, he found that a previous legislature had enacted a law disfranchising all persons who had served in the Confederate army, but this law was repealed by the legislature of 1865-66, and Captain Davis again became a citizen and voter.

In August, 1866, he was elected sheriff of Shelby County, and was re-elected in August, 1868. Under the laws of Kentucky he could not serve a third term as sheriff; but in 1870 he was elected clerk of the Shelby County Court by a good majority, after an exciting contest. He was twice re-elected to this lucrative office, declining to make another race at the expiration of his third term of four years, in 1882, but entered the race for the nomination of his party for clerk of the Court of Appeals, with eleven candidates, receiving a highly complimentary vote, but yielding the victory to Captain Tom Henry of West Liberty, Morgan County, for the nomination of his party.

In January, 1884, Captain Davis was appointed by Governor Knott Commissioner of Agriculture, Horticulture and Statistics, which office he held until May, 1888. He was also appointed State Statistical Agent for Kentucky by the Agricultural Department at Washington, serving in that capacity until August, 1888. In May, 1888, he returned to his farm in Shelby County, resuming the cultivation of the soil, until August, 1894, when he was appointed deputy collector of internal revenue by Hon. Benjamin Johnson, collector of the Fifth collection district of Kentucky, and is now serving in that office at Louisville.

Captain Davis was married June 17, 1869, to Mrs. Mary P. Gray, widowed daughter of Judge W. J. Steele of Versailles, Kentucky. He is the father of six children, one of whom, Andrew J. Steele Davis, died in 1875. His eldest daughter, Lizzie J., is the wife of Dr. W. T. Buckner of Shelbyville. William J. S. Davis is in business in Loogootee, Indiana. John C., George T. and Mary Stoddard Davis are in school in Louisville, where Captain Davis has purchased a homestead in which he expects to spend the remainder of his days.

WILLIAM EDWARD BATES of Georgetown, Judge of the Scott County Court, son of George W. and Maria (Burgess) Bates, was born in Scott County, Kentucky, August 8, 1830.

George W. Bates (father) was a native of Massachusetts, who came to Kentucky in 1826, locating in Scott County. In 1834 he removed to Indiana and after spending two years in that state he returned to his former home in Scott County, where he continued to reside until his death in 1886. He was a fuller by trade, but after coming to Kentucky he devoted his attention to farming. He was a major of militia under the command of General John T. Pratt. He was a highly respected citizen and a worthy and upright member of the Christian Church.

William Randall Bates (grandfather), also a native of Massachusetts, came to Kentucky in 1830 and located in Boone County, where he died in 1837. He was a merchant and a man of wonderful energy and enterprise. The Bates family is of English descent. Two brothers came over to this country in 1635, settling in Boston. Some of their descendants emigrated to the colony of Virginia. The late Honorable Edward Bates, who was President Lincoln's first attorney-general, belonged to the Virginia branch of the family.

Maria Burgess Bates (mother) was born in Scott County, and was a resident of her native county until her death, April 4, 1888. She was a most excellent woman, whose chief characteristic was her devotion to her religion and to the Christian Church, of which she was a member.

Edward Burgess (grandfather) was born in Culpeper County, Virginia, in 1783, and was one of the first settlers of Scott County, where he was a farmer and died in 1857. The Burgess family is descended from the Huguenots who were driven out of France by Louis XIV. in 1685, many of whom settled in Virginia and the Carolinas, and their descendants are everywhere highly honored and respected; being enterprising and intelligent, they are found in legitimate business pursuits and in the professions in almost every community. The ministers especially who belong to this sturdy race have wide influence in the South and West.

William Edward Bates lived on his father's farm until he was twenty-four years of age. He was educated in the common schools of his day, and by close application he became well advanced in many of the English branches. He was married in 1860 to Annie E. Reed, daughter of James Reed of Scott County, after which event he returned to the farm, where he remained until 1890, during a part of which time—about nine years—he served as justice of the peace.

In 1890 he was elected judge of the Scott County Court, and in 1894 was re-elected to that office, in both of which elections he was the candidate of the Democratic party.

Judge Bates is a man of great energy and force

of character, possessing many of those qualities without which few men rise to distinction. What is true in the wide field of universal history is none the less true in the limited range of a town or neighborhood. A determined and persistent purpose, practical sense and integrity, are traits which mark the outlines of Judge Bates' chief characteristics. He has been a member of the Christian Church since 1848.

Judge Bates is the eldest of twelve children—eleven sons and one daughter—of George W. Bates, eight of whom are now living. During the Civil strife the family was divided; two of the sons were in the Federal and two in the Confederate army, the latter two serving under General John Morgan. Two other brothers served for a short time only, one on each side of the conflict.

JOHN W. BREATHITT of Hopkinsville, Judge of the Christian County Court and ex-postmaster of that city, was born in Hopkinsville, Christian County, Kentucky, January 9, 1825. His father, James Breathitt, was born in Virginia in 1794 and came to Kentucky in his youth; attended school in Christian County; subsequently read law and was admitted to the bar before he was twenty years of age. He was quite prominent as a lawyer and politician; had a large practice in different parts of the state as well as locally. For several terms he was commonwealth attorney for his district, and was an active and leading member of the Presbyterian Church. His father, William Breathitt, was a native of Virginia, who came to Kentucky in the early days of the century and located in Logan County.

Peyton Short (maternal grandfather) was a native farmer of Christian County. His daughter, Elizabeth Short, married James Breathitt.

John W. Breathitt attended school in Christian County until he was fourteen years of age, when he went to North Bend, Ohio, and lived with his uncle while attending school in that place. At the age of seventeen he went to Kenyon College at Gambier, Ohio, and studied for two years, after which he attended school for a short time in Augusta, Kentucky. In 1844, when only twenty years of age, he returned to his native place and engaged in merchandising, in which he continued three years, and then went to farming and devoted his time to agricultural pursuits until 1861, when he joined the Federal army and was major of the Third Kentucky Regiment of Cavalry. He participated in the battles of Shiloh, Pittsburg Landing, Stone River, Lookout Mountain and many other engagements during the four years of his active service in the field.

After the close of the war, he returned to his farm, and in 1874 was elected county clerk, which office he held for sixteen years; was appointed postmaster of Hopkinsville by President Harrison in 1890; served until October, 1894, and one month later was elected judge of the Christian County Court for a term of four years.

John W. Breathitt is connected with the Missionary Baptist Church, and is a member of the Masonic fraternity.

He married Catherine A. Webber in 1847 and they have had nine children, seven of whom are living: Peyton S., Augustine Hatvie, Harry W., James, Elizabeth S., Mary Caroline and Catherine A.

WILLIAM E. AUD, one of the talented young lawyers of Owensboro, was born in Knottsville, Daviess County, Kentucky, March 19, 1870.

His father, Hilliary T. Aud, was also a native of Daviess County, and was educated at St. Mary's College, graduating when quite young. He began as a clerk in a store in Knottsville, and after serving in that capacity for four years, in 1860 he and his brother purchased the property of his employer and established the firm of J. B. Aud & Brother, which is still in existence, and is the oldest mercantile establishment in that town. Mr. H. T. Aud was married September 29, 1863, to Victoria Jarboe, and they had seven children: Guy G., Henry T., William E., Regina, Mary Joseph, Mary Rock and Victoria. Of these Guy G., Regina and Victoria are deceased.

Thomas C. Aud (grandfather) was a native of Nelson County, Kentucky, a highly educated man and a practicing physician in Knottsville, Daviess County, where he died in 1853. He married Alice Birkhead of Nelson County, Kentucky, daughter of Abraham Birkhead, and had seven children: Joseph B., Ellen, Maggie, Hillary T., Charles Z., Atha Matilda J. and George, all of whom are living except George and Matilda.

Ignatius Jarboe (maternal grandfather) was born in Nelson County, Kentucky, about 1805, and was a farmer in that county until a short time prior to the Civil war, when he removed to Daviess County and located about three miles from Knottsville and was a farmer there until the time of his death in 1884. His wife was a Miss Martina Speaks of Nelson County, and they had six children: Raymond, Henry, Benjamin, Victoria, Josephine and Edward, all of whom are dead except Victoria and Edward.

The parents and grandparents of the subject of this sketch and their antecedents were members of the Catholic Church. His grandfathers were Democrats, but his father is a Republican and is very active and influential in his party.

William E. Aud was educated in Jasper College, which is a branch of St. Meinrad College, Indiana, and in Cecilian College, Hardin County, and also graduated from the commercial department of Cecilian College in 1890.

He began the study of law in the office of Powers & Achison in Owensboro, and was admitted to the bar in March, 1891, when twenty-one years of age, and began the active duties of his chosen profession in 1893, and in the same year was appointed public administrator for Daviess County. He at once met with encouragement and has enjoyed a young lawyer's full share of business at the Owensboro bar; and being attentive to business, a diligent student and an industrious worker in behalf of his clients, he has the promise of a brilliant future. Mr. Aud is a Democrat in politics, but is modest in his ambition for political preferment.

HON. CURTIS F. BURNAM, senior member of the Madison County bar, was born in Richmond, Kentucky, May 24, 1820.

His father, Thompson Burnam, was born near Raleigh, Wake County, North Carolina, February 4, 1789. At the age of about thirteen years he was employed as a clerk in a store in Richmond, his father having removed to that place from North Carolina. He soon developed superior business qualifications and tact; was a man of fine intelligence and took a deep interest in the development of the new country and in the improvement of the educational facilities in the community, and took especial care in the education and training of his children. He was an old-line Whig of pronounced views, and while he never sought political preferment, honors were frequently thrust upon him. He represented Madison County in the Legislature in 1843. In early life he was a successful merchant, but the closing years of his life were spent on his farm of five hundred and sixty acres, one of the finest blue grass farms in Madison, in which county he died May 4, 1871. His wife's maiden name was Lucinda Field. Five of their children are living: John Field Burnam, a prominent business man of Pueblo, Colorado; Mrs. Mary Wilson, widow of Nathaniel Wilson of Columbia, Missouri, now a resident of Washington City; Rev. Edmond H. Burnam of Luray, Virginia, one of the ablest ministers in the Baptist Church, and one of the most accomplished scholars in this country; Mrs. Eugenia Hume, widow of William Stanton Hume, who was a large distiller and capitalist of Silver Creek, Kentucky, and Major Curtis F. Burnam, the principal subject of this sketch.

John Burnam (grandfather) was born in Cecil County, Maryland; was a soldier in the Revolutionary war; fought at Guilford Court House, North Carolina, and after receiving his honorable discharge from service in the patriot army, returned to his home in Maryland.

Thomas Burnam (great-grandfather), a native of England, came to this country and settled on the eastern shore in Maryland, near Georgetown, now in the District of Columbia, and acquired a large landed estate, from which, however, his descendants never reaped any benefit.

Lucinda Field Burnam, Major Burnam's mother, was born on the banks of the Rappahannock in Culpeper County, Virginia, and was a daughter of John Field, who removed to Kentucky in 1800, or about that time, and located in Bourbon County. He was a Whig and a great admirer and supporter of Henry Clay, and represented Bourbon County in the Legislature a number of terms.

Colonel John Field (great-grandfather) was a native of Virginia and a member of a distinguished family whose people were identified with the early development of that state. He was killed at Point Pleasant.

Major Curtis F. Burnam was prepared for college in the Madison Seminary and graduated from Yale College in the class of 1840, receiving the degree of A. B., and was valedictorian at the departure of the senior class from college. Two years later, in 1842, he graduated from the law department of old Transylvania University at Lexington, Kentucky. He was admitted to the bar in the same year and began his brilliant career as a lawyer in Richmond, which has been the scene of his labors ever since.

He was a member of the Legislature in all the sessions of 1851-2, 1859-60 and 1861-2, being three times elected to that body, in which he served with honorable distinction. In the Presidential campaign of 1851 he was elector on the Scott and Graham ticket, and cast his vote for them in the electoral college. In 1853 he declined the nomination for Congress when a nomination by the Whig party was equivalent to an election. In 1875 and 1876 he was assistant secretary of the treasury under President Grant, and in the absence of Secretary Bristow, was acting secretary of the Treasury and member pro tempore of the President's Cabinet.

He was honored in 1884 by his election as president of the Kentucky Bar Association, which held its annual session at Louisville.

In 1890-1 he was a delegate to the convention which framed the present Constitution of Kentucky, and was one of the most active and able members of that honorable body.

In 1846 he received from Yale the degree of A. M., and at later dates received from Center College and from Ogden College the degree of LL.D.

He has been for more than fifty years a member of the regular Calvinist Baptist Church.

He was during the great war for the preservation of the Union a devoted Union man, and has been a Republican in politics at all times since. In the Legislature of 1863 he received for thirty-five ballots the unbroken vote of his party for the office of United States Senator. His last public service was as delegate to the convention at Minneapolis in 1892, in which body he was chairman of the Kentucky delegation, and voted for Harrison for nomination to the Presidency.

Major Burnam has applied himself assiduously to the practice of his profession, in which he has enjoyed a liberal share of the more important cases in the higher courts and has seldom indulged in recreation, but in 1883 he took a holiday and made a tour of Europe.

He has acquired a handsome estate, including many valuable tracts of land in Madison County and his elegant homestead, which is situated in the suburbs of Richmond.

Major Burnam was married in 1845 to Sarah H. Rollins, daughter of Dr. A. W. Rollins, and sister of Hon. James S. Rollins, who was twice elected to Congress from Missouri, a brilliant orator and patriotic statesman.

They celebrated their golden wedding May 6, 1895. They have eight children, five sons and three daughters: A. R. Burnam, who was collector of internal revenue of the eighth collection district under President Benjamin Harrison, and is one of the ablest lawyers in the state; Thompson Burnam, a farmer and the owner of one thousand or twelve hundred acres of fine land in Madison County; James R. Burnam, judge of the Madison County Court and an ex-member of the Kentucky Legislature; Robert Rodes Burnam, teller in the Farmers' National Bank of Richmond; Hon. E. Tutt Burnam, now a member of the Legislature; Mary C., wife of Waller Bennett of Madison County, now in Europe; Misses Sallie and Lucy, who are at home, ladies of the highest social rank and influence in their community.

MALCOLM McNEILL, deceased, who was a prominent citizen of Christian County, Kentucky, was born in North Carolina, February 18, 1786. He was the seventh child of Henry and Dorothy McNeill. His father was born in Scotland, and coming to this country, landed at Charleston, South Carolina, and engaged in mercantile pursuits with his brother John, afterward marrying Miss Dorothy Pryor of North Carolina. The children of Henry and Dorothy were: Hector, Alexander, Angus, Pryor, John Pryor, Malcolm, Margaret, Elizabeth, Amanda, Catherine and Henrietta. Henry McNeill (father) died near Hopkinsville, Kentucky, November 3, 1820. Dorothy, his wife, died March 17, 1824, at the same place.

Malcolm McNeill moved to Kentucky from North Carolina in the fall of 1816, going to Christian County, near Hopkinsville, purchasing a large tract of land with his two brothers, and brought his father and mother from North Carolina to his place, which was known as the White House, seven miles from Hopkinsville on the Princeton pike. This house was built about 1816. Malcolm and John Pryor and their father owned at that time about ten thousand acres of land. Malcolm afterward purchased his brother John's interest, and became owner of other land in Christian County, living on this place until he sold it and moved near LaFayette. He purchased large lands in that vicinity, and there lived until his death, February 21, 1875.

Malcolm McNeill was educated at Chapel Hill University, in North Carolina; studied law but never practiced, turning his attention to farming and commercial life. He also purchased lands in Mississippi and engaged extensively in cotton raising.

His first wife was Miss B. Branch; his second wife Miss Juda Branch. There are no living children by these two wives. His third wife was Martha Rivers, daughter of Samuel Henderson and Eliza Culloney. This marriage was blessed by three children, two girls and a boy, Elizabeth and Martha, and Thomas Henry. His fourth wife was Miss Lizzie Lynch, and his fifth a Mrs. Bell, having no living children except by his third wife. He made large investments in Chicago, the first of which was in 1843, when he was compelled to reach Chicago by private conveyance—in a buggy or on horseback. In politics he was a Whig but opposed secession, but after the beginning of the war sympathized with the South. After the war he became a Democrat. He lost a great deal of property by the depredations of the soldiers. He gave largely to charitable institutions and supported several Methodist churches, being of that faith. He was beloved and respected by all who knew him. His business methods were exact and precise, meeting all obligations at the time specified, accumulating property worth one million dollars or more, which was equally divided among his grandchildren.

The oldest daughter of Malcolm McNeill, Elizabeth, married John P. Caruthers of Memphis, Tennessee. Martha, the second daughter, married Wiley P. Boddie.

HON. NORVAL L. BENNETT of Newport, Judge of Campbell County Court, is the son of George W. and Louisa (Perry) Bennett. His father is a native of Culpeper C. H., Virginia, and came to Kentucky with his parents when fifteen or sixteen years of age. He now resides on his farm at Cold Springs, Campbell County, where he has lived for the past thirty years. He is now eighty-one years old and has always been a farmer and is a stanch Republican.

George W. Bennett, Sr. (grandfather) was also a native of Culpeper County, Virginia, but removed to Kentucky in 1827 and owned a line of flatboats which ran between Pittsburgh and New Orleans. The Bennetts belonged to an old Virginia family whose ancestors came from Germany.

Louisa Perry Bennett (mother) was a native of Kenton County. She died in 1872, aged fifty-two years.

Charles Perry (grandfather) was a native of England; came to America when a youth; was a soldier in the War of 1812, and was a farmer, miller and a millwright. He died at his home in Covington in 1860.

Judge Norval L. Bennett was born near Latonia Springs, Kenton County, July 17, 1853. He was educated in the common schools of the county and was a farmer until 1878, when, having an adventurous spirit, he enlisted in the regular army. At the time of his enlistment there were thirty-three men examined and he was one of three who were accepted. He served five years, the full term of his enlistment, doing duty in the west, and from Canada to Mexico. He was all through the Rocky Mountain regions and was with his command through the Ute campaign. During the last three years of his service he was first sergeant, Company H, Sixth Regiment United States Infantry. He was discharged at Salt Lake City April 28, 1883. After returning home he read law, graduated from the Cincinnati Law School and was admitted to the Newport bar in 1889.

In 1894 he was the Republican candidate for county judge and was elected, assuming the duties of the office January 7, 1895.

Judge Bennett and Mattie A. Dodsworth, daughter of Robert Dodsworth of Cold Springs, were married in 1883, soon after his return from the army. He is president of the board of deacons of the Christian Church; an active member of the Young Men's Christian Association; a Knight Templar; member of the Junior Order of United American Mechanics; the Maccabees, Order of Ben Hur, K. A. E. O., and commander of the Regular Army and Naval Union.

THOMAS HENRY McNEILL, son of Malcolm McNeill, was born in Kentucky in 1821. He graduated from Yale College at the age of eighteen, and at the age of twenty married Miss Rebecca Tuck, daughter of Dr. Tuck, who lived on an adjoining farm, and settled near his father's farm, near LaFayette, Kentucky. This marriage was blessed by the following children: Flora, Harry, Malcolm, Ellen Mesha, Thomas Henry, John Pryor, Benjamin Franklin and Rivers. His wife, Rebecca, died November 20, 1859.

His second marriage, to Miss Ann Eliza Arthur of Mississippi, resulted in two children: W. A. and Alexander C. McNeill.

For several years Thomas Henry and his father were acquiring large tracts of land in Mississippi, which he took charge of, and devoted his time to raising cotton until 1866, and was known as the largest cotton planter of the South. He was a man of great business ability and large acquaintance, and entertained his friends in the most elaborate style. His family spent the winter on his plantation in Mississippi; the fall and spring months in Memphis, Tennessee, and the summer months traveling. After his death the younger children were taken by Malcolm McNeill, their grandfather, to his home in Christian County, where they went to school during the winter months, and were required to work on the farm in the summer. After the death of Malcolm, the younger children, Benjamin Franklin, Rivers, William and Alexander, moved to Chicago.

Flora, the daughter of Thomas Henry, married John P. Caruthers of Memphis, Tennessee. Several children were born to them.

Harry married, but had no children; died in 1883.

Malcolm married a Miss Burk of Mississippi, and was blessed with five children. Malcolm's second wife was a Miss Gillmore.

Ellen Mesha married John P. Crudup of North Carolina and had two children.

Thomas Henry married Miss Nannie Hammond of Chicago and had two sons.

John Pryor died young.

Benjamin Franklin married Miss Martha C. West of Chicago. The result of this marriage is five living children.

W. A. McNeill married Miss Rebecca Medcalf of Tennessee.

Alexander C. married Miss Humes.

PARIS C. BROWN, Mayor of Newport, was born in Concord, Lewis County, Kentucky, May 5, 1838, and is a son of Thomas L. and Mary (Rowland) Brown.

His father was a native of Washington, Mason County, and died in De Witt County, Illinois, in 1866. His grandfather's name was James Brown, a well-known resident of Mason County.

Mary Rowland Brown (mother) was born in Adams County, Ohio, and died in Concord, Kentucky, in 1845. Her father's name was William Rowland.

Paris C. Brown was educated in Concord, where he attended the common schools and graduated from Smith's Commercial College in Cincinnati, in 1854. From 1859 to 1865 he was engaged in steamboating, first as a clerk and later as captain in charge of different boats running from Cincinnati to New Orleans and other points along the western rivers, and in this way became one of the best known and most popular men on the river.

In 1866 he abandoned the river proper and accepted a position as bookkeeper for the Consolidated Boat Store Company of Cincinnati, then known as Harry Davidson & Co., of which he has been the efficient manager since 1870.

He was married in 1864 and became a resident of Newport, since which time he has been one of the most progressive and enterprising citizens of that flourishing city.

He is no politician, but has affiliated with the Democratic party, which has honored him by electing him to positions of honor and trust. He was a member of the School Board, in which he served for eight years, and was president of the board for two years. In November, 1893, he was elected mayor of the city of Newport, an office for which he was chosen on account of his business ability and splendid character as an upright and honest man, whose ideas of reform in municipal government were commended by the business men and substantial citizens. During the two years or more of his administration he has conducted the affairs of the city on business principles and with credit to himself, and the expectations of those who elected him have been more than realized. His official deportment has been characterized by a faithful and conscientious discharge of his duties and by excellent business judgment.

Mr. Brown was married January 17, 1864, to Margaret E. Cummings, daughter of William and Eliza Cummings of Lewis County. They have four sons and one daughter: Frank M., Thomas C., George W., James G. and Nannie.

ROBERT S. COLEMAN, M. D., leading physician of Princeton, was born in Stewart County, Tennessee, March 8, 1830.

His father, William H. Coleman, was born in Rockingham County, North Carolina, in 1800, and removed to Stewart County, Tennessee, in 1818, and was a farmer in that county until his death, in 1850.

Robert S. Coleman (grandfather), a native of Rockingham County, North Carolina, removed to Stewart County, Tennessee, in 1820, and was a highly respected farmer there until the time of his death, in 1853. His father was a soldier in the Revolutionary war. The Colemans were descended from an old Anglo-Saxon family of England.

Mary Gatlin Coleman (mother) was a native of Stewart County, Tennessee, and died at Murray, Calloway County, Kentucky, in 1881. She was a member of the United Baptist Church, in which denomination her father, Rev. Ephraim Gatlin, was a distinguished minister. Her ancestors were from South Carolina.

Dr. Robert S. Coleman received his early education in private schools and by hard study at the home of his parents in Stewart County, Tennessee. He then read medicine with Dr. A. J. Weldon, in Henry County, Tennessee, and subsequently attended the medical department of the University of Nashville, graduating in 1862. He was immediately ordered to report to General Pillow at Fort Donelson and was in the hospital service in the Confederate army until September 23, 1863, when he was captured in Henry County, Tennessee, and taken to Fort Heiman, Kentucky, where, in a few days, he was paroled, this ending his military career.

He then formed a partnership with his former preceptor and practiced medicine with Dr. Weldon in Henry County, Tennessee, for six years, when the firm was dissolved. Dr. Coleman continued his professional work in Henry County until 1872, when he removed to Murray, Calloway County, Kentucky, and practiced there until September, 1887, when he removed to Princeton, the scene of his present labors.

He was a member of the Board of Health in Calloway County from the time of its organization until he left that county in 1887, and is now a member of the Board of Health of Caldwell County. He was appointed a member of the Board of Medical Examiners for the First district by Governor Knott; is a member of a number of medical societies, including the Southwestern Kentucky Medical Association, and the Calloway County (Kentucky) Medical Association; is prominent in every movement for the promotion of the public health; and is a leading member of the Masonic fraternity and of the Knights of Honor.

Dr. Coleman was married in 1855 to Frances Williams, daughter of John H. and Anna Williams of Henry County, Tennessee, and has three sons and two daughters living: Dr. John R. Coleman, a physician and surgeon of Murray, Kentucky; James H. Coleman, an attorney-at-law in the same place; Thomas E. Coleman, a dry goods salesman in Princeton; and the two daughters, Mary and Frances Coleman, who are at home with their parents.

GEORGE NEWMAN BROWN, lawyer, statesman and jurist, was born September 22, 1822, on the banks of the Ohio, in Cabell County, West Virginia, on the site of the present City of Huntington.

His father, Richard Brown, was a native of Prince William County, Virginia, and an early pioneer with his brothers, Henry and Benjamin, to the Ohio Valley, between the Rivers Guyandotte and Great Tattaroy, now Big Sandy, where they settled in the wilderness. There Richard built his log cabin in the forest, and later, about 1810, the first brick residence ever erected in the County of Cabell, which was formed in 1809 out of part of Kanawha County. There his hospitality became proverbial.

That house is still standing, and in it Judge G. N. Brown was born and reared, and two of his sisters. His mother, grandmother and his uncle, Benjamin Brown, died in it.

Richard Brown was the fifth son of George Newman Brown of Prince William County, Virginia, a son of George Brown of King George County, Virginia, and he the son of Maxfield Brown of Richmond County, Virginia, who was a son of William Brown of old Rappahannock County, Virginia, member of the Virginia House of Burgesses in 1659-60 from Surry County. He was the son of Colonel Henry Brown of Surry County, Virginia, member of the Virginia Council of State, and of the Grand Assembly from 1642 to 1651, and who was son of Sir William Brown of England, one of the original grantees and adventurers in the Virginia charter granted May 23, 1609, by King James I. to Robert, Earl of Salisbury, and several hundred others named therein, of whom the said Sir William Brown was the fortieth on the long list.

Thus the Brown family has been coeval with the colony of Virginia and the settlement of the New World. And Richard Brown, a pioneer in the wilds of Western Virginia, where he and his brothers settled on lands held by them in the military survey of 28,527 acres, as run by George Washington under Governor Dinwiddie's proclamation of 1754, and granted by Virginia to Captain John Savage and his company of sixty men for military services rendered in the Indian and French wars.

George Newman Brown (grandfather) was a Virginia soldier in the War of the Revolution and was in the siege of Yorktown. His wife, Sarah, was a daughter of Henry Hampton of Prince William County, Virginia, and a near relative of the first General Wade Hampton of South Carolina.

His sons, Captain John, Captain Robert of the Cavalry, William, George Newman, James and the son-in-law Reno, were in the War of 1812 with Great Britain in the east; John and Robert were cavalry officers, and Richard a lieutenant and major under General Harrison in the northwest and at Fort Meigs; while Benjamin, in the same war, was United States collector of internal revenue for Western Virginia, appointed by President Madison.

Judge Brown's mother, Frances H. was a daughter of Henry Haney of Bourbon County, Kentucky. She died in 1838, and is buried at Huntington, West Virginia.

Sarah, his grandmother, widow of George Newman Brown, Sr., after the death of her husband in 1814, removed from Prince William to Cabell County and resided with her son Richard till her death about 1828 or 1830, aged about eighty; and is also buried at Huntington, West Virginia. All her children died without issue except Richard, Benjamin and Elizabeth.

Richard Brown was born January 28, 1782; died August 8, 1843.

George Newman Brown, the subject of this sketch, was twice married, and had twelve children, five by the first marriage and seven by the second. The first marriage, November 18, 1847, to Sophia, daughter of Thomas Cecil of Pike County, Kentucky. She died June 6, 1858; was the mother of first Nancy Frances, born August 31, 1848, died January 3, 1878; married Alexander Martin July 1, 1873, son of John P. Martin, and was mother of two children, viz.: Elizabeth Sophia Martin, born August 8, 1874, educated at Staunton, Virginia, and George Brown Martin, born August 18, 1876, a graduate of Central University, Richmond. Margaret Matilda, born November 20, 1849, married to Rev. John D. McClintock June 26, 1871. He died in Columbus, Mississippi, December 12, 1881. She resides in Catlettsburg with her children, viz.: Wallace Cecil McClintock, born May 5, 1872; George Bayless McClintock, born October 18, 1875, and John David McClintock, born November 6, 1878; Paul Brown McClintock, born December 10, 1880, and died September 11, 1881. John William Brown, born May 31, 1851, died July 1, 1851. Eliza Taylor Brown, born May 24, 1852, lives in Catlettsburg; unmarried. Thomas Richard Brown, born June 2, 1854, in Pikeville, Kentucky; educated in Catlettsburg, and at Danville Collegiate Institute. In 1872 he entered the University of Virginia, afterward attended the Louisville Law School, from which he graduated in 1876, and at once began the practice of law in Catlettsburg, in partnership with his father. He soon took high rank in his profession, and is one of the first lawyers at the bar; was appointed commissioner of public schools; elected president of the Big Sandy National Bank, and was one of its charter members. He married Mary, daughter of Greenville Lacky of Louisa, Kentucky, December 11, 1878. She was born December 13, 1859; educated in Wesleyan College, Cincinnati, Ohio. They are members of the Presbyterian Church, and enjoy high social standing in the community; have four children, viz.: Alexander Lackey, born December 6, 1879; Nannie McClintock, born April 19, 1883, died July 29, 1890; Mary Quinn, born October 26, 1887, and Florence Huston, born August 20, 1892.

The second marriage of Judge Brown was with Maria, daughter of William Poage. She was born November 6, 1829. The children by this marriage are: James Henry, born May 13, 1859, died January 16, 1861; Colbert Cecil, born October 25, 1861, died March 27, 1864; Lucy Murray, born April 16, 1863, educated at Staunton, Virginia; George Newman, born August 25, 1865, an attorney, who, upon beginning of his profession, died July 12, 1892; Sarah Elizabeth, born September 28, 1867, educated at Staunton, Virginia; Edgar, born October 16, 1872, died November 9, 1872; Benjamin Bernard, born November 24, 1873, educated at Catlettsburg, and studied law with his father and brother.

George Newman Brown was the eldest son and seventh child of Richard and Frances Brown; educated in the schools of the neighborhood, at Marshall Academy, Virginia, and Augusta College, Kentucky. After returning from college in the fall of 1840, he soon began the study of law in the office of Judge James M. Rice of Louisa, and was admitted to the bar in October, 1844. He practiced law in Pike and adjacent counties for sixteen years, during which time he was county attorney for four terms, and represented the counties of Floyd, Pike and Johnson in the Legislature of Kentucky in 1849-50.

In 1860 he removed to Catlettsburg and entered into partnership with Judge Rice. In the Civil war he was a non-combatant, but his sympathies were with the Southern people.

In 1880 he was elected by the people judge of the Circuit Court and served six years on the bench, when he returned to his law practice with his son, Thomas R. Brown, a brief sketch of whom has already been given. During his residence in Catlettsburg he served repeatedly on the Board of Trustees of the city; took an active part in every enterprise for promoting the public weal of county and city, and in the conduct and management of his business, mercantile, agricultural and professional. In Ely's History of Sandy Valley it is said he, Judge Brown, "was for thirty years one of the foremost men of business in the Sandy basin." In 1884, in a warm and close contest for the judgeship between him and W. C. Ireland, the latter was elected.

As judge on the bench Mr. Brown was courteous, patient and impartial to hear both sides and counsel fully, then firm and fearless to decide and enforce the mandates of the law. On the bench he won the reputation of being one of the ablest, purest of Kentucky.

As a man of business he has proved a success; as a farmer and patron of husbandry an example worthy of imitation in the improvement of his lands and varied systems of agriculture. Generous and liberal to the needy.

He was appointed by the Legislature of Kentucky one of the commissioners to expend $75,000 appropriated to Sandy River in improving the navigation thereof, a work of great importance to the prosperity of the people of that section.

CLAUDE CHINN, the efficient County Clerk of Fayette County, was born in the City of Lexington, Fayette County, Kentucky, August 14, 1842, and is the son of the late Dr. Joseph G. Chinn and Barbara (Graves) Chinn.

Dr. Chinn practiced medicine in Jessamine County in 1835-6, removing to Lexington in the latter year, where he was a successful practitioner for many years. He was a good and honored citizen and did more charity practice than probably any other physician in Lexington. He was a kind-hearted man and a spirit of meekness seemed to rule his conduct. In his daily life he was sensibly alive to every claim of his fellow-citizens and his voice in behalf of benevolence was emphatic and strong. The results of his efforts, as a true Christian gentleman, although limited as they were, in his old age, were appreciated by the people of Lexington, who will not soon forget him. He was born in Virginia and his father was one of the pioneer settlers of Harrison County. Dr. Chinn was a soldier in the War of 1812 in the capacity of assistant surgeon. He made a specialty of the diseases of women in the latter part of his life, but became almost blind and was retired for several years previous to his death, which occurred in Lexington in 1893, at the remarkable age of ninety-three. He was three times married: His second wife was Mrs. Shepherd and his third wife Mrs. Katherine Lawson of Lexington; his last wife died in 1892, at the still more remarkable age of one hundred and four. She was ninety-six years of age when she married Dr. Chinn; she was a refined lady and was particularly well versed in the principles of Christianity. It is supposed that they were the oldest couple ever married in Lexington. Dr. Chinn was mayor of Lexington many years and a stanch Democrat and was a lifelong member of the Christian Church. He built a church in Missouri, the cost of which he paid out of his private funds. He was an elder and exhorter in the church and a well known writer for the religious papers of his denomination, and no member was more highly respected by his brethren than Dr. Chinn. The Chinns are of Scotch ancestry.

Claude Chinn was reared in the City of Lexington and was principally educated at the old Transylvania University, and after leaving that institution he removed to Missouri, where he became deputy sheriff of Lafayette County under his brother-in-law, Colonel John P. Bowman, where he remained until the time of the breaking out of the war between the States.

Mr. Chinn was not long in entering the Confederate army, enlisting in a Missouri battery and served as a private until the close of the war. With the exception of one year he was with General John Morgan. He was slightly wounded at the battle of Blue Mills, Missouri, and at the close of the war returned home to Lexington and was engaged in farming in Fayette County for four years. At the expiration of that time he went to Arkansas, where he operated a plantation on the Mississippi River, raising cotton, and remained there for a year and then returned to Lexington and was agent there for the omnibus lines for some ten years. In 1894 Mr. Chinn received the Democratic nomination for County Clerk of Fayette County, defeating Theodore Lewis in the primary convention. He was then endorsed by all the political parties and elected without any opposition.

In 1866 he was united in marriage to Nannie Petett, daughter of William B. Petett of Fayette County. Mr. and Mrs. Chinn have four daughters and one son: Dixey, who married Colby Young; Nannie, wife of William Anderson of Bell County; Joseph W. and Edward. Mr. Chinn is a member of the Confederate Veteran Association and one of the leading Democrats of Fayette County.

RICHARD H. GRAY, Attorney-at-Law, Covington, son of Andrew J. and Catherine (Galbaugh) Gray, was born in Covington February 22, 1853. His father is a native of Covington

also, and has resided in Covington and in the County of Kenton all his life, being at present a resident of Milldale, near Covington. He was a large tobacco manufacturer until 1873, when he removed to his farm in the county, where he lived until 1893. He then retired and took up his residence in Milldale. He is now in his sixty-sixth year.

John Gray (grandfather) was born in Erie, Pennsylvania, who removed to Covington when a young man and resided there until the time of his death. His ancestors were from Scotland.

Catherine Galbaugh Gray (mother) was a native of Covington, where she resided all her life, and died in 1865.

John Galbaugh (grandfather) was a native of Harrisburg, Pa., but removed to Covington when he was a young man.

Richard H. Gray is a graduate of the public schools of Covington, and for a time attended the University of Virginia. He read law with John N. Furber of Covington and was admitted to the bar in 1875, since which time he has been successfully engaged in the practice of law in Covington. In 1884 he formed a partnership with James M. Tisdale and at this time the law firm of Tisdale & Gray is one of the oldest and most popular firms in the city.

Mr. Gray takes a lively interest in politics from a Democratic standpoint without seeking the honors of his party. He belongs to a number of benevolent orders, including the Masons, Odd Fellows and Knights of Pythias. He was married in 1877 to Cora B., daughter of John and Mary Dye of Cold Spring, Campbell County. Their residence is in Milldale, a suburb of Covington.

HON. LOUIS P. FRYER, Attorney-at-Law, Falmouth, Kentucky, is the son of John H. and Frances A. (Norris) Fryer of Butler, Pendleton County. His father is also a native of Butler, where he still resides, and is now in the sixty-third year of his age, and is still actively engaged in the practice of law. He is a Republican in politics, although not active, and is a faithful and zealous member of the Methodist Church.

Walter Fryer (grandfather) was a native of Scotland, who came to the United States when he was a young man and became one of the earliest settlers of Pendleton County. He was a farmer, and one of the best citizens of the county.

Frances A. Norris Fryer (mother) was a native of Pendleton County. She died in 1889.

William Norris (grandfather) was a native of Maryland and was one of the earliest settlers of Pendleton County.

Judge Louis P. Fryer was born in Butler, January 10, 1864. After leaving school he read law with his father and was admitted to the bar in 1886 and at once located in Falmouth, where he has been engaged in the practice of his profession with unusual success. He was police judge of Falmouth from 1886 to 1888; was city attorney in 1888 and 1889 and was county attorney for two years—1893 and 1894. Unlike his father, he is a Democrat and takes a lively interest in political affairs, having served as a delegate to several state conventions, and otherwise aiding in the party organization.

Judge Fryer and Mattie B. Barton, daughter of T. M. Barton of Butler, were married in 1888, and have one daughter, Mabel L.

RIVERS McNEILL, son of Thomas Henry and grandson of Malcolm McNeill, was born November 12, 1858, in Christian County, Kentucky, near LaFayette, and lived there until 1876, when he left for Emory and Henry College in Virginia. He graduated in 1879 and then studied medicine, but not being able to finish the course he desired, he abandoned the study of medicine and turned his attention to commercial life. He went to work in Chicago for a general mercantile house, and after being with them a short time was promoted to the management of one of the departments, afterward accepting a position as auditor for one of the largest publishing houses in the West.

He married Miss Stella Elizabeth Corby of Chicago, and has three living children: Malcolm Rivers, Cherrill and Dorothy Mesha. His oldest child, a daughter, died in infancy.

Stella Corby is a descendant, on her mother's side, of John Hampden, and on her father's side of the Banning family, early settlers of New York.

In 1885, Rivers McNeill and his brother, Thomas Henry, engaged in the real estate business and took charge of the estate left them by their grandfather, Malcolm McNeill, improving and looking after it in a general way. He has built several large modern houses in Chicago and is known as a reliable and competent business man. He has been identified with the reform movements and advanced ideas; has been successful in business and has established a good name among the business men of Chicago. He attributes his success to hard work and attentiveness to business, and to the strictest honesty in all transactions. He has never solicited any public office, but takes a great interest in the welfare and politics of his country. He is a member of several charitable institutions and of the Iroquois and Waubansee clubs. Retiring and reserved in disposition, he cares little for society and devotes most of his spare time to his home and family.

ELI H. BROWN, Corporation Attorney and prominent citizen of Owensboro, was born in Brandenburg, Meade County, Kentucky, November 13, 1843. He received his primary education from private teachers in Hawesville, and attended the high schools of Lewisport, then taught by Professors Gregg and Trimble, and graduated in June, 1863. He studied law for two and a half years in the office of Judge George Williams, and was licensed to practice law by the judge of the Circuit Court. He located in Hawesville and practiced alone until 1878, when he became associated with Judge Williams, a partnership which continued until October 1, 1878, when he removed to Louisville and was a prominent member of the bar in that city for nearly ten years. During a part of that time he was in partnership with D. M. Rodman. He acquired a lucrative business and was one of the most energetic and prominent lawyers at the Louisville bar. In March, 1891, he removed to Owensboro, where he has been steadily and successfully engaged in the practice of his profession, and is now one of the leading attorneys of that city, which is so distinguished for legal talent.

During his residence in Hawesville Mr. Brown was prosecuting attorney for two terms, and has frequently served as special judge of the Circuit Court, but has never sought political preferment. He was presidential elector for his district in 1872 on the Democratic ticket and made a spirited canvass, but has not turned aside at any time from strictly professional work. During the past fifteen years he has devoted himself almost exclusively to the legal work of various corporations, and is at present the attorney for the Glenmore Distillery Company, the Eagle Distillery Company, the Daviess County Distillery Company, and the Owensboro Woolen Mills Company.

One of the most important cases in which he has been engaged was that of a railroad company against the taxpayers of Muhlenberg County, in which he won the suit for the railroad company. In 1868 bonds were voted by Muhlenberg County to the amount of four hundred thousand dollars to secure railroad facilities in the county. The taxpayers refused to pay their assessments and in order to prevent the collection of the tax all of the magistrates in the county were induced to resign. The railroad people employed some of the most prominent legal lights in the state to prosecute their claim, but they gave it up as a bad job. Finally Mr. Brown undertook the case for the railroad company and secured judgment for the tax with interest at seven per cent for five years. The case was decided in the United States Circuit Court by Judge Lurton, who issued an order to Marshal Blackburn to go into the county with an armed force and collect the tax from the people at the point of the bayonet if necessary. The amount of the bonds, with interest, was collected. This case attracted universal attention, especially among the lawyers of the state, as it was of exceptional interest.

Mr. Brown has been signally successful as a corporation attorney, being greatly devoted to his profession and always faithful to the interests of his clients. He is a man of fine personal bearing, dignified in appearance, but genial and cordial in his intercourse with others, and is an exceedingly popular citizen. He is a Mason of high degree and a most excellent member of the Christian Church.

Mr. Brown was married February 3, 1870, to

Nancy W. Dorsey of Nelson County, daughter of Dr. Washington Dorsey, a native of Kentucky, and a very celebrated physician, who lived for many years at Yazoo, Mississippi. Mrs. Brown was born October 31, 1847, and died in Louisville, December 6, 1885, leaving four children: Horace Stone, born June 21, 1871, died March 6, 1894; Eli Houston, born May 3, 1875, graduated at the Kentucky University in the class of 1895; Washington Dorsey, born January 3, 1877, now in the senior class of the Kentucky University; and Sarah Ellen, born December 7, 1879, now studying under a governess in Nelson County.

At the time of his death Horace Stone Brown, eldest son, was city editor of the Louisville Daily Commercial, and the members of the press of that city paid a beautiful tribute to his worth and popularity.

Eli H. Brown is a son of John McClarty and Minerva (Murray) Brown. His father was born in Nelson County, May 7, 1799, and was educated in Bardstown. He was engaged in merchandising in Hardinsburg, in partnership with two of his uncles, Samuel and James McClarty, until 1823, when he married Minerva Murray and removed to Brandenburg and was the first merchant in that place. He was also interested in the tobacco business at Cloverport, Hawesville, and Leitchfield during the time of his stay in Brandenburg. In 1851 he removed to Hawesville and was secretary and treasurer of the Trabue Coal Mining Company until 1857. He was county judge of Hancock County for two terms, ending August 3, 1865. He was a man of splendid literary attainments, and was one of the best and most highly respected citizens of his county, a prominent Mason, and a leading member of the Presbyterian Church.

Robert J. Brown (grandfather), a native of Maryland, was one of the earliest settlers of Nelson County, where he was a farmer and trader. He married a Miss McClarty, and died when his son, John McClarty Brown (father), was an infant. His widow married a Mr. Hughes, and died in 1852. The Browns are of Irish descent, but have been in this country a long time.

Minerva J. Murray Brown (mother) was born in Breckinridge County, November 23, 1807, and was educated at Hardinsburg. She was a member of the Methodist Church and a woman of the most noble traits of character, whose death in 1871 was mourned by a host of loving and devoted friends.

John Murray (grandfather) was a native of Washington County, where he was a merchant for a great many years. He subsequently removed to Rumsey, McLean County, and continued in active business until 1864, when he returned and spent the remainder of his useful life with his daughter, Mrs. (Brown) Hughes. He was quite a figure in politics and was known as a "Constitutional Union" man during the war and in the days of reconstruction. His wife's name was Patsey Walker, who was a native of Washington County. She died, and Mr. Murray survived her until 1869, when he died in McLean County.

WILLIAM S. CASON, Lawyer, of Cynthiana, was born in Harrison County, November 23, 1856. His father, Benjamin C. Cason, was also born in Harrison County, in 1824, and has been a farmer and a resident of the county all his life.

Nelson Cason (grandfather) was a native of Spottsylvania County, Virginia, and was one of the pioneer farmers of Harrison County. He belonged to an old Virginia family of Scotch descent.

Mrs. Rochiel Elker Cason (mother) is a native of Harrison County, and is a prominent member of the Baptist Church. Her father, Samuel Elker, was born in Maryland, in 1792. He removed to Harrison County when quite young; lived in Cynthiana for some years, but devoted the latter part of his life to agricultural pursuits. He died in 1865, aged seventy-three years. His father was a native of Germany.

William S. Cason improved all of his opportunities in the way of country schools while assisting his father on the farm. He also attended the public schools of Cynthiana, graduating in 1876. He then went to Lafayette College, Easton, Pennsylvania, and graduated in 1880 with the degree of A. B., and three years later received the degree of A. M. from the same college. He attended the law department of the University of

Louisville, graduating in 1882. He began the practice of law in Cynthiana in August, 1882, and has acquired a large practice, to which he devotes his entire attention. He is not in politics but votes the Democratic ticket.

He was principal of the city schools of Cynthiana in 1885-86, having been elected to fill a vacancy caused by the death of Professor Marshall. He was county superintendent of schools from 1886 to 1890.

Mr. Cason married Ella N. Bowman, daughter of Jacob Bowman of Harrison County, in 1880, and has two sons: Hervey M. and Edgar B. Cason.

J. IRVINE BLANTON, attorney-at-law, of Cynthiana, was born in Boyle County April 21, 1860. He is a son of Lindsay H. and Elizabeth (Irvine) Blanton. His father is a native of Cumberland County, Virginia. He came to Kentucky in 1856, and attended the Danville Theological Seminary. After entering the ministry, his first charge was the First Presbyterian Church of Versailles. In 1866 he moved to Paris, Kentucky, and built the Second Presbyterian Church in that city, and continued as pastor until 1879, when he went to Richmond and assumed charge of Central University, of which he is now chancellor. He was with General John C. Breckinridge in his campaigns through Virginia and Kentucky.

Joseph Blanton (grandfather) was a native of Cumberland County, Virginia, and was an extensive farmer of that county. He died in 1882 in the eightieth year of his age. He was a leading member of the Presbyterian Church. He belonged to a well-known Virginia family who originally came from England.

Elizabeth Irvine Blanton (mother) is a native of Boyle County; a devoted member of the Presbyterian Church, and a lady of unusual intelligence and great force of character. Her father, Abner Irvine, was a native of Fayette County, who removed to Boyle County, where he was a large land owner and prosperous farmer up to the time of his death in 1868. The Irvines are of Scotch-Irish descent and came to America with the McDowells and Lyles, well-known Virginia families.

J. Irvine Blanton spent his boyhood in Paris and Richmond and graduated from Central University in 1880. He taught in the preparatory department for one year, and then studied law in Central University, law department, graduating in December, 1883. He located in Cynthiana the same year and formed a partnership with Judge John Quincy Ward, the firm name being Ward & Blanton. In 1886 his distinguished partner was elected judge of the Superior Court and the business relation was necessarily dissolved. Mr. Blanton continued to practice alone until 1893, when he became the partner of Baily D. Berry, under the firm name of Blanton & Berry, who are at this time associated in a general practice with a large clientele. No law firm in this section of the state stands higher or enjoys a more lucrative practice.

Mr. Blanton was married in October, 1886, to Sallie McDowell, daughter of Judge William C. and Bettie (Breck) McDowell of Richmond. Mrs. Blanton's grandfather was General Joseph McDowell of Hillsboro, Ohio.

They have one son and two daughters: Elizabeth, Lindsay H., Jr., and Mary Irvine Blanton. Mr. and Mrs. Blanton are members of the Presbyterian Church.

DR. ALEXANDER P. CAMPBELL, dentist, of Hopkinsville, Christian County, Kentucky, was born in that city May 9, 1865. His father, Dr. Alexander P. Campbell, Sr., was a native of Todd County, Kentucky, and was born February 11, 1826, and educated in the common schools of that county. He was a farmer until thirty-two years of age, when he removed to Hopkinsville, where he practiced dentistry until the time of his death, February 10, 1886. He was a graduate of the Baltimore Dental College.

Dr. Alexander P. Campbell was a student in the schools of Hopkinsville until eighteen years of age and obtained a good, practical knowledge of dentistry in his father's office before entering Vanderbilt University at Nashville, where he spent three years, and was graduated in the class of 1886. He was assistant demonstrator of dentistry in that institution for five months, when he resigned and began the practice of dentistry in Hopkinsville, where he has made a reputation as one of the best dentists in the state, and has secured the patronage of many of the best people in the city and county.

He was married December 7, 1886, to Jennie A. Mills, and they have two children: Fletcher Mills and Fay Ellis. Mrs. Campbell is a niece of Senator Roger Q. Mills of Texas.

HENRY STITES BARKER, city attorney of Louisville, was born in Christian County, July 23, 1850. His father, Richard H. Barker, was a native of Todd County, who practiced law in Clarksville, Tenn., for a number of years. His death, at the age of about thirty-six years, was caused by yellow fever which he contracted on a steamboat, on his way home from New Orleans in 1853. His ancestors belonged to an old Virginia family, some of whom came to Kentucky from Virginia soon after the Revolutionary war, and were of English extraction. Mr. Barker's mother, Caroline M. (Sharp) Barker, is a native of Christian County, now residing at Crescent Hill, near Louisville. Her father, Dr. Maxwell Sharp, was a native of Virginia, of Scotch-Irish descent, who came to Logan County, near Russellville, in the early settlement of that section, where he practiced medicine. He afterward removed to Christian County, Kentucky, where he owned and operated a large farm. He died in 1864, aged eighty-nine years.

Mr. Henry S. Barker removed from Christian County to Louisville at the age of thirteen. He received his college education in the Kentucky University at Lexington, after which he read law and was admitted to the bar in Louisville in 1875. After three or four years of practice in partnership with his brother, Maxwell S. Barker, the latter removed from Louisville and Mr. Barker entered into partnership with Aaron Kohn under the style of Kohn & Barker, which relation continued until 1888, when Mr. Barker was elected city attorney, and the popular law firm was dissolved. Mr. Barker has been re-elected to this position for the third term, which will expire in 1897. He is an active worker in local and state politics and has great influence in the Democratic party, which has unbounded confidence in his integrity and good judgment, as shown by the repeated honors conferred upon him. He is a member of the Louisville Commandery, F. & A. M.

Mr. Barker was married in 1886 to Kate Meriwether, daughter of Captain Edward Meriwether, of Todd County. They are members of the First Christian Church of Louisville.

ALEXANDER F. BUEREN, a popular physician, who has an extensive and important practice in the eastern portion of the city of Louisville, is a son of Francis and Catherine (Van Veen) Bueren, and was born in Papenburg (now Hanover), Germany, December 13, 1849. He was educated in the excellent high schools of his native city and subsequently studied chemistry in Papenburg. He came to the United States in 1872 and at once located in Louisville and began the study of medicine in the medical department of the university of that city, from which he was graduated in 1874.

After obtaining his license he opened an office at 1420 Story Avenue and began his professional career a stranger in a strange land, under circumstances that would have disheartened a man of less perseverance. But he had the happy faculty of making friends, and his ability as a physician was soon recognized, and he is now one of the most popular physicians in the "east end."

In the twenty-one years of his active professional life, Dr. Bueren has established himself in the confidence of his numerous patrons, who firmly believe in him as a man of honor and a physician of marked ability. He attends strictly to his large practice and is not interested in any other kind of business or carried away with politics or money-making schemes. Of a genial disposition and social nature, he is popular in the society of his friends and in the benevolent orders, to a number of which he belongs, including the Masons, Knights of Pythias, Knights of Honor, and Elks.

His father, Francis Bueren, was a native of Germany, and a well-to-do merchant, a highly-respected and intelligent citizen of Papenburg.

He never left his native country, but died there when Dr. Bueren was only seven years of age. His mother, Catherine (Van Veen) Bueren, died in 1852. Francis and Catherine Bueren had three children: Godfrey Bueren, who is still a resident of Papenburg, where he is engaged in naval insurance; Margarette, wife of Arnold Bruggmann, a brewer and lumber merchant of Ippenbueren, Westphalia, Germany; and Alexander F. Bueren.

STANLEY ADAMS, an enterprising young business man of Louisville, son of James L. and Martha L. (Jordan) Adams, was born in Brooklyn, New York, December 27, 1864. His father is a native of Petersburg, Virginia, who was for many years a manufacturer of tobacco in Montreal, Canada, and later in New York City, but has lived in Louisville since 1883, where he is in the life insurance business.

Thomas Adams (grandfather) was a native of Petersburg, Virginia, and a resident of that place all of his life. He was a planter and a large property owner and one of the successful business men of that section in ante-bellum times.

Martha L. Jordan Adams (mother) was born near Petersburg, Virginia, and is now a resident of Louisville. Her father was a large planter and land owner near Petersburg, Virginia, and was a native of that place.

Stanley Adams lived with his parents in Montreal for thirteen years, and then in New York until nineteen years of age. He enjoyed the benefits of the best private schools of those cities, and after coming to Louisville in 1883, began a successful business career as collector for the Picket Ice Company. Later accepted a position as collector and assistant bookkeeper for the coal firm of Byrne & Speed. In 1887 he was employed by George S. Moore & Co., pig iron merchants, as a traveling salesman, and after serving his employers for four years in that capacity, he was made general manager of their business, which position he held until 1892, when he began business in the same line on his own account, under the firm name of Adams, Watkins & Co. He withdrew from this firm in 1893 and engaged in the pig iron, coal and coke commission business alone, but under the style of Stanley Adams & Co. His long experience in this line of merchandise and his extended acquaintance among the large manufacturers of the South, together with his superior business tact and indomitable energy, has enabled him to establish himself within a comparatively short time, in one of the largest trades enjoyed by any house of the kind in Louisville. This is particularly true in reference to the coke trade, as he sells more of that commodity than any other commission house in the city. He is also a member of the Hartwell Coal Company, and is making his way to the front among the wide-awake young men of the Falls City.

In 1893 Mr. Adams was elected a member of the Louisville Board of Common Councilmen and in 1894 he was chosen president of the Board, being the youngest man who had ever held that responsible office in Louisville, and he performed its duties with dispatch and excellent good judgment. Being affable, of pleasing address and always gentlemanly in his demeanor, he made many friends in a very trying position. He is a popular member of a number of benevolent orders, including the Odd Fellows and Knights of Pythias, and is vice grand chancellor of Kentucky for the latter order. In this he enjoys the distinction of being the youngest man upon whom that honor has ever been conferred in the state. He is a consistent church member in connection with the Baptist denomination and in all of his church, society and business relations he is greatly esteemed as an exemplary young man.

Mr. Adams was married October 31, 1889, to Fannie E. Miller, daughter of Len S. Miller of Louisville.

DR. WILLIAM BOWMAN of Tolesboro, Lewis County, was born in Brown County, Ohio, February 22, 1843. His father, Benjamin Bowman, was a native of Pennsylvania and was a farmer near Ripley, Ohio. He was a volunteer soldier in the Mexican war. He died of cholera in 1850 in the fifty-fifth year of his age. His father, George Bowman, was a native of Pennsylvania and was one of the pioneers of the Ohio Valley. His son, Philip (uncle), served in the war of 1812.

Mary McElwee Bowman (mother) was a native of Brown County, Ohio. She died in 1893, aged seventy-six years. Her father, Patrick McElwee, was born in Ireland. He came to America when a youth and married Mary Crossley, who was born near Hagerstown. Her father and brothers were Revolutionary soldiers. She was one of the first settlers in Brown County, and was personally acquainted with Daniel Boone and Simon Kenton.

Dr. William Bowman attended the best schools in his native county, and on the 9th of July, 1861, when eighteen years of age, he enlisted as a private in an independent company of picked men from Brown County, who served as a body guard for Generals Halleck, McPherson and O. O. Howard. He served three years in this capacity and then entered the secret service. He received a flesh wound in the battle of Silver Creek, but otherwise escaped serious injury.

After returning from the war he studied Latin and Greek under a private teacher, at the same time reading medicine and teaching school. He was thus engaged in the dual capacity of teacher and pupil for three years. He then went to Michigan University, Ann Arbor, for three years, taking a literary and medical course, graduating in the medical department in 1873, and during the following year attended the Ohio Medical College.

In 1870 he removed to Tolesboro, Lewis County, Kentucky, which has been his home until the present time.

Dr. Bowman has been a very active politician, and although against his inclination and detrimental to his professional work, he has not been able to keep out of office all the time. He was elected to the legislature in 1881 and re-elected two years later. He was the Republican elector at large in the presidential campaign of 1888, and was appointed consul at Tien-Tsin, China, by President Harrison in 1889, and on his return in 1893 he was again elected to the legislature and was a member of the committee on education, in which he rendered valuable service.

Dr. Bowman is well and favorably known throughout the state and stands well in the estimation of the leading men in all parties. His name was prominently mentioned as the Republican candidate for lieutenant governor in the last convention. He stands at the top of the medical profession in the state and has quite an enviable reputation as a surgeon. He is a member of the State Medical Association and of the National Medical Association. Dr. Bowman was married in 1864 to Maggie McKinley of Ohio, a relative of Governor William McKinley.

HON. JACOB T. SIMON, Commonwealth Attorney, Cynthiana, was born in Grant County, September 9, 1846.

His father, Francis Simon, was a native of the northern part of France, and was engaged in agricultural pursuits all his life. He emigrated to the Island of Martinique in the Lesser Antilles in 1823, where he resided until 1834, when he came to the United States and settled in Grant (then Owen) County, where he was one of the most thrifty farmers of the county, until the time of his death, which occurred July 29, 1892, at the advanced age of eighty-six years. He was a Democrat in politics and served his country in some of the minor offices.

John Simon (grandfather) was a native of France and a soldier under the first Napoleon.

Eliza (Musselman) Simon (mother) was born in Grant County in 1821 and is now living in the old homestead. Her father, Jacob Musselman, was a native of Harrison County, who removed to Grant (then Owen) County in 1820, where he followed farming and was one of the leading citizens of the county. He died at the age of seventy-six years, in 1867. He was a soldier in the war of 1812, being at that time about twenty-one years of age. He was of German descent.

Hon. J. T. Simon enjoyed but limited opportunities in the way of education when a boy, but he was studious and ambitious, and after leaving the county schools attended an excellent seminary at Greenup Fork, Owen County, and afterwards took a thorough course in a commercial college. In 1868 he began the study of law under Hon. H. P. Montgomery of Owenton. He was admitted to the bar in 1868, and located at Williamstown, where he remained one year and then formed a partnership with the late Judge O. D. McManama of Falmouth. He remained in Falmouth until 1888, when he removed to Cynthiana, and has continued the practice of his profession with great success until the present time.

In 1874 he was elected county attorney of Pendleton County. He was elected city attorney of Falmouth in 1875 and was twice re-elected to that office. In 1881-2 he represented Pendleton County in the legislature and in 1885-6 he represented the Twenty-sixth Senatorial District, composed of Bracken, Pendleton and Grant Counties, in the Kentucky Senate.

He was elected commonwealth attorney for the Eighteenth Judicial District in 1892, after removing to Cynthiana. In all of his elections he has been supported by the Democratic party, in which he is a most active and successful leader.

Mr. Simon was married September 17, 1872, to Maggie T. McClure, daughter of John McClure, one of the most worthy and successful farmers of Grant County. She is a lady of great intellectual and moral worth. They have one daughter, Stella Simon.

Mr. Simon is a gentleman of fine personal habits, of exceptional business and professional ability; greatly devoted to his profession, in which he is remarkably successful, and is one of the most able and worthy self-made men in his section of the state.

LINDSEY B. RUGLESS of Vanceburg, son of Thomas Rugless, was born in Lewis County, Kentucky, January 1, 1818. His father was a native of Pennsylvania, who came to Lewis County with his father, one of the first settlers on Cabin Creek, eight miles south of Vanceburg. Thomas Rugless married Amelia Burriss, daughter of Mathew Burriss, also one of the pioneers of Lewis County. She was the mother of sixteen children, including the subject of this sketch. After her death her husband married again and two children were the result of that union, making a full dozen and a half to the credit of Thomas Rugless.

The ancestors of Lindsey B. Rugless on the maternal side were patriots and pioneers. His great-grandmother's maiden name was Forshee, and she married a Mr. Scott, a soldier in the Revolutionary war, which he survived only to be killed by Indians. The result of that marriage was one daughter, named Ruth, and who married Mathew Burriss, and to whom were born eleven children, five boys and six girls. One of the latter was named Amelia, above referred to. His great-grandfather Forshee settled in Lewis County about the time Kentucky was admitted into the Union. Lindsey B. Rugless is a man of unusual attainments, especially considering the difficulties he experienced in obtaining even an ordinary education. His only schooling was such as he could find in a primitive school house, built of round logs with oiled paper for "window glass." He was an industrious and energetic boy, with laudable ambition, and at the age of eighteen was as well qualified to teach school as any of the pedagogues of that time. He then got up a subscription school in the neighborhood and taught for eight years. It is with a good deal of pride that he now recalls the fact that he never whipped a scholar, although the rod was considered a very necessary appliance in the school room in those days. He was an expert penmaker, and with his pocket knife made and "mended" the quill pens for the entire school, and wrote all their copies. He struggled along through poverty and hardship, gradually gaining a little and eventually accumulating a competency, most of his undertakings proving successful. He has always prided himself on being a Jeffersonian Democrat, and was a Douglas man in the presidential campaign just prior to the war, rather bitterly opposing Lincoln and Breckinridge. In 1862 he was the Democratic candidate for the legislature against Judge G. M. Thomas, and was arrested for being a constitutional states right Democrat and placed under a bond of $15,000; but he was at heart a Union man and in 1863 joined the Federal army, served two years and was honorably discharged at the close of the war. He has been executor, administrator, assignee, trustee, guardian, arbitrator and processioner in a greater number of instances than any other man in the county and has settled many differences between man and man, possessing the confidence of his fellow citizens to an extent few men enjoy in any community. He has never united with any religious institution or secret order; but acknowledges a Fatherhood in God and every man his brother. The Golden Rule is his religious creed. He has always been a good friend to the poor; and has the deserved reputation of having bailed more men out of jail than any other citizen of the county, in some cases giving his bond for as much as $10,000. Mr. Rugless was married March 22, 1840, to Calista Lee, daughter of Barton Lee, a neighbor, who was one of the pioneers of Lewis County. She died March 5, 1887, and after her death Mr. Rugless divided his property between his two children, retaining only a small portion for himself, but to this he has added considerable in later years and is in excellent circumstances. This division was made before his second marriage in 1888, but in view of it. He married Mrs. Sarah A. Ewing, widow of Thomas Ewing of Vanceburg. His son, Socrates Rugless, died January 5, 1895, at the age of fifty-three years, leaving his children and his children's children, who were left orphans at a tender age, under the guardianship of his honored and aged father. Mr. Rugless' declining years have been full of sorrow, his son, two of his grandchildren, two of his great-grandchildren and a sister-in-law having died within a few months, leaving him laden with grief; still he exclaims, "All is right, in God I trust."

> God, in his wisdom, brought us here;
> God in his kindness takes us home;
> So we, His children, should not fear;
> He is but gathering up his own.

DR. C. B. SCHOOLFIELD, one of the most progressive physicians in Campbell County and one of the best known citizens of Dayton, was born near Foster, Kentucky, March 6, 1846; son of George T. and Mary (Maxwell) Schoolfield. His father was born in Maryland, December 31, 1799, and, at the age of fourteen years, emigrated with his father to Kentucky and settled on a farm in Bracken County near Augusta. He remained on the farm a few years, when he engaged in flatboating between Augusta and New Orleans. In 1838 he retired from the river and again engaged in farming in Bracken County, and there remained until 1873, when he removed to Dayton, Kentucky, and after one year's residence there removed to Missouri, where he died. He was for many years an extensive trader in live stock and general produce, which he shipped to New Orleans. In politics he was a Whig, prior to the Douglas campaign, when he became a Democrat. He was a son of Isaac Bosman Schoolfield (grandfather), who was also born in Maryland, emigrated to Kentucky in 1814 and settled on a farm in Bracken County. His wife was Mary Atkinson (grandmother), who also was a native of Maryland. The Schoolfield family in America is traced to the widow Schoolfield, who brought her three sons to Baltimore, Maryland, in 1632, from England. One of these brothers settled in Virginia, one in Maryland, and the other son pushed on further west. They brought with them their coat-of-arms, which is still in the family. George T. Schoolfield (father) married Mary Maxwell in 1840. She was born in Bracken County, February 24, 1819; was well educated in the private schools of her native county and is a most estimable lady, residing at present in Dayton. Her father was William Maxwell, a native of Pennsylvania, who later in life came to Kentucky and located on a farm in Bracken County, where he died in 1860. His wife was Rachel Adams.

Dr. C. B. Schoolfield received an academical education at Foster and Falmouth, Kentucky, and subsequently studied medicine, entered the Medical College of Ohio at Cincinnati and received his diploma from that institution in 1873. He located at once in his present home in Dayton, where he soon succeeded in building up a lucrative practice and in making an enviable reputation in his profession. He is a member of the Cincinnati Society of Medicine; Cincinnati Obstetrical Society; of the Kentucky State Medical Society; of the Ohio State Medical Association, and American Medical Association. Dr. Schoolfield is a practitioner of Gynecology in the Good Samaritan Hospital, and is one of the trustees of the Speers Memorial Hospital, which is nearing completion in Dayton. The fund for this hospital, which was left by Mrs. Elizabeth Speers of Dayton, amounts at present to nearly $100,000.

Upon the completion of this hospital Dr. Schoolfield will be gynecologist and surgeon.

Dr. Schoolfield is a member of the Baptist Church, a member of the Masonic order and votes the Democratic ticket.

He was married to Florence Holms, daughter of George B. and Mary Holms of Newport, August 18, 1868. Her death occurred May 27, 1889. Dr. Schoolfield was again married May 5, 1892, to Mrs. Ida Lee Arthur, a daughter of J. M. McArthur. She died March 17, 1894. There are three children by his first marriage: Dr. George Clarence, who graduated from the Cincinnati Medical College and is now practicing his profession in Charleston, West Virginia; Edna Pearl and Edward Raymond. By the second marriage he has no children.

Dr. G. Clarence Schoolfield is married and has one son, John Charles, the only grandson of the subject of this sketch.

JOHN E. PACK, M. D., Mayor of Georgetown and one of the leading physicians of that city, is a son of Richard F. Pack and Sallie M. Emison, his wife, and was born in Scott County, Kentucky, May 11, 1849.

Richard F. Pack was also a native of Scott County, where he was an industrious and extensive farmer nearly all his life. He was a very successful breeder of saddle horses and other high bred stock, and was an honorable and enterprising citizen. He died in his native county, March 4, 1892.

John Pack (grandfather), also a native farmer of Scott County, served as a soldier in the Mexican war, lived to a good old age and died a few years ago, near the scene of his birth. The Packs were of Irish descent, the first of whom in America settled in Virginia, from which state the great-grandfather of Dr. Pack came to Kentucky and settled in Scott County, about the time Kentucky was admitted to the Union.

Sallie M. Emison Pack (mother) was born in Scott County, and died in 1895, aged sixty-eight years.

William Emison (maternal grandfather) was also a native of Scott County, and was a leading farmer until the time of his death in 1875, when he was seventy-nine years of age. The Emisons were of Scotch-Irish descent and were among the early settlers of Scott County, coming to this state from Virginia.

Dr. John Pack spent his youthful days in the usual routine of the farmer boy, attending school and helping his father on the farm. He received his collegiate education in the Kentucky University; read medicine with Dr. W. O. Sweeney of Lexington and attended the Belleview Medical College of New York City, graduating in 1873.

He began his professional career in the northern part of Scott County, which was the field of his labors until 1888, when he removed to Georgetown, where he has enjoyed a very extensive practice and has found a wider field of usefulness.

He was elected to the legislature in 1887, and was a most able and efficient member of that body; was a member of the City Council of Georgetown from 1891 until the fall of 1893, when he was elected mayor of the city for a term of four years, taking charge of the office January 1, 1894. He is a member of the Kentucky State Medical Society, and other associations for the advancement of medical science; is an enterprising citizen and a man and physician in whom the people have great confidence.

Dr. Pack was married in 1879 to Laura Stevenson, daughter of Reverend Evan Stevenson, formerly of Georgetown, now of Oxford, Maryland.

CAPTAIN BENJAMIN C. MILAM.—Among the descendants of the brave and enterprising men who settled in the valley of Virginia, and who afterwards settled in Kentucky, were the "Milams," and were the descendants of the Welsh immigrants who came over from Wales with William Johnson to Virginia in 1722, grandfather of R. M. Johnson, and the ancestors of Henry Clay.

Captain Benjamin C. Milam was the son of John Milam and Lucy Bradley. His mother was of Scotch-Irish descent, and was born in Scott County, Kentucky, and died in 1831. Captain Milam was born in Franklin County on the first day of July, 1821. When war was declared to exist between Mexico and the United States in 1846, Captain Milam was twenty-five years old.

He immediately raised a company of cavalry, which was attached to the regiment of mounted men commanded by the late General Humphrey Marshall. Captain Milam was engaged in the battle of Buena Vista, when General Taylor ordered Colonel Marshall to charge the large body of Mexican lancers led by General Torrejon. Captain Milam's company took a conspicuous part in driving the enemy from the field with a loss of over two hundred. It was in this charge of the Mexican lancers that Colonel McKee, Lieutenant Colonel Henry Clay and Captain William T. Willis were killed at the battle on the 23d of February, 1847. Captain Milam served as a twelve months' volunteer in the Mexican war.

John Milam, the father of Captain Milam, was an upright farmer of Franklin County until the time of his death, which occurred in 1844, aged sixty years. He was a soldier of the war of 1812, serving under Governor Shelby when he assumed command of the Kentucky troops at that time. Moses Milam (grandfather) settled in Kentucky about the year 1787. He was also a farmer and died at a ripe old age many years ago.

Captain Benjamin C. Milam was reared on his father's farm until he had reached the age of fourteen years, when he went to Frankfort and learned the trade of watchmaking and silversmithing with J. F. & B. F. Meeks. He received only the advantages of a common school education, but being of robust physique and strong common sense, he overcame every obstacle and has succeeded where many would have failed. At the expiration of his apprenticeship the firm name of J. F. & B. F. Meeks was succeeded by J. F. Meeks & Company, which continued only twelve months, when B. F. Meeks withdrew and the old firm was succeeded by Meeks & Milam, J. F. Meeks giving his time and attention to the watch and jewelry business, while Captain Milam devoted most of his time to the manufacturing of fishing reels. This partnership lasted until 1854, when it was dissolved by mutual consent, Mr. Meeks taking the jewelry and watch department and Captain Milam the reel department, and in this line he continued successfully and built up quite a reputation and is known throughout the country as a maker of fishing reels. In later years his son John W. has been in partnership with him, the firm name being at present B. C. Milam & Son. In January, 1893, Captain Milam was elected president of the Deposit Bank of Frankfort, succeeding the late William J. Chinn, Sr., which position he now holds.

After returning from the Mexican war, Captain Milam was married in 1848 to Martha Shockley, daughter of Thomas Shockley of Frankfort. She died in December, 1885, leaving one son and a daughter, Annie, who is now the wife of Uberto Keenon of Frankfort; and John W. Milam, who is now in partnership with his father. Captain Milam is descended from a patriotic ancestry. He is a nephew of the celebrated General Benjamin R. Milam, who was one of the most daring men in the Texas Revolution of 1836, when the independence of Texas was won at the battle of San Jacinto. History does not mention more daring acts of bravery and hair-breadth escapes made in defense of the people of Texas than is recorded of General Milam in the annals of that state. He was a man of invincible courage, to which was added coolness in action and perseverance in effort. The predominant inclination of his mind was to a military life, and by close attention to the studies connected therewith he prepared himself to perform those duties which afterward devolved upon him, and thereby established his character as one of the great heroes of Texas freedom. Milam County in that state perpetuates his memory.

D. HARRY STINE, Deputy County Clerk of Campbell County, Kentucky, son of Frederick A. and Glorvina (Carlisle) Stine, was born in Lewistown, Pennsylvania, May 7, 1857.

His father, Frederick A. Stine, was born in Harrisburg, Pennsylvania; came to Newport in 1859 and is still a resident of that city. He was for many years connected with the lumber firm of I. W. Livezey & Company, and for thirteen years was engaged in the internal revenue service in the Sixth District of Kentucky. He is a stanch Republican and takes a lively interest in all political contests. His antecedents were of German extraction and have lived in Pennsylvania for several generations.

Glorvina Carlisle Stine (mother) was a native of Philadelphia, Pennsylvania, where her father, William Carlisle, Jr., was a leading merchant prior to 1854, when he became identified with the Pennsylvania Railroad and was auditor of the canal department of the Pennsylvania Railroad Company for many years. He died in Philadelphia in 1889, aged eighty-eight years.

D. Harry Stine came to Newport with his parents in 1859, when he was two years of age. He received a liberal education in the public schools of Newport; and after leaving school, was employed with his father in the lumber establishment of Livezey & Company. Beginning as an errand boy, he remained with the firm for twenty years and was promoted from time to time until he was manager of the establishment, in which capacity he was employed the greater portion of his long term of service with Livezey & Company.

In January, 1895, he was appointed deputy clerk of the Campbell County Court, a position in which he has proven a very accommodating and efficient officer.

He is now, and has been for several years past, secretary of the Republican State League of Kentucky and takes an active interest in state and local politics. He is also secretary of the Commercial Club of Newport, Kentucky.

In 1890 he was elected mayor of Newport over Albert S. Berry, but was counted out. He contested the election and was declared to have been elected by the Circuit Court. The case was carried to the Court of Appeals, and the term of office had expired before the case was reached. In 1892 he was a candidate for the office of clerk of the Circuit Court, but everything went Democratic that year, and he was not elected.

While Mr. Stine has not been successful in getting into office by election, he has accomplished a great deal for his party and has helped to elect other Republicans to office, and enjoys this as much as if he had been the favored candidate. Mr. Stine is very popular in his party and enjoys a very large acquaintance in the city, county and state in which he has lived nearly all of his life.

He is a member of the Robert Burns Lodge No. 163, F. and A. M., and has served as master of the lodge for four years. He is also a popular member of the Knights of Pythias.

Mr. Stine was married September 25, 1878, to Nellie Georg Holt, daughter of William Holt of Newport, formerly a wholesale grocer of Cincinnati.

STEPHEN GARLAND SHARP of Lexington is a son of Allenton B. and Mary (Gentry) Sharp and was born at the "Indian Old Fields" in Clark County, Kentucky, April 2, 1843. Allenton B. Sharp (father) was born and reared in Fayette County, where he resided all his life, excepting the short time he lived in Clark County. He was a tailor by trade, and for several years carried on merchant tailoring at Athens, Fayette County. He died at the age of fifty-four years, in 1874. He was the son of Stephen Sharp, who was also born in Fayette County and was a farmer by occupation.

William Sharp (great-grandfather) was a native of Virginia, who emigrated to Fayette County and was one of the earliest pioneers of that section, and was one of the first teachers in Kentucky, teaching at Boonesboro several terms. The father, grandfather and great-grandfather of Stephen G. Sharp lie buried on a farm, adjoining the old Sharp homestead, in Fayette County. The Sharps are descendants of Scotch-Irish ancestry. Mary Gentry Sharp (mother) was born in Fayette County and died in 1894, in the seventy-second year of her age. She was a daughter of Garland Gentry, a native of Fayette County, and one of the industrious and well-known farmers of his section. The Gentrys were of Scotch descent and, like the Sharps, were among the early settlers of Fayette County.

Stephen Garland Sharp was reared near Athens and was educated in the country schools, and in 1861 he entered the Confederate army, under the command of General Zollicoffer, as a private soldier, and served till the 30th of September, 1864, when he was severely wounded. In March, 1865, he was again wounded while serving with General Morgan in the second battle of Cynthiana and was wounded at Carter Station, East Tennessee, while under the command of General Duke. The wounds he received at Carter Station were severe and painful, being shot through the lung and liver, and receiving a severe sabre wound on the head. There was no braver man nor more devoted soldier to the "lost cause" than Captain Sharp. In every battle his bravery and daring were conspicuous, and in all the positions he was called to fill he did his duty like a soldier and with marked ability. He was captured in 1862, and when General Kirby Smith invaded Kentucky, Mr. Sharp made his escape and joined Smith's army in its march through the Cumberland Gap. In the spring of 1863 he joined Colonel Roy Cluke's regiment of cavalry. It was with Cluke's regiment that he was captured on the Ohio raid when the rear of Morgan's command was firing on the Federals. Senator Rodney Haggard of Winchester and Colonel Calvin Morgan rode back and informed Mr. Sharp not to fire any more, that General Morgan had surrendered. After the surrender many of the soldiers of General Morgan were sent to four different prisons: Rock Island, Camp Douglas, Fort Delaware and Camp Chase. Mr. Sharp was sent to Camp Chase, where he remained in prison for six weeks, when he was transferred to Camp Douglas, and from there made his escape on the night of March 18, 1864. Passing through Kentucky and Virginia, he rejoined a part of the command of General Morgan, who succeeded in making their escape across the Ohio river at Buckingham Island. He remained with Morgan until the latter was killed at Greeneville, Tenn.

In March, 1865, without his knowledge or consent, he was retired from the army on account of his severe wounds, and in the spring of 1865 returned to his home in Fayette County. The many severe hardships and sufferings endured by Mr. Sharp, in prison, and the painful wounds received in battle reduced his weight from one hundred and sixty pounds to ninety-eight pounds. In the fall of 1865 he returned to Virginia and there wedded Jennie Hill, daughter of Elijah Hill of Jonesville. He soon returned to Kentucky and engaged in school teaching on Marble Creek in Jessamine County. In 1866 he was appointed deputy jailer of Fayette County. In 1870 he was graduated from the law department of Transylvania and practiced law at the Fayette County bar until 1874, when he was elected jailer of Fayette County; in 1880 he was elected city attorney, which office he filled for one year; was elected county attorney in 1884 and served four years, and in 1886 was elected county judge, which office he resigned two years later, to accept the office of state treasurer to fill out the unexpired term of James W. Tate, to which he was appointed by Governor Buckner. After serving the nineteen months of his term by appointment, he was elected to that office for a term of two years, but resigned the office of treasurer in March, 1890, to accept a position as general manager of the Pine Mountain Iron & Coal Co., at Pineville, and after holding that position for one year he resigned and returned to Lexington, since which time he has served one term as president of the City Council; and in the spring of 1892 was elected city collector.

Judge Sharp has three children living, whose names are Virginia, Leslie and Stephen G. Sharp, Jr.

THEODORE M'DONALD HILL of Newport, Kentucky, ex-judge of the Campbell County Court, is a self-made man in the true sense of that term; born and reared in humble life on a farm in Campbell County, he prepared himself for the legal profession unaided and was admitted to the bar and commenced the practice of law in 1871.

He was elected police judge of Alexandria in 1872, to the state legislature in 1877 and re-elected in 1879. After retiring from the legislature, he devoted himself exclusively to the law until the death of County Judge Makibben in April, 1888, when the Board of Magistrates appointed him to fill the vacancy. His party since that time has twice nominated and elected him to that office by sweeping majorities. His practice as a lawyer from 1871 to 1888 was largely of a nature to acquaint him with county affairs, and he met every requirement of his important office. His popularity is attested by his several nominations without opposition in his own party and by the liberal vote he has always received from the people at the polls. Looking carefully after every detail of county affairs, keeping county taxes at the lowest possible figure; correcting errors of the assessments for hundreds of people; appearing with the assessor twice before the State Board of Equalization and by argument, facts and figures, he prevented in part the threatened increase of land and lot valuations over the assessors' figures that would have been very oppressive upon the taxpayers of Campbell County. In brief, Judge Hill performed all the duties and requirements of the people's court with marked ability. Since his retirement from the bench he has been engaged in the practice of law in Newport.

In 1861 he left school to join the Confederate army and enlisted in the Fifth Kentucky Infantry as a private, serving under different commanders —notably Colonel Giltner of Morgan's command —until the close of the war. He was with General Lee at Appomattox, and received his parole at Charleston, West Virginia, when on his way home. After arriving at Alexandria, Kentucky, he read law with Honorable R. T. Baker, a noted lawyer and Republican politician, and was admitted to the bar February 22, 1871.

January 1, 1868, Judge Hill was united in marriage to Mary Isaphine White, a daughter of H. E. White of Campbell County, Kentucky. Of the five children born of this marriage only one survives, Fay Fern Hill.

Theodore M. Hill is a son of William and Elizabeth (Nation) Hill. William Hill was born in Cincinnati, Ohio, in 1794, and removed to Campbell County in 1841, where he remained a resident until his death, which occurred in 1873. He was a stone mason and bricklayer by trade and a Democrat in politics. He was a soldier of the war of 1812 and of the Mexican war. In the war of 1812 he was at the massacre at River Raisin, the battles of the Thames and Lundy's Lane and others, and in Mexico with General Scott from Vera Cruz to the City of Mexico.

He married Elizabeth Nation, daughter of Joel Nation and Mary Albright of Eaton, Ohio, to which place they had removed from North Carolina.

William Hill (grandfather) was a native of County Antrim, Ireland, and his wife, Jane MacDonald, of the Isle of Skye, off the west coast of Scotland. Both of them were first cousins of the celebrated Scotch beauty, Flora MacDonald, the plain narrative of whose life touches all hearts.

William Hill and his wife came to America in colonial days (1767) and first settled in Pennsylvania, and, during his residence there, he was in the Continental army in the war of the Revolution. In 1794 he came with his family to Cincinnati, Ohio, where he lived until some time prior to his death in 1833, having reached the remarkable age of one hundred and three years. For some years after his settlement at Cincinnati, he kept a tavern known as the "Black Bear," which was one of the pioneer inns of that city. The latter years of his life were spent on a farm in Butler County, Ohio.

Mrs. Elizabeth Hill (mother) was born in East Tennessee, while her parents were en route from North Carolina to Ohio. She died in Campbell County at the early age of twenty-four years. She was a daughter of Joel Nation, a native of North Carolina, who removed to Prebble, and later to Champaign County, Ohio, where he died in 1864.

Mr. Hill is now engaged in the practice of law in Newport, Kentucky.

DR. JOHN W. SCOTT, deceased, of Lexington, was the son of the late Matthew T. and Winnie (Webb) Scott. He was born in Fayette County, Kentucky, January 6, 1821. He received a fair primary education and at the age of fourteen entered the Transylvania University and was graduated from there in the class of 1838, while that college was under the temporary presidency of Dr. Louis Marshall. Afterward he studied medicine with Dr. Benjamin W. Dudley and James M. Bush; and received his degree of M. D. from the medical department of Transylvania in 1842. In the same year he went to New York City, and after spending one year in general hospital practice settled down there in general practice of his profession, where he remained for about twelve years. In 1855 he purchased a country seat on Long Island, where he removed and resided until 1866, when he returned to Kentucky and lived in quiet retirement at Lexington until his death, which occurred July 22, 1888. He was twice married: First to Jane Heyer Suydam,

daughter of Cornelius R. Suydam, a prominent merchant of New York, by whom he has one child surviving, Cornelius Suydam Scott, a lawyer at Lexington, Kentucky. The only other child, Matthew Thompson Scott, was a prominent and successful physician at Lexington, Kentucky, and died in the thirty-ninth year of his age, on January 25, 1894. He was married the second time, in 1874, to Elizabeth B., daughter of Abraham T. Skillman, who was an old and prominent citizen of Lexington, and an uncle of Dr. H. M. Skillman. By the second marriage, there are three children living: John W., a graduate of Center College and of the College of Physicians and Surgeons. He is now in his twentieth year, and when a little past his eighteenth year he was graduated from Center College. The other living children are Henry Martyn Skillman Scott and Margaret Skillman Scott. Dr. Scott was an elder in the Second Presbyterian Church of Lexington, and took a great interest in church affairs; a decided believer in the doctrines of the Calvinistic faith and system; enthusiastic and public-spirited and a man of marked individuality. He never aspired to public office and had no taste for politics. He gave largely and liberally to the boards and objects of his church, to the Center College at Danville, Kentucky, and to other forms of social, educational and religious beneficence. He was deeply interested in the moral, religious and general elevation of the freedmen, and established and long conducted the first Sunday school for their benefit, managed by white persons in Lexington, Kentucky; was a student all his days and was accurately informed on a great variety of subjects.

His father was Matthew T. Scott, born at Shippensburg, Pennsylvania, January 5, 1786, of Scotch-Irish parents, both of whom died when he was quite young, and he came to live with his relative, Dr. John M. Scott of Frankfort, before the town plat of the present capital had been placed on record. In 1808 he became a clerk in the Bank of Kentucky and was transferred to the Lexington branch of the same institution about two years later. In June, 1810, soon after his arrival in Lexington, he wedded Winnie Webb, daughter of Isaac Webb, who had recently emigrated from Virginia. Mr. Scott subsequently occupied the positions of teller and cashier of the United States Bank, and when the paper of that institution was taken by the Northern Bank of Kentucky, which was founded in 1833, he became cashier of the new bank, and was an officer in the Northern Bank until his death in 1858, having for the last six years of his life been the president of the bank. He came to Kentucky a poor boy, but by good judgment, honesty and industry, attained a comfortable position in later years, and during his residence of a half century in Lexington had the respect of the best families in that section. He was one of the original subscribers of $500 to the cemetery fund and the first treasurer of the Lexington Cemetery Company. He was the father of fifteen children, nine of whom reached maturity: James, Isaac W., Joseph N., Mary, the widow of Dr. E. L. Dudley, John W., Winnie, deceased; Margaret, wife of Dr. H. M. Skillman; Lucy W., Matthew T., Joseph and William T., who was colonel of the Third Kentucky Infantry, and who led his regiment through the war, died at Frankfort in 1875, leaving a widow and three children. In the early history of the country the Scotts were Federalists and in more recent times were all Republicans. The father was an old line Whig. For many generations the Scotts have been of the same religious faith and the younger representatives may not inaptly be termed "hereditary Presbyterians," but are none the less members by conviction.

Matthew Scott, the grandfather of Dr. John W. Scott, was a lieutenant in Miles' Pennsylvania Regiment in the War of the Revolution. He volunteered March 5, 1776; was taken prisoner at Long Island August 27, 1776, exchanged December 8, 1776, and promoted to captain in a Pennsylvania State regiment April 18, 1777, to rank from October 24, 1776. The regiment was designated as the Thirteenth Pennsylvania, November 12, 1777; retired July 1, 1778. His brother, Moses Scott, was in the same war, and lived and died in New Brunswick, New Jersey, and William Scott, another brother, was commissary.

John Scott (great-grandfather) was a son of Robert Scott, who was a member of the old Scottish parliament, and opposed the union of the crown during the reign of Queen Anne; the ignoring of the Scottish crown and name in the new parliament of Great Britain was further offense to him, and he, with a number of others, who were members of the two houses of the old parliament, suffered in the Tower of London, with the risk of their heads, until they were released by an amnesty of George I., when he was brought over from Hanover to take the throne, by virtue of being descended of the Stuarts. Robert and his friend, the Earl of Belhoven, a member of the Upper House of the old parliament, emigrated in disgust to the North of Ireland. John W. Scott was a double cousin of Mrs. Lucy Webb Hayes, the wife of President Hayes, who was a daughter of Dr. James Webb of Fayette County, and a first cousin of Dr. Scott, the father of Mrs. Benjamin Harrison.

ANDREW JACKSON CASEY, President of the Inquirer Publishing Company of Owensboro, son of A. W. and Mary (Cagle) Casey, was born in Russellville, Kentucky, November 15, 1860. His father was born in De Kalb County, Tennessee, August 19, 1827; married Mary Cagle August 19, 1846; was a farmer; served in the Confederate army and was colorbearer in Colonel J. W. Caldwell's regiment, and was killed in the battle of Shiloh April 6, 1862.

His mother, Mary Cagle Casey, is a daughter of Charles Cagle, whose wife was Mary Demonbreun, daughter of Timothy Demonbreun, who lived near Nashville, and for whom Demonbreun street in that city was named. She was educated in the public schools; is now a resident of Russellville, Kentucky, and although past seventy-two years of age, still retains a vigorous intellect. Her grandfather, Timothy Demonbreun, was a soldier in the Revolutionary war.

Andrew J. Casey, after leaving school, which he did at an early age, found employment in the office of the Russellville Herald, and beginning as an office boy he was promoted step by step, learning the duties and how to perform them, in every department of the newspaper office, until, in 1885, he bought a half interest and became the editor of the Herald. He sold his interest in that paper in 1891 and purchased the Owensboro Inquirer, a daily and weekly Democratic newspaper, which, under his able management, has become one of the best papers published in the western part of the state, and a valuable property. Mr. Casey is of a retiring disposition, and has never sought political preferment or distinction, though he has numerous friends who would gladly thrust these honors upon him. His legion of admirers is the best evidence of his popularity. Mr. Casey was married April 17, 1894, to Lida Walker, daughter of the illustrious Judge E. Dudley Walker of Hartford, whose biography is given in this volume. She is of that type of woman who have made Kentucky famous. They have one son, Walker Casey.

HOMER HUDSON, formerly a prominent business man, but now retired, of Covington, was born in that city March 5, 1824, and is a son of John and Ann (Chance) Hudson. His father was born near Staunton, Virginia, in 1787. He received his education in his native county and emigrated from there to Kentucky in 1818, or about that time. For many years he was one of the leading merchants of Covington. His store was on the corner of Third and Garrard streets, and he owned a block of buildings known as Hudson Row. He served for a time as magistrate, but his principal ambition was to succeed in commercial pursuits, and to this he gave his entire time until his death, which occurred in 1825. James Hudson (grandfather) was a native of Virginia, and died in Staunton. He was a lineal descendant of Hendrick Hudson, the Holland nobleman who discovered the Hudson River and Hudson Bay.

Ann Chance Hudson (mother) was a native of Maryland, whose first husband was a Quaker, and after her marriage came west with her husband and located in Cincinnati. After the death of her first husband she married John Hudson in 1820. She died in 1886 aged eighty-seven years, and is buried in Highland Cemetery.

Homer Hudson received his education in the private schools in Boone County, and also at Kempt's Academy. After leaving school Mr. Hudson studied law in the office of Judge James Prior of Carrollton, who is the uncle of Chief Justice Prior of the Court of Appeals. In 1846 he was admitted to the bar and immediately entered upon practice. Finding that the law was not congenial to his tastes, Mr. Hudson, after two years' practice, abandoned the law and commenced merchandising, which he carried on successfully for seven years. At the expiration of this time he became the owner of the Empire Tobacco Works at Covington, which he operated for many years, becoming one of the best known tobacco manufacturers in the state. From 1850 to 1855 he was engaged in business in Louisiana, Missouri, in partnership with a Mr. Van Horn, under the firm name of Van Horn & Hudson.

In 1867 Mr. Hudson served as president of the City Council of Covington. He spent two years (1881 and 1882) with his family in Europe, visiting London, Paris, Brussels, Cologne, Switzerland, Italy and other interesting points on the continent. Mr. Hudson's beautiful home on Fifth street is largely furnished with rare specimens of bric-a-brac which were gathered on this European trip. In 1885 Mr. Hudson retired from active business. He is a director and stockholder in the Suspension Bridge Company, and has been for many years; a director of the First National Bank of Covington, and a director in the Covington Cemetery.

In 1857 Mr. Hudson was married to Esther Fowler, daughter of Edward Fowler and granddaughter of Major Jacob Fowler. She was born June 4, 1826, in Covington, Kentucky, and died April 31, 1894, leaving three children: John Shelley Hudson, a tobacconist of Covington; Ida Dell, now Mrs. Ida Prettyman, and Dr. Clifford Hudson, who studied medicine in the Ohio Medical College, and took a post-graduate course in a medical college in New York City. Mr. Hudson is well informed on all important questions and is liberal and independent in his opinions and in politics.

JOHN BUFORD HENDRICK was born in Frankfort, Kentucky, June 3, 1864, and is the son of John R. and Mary (Swigert) Hendrick, and is descended on his father's side from the Dutch Burghers of Holland, who in the sixteenth century fought Philip II. of Spain for fifty-one years and established the freedom and independence of Holland, and that Dutch republic was the fruit of their heroic resistance to the tyranny of Philip in that century.

John R. Hendrick (father) was born in Campbell County, Virginia, February 10, 1827, and emigrated to Kentucky when a young man. His education was received at Center College. He afterwards took a theological course at Princeton, and after entering the Presbyterian ministry, he removed to Frankfort, which was his home until the day of his death, November 28, 1881.

Phillip Swigert (maternal grandfather), in his day one of the most distinguished citizens of the state, was born May 27, 1798, and died in Frankfort, December 31, 1871, in the seventy-fourth year of his age. For fifty years he lived in that community and was one of its most active, useful and distinguished men. The farm on which he was born lies eight miles southeast of Lexington, in the present limits of Jessamine County, and is now owned by Thomas A. Davis. When quite young he wrote as a deputy in the Woodford Circuit Court under John McKinney. In 1822 he removed to Frankfort, and received the appointment of clerk of the Circuit Court of Franklin County, and was the successor of Francis P. Blair, Sr. He continued as circuit clerk by appointment and then by election, under the Constitution of 1849, until 1862, a period of thirty-two years. At the expiration of that time, wishing to embark in other pursuits, he declined being a candidate for further re-election to that office. He was elected to the state senate of Kentucky from the district composed of the counties of Franklin, Anderson and Woodford in 1865, for the term of four years. He was a man of remarkable financial ability, which was proven sufficiently when opportunities were afforded him for action. He was chairman of the State Board of Internal Improvements and was for many years president of the Farmers' Bank of Kentucky. Soon after his removal to Frankfort he was appointed commissioner, or agent, for the old Bank of Kentucky, the duties of which were to collect its assets and settle up its affairs, which he performed in the most satisfactory manner, and in the prosecution of which he visited nearly every county in the state.

He was one of the most distinguished members of the Masonic fraternity and was more widely known in that relation than any other man of his day. He became a Mason in 1819, at the age of twenty-one, and in the following year represented Landmark Lodge No. 41 in the Grand Lodge of Kentucky, which was in the same year that Henry Clay was elected and installed Grand Master of Masons in Kentucky. He was a lifelong friend of Henry Clay. After serving alternately as Grand Junior and Grand Senior Deacon he served some years as Grand Treasurer, and for twenty consecutive years afterwards acted as Grand Secretary of the Grand Lodge. Upon his retirement from office, as a testimonial of the high esteem in which he was held by his brethren, he was presented with an elegant Grand Secretary's jewel of gold. In 1858 he was elected Grand Pursuivant of the Grand Council, and held the same for several terms. He was elected Grand Master of the Grand Lodge of Kentucky in 1857; elected Grand Secretary of the Grand Chapter of Royal Arch Masons in 1822 and held the office with an interval of only two years until his death. For a period of forty-three years he was a constant and efficient member of Hiram Lodge No. 4 of Frankfort; was a Knight Templar, the members of which order, together with all other Masons in convenient distance, were present at his funeral, with all the imposing honors and ceremonies of that ancient and time-honored fraternity. He was a man of great energy of purpose, untiring industry and methodical habits. It did not matter how multifarious were his duties, he undertook them and accomplished them with great ability and fidelity. Whether of minor or greater importance, it made no difference; he did his duty and did it well. During his life he was nearly always one of the chief and directing spirits in the public affairs pertaining to his county and town, and his devotion to duty and his high moral rectitude were never questioned. No man enjoyed more fully the confidence and respect of the community in which he lived. For twenty years he was mayor of Frankfort; was a successful business man and left a large estate to his children. The ancestors of Phillip Swigert were from Zurich, Switzerland.

J. Buford Hendrick, his grandson, was reared in the city of Frankfort, and was educated in private schools. After leaving school he accepted a position in the Deposit Bank of Frankfort, where he also successfully managed the business affairs of his mother. In 1893 he was elected vice-president of the bank, which office he still holds. In 1889 he wedded Georgia, daughter of Jesse P. Lyons of Missouri, and has two children, Mary S. and J. Buford. Mr. Hendrick is a member and deacon in the Presbyterian Church, and a member of Hiram Lodge No. 4, Frankfort Chapter, Grand Consistory of Kentucky. In politics he is a Republican. The ancestors of the name of Hendrick are land owners in Holland. Henry Hudson, who, in the service of Holland, discovered the Hudson River and afterward became a land holder in the Dutch Republic, changed his name to Hendrick Hudson.

JAMES GUTHRIE COKE, editor of the Herald-Enterprise, Russellville, son of Richard Henry and Mary Elizabeth (Guthrie) Coke, and grandson of Honorable James Guthrie, was born in Louisville, Kentucky, June 18, 1841.

His father was born in Washington County, Kentucky, August 13, 1815; was a graduate of Miami University, Oxford, Ohio; studied law in old Transylvania University; began the practice of his profession in Springfield, Kentucky; moved to Louisville, Kentucky, in 1840, where he practiced law until his death, May 18, 1845. He was a member of the state legislature in 1837 and 1838; was married June 2, 1840, to Mary Elizabeth Guthrie, daughter of Honorable James Guthrie and Elizabeth Prather, his wife, of Louisville. She was born January 6, 1823, and was educated at Nazareth College, Nelson County. James Guthrie Coke is the only child of this union.

Mrs. Coke (mother) was married again in 1854 to John Caperton. He was born in Virginia and educated in the University of Virginia. He studied law in his native state and afterward continued his legal studies in New Orleans. In 1849 he moved to California. He was a deputy under

Colonel Jack Hayes, the first sheriff of San Francisco County, and as such opened the first court ever held in California. After his marriage he wound up his business in California, moved to Louisville, retired from active business, and took up his residence in the Guthrie homestead, which fell to his wife's share in the settlement of her father's estate. By this union there were four children: John H., Mary Eliza, Julia and Hugh Gaston; all of whom are dead but John H., who is a successful business man in Louisville, Kentucky.

Richard Coke (grandfather) was a native of Virginia, and one of the pioneers of Washington County, Kentucky.

James Guthrie (maternal grandfather) was born in Nelson County, Kentucky, December 5, 1792. He was educated at St. Mary's College and at Bardstown Academy. After a few years spent in flatboating to New Orleans, he studied law with Judge John Rowan; was admitted to the bar and began to practice at Bardstown.

He was appointed commonwealth attorney, under the old constitution, but resigned; removed to Louisville, where he soon acquired a lucrative practice; was a member of the City Council for many years; served repeatedly in both branches of the legislature; was a member of the constitutional convention and its presiding officer in 1849; was secretary of the United States treasury under President Pierce from 1853 to 1857; was a candidate for the nomination to the presidency before the Democratic national convention at Charleston, South Carolina, in 1860; was a delegate to the peace conference at Washington in 1860; also to the border state convention at Frankfort soon afterward; was offered a position in President Lincoln's cabinet, and afterward a major general's commission, with command of the division embracing Kentucky, both of which positions he declined to accept; was elected to the United States senate in 1865, but owing to feeble health, resigned in 1868, and died in Louisville, March 13, 1869.

His ability as a financier was illustrated in the management of his own affairs, no less than that of the national treasury and the Louisville & Nashville Railroad, in whose early history he was one of the master spirits, and by his indomitable energy and wise judgment the success of that road was attained after many years of threatened failure.

James Guthrie Coke was partly educated in Louisville, and when twelve years of age went to Washington City to live with his grandfather Guthrie, who was at that time secretary of the treasury. After attending private schools in Washington he went to Georgetown College, District of Columbia, and in 1857 to Georgetown College, Kentucky, and would have graduated in 1861, the same year that institution suspended on account of the war. He attended the law department of the University of Louisville; graduated in 1863, and began the practice of his profession in Louisville; was in the City Council for two years; served in the legislature from Louisville in 1871-72; was a director of the Louisville, Cincinnati & Lexington Railroad, and helped to organize, and was one of the first directors of the Manufacturing and Financial Company. He moved to a farm in Logan County in 1872; was twice elected on the board of magistrates; was elected a director of the Louisville & Nashville Railroad Company, and was elected a delegate from Logan County to the convention of 1890-91, which framed the present constitution of Kentucky. In 1884 he moved to Russellville and practiced law in the civil courts until 1888, in which year he connected himself with the Russellville Herald-Enterprise, of which he is editor. His paper is one of the best in the state, and Mr. Coke's strong, vigorous editorials wield a healthful influence on public opinion.

Mr. Coke is an able editor, as he was a distinguished lawyer, business man and public servant, before his newspaper work absorbed his attention; and is a man of sound judgment and unswerving principle, devoted to the progress and enlightenment of the people of his community. He is a trustee of Bethel College, a member of the Baptist Church, and a highly esteemed citizen.

Mr. Coke was married, first, September 27, 1865, to Jennie Winston, a native of Kentucky, daughter of David Y. and Elizabeth Winston. She was educated in Mrs. Nold's Louisville Female Seminary. By this union there was one son, James Guthrie Coke, born July 29, 1866. Mrs. Coke died October 9, 1870. His second marriage was celebrated November 5, 1873, to Queenie Marshall Blackburn, daughter of General Samuel Davis Blackburn. She was born in Bowling Green, Kentucky, June 3, 1855; was educated at Bowling Green and Nazareth College in Nelson County, and is one of the most cultured and refined ladies in Southern Kentucky.

They have three children: John Caperton, Elizabeth Blackburn and Richard H. Coke.

SPENCER C. LONG of Georgetown, son of Nimrod Long and Elizabeth (Curd) Long, was born in Russellville, Kentucky, March 3, 1835.

His father, Nimrod Long, was a native of Logan County, and died in Russellville in 1887, in the seventy-fifth year of his age. It was said of him that Logan County never produced a more honorable and upright man. He was a farmer of the most progressive class, a man of rare business qualifications, and was known as one of the wealthiest men in the county. For some years before his death he was engaged in the banking business in Russellville, and in 1868 the notorious bank robbers known as the James brothers robbed the bank and wounded Mr. Long; but fortunately the wound did not prove fatal, and he continued the business without loss to his depositors.

He was a faithful member of the Baptist Church, and was liberal in his support of the gospel. He was also one of the largest contributors to Bethel College, and his charities were innumerable and were chiefly unknown to others.

John Slaughter Long (grandfather) was born in Culpeper County, Virginia, and coming to Kentucky, was among the pioneers of Logan County. He was a farmer and one of the best citizens of his county. He died in 1839, having reached the age of seventy-six years.

Gabriel Long (great-grandfather) was a major and served under Generals Washington and Greene in the Revolutionary war. With Colonel James Slaughter and Chief Justice John Marshall, he had the honor of being in the battle of the "Great Bridge," the first battle that was fought in Virginia, and was present at the last, the surrender of Lord Cornwallis.

In 1777 Gabriel Long was assigned to the Eleventh Regiment, commanded by General Daniel Morgan. He was one of the sufferers at Valley Forge in 1778. Among his messmates was John Marshall, who was afterward Chief Justice of the United States Supreme Court. Gabriel Long was a gallant soldier, a true patriot, and lived to a great age and died in Virginia. The Longs were of English and Norman descent, and were among the earliest settlers of Virginia.

Elizabeth Curd Long (mother) was born in Logan County, in 1814, and died in 1845. Her father, Spencer Curd, was a native of Shelby County and was for twenty years circuit and county clerk of Logan County. During a part of that time the circuit embraced all of the southern part of Kentucky, a territory larger than the states of Rhode Island and Connecticut combined. Mr. Curd died in Russellville in 1833.

John Curd (maternal grandfather) was a native of Virginia, a soldier in the Revolutionary war and was taken prisoner by the British at the battle of Germantown. The ancestors of the subject of this sketch on both sides were patriotic citizens and soldiers in the war of independence.

Spencer C. Long spent his boyhood in Russellville, and attended Georgetown College, graduating in the class of 1854. His first business venture was as a wholesale grocer in Louisville, where he was a member of the firm of Hall & Long for six years. The firm dissolved about 1866; and he was then engaged in the tobacco business in Louisville until 1878, when he went to Russellville and took charge of his father's bank, in which business he remained until his father's death.

In 1887 he organized the Deposit Bank of Russellville, of which he was president until 1891, when he resigned and removed to Georgetown. He owns a fine farm almost within the limits of Georgetown, and is deeply interested in its cultivation, while having other investments of various kinds in the city.

During his residence in Louisville he was a member of the school board, and while in Russellville he served three times as mayor of that thriving city, and was, and still is, treasurer of Bethel College. He is a member of the Baptist Church, and in all respects is an exemplary and enterprising citizen.

He was married in 1856 to Camelia Gano, daughter of Dr. Stephen Gano of Georgetown. They have two sons and three daughters: Stephen G. Long is a lawyer in Los Angeles, California; Nimrod Long is in the grocery business at Owensboro; Nelly Long married Church Blackburn of Georgetown; Mary Long married Dr. Walter Byrne of Russellville; and Bessie Long married Robert Finnell of Georgetown.

CHARLES O. REYNOLDS, Register of the Land Office, son of O. A. and Catherine (Rice) Reynolds, was born in Lexington, Kentucky, March 23, 1856.

His father was born in Anderson County, Kentucky, in 1823, and died in Lexington, July 22, 1883. He was a well-known business man of Lexington, where he was in the grocery business for thirty-two years; was a leading member of the Baptist Church, a Republican in politics and a member of the Odd Fellow's fraternity, in which he was prominent for many years.

Catherine Rice Reynolds (mother) was a native of Rose Hill, Fayette County, daughter of Solomon Rice; was educated in the county schools; was a very active member of the Christian Church, in which her father was one of the organizers in Lexington. She died in 1866.

William Reynolds (grandfather) was born in Kentucky, in 1800, and was educated in Anderson County; married Margaret Abbott of that county; was a farmer, industrious, successful and highly esteemed, and was a leading spirit in the Old Pisgah Church. He died in 1868, and his wife in 1888.

William Reynolds (great-grandfather) and his father, Aaron Reynolds, were famous Indian fighters in the pioneer days of Kentucky, and William was awarded a land grant by Virginia for his three years' service in the Virginia State Line troops.

Charles O. Reynolds went into his father's grocery as a salesman before he could see over the counters and learned something about business before completing his education. He attended the city schools and won a scholarship in the Agricultural and Mechanical College, and completed his schooling in that institution.

When twenty years of age he embarked in the grocery business with his brother William, and was thus engaged until 1882, when he was appointed to a position in the United States internal revenue service by Colonel A. M. Swope, remaining until 1885. In the examination of revenue employes Mr. Reynolds was one of two men in the district who received a perfect mark, which resulted in his promotion to the position of division deputy under T. C. McDowell, Colonel W. C. Goodloe's successor having been the first man appointed by Collector Goodloe. He resigned in January, 1893, and was employed as superintendent of the new distillery of J. E. Pepper, and remained with that establishment until it shut down, temporarily, after which he was engaged in the coal business until his election as register of the land office.

His nomination for that office in the Republican convention was a surprise to him as he had not sought the nomination, which was secured by his personal friends. His selection was most fortunate, as he was well known throughout the central portion of the state and popular with the rank and file of the party, and by his gentlemanly, pleasing manner and striking personality he made many votes for his ticket. He made an active canvass and proved himself a worthy leader and a competent man for the office. In the November election, 1895, he received the largest majority in the state, having a plurality of 9,878 votes which was 966 votes ahead of the ticket. In his new position he has demonstrated his fitness for the office to which he was elected and has made many friends for himself and for his party.

Mr. Reynolds was married September 23, 1884, to Josephine DeLime of Frankfort. She was born November 10, 1866; educated in Frankfort schools and died July 11, 1888, and is buried at Lexington. Her father, Professor Louis A. DeLime, was sent to this country by the French authorities to investigate the culture of sugar beets. In France he was a noted chemist and the author of several scientific works. He was awarded the first prize at the Louisville Exposition for the best apparatus for aging whiskey.

The five children of O. A. and Catherine Rice Reynolds (parents) were: William, who accompanied the Greely relief expedition and traveled extensively over the world, now a resident of Lexington; Charles O., subject of this sketch; Mollie, married Reed Taylor, went to Chicago and died there in 1881, and Addie and Frank, who are living in Lexington.

CHARLES LATHAM, a prominent and highly successful merchant of Hopkinsville, is a native of that city, Christian County, Kentucky.

His father, John C. Latham, was born in Russellville, Kentucky, November 6, 1814, and removed with his parents to Christian County when he was five years of age. He was educated in Hopkinsville, and after leaving school was clerk of the Circuit Court of Christian County for several years. He was then engaged in mercantile pursuits for fifteen years, and in 1865 organized the Bank of Hopkinsville; was elected president of the bank and served faithfully in that capacity until the day of his death, 1885. His estimable widow, whose maiden name was Virginia Glass, is still living in Hopkinsville. His family consisted of three children: John C. Latham, Jr., Mary R. and Charles M. Latham, the subject of this sketch.

John and Nancy (Moorehead) Latham (grandparents) were Virginians, who came to Kentucky and located in Logan County in the earlier years of the present century and removed to Christian County in 1819. They belonged to that sturdy and intelligent class to whom the county in which they lived owes its high moral and intellectual standing at the present day.

Charles M. Latham secured a good practical education in the excellent schools of Hopkinsville and Bethel College, Russellville, Kentucky; engaged in business while still in his teens, and at once developed a remarkable aptitude for business, to which he gave his undivided attention, and in the course of the eighteen years of his mercantile experience he has steadily risen step by step until he is counted one of the leading merchants in his section of the state, and one of the most enterprising, industrious and substantial citizens of Hopkinsville.

He has made a careful study of all the details in the various lines of his trade, being particular to buy the best qualities of salable goods so that he can give his personal guarantee with each sale. His well known integrity and honesty of purpose have won for him the implicit confidence of the people.

Mr. Latham has been directly or indirectly identified with the general prosperity of his native city, being always ready to assist in any movement that promises to add to its further development and growth. He has investments in bank, hotel and turnpike stock; has never held office or had any aspirations in that direction, but he uses his influence and casts his vote for men and measures which tend to the improvement and elevation of the public service.

GEORGE HENRY MOORE, deceased, who was a leading and influential merchant of Louisville, was the son of George J. and Catherine (Fonda) Moore, and a native of Louisville, born January 10, 1835; died January 14, 1896.

His father was a native of Ashford, Connecticut, who came to Louisville in 1833, where he resided until his death, which occurred in 1875, aged sixty-five years. He was for some time a private banker; and subsequently engaged in the wholesale grocery business as a member of the firm of Fonda, Moore & Company, in which he continued for a number of years. He was a Whig in the days of Henry Clay, who always received his vote when Mr. Clay was a candidate. In 1856 he became a Democrat and affiliated with that party until his death, in 1875, although persistently refusing to accept any office, political or otherwise. The ancestors of the Moores were English.

Catherine Fonda Moore (mother) was a native of Troy, New York. She died in 1892, aged seventy-five years. The Fondas were originally from Holland. On coming to America they settled near Troy or Albany, New York.

Mr. Moore received his education principally in a private school in Shelbyville, taught by S.

B. Womack. After leaving school he entered his father's wholesale grocery as a salesman or clerk, continuing until 1858, when he went to Jackson, Mississippi, and accepted a position as bookkeeper in a large wholesale house, where he remained until the beginning of the war. Then he enlisted in the Confederate army and was made captain of Company I, Thirty-ninth Mississippi Infantry. After the surrender at Port Hudson he had command of his regiment. He was captured by the Federal soldiers at Altoona, Georgia, and was held a prisoner of war at Johnson's Island until the close of the war.

He then returned to Louisville and accepted employment as a clerk in the wholesale whiskey house of his uncle, Jesse Moore; and in 1868 became a partner in the house, the firm name being changed to Jesse Moore & Co. In 1892 Mr. Moore purchased his uncle's interest and conducted the business alone until his death.

He was also for many years engaged in the distilling business in partnership with Mr. Max Selliger, under the firm name of Moore & Selliger, having two large distilleries in Louisville, where the popular brands of whiskey known as Bellmont, Astor and Nutwood are manufactured.

Mr. Moore was also the senior member of the firm of Moore, Hunt & Company, wholesale liquor dealers in San Francisco.

He was for many years president of the People's Bank of Louisville until its liquidation in 1893; a director in the Fidelity Trust Company of Louisville, and for many years director in the Masonic Widows' and Orphans' Home, an institution in which he was deeply interested, as indeed he was in all worthy charities. He gave liberally to the poor, and said nothing about it. Few men have done more to assist his fellow men than did George H. Moore.

He was a Democrat and took a lively interest in the election of capable men to office; but refused to accept any office himself. He was a public-spirited citizen, who felt a great pride in his city, and was always interested in and ready to promote any enterprise that he deemed beneficial to the city.

He was married in 1867 to Florence, daughter of Cornelius Deweese of Carroll County. Two sons and two daughters were the result of this union: Jessie, wife of George D. Moore of Worcester, Massachusetts; Shirley Moore, who married Frankie, daughter of the late B. F. Guthrey of Louisville; and Percival and Georgie.

Mr. Moore was a great lover of art and had the finest private gallery in the city, containing about seventy-five very fine and costly oil paintings; a rich legacy to his surviving family.

L. FRANK JOHNSON, State Auditor's Agent and an able Attorney-at-Law of Frankfort, son of William P. and Mary Elizabeth (Cardwell) Johnson, is a native of Franklin County, Kentucky.

His father was a descendant of Presbyterian stock from the North of Ireland. The farm on which he was born and reared, in Franklin County —four miles from Frankfort—has belonged to the Johnson family since about the time of the Revolutionary war. William P. Johnson learned the trade of house carpenter and was a lifetime resident of his native county; was an elder in the Southern Presbyterian Church; an honest business man and one who loved and honored the religion which he professed. He died in 1875, at the age of fifty-six years.

William Johnson (grandfather) was born in the northern part of Ireland; came to America and located in Franklin County, Kentucky, at a very early day; married Sallie Arnold, daughter of John Arnold, who was sheriff of Franklin County in 1802, and a granddaughter of Colonel William McBride, a noted Indian fighter, who perished at the bloody battle of Blue Lick Springs in August, 1780. The first house built between Frankfort and Harrodsburg was the work of Frank Johnson's ancestors.

Mary Elizabeth Cardwell Johnson (mother) is a descendant of a Welsh family of Baptists, who, with the Broaduses, Brevards and the family of Colonel Richard M. Johnson, settled in Virginia in 1722. She was born in Franklin County in 1830, on the farm upon which she is now living. She is a faithful adherent of the religion of her ancestors.

John Cardwell (maternal grandfather) was born in Culpeper County, Virginia, and was closely related to the Crockett families of Virginia and Kentucky. He located in Franklin County when he was a young man and volunteered as a soldier in the Northwestern army in the War of 1812. He was an industrious and enterprising farmer, and died at the ripe age of ninety-three years.

L. Frank Johnson was reared on his father's farm, and obtained his education by his own exertions, working his way through Forest Academy, which he attended one year, and through the Kentucky Military Institute (three years), graduating from that institution in 1880. After teaching school one session he began the study of law with Judge Patrick N. Major, and was admitted to the bar in 1883.

In 1886 he formed a partnership with his former preceptor, Judge Major, and this relation continued until 1890, when Mr. Johnson was elected county attorney. He held this office for four years and four months, performing its duties with great credit to himself and to the satisfaction of the people who honored him with their suffrage. At the expiration of his term he was appointed state auditor's agent for Franklin County, which office he still holds in connection with the practice of his profession.

In speaking of Mr. Johnson's characteristics an acquaintance of his said: "His mind is methodical; untiring industry combined with clear judgment qualify him for the management of legal business in a degree that points to a bright future."

He is a steward in the Methodist Church, faithful in his duties and firm in his religious convictions.

He was married in 1882 to Mary S. McEwin, daughter of William McEwin of Frankfort, and has one daughter, Mary, and two sons, William F. Major Johnson and Benjamin P. Johnson.

JAMES M. GRAVES, Cashier of the Lexington City National Bank, and a well known business man of that city, son of William W. and Polly C. (Graves) Graves, was born in Fayette County, Kentucky, December 7, 1834. William, W. Graves was born in Culpeper County, Virginia, October 5, 1787, and emigrated to Kentucky with his parents when very young and settled in Woodford County on a farm. After receiving an ordinary English education in Woodford County he went to Lexington and engaged in the dry goods business, in which he continued for several years, when he returned to the farm. In 1850 he returned to Lexington, where he engaged in horse breeding, and continued in this until his death, which occurred March 8, 1871. He served as a private soldier in the War of 1812, remaining in the army until the close of the conflict. In 1852 he was elected magistrate and held this office as long as he lived. He was a Democrat, an active politician and a member of the Baptist Church. His father was Richard Grant Graves, who was born in Culpeper County, Virginia; came to Kentucky and settled in Woodford County, where he died in 1843. William W. Graves wedded Polly C. Graves, daughter of John Graves, of Fayette County. She was born February 15, 1797, and is now living at the age of ninety-eight years, and is in full possession of all her faculties. Since 1871, she has made her home with her son, J. M. Graves.

John Graves (maternal grandfather) was a native of Louisa County, Virginia; born March 2, 1775, and came to Lexington, where he was engaged in farming until his death in 1848. He was a Henry Clay Whig; was in the War of 1812, and served as colonel in the state militia. His father, Thomas Graves, was also a Virginian by birth and came to Kentucky as a major on the staff of General Lafayette; after the close of the War of the Revolution he settled near Lexington on a very large tract of land, where he died in the fall of 1801.

James M. Graves received his education in the Fayette County common schools and entered Transylvania University in 1851, where he studied for two years and then engaged in business with his father in the horse and stock business until 1861, when he entered the Confederate service as a member of General Abe Buford's Brigade in the Signal Service, in which capacity he continued until 1863, when he was transferred to the command of General John C. Breckinridge, and was afterward assigned to the Signal Service of the Army of the Tennessee, where he remained until the close of the war, when his command surrendered at Greensburg, North Carolina, to General

Sherman. Returning home, he again turned his attention to horse breeding, and continued in this until 1880, when he accepted the office of president of Lexington City National Bank, and served one year, when he was elected to his present position as cashier of that bank. He is an ardent Democrat and has filled several political offices; was appointed magistrate to fill out the unexpired term of his father; was elected county supervisor in 1870 and held the office until 1878. In 1890, after having served for twenty years as a member of the City Council, he resigned and was immediately re-elected by the people. Mr. Graves is director in the Security Safety Vault & Trust Company, president of the Southern Building & Loan Company (a branch of the Knoxville, Tennessee, Company of that name), treasurer of the Southern Mutual Investment Company, and is also connected with the hardware company of Kidd & Graves, Lexington. Mr. Graves is a member of the Baptist Church and has always been interested in the advancement of the educational, religious and business interests of Lexington.

J. M. Graves was married July 25, 1867, to Addie G. Allen, daughter of Rev. Buford E. Allen, a Baptist clergyman, and Elmira B. (Graves) Allen, his wife, and granddaughter of Rev. Joseph Craig, the pioneer Baptist minister of Kentucky. Mrs. Graves is a native of Kentucky and was educated at Georgetown College. They have four children: Mary Elenora, Buford Allen, J. Madison and George Thomas Graves.

MAJOR HENRY S. HALE, ex-State Treasurer, son of Nicholas and Rhoda (Crouch) Hale, was born near Bowling Green, Warren County, Kentucky, May 4, 1836. Nicholas Hale came from Virginia with his father and settled in Graves County and was a soldier in the War of 1812. The Hales are of English descent. Rhoda Crouch Hale (mother) was a daughter of David Crouch, who was a private in the Mexican war, and died in Graves County. The Crouches are of Scotch-Irish descent. Major Hales' family moved to Graves County when he was a mere boy, and he received his education in the county schools. Both of his parents died just as he was entering his teens. He had the true Southern spirit, and with a heart full of love for the "Sunny South," he espoused the cause of the Confederacy, and fought gallantly through the rebellion. He entered the army as captain of a company in the Seventh Kentucky Regiment, and was soon promoted to major, and was in command of the regiment in several hard-fought battles. He was severely wounded in the left hip at Harrisburg, Mississippi, and disabled for several months, when he was recalled by General Forrest, and for gallantry on the battlefield of "Brice's Cross Roads" was promoted to the rank of lieutenant-colonel and assigned to the Third and Seventh Consolidated Regiments.

The following extract from a Mayfield paper, describing Major Hale as a soldier, is worthy of publication: "Major Hale was a young man of about twenty-four years of age. He was as full of zeal and chivalry as the fine climate and good soil of Southern Kentucky could make one. He was a live, wide-awake officer, a man for emergencies, and would undertake anything he was commanded to do by his superior officers. Nothing was impossible with him. He had a loud, clear voice and a fine presence, and made a fine impression; in short he was a model soldier. He commanded the regiment in some of the hardest fought battles and always did it elegantly and knightly. His conduct in the face of the enemy was always inspiring to others. At one time when the regiment showed signs of wavering he snatched the colors and ran forward, flaunting them in the face of the enemy. The effect was magical; every man moved forward and the enemy was driven from its position."

In 1866 Major Hale was elected sheriff of Graves County, which office he held four years, and in 1871 he was elected State Senator and served his constituents faithfully. He was the chairman of the Democratic Committee of Graves County for a number of years. In 1876 a National Bank of Mayfield was organized, and at its first election Major Hale was made president, which place he held sixteen years, when he was chosen by Governor Buckner to fill out the unexpired term of Judge Sharp, who resigned the office of state treasurer. At the expiration of his term he became a candidate before the people and was elected by a very complimentary vote. The manner in which he has managed the affairs of office, the ability he displayed as a financier, and the general official conduct of Major Hale and as a private citizen are well known to the business men of the state.

Major Hale was a leading spirit in founding the West Kentucky College, an institution of learning, of which the people of Mayfield are justly proud. He is a man of sterling worth to the state, the church and the country. His integrity and true manhood have won for him the love and respect of all who know him.

Major Hale was married November 8, 1865, to Miss Virginia A. Gregory of Mississippi. They have six living children, four sons and two daughters: Nathan A., assistant cashier of the First National Bank of Mayfield; William Lindsay, who was assistant treasurer of the state during his father's term of office; Henry S., Jr., a student in the Military Academy at Danville, and Joseph Theodore. The daughters are Annie B. and Mary E.

Major Hale was a candidate for secretary of state in the late election (the constitution forbidding that he should hold the office of treasurer another term), but he went down with a great many other good men in the Republican year of 1895. He is a prominent member of the Christian Church, through his connection with which he performs many charitable acts and good deeds.

JUDGE FELIX GRUNDY was born in Berkeley County, Virginia, September 11, 1777; brought in early boyhood to Washington County, Kentucky; educated at Bardstown Academy; studied law, and began the practice at Springfield; in 1799, a month before reaching the age of twenty-two, was elected a member from Washington County of the convention which formed the second constitution of Kentucky; a representative in the Kentucky legislature, from the same county, in 1800, 1801, and 1802, and from Nelson County in 1804, 1805, and 1806; was commissioned, December 10, 1806, one of the judges of the Court of Appeals of Kentucky, and April 11, 1807, five months before he was thirty years old, chief justice of that high court; removed, in 1808, to Nashville, and took the highest rank at that bar; was a representative in Congress from Tennessee, 1811-14, and afterward for several years in the legislature of Tennessee; United States senator, 1829-38; in the latter year was appointed by President Van Buren attorney general of the United States; resigned that position in 1840, and was again elected United States senator, but did not take his seat—dying at Nashville, December 12, 1840, aged sixty-three. Judge Grundy was one of the most distinguished lawyers and statesmen of the western country; in the councils of the nation he had but few equals and fewer superiors.

WARNER ELMORE SETTLE, Judge of the Eighth Judicial Circuit, whose home is in Bowling Green, is descended from a worthy ancestry and the devotees of the theory that the law of heredity is applicable to the moral and intellectual as well as the physical man, have here strong evidence in support of their views. Mr. Settle was born in Green County, near Greensburg, Kentucky, January 21, 1850. His parents, Simon and Mary (Barnett) Settle, have been deceased many years, and his youth was spent on the farm of his maternal grandfather, Judge Thomas R. Barnett, a man of fine intellect, irreproachable character and of great influence in his community. He served the people of his county for twenty-four years as judge of the County Court, and represented them twice in the State Legislature. Young Settle, though unfortunate in the loss of his parents, was peculiarly fortunate in having the care and guidance of his grandfather. His educational training was such as the schools of Greensburg, his county town, afforded at that time, and they were excellent. He remained in school until eighteen years of age, and it was intended that he should have a collegiate education, but the emancipation proclamation of President Lincoln changed all that by liberating the slaves, which were about all the property his parents had left him, and his grandfather lost heavily by the same edict. But the young man was industrious and studious, and while he did not go to college he continued his studies so faithfully that he was well equipped before he reached his manhood, and having since then continued his studies he has acquired a fund of knowledge of which many collegiates can not boast. This knowledge not only pertains to the legal profession, but embraces a wide range of general information and literature, and he is particularly devoted to biography and history.

In 1869 Mr. Settle began the study of law and in January, 1870, he removed to Bowling Green and diligently pursued his legal studies while assisting in the office of the clerk of the Warren County Court. He was admitted to the bar, September 15, 1871, and in the same year formed a partnership with John B. Grider, the present judge of the Warren County Court, the style of the firm being Settle & Grider. This partnership was dissolved in 1875, when he formed a similar relation with Hon. Robert Rodes, an able lawyer and a member of the recent Constitutional Convention. W. O. Rodes, son of the senior member of this firm, came in later and the style of the firm was then Rodes, Settle & Rodes. Mr. Settle retired from this firm December 1, 1891, and became associated with John B. Rodes, a younger son of Robert Rodes, and this latter partnership was interrupted in 1892 by the elevation of Mr. Settle to the bench.

Warner E. Settle is learned in the law, accurate, able and eloquent as a pleader and advocate and was a very successful lawyer, his practice extending over his circuit and adjacent counties and to the Court of Appeals at Frankfort. He loved his profession and was equally at home whether pleading a cause before the chancellor or arguing a question before a jury, and retired from practice enjoying an enviable reputation. His nomination and election to the bench were exceedingly complimentary as both were without opposition, and this, too, in a district which abounds in "good timber for the bench." As a judge he has proven himself competent and popular and has reflected honor upon his profession by his quiet dignity, his pleasing manner and his correct and unbiased decisions. He is known as an "Honest Judge," and the members of the bar as well as their clients know that he will give them a patient hearing and a fair trial.

Warner E. Settle and Shelly Rodes were married November 2, 1875, an alliance which has added greatly to his happiness and usefulness. She is the eldest daughter of Hon. Robert Rodes, his former law partner, and is a very intelligent and highly accomplished lady, deservedly possessing the esteem of a large circle of friends and acquaintances. The family circle is enlivened by the presence of three sons and three daughters.

Judge Settle, on the paternal side, is of English descent. The first one of the family who came from England located in Virginia, where there are still many of the descendants. The great grandfather of Judge Settle, with an elder brother, came from Virginia to Kentucky in 1796, and the two settled on adjoining farms on Beaver Creek in Barren County. They were men of intelligence and of excellent character, and several of the Settle family, descendants, no doubt, of the English ancestor mentioned, have attained distinction, among whom may be mentioned Rev. H. C. Settle, D. D., of Louisville; Hon. Evan E. Settle of Owen County; Hon. Thomas Settle, deceased, late Judge of the United States District Court of North Carolina, and his son, Thomas Settle, present congressman from that state.

The paternal grandfather of Judge Settle's mother was a South Carolinian of Scotch-Irish descent, who served in the War of the Revolution under General Francis Marion, and received a bullet wound in each shoulder. Thomas Elmore, the mother's maternal grandfather, was of an excellent Virginia family and served through the Revolutionary war as a captain of Virginia infantry.

JOHN C. RUSSELL, lawyer, and enterprising citizen of Louisville, son of John W. and Ann M. (Julian) Russell, was born in Franklin County, Kentucky, June 30, 1849.

His father was a native of Rockbridge County, Virginia, and came to Kentucky with his father when he was nine months of age, in 1796, and located in Franklin County, where he made his home until his death in 1870. He was a man of influence in politics, in the Presbyterian Church—of which he was a member—in business and in public affairs; represented Franklin, Shelby and

Anderson Counties in the Kentucky Senate from 1846 to 1850; was a pioneer in steamboating on the Mississippi River; was superintendent of snag-boats on that river, and was chiefly and always an enterprising farmer in Franklin County. At the age of sixteen he enlisted for the War of 1812, and served his country faithfully for two years. He was a warm personal friend of John J. Crittenden—for whom his son was named—and was the companion, associate and the equal of many of the great Kentuckians who were better known only on account of the public positions which they held.

James Russell (grandfather) was a native of Rockbridge County, Virginia; removed to Franklin County, Kentucky, in 1796, where he completed his four score years and died in 1849. He was a soldier in the Revolutionary war, serving under Generals Washington and Greene at Yorktown.

The Russells who settled in the American colonies some twenty years before the beginning of the Revolutionary war were of Scotch lineage, and many of that name were natives of the North of Ireland, but these were also of Scotch parentage.

Ann M. Julian Russell (mother) was a sister of the father of John Julian of Frankfort, who died in 1890, aged seventy-three years. She was a very active and faithful member of the Presbyterian Church, and a most excellent Christian woman.

John C. Russell attended that excellent school in Frankfort taught by B. B. Sayre, and spent one year in the scientific department of Yale College; graduated from the law department of the University of Louisville in 1874, and began the practice of his profession in Louisville, and soon found his place as a thoroughly reliable and substantial lawyer.

His career has been one of uninterrupted success from professional, business and social points of view. Enjoying a very large practice in the civil courts, he has been able to command the capital for investment in a number of business and financial enterprises.

For ten years he was a director in the Merchants' National Bank, is a director in the Louisville Trust Company, for many years has been a member of the executive committee of that company; president of the Grahamton Manufacturing Company (cotton mill), director in the Southern Electric Railway Company of St. Louis, takes an active part in politics, and is now chairman of the Democratic Committee for the Eighth and Ninth Wards of the City of Louisville—not caring for office, but for the promotion of the best interests of the Democratic party. He has been urged frequently to accept office, but has always declined; is a member of the Sons of the American Revolution and of the Scotch-Irish Society of Kentucky; and is a member of the Second Presbyterian Church.

Mr. Russell was married June 27, 1882, to Lila P. Anderson, daughter of W. George Anderson of Louisville. She died in 1883, leaving one child, Lila, who died April 18, 1884.

Mr. Russell is a brother of Mrs. Mary B. R. Day, formerly state librarian, whose sketch will be found in this work.

THE HON. ROBERT TRIMBLE was born in Berkeley County, Virginia, and when three years old, his father emigrated to Kentucky. He received but the imperfect rudiments of an education—such only as could be had in a new settlement. He, however, improved himself, by teaching for a few years, and reading carefully the scanty libraries afforded by his neighborhood. After so imperfect a probation, he commenced the study of the law, under George Nicholas. That eminent man dying before he had completed his studies, he continued them under James Brown; and, in 1803, was licensed by the Court of Appeals to practice his profession. He commenced his career in Paris, and in the same year was elected a member of the legislature from the county of Bourbon. But the stormy life of a politician not being congenial to his disposition or taste, he ever afterward refused to be a candidate for political office—even to be nominated, on two occasions, for the United States' senate, when his assent only was necessary to secure his election. He devoted himself exclusively to his profession, and rapidly rose to the first class of jurists. In 1808, he was commissioned second judge of the Court of Appeals. He retained this place but a short time, but long enough to greatly distinguish himself in it by his rectitude, learning and ability. He was appointed chief justice of Kentucky in 1810, but, in consequence of his limited circumstances, declined the first judicial station of the commonwealth. After retiring from the bench, he resumed, with great assiduity, the practice of his profession; and, in 1813, was appointed a district attorney for the state. He continued at the bar, with eminent and profitable success, until 1816, when he was appointed by President Madison judge of the Kentucky district. He filled this office until 1826, when he was promoted by John Quincy Adams to the Supreme Court of the United States. He died the 25th day of August, 1828, in the fifty-second year of his age, and in the full vigor of his powers.

MAJ. GEN. JOSEPH WARREN, M. D., was one of the most distinguished patriots of the American Revolutionary war; was born at Roxbury, near Boston, in 1741—the son of a farmer; entered Harvard University, at fourteen, and was there remarkable for his talents, fine address, and bold and independent spirit; studied medicine, and had rapid and high success in the practice; on two occasions, delivered eloquent orations on March 5, the anniversary of the Boston massacre, and became prominent in politics, as a public speaker and writer; was president of the provincial congress of Massachusetts, in 1775; participated in the battle of Lexington, April 19, 1775; June 14, 1775, was appointed major general of the military force of Massachusetts province; and at the battle of Bunker Hill, in Boston, on June 17, 1775, when the American troops—after three times repelling the British troops—exhausted their ammunition and were compelled to retire, he was killed by a random shot, among the last to abandon the entrenchments. Congress passed a resolution to erect a monument to his memory, which long occupied the site of the present Bunker Hill monument.

THOMAS FRANCIS MARSHALL, eldest son of Dr. Louis Marshall, was born in Frankfort, Kentucky, June 7, 1801, and was educated chiefly by his parents, both of whom were accomplished scholars. His studies in history, as the basis of jurisprudence and moral and political philosophy, were completed in Virginia, under the direction of James Marshall, a relative and a man of erudition. On his return to Kentucky, he studied law in the office of Hon. John J. Crittenden. He again made a visit to Virginia, to attend a convention called to form a new constitution of that state, that he might improve himself by witnessing the intellectual strife in which were engaged those master minds, Chief Justice Marshall, John Randolph, James Madison, James Monroe, and other kindred spirits who were members of that body. He remained in Richmond five months. Thenceforward his mind took a political direction, he studied the political questions of the day, and entered upon their discussion.

His political career commenced with his election, in 1832, to the Kentucky legislature, from Woodford County, as a friend of Henry Clay. During that session he signalized himself by a very able report against "nullification," in answer to the communication on that subject addressed by South Carolina to the several states. In 1833, he removed to Louisville to practice his profession, but abandoned it to again enter the field of politics. He was elected to the legislature for two terms. In 1837 he was beaten for Congress by Hon. William J. Graves, and, mortified at the result, he once more returned to Woodford County, which sent him twice to the legislature.

Mr. Marshall was elected to the lower branch of Congress from the "Ashland district," in 1841. He spoke often in that body, but only two of his speeches were reported. Disgusted at the manner his speeches had been reported, he unwisely said to the reporters, they "must not pass on the public their infernal gibberish for my English." They took him at his word. Mr. Marshall had been elected as a friend of Mr. Clay, but took issue with that eminent statesman on the United States Bank charter and the Bankrupt bill, as he did subsequently on the question of annexation of Texas. The district he represented was devoted to Mr. Clay, and hence Mr. Marshall declined to offer for Congress for the next term, as his defeat was certain. He, however, "took the stump," and canvassed the state for Mr. Polk, for president. In 1845, he ran for Congress, but was beaten by

Hon. Garret Davis. He next served one year as captain of a cavalry company in the Mexican war. Some time after his return home, he was beaten for the convention to frame a new constitution for the state. He advocated the election of General Scott for president in 1852, and was elected to the legislature from Woodford County in 1853, which was his last public service.

Mr. Marshall never again aspired to public position, but devoted his time to the law. Occasionally he delivered a political address, but was hardly recognized as a politician. He gave a series of "Discourses on History," in various cities, and charmed his hearers by his wit, genius, eloquence, and learning. Civil war ensued. Its events followed each other in rapid succession, and Marshall, like all other civilians, was overshadowed by their tremendous importance. He appeared no more in public excepting in the courts. He died at the home farm near Versailles, Woodford County, Kentucky, on September 22, 1864.

Marshall was brilliant alike at the bar, on the stump, and in the forum. His powers of oratory and eloquence were unrivaled, matchless, and yet he was withal a pre-eminent logician, and was in truth a remarkable man, and such as we may "not look upon his like again."

JUDGE JOHN ROWAN was an able jurist and statesman, and one of the most distinguished men in the western country. He was a native of Pennsylvania. His father, William Rowan, at the close of the Revolutionary war came to Kentucky, in the hope of repairing the ravages made in his private fortune. Kentucky was then a wilderness, the choice hunting ground of many hostile tribes of savages—the field of hazardous adventure, the scene of savage outrage, the theater of ceaseless war, an arena drenched in blood and reeking with slaughter. In March, 1783, the father of John Rowan settled in Louisville, then an insignificant village. In the spring of 1784, when John was eleven years old, his father, with five other families, made a settlement at the Long Falls of Green River, then about one hundred miles from any white settlement. This region was resorted to by a band of the Shawnee tribe of Indians, as a hunting ground, and Mr. Rowan and his neighbors had many encounters with their savage foes. At the age of seventeen, he entered a classical school kept at Bardstown, by a Dr. Priestly. In this school were educated many of those men who have since figured conspicuously in the history of Kentucky, and on the broader theater of national politics. Here John Rowan was remarkable among his fellows for the facility with which he mastered the most difficult branches. He obtained an accurate and critical knowledge of the classical tongues. Guided by the advice of his friends he went, upon leaving this school, to Lexington, and commenced the study of the law. In 1795, he was admitted to the bar, and soon attained a high rank in his profession. Kentucky, even at that day, held many men eminent for talent, learning and eloquence; yet he was considered among the foremost. As an advocate, in criminal cases, he had few equals in the state. The Virginia act of 1779, constituting the basis of the celebrated land laws of Kentucky, though originally drawn and reported to the legislature by George Mason, one of Virginia's most able statesmen, was so amended before its passage, as to destroy all system in the procuring of patents, and the consequence was much litigation in Kentucky, arising out of conflicting land claims. Many of our most eminent lawyers acquired great wealth by buying up contested claims, and from contingent fees. In these things, Mr. Rowan never indulged, conceiving them to be inimical to the high moral tone which should be preserved by the profession, and tempting to oppression of the occupants of lands. At an early age, he was called into public life, and was a member of the convention that formed the present constitution of Kentucky, in 1799. He was appointed secretary of state in 1804, and in 1806 was elected to Congress from a district in which he did not reside. He took his seat in 1807, and served during the eleventh Congress.

He was frequently a member of the state legislature, and in 1819 was appointed a judge of the Court of Appeals. While on the bench he delivered a learned and forcible opinion on the power of Congress to charter the Bank of the United States in 1816. Not relishing the close confinement of the bench, in 1821 he resigned his seat.

In 1823, he was appointed by the legislature, in conjunction with Henry Clay, a commissioner to defend what were called the occupying claimant laws of the state, before the Supreme Court of the United States. The uncertainty of land titles under the Virginia laws before alluded to, had led to the enactment of laws by the Kentucky legislature more favorable to the occupant than the common law of England. These statutes were attacked before the Supreme Court, upon the ground that they violated the compact between Virginia and Kentucky. The petition of the commissioners was drawn by Judge Rowan, and is deemed the ablest vindication of those laws ever published.

In 1824, he was elected to the senate of the United States, in which body he served for six years. On the 10th of April, 1826, he delivered a speech of great ability, on a bill further to amend the judiciary system of the United States. In 1828, he made a learned and powerful speech on the subject of imprisonment for debt, under process issued from the courts of the United States. It had been abolished in Kentucky in 1821, and yet he had seen it practiced by process from the Federal courts in this state, in defiance of public sentiment.

The last public office Mr. Rowan filled was that of commissioner to adjust the claims of citizens of the United States against Mexico, under the convention of Washington of the 11th of April, 1839. Upon the organization of the Kentucky Historical Society in 1838, he was elected president of that institution, and held the office until the period of his death. He died, after a short illness, at his residence in Louisville, on the 13th of July, 1843, in the seventieth year of his age.

GEN. MARTIN D. HARDIN, one of the most distinguished citizens of Kentucky, was about six years old when his father, Colonel John Hardin, emigrated in April 1786, with his family, from the Monongahela country to a point on Pleasant Run, a branch of the Beech Fork, Springfield. He studied law with Colonel George Nicholas, and practiced at Richmond and afterward at Frankfort, with great success; indeed, was the leader of the bar at each place. He was a man of marked talent and of very decided character. In 1812, he was a major in the rifle regiment of Colonel John Allen, in the campaign on the northern border during the war with Great Britain, and approved himself a brave, vigilant, and efficient officer. He was secretary of state of Kentucky under Governor Isaac Shelby, 1812-16; and was appointed by Governor Gabriel Slaughter to fill a vacancy in the United States senate, serving one session, 1816-17. He died at Frankfort, October 8, 1823, aged forty-three. He was the father of the gallant Colonel John J. Hardin, an ex-member of Congress from Illinois, 1843-45, who fell in the battle of Buena Vista in Mexico, February 23, 1847.

WILLIAM WHITLEY, was one of the most distinguished of the early pioneers, whose adventurous exploits have shed a coloring of romance over the early history of Kentucky. He was born on the 14th of August, 1749, in that part of Virginia then called Augusta, and which afterward furnished territory for Rockbridge County. Unknown to early fame, he grew to manhood in the laborious occupation of tilling his native soil, in which his corporeal powers were fully developed, with but little mental cultivation. He possessed, however, the spirit of enterprise, and the love of independence. In 1775, having married Esther Fuller, and commenced housekeeping in a small way, with health and labor to season his bread, he said to his wife, he heard a fine report of Kentucky, and he thought they could get their living there with less hard work. "Then, Billy, if I was you I would go and see," was the reply. In two days he was on his way, with axe and plow, and gun and kettle. And she is the woman who afterward collected his warriors to pursue the Indians.

Whitley set out for Kentucky, accompanied by his brother-in-law, George Clark; in the wilderness they met with seven others, who joined them.

In the year 1813, being then in the sixty-fifth year of his age, he volunteered with the Kentucky militia, under Governor Shelby, and fell in the decisive and victorious battle of the Thames, on the 5th of October.

Colonel Whitley was a man above the ordinary

size, of great muscular power, and capable of enduring great fatigue and privation. His courage as a soldier was unquestionable, having been foremost in seventeen battles with the Indians, and one with a more civilized foe. In the battle of the Thames, he fell at the first fire. His memory is cherished throughout Kentucky with profound respect, as that of one uniting the characters of patriot and hero.

GEN. ORMSBY MACKNIGHT MITCHELL, a distinguished American astronomer, was born in Union County, Kentucky, August 28, 1810, and died of yellow fever at Beaufort, South Carolina, October 30, 1862, aged fifty-two. He received his early education in Lebanon, Ohio; was appointed to a cadetship at West Point in 1825; graduated in 1829, fifteenth in a class of forty-six—among whom were those distinguished Confederate chieftains, Robert E. Lee and Joseph E. Johnston. He filled the position of professor of mathematics in that institution for two years; subsequently studied law and practiced in Cincinnati until 1834; when he was elected professor of mathematics, philosophy, and astronomy in the Cincinnati College. In 1845, he succeeded in the establishment of an observatory in Cincinnati, raising the requisite amount of money therefor by his own exertions. In 1859, he was chosen director of the Albany, New York, observatory, and also retained his connection with that in Cincinnati. Among his published works are "Planetary and Stellar Worlds," "Popular Astronomy," and a treatise on algebra. He was commissioned a brigadier general in the Union army, August, 1861, and afterward promoted to major general.

REV. JOHN ALEXANDER McCLUNG, D. D., a distinguished scholar, orator, and divine, was born near Washington, in Mason County, Kentucky, September 25, 1804. He was the son of Judge William McClung, and grandson of Colonel Thomas Marshall; both of whom had emigrated from Virginia at an early day. Left at a tender age, by his father's death, to the care of a gifted and pious mother, he was, a few years after, sent to the academy of her brother, Dr. Louis Marshall, in Woodford County, Kentucky. There he exhibited unusual thirst for knowledge, and made great progress in his studies. In 1820, he became a member of the Pisgah Presbyterian Church in Woodford. In his eighteenth year he was entered as a student in the Theological Seminary at Princeton. In 1825, he married a lady of great piety and refinement, Miss Eliza Johnston, sister of Hon. Josiah Stoddard Johnston, and General Albert Sidney Johnston.

He was licensed to preach in 1828, and soon became one of the most popular young preachers of the West; but in a brief period, his religious convictions were disturbed, and he voluntarily withdrew from the ministry.

In 1830, he wrote and published "Camden," a tale of the South during the Revolution, and in 1832, "Sketches of Western Adventure"—both works of decided merit, the former published in Philadelphia, the latter by Judge Lewis Collins.

DR. DANIEL DRAKE, distinguished as physician, professor, and author, was born at Plainfield, New Jersey, October 20, 1785, and died at Cincinnati, Ohio, November 5, 1852, aged sixty-seven years. Brought to Mason County, Kentucky, June 10, 1788, before he was three years old, he grew up with that spirit and self-reliance which marked his whole life, receiving all the education the little village of Mayslick and surroundings could give him, theoretical and practical. In December, 1800, aged fifteen, he went to the village of Cincinnati with its population of seven hundred and fifty inhabitants, and became its first medical student—so faithful that, in after life, no medical man was more useful or reflected upon that city more varied renown. In May, 1804, aged nineteen, he began the practice of medicine in Cincinnati; spent the winter of 1805-1806 as a student in the Pennsylvania University, at Philadelphia, and the succeeding year in practice at his old home in Mayslick. Returning to Cincinnati in 1807, he made it his home for life, although much of his time was spent as a professor in Kentucky. In 1817, became professor of materia medica and medical botany in Transylvania University, Lexington, Kentucky;

November, 1820, founded and established the Medical College of Ohio, at Cincinnati, from which, after a bitter controversy, his connection was suddenly sundered, May 1822; resumed his professorship at Lexington, 1823-27; declined the professorship of medicine in the University of Virginia, 1830; was professor in Jefferson Medical College, Philadelphia, November, 1830-31; again in the Medical College of Ohio, 1831-32; founded a new medical school, as a department of Cincinnati College, June, 1835-39; was professor in the Louisville Medical Institute, afterward known as the University of Louisville, 1839-49; when he resigned and accepted a chair in the Medical College of Ohio, 1849-50. In 1827, he became editor of the Western Medical and Physical Journal, through which he continued to write for many years. His "Notices concerning Cincinnati," published 1810, enlarged as "The Picture of Cincinnati," 1815, were remarkable works. The great literary event of his life was his "Treatise on the Principal Diseases of the Interior Valley of North America," published 1850, an original work, a wonderful monument to American medical science.

CHARLES F. WING was a captain at the battle of the Thames, and saw Tecumseh after he was slain. He was clerk of the Muhlenberg courts from the organization of the county in 1798 to 1856—fifty-eight years; a longer period than any other man ever held a clerkship in Kentucky.

DON CARLOS BUELL, major general of volunteers, United States army, was born in Ohio, 1818; graduated at West Point Academy, 1841; was appointed second lieutenant in Third Infantry, regular service; promoted first lieutenant, June, 1846; brevetted captain for gallantry at the battle of Monterey, September 23, 1846. His regiment subsequently served under General Scott on the southern line of operations in Mexico, where Buell distinguished himself at Churubusco and Controras, and was brevetted major; in the latter battle he was severely wounded. He became assistant adjutant general with the rank of captain, January, 1848; relinquished his rank in the line, March, 1851, and was employed in the duties of his office until 1861, when he assisted in organizing the army at Washington. He was appointed brigadier general, and assigned to a division in the army of the Potomac, which soon became noted for its thorough discipline. In November, 1861, he superseded General Sherman, then in command of the army of the Cumberland —which he reorganized as that of the Ohio, with headquarters at Louisville, Kentucky.

General Buell assumed command of this army (if army it could be called) at a critical period in Kentucky. Sherman had notified the government at Washington that two hundred thousand men were necessary for the campaign in the southwest. His opinion was hooted at; he was considered a mad man, and this was the direct cause of his removal. Subsequent events justified his opinion and confirmed his sagacity. The people of Kentucky were divided, but at that period the sentiment for the South was intense and the preponderance was against the North. The army had to be organized. There were few reliable troops, most of the regiments were new, and many of them incomplete. Above all this, it was the policy of the Federal government, then, to conciliate the people of Kentucky—not alone to prevent an outbreak, but to win them to the Union cause. This seemed at least to be the object of Mr. Lincoln's administration. Its bad faith became apparent afterward. General Buell was, therefore, expected to enact the part of the soldier and the statesman. He did both well. His moderate course, his kindness and courtesy towards the non-combatants who were necessarily sufferers by the armed occupation of the state, won the respect of the Southern sympathizers and commanded the admiration of the best friends of the Union cause. During the winter of 1861-62, he organized his troops for the advance movement, which was to drive the Confederates from the state. He submitted his plan for this purpose to General McClellan, then at the head of the army. It secured his approval; and the result was the fall of Forts Henry and Donelson, the retreat of the Confederates from Bowling Green, and their subsequent evacuation of Nashville and ultimate withdrawal south of Tennessee River.

GEN. HENRY LEE, a native of Virginia, was one of the earliest pioneers who settled in the County of Mason. He was a man of considerable intelligence and remarkably strong natural powers of mind. He was a member of the Virginia legislature from the district of Kentucky, and also of the convention which adopted the Federal constitution. He served in the convention at Danville which met in 1787, and was one of the commissioners who located the seat of government at Frankfort. He was county lieutenant for all the territory north of Licking River, and was appointed judge of the Quarter Sessions Court, and associate judge of the Circuit Court for Mason County, and was president of the Washington Branch of the old Bank of Kentucky. He came to Kentucky originally as a surveyor, and acted in that capacity for many years. He was a very sagacious man, of fine business habits, and by his position and great application, amassed a very large fortune. He was tall and powerfully made, very erect, and a man of remarkably fine and imposing personal appearance. He died October 24, 1845, in the eighty-ninth year of his age.

COLONEL THOMAS MARSHALL, formerly commander of the Third Virginia Regiment on continental establishment, subsequently colonel of the regiment of Virginia artillery, during the Revolutionary war, was a gallant soldier—the friend and neighbor of Washington. Being appointed surveyor-general of the lands in Kentucky appropriated by Virginia to the officers and soldiers of the Virginia state line, he emigrated with his wife, Fanny Keith, and part of his children, to Kentucky in the year 1785, coming down the Ohio river to Limestone (Maysville.) They had fifteen children: Seven sons—John (chief justice of the United States), Captain Thomas (first clerk of the Mason County Court, Kentucky, and a member of the convention which formed the second constitution of Kentucky), James M., Charles, William, Alexander Keith (reporter to the Kentucky Court of Appeals in 1818), and Dr. Louis (of Woodford County, Kentucky, father of Thomas F. and Edward C., and president in 1855 of Washington College—now Washington-Lee University—Lexington, Va.); and eight daughters—Elizabeth (wife of Rawleigh Colston), Mary Ann or Polly (blind a considerable portion of her life, wife of Humphrey Marshall, United States senator from Kentucky, 1795-1801, and historian of Kentucky, 1812 and 1824), Judith (wife of George Brooke), Lucy (wife of Col. John Ambler), Susannah (wife of Judge William McClung), Charlotte (wife of Dr. Basil Duke), Jane (wife of George Keith Taylor), and Nancy (wife of Colonel Joseph Hamilton Daviess). John, and several brothers and sisters, remained in Virginia. The father died at his home in Woodford County, Kentucky, July, 1803.

GEN. CASSIUS MARCELLUS CLAY, son of General Green Clay, was born in Madison County, Kentucky, October 19, 1810; a graduate of Yale College, and a lawyer by profession; elected to the Kentucky Legislature from his native county, in 1835, and again in 1837; removed to Fayette County, which he represented in the Legislature in 1840, but was defeated at the next election on account of his anti-slavery views. In 1844 he canvassed the Northern States and denounced the annexation of Texas as a scheme for the extension of slavery.

In 1845 he established at Lexington a paper, the True American, in the interest of the abolition or anti-slavery party.

LEWIS COLLINS, third son of Richard Collins, a soldier of the Virginia army of the Revolutionary war, was born on Christmas day, 1797, near Grant's Station, several miles northeast of Bryan's Station, in Fayette County, Kentucky. Left an orphan when quite a youth, he took his first lessons at practical printing under Joel R. Lyle, of the Paris Citizen, during the year 1813; and in 1814 accompanied his old friend and teacher, David V. Rannells, to Washington, in Mason County, and assisted him first in the publication, and afterward in the editorial management of the Washington Union, until the fall of 1820.

On the 1st of November of that year he became proprietor and editor of the Maysville Eagle, a newspaper founded in 1814 by Richard and Joab

SIMON KENTON.

Corwine, who sold it in 1817 to Aaron Crookshanks, from whom Mr. Collins purchased in 1820. During the succeeding twenty-seven years, to November 1, 1847, he remained the owner and editor of that paper—conducting it, in conjunction with the book business, with much tact, ability, energy, and judgment. It was not only a financial success, but the Eagle exerted a wide influence for good over the whole community. It was a pure, truthful, elevated paper, conservative in its political views, and filled with sound and valuable instruction, adapted to the intellectual, material, and moral wants of the people.

On the 1st of April, 1823, he was married to Mary Eleanor Peers, daughter of Major Valentine Peers (an officer of the Virginia army of the Revolution, who was with General Washington at Valley Forge) and sister of Rev. Benjamin O. Peers. She became a true helpmate, a devoted, tender wife and mother, and still survives him (1877), an example and blessing to all around her, one of the noblest of her sex, a true "mother in Israel."

In the same year he retired from the Eagle, he edited and published "Collins' Historical Sketches of Kentucky"—a work of rare research, and a most authentic and comprehensive history of Kentucky. He died at Lexington, Kentucky, on the 29th of January, 1870, aged seventy-two years.

COLONEL JOHN SPEED SMITH, for forty years one of the leading lawyers and most prominent public men in Eastern Kentucky, was a native of Jessamine County, Kentucky; settled in Richmond when its bar was one of the ablest in the country, with Martin D. Hardin at its head, and rapidly rose to prominence; represented Madison County in the Kentucky House of Representatives 1819, '27, '30, '39, '41 and '45, and in the Senate 1846-50; was speaker of the former body, 1827; a representative in Congress during Monroe's administration, 1821-23; appointed by President J. Q. Adams secretary of legation to the United States Mission, sent to the South American Congress which was to assemble at Tacubaya; appointed by President Jackson United States attorney for the District of Kentucky; appointed by the Kentucky Legislature January 5, 1839, as joint commissioner with ex-Governor James T. Morehead to visit the Ohio Legislature and solicit the passage of laws to prevent evil-disposed persons in that state from enticing away or assisting in the escape of slaves from Kentucky, and to provide more efficient means for recapturing fugitive slaves by their masters or agents—which mission was entirely and handsomely successful. In the campaign of 1813, in the war with England and her Indian allies, he served as aide-de-camp to General Harrison, and proved himself a brave and vigilant officer.

GENERAL SIMON KENTON was born of obscure parents in Fauquier County, Virginia, April 13, 1755. His father was an Irishman; his mother of Scotch descent. The poverty of his parents caused his education to be neglected, most unfortunately for his future prosperity. His life, until he was sixteen years of age, appears to have run smoothly enough, distinguished by no uncommon events from that of the neighboring boys. About that age, however, a calamity befell him, which, apart from its irreparable nature, in the opinion of all young gentlemen of sixteen, gave a direction to his whole future life. He lost his sweetheart; not by death, or anything of that kind—for that could have been endured—but by means of a more favored rival. The successful lover's name was William Veach. Kenton, in utter despair and recklessness, having gone uninvited to the wedding, and thrust himself between the happy pair (whom he found seated cosily on a bed), was pounced upon by Veach and his brothers, who gave him, in the language of such affairs, "what he wanted." They, however, had mistaken his wants, for, meeting William Veach a short time afterward in a retired place, he informed him that he was not satisfied. A severe fight ensued which, after varied success, terminated in the complete discomfiture of Veach. In the course of the contest Kenton succeeded in entangling his antagonist's long hair in a bush, which put him entirely in his power. The desperate young man beat his rival with a severity altogether foreign to his subsequent amiable character. His violence appeared to be fatal; the unhappy man, bleeding at mouth and nose, attempted to rise, and fell back insensible. Kenton was alarmed; he raised him up, spoke kindly to him, and receiving no answer, believed him dead. He dropped his lifeless body and fled to the woods. Now, indeed, he thought himself ruined beyond redemption. He had lost the girl he loved, and had killed his former friend and companion, and therefore the society of civilized man must be not only repulsive, but dangerous. The Alleghanies and the wilderness of the unexplored west offered him a secure asylum, and he plunged at once into the woods. Traveling by night and lying concealed by day, after many sufferings, he arrived at Ise's ford, on Cheat River, some time in April, 1771. Here he changed his name to "Simon Butler." Thus, at the age of sixteen, this man, who, in the hands of the Almighty, was so instrumental in redeeming the great west from the savage, and opening the way for the stream of civilization which has since poured over its fertile plains, desolate in heart, and burdened with crime, was thrown upon his own resources, to struggle with the dangers and privations of the wilderness.

Kenton spent the winters of 1773-4 on the Big Sandy with a hunting party, and in the spring, when the war broke out with the Indians, he retreated into Fort Pitt with the other settlers. When Lord Dunmore raised an army to punish the Indians Kenton volunteered, and was actively employed as a spy, both under the expedition of Dunmore and that of Colonel Lewis. In the fall he was discharged from the army, and returned, with Thomas Williams, to his old hunting grounds on Big Sandy River, where they passed the winter. In the spring of 1775, having disposed of their peltries to a French trader, whom they met on the Ohio, for such necessaries as their mode of life required, they descended the Ohio in search once more of the "cane land." Although Yeager was now dead, the impressions left upon the mind of Kenton by his glowing descriptions of Kain-tuck-ee, which Yeager had visited with the Indians when a boy and a prisoner, were still fresh and strong; and he determined to make another effort to find the country. For this purpose he and Williams were now descending the Ohio. Accident at last favored them. While gliding along down "la belle riviere" (as the French had christened it), night overtook the young adventurers, and they were compelled to land. They put in with their canoe at the mouth of Cabin Creek, situated in the present County of Mason, and about six miles above Maysville. Next morning, while hunting some miles back in the country, the ardently sought "cane" burst upon Kenton's view, covering land richer than any he had ever seen before. Overjoyed at this piece of good fortune he returned in haste to communicate the joyful intelligence to Williams. Sinking their canoe, the pioneers, par excellence, of North Kentucky, struck into their new domain. In the month of May, 1775, within a mile of the present town of Washington, in Mason County, having built their camp and finished a small clearing, they planted about an acre of land with the remains of the corn bought from the French trader. The spot chosen by them for their agricultural attempt was one of the most beautiful and fertile in the State of Kentucky. Here, in due season, they ate the first roasting ears that ever grew by the care of a white man on the north side of the Kentucky River.

Kenton continued to range the country as a spy until June, 1778, when Major Clark came down the Ohio from Virginia with a small force, and landed at the Falls. Clark was organizing an expedition against Okaw or Kaskaskia, and invited as many of the settlers at Boonesborough and Harrodsburg as desired to join him. The times were so dangerous that the women, especially in the stations, objected to the men going on such a distant expedition. Consequently, to the great mortification of Clark, only Kenton and Haggin left the stations to accompany him on this expedition, so honorable to the enterprise of Virginia and the great captain and soldiers composing it, and so successful and happy in its results. After the fall of Kaskaskia, Kenton returned to Harrodsburg by way of Vincennes, an accurate description of which, obtained by three days' secret observation, he sent to Clark, who subsequently took that post.

Kenton, finding Boone about to undertake an expedition against a small town on Paint Creek, readily joined him. Inaction was irksome to the hardy youth in such stirring times; besides he had some melancholy reflections that he could only escape from in the excitement of danger and adventure.

The party, consisting of nineteen men, and commanded by Boone, arrived in the neighborhood of the Indian village. Kenton, who, as usual, was in advance, was startled by hearing loud peals of laughter from a cane brake just before him. He scarcely had time to tree before two Indians, mounted upon a small pony, one facing the animal's tail and the other his head, totally unsuspicious of danger and in excellent spirits made their appearance. He pulled trigger, and both Indians fell, one killed and the other severely wounded. He hastened up to scalp his adversaries, and was immediately surrounded by about forty Indians. His situation, dodging from tree to tree, was uncomfortable enough, until Boone and his party coming up, furiously attacked and defeated the savages. Boone immediately returned to the succor of his fort, having ascertained that a large war party had gone against it. Kenton and Montgomery, however, resolved to proceed to the village to get "a shot" and steal horses. They lay within good rifle distance of the village for two days and a night without seeing a single warrior; on the second night they each mounted a fine horse and put off to Kentucky, and the day after the Indians raised the siege of Boonesborough they cantered into the fort on their stolen property.

The winter of 1779-80 was a peaceful one to the Kentuckians, but in the spring the Indians and British invaded the country, having with them two pieces of cannon, by means of which two stations, Martin's and Ruddle's, fell into their hands; whereupon the allied savages immediately retreated.

When General Clark heard of the disaster he hastened from Vincennes to concert measures for present retaliation and the future safety of the settlements. Clark was no doubt one of the greatest men ever furnished by the west, of no ordinary military capacity. He believed the best way to prevent the depredations of the Indians was to carry the war into their own country, burning down their villages and destroying their corn, and thus give them sufficient employment to prevent their incursions among the settlements on the south side of the river. Accordingly an expedition consisting of 1,100 of the hardiest and most courageous men that the most adventurous age of our history could furnish, inured to hardships and accustomed to the Indian mode of fighting, assembled at the mouth of the Licking. Kenton commanded a company of volunteers from Harrod's Station, and shared in all the dangers and success of this little army. Commanded by Clark and piloted by one of the most expert woodsmen and the greatest spy of the west, Simon Kenton, the Kentuckians assailed the savages in their dens with complete success.

General Kenton lived in his quiet and obscure home to the age of eighty-one, beloved and respected by all who knew him; 29th of April, 1836, in sight of the place where the Indians, fifty-eight years before, proposed to torture him to death, he breathed his last, surrounded by his family and neighbors and supported by the consolation of the gospel.

JAMES GUTHRIE, LL.D., was born near Bardstown, Kentucky, December 5, 1792, and died in Louisville, March 13, 1869, aged seventy-six. Failing health, during several years, had compelled him, in February, 1868, to resign his seat in the United States senate, he being the oldest of the members of that body. He was educated at Bardstown Academy, and before he was grown became a flat-boat or produce merchant to New Orleans; afterwards studied law in the office of Judge John Rowan, and practiced in Nelson County; was made commonwealth's attorney in 1820; soon after, removed to Louisville, and obtained a lucrative practice; was a representative from Jefferson County in 1827, '28, 29, and from the city of Louisville in 1830, and senator from 1831-40; early in his political career was shot by an opponent, the wound confining him for three years to his bed; was a member of the convention which formed the present constitution of Kentucky, 1849, and its presiding officer; secretary of the treasury in President Pierce's cabinet, 1853-57; a candidate before the Charleston Democratic Convention for the presidency, 1860, and a delegate to the Democratic

National Convention in Chicago, 1864; elected by the Kentucky legislature a delegate to the Peace Convention which assembled at Washington City just before the outbreak of the Civil war, 1861, and afterwards was a delegate to the Border State Convention at Frankfort, 1861; United States senator from Kentucky, 1865-71, but resigned 1868, as above; was an earnest and consistent Union man during the war, and a member of the Union National Convention at Philadelphia, 1866.

HUMPHREY MARSHALL, the United States senator, was born in Virginia, the son of John Marshall and Jane Quisenberry, who were humble in fortune, and raised a large family. He had three children: John J., Thomas A., and a daughter who was killed by lightning in infancy, in Woodford County. The two brothers were well known to the people of Kentucky as men of ability, chiefly signalized by their judicial and political labors; for both were judges for many years, and both were repeatedly elected by the people to political stations. They were men of high mental culture, genial disposition and great amiability of character. They had early advantages of education, John having taken the first honors at Princeton College, New Jersey, while Thomas graduated with distinction at Yale. They entered life, each with a fortune which was colossal at the time, and each ran a career of great distinction. John represented Franklin County in the lower house of the legislature in 1815 and 1833, and in the senate, 1820-24; and was a judge of the Louisville Circuit Court for many years. John J. Marshall in 1809 married Anna Reed Birney, daughter of James Birney of Danville, niece of Thomas B. Reed, United States senator from Mississippi, 1826-27, '29, and sister of James G. Birney, who was for several times the "Liberty" candidate for President of the United States.

THOMAS A. MARSHALL was born in Woodford County, Kentucky, January 15, 1794, and died in Louisville, April 16, 1871, aged seventy-seven. When a boy, he spent some time in Washington City, while his father was United States senator. One day, dressed in homespun, he climbed up one of the huge posts in the vestibule of the old capitol and wrote his name. Some one inquired what he was doing. "I am writing my name," he replied, "and I want to see if it will be here when I come to Congress." He was but seven years old. In 1831-35 he came to Congress, from the Paris and Maysville District, but the name written in infancy had been painted out. He had previously, 1827, '28, represented Bourbon County in the Kentucky house of representatives, as he did the City of Louisville, 1863-65. From April, 1835, to August, 1856, and for a short period in 1866, he was upon the Court of Appeals bench, and from 1847-51, 1854-56, and in 1866 was chief justice. His claim to greatness and renown will be found in the twenty-four volumes of Kentucky Reports from 3d Dana to 17th Ben Monroe. From 1836, when he removed to Lexington, to 1849, he was a professor in Transylvania Law School. In November, 1816, he married Miss Price of Lexington, a niece of Mrs. Henry Clay. Several of their sons have attained distinction, Colonel Thomas A. Marshall of Charleston, Illinois, and Judge Charles Marshall of Paducah, Kentucky.

GENERAL HUMPHREY MARSHALL was educated at West Point Military Academy, New York, graduating in June, 1832, and promoted, upon his graduation, to the rank of second lieutenant in the army. His brief service in the army enabled him to make his mark, as will appear by the records of the War Departmental correspondence, for General Cass, then secretary of war, expressed officially the desire of the Government to retain him in the army, and offered to place him in any of the branches of the service he would prefer. Lieutenant Marshall had been mentioned honorably in the dispatches of Major General Winfield Scott, then in campaign against Black Hawk and the Sac Indians of the Northwest. But the country being in a state of profound peace, Mr. Marshall preferred to try his fortune in civic life. He studied law, and was admitted to the bar in April, 1833. He settled at Louisville, in November, 1834. In 1836, he was elected by the people of his ward to the city council, and was then elected to a captaincy of volunteers, called out by President Jackson to march to the Sabine to defend the frontiers of Louisiana against the approaching army of Santa Anna. He quit his profession and municipal honors to accept this new military position; but the battle of San Jacinto settled the fate of Texas, and rendered the march of these volunteers unnecessary.

In 1837, he became a candidate for the Kentucky legislature, and was defeated by Hon. S. S. Nicholas, who had just retired from the bench of the Court of Appeals, and whose services were demanded by the banks to insure the renewal of their charters, which they had forfeited by suspending specie payments in May, 1837. The canvass was quite animated. It was with difficulty, and only after a considerable expenditure of means, the defeat of Mr. Marshall was secured. It was the commencement of his political life; it was the beginning and end of that of his competitor.

Captain Marshall now, for the first time, sedulously addressed himself to his profession, and his increase of practice was the token of success. The Louisville bar was very strong—embracing such men as Guthrie, Thruston, Duncan, Benham, Loughborough, Pirtle, Field, Thomas Q. Wilson, Wat Wilson, and others, all in active practice; it was with difficulty younger lawyers struggled to the surface. The opening of the Mexican war in 1846 again drew Marshall away from his profession, to accept the command of the Kentucky cavalry regiment, which was mustered into the United States service at Louisville, June 9, 1846. Colonel Marshall embarked for Memphis early in July with his regiment, and marched thence, overland, to Mexico, arriving on the Rio Grande in November. At the memorable battle of Buena Vista the tide of adverse fortune was checked by the charge of the Kentucky cavalry.

On being mustered out of service, June 9, 1847, Colonel Marshall returned to Louisville. He was nominated for the state senate in September, 1847, but declined; and removed to Henry County, to try his fortune as a farmer. He was nominated as the Whig candidate for Congress from the Louisville district, in 1849, and elected, after a violent contest, by sixty-five votes, over Dr. Newton Lane, the Democratic candidate. He was re-elected, in 1851, over Governor David Merriwether, by a handsome majority—though Hon. Archie Dixon, the Whig candidate for Governor, failed to carry the district by more than two hundred votes. The death of General Taylor and accession of Mr. Fillmore to the presidency opened a schism in the Whig party upon the sectional questions which afterward led to the Civil war under Lincoln's administration. Colonel Marshall took an active part in favor of "The Compromise Measures of 1850," and his course was enthusiastically sustained by his constituency.

In June, 1852, a vacancy occurred on the bench of the Supreme Court of the United States by the death of Hon. John McKinley, to which the Louisville bar, the Court of Appeals of Kentucky, and the Kentucky delegation in Congress, of both parties, recommended Colonel Marshall. Several delegations from the western and southern states added their recommendations. President Fillmore was anxious to make the appointment, but was prevented from so doing by an administrative rule adopted by him at the time of Judge Woodbury's death, which limited the successor of a justice to the district to which the deceased had been assigned. This rule had been applied in the case of Postmaster General Hall, and now excluded Colonel Marshall. Mr. Fillmore tendered him the appointment of minister to the five states of Central America, which was declined. In August, 1852, he appointed him commissioner to China, with powers plenipotentiary, and Congress passed an act highly complimentary which raised the mission to the first class, after Colonel Marshall's appointment was confirmed by the senate. He left on the 2d of October, 1852, for England, and made his way to China, taking France and Italy in his journey, touching at Malta, and traversing the Egyptian desert between Cairo and Suez—an excellent opportunity of seeing what was notable in the Old World. He arrived at Canton, in China, about the first of April, 1853, and at once steamed on to Shanghai, where he resided as minister until 1854.

In 1855 he was returned by his old constituency to Congress, by a majority of more than 2,500, over Colonel William Preston, who had been elected during Colonel Marshall's absence from the country. This canvass was peculiarly animated, for the competitors were men of acknowledged talents, and the subject matter of discussion —Knownothingism—was new to the disputes of the political arena. Colonel Marshall was re-elected to Congress by some 1,800 majority, in 1857, over Mr. Holt; but the canvass was one of mere form—the result not doubtful from the beginning of it. In 1859 he was nominated by acclamation for re-election, but, not relishing the platform upon which the party convention placed him, he declined.

Colonel Marshall formed a partnership with ex-United States Senator James Cooper, of Pennsylvania, for the purpose of taking cases before the Supreme Court, before the Court of Claims, and the Departments of Washington City, until 1860.

The first battle of Manassas opened the trial by battle between the United States and the Southern Confederacy, and palsied the hands of all who hoped to save the Union by the intervention of the states themselves. Colonel Marshall retired to his farm in Henry County, Kentucky, intending to take such course as Kentucky might choose to pursue; but he was not destined to occupy this position long, for, in the fall of 1861, a coup d'état was planned and partially executed, of which the result would have embraced Colonel Marshall had he remained in the state. He withdrew, in September, to Nashville, Tennessee, and afterward accepted a brigadier's commission in the Confederate army. In this rank he was entrusted with a separate command, styled "The Army of Eastern Kentucky," with which it was at first designed to invade Kentucky through her eastern mountain passes. The surrender at Fort Donelson, in the winter of 1861-62 changed this plan, and threw the Confederacy on the defensive. In January, 1862, General Marshall came to action with General Garfield, of Ohio, at the forks of Middle Creek, in Floyd County, Kentucky, but neither lost many men. Both claimed victory. Marshall remained in the county—about seven miles from the field of battle—until about March; Garfield fell back to Paintsville, in Johnson County.

It was the occurrences in the West that commanded the management of the forces in the mountain passes. The campaign through the winter of 1861-2 by General Marshall's force was one of the hardest ever experienced by any soldiery. There were no roads through the country, and no mills to grind meal, except those on the mountain branches, which were barely sufficient to turn off about two bushels in twenty-four hours. The soldiers of General Marshall's command gathered the iced shucks in the fields, shelled the corn, and took it to these mills to be ground into meal. Many a time they lived on parched corn for days, though marching from morning until night. The typhoid-pneumonia took off hundreds of young Kentuckians and Virginians from this command in the spring of 1862.

In May, 1862, General Marshall surprised Major-General Cox at Princeton, Virginia, and, by an action, relieved the Lynchburg and Knoxville Railroad—indeed, Southwestern Virginia—of the presence of the Union troops. For this movement, General Robert E. Lee complimented General Marshall, in a letter written for the occasion.

The defeat of McClellan before Richmond, Virginia, seemed to open a chance for the invasion of Kentucky; and accordingly the president of the Confederacy directed General Marshall to prepare his column to move into Kentucky, promising that he should lead this invasion. Afterward this command was given to General Bragg, and amounted to nothing, for that officer knew nothing of the topography of Kentucky, nothing of her people, and chilled by his vacillation the spirit of revolt in Kentucky. General Marshall was opposed to the retreat from Kentucky, in the fall of 1862, by the Confederate army, but was alone in his opinion in the council of war which determined upon that measure.

In the winter of 1862-3 he pursued General Carter to the Kentucky line, when that officer penetrated to the railroad near Bristol, Tennessee, but only came upon his rear-guard at Jonesville, Lee County, Virginia, as they were entering the mountain passes in retreat. In the spring of 1863 General Marshall entered Kentucky with a cavalry force, to which it was designed to attach the commands of Generals Pegram and Jenkins, so as to make headquarters at Lexington, Kentucky, with some seven thousand cavalry; but the right and left wings of this force were exhausted by the independent movements of their chiefs, and this expedition effected nothing.

During his absence in Kentucky, the command of General Marshall was transferred to General William Preston of Kentucky, and General Marshall was ordered to report to General Joseph Johnston in Mississippi. This he did, but before a division was assigned to his command the president sent other generals of division to occupy the place designed by General Johnston for General Marshall; and as there was nothing left for the latter, but the broken brigade of Tilghman, who had been killed at Baker's Creek, General Marshall tendered the resignation of his commission in the army, which he insisted should be accepted by the government. This was reluctantly done when it was discovered that no other course could be pursued consistent with General Marshall's wishes.

General Marshall settled at Richmond, Virginia, to practice law in June, 1863; but the Kentuckians presented his name, and he was elected to the Second Congress of the Confederate States, in which he was placed upon the Committee on Military Affairs. He was re-elected, and occupied this place when Richmond was evacuated and the Southern armies surrendered. He crossed the Mississippi in July, 1865, but found the Confederate flag had yielded throughout the whole boundaries of the government. He spent the summer of 1865 in the valley of the Brazos, in Texas, and from this point obtained a permit to return to New Orleans, in November, 1865; but the public authorities would not consent to his return to Kentucky. He commenced practicing law in New Orleans, but left, in September, 1866, under a permit from President Johnson, to visit his family in Kentucky.

Once more on Kentucky soil, and in the midst of the people whom he had so long represented in the Congress of the United States, General Marshall was unconditionally pardoned by the President, and then settled to his profession in the city of Louisville. Congress subsequently removed all disability from his civic status, and restored him to the rights to which he was born.

In 1870 the friends of General Marshall induced him to present himself as a candidate for Congress from the Louisville District—and it is confidently believed he would have been elected had he continued a candidate to the poll—but the trickery which makes up the action of party conventions so disgusted him that he refused to submit to the convention, and declined the candidacy. After that time, he pursued the practice of law at Louisville energetically and successfully until his death, March 28, 1872, aged sixty. While General Marshall was by no means great as a military man, he was a statesman of considerable ability, and one of the strongest and most profound lawyers of Kentucky or the West.

JUDGE HENRY C. WOOD was born at Munfordville, Hart County, Kentucky, November 27, 1821, and died in Louisville, February 11, 1861, aged thirty-nine; graduated at Centre College, Danville, September, 1841, when the subject of his graduating address was the "Legal Profession;" studied law and began the practice in his native town—where, and on the circuit, he took high rank among the leading members of the bar, Honorable Joseph R. Underwood, Judge Elijah Hise, Jesse Craddock, Frank Gorin and others; was county attorney; representative from Hart County in the legislature, 1848; removed to Louisville, 1850, and in conjunction with William F. Barret soon became a leading law firm; in August, 1858, was elected a judge of the Court of Appeals for eight years, 1858-66, but in two years and a half was carried to his final rest, "worn out, with his harness on."

GENERAL LOVELL H. ROUSSEAU, a lawyer, soldier and political leader, was born in Lincoln County, Kentucky, August, 1818; died in New Orleans, Louisiana, January 7, 1869. His limited education, and the death of his father in 1833, leaving a large family in straitened circumstances, made manual labor a necessity; and, while employed in breaking rock on the Lexington and Lancaster turnpike, he mastered the French language. When of age he removed to the vicinity of Louisville and began the study of law; he was entirely without instruction, and had no conversation on the subject previous to his examination for license. In 1840 he removed to Bloomfield, Indiana; was admitted to the bar in 1841, and soon attained considerable success; was a member of the Indiana legislature in 1844, '45.

In 1846 he raised a company for the Mexican war, and took a prominent part in the battle of Buena Vista, his company losing fourteen out of fifty-one men. He was elected to the Indiana senate, four days after his return from Mexico; removed to Louisville in 1849, before the expiration of his term, but not being permitted by his constituents to resign, served them for one year while living out of the state. He immediately took a prominent position at the Louisville bar, his forte, like that of most lawyers who became prominent as successful commanders during the late war, being with the jury and in the management of difficult cases during the trial. He began recruiting for the United States army early in '61, but was obliged to establish his camp in Indiana; participated in most of the principal engagements in Kentucky, Tennessee, Alabama and Georgia; was early made a brigadier general; for gallant services at Perryville won a major general's commission. He served with distinction in the battles of Shiloh, Stone River and Chickamauga.

JAMES SPEED was born in Jefferson County, Kentucky, March 11, 1812; graduated at St. Joseph's College, Bardstown, Kentucky; studied law at Transylvania University and commenced practice at Louisville, 1833; a representative in the Kentucky legislature, 1847, and senator, 1861-63; November, 1864, appointed by President Lincoln United States attorney general, which he resigned July, 1866, and resumed the practice of law at Louisville.

GENERAL CHRISTOPHER RIFFE (pronounced Rife), the first settler of that part of Lincoln County which is now Casey County, was born of German parents, in Maryland, in 1765, married in Virginia before he was eighteen, and died March 25, 1852, aged eighty-five. He emigrated in 1784 to Bourbon County, Kentucky, lived awhile at Bryan's Station, at Boonesborough and at Logan's Station, and in 1788 settled at Carpenter's Station, two miles west of Hustonville, and one-fourth of a mile north of Green river (about one-half of a mile from Middleburg). Thence he removed eight miles southeast and built a cabin in the spring of 1793, where he spent the summer. In the fall, from Carpenter's Station was sent a warning of danger from Indians; which he was disposed to disregard, saying, "By shinks, I ain't afraid of 'em"—and this, notwithstanding he had, less than an hour before, killed a deer on the south side of the river, and while skinning it seen five or six Indians pass overhead on the cliff. He yielded, and took his wife and child to the station; but returning next day, found everything destroyed except his cabin —even the beds ripped and the feathers scattered; and a huge stone pipe, with a long stem or cane to it, stuck in a crack of the door, and these words written on the door with charcoal, "Ain't this the devil of a pipe!"

In 1808 General Riffe was a member of the Kentucky house of representatives, occupying a seat between Henry Clay and Humphrey Marshall, when the latter gave the insult which resulted in a duel. The former resented it on the spot, attacking Marshall, but Riffe (who was a tall, muscular and powerful man) seized each with one hand and held them apart, saying earnestly, "Come, poys, no fighting here, I whips you both," and closed the scene for the present.

THOMAS E. BRAMLETTE was born in Cumberland County, Kentucky, January 3, 1817; admitted to the bar in 1837; elected to the state legislature from the Counties of Cumberland and Clinton; appointed commonwealth's attorney by Governor Crittenden in 1848, and was the terror of violators of law in his district; resigned his position two years afterward and resumed the practice of law. In 1856 was elected judge of the Sixth Judicial District, where his decisions placed him among the foremost of Kentucky's expounders of law. Resigned the judgeship to go into the army, and, taking the Federal side, was elected colonel of the Third Kentucky Infantry. Appointed United States district attorney, vice James Harlan, deceased; but also resigned that position to accept the "Union" nomination for governor. He was elected for four years, from September, 1863, to September, 1867, and served through the entire time of many of the most trying scenes to which Kentucky was subjected after she became a state. Governor Bramlette afterward located at Louisville, where, until his death, January 12, 1875, he was a distinguished and successful lawyer.

GOVERNOR R. P. LETCHER was a native of Garrard County, where he resided and practiced law until 1840; was a representative in the legislature frequently; in Congress for ten years, 1823-33, and again in the legislature; was always a firm and consistent Whig, and in December, 1831, received the whole vote of the entire Whig representation for speaker of the house. In 1838 was speaker of the Kentucky house of representatives, and as such distinguished for energy and promptitude. As the Whig candidate, he was elected governor, August, 1840, for four years, by 15,720 majority over Judge Richard French. Although one of the most popular electioneerers in the state, he was beaten for Congress in the Lexington district, August, 1853, by Major John C. Breckinridge, by 526 majority—owing to the remarkable popularity of the latter in Owen County. He died in Frankfort, January 24, 1861.

EX-GOVERNOR JAMES T. MOREHEAD was born May 24, 1797, near Shepherdsville, Bullitt County, Kentucky, and died in Covington, Kentucky, December 28, 1854, aged fifty-seven; when three years old removed with his father to Russellville, Logan County, where he enjoyed the advantages of the village schools; was at Transylvania University, 1813-15; studied law with Judge H. P. Broadnax, and afterwards with John J. Crittenden, who was then living at Russellville; settled at Bowling Green and began the practice of law in the spring of 1818; was elected to the legislature, 1828, '29, '30; while attending the convention at Baltimore which nominated Henry Clay for the presidency and John Sergeant for the vice presidency, was nominated for lieutenant governor, and elected August, 1832; upon the death of Governor John Breathitt, February, 1834, was inaugurated governor, serving until September, 1836; was made ex-officio president of the board of internal improvement, February, 1835, and afterwards, under a change of the law, in 1838, commissioned by Governor Clark to the same office—having already, since March, 1837, been the state agent for the sale of bonds for internal improvement purposes; resumed the practice of law at Frankfort in the fall of 1836, and was elected to the legislature from Franklin County, August, 1837; in the winter of 1839-40, he and Colonel John Speed Smith were elected by the legislature commissioners to the state of Ohio, to obtain the passage of a law for the protection of the property of citizens of Kentucky in their slaves—which mission was entirely successful; was United States senator from Kentucky, 1841-47, and on his retirement resumed the practice of law at Covington. In the United States senate as a debater, few men ranked higher; whenever announced to speak, the lobbies and galleries were filled with spectators. As a speaker, he was remarkably fluent and energetic, with a manner eminently graceful and dignified. As a statesman, he was sound and conservative, and his political and general information was extensive and varied. His library, embracing the largest collection then known of works relating to the history of Kentucky, was purchased by the Young Men's Mercantile Association of Cincinnati. His address at the anniversary of the first settlement of Kentucky at Boonesborough, in 1840, was an invaluable historical summary, and rescued from oblivion a number of documents not elsewhere preserved.

CHARLES S. MOREHEAD was born in Nelson County, Kentucky, July 7, 1802. Graduated at Transylvania University, and removed to Christian County, where he commenced the practice of law. He was elected to the legislature in 1827, when barely eligible, receiving nearly every vote in the county; and was elected for a second term. On its expiration, he removed to Frankfort, as a more extended field for the practice of his profession. He was appointed attorney general of Kentucky in 1832, and held that office for five years. In 1838-39-40, he was returned to the legislature from Franklin County, the last year officiating as speaker of the house; was re-elected and made speaker in 1841; again in 1842; and, in 1844, for the third time he was chosen speaker. He was a representative in Congress from 1847 to 1851. Was again sent to the legislature in 1853, and chosen governor in 1855 for the term of four years. At the expiration of his term, in 1859, he removed to Louisville, and formed a law partnership with his nephew, Charles M. Briggs, Esq. His reception there was a perfect ovation. He was received at the railroad depot by a committee of citizens and escorted to the Galt House, formally welcomed, and made an address. After the secession of South Carolina, he was prominent among the conservatives of his state in laboring to avert civil war. He was a delegate from Kentucky to the "Peace Conference" at Washington, in February, 1861, and again to the "Border State Convention," at Frankfort, in May of that year.

HON. JOSHUA FRY BELL was born in Danville, Ky., Nov. 26, 1811, and died there, Aug. 17, 1870, aged nearly fifty-nine. His father was a leading merchant of Danville, a native of Newry, Ireland; his mother, Martha Fry, of Virginia, was the daughter of Joshua Fry, distinguished for his literary attainments and, after his removal to Kentucky, as an educator of many of the great men of the state, and the granddaughter of Dr. Thomas Walker, already spoken of under this county as the first white visitor to the interior of Kentucky (in 1750), and who in 1780 surveyed the boundary line between Kentucky and Tennessee. His great-grandfather, Col. John Fry, of Virginia, was commander of the American forces during the Colonial days, previous to the election of General Washington.

Joshua F. Bell graduated in 1828, when sixteen and a half years old, at Centre College, then under the presidency of Rev. John C. Young, D. D.; studied law at Lexington; spent several years in travel in Europe; at twenty-two, returned to Danville, and entered upon the practice of law, obtaining a large and lucrative practice, which he zealously cultivated until ill health prevented, a few months before his death; was representative in congress for two years, 1845-47; secretary of state under Governor John J. Crittenden, 1850; made a remarkable race as the opposition candidate for governor, in 1859, being beaten by Governor Magoffin; was chosen by the Kentucky legislature, by a unanimous vote in the senate and 81 to 5 in the house, one of six commissioners to the Peace Conference at Washington City, February, 1861, and there plead most earnestly for "peace between embittered and hating brothers;" March 19, 1863, was nominated by the Union Democratic state convention for governor, receiving 627 votes to 171 for acting-governor James F. Robinson.

SHADRACH PENN, Jr., one of the most distinguished of Kentucky editors, was born in Maryland, in 1790; brought when young to Scott County, Kentucky, where he assisted his parents on the farm; learned the printing business at Georgetown, and for a while published a newspaper at Lexington; spent some time at merchandising; was a soldier in the War of 1812; in 1818, started the Public Advertiser at Louisville, of which he was editor and one of the publishers until 1841; removed to St. Louis, and started the Reporter, a Democratic newspaper, editing it until his death in June, 1846, aged fifty-six. He was an earnest antagonist of Colonel Benton's favorite idea of an exclusive gold and silver currency for Missouri—preferring the safe system of Missouri banks with a limited issue, to the flood of doubtful bank issues from other states. Under the lead of his paper, the state bank system was continued, the district-plan for election of members to congress prevailed over the old general-ticket practice, and internal improvements by the state were sustained. He became a power in the politics of Missouri.

Mr. Penn had been a power in the politics of Kentucky, too—the champion of the Democratic party. On the "old court" and "new court" issues which convulsed the state, from 1822-27, he had vanquished the famous Amos Kendall, and scarcely an editor in the country had been able to cope with him. Indeed, the only exception was George D. Prentice, who out-generaled him, if at all, by bull-dog perseverance and terrific sallies of wit and ridicule. Prentice spoke of him, after his death, as an able and sincere man, but lacking in ready self-possession. He was too sensitive to the tortures of Prentice, and fled the field. Prentice said of him, then, that his removal would be regarded as a public calamity. Of all the history of newspapers in Louisville, the eleven years of controversy between those two is recounted with most zest and relish. Of all the prominent Democratic editors of his day, Penn alone seemed to care nothing for office or position. His life was one of controversy; he was fond of it. He was a great journalist, if not a great statesman.

CHANCELLOR GEORGE M. BIBB, born October 30th, 1776, in Prince Edward County, Virginia, was the son of Richard Bibb, an Episcopal clergyman of great learning. His earliest recollections were of the struggle for American independence, which began at his birth; and he died just before the war for the independence of his native state and the South had concentrated its unrecorded horrors around his birthplace. He was the last representative at the national capital of the "gentleman of the old school;" and, refusing to give up the fashion of his early life for the pantaloons of the present day, the "tights" or "small clothes" were not even odd in the elegant old-time gentleman, but added to the popular respect and reverence for him.

Judge Bibb was well educated, a graduate of Hampden Sydney and also of William and Mary Colleges—and in his latter days was the oldest surviving graduate of each. Studying his profession with that distinguished lawyer, Richard Venable, he practiced in Virginia a short time, and removed to Lexington, Kentucky, in 1798. He attracted business by his legal acquirements, solid judgment, and cogent reasoning, and was soon numbered among the ablest and soundest in a state already prominent for great lawyers. He was appointed by Governor Greenup one of the judges of the Court of Appeals, January 31, 1808; and by Governer Scott, its chief justice, May 30, 1809, but resigned in March, 1810; and again, by Governor Desha, was appointed chief justice, for the second time, January 5, 1827, but resigned December 23, 1828.

Judge Bibb was twice elected to the United States senate (the third of five Kentuckians who have enjoyed this distinction)—first in 1811, but resigned in 1814, and second in 1829, serving the full term of six years, to 1835. During the war of 1812, he, in the senate, and Wm. Lowndes and John C. Calhoun, of South Carolina, and Henry Clay, in the United States house of representatives, formed what was called the "War Mess" of the Madison administration—from having supported the war and the President with such great talent, vigor, and zeal. He settled in Frankfort in 1816. From 1835 to 1844, Judge Bibb held the important position of chancellor of the Louisville Chancery Court; but resigned, to become United States secretary of the treasury in the cabinet of his old colleague in the United States senate, President Tyler, holding it to the close of his presidential term, 1844 to March 4, 1845. Thenceforward, until his death, April 14, 1859, aged eighty-three years, he practiced law in the courts of the District of Columbia, most of the time in the position of chief clerk in the department of the United States attorney-general, but really doing the duties now required of the assistant attorney-general, an office established for the very labors performed by him.

GEORGE DENISON PRENTICE, a distinguished editor and poet, born December 18, 1802, in New London County, Connecticut (one account says in Griswold, and another in Preston, towns within eight miles of each other); died a few miles below Louisville, Kentucky, January 21, 1870, aged sixty-seven; a fluent reader at four years of age; could translate and parse any verse in Virgil or Homer at fifteen, and was ready for college, but want of means compelled him to teach school two years; entered the sophomore class at Brown University, Providence, Rhode Island, in 1820, and graduated in 1823; studied law, but finding the practice uncongenial, abandoned it; editor of the Connecticut Mirror, 1825; associated with John G. Whittier in the publication of the New England Weekly Review,

1828-30; visited at Ashland and wrote the Life of Henry Clay, 1830; removed to Louisville, September, 1830, and issued the first number of the Louisville Daily Journal, November 24, 1830, which he continued to conduct until November 8, 1868, when it was merged in the Courier, and the two issued thenceforth under the name of the Courier-Journal, Mr. Prentice continuing to aid in editing until the sickness which resulted in a few weeks in his death.

In college, Mr. Prentice was recognized as a fine scholar and distinguished as a writer of both prose and verse, his college essays exhibiting marked vigor of thought, beauty of diction, correctness of style, and purity of English; some of his sweetest productions in verse were written while in the university. He relinquished the law because he liked Addison and Byron better than Chitty and Blackstone; there was too much of poetry in him for the dry formulas of the court room. His "Biography of Henry Clay"—much of it written in the home of the great statesman—was finished just ten days before he entered upon the great work of his life as editor of the Louisville Journal. It was written in a glowing and ardent style, reflecting the true life of one in the unalloyed admiration of the other.

During the thirty-eight years of editorial life in the Journal, he perhaps wrote more, and certainly wrote better, than any journalist that ever conducted a daily paper in this state. He made the Journal one of the most renowned papers in the land, and many articles from his pen would have done honor to the highest literary periodical of the day. The Journal under his guidance made and unmade the poets, poetesses, essayists, and journalists who appeared in the West for the third of a century which preceded his death. His humor, his wit, and his satire were the best friends and the worst enemies that aspirants to fame in his region could have.

In 1835 Mr. Prentice was married to Miss Henriette Benham, daughter of Colonel Joseph Benham, a distinguished member of the Kentucky bar. They had two sons: William Courtland Prentice, who was killed while bravely leading his company of Confederate soldiers at the battle of Augusta, Kentucky, September 18, 1862; and Clarence J. Prentice, also a Confederate officer, who was killed by the upsetting of his buggy, near Louisville, November, 1873. Mrs. Prentice died in April, 1868, at the family residence in Louisville.

In 1860 he published a book under the title of "Prenticeana," made up of his humorous, witty, and satirical paragraphs as they appeared in the Journal. To this style of composition, perhaps more than to anything else, Mr. Prentice owed his fame as a journalist. He was a paragraphist of unparalleled ability.

At the breaking out of the rebellion in 1861, Mr. Prentice took sides and used his powerful pen against the South, in the conflict which ended so disastrously to that section. And yet, during the war he performed numerous kind and generous acts to individual sufferers on the rebel side, and proved a friend to many in times of need.

The disease of which Mr. Prentice died was pneumonia, the result of violent cold taken in riding in an open carriage, on the coldest day in the year, from Louisville to the residence of his son Clarence, some miles below the city. He struggled with it for a month, retaining his mental faculties to the last. Just before he drew his last breath, he exclaimed, "I want to go, I want to go." His grave at Cave Hill cemetery is yet without a becoming monument.

A eulogy of singular beauty and power was pronounced by Henry Watterson, editor of the Courier-Journal, by invitation of the legislature of Kentucky. His poems had been collected by his son, with a view to publication in a volume—to which, it is hoped, some of his most marked prose contributions will be added. As an author and poet Mr. Prentice had few equals; but he was a journalist of pre-eminent ability and versatility.

MAJ. PHILIP NORBOURNE BARBOUR, born near Bardstown, Kentucky, in 1817; raised and educated in Henderson County, Kentucky; graduated at West Point, 1834; made second lieutenant in Third Infantry; soon after made first lieutenant and became regimental adjutant until 1845; for bravery in defending Fort Waggoner in East Florida, made brevet-captain;

and for services at Palo Alto and Resaca de la Palma made brevet-major May 9, 1846; and was killed in action September 19, 1846, while leading his company at the storming of the breastworks of the city of Monterey. He was a man of great amenity of manners and of much talent—reputed one of the most energetic officers of the war with Mexico.

WILLIAM LYLE SIMMONS of Lexington was born in Frederick County, Maryland, October 9, 1829, and is a son of John E. H. and Martha (Lillard) Simmons. The family originally came to this country with Lord Baltimore. Brigadier-General Morris of Revolutionary fame, who contributed generously to the Continental Congress, was the maternal grandfather of the subject of this sketch. His grandfather Simmons and his father, John E. H. Simmons, were the owners of a large number of slaves in Frederick County, Maryland, and, about thirty years before the late war, foreseeing the inevitable conflict, they set their slaves free.

John E. H. Simmons left Maryland and went to New York City when his son, William L., was five or six years of age, and engaged in the wholesale manufacture of whips, in which trade he made a national reputation. William attended the grammar and high schools of New York and obtained a good education. At the age of fourteen he entered the office of B. Wood & Company and was with them for twenty years, becoming a partner within a few years after entering the house. He operated in Wall street and quite largely at times, but not frequently, and laid the foundation for the large fortune which he very nearly lost by the panic of 1873. He paid out and quit, which afterwards proved a very wise conclusion.

While he was in the possession of large means he had established his noted stables of thoroughbred horses, merely for the pleasure he could find in the ownership of them. He had done this, as he said, for a "plaything," expecting it to yield him nothing but expense. But when the tide of fortune turned he found that he had an exceedingly valuable property in his thoroughbreds, and in 1872 he brought them to Lexington, with a result that is well known to horsemen throughout the country.

Mr. Simmons, popularly known as "George Wilkes" Simmons, is in many ways a remarkable man. Besides being the owner of "George Wilkes"—champion in his day and progenitor of the greatest family of trotters the world has ever seen—he is the breeder and owner of Jay Bird, the sire of Allerton, the thrice-crowned king, who was also the four-year-old champion and was the fastest five-year-old of any sex; he bred Eagle Bird, sire of the two-year-old champion, Monbars; also bred and owns William L., the sire of Axtell, the three-year-old champion; bred and owns Betterton, sire of George St. Clair, the three-year-old champion of Michigan.

Such marvelous results do not come by chance. To breed the sire of one champion requires a vast amount of experience, intelligent thought and much more than ordinary ability. Few men have bred the sire of one champion. Mr. Simmons has bred and owned five or six champion stallions or sires, and in doing so became a public benefactor.

No mathematician is able to compute the amount of money the breeding establishment of Mr. Simmons has brought to this country. The commonwealth of Kentucky has gained untold millions by his enterprise.

PROFESSOR ARTHUR YAGER of Georgetown College, son of Dr. Frank J. and Diana (Smith) Yager, was born in Campbellsburg, Henry County, October 29, 1858. His father is a native of Oldham County, who removed to Campbellsburg in 1852, where he has ever since been engaged in the practice of medicine, and is still quite active for a man of seventy-eight years of age. He is a graduate of the Medical University of Louisville.

Daniel Yager (grandfather) was a native of Madison County, Virginia. He came to Oldham County in 1817 and resided there until he was eighty years of age, and died in 1860. He was a farmer on a very extensive scale. The Yagers are of German origin, but have been in this country for more than a century.

Diana Smith Yager (mother) is a native of Oldham County, and she and Dr. Yager are members of the Baptist Church.

Fountain Smith (grandfather) was a native of Virginia. When he first came to Kentucky he located in Oldham County, but afterwards removed to Henry County, where he died in 1843 at the age of forty years.

Professor Arthur Yager received his primary education in his native town and entered Georgetown College in 1875, graduating in 1879, after a four years' course, after which he had charge of the College Academy for three years. He then spent two years in the Johns Hopkins University at Baltimore, graduating with the degree of Doctor of Philosophy in 1884. He then returned to Georgetown and was elected Professor of History and Political Science, which position he holds at the present writing. He was for a time secretary of the Kentucky College Association and has been, since its organization, a director in the Kentucky Chautauqua at Lexington, and is a member of a number of historical and scientific associations.

Professor Yager was married in 1892 to Estill, daughter of Dr. James Lewis of Virginia. She was born in Louisiana, where her father was for a time located. They have one son, Rodes Estill Yager.

T. FERDINAND BEYLAND, a prominent citizen and business man of Bellevue, was born in Gardelegen, Germany, October 1, 1847. His father and mother, D. G. and Caroline (Meyer) Beyland, were natives of Wurtemberg, Germany, who came to America in 1850 and located in Cincinnati; and in 1856 went to Kansas and settled within about fifty miles of Kansas City, Missouri, in a part of the state which was then considered the western border of civilization. The inhabitants were principally Indians, and as they were not the most desirable neighbors, and as Mr. Beyland was a coppersmith, in which capacity he found little to do in the new country, and being unused to the life and work of the agriculturist, he remained there only about nine months and returned to Cincinnati, and finally took up his residence in Newport. Mr. Beyland was an industrious man and a good citizen. He and his wife were members of the Lutheran Church. He died in Newport in 1867, in the fifty-fourth year of his age. His estimable companion survived him until 1882, continuing her residence in Newport, and died at the age of sixty-six years.

After returning from Kansas, Ferdinand, now about ten years of age, joined a theatrical company and traveled through nearly every state in the Union, gaining a knowledge of the country and of human nature which, together with a good primary education, has been of great advantage to him in business. This was supplemented by three years' experience in the army. At the beginning of the war, he enlisted as a drummer boy and served in the armies of Generals Buell, Rosecrans and Sherman; participated in the famous battles of Shiloh, Stone River, Chickamauga and Missionary Ridge and was in the Atlanta campaign, and was honorably discharged from the service at Fort Adams, Rhode Island, in 1864, when he was not yet eighteen years of age. By this time he knew something about his adopted country, but he felt that his education was not complete, and he became a sailor on the Gulf and lived on the water during 1866. During the following year he traveled in Texas in a business capacity, and saw all that was to be seen of life in that state. He then became a commercial traveler for the George D. Winchell Manufacturing Co. of Cincinnati, covering the whole country from the lakes to the Gulf and from the Atlantic Ocean to the Rocky Mountains. This occupied his attention for ten years, when he concluded to settle down and put his education to practical use; and, in 1878, he became a citizen of Bellevue.

He at once interested himself in the development of that flourishing little city. He organized two of the most reliable building and loan associations; was president of one of them for a time and is, and has been, secretary of the Home Savings and Loan Association since its organization, April 4, 1889. In 1883 he was elected president of the City Council and served two years, having served as a member for a term of two years previous to that, and was City Treasurer of Bellevue in 1894.

In January, 1894, he became a partner of C. W. Nagel in the real estate business, in which they have met with gratifying success. He has accumulated considerable valuable property in his own name in Bellevue and vicinity.

Mr. Beyland was married in 1874 to Clara M. Smith, daughter of M. V. Smith of Newport, Kentucky, and they have an interesting family, consisting of two sons and four daughters: Walter, Agnes, Clifford, Alice, Dorothy and Beatrice.

Mr. Beyland is a member of the Granville Moody Post, G. A. R., and was the founder of the Bellevue Lodge of Knights of Honor in 1878. He is a Republican and a leader in local politics.

JOHN P. CAMPBELL, Secretary and Treasurer of the Fowler Wharfboat Company, and one of the most prominent young business men of the flourishing city of Paducah, was born in Martinsburg, West Virginia, September 15, 1867; and is a son of John P. and Mary Boyd (Faulkner) Campbell. His father was educated for the legal profession and practiced law for some time; was a member of Congress for one term, immediately preceding the Civil war, in which he took no active part; and was not thereafter engaged in the practice of law, but interested himself in a number of large business enterprises. He was interested in the Henderson & Nashville Railroad from its organization, and was president of that company during the construction of the road. He organized the Mastodon Coal & Iron Company, which was succeeded by the St. Bernard Coal Company. Soon afterwards he retired and gave his attention to his large landed estates during the latter years of his life; and died in 1887, aged sixty-seven years.

John P. Campbell (grandfather) was born in Virginia in 1778, and removed to Hopkinsville, where he organized the Branch Bank of Kentucky, the first bank in Hopkinsville, of which he was president as long as he lived; and was also proprietor of a large tobacco stemmery and a dealer in tobacco, shipping large quantities to London. He was of Scotch-Irish descent.

Mary B. Faulkner Campbell (mother) was a daughter of Honorable Charles James Faulkner, a native of Virginia, lawyer, politician and diplomat, who was minister plenipotentiary and envoy extraordinary to France under President Buchanan, and was on General Stonewall Jackson's staff during the Civil war. He was a member of Congress for twenty years, representing the Martinsburg, Virginia, District, serving before and after the war; was chairman of the Commitee of Ways and Means and of the Committee on Foreign Relations, and served on various other committees. His death occurred in 1886, when in the seventy-sixth year of his age. Mary B. (Faulkner) Campbell (mother) is a sister of the present Senator Faulkner of Virginia.

John P. Campbell was named for his father and grandfather. He attended school in Hopkinsville and finished his studies at Berkeley Academy at Martinsburg, West Virginia. He spent the first ten years of his business career in the Bank of Hopkinsville; and on May 1, 1892, removed to Paducah, where he became interested in the Wharfboat Company, of which he is now secretary and treasurer; in 1894 organized the Campbell-Mulvihill Coal Company, of which he is president; in January, 1895, organized the Merchants' Transfer, of which he is also the president. Later in the same year he established the general commission and grocery house of J. P. Campbell & Company, and is pushing to the front in a way that is surprising to the business men of Paducah.

John P. Campbell and Birdie E. Fowler, daughter of the late Captain Gus Fowler, who was one of the most prominent citizens of Paducah, were married October 27, 1891.

HENRY FIELD DUNCAN, Ex-Commissioner of Insurance, Frankfort, Kentucky.— The Reverend William Duncan, who was born in Perthshire, Scotland, January 7, 1630, was the progenitor of the Duncan family that settled in the colony of Virginia in 1690. Reverend William Duncan lost his life for refusing to take the Jacobite oath in the reign of Charles II.; he married in 1657 Sarah Haldane. His oldest child, William Duncan, was born October 1, 1659; Charles, another son, September 6, 1662; Henry, January 11, 1664; Thomas, January 28, 1665; Mary, February 1, 1667. William Duncan, born April 19, 1690, was the grandson of the Reverend

William Duncan who left Scotland, accompanied by his two sisters and brothers. He arrived in Culpeper County, Virginia, on January 23, 1722. On February 11 of the same year he took to wife Ruth Raleigh, daughter of Matthew Raleigh, who was born in England of Welsh parentage. Raleigh Duncan, their eldest son, was with General Washington at Braddock's defeat in 1755; also at Point Pleasant in 1774, where he was severely wounded, and was in all attacks made by the colonial troops against the invasion of Virginia by the traitor Arnold in 1781. The old Scotch families thus settled in the northern neck of Virginia were true to the cause of freedom during the great struggle for independence; no family was more true to the American cause than the children and grandchildren of William Duncan, who was the founder of this family in the colony of Virginia and the ancestor of the various branches of the Duncans who have scattered themselves over the South and West within the last seventy years.

Henry F. Duncan is the son of Joseph Dillard and Jane (Covington) Duncan, and was born near Bowling Green, Kentucky, March 13, 1854. Joseph Dillard Duncan was born in Culpeper Court House, Virginia, and with his father came to Kentucky in 1818. His father was a farmer in Warren County, and was for a number of years engaged in merchandising in Bowling Green in connection with his other interests. He is a member of the Baptist Church; has served as magistrate, and has always taken an active part in politics, and he is now chairman of the Democratic Committee of his district, although in the eightieth year of his age.

Edmund Duncan (grandfather) was a native of Culpeper County, Virginia, and made his settlement in Warren County, Kentucky, about the year 1818, where he was a farmer until the time of his death, which occurred in 1859. He had been a Whig in his political tenets in the old days of Whigs and Democrats, and filled the office of magistrate.

Joseph Covington (grandfather) was a native of Raleigh, North Carolina, who came with his father when a child and settled in Warren County, where his death occurred in 1858, aged seventy years. The Covingtons were of Scotch-Irish extraction.

Henry F. Duncan remained on a farm until he was twelve years old, receiving his education in the public schools, which was supplemented by one year at Georgetown College and one year at the State University of Michigan. After leaving school he commenced the study of law, but in May, 1876, he received an appointment in the State Auditor's office when he relinquished the study of law. He remained in this capacity for three years, at the end of which time he accepted a position in the quartermaster-general's office, and continued there for eight months. On January first, 1880, he was again appointed clerk in the state auditor's office under General Fayette Hewitt, and remained in that capacity for two years and five months. In June, 1882, he received an appointment of clerk in the Insurance Department and held the same until January 1, 1888, when he was appointed deputy insurance commissioner. On November 11, 1889, he received the appointment of insurance commissioner and held that important office until the expiration of his term in January, 1896.

Henry F. Duncan was married in 1876 to Sallie Childs Buford, a daughter of Temple Buford of Georgetown, Kentucky.

HAWES B. EAGLES, Assistant Cashier of the Owensboro Banking Company, son of Albert James and Kate Coleman (Hawes) Eagles, was born in Daviess County, Kentucky, February 28, 1867. He received his education in Hopkinsville, principally in Major Terrell's private school, and prepared himself for the occupation of civil engineer, which work he began in 1885, but was offered his present position as assistant cashier in the Owensboro Banking Company, which he accepted and has filled with efficiency for more than ten years.

He was married August 3, 1893, to Anna Belle Deane, an accomplished young lady who was educated in the best schools of Owensboro.

Mr. Eagles is attentive to business, of industrious habits and affable manners, obliging and courteous in business matters, and though quite popular, is unassuming and modest. He has

KENTUCKY BIOGRAPHIES.

made a good record as a banker and has a promising future. He is a Democrat in politics, but does not seek prominence in his party; is a member of the benevolent order of Elks, and a consistent member of the Baptist Church.

His father, Albert James Eagles, was born in Kent, England, June 26, 1835; was educated in Oxford College, and came to America in 1854. He was for some years engaged in teaching in Missouri and Kentucky, and after his marriage to Kate C. Hawes, October 26, 1864, he engaged in merchandising in Yelvington, in which he continued until his death, June 13, 1881. He was never naturalized as a citizen of the United States, but, being associated with the Southern people, he was an ardent sympathizer with the South in the Civil war. He was a man of superior education, highly cultured and was quite prominent and much respected in the community in which he lived. He was a member of the Episcopal Church and an exemplary Christian gentleman. He married Kate C. Hawes, and they had three children: Hawes, William, now with Fairleigh & Straus, attorneys of Louisville, and Marianne.

William Eagles (grandfather) was a gentleman of leisure, being very wealthy. He lived and died in Kent, England, his native place.

Kate Coleman Hawes Eagles (mother) was born in Kentucky, October 4, 1841. She was educated in a private school taught by Reverend Beckett, an Englishman and a minister in the Episcopal Church. She is a resident of Owensboro, and a member of the Baptist Church.

Benjamin Hawes (grandfather) was born in Virginia, April 8, 1810, and was educated in Owensboro, Kentucky; was a farmer in Daviess County; married Mary Ann Taylor of Clarke County in 1832, and died October 17, 1861. His wife was a daughter of Samuel M. and Mildred Martin Taylor, and a sister of Jonathan Gibson Taylor. She was born July 3, 1813, and was educated in private schools in Lexington; married Benjamin Hawes in 1832, and died February 11, 1862. Mildred Martin Taylor was a daughter of Colonel John Martin of Clarke County, whose father was one of the early pioneers and was contemporary with Daniel Boone. He took part in all of the Indian wars of his day.

Samuel M. Taylor was born in Virginia in 1785. He married Mildred Martin in 1810. His father, Jonathan Taylor, lived in Caroline County, Virginia, prior to the Revolution, and afterward came to Kentucky.

Richard Hawes, a brother of grandfather Hawes, was Confederate governor of Kentucky during the war between the states after the death of George W. Johnson, the first Confederate governor.

Richard Hawes (great-grandfather) came to Kentucky from Virginia in 1810, and located first in Fayette County, later in Jefferson County, and finally in Daviess County, in 1819; and at that time purchased large tracts of land in Daviess and Hancock Counties. He bought three thousand acres of land on the Ohio River in the Yelvington precinct; one thousand acres adjoining the village of Yelvington and one thousand acres bordering on Hancock County, embracing the site of Hawesville, which town was named for him. He married Clara Walker, and was the father of eleven children. He died in 1829, ten years after acquiring his large landed estate. His wife's maiden name was Clara Walker, and they had seven sons and four daughters: Richard, Samuel, Walker, Albert, Aylett, Benjamin, William, Ann, Kitty, Susan and Clara.

Albert Hawes was the first Democratic candidate elected to Congress from the Owensboro district, as up to that time the Whigs prevailed in every election.

H. THOMAS LLOYD, a prominent farmer of Bracken County and well-known citizen of Augusta, son of Richard and Elizabeth (Adamson) Lloyd, was born in Bracken County, Kentucky, May 24, 1836. His father was also born in Bracken County, February 2, 1797. He received his education in the county schools; was a farmer of progressive ideas; was interested in politics, first as a Whig of pronounced views, then as a Union man during the Civil war, and as a straight-out Democrat from 1865 until his death, June 23, 1874. He was a member of the Christian Church, and a man of most positive character, honored and respected by a large circle of friends and acquaintances.

The grandfather Lloyd was a native of Maryland, who came to Kentucky in 1788, and settled first in Fayette County, four miles from Lexington; removed to Bracken County in 1795. He married Susan Winter of Lexington, who was born in 1767; lived one hundred and one years, and died in 1868.

Elizabeth Adamson Lloyd (mother) was born in Mason County, in 1800; married Richard Lloyd in 1826; died in Bracken County in 1870; was a member of the Christian Church, and a noble Christian woman.

John Adamson (grandfather) was a native of Philadelphia, Pennsylvania; removed to May's Spring, Mason County, Kentucky, in 1786 or 1787, and was a farmer in that county. His wife, Ruth, died in Mason County in 1840.

H. Tom Lloyd, as he is familiarly known, was educated in public schools; finished his studies in 1855; went to Missouri in 1856 and bought a half section of land near the town of Mexico, but having inherited his father's estate, he returned to Bracken County; has purchased other property, including the Garrett Perrine farm, upon which he resides, and has recently purchased a one-twelfth interest in sixteen thousand acres of land—known as Kentucky colony—on which they have a proposed town site section near Phoenix, Arizona.

Mr. Lloyd is quite active and prominent in all matters relating to improvement in agriculture in his county and state; has been president two years and director twenty-six years, and always a leading spirit in the Union Agricultural Society of Mason and Bracken Counties since 1870; vice-president of the Bracken County Fair Association since 1893; was a member of the World's Fair Auxiliary Congress of 1893; was appointed and commissioned by Governor Buckner a member of the National Farmers' Congress at Council Bluffs, Iowa, in 1890; was alternate to the national Democratic convention at Chicago in 1892; is a county infirmary commissioner and receiver for the same; and has at frequent and divers times represented his county and section in conventions and societies. He has been superintendent of the Augusta and Brookville turnpike alternately for twenty-five years, and is the acknowledged representative progressive farmer in one of the best agricultural districts in the state. In politics Mr. Lloyd is a Democrat, and he is a liberal supporter of the Christian Church.

Mr. Lloyd was married November 30, 1865, to Lucy Perrine of Bracken County. She was born March 13, 1846, and is a daughter of Garrett and Amanda (Myers) Perrine, and granddaughter of Thomas and Elizabeth (Davidson) Myers. Mr. and Mrs. Lloyd have one daughter, Julia, who was born October 5, 1866, and married Nicholas C. Taliaferro, October 4, 1888.

DR. BUSHROD FOLEY LAIRD of Covington, one of the most distinguished men of the medical profession in Kentucky, was born in Covington, January 5, 1847. He is a graduate of the city high school, class of 1865; attended the Western Military Academy of Dayton, Ohio, in 1866 and 1867 as cadet captain, and the University of Leipsic, Saxony, in 1868 and 1869; and having returned to his home, he continued the study of medicine in the Cincinnati Medical College in 1872, graduating in 1874. He entered into the practice of medicine in the Good Samaritan Hospital in Cincinnati in the year 1875, and was winner of the Dawson and Bartholow prizes. While in Leipsic he studied music in the Kessler Musical Institute, from which he received a certificate. In 1888 he received the premium from the Centennial Exposition of the Ohio Valley and Central States for an automatic car coupler, and in 1889 the same device was awarded the medal at the Exposition Universelle, Paris.

In 1861, when only fifteen years of age, he was awarded a prize as the best mathematician in the public schools of Covington. The examiners in the contest were Mr. Meade, father of the late Admiral Meade; A. M. Randolph, ex-attorney-general of Montana and the high school faculty.

Dr. Laird is a member of the Cincinnati Academy of Medicine, member of the Kentucky State Medical Association, of the Mississippi Valley Medical Association and the American Association.

He was married, November 15, 1877, to Ellen Zimmerman, daughter of Solomon Zimmerman of Clifton, Ohio. She was educated in a convent in Brown County, Ohio. She is a sister of Eugene Zimmerman, vice-president of the Cincinnati, Hamilton & Dayton Railroad Company. Dr. and Mrs. Laird have two children: Martina and Eugenea.

Dr. Laird has a distinguished ancestry. His father, Samuel Boden Laird, was born in Edinburgh, Scotland, October 15, 1815. He came to America when quite young and was educated in the common schools of Pittsburgh. He was a tobacco manufacturer in that city for some years, and took his tobacco to New Orleans on flatboats. After selling his tobacco he would buy a horse and return overland. In 1837 he was returning from New Orleans and stopped in Covington, where he concluded to locate. He was the largest manufacturer of tobacco in the city for a number of years, and was inspector of tobacco in the Bodman House, and was acknowledged to be the best judge of tobacco in Kentucky. He was awarded the premium a number of times for work in this respect.

He was also a manufacturer and dealer in firearms during the early days of the war, and in 1861 he was the only man in Covington who was allowed to sell ammunition and firearms, and in this way he became known as the "Uncle Sam" of Covington. At the time of his death he was the richest man in Covington. The principal school buildings in the city stand on ground that was owned by "Uncle Sam" Laird.

He was independent in politics, but his sympathies were with the North during the Civil war. He attended strictly to business, caring little for politics. He was an Odd Fellow. He was related to Rev. Charles Laird, a distinguished divine of Pittsburgh, and was a member of the Presbyterian Church. He died October 2, 1863, and is buried in Linden Grove Cemetery. His parents died soon after their arrival in Pittsburgh, leaving three sons and three daughters, who made their home with a family by the name of Wilson, Mr. Wilson being a leading citizen and at one time mayor of Pittsburgh.

Dr. Laird's mother, Cordelia (Whitaker) Laird, was born of Scotch parents in London, England, August 1, 1825. The family came to America when she was twelve years old and located in Cincinnati. She received her principal schooling in Dr. Orr's Ladies' Seminary in Covington, and was married to Samuel B. Laird in 1844. She is one of the oldest members of the First Presbyterian Church in Covington. Her father, William Whitaker, was born in Scotland, but lived for a time in London. He was a steamboat painter and one of the largest contractors in that line in this country. He retired from business in 1850, and lived with his daughter, Mrs. Laird, until 1863, when he died. His son, William Whitaker, Jr., was one of the organizers and founders of the Cincinnati Gymnasium.

HENRY MARSHALL BUFORD, a leading lawyer of Lexington, son of Henry and Bettie (Marshall) Buford, was born in Paris, Kentucky, November 20, 1845. When twelve years of age he entered Center College at Danville, and graduated in 1864, receiving the highest honors of his class. He studied law with Garret Davis, of Paris, and attended Harvard Law School, from which he graduated in 1866. He was elected by his class to write a prize essay, and this effort, at the age of twenty-one, gave him at once a reputation as a writer and as a scholar of superior ability.

In 1867 he began the practice of law in Lexington and soon took rank as one of the brightest young lawyers of the blue grass capital. His success was at once assured, and for nearly thirty years he has maintained the dignity of his profession and the honor of his illustrious ancestors, whose names are written on almost every page in the history of Kentucky and of the southwest.

Aside from his practice at the bar, which has always been of the first consideration and has received his best attention, he has once or twice held public office. He was master commissioner of the Circuit Court from 1877 to 1880, and was judge of the Common Pleas Court from August, 1886, to August, 1890. His record as lawyer, officer and judge is without stain or blemish, and much might be said of his busy career, but the main purpose of this sketch is to record the history of the several families from which he is descended.

Henry Buford (father) was a native of Scott

County, Kentucky. Afer reaching maturity, he removed to Fayette County, where he made his home until his death, which occurred in 1849, in the twenty-seventh year of his age. He was a farmer by occupation, and a Henry Clay Whig in politics.

He was the son of Charles Buford (grandfather), who was born in Scott County, Kentucky, and in 1853 removed to Rock Island, Illinois, where he died in 1866, in the sixty-seventh year of his age. He was one of the enterprising farmers of Scott County, and owned one thousand acres of valuable land there. At Rock Island he led a retired life, but was president of a short coal line railroad, in which he was interested. For many years before going to Illinois, he was president of the Kentucky Racing Association and a breeder of thoroughbred race horses.

His father was Abraham Buford (great-grandfather), a native of Virginia, who emigrated to Scott County in 1788 and was an extensive farmer and large land owner. The ancestors of the Bufords, who settled in Virginia in 1697, were of Norman-English descent, and were as brave and fearless a race of men as ever lived in Kentucky. The descendants of the Bufords, who left Virginia in 1786, 1787 and 1788, are now living in various portions of the south and west. The Bufords of Illinois were a branch of the Virginia family who settled there some years prior to the admission of Illinois into the Union, in 1818. John Buford was the founder of the Illinois branch.

Bettie Marshall Buford (mother) was a native of Mason County, daughter of James Keith Marshall, and is now a resident of Lexington.

Henry Marshall Buford's grandmother Buford was a daughter of Governor Adair, who was descended from Huguenots, who settled in South Carolina in 1696. Governor Adair was a soldier in the War of the Revolution, and settled in Kentucky in 1786. He served as aide to Governor Isaac Shelby at the battle of the Thames in the year 1813. His conduct during this war was such as to elicit from his superior officers an expression of the highest admiration. Governor Shelby afterwards conferred upon him the appointment of adjutant general of Kentucky troops, with the rank of brigadier general, and in that capacity he commanded the soldiers of Kentucky in the battle of New Orleans. In 1820 John Adair was elected governor of Kentucky in opposition to Judge Logan, Governor Desha and Colonel Butler. He often served as a member of the State Legislature of Mercer County, and was more than once speaker of that body. In 1825 he was elected to the United States Senate; was elected to Congress in 1831, and served as a member of the House for three years. He was born in Abbeyville, South Carolina, in 1757, and died May 19, 1840, at the age of eighty-three years.

J. K. Marshall (maternal grandfather) was a native of Mason County; removed to Bourbon County in 1837; thence to Milwaukee, Wisconsin, in 1855, where he resided some years and then returned to Kentucky, and died in Mason County in 1866, aged sixty-five years. He was an able lawyer, and during his residence in Bourbon County, served as county judge. He was a man of exalted character, of fine judgment and wonderful energy and liberality.

He was the son of Alexander K. Marshall (great-grandfather), a native Virginian, who settled in Kentucky in 1785, and was reporter of the Kentucky Court of Appeals in 1818.

His father was Colonel Thomas Marshall (great-great-grandfather), who was a brother of Chief Justice John Marshall. He was a noted orator, and like many members of his family, a great lawyer, and was distinguished for his strong common sense.

JESSE E. FOGLE, a well-known lawyer of Hartford, was born in Liberty, Casey County, Kentucky, April 7, 1848.

His father, Hon. McDowell Fogle, one of the foremost lawyers of the state, was born in Lebanon, Kentucky, December 30, 1815, and was the second child, and first male child, born in that now flourishing city. He was educated in the district and private schools and in St. Mary's College in Marion County; adopted the legal profession and studied law privately and under the direction of one of the learned lawyers of that locality, and after being admitted to the bar, he began the practice of his profession at Liberty, the county seat of Casey County; continued there until about 1853, when he removed to Owensboro, accompanied by his brother-in-law and pupil, the late William N. Sweeney, who became one of the most prominent and powerful pleaders at the bar in Western Kentucky. Mr. Fogle practiced law in Owensboro for only a short time, when he returned to Liberty and resumed the practice there and in adjoining counties until 1872, and then retired from regular practice. For many years he was a member of the firm of Fogle & Fox, the latter subsequently becoming judge of the Eighth judicial district. He was also for many years associated in the practice of the law with Colonel Silas Adams—who has since represented the Eleventh district in Congress—under the firm name of Fogle & Adams. His party frequently honored him by electing him to office; he served two or three terms as county attorney; was appointed master commissioner and receiver of the Casey Circuit Court; was a member of the Kentucky legislature in 1855-57 and 1859-61, representing the counties of Casey and Russell; and Democratic elector for his district.

When he gave up the practice of law in 1872 he retired to his farm in the country—but a short drive on the turnpike road leading from Liberty to Middleburg—where he is independently situated, and with his interesting family is enjoying the fruits of an honorable and well spent life. He was quite successful in his profession and succeeded in accumulating a large property, and is now one of the largest land owners of his county. He is a member of the Methodist Church, as was his wife, the mother of the subject of this sketch, and his home has always been a hospitable retreat for the ministers of his church and for others, who have been royally entertained thereat.

He married Miss Emily J. Sweeney of Liberty, February 17, 1841, who was born there June 4, 1821, and died at Liberty, October 14, 1852, and is buried in the Liberty cemetery, near her father and mother. She was the mother of six children: Marietta, Isabelle, Sarah Frances, Jesse Edwin, William McDowell, and a daughter who died in infancy, a few days preceding the death of its mother.

Subsequently Mr. Fogle married Miss Sallie Barger of Russell County, who died after about a year of wedded life.

His third marriage was to Miss Martha J. Murphy of Casey County. By this marriage there were seven children: James M., Elizabeth A., Robert B., Joel, Lena J., D. Edgar and George Preston.

Joel died in infancy, and William McDowell died September 3, 1883.

Robert H. Fogle (grandfather) was born in Maryland, May 1, 1788, and came with his parents to Marion, then Washington County, Kentucky, in 1792, with the pioneers; he helped to clear the land where Lebanon is located, and built the first house that was erected in Lebanon, and when the town was established was one of its first trustees; and was appointed the first postmaster of that place. He was a saddler by trade; gained considerable wealth, and in 1829 quit the saddlery business and invested his money in lands near Lebanon and engaged in agricultural pursuits; he owned a great many slaves, but gave them their freedom before he was compelled to do so by the emancipation proclamation. He removed to Daviess County in 1849 and purchased a large, valuable farm near Owensboro, whereon is now located Elmwood cemetery, and there was interested in farming until the death of his wife, in 1860, when he sold his land, liberated his slaves and divided his wealth among his children, and made his home amongst them until his death, which occurred February 17, 1884, in the ninety-sixth year of his age.

He married Miss Rachel Shuttleworth, who was the mother of five children: Ebenezer, McDowell, Sallie Ann, who married Milford Purdy of Daviess County, and Mary, who married W. B. England of Lebanon, and one who died in boyhood.

His second wife was Sallie Newbold. There were two children of this marriage: Catherine, who married Thomas England of Lebanon, and Rachel J., who married John Murphy, deceased, of Owensboro.

Mr. Fogle was a member of the old school Presbyterian Church, and during his stay near Owensboro was the superintendent of the Sunday school of the First Presbyterian Church of that city. He was loved and respected by all and his buoyant spirits and his kind and unselfish nature made his coming always a source of pleasure to his children and grandchildren.

The great-grandfather Fogle married Sarah Hammet.

Joel Sweeney (maternal grandfather) was a native of Casey County and was educated in the private schools; was bred a lawyer, but did not practice law; was elected, when quite a young man, clerk of the Casey County Court and Circuit Court, and held this dual position during life; he was a man of wealth, owning a great deal of land, including a large and valuable farm adjacent to Liberty, numerous slaves, a large mill in the town, and much valuable real estate, besides being interested in the mercantile business; he was an upright, honorable and respected citizen; a man of exemplary character; generous to the poor and needy, and highly esteemed by the people of his county.

He married Obedience Edwards of Garrard County, and they had eight children: Elizabeth, married Major G. W. Sweeney of Casey County; Amanda, married Dr. Martin Adams of Somerset; Jesse G. Sweeney, a merchant of Lancaster; Emily J., who married McDowell Fogle; W. N. Sweeney, deceased, the eminent lawyer of Owensboro; Anna Eliza, married Captain C. M. Whipp of Liberty; Marietta, married Dr. D. S. Parker of Arkansas, and James, who was killed by an accident during boyhood.

Joel Sweeney died at his home in Liberty, in 1869, and his wife died while on a visit to her son, Hon. W. N. Sweeney, in Owensboro, in 1873, and is buried beside her husband at Liberty.

Charles Sweeney (maternal great-grandfather) was a native of Virginia, who came in early life to Casey County, and married Frances Shachelford there. His principal occupation was that of a farmer.

Jesse Edwin Fogle attended the Seminary at Liberty, and the Parochial Academy at Houstonville, Lincoln County, and taught school in Casey County, and clerked in the general store of his brother-in-law, George G. Fair, in Middleburg, Casey County, before going to Kentucky University at Lexington, where he concluded his school days in 1870. It had not occurred to Mr. Fogle to enter the law, but, "a competent knowledge of the laws of that society in which we live is the proper accomplishment of every gentleman and scholar, and highly useful, I had almost said essential, part of liberal and polite education." This quotation from the first chapter of Blackstone's Commentaries, picked up in his father's library and read out of curiosity, so impressed him that he became interested therein and after having completed the reading of the work determined upon the study of the law, which he did in his father's office and under his instruction. He was admitted to the bar at Liberty, May 25, 1871, and began the practice in partnership with his father. It was a severe trial for him to separate himself from his father and boyhood home, but it appeared to him that it would be the best for him to do so, and, thereupon his maternal uncle and namesake, Jesse G. Sweeney, volunteered his kind assistance and made known his inclination to his brother, the late William N. Sweeney of Owensboro, who then represented his district in Congress, and he kindly expressed his willingness to assist him, either in Owensboro or elsewhere. At that time Mr. Sweeney had a son preparing for the law, and his law partner, the late Judge James Stuart, had also a son just entering law, and under these circumstances Hartford seemed to be the best point to begin and have his uncle's assistance and to abide future developments, and it was at his kind suggestion that he came to Hartford, September 4, 1872, and there associated Mr. Sweeney and Judge Stuart with himself in the practice, and thereafter had the benefit of their assistance and friendship during their lives.

Mr. Fogle's success in the practice of his profession demonstrates the wisdom of his choice, yet he never forgets an overruling Providence and the valuable and unselfish assistance rendered him by his distinguished uncle and law partner. He is considered one of the best lawyers at the Hartford bar, made up of good lawyers, and by his industry and good management has become financially independent. Besides owning one of the most desirable residences in Hartford, he owns other valuable property in the city, and an extensive mercantile establishment, over which are his law offices. Adjacent to the town he has a valuable farm, and is also one of the stockholders of the Bank of Hartford.

While at Liberty he joined the Christian Church. Still, the church of his father and mother and his wife's church, are alike the objects of his solicitude; he has been a friend to the temperance cause from his boyhood.

Mr. Fogle was married June 6, 1877, to Miss Lelia Addington, only child of the late Virgil P. Addington, a merchant of Hartford. She was born in Hartford, October 15, 1856. She is a member of the Methodist Episcopal Church, South, refined and cultured and has rare good judgment. Mr. Fogle attributes no small amount of his success to the faithful assistance of his wife, and is very much attached to his home and family. They have two children: Annie, born April 14, 1878, and now in Hartford College, from which she will graduate June, 1896, and McDowell Addington Fogle, born June 22, 1888.

JAMES RODMAN, M. D., retired physician of Hopkinsville, one of the ablest men in any profession in Kentucky, son of John and Patsy Foré Rodman, was born in New Castle, Henry County, Kentucky, March 6, 1829.

His father, John Rodman, who was prominent in Kentucky politics, was a native of Berks County, Pennsylvania, an officer in the War of 1812, and was made a prisoner at the battle of the River Raisin. The progenitor of the Rodman family was John Rodman, a well born, educated Irishman, a member of the Quaker Society, who was banished from his home on account of his religious views to the island of Barbadoes, and died in 1690. His sons, John and Thomas Rodman, were the progenitors of the Rodman family in this country.

Patsy Foré Rodman (mother) was born in Prince Edward County, Virginia. Her ancestors were Huguenots, who came to this country on the revocation of the Edict of Nantes, landed in South Carolina, and subsequently removed to Virginia. Her father, William Foré, was born in Virginia, and came to Henry County in 1801. He was a farmer and a man of affairs, taking great interest in the welfare of the community and in the material progress of his state and country. His father, Peter Foré, was among the very early emigrants from Virginia to Kentucky; was a Revolutionary soldier, died in a blockhouse in what is now Harrison or Bourbon County, Kentucky, on the day it was taken by the British and Indians under Colonel Byrd. His children, seven in number, with him at that time, were made prisoners and taken to Detroit. The sons returned to Kentucky, living long and reputable lives. The daughters remained, marrying officers in the British army—Wykoff and Smith by name.

James Rodman was educated in the Henry County Academy, one of the best schools of that day; read medicine with his brother, Hugh, who removed to Frankfort in 1850, where he distinguished himself as one of the best physicians in the state, and was accidentally thrown from his carriage and killed in 1872, when fifty-two years of age.

Dr. Rodman, after leaving his brother's office, attended the medical department of the University of Louisville, and was graduated from that institution in the class of 1849, before he was twenty years of age. He was fortunate in having the oversight in his studies of such men as Dr. L. P. Yandell, Sr., who was then dean of the faculty, as well as Drs. S. D. Gross, Daniel Drake and others, among the most eminent physicians and surgeons and able instructors in the profession.

After receiving his diploma Dr. Rodman began the practice of his calling in Hopkinsville, where he remained three years, and then returned to his native county; and from there he went to Frankfort, where, in 1860, he erected the first building for the Feeble Minded Institute. After three years of labor in behalf of this institution, he was made superintendent of the Western Kentucky Lunatic Asylum, and returned to Hopkinsville. He remained in charge of this asylum until April 20, 1889, since which time he has been retired, acting only as consulting physician, and in this capacity only in exceptional cases.

During his long term of service in the asylum, he saw it grow from small dimensions, accommodating only one hundred patients, to a magnificent institution, thoroughly equipped, with nearly six hundred inmates. It is no flattery to Dr. Rodman to say that the Western Kentucky Asylum was among the best institutions in the country, under his management. He was urged by the governor of Kentucky to remain in charge, but declined a reappointment, feeling that he had earned a much needed respite from his labors.

James Rodman was married in 1853 to Henrietta Thomasson, daughter of Captain Joseph M. Thomasson of Henry County, Kentucky. She was a worthy and efficient helpmate in all of the work to which Dr. Rodman devoted his life, and her death on December 20, 1894, was lamented by a host of relatives, friends and acquaintances.

Dr. Rodman has one son, Thomas, and one daughter, Mary, who married Lieutenant W. H. H. Southerland of the United States Navy, on August 1, 1877, who is now residing in Washington.

EDWARD O. LEIGH, late Assistant Secretary of State, and a representative of the young Democracy of Kentucky, is a native of Shelby County, Tennessee, where he was born June 23, 1859. His parents were Rev. William H. and Mary (Brooks) Leigh.

Rev. William H. Leigh was born in Virginia, December 28, 1826, and for forty-five years was a minister in the Methodist Episcopal Church, and for thirty years of that time he was presiding elder, preaching in Kentucky, Tennessee, Mississippi and other states. He was a man of wonderful force of character and of great executive ability. He was self-educated, and at the age of twenty commenced preaching the gospel, and soon became one of the leading lights of his church; a man of earnest convictions, whose reputation as a minister was confined to no one state. In 1879 he removed to Paducah, Kentucky, where he labored in the church until a short time before his death, which occurred in March, 1880.

Dr. James Walker Leigh (grandfather) was a native of Virginia, and died of the cholera at Eddyville, Kentucky.

Ferdinand Leigh (great-grandfather), son of William B. Leigh, was born in Virginia, and was a soldier in the war of the Revolution. James Brooks (maternal grandfather) was a native of North Carolina, of English descent, who subsequently settled in Tennessee, where he died. The maternal great-grandfather of Edward Leigh's mother was a Polk and a first cousin of James K. Polk.

Edward O. Leigh received his certificate of graduation from Odd Fellows College, Humboldt, Tennessee, at the age of sixteen years, at which time he commenced business on his own account, associating himself with his brother, Robert W., who bought out the Humboldt Journal. They published this paper for about two years, when he sold his interest to his brother and went to Memphis. At that place he worked at proof reading for a short time, and in 1884 removed to Paducah and founded the Daily Standard. He was the editor and publisher of this paper until the close of the year 1889, when he sold out to Dilday and Van Senden and went to Frankfort, June, 1890, where he afterward accepted the position of assistant clerk in the state senate. At the close of the session he was appointed by Governor Buckner as assistant secretary of state, and re-appointed by Governor Brown, in which position he served until the close of Governor Brown's administration.

SAMUEL W. BEDFORD, special agent of the Mutual Life Insurance Company of New York and a popular citizen of Owensboro, was born in Washington County, Kentucky, December 7, 1861, and is a son of Dr. Thompson Ware Bedford and Mildred (Houtchens) Bedford.

His father was born in Bourbon County, Kentucky, November 27, 1836; graduated from the medical department of the University of Louisville in March, 1861; began the practice of medicine in Washington County, in April, 1861, since which time he has devoted his whole time to his profession, practicing in Daviess County, in Louisville and in Nelson County, being at present located at Chaplin in that county. He is an elder in the Christian Church, a scholarly gentleman, and a man of high Christian character. He was married in October, 1860, to Mildred Houtchens. They have five children: Samuel W., Ella S., William K., Hattie O. and Henry W.

Asa Kentucky Lewis Bedford (grandfather) was born in Bourbon County, December 14, 1811, and died June 7, 1847. He was a farmer in his native county; a man of very pronounced character, who had the courage of his convictions and yet, with his strong force of character, an amiable man and highly esteemed by his neighbors.

Archibald Bedford (grandfather) was a native of Bourbon County, who married a Miss Clay, a member of the prominent family in that county.

Samuel W. Bedford's paternal grandmother, wife of Asa Kentucky Lewis Bedford, was Davidella Ware, daughter of Colonel Thompson and Sallie Ware of Bourbon County. She was born February 18, 1812, and died June 22, 1875.

A member of the Bedford family in Boston has traced the genealogy of the family to England and sent it to England in order to obtain a legacy that was said to belong to the Bedford heirs in the United States.

Colonel Thompson Ware (great-grandfather) was a son of James Ware and married Sallie Conn. William E. Houtchens (maternal grandfather) was a farmer in Nelson County, whose first wife was a daughter of Bishop Medley, and his second wife a daughter of Colonel Wood of Bloomfield, Nelson County.

Samuel W. Bedford was educated in the common schools of Daviess County and Owensboro, his parents having removed to that county when he was seven years of age. At the age of twelve years he left school, but continued his studies while clerking in a store.

He left Owensboro and went to Louisville, where he was employed a short time before going to Fulton, Kentucky, where he engaged in the clothing business. He became quite popular in that city and was elected mayor of Fulton, May 7, 1892. After serving one year he resigned his office and disposed of his clothing business to accept the agency for a life insurance company, and in 1893 he resigned that agency to accept a better position as special agent in Kentucky and Tennessee for the Mutual Life Insurance Company of New York, with headquarters at Owensboro, a business in which he has been very successful and is still engaged. He is a member of the Christian Church, an Odd Fellow and is popular among a host of friends and acquaintances.

Mr. Bedford was married in 1889 to Winefred M. Bowden, daughter of 'Squire Turner Bowden of Weakley County, Tennessee. She is a graduate of Gallatin College, class of 1888, and is a lady of fine accomplishments. Their only child, Kernan Ware Bedford, was born in August, 1890.

ADAM S. ADAMS, a successful farmer of Mercer County, son of John W. and Elizabeth (Sharp) Adams, was born in Mercer County, December 26, 1823. His father was born in the same county, April 29, 1792; was educated in the county schools; enlisted for the War of 1812, but was not called into active service; was a farmer in his native county, where he died September 15, 1855. He was a member of the Presbyterian Church and a man of most exemplary character. He was married January 30, 1823, to Elizabeth Sharp, of the same county, who was born October 29, 1793; educated in the schools of Mercer County and was a devout member of the Presbyterian Church. She died January 13, 1831. The four children of John W. Adams and Elizabeth Sharp, his wife, were: Adam S., born December 26, 1823; David Adams, born June 24, 1827, married Emma Crawford, May 24, 1870; Precilla, born December 24, 1828, and married Simon Stagg, October 5, 1848; Martha E., born November 10, 1830, married George Vanarsdale, November 17, 1853.

Mr. Adams' second wife, to whom he was married January 29, 1835, whose maiden name was Jane Adams, was born October 8, 1804, died August 16, 1864. She was the mother of six children: Ebenezer, born September 14, 1837, married Sallie Vananarsdall, December 10, 1863; Thomas, born December 14, 1835, married Sadie Adams, March 13, 1867; John W., born July 7, 1839, married Jane Thompson, January 2, 1865; Caleb, born October 8, 1841, married Lettie Terhune, January 10, 1888; Joshua, born September 7, 1843, and married Nannie Leachman, November 5, 1868; William J., born November 8, 1845, married Mary Smith, October 13, 1869.

David Adams (grandfather) was born in Virginia in 1754; was reared and educated in his native county; came to Kentucky in 1775 and settled in Mercer County, on land granted him by the state of Virginia, upon which his grandson, Adam S. Adams, is now living. He died January 19, 1823. His wife was Elizabeth Wood of Virginia, who was born in 1756, and died in Mercer County, April 24, 1840. Great-grandmother Sharp was slain by Indians. The children of David and Elizabeth Wood Adams (grandparents) were: Mary, born December 1, 1778, married Josiah J. Mann; Margaret, born March 21, 1781, married David McCamy; Martha, born July 16, 1783, married William Bard; Archibald, born September 25, 1786, married Pheba Caldwell; Elizabeth, born June 4, 1788, married Samuel Irvine; William, born November 15, 1790, married Percilla Armstrong; John Wood, born April 29, 1792, married Elizabeth Sharp; Ann, born September 7, 1795, married Cornelius Vanice; James, born July 18, 1798, married Rebecca Rose.

Adam S. Adams' educational opportunities were limited, as there were no schools that he could attend, except a subscription school, which was taught during the winter months. He learned the carpenter trade in his youth and followed that occupation industriously for fourteen years. In the fall of 1855 he removed to Parke County, Indiana, and engaged in farming and in buying horses and mules for the southern market. At the beginning of the war he lost all he had made and resumed his occupation as carpenter and builder, and followed it successfully for three years; was drafted in 1864, but furnished a substitute and was released from service.

After his father's death he purchased a part of the homestead farm, to which he subsequently removed, and upon which he is now living.

During the past six years Mr. Adams has been a director in the Mercer National Bank. He was a member of the fiscal court from 1875 to 1879, but has neither held nor sought any other office. He was a Whig until 1856, since which time he has voted with the Democratic party. He is a member of, and a deacon in the Presbyterian Church, and is one of the most honored and substantial citizens of Mercer County.

Mr. Adams was married March 11, 1863, to Martha Ann Watson, daughter of Wesley and Miranda (Burford) Watson, then of Parke County, Indiana. She was born September 30, 1836. They have no children.

Wesley Watson was a Virginian by birth; came to Kentucky with his parents when quite young; married Miranda Burford and removed to Parke County, Indiana, in 1832.

JOHN L. CASSELL, cashier of the Mercer National Bank, Harrodsburg, son of Thomas J. and Susan M. (Daniel) Cassell, was born in Jessamine County, Kentucky, October 7, 1834.

Thomas J. Cassell was born in Fayette County, Kentucky, in 1802; studied under private tutors and was one of the most thoroughly educated men in the state; read medicine under Dr. Satterwhite of Lexington, but his health failing he never practiced his profession; was a druggist for many years, but retired some ten years before his death, in 1867. In religion he was a Methodist; in politics a Whig.

Abram Cassell (grandfather), the son of Henry Cassell, who came to the United States from Hesse Cassel, Germany, the early part of the seventeenth century, was born near Fredericksburg, Maryland; was a lieutenant in the Revolutionary war; came to Kentucky and settled in (now) Jessamine County, on land for which he received a patent from the state of Virginia. This land is still owned by some of his descendants. He drew a pension from the government for military services until his death in 1845, at the advanced age of ninety-two years. His wife was Catherine Lingenfelder of Frederick, Maryland, who also reached the age of ninety-two years, and died in 1847. They were Presbyterians. Her father came from Germany and settled in Maryland. The sword used by Abram Cassell in the Revolutionary war and part of the continental money paid him is now in the possession of his grandson, J. L. Cassell, the principal subject of this sketch.

Susan M. Daniel Cassell (mother), a native of Pendleton County, was reared and educated near Lexington; died in 1867. She was a member of the Methodist Church.

Enos Daniel (maternal grandfather) was a son of Charles Daniel and Sarah Tate of Louisa County, Virginia. Charles Daniel was the son of John Daniel, the grandfather of Peter Daniel, one of the judges of the Supreme Court of the United States. The family came from England about 1750. Under the old constitution Enos Daniel was high sheriff of Pendleton County, Kentucky, for many years, and was a pioneer planter of that county; he died in Jeffersontown, Kentucky, at the home of his son-in-law, Dr. W. W. Senteny, June 6, 1857. He was married April 4, 1779, to Mary Nelson, the grandmother of John L. Cassell.

The children of Thomas J. and Susan M. (Daniels) Cassell are: William H. of Canton, Mississippi; John L. of Harrodsburg; Albert G. of Vicksburg, Mississippi; Thomas J. of Lexington; James D. of Lampasas, Texas, and Lizzie, wife of John Nicholas of Georgetown. Benjamin F. Cassell, the third son, was colonel of the Eighteenth Mississippi Regiment, Confederate army, Barksdale brigade, and fell at the front of that brigade, on Cemetery Hill, in the battle of Gettysburg.

John L. Cassell was educated in Nicholasville, in the excellent school then known as Bethel Academy; went to Lexington, Kentucky, in 1850, and was a clerk in the dry goods store of Allen & Plunkett for four years; then engaged in the same business in Lexington with James H. Shropshire, under the firm name of Shropshire & Cassell, until 1860, when he visited Mississippi with the view of purchasing a cotton plantation. But the war coming on returned to Kentucky and engaged in farming in Fayette County until 1872, when, in company with Messrs. Shropshire and Berkley, he established a wholesale grocery in Lexington, which business was conducted with few changes until 1879, when he purchased Avondale and removed to Mercer County and engaged in planting; was a director in and vice-president of the Mercer National Bank (capital $100,000), of which he was elected cashier in 1891, and to which business he has given his best attention until the present time. Has interests in other corporations and owns farms in Mercer and Jessamine Counties.

He is a member of the Christian Church, and in politics is a Democratic voter, but is not a politician.

Mr. Cassell was married (first) December 13, 1858, to Phoebe Elizabeth Bryan, daughter of Thomas Bryan of Fayette County, Kentucky. She died April 11, 1880, leaving six children: Robert, educated at the University of Virginia, married Gertrude Johnson of Michigan, now practicing law in Harriman, Tennessee; Henry B., hemp and grain dealer and postmaster of Burgin, Kentucky; Joseph, now studying medicine in the University of Louisville; Albert, now a student in the college at Harriman, Tennessee; Thomas B. Cassell died in Lampasas, Texas, aged twenty-nine years; Dr. John B. Cassell died in San Antonio, Texas, aged twenty-eight years.

Mr. Cassell was married (second time) September 14, 1882, to Virginia Bowman, daughter of Dudley and Virginia Smith Bowman of Mercer County, who is the mother of three children: Virginia and Susan, who are being educated at Daughters' College, and Carrie, who is at home.

The family residence is on Lynden street, Harrodsburg, Kentucky.

WILLIAM CARROLL, Judge of the Circuit Court of the Twelfth district, a resident of New Castle, was born in Arkansas, November 9, 1836.

His father, Owen Carroll, was born in Parish Killmallock, Ireland; came to New York, where he met and married Ellen Kirk; came to Kentucky in 1837, and located in Louisville. He was a railroad and turnpike contractor, and built portions of the Louisville, Frankfort & Lexington Railroad; also built the Muldraugh Hill turnpike, and other public roads. He removed from Louisville to Frankfort some time previous to his death, which occurred at Simpsonville, Shelby County, in 1842. He and his wife were members of the Catholic Church. Their two children were Judge Carroll and his sister Mary, wife of John W. Hall.

Judge Carroll's early education was obtained in Anderson College, New Albany, Indiana. After leaving school at the age of sixteen, he followed civil engineering for a time and then taught school in Kentucky for five years. While teaching he was an active member of a debating society in the neighborhood, and a friend who was also a member of the society advised him to study law, assuring him that he had unusual talent for argument. This turned his attention to the legal profession, and he began to read law—indifferently and in a desultory way, at first—but soon became intensely interested and then he knew that he had found the profession in which he could hope to be successful, and determined to prepare himself for the practice of law; a decision which he has had no occasion to regret, and the wisdom of which has never been questioned.

At the age of twenty-four he entered the law office of Judge DeHaven of LaGrange (whom he succeeded in the office of circuit judge), remaining with him for eight months, when he was admitted to the bar of Oldham County. After practicing one year he was elected county attorney in 1862. This office he resigned in 1864 to enter the Federal army as captain of Company E, Fifty-fourth Regiment Kentucky Volunteer Infantry; was in the army but a short time when matters of importance demanded his attention at home, and returning to LaGrange he continued in the practice of law at that place until 1873, when he removed to his present home in New Castle.

In 1871 he formed a partnership with Judge DeHaven, which continued until the election of the latter as circuit judge. In 1877 he formed a partnership with Judge Barbour, and was associated with him until 1884, when Mr. Barbour was elevated to the bench of the Superior Court.

In November, 1892, he was elected judge of the Circuit Court for the Twelfth Judicial District, composed of the Counties of Anderson, Shelby, Spencer, Oldham, Trimble and Henry, and in this capacity he has proven one of the ablest jurists in the state. With commendable firmness and decision of character, self-poised and self-reliant, yet modest and unassuming, of pleasing and courteous address, he is highly respected by the members of the bar.

Judge Carroll is a Democrat, and was quite active and prominent in local and state politics before his elevation to the bench.

Although not a member of any church, he believes in the tenets of the Christian religion, and has a high regard for the church as a great moral agent in society.

Judge Carroll was married in 1870 to Mrs. Mary J. Jackson, whose maiden name was Mary Smart, daughter of Benjamin P. Smart, a native of Mercer County. She was born in Louisville, and was educated there. Her first husband was William Jackson, by whom she has one son, William O. Jackson.

The children of Judge and Mrs. Carroll are Dr. Owen Carroll, a graduate of the Kentucky School of Medicine at Louisville, and Benjamin, a farmer, of Henry County, and Louise, who is now a pupil in Dr. Poynter's Science Hill Academy at Shelbyville.

WILLIAM L. CRABB, President of the Fible & Crabb Distilling Company of Eminence, son of Stephen D. and Nancy B. (Poston) Crabb, was born in Henry County, Kentucky, August 17, 1844.

His father, Stephen D. Crabb, was born in Shelby County, April, 1802, and received an ordinary education in the schools of his day; and was a farmer and stock raiser in Henry County nearly all his life. He was quite prominent in his sphere; an ardent Democrat, but never held or sought any public position; was a member of the Baptist Church, in which he was even more interested than he was in politics, and was well known for his uprightness and integrity. He was married in 1823 to Nancy B. Poston, and raised a family of eight children, whose names in the order of their birth were: John P., Ellen, Susan M., James M., Edward D., Emily C., Stephen T. and William L.

Nancy B. Poston Crabb (mother) was born in Clark County, February, 1802, and died May 7 1888. She was a devout member of the Baptist Church, and a noble Christian mother. She was a daughter of John Poston, a farmer of Henry County, whose wife was a Miss Yates of Shelby County.

Jeremiah Crabb (grandfather) was born in Frederick County, Maryland, September 17, 1769 and died March 21, 1840. Coming down the Ohio River with others in canoes in 1800, they landed at the present site of Louisville, and from there he "drifted" out into the country and finally settled in Shelby County. However, before leaving his native state, he had done what he could in the war of the Revolution; being too young to bear arms, he was assigned to duty—with those who were too old, or, like himself, too young, for active warfare—as a guard for the prisoners of war. He married Eleanor Compton, a native of Virginia, and was the father of seven children, viz.: Stephen D. (father), Ralph, Jeremiah, Priscilla, Elizabeth, Samuel and Alexander C.

He was quite prosperous and accumulated considerable property, including a number of valuable slaves, whom he bequeathed to his wife; and, before her death, she gave all of the slaves, who were over twenty-one years of age their freedom, and provided that the younger ones should be made free upon reaching their majority.

The Crabb family originally came from England. In the life of John Wesley, he tells of his great-grandfather attending a certain college in England of which John Crabb was the dean. Various branches of the family appear to have settled in Norfolk, England, and at different seaports along the coast of Suffolk; and history tells us that a pilot of great experience named Crabb of Walton, was consulted in reference to the voyage of Edward III. before the battle of Crecy, which was fought in the year 1346.

George Crabb was a philologist of distinction and author of a book of English synonyms. He was born in 1778 and died in 1851, and some of his writings, especially his synonyms, are standard authority at the present time.

John Compton, Sr. (great-grandfather), was born February 28, 1747; died January 10, 1803. Elizabeth, his wife, died November 4, 1809. Their children were: Phillip Brisco Compton, born April 27, 1772; Elenor Williamson Compton (grandmother), born September 4, 1774, died December 26, 1851; Alexander Compton, born July 10, 1777, died March 5, 1796; John Compton, Jr., born June 20, 1779, died September 18, 1855; Leonard Brisco Compton, born September 3, 1781, died February 5, 1841; Samuel Compton, born February 2, 1789, died June 1, 1826.

The children of Jeremiah Crabb (grandfather) and Elenor W. Compton, were: Elizabeth Compton Crabb, married James Carter, December 21, 1815; Stephen Drane Crabb (father), married Nancy Poston, December 11, 1823; Jeremiah Crabb, Jr., married first Emily Poston, second Lucy Dawson, third Miss Boker; Samuel Compton Crabb, married Hemia Thompson; Priscilla Spigg Crabb, married Richard Young; Alexander Compton Crabb, married first Sarah Barnett, August 23, 1842, second Lucy B. Rees, April 8, 1857.

William L. Crabb was educated in the district schools of Henry County, and was taking a course preparatory for college when the Civil war began. At the age of eighteen he enlisted in General John H. Morgan's command, Company H, Fourth Kentucky Cavalry, and was in almost every engagement in which that famous cavalry command fought, and was in a fight at New Castle, Kentucky, in which all on the Confederate side were killed or wounded except himself.

He served all through the war and carried the flag that surrendered the last armed force of the confederacy east of the Mississippi River at Mt. Sterling, nearly a month after General Lee's surrender.

Returning after the war was over, he followed farming in Henry County for two years, and was interested in milling. From 1868 to 1872 he was engaged in mercantile pursuits in Eminence, dealing principally in hardware and agricultural implements. Since 1872 he has been engaged in distilling, as a member of the firm of Fible & Crabb, until 1890, when the company was incorporated as the Fible & Crabb Distilling Company, of which Mr. Crabb was elected president. While the business of this company demands much of his time and attention, he is largely interested in farming and stock raising, giving special care to fine horses, in which he takes great pride and pleasure, and from which he derives handsome returns.

There are few more active, energetic and enterprising men than Mr. Crabb in Henry County. With large business interests of his own, which are conducted with conservative enterprise and with good business judgment, he is one of the foremost men in matters concerning the public weal, and his interest in the welfare of his fellow-citizens is manifested by his willingness to enter into any measure for the general advancement of the people with that energy and enthusiasm which are characteristic of the man.

In politics he is zealous for the success of his friends and of the Democratic party, in which he is a wheel-horse. He has no predilection for office or public recognition; but he can take off his coat and work for a friend as if he were the candidate himself. He received an appointment from Governor Knott on his staff with rank of colonel.

Mr. Crabb was married October 31, 1866; to Mattie V. Owen, daughter of Grandison P. Owen and Mary Ann Thomas, his wife, who was a native of Shelby County, but located at Eminence in Henry County.

There were two sons born to Mr. and Mrs. Crabb: Lindsey T. Crabb, born November 5, 1867, and William Owen Crabb, born March 31, 1871, died December 13, 1871.

Grandison P. Owen's father, Edward Owen (Mrs. Crabb's grandfather), came from Virginia to Harrison County, Kentucky, in 1825; and his father was Edward P. Owen of Virginia.

Mary Ann Thomas (Mrs. Crabb's mother) was a daughter of Lindsey Thomas, who was a son of Oswald Thomas, one of the pioneers who came from Virginia and located in Mercer County, Kentucky. Oswald Thomas married Mary Pogue, youngest daughter of General William Pogue, who was killed in Mercer County by the Indians. She was born in the fort at Harrodsburg, Kentucky. Oswald Thomas was an intimate friend and comrade of Daniel Boone, and was with him in many of his excursions and conflicts with the Indians. The descendants of Oswald Thomas embrace many of the old and numerous families of Shelby County, where he located after leaving Mercer County.

WILLIAM LEROY DULANEY, ex-judge of the Circuit Court and a prominent attorney of Bowling Green, son of Woodford and Eliza (Archer) Dulaney, was born at York, Illinois, July 31, 1838.

His father, Woodford Dulaney, a native of Culpeper County, Virginia, came to Kentucky in 1819, and located in Bowling Green, where he lived until 1825, when he removed to Louisville. In 1827 he took a boat-load of merchandise up the Wabash river, and, while on this trip, the Blackhawk war broke out and Mr. Dulaney went into the war as captain of a company which he recruited in Illinois. He served with Lincoln, Jeff Davis and others, and in the regiment of his father-in-law, Colonel William B. Archer. After the war was over Mr. Dulaney returned to his plantation in Warren County, near Bowling Green, where he was engaged in farming until his death, which occurred in 1878, at the age of seventy-nine years.

LeRoy Dulaney (grandfather), a native of Culpeper County, Virginia, came to Warren County, Kentucky, in 1820, and located on a plantation, where he resided until his death, in 1841. The Dulaneys are of French origin, and the ancestors of the family in this country came to the United States by way of Ireland.

Eliza Archer Dulaney (mother) was born near York, Illinois, in 1818, and died of cholera in 1849, in the thirty-first year of her age.

Colonel William B. Archer (maternal grandfather) was born in Scott County, Kentucky. He was a colonel in command of an Illinois regiment during the Blackhawk war. He died in Marshall, Illinois, in 1883, aged about ninety years.

William LeRoy Dulaney spent the earlier days of his boyhood in the country near Bowling Green, and attended Centre College at Danville, from which he graduated in the class with Senator Blackburn, ex-Governor McCreary, and other distinguished Kentuckians in 1857. He read law with Judge William V. Loving of Bowling Green, and was admitted to the bar in 1861.

In the same year he enlisted in the Confederate army as a private soldier in the "Buckner Guides," but was soon transferred to General Morgan's command in Colonel Breckinridge's regiment, and served as a private. He had learned something about military tactics prior to the war, having been captain of a company of state guards. His brother, Hiram W. Dulaney, was also a soldier in the Confederate army, and served throughout the war.

After peace was declared Mr. Dulaney returned to his home in Bowling Green and took up the business of his profession, and to this he has been faithfully devoted, without interruption, for more than thirty years.

In 1869 he was elected judge of the Common Pleas Court, and acted in that capacity for two terms. In 1880 he was elected judge of the Circuit Court, and served one term of six years, declining a re-election at the expiration of the term.

Judge Dulaney has been quite prominent in local and state politics, having served on important committees and as delegate to several Democratic national state and district conventions, but in this he has been actuated by a sense of duty to the public rather than by any political ambition on his part. He is exceedingly fond of sport, and takes particular delight in fox hunting, having a pack of the finest hounds in the state.

Judge Dulaney was married in 1860 to Jane Barclay, daughter of Samuel A. Barclay, of Bowling Green. They have no children of their own, but have one adopted son, Paul LeRoy Dulaney. They are members of the Presbyterian Church, and Judge Dulaney is an Odd Fellow and a Knight Templar.

ISAAC WESLEY KELLY, a leading citizen of New Castle, and one of the largest taxpayers in Henry County, son of Griffin and Rebecca (Smith) Kelly, was born in Henry County, Kentucky, May 16, 1837.

His father, Griffin Kelly, was born in Clark County, Kentucky, January 25, 1810, and removed to Henry County with his parents when he was fourteen years of age. His educational advantages were limited to one term of six months in a country school, but he was a man of sound judgment and remarkable ability. His chief business was that of a farmer, but he was a judicious speculator and a successful financier. A man of wonderful natural resources, prudent and sagacious, he would have made his mark in any avocation, and had he received an education in accordance with his natural ability he could have reached fame and distinction in public life. But he had no ambition for political preferment, and declined frequent calls to represent his county and district in Congress and other positions of honor and trust.

The first money he made was fifty cents which he received for stripping blue grass, and at his death his estate was worth over one hundred thousand dollars. He attributed his success to the fact that he attended to his business affairs himself and never asked any one else to do for him anything he could do himself. He was a director in the Bank of Shelbyville for more than twenty years, and for a long time a director in the Bank of New Castle. He was a member of the regular Baptist Church, and his business was conducted upon principles that were consistent with his profession, and he was known and respected as a man of exemplary piety and upright character.

He was married September 25, 1834, to Rebecca Jane Smith, who was born near Brownsborough, Oldham County, September 14, 1815, and died December 22, 1894. She was a woman of extraordinary energy, of strong, vigorous intellect, who exerted a great influence over her children and commanded the love and admiration of her neighbors. She was in every sense a noble woman, a dutiful and helpful wife, an affectionate mother and a pious member of the Baptist Church. Her father was Isaac Smith, born in Blue Ridge, Virginia, a descendant of Captain John Smith. His wife, Susan Schmidt, was from Baden-Baden, Germany.

Griffin and Rebecca Kelly had five children who reached maturity:

Elizabeth, married William H. Forwood; died at the age of forty years.

Isaac W., subject of this sketch.

Joseph, died at Eminence in 1885.

Helen, married, first, George Kilpatrick, who was of English birth, graduated with honor at Toronto, Canada, and was a successful practitioner at the Louisville bar and died at the age of thirty-four years. Her second husband is William Swift of Bourbon County, Kentucky. She is a woman of great strength of character, of fine intelligence and of unusual business ability.

Clinton Wayne, educated at Kingston and

Montreal, Canada, and Berlin, Prussia; is one of the leading physicians of Louisville; dean of the Louisville Medical College, which he founded in 1869, and is known throughout the South and Southwest as one of the most distinguished men in the medical profession.

Joseph Kelly (grandfather) was born in Spottsylvania County, Virginia, January 29, 1767; came to Kentucky in 1824; was a captain in the war of 1812 under Generals George Rogers Clarke and William H. Harrison, and was in the terrible battle at River Raisin. At one time with three hundred soldiers he held at bay eighteen hundred English soldiers and Indians, accomplishing this by strategy; when the enemy advanced he commanded his men to fall on their faces and reserve their fire until they could see the white of the enemies' eyes. By this means they held the British at bay until their ammunition gave out and they were captured. It was Joel Hume, one of Captain Kelly's men, who killed the Indian Chief Tecumseh, instead of Johnson, as history claims. Hume was in line of battle with Captain Kelly's company. He found he had three loads in his gun. He discharged them all at once at a tall Indian chief. After the battle Tecumseh was found with three bullets in his body. Captain Kelly was detailed by General George Rogers Clarke to make a road from near Louisville to Vincennes, Indiana. Joseph Kelly married Elizabeth Mallory, born March 24, 1771; died March 30, 1850.

Isaac W. Kelly began his studies in the typical log school house in Henry County. At the age of fourteen he removed to New Castle with his parents; graduated from Georgetown College in 1860, accomplishing a four years' course in two years, the first instance of the kind in the history of that institution; taught school in Henry County for two years; went to Louisville in 1863, and was engaged in brokerage business there for four years. In 1869 he returned to New Castle and attended to his father's business until 1871. He was in the internal revenue service under President Cleveland's first administration and has had large landed and other business interests to occupy his attention; is president of the New Castle Creamery Company; president of the Eminence & New Castle Turnpike Road Company; vice president of the Bank of New Castle; trustee of the Henry Male & Female College of New Castle. He owns a beautiful home in New Castle, from which he directs the affairs of his large farming and other interests in the county; is the largest tax-payer, with but two exceptions, in the county; and is a leading, progressive and influential citizen.

He never sued a debtor, and has never been sued; strictly honest and true, he is greatly respected and honored by the people, who have the utmost confidence in his fidelity and integrity.

Mr. Kelly is an ardent member of the Baptist Church; a deep student of the Bible, explaining many of the mysteries of the scriptures with a power and force that carries conviction, and in the absence of the pastor often takes his place in the pulpit, in which capacity he displays unusual ability as a teacher of the Word.

He has traveled extensively in the United States and Canada, and has been a close observer and careful student of men and affairs and is well informed upon local, state and national politics; is a Democrat and the author of his own platform: "The greatest good for the greatest number." He was in sympathy with the South, but took no active part during the Civil war.

He was associated with his brother, Dr. Clinton W. Kelly of Louisville, in the settlement of their father's large estate, and this they accomplished without the aid of a lawyer, the total expense amounting to $18. Isaac W. Kelly was married October 12, 1871, to Thermuthis Hannah Webb, daughter of Honorable Isaac N. and Levian (Gist) Webb. She was born in New Castle and educated in the college at that place.

Her father was an eminent lawyer of New Castle; a graduate of Hanover (Indiana) College; was an able draughtsman and distinguished scholar; served in the Kentucky legislature and was a man of fine personal appearance and gentlemanly bearing. His wife, Levian Gist Webb, was a native of Northern Alabama, a graduate of a Nashville college; a woman of great strength of character, moral courage and fine literary attainments, intensely religious and very active in church work. The children of Isaac W. Kelly

KENTUCKY BIOGRAPHIES.

and his wife are: Levian, wife of Dr. John R. Smith, now a resident of Carmi, Illinois; Rebecca Jane, wife of Robert Lee Samuells of New Castle. The other children, Griffin, Isaac Newton, Washington Irving and Sallie Barbour, are at home, the greatest care being given to their education and training.

GEORGE W. JOLLY, a member of the Owensboro bar, son of John B. and Rachel (Hardin) Jolly, was born in Breckinridge County, near the town of Stephensport, February 22, 1843.

His father was born in Breckinridge County, July 20, 1815; was educated in private schools in the vicinity of his home. He was engaged in agricultural pursuits until his death, March 10, 1896. He was a consistent member of the Methodist church and an honored citizen, whose quiet and unostentatious life won for him the love and confidence of his neighbors. He was married May 9, 1842, to Rachel Hardin, who was born in Breckinridge County in 1817. They were the parents of eight children: George W.; William Henry Harrison, who died in 1864; Nannie; John L., who also died in 1864; Gideon N.; Thomas and Sarah. Mrs. Jolly died December 7, 1893.

Nelson Jolly (grandfather) was born in Hines' Fort, near Elizabethtown, Kentucky, February 20, 1786, and removed to Breckinridge County with his father when a child. He married Barbara Barr, a native of Breckinridge County, and they were pioneer Methodists, as well as citizens of a new and but partially settled country.

Nelson Jolly, the elder (great-grandfather), was born at Londonderry, Ireland, and came to this country in 1755 with his father, who settled in Bucks County, Pennsylvania. He married a Miss Graham of Maryland, and came to Kentucky in 1780, or about that time; settled near Hardinsburg in 1790, and made his home in Breckinridge County until 1819, when he died.

The progenitor of the Jolly family in America (the father of the great-grandfather), was of Scotch-Irish extraction, and settled in Bucks County, Pennsylvania, thirty miles east of Philadelphia. He enlisted under Paul Jones and was killed in a naval battle off the Irish coast. He left a widow and two children, Nelson and Alcey Jolly. Nelson Jolly brought his mother and sister with him (having married Miss Graham before coming) to Kentucky. Alcey married John Combs and lived in Nelson County, Kentucky, after her marriage.

Henry Hardin (maternal grandfather) was the youngest child of William Hardin (great-grandfather) who was a native of Virginia, and subsequently became a citizen of Westmoreland County, Pennsylvania, whence he came to Kentucky. He was in the Revolutionary war, in command of Virginia troops, and he received land patents in Kentucky as a compensation for his services. These patents were issued by Governor Patrick Henry and Benjamin Harrison. He brought his own and several families from Westmoreland County, Pennsylvania, by water in flat boats, to the mouth of Bear Grass Creek (now Louisville), in the fall of 1779, and took his settlers to Breckinridge County in March, 1780, and there made a settlement. Block houses and stockades were erected as a defense against the Indians, and in 1782 he founded the town of Hardinsburg, donating the land on which the town now stands. He was appointed colonel of the militia of the county, and soon became known as an Indian fighter. He was a man of large frame and great strength, of dauntless courage, skilled in all of the arts of border warfare.

George W. Jolly received his education in private schools. His principal tutor was the Rev. R. G. Gardiner of Hardinsburg, by whom he was sufficiently advanced for the study of law. He then began his legal studies with Judge Kincheloe in Hardinsburg, and was afterwards a pupil of Judge G. W. Williams of Hawesville (a sketch of whom is given elsewhere in this volume). Mr. Jolly was admitted to the bar in 1867, and began the practice of law at Hardinsburg, where he remained until 1872, when he removed to Owensboro. In this larger and more inviting field he has met with success and has enjoyed a share of the important litigation.

August 5, 1889, he was appointed United States Attorney for the District of Kentucky by President Harrison, and at once assumed the duties of that office. He was re-appointed January 27, 1890, and served until the appointment of his successor, January 27, 1894. In the performance of his duties in that office he was indefatigable, and he served the government with fidelity. After the expiration of his term of office he resumed his practice in Owensboro.

Mr. Jolly was married February 16, 1871, to Miss Sue E. Henderson, who was born in Breckinridge County, November 7, 1843. She is a daughter of P. J. and Elizabeth (Orendorf) Henderson, and was educated in the schools of Breckinridge County. They have five children: Horace, born April 17, 1873; Marian, born August 27, 1876; Jessie, born January 23, 1878; Percy, born October 25, 1880, and Susie, born November 4, 1884. (For interesting lineage of Mrs. Jolly, see sketch of Dr. Henry Orendorf in this volume.)

JAMES ROBERT MINOR of Augusta, son of Ezekiel and Nancy (Sallee) Minor, was born August 6, 1840. His father was born in Mason County, October 11, 1801. In early manhood Ezekiel Minor engaged in trading on the Ohio river between Pittsburg and New Orleans, but retired from active trading in 1832 and spent the remainder of his life on his farm. During the War of 1812, when only eleven or twelve years of age, he took care of the family while his father was fighting for his country. He enlisted in the Mexican war, but was not called into active service. He was a genial and hospitable man and was never so happy as when his home was filled with guests.

Ephraim Minor (grandfather) was a native of Virginia who came to Kentucky, Mason County, in 1794, when he was twelve years of age, with his mother, then a widow, who brought with her from Virginia a number of slaves. The old English law of primogeniture which gave the real property to the eldest son prevailed in Virginia at that time, and on that account Mrs. Minor determined to remove to Kentucky. Ephraim took part in the War of 1812, serving as a private soldier. He engaged in farming in Kentucky until 1832, when he removed to Illinois and died there about 1834. He was a member of the Methodist Church. He married Rachel, daughter of William Lamb, a native and the first sheriff of Mason County. She died in 1846. The Minors were originally from England.

Nancy Sallee Minor (mother) was born in Mason County, March 5, 1802. She was educated in one of the old seminaries of Lexington and was married to Ezekiel Minor December 8, 1831. She was a consistent member of the Christian Church and died in 1888. Her father, Jacob Sallee, was a native of Virginia who came to Kentucky before the beginning of the present century and located near what is now known as Bryant Station; he afterwards moved to Mason County, where he died in 1830. He married Lucy Hayden of Virginia, who survived him many years and died in 1861 at the advanced age of ninety-three years.

James R. Minor was educated at Augusta College and taught school in 1869 and 1870 while studying law; was admitted to the bar in 1871 and at once commenced the practice of his profession in Augusta, where he has continued to reside until the present time.

He has served two years as mayor of Augusta; was city attorney for several terms and county attorney from 1884 to 1894. He is a Mason, an Odd Fellow and a member of the Christian Church. He married Minerva A., daughter of Richard D. and Catherine (Walton) Smith, August 16, 1869. Mrs. Minor was born November 26, 1845, and was educated at Augusta College. They have seven children living: Florence Salle, Mary Ware, John Lamb, Carrie Rule, Nancy Lou, Anna Clay and Emma Bertell.

JAMES H. MOORE, M. D., a retired physician and merchant of Harrodsburg, a descendant of one of the oldest and most respected families, son of Lawson and Jane Murray (Rochester) Moore, was born near Danville, Kentucky, October 3, 1819.

Lawson Moore (father) was born in Westmoreland County, Virginia, in 1771, and died in Boyle County, Kentucky, September 15, 1858. He came to Kentucky in 1798 and purchased a large tract of land near Danville, where he was a farmer and stock raiser on an extensive scale. He was married January 2, 1794, to Elizabeth Rochester, who died July 26, 1815; January 22, 1817, he married Jane Murray Rochester, a sister of his first wife, with whom he lived until April 14, 1855, when she died. There were eleven children by the first marriage, and the five children of his second wife were: Christopher Collins, James H., Thomas R., Charles O. and Joseph L.

Lawson Moore was a man of large frame, of commanding presence, more than six feet high, of powerful physical strength, of strong intellect, well read, thoroughly posted in history and abreast of the spirit of the times. Having a large family, he fully appreciated the advantages of education and was one of the active promoters in establishing Centre College; a man of influence and high moral standing, who left his impress upon the community and helped to provide many advantages for future generations

Elijah Moore (grandfather)—son of William Moore and Sarah Lawson—was married when he was nineteen years of age to Judith Harrison of Northumberland County, Virginia, and had three sons: Lawson, George and William. He was a large and powerful man, of unusual perseverance and energy, and gave promise of a useful life. Shortly after the birth of his son William he was killed by lightning, when twenty-six years of age. His wife survived him only eighteen months and died leaving three sons, who were placed under the guardianship of Christopher Collins, a merchant of Westmoreland County, Virginia, who proved an efficient and trustworthy protector and guide, whose noble traits of character were cherished by his wards.

William Moore (great-grandfather)—son of Thomas Moore—married Sarah Lawson and spent his life on his patrimonial estate. He had two sons, Elijah and Vincent. The latter married and reared a family in Northumberland County, Virginia, where he died.

Thomas Moore (great-great-grandfather), the progenitor of the numerous and influential family, came from England at a very early period in the history of this country, and settled on the banks of the Nomonee River in Westmoreland County, Virginia, where, as one of the pioneers, he lived in peace and friendship with the Indian tribes with which he was surrounded. He left two sons, William and Thomas, between whom he divided his estate. Thomas died on his portion of the old farm, leaving two sons, Thomas and James, who disposed of their property and removed to North Carolina, where they are now represented by numerous descendants.

Dr. Moore's lineage on his mother's side is traced back for more than two hundred and fifty years.

Nicholas Rochester (great-great-great-grandfather), the first ancestor who came to America, was born in Kent County, England, in 1640. The time of his settlement in Virginia is not recorded, but he had been there many years before his death in 1719.

William Rochester (great-great-grandfather), son of Nicholas, was born in 1680, died October 23, 1750. He married Mrs. Frances McKinney, and they had two children: John, born in 1708, died November, 1754; William, born in 1710, died in July, 1767.

John Rochester (great-grandfather)—son of William—married Hester Thrift, who died in 1773. Their children were: William, who died in infancy; John, born 1746, died December, 1794; Ann, born 1748; Phillis, born 1750; Nathaniel, born February 21, 1752, died May 14, 1831; Esther, born 1753. John Rochester was married the second time to Mrs. Annie McClanahan, nee South, June 9, 1793, and their only child was William Rochester.

John Rochester (grandfather)—son of John—married Anne Jordan in 1766. She died in 1789. Their children were: William John, Elizabeth (Lawson Moore's first wife), Robert, Nancy, Esther, Hannah, Nathaniel, Jane Murray (Lawson Moore's second wife), Sophia and Artemisia.

Dr. James H. Moore received a classical education, attending Centre College until he was ready for the senior class; went to St. Mary's College for a short time; was then under a private tutor and subsequently returned to Centre College; studied medicine with Drs. Fleece and Weisiger and graduated from Transylvania in 1841; at the age of twenty-one went to Mississippi, and practiced medicine successfully for five years; returned to Kentucky in 1845 and located in Harrodsburg, April, 1846. Here he engaged in merchandising with his brother, Christopher Collins

Moore, in which business they were very successful. In 1852 he retired to his farm and engaged in raising and importing fine sheep, cattle and horses. He has been an active and leading member of county fair associations; was president of the Mercer County Association and director for a number of years; was sent as delegate to the Second Congress of Agricultural Associations, which met in Selma, Alabama, and has always taken a deep interest in agricultural matters; and besides his farm in Mercer County is engaged in cotton planting in the delta between the Mississippi and Yazoo rivers on Deer Creek, about forty miles from Vicksburg, where long staple cotton is grown.

During the war his property was destroyed, amounting to between $200,000 and $300,000, consisting of 1,200 bales cotton, new and costly steam gins, corn crib frames, quarters for 100 slaves, but he was not a man to be discouraged by misfortune, and he set to work earnestly to recuperate his fortune. He was one of the organizers of the Mercer County National Bank, and was its president from the time of its organization until he resigned in 1894; was a useful and diligent member of the Constitutional Convention of 1890-91, having been elected over four opposing candidates by a majority of over one thousand votes. He has been an elder in the Presbyterian Church for many years, and has represented his presbytery in the Synod and General Assembly a number of times; is liberal in his views of church doctrine and charitable toward those who differ with him; is a man of great strength of character and greatly honored and respected by the people who have known him during his long residence in Mercer County. Although advanced in years, he is active, energetic and enterprising, and is thoroughly imbued with the spirit of progress, an advocate for advancement in every direction, an exemplary Christian, a model gentleman and a valuable citizen. He has educated a number of poor young men who are now filling honorable positions, of whom the county is proud.

In 1891, when his time was up, according to the scriptural estimate of human life, he built him a beautiful home in Harrodsburg, a lovely place which he has christened "Hillsdale," and in this he hopes to spend the remainder of his life.

Dr. Moore was married February 13, 1845, to Mrs. Mary S. Foster, nee Messinger, daughter of Hon. Daniel T. and Mary Messinger of Berkshire County, Massachusetts. Her father, Daniel Messinger, was a farmer and merchant in Massachusetts. His father was George Messinger, who was a son of Nehemiah Messinger, who purchased lands in Massachusetts from the Indians. His brother Samuel was a surveyor of land in Massachusetts in colonial days. Her mother was Mary Bacon, a noble Christian woman from one of the oldest and most prominent New England families.

Dr. and Mrs. Moore, like many of the elder Moores, have two sons: Hon. Daniel Lawson Moore, born January 31, 1847; and Bacon Rochester Moore, born June 13, 1850.

Daniel Lawson Moore (elder son) was educated under private tutors and at Centre College; studied law under Phil B. Thompson, Sr.; was state senator in Capital District; has large business interests in Colorado, Florida, Mississippi and New Mexico, and is president of the Mercer National Bank, succeeding his father; married Henrietta, daughter of Judge William H. McBeyer, by whom three children were born: May Messinger, Wallace and William H.; married a second time to Minnie Ball, who is the mother of one child, Anneta.

Bacon Rochester Moore (younger son) was educated under private tutors at Centre College and at Washington and Lee University, Virginia; studied law with John Charles Thompson; was an extensive planter in the South; was appointed under Governor Knott delegate to Mississippi River Convention held at Vicksburg, and elected by his county as a director of the Levee Board and received the highest commendation on retiring; married Nannie Bowman of Mercer County and had five sons and two daughters: Dudley Bowman, Mary Bacon, James Harrison, Virginia, Daniel Lawson, Bacon Rochester and John Bowman. Bacon R. (son) died at Harrodsburg, August 20, 1889, and at a meeting of the bar at that place on the day following his death the committee appointed to prepare resolutions testified to the high standing in private and social life which he had reached through true merit; that his official career was marked by a strict observance of duty; that he was a true friend; a perfect husband and father; a dutiful son; a Christian gentleman; an estimable citizen and member of the bar and officer of the Court. His death was sincerely deplored by all who had known him at home and abroad. He was bright, quick of perception; possessed great firmness and sound judgment.

JUDGE ALNEY McLEAN, in honor of whom McLean County was named, was a native of Burke County, North Carolina; emigrated to Kentucky, and began the practice of law at Greenville, Muhlenberg County, about 1805; had but little to do with politics before 1808; was a representative from that county in the legislature, 1812-13; a captain in the War of 1812; a representative in Congress for four years, 1815-17 and 1819-21; one of the electors for president in 1825, casting his vote and that of the state for Henry Clay; again in 1833 an elector for the state at large, when the vote of the state was cast a second time for the same distinguished citizen; and appointed a circuit judge, and for many years adorned the bench.

FRANK H. SOUTHGATE, M. D., Pension Examiner and a popular young physician of Newport, son of James and Emma (Hills) Southgate, was born in the Highlands, near Newport, Kentucky, April 12, 1869.

His father, now a resident of Newport, was born in that city in 1848. He returned to Newport after a long residence in the Highlands a few years ago, and is engaged in the manufacture of shingles; a member of the board of aldermen and president of the Newport Commercial Club. He has been a director in the German National Bank ever since its organization and is now vice president.

Edward L. Southgate (grandfather) was also a native of Newport, where he lived until his death in 1852, when thirty-eight years of age. He was a lawyer by profession, and in addition to his law practice looked after his father's extensive business.

Richard Southgate (great-grandfather) was born near Richmond, Virginia, and came to Newport, Kentucky, in 1776. He was a lawyer by profession, but was more extensively interested in mercantile pursuits, in which business he accumulated a large fortune in money and realty. He owned about ten thousand acres of land in Campbell and Kenton Counties, and was considered one of the wealthiest men in the state. He was at one time a representative of his district in the Kentucky legislature. His wife was a Miss Hinde, daughter of the celebrated physician, Dr. Thomas Hinde, who was a native of England and a surgeon in the English navy. He attended General Wolfe at the time of his death in Quebec, and was the physician of Patrick Henry of Virginia; also served throughout the Revolutionary war as a surgeon. He was well known as a physician in Virginia and Kentucky.

Emma Hills Southgate (mother) is a native of Newport, of which city she is still a resident. Her father, B. F. Hills, a native of Massachusetts, came to Newport, Kentucky, in 1814, and is still a resident of that city. Although about eighty-eight years of age, he is a stout man, in perfect health, and has never known what it is to have to endure illness. Most of his life has been spent in farming in the South. He went to Louisiana in 1867, and lived in that state for twenty years, when he retired from business and returned to his old home in Newport.

Dr. Frank H. Southgate spent the days of his youth in the Highlands and attended the excellent schools in Cincinnati, Ohio. After acquiring a good education, he entered upon his professional studies under Dr. B. K. Rockford of Cincinnati; and attended the Medical College of Ohio, from which he was graduated in 1892. He then took a post-graduate course in Germany, at the University of Berlin.

In 1894 he began a general practice of medicine in Newport, and in the short time in which he has been known as a practicing physician, he has met with encouragement and every assurance of success.

Few men have been better prepared for the responsible duties of the physician; and this fact, together with genial manner and kindly disposition, has won the favor and confidence of a host of friends. While doing a general practice, his special work, for which he has more fully prepared himself, is the treatment of diseases of children. He is assistant professor of physiology and clinician in the Medical College of Ohio at Cincinnati, two very responsible positions which are usually filled by older men. Dr. Southgate is a member of the Academy of Medicine of Cincinnati, and a member of the United States Board of Pension Examiners of Newport, and it is hardly necessary to add that he is a Democrat in good standing with Mr. Cleveland's administration.

GOVERNOR NINIAN EDWARDS was born in Montgomery County, Maryland, in March, 1775, and died of cholera at Belleville, St. Clair County, Illinois, July 20, 1833—aged fifty-eight. His early education was in company with, and partly under the tuition of, the celebrated William Wirt, whose bosom friend he was for forty-three years. His academic education was continued under other tutors, and at Dickinson College, Carlisle, Pa. He studied law and medicine together, and became proficient in both. In 1794, at the age of nineteen, he was sent by his father to take care of his landed estate in Nelson County, Kentucky, where he opened and improved a farm (upon which his father settled in 1800), built distilleries and tanyards, and showed great capacity for business. Before he was quite twenty-one he was elected to the Kentucky house of representatives in 1796, and re-elected in 1797 by an almost unanimous vote. From the time he was nineteen until twenty-two, he indulged in habits of dissipation and gambling; but by a determined resolution broke loose from old associates, removed in 1798 to Russellville, Logan County, and began the practice of law, both in Kentucky and Tennessee. Without a dollar of his own in 1799, in four years' practice and judicious investment of what he made, he became rich; then went upon the bench as presiding judge of the General Court, and filled in rapid succession the offices of circuit judge in 1804, fourth judge of the Court of Appeals on December 13, 1806, and chief justice of Kentucky on January 5, 1808 —all before he was thirty-three years of age. In 1804 he was chosen one of the presidential electors who cast the vote of the state for Thomas Jefferson. "The great secret of his success was owing to his powerful intellect, and to his energy and untiring industry."

On the 24th of April, 1809, he was appointed by President Madison governor of Illinois territory, which he accepted; he was twice re-appointed, November, 1812, and January, 1816. In advance of any action by Congress, he organized companies of rangers, supplied them with arms, built stockade forts, and established a cordon of posts from the Wabash river to the mouth of the Missouri—thus preparing with extraordinary energy for defence against the Indians. In 1816, he was a commissioner to treat with the Indians; in 1818, when Illinois became a state, was sent to the United States senate for six years; then appointed minister to Mexico, but declined; in 1826, was elected governor of Illinois for four years, retiring in 1831 to private life.

JOHN CLAY THOMASSON, M. D., leading Homeopathic physician of Georgetown, son of Julius V. and Mary W. (Yelton) Thomasson, was born in Butler, Pendleton County, Kentucky, April 21, 1857.

His father was born in Virginia in 1800; went to Cincinnati, Ohio, in 1819, where he lived and followed the trade of a plasterer until 1836, when he removed to Butler, Kentucky; and he spent the remainder of a long, industrious and useful life on a farm, and died there in 1890. He was a true man and a good citizen, and a member of the Christian Church for sixty years. He was provost marshal during the war, and served several terms as magistrate in Butler County. He was a stanch Republican and an enthusiastic Union man during the war, and was descended from a line of noble English ancestors who were greatly distinguished in the early history of Virginia.

Mary W. Yelton Thomasson (mother) was a native of Virginia, a devout and earnest member of the Christian Church, and died in 1893, aged seventy-seven years. Her father was a Virginian by birth, and an early settler of Pendleton County, Kentucky.

Dr. John Clay Thomasson was educated in the schools of Butler; read medicine with Dr. William Hunt of Covington, and graduated from the Pulte Medical College (Homeopathic) of Cincinnati. He began the practice of medicine the same year in Georgetown. In 1866 he took a post-graduate course in Hahnemann Medical College, Chicago, and claims Homeopathy as the true science of medicine. He is a man of great energy and persevering industry, greatly devoted to his vocation, and is one of the most skillful and popular physicians in Scott County. He is a member of the Kentucky State Homeopathic Medical Society, and is one of the most earnest advocates of that school of medicine in the state. He is not greatly interested in politics, but votes the Prohibition ticket, and has strong convictions on the temperance question.

Dr. Thomasson was married in 1881 to Rena Lucas, daughter of Mrs. Rebecca Lucas of Georgetown. They are active and influential members of the Christian Church, and enjoy a fine social position in the most cultured society.

ALEXANDER SCOTT BULLITT was born in Prince William County, Virginia, in the year 1761. His father, Cuthbert Bullitt, was a lawyer of some distinction and practiced his profession with success until he was appointed judge of the Supreme Court of Virginia, which office he held at the time of his death. In 1784 he emigrated to Kentucky, and settled in what is now Shelby County. Here he resided but a few months, being compelled by the annoyances to which he was subjected by the Indians to seek a less exposed situation. This he found in Jefferson County, in the neighborhood of Sturgus' Station, where he entered and settled upon the tract of land on which he continued to reside until his death.

In the year 1792 Colonel Bullitt was elected by the people of Jefferson County a delegate to the convention which met in Danville, and framed the constitution of Kentucky. After the adoption of the constitution, he represented the county in the legislature, and was president of the senate until 1799, when he was again chosen a delegate to the convention to amend the constitution, which met in Frankfort. Of this convention, he was chosen president. The year following this convention (1800) he was elected lieutenant governor of the state, in which capacity he served one term. After this, his county continued to send him to the legislature, of which body he served either as a representative or senator, until about 1808, when he retired from public life, and resided on his farm in Jefferson County until his death, which occurred on the 13th of April, 1816.

JAMES ELLIOTT STEWART, attorney at law, of Louisa, Kentucky, son of Ralph and America (Canterbury) Stewart, was born in Lawrence County, Kentucky, October 1, 1832.

His father, Ralph Stewart, was born in Virginia, March 4, 1799, and was educated in the county schools. When about twenty years of age he came to Lawrence County, Kentucky, and was a prominent farmer and citizen of that county until his death, April 15, 1882. He was a colonel of militia, having been promoted step by step from the ranks, and was familiarly known as Colonel Stewart. He was a Democratic voter and took some interest in political matters without seeking office. He was more deeply interested in religious matters than in politics; exceedingly hospitable, his house was always open to the itinerant preachers of the Methodist Church. He was a highly cultured gentleman and sought the society of educated and refined people, who always found a genial companion and a hearty welcome in his home.

James Stewart (grandfather) was born in Virginia, where he was a farmer and trader. In the War of 1812 he served as a private soldier; removed to Lawrence County, Kentucky, late in life, and died at the home of his son. His father was a native of Ireland.

America Canterbury Stewart (mother) was born in Greenup (now Lawrence) County, September 13, 1813. She was a lady of education and culture and a devout Christian; was married to Ralph Stewart July 2, 1829.

Reuben Canterbury (grandfather) was born in Southern Kentucky; settled near the Big Sandy River and cleared a farm from the canebrake and underbrush. This farm he cultivated with success, and was no less fortunate in the rearing of a family of twelve children. He first married a Miss Hornback, of Southern Kentucky, by whom he had three children: Jackson, Benjamin and Nancy. His second wife was a Miss Lykens, who was the mother of nine children: Jeremiah, Ben Franklin, Milton, Lawrence, Washington, America, Flora, Sarah and Elizabeth. Mr. Canterbury was one of the commissioners appointed by the legislature to locate the official seat of Lawrence County. The Canterbury family were of English extraction.

James Elliott Stewart was reared on his father's farm, attending the common schools when opportunity afforded. He left home when twenty years of age and was employed as a clerk in the store of William L. Geiger at Cannonsburg, Boyd County, and in August, 1853, he went to Louisa and began the study of law in the office of Ben F. Canterbury, and was admitted to the bar in October, 1854. He went to Paintsville December 31, 1854, and opened a law office. He remained there until October 11, 1871, when he returned to Louisa. In 1868 he was elected commonwealth attorney for the Sixteenth judicial district, and served six years. In 1876 he was elected judge of the Criminal Court for the Sixteenth judicial district, and served for four years.

Since his return to Louisa Judge Stewart has aspired to no office, but has devoted his time to the practice of law. He has never posed as a politician and would accept no office that was not strictly in the line of his chosen profession. He is one of the best known and most popular lawyers in his section of the state. He is a prominent Mason and a member of the Methodist Church, and a liberal supporter of all religious work, especially that in connection with that denomination.

Judge Stewart was married January 11, 1860, to Cynthia F. Mayo, daughter of Lewis and Maria (Jones) Mayo of Fluvanna County, Virginia. The Jones family were wealthy planters of Virginia. Lewis Mayo was a highly cultured gentleman, a fine scholar and linguist, and taught school for thirty years.

Mrs. Stewart was born December 22, 1840, and is a lady of culture and refinement.

Judge and Mrs. Stewart have had five children: James Lewis, born October 31, 1861, died July 18, 1884; John Wesley Mayo, born December 13, 1863; Forrest L., born November 25, 1870; Warren Franklin Canterbury, born July 16, 1868, died July 11, 1869; Neva Sharon, born December 5, 1874.

John W. M. Stewart (son) is a graduate of the Michigan State University law department at Ann Arbor, and previously attended Vanderbilt University at Nashville, Tennessee, and was admitted to the bar in 1887. He married Eva S. Southgate, daughter of W. W. Southgate, November 28, 1887. She was born September 19, 1867, and was educated in Wesleyan College, Cincinnati, Ohio.

James Lewis Stewart (deceased) was a graduate of the Michigan State University law department —having previously attended Vanderbilt University—and was admitted to the bar before he was seventeen years of age. According to the United States census, he was the youngest attorney in the United States.

Neva Sharon Stewart graduated at Belmont Female College with high honors, May, 1896.

Forrest Lee (son), after attending the schools of his native town—studying civil engineering in the field—completed his education at Michigan University, since which time he has been in the mercantile business.

GENERAL WILLIAM ORLANDO BUTLER was born in Jessamine County, Kentucky, April 19, 1791; graduated at Transylvania University, 1812; postponed the study of law to volunteer as a private in Captain N. S.-G. Hart's company at Lexington; was elected corporal and marched to the relief of Fort Wayne; promoted to ensign in Colonel Wells' Seventeenth United States Infantry; in the two battles of the River Raisin, January 18 and 22, 1813, he signalized himself by self-devotion and daring, was wounded and taken prisoner; captain of the Forty-fourth United States Infantry, in the attack at Pensacola; in the battles at New Orleans, December 23, 1814, and January 8, 1815, General Jackson says he "displayed the heroic chivalry and calmness of judgment in the midst of danger, which distinguish the valuable officer in the hour of battle;"

received therefor the brevet rank of major; was aide to General Jackson, 1816-17; resigned, studied law and practiced at Carrollton; married a daughter of General Robert Todd; was representative from Gallatin County in the Kentucky legislature, 1817, '18; in United States Congress for four years, 1839-43, and refused to be a candidate for a third term; was the Democratic candidate for governor in 1844, and reduced the Whig majority to 4,624; June 29, 1846, was appointed major-general of the volunteers raised to support General Taylor in his invasion of Mexico; acted an important part (and was wounded) in the battle of Monterey, September 19-24, 1846, and in subsequent events in that part of Mexico; February 18, 1848, succeeded General Scott in the chief command of the army in Mexico, until the treaty of peace, May 29, 1848; May, 1848, was nominated for vice president of the United States on the Democratic ticket with General Cass, but defeated by Taylor and Fillmore; 1851, supported by the full party vote for United States senator, but not elected; January 29 to February 27, 1861, one of six commissioners from Kentucky to the "Peace Conference" at Washington City.

GENERAL JOHN ADAIR was born in South Carolina in the year 1757. His character was formed in the trying times and amidst the thrilling incidents of the Revolution. At an early age he entered the army as a volunteer, and was made prisoner by the British.

In 1786 he emigrated to Kentucky and settled in Mercer County. In the border war which raged with so much fury on the northwestern frontier, General (then major) Adair was an active and efficient officer, and frequently engaged with the Indians. On the 6th of November, 1792, Major Adair, at the head of a detachment of mounted volunteers from Kentucky, while encamped in the immediate vicinity of Fort St. Clair, twenty-six miles south of Greenville, near where Eaton, the county seat of Preble County, Ohio, now stands, was suddenly and violently attacked by a large party of Indians, who rushed on the encampment with great fury. A bloody conflict ensued, during which Major Adair ordered Lieutenant Madison, with a small party, to gain the right flank of the enemy, if possible, and at the same time gave an order for Lieutenant Hall to attack their left, but learning that that officer had been slain, the major with about twenty-five of his men made the attack in person, with a view of sustaining Lieutenant Madison.

The pressure of this movement caused the enemy to retire. They were driven about six hundred yards, through and beyond the American camp, where they made a stand, and again fought desperately. At this juncture about sixty of the Indians made an effort to turn the right flank of the whites. Major Adair foreseeing the consequences of this maneuver, found it necessary to order a retreat. That movement was effected with regularity, and as was expected, the Indians pursued them to their camp, where a halt was made and another severe battle was fought, in which the Indians suffered severely and were driven from the ground. In this affair six of the whites were killed, five wounded, and four missing. Among the wounded were Lieutenant (afterwards governor) George Madison and Colonel Richard Taylor, the father of the President, Major General Zachary Taylor, the hero of Palo Alto, Monterey, Buena Vista, etc.

The Indians on this occasion were commanded by the celebrated Little Turtle. Some years afterward, in 1805-6, when General Adair was register of the land office in Frankfort, Captain William Wells, Indian agent, passed through that place on his way to Washington City, attended by some Indians, among whom was the chief, Little Turtle. General Adair called on his old antagonist, and in the course of the conversation the incident above related being alluded to, General Adair attributed his defeat to his having been taken by surprise. The Little Turtle immediately remarked with great pleasantness: "A good general is never taken by surprise."

In the campaign of 1813 he accompanied Governor Shelby into Canada, as an aide, and was present in that capacity at the battle of the Thames. His conduct during this campaign was such as to draw from his superior officers an expression of their approbation, and his name was honorably mentioned in the report to the war department. Governor Shelby afterwards conferred upon him the appointment of adjutant general of the Kentucky troops, with the brevet rank of brigadier general, in which character he commanded the Kentuckians in the glorious battle of New Orleans. The acrimonious controversy between him and General Jackson, growing out of the imputations cast by the latter on the conduct of the Kentucky troops on that eventful day is fresh in the recollection of all.

In 1820 he was elected governor of Kentucky, in opposition to Judge Logan, Governor Desha and Colonel Butler. He was often a member of the state legislature, and on several occasions was speaker of that body. In 1825 he was elected to the senate of the United States from Kentucky for the term of one year. In 1831 he was elected to Congress, and served in the house of representatives from 1831 to 1833, inclusive.

General Adair was a brave soldier, an active, vigilant and efficient officer—a politician of sound principles and enlarged views, and an ardent patriot. Among the early pioneers of Kentucky, he deservedly occupies a prominent place and a high rank. He died on the 19th day of May, 1840, at the advanced age of eighty-three years.

PRESTON H. LESLIE, Twenty-sixth Governor of Kentucky, was born in that part of Wayne which now forms Clinton County, Kentucky, March 2, 1819. Left an orphan at an early age, his fellow citizens are proud of that self-relying spirit and indomitable energy which made him, in his poverty, a cart-driver in the streets of Louisville at the age of thirteen, a wood-chopper at fourteen, a ferryman, farmer's boy and cook for tan-bark choppers at fifteen, a lawyer at twenty-two, a representative in the legislature at twenty-five, a senator at thirty-one, and governor of the eighth state in population of the American Union at fifty-one. He began the practice of law in Monroe County and represented that county in the legislature in 1844 and 1850, and the counties of Monroe and Barren in the senate in 1851-55. After removing to Barren, he was again in the senate, in 1867-71; in December, 1869, was chosen speaker of the senate, and thereby acting lieutenant governor; on February 13, 1871, upon the resignation of Governor Stevenson, was inaugurated for the unexpired term, until September, 1871; in August, 1871, was the Democratic candidate and elected governor for four years, from 1871-75, by the remarkable majority of 37,156.

WILLIAM KRAUS, the efficient manager of the Rehkopf Horse Collar Manufacturing Company of Paducah, is a son of Philip and Louisa (Keyser) Kraus, and was born in Baltimore, Maryland, September 2, 1846.

His father was born in Hanover, near Bremen, Germany, and was a glass stainer, who came to America, and was the first man who engaged in that business in this country. He first went to Fredericksburg, Virginia, in 1834, and removed to Baltimore, Maryland, in 1840, where he followed his trade industriously until his death in 1872. He was a strictly honest and upright man and left no estate. His wife was a native of Saxony and was a woman of superior intelligence who took especial care and pride in the education and proper training of her son.

William Kraus was reared in Baltimore and was educated at Irvin College, Hanover, Lancaster County, Pennsylvania. After spending seven years in that institution, he entered the government service in the ambulance department and served for four years, during the war of the '60's.

When the war was over he returned to Baltimore and served an apprenticeship of three years with John D. Hammond & Company, learning the trade of horse-collar making, and then accepted a position with John D. Lemp of Wheeling, West Virginia, and, after spending a short time there, made a tour of the west.

He first came to Paducah in April, 1876, and after spending about three months there, went to Jefferson City, Missouri, where he was employed in the State Prison for a short time, when he was induced to return to Paducah and to accept his present position as manager of the Rehkopf Horse Collar Manufacturing Company, the plant of which was established by E. Rehkopf in 1858. Under Mr. Kraus' management, the business of the concern has greatly increased and the present average product of the factory is about two hundred dozen collars a week. Nine traveling salesmen are employed who cover the entire southern trade and as far north as Michigan. This manufactory has a reputation all over the country for the excellence of its collars, and it is probably one of the largest establishments of the kind in the country. Much of its success is due to the excellent management of Mr. Kraus, whose thorough knowledge of the details of the work in the shop and of the wants of the trade throughout the country enables him to keep abreast with the demands of the trade and to produce a class of work that cannot be excelled. Mr. Kraus is an educated gentleman, of most agreeable manners, and is popular among a host of acquaintances. He has frequently been called upon to serve the city in the capacity of Councilman and School Trustee, to which offices he was elected on the Democratic ticket. He is a popular and active member of a number of the benevolent orders, including the Masons, Odd Fellows, Knights of Honor and the "Sapient Screechers," Nest No. 17; has served as master of his Masonic lodge; as dictator of Rapidan Lodge of Knights of Honor and past Grand Sire of I. O. O. F. Lodge No. 19. Mr. Kraus was married January 31, 1876, to Anna E. Earhart of Cincinnati.

COLONEL DANIEL BOONE, who was the first white man who ever made a permanent settlement within the limits of the present State of Kentucky, was born in Bucks County, Pennsylvania, on the right bank of the Delaware River, on the 11th of February, 1731. Of his life, but little is known previous to his emigration to Kentucky, with the early history of which his name is, perhaps, more closely identified than that of any other man.

It is said that the ancestors of Daniel Boone were among the original Catholic settlers of Maryland; but of this nothing is known with certainty, nor is it, perhaps, important that anything should be. He was eminently the architect of his own fortunes; a self-formed man in the truest sense— whose own innate energies and impulses gave the moulding impress to his character. In the years of his early boyhood his father emigrated first to Reading, on the headwaters of the Schuylkill, and subsequently to one of the valleys of South Yadkin, in North Carolina, where the subject of this notice continued to reside until his fortieth year.

In 1767, the return of Findlay from his adventurous excursion into the unexplored wilds beyond the Cumberland mountains, and the glowing accounts he gave of the richness and fertility of the new country, excited powerfully the curiosity and imaginations of the frontier backwoodsmen of Virginia and North Carolina, ever on the watch for adventures; and to whom the lonely wilderness, with all its perils, presented attractions which were not to be found in the close confinement and enervating inactivity of the settlements. To a man of Boone's temperament and tastes, the scenes described by Findlay presented charms not to be resisted; and, in 1769, he left his family upon the Yadkin, and in company with five others, of whom Findlay was one, he started to explore that country of which he had heard so favorable an account.

Having reached a stream of water on the borders of the present State of Kentucky, called Red River, they built a cabin to shelter them from the inclemency of the weather (for the season had been very rainy), and devoted their time to hunting and the chase, killing immense quantities of game. Nothing of particular interest occurred until the 22d of December, 1769, when Boone, in company with a man named Stuart, being out hunting, they were surprised and captured by Indians. They remained with their captors seven days, until, having by a rare and powerful exertion of self-control, suffering no signs of impatience to escape them, succeeded in disarming the suspicions of the Indians, their escape was effected without difficulty. Through life Boone was remarkable for cool, collected self-possession in moments of most trying emergency, and on no occasion was this rare and valuable quality more conspicuously displayed than during the time of this captivity. On regaining their camp, they found it dismantled and deserted. The fate of its inmates was never ascertained, and it is worthy of remark, that this is the last and almost the only glimpse we have of Findlay, the first pioneer. A few days after this they were joined by Squire Boone, a brother of the great pioneer, and another man, who had followed them from Carolina, and accidentally stumbled on their camp. Soon after this accession to their numbers, Daniel Boone and Stuart, in a second excursion, were again assailed by the Indians, and Stuart shot and scalped; Boone fortunately escaped. Their only remaining companion, disheartened by the perils to which they were continually exposed, returned to North Carolina, and the two brothers were left alone in the wilderness, separated by hundreds of miles from the white settlements and destitute of everything but their rifles. Their ammunition running short, it was determined that Squire Boone should return to Carolina for a fresh supply, while his brother remained in charge of the camp. This resolution was accordingly carried into effect, and Boone was left for a considerable time to encounter or evade the teeming perils of his hazardous solitude alone. We should suppose that his situation now would have been disheartening and wretched in the extreme. He himself says that for a few days after his brother left him he felt dejected and lonesome, but in a short time his spirits recovered their wonted equanimity, and he roved through the woods in every direction, killing abundance of game and finding an unutterable pleasure in the contemplation of the natural beauties of the forest scenery. On the 27th of July, 1770, the younger Boone returned from Carolina with the ammunition, and with a hardihood almost incredible, the brothers continued to range through the country without injury until March, 1771, when they retraced their steps to North Carolina. Boone had been absent from his family for near three years, during nearly the whole of which time he had never tasted bread or salt, nor beheld the face of a single white man, with the exception of his brother and the friends who had been killed.

On the 25th of September, 1773, having disposed of all his property, except that which he intended to carry with him to his new home, Boone and his family took leave of their friends and commenced their journey west. In Powell's valley, being joined by five more families and forty men, well armed, they proceeded towards their destination with confidence; but when near the Cumberland mountains they were attacked by a large party of Indians. These, after a severe engagement, were beaten off and compelled to retreat, not, however, until the whites had sustained a loss of six men in killed and wounded. Among the killed was Boone's eldest son. This foretaste of the dangers which awaited them in the wilderness they were about to explore so discouraged the emigrants that they immediately retreated to the settlements on Clinch river, a distance of forty miles from the scene of action. Here they remained until 1775. During this interval Boone was employed by Governor Dunmore of Virginia, to conduct a party of surveyors through the wilderness, from Falls of the Ohio, a distance of eight hundred miles. Of the incidents attending this expedition, we have no account whatever. After his return he was placed by Dunmore in command of three frontier stations, or garrisons, and engaged in several affairs with the Indians. At about the same period, he also, at the solicitation of several gentlemen of North Carolina, attended a treaty with the Cherokees, known as the treaty of Wataga, for the purchase of the lands south of the Kentucky river. It was in connection with this land purchase, and under the auspices of Colonel Richard Henderson, that Boone's second expedition to Kentucky was made. His business was to mark out a road for the pack-horses and wagons of Henderson's party. Leaving his family on Clinch river, he set out upon this hazardous undertaking at the head of a few men, on the 10th of March, 1775, and arrived, without any adventure worthy of note, on the 25th of March, the same year, at a point within fifteen miles of the spot where Boonesborough was afterwards built. Here they were attacked by Indians, and it was not until after a severe contest, and loss on the part of the whites of three men in killed and wounded, that they were repulsed. An attack was made on another party, and the whites sustained a loss of two more. On the 1st of April they reached the southern bank of the Kentucky river, and began to build a fort, afterwards known as Boonesborough. On the 4th they were again attacked by the Indians, and lost another man; but, notwithstanding the dangers to which they were continually exposed, the work was prosecuted with indefatigable diligence, and on the 14th of the month finally completed. Boone shortly returned to Clinch river for his family, determined to remove them to this new and remote settlement at all hazards. This was accordingly effected as soon as circumstances would permit. From this time the little garrison was exposed to incessant assaults from the Indians, who appeared to be perfectly infuriated at the encroachments of the whites, and the formation of settlements in the midst of their old hunting grounds; and the lives of the emigrants were passed in a continued succession of the most appalling perils, which nothing but unquailing courage and indomitable firmness could have enabled them to encounter. They did, however, breast this awful tempest of war, and bravely and successfully, and in defiance of all probability the small colony continued steadily to increase and flourish, until the thunder of barbarian hostilities rolled gradually away to the north, and finally died in low mutterings on the frontiers of Ohio, Indiana, and Illinois. The summary nature of this sketch will not admit of more than a bare enumeration of the principal events in which Boone figured in these exciting times, during which he stood the center figure, towering like a colossus amid that hardy band of pioneers, who opposed their breasts to the shock of that dreadful death struggle, which gave a yet more terrible significance, and a still more crimson hue, to the history of the old dark and bloody ground.

In July, 1776, the people at the fort were thrown into the greatest agitation and alarm, by an incident characteristic of the times, and which singularly illustrates the habitual peril which environed the inhabitants. Jemima Boone and two daughters of Colonel Callaway were amusing themselves in the neighborhood of the fort, when a party of Indians suddenly rushed from the surrounding coverts and carried them away captives. The screams of the terrified girls aroused the inmates of the garrison; but the men being generally dispersed in their usual avocations, Boone hastily pursued with a party of only eight men. The little party, after marching hard during two nights, came up with the Indians early the third day, the pursuit having been conducted with such silence and celerity that the savages were taken entirely by surprise, and having no preparations for defense, they were routed almost instantly, and without difficulty. The young girls were restored to their gratified parents without having sustained the slightest injury, or any inconvenience beyond the fatigue of the march and a dreadful fright. The Indians lost two men, while Boone's party was uninjured.

From this time until the 15th of April, the garrison was constantly harassed by flying parties of savages. They were kept in continual anxiety and alarm; and the most ordinary duties could only be performed at the risk of their lives. "While plowing their corn they were waylaid and shot; while hunting, they were pursued and fired upon; and sometimes a solitary Indian would creep up near the fort during the night, and fire upon the first of the garrison who appeared in the morning." On the 15th of April, a large body of Indians invested the fort, hoping to crush the settlement at a single blow; but, destitute as they were of scaling ladders, and all the proper means of reducing fortified places, they could only annoy the garrison, and destroy the property; and being more exposed than the whites, soon retired precipitately. On the 4th of July following, they again appeared with a force of two hundred warriors, and were repulsed with loss. A short period of tranquillity was now allowed to the harassed and distressed garrison; but this was soon followed by the most severe calamity that had yet befallen the infant settlement. This was the capture of Boone and twenty-seven of his men in the month of January, 1778, at the Blue Licks, whither he had gone to make salt for the garrison. He was carried to the old town of Chillicothe, in the present state of Ohio, where he remained a prisoner with the Indians until the 16th of the following June, when he contrived to make his escape, and returned to Boonsborough.

During this period, Boone kept no journal, and we are therefore uninformed as to any of the particular incidents which occurred during his captivity. We only know, generally, that, by his equanimity, his patience, his seeming cheerful submission to the fortune which had made him a captive, and his remarkable skill and expertness as a woodsman, he succeeded in powerfully exciting the admiration and conciliating the good will of his captors. In March, 1778, he accompanied the Indians on a visit to Detroit, where Governor Hamilton offered one hundred pounds for his ransom, but so strong was the affection of the Indians for their prisoner, that it was unhesitatingly refused. Several English gentlemen, touched with sympathy for his misfortunes, made pressing offers of money and other articles, but Boone steadily refused to receive benefits which he could never return.

On his return from Detroit, he observed that large numbers of warriors had assembled, painted and equipped for an expedition against Boonsborough, and his anxiety became so great that he determined to effect his escape at every hazard. During the whole of this agitating period, however, he permitted no symptom of anxiety to escape; but continued to hunt and shoot with the Indians as usual, until the morning of the 16th of June, when, making an early start, he left Chillicothe, and shaped his course for Boonsborough. This journey, exceeding a distance of one hundred and fifty miles, he performed in four days, during which he ate only one meal. He was received at the garrison like one risen from the dead. His family supposing him killed, had returned to North Carolina; and his men, apprehending no danger, had permitted the defenses of the fort to fall to decay. The danger was imminent; the enemy were hourly expected, and the fort was in no condition to receive them. Not a moment was to be lost: the garrison worked night and day, and by indefatigable diligence, everything was made ready within ten days after his arrival, for the approach of the enemy. At this time one of his companions arrived from Chillicothe, and reported that his escape had determined the Indians to delay the invasion for three weeks. The attack was delayed so long that Boone, in his turn, resolved to invade the Indian country; and accordingly, at the head of a select company of nineteen men, he marched against the town of Paint Creek, on the Scioto, within four miles of which point he arrived without discovery. Here he encountered a party of thirty warriors, on their march to join the grand army in its expedition against Boonsborough. This party he attacked and routed without loss or injury to himself; and, ascertaining that the main body of the Indians were on their march to Boonsborough, he retraced his steps for that place with all possible expedition. He passed the Indians on the 6th day of their march, and on the 7th reached the fort. The next day the Indians appeared in great force, conducted by Canadian officers well skilled in all the arts of modern warfare. The British colors were displayed and the fort summoned to surrender. Boone requested two days for consideration, which was granted. At the expiration of this period, having gathered in their cattle and horses, and made every preparation for a vigorous resistance, an answer was returned that the fort would be defended to the last. A proposition was then made to treat, and Boone and eight of the garrison, met the British and Indian officers, on the plain in front of the fort. Here, after they had gone through the farce of pretending to treat, an effort was made to detain the Kentuckians as prisoners. This was frustrated by the vigilance and activity of the intended victims, who springing out from the midst of their savage foemen, ran to the fort under a heavy fire of rifles, which fortunately wounded only one man. The attack instantly commenced by a heavy fire against the picketing, and was returned with fatal accuracy by the garrison. The Indians then attempted to push a mine into the fort, but their object being discovered by the quantity of fresh earth they were compelled to throw into the river, Boone cut a trench within the fort, in such a manner as to intersect their line of approach, and thus frustrated their design. After exhausting all the ordinary artifices of Indian warfare, and finding their numbers daily thinned by the deliberate and fatal firing from the garrison, they raised the siege on the ninth day after their first appearance, and returned home. The loss on the part of the garrison, was two men killed and four wounded. Of the savages, twenty-seven were killed and many wounded, who, as usual, were carried off. This was the last siege sustained by Boonsborough.

In the fall of this year, Boone went to North Carolina for his wife and family, who, as already observed, had supposed him dead, and returned to their kindred. In the summer of 1780, he came back to Kentucky with his family, and settled at Boonsborough. In October of this year, returning in company with his brother from the Blue Licks, where they had been to make salt, they were encountered by a party of Indians, and his brother, who had been his faithful companion through many years of toil and danger, was shot and scalped before his eyes. Boone, after a long and close chase, finally effected his escape.

After this, he was engaged in no affair of particular interest, so far as we are informed, until the month of August, 1782, a time rendered memorable by the celebrated and disastrous battle of the Blue Licks. On this fatal day, he bore himself with distinguished gallantry, until the rout began, when, after having witnessed the death of his son, and many of his dearest friends, he found himself almost surrounded at the very commencement of the retreat. Several hundred Indians were between him and the ford, to which the great mass of the fugitives were bending their way, and to which the attention of the savages was particularly directed. Being intimately acquainted with the ground, he together with a few friends, dashed into the ravine which the Indians had occupied, but which most of them had now left to join in the pursuit. After sustaining one or two heavy fires, and baffling one or two small parties who pursued him for a short distance, he crossed the river below the ford by swimming, and returned by a circuitous route to Bryant's station.

Boone accompanied General George Rogers Clark, in his expedition against the Indian towns, undertaken to avenge the disaster at the Blue Licks; but beyond the simple fact that he did accompany this expedition, nothing is known of his connection with it; and it does not appear that he was afterward engaged in any public expedition or solitary adventure.

The definitive treaty of peace between the United States and Great Britain, in 1783, confirmed the title of the former to independence, and Boone saw the standard of civilization and freedom securely planted in the wilderness. Upon the establishment of the court of commissioners in 1779, he had laid out the chief of his little property to procure land warrants, and having raised about twenty thousand dollars in paper money, with which he intended to purchase them, on his way from Kentucky to the city of Richmond, he was robbed of the whole, and left destitute of the means of procuring more. Unacquainted with the niceties of the law, the few lands he was enabled afterward to locate, were, through his ignorance, swallowed up and lost by better claims. Dissatisfied with these impediments to the acquisition of the soil, he left Kentucky, and in 1795, he was a wanderer on the banks of the Missouri, a voluntary subject of the king of Spain. The remainder of his life was devoted to the society of his children, and the employments of the chase—to the latter especially. When age had enfeebled the energies of his once athletic frame, he would wander twice a year into the remotest wilderness he could reach, employing a companion whom he bound by a written contract to take care of him, and bring him home alive or dead. In 1816, he made such an excursion to Fort Osage, one hundred miles distant from the place of his residence. "Three years thereafter," says Governor Morehead, "a patriotic solicitude to preserve his portrait, prompted a distinguished American artist to visit him at his dwelling near the Missouri river, and from him I have received the following particulars: He found him in a small, rude cabin, indisposed, and reclining on his bed. A slice from the loin of a buck, twisted round the rammer of his rifle, within reach of him as he lay, was roasting before the fire. Several other cabins, arranged in the form of a parallelogram, marked the spot of a dilapidated station. They were occupied by the descendants of the pioneer. Here he lived in the midst of his posterity. His withered energies and locks of snow, indicated that the sources of existence were nearly exhausted."

He died of fever, at the house of his son-in-law, Flanders Callaway, at Charette village, on the Missouri river, September 26, 1820, aged eighty-nine. The legislature of Missouri in session at St. Louis, when the event was announced, resolved that, in respect for his memory, the members would wear the usual badge of mourning for twenty days, and voted an adjournment for that day. It has been generally supposed that Boone was illiterate, and could neither read nor write, but this is an error.

The following vigorous and eloquent portrait of the character of the old pioneer, is extracted from Governor Morehead's address, delivered at Boonsborough, in commemoration of the first settlement of Kentucky:

"The life of Daniel Boone is a forcible example of the powerful influence which a single absorbing passion exerts over the destiny of an individual. Born with no endowments of intellect to distinguish him from the crowd of ordinary men, and possessing no other acquirements than a very common education bestowed, he was enabled, nevertheless, to maintain through a long and useful career, a conspicuous rank among the most distinguished of his contemporaries; and the testimonials of the public gratitude and respect with which he was honored after his death, were such as are never awarded by an intelligent people to one undeserving. * * * * He came originally to the wilderness, not to settle and subdue it, but to gratify an inordinate passion for adventure and discovery—to hunt the deer and buffalo—to roam through the woods—to admire the beauties of nature—in a word, to enjoy the lonely pastimes of a hunter's life, remote from the society of his fellow men. He had heard, with admiration and delight, Finley's description of the country of Kentucky, and high as were his expectations, he found it a second paradise. Its lofty forests—its noble rivers—its picturesque scenery—its beautiful valleys—but above all, the plentifulness of 'beasts of every American kind'—these were the attractions that brought him to it. * * * * He united, in an eminent degree, the qualities of shrewdness, caution, and courage, with uncommon muscular strength. He was seldom taken by surprise—he never shrunk from danger, nor cowered beneath the pressure of exposure and fatigue. In every emergency, he was a safe guide and a wise counsellor, because his movements were conducted with the utmost circumspection, and his judgment and penetration were proverbially accurate. Powerless to originate plans on a large scale, no individual among the pioneers could execute with more efficiency and success the designs of others. He took the lead in no expedition against the savages—he disclosed no liberal and enlarged views of policy for the protection of the stations; and yet it is not assuming too much to say, that without him, in all probability, the settlements could not have been upheld, and the conquest of Kentucky might have been reserved for the emigrants of the nineteenth century. * * * * His manners were simple and unobstrusive—exempt from the rudeness characteristic of the backwoodsman. In his person there was nothing remarkably striking. He was five feet ten inches in height, and of robust and powerful proportions. His countenance was mild and contemplative—indicating a frame of mind altogether different from the restlessness and activity that distinguished him. His ordinary habiliments were those of a hunter—a hunting shirt and moccasins uniformly composing a part of them. When he emigrated to Louisiana, he omitted to secure the title to a princely estate, on the Missouri, because it would have cost him the trouble of a trip to New Orleans. He would have traveled a much greater distance to indulge his cherished propensities as an adventurer and a hunter. He died, as he had lived, in a cabin, and perhaps his trusty rifle was the most valuable of his chattels.

"Such was the man to whom has been assigned the principal merit of the discovery of Kentucky, and who filled a large space in the eyes of America and Europe. Resting on the solid advantages of his services to his country, his fame will survive, when the achievements of men, greatly his superiors in rank and intellect, will be entirely forgotten."

MATTHEW WALTON, one of the leading attorneys of Lexington and a man of prominence in business and public affairs, was born near Germantown, Mason County, Kentucky, February 16, 1852, and is a son of John H. and Susan Isabelle (Frazee) Walton.

His father was a native of Bracken County, who removed to Mason when he was a young man and is still a resident and a large land owner and tobacco grower of that county; an influential man in his community and highly esteemed for his integrity and noble Christian character. He is a faithful member of the Christian Church and his chief characteristic is his devotion to his church and its good work.

Matthew Walton (grandfather) was a native of Boone County, but removed to Bracken County, where he was engaged in farming and died there in 1843, aged forty-eight years. His father—the great-grandfather of the subject of this sketch—was a near relative of George Walton, a delegate in the Continental Congress and one of the signers of the Declaration of Independence. This distinguished patriot was born in Frederick County, Virginia, his parents having removed from Culpeper to that county. His educational facilities were limited, but he was a diligent student and under the most adverse circumstances he overcame all difficulties, and few young men of his time were better informed than he when he reached his majority. At the age of fourteen he was apprenticed to a carpenter, an ignorant man who considered the time spent in reading and study as time wasted, and he denied the boy any time for his studies; but Walton, using pine torches for candles, spent his evenings in studies, which prepared him for the important part he was destined to take in the affairs of the nation. After serving his time he went to the Province of Georgia and began the practice of law in 1774, a time when the colonies were ablaze on account of the various acts of the British Parliament, and he espoused the cause of independence. He boldly opposed the movements of the loyalists and soon called down upon his head the denunciation of the ruling powers. He labored assiduously to persuade the people of the province to take steps toward independence and freedom, which the parish of St. John had chosen. At first it seemed his labors would be in vain, but at length his zeal and enthusiasm began to bear fruit, and in the winter of 1776 the Assembly of Georgia, through his earnest labors, declared for the cause of the patriots, and in February appointed five delegates to the Continental Congress, and of these George Walton was one who signed the Declaration of Independence. When he died, February 2, 1804, aged sixty-four years, the State of Georgia went into mourning for twenty days.

George Walton's ancestors had come to this country from Norway just one hundred years before he died, settling in Virginia in 1704. Many branches of the family are now scattered over the South and West.

Susan Isabelle Frazee Walton (mother) was born in Mason County, Kentucky, in 1829, and is now a resident of her native county, a zealous member of the Christian Church, and a lady of rare intelligence and amiability.

Joseph Frazee (maternal grandfather) was a large land owner in Mason County, and a highly respected citizen, who held many responsible positions in that county.

Matthew Walton was educated principally in the Kentucky State University at Lexington, and read law with the late Judge Owsley and Benjamin M. Burdett of Lancaster; was admitted to the bar in the fall of 1874; practiced law in Lancaster nearly seven years; was appointed master commissioner of the Circuit Court in 1877; was an active and interesting correspondent of some of the leading newspapers of the state; was chairman of the Garrard County Democratic Committee for four years; represented the Eighth Congressional District in the National Convention that nominated General Hancock for the Presidency; and was prominent in the politics of his county and district.

He removed to Lexington in 1881 and located there permanently in the practice of his profession. His reputation had preceded him and he was by no means a stranger in the Blue Grass Capital, so that he at once stepped into a lucrative practice and into prominence among the many distinguished members of the bar. In 1885 he was elected judge of the Recorder's Court of the City of Lexington, which office he filled with credit and marked ability until 1890.

For seven or eight years past he has been one of the commissioners of the Eastern Asylum for the Insane, and is president of that board; is a director in the Safety Vault & Trust Company of Lexington; is attorney for the Phoenix National Bank, in which he is also a director; is attorney for a number of financial and industrial corporations and president of the Lexington Charity Organization, of which he was one of the leading promoters. He is well informed in all matters of public interest and is frequently called upon to represent Fayette County in political and other conventions. He is by no means a partizan in politics, but his ability and wide scope of information have brought him into prominence in his party, which has implicit confidence in his integrity, wisdom and sound judgment.

After serving out his term as judge he formed a law partnership with J. H. Beauchamp, under the firm name of Beauchamp & Walton, which at present is one of the most successful firms in Lexington.

Judge Walton and Carrie Farra, daughter of B. F. Farra of Jessamine County, were married October 3, 1878. They worship in the New Central Christian Church, one of the most beautiful church edifices in the Blue Grass region, the erection of which was under the supervision of a building committee of which Judge Walton was one of the most industrious members.

Judge and Mrs. Walton have only one child, a daughter four years old, Clara Belle Walton.

ROBERT ALLEN BURTON, President of the Farmers' National Bank of Lebanon, son of John Allen and Louisana (Chandler) Burton, was born in Boyle (then Mercer) County, Kentucky, near the battle ground of Perryville, June 11, 1834.

His father was born in Mercer County, April 3, 1801; was educated in the ordinary schools of his day and was a farmer and merchant at Perryville for forty years; retired in 1860, and died in 1874, aged seventy-three years. He was one of the stanchest Democrats of his time—not for the sake of office, which he did not seek, but from principle. He had large commercial interests and was a man of superior judgment and excellent business qualifications and was quite successful in business.

Robert Burton (grandfather) was a native of Virginia; came to Kentucky at a very early day, and married a Miss Ferguson, who was born in a fort at Harrodsburg.

Louisana Chandler Burton (mother) was born in Washington County, in 1810; was an amiable, Christian woman, greatly admired and respected by her acquaintances and revered by her children. She survived her husband about five years, and died in 1879.

Richard Chandler (grandfather), a native of Maryland, came to Kentucky when he was a young man and located in Washington County, where he was a farmer and blacksmith. He married Elizabeth McNeal of Fayette County and died in 1855.

Judge R. A. Burton was educated in Boyle County, finishing at the Perryville Seminary in 1856; was engaged in farming while studying law, which he did without an instructor, and was admitted to the bar in 1858; removed to Marion County in the same year and continued farming; was elected to the Legislature in 1859; elected county judge in 1862 and was twice re-elected; elected State Senator in 1869 and served four years; was division deputy collector of internal revenue during President Cleveland's first administration; was again elected county judge in 1890 and again in 1894 for a term of three years under the new constitution; represented his district in the Democratic National Conventions of 1874 and 1888, and was elected president of the Farmers' National Bank of Lebanon in 1890, a position which has required his best attention since that time.

Judge Burton has been a leading spirit in the Democratic councils of his county and section for many years, and his popularity is so great that he could have any office in the gift of the people. All men who know him have the utmost confidence in him; dignified and courtly, he is easily approached, and while his polished manner is such that a stranger will instinctively take off his hat to him, he is open and free with those who know him and is a friend who is always steadfast and true.

Judge Burton was married May 17, 1860, to Margaret Lowry, daughter of Hon. James Lowry of Jessamine County. She was born June 11, 1837; was educated in St. Catherine Academy, Washington County, and in Lexington. They have four children living: John A. Burton, general deputy internal revenue agent for Kentucky under Colonel Yates; Mary A., educated at Daughter's College, Harrodsburg, and at Science

Hill Academy, Shelbyville; Robert Lee, in college at Richmond, Kentucky; and Marion County Burton, who is in school at Lebanon.

Judge Burton has shown his high regard for his county, the scene of his many political triumphs and business successes, by naming his youngest son for his county.

Colonel Richard G. Burton, the only brother of Judge R. A. Burton, who lived in Richmond, Kentucky, is now dead. His sister, Belle, now deceased, married Lee Irvine of Boyle County. Augusta Celesta (sister), married Dr. W. O. Robards of Mercer County. Eusebrie (sister), married J. G. Phillips of Lebanon.

MATTHEW HEROLD, City Attorney of Bellevue, a popular young lawyer and Democratic politician, was born in Cincinnati, Ohio, March 3, 1859.

His father, Andrew Herold, was a native of Germany, who came to this country in 1835 and located in Cincinnati, where he was engaged in organ building until his death in 1860.

His mother, Susan (Barwick) Herold, now a resident of Cincinnati, is a native of Germany.

Matthew Herold was educated in the excellent public schools of Cincinnati. From 1882 until 1888 he was engaged in the grocery business in Bellevue, which he abandoned for the legal profession. After reading law for two years he took a two years' course in the Cincinnati Law School, from which he was graduated in 1892. He was admitted to the bar and began the practice of law in Newport in the same year, and has met with great encouragement and a good degree of success in a field that he found pretty well occupied when he embarked in his new profession.

He takes quite an active part in politics, and being a resident of Bellevue he was elected a member of the City Council in 1890; served until 1892, when he was elected city attorney; was re-elected to this office in 1893, again in 1894, and again in 1896, a very high testimonial of his efficiency and personal popularity inasmuch as he is a Democrat and Bellevue is a stronghold of the Republican party. Mr. Herold was a member of the convention held in Winchester in 1891 to frame charters for cities of the fourth class.

He is attorney for a number of corporations, including three building associations in Bellevue and one in Cincinnati, and has given much attention to the legal business of these organizations.

Mr. Herold was married in 1885 to Caroline Herbert, daughter of Andrew Herbert of Cincinnati, and they have three sons: Matthew, George and William Herold.

UREY WOODSON, Editor of the Owensboro Messenger and president of the Kentucky Press Association, was born at Madisonville, Kentucky, August 16, 1859. Six years later his parents moved to Evansville, Indiana. In 1877, when only eighteen years of age, his spirit of independence began to assert itself, and he left home and started the Muhlenberg Echo, a small weekly, at Greenville, Kentucky. This paper still lives, a monument to the "nerve" displayed by its founder, though it soon became too small a medium for the exercise of his talent for journalistic work.

At the annual meeting of the Kentucky Press Association, at Hopkinsville, in 1878, Mr. Woodson, who was then only nineteen and looked five years younger, was christened "The Baby Editor," which appellation clung to him for several years. In September, 1881, Mr. Woodson sold his paper at Greenville and moved to Owensboro, becoming a part owner of the Messenger, then a semi-weekly. The editorial control of the paper was in his hands, and there has been no interruption to the career of prosperity and increasing influence it at once entered upon.

He has since become sole owner of the Messenger, which is now said to be the most valuable newspaper property in Kentucky, using Merganthaler type-setting machines and all modern improvements. Mr. Woodson's capacity for work is without limit. He is tireless, alert and never resourceless.

He was the first man in Kentucky to give an intimation of the looseness about the office of James W. Tate, state treasurer, four years before he was proven a defaulter. With that instinct for news that amounts almost to intuition with him, he got an inkling of something wrong at Frankfort, and suggested that an investigation would be a good thing. The matter was laughed at and hushed up by Tate's associates, who declared that they knew his affairs were all straight, and for four years longer the stealing went on.

In his writings sarcasm and ridicule are his favorite weapons, and while he is personally jovial and witty, he makes but little pretensions to humor with his pen. He prefers to deal in a plain-spoken, business like style that is seldom mistaken for the "lighter vein." There is no more conscientious or influential editor in the smaller cities of Kentucky than Mr. Woodson.

His paper is a power in the politics of his state, and Democracy has no more ardent champion than he is.

When Governor John Young Brown was elected he tendered Mr. Woodson the appointment of railroad commissioner, which position he filled for four years.

For eight or ten years he has been a member of the Democratic state central committee, and was for a term president of the Kentucky Press Association.

JAMES A. VIOLETT, Attorney-at-Law of Frankfort, and a member of the legislature, representing Franklin County, is a son of Leland and Polly (Walker) Violett. His father was a native of Owen County, where he was a farmer in good circumstances and a highly respected citizen of the county. He was a man of exemplary habits, industrious and frugal, and was an active and energetic man until his death in 1882. His father's people were of French extraction.

Polly Walker Violett (mother) was a daughter of a Mr. Walker, who came to America from England and lived in Owen County until he reached the unusual age of ninety-seven years.

James A. Violett was born in Owen County, Kentucky, July 20, 1852, and lived the life of a farmer's boy until he was eighteen years of age, when, having obtained a good common school education, he attended the excellent school at Harrodsburg under the tutorship of Professor Edward Porter Thompson and then taught school in Owen and Franklin Counties, at the same time studying law without an instructor until 1876, when he placed himself under the care and instruction of Judge Coffee, one of the most eminent judges of the Court of Appeals. He was admitted to the bar in Frankfort in 1879, and at once entered upon a career which has thus far proven highly successful and promises a brilliant future.

He was elected county attorney of Franklin County in 1882, serving four years, and in 1895 was elected on the Democratic ticket as representative of Franklin County in the legislature. In the remarkable contest for the United States Senatorship in the General Assembly of 1896, Mr. Violett was one of five sound-money Democrats who refused to support Senator Blackburn, the Democratic caucus nominee. He did this in spite of the tremendous pressure the friends of Blackburn brought to bear upon him. Believing, however, that the majority of his constituents and the good of the state demanded the defeat of Blackburn, he steadily refused to cast his vote for that candidate.

Mr. Violett is one of the most active and able members of the legislature, and a faithful representative of his constituents.

He was married to Alice Bell Deakins, daughter of John T. and Polly (Woodsides) Deakins of Shelby County, and they have three children: Luther Francis, now in college at Georgetown; Mary Hill and Walter.

WILLIAM WELLS CLEAVER, M. D., a leading physician of Lebanon, son of David and Lucy (Kirk) Cleaver, was born in Lebanon, Kentucky, March 15, 1827.

His father was born in Marion County, in 1804; was educated at St. Mary's College, and was a man of superior intelligence. He married Lucy Kirk in 1824, and they were members of the Presbyterian Church. He followed farming and stock trading and was prosperous in his business. He was identified with the Democratic party, but merely as a voter. Having reached the age of seventy-seven years, he died in 1885, and is buried in the cemetery at Lebanon.

David Cleaver (grandfather) was a native of New Jersey, who came to Kentucky in 1788 and settled in (now) Marion County. Three brothers came with him; and after living as neighbors for

JUDGE CHAS. G. RITCHIE.

a while, two of them removed to Missouri and one went to Alabama, and thence to Arkansas. David remained in Kentucky and spent the remainder of his days on the farm upon which he located as one of the pioneers of the county. His wife's name was Lettitia Griffey, who was of Irish parentage.

Lucy Kirk (mother) was a daughter of James and Annie (Horton) Kirk; a devout Christian and a member of the Presbyterian Church. She died in 1827, and is buried beside her husband at Lebanon. Her parents were of Scotch-Irish extraction.

James Kirk (grandfather) was a native of Stafford, Virginia, came to Kentucky in 1788; was a soldier in the war of the Revolution; married (first) Annie Horton, who was the mother of his twelve children. He lived to the extreme age of ninety-nine years; and when he was eighty-one years of age he married his second wife, who was then twenty-two years of age.

Dr. William W. Cleaver was educated in Lebanon Seminary and studied medicine in the University of Louisville, from which he was graduated in 1850. He practiced in Lebanon for a short time and in 1853 went to Louisville and followed his profession in that city until 1855, when he returned to Lebanon and located permanently. He had attained gratifying success when, in 1862, he recruited a company and joined Morgan's cavalry; was in command of his company at the battle of Perryville and other stirring engagements; was subsequently appointed surgeon; was with General Morgan in his celebrated Indiana and Ohio raid; was captured with the rest and taken to Fort Delaware, where he remained about five months, doing duty as a surgeon in a hospital while there.

After the close of the war he resumed his professional work at Lebanon, since which time he has given his whole time to the exacting duties of a very extensive practice.

Long experience and faithful attention to business have made him an enviable reputation as one of the most skillful physicians in his city and county. His services are in demand in almost all extreme cases within his reach. He is one of the pillars in the Presbyterian Church and is a Mason of long standing and high degree; a member of the Marion County Medical Society, of the Kentucky State Medical Society, ex-member of the National Medical Association; and is known in politics merely as a loyal voter of the Democratic ticket. Nevertheless, he was elected to the legislature in 1893, representing his county for one term of two years.

Dr. Cleaver was married (first) in 1850 to Joanna Grundy, daughter of Felix B. Grundy and Esther McElroy. She was a native of Lebanon, a woman of superior mind and culture and a devout member of the Presbyterian Church. She died in 1894. Their seven children were named: Dr. J. F. Cleaver, deceased; George Hannibal, deceased; Esther, wife of Dr. A. Rose of Utah; Lucy Hemans, wife of G. W. McElroy of Lebanon; Willie Elizabeth, wife of Rev. George A. Blair of Portland, Oregon; Thomas Foster, physician of Lebanon; and David Irvin, deceased.

Dr. Cleaver was married (second) November 28, 1895, to Miss Minnie McElroy, daughter of Abraham B. and Mary Buckner McElroy.

HONORABLE CHARLES G. RICHIE, Judge of the Jefferson County Court, is probably the youngest man ever elected or appointed to a judgeship in the state, and is one of the ablest of the numerous gentlemen who adorn the bench in the city of Louisville. He was elected to this office in November, 1893, before he was twenty-seven years of age, receiving a majority of two thousand votes over Judge Hoke, his Democratic opponent, who had held that office during the lifetime of the successful candidate. He had been made the nominee of the Republican party and went into the race with the support of his own party and of a host of friends, and with a reputation as an exemplary young man, as a lawyer of marked ability and of the highest integrity, and his success was due to the fact that he was admirably adapted for the position as well as to the general impression that a change in the office would be for the public good. In the one year or more in which he has presided over the judicial affairs of the county, he has more than met the expectations of his most sanguine friends, having rejuvenated the office and corrected many errors, which had naturally and perhaps inadvertently crept into the methods of the court under an administration of too long standing. Of commanding and prepossessing appearance, being over six feet in stature, of large manly frame, surmounted by a large brainy head, no one would think of his age in taking the measure of the man. He is industrious, painstaking, conscientious and determined; thoroughly conversant with the law, with sufficient self-reliance to depend upon his own judgment in the disposition of business. Personally, a very affable gentleman, he has clothed his office with a new dignity and respect which has been favorably commented upon by the habitues of the court house. A Republican of the most pronounced convictions and a partisan in politics, he is fair and impartial as a judge and in legal matters his bitterest political opponent knows that he will receive an unprejudiced hearing and a just decision in the court over which the jurist and not the politician presides.

The newspapers have complimented him upon his admirable manner of conducting the affairs of his office, and have shown him courtesies which few men in his position would be able to command from political opponents. He has charge of the entire election machinery of the county, and while the one general election held under his administration was of the most exacting character, no charge has ever been made by his political opponents that his course has been in the least partial to his party.

Judge Richie was born in Louisville, Kentucky, January 18, 1868, and was graduated from the high school in the class of 1887. He then attended the Louisville Law University and graduated in 1889, after which he entered the office of Honorable Walter Evans, with whom he was associated in the practice of law for three years. In 1893 he formed a law partnership with A. J. Speckert, which business relation continued until Mr. Richie's elevation to the bench in January 1895.

Judge Richie is exceedingly popular, especially with the younger people of Louisville, with whom he has mingled all of his life. As a lawyer he occupies a place in the front rank of the profession, and is held in the highest esteem by the members of the bar. As a judge he has the utmost confidence and respect of the legal fraternity who have business in his court. As a citizen he is known as a man of the highest integrity, and his relation to the Methodist Church, of which he is a member, is that of an upright Christian gentleman.

Judge Richie's father, H. C. Richie, is a native of New Albany, Indiana, and a well-known citizen of Louisville, who has been sole traveling agent for the Eclipse Woolen Mills for twenty years. He is a man of fine education and unusual business ability, a vigorous writer and speaker, an enthusiastic Republican and protectionist, and is well-informed in national politics.

William H. Richie (grandfather) was also a native of New Albany, Indiana, and a lifetime resident of that city. He was a pilot on the western rivers and continued his work upon the river until a short time before his death, in 1884.

Sophia Spurrier Richie (mother) is a native of Sumner County, Tennessee; a leading spirit in the Methodist Church and a lady of fine attainments, and is especially noted for her many "good works."

Edward Sperrier (grandfather) was for many years a resident of Clarksville, Tennessee. He removed to Cave City, Kentucky, in 1865, where he kept a hotel for a short time, subsequently removing to Hardin County, where he died in 1882. He was of Scotch-Irish descent.

Judge Richie was married August 29, 1895, to Margaret Pierce, daughter of LaFayette and Nannie (Lyles) Pierce. Mrs. Richie was born in Sumner County, Tennessee, September 1, 1873.

CHARLES F. WEAVER, Secretary and Treasurer of the Ashland Foundry and Machine Works, was born in Cochran, Indiana, March 10, 1858. His father, Daniel L. Weaver, was born in Gordonsville, Pennsylvania, February 25, 1835, and was a master mechanic in the Baldwin Locomotive Works at Philadelphia, and an excellent workman. He served eighteen months on the gunboat "Carondalet" in the Mississippi squadron in the Civil war, and after his honorable discharge, continued in the service of the government as master mechanic during the remainder of the war, after which he held a similar position with the Ohio & Mississippi Railroad Company for fourteen years. He was then master mechanic of the Chesapeake & Ohio Railroad Company at Lexington for four years. He removed to Ashland in November, 1886, and established the Ashland Foundry and Machine Works, which he operated successfully until the time of his death, December 11, 1894. He was a very popular man and a public-spirited citizen, who made many personal friends and enjoyed the confidence of the business community, by whom he was regarded as a man of the highest integrity. He was a Republican in politics, and took a hand in all important elections but would accept no office. He was a general favorite among his acquaintances, particularly as a member of benevolent societies, including the Masons, in which he was an officer and an enthusiastic and zealous worker.

Jonathan Weaver (grandfather) was a native farmer of Lancaster County, Pennsylvania, where he owned a large tract of valuable land, and where he died. His wife, who survived him, was Nancy Lefevre, a native of the same county, and died there in 1888. His father was a soldier in the Revolutionary war, and was wounded at the battle of Brandywine.

Henry W. and Jonathan R. Weaver (uncles) served in the war of the Rebellion, enlisting in the naval service at Aurora, Ind., and were discharged at Helena, Arkansas, in 1864.

Charles F. Weaver's mother, Arjyra Daniels, was born in Portsmouth, Virginia, December 16, 1838, and was educated in Philadelphia; married Daniel L. Weaver June 7, 1857, and is now living in Ashland. She is a member of the Methodist Episcopal Church and a devout Christian woman, who is loved and respected by a large circle of friends.

Abel Davis (grandfather) was a native of Baltimore, Maryland, where he received a good education and was engaged in the drug business for a time, and was for some years traveling salesman for the Baltimore Steam Packing Co., and subsequently kept books for a hotel in Charlestown, South Carolina, and suffered a paralytic stroke in that city. He went to Philadelphia and opened a Home for Southern Students, who were numerous in the educational institutions in that city, and died there January 28, 1861. He was married January 14, 1838, to Eliza Whittis, a native of Elizabeth City, North Carolina; educated in Norfolk, Virginia; died June 7, 1853, and is buried in the Odd Fellows' Cemetery at Philadelphia.

Daniel L. and Arjyra Weaver were the parents of six children: Charles F., born March 10, 1858; Elizabeth, born March 25, 1860, wife of B. F. Myers; Hattie A., born July 8, 1862; Harry Marion, born May 13, 1864; Maggie Rose, born February 24, 1866, and Jerrie Arjyra, born November 28, 1877.

Charles F. Weaver began business as a civil engineer, for which he was prepared by a splendid education, and was employed on the staff of the engineer who built the Kentucky Central Railroad from Paris to Richmond. Being a Republican he accpted the position of chief clerk to Major D. J. Burchett, United States Marshal of Kentucky, at Louisville, and served during President Harrison's administration, after which he returned to his home in Ashland and was made secretary and treasurer of the Ashland Foundry and Machine Works. In 1892 he was elected to the legislature from the Ninety-eighth District and served one term, but is now out of politics, except for the lively interest he takes in the success of the Republican party.

THOMAS FOSTER CLEAVER, M. D., son of Dr. William W. and Joanna (Grundy) Cleaver, was born in Lebanon, Kentucky, November 25, 1865, and was educated in the best schools of his native city and in the Commercial College at Lexington, under Colonel Wilbur F. Smith; studied medicine in the University of Louisville, from which he was graduated March, 1887. He at once engaged in the practice of medicine with his distinguished father, making a specialty of the treatment of diseases of eye, nose and throat, in which he has been highly successful, while attending to a large share of the general practice of the firm.

He is a member of the Marion County Medical

Society; is a prominent member of the Presbyterian Church and is noted for his interest in good works, and his many deeds of charity. He is very able and skillful as a physician, and is deeply interested in his profession.

He was married in March, 1888, to Mamie Nutting, daughter of J. P. Nutting of Indianapolis, Indiana.

JOSEPH B. SIMRALL, Mayor of the city of Lexington, son of the late Rev. John G. Simrall, was born in Fayette County, Kentucky, February 4, 1844. He is a brother of Judge John G. Simrall, the eminent jurist of Louisville, whose sketch with a brief history of the family will be found in this volume. Mayor Simrall was pursuing his studies in the academy at Walnut Hills, near Lexington, when the North and South crossed swords and prepared for the four years' conflict that followed, and the young student, fired with a love for the Sunny South and with zeal in behalf of the cause of his people, enlisted early in the conflict as a private in Company B, Eighth Regiment of Kentucky Cavalry, under General Morgan. His career as a soldier was very brief, except as a prisoner of war, in which capacity he served an unusually long term, enduring privations and sufferings in body and mind which he would gladly have exchanged for the dangers of the battlefield. He was taken prisoner at Buffington Island in 1863, and confined in Camp Chase, Columbus, Ohio, where he remained for six months, and was then removed to Delaware prison, from which he was not released until after the war was over, in June, 1865.

He returned to his home in Fayette County and soon afterwards engaged in the drug business in Lexington, in partnership with Mr. Richardson, under the firm name of Richardson & Simrall. This relation continued for about twenty years, when, in 1886, Mr. Simrall became sole proprietor of one of the most popular, enterprising and reliable drug houses in the city, an establishment of which he is still proprietor.

As a business man, rather than a politician, Mr. Simrall has taken a lively interest in municipal affairs and has always been ready to participate as far as possible in all public enterprises and has been found on the right side of all public interests. He was a member of the Board of Aldermen from 1888 until 1892, and in November, 1895, he was elected chief executive of the city, an office into which he was installed but a short time previous to the writing of this sketch. He brings to his office a thorough knowledge of the needs of the city, a mind well trained in business affairs and a strong and abiding purpose to do the right, with the moral courage to obey the dictates of his conscience. He is a member of the Presbyterian Church and the graces and virtues of the Christian religion are so pronounced in his character that all men have confidence in him, and predict for him a wise and progressive administration of the city's affairs.

Mayor Simrall and Ellen Harrison were married November 23, 1871. Mrs. Simrall died August 11, 1892, leaving four children living: Sarah, Harrison, John and Ellen. Margaretta, the oldest child, is deceased.

Harrison Simrall (son) is pursuing his studies in the Kentucky State University, and John is in the city schools.

Mrs. Simrall's father, Hon. James O. Harrison, was one of the most distinguished attorneys of the Lexington bar. He was born April 11, 1804, and died August 1, 1888.

HENRY CHRISTIAN SULLIVAN, a young lawyer of the highest integrity of Louisa, Kentucky, was born in Ashland, Kentucky, in 1863, and is a son of Christian Mills and Chattie Clifford (Moore) Sullivan. His father was born in Mason County and educated in Lexington, and was a prominent minister in the Methodist Episcopal Church, South, being a strong Southerner in all of his opinions. He was presiding elder for many years of the district in which he lived, and at different periods of his ministry he preached at Ashland, Kentucky, Charleston and Clarksburg, West Virginia, and Greenup and Louisa, Kentucky.

Henry C. Sullivan, after leaving school, in 1880, engaged in railroading in Georgia, and from 1881 to 1884 he was fireman on an engine running between Rome and Macon; when not on the road he worked in the shops and assisted in building engines. Returning to Louisa, he clerked in a grocery and was assistant postmaster for several years before entering the office of Alexander Lackey as a student at law. He was chairman of the Lawrence County Democratic Executive Committee from 1888 to 1892, and during the first year of his service on that committee the county went Democratic for the first time in seven years.

He was admitted to the bar in 1891, and during the following year he attended the University of Michigan. It was in that year that the one-year class was organized. A Kentuckian was elected valedictorian of that class, this being the first time that honor had been conferred upon a student who lived south of Mason and Dixon's line. Mr. Sullivan was the originator of a political movement in the class which resulted in great advantage to the Southern students.

In 1893 he began the practice of law, and having a large acquaintance and excellent standing in the community, he at once stepped into a lucrative practice, which has grown rapidly. He is one of the brightest young men in the profession in Louisa, and undoubtedly has a brilliant future before him. He is a member of Louisa lodge No. 270, I. O. O. F., which he has represented in the Grand Lodge of Kentucky, and served in every official position in his lodge, being its treasurer at present. He is also a Knight of Pythias and a member of the Methodist Episcopal Church, South.

Mr. Sullivan was married October 11, 1893, to Nora K. Borders of Louisa, Kentucky. She was born in Catlettsburg in 1868, and is a graduate of Wesleyan College, Cincinnati, Ohio, and was a teacher in the Louisa and Lawrence County schools before her marriage.

WILLIAM EDWARD RAGSDALE was born near Lafayette, Christian County, Kentucky, July 31, 1847. His father, William Jones Ragsdale, a farmer and native of Virginia, moved to Tennessee near the state line in 1839, and afterwards removed to Kentucky, where he died. Reverses consequent upon the war left his widow, Emily (Tillotson) Ragsdale, in moderate circumstances, with seven children, whose names were as follows: Elizabeth Rogers, Lucy Cooper, Mary Rives, James S., Emily Foster, Rebecca Hancock and William E.

With a very incomplete education, the youngest son found himself confronted with the problem of life. Bright, energetic and determined, he bravely faced the difficulties of his position and decided to carve out a career for himself. He was descended from fine old Scotch-English ancestry and had a grand, good mother, who reared a family of children who were noted for their honor, culture and true citizenship. In strength of character, resolute and inflexible devotion to principle, her devotion to family, church and her section was evidenced by tireless ministrations, and during the war she did much to relieve the sick and wounded soldiers. Under the influence of such a mother, he acquired naturally honor, charity and a love of liberty and a spirit of independence.

His maternal grandmother was Mildred (Gold) Tillotson, the only daughter of Jack and Marion Gold of Mecklenburg County, Virginia, who married a descendant of Sir John Tillotson, who left her a widow at the age of twenty-six and the mother of six children, viz.: Nancy Yancey, Sarah Blaine, Joyce Wilkinson, Emily Ragsdale, Eleanor Rives and Rebecca Baynham. She never married again and died at the advanced age of eighty.

His paternal grandfather was William Jones Ragsdale, Sr., of Virginia, a planter, merchant and money lender, who possessed vast wealth before the war, a considerable amount of which was invested in slaves. He married Miss Young, a daughter of General Young, a distinguished soldier and statesman. Being a man of quiet habits and vigorous health, he was as free from contagions and infections as "the sound oaks are, and the stars," and lived to the ripe age of eighty-one, leaving five children, viz.: John H., Smith, William J., Elizabeth Mann and Frances Hester.

Before he was quite twenty years of age, William E. Ragsdale married Achilles Collins, November 20, 1866, and had other responsibilities in addition to his widowed mother and sisters to call forth his energies.

Old men now in the vicinity of his boyhood tell

how Will Ragsdale made his first speculation in tobacco when only twelve years old. Stephen Rogers, an old negro man, had a crop to sell, and the boy asked what he would take for it. The darkey, doubtless knowing the state of his finances, said, "I'll take five dollars, your silver watch (which, by the way, ran backward and forward with equal energy) and a squirrel and cage." This was exactly what Will owned, so they "traded."

The investment netted him $36, and he was stimulated to try again and again until, finally, he became a capable judge of tobacco. After dealing in tobacco five years in Lafayette, Kentucky, he removed in 1872 to Hopkinsville, Kentucky, which is now the first dark tobacco market in the world. He purchased the Main Street Warehouse and conducted an enormous business of buying and selling the weed in that and in New York markets. In 1874 he cleared $116,000. The year following he sold his warehouse to Buckner & Wooldridge and bought of S. G. Buckner "Woodlawn," a fine farm of 526 acres seven miles from the city, and began farming on a large scale, at the same time continuing a broker's business in Hopkinsville. In this he was successful and did a more extensive business than any other one man there.

He was also the owner of fine horses. In 1879 he bought a colt for $500 and named her Minnie R., had her trained upon his own track, then raced her for two years, winning in more than half the rings she entered. In Chicago, Illinois, July 17, 1882, she won a purse of $3,000, and even before the race was done he sold her to Commodore Kittson of St. Paul for $10,000. He was the owner of "Arlington Denmark," a combined saddle and harness horse; "Highflyer," "Toppy" and "William Singerly," a pacer with a record of 2:16¼.

"Arlington Denmark" was shown at fairs for four years all over the state and never lost a race. In St. Louis he captured first prize out of thirty-six starters.

In 1884 Mr. Ragsdale sold his farm to Joe F. Garnett and again bought a home in Hopkinsville, where he still lives. He repurchased Main Street Warehouse and does a splendid business under the firm name of Ragsdale, Cooper & Co. He has scores of premiums which he has won from time to time as the best judge of tobacco.

The foundation of his active life was laid in Hopkinsville and the people both of that city and country entertain for him the highest regard and admiration as a business man and a Christian gentleman. Firm and conscientious in all his convictions and bold and fearless in the defense of them, he has always commanded the respect of those who honestly differed with him in political faith. He is the father of twelve children: Manfred, Lucy, Will, Roy, Clark, James, Achilles, Howell, Thomas, Douglas, and two died in infancy.

DR. C. M. PAYNTER of Lawrenceburg, one of the most successful and popular physicians in Central Kentucky, was born in Washington County, Indiana, December 23, 1854. His father, C. M. Paynter, was a lifetime resident and farmer of Washington County, Indiana. He was a member of the Methodist Episcopal Church, a good neighbor and a man of the highest integrity.

John Paynter (grandfather) was a Virginian, who belonged to an old and highly respected family in that state, and who became a pioneer in what was then considered the "far west," in Washington County, Indiana.

Margaret Coffman (mother) was born in Washington County, Indiana, and died there January 23, 1855. Her father, M. Coffman, emigrated from Ireland in 1820, and made his home in Washington County, Indiana.

Dr. C. M. Paynter was educated with a view to professional life, and after leaving the country schools attended the graded schools in Salem, and finally graduated from J. G. May's private school in 1874, after taking a four years' course. He taught school one year in Salem before entering directly upon the study of medicine with Dr. C. L. Paynter of Salem. After studying in the office one year he went to the Medical University of Louisville and took a graded course of three years, graduating with the highest honors, February 25, 1881.

His first work as a practicing physician was

done at Orr, Anderson County, but he remained there only a short time, when he removed to Fox Creek and remained there until March, 1891, and then removed to his present location in Lawrenceburg. His skill as a physician has been recognized in every community in which he has practiced, and he is one of the busiest physicians in the county. He is very popular, personally, being of a kindly, sociable disposition; does not meddle in politics except to vote as a Democrat and to do his duty as a citizen; is a member of the Methodist Church and is interested in all matters pertaining to the good of the community in which he lives. He was united in marriage December 28, 1880, to Lelia D. Fiddler of Anderson County, and they have three children: Norah L., Walker B. and Charles A. Paynter.

JAMES WILLIAM RICE, Attorney-at-Law, Louisa, Kentucky, son of ex-Congressman John M. Rice, was born in Louisa, Lawrence County, Kentucky, July 21, 1861. His father, John McConnell Rice, enjoyed limited advantages in the way of schooling and was for the most part a self-educated man. He attended the Louisville Law School and after graduating began the practice of law in Pike County. So well had he progressed in his reading and studies he was made superintendent of schools; was elected county attorney and served one term in the Kentucky legislature. In 1861 he removed to Louisa, and was again elected to the legislature. In 1869 he was elected to Congress, defeating George H. Thomas, the Republican candidate, by 3,600 majority; and was re-elected in 1871 by 3,900 majority, but Colonel Zeigler, his opponent, contested his election. James G. Blaine was speaker of the House and John A. Logan and James A. Garfield were members, and each of them made a speech in favor of Mr. Rice, who received 247 votes, while Colonel Zeigler received 7.

In 1883 he was appointed judge of the Lawrence County Criminal Court by Governor Proctor Knott, and in 1884 he was elected to that office by the people without opposition; was re-elected in 1890, defeating J. F. Stewart, the Republican candidate, by a majority of 210 votes, notwithstanding the district had given a Republican majority of 1,100 votes in the preceding presidential election.

During the past seven years Judge Rice has been an invalid and has visited many of the leading health resorts in the hope of finding relief.

He was married to Sarah Pogue, daughter of William Pogue. His children are: Ida, wife of Judge McConnell of Catlettsburg; Ada, wife of B. F. Thomas, United States engineer in charge of the Big Sandy Railroad; James W. (subject of this sketch); and John M., Jr., a clerk in the auditor's office at Frankfort.

James W. Rice received a good education in the schools of Louisa; studied law in his father's office; was admitted to the bar in 1883, and at once began the practice of his profession in his native city. In 1885 he was elected chairman of the board of trustees of the city of Louisa, and in 1890 was elected police judge. He is quite prominent in local politics, being a leader in the Democratic party, popular as a citizen, and a lawyer of acknowledged ability.

He was married March 18, 1884, to Josie Abbott, daughter of James Abbott of Louisa, and has two children living: Carrie Frances, born September 10, 1886; and James William, Jr., born May 18, 1893. One child, Greenway, born July 4, 1888, died December 14, 1891.

LAWSON RENO, Cashier of the Owensboro National Bank, son of Lawson R. and Mary T. (Campbell) Reno, was born in Greenville, Kentucky, February, 1849. His father was born near Norfolk, Virginia, and came with his parents to Muhlenberg County when he was about fifteen years of age. He received his education in private schools of Virginia and Kentucky. In 1840 he embarked in the hotel business in Greenville and was proprietor of the Reno House in that place for fifty-five years. He was for a long time a trustee of the Greenville Female Academy, a school which was conducted for many years under the auspices of the Presbyterian Church, and to the support of which Mr. Reno was a liberal contributor. Before the war he was a Whig, and after the disruption of that party he became identified with the Republicans and always took a lively interest in the political issues of the day, caring nothing, however, for office. He was sheriff of Muhlenberg County at one time, but with that exception he has not held or sought any official position. His wife's maiden name was Mary Campbell, a native of Norfolk, Virginia, and is now living in the family homestead in Greenville. Mr. Reno died in 1895. He was the father of seven children: Mary, William, Amanda, John, R—— T., Cordelia and Lawson.

John R. Campbell (maternal grandfather) was an eminent educator of Virginia, his native state.

Lawson Reno was educated at Greenville College, chiefly under the instruction of Professor E. W. Hall, who was employed by the prominent men of Greenville to impart special instruction to their sons. Mr. Reno was a delicate youth, and while his education was very thorough, there were times when his studies had to be thrown aside, and for this reason he did not leave school until he was twenty years of age.

In 1871, when twenty-two, he went to Owensboro and was employed in the revenue service as deputy collector under his brother, who was collector for the Second district of Kentucky. After the expiration of his brother's term as collector he was re-appointed by William A. Stewart, the incoming collector, but resigned to accept the appointment of postmaster of Owensboro, which office he filled for seven years, discharging its important duties with credit to himself and to the entire satisfaction of the community. He resigned in 1886 and organized the Owensboro National Bank, accepting the position of cashier, which he has held until the present time.

In all of his business relations with the public, as well as in the wide circle of personal friends, Mr. Reno has enjoyed great popularity, his genial, courteous manner, obliging disposition and natural kindliness towards others winning him a host of friends, while his splendid business qualifications and methods have won the esteem and confidence of the business community.

Mr. Reno has been twice married; first to Mary Frey, daughter of William H. and Martha (Campbell) Frey, of Owensboro. She died in 1883, leaving three children: Cordelia, educated in the Owensboro high school and at Nazareth; William, now a student in Center College, Danville, and Campbell, who is at school in Owensboro. In June, 1894, Mr. Reno married Mrs. Virginia Berry, widow of James I. Berry, of Marion County, Kentucky, who was a son of John B. Berry of that county. Mrs. Reno's maiden name was Wrinn, whose father's name was Paul Wrinn, a wholesale liquor merchant of Baltimore. He married Julia Berry, daughter of Jeremiah Berry of Maryland. Mrs. Reno is a descendant of the Berrys, Miles, Wathens and Snowdowns, families who were prominent in Maryland during and after the colonial times, and is a highly cultivated lady, exceedingly dainty, kind and sweetly sympathetic, and has found herself in the midst of a charmed circle of friends in the city to which she recently came as a stranger.

JERE P. O'MEARA, one of the prominent young lawyers of the Elizabethtown bar, son of the late Thomas O'Meara and Mary (Dooley) O'Meara, was born in Hardin County, Kentucky, near Elizabethtown, July 3, 1867. He was reared on his father's farm, but he had the capacity for an education and his parents gave him every advantage at their command. After passing the usual routine of the district schools, he entered St. Joseph College at Bardstown, and was graduated from there in the class of 1885. He then taught in the public schools of Elizabethtown for a short time, after which he began to read law with J. P. Hobson of Elizabethtown, whose sketch is given in this work.

He made a thorough and careful preparation for the law and was so diligent and studious that upon his admission to the bar in 1888 his preceptor took him in as a partner, under the firm name of Hobson & O'Meara. This business relation continued until the first of May, 1895, when Mr. O'Meara withdrew from the firm and engaged in a general civil practice by himself.

Mr. O'Meara was elected to the legislature in 1891 and served during the "long term" until July, 1893. He was chairman of the committee on Court of Appeals and Superior Court and a member of the committee on general statutes, codes of practice and criminal law. His appointment on these important committees was a deserved recognition of his marked legal ability, and he distinguished himself in the discharge of his duties as one of the brightest young lawyers in the state.

Mr. O'Meara is a very active Democratic politician and a leader in party affairs in his section of the state, and no young man is better known in Hardin County.

His father and mother were born in County Waterford, Ireland, and came to this country in 1862, before their marriage. Mr. O'Meara first located in New York, where he spent a year and came to Kentucky in 1863. He was engaged in railroading for some time, but subsequently bought a farm in Hardin County and was engaged in agricultural pursuits until the time of his death, July 3, 1890. His widow is a resident of Hardin County.

REV. JOHN D. JORDAN, Pastor of the Baptist Church, Decatur, Illinois, and one of the most distinguished young ministers in that denomination, was born in Caldwell County, Kentucky, February 9, 1861. His parents were of Scotch-Irish descent, and the progenitor of the family in this country settled first in Virginia, subsequently removing to North Carolina, whence his grandfather removed to Kentucky, about the time of his father's birth. Mr. Jordan's father died in 1862, leaving no estate, so that there was small chance for education, as the widowed mother of the boy needed his assistance in keeping the wolf on his own side of the door. Young Jordan worked faithfully for his mother until he was nineteen years of age, and then started out to educate himself. He could read fairly well and "write and cypher" a little, and had a cash capital of four dollars. After spending one year in the district school he went to the Princeton High School, working his way while taking a four years' course. At that time it was his purpose and ambition to study law and enter politics.

He taught school for two years in his native county—the two terms covering twenty months—at $40 a month, and during these two years he began to conduct public religious services. The meetings were well attended, and one hundred persons were converted by his preaching during the first few months of his work in that direction.

This determined his course for the future, and he began his studies with a view to the ministry in Bethel College September 1, 1886, and spent four years in that institution, during which time he preached at Leitchfield, Allenville, Madisonville, and other places, in connection with his college work, and thus made money to defray his expenses, help his mother and educate his half-brother, Rev. B. F. Hyde, besides assisting many a poor and worthy student. He took the degree of A. B. in June, 1890, and the degree of A. M. in June, 1893. During his last year in college he had charge of the mental and moral science department. In 1895 he delivered the alumni oration, being the youngest graduate ever honored by that election.

For two years he was pastor of the First Baptist Church of Paducah, and when he resigned that charge, September, 1891, to attend the Southern Baptist Theological Seminary at Louisville, it was against the protest of his congregation. He spent three years in the seminary and graduated in nine of the most important classes of that institution. During these three years he preached in the Elizabethtown and Gilead Baptist Churches.

While a student in the seminary he was elected to the presidency of a college in Texas at a salary of $2,000 a year, but declined. He was also recalled to the First Church in Paducah and declined that; was offered the pastorate of the First Baptist Church of Evansville, Indiana, but this and other important calls he declined, hoping to complete his studies in the seminary before entering upon stated work; but in the fall of 1894, following the advice of a leading specialist, he gave up his studies on account of an affliction in his eyes. At this time the First Baptist Churches of Ocala, Florida, and of Decatur, Illinois, were tendered him, and he accepted the call to Decatur, which congregation has a membership of seven hundred and fifty and church property worth $60,000 in a city of 30,000 population. It is one of the best churches in the state. Prof. John P. Fruit, Ph.D., who was in Leipsic, Germany, at the time, writing to a friend in Decatur, said: "I am delighted that Mr. Jordan has gone to Decatur. I have known the man thoroughly; have seen him tried and therefore know him to be one of the most promising young preachers we have ever had at Bethel College. He is a man, every inch of him. There is nothing little in him; no common streak such as you find in many a man." A minister of the gospel could hardly wish for a higher compliment than this, but it is only one of many which could be given to show the popularity, high standing and ability of Mr. Jordan as a man and a preacher. In his present field his work has been greatly blessed, as it has been wherever he has labored.

Mr. Jordan is an indefatigable worker, a fine speaker, and a good mixer—genial in manner and kindly considerate for others. His popularity and magnetism as a speaker have led him to enter the lecture field on special occasions, and he has already made an enviable reputation upon the platform.

His wife, to whom he was married July 8, 1891, was Ray Griffin of Mississippi.

JOHN P. NEWMAN, a prominent Attorney-at-Law and a well-known and highly popular citizen of Newport, son of John and Catherine (Charde) Newman, was born in the village of Upton, Worcester County, Massachusetts, September 21, 1851.

John Newman (father) was born in Trenton, New Jersey, in 1820; received a good education and taught school in early life. He is now a resident of Boston, Massachusetts, which has been his home and where he has been engaged in commercial and manufacturing enterprises for many years. At present he is interested in the Boston Type and Stereotype Foundry. He is a member of the Episcopal Church, a consistent Christian, and stands well in the business community; has reached his seventy-sixth year and is still active and energetic for one of his age. He enlisted in Company G, Twentieth Regiment Massachusetts Infantry, in the Civil war, being elected first lieutenant, and was afterward promoted to captain of his company.

He married Catherine Charde, daughter of Lawrence Charde of Massachusetts. She was born in 1829 and died in 1852. She was descended from Irish ancestry.

Samuel Newman (grandfather) was a native of the southern part of Ireland, who came to the United States when twenty-five years of age and located, first, in New York City. He afterward removed to Trenton, New Jersey, and thence to Scranton, Pennsylvania, where he died.

John P. Newman received his primary education in the common schools of Worcester County, and attended the Newtonville Academy in Massachusetts, from which he graduated in 1871. At the age of twenty-one years he came west and entered the Cincinnati Law School, and was graduated from that institution in 1878. He at once commenced the practice of law at the Newport bar, and has given his best attention to his large clientele, while serving the public in the various capacities to which he has been called from time to time. He has been mayor and president of the City Council of Bellevue; has served five years in the legislature, where he took an active and leading part in behalf of the labor organizations; was tendered the nomination of the Union Labor party for attorney-general of the state, which honor he declined. He is a stanch Democrat, faithful and true to the principles of the party, and while he has always been a friend of and sympathized with the laboring classes he could not go outside of his party, which had frequently honored him by election to office, to accept a nomination by a third party organization.

He is a member of the Knights of Honor, Knights of Pythias, of the Masonic fraternity and of the Benevolent Order of Elks, and in all of these he is a popular and useful member and has received his share of honors at their hands.

Mr. Newman was married in 1877 to Bertha Houser, daughter of Mathias Houser, one of the old pioneers of Cincinnati. They have two children, Oliver and Stella.

COLONEL WILLIAM M. MOORE of Cynthiana, was born in Harrison County, near Cynthiana, in 1837. His father was also a native of Harrison County, who removed with his family to Lewis County, Missouri, in 1839, where he spent the remainder of his life, and died in 1858 at the age of forty-six years. He was a farmer and a large owner of land in Lewis County, which he cultivated with great care and success, raising large quantities of wheat, at the same time devoting much attention to stock raising.

Moses Moore (grandfather) was born in Rockbridge County, Virginia, and removed to Harrison County, Kentucky, in 1808. He was a farmer and a man of unusual intelligence. He died at the early age of thirty years. He belonged to an old and highly respected family of Rockbridge County, Virginia, who were of Scotch-Irish extraction.

Colonel Moore's mother, Mary (Magee) Moore, was born in Harrison County in 1813, and died in Missouri in 1890. Her father, William Magee, was a native of Virginia, who settled in Harrison County in 1807, and his farm adjoined that of Moses Moore. When he was a lad of fourteen or fifteen he served as orderly or messenger for General Washington in the Revolutionary war. The Magees were from Ireland, and were Protestants. The Moores and Magees were Methodists, and as far back as known until the present time they were Democrats.

Colonel William M. Moore was two years old when his father removed to Missouri, which was at that time a new country and on the frontier of civilization, where the educational advantages were nothing to boast of. However, with the aid of his parents, he was prepared for college and was a member of the junior class of the Missouri State University in 1860. When the Civil war broke out he was one of the first to offer his services, and he enlisted as a private soldier in May, 1861. He received his first wound in the battle of Lexington. In December, 1861, he was made adjutant, and in May, 1862, he was promoted to the rank of lieutenant-colonel. He resigned in August, 1862; re-enlisted and was made captain of his company, and in the same year was made lieutenant-colonel again; and in April, 1863, he was promoted to the rank of colonel, and during the last year of the war he commanded a brigade, refusing a commission as brigadier-general in order to stay with his men. He was wounded at Helena and again at Jenkin's Ferry; was in the battles of Mansfield and Pleasant Hill; was officer of the day in command of the guards when Shreveport was surrendered to General Canby, whose parole Colonel Moore still has in his possession

July, 1865, Colonel Moore returned to his home in Missouri after four years' service in a cause to which he had sacrificed everything he had, and settled down to the quiet life of the farmer.

He was elected sheriff of Lewis County in 1875, and in 1877 he was elected to the State Legislature. In 1882 Colonel Moore returned to his native county and located near the place of his birth, about six miles north of Cynthiana, where he engaged in farming extensively and in raising stock. He owns over seven hundred acres of land, with modern improvements.

He was elected to the Kentucky Legislature in 1889 and again in 1891, and was Speaker of the House of Representatives during the session of 1891-2. His public career has been singularly fortunate, especially in view of his unprofessional life. He is essentially a leader, having a strong will, firm convictions, with courage to assert his views and the intelligence to forcibly present them before the people. He enjoys the confidence of his friends not only in the Democratic party, to which he belongs, but among his neighbors and acquaintances.

Colonel Moore married Fannie Garnett in 1870. They have two daughters, Mary L. and Jennie Moore. Mrs. Moore is the daughter of Thomas T. Garnett, a Harrison County farmer, who came from Virginia with his parents when he was one year old.

WILLIAM CRAWLEY LANG, a well known business man and at present coal oil inspector of Paducah, although seventy-four years of age, is an active and industrious citizen, who has been closely identified with the business interests at Paducah for more than forty years. He was born in Manchester, Virginia, September 15, 1821, and after receiving a fair common school education was a manufacturer of and dealer in tobacco in his native city until 1852.

He removed to Paducah in 1854 and established a tobacco manufactory in that city, in which he continued with remarkable success until 1863, a time in which many fortunes were wrecked, and Mr. Lang, with many others, lost all he had, and was compelled to abandon his business for a time.

In 1865 he retired to a farm and in the course of

ten years had recovered from his embarrassment and gained sufficient capital to resume business in the city.

In 1875 he became associated with Thomas Lyle in the grocery business, and was thus engaged until 1893, when he was appointed coal oil inspector, a lucrative position, for which he is well qualified, and to which he was called through the influence of the leading business men of Paducah.

Mr. Lang was married April 5, 1846, to Martha Muse, with whom he lived for nearly half a century. She was born in Gloucester County, Virginia, in 1825, and died January 9, 1895. She was a member of the Methodist Church for fifty-three years, and a most exemplary Christian woman.

Mr. and Mrs. Lang were the parents of six children: James Maynard, deceased; Mollie, wife of William Allen of Paducah; James Maynard, of whom a brief sketch is given herewith; Wallie Lee, Nellie and Addie.

James Maynard Lang, the third child, and second son of that name, was born in Paducah, July 15, 1857, and was carefully educated in the public schools of the city until he was seventeen years of age, when, in 1874, he was apprenticed to A. B. Kincaid, a druggist of Paducah, for a term of three years. In this capacity he learned the intricacies of chemistry and pharmacy, and by careful study prepared himself for the responsible duties of the modern druggist. After a rigid examination in Louisville, having complied with the regulations of the State Board of Pharmacy, he became a duly registered pharmacist in 1881, and to this work he has applied himself in his native city without interruption until the present time.

He has been a member of the Board of Education for three consecutive terms, and in November, 1894, he was elected president of the Paducah Fair Association, a post to which only the most capable business men of the city are called. He is a Democrat, but not for revenue or office; a member of the Knights and Ladies of Honor and of the Odd Fellows.

James Maynard Lang and Georgie McKee, daughter of George McKee of Paducah, were married October 15, 1882, and they have one child, India, who was born July 22, 1890.

William Lang, father of William Crawley Lang, was born in Manchester, Virginia, and was a private in the War of 1812. He was a merchant tailor in his native city and an enthusiastic Democrat, but sought no political office. He was a faithful member of the Methodist Church, to which faith his descendants have adhered until the present generation. His father, Archibald Lang, was a Scotchman, who came to Virginia during the latter part of the eighteenth century. His wife, Sarah Lang, was a Huguenot. The ancestors of Martha Maynard Lang (mother of William C. Lang) were also from Scotland.

A. T. LACEY, grain dealer and a popular citizen of Paducah, son of Charles Smith and Mary Jane (Baker) Lacey, was born in Halifax County, Virginia, March 28, 1858. His father, Charles Smith Lacey, was also born in that county, in 1819, where he received a fine education, and although he led a non-professional life, was one of the most intelligent and cultured men of that section. He began life as a merchant, but soon found he had a preference for agricultural pursuits and became an extensive planter, owning many acres of valuable land and a great number of slaves. During the struggle between the North and the South his sympathies were decidedly with the people of his own section and he contributed generously to the cause, furnishing provisions and clothing for the Confederate soldiers and aiding them in every way except by taking up arms. His generosity during the war was one of the characteristics of the man, for he has been a philanthropist, whose aim in life has been to minister to the needs of others. He is now living a retired life, in his native county, loved and honored by his fellowmen on account of his superior mind, gentleness of spirit, generosity, goodness of heart and many other noble traits of character.

Robert Dudley Lacey (grandfather) was a native of England, who came to this country after his marriage to a Miss Stubblefield, a member of a distinguished English family, and settled in Halifax County, Virginia, where they became fully identified with the progressive and cultured people of that part of the state.

Mary Jane Baker Lacey (mother) was born in

Halifax County, Virginia, in 1829, and married Charles S. Lacey in 1847. She is living with her honored husband in her native county, a member of the Baptist Church and a devout Christian woman, greatly loved and admired by a host of friends and relatives.

Elijah Baker (grandfather), a planter and slave owner of Halifax County, Virginia, married Susan Barkstead of the same county. He was noted for his wealth and intelligence, and was one of the best citizens of the county.

A. T. Lacey, a worthy descendant of these first families of Virginia, received a liberal education in Halifax County, attending the best schools in the vicinity, completing his studies in 1876, when eighteen years of age. He began his business career as a merchant in Boydsville, Kentucky, where he sold dry goods, and also dealt in tobacco for three years. He then removed to Paducah and was bookkeeper for a wholesale saddlery house for three years, and traveled throughout the South for six years for the same firm. He was then engaged in the milling business for five years, which led to his present business as a dealer in grain, in which he has been engaged since 1891. In this line of business he has established a very extensive trade and made a reputation as one of the most reliable and successful grain brokers in Southwestern Kentucky.

Mr. Lacey was married June 4, 1884, to Kate I. Baker, daughter of T. A. Baker, cashier of the First National Bank of Paducah. Mrs. Lacey died May 29, 1895, leaving one child, Cecil Baker, born May 24, 1895.

Mr. Lacey is not a partisan, but votes the Democratic ticket, taking very little active interest in politics. He is more interested in church work, being a member of the Presbyterian Church and an honored and useful citizen.

MILLARD FILMORE HAMPTON, for many years Clerk of the Circuit Court and at present a practicing attorney in Catlettsburg, was born in that city June 15, 1849.

His father, Levi Hampton, was a native of Cabell County, Virginia, who removed to Boyd County, Kentucky, and subsequently to Brown County Ohio, where he married Elizabeth Henderson in 1845, and returned to Catlettsburg, at which place he made his home during the remainder of a busy and useful life. He was at different times engaged in various enterprises—lumbering, farming, trading and hotelkeeping—and was a man of affairs, and of wide influence in his county. When war was declared between the North and South he enlisted in the Union army, joining the Thirty-ninth Regiment, Kentucky Volunteer Infantry. In 1862 he was appointed quartermaster, and in December of the same year he was killed at Wireman's Shoals while defending his stores. He was a friend of education, civilization and progress, and was instrumental in bringing Catlettsburg up to its present high moral and educational standard. He left a widow and five children: Julia, Amelia, Mary, Lizzie and Millard F. Hampton. Mrs. Hampton survived her husband but one year, and died in 1863.

Henry Hampton (grandfather) was a native and lifetime resident of Wayne County (now West Virginia). His ancestors were English people, some of whom came to the new world before the American Revolution, and settled, some in New York, some in Pennsylvania, and others in Virginia and other southern states.

Millard Filmore Hampton was educated in the public schools of his native town and at Asbury, now De Pauw University, Indiana. Returning from college in 1867, he engaged in merchandising, at the same time pursuing his studies for the legal profession; in 1868 he was appointed deputy clerk of the Circuit Court, and after serving six years in that capacity was elected clerk in 1874. He held this office by re-election until 1892, when, twenty-five years after first taking up his legal studies, he was admitted to the bar as a practicing attorney. His experience of a quarter of a century in the clerk's office, attended with a purpose to practice law, together with his reading from time to time, qualified him for successful labor in the profession of his choice, and the extended acquaintance with legal matters and with the people, formed during his long public service, enabled him to command a lucrative practice at the outset, and he is to-day one of the most popular attorneys in Catlettsburg.

He was married June 20, 1873, to Katherine Hornshell, eldest daughter of Captain Washington Hornshell. They have one son, Gus Hornshell Hampton, born March 5, 1874, a graduate of Washington and Lee University of Lexington, Virginia, a bright, industrious and exemplary young man, now employed as bookkeeper in the Catlettsburg National Bank. All of the members of the family are members of the Presbyterian Church.

Captain Hornshell is a native of Ohio, and married in Burlington and removed to Catlettsburg, where he was for many years engaged in steamboat building, but is now retired. By industry, perseverance and honesty of purpose he carved an honored name and acquired a handsome fortune. He had the reputation of having built the best steamboats that ever plied the waters of the western rivers; was interested in a number of business enterprises, and is now vice-president of the Catlettsburg National Bank and a highly honored and public-spirited citizen.

JOHN M. HUTTON, Cashier of the Second National Bank of Ashland, Kentucky, son of James and Luvenda (Jones) Hutton, was born April 24, 1865. His father was born at Pond Run, Scioto County, Ohio, November 5, 1828, and after receiving a good common school education spent the earlier years of his life on his father's farm in that county. In 1853 he removed to Ashland, Kentucky, and was a merchant there for two years, when he went to Catlettsburg, where he was in the same line of business for six months, and in 1855 he embarked in a new business known as "store-boating," taking a large stock of merchandise on a boat and stopping at different points along the river. After reaching Memphis with fair success he returned to Ashland, but soon removed to the farm in Scioto County, Ohio. He did not remain there long, and returned to Ashland to accept a position with the A. C. & J. R. R. Company. In 1857 he embarked in the grocery business in Ashland, in which he continued until 1889, when he retired, having sold out to his son, the subject of this sketch, and J. H. McCleary. He was always devoted to his business and cared little for politics. He was a Democrat until the election of President Buchanan, for whom he voted, but after that he was an ardent Republican. During the war he was a strong Union man.

John Hutton (grandfather) was born in Scioto County, Ohio, in 1805, and spent his life as a farmer in his native county. He married Frances Burress, a native of Maryland, but of German descent. He died in 1871, and his wife died in 1881. They were members of the Methodist Church.

James Hutton (great-grandfather) was also a native of Scioto County, Ohio, and was a soldier in the War of 1812. He married Anna Hamilton of the same county, and they made their home there during their lifetime.

George Hutton (great-great-grandfather) was a native of Ireland, who was one of the first settlers in Scioto County.

James M. Hutton's mother, Luvenda (Jones) Hutton, was born near Vesuvius Furnace, Lawrence County, Ohio, in 1836. She received a superior education in the county schools and at Ashland, Kentucky, and was married to Mr. Hutton August 2, 1853. She is the mother of seven children, four of whom are living, and is now a resident of Ashland, the center of a large circle of devoted relatives and friends.

Richard Jones (grandfather) was born in Marietta, Ohio, March 22, 1800. He was a foundryman by trade, and had charge of Hecla Furnace for a great many years, and afterward was manager of Vesuvius Furnace until 1840, when he removed to Clinton Furnace in Boyd County, Kentucky, of which he was manager for six years. He bought from James Biggs the farm which is now the site of Ashland, and which was in what was then known as the Poague settlement. He was elected to the legislature in 1851, and served one term, after which he sold his farm and went to Missouri to buy land near St. Louis, and while there he was thrown from a carriage, receiving injuries which terminated fatally August 10, 1856. He was married in 1827 to Jane Coyle, daughter of Stephen and Clara Coyle, who was born October 21, 1804, and died December 26, 1874.

William Jones (great-grandfather) married Margaret Jones; they were both of Irish descent and were among the pioneers of Marietta, Ohio.

John M. Hutton was graduated from the public schools of Ashland in 1883, after which he was a clerk in his father's store for a year before going to Duff's Commercial College in Pittsburgh and again for six months after his return. He was then employed as bookkeeper in the wholesale hardware house of Thomas Henderson for a few months, resigning to accept a similar position with the Great Western Mining & Manufacturing Company, where he was employed until he was elected cashier of the Second National Bank of Ashland, a position he has held until the present time and in which he has developed unusual financial ability, and has distinguished himself as a very capable manager of the important interests of the bank.

He is not active in politics, but is a voter of the Republican ticket, and a useful member of his party. He is a member of the Masonic Order and of the Mystic Shrine, and is an officer in the Supreme body of the Knights of the Golden Eagle.

Mr. Hutton was married April 15, 1891, to Mary Kinner, daughter of Judge S. G. Kinner of Catlettsburg, where she was born November 14, 1871. She was educated in the best schools of Catlettsburg and at Bellewood Seminary, near Louisville, finishing in the Convent of the Sacred Heart, Cincinnati.

DR. J. B. HADDAN, Dentist, Lawrenceburg, was born in Freeport, Louisiana, October 5, 1866. His father, Samuel Haddan, was born in Owen County in 1846 and at the age of twenty-six years he removed to Louisiana and engaged in planting. He died there in 1873, when only twenty-seven years of age.

Margaret Brown Haddan (mother) was born in Owen County, a daughter of Joseph Brown, who was also a native and lifetime resident of Owen county, where he died in 1863.

Dr. J. B. Haddan, after enjoying all of the advantages of the common schools, was a student in Georgetown College for two years. Having chosen dentistry as his profession he studied and worked in the laboratory of Dr. Foster of New Albany, Indiana, for two years and then completed his course by two years of study in Vanderbilt University, Nashville, Tenn., and graduated with a class of sixty-six pupils in 1889. He then went to the town of Monterey in Owen County and began the practice of his profession, but at the end of one year he removed to Lawrenceburg, in 1890, where he has met with gratifying success, and has won the confidence and esteem of the entire community as well as of his numerous patrons. He is a member of the Monterey Lodge of Odd Fellows, and of the Lawrenceburg Lodge of Free Masons, in both of which orders he is actively interested and popular. He is a communicant of the Baptist Church and a regular attendant.

Dr. Haddan was married July 10, 1889, to Mollie Sullivan, who died June 29, 1895, leaving three children: Thomas, Samuel D. and Blanche.

ALFRED HERR HITE of St. Matthews, Superintendent of Public Schools of Jefferson County, is the son of Samuel S. and Jennie (Herr) Hite, and was born at St. Matthews November 6, 1865. His father was born in Jefferson County in 1829, and resides at St. Matthews. He is actively engaged in the real estate business in Louisville. He served one term as sheriff of Jefferson County and was deputy commissioner of the Louisville Chancery Court for many years. He is a man of sterling integrity and honesty and a Democrat in politics.

Jacob Hite (grandfather) was also a native of Jefferson County, and was a prosperous farmer on the land now partly occupied by the Central Asylum. He served in the Mexican war. Died aged eighty-two years.

Isaac Hite (great-grandfather) was a native of Virginia, and was a surveyor, tanner and miller. He was a member of the colony that Daniel Boone brought to Jefferson County, and his name and many of the experiences of the colony are mentioned in Collins' History of Kentucky.

Mr. Hite's mother was born in the house now occupied by him. Her family came from Pennsylvania to Jefferson County soon after the arrival of Daniel Boone.

Alfred Herr (grandfather) was a native farmer of Jefferson County.

John Herr (great-grandfather) was born in Lancaster County, Pennsylvania, where he was a cabinet-maker, but after coming to Kentucky he became a successful farmer, and acquired a very large estate.

Mr. Hite was reared on the farm near St. Matthews, and received his education in the country schools and in the Louisville High School, graduating in 1886 with the degree of Bachelor of Arts. He taught school in the county for several years and in November, 1893, he was elected county superintendent of schools, taking the office in August following. He married Ninette, daughter of John L. Herr of Jefferson County, April 9, 1895. He resides on the old homestead, which is owned by his brother and himself.

He has a fine library and a valuable collection of Indian relics, besides some fine old china and silverware, which he prizes very highly. He is a member of the Christian Church. He belongs to a fine family, whose members have always stood well in the community, and the young man is doing his part to sustain the good name of his ancestors.

ABRAHAM LINCOLN, President of the United States, born in Hardin County, Kentucky, in that part since included in Larue County, February 12, 1809; removed to Spencer County, Indiana, in 1816; received but a limited education; worked at splitting rails and was a boatman on the Ohio and Mississippi rivers; removed to and worked on a farm in Illinois, 1830; served as a volunteer captain in the Black Hawk war, 1832; for four terms, 1834-36-38-40, a member of the Illinois Legislature; studied law in the interim; a delegate to the national convention which nominated General Taylor for President, 1848; a representative in Congress from Illinois, 1847-49; President of the United States, 1861-65; re-elected November, 1864; assassinated by John Wilkes Booth on April 14, 1865, "Good Friday," while seated in a private box in Ford's Theater, in Washington City. Such, in brief, is the public record of Abraham Lincoln.

The historian of this day can not do justice to this remarkable man. The Northman would draw his character in terms of glowing eulogy; the Southron would point his pen with bitterness and gall. The one would absurdly ascribe to him the lofty virtues of Washington, the other would class him with Grimaldi the clown. And both would be wide of the mark. He was a man of quaint humor and genial disposition, patient, calm, self-poised and thoroughly honest. His administration of the government was for no selfish or personal ends, but meant for the general good. The rectitude of his public conduct was above suspicion, and his love of country must ever challenge admiration.

COL. REUBEN T. DURRETT was born in Henry County, Kentucky, January 22, 1824; graduated at Brown University, R. I., 1846, and at the Louisville Law School, 1850; editor of the Louisville Daily Courier for two years, 1857-59; and just two years later, September 18, 1861, because prominently on the side of the South, was arrested by the military and sent to Fort Lafayette—the first political prisoner in Kentucky. As a lawyer, editor, scholar, writer, Colonel Durrett has made his mark. But the crowning glory of his life, so regarded, is the unparalleled success of his favorite scheme for a great "Public Library of Kentucky" at Louisville, open and free to all; permanently established (January, 1874) in a magnificent building, 168 feet front and four stories high, which cost $210,000, and with a library of over 40,000 volumes and a museum of over 100,000 specimens and curiosities.

S. GRABFELDER, son of Emanuel and Rena (Driefus) Grabfelder, was born September 2, 1844. His father was a native of Bavaria, Germany, and was engaged in mercantile business there until November, 1848, when, on account of his somewhat decided republican principles, nearly all of his property was confiscated. He died in 1855, at the age of sixty-five, and was buried within a short distance of Nuremberg, Germany. Shortly after the death of his father Mr. Grabfelder's mother determined to come to America, and with her three sons landed in New York in 1856. Mr. Grabfelder came to Louisville with one of his brothers in 1857, leaving his mother in New York, where she died in 1887. He clerked in a large wholesale dry goods house until 1866, when he engaged in the distillery business, to which he has successfully given his attention uninterruptedly for nearly thirty years, and for many years holding the important office of president of the Temple Adas Israel.

Mr. Grabfelder married Miss Delia Griff, daughter of Samuel Griff of Louisville, in 1871. Mrs. Grabfelder was educated in a convent in Lorado. They have a fine residence on Broadway, where, with no children of their own, they enjoy the society of their many friends and visitors.

Mr. Grabfelder is an ardent Republican, always liberal in his support of his party, but has never sought nor would he accept any political office.

WILLIAM LINDSAY, one of the present senators in Congress from Kentucky, and one of the leading members of the Democratic party of the nation, is a lineal descendant of an old Scotch-Irish family, the progenitor of which in this country was James Lindsay (grandfather), who was a native of Dykehead Farm, Lanark County, Scotland. He was born in September, 1773, and emigrated from his native land in 1790 and located in Rockbridge County, Virginia, where he engaged in farming. On June 30, 1797, he wedded Agnes McCambell, who was born in that county on December 24, 1775, and was descended from Scotch-Presbyterian ancestry. Of this marriage were born nine children: Five girls and four boys, of whom Andrew (father) was the fifth child and third son. Andrew Lindsay was born October 6, 1809, and died July 4, 1883. His entire life was spent in his native county engaged in the peaceful pursuits of the farm. He enjoyed the reputation of an industrious, upright and leading citizen. His first wife, whom he married in January, 1834, was Sally Gilmore Davidson, whose ancestors were Scotch-Presbyterians, and settled in Virginia as early as 1745, where they became identified with the pioneer settlement and development of the state. She was born October 7, 1809, and died January 7, 1845. To Andrew and Sally Gilmore Lindsay were born four children: William, born September 4, 1835; James, April 1, 1837; Polly G., October 4, 1839, who became the wife of Daniel A. Teaford of Rockbridge County, and Sally D.

who married James Kirkpatrick of the same county.

Andrew Lindsay in the year 1847 took for his second wife Mary F. Gilmore. The children born to this marriage were: Marion, born February 22, 1851; Charles, October 14, 1855; Andrew W., February 28, 1861, and Bruce, July 26, 1865. The death of the second Mrs. Lindsay occurred April 16, 1878.

Senator William Lindsay received his education in the high schools of Lexington, Virginia, and after completing his academic course there entered the office of Judge John W. Brokenborough of that city as a student at law. In November of 1854 he migrated to Kentucky and located in Hickman County, where he continued his legal studies under the tutelage of Judge Edward Crossland of Clinton, and was duly admitted to the bar to practice law in 1858. He at once engaged in the practice in Hickman and the surrounding counties, meeting with success from the start, but he had no sooner become fully established with a promising career ahead of him when the breaking out of the Civil war between the States compelled a change. Mr. Lindsay being in warm sympathy with the South, enlisted as a private in the Confederate army in May, 1861; in July of the same year was made lieutenant of Company B, Twenty-second Tennessee Infantry, a company composed entirely of Kentuckians. He commanded it as captain in the battle of Belmont, Missouri, in November, 1861, and at Shiloh in April, 1862. After that battle the company was transferred to a Kentucky regiment, and Judge Lindsay was thereafter connected with the Seventh Kentucky Infantry, and served as staff officer with the brigade commanders, General Abe Buford, General H. B. Lyon, Colonel Thompson and Colonel Crossland. He was paroled at Columbus, Miss., May 16, 1865, at the close of the war. Returning to Hickman County, Judge Lindsay was elected to the State Senate in August, 1867, to represent the counties of Hickman, Fulton and Graves, and performed his duties in a capable and able manner, and to the satisfaction of his constituents. In August, 1870, he was elected one of the judges of the Court of Appeals, occupying that distinguished position until September, 1878, serving as chief justice the last two years of his term, when he declined a re-election, and, retiring from the bench, commenced the practice of law at Frankfort, where he at present resides. Perhaps no lawyer in Kentucky is better known or more highly esteemed, both in his profession and among the people, than Judge Lindsay. As a lawyer he stands in the front rank of his profession, and enjoys a large and remunerative practice. As a judge his career was of the highest order. He wrote the opinion in the case of the Commonwealth vs. Hawes, which involved the question of extradition, and the construction of the treaty upon that subject between Great Britain and the United States, in which it was the first time decided by a court of last resort that a person extradited for one of the causes named in the treaty could not be lawfully tried for an offense not named in the warrant of extradition, without first being afforded an opportunity to return to the country from which he had been taken. This decision has been followed by the courts of the other states and by the Federal courts, and the doctrine was affirmed and approved by the Supreme Court of the United States during the session of 1886-7 in the case of United States vs. Rauscher (119 U. S. 407). Judge Lindsay also wrote the opinion in the case of the Covington & Lexington Railroad Company against Bowler, in which it was held that the directors of a railroad company could not assist in bringing the property of the corporation to sale, and then claim the benefits of such sale as purchasers. Judge Lindsay has always been a consistent member of the Democratic party, and faithful to its principles and doctrines. In 1889 Judge Lindsay was elected to the Kentucky State Senate from the district composed of the Counties of Franklin, Anderson and Mercer. In 1891 he was appointed a member at large of the World's Columbian Commission, and served as such until February, 1893, when he resigned. In January, 1892, he was appointed by President Harrison a member of the Inter-State Commerce Commission, and his appointment was at once confirmed by the senate of the United States. But not having been an applicant for the place, Judge Lindsay felt at liberty to decline, and did decline to accept the appointment. In February, 1893, he was chosen by the Kentucky Legislature United States Senator to serve out the unexpired term of Senator John G. Carlisle, ending March 4, 1895. In January, 1894, he was re-elected to the United States Senate, without opposition, for the full term, that commenced March 4, 1895, and will end March 4, 1901.

In December, 1893, Judge Lindsay was united to his present wife, Miss Eleanor Holmes, a lady of great beauty and many rare excellencies of character, prominent in church and society, in which she is distinguished for the character of her receptions and entertainments, and who presides with grace and tact over the hospitable home of her husband. Senator Lindsay has one living child: Miss Marion Semple Lindsay, a daughter by a former marriage.

DR. JOHN C. WELCH (father) was a native of Jessamine County, born July 3, 1823; the degree of Bachelor of Arts was conferred upon him by Transylvania University in 1844 and the degree of Doctor of Medicine by same institution in 1846.

For forty-one years he practiced his chosen profession in his native county with the exception of four or five years, during the war. In 1861 Dr. Welch espoused the cause of the Union and entered the service as surgeon of the Twentieth Kentucky Volunteer Infantry. In 1863 he was made brigade surgeon and served in that capacity until the close of the war. He was an able physician, whose skill was known throughout the state.

In 1877 and 1879 he represented his county in the lower house of the legislature, and was chairman of the committee on charitable institutions and a member of the committee on education.

JOHN BREATHITT, late Governor of Kentucky, was a native of the State of Virginia. He was the eldest child of William Breathitt, and was born on the ninth day of September, 1786. His father removed from Virginia and settled in Logan County, Kentucky, in the year 1800. The old gentleman was a farmer, possessed of a few servants and a tract of land, but not sufficiently wealthy to give his children collegiate educations. The schools of his neighborhood afforded but few opportunities for the advancement of pupils. John made the best use of the means for improvement placed within his reach, and by diligent attention to his books, made himself a good surveyor.

He taught a country school in early life, and by his industry and economy, as teacher and surveyor, he acquired property rapidly, consisting mostly in lands, which were easily obtained under the acts of the assembly appropriating the public domain. After his earnings had secured a capital capable of sustaining him a few years, he resolved to read law, which he did under the direction of the late Judge Wallace. He was admitted to the bar in February, 1810. His industry and capacity for business soon secured him a lucrative practice, and from this time he rapidly advanced in public estimation.

In 1810 or 1811 he was elected to represent the County of Logan in the House of Representatives of the General Assembly, and filled the same office for several years in succession. In 1828 he was elected lieutenant-governor of the commonwealth, the duties of which station he filled with great dignity and propriety. In 1832 he was elected governor, but did not live to the end of his official term. He died in the governor's house, in Frankfort, February 21, 1834.

BENJAMIN B. WILSON, a popular young business man and Treasurer of the City of Lexington, son of Reuben B. and Elizabeth M. (Dunbar) Wilson, was born in Barnwell County, South Carolina, April 28, 1858. Reuben B. Wilson was born in Barnwell County, South Carolina, March 3, 1831; was educated at Charleston, South Carolina, at the Citadel Academy, from which he was graduated in the class of 1853. He was engaged in the occupation of farming until 1875, when he removed to Augusta, Georgia, where for two years he was engaged in the grocery business, and was then in the cotton commission business. His health failed in 1888, when he removed to Lexington, and died there in 1889. He was a devoted member of the Baptist Church and held a license to preach, but never had any regular charge. He was an enthusiastic worker in church affairs, and at the age of seventeen years was clerk of the congregation of which he was a member, and in 1853 was elected a deacon.

He enlisted in the First Georgia Confederate Regiment of Infantry under Colonel Johnson Haygood, and was at Charleston when the first gun was fired on Fort Sumter. He subsequently joined a cavalry regiment under Colonel Colcott, with whom he served during the war.

James J. Wilson (grandfather) was a native of South Carolina, and was well educated, but had to work hard for it; was a member of the House of Representatives in the Legislature for several terms, and later a member of the State Senate. He was a lawyer by profession, but on account of ill-health relinquished the work of his profession and retired to his farm and finally gave up business and went to live with his son, and died April 28, 1876.

James Wilson (great-grandfather) was one of the immortal signers of the Declaration of Independence, who was afterward one of the judges of the Supreme Court of the United States.

Elizabeth Dunbar Wilson (mother) was born in Barnwell County, South Carolina, August 17, 1835. She was educated in the high school of Barnwell Village, and this was supplemented by a course in Augusta Female Academy in Georgia, taught by William Hard, a Baptist minister and a teacher of distinction. She was a member of the Baptist Church and a most excellent Christian woman.

Frank F. Dunbar (maternal grandfather) was a native of Barnwell County, South Carolina, where he received a common school education, and was for sixteen years tax collector of his county, and was familiarly known as Major Dunbar.

George R. Dunbar (great-grandfather) was a native of the same county and a farmer by occupation. He accumulated considerable property; was modest and unassuming in his manner, and an elegant gentleman of the old school.

Benjamin B. Wilson is a native of Barnwell

County, South Carolina; received his education in the best private schools of that section. At the age of seventeen years, he went to Augusta, Georgia, where he became engaged as a salesman in his father's grocery, where he remained for several years, afterwards becoming a partner, in which he continued for two years, and came to Kentucky with his father, in 1881.

After arriving in Lexington he became interested in the livery business, in which he is now engaged. He was elected city treasurer of Lexington, of which office he is the present incumbent. Mr. Wilson is Past Grand Master of the Odd Fellows of the state and a member of several other secret and benevolent orders. He owns and manages a stock farm near the city limits in which he takes especial pride.

Mr. Wilson was married May 9, 1883, to Alice Hancock of Lexington, a graduate from Sayre Institute, class of 1882, taking the first honors of her class. They have four children: George H., Horace H., Benjamin Dunbar and Ethelbert Reed.

BENNETT H. YOUNG, one of the most distinguished citizens of Louisville, was born in Nicholasville, Jessamine County, Kentucky, May 24, 1843. He received his early education in Bethel Academy in Nicholasville and spent two years in Center College, Danville, leaving college to enter the Confederate army, in which he served with distinction, and spent three years following this service in Europe, completing his studies in the Scotch and Irish universities. He took the highest honors in the law department, and the third distinction in the literary department of the Queen's University. He began the practice of law in Louisville in 1868, and in a very short time acquired a large and lucrative practice. In 1872 he formed a partnership with St. John Boyle, with whom he became associated in the construction of railways in 1878. When Mr. Boyle was receiver of the Henderson railroad Colonel Young was his legal adviser, and they united later in the construction of the New Albany & St. Louis Air Line Railroad, which is now controlled by the Mackey syndicate. The construction of this road was due to the energy and enterprise of these two men. Later Colonel Young accomplished the reorganization and purchase of the Louisville, New Albany and Chicago Railroad, now known as the "Monon Route," and was its general counsel until 1883, when he was elected president of the company, which office he resigned in 1884. He was president of the Southern Exposition in 1884, and in the following year undertook the construction of the Kentucky and Indiana bridge, an enterprise which was carried on with an expenditure of over two and a half million dollars, and with its terminals has proven one of the most important features in the development of the commercial interests of Louisville. The bridge itself is a remarkable structure and contains the largest cantilever system in the world. It has a length of 2,453 feet, with two spans of 500 feet each. Its five spans form a cantilever system extending a distance of 1,843 feet. The draw span is 370 feet in length and is a marvel of mechanical exactness and can be opened and closed by one man in three minutes. The terminal lines include about sixteen miles of road in New Albany and Louisville, making one of the best terminal systems in America.

On the Indiana side the bridge connects directly with the Ohio & Mississippi (or B. & O.) Railway, the Louisville, New Albany & Chicago Railroad (or Monon Route), the J. M. & I. R. R. (or Pennsylvania system), and the Louisville & St. Louis Air Line Railroad; on the Kentucky side with the Louisville & Nashville R. R., the Chesapeake, Ohio & Southwestern Railway, the Louisville, St. Louis & Texas Railway, and the Louisville Southern Railway. It operates about sixty passenger trains daily between Louisville and New Albany. The belt lines of this company have been largely instrumental in developing and building up manufactories in the western portion of the city, while the construction of the bridge caused a large reduction in tolls, and has relieved the traffic of Louisville of an expense of several hundred thousand dollars per annum. It has restored Portland to prosperity, added millions of dollars to the taxable wealth of Louisville and has given the western portion of the city an impetus and growth that could never have been accomplished without the conception and completion of this enterprise whose chief promoter, director and president was Colonel Bennett H. Young. He had the able co-operation of such men as W. S. Culbertson, Vernon D. Price, W. T. Grant, Thomas W. Bullitt, Morris McDonald and James M. Fetter. John McLeod was the chief engineer and the Union Bridge Company was the contractor. The present officers of the company are Colonel Bennett H. Young, president; W. T. Grant, vice-president; Charles P. Weaver, secretary and treasurer, and W. R. Woodard, general manager.

In 1886, upon the completion and opening of the bridge, seeing that its great value depended upon a southern connection, Colonel Young, in conjunction with some of the leading capitalists of Louisville, undertook the construction of the Louisville Southern Railroad, the building of which marked a new era in the development of the City of Louisville, and gave life and prosperity to a section of country tributary to Louisville which had no railroad facilities previous to the completion of this enterprise. It was built without aid from the state and gave Louisville a trunk line into the south similar to that which cost Cincinnati nearly $2,000,000. In these two gigantic enterprises alone Colonel Young probably accomplished more for the substantial growth and prosperity of the City of Louisville than any other individual has ever undertaken, and he did this at a great personal sacrifice, as he came out of the hard struggles which they cost him with less money than he had when they were undertaken. But this is not all that he has done. He reorganized the Polytechnic Society and inaugurated a business policy which relieved it of embarrassment, made its valuable property pay handsome rentals, increased the number of valuable volumes in its great library, systematized, classified and catalogued its books, reconstructed its quarters and provided accommodations for visitors, increased its membership and made it a library worthy of the great City of Louisville, and thus placed the means of education by reading and research within the reach of all who desire to avail themselves of its advantages. Few institutions have ever proven more beneficial to a community; with its extensive library, its scientific lectures and its instructions in art, etc., it has met a great need, for until Colonel Young gave it his attention it was not known as a valuable property or as a great library.

Colonel Young also organized and chiefly endowed Bellewood Seminary and the Kentucky Presbyterian Normal School, both of which have become successful and famous institutions.

In the face of many solicitations Colonel Young has steadily declined public office, except as a member of the State Constitutional Convention of 1890-1, to which he was elected, and which he accepted believing that he could serve his state to some advantage. In this body he occupied a distinguished position, and probably wielded as much influence as any individual member in forming the present organic law of the state.

He is a strong and vigorous writer; was editor of the Evening Post for some time, giving it a force of character that no other newspaper in the city has ever enjoyed; is the author of a valuable book entitled "History of the Three Constitutions of Kentucky," also several pamphlets —one on evangelical work in the State of Kentucky, and another the "History of the Division of the Presbyterian Church in Kentucky."

His valuable work in building the K. & I. bridge and the Louisville Southern Railroad and other public-spirited labors in behalf of his city has been recognized by the merchants and business men through their principal organization, the Board of Trade, by his unanimous election as an honorary member of that body. He was the youngest man upon whom this great honor was ever conferred.

Colonel Young is a man of great benevolence, and his kindness to the poor and needy is well known throughout the city in which he lives. He possesses qualities of no uncommon kind. His capacity for the transaction of business is remarkable. His mind is naturally capable of great research; he can divest difficult subjects of their obscurity, see readily through the mazes of intricate questions and propositions, and arrange and methodize a multifarious business and conduct doubtful plans to a successful issue. He is a warm friend and a generous opponent; has never been afflicted with the spirit of envy or jealousy, and the desire to be great among his friends and neighbors has never disturbed his equanimity. His chief characteristic is a desire to do all the good he can for his fellowmen.

Colonel Young was married in 1866 to Martha Robinson, eldest daughter of Rev. Dr. Stuart Robinson, the eminent Presbyterian divine. Mrs. Young died December 14, 1890.

Colonel Young was married again June 29, 1895.

Colonel Bennett H. Young is descended from a Scotch ancestry that settled in the American colonies thirty years before the Revolution. His father, Robert Young, was born in Fayette County, Kentucky, in 1803, and died November 28, 1889. During the many years he lived in Jessamine County, no spot or blemish tarnished his good name. His high integrity as a man and his devotion to his church were unquestioned. All of the duties which society imposed upon him he discharged with scrupulous fidelity; as a husband and father no one could have been more tender; as a friend none were more faithful. Religion with him was an ever living and pure principle of action, prompting not only his duties as a professed Christian, but controlling and tempering his intercourse with his fellowmen. He married Josephine Henderson, daughter of Bennett Henderson, a native of Albemarle County, Virginia, and granddaughter of Colonel Joseph Crockett, a distinguished officer under General Washington in the Revolutionary war, who settled in Kentucky in 1784, and died in Jessamine County in 1829.

John Young (grandfather), son of Joseph Young and Hannah McCraney, was born November 15, 1760. He and his brothers, Thomas and Robert, were soldiers in the Revolutionary war, serving in all the campaigns with General Greene against Lord Cornwallis in 1781 and 1782, in North and South Carolina. Robert Young was a sharpshooter at the battle of Kings Mountain, and shot and killed Colonel Patrick Ferguson, the British commander. (See Draper's Kings Mountain, page 275.) Soon after the close of the Revolutionary war John Young (grandfather) left North Carolina and went to Brunswick County, Virginia, where he married Nancy Rymond, who died after the birth of her only child—John Young—in 1788, and in 1789 he came to Fayette County, Kentucky, and married Cynthia McCullough, sister of Captain S. D. McCullough. The late Dr. Archibald Young of Jessamine County was his eldest child by his second marriage, and Robert Young (father) was the youngest.

Joseph Young (great-grandfather) married Hannah McCraney in 1754. Their children were: Hannah Ann, born in Lancaster, Pennsylvania, August 30, 1755; Thomas, born December 23, 1757; Mary Haddon, born January 30, 1759; John (grandfather), born November 15, 1760; Tabitha, born October 29, 1763, and Robert, March 15, 1765.

Archibald Young (great-great-grandfather), married Elizabeth McMurds in 1729. She was a daughter of Andrew McMurds and Margaret Hanford, and was born January 1, 1705. She was three years her husband's senior. Their children were: Nancy Elizabeth and Thomas (twins), born February 2, 1728; Clotilda, born March 6, 1730; Andrew, born December 6, 1732; Joseph (great-grandfather) and Martha (twins), in Philadelphia, November 14, 1734.

Archibald Young (great-great-great-grandfather), son of Archibald Young of Dundee, Scotland, was born in Dundee January 26, 1708, and was married to Martha Drennan, also a native of Dundee.

CHARLES WALTER YUNGBLUT, a citizen of Dayton, Kentucky, and a bright and promising young attorney, whose office and principal business is in Cincinnati, was born in Newport, Kentucky, September 5, 1868. He is a son of John R. and Anna (Sweitzer) Yungblut, well known citizens of Dayton.

His father was born in Canton, Ohio, in 1835, and was partly educated before leaving his native place. He came to Newport early in life, and after serving his time as an apprentice in a drug store engaged in that business on his own account, and was a successful druggist in Newport for a period of forty years. He is now retired and is living in Dayton. His ancestors came to this country from Belgium.

Annie Sweitzer Yungblut is a native of Lorraine, France, now a province in Germany. She was born in 1843, and came with her father's family to this country when she was a child. They lived for a time in Cincinnati and then removed to Newport. Her father married a Miss Mignot of Lorraine.

Charles Walter Yungblut received his education in the public schools of Newport, graduating with honors in the class of 1887. He then began the study of law in the Cincinnati Law School, from which he was graduated in 1890, taking the forensic prize of his class.

He at once opened his office in Cincinnati, and in the five years or more of his professional career he has distinguished himself as a lawyer of ability, having already established a good business, which by careful attention and study and the wise and judicious management of his cases, has grown steadily in the number and importance of the cases entrusted to his care.

He was appointed city attorney of Dayton in 1893, and in that capacity has served the city in which he makes his home with credit to himself and with the approval of the people.

Mr. Yungblut is an ardent Republican, and is one of the most prominent young men in local politics. Modest and unassuming, yet progressive and aggressive in politics and law, he is steadily preparing the way for a brilliant and useful career.

THOMAS CRYSOSTROM BIRGE, Attorney-at-Law, Maysville, son of Ellen (Spellman) and William C. Birge, was born in Northampton, Massachusetts, December 3, 1857. His father was born in the same city in 1823 and after completing his studies went to the Sandwich Islands as a sailor; returned and enlisted in the Thirty-seventh Massachusetts Volunteer Infantry and was with the Army of the Potomac throughout the Civil war. When the war was over he returned to his old home and was a farmer the rest of his life. He was a man of fine intellect, a scholarly gentleman, a brilliant conversationalist and highly respected by all who knew him.

Thaddeus Birge (grandfather) was born in Northampton in 1785; he was a merchant and farmer; died in 1872. The Birge family came from Scotland and first settled in Worcester, Massachusetts.

Ellen Spellman Birge (mother) was born near Lake Killarney, Ireland, and came to America when she was fourteen years of age, and lived in Worcester, Massachusetts. She married William C. Birge in 1851, and is now living in her old home. Her father, Thomas Spellman, was born in Ireland in 1770, and died in 1870, aged one hundred years. He was the manager of large estates which belonged to the nobility. Great-grandfather Spellman was an Englishman who went to Ireland in the early part of the eighteenth century.

Thomas C. Birge was educated in the Northampton schools; came to Kentucky in 1879, and afterwards went to Cincinnati, and remained there a short time before removing to Covington, where he studied law with Judge Shine. He was admitted to the bar in Covington September 6, 1890, and in the same year formed a partnership with T. B. Wise, which continued until June 30, 1894, when Mr. Birge came to Maysville, where he has already taken a position of prominence at the bar.

Mr. Birge married Mary Cunningham, daughter of William Cunningham, April 27, 1882. She was born in Cincinnati in January, 1860, and was educated in her native city. They have five children: Ida, Nellie, Mary, William and Benjamin.

Mr. Birge is a Democrat without seeking prominence, and has accepted the religious belief of his mother, who is a Catholic, while his father was a Republican and a Protestant.

ALEXANDER JEFFREY, President of the Lexington City Gas Company, was born in the City of Edinburgh, Scotland, May 10, 1815, and is the son of John and Elizabeth (McConnell) Jeffrey.

His father was also a native of Scotland, a barrister by profession and solicitor for the Supreme Court of Edinburgh. He was the father of nine children, of whom the subject of this sketch was next to the youngest. He wedded Elizabeth McConnell, a native of Scotland and a member of the Church of England. She emigrated to the United States several years after her husband's death and after her son Alexander had arrived in this country and located at Canandaigua, New York, where she died.

At the age of sixteen, having previously attended college in Edinburgh, Alexander Jeffrey came to this country with his aunt, Mrs. George Ross, who located on a farm in the vicinity of Canandaigua, New York, where he remained three years. He then accepted a clerkship in a bank in New York City, remaining there for about six months, and then returned to Canandaigua and was a clerk in the land office under ex-Congressman John Greig for about one year; was teller in a bank in Canandaigua for several years, when he became associated with his brother, John Jeffrey, who was a civil engineer and contractor and builder of gas works. They constructed the gas works of Cleveland, Ohio, Nashville and Memphis, Tennessee, Covington, Kentucky, and in other cities throughout the country. In 1853 Alexander Jeffrey built the gas works at Lexington and has been a resident of that city and president of the Lexington Gas Company since that time.

Mr. Jeffrey was married (first) to Delia Granger, a daughter of General John A. Granger of Canandaigua. She died, leaving three daughters and one son.

His second wife was a well-known poetess, Mrs. Rosa Vertner (Griffith) Johnson of Lexington, who died October 6, 1894. She was born near Natchez, Mississippi, where her father, John T. Griffith, a gentleman of literary culture and a graceful writer in both prose and verse, lived for many years. Some of his Indian tales have attained celebrity on two continents. Her mother was a beautiful and accomplished woman, daughter of Reverend James Abercrombie, who was for forty years rector of old St. Peter's Episcopal Church of Philadelphia. She died of yellow fever, leaving four little children. The youngest, Rosa Vertner, being only nine months old, was adopted by a maternal aunt, whose husband, Daniel Vertner, became the foster father of the little orphan. Daniel Vertner was born in Pittsburg, Pennsylvania, in 1768, and in early manhood removed to Lexington and became a successful business man of that city. He married a Miss Langhorn of Maysville, who died, leaving one son; removed to Mississippi, where he became extensively engaged in cotton planting and married a Mrs. Sparks, a lady of distinguished social reputation who is referred to in Mrs. Elliott's "Court Circles of the Republic." Some years after the death of his second wife, Mr. Vertner married Rosa's aunt, then the widow Harding of Natchez.

With two fathers and a foster mother, the young girl passed her childhood in the midst of tender affection, luxury and refinement at "Burlington," Mr. Vertner's beautiful country seat near Port Gibson, Mississippi, to which she paid a loving tribute in her poem, "My Childhood's Home." Beneath the glow of the Southern skies and amid the balmy fragrance of Southern flowers, the poetic fire inherited from her gifted father began to burn within her breast and move her mind to musical pulsations, even in her childhood. Before she could write well enough to give her verses shape on paper, Mrs. Vertner wrote them down, and the poetess in after years cherished one of these childish efforts as a memory of the loving hand that had traced the lines.

Rosa's education was begun in the South under private tutors, but when she was ten years of age, in the summer of 1836, Mr. Vertner moved to Lexington, Kentucky, to give her the benefits of further instruction. His home there was noted for its elegant hospitality, and none were more popular than he and his wife. As the guardian of several young girls, he was also a father to them, and they clung to him with touching devotion during his life. Between him and the great statesman, Henry Clay, there existed a warm feeling of friendship.

Rosa was educated at Bishop Smith's seminary, and at the age of seventeen became the wife of Claude M. Johnson—a gentleman of fortune and a resident of Louisiana; and, for a number of years after her marriage, she spent her summers in Kentucky and her winters in Louisiana.

In 1850 she became a contributor to the Louisville Journal, in which the greater number of her poems made their first appearance, and through that popular paper "Rosa" became favorably known to the readers of the principal periodicals of the country. In 1859 her father died, and this grief, together with the cares of motherhood, soon gave to her writings a more spiritual vein, revealing the deep and tender mercies of the heart. Her poems, first published in book form in 1857, elicited warm encomiums from the press and gave her at once a high place as an American poet.

In 1864 there appeared a novel from her pen, entitled "Woodburn," somewhat sensational, but finely descriptive of past social life in the South. She afterward wrote several tales and a long narrative poem, "Florence Dale, a Tale of Tuscany," besides occasional shorter lyrics.

She was the mother of two children: Alexander Jeffrey, Jr., and Virginia A. Jeffrey, and was one of the handsomest women of her day.

REV. WILLIAM MOODY PRATT, one of the oldest and certainly one of the most distinguished ministers in the Baptist Church, whose personal history is one of deep interest and whose ancestry is most remarkable, was born in Fenner, Madison County, New York, where he received his primary schooling; was prepared for college at Casenovia, and then attended Madison, now known as Colgate University—the name having been changed by reason of large endowments from a family of that name; graduated in 1838; went to Crawfordsville, Indiana, to preach; returned to college to complete his course in theology, and graduated from the theological department in 1839. On leaving the seminary a most valuable and unusual recommendation, signed by all the members of the faculty, was presented him, and this he has kept and held good and true for fifty-seven years.

After completing his studies he returned, with his wife, in a buggy—a distance of 800 miles—to Crawfordsville, Indiana; he remained there as pastor of the Baptist Church for some years, also teaching in a female school; went from there to Logansport, and from there to South Bend, Indiana; went to Lexington in 1846, and his wife having died, was married again to Mary Elise Dallard, great-granddaughter of Ambrose Dudley, who was one of the first settlers at Bryan Station and a distinguished minister, who, with his son, Thomas Dudley, covered a period of nearly one hundred years in the ministry. Mr. Pratt remained in Lexington for seventeen years, and then, during the Civil war, was stationed in Louisville and New Albany, in the interest of church erection; was stationed at Shelbyville for several years; returned to Louisville and has made his home in that city since 1885, and is still engaged in church work.

His is a most remarkable record; in the ministry for fifty-seven years; traveled 24,000 miles in a buggy in Indiana and Kentucky; preached about 8,000 sermons; officiated at 600 funerals, and has joined hundreds of couples in the holy bonds of matrimony.

Only an outline of his work can be given in this brief sketch; many interesting volumes have been written with fewer facts of smaller import than the busy life of Dr. Pratt could furnish. He is an old man now, having almost rounded out his four score years, nearly three score of which have been in the service of the Master; but he is hale and vigorous still, and his zeal knows no abatement. He was a member of the board of trustees of Georgetown College for forty years and president of the board many years, and is a member of the board of trustees of the Southern Baptist Theological Seminary at Louisville.

He is a brother of Daniel D. Pratt of national reputation, who was United States senator and commissioner of internal revenue.

Dr. Samuel Pratt (father) was born in Belcher, Mass., December 26, 1779, where he received his preliminary schooling. He was highly educated and was very proficient in the languages; studied medicine in New York City; began to practice his profession in Maine; returned to New York and located at Fenner—five miles from Petersburgh, and was appointed surgeon by the governor of Massachusetts in the War of 1812. He was a very successful physician, greatly beloved by his friends and those to whom he brought relief in suffering; was a good, pure and noble man; an intense partisan of the Whig stripe; and living in a time when there was opposition to Masonry, he bitterly opposed that order. He died in 1864 at the age of eighty-four years.

David Pratt (grandfather) was a native of Massachusetts; served as captain in the Revolutionary war, and was present at the surrender of General Burgoyne at Saratoga. He was not a professional man, but spent most of his life in farming. He was a son of Nathaniel and Sallie (Rundall) Pratt.

A great-great-grandfather of Rev. William M. Pratt was Josiah Coldridge, who lived near Boston.

Sallie Hill Pratt (mother) was born in Kittery, Maine, September 14, 1775. She first married Dr. W. D. Moody of York, Maine, who died, and she became the wife of Dr. Samuel Pratt and died in 1849, in the seventy-fifth year of her age. Her mother was a direct descendant of John Rogers, the martyr. She was a daughter of Elephalet Rogers, who was a son of Rev. John Rogers, pastor of the first church at Ipswich and president of Harvard College, who died July 2, 1684; he was the eldest son of Rev. Nathaniel Rogers, who came from England in 1636 and settled in Ipswich—as co-pastor with Rev. Nathaniel Ward—and died July 2, 1655. Nathaniel Rogers was a son of Rev. John Rogers of Dedham, England, who died October 18, 1639, aged sixty-seven years, and this John Rogers was a grandson of the Rev. John Rogers who was burned at the stake at Smithfield February 6, 1555.

WILLIAM LOWTHER JACKSON, deceased, late judge of the criminal division of the Jefferson Circuit Court of Louisville, was born in St. Mary's, (now West) Virginia, August 12, 1854, and died December 29, 1895. He was the youngest child of Judge William L. Jackson and Sarah (Creel) Jackson. He secured his education in the public schools of Louisville, graduating from the high school in June, 1875; was valedictorian of his class, and was one of the brightest and best informed young men who have been educated in that school. While engaged in his studies, he laid the foundation for the great popularity which distinguished him in after years. He began the study of law in 1876, graduated from the Louisville Law School in 1887, and at once began the practice of his profession, in which he had a most successful career until May 19, 1890, when he was inducted into the office of judge of the old Jefferson Circuit Court, and in November, 1892, was elected judge of the criminal division of the Jefferson Circuit Court—which, under the new constitution, succeeded the old Jefferson Circuit Court—and this office he held until his death, which occurred at his home after a long and painful illness, December 29, 1895.

For three consecutive terms—1881 to 1886—he was a member of the house of representatives in the Kentucky legislature, and served with great distinction on the judiciary, the revenue and taxation, and other important committees.

Returning from his duties in the legislature, he formed a partnership with Mr. Zack Phelps, and they were joined later by Mr. J. T. O'Neal, making one of the strongest legal firms in the city or state. Judge Jackson remained with these gentlemen until the death of his father, when he was appointed to succeed him on the bench. He accepted that office with reluctance and at a personal sacrifice, as he had a most valuable practice.

Few men have a greater faculty of making friends and keeping them than Judge Jackson had, and he had all of the requirements of the successful lawyer and politician, but he was eminently qualified by training, study and natural aptitude for the higher duties of the judge, and he filled that office with ability and with such fidelity that he was frequently in his place on the bench when his sufferings from a lurking disease were so great that his physicians were compelled to interfere with his strong will and order him to abandon his work for some months before his death. Even against the protests of his friends and physicians, he insisted on being carried to the court room in a chair, and he frequently performed his duty as judge while suffering excruciating pain.

He was a man of firm, honest purpose, and successfully carried out his plans and purposes, overcoming all difficulties until he was compelled to yield to the hand of death. His popularity was shown in his last illness by the vast numbers who offered him and his family the sincere sympathy and condolence of loving friends and associates.

He was an able lawyer, a wise statesman, an honest judge, an honored citizen, a dutiful son, a devoted husband and a loving father.

His father, Judge William L. Jackson, Sr., was a native of (now West) Virginia, in which state he was judge of the Nineteenth Judicial District; second auditor of the state, and lieutenant governor. He came to Louisville January 1, 1866, and was a successful practitioner at the bar until January, 1873, when he was appointed judge of the old Jefferson Circuit Court by Governor T. H. Leslie. He was elected to succeed himself, and was re-elected again and again, holding his office until his death in 1892. His wife was a daughter of Alexander H. and Lucy (Neal) Creel. Her father was distinguished for his intellectual attainments. Her mother came from the Lewis family, and the Lewises and Neals owned what was called Washington's Bottom, near Blennerhassett Island, and took an active part in Revolutionary annals.

RICHARD D. DAVIS, President of the Second National Bank of Ashland, and one of the leading business men of that city, is a son of Elias P. and Myrtilla A. (Winn) Davis, and was born in Carter County, Kentucky, September 22, 1844.

His father was born in Prince William County, Virginia, February 14, 1810; was educated in his native county; removed to Kentucky and was a resident of Fleming County for ten years; removed to Carter County in 1837; was sheriff of that county (1851); circuit clerk from 1851 to 1884, and clerk of Carter County Court from 1854 to 1882; enlisted in the Union army in 1863, and was captain of Company D, Fortieth Regiment Kentucky Volunteer Mounted Infantry; was prominent in politics as Whig and Republican, and was a leading citizen in his county; died March 8, 1884.

Richard Davis (grandfather), a native of Virginia, was a farmer in Fleming County, where he died in 1840. He was passionately fond of hunting, and was familiarly known as "Hound Davis," on account of the number of hounds he owned. His father, Elias Davis, was a native of Wales, who settled in Virginia before the Revolutionary war.

Myrtilla A. Winn Davis (mother) was born in Champaign County, Ohio, October 25, 1812; was educated near Urbana; was married in 1836; died in Carter County, Kentucky, July 25, 1886. She was a devout member of the Christian Church, a faithful wife and mother and a woman of great influence and strength of character.

Douglass I. Winn (grandfather), a native of Virginia, went from that state to Champaign County, Ohio; afterwards removed to Kentucky, and finally to Calloway County, Missouri, where he died. He was a fine scholar, a noted mathematician and a professional teacher; a member of the Christian Church and a courtly gentleman. He married Elizabeth Triby Rawlins, who was born in Champaign County, Ohio, and died in Calloway County, Missouri, in 1876. Her mother was a Miss Triby, a native of France. The Davis and Winn families were originally from Wales, and the Rawlins branch of the family are distinguished citizens of several American states.

Richard D. Davis of Ashland was educated in Carter County and was well advanced in his studies in 1862, when he found his first employment in the office of the clerk of the Circuit and County Courts of Carter County; was afterwards deputy circuit clerk in Winchester for nineteen months; was for a short time in the office of Collector of Internal Revenue at Richmond; was then in charge of the circuit clerk's office in Richmond from February 20, 1865, to 1867—serving a part of that time as deputy clerk—when the clerk resigned and he was appointed clerk, serving until 1868, when, having been admitted to the bar, he returned to Carter County and began the practice of law, in which he continued successfully until 1889.

He was county attorney of Carter County from September, 1870, to August, 1873; resigned, having been elected to the legislature as representative from Carter and Boyd Counties; was county judge of Carter County from October, 1881, to September, 1882. These offices were merely incidental to a busy career as an attorney-at-law, and furnish some evidence of his popularity, especially as he has no ambition for political preferment.

Having organized the Second National Bank of Ashland in 1888, of which he was chosen president, he removed to Ashland in 1889 and assumed the duties of that position, which now demand his best attention. He also has other interests and investments, which combine to make him a very busy man. He is a very genial and warm hearted gentleman, and is regarded as one of the best and most enterprising citizens of Ashland. He is a popular and helpful member of the Masonic and Odd Fellows orders and also of the "Concatenated Order of Hoo Hoo," an association of railroad and lumber men.

Mr. Davis was married November 8, 1870, to Mary Lewis, daughter of C. N. and L. A. (England) Lewis of Kansas City, Missouri. Mrs. Davis was born in Carter County, Kentucky, May 25, 1851; is a member of the Christian Church and a lady of culture and fine personal attractions. They have four children: Lewis N., born October 31, 1871; Roscoe C., born October 19, 1878; Myrtilla Annie, born February 15, 1883; and Richard D., born July 15, 1885.

PETER CALDWELL, Superintendent of the Industrial School of Reform, Louisville, Kentucky, was born in Huntingdon, near Montreal, Canada, April 23, 1836. He is a son of William and Jeanette (Elder) Caldwell. His father was born in Glasgow, Scotland, in 1808 and emigrated with his father and others when quite young to Huntingdon, Canada. They were among the first settlers of a section near Montreal that was then nothing more than a wilderness. William Caldwell became a prosperous farmer and a highly respected citizen who took a lively interest in the development of the new country. He was a man of strong convictions, and of sterling integrity, and a strict member of the Presbyterian Church. He died in 1893, aged eighty-four years. He had three elder brothers, each of whom lived to be eighty-four years of age.

William Caldwell (grandfather), native of Glasgow, Scotland, removed to Canada, as before stated; was a soldier in the War of 1812. He died in Huntingdon when eighty-two years of age, his death occurring in the morning of his birthday.

Jeanette Elder Caldwell (mother) is now a resident of Huntingdon, Canada, where she has lived since her childhood, and is now eighty-five years of age. Her father, George Elder (grandfather), was a native of Glasgow, Scotland, and removed to Canada, crossing the ocean in the same ship with the Caldwells; and the two families were neighboring farmers in Huntingdon and brethren in the Presbyterian Church.

Peter Caldwell, after attending the schools in his neighborhood, was graduated from the Middleberry, Vermont, College in 1863. When he was seventeen years of age, he began teaching, and was thus employed in Canada for three years, when he came to the United States and spent seven years in teaching and studying, taking special courses in various institutions. He was at one time principal of the Hinsdale College in Massachusetts. In the spring of 1864 he was appointed principal of the Reform School of Chicago, and three months later was made assistant superintendent of that institution, a position which he resigned in 1865 to accept the superintendency of the "House of Refuge," as it was then called, in Louisville. He has been engaged in this important work for the reformation of the youth of Louisville for over thirty years and his tenure of office depends upon the number of years that he may live. As he belongs to a family noted for longevity, it is to be hoped that he may at least complete his half century as superintendent of this institution, which has grown from a small beginning until, under his able management, it is now one of the largest and most complete schools of the kind in the United States and is in many respects regarded as the model reform school in the country.

SILAS EVANS, M. D.

When Mr. Caldwell took charge of the school, there was but one building, which was used for all purposes; now there are fourteen buildings, each one adapted to the department for which it was constructed and is now used. Then, the number of children in the school was limited, as were the advantages given them. Now, the average number of inmates is about three hundred, and the accommodations for their care and instruction are the best the board of directors can afford with the means at hand. The material growth of the institution, together with the wonderful advancement that has been made in the educational and industrial work of the school, are due in a large measure to the indefatigable labor and wise management of its able superintendent.

The grounds of the school embrace eighty acres of valuable land within the city limits, twenty-five acres of which are occupied by the buildings and campus, while a large portion of the ground is cultivated for the use of the school. The grounds surrounding and adjacent to the buildings are beautified by trees, shrubbery, flowers and rare plants, all of which are tenderly cared for by the children under the direction of competent employes who are practical florists and gardeners. This was the first school of the kind in the country to give attention to the cultivation of flowers and plants in greenhouses, and was the first to abandon the system of giving out the labor of the school under contract. It was the first to build a chapel to be used exclusively for worship and Sunday school, and the progress made in these and other matters has led other institutions to advance in the same directions.

The Industrial School of Reform is, first of all, a school in which the English branches are thoroughly taught and second in importance is the manual training departments, in which the children are instructed in the trades. Mr. Caldwell regards the moral and religious training of the inmates of the highest importance and is devoted to his Sunday school and other religious work among the boys and girls, and in this respect he has accomplished a work the value of which cannot be estimated.

Mr. Caldwell was married in 1865 to Mary Wells, daughter of Rev. Edward Wells of Chicago; and they have three sons and four daughters: Nettie A., Addie, Carrie C., Willie E., Mary E., Hamilton Peter and David C. All of the family are members of the Presbyterian Church.

SILAS EVANS, M. D., one of the ablest young physicians of Lexington, is a descendant of a Welsh family who settled in Virginia and Pennsylvania in 1722. He is a son of Silas and Parmelia (Quisenberry) Evans, and was born in Fayette County, Kentucky, April 2, 1858.

Silas Evans (father) was also a native of Fayette County, and was an extensive farmer and large trader in live stock prior to the Civil war. He died in Scott County, Kentucky, in 1879. He was a life-time member of the Baptist Church and was a Democrat in politics.

Peter Evans (grandfather) was a Virginian by birth who emigrated to Fayette County, where he became one of the first distillers in that vicinity. He was a son of Peter Evans (great-grandfather), who was a captain in the war of the Revolution and fought in the battles of Monmouth, Princeton, Germantown, and was present at the capture of Lord Cornwallis at Yorktown, October 19, 1781. After the war he returned to his Virginia home, where he died. He served under Colonel Lewis in the battle of Point Pleasant in 1774.

The following facts are taken from the records in the pension office at Washington:

"Captain Peter Evans, born in Prince William County, Virginia, October 25, 1758; removed to Clark County, Kentucky. He married Ann, daughter of Captain John Newman of Prince William County, Virginia, December 11, 1777. She was born April 6, 1755, died July 8, 1836, in Clark County, Kentucky. Captain Evans' will, dated February 12, 1814, was probated July, 1814.

"He enlisted as a private in Prince William County, February, 1776, Colonel Bland's Regiment Dragoons, service certified to by Captain Lee of his company. He was commissioned lieutenant by Governor Thomas Jefferson August 3, 1779, in Captain Charles Lee's company, and served as such in Captain Valentine Peyton's company, Colonel Ewell's command; joined main army near Philadelphia; was on guard on the line three months, discharged December, 1779; was commissioned captain by Governor Thomas Jefferson May 1, 1780, and joined the regiment of Colonel Wheeden; was at the siege of Yorktown and surrender of Cornwallis, October 19, 1781; rendered service five or six years. 'Witnesses allude to him as a brave and intrepid officer.'

"He was at the battle of Princeton, New Jersey, January 3, 1777, and was with Light Horse Harry Lee, attending the burial of General Mercer, who was mortally wounded in that battle.

"He was wounded in a skirmish near Morristown, New Jersey."

Hickman and Oliver P. Evans appear in the widow's papers.

Belam P. Evans, son of Captain Evans, was born in Prince William County, Virginia, September 25, 1778, died in Jessamine County, Kentucky, October 30, 1843.

Parmelia Quisenberry Evans (mother) was born in Clark County, Kentucky, and was a member of a large and influential family of that county. She died in 1860.

Doctor Silas Evans' collegiate course was taken in Central University at Richmond. He read medicine and was graduated from the Hospital College of Medicine at Louisville in 1882, going thence to New York City, where he took a post graduate course at Polyclinic College and immediately afterwards located in Lexington.

He was appointed by President Arthur to the position of United States examining pension surgeon, and was for some time visiting surgeon to St. Joseph Hospital. In 1883 he was appointed by the Board of Commissioners under Governor Knott assistant physician in the Eastern Kentucky Asylum for the Insane; and was also assistant physician in the Cincinnati Sanitarium for one year. Governor Buckner appointed him assistant physician in the Hospital for the Insane at Lakeland, where he remained during Governor Buckner's administration; then, returning to Lexington, he became superintendent of High Oaks Private Sanitarium for mental and nervous troubles. He is a member of the Kentucky State Medical Society and of the American Medico-Psychological Society.

Doctor Evans was married April 17, 1889, to Pearl Chenault, a daughter of Doctor R. C. Chenault of Madison County. Dr. and Mrs. Evans are members of the First Presbyterian Church at Lexington.

The name of Evans is an honored one in this country, having lost none of the lustre that clusters around it in Wales. The Welsh are descended from the ancient Britons who fought the Roman legions under Caesar with more undaunted courage than any other people in the Isle of Great Britain, and it is the old Welsh barons who forced King John to sign the Magna Charta on the field of Runnymede, June 15, 1215.

DRURY JAMES BURCHETT, President of the Bank of Louisa, one of the best known and most popular Republicans in the state, son of Armstead and Rebecca (Pigg) Burchett, was born in Floyd County, Kentucky, August 15, 1843.

His father was born in the same county, May 12, 1818, and was a prominent citizen, farmer, soldier and business man in his native county until his death, which occurred on his birthday, May 12, 1894. He was a Democrat before and a Republican after the Civil war; enlisted in the Union army and was a sergeant in the Fourteenth Regiment Kentucky Infantry, and was not actively engaged in business thereafter.

Drury Burchett (grandfather) was a native of Virginia; married a Miss McCowan; removed to Kentucky and was a farmer in Floyd County. His father and four brothers were soldiers in the Revolutionary war. The family is of Scotch-Irish origin, the progenitor coming to this country in colonial times.

Rebecca Pigg Burchett (mother) was born in Floyd County, Kentucky, in 1820; was educated in the county schools; married Armstead Burchett in 1841, and is now a resident of Louisa.

James Pigg (maternal grandfather) was a native of Virginia; married a Miss Ratliff of that state; removed to Kentucky and was a farmer in Floyd County. His ancestors were of Scotch-Irish extraction.

Major D. J. Burchett left the school room in Louisa to enlist as a private in Company K, Fourteenth Regiment Kentucky Infantry, June 30, 1861; was promoted to the rank of first lieutenant November 8, 1861; promoted to the captaincy of the company February 1, 1862, and to the rank of major August 6, 1864, and served until the close of the war. During eighteen months of his service as captain, he was in command of a battery of eight guns on the border between Virginia and Kentucky.

He was in several battles of the Eastern Tennessee campaign, and went from there on to Atlanta; returned with General Thomas to Nashville; was in command of the regiment from Gaylesville to Rome, Georgia, and of the brigade from Chattanooga to Pulaski and Nashville, and thence to Johnsville. Few men saw more active service during nearly four years of the war, and have had as little to say about it since the smoke cleared away.

Returning to Louisa, he was mustered out of the service January 31, 1865. For fifteen years following he was engaged in mercantile pursuits in Louisa, during which time he was a prominent figure in the Republican party in his county and district; was elected to the legislature August, 1865, and returned in 1877 and again in 1879, representing Boyd and Lawrence Counties; was chairman of Committee on Banks and a member of the Committee of Ways and Means; was tendered the nomination for Congress in 1884, which he then declined, but accepted the candidacy of his party in 1888, and was defeated by only two hundred and twenty-nine votes; was appointed United States marshal for the District of Kentucky by President Harrison in 1889 and served the full term of four years; was a delegate to the Republican National Convention at Minneapolis in 1892, and was an ardent supporter of President Harrison, who was renominated. It is hardly necessary to add that he is uncompromising in his loyalty to the Republican party.

The Bank of Louisa was organized in 1890 and Major Burchett, who was then serving as United States marshal, was elected president of that corporation. This is the nearest banking point for the Counties of Lawrence, Johnson and Martin in Kentucky and Wayne County, West Virginia. The extensive lumbering and mining interests of that section are greatly facilitated by the establishment of a bank at Louisa.

He is also president of the Louisa Milling Company; is interested in a wholesale grocery establishment; has investments in real estate and is a very active and enterprising citizen of the thriving city of Louisa.

Major Burchett was married March 15, 1865, to Addie Jones, daughter of Daniel D. Jones of Lawrence County. She was educated in the schools of her county; was a very intelligent and attractive woman, noted for piety and Christian charity; a devout member of the Methodist Episcopal Church; died February 7, 1890. Major Burchett's children are: Mary, wife of J. F. Ratcliff; Emma D., wife of G. R. Vinson, cashier of the Bank of Louisa; Harlan Geiger, now employed in the bank; John, a student in Centre College at Danville; and Addie and Drury, who are at home.

WES. B. WILSON, Clerk of the Kenton County Court, Covington, was born in Kenton County, Kentucky, December 12, 1852. He was a typical farmer's boy and attended the common schools when he had nothing else to do, and later attended a private school at Independence in Kenton County; was for a time a matriculate in the Kentucky University at Lexington, where he advanced rapidly, and was subsequently admitted to West Point, where he spent one year. After leaving school as a pupil he became a teacher, and followed that profession for seven years, being well equipped and quite successful. While thus engaged he was appointed deputy clerk of the Circuit Court at Independence, the old county seat of Kenton, and filled that position from 1879 to 1888. In 1885 he represented his district in the Legislature, and in 1890 he was elected clerk of the County Court for a term of four years. He was re-elected in 1894, and is the present incumbent of that office. He is a leader in the Democratic party, and enjoys the friendship and good will of men of all parties. He is a prominent member of the Knights of Pythias and of the Elks; is a man of influence in business matters, being a director in the Farmers & Traders' Bank and a director in the Covington Trust Company.

Mr. Wilson was married in 1876 to Lyda Miles of Covington, and they have four sons and one daughter: Grace, Miles, Hansford, Earl and L. B.

Mr. Wilson's father, Walker H. Wilson, was born in Kenton County, of which he was a resident until the time of his death in April, 1895, when he was seventy-two years of age. He was a prosperous farmer and dealer in live stock. He was a devout member of the Christian Church.

Aquilla Wilson (grandfather) came to Kenton County from Virginia in 1800, and was one of the pioneer farmers of that county. He died in 1839. The Wilson family is descended from Cavalier English stock.

W. B. Wilson's mother, Mary J. (Hansford) Wilson, was born in Bourbon County, Kentucky, in 1828, and died at the age of sixty-five years, in 1883. She was a member of the Christian Church, a woman of superior intelligence and loveliness of character.

NAPOLEON M. DURBIN, deceased, was born near Claysville, Harrison County, Kentucky, April 1, 1815. His father, Daniel Durbin, with two brothers, came from the vicinity of Baltimore, Maryland, descending the Ohio river on flatboats and landing at Maysville before there was any town there. Daniel found his way through the wilderness to Bourbon County, where he bought a large tract of land near Paris. He also owned a grist mill on Stoner Creek, which is still in operation, about three miles from Paris. After some years' residence in Bourbon County, he sold his property and purchased a large tract of land near Claysville, Harrison County, where he died in 1827, aged eighty-six years. He was the grandfather of Rev. John P. Durbin, D. D., deceased, a noted divine of the Methodist Episcopal Church and Eastern traveler, who was president of Dickinson College, Carlisle, Pennsylvania. He is buried in Forest Hill Cemetery, Philadelphia.

Daniel Durbin (father) was twice married; first to a Miss Nunn of Bourbon County, Kentucky, by whom he had several children, one of whom, a son, Hosier, was the father of Rev. John P. Durbin. Hosier is buried at Cane Ridge, Bourbon County, Kentucky. The other children were daughters: Cassie, who married a Dr. Sappington, and Nancy, who married General Eastin of Fayette County. Elizabeth Pursell was the second wife of Daniel Durbin, and she was the mother of three children: Napoleon M. Durbin, John Bonaparte Durbin and Corilla Boracea Durbin. John B. died without issue. Corilla B. married John C. Wilson, the father of N. B. Wilson, now a resident of Cynthiana.

Napoleon M. Durbin enjoyed but limited advantages in getting an education; but he was an ambitious and faithful student, and with his natural qualifications was well equipped for almost any position in public life. In starting out he found lucrative employment as a surveyor and he soon acquired property in two grist mills and a woolen factory, which were the beginning of a handsome fortune.

A man of his intelligence could not be kept out of public life, although he sought no office. He represented his county in the legislature in 1846, being elected by the Whig party. He served in that body with General Lucien Desha, they having defeated Hugh Newel and Joseph Shawhan.

He was a very fluent speaker and was one of the most popular campaigners of his time. He became a Democrat before the war and was outspoken in his sympathies for the South during the war; and on that account he spent a good portion of his time in prison, while his friends were fighting for the South.

The primary cause of his long imprisonment was the fact that he organized a company, and when about to depart with his company to join the Confederate forces, was captured and taken to Lexington.

He was a formidable and successful opposer of taxation for private or quasi-public enterprises. He strongly and vigorously fought the proposed levy of a tax on Harrison County property to aid in the construction of the Kentucky Central Railway. The proposition was defeated, to the great gain of the county.

He owned a large number of slaves, every one of whom praised and willingly obeyed him. Those of them who are still living speak of him as the kindest, noblest and best hearted man who ever lived. He was just, generous and benevolent, noble in his bearing and gentlemanly in his deportment; true and ever faithful to his friends; fierce and bordering almost on the terrible when aroused, yet magnanimous to his enemies.

He died March 12, 1871, at the old homestead near Claysville in Harrison County, which had been the home of his father for many years.

Mr. Durbin was married in 1860 to Cynthia Hill, daughter of James Hill, of Fayette County. She died in October, 1888, aged fifty-nine years.

His son, Daniel Durbin, attorney-at-law of Cynthiana, was born at the family homestead in Harrison County, November 27, 1862. When fifteen years of age he entered Prof. Smith's classical school, which he attended for four and a half years, and then went to Ann Arbor College, Michigan, for one year. He studied law in the Cincinnati Law School for two years, graduating in 1889, and at once entered upon the practice of his profession in Cynthiana.

He was married in 1887 to Mary L. Fisher, daughter of John W. Fisher of Bourbon County. They have two sons and two daughters: Cullen, Bessie, Laura and one other.

Daniel Durbin has two sisters: Mary, wife of Darwin E. Fisher of Bourbon County; and Elizabeth, wife of Dr. James B. Adams, a dentist of Cynthiana. He also had a brother John, who died in December, 1870.

The large estate of Napoleon Durbin has been kept intact by his children.

JOHN CALVIN HOPKINS, a leading business man of Catlettsburg, was born in Tazewell County, Virginia, January 25, 1849.

His father, John Calvin Hopkins, was born in Bedford County, Virginia, August 13, 1812; was educated in Lynchburg and was a merchant in Tazewell County, Virginia, where he died July 20, 1889. Prior to the war he was a Whig and afterwards a Republican; a member of the Presbyterian Church; a good and exemplary citizen and an upright and honest business man.

John Hopkins (grandfather) was a native farmer of Bedford County, Virginia. His ancestors were of Scotch-Irish descent.

Elizabeth Tabler Hopkins (mother) was born in Frederick City, Maryland, in 1820; educated in the best schools of that city; married John C. Hopkins in 1847, and died in 1880.

William Tabler (maternal grandfather) was sheriff of Frederick County, Maryland, a hotel keeper and a prominent politician. He was of German extraction.

John Calvin Hopkins of Catlettsburg was educated in Jeffersonville, Virginia; began business as traveling salesman for the hat house of R. G. Lampkins and was with that house from 1871 till 1873; went to New York and was engaged in real estate business with his father in 1874; removed to Kentucky and married Monsie L. Martin, October 20, 1874; lived in Prestonsburg about two years and removed to Catlettsburg February 15, 1876; was engaged in the retail grocery business for one year, when he became interested in steamboating, as captain and owner of a fine line of steamboats, which he has continued to operate with marked success until the present time; has also a retail gentlemen's furnishing establishment in Catlettsburg; has been a member of the city council for ten years; was elected mayor of the city in 1893, the first mayor under the present city charter; was master commissioner of the Circuit Court for eight years; is a director in the Catlettsburg National Bank; and in many ways identified with the material interests of his city and county.

His wife, Monsie L. Martin Hopkins, a descendant of a very distinguished family whose antecedents are given herewith, was born August 7, 1848. They have four children:

Elizabeth, born in Prestonsburg, July 16, 1875; Mary Grau, born in Catlettsburg, June 24, 1877; Nellie, born in Catlettsburg, January 3, 1880; John Martin, born in Catlettsburg, June 30, 1884.

John P. Martin, Mrs. Hopkins' father, was born in Jonesville, Lee County, Virginia, October 17, 1811; removed to Prestonsburg, Kentucky, in 1828 and soon rose to distinction as a lawyer, politician and statesman. He was twice elected to the Kentucky house of representatives, twice to the Kentucky senate and once to Congress. He was one of the best informed and most brilliant men of his time and exerted a wonderful power over the people whom he represented in public affairs; was a most eloquent speaker; of elegant manners, courteous towards others who looked up to him, and universally popular with all classes. One of the secrets of his power was the fact that he had a very fine library and was a constant reader and tireless student; and he thus equipped himself for the battle of life and was ever ready to inform and enlighten his constituents and to combat the errors of those who opposed him.

His daughter, Mary W. Martin, who was his constant companion, was hardly less distinguished than her father. Born in the little town of Prestonsburg, September 13, 1837, she became one of the brightest women of Kentucky or of any state. She was educated in a school for girls in Alexandria, D. C., and in the female seminary at Steubenville, Ohio. She spent much of her time in Washington, where she was associated with the most intelligent people, who appreciated her talents and admired her qualities of mind and heart, and her many personal attractions. She never lost her identity with Kentucky. She loved the people of her native state and was greatly loved and admired by them.

She was married in 1868 to Major James Trimble and removed to Harrisonville, Missouri, where she died in 1880.

Her brother, Alexander L. Martin, was a very prominent and popular man in his day. He was a member of the Kentucky senate, and the county of Martin was named for him. His wife was a daughter of Judge George N. Brown (see sketch in this work).

John P. Martin (Mrs. Hopkins' grandfather) was a merchant, lawyer and politician of Prestonsburg, where he died in 1863. He was a member of the Kentucky legislature in 1840, and was the only Democrat in that session, "the whole legislature being a den of Whigs;" was a candidate for lieutenant governor with Linn Boyd, in opposition to Helm and Stephenson; was a very strong Southern sympathizer, and often contributed blankets and bedding to the Confederate soldiers. He was married May 14, 1835, to Elizabeth Lackey, daughter of Alexander and Mary (Morgan) Lackey. Mrs. Martin died June 18, 1889.

WILLIAM ALONZO TALIAFERRO, a leading farmer of Bracken County, son of Nicholas and Elizabeth (Kelsey) Taliaferro, was born in Bracken County, Kentucky, September 9, 1834.

His father was a native of Bracken County and was educated in the county schools; was a tanner, and had a very large trade in early days, but when the eastern manufacturers began to send their goods into his section of the country he gave up tanning and spent the remainder of his days on a farm. He was a man of fine intelligence; a Whig in politics; a Southern sympathizer during the war, and after that a Democrat; was a member of the Sons of Temperance, a Mason and a member of the Presbyterian Church. His chief characteristic was his love of home, and his highest ambition was to be a successful farmer. He died November 6, 1867, and is buried in the family burying ground on the old homestead.

Nicholas Taliaferro (grandfather) was a native of Virginia, who came to Kentucky about one hundred years ago and bought a farm of one hundred and fifty acres in Bracken County, which place he called "Grampion Hill." He served as a cavalryman in the Revolutionary war.

The genealogy of the Taliaferro family as far back as the great-grandfather of the subject of this sketch is given as follows:

Colonel William Taliaferro and his wife, Mary, daughter of Nicholas Battaile of "Hay," Caroline County, Virginia, had issue: Nicholas, born October 30, 1757, died February, 1812; married, first, Annie, daughter of Colonel John Taliaferro of "Dissington"; second, Frances Blassinggame. John, born July 31, 1753, married Ann Stockdell. Lucy, born December 15, 1755.

Nicholas had issue by his first marriage: Lucy Mary, born August 6, 1789; married Captain William Buckner of Augusta, Kentucky. John Champ, born October 12, 1784; married Susan

Buckner. Matilda B., born September 3, 1787; married Martin Marshall of Kentucky. Mary Willis, born August 11, 1789; died January 25, 1797. George Catlett, born March 21, 1792; died March 23, 1823; married Mary King. William T. (Dr.), born January 16, 1795, soldier of 1812, and a distinguished physician; married Elizabeth Ramsay. Nicholas had issue by his second marriage: Lawrence, born October 28, 1800. Nicholas, born August 14, 1806. Marshall, born March 9, 1808.

George Catlett and Mary King Taliaferro had issue: Matilda Ann, born December 28, 1814, married Colonel Alfred Souard.

John and Annie Stockdell Taliaferro had issue: Hay and John, who married, had a son, who died young, and three daughters: Anne, married Isaac Walters, and had John L., George and Alfred. Lucy, married James Bosnell, had several children. Mary, married James Bosnell; had no children.

Elizabeth Kelsey Taliaferro (mother) was born in Bracken County, January 1, 1807; was educated in the county schools; married Nicholas Taliaferro, November 5, 1829; died March 21, 1893, and lies in the family burying ground by the side of her husband.

William Kelsey (maternal grandfather) was born in Virginia, September 9, 1777, and was a farmer in Bracken County. He was married November 2, 1805, to Sallie Fee, who was born May 23, 1786. There were two children of this union: Elizabeth (mother) and Caroline, born July 6, 1810. William Kelsey died May 17, 1852, in the seventy-fifth year of his age, his wife, Sarah (Fee) Kelsey, having died on the 23d day of the preceding month, in her sixty-seventh year.

Sallie Fee Kelsey (grandmother) was a daughter of John Fee and Elizabeth Bradford Fee, who were married February 18, 1783. Elizabeth Bradford (great-grandmother) was born March 13, 1757. She was the mother of nine children. She died November 15, 1839, having survived her husband, John Fee, who died November 7, 1822.

W. A. Taliaferro's only sister, Laura Augusta Caroline Taliaferro, was born September 23, 1836. He was educated in the schools of Bracken County; bought the old Charles Gibbons farm, which has been the scene of his prosperous labors since his early manhood.

He was married November 5, 1860, to Anna J. Curtis, daughter of Nicholas and Rebecca (Petticord) Curtis. She was born November 16, 1835, and died January 10, 1865. There were three children by this union: Lizzie, born October 11, 1861; died May 28, 1862. Nicholas C., born July 24, 1863; died July 14, 1891. William A., born October 28, 1864; died July 10, 1894.

Nicholas C. Taliaferro, the second son, was a young man of superior business qualifications, very talented and highly educated, having graduated from Richmond University in the class of 1884 with the highest honors of his class. His early death was a heavy blow to the hopes of his family and many friends and admirers.

Mr. Taliaferro was married a second time, May 7, 1868, to Lizzie Pinkard, daughter of Stanfield and Rebecca (Harmon) Pinkard. She was born December 3, 1841. They have one child, Mattie, born November 26, 1869; married Carroll Asbury, May 3, 1894.

Stanfield Pinkard, Mrs. Taliaferro's father, was born March 29, 1798; died October 17, 1846.

Rebecca Harmon Pinkard was born March 26, 1803; died March 29, 1879.

Mr. Taliaferro is an elder in the Presbyterian Church; takes the part of a good citizen in the matter of politics, voting the Democratic ticket, but has never sought any position or favor at the hands of his party.

L. WESLEY GERMAN, D. D. S., M. D., a leading dentist of Louisville, an industrious worker in the Young Men's Christian Association and in the church and Sunday school, a director of one of the city missions and a member of the City Council of Louisville, is a native of Pennsylvania. He was born in Harrisburg, September 7, 1855, and is a son of E. S. and Sarah J. (Westfall) German, he a native of Harrisburg, where they now reside, and she of East Liberty, Pittsburgh, Pa.

His father was born August 3, 1822, and after learning the printer's trade and reading law he embarked in the book business in 1856, dealing principally in works of a religious character, from which occupation he retired in 1878, being succeeded by his sons, Philip and John. The latter subsequently sold out and the establishment is now conducted by Philip German. E. S. German (father) is a prominent member of and an office-bearer in the Lutheran Church. He has always been active in religious work in connection with that church; and is noted for his remarkable knowledge of the Bible, in the study of which he takes great delight, as he says, "amidst the labors of the day and in the watches of the night." Few men have a more extended and valuable knowledge of religious publications. He was twice elected to the School Board of Harrisburg, but has never aspired to political honors. His ambition has been to be useful in the promotion of true life according to the teachings, example and spirit of Christ, and has recently organized the New Church (Swedenborgian) in Harrisburg.

Philip German (grandfather) was a native of Meyerstown, Pennsylvania, and became a brewer in Harrisburg. He was a volunteer soldier and corporal in the War of 1812, and marched to Baltimore with others at the time of the attack of the British on that city. His regiment was quartered outside of the city ready to participate in the battle when the English commander was shot and the victory won by the patriots. Following the war, he removed to Harrisburg, where he was engaged in his former business until his accidental death in 1855. He married Mary Elizabeth Hirsh, whose mother was Catherine Seltzer and her grandmother was Catherine Linde of Stockholm, Sweden. Her father was from Wittenberg, Germany. The father of Philip German (grandfather) and his father's father were natives of Germany, near Heidelberg; and it is definitely known that they were members of the Lutheran Church.

Sarah J. Westfall German (mother) was born in East Liberty, Pittsburgh, Pennsylvania, June 12, 1823, and is now a resident of Harrisburg, a member of the Lutheran Church, and has been a willing helper in the work in which her husband has been engaged in the church and in the Sunday school.

Simeon Westfall (grandfather) kept a shoe store in Wilkinsburg. He left that business and engaged in hauling merchandise between Philadelphia and Pittsburgh before the day of canals and railroads. He married Hannah Barr of Harrisburg, and after living for a time in East Liberty, where Dr. German's mother was born, he removed to Harrisburg and spent the remainder of his life there.

Robert Barr (great-grandfather) was a Scotch-Irish Presbyterian, a stone mason by occupation, who came to America in 1770. The oath of allegiance which he took before the formation of the government is framed and kept as an heirloom by a member of the family.

L. Wesley German was educated in the High School of Harrisburg and at Pennsylvania State College, Pennsylvania. In November, 1874, he began the study of dentistry and was graduated from the Philadelphia Dental College in 1878. He had charge of a dental office in Polo, Illinois, for one year prior to this. After completing his course in the Dental College he returned to Polo, Illinois, and practiced dentistry there for one year; and in the fall of 1879 he located permanently in Louisville, where his success was at once assured.

He identified himself with religious work in the Lutheran Church and in the Young Men's Christian Association, and in 1880 was elected a member of the Board of Managers of the Y. M. C. A. One year later he was elected one of the secretaries of that association, which office he held for three years, when he was again elected a member of the Board of Managers, and one year after was made treasurer, in which capacity he served for three and a half years.

Dr. German is a hard working member of the Lutheran Church and is the teacher of a large young men's Bible class in the Sunday school, and has been particularly active in missionary work, having helped to organize three congregations as the result of work in which he has been associated with others. He was a deacon in the First Lutheran Church and assistant superintendant of the Sunday school; was an elder in St. Paul Lutheran Church, having assisted in the organization of the two last named and also one other church.

Dr. German is an active member of a number

of benevolent orders, having been several times dictator in the Knights of Honor and a member of the State Grand Lodge of that order, and was regent for several terms in the Royal Arcanum. He is also a member of the Masonic fraternity.

He was one of the fifty citizens who went to Pittsburgh to secure the Twenty-ninth Annual Grand Army Encampment of the Republic for Louisville, and was an indefatigable worker in the preparations in the city for that notable event.

In November, 1895, Dr. German was elected a member of the City Council, representing the Sixth Ward, and was urged to accept the presidency of the board, but declined the honor.

He is not only a dentist, but is also a graduate of the Kentucky School of Medicine, class of 1888, and was for a time a practicing physician until his dental work required all of his time. He is still a diligent student of medicine and dental surgery, keeping up with the times through the best medical literature of the day.

Dr. German was married July 18, 1889, to Orrel M. Davis, daughter of George Davis of Louisville, and they have one child, Marguerite Elizabeth.

JAMES H. PARRISH, Banker and Insurance Agent of Owensboro, son of Isaac Newton and Elizabeth (Givens) Parrish, was born in Bullitt County, Kentucky, February 28, 1855. His father was born in Goochland County, Virginia, April 4, 1818. His education was obtained by his own efforts, as the sum total of his schooling was one month in the common school. He came to Kentucky with his father in 1822, who settled in Jefferson County, afterward a part of Nelson, and still later a part of Bullitt County, and was a resident of three different counties without changing his location. He went to Louisville when sixteen years of age and learned the tailor's trade; returned to Bullitt County, and followed that occupation until 1865. He was drafted during the war, but was exempted on account of having artificial teeth. After the close of the war he removed to Owensboro and was engaged in tailoring there until 1878, when he became interested with his son in the wholesale and retail book business, the firm name being W. E. & I. N. Parrish. He was a prominent member of the Methodist Church, and a trustee of Settle Chapel. He was twice married, first to Martha Amos, a native of Jefferson County, Kentucky. Two children of this union died in infancy. The second wife, to whom he was married in October, 1846, was Elizabeth Givens. Their children were: Jane Givens, wife of William A. Brotherton, of Owensboro; George W. and John Otis, wholesale book dealers in Owensboro; James Howard, the subject of this sketch; Arthur Lee, assistant cashier of the Owensboro Savings Bank; Lizzie Sue, now living with her mother in Owensboro; William E., wholesale book dealer. Isaac N., who began business as a newspaper carrier, graduated from the Owensboro High School at the age of sixteen, and in 1890 was elected cashier in a bank. He was married February 10, 1895, to Mattie B. Haney; Walter Benjamin, died March 1883, and Mary Martha.

Nelson Parrish (grandfather) was a native of Goochland County, Virginia; came to Jefferson County in 1803; was a farmer and cooper, and married a Miss Cosby of Virginia, who died in Bullitt County. He was the father of eight children: Milton W., Marion, Lester, Edwin, Elizabeth, Isaac N., Rebecca and Lucien.

George Givens (maternal grandfather) was born in Lincoln County in 1792. He was a farmer, a Democrat in politics and member of the Baptist Church. He married Mary Simpson and was the father of seven children: Elizabeth (mother), William, Joseph, Agnes, Samuel, Jane and Sallie: They removed from Lincoln to Daviess County in 1860 and he died there in 1864, aged seventy-two years.

The great-grandfather Givens was a native of Virginia, who emigrated to Kentucky and lived on a farm at Fort McKinney, in Lincoln County, and the widow of one of his sons is still living on that farm at a greatly advanced age.

James H. Parrish was educated in the schools of Owensboro; learned the printing trade in the office of the Owensboro Monitor, when Thomas H. Pettit was proprietor; remained in that office five years; was employed in the office of the Examiner, of which Lee Lumpkin was editor; became clerk in the Owensboro Savings Bank in

1877, and within one year was made cashier. T. S. Anderson, president of the bank, withdrew in 1884, and Mr. Parrish and others bought his interest, since which time he purchased the other stockholders' shares and is now the owner and cashier of the bank in which he began as a clerk. He is a member of the insurance firm of Stirman & Parrish, and is one of the most progressive business men of the city.

In past years he was a Democrat, but is not associated with any political party, preferring to vote according to his judgment and to support the best man regardless of his political affiliations.

He has been a member of the Baptist Church since he was twelve years of age and a deacon for many years; has been superintendent of and is teacher of a primary class in the Sunday school, and is greatly interested in the work of the school and the church.

Mr. Parrish was married June 14, 1881, to Jessie Moorman, daughter of Silas Mercer Moorman, who was for many years a merchant in Breckinridge County; was in the Confederate army as quartermaster under General Buckner, and was promoted to the rank of major; was in the service three years and died of camp fever at La Grange, Georgia, in 1863, and is buried there. His wife was Sarah Talbott, who was born in New Market, Tenn. Their children were: George, Edward, Sallie, Henry, Hetty, Belle, Guy, Tennessee and Jessie (wife).

Mrs. Parrish was educated in Owensboro, and at a private school in New Orleans. Of the four children born to Mr. and Mrs. Parrish, Moorman, who was born March 12, 1886, is the only one living. Nora, born July 24, 1882, died June 21, 1890; Sarah Moorman, born June 25, 1884, died August 31, 1884; Maria Louise, born March 8, 1890, died March 31, 1890.

MILTON C. RUSSELL, wholesale grocer of Maysville, one of the most conspicuous and successful business men of Northern Kentucky, was born in Maysville April 6, 1844.

His father, Christopher Russell, was born in England in 1814 and came to America in 1821, locating in Wilmington, Delaware, from which place he removed to Maysville in 1839. He was one of the leading contractors and builders of his time and built many houses in Maysville. Having reached his eightieth year, he died in 1894. His wife was Mary Maule, a native of Pennsylvania. Her father, John Maule, was also a native of that state and a son of John Maule, who was a native of Scotland.

Milton C. Russell was educated principally in Rand and Richeson's Seminary in Maysville. Leaving school when sixteen years of age he began his business career as a salesman in the grocery of John H. Richeson, with whom he remained for four years, when he accepted a similar position with Dudley A. Richardson, remaining with him as salesman until 1881, when he acquired an interest in the house. This partnership continued until July, 1886, when the whilom clerk bought out the proprietor, and from that time he has been the controlling spirit in the affairs of an ever increasing business.

In 1892 the old house was torn away and the present elegant five-story building was erected in its stead, giving Mr. Russell and his sons more room and better facilities and adding a valuable improvement to the city. This house, 42x80 feet, is filled with goods, embracing a stock of about $50,000 in value, and is one of the best equipped and most thoroughly stocked jobbing houses in the state. The trade, while not far reaching, being confined chiefly to adjacent counties, is kept well in hand by traveling salesmen. In 1890 his son, James B. Russell, became a partner in the establishment, and another son, Thomas M. Russell, is now associated with him in business.

Mr. Russell is president of the Union Trust Company (capital $50,000), of which he was one of the organizers. He is secretary of the Mason County Building & Loan Association, one of the most substantial associations of that character in the state. Beginning life as a clerk without any pecuniary assistance and without capital, save industry and a marvelous capacity for business, he has forced himself to the front, and is now recognized as one of the most progressive and substantial business men of Maysville, thoroughly respected and trusted and greatly admired for his fine traits of character and superior business acumen.

He is prominently identified with the leading benevolent fraternities, being a Knight Templar in Masonry, an Odd Fellow and a Knight of Pythias and Red Men.

Mr. Russell was married in 1865 to Elexene P. Johnson of Maysville, and has three sons, two of whom are associated with him in business. Christopher D. Russell has embarked in business on his own account as wholesale and retail dealer in queensware, glassware, in Maysville.

REV. WALLACE L. NOURSE, pastor of the Ninth Street Presbyterian Church of Hopkinsville, was born in Bardstown, Kentucky, November 30, 1834. His father, Charles Nourse, was also born in Bardstown, was educated in the schools of that place, and engaged in mercantile business there when twenty-two years of age. He was a man of great force of character, a prominent and influential member of the Presbyterian Church, a Whig in politics, whose convictions were as freely and openly expressed as they were firm and decided. He spent most of his life in Bardstown, but removed to Jefferson County, where he died in 1865, in the seventy-fifth year of his age.

James Nourse (grandfather) was born in Virginia, emigrated to Kentucky when he was a young man and became a prominent lawyer of Harrodsburg. He was a man of great influence and personal magnetism and made friends wherever he was known. He was agent of a Kentucky Land Company and transacted a great deal of business for the early settlers of the state.

James Nourse (great-grandfather) was a native of England, who emigrated to Virginia, and died there in 1780.

Rosa Logan Nourse (mother) was a daughter of Judge William Logan and Priscilla Wallace, and was born in Shelby County in 1802. She lived to the extreme age of ninety-one years, and was hale and hearty and was an interested reader of the newspapers and the literature of the day until within a short time before her death, which occurred in Louisville, November, 1895.

William Logan (maternal grandfather) was born in Fort Asaph, near Harrodsburg, December 8, 1876, and was the first white child born in the State of Kentucky. Collins states that of the early born sons of Kentucky "he was the most gifted and eminent." He was a judge of the Court of Appeals for many years; was United States Senator in 1819-20, resigning his seat in the Senate to become a candidate for governor of Kentucky during the old and new court controversy, but was not elected; was a member of the Constitutional Convention in 1799 and frequently a member of the Kentucky Legislature from both Lincoln and Shelby Counties, and three times speaker of the house. He died August 8, 1822, aged forty-six years. His father was General Ben Logan of pioneer fame.

Wallace L. Nourse was educated in the Presbyterian schools of Bardstown and attended the Presbyterian Theological Seminary at Danville, teaching school in the meantime, and was licensed to preach by the Presbytery of Louisville in 1862. He began his work in the ministry in Daviess and Hancock Counties. In connection with the Synod of Kentucky he removed to Rockport, Indiana, in 1869; remained there for sixteen years, and was instrumental in building several churches in that vicinity, to which he made liberal contributions in time, labor and money. In 1885 he went to Hopkinsville, where he has accomplished a good work in building up the church, and has sustained his reputation as one of the ablest preachers and finest pulpit orators in that section of the state.

He married (first) Louisa Bell of Owensboro, in 1864, by whom he has two children living and one deceased. In 1875 he married (second) Sadie, daughter of James Bartrim of Rockport, Indiana, who is the mother of eight children.

HUGH RAY RIFFE, druggist of Bellevue, son of Dr. John M. and Mary A. (Ray) Riffe, was born in Winchester, Clark County, Kentucky, September 17, 1858. His father, Dr. John M. Riffe, is a native of Liberty, Casey County, and is now living in Covington, where he has been a practicing physician for more than a quarter of a century. He is a man of great piety and is loved and respected by a host of friends, not only in the Christian Church, of which he is a member, but in the entire community. He is now well advanced in years, having passed three-score and ten, but he is quite active and is greatly devoted to his profession, in which his services are as much in demand as when he was younger.

George Chilton Riffe (grandfather) was born in Casey County in 1802. He was educated for the medical profession, and studied medicine under Dr. Ephraim McDowell of Danville, but his preference was for agricultural life, and he never entered the active profession of medicine. He was a farmer all his life after completing his studies, but being a man of more than ordinary intelligence and of excellent education he was frequently elected to the legislature, serving in the lower house in 1838-40, and in the Senate from 1862 to 1870. He was magistrate in Casey County for many years, and was prominent in all of the affairs of interest to his county. He was married March 17, 1823, to Elizabeth Blaine Anderson, daughter of Walter Anderson of Virginia, and was the father of nine children, of whom Dr. John M. Riffe was the eldest. He was a man of great strength of character and a member of the Christian Church, whose daily life was in keeping with his profession.

Christopher Riffe (great-grandfather) was born in Pennsylvania in 1765. At the age of seventeen he was married to Polly Spears of Virginia, and came to Kentucky, at first locating in Harrodsburg, but he subsequently removed to Casey County. He served in the War of 1812 under General Shelby, in the commissary department, receiving the title of general. He represented the counties of Casey and Russell in the Legislature for sixteen years. He was a very intimate friend of Daniel Boone, Simon Kenton and other distinguished Kentucky pioneers. He died in 1850 in the eighty-fifth year of his age.

Walter Anderson (maternal grandfather) was a Virginian and a Baptist minister, but connected himself with the Christian Church about the time of its organization. He married Sarah Ann Blaine, daughter of Alexander Blaine. He died in 1862, aged ninety-one years, and she in 1877. Her father was aide-de-camp to General Washington, and was a relative of James G. Blaine. The family was originally from Ireland.

Hugh R. Riffe was educated principally in the public and high schools of Covington, to which place his parents had removed when he was twelve years of age. He began business as a clerk in the drug store of his brother, John M. Riffe, Jr., and at the age of nineteen began business in the same line on his own account. In 1887 he removed to Bellevue, where he has continued in the drug business, at the same time trading more or less in real estate, and has acquired some valuable property.

He was married April 24, 1883, to Mamie Lee Cassiday, daughter of the late James A. Cassiday of Covington, and they have three children: James M., Hugh Ray, Jr., and Laura Cassiday.

A. F. GOETZE, a leading druggist of Dayton, was born in Cincinnati, October 21, 1858. He is a son of August and Sophia (Hartman) Goetze. His father was born in Cassel, Germany, June 9, 1829, and came to America and located in Cincinnati, July 16, 1854. He received a good education in Germany and at once stepped into prominence in Cincinnati, where he was engaged in the wholesale hat business until 1882, when he removed to Dayton, Kentucky. In 1883 he was elected city treasurer of Dayton, and when he took charge of that office the little city was overwhelmed with debt. Its bonds were held at from 60 to 75 cents on the dollar, and there were no purchasers willing to take them at any price. Mr. Goetze proved a very able financier, and in ten years he paid every debt, including bonds to the amount of $40,000 in the Jamestown district. There are few more popular or useful citizens of Dayton than August Goetze.

Herman Goetze (grandfather) was born in Cassel, Germany, June 29, 1778, and was a resident of that country all his life.

Sophia Hartman Goetze (mother) was born in Cassel, Germany, May 14, 1830, and received a fine education in that country. Her marriage to Mr. Goetze took place on his arrival in this country in July, 1854, and they have spent over forty years of married life together. She is a daughter of Valentine Hartman, who was born in Germany May 13, 1779, and died there May 17, 1846. His wife, Sophia, was born August 22, 1800, and died May 22, 1830.

A. F. Goetze was educated in the public schools of Cincinnati, finishing with credit to himself when sixteen years of age. He attended the Cincinnati College of Pharmacy in 1876, and was graduated in 1878, and while pursuing his pharmaceutical studies was employed in a drug store in Dayton, and after completing his course located in that city permanently, and has now one of the best retail drug stores in Campbell County.

Mr. Goetze is a Republican in politics, as is his venerable father, and is prominent as a Mason and Knight of Pythias.

He was married March 12, 1884, to Lula M. Jones, daughter of Thomas Jones, a prominent politician of Dayton. Mrs. Goetze was born April 15, 1863. Their only child, Earl, was born December 24, 1884.

JOHN C. HOOE, Railroad Ticket and Freight Agent and Agent of the Adams Express Company at Lawrenceburg, was born in Mercer County, Kentucky, August 21, 1860. His father, William Archer Hooe, was born in Virginia, in 1809, and at the age of twenty-two years came to Harrodsburg, and after studying law began the practice of his profession in Harrodsburg. He retired from active work a few years before his death in 1869. He was twice a member of the Kentucky Legislature and was a prominent and popular man in political affairs. His father was a Virginian, who died in his native place.

Sue B. (Burford) Hooe, mother of the subject of this sketch, was born in Harrodsburg August 24, 1843, and is still a resident of that city.

Elijah Burford (maternal grandfather) was born in Indiana in 1801, and removed to Harrodsburg in 1820, where he lived to be eighty-six years old. He was a general merchant in Harrodsburg for fifty years.

John C. Hooe enjoyed the usual advantages of the country boy in the way of schools, and completed his studies at Daughters' College, Harrodsburg. At the age of seventeen began a successful business career as clerk in a store. After one year of service in this capacity he accepted a position as clerk in the office of the Southwestern Railroad Company. Three years later he was appointed agent of the company at Harrodsburg, which position he resigned five years later to become superintendent of the Southwestern Railroad. He held this important office for seven years and resigned to accept the office of superintendent of construction on the Louisville Southern Railroad, and held that position for eighteen months, when he was made general agent of the Louisville Southern, with headquarters at Harrodsburg. When the Monon people leased the road he was made traveling auditor of the Louisville Southern line, and after two years of service as auditor he resigned and became superintendent of the T. B. Ripy Distillery at Lawrenceburg, and was there for six years when he again resigned to accept the position of ticket and freight agent in connection with the Adams Express Company's agency at Lawrenceburg, and this is the only position he has ever held that he has not resigned.

Mr. Hooe was married November 23, 1884, to Mary V. Roemer of St. Louis. She died September 30, 1885. He was married again November 3, 1891, to Maggie Crenshaw of Georgetown, and she died May 19, 1895.

Mr. Hooe is an active and influential member of the Christian Church, and a member of the Order of Maccabees. He has one son, R. B. Hooe, the child of his first wife.

C. B. HAYGOOD, City Clerk of Dayton, son of Susan (Von Gundy) and Plato Haygood, was born in Cincinnati, January 28, 1852. His father was born in Geneva, New York, in 1816; spent his school days in Cleveland, Ohio, and was a clerk in many of the leading hotels in the large cities, including Cleveland, Columbus, Ohio, St. Louis and New Orleans. He was a pure, good man, a member of the Presbyterian Church, an Odd Fellow and a thirty-second degree Mason. He died in Cincinnati in 1876, at the age of sixty years, and is buried near that city in Spring Grove Cemetery. His ancestors came from Scotland.

Susan Von Gundy Haygood (mother) was born in Hamilton County, Ohio, in 1827, and was educated in the common schools. She and Plato Haygood were married in 1850, and she survives him, being now a resident of Dayton. Her father, Christian Von Gundy, was a native of Germany.

C. B. Haygood, subject of this sketch, was educated in the splendid schools of Cincinnati, graduating from the high school in 1868. He began business as a clerk in the well known wholesale grocery establishment of Babbitt, Harkness & Co. of Cincinnati and was with them for ten years. He then engaged in the retail grocery business on his own account in Dayton and was thus engaged for seven years.

In 1879 he was elected city assessor; was a member of the City Council from the Third Ward in 1885; was elected city clerk in 1886, and has held that office four consecutive terms, rendering service that has given entire satisfaction to the citizens. He takes an active and leading part in Republican politics; is a Mason, Odd Fellow, Knight of Pythias and a member of the Presbyterian Church, in all of which organizations he takes a lively interest.

Mr. Haygood and Mary Brooks, daughter of Samuel Brooks, were married June 19, 1873. She is a native of Columbus, Ohio. They have four children: Clarence, born May 8, 1876; Walter, born October, 23, 1878; Alma, born July 22, 1889, and Dallas, born April 26, 1893.

MARTIN J. BROWN, a popular lawyer of Newport, was born in Warsaw, Ohio, May 30, 1860. His father, Frederick Brown, was born in Germany in 1822 and came to America in 1847. He lived in Cincinnati until 1869, when he removed to Newport. He was a blacksmith and followed his trade with great industry and success. He died in 1883, aged sixty-one years. He married Margaret Miller, a native of Germany, near Baden, who survives him.

Martin J. Brown came to Newport with his parents when nine years of age, and received his primary education in the Catholic schools of Delhi, Ohio, and at St. Michaels in Cincinnati. He then spent some time at St. Vincent, Westmoreland County, Pennsylvania, finishing at Xavier College, Cincinnati; studied law with A. T. Root, then city attorney of Newport, and was admitted to the practice of law September 25, 1880. He has had a very successful career as an attorney at law, having a large general practice and being attorney for a number of building associations, to which he has given much attention. He is a Democrat, but takes no active part in politics. He and his mother are members of the Roman Catholic Church, as was his father.

Mr. Brown was married January 10, 1882, to Hattie Kearney, daughter of James Kearney, deceased, of Newport. She died in 1892, leaving two sons and three daughters: Hattie, Mary, Lilian, George and Martin J. Brown, Jr.

ISAAC P. GOULD, M. D., one of the rising young physicians of Bellevue, was born in Newport, Kentucky, April 28, 1871, and is the son of Isaac P. and Dora A. (Martin) Gould. His father was a native of Raleigh, North Carolina, who came to Newport in 1865, and while living there was engaged for twenty years in the wholesale shoe business in Cincinnati. He subsequently removed to Lexington. He was a member of the Methodist Episcopal Church, and was Grand Master of the State Lodge of Free and Accepted Masons. He died in Bellevue in 1895, aged forty-five years. His father was a native of Raleigh, North Carolina, and a minister in the Methodist Episcopal Church. He died in Cincinnati, Ohio, in 1867, while on a visit to that city, aged forty years. The Goulds are of English descent.

Dora A. Martin Gould (mother) is a native of Newport, now living in Bellevue, and is one of the honored members of the Methodist Episcopal Church.

John Martin (grandfather) was a native of Memphis, Tennessee. He came to Newport in 1860 and made that city his home most of the time until his death. He was a ship builder, and built gunboats during the war, and was extensively engaged in shipbuilding in Baltimore. He reached the age of seventy-eight years and died in 1893 at Dayton, Kentucky. He was of Scotch-Irish extraction. Mr. Martin was a Republican and a man of great force of character. He was quite prominent during the war, serving his country in the line of his business as faithfully as many who served upon the battlefield.

Dr. Isaac P. Gould is a graduate of the Bellevue High School and spent several years in college. After leaving school he read medicine with Professor Fred Kabler of Cincinnati for a time, and then attended the Ohio Medical College at

Cincinnati, graduating in 1891. He then took a year's course in the New York Polyclinical Medical College, and in 1892 began the practice of medicine in Bellevue. His thorough preparation for his high calling enabled him to take rank almost at once among older and more experienced physicians, and he has met with phenomenal success, both from a business point of view and as a physician of the highest qualifications.

JOHN H. LEATHERS, Cashier of the Louisville Banking Company, son of William and Elizabeth (Hess) Leathers, was born in Middleway, a small town in Jefferson County, near Martinsburg, now West Virginia, April 27, 1841. There are few business men in Louisville or elsewhere who have been more successful through strictly honest and legitimate means than has Captain Leathers. He holds many offices of trust and honor, which have been thrust upon him on account of his business qualifications, fine judgment and his unswerving integrity, and, as will be seen from this brief sketch, he has reached his present enviable position among the first men of the city by his own efforts and without financial aid from friends or relatives.

His father, William Leathers, was born in Orange County, Virginia, where he was a farmer for some years, but removed to Berkeley County (now West Virginia), in 1850, and died there in 1872. He was a member of the Methodist Church and was licensed as a local preacher. His sympathies were with the South during the Civil strife, but he was then past the military age and did not enlist.

Captain Leather's mother was a daughter of Peter Hess, a sturdy German blacksmith of Berks County, Pennsylvania, who removed about the year 1810 to the Shenandoah Valley, where there was a large settlement of Pennsylvania people. She was educated in Virginia and during her early years was a member of the Lutheran Church, but after her marriage she joined the Methodist Church, of which she was a faithful member until her death, which occurred in Martinsburg in 1870.

The Hess family came from Germany and settled in Pennsylvania. The Leathers are of English descent.

Captain John H. Leathers was educated in Martinsburg, Virginia, receiving the best instruction afforded in the common schools, and then pursuing his studies in the higher branches under the teaching of his uncle, John Hess, a man of great learning, who held the office of county surveyor almost during his whole life and taught school in connection with his duties as surveyor. He belonged to the old school and was a thorough teacher, under whose guidance some of the most distinguished men of Virginia—who will remember him most kindly and gratefully—received their early training.

When about fifteen years of age Mr. Leathers began his business career in a country store, and after about two years' experience there he came to Louisville in 1859. He lost no time in finding employment in the drug store of Cary & Talbot, then located on Market, near Fourth street, and after working for that firm about eighteen months, he secured a place as bookkeeper for William Terry & Company, wholesale clothiers, Sixth and Main streets. He held that position until the spring of 1861, when the war began, and went back to his home in Virginia and enlisted as a private in Company D, Second Regiment Virginia Infantry, which was afterward a part of the famous Stonewall Brigade. Mr. Leathers served with this regiment in most of its campaigns; was taken prisoner at the battle of the Wilderness and was released only a month or two before the final surrender. He was a prisoner at Point Lookout, Maryland, and Fort Delaware. He was wounded in battle at Gettysburg, after two days' fighting, and had many other thrilling experiences, escapes and exploits. The highest rank he attained in actual service was that of sergeant-major of his regiment, which rank he held at the time of the surrender, his present military title of captain, by which he is familiarly known, having been earned in the militia in the service of his state.

After the close of the war he returned to Louisville and secured employment as bookkeeper for the wholesale clothing house of Jones & Tapp, and after two years became a member of the firm of Jones, Tapp & Company. Mr. Jones retired in about a year and the firm name was changed to Tapp, Leathers & Company, in which he continued an active member until 1885, when he was offered the position of cashier of the Louisville Banking Company. This he accepted, retaining his interest in the firm of Tapp, Leathers & Company for several years, but finally sold out, the firm still continuing in the same name.

Captain Leathers is a deacon in the Second Presbyterian Church and president of the Board of Trustees of that congregation; vice-president of the Kentucky Humane Society; president of the Board of Managers of the School of Reform (House of Refuge), president of the Newsboys' Home, grand treasurer of the Grand Lodge of Masons, president of the National Building & Loan Association of Kentucky, resident vice-president of the National Security Company of Kansas City, Missouri, and many equally important offices, mostly of a financial and business nature, which have not been sought by him, but have been urged upon him.

Captain Leathers was married March 12, 1868, to Kate Armstrong, daughter of C. Q. Armstrong of Louisville. She was educated in Mrs. Nold's Louisville Female College, graduating in 1867. They have four children: Charles F., employed by the Louisville Banking Co.; Annie, graduate of Hampton College, Louisville; Allen, assistant superintendent of the registry department of the Louisville postoffice, and Stuart Robinson, now in the public schools.

WALTER HOLLADAY DADE, physician and surgeon of the penitentiary at Frankfort, and practicing physician in that city, was born February 28, 1865, in Edgehill, Louisa County, Virginia, a small village near the head of the Shenandoah Valley.

His father, Henry Fitzhugh Dade, is a native of Albemarle County, Virginia, whose wife and General Fitzhugh Lee's wife were cousins. He entered the Confederate army at the beginning of the Civil war and was captain of the Monticello Guards from Charlottesville, and was with General Lee throughout the war and at the final surrender at Appomattox. His father, Albert Gallatin Dade, would have been exempt from military service on account of his age, but he served throughout the war as chief of the commissary department of General Lee's army. He was a very wealthy man when the war began and had great confidence in the success of the Confederacy, contributing largely to the cause, and this, with the ravages of war, left him almost penniless when the war was over.

The Dades are of pure Anglo-Saxon ancestry, which is traced to William, Earl of Sterling. The family was one of the most prominent in Virginia, where they were among the very earliest settlers.

Captain Jack Dade (uncle) is mentioned in Ridpath's History of the World as having been killed in the Seminole war. He and several others were on a reconnoitering expedition when they were surprised and surrounded by the Indians and every one of the party was killed. Captain Dade was one of the bravest men of his time and was a principal in a number of duels, surviving his chivalrous antagonists only to be slain by the sneaking Indians.

Mary Holladay Dade (mother) was a daughter of Walter and Sallie Barrett Holladay of Louisa County, Virginia. Her father's parents were natives of Scotland.

Dr. Walter H. Dade left Virginia when seven years of age and removed with his parents to Henderson, Kentucky, where he attended Reubelt's select school and the Henderson High School, graduating when sixteen years of age. He was a clerk in a shoe store in that city for three years when he began the study of medicine with Dr. Archibald Dixon; went to college two years and in the spring of 1886 entered Bellevue Medical College, from which he was graduated in 1888. He served two years in the Harlem dispensary of Bellevue Hospital doing surgical work exclusively, after which he served on the New York Board of Health, an appointment which he received after a competitive examination, in which there were one hundred and sixty-two applicants for the seventeen places which were to be filled. Dr. Dade stood second in this examination and received the highest compliment from the Board of Examiners. He held this important position in New York City for one year, when, on account of failing health and at the instance of Governor

Brown, he removed to Frankfort, February 10, 1892. There he accepted the appointment of the sinking fund commissioners as physician and surgeon of the State Prison, which position he holds at present. Dr. Dade, although a general practitioner, has been remarkably successful in surgery, making that his specialty; and there are few more skillful surgeons in the state. In order to improve his knowledge and proficiency in that important branch of his profession he contemplates taking a full course in surgery and in the treatment of diseases of women in the University of Vienna.

Dr. Dade is a member of the Knights of Pythias, a member of the New York County Medical Association, of the Kentucky State Medical Society and the Franklin County Medical Society. He is a regular contributor to the medical journals, writing about one article a month, and lectures on physiology in the Frankfort High Schools.

Dr. Dade was married June 1, 1893, to Blanche Farra of Lexington, and she died April 22, 1894.

CHURCHILL HADEN BLAKEY was born August 26, 1829, on his father's farm near Shakertown, Logan County, Kentucky, in the first brick house ever built in the county. He spent his boyhood days there, and was educated at Russellville, Kentucky, Academy, first under the superintendency of Mr. French and later under Professor William Wines. He married Mary C. Becker in March, 1855, daughter of Theodore Becker, who was a native of France, and a soldier under Bonaparte, having been brought to America by the English as a prisoner of war. Their children were: Thomas W., Theodore B., Churchill, Nellie, Hubert, Clayton B., George D., Lou and Mary. He was a farmer, and served as magistrate for a number of years, succeeding his father; was elected three times as member of the Kentucky Legislature as a Democrat, first in 1871, serving contemporary with John G. Carlisle, J. C. S. Blackburn and James B. McCreary; was chairman of Committee on Charitable Institutions and other important committees. He was distinguished for his quaint humor, and had an inexhaustible supply of anecdotes, which he could relate with great zest and with good effect to illustrate a point or entertain his friends. While in the Legislature he opposed the bill for establishing an immigration bureau, and in his speech said: "I am in favor of keeping Kentucky for Kentuckians." He was credited with being the originator of the expression, "He bit off more than he can chaw."

He was a Master Mason, a member of the Baptist Church, superintendent of the Sunday school, and served as moderator of the Baptist Association for several years, an office seldom conferred upon a layman; was a strong advocate of the temperance cause, and secured while in the Legislature the prohibition of the liquor traffic in Auburn, Logan County, Kentucky. He died at his home in Auburn, Kentucky, April 28, 1895. His parents were Ann Whitsitt and Thomas Blakey, early settlers of Logan County, Kentucky. His father was a physician and farmer. Also served as magistrate under the old constitution for a number of years, and also by succession as sheriff of the county. He lived and died on the old Blakey homestead, near Shakertown, in 1842, aged sixty-three years.

George Blakey (grandfather) was born in Culpeper County, Virginia, November 22, 1749, and married Margaret Whitsitt. He was a soldier of the Revolution under Washington, and died on his farm, "Rural Choice," Logan County, Kentucky, September 8, 1842, aged ninety-four years. His maternal grandmother was Margaret Douglas of Scotland.

George Douglas Blakey, a son of George and Margaret W., and uncle of Churchill H. Blakey, was quite prominent as a politician and statesman. He was one of the early advocates of the abolition of slavery, and being a large slave holder emancipated them several years before the war of the rebellion. He was a candidate for governor of Kentucky on the abolition ticket with Cassius M. Clay; was a member of the Constitutional Convention in 1849, and was internal revenue collector under Lincoln. He died at Bowling Green, Kentucky, in 1885, aged seventy-five years. Thomas and Ann Hadin Blakey (great-grandfather and mother) emigrated from England to America and settled in Virginia.

Churchill Blakey (great-great-grandfather)

married Miss Sallie George of Wales. Churchill H. Blakey had no brother, but a cousin, George T. Blakey, was raised in his father's family. And they loved and esteemed each other as brothers during their entire lifetime. George T. Blakey, being the elder, was born in Logan County, Kentucky, in 1821. He was sheriff of his county, and though of different political faith (being a Republican) they alternated as members of the Kentucky Legislature. He was several times a delegate to the National Republican Conventions, and was one of the faithful three hundred and six who stood by General U. S. Grant in his memorable contest for a third term in 1880. He lives at Auburn, Logan County, Kentucky.

JAMES D. BLACK, leading lawyer of Barboursville, son of John C. Black and Clarissa Jones, was born in Knox County, Kentucky, in 1850. His father was born in South Carolina in 1805 and came to Knox County with his father when three years of age and became a well-to-do farmer in that county, in which he made his home until his death in 1876. He was devoted to farming and held no office except that of justice of the peace, in which he served his county for many years.

Alexander Black (grandfather) was a native of Ireland, who came to South Carolina when he was a young man, and removed to Knox County, Kentucky, about 1808, and was a farmer there during the remaining days of a well spent life.

Clarissa Jones Black (mother) was a native of Clay County, Kentucky, and died in Knox County in 1862, aged sixty-five years. Her father, Isaac Jones, was a prosperous farmer in Clay County. The great-grandfather of the subject of this sketch, on his mother's side, came from France to this country during the Revolutionary war, it is said, with Lafayette, and was a soldier on the side of the colonies in their struggle for independence. So there is an intermixture of French and Irish blood in Mr. Black's veins.

James D. Black found time during his farm life to attend such common schools as were then in his neighborhood, and by close application he acquired such education as these scanty opportunities afforded. He was never known to ignore any chance within his reach to learn, and before he reached his legal age he was employed as a teacher. By this means he acquired sufficient means to enter college. He did not miss this opportunity, for from early boyhood he was possessed with a strong and abiding ambition to enter the profession of the law, and applied himself with much zeal to preparing himself for this higher pursuit. He attended school at Greenville and Tusculum College in East Tennessee, where he reached a high standing in scholarship. Returning home he again went to teaching for the purpose of replenishing his finances and to enable him to take up the study of law. He began reading law; was duly admitted to the bar, and subsequent events have shown the wisdom of his choice in selecting that profession, for no man in his section of the state has achieved greater success than has come to him. He is a profound civil lawyer, and a fine practitioner. As an advocate he has no superior within the range of that entire section of the state, if, indeed, he has an equal. He has never shown any predilection to politics, having time and again been urged by admiring friends to enter the arena of politics, but he has uniformly declined. But notwithstanding his aversion to office seeking for himself he has many times done valuable services in that direction for his friends. When barely of eligible age he was, even against his own desire, taken up by his friends and elected to the Legislature of his state over an adverse political majority of more than one thousand votes, and after one of the most exciting and hard fought battles ever known in that legislative district. In the Legislature he at once took a high standing, and maintained a commanding prestige during the entire session, giving to his constituents universal satisfaction. He was petitioned by leading men of both parties to announce himself for re-election, but declined to do so. He then began actively the practice of law, and from that time till now his career has been brilliant and successful, bringing to him not only more than a competency but a constantly widening and increasing practice. His people still recognizing his merits elected him school commissioner of his county, giving him the vote of every elector over a number of opponents. In 1873 he became a member of the Masonic fraternity, and in 1886 was elected Grand Junior Warden and successively Grand Senior Warden, Deputy Grand Master and Grand Master of the Grand Lodge of Kentucky. While holding the highest office within the gift of the Masons of Kentucky a serious question of Masonic jurisdiction came up for adjudication by him, and by his able handling of that question he permanently settled the contest, and his decision was sustained by the Grand Lodge when that exalted body assembled to pass upon the acts of the Grand Master.

In 1893 the governor of Kentucky, recognizing Mr. Black's worth, made him commissioner to the World's Fair for the State of Kentucky. By the division of the duties among the members of that commission the Departments of Minerals and Forestry were given to Mr. Black. When the great fair was opened but few states in the Union had any better exhibit in minerals or timber than Kentucky. This gratifying result was largely due to the efficient services of Mr. Black.

It may be truthfully said that in all the varied experiences and wide range of this man's active life he has never failed to do his whole duty.

James D. Black and Nettie Pitzer, daughter of Thomas J. Pitzer of Barboursville, were united in marriage December 2, 1875. Mrs. Black belongs to old Virginia families on both sides and is a most accomplished and refined lady. The children of this union are: Pitzer D. Black, Gertrude D. and Georgia C.

LEWIS MAJOR SANFORD, a wealthy and worthy citizen of Henry County, son of Charles and Martha (Major) Sanford, was born in Henry County, Kentucky, September 15, 1824.

Charles Sanford (father) was born in Virginia February 6, 1790. When he was eight years of age his parents removed to Bourbon County, Kentucky; subsequently moved to Henry County, where he lived until his death, January 24, 1867. He devoted his life to agricultural and kindred pursuits, and was the leading farmer and one of the most prominent citizens of the county. He married (first) Sallie Foree, daughter of Berry Foree, a native and wealthy planter of North Carolina, who removed to Henry County. Mrs. Sanford was born in North Carolina and was educated in the best schools of Henry County. She was the mother of one child, Berry Foree Sanford.

Mr. Sanford was married (second) to Martha Major (mother), who was a native of Woodford County, daughter of John Major. Her two children were Lewis Major and Charles B. She died in September, 1836, and Mr. Sanford survived her for thirty-one years, but did not marry again. Charles B. Sanford (brother) died December 20, 1851.

Daniel Sanford (grandfather) was a native of Virginia, who came to Bourbon County in 1798, and subsequently removed to Henry County, where he owned large and valuable tracts of land. He was a schoolmate of George Washington and his brother in Virginia, and was a captain in the War of the Revolution. After coming to Kentucky he was wholly engaged in the cultivation of his lands. He was a son of Richard Sanford of Virginia.

John Major (maternal grandfather) was also a native of Virginia, who became a successful farmer in Woodford County, where he died many years ago.

Lewis Major Sanford, familiarly known by his middle name, which has no military significance, was educated in the best schools of his day and was hurried from the school room at the age of seventeen to take charge of his father's farming interests. This proved a valuable part of his education, affording business experience which, with great industry and good management, has made him one of the most prominent and wealthy farmers in Henry County. The life of the farmer is uneventful, and Mr. Sanford has found his chief pleasure in the quiet and peaceful pursuit of an occupation which is first in importance, but in which notoriety is seldom sought and less frequently attained. He has other business interests and investments, however, and has been president of the Bank of New Castle for many years.

He was married in 1869 to Fannie M. Smith, daughter of A. O. Smith and Harriet L. Hunter Smith, natives of Virginia and residents of Henry

County, where Mrs. Sanford was born July 26, 1846. She was educated in convent schools in St. Louis and Louisville. She was a member of the Christian Church, of which she was a liberal supporter and faithful in good work until the day of her death, February 16, 1892.

The children of L. M. and Fannie M. Sanford are: Charles, Abram, who married Mary Pryor, daughter of Chief Justice Pryor, of the Kentucky Court of Appeals; Lewis Major, Jr., Hallie Hunter, who married John D. Carroll, whose sketch is given in this work; Robert Hunter, Daniel Lawrence, James Goslee, Francis Symmes, Marie Humes and Martha Major.

ROBERT BENJAMIN LANCASTER, banker, distiller, miller and a leading citizen of Lebanon, son of Benjamin and Ann (Pottinger) Lancaster, was born in Marion County, Kentucky, May 26, 1835.

His father was born in the same county in 1799; educated in the local schools; was a farmer and devoted his entire attention to agricultural pursuits; married Ann Pottinger of the same county; died in 1839, and is buried at St. Charles, Marion County.

John Lancaster (grandfather) was born in Maryland and came to Hardin Creek Catholic Settlement in 1788. He was a man of superior capabilities and extraordinary strength of character; a recognized leader in the community and was first in every movement for the material prosperity of the people. He was married in 1790 to Catherine Miles, daughter of Philip Miles of Pottinger Creek Settlement. Their children were: Joseph B., married Anna Blair; Raphael, married Caroline Carter, niece of Reverend Charles Carter of the arch-diocese of Philadelphia; Philip Henry, married Catherine Hagan; John, married Mary Hayden; Benjamin, married Ann Pottinger (father and mother); Ellen, married Judge A. H. Churchill; Ann, married E. B. Smith; James Madison, priest; William, married Malvina Churchill; Catherine, married Leonard A. Spalding, brother of Archbishop Spalding of Baltimore.

John Lancaster (grandfather) represented Washington County in the Kentucky Legislature from 1799 to 1802, and again in 1820. He amassed a large fortune for the times in which he lived. His death occurred in the spring of 1838.

Family tradition says that the first of the name of Lancaster who came to America was John—a son of a Lancastershire landlord of the same name—who offended his father by marrying Fannie Jarnigan, a portionless Irish girl. The young man and his wife came to America and settled on the lower Potomac in a locality then known as "Cob Neck," where they reared a family. One of their sons, Raphael Lancaster, married Eleanor Bradford, whose mother was a Darnell, sister of the mother of Dr. John Carroll, first bishop, and subsequently archbishop, of Baltimore. Two of Raphael Lancaster's sons, John and Raphael, removed from Maryland to Kentucky in 1788, John (grandfather) settling on Hardin's Creek, as before stated, and Raphael near Bardstown.

Ann Pottinger Lancaster (mother) was a daughter of Samuel Pottinger and a Mrs. Logan, whose maiden name was Caldwell. The Pottingers came to Kentucky from Virginia in 1781.

Robert B. Lancaster, the subject of this sketch, was educated in St. Joseph College, Bardstown, and was engaged in farming near that place, and also in distilling until 1860, when he removed to Lebanon and was employed in merchandising until the beginning of Civil war, in which he took no active part, being absent in Brazil.

Returning after the war he again engaged in farming, and was at different times the owner of some of the finest horses in Kentucky. Among others were Marion C., Longbow, Trafalgar, Emma Mc, Lizzie Hayden, Bettie Magruder, Zuma and Linna.

In 1874 he established the Maple Grove Distillery Company near Lebanon, of which he is sole proprietor; is also the owner of the S. P. Lancaster Distillery Company at Bardstown. In 1886 the firm of W. Q. Emison & Company, wholesale liquor dealers and distillers, was organized, Mr. Lancaster having a half interest in the company; has been a director in the Citizens' National Bank of Lebanon for ten years and president since 1891; was one of the promoters of the local telephone exchange of Lebanon, and is a director in the company; has been president of the Springfield

& New Market Turnpike Company for twelve years; is president of the Lebanon Roller Mill Company, and has other large business interests in the city and county; is not prominent in politics, but is a Democrat in favor of bimetallism; is a leading member of the Catholic Church, and very generous in his charities, and a most worthy and highly honored citizen.

Mr. Lancaster was married May 7, 1867, to Mary T. Abell, daughter of John and Mary Jane (Spalding) Abell, and she was the mother of six children: Mary J., wife of T. A. Mattingly of Lebanon; Annie E., Joseph S., Benjamin H., married Rose Brown of Lebanon; John A. and Mary T.

Mr. Lancaster was married a second time, June 22, 1881, to Sally Dougherty of Louisville, and by this marriage he has one son, Robert B. Lancaster, Jr.

JOHN D. CARROLL, a leading attorney at law and distinguished politician of New Castle, son of Anthony J. and Eliza (Collins) Carroll, was born in Oldham County, Kentucky, in 1854.

His father was a native of Ireland; came to Kentucky in 1848, and soon thereafter located in Oldham County, near Buckner's Station, where he resided until his death in 1867; he was a man of strong common sense, excellent judgment and fine business capacity and at the time of his death and for several years prior thereto, was engaged in the business of farming and railroad building. In 1852 he was married to Eliza Collins, who died in 1885. Mrs. Carroll was highly esteemed as a good Christian woman, was devoted to her home and family, and enjoyed the love and respect of a large circle of friends. Four children now living —John D., Thomas, Charles and Anthony J.— were the result of this union.

Few men have risen from humble surroundings in childhood to such prominence in public life and in the legal profession, in both of which relations John D. Carroll is one of the first men in Kentucky to-day. Modest and unconscious of his own worth, unwilling to speak of his achievements, a mere outline of his life is all that can be given in this brief sketch.

He attended school in La Grange, and this is all that can be said of his early education. But he was studious and ambitious, and followed his limited opportunities in the school room by a careful course of reading and study of the higher branches, improving his time to the best advantage while performing manual labor on his father's farm, on which he worked from 1869 to 1875. Following his inclination he began the study of law regularly in 1875 with Judge William Carroll of New Castle, now circuit judge; was admitted to the bar in 1876 and began the practice of his profession in New Castle; was a law partner of C. M. Harwood of Shelbyville—one of the finest lawyers in the state—until his death in 1882; was then associated with R. W. Masterson, an excellent attorney, now residing in Carrollton, Kentucky, and has recently been associated with Honorable Joseph Barbour, late judge of the Superior Court.

In all of these professional relations he was eminently successful and soon became known as a leading lawyer of his section; and as a matter of course he became a leader in Democratic politics; was elected to the Legislature in 1881 and again in in 1883, serving four years, in which capacity he made himself known throughout the state; was a member of the Constitutional Convention of 1890-1, to which he was elected without opposition, and in which he further distinguished himself as a man of superior ability; was appointed in 1891 by Governor John Young Brown as one of three commissioners to revise the laws under the new constitution—a just compliment to his superior knowledge and fitness for the work in hand; subsequently, in conjunction with Judge Joseph Barbour, he prepared the Kentucky statutes, which is the only compilation of the statute laws in use in Kentucky, and is invaluable to the profession. He is also the editor of Carroll's Kentucky Codes of Practice, a work that has been received with great favor by the profession. However, his public services have been merely incidental to his labors in the legitimate pursuit of his vocation, in which he excels and to which he is earnestly devoted.

His leadership in his party was recognized by his selection in 1892 as chairman of the Democratic State Central Committee, in which capacity he served faithfully and with signal ability until 1895.

He is a prominent and helpful member of the Odd Fellows fraternity, with which he has been associated since 1876.

Mr. Carroll was married in 1894 to Harriet Hunter Sanford, daughter of Lewis M. Sanford, whose sketch will be found in this volume. Mrs. Carroll was born in Henry County, Kentucky, and was educated at St. Mary's College, South Bend, Indiana.

HENRY CLAY, the son of a Baptist clergyman of respectable standing, was born in Hanover County, Virginia, on the 12th of April, 1777. His father died when young Henry had attained his fifth year, and the care of superintending his education devolved on his widowed mother. She appears to have been a lady of sterling worth, singular intelligence and masculine vigor of intellect.

The boyhood of Henry Clay was furnished with few of those facilities for obtaining a literary education, which are now accessible to almost all. His mind was left to develop its powers and attain its growth through the force of its own innate energies, with but little aid from books or competent instructors. Those rich treasures of intellectual wealth, which are to be found in well selected libraries and properly organized schools, were to him a sealed fountain. The extent of his boyish attainments in literature consisted of the common elements taught in a country school of the most humble pretensions. Even these slender advantages were but sparingly enjoyed, and the future orator and statesman was compelled, by the straitened circumstances of his family, to devote a considerable portion of his time to manual labor in the field. The subsequent brilliant achievements of that master mind derive increased luster from the contemplation of the obstacles thus early interposed to its progress, and no more honorable testimony can be offered to the ardor, energy and invincibility of that towering intellect and imperial spirit, than the severe trials which at this period it encountered, and over which it triumphed. It is probable that this early familiarity with the sternest realities of life contributed to give to his mind that strong practical bias, which has subsequently distinguished his career as a statesman; while there can be no doubt that the demands thus continually made upon his energies tended to a quick development of that unyielding strength of character which bears down all opposition, and stamps him as one of the most powerful spirits of the age.

At the age of fourteen he was placed in a small drug store in the city of Richmond, Virginia. He continued in this situation but a few months, and in 1792 entered the office of the clerk of the High Court of Chancery. While in this office he attracted the attention of Chancellor Wythe, who, being very favorably impressed by his amiable deportment, uniform habits of industry, and striking displays of intelligence, honored him with his friendship, and employed him as an amanuensis. It was probably through the advice of Chancellor Wythe that he first conceived the design of studying law, and he has himself borne testimony to the fact, that his intercourse with that great and good man exercised a decided and very salutary influence in the development of his mental powers, and the formation of his character.

In the year 1796, he went to reside with Robert Brooks, Esq., attorney-general of Virginia. While in the family of this gentleman his opportunities for acquiring a knowledge of the profession to which he had determined to devote his life, were greatly improved, and he appears to have cultivated them with exemplary assiduity. The year 1797 seems to have been devoted by Mr. Clay exclusively to the study of his profession. It is worthy of remark that this was the first year in which his necessities permitted him to pursue an uninterrupted system of study, and so eagerly did he avail himself of the privilege, and such was the ardor and vivacity of his mind that near the close of the year he obtained from the Virginia Court of Appeals a license to practice. Of course the acquisitions made in the science of law, in the course of these irregular and broken efforts to master that intricate and complex system, were somewhat desultory and crude, and it is not the least striking evidence of the wonderful resources of Mr. Clay's genius, that he was enabled, notwithstanding these disadvantages, to assume so

HENRY CLAY.

early in life a high rank in his profession, at a bar distinguished for the number, ability and profound erudition of its members.

When Mr. Clay entered upon the duties of his profession, the Lexington bar was noted for talent, numbering among its members some of the first lawyers that have ever adorned the legal profession in America. He commenced the practice under circumstances somewhat discouraging, and as appears from his own statement, with very moderate expectations. His earliest efforts, however, were attended with complete success; his reputation spread rapidly, and, to use his own language, he "immediately rushed into a lucrative practice." This unusual spectacle, so rare in the legal profession, is to be ascribed mainly to Mr. Clay's skill as an advocate. Gifted by nature with oratorical genius of a high order, his very youth increased the spell of that potent fascination which his splendid elocution and passionate eloquence threw over the public mind, and led the imagination a willing captive to its power. It was in the conduct of criminal causes, especially, that he achieved his greatest triumphs. The latitude customary and allowable to an advocate in the defense of his client, the surpassing interest of the questions at issue, presented an occasion and a field which never failed to elicit a blaze of genius, before which the public stood dazzled and astonished.

A large portion of the litigation at that day in Kentucky grew out of the unsettled tenure by which most of the lands in the country were held. The contests arising out of those conflicting claims had built up a system of land law remarkable for its intricacy and complexity, and having no parallel in the whole range of the law of real property. Adapted to the exigencies of the country and having its origin in the necessities of the times it was still remarkable for its logical consistency and sound principle. Kentucky, at that day, could boast some of the most profound, acute and subtle lawyers in the world.

In 1803 he was elected to represent the County of Fayette in the most numerous branch of the State Legislature. He was re-elected to that body at every session until 1806. The impression made upon his associates must have been of the most favorable character, since, in the latter year, he was elected to the Senate of the United States to serve out the unexpired term of General Adair. He was elected for one session only.

During this session Mr. Clay, as a member of the Senate, had occasion to investigate the extent of the power of Congress to promote internal improvements, and the result of his examination was a full conviction that the subject was clearly within the competency of the general government. These views he never changed; and profoundly impressed with the policy of promoting such works, he at the same session gave his cordial support to several measures of that character.

At the close of the session Mr. Clay returned to Kentucky and resumed the practice of his profession. At the ensuing election in August he was returned as the representative from Fayette to the Legislature. When the Legislature assembled he was elected speaker of the house. In this station he was distinguished for the zeal, energy and decision with which he discharged its duties. He continued a member of the Legislature until 1809, when he tendered his resignation, and was elected to the Senate of the United States for two years, to fill the vacancy occasioned by the resignation of Mr. Thurston.

The principal matters which came before the Senate during Mr. Clay's second term of service, related to the policy of encouraging domestic manufactures; the law to reduce into possession, and establish the authority of the United States over the territory between the Mississippi and Perdido Rivers, comprehending the present States of Mississippi, Alabama and Florida, and the question of a re-charter of the Bank of the United States.

At the session of 1810-11 the question of a re-charter of the Bank of the United States was brought before the Senate, and became the subject of a debate, noted in our congressional history for its intemperate violence and splendid displays of eloquence. On this occasion Mr. Clay was found opposed to the re-charter of the bank, and maintained his views in a speech of great ingenuity and power.

When, at the expiration of the term of service

for which he had been elected, Mr. Clay retired from the Senate, he left behind him a character for general ability and sound statesmanship which few men of the same age have ever attained.

In 1811, the same year in which he retired from the Senate, he was elected by the people of the Fayette district to represent them in the House of Representatives of the United States. In 1813 he was re-elected, and continued a member of the House until he was sent to Europe as one of the commissioners to negotiate a treaty of peace with Great Britain. During the whole of this period he filled the speaker's chair in the House, having received the high and unusual compliment of being chosen to that responsible station the first day on which he appeared in his seat in Congress.

Mr. Clay consequently presided over the Twelfth and Thirteenth Congresses, and participated largely in those measures adopted to vindicate the honor and assert the rights of the country against the usurpations and aggressions of Great Britain. He gave a warm and hearty co-operation in all those efforts that were made to put the country in a state of defense, and contributed as much, if not more, by his sleepless energy and unrivaled eloquence, to infuse a proper spirit into the deliberations of Congress, than any other man. His speeches on the subject of our difficulties with Great Britain exhibit some of the most brilliant specimens of parliamentary eloquence extant, and their effect at the time in arousing the country to a sense of its wrongs, and a determination to redress them, is said to have been unequalled. As strange as it may sound in the ears of the present generation, there was a large and respectable party at that period, both in and out of Congress, which was averse to war with Great Britain, and disposed to submit to almost any outrage rather than distract her efforts to put down the power of Napoleon, then in the midst of his extraordinary career. It was in opposition to what he considered the parricidal efforts of these men that the transcendent genius of the Kentucky statesman displayed its most brilliant, powerful and commanding attributes. He was the life and soul of the war party in Congress—the master spirit around whom all the boldness and chivalry of the nation rallied in that dark hour, when the gloom of despondency hung heavy on every brow, and the generous pride of a free people drooped under the withering sense of the unavenged insult that had been offered to the national honor. In 1814 he resigned his place in Congress to accept an appointment as commissioner and minister plenipotentiary to Ghent. At this period the control which he had acquired in Congress was unlimited. In the house it was probably equal to that he had obtained a few years before in the Kentucky Legislature.

In 1814, having been appointed in conjunction with Messrs. John Q. Adams, James A. Bayard, Albert Gallatin and Jonathan Russell, a commissioner to meet commissioners appointed on the part of Great Britain, he proceeded to Europe. On the sixth of August the plenipotentiaries of both nations met in the ancient city of Ghent, prepared to proceed to business. The plan of this sketch does not require, nor would it admit, of a detailed account of the negotiations, extending through several months, which finally resulted in a treaty of peace between the two nations. These are to be found related at large in the public histories of the time, and to them we refer the reader for a full knowledge of those transactions. Let it suffice to say that on this, as on all other occasions, Mr. Clay mingled controllingly in the deliberations of his distinguished colleagues, and exercised a very commanding influence over the course of the negotiation. There is, indeed, reason to believe that, but for his firmness and tact, the right to the exclusive navigation of the Mississippi River would have been surrendered for a very inconsiderable equivalent. His colleagues in the negotiation have always borne the most honorable testimony to the ability and comprehensive knowledge displayed by Mr. Clay in those memorable transactions, and he returned to the United States with a reputation materially enhanced.

He found upon his arrival in Kentucky that during his absence he had been nominated by his friends and elected to Congress; but as there arose doubts as to the legality of his election he resigned, and the canvass was opened anew. This resulted as the previous vote, in his being returned by an overwhelming majority. He was re-elected in succession to every Congress that assembled until the session of 1820-21, when he retired to repair the inroads made in his private fortune by his long devotion to public affairs. During this period he was thrice elected speaker of the house, and presided over the deliberations of that body during the whole period which intervened between 1815 and 1821.

On his re-entrance into Congress Mr. Clay was called to defend the treaty, in the formation of which he had participated so largely, against the animadversions of his old enemies, the Federalists. That treaty was made the subject of unbridled criticism by those who had opposed the war, and with the magical astuteness of hatred they discovered objectionable features in every clause. In the course of the discussions which thus arose he had frequent occasion to review the origin, progress and termination of the war, which task he performed with masterly ability, exposing the inconsistency and malignity of his adversaries to deserved odium. He met them at every point, and never failed to make their rancorous virulence recoil on their own heads with tremendous effect.

During the time of this, Mr. Clay's second incumbency in the House of Representatives, many questions were presented for its deliberation of surpassing interest, and closely touching the permanent welfare of the republic. The finances of the country were found to be in a condition of ruinous embarrassment; the nation was deeply involved in debt and the little money left in the country was being continually drained away to pay for foreign importations. It was in this gloomy conjuncture of affairs that the session of 1815-16 opened, and Congress was called to the arduous task of repairing the breeches which thus yawned in the public prosperity. In all those measures recommended by Mr. Madison's administration, with a view to the accomplishment of this end, Mr. Clay heartily co-operated. Among other things, he gave his support to a proposition to reduce the direct tax of the United States. He advocated, as has been already stated, the incorporation of a United States bank.

The recognition of the South American republics by the government of the United States, a measure which was almost entirely attributable to the indefatigable exertions, personal influence and powerful eloquence of Mr. Clay, while it shed lustre on the Monroe administration, surrounded the brow of the great statesman with a halo of true glory which grows brighter with the lapse of time.

At the session of 1816-17 the subject of the Seminole war was brought before Congress, and Mr. Clay, in the course of his speech on that occasion, found it necessary to speak with some severity of the conduct of General Jaickson. This was the origin of that inveterate hostility on the part of the old general towards the great Kentuckian, the consequences of which were deeply felt in after years.

The only remaining measure of importance with which Mr. Clay's name is connected in the history of those times, was the great and exciting question which arose on the application of Missouri for admission into the Union. Probably at no period of our history has the horoscope of our country's destiny looked so dark and threatening. The Union was convulsed to its center. An universal alarm pervaded all sections of the country and every class of the community. A disruption of the Confederacy seemed inevitable—civil war, with its attendant horrors, seemed to scowl from every quarter, and the sun of American liberty appeared about to set in a sea of blood. At this conjuncture every eye in the country was turned to Henry Clay. He labored night and day, and such was the excitement of his mind, that he has been heard to declare that if the settlement of the controversy had been suspended three weeks longer, it would have cost him his life. Happy was it for America that he was found equal to the emergency, and that the tempest of desolation which seemed about to burst upon our heads was, through his agency, permitted to pass away harmless. At the close of the session of Congress in 1821, Mr. Clay retired, and resumed the practice of his profession. He did not again enter Congress until 1823.

Upon resuming his seat in Congress at the commencement of the session of 1823-4, Mr. Clay was elected speaker, over Mr. Barbour of Virginia, by a considerable majority. He continued speaker of the House until he entered the cabinet of Mr. Adams, in 1825. During this time, the subject of the tariff again came before Congress, and was advocated by Mr. Clay in one of the most masterly efforts of his life. His speech on the occasion was distinguished for the thorough knowledge of the subject which it displayed; for its broad, comprehensive and statesmanlike views, and for its occasional passages of impressive and thrilling eloquence. He also advocated a resolution, introduced by Mr. Webster, to defray the expenses of a messenger to Greece, at that time engaged against the power of the Turks in an arduous and bloody struggle for independence. A spectacle of this kind never failed to enlist his profoundest sympathies and elicit all the powers of his genius.

Toward the close of the year 1824 the question of the Presidency was generally agitated. As candidates for this office Messrs. J. Q. Adams, Andrew Jackson, Henry Clay and W. H. Crawford had been brought forward by their respective friends. Mr. Clay had been nominated by the Kentucky Legislature as early as 1822. The people failing to make a choice, the election was thrown into the house. Mr. Clay, being the lowest on the list, was excluded from the house by the constitutional provision, which makes it the duty of Congress to select one of the three highest candidates. His position in the house now became exceedingly delicate as well as important. He had it in his power, by placing himself at the head of the party who went with him in the house, to control its choice of the three candidates before it. When the election came on he cast his vote for Mr. Adams, who thus became President of the United States. This vote of Mr. Clay has been made the subject of much calumny and misrepresentation. At the time it was charged that he had been bought up by the offer of a seat in the cabinet. Efforts were made to produce evidence to this effect, but it was attended by signal failure. The charge was reiterated by General Jackson, the defeated candidate, which led to an investigation of the whole affair. The result of this was the exposure of one of the darkest conspiracies ever formed to ruin the character of an individual. Our limits forbid an attempt to array the evidence on this subject, and we must content ourselves with the remark that there is probably not one man of intelligence now in the Union who gives to the charge of "bargain and corruption" the slightest credit.

During Mr. Adams' administration Mr. Clay occupied a seat in his cabinet as secretary of state. The various official documents prepared by him while in his office are among the best in our archives. While secretary of state he negotiated many treaties with the various foreign powers with whom this country maintained relations, in which he approved himself as superior as a diplomatist, as he had been before unrivaled as a legislator and orator. He was a universal favorite with the foreign ministers, resident at Washington, and contributed much, by his amenity and suavity of deportment, to place the negotiations on a footing most favorable to his own country.

At the expiration of Mr. Adams' term of office Mr. Clay retired to Ashland, his seat near Lexington. He continued engaged in the avocations of his profession until 1831, when he was elected to the Senate of the United States for the term of six years. About the same time in a national convention at Baltimore, he was nominated to the Presidency in opposition to General Jackson.

The subjects brought before the Senate during this term of Mr. Clay's service were of the most important and exciting character. The subjects of the tariff, the United States bank, the public lands, etc., embracing a system of legislative policy of the most comprehensive character and the highest importance, constantly engaged the attention of the country and of Congress. During the period signalized by the agitation of these great questions, probably the most exciting in the political annals of America, no man filled a larger space in the public eye than Mr. Clay. He was the center of a constellation of genius and talent, the most brilliant that has ever lighted this western hemisphere. Although defeated when the election for President came on, that circumstance appeared but to increase the devotion of his friends, and perhaps the star of Henry Clay never blazed with a luster so bright, so powerful and far-pervading as at this moment, when all the elements of opposition, envy, hatred, malice and detraction conglomerated in lowering masses, seemed gathering their forces to extinguish and obscure its light forever.

General Jackson's veto of the bill to re-charter the Bank of the United States, while it clearly indicated the unsparing temper in which this war of parties was to be prosecuted, produced an effect on the financial condition of the country, which resulted in the most disastrous consequences to trade, commerce and business in all its branches. The establishment of the pet bank system but aggravated and hastened the evil, and in those first measures of General Jackson's second term of service were sown the seeds which, at a future day, were reaped in a harvest of woe and desolation. As in 1816, Mr. Clay advocated the re-charter of the bank, and denounced the veto in unmeasured terms. He predicted the consequences which would result from the measure, and subsequent events fully verified his anticipations.

In 1840 General Harrison, the Whig candidate for the Presidency, was elected by one of those tremendous and irresistible popular movements, which are seen in no other country besides this. During the canvass Mr. Clay visited Hanover county, the place of his nativity, and while there addressed an assembly of the people. It was one of the ablest speeches of his life, and contained a masterly exposition of the principles and subjects of controversy between the two parties.

After the election of General Harrison, when Congress assembled, it set itself to work to repair the ravages made in the prosperity and institutions of the country by twelve years of misgovernment. Unfortunately, however, the work had scarcely commenced before death removed the lamented Harrison from the scene of his usefulness, and Mr. Tyler, the Vice-President, succeeded to his place. Then followed, in rapid succession, veto after veto, until all hope of accomplishing the objects for which the Whigs came into power were extinct.

During this period Mr. Clay labored night and day to bring the President into an accommodating temper, but without success. He seemed resolved to sever all connection between himself and the party which brought him into power. He will go down to posterity with the brand of traitor stamped upon his brow, and take his place with the Arnolds of the Revolution.

On the 31st of March, 1842, Mr. Clay executed his long and fondly cherished design of retiring to spend the evening of his days amid the tranquil shades of Ashland. He resigned his seat in the Senate and presented to that body the credentials of his friend and successor, Mr. Crittenden. The scene which ensued was indescribably thrilling. Had the guardian genius of Congress and the nation been about to take his departure deeper feeling could hardly have been manifested than when Mr. Clay arose to address, for the last time, his congressional compeers. All felt that the master spirit was bidding them adieu; that the pride and ornament of the Senate and the glory of the nation was being removed, and all grieved in view of the void that would be created. When Mr. Clay resumed his seat the Senate unanimously adjourned for the day.

In May, 1844, the National Whig Convention nominated Mr. Clay as a candidate for President of the United States. The nominee of the Democratic party was Colonel James K. Polk of Tennessee. The canvass was probably one of the most exciting ever witnessed in this country. In addition to the old issues, a new one was formed on the proposition to annex the Republic of Texas to the American Union. This question, intimately involving the exciting subject of slavery, gave to the Presidential canvass a new character and an unforeseen direction. It would be out of place here, although not without interest and instruction, to trace and analyze the causes which operated to defeat the Whigs. Suffice it to say, that Mr. Polk was made President. Texas became one of the United States. War ensued with Mexico; and the armies of the United States swept the fertile provinces of that sister republic from the mouth of the Rio Grande to the western base of the Rocky Mountains. Governments were abrogated and new ones established in their place by the fiat of subordinate militia officers; and throughout the whole extent of that rich and beautiful region scenes were enacted which carry the mind back to the days of romance, and revive the memory of those tragedies which have crimsoned the pages of European and Asiatic history.

Defeated for the Presidency, with apparently no chance to ever reach that high place, Mr. Clay resolved to remain in private life. He had spent more than forty years in public service. He had nearly lived out the years allotted to man. All the honors his state could bestow had been lavished upon him. He commanded alike the love of his friends and the respect of his foes. During the period of his retirement Ashland, his home, was visited by thousands of persons from all sections of the country, and even from abroad, who came to testify their admiration or esteem for the statesman and the patriot. Now and then he appeared professionally in court, at the solicitation of an old client; but most of his time was devoted to casual visitors, or to the enjoyment of the society of his friends. In 1847 Mr. Clay joined the Protestant Episcopal Church of Lexington—thus consummating a purpose he had cherished for years.

A year before the Presidential election of 1848 the two great political parties began preparations for the contest. No one could conjecture who were to be the chiefs of the opposing forces. There were dissensions in the Whig party, and Mr. Van Buren's defection threatened to disrupt the Democracy. He did finally accept the nomination of the "Free Soilers" for the Presidency, which brought disaster on the Democratic party. The Whigs would not unite on Mr. Clay. They had followed his fortunes with singular devotion, but the exigencies of the party were great—so great, indeed, that its dissolution seemed imminent. In the national contests he had often led to defeat—never to victory. They determined to sacrifice him for success, and ventured upon the fatal policy of expediency. General Zachary Taylor, already famous for other achievements in Mexico, had won the battle of Buena Vista against immense odds; and he who before that war was scarcely known beyond army circles became the object of popular adoration. The opponents of Mr. Clay's nomination concentrated on Taylor, who received the nomination of the Whig Convention held in Philadelphia in June, 1848. Mr. Clay, probably, was not surprised at the result, but he was keenly affected by the action of a portion of the Kentucky delegation, who, at a critical moment, abandoned him, and cast their vote for General Taylor. They were accused of treachery by the disappointed and incensed adherents of Mr. Clay, who himself believed that he was betrayed. The occurrence led to a temporary alienation of friendship between Mr. Clay and a lifetime friend who had been one of the chief actors. But Mr. Clay's resentment was of brief duration, for they met subsequently with the usual cordial greeting.

Mr. Clay was married in 1799 to Lucretia, daughter of Colonel Hart of Lexington, Kentucky, with whom he lived happily for fifty-three years.

GENERAL JOHN HUNT MORGAN—distinguished as the greatest partisan ranger (perhaps excepting General Francis Marion) of all American wars—was born June 1, 1825, at Huntsville, Alabama. His father, Calvin C. Morgan (a Virginian by birth, and a relation of General Daniel Morgan, of the Revolutionary war), was a merchant there; his mother, the daughter of John W. Hunt, a leading merchant of Lexington, Kentucky. In 1829 they removed to a farm near the latter place. John was the eldest of six sons, of whom five devoted themselves to the cause of the South: Calvin C. Morgan, who always acted as agent in Kentucky for his brother John; Colonel Richard Morgan, on the staff of the great General A. P. Hill as adjutant-general; Major Charlton Morgan, in his brother's command (formerly representing the United States government abroad); and Lieutenant Thomas Morgan, also in his brother's command, and twice captured. A cousin was one of the bravest private soldiers in the same command.

John H. Morgan's first war experience was as first lieutenant of Captain Oliver H. P. Beard's company, of Colonel Humphrey Marshall's regiment of Kentucky Cavalry, in the Mexican war; and his first battle experience, of the terribly-in-earnest type, at Buena Vista, February 22 and 23, 1847, with his men dismounted and fighting as infantry. In 1857 he was made the first captain of a volunteer infantry company, the Lexington Rifles, which became prominent for its drill and efficiency, and was afterward incorporated into the "state guard." September 20, 1861, having determined to link his fortunes with the South, he succeeded—although a Federal regiment was encamped within a mile, with orders to next day seize the armory and guns of Captain Morgan's company—in eluding their vigilance, and escaping with all his guns and a number of his men toward the Confederate lines. After a few weeks' service his company was regularly organized as Company A, of Morgan's Squadron; and the dashing independent service to which his life was henceforth devoted began. We have not space to follow him in all his brilliant and dangerous exploits—generally successful and forward, but often of the hurriedly retrograde kind.

April 4, 1862, he received from General Albert Sidney Johnston his commission as colonel, and positive encouragement that his field of action would be enlarged, his force increased and his desire to act independently gratified. The victory at Hartsville, Tenn., in December, 1862, brought him a long-ago-won and long-delayed commission of brigadier-general, which General Hardee urged should be that of major-general at once; but President Davis could only overcome by slow degrees what seemed an unreasonable prejudice against Kentuckians—possibly because he was too rigid a disciplinarian to encourage the brilliant independency of Morgan's men and movements. May 17, 1863, the Confederate Congress recognized the invaluable services of General Morgan in a handsome resolution of thanks. His great raids through Kentucky were in July, 1862, August and September, 1862, December, 1862, and June, 1864. His wild raid or ride from Tennessee, across Kentucky, and through the southern part of Indiana and Ohio, to his capture in Columbiana County, Ohio, was in July, 1863. His imprisonment in the penitentiary at Columbus lasted only four months; his escape was as startling as it was ingenious; and on November 28, 1863, he was again working his way southward.

JAMES G. BIRNEY, the first "Liberty" candidate for President of the United States, was born in Danville, Kentucky, February 4, 1792; died at Perth Amboy, New Jersey, November 25, 1857, aged sixty-five years. After studying law he settled in Alabama, was district attorney and quite successful. Returning to Kentucky in 1833 he assisted in organizing the Kentucky Colonization Society, and was made president of it—while holding the position of professor in Center College. His views, at first conservative, then progressive, rapidly changed to "anti-slavery" of the demonstrative kind; he advocated in a public letter in 1834 immediate emancipation, and set the consistent example of freeing his own slaves; then removed to Cincinnati and established a newspaper, The Philanthropist, of a type not prudent to publish in Kentucky. But there he ran so far and so obnoxiously in advance of public sentiment, that his press was thrown into the river; he revived it, however, in connection with Dr. Bailey. In 1836 he became secretary to the American Anti-Slavery Society at New York, and continued to press the idea of a political party for "freedom." The "Liberty" party nominated him in 1840, and again—after he had become a resident of Michigan—in 1844, as its candidate for the Presidency.

GARRET DAVIS was born in Mount Sterling, Kentucky, September 10, 1801. His father, in early life a blacksmith, was a man of energy and good sense, gained a competency, and served one term in the Legislature. Two of his brothers, Singleton and Amos, were brilliant young men—the latter a member of Congress, 1833-35, and dying June 5, 1835, before he could be re-elected. Garret Davis in his boyhood was a deputy in the circuit clerk's office at Paris; admitted to the bar in 1823; a representative in the Legislature in 1833, '34 and '35; elected to Congress from the Maysville district in 1839-41, and was thrice re-elected, 1841-47, from the Ashland district, Bourbon County having been transferred to the latter; was a member of the Constitutional Convention in 1849, and so determinedly opposed to an elective judiciary that, solitary and alone, on December 21, he voted against the new constitution, refused to sign it, and left the convention (Richard H. Hanson being elected to fill the vacancy, who signed the constitution); was elected United States Senator, 1861-67, and re-elected, 1867-73, but died September 22, 1872, aged seventy-one years and twelve days. In Congress he acquired distinction by his earnest advocacy of the principles and measures of the Whig party; and when about to retire in 1847 Henry Clay appealed to him as a personal favor to make the race for another term, but he had invited Charles S. Morehead to take the field, and could not honorably consent. He was a prominent leader in the "Native American" movement, as he was afterward in the "Know-Nothing" or "American" party; and his anti-Catholic views, boldly and ably expressed in a speech in the Constitutional Convention in 1849, gave him considerable notoriety; he was nominated in 1856 as the American party candidate for the Presidency, but declined. He was nominated for lieutenant-governor in 1848 on the Whig ticket with John J. Crittenden for governor, but declined; and when nominated for governor by the American party in 1855, also declined; thus he declined more good positions, even when election was certain, than most ambitious men succeed to. He was among the few leading Kentuckians who opposed secession in 1861.

GENERAL CHARLES SCOTT, from whom Scott County received its name, a distinguished officer of the Revolution, was born in Cumberland County, Virginia. He served as a corporal in a volunteer company of militia in the memorable campaign of 1755, which terminated in Braddock's defeat. Upon the breaking out of the Revolutionary war he raised the first company of volunteers south of James River that entered into actual service, and so distinguished himself that when the County of Powhatan was formed in 1777 the County of Scott was named in honor of him. Having been appointed by General Washington to the command of a regiment in the Continental line, he was with General Wayne at the storming of Stony Point. He was in Charleston when it surrendered to Sir Henry Clinton. When marching out of the gate a British officer spoke to him very abruptly; ordered him to march faster to give room for others. Scott turned upon him, ripped out a tremendous oath (one of his characteristics), and shamed the officer for having let so few men stand out so long against so large an army. The officer molested him no further. After the war terminated he removed to Kentucky, and in 1785 settled in Woodford County. He was with General St. Clair in his defeat on the 4th of November, 1791, when there were about six hundred men killed in one hour. In 1791 he and General Wilkinson conducted a corps of horsemen against the Indian towns on the Wabash, killed some of the warriors and took a number of prisoners. In 1794 he commanded a portion of Wayne's army at the battle of the Fallen Timber, where the Indians were defeated and driven under the walls of the British fort. In 1808 he was elected to the office of governor of Kentucky, and discharged his duties faithfully.

JEFFERSON DAVIS was born in Christian County, Kentucky (in that part now included in Todd County), June 3, 1808; but with his father removed to Mississippi in his infancy. He returned to Kentucky for awhile as a student at Transylvania University; was a cadet at West Point Military Academy, 1824-28, and graduated 1828; second lieutenant infantry, 1828-33; first lieutenant of dragoons, 1833-35; served in various campaigns against the Indians, and was distinguished as a subordinate officer in the Black Hawk campaign; resigned his army commission, 1835, and became a planter in Mississippi. Mr. Davis began his political career as Presidential elector, 1844; was elected to Congress, 1845-47, but resigned, 1846, to take a colonelcy of a Mississippi regiment enlisted for the Mexican war; was promoted brigadier-general for gallant conduct at Buena Vista—where, it was claimed, his regiment, by its steadiness and valor in repelling the final charge of the enemy, turned a doubtful battle into a great victory; in 1847 was appointed by the governor of Mississippi to fill a vacancy in the United States Senate, and subsequently was unanimously elected by the Legislature to the same, 1847-51; resigned, 1850, to make the race for governor of Mississippi against Henry Stuart Foote; was re-elected United States Senator, 1852, but resigned to accept the position of secretary of war under President Pierce, 1853-57; in 1857 was again elected to the United States

Senate, from which he withdrew January 8, 1861, Mississippi having seceded from the Union.

On February 4, 1861, the delegates from the cotton states met at Montgomery, Alabama, organized a provisional government, adopted a constitution for the Confederate States, and chose Jefferson Davis President, and Alexander H. Stephens Vice-President.

Jefferson Davis died at his home in Mississippi in 1888.

GOVERNOR JOHN POPE, one of the most distinguished politicians and statesmen of Kentucky, and for many years a resident of Washington County, was born in Prince William County, Virginia, in 1770, but brought to this state when quite a boy. In early life, while attending a cornstalk mill, he had the misfortune to lose his arm—an accident which turned his attention to the profession of the law. Being a young man of great native vigor of intellect, he soon attained eminence. He settled in Shelby, which county he represented in the Kentucky Legislature in 1802; then removed to Lexington, and in 1806-7 was a representative in the lower house from Fayette County, a colleague of Henry Clay and Colonel William Russell. Of that body his great talents rendered him an eminently conspicuous and influential member. He was United States Senator from Kentucky for six years, 1807-13—a colleague of Henry Clay, Buckner Thruston and George M. Bibb; and twenty-four years later a member of the lower house of Congress from the Springfield district for six years, 1837-43. In the meantime he was appointed by President Jackson governor of the territory of Arkansas, which office he held for six years, 1829-35. He died at his residence in Washington County July 12, 1845, aged seventy-five years.

PHIL J. VEITH, Clerk of the Campbell County Court, Newport, was born in Newport, January 17, 1864. He received a good education in the public schools, and after taking a business course in a commercial college, commenced bookkeeping for a planing mill when eighteen years of age. He remained with that firm nine years, and in 1891 took charge of the Phil J. Veith Planing Mill & Lumber Company of Newport, which employs about forty people. While the business is conducted in his name the firm is Stone & Veith. Very few young men have met with such signal success, and this is due in a large measure to his careful attention to business and well directed energy. Although an active, pushing business man he has had time to look after politics on the Republican side, and his party honored him with the lucrative office of clerk of the Campbell County Court in November, 1894. He is an active member of a number of benevolent orders, including Knight Templars, Knights of Pythias and Odd Fellows, and is one of the prominent members of the Newport Commercial Club, from all of which it may be inferred he is a busy man.

Mr. Veith and Annie Burke of Cincinnati were married in 1886, and have two children, Carl and Helen. Mr. Veith's father, Frederick Veith, was born in Germany in 1831, and came to the United States when eighteen years of age. After living in Cincinnati two years he removed to Newport, where he engaged in the grocery business until the time of his death in 1885. He was a member and one of the organizers of St. John's Lutheran Church in Newport. His wife, Catherine (Schmidt) Veith, who survives him, was born in Cincinnati in 1837, and is a faithful member of St. John's Lutheran Church.

COLONEL ROBERT JOHNSON (the father of Colonels Richard M., James and Major John T. Johnson), was a native of Virginia, and emigrated to Kentucky, then a county of that state, during the stormy period of the revolution. He was distinguished for that high-toned integrity and courage which marked the age and country in which he lived; and took an active and prominent part in the sanguinary conflicts which raged between the settlers and natives in the early settlement of Kentucky. So great was the confidence reposed in his skill and courage by the adventurers of that age, by whom he was surrounded, that he was called to take a conspicuous position in almost every hazardous enterprise. The sentiments of patriotism and integrity which marked the history of his active life he did not fail to inculcate upon the minds of his children; and the character of those children, as developed, shows that they were not without their proper effect. Of Colonel Richard M. Johnson, the eldest son, a sketch will be found under the head of Johnson County. Colonel James Johnson was the lieutenant-colonel of the mounted regiment of Colonel R. M. Johnson, during the late war, and distinguished himself at the battle of the Thames, as well as on several occasions while in the service. He subsequently served several sessions in the Congress of the United States with general acceptance. At the time of his death, which occurred many years since, he was in communion with the Baptist Church, and was esteemed a zealous and devoted Christian. Major John T. Johnson was for nine months a judge of the "New Court" of Appeals; for five years a Representative in the Legislature; from 1821-25 a member of Congress; and from 1831 until his death in 1856, a distinguished minister of the Christian Church.

GOVERNOR GEORGE W. JOHNSON—son of William Johnson and grandson of Colonel Robert Johnson (one of the early settlers and defenders of Bryan's Station, and the ancestor of a large and distinguished family in Kentucky and other states in the South and West)—was born near Georgetown, Kentucky, May 27, 1811, and died April 9, 1862, aged nearly fifty-one years. He was a graduate of Transylvania University; studied law, and practiced at the Georgetown bar; abandoned the law for agricultural pursuits—farming in Kentucky and cotton-planting in Arkansas; represented Scott County in the Kentucky Legislature for three years, 1838, '39 and '40; was twice a candidate on the Democratic ticket for Presidential elector, but defeated. In 1861 he labored earnestly to place Kentucky by the side of the Southern States in the Civil war; and went, in September of that year, in company with General John C. Breckinridge and others, to the South. He set on foot the organization of a provisional government for Kentucky, which was effected by the convention at Russellville, Logan County, November 18-21, 1861. A constitution was adopted, Mr. Johnson elected provisional governor, and December 10 Kentucky admitted as a member of the Confederacy. He was mortally wounded at the battle of Shiloh, April 7, 1862.

BENJAMIN HARDIN, one of the great lawyers of Kentucky, was born in 1784 in Westmoreland County, Pennsylvania; was the son of Ben and Sarah Hardin, cousins, the latter a sister of Colonel John Hardin. He was brought, in 1787, to the neighborhood of Springfield, Washington County, Kentucky; received his early education from Ichabod Radley, and then at Bardstown, and at Hartford, Ohio County, from Daniel Barry, an Irish linguist; studied law in 1804 at Richmond, Kentucky, with Martin D. Hardin, and in 1805 at Bardstown with Judge Felix Grundy; in 1806 was licensed, married to Miss Barbour, and settled at Elizabethtown, where he remained not quite two years. Some friends of William Bray, under arrest on a charge of murder, employed young Hardin to defend him "until the big lawyers came down from Bardstown." The full meaning of that expression and qualified employment flashed upon Hardin at once; going immediately home he told his wife they must pack up forthwith and remove to Bardstown, or he would never be called a big lawyer; and before Bray was indicted, at spring term, 1808, Mr. Hardin was a resident of Bardstown, and continued to live there until his death; yet in about forty-six years he was not absent from more than six terms of the Hardin Circuit Court and frequently attended the County Court. He was an indefatigable practitioner in the Counties of Nelson, Washington, Hardin, Bullitt, Meade, Grayson, Marion, Breckinridge and sometimes Spencer, and in winter time in the Court of Appeals, and at special calls in Louisville and in the State of Indiana. His practice yielded him a handsome revenue and a consequent handsome fortune, in spite of the extremely low fees he charged. At full prices for his services his fortune would have been immense, for he had one side or other of nearly every seriously contested case. His consultations with his clients were very brief; he seemed to catch the points and facts of a case by intuition; this enforced brevity sometimes gave offense, but on the trial no client ever complained that he did not fully understand his case. His memory was extraordinary, and was cultivated and relied upon; he steadily refused to take a single note, and yet, in the concluding argument, was often known to trace correctly the evidence of a dozen witnesses, repeat what each witness swore, and answer all the points made by the two opposing counsel. He seldom dealt in figures of speech or fancy sketches; his force lay in his perspicuity, in clearly arraying facts and fitting the evidence to sustain each fact in its proper place; he was an animated speaker, always commanding the closest attention, even if not carrying conviction.

Mr. Hardin served his county in the House of Representatives of Kentucky in 1810, 1811, 1824 and 1825, and in the Senate from 1828 to 1832; and represented his district in Congress from 1815 to 1817, from 1819 to 1823 and from 1833 to 1837—ten years in all. From September, 1844, to February, 1847, he was secretary of state, under Governor Owsley, with whom he had one of the most heated controversies which has ever taken place among the public men of Kentucky; his speech defending himself before the senate committee on executive affairs in January, 1847, was remarkable for its length, power and keenness. His last public service was in the convention that formed the present constitution of Kentucky in 1849-50.

GENERAL JOSEPH DESHA was a descendant of the Huguenots of France, his paternal grandfather being one of that persecuted sect, who in the middle of the seventeenth century fled to America to avoid the fury of intolerance, and enjoy unmolested the religion of their choice. The subject of this notice was born December 9, 1768, in Monroe County, in the eastern part of the then colony of Pennsylvania. In July, 1781, his father emigrated to Kentucky, and in the following year removed to that part of the present State of Tennessee, which was then known as the Cumberland District. In the month of December, 1789, Joseph Desha was united in marriage with the daughter of Colonel Bledsoe, and in the year 1792 settled permanently in Mason County, Kentucky.

As early as the year 1794 he volunteered under General Wayne, and served in his campaigns against the Indians with distinction. Indeed, at the early age of fifteen, and between that age and twenty-two, he took an active part in various skirmishes with the foe, who at that period in the early history of the west proved so fatal an annoyance to the settlers. In one of these skirmishes he had the misfortune to lose two of his brothers, who were killed in Tennessee, an event which no doubt stimulated his courage and greatly excited his vengeance against the perfidious enemy. His gallant bearing as a soldier and amiable qualities as a man, rendered him justly popular with the people, and for nine years previous to 1806 he represented the County of Mason in the State Legislature. In 1816 he was elected to Congress, and by successive re-elections was continued in that body until the year 1819.

GOVERNOR CHARLES ANDERSON WICKLIFFE, the youngest of nine children of Charles and Lydia (Hardin) Wickliffe, and brother of the late Robert Wickliffe of Lexington, was born June 8, 1788, in a log cabin on Sulphur Run, a branch of Cartwright Creek, six miles southwest of where now stands Springfield, Washington County, Kentucky; and died at the residence of his son-in-law in Howard County, Maryland, October 31, 1869, aged eighty-one years. His mother was a sister of Colonel John Hardin, so celebrated in the traditions of the west for his heroism and tragic fate.

His early education was limited. He remained at home until his seventeenth year, then spent a year at a grammar school in Bardstown under Rev. Dr. Wilson, and the ensuing nine months under the instruction of Rev. Dr. James Blythe, acting president of Transylvania University. He studied law in the office of his cousin, General Martin D. Hardin. The bar of Bardstown, when he settled there and began his professional career, was the ablest (perhaps excepting Lexington) west of the Allegheny Mountains. It comprised such men as John Rowan, an advocate unexcelled and rarely equaled in his day—afterward a judge of the Court of Appeals and United States Senator; John Pope, one of the strongest debaters that this country has ever produced; Ben Hardin, one of the great lawyers of the state; and at a subsequent period that prodigy, John Hays, whose marvelous eloquence is never spoken of without enthusiasm by those who had the good fortune to hear him. In this battle of the giants Mr. Wickliffe, by fair and honorable exertion, forced his way to a high place in public estimation.

After war had been declared in 1812, Mr. Wickliffe volunteered as a private, but was soon appointed aid to General Winlock. He was elected to represent Nelson County in the Legislature in 1812, and re-elected in 1813. When the news of the appalling disaster at the River Raisin, which covered the state with mourning, reached Frankfort, the Legislature requested the venerable Colonel Isaac Shelby, then governor for the second time, to take command of the Kentuckians and lead them to victory and vengeance. Governor Shelby by proclamation invited his fellow-citizens to meet him at Newport; Mr. Wickliffe again volunteered, was appointed aid to General Caldwell, of the Kentucky troops, and rendered valuable service at the battle of the Thames.

In 1820 and 1821 he was again a member of the Legislature, and for ten years consecutively, 1823 to 1833, represented his district in Congress. In 1825, when the choice of President of the United States devolved upon the United States House of Representatives, Mr. Wickliffe, in opposition to most of his colleagues, voted for General Andrew Jackson in preference to John Quincy Adams—which action his constituents sustained by a re-election with over 2,000 majority. He was chosen by the house one of the managers of the impeachment of Judge Peck before the United States Senate, and made one of the ablest speeches reported in the proceedings of that trial.

In 1833, 1834 and 1835 Mr. Wickliffe was again a member of the Kentucky House of Representatives, and in 1834 was chosen speaker after an animated race, over Daniel Breck and John L. Helm. In 1836 he was elected lieutenant-governor, upon the Whig ticket, with Judge James Clark for governor—receiving 35,524 votes to 32,186 cast for Elijah Hise, the Van Buren candidate. By the death of Governor Clark, Mr. Wickliffe became governor, October 5, 1839, until September, 1840. He was United States postmaster-general in the cabinet of President Tyler, September 13, 1841, to March 3, 1845; during which time, August 1, 1843, an attempt was made to assassinate him by a crazy man.

COLONEL GABRIEL SLAUGHTER, Governor of Kentucky, was a native of Virginia, but emigrated in his youth to Kentucky, and settled in Mercer County, some few miles from Harrodsburg. His residence was widely known under the attractive name of "Traveler's Rest."

Early in life he became a member of the Baptist denomination of Christians, and was extensively known as a prominent and useful member of that numerous and respectable society. He was frequently employed as messenger to its associated churches, and generally presided as moderator of their assemblies.

He rendered gallant and distinguished service in the battle of New Orleans on the 8th of January, 1815, as a colonel of a regiment of Kentucky troops. On one occasion, while acting as president of a court-martial—whose decision was not in accordance with the views of General Jackson—the court were ordered to reverse their proceedings; but Colonel Slaughter declined to comply, saying, "He knew his duty, and had performed it." General Jackson entertained the highest respect for his character as a soldier and patriot.

Colonel Slaughter was elected in 1816 to the office of lieutenant-governor, and upon the death of George Madison, succeeded him in the executive chair, and administered the government as acting governor of Kentucky for the four years of Madison's term. He appointed John Pope, Esq., secretary of state, who, at that time, was somewhat unpopular in Kentucky, on account of his opposition to the war with England while

Engraved by J.R. Rice & Sons Phila.

Senator of the United States. In consequence, it is thought, of this unexpected appointment, the new election question was fiercely agitated during the first session of the Legislature after Governor Slaughter's inauguration, and at the succeeding session also. The new election movement failed, and the construction or exposition then given to the constitution, in regard to the succession of the lieutenant-governor to the office of governor, upon the "death, resignation, or refusal to qualify," of the governor-elect, has been acquiesced in ever since, and regarded as a settled precedent.

DANIEL JAMES FALLIS, of Covington, was the late president of the Merchants' National Bank of Cincinnati, and also vice-president (for Ohio) of the National Bankers' Association of America. He was born near Fredericksburg, Fauquier County, Virginia, August 19, 1809, and the place of his nativity abounds in historic associations. Mr. Fallis was descended from Scotch-Irish ancestry, and his great-great-grandfather presided at a manufacturers' meeting in Dublin in 1698, for which he was compelled to sell his glass manufactory to avoid ruinous taxation, and finally was executed for treason. In the same year his great-grandfather, Thomas Fallis, came to the American colonies and landed in Philadelphia, and nine days after his arrival George Fallis (grandfather) was born. Remaining there twenty-three years, they emigrated to Virginia, where they purchased a large landed estate in Stafford County. There was a community of Quakers in that vicinity, to which the Fallises belonged, owing to which fact they were non-combatants during the revolution.

George Fallis was personally acquainted with and a friend of General Washington; and, learning of the suffering of the Continental soldiers, he wrote letters of sympathy offering to render him any service, except bearing arms, in his power for the relief of the army. Much of his property, consisting of many farms, was sold for the purpose of raising money to make good his offer. At one time the Continental money on hand from a portion of these sales amounted to one hundred and one thousand dollars ($101,000).

In 1797 Thomas Fallis (son of George) married Mary James; and, of the eight children born to them, Daniel James was the sixth.

Mr. Fallis remained in Virginia until 1824, when he followed two uncles to Wilmington, Ohio; and in 1826 went to Hillsboro, Ohio, where, until 1853, he was engaged in the mercantile business, but sold out preparatory to commencing business in Cincinnati.

In 1854 he began banking, and was the head of the firm of Fallis, Brown & Company, Third street, Cincinnati; but later Mr. Fallis bought his partner's interest and carried on the business under the firm name of Fallis & Company, until December, 1859, when the firm Fallis, Young & Company was created, continuing until 1865, and then merged into the Merchants' National Bank, with a capital of five hundred thousand dollars ($500,000). In 1867 this bank purchased the stock of the Ohio National Bank, thus increasing the capital to $1,000,000. Of this bank Mr. Fallis was the president until he tendered his resignation on his eighty-second birthday, August 19, 1891. He was therefore in the banking business uninterruptedly over thirty-seven years, and twenty-six years as president of the Merchants' National Bank. He was the oldest banker in Cincinnati who had steadily continued in the business, having passed safely through all the financial crises, never suspending or failing to meet the demands of his depositors and creditors.

One of his partners, John Young, was a warm personal friend of Secretary Chase. From this arose the fact that Mr. Fallis' judgment was also invoked touching the financial measures of the government, and had great weight upon the public mind. It was from this intelligent and unfaltering support of the leading bankers of the nation, of whom Mr. Fallis was a representative, that the government, through the treasury department, derived the wisdom and courage to take the steps which finally led to the crowning consummation of the specie payment; and the glory that surrounded the names of Chase and Sherman is none the less enduring because they were great financiers and not generals. These great secretaries, supported by their lieutenants, the representative bankers of the nation, their judgment and co-operation, commanded the revenues and marshaled the resources that constituted the sinews of the war.

Mr. Fallis was president of the Cincinnati Clearing House, an important institution, which he and John W. Ellis, Esq., now of New York City, were chiefly instrumental in organizing. He was a large stockholder, director and chairman of the executive committee of the pioneer iron establishment of Alabama, known as the Eureka Company; was director and president of the Western Tract Society of Cincinnati. Besides these interests he invested his capital in other enterprises, which yielded profitable returns while they gave employment to many men.

In politics Mr. Fallis was first an old line Whig, then a Know-Nothing, and finally an ardent Republican.

At the age of nineteen he became a member of the Presbyterian Church, and for many years was one of the ruling elders. At the time of his death, and for many years previous, he was connected with the old First Presbyterian Church, Cincinnati, and was its most able supporter. Mr. Fallis never hesitated to say that he owed his success in life to the Bible and its Author. These constituted the foundation of his character. Add to these experience, judgment, quick perception, a fine moral sense, unquestioned integrity, and we have the main reasons for a business career which was as honorable as it was successful. His interest in the world at large, and especially in his own country and in the church of his choice, had not abated as his years increased. It can be said that he was a very quiet man; and, while pursuing his business, he unostentatiously dispersed his charities.

October 30, 1835, Mr. Fallis married Miss Ann Poage, daughter of General John Poage, of Greenup County, Kentucky, and granddaughter of Colonel George Poage, who commanded under General Washington at the siege of Yorktown.

Colonel Poage's father (John Poage) came to the American colonies with his parents in 1740, and occupied a high civil office throughout the Revolutionary war.

Mrs. Fallis most emphatically belongs to one of Kentucky's oldest families, as her mother was the fourth white child born in this state, and at Harrodsburg, when it was only a fort, in the year 1777.

Mr. and Mrs. Fallis had but two children, a daughter, now Mrs. Charles G. Rodgers, and son, the Honorable John T. Fallis, who was a member of the Cincinnati bar and represented Hamilton County in the Ohio Legislature. From March, 1861, until his death, Mr. Fallis resided in Covington, in a beautiful home that has been the scene of hospitality and domestic happiness, but alas! the Angel of Death hovered over it, and on May 7, 1893, the only and beloved son was taken from it. This was a very great shock to Mr. Fallis and one from which he never recovered, yet he claimed to be sufficiently well to undertake a journey, so on the evening of June 7 (just one month after his son's death) he left home, but on the following morning was suddenly and fatally attacked with heart disease at Jamestown, New York, his sickness and death both occupying but a few minutes. His remains were brought to the home he so much loved, and there his funeral took place. Beside his son he was laid in Highland Cemetery, back of Covington, and a handsome monument marks their resting place. At this writing Mrs. Fallis, with her daughter, Mrs. Rodgers, occupies the old homestead.

EDMUND HAYNES TAYLOR, Jr., of Frankfort, Kentucky, is descended from one of the pioneer families of Kentucky and Virginia.

The progenitor of this family in America was James Taylor, who came from England and settled in what was then New Kent County, Virginia, about the year 1650. He was a wealthy man for that time and invested largely in land, and died in 1698, leaving a large family.

The oldest son of the first James Taylor, also named James, was one of the earliest surveyors of Virginia, who ran out the lines between Hanover, Spottsylvania and Orange Counties and located about 10,000 acres of land in the latter county, to which he removed at a very early date, as he was living there at the time of his death in 1729. He married Martha Thompson and left a family of nine children; the eldest child, Frances, married Ambrose Madison and was the grandmother of President James Madison. The third child and oldest son was named James, and was the ancestor of the large Taylor family of Newport, Kentucky.

The fourth child and second son was Zachary Taylor, father of the gallant Lieutenant Colonel Richard Taylor of the Revolution, and his brother, Hancock Taylor, who together made the first journey down the Ohio and Mississippi rivers from what is now Pittsburg to the mouth of the Mississippi, returning through the unknown Indian country overland in 1769. Lieutenant Colonel Richard Taylor was the father of Major General Zachary Taylor, President of the United States.

The fifth child, and third son, of James and Martha Thompson Taylor was George Taylor, born in Orange County, Virginia, in 1711.

He was appointed deputy clerk of Orange in 1749 and in 1750 was appointed clerk, which position he held until 1772, when he was succeeded by his eldest son, James Taylor.

George Taylor was appointed colonel of the Orange County militia by Governor Dinwiddie, during the French and Indian war, and at the outbreak of the Revolution was a member of the Orange County Committee of Safety. He was a member of the House of Burgesses from Orange from 1748 to 1758, and member of the Virginia Convention of 1775. He married, first, Rachel Gibson, daughter of Jonathan Gibson, at one time clerk of Orange County, who bore him eleven sons: James, George, Jonathan, Edmund, Francis, Richard, John, William, Charles, Reuben and Benjamin.

Of these sons, George died in 1761, but all of the other ten served either in rank or file of the Revolution.

James was a sergeant; Jonathan was lieutenant; Edmund an officer of Virginia militia; Francis, colonel of the Regiment of Convention Guards; Richard, captain in the Navy of the Commonwealth; John, a lieutenant in the navy, was captured by the British, carried to New York and confined in the old prison ship "Jersey," and died while a prisoner; William was major in the Second Virginia Regiment; Charles, surgeon in the Regiment of Convention Guards; Reuben at first a private in the Minute Men and later captain; Benjamin was midshipman in the navy and served with his brothers Richard and John.

After the death of Rachel Gibson, his wife, Col. George Taylor was married a second time to Mrs. Sarah Conway, nee Taliaferro, and had one son, George Conway Taylor, who was at one time a member of the Virginia Council.

Edmund Taylor, the third son of Col. George Taylor, served throughout the Revolution as a soldier and officer of militia; he received for his services several thousand acres of bounty land, which he located in Jefferson County, Kentucky, and to which he removed shortly after the close of the war. He died in 1784-5, leaving ten children, one of whom, Mary Taylor, married her first cousin, Richard Taylor, Jr., son of Captain Richard Taylor of the Virginia Navy.

Richard Taylor, the fifth son of Col. George and Rachel Gibson Taylor, was born in Orange County, Virginia, January 6, 1749. On the recommendation of General Washington he was appointed a captain in the Virginia Navy of the Revolution in 1776 and served until the close of the war. He commanded at various times the state boats "Liberty," "Patriot" and "Tartar," and captured several armed British cruisers, one of which, the "Speedwell," was afterward sent to the West Indies for ammunition and supplies so badly needed by the Patriot army.

At one time Captain Taylor's boat was becalmed just inside of the Virginia Capes, in sight of a British ship, and he determined to attempt the capture of the ship in his open boats, and made the attack. The British fired on his boats, killing six of his men and putting a ball through his thigh, which lamed him for life, but he urged his men on to the attack and finally overpowered the British crew and took them into Norfolk harbor.

For his services during the war he received several thousand acres of bounty land, most of which he located in what was then Jefferson County, Kentucky, about twenty miles above the Falls of the Ohio, and in 1794 removed to his land with his large family.

In addition to bounty land, Captain Taylor received a pension of $300 per annum on account of the wounds received in action.

Captain Richard Taylor married Catharine Davis of Orange or Culpeper County, Virginia, and left a very large family; his son, Col. Richard Taylor, was appointed surveyor of the lands set apart for the officers and soldiers of the Revolution, west of the Tennessee river, in Kentucky, and settled at Columbus, Kentucky.

Col. Richard Taylor, Jr., married his first cousin, Mary, daughter of Edmund Taylor, and had, among other children, John Eastin Taylor, who married Rebecca Edrington, and was at one time clerk of Hickman County, Kentucky; born 1803; died at Point Coupee, Louisiana, February, 1835, leaving three children, the eldest of whom is living.

Edmund Haynes Taylor, son of John Eastin and Rebecca (Edrington) Taylor and grandson of Richard Taylor, Jr., and Mary Taylor, was born in Columbia, Kentucky, in 1832. He was left an orphan at an early age and was adopted, raised and educated by his uncle, Col. Edmund H. Taylor of Frankfort, who gave him every educational facility, and who started him out in his business life as he did his own son.

In early life, with limited patrimony, but with an ambition born of laudable desire, he began to carve out the career which has achieved success and given him distinction and prominence as a leader among men. The foundation was fortunately laid in a good education and personal discipline under that master of his art, B. B. Sayre, who was not surpassed as an educator in Kentucky. His training applied to the entire personality of the pupil, and to this Mr. Taylor owes, besides his mental culture, that grace and dignity of address and that suavity and charm of expression which adds so much to the popularity of character and potency.

At the age of twenty-one he was united in marriage with Fannie, daughter of William Stapleton Johnson of Frankfort. He was at that early age cashier of the Commercial Bank of Kentucky at Versailles. Soon after he was engaged with men of capital in private banking in Lexington. The great disturbing event of the Civil war led his adventurous spirit to embark in other enterprises of the troublous times. In 1868, with little more than his business qualifications to bank on, he began the manufacture of whiskey at Frankfort, and in this struck the flood-tide of his career. His ready intuitions soon mastered all details of the science of distilling and its products, and placed him far in advance of the day in perfecting his novel and improved methods which have acquired fame for superior purity and excellence wherever fine Bourbon whiskies have become famed over the world. Since 1868, barring some incidents of reverses and financial troubles, this great enterprise has steadily grown in prestige and prosperity, and to-day stands unsurpassed by any other in the distilling interests in the United States. From 1871 to 1891 he was repeatedly elected mayor of the city of Frankfort, serving in all sixteen years, and until he removed to his new and beautiful residence one mile beyond the city limits. On his resignation as mayor he was elected with unanimity by the people of the county to serve them in the legislature of 1891-2, at a period of supreme interest and importance to his constituents and to the state. He was subsequently elected to the state senate to complete the unexpired term of Judge Lindsay, who was elected to the United States Senate, and narrowly escaped membership in the present (1896) legislature, having been happily defeated in the nominating convention of his party.

Few men have shown the qualities of high courage and invincible power of will of Edmund H. Taylor, Jr., and these have given him a force of character and prestige that make him an acknowledged leader of men. His generosity is equal to his splendid abilities, and his charity and public beneficence are as notable as his other traits of character. Mr. Taylor's ample fortune enables him to dispense in munificent style that old fashioned Kentucky hospitality in which he has always taken a delight and pride.

JUDGE HORATIO W. BRUCE, son of Alexander and Amanda (Bragg) Bruce, was born February 22, 1830. His father was born in Garrard County, Kentucky, in 1797, and received a thorough education in the academy in Lancaster; studied law in the office of Samuel McKee, and after his admission to the bar he

JUDGE H. W. BRUCE.

practiced law for a short time and then removed to Vanceburg, Kentucky, and engaged in merchandising. He accumulated a handsome fortune, which was largely invested in farms and timberlands, and for many years he gave his attention to his farms and his several saw mills. He was an intense Whig and took an active part in state and national politics, serving his country in the State Legislature in 1825 and 1826. He died in 1851 and was buried at Vanceburg, Kentucky.

John Bruce (grandfather) was born in Pittsylvania County, Virginia, in 1748. He was a farmer, of good education, and a patriot, serving as a soldier in the Revolutionary war within the Virginia State line. After the war he removed to Kentucky and settled in Bourbon County, but afterward removed to Garrard County, where he died in 1827. His wife was Elizabeth Clay, daughter of Henry Clay, Jr., of Mecklenburg, Virginia, who survived him a few years. His father, H. W. Bruce's great-grandfather, was a native of Scotland, who came to this country and settled in Virginia.

Mrs. Amanda (Bragg) Bruce (mother) was born in Lewis County in 1805. She and Alexander Bruce were married in 1818. She died and was buried at Vanceburg in 1852. She was a member of the Methodist Episcopal Church. Her father, Thomas Bragg, was a native of Fauquier County, Virginia, who came to Kentucky and located in Nelson County in 1800, and afterward moved to Lewis County. He served in the Revolutionary war; was a farmer and a member of the Episcopal Church. His wife, Lucy Blakemore, daughter of Thomas Blakemore, who married Anne Nevil, was born near Battletown (now Berryville), Frederick (now Clark) County, Virginia. She was born in March, 1764, and died in November, 1862, so that, if she had lived until the following March, she would have been ninety-nine years of age. She was reared in the Episcopal Church, but was for many years member of M. E. Church. Her father, Joseph Bragg (maternal great-grandfather), was a native of and was reared on Albemarle Sound, not far from Norfolk, Virginia. His brother, Peter Bragg, was the great-grandfather of Walter L. Bragg of the Interstate Commerce Commission. The Braggs belonged to the old English Newport family, for whom Newport News and the City of Norfolk were named.

Hon. H. W. Bruce is a native of Lewis County. He was educated in private schools in Kentucky and in Manchester, Ohio; studied law in the office of L. M. Cox of Flemingsburg and after admission to the bar, at the age of twenty-one, practiced law in Flemingsburg until Christmas, 1858, when he came to Louisville, which has been his home ever since, although voluntarily absent during the war. While living in Flemingsburg he represented his county in the Legislature in 1855 and 1856; and in 1856, when twenty-six years of age, he was commonwealth attorney for that district. He was also a member of the Board of School Trustees of Flemingsburg.

When he came to Louisville he formed a copartnership with his brother-in-law, Ben Hardin Helm, under the firm name of Helm & Bruce. Mr. Helm was afterward a general in the Confederate army. He was a brother-in-law of President Lincoln, having married Miss Emily Todd, a sister of Mrs. Lincoln. Mr. Helm went into the Confederate army as a colonel and was promoted to the rank of brigadier-general on the recommendation of Albert Sidney Johnson. He was desperately wounded in the battle of Baton Rouge and was killed in the battle of Chickamauga.

Judge Bruce also cast his lot with the Southern Confederacy, but in a civil capacity, after having been a States' Rights candidate for United States Congress in 1861 in opposition to Robert Mallory, the successful candidate. He was a member of the Russellville conventions, the second of which passed the ordinance of secession, declaring Kentucky out of the Union. That convention established a provisional government for Kentucky, the Legislature of which was called the Provisional Council. He was a member of that council, and during his term of service in the council, Kentucky, by act of the Congress of the Confederate States, was admitted as a member of the "Confederate States of America."

Judge Bruce was elected a member of the

House of Representatives of the Confederate Congress, in which capacity he served until the end of the war. In 1861, at Montgomery, Alabama, eleven states (not embracing Kentucky, Missouri, Delaware and Maryland) formed a provisional government under a provisional constitution as the Confederate States of America on an equal footing. The first congress was organized at Montgomery, Alabama, but was transferred to Richmond, Virginia. It was of one body and was known as the Provisional Congress. It adopted a constitution for the Confederate States of America, which was accepted by those states. The constitution provided for a Legislature designated as the "Congress of the Confederate States of America." That congress was bicaudal in character. It was ordained that that congress should assemble in Richmond, Virginia, on the eighteenth day of February, 1862, when its House of Representatives should elect a speaker and other officers. It was also ordained that the President and Vice-President of the C. S. A. should be inaugurated on the 22d day of February, 1862.

As stated, Judge Bruce, who was then thirty-two years of age, was elected a member of that House of Representatives which assembled February 18, 1862. The Congress of the permanent government also assembled on that day. About one hour previous to the assembling of the House of Representatives, the Provisional Congress, with Howell Cobb as President, adjourned sine die. Immediately after the adjournment of the Provisional Congress, the first session of the House of Representatives convened, and Thomas S. Bocok of Appomattox Court House, Virginia, was elected speaker. The President, Jefferson Davis, and the Vice-President, Alexander H. Stephens, were to be formally inaugurated on the 22d of February, four days later; and a resolution was adopted by the house directing the speaker to appoint a committee of thirteen, one from each state, on inaugural ceremonies, which committee was charged with the duty of arranging and conducting all the ceremonies incident to the induction of the President and Vice-President into office. The State of Kentucky was represented on that committee by Judge Bruce, whose career as a member of Congress of the C. S. A. during the remaining years of its existence has long passed into history.

He left Richmond April 2, 1865, with the other members of Congress, and with President Davis, and went to Danville, Virginia, where he remained until the surrender at Appomattox Court House; and after remaining for a while at Greensburg, North Carolina, and Augusta, Georgia, he returned to Richmond. President Johnson had issued his amnesty proclamation, and the attorney-general, Hon. James Speed of Kentucky, being a personal friend of Judge Bruce, he determined to go to Washington and have a settlement with the United States government. When he arrived in Washington Mr. Speed informed him that he had been pardoned.

In August, 1865, he resumed the practice of law in partnership with a former pupil, Mr. Samuel Russell (late president of the Bank of Louisville), under the firm name of Bruce & Russell. This partnership was dissolved in August, 1868, when Mr. Bruce was elected judge of this judicial district, which he held as circuit judge until 1873, when he was appointed chancellor of the Louisville Chancery Court by the governor of Kentucky. He remained chancellor, by election, until March 10, 1880, when he resigned to accept his present position of attorney for the Louisville & Nashville Railroad Company, the duties of which demand his exclusive attention.

From 1872 to 1880 he was a professor in the law department of the University of Louisville, holding the chair of history and science of law, the law of real property, contracts and criminal law. He was not a graduate of any college or university, which is usually required of professors in chartered institutions of learning. He was for a number of years president of the Louisvill Medical College.

Judge Bruce married Miss Lizzie Barbour Helm, June 12, 1856. She was a daughter of John L. and Lucinda Barbour Helm. Her mother was a daughter of Ben Hardin. Mrs. Bruce was born at Helm Place, Hardin County, April 11, 1836, and was educated in Elizabethtown and Louisville. She is a member of the Presbyterian Church. They have five children: Helm, Lizzie Barbour, Maria Preston Pope, Mary and Alexander.

Helm Bruce is a lawyer in Louisville in partnership with his uncle, James P. Helm, who is a brother of General Ben Helm—the former partner of Judge Bruce—and the firm name of Helm & Bruce is the same as that which existed before the war. Young Mr. Bruce is a graduate of Washington and Lee University, taking two scholarships, one in moral philosophy and one in mathematics, in both of which he received very high honors. He was orator of the literary society to which he belonged at college, and when he graduated in the law department of the University of Louisville he received the medal for the best essay, choosing for his subject "Contributory Negligence."

Two daughters of Judge Bruce, Preston and Barbour, after receiving the best instruction in the schools at home, spent three years in Europe studying the languages, arts and literature.

WILLIAM J. RANKINS, retired merchant of Augusta, was born in Mason County, September 1, 1823; son of Blackstone H. and Elizabeth (Barker) Rankins. His father was born in Virginia, November 4, 1794, and removed to Mason County when a boy, receiving a part of his education in Mason County, where he died August 31, 1868. In politics he was a Whig and in religion a Universalist. His father, William Rankins, came from Virginia and located in Mason County early in the present century, where he was a successful farmer. He died April 12, 1838. His ancestors came from Ireland.

Elizabeth Barker Rankins (mother) was born in Maryland, June 26, 1797, and died in Bracken County, November 20, 1853. Her father, Joseph Barker, was born July 25, 1759; died May 10, 1821. His wife (maternal grandmother) was a sister of John Quincy Adams; born June 2, 1769; died May 11, 1854.

William J. Rankins received a good education in the Mason County schools, after which he engaged in a general merchandising, commission and forwarding business, having large transactions on the Ohio river, in which he continued from 1849 until 1884, when he retired. During the war his sympathies were with the Union, but he took no active part, giving attention to commercial affairs and having little interest at any time in politics. He is an elder in the Presbyterian Church, and one of the most honored and substantial citizens of Augusta.

He was married July 5, 1852, to Hannah J. Silverthorn, daughter of Samuel and Isabella Silverthorn. She was born December 1, 1831; died July 22, 1878.

He was married the second time, in Brooklyn, New York, September 20, 1883, to Mary Ann, daughter of James and Mary (De Cue) Sproule. She was born February 9, 1853.

CHARLES WILLIAM AITKIN, M. D., of Flemingsburg, Kentucky, son of Dr. George and Jennie Holiday (Duty) Aitkin, grandson of George Aitkin, was born December 16, 1859, at Sherburne, Kentucky. He was educated in the public schools of Fleming County, Kentucky, and at Threlkeld's Select School, Lexington, Kentucky. Commenced the study of medicine in 1877 at Sherburne under his father, George Aitkin, A. M., M. D.; attended two courses of lectures at the Medical College of Ohio, Cincinnati, and was graduated March 2, 1880; he also took a post-graduate course of instruction in microscopy, bacteriology, physical diagnosis and ophthalmology at the Ohio Medical College in 1890, and at the New York Polyclinic in 1891. He practiced his profession in Sherburne, Kentucky, with his father from the time of his graduation until 1889, then alone till September, 1890; since April, 1891, in Flemingsburg in partnership with Drs. McDowell & Garr, with whom he is now associated under the firm name of McDowell, Garr & Aitkin. (See sketch of Dr. Charles R. Garr in this volume.)

Dr. Aitkin is a member of the Fleming County Medical Society; Northeastern Kentucky Medical Association; was treasurer of the same in 1893, and re-elected at the May meeting, 1894; was elected president of the Northeastern Kentucky Medical Association in January, 1896; member of the Kentucky State Medical Society, elected first vice president at June meeting, 1894; member of Alumni Association of the Medical

College of Ohio; member of the American Medical Association; secretary of the Fleming County Board of Health, 1891-98;. secretary of the Flemingsburg Board of United States Pension Examiners, 1890-93; president of the Fleming County Farmers' Bank since August, 1892; director of local board of the Blue Grass Building & Loan Association; member of Board of Missions, and of the Board of Church Extension of the Kentucky Conference, Methodist Episcopal Church, South.

He has published articles on "Pleuritic Effusions," Medical Progress, July, 1890, and American Practitioner and News; "Diagnosis and Treatment of Diphtheria," Transactions of Kentucky State Medical Society, New Series, Vol. I.; "Wound Closure After Empyema Operation," Ohio Medical Journal, April, 1892; "Some Points on Physical Examinations of the Chest," ibid., January, 1894; "A Complicated Pleurisy," ibid., July, 1894. He is also the author of a paper on "Post-Scarlatinal Nephritis," "Report of Three Atypical Cases of Cancer of the Stomach," read before local societies; also a paper on "The Clergyman, the Doctor and the Religious Press," Ohio Medical Journal, October, 1895.

Dr. Aitkin was married September 20, 1881, to Miss Ida J. Browning of Mason County, Kentucky. Mrs. Aitkin is a daughter of William Reed Browning and Mary A. Ball, his wife, natives of Mason County. The children of Dr. and Mrs. Aitkin are Jennie Browning, born November 13, 1883, died October 25, 1888, of diphtheria; and Maurice Duty Aitkin, born April 8, 1890.

Dr. Aitkin is a man of great energy and industry, devoted to his profession and to the important work of the church which is entrusted to his care; an exemplary Christian gentleman, whose professional and other business interests are conducted upon correct principles, and in every relation of life his deportment is characterized by the faithful and conscientious discharge of duty.

George Aitkin, A. M., M. D. (father), was born near Knoxville, Tennessee; was a graduate of the academic, theological and medical departments of Transylvania University; taught as a supply in academic department for one term; practiced medicine at Sherburne, Kentucky, during his whole professional career, and died there in 1889. For a number of years he preached to Presbyterian congregations at New Hope, Gilead and Battle Run; was president of the Sherburne Board of Trustees of the public schools and of the Town Council for many years; owned a farm near Sherburne, which was used principally for grazing; was a Republican in politics until four years before his death, when he became associated with the Prohibition party; was married in 1848 to Jennie Holiday Duty, who was born in Bath County, Kentucky, and was educated in private schools in Sharpsburg. They had four children: Nathan Rice, Emma, wife of Charles H. Daugherty, Daniel D. and Dr. Charles W. Aitkin.

George Aitkin (grandfather) was born in Scotland about 1770; graduated in medicine at Edinburgh; emigrated to America in 1800 and located in Tennessee; was not fond of his profession and virtually abandoned the practice of medicine and followed farming. He removed to Lexington, Kentucky, where he died some years later. He was a member of the Presbyterian Church and a devout Christian gentleman.

Rev. William Aitkin (great-grandfather), a native of Scotland, was educated in Edinburgh College, and was a Presbyterian minister. His two sons were also educated in the University of Edinburgh.

Littleton Duty (maternal grandfather) was a native of Virginia; came to Kentucky about 1810 and located in Bath County, where he died; was a member of the Methodist Episcopal Church; married Sallie Lyle McAllister, who was a native of Richmond, Virginia, daughter of Charles McAllister and Jennie Holiday, his wife, both of whom were members of the Methodist Episcopal Church.

JAMES C. CARRICK, a leading physician of Lexington, is of Scotch-Irish origin. He is a grandson of Robert Carrick, who served in Colonel Richard M. Johnson's mounted regiment, and is a son of Alexander and Mary Helm (Cantrill) Carrick, and was born in Scott County, Kentucky, January 25, 1867.

Alexander Carrick was also a native of the same county and was a well-known farmer and breeder of thoroughbred horses for many years. He was born in 1802 and died in 1875. He was a member of the Christian Church in New Town, and performed his duties in every relation of life well. He was a Democrat and espoused the cause of the Confederacy and served through that struggle as a captain of a company. He was the owner of three thousand acres of land in Scott County at the time of his death.

His father, Robert Carrick, died in the same year, 1876, and was also a member of the Christian Church, and held the office of magistrate. He was born in 1791. He father was a native of Scotland and, when a young man, emigrated from his native land and settled in Kentucky.

Alexander Carrick married Mary Helm Cantrill (cousin of Lieutenant Governor Cantrill), who was born in Scott County, Kentucky, and is now living in the old homestead in that county. Her father was John F. Cantrill, a native Kentuckian, and during the greater part of his life an extensive farmer and stock breeder of Bourbon County, where his death occurred in 1890, in the eighty-third year of his age. He was a worthy member of the Baptist Church. He married a Miss Barlow, a member of an old Virginia family who settled in Bourbon County. He had four sons, who served in the Southern army under Generals Morgan, Forrest and Wheeler. The Cantrills are descended from the Huguenots who settled in England in 1695, when Louis XIV. issued an edict forbidding the return to France of all refugees who had fled to England to escape being publicly burned alive for the crime of heresy. The Cantrills were silk dyers in France, and followed that profession when exiled in England from 1695 to 1698. Peter De Cantrill settled in Virginia in 1728.

James C. Carrick, at the age of fourteen, entered the Kentucky University at Lexington and graduated therefrom in 1884. He subsequently accepted a position in a drug store in Louisville, where he remained for two years, and 1888 was graduated from the Hospital College of Medicine of that city. He then took a post-graduate course at Bellevue Hospital College, New York City, and received the degree of M. D. in 1889. While there he was house surgeon of the Polyclinic Hospital for twelve months. In 1890 Doctor Carrick located in Lexington, where he has become well established as a leading member of his profession, being an industrious student and having a large practice.

He is a member of the Fayette County Medical Society and of the State Medical Society. He recently contributed an article to the Medical press on Diphtheria, which has been widely read and favorably commented upon by the profession. Doctor Carrick is a member of the Masonic order, Knights of Honor and Odd Fellows, and is a member of the Broadway Christian Church, and is a Democrat in politics.

He owns a fine farm in Scott County and raises many valuable horses.

JOHN GRIFFIN CARLISLE, the present Secretary of the Treasury, was born in Kenton County, Kentucky, September 5, 1835; educated in the best schools of the neighborhood, and himself a teacher at fifteen and for five years afterward; studied law in Covington with ex-Governor John W. Stevenson and Judge William B. Kinkead; as the partner of the latter began the practice in March, 1857, and took rank at once as one of the most analytical and clearest legal minds among the young men of Kentucky; was elected to the lower house of the Legislature, 1859-61; took a "back seat" during the War of the Rebellion because of certain differences of opinion which were inconsistent with his promotion; but in August, 1865, again came to the front as the Democratic candidate for the State Senate from Kenton County, but was beaten at the polls by Mortimer M. Kenton. In February, 1866, the Senate declared the seat of the latter vacant, because the election was "neither free nor equal in the sense required in the constitution, being regulated, controlled and unduly influenced by armed soldiers in the service of the United States, in utter disregard of the law." Mr. Carlisle was elected to fill the vacancy, 1866-69, and triumphantly re-elected for another term, 1869-73, but resigned in 1871 to accept the Democratic nomination for lieutenant-governor of the state—to which office he was elected August, 1871, for four years, receiving 125,955 votes to 86,148 cast for the Radical nominee. In 1872, for a few months, he was the leading editor of the Louisville Daily Ledger. He was several times sent to Congress from the Sixth (Covington) District; twice elected speaker, and upon the death of Senator Beck was appointed to fill out the unexpired term of Beck; was elected for a full term of six years as United States Senator at next meeting of the Legislature. In March, 1893, when President Cleveland came into office, Mr. Carlisle resigned to accept the treasury portfolio, a position he at present occupies.

Mr. Carlisle is generally regarded by his countrymen as being the highest authority on questions of finance and the currency.

JOHN BODINE OWSLEY, M. D., cashier of the Farmers' Bank and Trust Company of Stanford, son of Walter Williams Owsley and Martha Hays, was born in Pulaski County, near Somerset, Kentucky, November 3, 1833.

His father was born in Lincoln County, Kentucky, April 12, 1808; educated in his native county; attended medical lectures at Transylvania University; practiced medicine in Pulaski County; removed to Lincoln County, on Dick's river, near Lancaster, in 1853, where he followed his profession during the remainder of his life; died in 1887, and is buried in Buffalo Cemetery at Stanford. He was married in 1831 to Martha Hays, daughter of Charles and Catherine Hays, who was born in Pulaski County in 1810. She was carefully educated, and spent a portion of her early life with her aunt, Mary Owsley, who was a daughter of William Finley. Mrs. Martha Hays Owsley (mother) died in 1839, and Dr. Owsley was married again in 1849 to Isabella Ann Pennington, who died in 1889.

Of the six sons of Doctor and Martha Hays Owsley, but one, the subject of this sketch, is now living; and of the two children of Isabella Pennington Owsley (stepmother) one remains, Stephen Ephraim Owsley.

Dr. W. W. Owsley (father) was an elder in the Presbyterian Church, a leading citizen and an exemplary Christian gentleman.

Ebsworth Owsley (grandfather) was born and reared in Lincoln County; was a son of Harry Owsley (great-grandfather), a citizen of Lincoln County, who was a descendant of Thomas Owsley, a native of Virginia, who surveyed and cut the famous Wilderness road under a territorial contract, receiving his compensation from the tolls collected on the road. One of the original toll-gates is still in existence.

Ebsworth Owsley's mother was Martha Bodine, whose parents were of Welsh and German origin. The Owsleys were originally from England, where the family was quite noted for intelligence and good citizenship. Governor William Owsley was a cousin of Dr. J. B. Owsley of Stanford.

Charles Hayes (maternal grandfather) was one of the leading men in Pulaski County, a very prominent Presbyterian—as were all of his family and all of the Owsleys—and a most liberal contributor to the extension and support of the church. He donated the ground and erected a building, which is still in good repair, a monument to his memory, and in which his "good works follow him."

Catherine Logan (grandmother), wife of Charles Hayes, was a daughter of William Logan, who was a brother of General Benjamin Logan.

Dr. J. B. Owsley was graduated from Center College, Danville, in the class of 1853. During the next two years he attended the medical department of the University of Louisville, and in 1855 attended medical lectures in the New York State University, known as the College of Physicians and Surgeons, and finishing before he was twenty-one years of age, did not receive his diploma until he had reached his majority, and in the meantime served as an assistant in Bellevue Hospital in New York; was appointed assistant physician on one of the United States war ships, but declined; returned to Kentucky in the fall of 1856 and began the practice of medicine at Crab Orchard Springs, where he was quite successful for six years. His Grandfather Hayes having died about that time (1862), leaving a large estate, he was called away from that field of labor to attend to the settlement of the estate, and this closed his professional career. He gave his attention to farming for some years, and in 1870 organized the Farmers' National Bank of Stanford. This was succeeded by the Lincoln County National Bank, which was succeeded by the present Farmers' Bank and Trust Company, operated under state authority, of which he is cashier.

From 1884 to 1886 Dr. Owsley was engaged in pork packing in Louisville, being a member of the firm of White, Akin & Company, of that city. Following his inclinations, however, and having business interests in his former home, he returned there and has since been identified with the banking business in Stanford.

He is a man of the highest integrity, of superior business ability, highly respected and implicitly trusted by all who know him. His opinion and judgment in business matters is regarded by his associates as almost infallible.

Dr. Owsley was married (first) to Sabra Pennington, daughter of Ephraim Pennington. She died in 1862, and he was married (second) to Mary F. Welch, daughter of John M. and Elizabeth Welch.

JOHN FELAND, Attorney-at-Law of Hopkinsville, son of Samuel and Nancy (Hamill) Feland, was born in Barren County, near Glasgow, December 23, 1837. His parents removed to Christian County in 1848, and he was educated in the schools at Hopkinsville and at Center College, attending college in 1858, contemporary with Blackburn, Dulaney and others who have distinguished themselves in public life. After leaving Center College he read law with Colonel James F. Buckner, who was for many years collector of internal revenue in Louisville, and was licensed to practice law by Judges Henry C. Stites and Thomas C. Dabney in 1859. He has been a citizen and lawyer of Hopkinsville ever since, except at short intervals.

He was elected to the legislature, August, 1875, and was re-elected in 1877 and 1879; and, notwithstanding the fact that he was one of the minority of Republicans in the house, he served on more committees than any other member. He was elected to the senate of Kentucky in 1885, to fill out the unexpired term of Hon. Austin Peay, resigned.

In 1889 President Harrison appointed him collector of internal revenue for the Second Collection District of Kentucky, with headquarters at Owensboro; and he held that office for four years.

John Feland and Sarah Kennedy of Todd County were united in marriage February 12, 1863, and they have four children: William S., civil engineer; John, Jr., lawyer; Logan, architect, and Mary, wife of John Gilmour, all of whom are now residents of Owensboro.

Samuel Feland (father) was born in Barren County, January 21, 1811, and was reared in that county as a farmer; but afterwards was a brickmason and builder. He removed to Christian County in 1848; married Nancy Hamill, daughter of John Hamill, a native of Ireland, who came to Kentucky from Pennsylvania about the time the Felands moved to the Green River country, and the families were neighbors. The date of their settlement in Kentucky is not known precisely, but it was about the beginning of the Revolutionary war.

Thomas Feland, the progenitor of the Felands who came to Kentucky, was of Scotch-Irish descent. He, with several brothers, came to America when the country was new, and located in Campbell County, Virginia. With the first tide of emigration to Kentucky, he removed to Lincoln County and lived there until he reached the unusual age of one hundred and fifteen years, when he died and was buried in Lincoln County. His sons, James and John, lived and died in that county. Andrew removed to Missouri and Samuel went to Tennessee. Thomas Feland (great-grandfather) was killed by the Indians. He left a widow and eight children. His son, William Feland (grandfather) was then fourteen years of age. He removed to the Green River country, first to Barren and then to Warren County, where he died in 1839. He left six sons and eight daughters. The sons were: David, Thomas, James H., Joseph, Samuel (father) and John. William Feland married a daughter of David Culbertson of Culbertson's Valley, Pennsylvania.

After quitting the revenue service at Owensboro in 1893, John Feland returned to Hopkinsville and resumed the practice of law. He is one of the leading men in his profession and has an extensive practice in the courts of Hopkinsville and in the adjacent counties, and in the Court of Appeals and the United States Courts at Louisville and Paducah.

JOHN WILLIAM RESPESS CORLIS, M. D., a prominent physician of Brooksville, son of John and Maria (Rice) Corlis, was born in Bracken County, Kentucky, August 14, 1833.

His father was a native of Providence, Rhode Island, who came to Lexington, Kentucky, when he was seventeen years of age; graduated from the medical department of Transylvania University, and was a practicing physician in Bracken County for about thirty-five years; was one of the best known and most popular men in the county; prominent in the Masonic order; active in charitable work; a Democrat in politics, but was too loyal to his profession to take an active interest in political affairs. He died September 15, 1867, and is buried at Brooksville.

John Corlis (grandfather) was born in Providence, Rhode Island, January 3, 1767, where he was a merchant and importer of fine silks. Many of his ships were lost at sea, and from these disasters and other losses he was threatened with bankruptcy; removed to Lexington, Kentucky, where he lived in retirement, having saved a competency from his former wealth.

He married (first) Susanna Condie Russell, who was born in Providence, Rhode Island, October 22, 1767, daughter of Joseph Russell, and died September 26, 1824.

George Corlis (great-grandfather) was born in Shrewsbury, New Jersey, October 24, 1717; died June 16, 1790. His wife, Waitstill Rhodes, was born in Pawtucket, Rhode Island, February 8, 1723; died in Providence, October 23, 1783, and was buried on her father's plantation at Pawtucket.

George Corlis (great-great-grandfather) came from England about 1675 or 1680, and married Exercise Shattuck, daughter of William Shattuck, a Massachusetts Quaker, who was driven from his home by the intolerance of the Puritans and settled at Shrewsbury, New Jersey.

Maria Rice Corlis (mother) was born in Bracken County, Kentucky, February 2, 1817; was educated in the common schools; married Dr. John Corlis September 27, 1832; died December 12, 1861, and is buried at Brooksville. Her father was Hudson M. Rice, a native of Virginia, who came to Kentucky in his early manhood; was a farmer in Bracken County, and subsequently removed to Missouri, where he died.

Dr. J. W. R. Corlis was educated in the schools of Bracken County, and prepared for his vocation in the Ohio Medical College, Cincinnati, from which he graduated in March, 1855. He at once began the practice of medicine at Brooksville, in which he has continued with most excellent success for more than forty years, having at this time a very large practice. He also has a fine farm in which he takes a lively interest, being quite devoted to improved methods of farming. His home in Brooksville is noted for genuine Kentucky hospitality and good fellowship.

Dr. Corlis was married July 2, 1857, to Mary Eleanor Kemper Linn, who was born December 13, 1834; daughter of E. W. and Octavia (Pearl) Linn. They have two children living:

Eva, born November 30, 1859, and Octavia, born April 28, 1865.

Eva married R. E. Staton, January 19, 1887, and has three children: Octavia Jane, born December 16, 1887; John Edgar, born October 31, 1889; William Linn, born March 24, 1894.

Octavia married Rev. J. G. Tucker of the Methodist Episcopal Church, November 20, 1895.

JOHN VOSE, County Clerk of Boyd County, a popular official and excellent citizen of Catlettsburg, son of John and Christina Vose, was born in Pomeroy, Ohio, August 9, 1854.

His father was born in Krembendorf, Prussia, December 16, 1824; came to America when about twenty-five years of age; lived in Pittsburg about a year; then removed to Pomeroy; married Christina Strohmeier in 1853; was a manufacturer of vinegar and was an educated and highly intelligent man; industrious, honest and much respected; a member of the German Methodist Church; a Whig, and afterwards a Republican in politics; and a naturalized citizen of the United States. He died in Pomeroy, April 12, 1860.

Christina Strohmeier Vose (mother) was a native of the southern part of Germany; came to America with her parents and completed her education—which had been begun in Germany—in Pomeroy, Ohio; married John Vose in 1853; after his death she was married, July, 1865, to Frederick Bruns of Pomeroy, and subsequently removed to Catlettsburg, her present home. She is a devout member of the Methodist Church and a woman of superior intelligence and of noble Christian character.

John Vose of Catlettsburg was educated in the schools of Pomeroy, Ohio, and in Catlettsburg. After leaving school he returned to Pomeroy in 1870 and sold goods in a mercantile establishment for about a year and a half; returned to Catlettsburg in 1872 and some months later went to Ashland and engaged in mercantile business until 1886, when he became bookkeeper in the flour mill of R. C. Poage & Son, which position he held for eight years. In 1894 he became the Republican candidate for the office of county clerk and was elected to his present position, which he has filled with splendid ability and to the entire satisfaction of the members of the bar and others who have business in the county court. He is a very clever and obliging gentleman and an efficient official. He is a member of the Methodist Church, the Masonic order and the Ancient Order of United Workmen.

Mr. Vose and Jennie Eba, daughter of D. W. Eba, were united in marriage November 29, 1877. Mrs. Vose was born August 11, 1856; educated in the best schools of Catlettsburg; is a member of the Methodist Church and a lady of the highest Christian character. They have two children living: Clarence Eba, born November 25, 1878, died July 23, 1887; William Wentworth, born August 9, 1881; and John Raymond, born June 5, 1885.

D. W. Eba (Mrs. Vose's father) was born in Butler County, Pennsylvania, in 1819, and died October, 1887; was educated in his native county; came to Catlettsburg about 1850, and engaged in general merchandising, in which he was very successful, and built the Alger House in 1878, one of the best equipped hotels in eastern Kentucky.

He married Isabella Henderson, daughter of Duncan Henderson, a native of New York. She was raised in the Presbyterian Church, but after marriage together with her husband united with the Methodist Episcopal Church in Catlettsburg, and now resides with her daughter at Ashland, Kentucky.

WILLIAM W. HITE, President of the Louisville, Evansville & Henderson Packet Company and of the Louisville & Jeffersonville Ferry Company, and interested in many business enterprises in his native city, was born in Louisville, Kentucky, November 14, 1854.

His father, William Chambers Hite, was born in Jefferson County, Kentucky, July 23, 1820, and was a resident of Louisville nearly all of his life. He was a man of superior business qualifications and was interested in a number of enterprises which were of great public benefit and which brought him a handsome fortune. He was an exceedingly affable and popular man, and was unerring in business tact and judgment. At the time of his unfortunate and accidental death he was president of the Louisville, Evansville & Henderson Packet Company; a director in the Bank of Kentucky and the Louisville Gas Company, besides having investments and taking an active interest in a number of other profitable enterprises.

Lewis Hite (grandfather) was a native of Jefferson County, Kentucky, a farmer and resident of the county all his life. He was a son of Joseph Hite, who was a son of Abraham Hite, who was a son of Yost or Jost Hite, the histories of all of whom are given in W. H. English's Life of George Rogers Clark.

Mary Rose Hite (mother) is a native of Jefferson County, a resident of Louisville, a member of Christ Church Cathedral, and a most exemplary Christian woman, who is still in the vigor of youth, although now well advanced in years.

William W. Hite, eldest son of W. C. and Mary (Rose) Hite, was educated in the public and private schools of Louisville, and began his business career as a salesman in the wholesale dry goods house of Joseph T. Tompkins & Company, at that time the largest establishment of the kind in Louisville. He was employed with them for five years, when he was made secretary and treasurer of the Louisville, Evansville & Henderson Packet Company, which official position he held until the death of his father, when he was made president of that company, and also president of the Louisville & Jeffersonville Ferry Company; was elected director in the Bank of Kentucky and in the Louisville Gas Company, and, in short, took his father's place in all of the enterprises in which he had been interested, including the leading steamboat and railroad supply establishment in the city, in which the son, in 1878, became the senior member of the firm of W. W. Hite & Company. These heavy responsibilities, together with the settlement of his father's estate, fell upon the young man's shoulders before he was thirty years of age, and while he was yet relying upon his father's superior ability in the guidance of his various business interests; but he inherited and had learned wisdom from his father and rapidly developed qualities of head and heart for which his father was conspicuous. He has not only met every requirement to the satisfaction of his associates in business and of the members of his family—whose estate he has managed with ability—but has conducted the various branches of business so successfully and profitably that he is now as prominent among the capitalists of Louisville as was his illustrious father.

Mr. Hite was married in 1888 to Carrie Hope Pace of Richmond, Virginia, and has two sons, a namesake and James P. Hite, who represent the eighth generation of the Hite family as given in this brief sketch.

THOMAS SIDNEY ANDERSON, son of James B. and Mary Ann Martin (Robertson) Anderson, was born in Daviess County, that part known as the "Beech Woods," six miles east of Owensboro, Kentucky, July 8, 1842.

James B. Anderson (father) was born in Lexington, Kentucky, June 1, 1808; first engaged in business with Thomas Anderson & Company, commission merchants of Louisville, as a clerk, and after a few years he acquired an interest in the business. His health failing, he removed to Brandenburg, Kentucky, and was engaged in mercantile business there for several years, but returned to Louisville and engaged in the wholesale dry-goods business as senior member of the firm of Anderson & Evans.

A few years later he removed to Daviess County and bought a farm, upon which he lived until January 1, 1850, when he moved into Owensboro, having been in 1849 elected cashier of the branch of the Southern Bank of Kentucky there. He held that position until 1864, when he organized the Planters' Bank of Kentucky—now the First National Bank of Owensboro—of which he was cashier until his death, which occurred October 17, 1864.

He was a very decided Union man before and during the Civil war, and expressed his convictions openly; was an ardent advocate of the cause of temperance, and was an elder in the Presbyterian Church, he and his wife having been charter members of the first Presbyterian congregation that was organized in the county of Daviess.

John Anderson (grandfather) was a native of County Tyrone, Ireland. He came to America in his youth and settled in Lexington. His father was a sea captain; his wife was Sallie Quicksall, a native of New Jersey.

Mary Ann Anderson (mother) was born near Frankfort, Kentucky, January 2, 1811. Her marriage to James B. Anderson was celebrated in Louisville, December 30, 1828. She survived her husband nearly fourteen years and died in Owensboro, September 18, 1878.

The children of James B. and Mary A. Anderson, two sons and two daughters, were:

Matilda Robertson, who married Charles R. Tyler of Owensboro; Thomas Sidney, the subject of this sketch; Sallie Quicksall, who married Thomas S. Venable of Owensboro; William Kyle, who married Cornelia Cook of Detroit, Michigan.

Thomas Anderson (mentioned in the early part of this sketch) and James B. Anderson were not relatives. They became very warm friends, and the latter named his first son for his friend and his wife, whose name was Sidney.

Isaac Robertson (maternal grandfather) was educated at Princeton College, New Jersey. He was a lawyer in Frankfort, an upright, honorable gentleman; married Matilda Taylor, daughter of

Commodore Richard Taylor of Revolutionary fame; and met an untimely death at the hands of a portrait painter named Dearborn, who was arrested and imprisoned, but made his escape.

Donald Robertson (maternal great-grandfather) was an educator, mentioned in "Fisk's American Revolution" as "that most excellent Scotch school master," who numbered among his pupils President James Madison.

T. Sidney Anderson, the principal subject of this sketch, attended the University of Michigan at Ann Arbor, but while in his junior year his longer attendance was prevented by the death of his father, who named him executor of his will, and by the fact that he was elected cashier of the Planters' Bank of Kentucky, to succeed his father. This position he held from October, 1864, to September, 1871. He and his brother then organized the Owensboro Savings Bank, of which he was at first vice president and then president until 1887. In 1883 he removed to Detroit, Michigan, where he was the principal mover in organizing the State Savings Bank, of which bank he was vice president and manager till 1887, and then president until December 9, 1889, when he resigned voluntarily. While living in Owensboro, and president and principal owner of the Owensboro Savings Bank, his conscientious business policy was to lend no money to, or aid in any way, the liquor and tobacco trades, or any other business detrimental, in his judgment, to man's good. The same policy was pursued by the State Savings Bank at Detroit from its organization, and during his management. In December, 1889, the board of directors desired to change the policy of the bank, and lend the money to any one who offered good paper, financially, regardless of a moral consideration; and also wished to hire a special police force to patrol the bank premises on Sundays and Sunday nights, the same as on week day nights. To neither of these changes was he willing to be a party, preferring to sever his connection with the institution which he had founded, had managed successfully, and of which he was by far the largest individual stockholder.

He remained in Detroit until March, 1893, dealt in real estate successfully, and then moved back with his family to his old home, Owensboro, Kentucky, since which time he has been attending to his private business only.

Mr. Anderson is an elder in the First Presbyterian Church of Owensboro, and is superintendent of its Sabbath school. He is an ardent temperance man in principle and in practice, and since about 1885 has voted with the national Prohibition party. Previous to that time he voted the Republican ticket.

Mr. Anderson was married May 29, 1867, to Susan Elizabeth Harris, daughter of Giles Harris of Petersburg, Virginia. They have three children, daughters: Mary Ann, wife of William A. Underhill, a native of Brooklyn, New York; Pattie Bransford and Susan Harris.

Giles Harris, Mrs. Anderson's father, was born in Prince Edward County, Virginia, September 19, 1805; married Martha Williamson Bransford, December 24, 1828; died Sunday, March 15, 1874, in Owensboro. He was a prominent planter and tobacconist and was one of the leading citizens of his city.

Martha Williamson Bransford (Mrs. Anderson's mother) was born in Cumberland County, Virginia, February 15, 1807.

John Claibourn Harris (Mrs. Anderson's paternal grandfather) was a prominent planter in Prince Edward County, Virginia; married Polly Ganaway. Mrs. Anderson's maternal grandfather was Benjamin Bransford, who was born in Cumberland County, Virginia, December 15, 1769; was a planter; married Lucy Hatcher of the same county. He was a son of John Bransford and Judith Amonette Bransford, who had ten children; he was a grandson of John Bransford, who was the father of three daughters and two sons.

WILLIAM A. BYRNE, Attorney-at-Law, Covington, son of James and Margaret (Hughes) Byrne, was born in Louisville, November 16, 1854. His father was born in County Wexford, Ireland, where he received a good education, and where he followed farming. He came to Kentucky when a young man and lived in Louisville; but left that city in 1855 on account of the "Know Nothing" riot which occurred there on Monday, August 1, 1855, and removed to Covington, where he continued to reside until his death in 1892. He was an uncompromising Democrat in politics, and was a member of the Catholic Church.

James Byrne, Sr. (grandfather), was born in County Wexford, Ireland, and was killed in the revolution in Ireland, in which his family distinguished themselves. His wife was Johanna Cousins, who belonged to a prominent family in County Wexford.

Margaret Hughes (mother) was born in County Wexford, Ireland. Her father, William Hughes, was a highly respected farmer in his county. His daughter and two sons, Andrew and Thomas, came to America, and Andrew was killed in the Union army.

W. A. Byrne was educated in St. Xavier College, Cincinnati, graduating in 1875. He studied law with Hon. John G. Carlisle for two years; was admitted to the bar, and after practicing law for three years, was elected city attorney, and was re-elected for three terms, consecutively. At that time all of the civil and criminal cases were conducted by the city attorney; but the legislature changed this, making two offices and dividing the work between the city solicitor and the prosecuting attorney. Under this arrangement, Mr. Byrne was elected city solicitor for a term of four years, and was twice re-elected.

Under the new constitution there was a question whether he could hold the office until the expiration of the term for which he had been elected, and it devolved upon Mr. Byrne to decide this question. His decision was that he could not, thus depriving himself of two years of service. He became a candidate for re-election in 1893 and was defeated by W. McD. Shaw, the Republican candidate.

During his long service as city attorney and solicitor, the city did not lose an important case. In this way he saved the city large sums of money. Since giving up his office, the city has employed him as special attorney, which is probably the best evidence of the public appreciation of his legal services.

Mr. Byrne is president of the Alumni Association of St. Xavier College; and president and originator of the Catholic Institute and Gymnasium in Covington, which has over four hundred members and is well equipped with library, reading room, gymnasium, billiard room, bath rooms, etc. He is deeply interested in this work, especially in behalf of the young men of Covington.

He has been twice married; first to Mary Byrne of Newport, May 11, 1882. They had two children, James and William, both of whom are dead. She died in 1885. His second marriage, in 1892, was to Mrs. Anna McNamara, widow of George McNamara, of Covington. By the second marriage there were three children; Leo, who died, and Xavier and Martina, who are living.

DAVID JACKSON WALLIN, M. D., a popular gentleman and capable physician of Brooksville, son of John and Mary (Bridges) Wallin, was born in Montgomery County, near Mt. Sterling, Kentucky, May 2, 1840.

His father was born and reared near Cumberland Gap, Tennessee, and removed to Montgomery County, Kentucky, where he followed millwrighting; and being a most excellent mechanic, his services were greatly in demand far and near. After some years of successful business in the line of his trade, he studied medicine and practiced for one year. Returning to the Cincinnati Medical College in 1842 to take a second course, he accidentally cut his finger while dissecting a subject who had died of puerperal fever; blood poison resulted and he died within twenty-four hours after the time of the accident. He was a man of intelligence, excellent judgment and remarkable industry, and was greatly respected in every community in which he lived.

Mary Bridges Wallin (mother) was born in Montgomery County, Kentucky, and was the daughter of Hiram and Elizabeth Bridges. She died in 1850. She was an exemplary Christian woman, noted for her kind and loving disposition and her deeds of charity, and was greatly loved and admired for her many Christian graces.

After completing his literary studies in the Montgomery County schools, Dr. D. J. Wallin studied medicine in the Eclectic Medical Institute of Cincinnati, taking two courses, graduating in 1860 and commenced the practice of medicine in Brooksville in the same year.

In 1861 he entered the Confederate army, joining Captain Stoner's company in Major Bradley's battalion and General Humphrey Marshall's brigade. After serving one year he recruited a part of a company at Mt. Sterling and Captain Tipton having raised a part of another company, they consolidated and Dr. Wallin was made first lieutenant of Company I, Eighth Regiment, Kentucky Cavalry, which was commanded by Colonel Roy Clukes. They joined Morgan in October, 1862, and accompanied him in his raid through Indiana and Ohio in 1863. Dr. Wallin was taken prisoner with the rest, and sent to Camp Chase, where he remained a prisoner of war for three months and was then transferred to Johnson's Island—a prison for Confederate officers—and was held there for two years. While there he was surgeon of one of the departments, and in that way found something to do to prevent him from becoming rusty in his medical and surgical practice.

He returned to Brooksville in the fall of 1865 and resumed the practice of his profession, to which he has given his undivided attention for more than thirty years. He is a skillful and popular physician, and is a wide-awake and enterprising citizen, progressive and aggressive in his ideas, keeping fully abreast of the times in his knowledge of the great science of medicine. He is the physician of the County Infirmary, and a member of the Board of Examiners for Pensions, and secretary of the board; a member of the Christian Church, and is active in good work.

Dr. Wallin was married January 29, 1866, to Mary A. Corlis, daughter of Dr. John Corlis, and has two children living: William Bridges, born March 17, 1870, and Corlis, born July 22, 1872. Another child died in infancy. His sons are graduates of the medical department of the University of Louisville and are associated with him in the practice of medicine.

JOHN GIVENS CRADDOCK, editor and proprietor of the Paris Kentuckian-Citizen, one of the best newspapers in the state, was born in Harrison County, Kentucky, near the line of Bourbon County, nine miles northwest of Paris, August 28, 1825. He is a son of Richard Clough Craddock, a native of Virginia, who was making the journey from his home in Virginia to the Green River country in Kentucky, and, stopping in Paris, he met the widow Givens, who was the mother of six children, and married her. His trip to the promised land in the Green River country was abandoned or postponed indefinitely, as he doubtless thought the Blue Grass country would compare favorably with any other section of the state. So he settled down early in the '20's and became an industrious tiller of the soil in the vicinity mentioned above. He was the father of two children, the subject of this sketch and a daughter, Ann, who died when she was of tender years.

John G. Craddock, who has become so well known as a newspaper man and as the Nestor of the Kentucky press, studied for two professions before finding that his talents were best suited to the tripod. After his school days were over he studied medicine at Transylvania University, but before completing his course he joined Colonel Simm's company, Second Regiment Kentucky Infantry, for the Mexican war (1846) and served until that war was ended. He is one of a few remaining Mexican war veterans in Kentucky. In 1852, having read law with Governor Hawes, he began doing editorial work for the "Flag," and this latter work, which he began as an amusement, became so congenial, and his talent being recognized by the publisher of the paper, he virtually abandoned the idea of practicing law and became joint editor of the Flag with Colonel Simms. The paper was successful and grew in popularity until 1861, when the Civil war began, when it was compelled to discontinue on account of its sympathy with and advocacy of the cause of the Southern people.

Mr. Craddock took no part, personally, in the war, except to make an occasional reconnoiter as scout on the Confederate side, and spent most of the time during the four years of the conflict in Canada.

In 1866 he established the Paris True Kentuckian, which soon came to be known as the best local paper in Kentucky.

In 1886 this paper consolidated with "The Western Citizen," and in accordance with the custom in such cases, the hyphenated name of Kentuckian-Citizen was given the paper. The combined circulation of the two papers gave Mr. Craddock a larger audience than he had before, and under his leadership the new venture has prospered until it now has a circulation of about four thousand copies.

Mr. Craddock has for many years enjoyed the reputation of having the best local newspaper published in the state of Kentucky, and the editors and publishers throughout the state have endeavored to follow the pattern which he has given them, but few of them have succeeded in worthily imitating their leader. The main purpose of his paper has been to give the local news in pithy paragraphs, and this, in addition to the force of his editorials and a careful regard for general news and choice literary matter, has made his paper exceedingly popular with the people of Bourbon and adjacent counties, while among newspaper publishers and politicians it is regarded as first in importance and value among their exchanges. The Kentuckian-Citizen is published semi-weekly, on Wednesday and Saturday, by J. G. Craddock and William Remington.

In 1882 Mr. Craddock, who had made no profession of religion previous to that time, was the first of six hundred and two persons who confessed religious conviction under the powerful preaching of that eminent evangelist, Rev. George O. Barnes.

WILLIAM HENRY SWEENEY of Springfield, commonwealth attorney of the Eleventh Judicial District, son of Harvey Sweeney and Mary Edmondson, was born in Marion County, Kentucky, October 22, 1858, and was educated in the high school of Lebanon and at Forest Academy, near Anchorage, Kentucky; began the study of law with Russell & Averitt and received his license to practice law from Judge Wickliffe, August, 1879; began the practice of law in Springfield in February, 1880, since which time he has devoted his best energies to the legitimate labors of his calling. However, in 1885 he purchased the Leader, a weekly newspaper at Springfield, which he edited and published for about eighteen months. In the spring of 1886 he became a candidate for the nomination by the Democratic party for county judge, and received the nomination over Judge W. E. Selectman, the then incumbent, but was defeated at the ensuing August election by the Republican candidate, Judge Andrew Thompson, who was elected by a small majority, the county at that time being a Republican county.

In September, 1886, Mr. Sweeney was appointed master commissioner and receiver of the Circuit Court; in 1892 he became a candidate for the office of commonwealth attorney in the Eleventh Judicial District, embracing the counties of Green, Marion, Taylor and Washington, and in the primaries received a majority in each of the voting precincts except four. In his own (Washington) county out of a vote of over 1,200 cast he received every vote with the exception of six. His election followed in November without opposition and he is still attending to the duties of that office with fidelity and marked ability. His popularity, which was forcibly attested in his nomination and election, has suffered nothing from the vigorous and conscientious performance of his duties as prosecuting attorney.

One of the most noted cases which have come within the range of his official duties was his prosecution of the Louisville & Nashville Railroad Company in the Marion Circuit Court, May, 1895, in which the railroad company was charged with extortion in freight charges. In that celebrated case Mr. Sweeney met a number of the greatest railroad lawyers in the country, including Judges Edward Baxter of Nashville, Bruce of Louisville, Alcorn of Standford, Kentucky, and others, and despite this galaxy of legal talent and the powerful influence of that great railroad corporation, he won his case, the jury, after being out about thirty minutes, returning a verdict of guilty, assessing a fine of $500.

Mr. Sweeney has been very active in politics, as in everything else in which he takes an interest, especially as chairman of the Democratic County Committee for six years and until the close of 1895, when he declined further service in that place of honor.

W. H. Sweeney and Mary A. Leachman of Washington County were united in marriage February 22, 1882. Mrs. Sweeney was educated in Bellwood Seminary and is an estimable and cul-

COL. W. W. BALDWIN.

tured lady. Her father, Thomas Leachman, a Washington County farmer, was a very substantial citizen, who enjoyed the unbounded confidence of his neighbors. Emeline Thompson, Mrs. Sweeney's mother, was a daughter of James Thompson, a leading and influential citizen of Washington County.

Mr. and Mrs. Sweeney have five children: Ella, Harvey, Sue, Mary and William Sweeney, Jr.

The family history of Mr. Sweeney, which is a matter of record, is given as follows:

Moses Sweeney (great-grandfather) was born in Ireland and came with his parents to Virginia when about four years of age. He was a soldier in the Revolutionary war in General Putnam's command and died in Virginia in 1787.

Daniel Sweeney (grandfather) was the oldest child of Moses Sweeney and was born in Virginia in 1776; immigrated to Kentucky and settled in Lincoln County when about eighteen or twenty years of age and afterwards removed to Washington County, near Mackville, and resided there until 1837, when he moved to Boone County, Missouri, where he died in 1859.

Lizzie Sweeney (great-grandmother) was a Miss Johnson of New Jersey and an own cousin of Vice President Richard M. Johnson.

Elizabeth Sweeney (grandmother) was a Miss Jones, daughter of Evan Jones of Lincoln County. She was born in 1777 and died in Washington County in 1838.

Harvey Sweeney (father) was born in Washington County, February 15, 1809, and lived there until the fall of 1833, when he removed to Lebanon, Kentucky, where he is still living in good health at the advanced age of eighty-seven years. He is a mechanic by trade, but for a number of years operated a farm near Lebanon. He has been a strong, active, energetic man, and in early life took an active part in all matters connected with the town and county; has been a life-long Democrat and has always taken a lively interest in political matters; was a Confederate sympathizer during the war and no Southern soldier ever appealed to him for help in vain.

Joseph Edmondson (maternal grandfather) was born in Scotland and came to Virginia at an early age. He was a nephew of General Stevens, from whom he inherited a considerable tract of land situated on Cartwright's Creek in (now) Marion County. He married a Miss Watts in Virginia and removed to Kentucky in 1798, and settled on his land, as above stated.

Wilson Edmondson (grandfather) was born in Virginia in 1791 and came to Kentucky with his father and resided in (now) Marion County all of his life. He was a farmer by adoption and died in Lebanon, Kentucky, at the age of ninety-two years. He married a Miss Shelby (grandmother), daughter of William Shelby.

Mary Edmondson Sweeney (mother) was the oldest child of Wilson Edmondson and was born in 1812 in (now) Marion County and died December 4, 1884, leaving two children: Fannie, the wife of A. C. Van Cleave of Lebanon, Kentucky, and William H. Sweeney, the subject of this sketch.

Daniel Sweeney and Wilson Edmondson (grandfathers) were soldiers of the War of 1812 and served under General Jackson at New Orleans.

COLONEL WILLIAM W. BALDWIN of Maysville, who is popularly and universally known throughout Northern and Central Kentucky, was born one and one-half miles south of the city of Maysville, Mason County, Kentucky, January 23, 1827. His father, Garrison Baldwin, was a well known farmer and trader of his day and was a native of King William County, Virginia. He was a son of Henry Baldwin, who emigrated from his native State of Virginia to Kentucky and became one of the pioneer and prominent settlers of Mason County. Garrison Baldwin wedded Nancy Marshall Anderson, a native of Prince Edward County, Virginia, and a daughter of Worsham Anderson, who was also one of the early settlers of Mason County. Garrison Baldwin's death occurred in 1829, at about the age of forty years. He had three sons and two daughters, of whom Colonel Baldwin and one sister only survive. He was of Scotch-Irish descent.

Colonel William W. Baldwin at the age of two years was left an orphan by the death of his father, who had been in good circumstances, but having met with reverses, left no estate. Colonel Baldwin grew up on the farm, and received only the advantages afforded in the ordinary schools in the neighborhood of that day. He started out to make his way in the world with little money, but being endowed with good common sense and excellent judgment, he has reached a degree of success in business that few men have attained without aid. For many years he has been one of the most conspicuous figures in his section of the state, both in business and politics. His first venture in business was in buying and selling tobacco, which he conducted for some years in connection with general farming, and which he carried on successfully until 1866, when, in partnership with Charles E. Tabb, he purchased the Calhoun Plow Works at Maysville—which was at that time a very extensive and important industry of the city—and employed on an average two hundred operatives. These works were burned in 1873 and were never rebuilt. After their plant was burned they engaged quite extensively in the grain and stock business at Maysville, but the partnership was subsequently dissolved, and in 1884 he formed a partnership with Newton Cooper and engaged in the grain and tobacco business on Front street.

Colonel Baldwin has large turnpike interests, and owns a majority of the stock in the Maysville & Lexington Turnpike Company, of which he is president and superintendent, and which is one of the best managed roads in the country; he is also president of the Germantown Turnpike Company, and it has been through his management, principally, that these roads have been made profitable to the stockholders. In 1855 and 1856 he served as deputy sheriff of Mason County, and in 1858 to 1862 held the office of sheriff of the county. In 1871 he was elected from Mason County to the lower house of the State Legislature, and was re-elected, serving on the Committee of Ways and Means, since which time Colonel Baldwin has never sought for office.

In the Legislature, being a careful business man, of fine judgment, painstaking and far-seeing, he exercised those admirable qualities that have so signally advanced his private interests.

In politics he is a sound money Democrat, and wields a remarkable influence among politicians of his party. He owns a beautiful farm south of Maysville, containing six hundred acres of valuable land, where he resides and entertains his many friends with that hospitality so characteristic of old-time Kentuckians. He was united in marriage November 20, 1850, to Martha A. Tabb, a native of Mason County, and daughter of Edward and Letitia (Gill) Tabb. Her father was born in Virginia and her mother in Maryland. Of the children born to this marriage six are now living: Lucia, wife of C. W. Cartmell of Maysville; Nannie Marshall, wife of A. C. Respass, ex-postmaster of the same city; Sue B., who was the wife of Frank B. Ranson, and is now deceased; William W., Jr.; Mattie, wife of W. E. McCann of Lexington, and Robert Lee, who is a prominent young business man of Maysville.

While possessed of great firmness, and strength of character, Colonel Baldwin is of pleasing address, unassuming and affable in manner and popular with all classes, and although in his seventieth year is apparently in the prime of perfect manhood. Having been very successful in business he is by no means a gentleman of elegant leisure, but retains the vim, vigor and industrious habits of his earlier years, still devoting his energies to the management of the many enterprises in which he is interested.

Colonel Baldwin was never known to desert a friend; there is no deception in his nature; is bold and aggressive and is universally esteemed by the people of Northern and Central Kentucky.

JOHN R. PFLANZ of Louisville, Sheriff of Jefferson County, was born in Portland, now a part of the City of Louisville, July 15, 1855. His parents, John Reinhard and Mary F. Hollicher Pflanz, were natives of Germany, but were married in this country. His father died in Portland in 1868, when thirty-six years of age. He was a member of the Presbyterian Church, while his wife, who is still living in Louisville, is a communicant of the Catholic Church. Left an orphan at an early age, Mr. Pflanz did not enjoy the advantages of a thorough educaion. He attended the excellent ward schools for a while, but left his studies soon to assist his mother in her grocery, and the best part of his education was of the most practical nature. He regards his early business experience as being quite as useful as any schooling which he could have received after leaving the old Portland school.

After clerking for his mother for some time, he bought out the grocery and opened a bar in connection with it. This branch of the business proved quite successful, and his patronage increased so rapidly that he soon abandoned the grocery department and devoted his time to the bar exclusively. He continued in this until 1892, when he engaged in the manufacture of brick, but sold out after a brief experience in that line. His next venture was in the "Herald Tobacco Works," but at the same time he was incidentally and to some extent financially interested in a number of other enterprises which he was helping to push along. In November, 1894, he organized the Peerless Cider and Vinegar Works, in which he is the principal stockholder. The works are situated in a large brick building owned by Mr. Pflanz on Thirty-third street. This is one of the largest establishments of the kind in the country, having a daily capacity of two hundred barrels; and while interested in other enterprises, Mr. Pflanz is especially partially to his cider and vinegar factory and has great expectations for its future.

Few men in Louisville have been more active in politics than John R. Pflanz, who has the reputation of always accomplishing what he undertakes. He is one of the charter members and was for a term president of the Bandana Club, an organization which did valiant service for the Democratic party during Mr. Cleveland's first and second campaigns; was a member of the city executive committee for several terms, being chairman of the Seventh Legislative District Committee; was a member of the Board of Common Council for eleven years, and was easily promoted to the Board of Aldermen by election in November, 1893, and was a candidate for the presidency of that honorable body in opposition to Charles F. Grainger, who was finally elected after a deadlock for twenty days and nights, during which time over eleven hundred ballots were cast. This is probably the only instance in which Mr. Pflanz was ever defeated and that was not a contest before the people.

In November, 1894, he was elected sheriff of Jefferson County, receiving a majority of thirty-five hundred votes; and was one of two Democratic candidates for county offices who were not defeated by the Republican candidates. He assumed the duties of sheriff January 1, 1895, and is one of the best sheriffs the county and the metropolis of the state has ever had.

Mr. Pflanz was married in August, 1879, to Ida L. Wilkes, daughter of Captain Perry Wilkes, a river captain pilot, who was also captain in the Union army during the Civil war. They have a family of four children: Virgie, Willie, Stanley, and Grace.

ROBERT C. TALBOTT of Paris, Kentucky, a member of the Bourbon bar, was born in North Middletown, Bourbon County, August 2, 1862. He began his education in the common schools of the county and when sixteen years of age was placed under the charge of Professor W. L. Yerkes of Paris, under whose efficient training he formed a liking for study, and when at the end of the first year Professor Yerkes took leave of his school to spend a season in Europe Mr. Talbott attended Edgar Institute in Paris, then under the management of Withrow and Waddell, two scholarly gentlemen from Virginia. He continued his studies there for two years and each year received the gold medal for the highest general average. He then entered Kentucky University of Lexington, Kentucky, and at the close of three years graduated with the first honors of his class. He read the text books of law privately for a year and was admitted to the bar by the Court of Appeals of Kentucky. He began the practice of law in the fall of 1884 at Paris. Upon his twenty-first birthday he was elected superintendent of public schools of Bourbon County for a term of four years; was then re-elected, continuing the practice of law during these eight years, and after the expiration of his second term devoted his attention exclusively to the practice of law. He is now associated with W. H. McMillan, under the firm name of McMillan & Talbott.

Robert C. Talbott is a great-great-grandson of Samuel Talbott of Fairfax County, Virginia, who was a lineal descendant of the English family of Talbotts. Samuel Talbott married Mary Magdalene De Moville, and from their family most of the Kentucky Talbotts have descended. He died December 31, 1777, and his wife in 1791. His oldest son, De Moville Talbott (great-grandfather), was born July 25, 1754, and married Lee Ann Mason of the Mason family of Virginia. After her death in Virginia De Moville Talbott married Margaret Williams, who was born in Virginia, June 7, 1767. De Moville Talbott moved to Kentucky, and located in Bourbon County. He had in all sixteen children, a record of whose births, marriages and deaths were kept in the family Bible, which recites that De Moville Talbott died April 16, 1839. De Moville Talbott's third son, Samuel Talbott (grandfather), was born October 4, 1781, to his wife, Lee Ann Mason, in Virginia. He was twice married. His second wife was Miss Margaret Lauder (grandmother). Samuel H. Talbott, the father of Robert C. Talbott, was the son of Samuel and Margaret Lauder Talbott. From the early days when the settlers followed farming as a necessity, because little else was open to them, his forefathers continued this independent and honorable calling, which descended, like the lands, from father to son. Samuel H. Talbott married Anna McMillan (mother), daughter of Robert McMillan, late of Bourbon County, formerly of Clark County. There are but two children of this marriage: William F. Talbott and Robert C. Talbott, both of Paris, Kentucky.

Robert McMillan (grandfather) was born in 1813, and was a son of Colonel William McMillan and Elizabeth Frame McMillan, of Clark County, Kentucky. Colonel McMillan in the early days of the commonwealth served his people not only in peace, having represented them for twenty-four years in the State Legislature and in the Senate, but also in war; was engaged in the Indian war previous to 1812, and was colonel of the Seventeenth Regiment United States Infantry, in the War of 1812. He was a son of James McMillan and Margaret White, daughter of Dr. Robert and Helen White of Edinburgh, Scotland, a family made famous by Henry Kirk White, whose poetic genius attracted the attention of the literary world, although he died before arriving at the age of twenty-one years. From the union of James McMillan and Margaret White, besides Colonel William McMillan, were the following children: James and his brother, both of whom were killed in the Revolution; Robert was private secretary to George Washington, and Mrs. Trimble, the mother of Judge John Trimble of the Court of Appeals of Kentucky, and Robert Trimble of the Supreme Court of the United States.

Mr. Talbott's grandmother, Matilda Barclay, wife of Robert McMillan, was the daughter of William Barclay and Nancy Shelton, daughter of Commodore Shelton of the Revolution. William Barclay was a son of William Barclay and Nancy Ramsey of Pennsylvania. This William Barclay was a Revolutionary soldier, and after the war moved to Virginia. His son William was born in Virginia, but moved to Clark County, Kentucky, where he reared a family.

Robert C. Talbott was married in June, 1888, to Sara Grimes, daughter of William and Mary Hedges Grimes. Mrs. Talbott attended Hamilton College at Lexington, Kentucky, for four years, and was an honor student of that college of the class of 1887. While there she received three gold medals for proficiency in different branches. She is a great-great-granddaughter of John Grimes of Loudoun County, Virginia, who was a soldier of the Revolution in the Virginia State service. She is a descendant of the Scott, Shore, Stamps and Metcalfe families of Virginia, all of whom were descendants of English families of prominence, also of the Adams and Biggs families of Pennsylvania, and the Hedges and Troutman families of Maryland. Mr. Talbott is a Democrat; he and his wife are members of the Christian Church. They have three children: Robert C. Talbott, Jr., Edna Cecil and Ethel Allen Talbott.

William F. Talbott, son of Anna McMillan and Samuel H. Talbott and only brother of Robert C. Talbott (whose sketch is given above) was born in North Middletown, Bourbon County, Kentucky, February 27, 1857; was educated in the common schools of the county, and was also under the charge of Professor W. L. Yerkes of Paris, Kentucky, but owing to bad health was compelled to leave school. He engaged in farming; continued in this occupation until 1890, when he removed from his farm to Paris, and is now engaged in the livery business.

He was married in October, 1887, to Mattie Shipp, only daughter of Edwin T. and Blannie (Williams) Shipp. The Shipp family were formerly of Fauquier County, Virginia, and came to Kentucky in 1795, where they engaged in farming and were large land owners. Edwin T. Shipp was an old and prominent citizen of Bourbon County. The Williams family is of Welsh extraction. Mrs. Talbott was educated in the private schools of Bourbon. They have three children, Dorothy L., Gladys C. and William McMillan Talbott. Mr. and Mrs. Talbott are members of the Christian Church.

WILLIAM T. KNOTT of Lebanon, Kentucky, cultured gentleman and ripe scholar, son of Joseph Percy and Maria Irvine (McElroy) Knott, was born on Cherry Run, Washington (now Marion) County, Kentucky, October 10, 1822.

The genealogy of the Knott family begins with Thomas Percy Knott (great-great-grandfather), who was an Episcopal minister in Derbyshire, England. His only son, Thomas Percy Knott (great-grandfather) was educated for the ministry and had pursued his studies with that intent, until he chanced to meet a young lady named Jane Hart, who was to be sent to Baltimore, Maryland, to school, and the young man changed his purpose, or rather the young lady changed it for him, and after completing his classical course in England he came to America and married the same Jane Hart. The children of this marital relation were: Nancy, who married Anthony Bickett; Joseph Percy, married Frances Ray; Mary, married Richard Ray; Frances, married Stephen Briscoe; Thomas Percy, married Frances Rayne; Samuel, married Elizabeth Ray; Lloyd W., married Martha Allen; Jane Hart and Ellen, who never married.

Thomas Percy Knott (grandfather) was a teacher in Maryland before coming to Kentucky, and followed that profession in Marion (then Washington) County. Among his pupils were Ben Hardin, Colonel C. A. Wickliffe, Martin Ewing and others, whose names illumine the pages of Kentucky history. He continued to teach—being especially devoted to the languages and to surveying—until the time of his death in 1826. His remains were interred at Raywick, Marion County.

Joseph Percy Knott (father) was born in Maryland, near Elicott's Mills, March 31, 1794; came to Kentucky an infant, was educated by his father and was a teacher in Washington (now Marion) County, in the vicinity of Lebanon, and was also a teacher in Columbia Seminary, and on Cherry Run, near the place where he settled after his marriage. He was one of the contractors who constructed the famous turnpike over Muldrough's Hill, one of the first improvements of that kind in the state; resumed teaching in Shelbyville in 1846 and 1847, and later at West Point, where he died in 1851. He served as magistrate in Washington County (now Marion) for some years; was a member of the Legislature from Washington County in the years 1833-34, when Marion County was cut off from Washington, and an active, public-spirited and scholarly gentleman. He was a member of the Presbyterian Church and an exemplary Christian. He married Maria Irvine McElroy, and the names of their children were: William T. Knott, the subject of this sketch; Samuel Cleland, who married Sarah Gates; Margaret Marion, married Robert T. Nesbitt; James Proctor, ex-governor, married Sarah R. McElroy; Edward Whitfield, married Mattie McCoy, now living in Kirkwood, Missouri; Anna Maria, married Randolph Hudnall, and Joanna, who married Reverend Marcellus C. Gorin, a Presbyterian minister of St. Louis, Missouri.

Anna Maria Hudnall died in 1859, leaving a daughter, Anna Hudnall, who is the editor of a newspaper in Carson City, Nevada.

William T. Knott attended the schools in the county and in Lebanon; and is a graduate of Center College, in which institution he never spent a day or recited a lesson. He was teaching school in Lebanon and from some of his young friends who were attending Center College he obtained the curriculum, purchased the books and studied the full course at home. When the commencement was held and the graduates received their diplomas, Mr. Knott, who was in the audience, was called up by the faculty and presented with a diploma, and was thus placed on an equal footing with other graduates. The college conferred upon him the degree of Ph. D. in 1894, being the third person to receive that honor from old Center College.

He had charge of the Lebanon Seminary for ten years, losing but two days' time in all those years. In 1852 he became interested in promoting and building the Lebanon branch of the Louisville & Nashville Railroad, and when, after much diligent labor on his part, the road was completed to Lebanon, he was made general agent of the branch and located at Lebanon, and it was his duty to appoint and superintend local agents. He was connected with the Louisville & Nashville Railroad in one capacity or another from 1858 to 1890, when he resigned his position to accept an appointment as superintendent of county schools, an office to which he has since been elected and re-elected, and is now serving his third term, and in which he is deeply interested, having a fondness for children and being enthusiastically devoted to the cause of education. His qualifications for this work are unusual. Having been a professional teacher for ten years and a lifetime student, few men in the state are better prepared to direct the education of the rising generation than is Mr. Knott.

During the term of his brother, J. Proctor Knott, as governor of Kentucky, he was assistant state geologist under John R. Proctor, who was director of the geological survey of Kentucky. This line of study has always been of the deepest interest to him, and as a result of his researches he has one of the finest collections of geological specimens, outside of the large institutions, in the United States. He has made several trips to the Rocky Mountains, and his collection of specimens of the minerals and geological formations of that section of the country is one of great interest and value. His library embraces the largest private collection of scientific works in the country. At odd times he has made a careful study of the botany of Marion County, and knows every plant scientifically in that section. Has made a careful study of the archaeology of the county and has worked up the conchology of the state, the greater part of the land and fresh water shells and has them named and classified in his cabinet.

Mr. W. T. Knott was married (first) July 11, 1847, to Marion B. McElroy, by whom he has four children living: Joseph McElroy Knott, cashier of the Marion National Bank of Lebanon, married Mattie Ruble; William Sneed Knott, attorney at law of Los Angeles, California, married Lulie Pierce of Springfield, Illinois, a sister of William Pierce, ex-consul to Cuba; Kate Grundy Knott and Jennie Marion, who are at home.

Mrs. Knott died May, 1865, and Mr. Knott was married (second) January, 1867, to Mrs. Lydia McElroy, widow of Hugh Sneed McElroy, who was a brother of Mr. Knott's first wife. Her maiden name was Lydia Harrison, daughter of George S. Harrison. She is a native of England. She had two children by her first husband: Rosa, wife of James B. Shepard of Denver, Colorado, and George S. McElroy, now of San Antonio, Texas, whose wife was Louise Phillips.

The genealogy of the McElroy family is meager but interesting. The first now known of the name were contemporaneous with John Knox of Scotland, and they were the ancestors of the McElroys of Marion and Washington Counties. They have kept the tradition that their ancestors were active participants in the establishment of the "Solemn League and Covenant" of 1636. Being opposed in their desire to worship God according to the dictates of their consciences and being denied all offices of trust and all privileges, they became very bitter in their opposition to the British government. Consequently, early in the eighteenth century, they sought homes in the American colonies, settling for the most part in Pennsylvania, New Jersey, Virginia and the Carolinas.

From the best information at hand, it was about 1730 when James McElroy and Sarah McCue (or McHugh), his wife, first located in New Jersey.

They afterward removed to Pennsylvania and finally to Virginia, locating in (now) Campbell County, in 1760. All of their children were boys: John, Archy, Hugh, Samuel and James. The father was a farmer, whose principal crop was tobacco, which, for the want of money, was common currency in Virginia in those days. The father and his sons were ever ready to respond to frequent calls to arms on account of the French and Indian wars and the greater war of the Revolution. They were in many battles in Virginia and campaigns on the Pennsylvania border. Samuel and several of his brothers were present at the surrender of Lord Cornwallis.

John and Archy, sons of James McElroy, removed to South Carolina, and were the progenitors of the McElroys in the Carolinas, Georgia, Tennessee and some of the southern counties of Kentucky. Three of the sons of James married three sisters, who were daughters of John Irvine. Hugh married Esther, Samuel married Mary, and James married Margaret Irvine. These women were daughters of a Scotch-Irish Presbyterian minister.

Hugh McElroy and John Irvine, his brother-in-law, with their families, removed from Campbell County, Virginia, to Kentucky in 1787. McElroy settled in Nelson (now Washington) County, and Irvine in Lincoln (now Boyle) County, near Danville. In 1789, September 4, Samuel and James, with their wives, followed Hugh to the "wilderness of Kentucky," and settled in Nelson (now Marion) County, near Lebanon.

Of these Samuel (the great-grandfather of William T. Knott) and his wife, Mary Irvine, had issue as follows: Sarah, born 1767, married Alexander Handley; John, born 1769, married (first) Miss Copeland (second), Mrs. Simpson; James, born 1770, died young; Hugh, born 1772, married Miss Gilkie; Margaret, born 1773, married James Wilson; Abram, born 1774, died young; William, born 1776, married (first) Keturah Cleland, (second) Mary Kirk; Samuel, born 1777, married (first) Mary Briggs, (second) Jane B. Grundy; Mary, born 1778, married William McColgan; James, born 1780, married Esther Simpson; Abram, born 1780, married Miss Redford (James and Abram were twins); Elizabeth, born 178—, married George Wilson, and Nancy, born 178—.

The children of William McElroy (1776) and Keturah Cleland, his wife, were: Maria Irvine McElroy, born 1805, who married Joseph P. Knott, October 10, 1822 (parents of William T. Knott); Eliza, born 1807, married (first) Isaac Everhart, (second) T. P. Gibbs, (third) Isaac Withrow; Philip E., born 1809, married Lydia Gibbs; Harriet Paulina, born 1811, married A. S. Mays; Margaret, born 1814, married Samuel T. Ray. The children of William McElroy and his second wife, Mary Kirk, were: Paul Irvine, married Sue McElroy; Robert Lapsley, married Lizzie Hughes; Cecil Scott, married Fannie Brown; Lucy Ann, married Samuel T. Ray (after the death of his first wife, who was her half sister); William T., married Eliza Cassidy; James Franklin, married Mary Chapman; Samuel Rice, married Belle Reed; Keturah, married Dr. George Hubbard, and Sarah, who died young.

James Proctor Knott, son of Joseph Percy and Maria (Irvine) Knott and brother of William T. Knott—the principal subject of the foregoing sketch—was born in Marion County, Kentucky, August 28, 1830. After receiving a common school education, he was professor of natural science in the Lebanon Seminary; practiced law in Lebanon; removed to Missouri, where he practiced law; was a delegate to the Democratic National Convention in 1860; was elected to the Missouri Legislature; was attorney-general of that state during the Civil war; returned to Lebanon and was a member of Congress from that district for twelve years, 1867-71 and 1875-83; was governor of Kentucky, 1883 to 1887; and is now dean of the faculty of the law department of Center College at Danville, Kentucky.

THOMAS R. WELCH, M. D., an able and successful homeopathic physician and surgeon of Nicholasville, was born in that city, February 4, 1860, and is a son of the late Dr. John Welch, who died in Nicholasville, February 2, 1887, and Lizzie (Downing) Welch. Thomas R. Welch received his primary education in Bethel Academy, under the training of that eminent teacher, Professor A. N. Gordon, who is now principal of an academy in Fayette County. He afterwards attended Kentucky Wesleyan College and received the degree of A. M. In 1882 and 1883 he taught in the city schools and then read medicine with his father and graduated from the Hahnemann Medical College, Chicago, in 1885, and in the same year he began the practice of medicine in his native city, where he has become known as one of the best physicians in the county.

During all of that time he has been and is still a member of the board of examiners for the common schools; is a member of the Nicholasville Board of Education; is a member of the Kentucky State Homeopathic Association, of the Southern Homeopathic Association and the American Institute of Homeopathy; is a member of the Baptist Church; an Odd Fellow and a Knight of Pythias, and has served in all of the offices in these two orders.

Dr. Welch is a most scholarly gentleman and a student of great industry; of quick perception, a retentive memory and a close observer, he can rapidly acquire knowledge of every kind, particularly in the great science of medicine. As a physician and surgeon he has few superiors. He is faithfully devoted to his profession and has gained wide popularity by his prompt and courteous attention to business.

Dr. Welch was married in 1889 to Josephine Stanley, daughter of Elder William Stanley, a minister in the Christian Church, who is now living in East Aurora, New York. They have one daughter, Amanda.

John Welch (great-grandfather) was born in the north of Ireland in 1743, came to America and served under General George Washington in the Revolutionary war, after which he settled in Lincoln County. He subsequently removed within the present limits of Jessamine County, where he raised a large family of sons and daughters, whose descendants in Jessamine County are very numerous and are of the highest respectability. He died one mile south of Nicholasville in 1836, and is buried on the farm which he opened in 1784. His oldest son, Alexander Welch, was born in Virginia in 1778. Nathaniel Welch, his second son, was born in Lincoln County in 1783, and John Welch, his youngest son, who was the father of Dr. John C. Welch and grandfather of Dr. Thomas R. Welch, was born in Lincoln County in 1790, and died in 1842.

Lizzie Downing Welch (mother) was the oldest daughter of Armistead Downing, whose ancestors were from England and settled in Northumberland County, Virginia, in 1726, where many of the descendants are yet living. The Kentucky family of Downings are descended from this English branch, of whom three brothers, John, Thomas and Robert, are supposed to have settled in Virginia in the year above mentioned.

GEORGE HENRY MEADE, Circuit Clerk of Boyd County, son of Albert Gallatin and Elizabeth (Hornbuckle) Meade, was born September 9, 1862, in Boyd County, Kentucky. His father, Albert Gallatin Meade, was born in Bedford County, Virginia, in 1803, and came to Greenup (then a part of Boyd) County in 1828. He was a farmer and a prominent member of the Methodist Church and one of the most respected citizens of the county. He died at the age of sixty-nine in 1872, and is buried at McCormick's Chapel in Boyd County. His father was a native of Clay County, Virginia, and was a highly respected farmer of that county. The Meades are of Irish and German extraction.

George H. Meade's mother, Elizabeth (Hornbuckle) Meade was born and educated in Greenup County, Kentucky. She was a lady of noble Christian character, prominent and useful in the work of the church to which she and her husband belonged, and her death, which occurred on the twelfth day of March, 1864, was lamented by a large circle of loving relatives and friends.

Richard Hornbuckle (maternal grandfather) was a farmer in Greenup County, a man of great force of character and a gentleman of culture. He was an old-time Whig in his younger days, and later became a Republican of pronounced convictions. He was a native of North Carolina.

George Henry Meade, the subject of this sketch, was educated in the Boyd County district schools, and at Marshall College, Huntington, West Virginia, from which institution he was graduated in the class of 1883. He afterward took a commercial course in the Valparaiso (Indiana) Normal School, graduating in 1884.

He taught in the district schools of Boyd County for two years and then went to Lebanon, Ohio, and took a teacher's course in the Normal School, after which he resumed his professional work as teacher in his native county, and was thus employed until January, 1895, when he assumed the duties of the office of clerk of the Circuit Court at Ashland, to which he was elected on the Democratic ticket in November, 1894. In this change from one department of public service to another the educational interest of the county was the loser, but the legal branch of service gained an efficient and faithful officer.

Mr. Meade was married January 10, 1894, to Mary Edith Fannin, daughter of J. L. and Mary (Lock) Fannin, of Boyd County. She was born March 29, 1873. They have one child, Delbert Quigley, born January 25, 1895.

Mr. Meade has two sisters and five brothers: Mary E. Meade; Richard; William R. Meade, served in the Fourteenth Regiment Kentucky Infantry, Union army and married Melissa Shelton; Pierce L. Meade, married Ellen Ward; Anna Meade; Albert Gallatin Meade, married Pauline Molsvarger, and Luke Cullis, who has been twice married, first to Caroline Molsvarger, who died in March, 1888, and whose second wife was Addie Walters.

THOMAS HENRY HINES, ex-Chief Justice of the Kentucky Court of Appeals and distinguished attorney at law of Frankfort, son of Judge Warren W. and Sarah (Carson) Hines, was born in Butler County, Kentucky, October 9, 1838. His ancestors were of English and Scotch origin and were among the first settlers of Kentucky. Dr. McDowell states that these early settlers were the largest body of pure English stock that has been separated from Virginia in two hundred years. They were descended from Romans, Saxons, Celts and Normans, the two latter predominating, the characteristics of whom were impressed upon their English descendants. They were noted for their love of liberty and were men of strong individuality. It was the same principle that produced the American Revolution and made the people of the North American colonies free and independent.

Judge Hines is a true blue descendant of the old Roman and Norman blood of these English ancestors. His professional career has been successful and brilliant and his service on the appellate bench, for a term of eight years ending in 1885, was distinguished by the highest legal ability. The State of Kentucky never gave birth to a more daring and accomplished gentleman. Brave and generous, with that high sense of honor so characteristic of true representative Kentuckians, he has manfully performed his duty as soldier, advocate, judge and citizen, and is admired and honored by a host of friends and acquaintances.

In order to vary the monotony of a work of this character, as well as to show the daring and chivalrous courage of the man, an account of the escape of General Morgan, Captain Hines and six other Confederate officers from the Ohio Penitentiary during the war, which escape was planned by him and executed under his management, and is given in lieu of the usual details of his ancestry and the deeds and exploits of his fathers. History furnishes no more interesting facts, and romance is thrown in the shade by the reality of that most daring and successful venture.

In the exciting account of General Morgan's escape, in November, 1863, written by Samuel C. Reed, is seen the brave and defiant spirit of the old British blood in Captain Thomas H. Hines, who was then twenty-three years of age, of great nerve and endurance.

Merrion, the warden, feeling the importance of a little brief authority, on the morning of November 3, 1863, grossly insulted Captain Hines, who determined that he would neither eat nor sleep until he had planned some means of escape. Prison life had become intolerable, and the thought of breathing the free air of heaven once more was inexpressibly sweet. He was engaged in reading Victor Hugo's graphic description in "Les Miserables" of the subterranean passages of Paris, and of the wonderful escapes of Jean Valjean. He argued in his mind that the dryness of the cells must be owing to air passages or ventilators beneath, to prevent the moisture from rising, and that by removing the cement and brick in the cells they might strike the air chambers and thence escape by undermining the foundation walls. This plan was first communicated to Captain Samuel B. Taylor—a grand nephew of President Zachary Taylor—who was as agile, ingenious and daring as Captain Hines.

There were difficulties to overcome from the arrangement of the cells—five tiers or stories of solid stone masonry, six feet long, six feet high and three feet wide. General Morgan's cell was in the second story, and Hines' immediately beneath.

With two case knives, which had been sent from the hospital with food for some of the sick men, the work was begun November 4 in Hines' cell, he assuming the responsibility and alone taking the risk of discovery and its consequent punishment by imprisonment in the dungeon. With these tools two men could work at a time, relieving each other every hour and spending four or five hours a day in labor. It was a work of love and progressed steadily, Hines keeping strict guard, and by a system of knocks or raps upon the cell door, indicating when to begin and when to stop work and come out. The cement and bricks removed were hidden by the men in their beds. The prison guards were always suspicious and watchful, and some privileged convicts were sometimes set as spies to watch the Confederate officers.

After digging in each of the seven cells for eighteen inches square through six inches of cement and six layers of brick, the air chamber was reached and found to be sixty feet long and three by three feet in height and width. Thereafter the rubbish was removed to the air chamber, while the holes in the walls were carefully concealed by their beds. But their patient work was scarcely begun. They worked thence through twelve feet of solid masonry, fourteen feet of "grouting" (the stone and liquid cement) and five feet of graveled earth, and on November 25th reached the yard of the penitentiary.

For the first time General Morgan was now made acquainted with the mysterious underground avenue, and was greatly surprised and delighted upon examining the work. A consultation in Morgan's cell on the evening of the 27th determined them to attempt their escape that night. The weather for some weeks had been perfectly clear, and for several nights succeeding their escape the ground and penitentiary walls were covered by a heavy sleet, which would have made it impossible to scale them. Late in the evening of the 27th light fleecy clouds gathered in the west, which with the feeling of the atmosphere, betokened a cloudy sky and rain; and at nine p. m. a steady rain set in, lasting through the night. How to scale the outside wall, thirty-five feet high, was their greatest difficulty; besides, several sentinels were on post in the yard and two or three vicious dogs were unchained at night. Again, General Morgan was to be gotten out of his cell in the second story before the turnkey locked all the cell doors at five p. m. "Love laughs at locksmiths," and so did Morgan's men. Calvin Morgan, the general's brother, made out of his bed-ticking a rope seventy feet long, and out of a small iron poker a hook for the end of the rope. At five p. m. when the prisoners were ordered to their cells, Colonel Dick Morgan went to his brother's cell while the general was locked up in Dick's, one of the seven on the ground floor. General Morgan was allowed the exceptional privilege of a candle to read by after nine o'clock, and the turnkey on going his rounds, finding Dick Morgan with a book before his face reading, mistrusted nothing, but locked in the wrong prisoner.

In the stillness of the night, at 12:25 a. m., when even a whisper or the falling of a pin could be heard, Captain Sam Taylor dropped noiselessly into the air chamber, passed under the other six cells and touched the occupants as a signal to come forth, each one first so shaping his bed clothes as to resemble the sleeping form of a man, and prevent the suspicion of guards on their hourly rounds, until after daylight.

When they emerged from the hole under the foundation three sentinels stood within ten feet, but the steady rainfall drowned any noise from their footsteps. A few paces toward the wall were gone over when one of the huge dogs came running with a howl within ten feet of them, barked once, and then went off, doubtless mistaking them for sentinels. They reached in safety the last gate of the wall, a double gate thirty feet high, of iron outside and inside of heavy wooden cross-timbers with open spaces. Wrapping a stone in a cloth to prevent noise and tying it to one end of the rope, Taylor threw it over the top of the inside gate, the weight of the stone drawing down the rope. Securing the hook to one of the timbers one of the parties climbed to the top of the gate and thence to the top of the wall. The rope was hauled up, the hook fastened to the iron railing on the main wall, and in a few minutes they had descended to the open street, within thirty steps of a guard, who stood near a bright gaslight. The party immediately separated, General Morgan and Captain Hines going together. By a letter in cipher to a lady friend who sometimes loaned books to the prisoners, Hines' need of money had been supplied, the money being hidden within the folds or binding of a book. Morgan wore goggles loaned by a sore-eyed fellow-prisoner, and kept from the gaslight, while Hines went boldly up to the ticket office and purchased two tickets, just as the Cincinnati train, at 1:25 a. m., came thundering along. Once in the car without suspicion they felt equal to the emergency, and by care and ingenuity made good their escape to the South.

Those who made their exit from prison walls on that memorable night were General Morgan and six of his captains: Thomas H. Hines, Jacob C. Bennett, Ralph Sheldon, James D. Hockersmith, Gustavus McGee and Samuel B. Taylor.

The coolness and composure of Captain Hines was wonderful. He spent the evening from five to nine in reading one of Charles Lever's novels, and then slept soundly until aroused by Captain Taylor, just after midnight. He was too polite to part with his host Merrion without leaving his compliments and wrote a letter enclosing the tally of the time and labor expended in effecting the escape, which was as follows:

"Castle Merrion, Cell No. 27.

"Commencement, November 4, 1863; conclusion, November 20. number of hours for labor per day, three; tools, two small knives.

"'La patience est amere, mais son fruit est doux.' By order of my six honorable Confederates.

"THOMAS H. HINES, C. S. A."

Four days after Captains Taylor and Ralph Sheldon were captured near Louisville and returned to the penitentiary. Captain Taylor died several years after the war; General Morgan was slain; Gustavus McGee was killed near Cumberland Gap; Ralph Sheldon, a descendant of Ralph Sheldon, who was a member of the English Parliament in 1645, died a few years ago, and Captain Hines still lives to hear the story of the greatest exploit in American history told by others.

Collins' History states that General Morgan and Captain Hines, after getting on the train, went through Dayton to Cincinnati, where they crossed the Ohio at seven p. m. in a skiff to Ludlow, just below Covington, took breakfast at the residence of an enthusiastic lady friend, where they were furnished with horses and traveled twenty-eight miles to Union in Boone County, thence by easy stages, with volunteer guides, through Gallatin, Owen, Henry, Shelby, Spencer, Nelson, Greene and Cumberland Counties, arriving at Overton, Tennessee, December 8, where Hines by quick wit again saved Morgan; was captured December 13, but in five days made his escape. General Morgan escaped by way of Athens, Tennessee, across the mountains of North Carolina to Columbia, South Carolina, and thence to Richmond, Virginia. The governor of Ohio offered five thousand dollars reward for his capture.

GUY M. DEANE, one of the most energetic and promising young business men of Owensboro, son of Silas Mercer and Sallie Moorman Deane, was born in Owensboro, Kentucky, January 5, 1870.

His father was born in Breckenridge County, May 25, 1839; died June 14, 1894. He received a collegiate education and removed to Owensboro when a young man and found employment as a clerk in the old Planters Hotel. For a number of years he was engaged in the drug business in partnership with Mr. Courtney and became interested in the coal business; was the owner of several coal mines near Owensboro, and these being nearer the city than other mines, furnished most of the coal that was consumed in Owensboro for many years. He had been quite prosperous in business and had bright prospects for the future, but, as was common in the early tumult of the Civil strife, his heart was fired with zeal for the southern cause, and he abandoned his business and entered the Confederate army as a private in Captain Noel's Company, First Regiment, Kentucky Volunteers. He was with Captain Noel at Shiloh when that gallant officer received his mortal wound. He continued with the army until the spring of 1863, when he was forced to return to his home in Owensboro, on account of impaired health.

He resumed the operation of his coal mines, at the same time having an interest in the drug business with Pointer & Conway, in which he continued until 1887, at which time he was made president of the Owensboro Savings Bank, a position which he held until his death. He was one of the originators of the Falls of Rough Railroad, and was president of that company at one time.

Notwithstanding his many business interests and his contact with men of affairs, he was an extremely modest man, and accomplished more by his quiet and unassuming manner than others who made more noise in the world. He was always ready and willing to aid and foster any charitable undertaking, whether public or private; he gave liberally to the poor, but did it quietly and with the stipulation that it must not be mentioned publicly. In business his word was as good as his bond, and he adhered to that principle through life, no one ever having known him to fail to keep his promise. He was a living example of manliness, gentleness, integrity and truthfulness. His death was a public calamity, for he was a most useful citizen and greatly loved and respected by all classes.

He was baptised and received into the fellowship of the Baptist Church in 1869, and remained a consistent member until his death, being one of the most liberal supporters of the church and its work. He was a Mason of highest degree.

Mr. Deane was married October 4, 1866, to Sallie Moorman, a highly educated and accomplished lady, a graduate of the Georgetown Female Academy and a member of one of the most honored families of Kentucky. The names of the children of Mr. and Mrs. Deane are: Guy M., born January 5, 1870; Allen, born December 13, 1871; Anna Belle, born November 25, 1873; and Edward, born May 18, 1876.

Somers Deane (grandfather) was a native of Breckenridge County, a prosperous farmer and large slave owner. He was quite prominent as a member of the Baptist Church and was well known as a Democrat of decided convictions. He married Elizabeth Moorman, daughter of James L. Moorman. Guy M. Deane graduated from the high school of Owensboro in the class of 1886, and began business as a retail coal dealer, and in 1890, formed a partnership with Boyd Micheson in the same business; was bookkeeper in the Owensboro Savings Bank until April, 1895, when he began operating a coal mine at Deanefield, in which he is now successfully engaged; is also interested in real estate and is a stockholder and director in the Owensboro Savings Bank. He is one of the most enterprising young business men of the thriving city of Owensboro, well known for his energy, push, business sagacity, integrity and honesty.

Mr. Deane and Sue Griffith were married March 1, 1892, and their only child, Ruth Griffith, was born May 1, 1893. Mrs. Deane is a daughter of Honorable Clinton Griffith, and was educated in Oxford Female College, graduating in 1889.

CHARLES ALBERT BIRD, a director in the Louis Snider & Sons Paper Company of Cincinnati, and one of the substantial citizens of Dayton, Kentucky, was born November 4, 1842, in Milwaukee, Wisconsin, of English parentage. He left his home when ten years of age and went to Chicago and subsequently to St. Louis and took a position as clerk on a steamboat plying between St. Louis and New Orleans, and was in this service when the Civil War began. He enlisted in the First Missouri Infantry, C. S. A., commanded by Colonel Bowen, who was afterwards a brigadier general, and continued in the service until 1863, and was present at the surrender of Vicksburg. He then came to Cincinnati and secured employment in the well-known paper house of Louis Snider & Sons, which has since been incorporated, and in which company he is a stockholder and director.

Mr. Bird is deeply interested in the welfare and progress of the city in which he has made his home for many years, and was elected mayor of Dayton by the Democratic voters in 1893; has been an honored and trusted member of the city council for eight years; is courthouse commissioner of Campbell County; is a member and Past Master of the Henry Barnes Masonic lodge No. 607 of Dayton, and is one of the leading spirits in all affairs for the betterment of the community in which he lives.

Mr. Bird was married in November, 1873, to Isabella Twaddell, who was born in Cincinnati, April 17, 1852, and where she enjoyed unusual advantages in her school days. They have a group of five promising boys: Charles, Albert, Clarence, George and Nelson McKibben.

WILLIAM ROGERS CLAY, son of Samuel Clay, Jr., and Mary Rogers Clay; grandson of Colonel Littleberry Bedford Clay (C. S. A.) and Arabella Maccoun, daughter of James Maccoun, of the McAfee Company, first settlers of Mercer County, Kentucky; great-great-grandson of Dr. Henry Clay, who emigrated to Kentucky in 1787 from Mecklenburg County, Virginia, and who was a descendant of John Clay, who settled in what is now Chesterfield County, Virginia, in 1613; great-great-grandson of Dr. David Rice, founder of Hampden-Sidney College, Virginia, and Transylvania Seminary, Kentucky, which subsequently became Transylvania University, and a member of the Kentucky Constitutional Convention of 1792, who married Mary Blair, sister of Samuel Blair, Jr., President of Princeton College, New Jersey, and chaplain of the Continental Congress, and a daughter of Samuel Blair, founder of Fagg's Manor Seminary, Pennsylvania, and professor of divinity in Princeton College, who married Frances, the daughter of Judge Lawrence Van Hook, the first Dutchman to hold an official position in New Jersey. On his maternal side, William Rogers Clay is a grandson of Captain William S. Rogers (C. S. A.), and a great-great-grandson of Nathaniel Rogers, member from Bourbon County of the Constitutional Convention of 1798, who was the great-great-grandson of John Rogers, fifth president of Harvard College, and Elizabeth Denison, the only daughter of Major-General Daniel Denison, Governor of Massachusetts, and his wife, Patience, a daughter of Thomas Dudley, Governor of Massachusetts.

ERNEST LINNWOOD CRYSTAL, teacher and a student of theology of Chilesburg, Fayette County, son of George and Victoria (Deane) Crystal, was born in Fayette County, Kentucky, May 13, 1872.

His father, also, was born in Fayette County, January 8, 1845; was educated in the county schools; and at the age of sixteen, enlisted in the Confederate army under General John H. Morgan, in Company A, Eighth Regiment, Kentucky Cavalry; was with his command in the famous raid through Indiana and Ohio in 1863 and was captured, taken to Camp Chase and then to Camp Douglas, where he remained until the close of the war.

Returning to his home in Fayette County, he engaged in blacksmithing, and has followed his trade with commendable industry and good success until the present time. He is a Democratic voter, a member of the Confederate Veteran Association, a faithful member of the Christian Church and an honored citizen.

James E. Crystal (grandfather) was a native of Fayette County; married Mrs. Biven, whose maiden name was Sallie E. Hall. He was a devout member of the Baptist Church and followed the trade of blacksmithing at Brian Station.

Victoria Deane Crystal (mother) was born in Woodford County, March 9, 1844; was educated in the schools of her native county; married George Crystal in 1866 and died April 5, 1878. She was a member of the Christian Church.

Peter Francis Deane (maternal grandfather) was born near Culpeper C. H., Va.; removed to Kentucky and married Lucinda Smith of Jessamine County.

Ernest L. Crystal received his primary schooling at Briar Hill; attended the Kentucky State College from 1887 to 1889, inclusive, and was in Transylvania University from 1890 to 1892, inclusive. In the fall of 1892 he commenced teaching in Fayette County and taught one year; resumed teaching in 1894, continuing through 1895, since which time he has been a student in Bible College at Lexington, preparing for the ministry in the Christian Church.

Mr. Crystal has applied himself industriously in endeavoring to qualify himself for the high vocation which he has in view; his work has been very thorough and his friends and teachers speak of him as a young man who has the prospect of a bright and successful career.

JAMES BURNIE BECK, who was Senator in Congress for many years, was born February 13, 1822, in Dumfries-shire, Scotland. He received an academic education, and came to America in the spring of 1838, joining his father in Wyoming County, New York, where he had settled and engaged in agricultural pursuits many years previously, leaving his son to complete his literary education in Scotland. In 1843, he came to Lexington, Kentucky, and at once began to read law, and after a thorough preparation, graduated from the law department of Transylvania University, in March, 1846; and at once entered on the practice of his profession, at Lexington. In 1867, he was elected to Congress; was re-elected in 1869, and again in 1871 and 1873, serving eight years, consecutively, in the National House of Representatives; during the sessions of the Fortieth Congress he was member of the reconstruction committee, of which Thaddeus Stevens was chairman, and was conspicuous in his influence over the acts of that committee; was member of the Committees of Reconstruction and Appropriation during the Forty-first Congress; was member of the Committee of Ways and Means in the Forty-second and Forty-third Congresses and distinguished himself by his great industry, ability, and zeal. In January, 1876, he was elected to the United States Senate, being selected, without opposition, by the Legislative Democratic caucus. His name had previously appeared, on several occasions, in the party caucuses, for the same position. He was a member of the Charleston and Baltimore Conventions of 1860, and assisted, at the latter place, in the nomination of John C. Breckinridge. He was identified with the Whig party until its dissolution, casting his first presidential vote for Henry Clay, in 1844; was the law partner of John C. Breckinridge from 1854 to 1860, and supported Mr. Breckinridge in his race for the Presidency. Senator Beck was a man of powerful build and constitution, his whole make-up indicating a man of great strength, determination, and self-reliance. He was a speaker of uncommon powers, and was undoubtedly one of the ablest lawyers and most influential men of his adopted state. He was married February 3, 1848, at Louisville, to Miss Jane W. A. Thornton, of Loudoun County, Virginia, step-daughter of Governor James Clark, of Kentucky, and daughter of George W. Thornton, grand-nephew of General Washington. Senator Beck died in 1890.

CLARENCE CRITTENDEN CALHOUN, principal of the Lexington Business College, was born in Daviess County, Kentucky, September 13, 1863, being a descendant of a Scotch-Irish Presbyterian family, who on their arrival in America first settled in Pennsylvania but subsequently moved to Virginia. From this family John C. Calhoun, the immortal statesman of South Carolina, was descended. One branch of the family, in company with a body of settlers who were coming to Kentucky, were attacked by a band of Indians, and almost the entire party either killed or taken prisoners. Among the slain were the father and mother of George Calhoun, the great-grandfather of the subject of this sketch, and George, their son, was taken prisoner by the Indians at the tender age of three years, and held by them until he was seven years of age, when he was rescued by a party of settlers under Judge Cotton, by whom he was tenderly cared for until he was grown, when he repaid the kindness of Judge Cotton by marrying one of his daughters. After which time he spent a part of his life in Henry County, Kentucky, but finally moved to Daviess County, Kentucky, where he lived until his death in 1835. He was First Lieutenant of a company of Pennsylvania Rangers during the Revolutionary War, serving from June 8, 1776, to January 1, 1781. He was often called on to act as courier, carrying messages through the trackless wilderness from one army to another. Serving at one time in this capacity under General Washington, he was complimented on the field of battle by that illustrious leader and patriot, who entrusted him with a most important and perilous mission, telling him that he had never failed him and he felt that now he was the only man in his command who would be able to deliver his message, which was done at the risk of his life, thus saving the day.

Rev. Samuel Calhoun, grandfather of C. C. Calhoun, removed with his father, George Calhoun, to Daviess County, Kentucky, where he became profoundly and deeply impressed with a call to the ministry, and although his education had been neglected, on account of delicate health and poor facilities, yet with remarkable perseverance he prepared himself for his high calling, which he soon entered with his heart and soul full of love for his fellow-man and fired with enthusiasm to proclaim to them the glad tidings of the gospel of peace. He soon became one of the leaders of his church (the Cumberland Presbyterian), preaching all over Southwestern Kentucky for a term of fifty years. At all times and under all circumstances he absolutely refused to receive any salary for his work, yet his financial prosperity abounded largely above that of his fellows. He held his congregations solidly together during the exciting scenes of the Civil War; and at the ripe age of eighty-six years, he was called away from his earthly labors to receive an eternal reward at the hands of his Master.

His youngest son, John R. Calhoun, father of C. C. Calhoun, was born in Daviess County, Kentucky, March 17, 1839. Owing to delicate health, and much against his will, he was forced to give up his college course, in which he gave great promise and through the advice of his physicians he has devoted himself to farming, spending what spare time he could in the study of the Bible and sacred literature, and to the service of his church.

December 11, 1862, he was married to Miss Margaret N. Bosley, who was educated at Science Hill, Shelbyville, Kentucky. Mrs. Calhoun being possessed of high intellectual endowments, kind and gentle manner, unselfish and considerate of others, is loved and admired by all who know her. Her father, Nicholas G. Bosley, was born in Maryland, April 9, 1803, and came to Daviess County, Kentucky, in 1826. He possessed great enterprise and industry with the highest morality and integrity. By hard work and good management, he acquired a comfortable fortune, but had a large portion of it taken from him by the Federal forces during the Civil War.

Clarence C. Calhoun was the eldest of a large family, and the duty of looking after his father's business devolved upon him at an early age, so that he had neither time nor opportunity to acquire an education, although he endeavored to improve every opportunity which presented itself. He usually had a book with him studying while his team and the other workmen rested. In this way, while plowing, he mastered the subject of fractions so thoroughly and so well as to enable him to take a college course without again going over the subject. When twenty-one years old, he left the parental roof fully determined to obtain an education, although his capital, which he had saved up, amounted to the modest sum of $15.00. With a resolution to do or die, he went to work building patent fences, digging ditches, working in the harvest field or at anything else that was honorable until he had accumulated about $100. January 24, 1886, he entered the State A. &. M. College at Lexington, Kentucky, and was there three and one half years, taking a scientific and classical course. While taking his course the trustees of the college placed him in charge of the commercial department of that institution now known as the Lexington Business College. While attending college, or rather during vacations, he made the money to defray his expenses at manual labor or by selling books, making as much as $200 in one month.

He had been a student in this institution less than a year when he was called upon by the faculty to deliver an address on Commencement Day. This effort was made in the presence of Senator James B. Beck, Governor Proctor Knott and many of the most distinguished men of the state. At the conclusion Senator Beck arose to his feet and complimented the address in a most enthusiastic manner, which was heartily entered into by the other distinguished gentlemen present.

The Lexington Business College has had a

wonderful growth under his able management. When it started, less than seven years ago, the school was located in an old dwelling, almost entirely without equipment and with less than one dozen students. Since then thousands of young men and women have been given a business training, and placed in positions in which they are able to make comfortable livings. Through his influence and work a new building has been erected, especially adapted to the business college. This is situated on East Main street, near the Phoenix Hotel, and its magnificent and imposing front constructed of stone is the chief attraction in that part of the city. It is unequaled in the arrangement and equipment of its several departments, the planning and furnishing of which was done under the direction of Mr. Calhoun, whose management of the school has made it possible for this fine building to be erected. Thus by his energy and business tact he has built up an institution which is destined to stand among the most renowned business colleges on this continent. He is a hard worker himself, and expects all work done under him to be faithful and conscientious and based upon the highest principles of honesty and integrity.

When Mr. Calhoun was at home, occasionally attending the country common schools, they were so poor and the results of their work so unsatisfactory, he determined if ever in his power to do something for the improvement of the system and the advancement of the cause of education in Kentucky. Accordingly in January, 1892, in connection with Hon. A. L. Peterman, he began the publication of an educational journal known as "The Southern School," which has developed into the largest and most popular periodical of the kind west of the Allegheny Mountains. In a little more than two years it has gained a subscription list of over six thousand, and its weekly visits are hailed with delight by teachers in every state in the South. When it was projected its publishers did not expect it to be a success from a financial point of view, but in this they have been happily disappointed, while they have seen it grow and flourish until it has done more for the public school system in Kentucky than any other instrumentality. In conclusion it may be said of Mr. Calhoun that he has accomplished, within ten years, a work which few men have equaled in a lifetime.

"C. C. Calhoun, when a boy at home with his father, was noted for his stability of character, fixedness of purpose and close application to business. What he did was thoroughly done; he lost no time; when not engaged in physical labor his time was occupied in reading. He was ever trusty, faithful and punctual in attendance upon his father's business and immovable in his moral character." Written by his father as a just tribute.

SAMUEL P. AMENT, deceased, financier, business man, manufacturer, missionary preacher and soldier, for many years before his death a citizen of Louisville, was born in Jessamine County, Kentucky, May 12, 1801.

His father, Gabriel Ament, was a native of Germany who came to Kentucky and was a successful farmer in Jessamine County. He married Mary Metcalfe, sister of Governor Metcalfe, and was a man of education and of fine intelligence. Their son, Samuel, was reared on the farm and sent to the common schools, obtaining the rudiments of a fair education; but it was in the home under the wise and careful training of his gifted mother that he imbibed the knowledge and the principles which guided him in all the affairs of a remarkably busy and useful life.

He inherited very little of this world's goods, but received from his parents that which is more precious than wealth. Possessing unusual talent, he applied a vigorous intellect and an honest purpose with diligence, industry and wise discretion and was rewarded with a degree of success which few self-made men enjoy.

Leaving the parental roof before he was twenty years of age, he went to Nashville, Tennessee, and there laid the foundation for a large fortune, establishing a foundry as the nucleus of his business operations, and extending his interests on mercantile lines, at one time having a supply house for steamboats, and in the year of the cholera epidemic, he was proprietor of three or four drug stores.

While active, energetic, enterprising and successful in business, occupying a prominent and enviable position among the leading business men of Nashville, accumulating wealth and distinction as a man of the highest integrity, uprightness and enterprise, it was in the capacity of a Sunday school teacher and worker and as a missionary preacher of the gospel that he was most prominent and popular. In this line his success was co-equal with that of his business career.

In McFerrin's history of "Methodism in Tennessee" a detailed account of Mr. Ament's early work is given. In Redford's "History of Methodism in Kentucky" his father, Gabriel Ament, is mentioned as one of the earnest workers in the early days of the century in Kentucky. Dr. McFerrin says that Samuel P. Ament came to Nashville, June, 1820 (his nineteenth year), where he knew no one but Honorable Felix Grundy and his wife. Mrs. Grundy was a devout Presbyterian and having invited young Ament to her house, she informed him that a few friends had determined to establish a school for the purpose of educating poor children who wished to attend and for religious instruction of the children generally. He readily consented to become one of the teachers.

The first meeting was held on the first Sunday in July, 1820, in a little dilapidated building with no glass in the windows. The books used were Webster's spelling book and the New Testament. Meetings were held each Sunday morning at eight o'clock and the teachers became missionaries to solicit attendance, and for this they were subjected to persecutions in almost every concievable way. They were denounced as Sabbath-breakers and violators of the law, and were threatened with punishment as disturbers of the peace. The finger of scorn was pointed at them on all occasions, and the churches pronounced against them, declaring that they should not be countenanced. In fact, their greatest opposition came from the churches who refused them the use even of the basement rooms and thus compelled the abandonment of the school during the winter months. But it was revived in the following spring, and they obtained permission to use the basement of an old cabinet shop, which had been the resort of hogs and where they had wallowed and slept and where there were "innumerable little insects with hopping propensities." Other good people joined the little band of teachers and the good work was carried on.

Mr. Ament found two boys fighting, separated them, took them into the Sunday school where they were taught and reformed and both became men of superior talent and of high moral and Christian character.

Eventually the opposition gave way, and in November, 1822, they were invited into one of the churches. This was undoubtedly the first Sunday school in Nashville, and out of it grew some of the churches in that city. Among the fruits of this school and others which followed, Mr. Ament could point to many of the communicants in the various congregations in the city who were trained in the Sunday school, and many of the leading lights in the ministry were pupils of these earnest "Sabbath-breakers and violators of the law."

Dr. McFerrin writing (1879) before the death of Colonel Ament, says: "He still lives in the enjoyment of a green old age, full of zeal and constant in labor for the good of the rising generation. For the instruction of the children and the prosperity of the Sunday schools, his zeal knows no abatement."

Colonel Ament was not a man to exploit his own achievements, and the good work that he accomplished cannot now be estimated. It is known, however, that he built a mission church in Nashville, at his own expense, in which he preached regularly every Sunday night; that he was never too much engrossed with his large business interests to devote his time and contribute of his means for the work of the church and its nursery, the Sunday school.

Little is known of his record as a soldier, but he enlisted and fought in the Mexican war, and thus won the military title of Colonel, by which he was known.

He was for some time after the war a resident of Washington, District of Columbia, where he bought a fine home and practically retired from business pursuits.

He was married February 10, 1887, to Mary Ann Howard, daughter of Alfred Hoskins and Nancy Monroe.

Colonel Ament made his home in Louisville until his death in June, 1891. He is buried in Mount Olivet Cemetery at Nashville, Tennessee.

Alfred Hoskins, Mrs. Ament's father, was a native of Hardin County, whose parents came to this state from Virginia. He was a prosperous farmer and slave owner and for some years kept a tavern and stage office on the Louisville and Nashville turnpike, about five miles from Louisville. He died when Mrs. Ament was thirteen years of age. His wife, Nancy Monroe, was a native of Bullitt County, whose parents were from Virginia. Her father was the youngest brother of President James Monroe. Mrs. Ament survives her husband and is living in Louisville and has with her Daisy Lee Dyer her granddaughter.

FRANK E. DAUGHTERY, of Bardstown, Clerk of the Nelson County Circuit Court, son of Dr. Daniel Daughtery and Sarah Slevin, was born in Bardstown, July 5, 1871.

His father, a native of Philadelphia, Pennsylvania, came to Bardstown in 1840 and engaged in the practice of dentistry in which he continued until the time of his death, July 4, 1888, having reached the age of seventy-two years. He was a very learned man, especially in the science of dentistry, and his work was of the highest standard. He soon made a reputation for excellent work and gained a very large patronage from the best people in the county and established himself in the confidence of the people, by whom he was universally respected. He was a brother of Hon. M. A. Daughtery, who was Judge of the Supreme Court of Ohio for many years and both were devout Catholics.

Sarah (Slevin) Daughtery, who was a native of Somerset, Ohio, survives her husband and is a resident of Bardstown. The grandfathers of the subject of this sketch were natives of Ireland.

Frank E. Daughtery was educated in the Bardstown schools, at Bethlehem Academy and St. Joseph's College, and after quitting college was correspondent of Louisville and Cincinnati newspapers, in which he did special work of a very acceptable character.

In 1892 he was employed in the office of the Clerk of the Circuit Court under D. C. Hardin and in June, 1892, Mr. Hardin was appointed Secretary of the Railroad Commission by Governor Brown and Mr. Daughtery announced himself as a candidate for the office of Clerk of the Circuit Court. When the vacancy occurred Judge Russell expressed his desire to appoint Mr. Daughtery to the office, but he was not of legal age and the County Clerk, W. J. Dalmazzo, was appointed to serve until after the primary election, which was to be held August 1, 1892. Mr. Daughtery received the nomination over two opponents, and Mr. Dalmazzo resigned the Circuit Clerkship and the candidate took charge of the office to which he was easily elected in the following November for a term expiring in 1897.

Mr. Daughtery is quite active in politics and for one of his years has made a mark of considerable breadth. Few young men have accomplished as much before reaching their twenty-fifth birthday and he was hardly out of his teens until he was something of a wheel-horse in the political arena. His hustling qualities and his effective methods were soon recognized by the older politicians and they made him Chairman of the County Democratic Campaign Committee in 1895 and he led them to an easy victory, while other Democratic strongholds in the state were demolished by the Republicans and others who were clamoring for a change. Mr. Daughtery not only managed the campaign by virtue of his position as Chairman, but he took the stump and preached the gospel of Democracy with telling effect in every school house in the county.

He is the youngest Circuit Clerk in the state at present and one of the most efficient. He will go forward, not backward, and those who watch his career for another quarter of a century will see him away up in front.

STEPHEN A. YOUNG, Clerk of the Circuit Court and an exceedingly popular citizen of Henderson, was born in Union County, Kentucky, October 2, 1842.

His father, Judge Milton Young, removed from Nelson to Union County, where he was county judge for two terms, and represented his county for one term in the Kentucky Legislature. He was quite wealthy before the war, and owned a large number of slaves. He removed to Henderson in 1859 and spent the remainder of his days in that city.

Hon. Bryan R. Young, M. D. (grandfather), owned a large estate in Nelson County, and was the father of a large family, of whom Judge Milton Young was the junior member. Dr. Brown served the Bardstown district in Congress for one term, 1845-7. He was a successful physician, and astonished the neighbors by building the first brick house in Nelson County, which is still standing as a reminiscence of former days.

John Young (great-grandfather) was a native of London, England, who came to this country soon after the Revolutionary war.

C. M. Singleton (great-grandfather) came to Kentucky in 1796 and located in Nelson County, near Chaplin, where he owned a large tract of land. He was the father of ten sons and daughters, among whom was William Singleton (grandfather), who represented his district in Congress back in the '30's.

Stephen A. Young, son of Judge Milton Young and Maria Thompson Young, is a brother of Milton Young, the owner of McGrathiana of Lexington, and is a worthy descendant of an illustrious ancestry. He lived with his father in Union County until about eighteen years of age, attending the common schools, where he acquired the rudiments of a good education. After removing to Henderson he attended an excellent private school, where he advanced rapidly and soon completed a course which was deemed sufficient for one who was then inclined to agricultural pursuits. Leaving school, he was engaged in farming for four years, when he was elected constable in the Henderson district, serving two terms. He was then elected marshal and tax collector of Henderson, and performed this double duty for two terms.

In 1883 he was appointed clerk of the Circuit Court, to fill a vacancy, and in the following November was elected to that office, to which he has been re-elected the second time. Soon after his appointment as clerk he was also made commissioner of the Circuit Court, which office he held in connection with the clerkship for five years.

His frequent elections were due to his universal popularity, his admirable qualifications, and incidentally to his excellent standing in the Democratic party, in which he is a leader and an active worker.

He is one of the sinking fund commissioners of the city by appointment of the mayor, a deserved compliment to his excellent judgment and ability as a financier and to his unswerving integrity in business transactions.

Mr. Young is a member of the Methodist Episcopal Church, and is a Knight of Pythias, in both of which he is an active worker and a helper of others.

He was married in 1863 to Caroline Bank, daughter of David Bank of Henderson.

GEORGE D. TODD, Mayor of Louisville, vice-president of the Todd-Donigan Iron Company, president of the Kentucky Machinery Company, vice-president of the Kentucky Society of Sons of the American Revolution, vice-president of the Union Soldiers' and Sailors' Monument Association of Kentucky, and incidentally connected with other business, social, political and patriotic interests, a descendant of a long line of ancestors whose names are inscribed on the pages of history, was born in Frankfort, Kentucky, April 19, 1856. He is the tenth of twelve children—who reached maturity—of Harry Innes and Jane (Davidson) Todd, who were for many years well known citizens of Frankfort.

George D. Todd was educated in the public school of Frankfort, and in 1874, when eighteen years of age, went to Louisville and found employment as bookkeeper in the hardware establishment of W. B. Belknap & Company, and was thus engaged for six years, when the Todd-Donigan Iron Company was organized (1880) and he engaged in business on his own account. As a stockholder and vice-president of that company he has made his way to the front in commercial circles, built up a substantial and growing business, and has encouraged and assisted other enterprises and business men; has aided in the general growth and prosperity of the business interests of the city by his individual efforts and by his active interests in and labors for the Board of Trade, in which he was a director for many years.

With all of these interests and the many duties which they have imposed, he has given much of his valuable time and helpful assistance to the Kentucky Society of the Sons of the American Revolution, of which he is vice-president; to the Union Soldiers' and Sailors' Monument Association, of which he is also vice-president, and to the cause of the Republican party in Kentucky, being treasurer and one of the most active managers of the State Executive Committee, and a hard-working, successful and invincible leader in local and state politics.

His election by the Republican City Council to the office of mayor was a tribute to his worth as a business man and as a true friend of the commercial interests of the city, as well as to his wise leadership in his party. Henry S. Tyler, mayor, having died in office, the election of his successor became the duty of the City Council, both boards of which were solidly Republican for the first time in the history of the city, and Mr. Todd was the logical candidate, being supported by the better element in his party, and by the substantial, representative business men of all parties. He was inaugurated mayor January 31, 1896, and at once began to apply the wise and safe rules of business in the management of the affairs of the city. Without giving up his attention to other interests he has already done faithful service in his responsible position as chief magistrate of Louisville.

Mr. Todd is unmarried, being devoted to the care of his aged mother and a sister, who presides over his household affairs. His home is the depository of a fine collection of relics of early times in Kentucky, in which his forefathers figured prominently; and in addition to his association with Kentucky history and active work in that line, he is a member of the Virginia Historical Society. He is a Mason of the Thirty-second degree, and is a member of the Presbyterian Church.

Harry Innes Todd (father) was born in Frankfort, Kentucky, September 16, 1818; died in his native city May 12, 1891. He was educated in Frankfort, and when a young man went to Louisville and was employed as a clerk with Coleman & Ward for a few years. Returning to Frankfort he was engaged in steamboating as captain of one of the boats then plying the Kentucky and Ohio Rivers; was sheriff of Franklin County for two terms; was lessee of the state prison for eight years, and then warden of the same institution for one term, after which he retired from active business.

He represented Franklin County in the Legislature for two terms. During the Civil war he was an uncompromising Union man, and after that a Democrat—although a protectionist—and was very active and successful in politics; had a wide acquaintance throughout the state and enjoyed the happy faculty of remembering the face and name of every man he met, and thus secured the good will and warm friendship of a host of prominent people.

John Harris Todd (grandfather) was born in Frankfort, Kentucky, in 1796, and was a young lawyer of distinction with the promise of a brilliant career, but died in his twenty-eighth year. He married Maria K. Innes, daughter of Judge Harry and Anne (Harris) Innes. (See brief sketch of Judge Innes herewith.)

Thomas Todd (great-grandfather) was born in King and Queen County, Virginia, January 23, 1765. He was the youngest son of Richard Todd, who was descended from one of the most remarkable families in the colonies, his ancestors being among the early emigrants from England. Thomas Todd's mother was Elizabeth Richards. His father died when Thomas was eighteen years of age, leaving a considerable estate, which, by the laws of primogeniture, descended to the eldest son, William, but was swallowed up by mortgages and debts inherited. Thomas Todd received a good education, mainly through his own efforts; served as a substitute for six months in the Revolutionary war, and often referred to the incident in after life as the first opportunity he ever had of making any money. He afterward served in the cavalry in that war on his own account; came to Danville, Kentucky, in 1786 and was the guest of Judge Harry Innes and a teacher in his family while studying law. He was appointed clerk of the Federal Court prior to the admission of Kentucky into the Union, and was clerk of the Court of Appeals after that event, until December, 1801; was appointed judge of that court by Governor Garrard; was appointed chief justice by Governor Greenup; was appointed judge of the United States Circuit Court, embracing Ohio, Kentucky and Tennessee, by President Jefferson, and continued in that office until his death, February 7, 1826. He married Elizabeth Harris, who died in 1811, having borne him five children: Harry Innes, John Harris, Charles Stewart (who was minister plenipotentiary to Russia under President William Henry Harrison), Elizabeth Hanna and Ann Maria Starling.

He married (second) the widow of George Steptoe Washington (nephew of General Washington), whose maiden name was Lucy Payne, a sister of the wife of President Madison. There were three children by this marriage: James Madison, William Johnston and Madisonia. The Todds were originally from Ireland.

Jane Davidson Todd (mother) was born in Frankfort, Kentucky, September 19, 1821. She was educated in the schools of her native place and became the wife of Harry I. Todd, August 20, 1839. As before stated, she is now living with her son, Mayor Todd, in Louisville, and is a devout member of the Presbyterian Church.

Colonel James Davidson (maternal grandfather) was a native of North Carolina, and a twin brother of Michael Davidson. They came to Kentucky and were farmers and prominent men in Lincoln County. Each was elected to the Legislature—sometimes one would be in the Senate and the other in the House, and in the next term their positions in the Assembly would be reversed. James was finally elected state treasurer; was in the War of 1812; married Harriet Ballinger, daughter of Joseph and Jane Logan Ballinger. He died May, 1860, and she died in 1861. Jane Logan Ballinger died January, 1851. Her mother was Janet McClure, and her father was John Logan of Revolutionary fame, for whose brother Logan's Fort was named.

George Davidson (maternal great-grandfather) was a captain in the Revolutionary war. He came to Lincoln County, Kentucky, from North Carolina, while his brother William went to Tennessee. Davidson County—in which Nashville, the capital of the state, is situated—was named in his honor. The Davidsons are of Irish and the Logans of Scotch descent.

Judge Harry Innes, Mayor Todd's great-grandfather, was appointed judge of the Supreme Court of the District of Kentucky, October 13, 1782, by General Benjamin Harrison, then governor of Virginia; and in 1789, under the first judiciary law of the United States, was appointed United States judge for the District of Kentucky by President Washington, which position he held until his demise, September 20, 1816. July 18, 1792, Governor Isaac Shelby, "by and with the advice and consent of the Senate, appointed said Harry Innes chief justice of the Supreme Court of Kentucky," which he declined. He was born January 15, 1752, in Caroline County, Virginia; son of Rev. Robert Innes, who was a native of Scotland and a minister in the Episcopal Church. Judge Innes held many offices and performed public services which were of the highest importance to the people of Virginia and to the new State of Kentucky.

LUCIUS P. LITTLE, a well-known author and able attorney at law of Owensboro, son of Douglass Little, was born on his father's farm in the southern part of Daviess County, Kentucky, February 15, 1838.

His father was a native of what was then Ohio County, Kentucky, but in the part afterwards embraced in Daviess County. He was at various periods of his life engaged in farming, blacksmithing and wagon making and in the latter days practiced law. He held the offices of constable, justice of the peace, and county judge and was in office over twenty years and died in 1877. His father and mother, grandparents of Lucius P. Little, were natives of South Carolina, where they were married in 1798. They, with Judge Little's great-grandfather, George Little, emigrated from South Carolina to Kentucky in 1802. George Little was a native of Scotland, whence he came to America before the Revolutionary War, and during that time he served as a private in the Colonial army. He was a life-long cripple in consequence of a severe wound received in battle.

Judge Little's great-grandmother was a daughter of Alexander and Mary (Handley) Douglass, both of whom were natives of Scotland. His mother's maiden name was Martha Wright, daughter of John and Katherine (Weatherford) Wright of Charlotte County, Virginia. She came to Kentucky with her parents in 1820, and still lives in her eighty-fifth year.

Judge Little was the eldest of seven children, and his early years were spent on the farm where he was born and in the small towns of Rumsey and Calhoun. He attended school in these towns, but never enjoyed the advantages of collegiate training. When sixteen years of age he became a deputy clerk, remaining three years in the clerk's offices in Daviess and McLean Counties.

At the age of eighteen he began the study of law and in 1856 and 1857 attended law school at Cumberland University, Lebanon, Tennessee. He began the practice of his profession at Calhoun in 1857, in his twentieth year, continuing there until 1860; was appointed deputy United States marshal and took the census in McLean County in 1860. In the close of that year he removed to Louisville, and after practicing in that city for twelve months he went to California in 1861 and remained there a year, employed in a conveyancer's office. Returning to Kentucky in 1862 he spent some months in recruiting for the Confederate army, for which offense he was arrested by the United States authorities and imprisoned, first at Bowling Green, and then at Frankfort. Securing release, he went to Mexico in the fall of 1863, but returned to Kentucky in the spring of 1864 and after some time resumed his law practice at Calhoun.

He removed to Owensboro, February, 1867; where he has ever since resided. He was a candidate for Circuit Judge in 1874 and defeated; was again a candidate in 1880 and elected; and was re-elected in 1886. After serving twelve years on the bench, he resumed the practice of law in Owensboro in 1893, and is known as one of the leading lawyers in Kentucky.

Judge Little is much inclined to literary work and is a frequent contributor to the magazines and newspapers, his work always being acceptable. His most pretentious work, "Ben Hardin," published in book form in 1887, is a volume of rare merit and deep interest, and has had an extensive sale. It is a book that should be in the library of every Kentuckian.

He is a member of the Methodist Episcopal Church South, and is a Knight Templar Mason.

Judge Little has been three times married: First, to Lizzie Freeman of Woodford County, April, 1868; second, to Louise Holloway of Henderson County, October, 1875; and third, to Fannie Beach of New Jersey, January, 1889. He has eight living children.

ROBERT CARTER RICHARDSON, one of the senior attorneys of Covington, and an author of distinction, son of Samuel Q. and Mary H. (Harrison) Richardson and a descendant of some of the most distinguished patriots of Revolutionary times, was born in Louisville, Kentucky, May 18, 1826. His parents died when he was quite young, but he received a good education, graduating from the academical department of Transylvania University in 1846; and after reading law with Judge George Robertson of Lexington, graduated from the law department of his alma mater in 1848, and was admitted to the bar in Lexington.

He removed to Covington in 1850, and has been engaged in the practice of his profession in that city—his present home—for forty-six years; and during all that time has been regarded as one of the most successful and honored members of the bar.

He was a member of the Legislature from Kenton County from 1855 to 1859, and was succeeded by John G. Carlisle; was superintendent of public instruction from 1859 to 1863; register in bankruptcy from 1872 to 1883, and has been prominently identified with the public affairs of his city, county and state and the national government during all of the years of a busy and useful life. While yet a minor he served one year in the Mexican war in Cassius M. Clay's company, Colonel H. Marshall's regiment, as sergeant, and for a time as acting sergeant major. During the Civil war Mr. Richardson was an uncompromising Union man and had command of two companies of home guards.

Mr. Richardson was married in 1859 to Marie

Louise Harris, daughter of Colonel Henry C. Harris, who was for fourteen years a member of the Kentucky House of Representatives and Senate. He was a lawyer of eminence in his profession; was a Southern sympathizer during the war; made one or two races for Congress; married a Miss Davis of Virginia.

Samuel Q. Richardson (father), a distinguished lawyer, was a native of Fayette County, Kentucky; located first in Cincinnati, Ohio, then in Louisville, and finally in Frankfort, Kentucky, where he had a large practice in the Appellate Court. He died in the forty-fifth year of his age.

John Crowley Richardson (grandfather) was a native of Virginia and was ensign in a Baltimore regiment in the Revolutionary war.

William Richardson (great-grandfather) was born in Baltimore, and was colonel of a Maryland regiment in the Revolutionary war. The progenitor of the Richardson family in this country came from England in 1680, or about that time, and settled in Baltimore. The descendants have always been distinguished for their patriotism, loyalty and good citizenship.

Mary H. Harrison Richardson (mother) was born on the old Harrison estate in Virginia. Her father, Robert Carter Harrison, was a cousin of President William Henry Harrison, and a nephew of Benjamin Harrison, who was one of the signers of the Declaration of Independence and governor of Virginia. The mother of Robert Carter Harrison was Susannah Randolph. She was a sister of Jane Randolph, who married Peter Jefferson, and was aunt of President Thomas Jefferson.

Mr. Richardson is also an author of distinction, his name appearing in Allibone's Dictionary of Authors, published some time since in Philadelphia.

CHARLES STEWART BELL, Sr., born August 14, 1825, now resident at Lexington, Kentucky. A beautiful, a sweet and gentle yet a forceful life it has fallen to my lot to sketch, as the setting sun falls across it with mellow glow, and the twilight is modestly, yet wistfully, to come and fold the good man to its heart. I write of such a man, without an enemy, though placed in such position that another would have scores of them. He has held his own with sturdy strength, through every storm, without engendering animosities; he has been true to every trust—true to his God, his neighbor and himself, and faithful always. He has not found a man to speak one idle word against his character. Old as he is, with a long, a busy and a useful life behind him, there is no spot, nor smirch, nor stain upon his name. Shame has not known him nor disgrace abided in his house. Of him it might in truth be said:

"Sweet are the thoughts that savor of content,
The quiet mind is richer than a crown;
Sweet are the nights in careless slumber spent,
The poor estate scorns Fortune's angry frown.
Such sweet content, such mind, such sleep, such bliss,
Beggars enjoy when princes often miss.
The homely house that harbors quiet rest,
The cottage that affords no pride nor care,
The man that 'grees wi' country music best,
The sweet consort of Mirth, and Music's fare,
Obscured life sets down a type of bliss:
A mind content both crown and kingdom is."

The modesty and accuracy of his mind could not be better shown than in his own sketch of his family, which is reproduced almost literally as written by him for the purposes of this article. It is as follows:

My ancestors were natives of Annandale, Dumfries-shire, Scotland. The natives of Annandale were a warm-hearted race, proud of the common tie which binds them to their grand historic dale, and with feelings of attachment for the "glorious heritage of name and fame bequeathed to them by their forefathers."

My grandfather, William Bell, married Agnes Irving; they were born and lived in Annandale, near Annan. He was a descendant from the three connected Bells of Middlebie, Allenbie and Blackethouse, and was noted as a good farmer in his day. They had six children, four sons and two daughters.

My grandfather on my mother's side was John Moffat. He married Elizabeth Brown; they were also born in Annandale, near Lockerby, and had five children, two sons and three daughters. He was a mercantile man. Both families were Presbyterians. My father, George K. Bell, was the son of William and Agnes I. Bell, and married

Sybella Moffat, in 1820. They had twelve children, nine sons and three daughters. After they were married they lived at Hillside, near Lockerby. From there he removed to Jardine Hall, in the parish of Applegarth, and resided there for several years. In 1838 he took charge of the woods and forests on the Marquis of Queensberry's estates, and upon the resignation of James Stewart, Esq., as factor on the estates, he succeeded to that position, and continued to hold it until his death, which took place on the 26th of April, 1873, at Cummertrees House at the age of seventy-six years. My mother died on the 26th of October, 1873, at the age of seventy-four years.

I was born at Clughfoots, near Hillside, parish of Dryfesdale, August 14, 1823, and received most of my education at the School of Sandyholm, in the parish of Applegarth. I was fond of botany, and at the age of fourteen years wanted to follow horticulture. As soon as Sir William Jardine, the naturalist, knew of my wish he got his gardener to make a place for me in his gardens at Jardine Hall, and after working two years in them I went to the nurseries of Thomas Kennedy in Dumfries, then the largest in the south of Scotland, to learn something of nursery work. After remaining some time in these nurseries, a situation was offered me in the gardens of the Duke of Beccleugh, at Drumlanrig Castle, which were then undergoing some improvements, as it was expected that Queen Victoria would stop there on her way from London to Edinburgh, this being her first visit to Scotland. The gardens of Drumlanrig were then considered amongst the finest in Scotland. After remaining about two years at Drumlanrig, in the different departments of the gardens, I went to Liverpool in England, and was employed some time in the large nurseries of William Skirving.

While living in Liverpool I concluded to visit the United States, and sailed from Liverpool early in June, 1842, arriving in New York on the 6th day of July, not then eighteen years of age. I remained in New York City and vicinity and in Dutchess County, New York, for about a year, occasionally visiting some of the noted places on the banks of the Hudson River when not employed. In November, 1843, I sailed from New York to New Orleans, and spent part of the winter there, and then went to Mobile, Alabama. From there returned to New Orleans and took passage by steamboat for Cincinnati, Ohio, arriving at that city in June, 1844, where I soon found employment with a florist in his greenhouses. While there I was engaged to come to Lexington, Kentucky, by Henry Duncan, Esq., who was having greenhouses and vineries built for growing the fine varieties of foreign grapes at his then beautiful residence, Duncanan.

I arrived in Lexington on the 28th of November, 1844. On the 17th of February, 1846, I married Margaret Bunyan Smith, in Chillicothe, Ohio. Her father's name was William Smith and her mother's name Helen Scott. Her paternal grandfather was named William Smith. He was born, lived and died at Newstead, a village in Rosburyshire, Scotland. He married Margaret Bunyan in January, 1787. They had a family of three sons and four daughters. William, the oldest, my wife's father, was born in November, 1787, at Newstead. He was a direct descendant from John Bunyan, the author of the Pilgrim's Progress, a book which, next to the Bible, is more read in Scotland than any other. He had two uncles named Robert and Andrew. One was a surgeon in the British navy, and the other an "ensign." Her mother's name was Helen Scott. She was born February 2, 1792, near Hawick, Scotland. Her father's name was John Scott, and his wife's name Mary Riddle. They moved to a farm at Merton, near Abbotsford. Her father and his son were elders in the same church. Her uncle, John Scott, had a position in the office of Sir Walter Scott. They were distant relations of Sir Walter Scott's. William Smith and Helen Scott were married near Hawick, but left there in 1819 or 1820, and went to Dumfries-shire. He was employed for about twenty-two years at Drumlanrig in superintending the home farms and improvements on them for the Duke of Beccleugh. In the spring of 1842 he sold his property near Hawick, and emigrated to the United States with his family. They arrived in New York from Scotland August 4, 1842. From there went to Circleville in Pickaway County, Ohio, and in March, 1843, he purchased a farm in Ross

County, Ohio, near Chillicothe, where he lived until November 18, 1852, when he died, his wife following him February 13, 1857. They had twelve children, all born in Scotland.

On the first of April, 1849, I was chosen superintendent of the Lexington Cemetery, and from that date until September 1, 1866, continued to be superintendent. From September, 1866, to September 1, 1867, I was superintendent for the A. and M. College on the farms of Ashland and Woodlands, then the property of the Kentucky University and A. and M. College. When I left the A. and M. College it was my intention to have gone more extensively into the nursery and florist business and to devote my whole time to it, but when it became known to the trustees of the cemetery they made me a proposition to again take charge of the cemetery, and I again became superintendent of it on September 1, 1867, and have continued up to the present time (1896).

On the 24th of July, 1885, my wife died, in the sixty-fifth year of her age. At an early age she joined the Presbyterian Church in Scotland, and continued to be a member of that church until her death.

We had five children, four sons and one daughter: George K. Bell, born December 28, 1846, now agent for the Adams Express Company in Lexington, Kentucky; John Moffat Bell, born March 16, 1848, now cashier of the First National Bank of Lexington, Kentucky; William Smith Bell, born November 9, 1852, now a florist in Lexington; Charles Stewart Bell, born January 15, 1855, now in the wholesale fruit and commission business in Lexington, Kentucky; Ellen Scott Bell, born December 3, 1849, was graduated at the Sayre Female Institute in Lexington, and married T. V. Munson June 27, 1870.

Mr. Munson was born near the village of Astoria, Fulton County, Illinois, September 26, 1843. His father, William Munson, was a New Englander, his mother a Kentuckian. He took a full course in Bryant and Stratton's Business College of Chicago, getting his diploma in 1864. In 1866 he entered Kentucky University, taking the full scientific course, and graduated as B. S. in 1870. He was at once elected adjunct professor in the sciences. This position he held one year, when too long continued hard study in the schoolroom weakened his health, so that he chose to give up teaching for the pursuit of horticulture. He started a nursery in Lincoln, Nebraska, in 1873, and in 1876 he moved to a better location at Denison, Texas, where he now has a fine nursery, well stocked, of over one hundred acres. In 1888 he was honored by the Republic of France, which conferred upon him the title of "Chevalier du Merite Agricole," and presented him with the diploma and decorations of the Legion of Honor, for valuable information on the native grapes of North America, especially as to resistant stocks, and such as will grow well in dry, chalky soils. Only one other such decoration was given an American, Thomas E. Edison receiving that.

It is amongst the species of native grapes that he has achieved during twenty years of experimentation some most remarkable results in hybridization. This work he is still pursuing, and only future generations will be able to fully appreciate the broadening he has given to American viticulture. He has now associated with him his eldest son, William Bell Munson, in the management of his business, finding himself overloaded with the management of it.

"In May, 1895, the trustees of the cemetery granted me a leave of absence for two months to visit Scotland. I sailed from New York on June 8, 1895, and was absent nearly two months, never having been back to Scotland since I left there early in the spring of 1842, after an absence of fifty-two years. On visiting my old home I found all that was left was outside, the old trees, the grass, the house; but inside all was changed by time and death."

A life history, told in such simplicity, need not be classed as uneventful. To be born, to marry, to become a parent and to die is but the common lot of man; but to start like the trickling rivulet from mountain mosses on the cliffside, to form misty cataracts and limpid pools in the descent, to broaden into a meandering brook and fertilize the fruitful fields, to become part of the broadbreasted river which turns the whirring wheels of factories and bears its white-winged commerce to the sea and yet retain the purity and gentleness of mountain dew, is not the heritage of every man. To this man such a life has been—a life of usefulness, of gentleness, of grace and peace.

The Scotch race exhibits its sturdy tenacity in nothing more than its adherence to the idea of home, and its capacity for founding and perpetuating the family. Its favorite doctrine of predestination makes its people look upon the rooftree as especially the gift of God, and the Scotsman considers the corner stone of his dwelling as having been laid in the mind of the Almighty before the foundation of the world. To have about him a family of strong and brave children, self-reliant and devout, is the crowning glory of the old man as he looks into the setting sun.

But with all his sublime faith in the Higher Power he does not forget works, which are the fruit of faith. No matter how poor, he must strive to be better off in this world's goods; no matter how humble, he must seek to rise higher, so that in his old days he may be able to stretch a helping hand to the son, perhaps, of the man who helped him in his youth. Industry and persistent effort bring him to the front in every clime, and when he thinks his betterment demands it, he does not hesitate to leave his much beloved land behind him, turning his face toward a new soil where growth is rapider and skill and energy in more demand.

Such reasons brought Charles Stewart Bell to this country in 1842, a youth in years, but a mature man in experience. The instinct for home life, for cherishing and developing, for training the young in strength to resist rough blasts and flourish in rocky soil, is innate with his race and makes of the Scotchman the best nurseryman in the world. He makes the plant, as well as the child, thrifty and self-reliant. With four years' apprenticeship in the best gardens of his native land, with strong arms, stout heart and willing mind the young man found no difficulty in securing work. From the Gulf to the Ohio he wrought faithfully, studying with apt mind the changing conditions of soil and climate. Until he reached Lexington he had not realized his gardener's ideal. Here he paused, and his heart said to itself, "Eureka! I have found it."

In this chosen land he found at last perfection, and here he planted himself, and built the monument of his life, which still remains, and will remain for generations yet unborn—the Lexington Cemetery. In this his best thought has found expression, and the earth showeth forth his handiwork.

This country suited him; its fertile soil and blue skies incited him to faithful labor in this world, and firmer faith in a better world to come. He had roved enough, and while pruning the grape vines at "Duncanan," or watching the full clusters ripen into purple beauty, the strong young heart felt its warm blood stirred by the angel Love. He was young and impulsive, yet cautious, as his people are. Love with him meant an eternal union of two hearts; it meant the home, the hearthstone, the family, the frugal, honest life, the serene old age, the peaceful death. So he curbed his strong impulses, and labored on in silence for nearly two more years, his loneliness increasing all the time. Then when his future was assured his home was chosen and he ceased to be a wanderer, for the wedding day came quickly, and he was made happy by the hand of one who was to be a faithful friend, a wise counselor, a devoted mother, a loving, tender helpmate in all things, until death should part. Time has made good the wisdom of his choice, and death has made of that pure wife a blessed memory.

With his marriage the real life of the man began. Hitherto he had been a wanderer—an apprentice of destiny. Now, having chosen an abiding place, a home, his constructive nature began to assert itself. First he established a nursery of his own, where with his young wife he could begin to enjoy existence for the first time under his own vine and fig tree. But the capacity for work, the genius and skill for designing and executing was too great in him to be hidden in a private station. While his modest tastes and frugal habits made a quiet home life his ideal, yet there was a higher need for him, a broader sphere for his abilities. He was called in 1848 to the superintendency of his lifework,

THE LEXINGTON CEMETERY.

This beautiful place of rest had just been purchased by a company, and consisted of about forty acres of beautiful, undulating land on the outskirts of the city, which was then covered with virgin grass and shaded with mighty forest trees, most of them remaining. The area was increased from time to time, until now it comprises one hundred and six acres, the whole being a beautiful monument to the exquisite taste, the far-reaching thoughtfulness and the broad executive ability of this one man.

Nature had been not niggardly in her gifts to the favored spot, but the genius of Charles Stewart Bell has supplemented Nature, and builded beauty upon what was already beautiful. Every obstacle of unsightliness has been transformed into lines of grace, and the very defects of the situation and the soil have been made the handmaids of its perfection. Exuberant undergrowth has been cleared away, the long grass trimmed into a velvet sward, the native trees thinned so that sunlight may enter through their interspaces, depressions have been terraced, or transformed into crystal lakes, hills turned into gentle slopes, broad winding roads constructed so as to give access to every portion of the grounds, foreign trees, flowers, shrubbery, evergreens have been added to the perspective, until in all the land there is nowhere a more beautiful city of the dead. All this has been done by an humble, unobtrusive Scotchman, who has claimed no credit except that he has loved his work and been faithful to those who trusted him.

It is not given to all men thus to have written their life history, as it were, upon the face of Nature. It is true, the battlefield remains a memento of the conqueror, and the fortress a monument to the engineer, but it is sweeter far and better far to be remembered by the well trimmed hedge, the robust trees, the banks of violets, the roadway winding through the shadows, and the dell where the spring bubbles and the sunbeam loves to play at noon. This man has written upon God's footstool the serious depths and the happy hillocks of his earthly years, the meditations of his mind, the gentle graciousness of his heart. Longer than a granite tomb his work will last, for the lines of beauty upon Nature's face withstand the touch of Time. For centuries the Lexington Cemetery will be looked upon as the crowning work of Charles Stewart Bell, and its accurate conformity to every graceful attribute of landscape gardening will make of it a model to be striven for by his successors in the art. Cared for as tenderly as if it were an only child, with not a vagrant weed to mar its velvet sward, and not a twig nor fallen leaf to cumber up its winding paths or float upon the surface of its lakes, he will leave this lovely spot a sacred heritage to his successor, without spot or blemish on it. His talent has not been hidden in a napkin, but has been increased an hundredfold, and his reward shall be as great.

Blessed as he has been in the success of all his earthly undertakings, he has been equally as fortunate in his children. Of his son-in-law, T. Volney Munson, he has given a sketch more complete than this writer could pen. Mr. Munson is a man of rare ability in literature, both in and out of his chosen profession, and having married the only daughter and pet of the family it is natural that Mr. Bell should take pride in his achievements. To see his daughter well married and provided for must be indeed a solace to his declining years, the more so that her children have begun to follow in the forceful footsteps of their ancestors.

Each of the boys has carved out for himself an honorable niche in the community. Upright, honorable, their fidelity to every principle of justice has made them worthy of the good old stock from which they sprung, and the responsible positions which they fill. Each one has his home and hearthstone, and finds his delight there rather than in the mad rush of ambition, or the maelstrom of swirling politics. All are good citizens, and exercise their privileges at the polls with conscience for a guide and the best interests of all the people as a purpose. Yet from the wrangling of ward meetings they stand aloof, and of bribery and corruption and trickery they know nothing. The darker side of life, the weakness or venality of public men are to them, and will be ever, a sealed book.

The eldest, George Keatley Bell, attended the city schools of Lexington, and was also for two years a student of Transylvania University, at the same place. After leaving college he went into business in the grocery store of his uncle, Thomas M. Bell, where he remained as clerk, and partner for about ten years. On June 6, 1872, he entered the office of the Adams Express Company at Lexington as clerk, and in June 19, 1882, became agent, which position he continues to hold. On June 5, 1873, he was married to Miss Endora Smith, daughter of John M. Smith of Versailles, Kentucky. She died August 19 of the same year. On December 14, 1880, he was married to Miss Laura Stone, daughter of David Stone of Lexington. By her he became the father of three children, all now living: Walter Stone Bell, born August 17, 1882; Arthur Hampton Bell, born July 10, 1885; George Scott Bell, born November 22, 1887.

His second wife was born October 26, 1854. Her mother, Harriet N. Hampton, was married to David Stone (his second wife) February 22, 1840, and died June 15, 1855. David Stone was born February 14, 1807, married three times and died November 13, 1873. Mr. Bell and his wife are members of Central Christian Church.

John Moffat Bell, the second son, received the same education as his elder brother, except that he spent three years at Transylvania. Leaving college he entered the banking house of David A. Saye, where he remained until November, 1866, when he became individual bookkeeper in the First National Bank of Lexington, Kentucky. June, 1869, he was made teller and in July, 1887, was promoted to cashier, having been assistant cashier for several years previous. March 19, 1872, he married Mary H. Erd, daughter of Frank I. Erd of Lexington. Mr. Erd was a German by birth, but came to America at an early age, and was a prosperous furniture dealer in Lexington. She was born in Lexington, Kentucky, July 8, 1848, and educated at the celebrated private school of Mrs. Rhoten in that city. To them were born three children: Frank Charles Bell, born November 30, 1872, now bookkeeper in First National Bank; Lawrence E. Bell, born March 30, 1874, now with E. J. Curley & Company, Lexington office; John Lambert Bell, born August 25, 1875, and educated at the Kentucky State College at Lexington.

Mr. Bell and wife are not connected with any congregation, one being Presbyterian the other Christian in faith.

William Smith Bell, born November 9, 1852, is, like his father, a florist and nurseryman, and his success has placed him in the front rank of florists in Kentucky. He received only a common school education, and in 1868 entered business life with his father as florist. Their partnership continued until 1881, since which time he has been in business for himself. In 1871-72, however, he was with Scott & Son, prominent florists of Philadelphia. Since returning to Lexington he has become the fashionable florist of the city, and also ships his goods to all parts of the state, and to other states.

He was married October 12, 1875, to Miss Addie Lancaster, daughter of Henry Lancaster, a contractor and builder of Lexington, who died in 1876. His wife was born October 20, 1852. To them six children were born: Emily Scott Bell, October 4, 1877; Nellie Munson Bell, March 19, 1880; W. S. Bell, Jr., November 19, 1882; Adelaide Lancaster Bell, March 9, 1885; Flora Bunyan Bell, January 26, 1890; Charles Stewart Bell, April 7, 1893.

Mr. Bell is a member of the M. E. Church, South, and of several secret societies.

Charles Stewart Bell, Jr., is the youngest of the five children, having been born January 15, 1855. He was educated in the public schools and Transylvania University. After leaving school he was for a short time deputy county clerk and afterward clerk in Adams Express Company. He then went into the fruit business, first by retail, but since 1875 in the wholesale and commission fruit and vegetable trade, and is now one of the largest dealers of the state in both foreign and native lines. He also owns a wholesale and retail store in Frankfort, Ky., but resides in Lexington. On November 16, 1876, he was married to Miss Luella Keith, daughter of Dr. Marvel Lewis Keith, formerly of Greenville, South Carolina. Her mother was Miss Susannah Ball of Lexington. Mrs. Bell was born June 20, 1854, and is a graduate of Sayre Female Institute. Both are members of First Presbyterian Church of Lexington. They have three children living, the eldest having died at an early age. The living are: Margaret Elizabeth Bell, Lewis Keith Bell and Virginia Wickliffe Bell.

The sons of Mr. Bell, senior, are all Democrats in politics, and steady, church-going people. Of his daughter it can well be said, as of her mother, that she is indeed a helpmeet for her husband, and a guardian angel to her children.

And thus we come to the closing chapter to this successful life, for in the course of nature the last page in the precious volume must soon be turned. To such a life, however, death can have no terrors, and the tired body can sweetly sleep in the home which his hands have made so beautiful by the side of the wife whom he loved so well; and every tear which drops upon the sod above him will be as pure as the violets he taught to bloom upon the sunny slopes. He will die full of years and honors, with children and grandchildren about him and unsullied memories to speak his name when he has gone. Upon his monument it could be carved

"The earth has lost a man
Whom Heaven has claimed."

This sketch of the Bell family was written by J. Soule Smith, of Lexington.

WILLIAM J. DALMAZZO of Bardstown, Clerk of Nelson County Court, son of James Dalmazzo and Ann E. Price, was born in Vevay, Switzerland County, Indiana, December 7, 1844. His father was a native of Turin, Italy, who came to America when he was sixteen years of age for the purpose of completing his education. He became a citizen of Vevay and made his home there until the time of his death, which occurred in 1845, in the fifty-third year of his age. He was a very prosperous merchant and a highly respected citizen.

Ann E. Price (mother) was born in Nelson County, December 18, 1822, and is now a resident of Bardstown. After the death of Mr. Dalmazzo she married Francis Smith of Nelson County. There were four children by her first marriage, only one of whom, the subject of this sketch, reached maturity.

Ignatius Price (maternal grandfather) was a native of Nelson County, whose parents were from Maryland. He was an industrious blacksmith and wagonmaker in Bardstown in the days of the old stage coach and did a very thriving business. He died in 1840 in the forty-fifth year of his age.

W. J. Dalmazzo's mother returned to Bardstown after the death of his father and he was educated in St. Joseph's College. After leaving school, well advanced in the English branches, he found employment as a clerk in a dry goods establishment for some time, and in 1864 was appointed Deputy County Clerk by Edwin Turner, in which capacity he served for several years and was deputy in that office and in the Circuit Clerk's office and postoffice at different times until November, 1886, when he was appointed to his present position as County Clerk and expects to serve out his term—which expires January 1, 1898—when he proposes to retire, having acquired a considerable estate.

Mr. Dalmazzo has taken quite an active part in local politics and has held a number of minor offices in Bardstown, where he is one of the most popular citizens, and was Assistant Postmaster for three years, when not engaged in the Clerk's office. He has never married, but is living with his aged mother, for whom he has provided the comforts of a happy home. They are devout members of the Catholic Church and are highly respected by the people of Bardstown and of Nelson County.

WILLIAM P. THORNE, distinguished criminal lawyer and politician of Eminence, son of William Kimberland and Mary K. (Moody) Thorne, was born in Henry County, Kentucky, March 5, 1845.

William K. Thorne (father) was born in Shelby County, April 13, 1813; was educated in the common schools and applied himself to farming and raising fine stock, removing to Henry County in 1839, where he died August 1, 1889. He was a man of great force of character, but did not seek prominence; a Democrat in politics; a faithful member of the Christian Church and one of the best citizens of Henry County. He married the widow Ireland, whose maiden name was Moody, and who was the mother of five children by her first husband, including John Crit Ireland, who was a captain in the Confederate army and afterward for many years proprietor of the Euclid livery stable in Louisville, and Dr. J. W. Ireland, a prominent physician.

The children of William K. Thorne and Mary (Ireland) Thorne were Andrew J., William P. and Shelby T. Thorne.

John Thorne (grandfather) was a native of Virginia, who came with his father (John) to Shelby County when he was a child. His sister and two cousins (boys) were killed by the Indians. They had been sent out of the fort on an errand and were surprised and pursued by the Indians, and ran into Clear Creek for refuge at a particularly deep place, which has been known ever since as Thorne's Pool. For some time the children evaded the shots of the redskins by diving, but they could not remain long under water, and as they arose in the water they were struck by the Indians' arrows until all three were killed. W. P. Thorne has presented one of the arrows taken from the girl's body to the Filson Club, of which he is a member.

John Thorne (grandfather) married Elizabeth Kimberland (grandmother), a native of Virginia, and their children were: Levisa, who married Peter Laswell; Nancy, wife of W. Morrison; Ann, wife of William N. Perkins; William K. and J. J.

John Thorne (great-grandfather) came to Kentucky from Virginia; was one of the pioneers of Shelby County, and lived in the fort mentioned in the above tragic incident.

William P. Thorne graduated from Eminence College in 1865, under the able instruction of Professor Giltner; studied law with Judge George C. Drane, now of Frankfort and at that time a partner of Chief Justice Pryor; was admitted to the bar of Henry County in 1868, and at once began the practice of his profession, in which he has steadily risen until he is one of the most celebrated lawyers in the state.

In 1874 he was elected county attorney, serving until 1878; has frequently been chosen to the position of circuit judge and that of commonwealth attorney in the absence of those officials; and while serving as prosecuting attorney he succeeded in holding over the four men of the notorious Simmons' gang who were hung by a mob; and this brought him into notice all over the state as a fearless and capable prosecutor. He also prosecuted Alsop for the murder of Harrison in Jefferson County; defended Stivers, who killed Colonel Veal of Fayette County; with Colonel Wadsworth defended Shire, who was charged with poisoning his father-in-law, Colonel M. Gleason, of Grant County; defended Foreman in Montgomery County, who was charged with the murder of Cravens, which case was three times taken to the Court of Appeals; prosecuted Doome for killing Hughes at Bardstown; defended Mattox, who killed Jameson at Lakeland; and there has not been an important criminal case in Henry County since Mr. Thorne became a lawyer in which he has not taken an active part; and he has been employed in many important civil cases; was local attorney for the Louisville & Nashville Railroad Company for many years, and is attorney for the Farmers & Drovers' Bank of Eminence.

He has taken a lively interest in Democratic politics and is serving his county for the third time in the Legislature; has been assistant Democratic Presidential elector in four campaigns, and was a delegate to the National Convention in New York (1868), which nominated Seymour and Blair, and was an alternate delegate to the National Convention that nominated Cleveland the second time.

Mr. Thorne was united in marriage March 27, 1866, with Anna Dickerson, and their children are: Agnes Pearl, wife of Lindsey T. Crabb, son of W. L. Crabb, whose sketch will be found in this volume; Mary Bernice, wife of James E. Waugh of Pembroke, and William P. Thorne, Jr.

Mrs. Thorne's father, Richard A. Dickerson, was born in Grant County June, 1825, and was a prominent farmer and distinguished citizen of his native county; active and influential in the Democratic party; exerting great power over the minds and actions of others and enjoying the good will and confidence of all men. He was a son of Archibald and Harriet (Dictum) Dickerson; and his mother was a daughter of Captain

Richard Dictum, whose wife was a Miss McBride, whose two brothers fell at the battle of Brandywine, one of whom was General McBride.

Agnes Collins Dickerson, Mrs. Thorne's mother, was a daughter of Richard Collins and a niece of Lewis Collins, the historian of Kentucky. Richard Collins married Lucy Wilson, daughter of James and Agnes (Pickett) Wilson. James Wilson was a soldier in the Revolutionary war, as is shown by a land grant allotted to him January 31, 1786, and signed by Patrick Henry. Agnes Pickett belonged to a distinguished Virginia family, and was present at the surrender of Lord Cornwallis.

Mrs. Thorne has three brothers: R. T. Dickerson; Worth W. Dickerson, ex-congressman, of Williamstown, and Jefferson D. Dickerson, deceased.

JOHN SAMUEL OWSLEY, farmer of Stanford, Lincoln County, son of Samuel Owsley and Eliza W. Stephenson, was born in Walnut Flat, Lincoln County, Kentucky, October 3, 1840; attended Stanford Seminary for several years, and in 1855 entered Center College, Danville, where he pursued his studies for two years; returned to his father's farm and engaged in farming, stock raising and trading; was married October 15, 1861, to S. Malinda Miller, daughter of Thomas W. and Mary J. (Hocker) Miller of Madison County. She was one of the most cultured ladies in all that section of the state; a graduate (in 1859) of Mrs. Tevis' Science Hill Academy at Shelbyville; was a remarkably fine musician; a lady of very superior intellect and a devout member of the Cumberland Presbyterian Church. She died October 15, 1888, and is buried in Buffalo Cemetery at Stanford. She was the mother of eight children, all of whom are living: Mary E., wife of J. W. Manier of Nashville, Tennessee; John Samuel, Jr., commonwealth attorney of Stanford; Mattie H., wife of W. P. Walton, editor and proprietor of the Stanford Interior Journal; Maggie S., Linda, Thomas Miller, attorney at law of Bowling Green; Emma McGee, Michael, in school at Danville.

Maggie S., Linda and Emma McGee are at home with their father. All of their children are members of the Cumberland Presbyterian Church, and the voters are Democratic in politics.

After the death of his wife Mr. Owsley removed to Stanford, where he lived for four years, at the same time giving his attention to his farm, to which he has since returned. He was a member of the Legislature from Lincoln County in 1877-8, contemporary with Hon. James B. McCreary, who was Governor at that time; is a director in the Farmers' Bank & Trust Company, and is interested in other business enterprises, aside from his farming operations, which demand his first attention.

Samuel Owsley (father) was born in Virginia; came to Kentucky in 1781 with his parents, when he was about four years of age; was educated in the common schools near Crab Orchard; was a farmer by occupation; married Eliza W. Stephenson, daughter of George Stephenson, in 1839, and had one child, John Samuel, the principal subject of this sketch. He (father) died September, 1851, and is buried at the old homestead, now the home of his son. His wife died May, 1874, and is buried by his side.

William Owsley (grandfather) was a Virginian; came to Kentucky in 1781, and married Mary Bolin, and was a farmer in Lincoln County.

John Samuel Owsley, Jr., son of John Samuel and Melinda Miller Owsley, was born in Lincoln County, Kentucky, January 20, 1867. Is a graduate of the literary and law departments of Cumberland University. He commenced the practice of law in Stanford in the spring of 1889, and was elected Commonwealth Attorney by the people in the Thirteenth Judicial District in 1892, when he was only twenty-six years of age. He is associated in the practice of law with Judge Softly, and is one of the leading young lawyers practicing at the Lincoln County bar. He is a member of the Cumberland Presbyterian Church; a member of the Knights of Pythias and the K. U. T. M.; a Democrat in political affiliations and quite active and influential in party affairs.

He was married April 26, 1894, to Ella McElwain of Franklin, Simpson County, and has one child, James M. Owsley, born February 1, 1895.

The genealogy of the Owsley family is given as follows:

Reverend John Owsley (great-great-great-great-grandfather) born in 1663, married Ann Glaston of Virginia.

Captain Thomas Owsley (great-great-great-grandfather) was a native of Virginia.

Thomas Owsley (great-great-grandfather), married Ann West. Lived in Virginia.

Thomas Owsley (great-grandfather), born in 1731, married Mary Middleton.

William Owsley (grandfather), born in 1749, married Catherine Bolin.

Samuel Owsley (father), born February 2, 1778, married Eliza W. Stephenson.

John Samuel Owsley, born October 3, 1840, married S. Malinda Miller.

John Samuel Owsley, Jr., born January 20, 1867, married Ella McElwain.

James M. Owsley, born February 1, 1895.

DAVID L. EVANS, County Clerk, Cynthiana, son of Green D. and Emaline (Davis) Evans, was born in Harrison County, November 11, 1864. His father was born in the same county on the same farm, April 10, 1826. He was an active farmer until 1893, when he retired and removed to Cynthiana.

David Evans (grandfather) was a native of Virginia, who came to Harrison County when a boy with his father, Walter Evans, who purchased the farm now owned by Green D. Evans. The Evanses are of Welsh descent.

Emaline Evans (mother) was born in Hanover County in 1838. She and her husband and son, David L., are members of the Christian Church, the latter being clerk of the congregation in Cynthiana.

James Davis (grandfather) was a native of Harrison County, and for many years a well-known distiller, but the latter part of his life was devoted to farming.

David L. Evans, after attending the common schools, took a thorough course under the tutorship of Professor N. F. Smith, who had a private school in Cynthiana. He taught school in the county for one term and then removed to Garrard County and opened a general store at Point Lick. He remained there about two and a half years and then went to Kansas, where he commenced the study of law, returning in a short time to Cynthiana, where he completed his law course with M. C. Swinford, and was admitted to the bar in October, 1889. During the same year he became a partner of Mr. Swinford, under the firm name of Swinford & Evans, which relation has continued satisfactorily until the present time. The firm has a very large and lucrative practice.

In November, 1894, Mr. Evans was elected county attorney on the Democratic ticket, taking charge of the office January 1, 1895.

MRS. MARY B. R. DAY, who has been State Librarian for six years and whose present term of office expires June 1, 1896, is a native of Franklin County, Kentucky, and a daughter of John W. Russell, whose family name is found in many pages of the best histories of Kentucky. Mr. Russell was himself quite prominent in Kentucky politics, and was an intimate friend of President William Henry Harrison. He was a descendant of a Scotch-Irish family, whose ancestors came to Virginia prior to the Revolution, and, with the characteristics of their intelligent race, were true patriots in the struggle for American independence.

Mr. Russell married Ann M. Julian, of a Huguenot family, and a daughter of Charles Julian, who was one of the wealthiest men in the state. He moved to Kentucky from Fredericksburg, Virginia.

Mrs. Day was educated principally in Frankfort, and to the many liberal endowments of mind and heart she added those accomplishments which have distinguished her as a lady of unusual intelligence and refinement.

She was married in 1880 to W. E. Day, a traveling correspondent of the Chicago Journal, who died in 1881. Her health failed and she lived several years in Florida and the West. Mrs. Day spent near all of her living in her efforts to regain her health, and showed both pluck and ability from her first effort in politics; although defeated in her first race she made such friends as to give her great strength with the succeeding Legislature and she was elected against strong opposition. She served with credit through the Constitutional Convention and long Legislature which imposed more work on the librarian than any legislative bodies ever held in the state.

Returning to Kentucky she was one of the brightest women of the capital, and it was on account of her popularity and extensive acquaintance that she was elected State Librarian by the Legislature in 1890. It was a deserved recognition of her scholarly accomplishments and business ability—the highest official compliment that could be paid to a lady in Kentucky. She is now serving her third term, but withdrew from the last race before the caucus.

Mrs. Day is a member of the Daughters of the Revolution and is a sister of John C. Russell, a prominent attorney of Louisville, of whom see sketch.

"The penitentiary at Frankfort has no doubt the best Warden in America in the person of Colonel George. And he has with him the best of men to assist him. The writer was the guest of Captain Gervis Stone, who is the clerk of the prison. He needs no commendation. His name wherever known is enough to know that he is not there as the favorite of some one, but of worth and competency.

With such men at the head of our prison, they have turned what might be a hell on earth into a humane home for our unfortunate brothers. Rev. Mr. Cooper, the chaplain, is a small man, but as large as all out-of-doors. He is doing a noble work and tells me he has the co-operation of all the officers, and that the Warden never fails to worship with the prisoners.

I met on Sunday afternoon some of Frankfort's best women, among whom was the State Librarian, Mrs. Day, teaching the Sunday School. May God bless them and their labors. I believe many men are made better rather than worse."

Written by Rev. George Froh and published in the Spencer Courier.

JACKSON McCLAIN, of the real estate and insurance firm of McClain & Rogers of Henderson, eldest son of Colonel Jackson and Carrie (Hunt) McClain and elder brother of M. Hunt McClain, whose sketch is given above, was born in Henderson, Kentucky, June 16, 1870.

He received a liberal education in the Henderson schools and was well prepared for a business career when he engaged in the real estate and insurance business in his native city, to which employment he has given his attention with profitable results and has established a very extensive business. He is a man of strong individuality, with many of the characteristics of his father, whom he resembles in many respects, especially in his methodical habits and excellent business judgment. He is well posted in the value and history of property and is one of the most reliable appraisers in Henderson County. Although quite young, he has fully established himself in the confidence of his fellow-citizens, who predict for him a successful future. Few young men have handled their patrimony with finer discrimination or better results and he is constantly adding to the nucleus of a splendid fortune. He has been a member of the water works commission of Henderson for the past year.

Mr. McClain was married in April, 1891, to Myra Strother Hart, and they have one child, Carrie Lucelia.

THOMAS D. WILLIAMS, M. D., one of the most skillful and reliable physicians of Bardstown, son of Thomas H. Williams and Sarah T. Rodman, was born near Beechland P. O., Washington County, Kentucky, January 11, 1840.

His father was a native farmer of Washington County, in which he spent all the years of a useful life and died February 10, 1895, aged 82. He was an earnest Christian and is remembered as a very active member of the Methodist Episcopal Church South.

Samuel Williams (grandfather) was born in Maryland and was one of the earliest settlers of Washington County, where he was distinguished as a scholarly gentleman, an educator and a surveyor. He removed to Marion County late in life and died there at the advanced age of eighty-six years. The Williams family is of Welsh origin, the progenitor of whom came to Maryland in colonial days.

Sarah T. Rodman Williams (mother) was born in Washington County, Kentucky, in 1820, and died there May 22, 1890, aged seventy. She was also a member of the Methodist Episcopal Church

South and a woman of great piety and Christian benevolence.

David Rodman (grandfather) was a native of Maryland, of Scotch-Irish descent and was one of the pioneers of Washington County, where he followed farming and millwrighting principally and was for a time engaged in business as a merchant in Springfield. He was one of the most industrious and influential men of his times.

Dr. Thomas D. Williams came of a good stock of sturdy, intelligent people, who were the peers of their neighbors—not prominent in public affairs nor ambitious for public applause—but men and women who performed their duties with punctuality and lent character and stability to the community in which they shared the privations so familiar to the people who developed a new country and prepared the way for the comfort and enjoyment of their posterity. He was made acquainted with the rugged duties of farm life, and, as a boy, performed his share in the field and forest, attending school betimes, until he was sufficiently advanced to enter the Covington Institute in Springfield, where he was prepared for his collegiate course, which followed in Maxwell College, in the same county. After leaving college he was engaged in teaching, an avocation in which many eminent men have found the key to success and fame, and then attended the Bellevue Medical College in New York in 1867 and 1868, from which he received his diploma and began the practice of his profession in Washington County, removing to High Grove, Nelson County, after one year's practice, and there continued the exacting labors of the country physician for seven years. Leaving that field he went to Maud, Washington County, and practiced in that vicinity until 1886, when he sought a more inviting field in his present location at Bardstown. In the meantime, after practicing about eight years, he took a postgraduate course in the Hospital College of Medicine at Louisville, from which institution he also received the degree of M. D.

His success has been most gratifying, especially in his present location. Thoroughly qualified by study and long experience, he is one of the most reliable and popular family physicians in Nelson County or thereabouts. Devoted to his profession, industrious and energetic, faithful and prompt to answer the signal of distress, he has won the confidence of his patients and the public to a most gratifying degree. He is still a student and a careful reader of medical literature, keeping pace with the rapid progress of medical science and is a member of the Kentucky State Medical Society, and secretary of the Nelson County Medical Society. He was one of the founders of "The Buck Fork Medical Society (embracing the counties of Nelson, Marion and Washington), which was a most prosperous organization for eight years, four years of which time Dr. Williams was its active secretary and for three years its president.

In 1893 the Pan-American Medical Congress was held in Washington City, D. C. Dr. Chas. A. L. Reed, Chairman of Committee on Permanent Organization, appointed Dr. T. D. Williams Chairman on Organization for the Local Profession for Bardstown and Nelson County, which position he filled with ability and honor to himself and his profession. He has always been deeply interested in the success and advancement of his profession, and has, for many years, been an enthusiastic medical society man, always delighting in the discussion of medical topics. He has written several articles for the medical press, which received most favorable comment, especially his article or essay on "Puerperal Convulsions," read before the State Medical Society at Danville, Kentucky, in 1879.

He is a Mason and a member of the Methodist Episcopal Church South.

Dr. Williams was married (first) to Annie M. Burdette, daughter of Peyton Burdette of Mt. Washington, Kentucky, February 28, 1871. She died September 1, 1879, leaving two children: Lizzie, now deceased, and Nannie.

Peyton Burdette was one of the leading citizens of Bullitt County, a man of sterling worth and integrity, full of energy and enterprise, and did more than any other citizen to build up Mount Washington, and to advance the educational and commercial interests of the town. He lived to be a very old man and was escorted to his last resting place by one of the largest processions of sorrowing friends in the history of the town.

Dr. Williams was married the second time to Miss Theresa Reed of Springfield, Washington County. She was a daughter of Nelson Reed, deceased, who was one of the wealthiest and most prominent farmers of the county. Mr. Reed was a prominent member of the Presbyterian Church, and one of the most liberal supporters of Pleasant Grove Church, at which place he and all his family held their membership.

Miss Nannie Williams, only daughter and child of Dr. Williams, is now a pupil of Logan Female College, Russellville, Kentucky, and has been for three years. She will graduate from that institution in June, 1897.

Dr. Williams' brothers are: J. R. Williams, a prominent farmer of Washington County; John M. Williams, a merchant and farmer of the same county; Rev. James H. Williams of the Kentucky M. E. Conference and Samuel W. Williams, a farmer of Washington County, all of whom with their families are members of the Methodist Episcopal Church South.

The character of the parents may be judged from the excellent standing of their sons, among whom there is none who has not honored the father's good name.

MILTON YOUNG, the leading stock farmer and breeder of thoroughbred race horses in Kentucky, was born in Union County, Kentucky, January 10, 1851. He is a descendant of the family of Youngs whose progenitors came from the North of Ireland and settled in the Valley of Virginia and Pennsylvania after the close of the Revolutionary War.

His father, Judge Milton Young, was a native of Nelson County, Kentucky, who removed to Union County early in life, probably about the time of his marriage, and lived there until 1859 and then removed to Henderson, where he died at the age of forty-eight years. During his residence in Union County, he was County Judge for two terms and was a member of the Kentucky Legislature from Henderson County at the time of his death. He operated an extensive tobacco stemmery after removing to Henderson, and shipped tobacco to England. He was quite wealthy before the Civil War, and owned a large number of slaves. He was a Henry Clay Whig, and took an active interest in politics, and was an influential leader in his party. His early opportunities for obtaining an education were limited, but he acquired a wide range of useful knowledge, and mastered civil engineering and informed himself on all questions of practical use in his sphere of life. He possessed a strong mind, great firmness, decision and force of character and was a highly respected citizen of his county. He married Maria Thompson, whose father, Stephen Thompson, was a farmer in Washington County, Kentucky.

Bryan R. Young (grandfather) was a native Virginian, who removed to Kentucky in 1796, and was one of the first settlers of Nelson County. His father's old farm in that county was opened in 1793, or about that time, and is still known as the "John Young Farm," upon which stands the first brick house that was built in the state. His daughter, Elizabeth Young, sister of Judge Milton Young, married Thomas Brown, and was the mother of ex-Governor John Young Brown. Bryan R. Young was a practicing physician in Nelson County, a leading citizen and politician, and was a member of Congress in 1845-7.

Milton Young of Lexington was nine years of age when his father, Judge Milton Young, removed from Union County to Henderson, and he lived there until 1884, except during two years when he was in Hopkinsville. For several years he was successfully engaged in the cigar and tobacco business, and subsequently was in the hardware and implement business for five years at Henderson.

In 1881 he was married to Lucy Spalding, daughter of Honorable I. A. Spalding (ex-Railroad Commissioner) of Union County, and they have five children: Sue Spalding, Alice, Mamie, Milton and Jack Spalding.

In 1884 he removed to Fayette County, where he has ever since been engaged in breeding thoroughbred horses. He bought the celebrated stock farm, "McGrathiana," situated three miles from Lexington on the Newtown pike. This is one of the finest and most extensive stock farms in Kentucky, consisting of seven hundred and fifty acres of the finest blue grass land. He keeps three hundred brood mares, which, in 1894, furnished the turf with one hundred and seventy-four winners, whose combined winnings amounted to $346,283 in stakes and purses. In the last two years sons and daughters of the McGrathiana stallions have won $710,496 on the American turf, a marvelous unbeaten record of a wonderful thoroughbred breeding plant.

Though the stallions, living and dead, representing McGrathiana Stud Farm had fourteen less winners, that captured $17,930 less in 1894, than did the same representative horses in 1893, the showing last year is even better than during the season of the World's Fair Carnival. In 1893, race meetings were held at Monmouth Park, Gloucester and Guttenberg, while in 1894, adverse legislation closed the above named tracks, with their half a million dollars in stakes and purses, a part of which the horses bred at McGrathiana have always been lucky enough to win. With the chances at the same valuation of stakes and purses in 1894 as was offered in 1893, last year would have, no doubt, witnessed horses by McGrathiana sires winning fully $400,000. As it is, the mark they made in 1894 has only been beaten by the McGrathiana stallions the previous year, and the combined winnings of two seasons constitute an unbeaten record in the annals of American racing. They had out a winner every day, on an average, for nearly six months, and they won, on an average, over one and a half races per day during the entire year. Had a man followed the sons and daughters of these horses for two years he would have had nothing but money, as in 730 days (two years), they have won 1,268 races, that in valuation equaled an average of nearly $1,000 per day. The following resume gives a condensed record of Mr. Milton Young's famous sires which, in 1894, made such a remarkable showing. It is worthy of note, too, that the now famous McGrathiana Stud has been in the hands of Mr. Milton Young for thirteen years only.

Hanover's get have shown this year again their high class as three-year-olds. Halma has developed into a great stake winner. He landed the Phoenix Hotel Stakes, one and one-eighth miles, in 1:52½ (a second slower than the record); the Kentucky Derby and the Clark Stakes. In the Phoenix Hotel Stakes the contending horse was The Commoner, another son of Hanover, who was giving Halma five pounds. At even weights it is doubtful which would have won, and it was a feather in Hanover's cap that his two sons should have run such a bruising race in fast time. It proves conclusively that the Hanovers train on and stay as three-year-olds. Other three-year-olds that have been returned winners this season are The Commoner, Hallowe'en, Urania, Hollywood, Buck Massie, Sligo, Miss Young, Whyota and Handspun, winner of the Tennessee Oaks, etc.

Among Hanover's two-year-olds are the highly tried Handspring and the winners Hand Maid, Lela Dell and Helen Mar.

Where is a sire in America that can boast of a Derby and an Oaks winner in the first season? There is no doubt that Hanover will in a short while be at the head of our winning stallions, and perpetuate the famous line of Glencoe, who sired the greatest of all mares, old "Pocahontas."

In spite of the decrease of racing in 1894 as compared to 1893, the get of Duke of Montrose won only 1,996 less in 1894 than they did in 1893, and out of forty-seven starters thirty-five of his get were money winners, while twenty-six captured one or more races. His son, Henry Young, broke the one and three-sixteenths mile record in the Columbus Handicap, at Washington Park, Chicago, in which he defeated a great field, including Yo Tambien, Cash Day, Rudolph and Dr. Rice, in 1:58½. Saragossa beat all kinds of horses last year, while Pocahontas was easily the best of the Western three-year-old fillies and Ta Ta was a very smart two-year-old. Duke of Montrose up to the close of 1894 has had out ninety-five starters during his stud career and sixty-eight of these performers have proven winners. Just half of the two-year-olds by him that were out last year were winners and one of these performers won eight races.

Macduff's record of thirty-two winners in forty-three starters was a grand one, inasmuch as only eight starters by him failed to earn money in 1894. Out of thirteen two-year-old starters he had ten winners, and in that lot were Kitty Clive, Satsuma and Katherine, all high class performers. Of sixty-two performers that represent all of Macduff's get that have appeared on the turf as yet, fifty-three have won races, making his percentage of winners reach a shade over 90 per cent. It is hard to find a stallion with as good a showing in this respect, considering the number of starters by him that have faced the red flag.

Strathmore is another wonder as a sire of winners. In twenty-four starters out last year, he was represented by eighteen winners, and two others of his six non-winners landed money. Cash Day, a grand three-year-old, equalling the record of Wildwood and Faraday (one mile seventy yards in 1:44), was his brightest star, though his old timers Strathmeath, Monrovia and Soundmore, as usual, have done well. Strathmore had six winning two-year-olds in ten starters, among them being Queen May, Glad and Ashland, all of which were good class. Strathmore would have been higher up in the list of winners had Strathrol not turned out a sulker, as the colt showed high class in the spring, running the $10,000 Ducat to a head, a mile in 1:40 flat, the fastest time ever scored in a mile race in Kentucky. Ten Broeck's mark, a quarter of a second faster, also scored in that state, being made against time. During his career in the stud Strathmore has furnished the turf with forty-seven starters, thirty-three of which have won races. He also has the distinction of being one of the few living horses that has sired a winner of $100,000 or over, his son Strathmeath having won $109,772 in stakes and purses.

Imp. Pirate of Penzance had no big money winners out last year, but he had a great array of winners, only three of his fifteen starters failing to earn brackets. One of these won in 1893, so in all his starters last season he had but two maidens. Little Cripple turned out a very fine selling plater, while Rhett Goode was a stake winner and Bandit scored several fine victories. He had but four two-year-old starters, and three of them proved race winners. But nineteen of this son of imp. Prince Charlie's get have as yet started in the two seasons he has been represented on the turf, and fifteen of these performers have proven winners. This showing is all the more remarkable inasmuch as, with but one or two exceptions, he has been favored with a very inferior lot of mares.

Favor had nine winners in his list of starters last year, Fertile being the best class of the lot. In the two seasons he has been represented on the turf by thirty-one starters. Of these seventeen proved winners, a fair average considering his chances, he having been favored with few good mares. Of thirteen two-year-old starters out by him last year six won races, and nine proved money winners.

Imp. Simple Simon is a son of the great St. Simon, who was unbeatable on the turf, and whom Fred Archer, the greatest jockey of all time, pronounced the best race horse he ever threw a leg over.

Since St. Simon's retirement from the turf his success at the stud has been unprecedented. The first of his get appeared on the turf in 1889, and with the disadvantage, compared with older sires, of having only two-year-olds to represent him he was third on the list of winning stallions. The premier position that season was occupied by his sire, Galopin, with Hampton second and St. Simon a good third. Every year since 1889 St. Simon has been the undisputed champion stallion.

The following statistics show the amounts won each year by the sons and daughters of St. Simon in first money only:

1889. $121,500............3d on the list of winning sires.
1890. 164,000............1st on the list of winning sires.
1891. 134,500............1st on the list of winning sires.
1892. 266,250............1st on the list of winning sires.
1893. 183,000............1st on the list of winning sires.
1894. 210,000............1st on the list of winning sires.

T'tal.$1,079,250

Such figures speak for themselves.

To refer at length to the cracks by St. Simon would be almost equivalent to writing a history of the principal events of the English turf since 1889, which would take up too much space. In 1890, when the oldest of his get were three years old, a larger proportion of first-class stakes fell to their share than to the first get of any stallion before or since. Their wins included the St. Leger, the Oaks, the 1,000 Guineas, the Epsom Grand Prize, the Newmarket Stakes, the Newmarket Oaks, the Rous Memorial Stakes, the Sussex Stakes, the Zetland Biennial Stakes, the Brocklesby Stakes, the Ascot Biennial Stakes, etc.

Lady Gladys, the dam of Simple Simon, was by Gladiateur, one of the greatest race horses ever foaled, winner of the 2,000 Guineas, Derby, St. Leger, etc. Lady Gladys threw the winners Gallant, Gayland and Laddie. Gladiateur is the sire of Lord Gough, he the sire of the dams of Kilwarlin (winner of the St. Leger, etc.), and Bendigo, another crack. Margery, the granddam (sister to Scottish Queen, winner of the 1,000 Guineas), was by Blair Athol, winner of the Derby and St. Leger.

Edith, the third dam, threw Lord Ronald, a superior race horse, sire of Master Kildare, he the sire of Melton, Derby and St. Leger winner.

The fourth dam Deidamia, by Pyrrhus I. (winner of the Derby), was out of Wiasma, the granddam of imp. Blairgowrie (the dam of the crack mares Breeze and Blossom), by Hetman Platoff, sire of The Cossack (winner of the Derby) and Maltese, the dam of imp. Knight of St. George. Klarnet, Klarinska (winner of the Great Yorkshire Oaks) and Klarikoff, were also out of Wiasma. Mickleton Maid, the sixth dam, was the granddam of imp. Wombat, the dam of Warwickshire, Princeton, Pouch (dam of Boulotte, Airshaft, Fiddlehead, etc.), Lillian, etc.

Maid of Lune, the seventh dam, was an own sister to Emma, the dam of imp. Trustee, Mundig (winner of the Derby), Cotherstone (winner of the 2,000 Guineas and Derby) and Mowerina, the dam of West Australian, winner of the 2,000 Guineas, Derby and St. Leger.

The following creditable winners, which failed to win as much as $5,000, were also bred by Mr. Young at McGrathiana. They number one hundred and forty-five, which, with the fifty-five stars above noted, makes 200 performers hailing from their great establishment that have earned winning brackets in the last eleven years. As a majority of these horses won from $1,000 to $4,000 or over in their turf career, it is no wild hazard to say that the winning product of McGrathiana have captured over 1,000 races and won in money between $1,500,000 and $2,000,000, all of which was earned on the American turf.

Hanover, the matchless race horse, still the largest winning three-year-old in American turf history, who heads the list, has made a wonderful record. No stallion can be recalled that ever before in his first season in the stud or any other year sired twenty-one winning two-year-olds. The class of performers he got was also remarkable, Halma, Handsome, The Commoner, Handspun, Urania, Hessie and Levina, being among the lot. The Hyde Park Stakes, the Essex Stakes, the Mumm Handicap, the McGrathiana Stakes, the Thora Stakes, the Lassie Stakes, the Willow Stakes, the Kentucky Stakes, the Maiden Stakes and the Covington Autumn Stakes were among the important events his sons and daughters won, while Handspun ran a dead heat for the Pepper Stakes, and in the rich Matron Stakes was only beaten three parts of a length, with a classic field of fourteen behind her.

Hanover earned fourth place among the winning sires of the year, being only beaten out by stallions who have had representatives out for five and six years. Handsome, one of his sons, sold for $10,000; Handspun, one of his daughters, brought $7,500 at auction, while $11,000 was offered and refused for The Commoner, and Halma sold for over $6,000 privately. Before her sickness in the spring Handspun was absolutely unbeatable, while Hessie lost but one race. Handsome beat all the best colts in the West, including Laureate, Frank K., Rey del Carades and Lissak, while Levina won a greater number of races than any two-year-old filly of the year.

A glance at the table of his winners which follows, shows that Hanover got a number of his most creditable performers out of mares without records as producers, and many untried as stud matrons. Going over his maiden list, it will be seen that three of the eleven won money, while the remaining eight together only faced the starting post twenty-two times. One of these, Niagravela, a filly with a very high private reputation, who started twice, was upon both occasions left standing at the post.

The consistent sire Onondaga made a good showing again in 1894, his twenty-seven winning sons and daughters taking into camp 101 races. Dr. Rice beat all the cracks of the year in the Brooklyn Handicap, including Henry of Navarre, Sir Walter, Banquet and Clifford. His performance at Washington Park, Chicago, when he ran a mile in 1:40¼, was also a brilliant achievement, inasmuch as he carried the crusher of 127 pounds. Peacemaker was class enough to win the United States Hotel Stakes, at Saratoga, in which race he defeated Dobbins. Derfargilla and Ottyanna were good sprinters, while Outlook, Brodhead and Beatifice did well in the selling plate class. Onondaga's get have now raced nine years, during which time he has been represented on the turf by 118 winners, that have won a total of eight hundred and nineteen races and $555,821 in stakes and purses.

Number of starters, 47; number of winners, 26; number of non-winners, 21; number of these non-winners that were winners previous to 1894, 12; number of maidens, 9; times started, 570; times first, 85; times second, 98; times third, 67; times unplaced, 320. Total amount won, $56,320.

Number of starters, 43; number of winners, 32; number of non-winners, 11; number of these non-winners that were winners previous to 1894, 7; number of maidens, 4; times started, 615; times first, 91; times second, 90; times third, 73; times unplaced, 361. Total amount won, $45,932.

BENJAMIN ULEN STEELE, Deputy Clerk of Boyd County, a well-known citizen of Catlettsburg, brother of Daniel W. Steele, was born September 17, 1869. After attending school in the county and in Ashland, he found his first employment, in 1889, as a clerk in the office of the Norton Iron Works and remained there eighteen months. In October, 1891, he was appointed clerk of the Circuit Court at Catlettsburg, holding that office until January, 1893. In 1892 he was elected to the office which he was then filling by appointment, but his election was contested. Judgment was rendered in his favor in the Circuit Court, but was reversed by the Court of Appeals, and his competitor took the office. In 1895 he was appointed to his present position as deputy clerk of the Boyd County Court. He is a young man of exemplary habits, of indefatigable industry and possesses every qualification for the proper discharge of his official duties, is quite popular in the community and admired by his friends and acquaintances.

Mr. Steele and Leona Brown Porter, daughter of John Marshall Porter, were married April 7, 1894. Mrs. Steele was born in Pike County, November 12, 1873. Her father is also a native of Pike County, where he was a farmer, but subsequently removed to Catlettsburg and was proprietor of a hotel for some time, but retired from active business in 1886, and is now living in Catlettsburg. He married Amanda, daughter of Judge Thomas Brown, and a sister of Mrs. Samuel P. Hager, of Ashland.

GEN. JOHN CALDWELL was a native of Prince Edward County, Virginia. He removed to Kentucky in 1781, and settled near where Danville now stands. He took an active part in the conflicts with the Indians, and rose by regular steps from the rank of a common soldier to that of a major-general in the militia. He served as a subaltern in the campaign against the Indians in 1786, under General George Rogers Clark. He was a prominent man of his day—esteemed in private and political, as he was in military life. He was a member, from Nelson County, of the conventions held in Danville in 1787 and 1788. In 1792 he was elected from the same county a senatorial elector, under the first constitution; and in the college of electors, he was chosen the senator from Nelson. He took his seat in the senate at the session of 1792-3. He was elected lieutenant-governor of the state in 1804, and during his term of service removed to the lower part of the state. He died at Frankfort, November 19, 1804, while the Legislature was in session.

SELDEN Y. TRIMBLE, of Russellville, one of the brightest and most successful young attorneys of Southern Kentucky, was born in Caldwell County, Kentucky, April 19, 1867.

His father, Rev. Selden Y. Trimble, was born in Logan County, and educated in private schools in his native county and at Murfreesboro College, Tennessee, from which institution he graduated with the degree of A. M. He then studied for the ministry in the theological department of the same college, and after his ordination began preaching in the Baptist Church in Logan County. In 1855, having previously married, he and his wife went as missionaries to Liberia, under the auspices of the Baptist Missionary Society. There were three men, but Mrs. Trimble was the only lady in the party. They spent two years in missionary work there, when Mrs. Trimble was thrown from a horse, receiving injuries which disabled her for life and compelled their return to Kentucky. Mr. Trimble preached in the counties of Logan, Caldwell, Lyon and Trigg and devoted the remainder of his life in securing aid for the support of Baptist missionaries in foreign fields.

Mary E. Morehead Trimble (mother) was born in Kentucky, educated in private schools of Keesburg, Logan County, was a most excellent Christian woman, joined heartily in her husband's work until permanently disabled by the accident in Liberia and was an invalid and great sufferer for thirty years following her return. She bore her sufferings with that Christian fortitude and faith which characterized her noble self-sacrificing life. She entered upon the reward of the just.

Rev. and Mrs. Trimble had seven children: Sue was educated at Princeton (Kentucky) College, and married John P. Garnett; Bettie married Selden Lyne; Grace married Professor Henry L. Garretson, of Bethel College, Russellville; Mary died young, and Nellie died at the age of eight years. The only son is the subject of this sketch.

William Trimble (grandfather) was a native of Logan County and a son of one of the first settlers of Kentucky.

James Morehead (maternal grandfather) was also a native of Logan County, a farmer and quite prominent as a Whig in politics and a faithful member of the Baptist Church. He married a Miss Poor, who was born in Logan County in 1813; her father was quite prominent in Logan County politics, held several county offices, and was at one time a member of the Legislature. She was a cousin of Governor Morehead, although it does not appear that her husband, James Morehead, was a relative of the governor. Mrs. Morehead reached the advanced age of four score and two years and died in 1895.

Presley L. Morehead (great-grandfather), a native of Virginia, came to Logan County at a very early day and was one of the pioneers of the county, was a prominent and influential citizen, and served his county in the Legislature.

Selden Y. Trimble was educated in Princeton College, in his native county, and at Bethel College, Russellville, graduating from the last named college in the class of 1886; taught school for two years in Logan County and one year in Macon County, Tennessee, and while teaching studied law. In 1888 he entered the office of Scyon A. Bass, whose biography is given in this volume, and was admitted to the bar in 1889. He at once opened an office and entered upon a career that has been marked by success and has attracted the attention and won the respect and confidence of the members of the bar and of the community.

He began his professional career under rather discouraging circumstances. Having paid his way through college, he was entirely without means when he entered the practice of law, but he asked no one for assistance, and with singleness of purpose and by close attention to his studies and his work he soon acquired a lucrative practice, and in the language of one of the oldest lawyers of Russellville, "his success has been wonderful considering the difficulties which he had to contend with at the outset, and he is one of the most promising young lawyers at the Logan County bar."

Mr. Trimble was elected a member of the Legislature in 1893 by the Democratic party, and although one of the youngest members of that body, he was one of the most diligent and useful representatives the county has ever had.

He was married November 14, 1895, to Maria Perkins, daughter of Judge Ben. G. Perkins, an eminent lawyer of Todd County.

DR. WILLIAM G. MOORE, M. D., of Georgetown, was born in Scott County, Kentucky, September 5, 1847. His father, William Moore, was also born in Scott County, February 2, 1802. After obtaining the best education possible in the new settlement, at the age of twenty years he chose the independent life of the farmer, and continued in that occupation until the time of his death, in 1873. He was a man of excellent character and a prominent member of the Christian Church. His wife, Anna Miller Moore, was born in Scott County in 1809. Her father's name was Adam Miller, one of the pioneers of the county.

Dr. William G. Moore received his early education in the county schools and was much inclined to follow in his father's footsteps. He remained on the farm until he began to study medicine in 1870, when he entered the Kentucky School of Medicine in Louisville. He studied from September until the following March, when he returned to the farm and remained till 1873, and then attended a course of lectures in the Medical University of Louisville, receiving his diploma in March, 1874. He practiced medicine in connection with farming until September, 1883, when he returned to the Medical University and graduated in February, 1884. Having no longer any hesitation between farming and medicine, he practiced his profession at Kincaide for three years, at Oxford for five years, and then returned to Georgetown in 1892 and located permanently.

Dr. Moore has been appointed county physician for a term of four years and has been a member of the local board of health for two years. He is a prominent member of the Masonic fraternity and has been master of the lodge at Oxford for ten years, is president of the National Fraternal Union of Georgetown and a member of the Baptist Church.

Dr. Moore and Sallie E. Ford, of Scott County, were married October 18, 1887. They have two children living, Jessie Gano and Hugh Adams. Two other children are dead.

WILLIAM H. NETHERLAND, owner of "Idlewild," in Bullitt County, and veterinary surgeon of Louisville, son of Robert H. and Maggie (Hegan) Netherland, was born in Louisville, Kentucky, October 19, 1866. His father was born in Culpeper County, Virginia, and came to Louisville in 1856, where he became one of the most prominent and wealthy business men of the city. He had no capital when he reached Louisville and was an entire stranger in the city, but by his remarkable energy and business tact he built up the fine establishment now known as the Hart Hardware Co. He was first interested in business with Mr. John Neal, who is now engaged in raising thoroughbred horses at Bowling Green, the firm name being Neal & Netherland. Mr. Neal subsequently retired from the firm and the name was changed to Netherland & Hart. After Mr. Netherland's death, in 1876, the Hart Hardware Company was incorporated. Mr. Netherland was a very kind and generous man, liberal to a fault and greatly loved and respected by those who were associated with him in business and by a large circle of friends and acquaintances. He was a member of the Broadway Baptist congregation and was devoted to his church and his home. He was only forty-six years of age when he died, but he had accumulated a handsome estate in the twenty years of his residence in Louisville. His father was a native of the Netherlands, who came to America and settled in Virginia, where he spent the remainder of his years.

Margaret Hegan Netherland (mother) is a member of the well-known Hegan family of Louisville and is still a resident of her native city.

Francis Hegan (grandfather) was a native of Ireland, who came to the United States and a few years later located in Louisville and established a show case and picture frame factory near the corner of Fourth and Main streets. He made the first show case ever manufactured in Louisville and did a thriving business in that line and in the manufacture and sale of picture frames. He was a great lover of art and one of the best art critics in the whole country, and besides dealing largely in fine pictures he had a fine collection of the best pictures he could procure in his private gallery. He began business in a small way, but he was frugal and industrious and he met with great success, leaving a large estate at the time of his death in 1865.

William H. Netherland was educated in the public schools of Louisville and at the Kentucky Military Institute at Frankfort, from which he was graduated in 1884. He engaged in farming and stock raising and bought "Idlewild," the most beautiful stock farm in Bullitt County, and made a business of breeding fine trotting horses, which proved quite profitable for some years, but the value of horses depreciated a few years ago, and Mr. Netherland took up the study of the treatment of diseases of horses, to which he had given much attention, and for which he had a fancy; and attended the Chicago Veterinary College, from which he graduated in 1893, since which time he has devoted most of his time to his veterinary practice in Louisville, although still residing at "Idlewild," where he has a large number of fine horses and raises some of the best trotters in the state. His veterinary practice has grown rapidly. In fact, he at once met with remarkable success, his extensive acquaintance among the horse men of the county and state giving him a great advantage. His experience in the treatment of his own horses made him a very good horse doctor before he undertook it as a profession. While he still resides on his ideal farm in Bullitt County, his practice, together with his shoeing forge—in which the shoeing of horses is done on scientific principles—requires all of his time and attention in the city.

Dr. Netherland was married in 1887 to Lillie P. Rogers, daughter of John Rogers of Jefferson County, and has one child. He is a member of the Broadway Baptist Church, as was his father and mother and his Grandfather Hegan before him.

DUDLEY SHARPE REYNOLDS, A. M., M. D., physician and surgeon, and one of the members of his profession in Louisville who has achieved unusual distinction, was born near Bowling Green, Kentucky, August 31, 1842; only son of Rev. Thomas and Mary (Nichols) Reynolds. Both his parents were natives of Kentucky, and his father was a son of Dr. Admiral and Sarah Freeman Reynolds, and grandson of Nathaniel and Catherine Vernon Reynolds. In 1839 Thomas Reynolds and Mary Nichols eloped from Kentucky to Gainesville, Tennessee, and were married there, after which they went to live in Barren County, Kentucky, on a tract of land owned by the Reynolds family, and on which Nathaniel Reynolds, of Revolutionary fame, settled in 1791. He had joined the Baptist Church in 1841, and in 1850, the Blue Springs Baptist Church, of which the Rev. James L. Brooks was pastor, licensed him to preach. On the 30th day of May, 1852, he was ordained minister by the presbytery, composed of the Rev. Jesse Moon, Rev. William Skaggs, and Rev. Theodore Meredith, and labored faithfully as a preacher of the gospel to the end of his life. He was employed as a church missionary for nearly fifty years, and was the chief organizer and founder of the Corn Creek, Poplar Ridge, and Middle Creek Baptist Churches, of Trimble County; established the Covington, Liberty and other churches in Oldham County, and is said to have organized more Baptist churches than any other minister who has labored in Kentucky. During the last forty years of his life he lived at Westport, in Oldham County, and built up a large congregation there. In 1876 he also organized there a Union Sunday School, which included in its membership the representatives of nearly every family within a radius of five miles, and embraced Presbyterians, Episcopalians, Christians, Methodists, and Unitarians, being the largest single Sunday school organization in the state. His life was one of great usefulness, and he was revered, honored, and beloved by the Baptist Church of Kentucky and by all who knew him. He died at the residence of his son, December 30, 1895, aged seventy-four years, and on January 1, 1896, he was buried in the family cemetery at Westport, Kentucky.

Dudley S. Reynolds, the son, was educated at the private schools of Professors Arnold and Allman, at the Trimble High School, of Kentucky, and at Irving College, of Tennessee. Ogden College, of Bowling Green, Kentucky, conferred upon him the degree of master of arts, and he was graduated in medicine from the University of Louisville, March 3, 1868.

In January, 1869, Dr. Reynolds was elected surgeon to the Western Dispensary, resigning his position in October, 1871, to engage in specialism. From October, 1871, to June, 1872, he was engaged in study at the New York Eye and Ear Infirmary, at the Wills Eye Hospital, of Philadelphia, and at the Royal London Ophthalmic Hospital, in Moorefields. On returning to Louisville, in 1872, he devoted his attention exclusively to ophthalmology and otology.

When the Central University of Kentucky established its medical department at Louisville, in

1875, Dr. Reynolds was appointed to the chair of ophthalmology and otology, and took an active part in the organization of the Hospital College of Medicine. He represented the college at the meeting of medical teachers at Chicago, in 1877, and participated in the organization of the Association of American Medical Colleges. At the joint convention of teachers and governing boards of medical colleges, held at Atlanta, Georgia, May, 1879, he represented the faculty of the Hospital College of Medicine, and was its delegate to each of the succeeding annual meetings of the College Association. At the meeting held in Washington, D. C., May, 1891, he took a leading part in the reorganization of the Association of American Medical Colleges, was elected chairman of its judicial council, and re-elected at Detroit, in 1892, for a term of three years, and again at Baltimore, May 8, 1895.

Dr. Reynolds is a member of the American Medical Association, and was elected president of the Section of Ophthalmology, at New York, in 1880. At Detroit, 1892, he wrote the preamble and resolutions, which were unanimously adopted, pledging the support of that body to the Association of American Medical Colleges, and demanding that all the colleges in the United States should observe a standard of requirement not to fall below the minimum standard adopted by the College Association. In conjunction with Drs. X. C. Scott of Cleveland, Ohio, and J. M. Bodine of Louisville, Kentucky, he formulated the plan for establishing the Section on Ophthalmology in the American Medical Association, which was presented to the meeting at Louisville, in 1875, and subsequently adopted at Chicago, in 1877.

In 1879 the property of the Public Library of Kentucky was directed, by decree of the Chancery Court of Louisville, to be sold by the sheriff, to satisfy judgments amounting to about thirty thousand dollars. Dr. Reynolds conceived the idea, and successfuly undertook the re-organization of the Polytechnic Society of Kentucky, which, by special act of the legislature, had been empowered to take charge of the old Public Library property; but, owing to the decree of sale in chancery, the society had abandoned its trust. The re-organization was accomplished January 3, 1879, and a new executive council was elected. Dr. Reynolds, with four other gentlemen, having gone into bank and borrowed the money and paid off all the executions and judgments in court, announced to the society at its re-organization the purpose to take possession of the property at once. This met with unanimous approval, and the gentlemen who had procured the necessary funds for relieving the financial obligations were elected members of the board of directors to serve for five years. Dr. Reynolds was made chairman of the library committee, and continued in that office until April, 1894. In November, 1879, the building had been remodeled and a new library room provided, and about twenty thousand volumes of useful literature were opened to the public. This plan of arrangement was continued until 1891, when the work of re-arranging and cataloguing was begun; it was completed in 1894, and the last fasciculus of the subject catalogue, according to the Dewy system, was published. Under Dr. Reynold's management, the library grew from a little more than twenty thousand to fifty thousand volumes.

In 1879 he became editor of the "Medical Herald," a monthly magazine, which was well supported by the profession and attained a wide circulation. He sold the magazine and retired with the close of the year 1883. In March, 1886, Mr. D. W. Raymond established "The Medical Progress," a monthly magazine for students and practitioners; he secured the services of Dr. Reynolds as editor-in-chief, and, after a successful career of five years, the publishers, the Rogers-Tuley Company, having failed in business, the magazine was sold by the assignee, and Dr. Reynolds ceased his connection as editor.

He has been appointed by the Kentucky State Medical Society as one of its delegates to the American Medical Association, annually, 1872-96, inclusive. In 1878, at the request of the Hon. James B. McCreary, governor of Kentucky, he was appointed by the President of the United States an honorary commissioner from Kentucky to the International Industrial Exposition at Paris, France. He represented the American Medical Association in the International Medical Congress of 1881, and in the British Medical Association at Ryde, Isle of Wight, August, 1881; was one of the vice presidents of the Section on Ophthalmology of the Ninth International Medical Congress, 1887; was honorary president of the Sections on Ophthalmology and Medical Pedagogics in the first Pan-American Medical Congress, Washington, D. C., September, 1893; delivered the annual oration of the Alumni Association of the Medica-Chirurgical College of Philadelphia, April 7, 1887, and was made a fellow of that college; was president of the Mississippi Valley Medical Association, 1887-88; president of the Academy of Medicine and Surgery in the Polytechnic Society of Kentucky, 1880; chairman of the board of censors of the Kentucky State Medical Society, 1881-90; was president of the joint faculties of the medical and dental departments of the Central University of Kentucky, 1891-93. He is a member of the Mitchell District Medical Society of Indiana, and in July, 1892, was elected its president, a position never before occupied by a non-resident of that state; is a member of the Filson Historical Club, and of the Watterson Club, of Louisville.

Dr. Reynolds is professor of ophthalmology, otology and medical jurisprudence in the Hospital College of Medicine, medical department of the Central University of Kentucky. He was professor of general pathology and hygiene from 1883 to 1890. He conducts the largest clinic in Louisville at the Hospital College every Monday and Thursday during the year, and has been surgeon to the eye and ear department of the Louisville City Hospital almost continuously since 1873. He is the author of many essays and clinical reports, embodying a great variety of subjects and many original devices in ophthalmic surgery.

On May 7, 1865, Dr. Reynolds married Miss Mary F. Keagan of Louisville. Their children are Dr. Dudley S. Reynolds, Jr., who lost his life by accident, at Collinsville, Illinois, October 22, 1894, and Mary A., wife of Professor P. Richard Taylor, M. D., dean of the faculty of the Hospital College of Medicine.

Mrs. Reynolds died March 3, 1876. He was married again, July 13, 1881, to Miss Matilda L. Bruce of Covington, Kentucky, daughter of Hon. Eli M. Bruce, a distinguished member of the late Confederate States Congress. Of this union there are two children: Eli M. Bruce, aged thirteen years, and Elizabeth, aged ten years.

M. HUNT McCLAIN, Attorney at Law of Henderson, Kentucky, was born in that city November 22, 1871, and is a son of the late Jackson and Carrie (Hunt) McClain. His father, Colonel Jackson McClain, was born in Henderson October 5, 1816. At the age of twenty-three years his father died, leaving a large estate for his son to look after. The settlement of the estate was accomplished with marked ability and to the satisfaction of all concerned. He was a large land owner and gave attention to the cultivation of his crops for many years. He owned a number of slaves before the war, and their freedom, combined with other losses resulting from the war, crippled him financially for a time; but he overcame this by his indomitable will power, energy and business tact, and fully recovered and increased his fortune. He was a man of superior intellect and fine judgment who applied himself strictly to the management of his business, and this chief characteristic was in a large measure the secret of his success in life. He was interested in a number of large enterprises and was a director in the Farmers' Bank, of which he was president for a time during the war. He was also a director in the Henderson & Nashville Railroad and was largely instrumental in making a success of that enterprise. For several years he was a member of the School Board and was frequently called upon to handle trust funds, settle estates, etc. In 1841 he married Mary Watson, who died leaving one child, Annie, who married the late Colonel A. H. Major. In 1869 Jackson McClain married Carrie S. Hunt of Warsaw, Illinois, who died leaving five sons: Jackson, born June 16, 1870; M. Hunt, born November 22, 1871; William, born September 19, 1873; James Henry, born March 4, 1877, and George, born August 6, 1879. Mr. McClain's third wife, who survives him, was Mrs. Helen Trafton. He was paralyzed in 1888, an attack from which he did not fully recover, and died in 1892.

James McClain (grandfather) was a native of

JACKSON McCLAIN.

Henderson, a farmer and large land owner in the county, and was one of the most influential citizens of his day. He died in 1839. His wife (grandmother) was a Miss Butler, daughter of a Henderson County farmer.

M. Hunt McClain, after attending the Henderson schools to the limit, received his collegiate education in the Cumberland College at Lebanon, Tennessee, graduating in the class of 1892. He was admitted to the bar and began the practice of his profession in Henderson in the same year. In the short time in which he has been in actual business he has devoted much of his time to the further equipment for the lifework before him, and at the same time has met with remarkable success in his vocation. He is the owner of one hundred and seventy-five acres of land on Green River Island, five miles from Henderson.

In 1892 he married Minnie Wilson Hoskins, daughter of W. T. Hoskins of Henderson. They have one child, Elizabeth Hunt, born April 14, 1893.

THOMAS PATRICK CAROTHERS of Newport, a prominent attorney and Democratic politician, son of Robert Barr and Elizabeth (Abbott) Carothers, was born in Campbell County, Kentucky, March 30, 1857. His father, Robert Barr Carothers, is a native of Carlisle, Cumberland County, Pennsylvania, who came to Kentucky in 1856, locating in Campbell County—which has been his place of residence ever since—and is now actively engaged in contracting for and building water works. He is a Republican of liberal views and a man of superior intelligence and business ability.

Patrick F. Carothers (grandfather) was born in Huntingdon County, Pennsylvania, in 1802 and lived in Dayton, Ohio, where he was a railroad master mechanic and a man of great strength of character and something of a Democratic politician, being greatly devoted to the interests of his party. He died in Dayton, Ohio, in 1880. The progenitor of the Carothers family in America came from Scotland about one hundred and fifty years ago.

Elizabeth Abbott Carothers (mother) is a native of Covington, and was born before that part of Kenton was taken from Campbell County. Her ancestors came from England more than two hundred years ago. Her father, Thomas Helm Abbott, was born in Mason and reared in Campbell county, where he was a prosperous farmer and a prominent member of the Baptist Church. He died in 1892 at the age of eighty-eight years.

Thomas P. Carothers was educated in the public schools of Newport and Cincinnati, and after leaving school was engaged in business with his father for several years. He then attended the Cincinnati Law School, from which he graduated in May, 1878. He at once began the practice of law in Newport and soon built up a large general practice, to which he is earnestly devoted.

He was a member of the state legislature in 1883-4; was elected city attorney in 1891 and 1892, and again in 1894 and 1895.

He has always taken quite an active interest in local and state politics, serving his time as a member of the Democratic state central committee; was for several terms chairman of the Campbell County Democratic executive committee, and was a delegate to a Democratic state convention before he was twenty-one years of age.

He is a member of the Protestant Episcopal Church, belongs to Robert Burns Lodge No. 163, Free and Accepted Masons, and member of the Kentucky Society of the Sons of the American Revolution.

Mr. Carothers was married in 1866 to Caroline Butler Powell, daughter of Charles Powell of Louisville, and they have two daughters: Mary Belle and Caroline Thomas. Mrs. Carothers is a member of the distinguished Butler family of Carrollton, of whom Gen. William O. Butler was the most conspicuous.

FRANCIS WILLIAM BUCKNER, deceased, for many years a prominent merchant of Hopkinsville, Kentucky, was born in Virginia, in 1809. He came to Kentucky with his parents when he was a youth. His father's name was George B. Buckner, who married Martha Upshaw, both of whom were natives of Virginia. Francis W. Buckner was for some time a merchant at Oak Grove, Christian County, and subsequently removed to Hopkinsville, where he continued in the same line of business until his death. He was married April 9, 1835, to Sarah Gordon, daughter of Samuel Gordon, a native of Buckingham County, Virginia, who was one of the first settlers of Christian County, where he died in 1852. Mrs. Buckner was born December 2, 1819, and still lives to enjoy the results of her noble life work. She is the mother of four sons and one daughter, all of whom she brought up to be useful and influential citizens. Her sons are among the most prominent and respected men in the community in which they live.

Samuel Gordon Buckner, her eldest son, a leading tobacco merchant of Hopkinsville, was for some years the senior member of the firm of Buckner, Wooldridge & Co., tobacco warehousemen of Hopkinsville, and is now a member of the firm of Abernathy & Co., one of the largest tobacco houses in the city. He is a great admirer of fine horses and has from time to time owned some of the best thoroughbred horses in Kentucky. He married Kate Wooldridge, a most highly cultured lady and a member of one of the best families of Virginia, and they have six children: Thomas, Frank, Joseph, Sherwood, Robert and Mattie Owsley.

Frank Buckner, second son, was born June 15, 1843. When the Civil war began he enlisted in the Oak Grove Rangers, commanded by Captain Woodward, and in 1862 was made second lieutenant in the Second Kentucky Cavalry, and served in that capacity until the war was ended. He was a brave soldier and uncomplainingly endured many hardships. He is now a tobacco commission merchant of Clarksville, Tennessee; a man of sterling worth, Mason and Knight of Pythias. He was married in 1867 to Hattie Elliott, daughter of Col. William H. Elliott, and they have four children: Elliott, Gordon W., Annie and Lewis.

Harry Buckner, third son, is one of the finest farmers in Christian County, and a man of wide influence in his section. He married Elizabeth Monroe, a most estimable lady, who died in 1889, leaving two little girls, who are living with their father and devoted grandmother.

Upshaw Buckner, youngest son, was born January 17, 1858, and is a farmer near Longview, where he owns 800 acres of land, nearly all of which is in a high state of cultivation. He was married in 1894 to Mary Kelly.

Annie Wooldridge Buckner is the only daughter of Francis W. and Martha (Upshaw) Buckner.

WILLIAM P. M'CLAIN, a leading attorney of Henderson and native of that place, is the son of William McClain, who was also a native of Henderson and an extensive and wealthy farmer of Henderson County. He had large possessions in land and other property, including one hundred and eighty-five slaves, whom he set free of his own volition. His tobacco crop alone for one year sold for seventy-five thousand dollars. He married Virginia Pollitt of Henderson, daughter of James Pollitt, one of the first merchants in Henderson, who died of cholera in 1832. William McClain (father) died in 1885, aged sixty-one years.

James McClain (grandfather) was a native of Kentucky and his father was from Maryland. Col. Jackson McClain (uncle), brother of James, a colonel on Governor Powell's staff, died in 1891.

Virginia Cabell McClain (grandmother) was a member of the noted Cabell family of Virginia, who were descended from Pocahontas. She was left a widow and married Governor Dixon of Kentucky.

W. P. McClain, after his primary schooling in Henderson, attended Notre Dame College, in Indiana, graduating with the degree of A. B., in 1869. He then attended the University of Virginia and graduated from the law department of that institution in 1872; remained there two years longer; was licensed to practice in the Supreme Court of Missouri; subsequently began the practice of law in Henderson. He was elected city attorney in 1880, and resigned that office in 1881 to accept the office of county attorney, which he held for fourteen years consecutively, at the same time attending to a growing general practice in all of the courts.

He was a candidate before the Democratic convention for the nomination for congressman in 1894 and made a brilliant campaign, but was defeated in the convention by a small vote. He received 9½ of the 11 votes of the Henderson

County delegation, while Mr. Vance, his local opponent, received 1½ votes, throwing the nomination to John D. Clardy of Christian County. His friends will urge him to become the congressional candidate of his party in 1896.

Mr. McClain is one of the foremost men at the Henderson bar; a leader in the Democratic party and one of the prominent citizens of Henderson.

He was married to Mary Garland, daughter of Dr. Richard Garland of Henderson.

REVEREND JAMES VENABLE LOGAN, D. D., LL.D., president of Central University, Richmond, son of James Hervey and Mary Venable Logan, was born in Scott County, Kentucky, July 11, 1835.

His father was a native of Shelby County, where he died, January 1, 1856, in his fifty-sixth year. He was a Presbyterian minister and had charge of Bethel Church in Scott County during the twenty years of his ministry.

Alexander Logan (grandfather) was a native of Augusta County, Virginia, and was one of the early settlers of Shelby County, Kentucky. He was a farmer by occupation and a leading member of the Presbyterian Church. There is an interesting account of the Logans in Thomas M. Green's "Historical Families of Kentucky."

Mary Venable Logan (mother) was born in Shelby County in 1810 and was a most exemplary Christian woman of the Presbyterian faith. She survived her husband many years, and died in 1892.

James Venable (maternal grandfather) was a native of Prince Edward County, Virginia, who came to Kentucky with the pioneers and located in Shelby County, where he was a farmer and died well advanced in years. He was a soldier in the War of 1812. He was descended from the Huguenots, of which sturdy race much is said in other sketches in this work.

Rev. James V. Logan, D. D., was prepared for college in primary and classical schools in Scott County, and graduated from Center College in the class of 1854. He then attended the Presbyterian Theological Seminary at Danville, finishing that course in 1860. He received and accepted a call from the Harrodsburg congregation and was installed as pastor of that church in October, 1860, remaining there until 1868, when he was released from that charge to assume the editorial chair of the Free Christian Commonwealth at Louisville, and was engaged in that work until the union between the Synod of Kentucky and the Presbyterian Church South was effected. In 1872 the Kentucky Synod undertook to establish a school of learning and Dr. Logan was occupied in the work looking to that end until 1874, when his labors, in connection with others, culminated in the establishment of Central University, College of Philosophy, Letters and Science, at Richmond, Kentucky.

In the memorial of the Educational Convention held at Lexington, May 7 and 8, 1872, and which inaugurated the movement which resulted in the establishment of this university, the following language occurs: "It is the sense of this convention that steps be taken to at once establish, on a broad and liberal basis, an institution of the highest order, under the auspices of the Synod of Kentucky, and thus carry out the earnest wishes of the fathers, as demonstrated by the establishment of Center College, now lost to this church."

Dr. Logan was elected to the chair of ethics, the only chair then appointed by the Synod. In 1880 he was elected to his present position, in which he presides over and conducts the deliberations of the faculty and sees that their decisions are enforced. He is also vice chancellor of the university and discharges the duties of the chancellor in his absence or inability to act. This institution has prospered greatly under the wise management and direction of President Logan, and now has over two hundred students enrolled. The university grounds are beautifully situated in the suburbs of Richmond, and are nearly square, about one-fourth of a mile to the side. The Hospital College of Medicine of Louisville, the Louisville College of Dentistry, the Collegiate Institute of Jackson, Kentucky, and Hardin Collegiate Institute of Elizabethtown are departments of Central University, and all are in a most flourishing condition. But Dr. Logan's duties are confined to the College of Philosophy, Letters and Science at Richmond, with which he has been connected since its inauguration in 1874, and of which he has been president for sixteen years past.

Dr. Logan was married (first) in December, 1863, to Martha E. S. McBrayer, daughter of Sandford McBrayer of Harrodsburg. She died January, 1888, leaving two sons and three daughters: Sandford V. M.; Mary McBrayer; Martha E., wife of Franklin H. Kean of Louisville; Susan Magoffin, wife of Thomas Burnam of Richmond, and James Venable, Jr., who married Jessie Taylor of Richmond.

Dr. Logan was married (second) November 7, 1895, to Mrs. Mary Lee Herndon of Richmond.

The degree of D. D. was conferred upon Rev. James V. Logan in 1880 and the degree of LL. D. in 1890, by Hampden Sydney College of Virginia.

I. W. BERNHEIM, senior member of the large wholesale liquor house of Bernheim Brothers, Louisville, although a comparatively young man, has gone from the bottom to the top of the financial ladder; has won success against great and opposing odds, and for a number of years back has given a very large portion of his time, and liberally of his money, to aid other young men to whom fortune has made small endowment.

I. W. Bernheim is by no means an ordinary, or a commonplace man; he exhibits great genius as a manufacturer, a merchant, and as a money maker, but he also exhibits towards public and private charities, without regard to sect or creed, a liberality that stamps his as a philanthropic spirit.

With small opportunities for study, he is nevertheless in touch, and in sympathy with the best English and German literature, and no friend to culture could find in him aught to offend the most delicate taste. Although his boyhood and earlier manhood were fully taken up with the struggles of a pathetic poverty, a poverty that might have been expected to harden and deface the man, Mr. Bernheim has never allowed the love of the beautiful in his nature to die out, and since fortune has smiled upon him he has patronized art, not through affectation or stintingly, but liberally, and because he is fully persuaded that art is one of the most glorious fruits of human civilization. Among the business men of Louisville, the name of I. W. Bernheim is an influential one; for it is synonymous with success, and his indorsement of an enterprise is recognized always as a most important factor, doing much to insure success. As a business man he is genial, exhibiting at all times a breadth, a comprehension and a confidence that at once stamps his as a master mind. He is an enthusiast, loving his work, rejoicing in the development of his ideas, and glorifying in the reputation, international in character, that he wins from a busy world. He is a man of detail, possessing in a phenomenal degree the faculty of keeping in touch with the most minute affairs of his great enterprise, and wisely holding that a really great business rests upon a foundation of details, even as the calcareous secretion deposited by coral insects forms the base for future continents.

When he landed in America from Freiburg, Germany (the place of his birth), in 1867, it was with but twenty francs in his pocket, and only to find that the house he was to work for had failed during his coming over. His indomitable nature had already developed, however, and quickly his small capital was invested in a stock of goods, shouldering which he started on foot, an itinerant trader, toward the, to him, unknown and boundless West. A year later found him in Paducah, Ky., where he secured a position as bookkeeper for a house with which he remained until 1872. In 1869 he sent for his brother, Bernard, and three years later the house of Bernheim Bros., a small craft then, but a large one now, was launched upon the sea of commerce. It is interesting just here to note that I. W. and Bernard Bernheim had won already the esteem of Mr. Elbridge Palmer, president of the City National Bank of Paducah, a gentleman of wealth, culture, of discernment and of great liberality, and by his assistance they were enabled to enter upon a career that he has lived to see become in all particulars a successful one, and he has the further satisfaction of knowing that Bernheim Bros. will never and could never forget the friend of their earlier and struggling days.

Isaac W. Bernheim feels that he owes much to America, and although he makes trips from time to time to Europe and to Oriental countries, he loves no country as he does this, and the spirit of no other people as he does the American spirit. It is, therefore, not only a duty to him, but a pleasure to subscribe liberally and systematically to all charitable enterprises with which he is familiar, and to all movements that seem to him for the betterment of the masses, or for the improvement of our institutions.

To him the Young Men's Hebrew Association of Louisville owes its origin and its steady growth, and of this association he has been unanimously elected president every year since it was founded. In giving, however, Mr. Bernheim is bound by no sectarianism nor controlled by any prejudice, for the struggles of his early days, and the sunshine that fell across his path when a kind word was spoken or a helping hand given, has inspired him with a firm belief in the "Fatherhood of God," and the "Brotherhood of man."

HON. EPHRAIM T. LILLARD of Nicholasville, Kentucky, son of Stephen and Rosanna (Hudgons) Lillard, was born in Mercer County, Kentucky, June 23, 1847. His father, Stephen Lillard, was born in Lawrenceburg, Kentucky, June 23, 1808; was a farmer until 1861, when he went out as captain of a squadron of volunteers at the time Morgan organized his forces, before any general organization had been effected in the South. After several months service he returned to his farm in Mercer County, where he was shot down in his own house by the Federal soldiers, but he survived his wounds and lived until September 30, 1889. He was an intense Democrat and often boasted that he never scratched his ticket. He was a member of the Methodist Church, and very domestic in his disposition. He was the son of Ephraim Lillard, a native of Virginia, who came to Anderson County, Kentucky, when quite young, and engaged in farming.

Mrs. Rosanna Hudgons Lillard, mother of Ephraim T. Lillard, was born in Lawrenceburg, Kentucky, in 1816; was married to Stephen Lillard in 1832, and was the mother of twelve children, six sons and six daughters. She died February, 1896; was buried beside her husband at their old homestead in Mercer County, Kentucky.

Her father, William Hudgons, a native of Virginia, married Miss Nancy Blake, a direct descendant of Lord Dudley Blake of England. William Hudgons removed from Virginia to Lawrenceburg, Kentucky, and was several times elected judge of the Anderson County Court; and afterwards removed to Richmond, Missouri, where he died.

Ephraim T. Lillard was educated in the common schools and in the Confederate army, which he joined at the age of fourteen years. He was wounded at the battle of Cross Roads, near Wild Cat, Kentucky, and was in the battles of Perryville, Stone River and other engagements; was with John Morgan on his raid through Indiana and Ohio; was captured at Buffington Island, Ohio, imprisoned, and, after being exchanged, entered Lee's army, served through the war and received his parole at Appomattox Court House.

After the war he returned to his father's farm; married Miss Bettie Nooe, daughter of Nimrod and Lucy P. Nooe, June 22, 1870; was elected to the legislature from Jessamine County, whence he removed in 1875; was one of the original fourteen in the house who voted for Joe C. S. Blackburn in his race for the United States Senate and says, "I'm still for Joe." It is hardly necessary to say that Mr. Lillard is a Democrat. He and his wife are members of the Christian Church. They have three children living, and two have died.

Mr. Lillard is now in the internal revenue service in Louisville under appointment of Ben Johnson, collector of the Fifth district. He was special deputy appointed to superintend the income tax collection, before that law was declared unconstitutional, and after that was transferred to duty in the internal revenue service in same district.

EUGENE K. WILSON of London, county attorney of Laurel County, son of Dr. John M. Wilson and Nancy Kerr, was born in Williamstown, Grant County, Kentucky, February 2, 1869.

Dr. John M. Wilson was born in Pendleton County, Kentucky, in 1832, and has been a resident and practicing physician of Williamstown for forty years. He is very prominent in his profession, useful as a citizen and vigorous and aggressive as a Republican politician; has been chairman of the county committee for twenty-five years, and three times a delegate to national conventions; is still active and skillful in his profession and always ready for a campaign, in which he is a foe worthy of the best of the Democrats in his bailiwick. He is, moreover, a Christian gentleman and a consistent member of the Methodist Episcopal Church.

Dr. James M. Wilson (grandfather), a native of Culpeper County, Virginia, came to Kentucky when he was a young man, locating at Falmouth, where he practiced medicine and took a lively interest in political affairs. He served his county and district in both branches of the legislature; was a captain in the Mexican war, and was in all things faithful, honest and true, living up to his religious profession as a member of the Methodist Church. He reached his full seventy-eight years, and died in 1880.

James Wilson (great-grandfather) was a native of England. He was a major in the patriot army during the Revolutionary war and was among the slain in that great conflict.

Nancy Kerr Wilson (mother) was born in Fayette County, Kentucky, in 1839; is now living in Williamstown and is a member of the Presbyterian Church.

James Kerr (grandfather), a native of Henrico County, Virginia, came to Kentucky with his father, James Kerr, who came with Simon Kenton, and was killed by the Indians near Lexington. He was a lineal descendant of Robert Bruce. His son, James Kerr, became a farmer in Fayette County; was a large slaveholder; a Union man during the Civil war and a citizen of the highest respectability.

Eugene K. Wilson was reared in Williamstown and received his primary education in the schools of that place; attended Center College, from which he graduated in the class of 1887; read law and attended the law department of the University of Louisville, graduating and receiving his diploma from that institution in 1889; edited and published "The Eagle," a weekly Republican newspaper in Williamstown, for one year, while waiting to reach his majority; went to London in 1890 and began the practice of law, meeting with encouragement and a liberal share of the legal business in the Civil Courts; was Republican elector for the Eleventh Congressional district in the presidential campaign of 1892, making a brilliant canvass, and establishing a reputation as a young politician of more than ordinary ability; in November, 1894, was elected to his present office as county attorney, which will require his attention until January, 1898.

This is a fine record for a young man, now in his twenty-seventh year, but it is only the preliminary work for future honors and successes that must come to one of Mr. Wilson's ability and industry. He is also a star-route mail contractor, in which he has large interests, London being a point of great interest in that line of government work. There were twenty thousand contracts let during the past year from London. Mr. Wilson is a member of the Methodist Church, and is a leading Knight of Pythias, having been twice elected chancellor commander of London Lodge No. 102.

CHARLES BRIDGES PEARCE, Cashier of the State National Bank of Maysville and one of the ablest financiers in the state, was born near Flemingsburg, Kentucky, May 7, 1823. For nearly half a century he has been closely identified with the growth and development of Maysville, where he is highly esteemed as a citizen and recognized as one of the most successful business men in all that section of the state.

His father, William Pearce, was a native of England, and one of the most prosperous merchants of his day. He received only an ordinary education, but was a man of strong character and remarkable individuality. He was a merchant, private banker and farmer, and became one of the wealthiest men in northern Kentucky. He died of cholera, aged forty-eight years, June 14, 1833.

Mary Bridges (mother) was a Virginian, daughter of a Welshman who, coming from Virginia, settled in Flemingsburg, Kentucky, before the Revolutionary war.

Samuel Pearce (grandfather) was a native of

England who came to this country and settled at Little Egg Harbor, New Jersey, and was a soldier in the war for American independence, as was also his brother William, who came to this country with him. Samuel Pearce removed from Pittsburg to Kentucky, and for a time lived in the vicinity of Lexington, subsequently removing to Flemingsburg, where he spent the remainder of a useful life.

Hiram T. Pearce (brother) was born in 1813 and was the guardian of Charles B. Pearce. He died in 1866 or 1867, leaving an estate worth half a million dollars, which was considered a very large fortune, as there were few wealthier men at that time.

Charles B. Pearce was only seventeen years of age when he became associated with his elder brother, Hiram T. Pearce, in the wholesale dry goods business at Maysville, under the firm name of L. C. & H. T. Pearce. This firm was succeeded by Pearce & Company, and afterwards by Pearce, Wallingford & Co., and the jobbing business was removed to Cincinnati in 1861.

In 1860, principally through the efforts of Charles B. Pearce, the banking house of Pearce & Wallingford was formed, and in 1866 H. T. Pearce was admitted to the firm, which became Pearce, Wallingford & Co.; in 1872 Charles B. Pearce and Joseph Wallingford bought the bank stock belonging to the estate of Hiram Pearce and continued in business until 1882, when Mr. Pearce purchased Mr. Wallingford's interest and organized the State National Bank of Maysville, the capital stock of which is $150,000, while the average deposits show it to be equal in point of business to any bank in that section. Its predecessors were the banking house of Pearce, Wallingford & Company and the branch of the Farmers' Bank of Kentucky, the assets of which Mr. Pearce bought.

Mr. Pearce was made cashier of the State National Bank at the time of its organization and has been at the head of its management until the present time, being the owner of one-half of the stock. Of all the members who constituted its board of directors in 1882, Mr. Pearce alone survives.

He is largely interested in other business enterprises and is sole proprietor of the Limestone Flouring Mills, which cost him $85,000.

From 1843 to 1858 he was a leading dry goods merchant and it is no vain boast to say that in those years he sold more dry goods throughout northern Kentucky and southern Ohio than any other jobber. He made regular journeys to and from Philadelphia to buy goods, by stage coach on the old National Pike, and found no better mode of travel until 1847.

He has never aspired to office, having no time to devote to politics, but has performed his duty as a citizen at the polls with commendable punctuality.

Mr. Pearce was married in 1848 to Maria Shultz, daughter of Christian Shultz, who came from York, Pennsylvania, to Maysville, where he established a large bagging factory and also owned a commission house in New Orleans. Mrs. Pearce died in 1885, leaving five children: L. E. Pearce; Christian S. Pearce of Nashville; Charles D. Pearce, whose first wife was a daughter of W. N. Haldeman and who was business manager of the Louisville Courier-Journal for many years; and two daughters, residents of Louisville.

GEORGE FRANKLIN THOMPSON, M. D., an eminent and popular physician of Frankfort, son of William B. Thompson and Sarah Franklin, a native of Virginia, was born at Bryant Station, Fayette County, Kentucky, June 20, 1848. His father was for forty years a large stockholder in the celebrated Phoenix Hotel of Lexington, and died in March, 1891.

Dr. Thompson was educated in the schools of Lexington and under Professor Smith at Versailles, but his studies were interrupted by the war, and in 1862, when only fourteen years of age, he enlisted in Company A, Fifth Regiment Kentucky Cavalry, C. S. A., and was detailed as escort to Gen. Abe Buford. He followed the varying fortunes of the Confederacy until the last and was in the thickest of the battles of Murfreesboro (Christmas, 1862), and later at Chickamauga and Mission Ridge and other important engagements in that vicinity. He was with Gen. Morgan in his raid through Kentucky, Indiana and

Ohio, and on this excursion he rode an excellent horse, covering 109 miles from four o'clock in the morning until nine in the evening. The trip was through a section of the country in which it would not have been safe for a man (or boy) of his views to venture alone, but he was of a daring spirit and rather enjoyed the excitement and especially the consternation of the people.

He was wounded in the left breast at Mt. Sterling (1864); escaped to Cynthiana, where he was captured on Sunday; escaped the same day and was recaptured the following Sunday at Hall's Gap; escaped again the same day and joined his command at Alberene, Virginia, with which he remained until paroled at Athens, Georgia, in May, 1865.

Returning to his home, he resumed his studies at Danville, where he completed his literary course in 1867, and began the study of medicine with Dr. J. W. Foster of Lexington; attended the Hospital College of Medicine in Louisville, from which he was graduated in 1874.

In the following year he located in Frankfort and began a professional career which has been eminently successful. Among the physicians with whom he has labored for over twenty years he stands in the front rank, while the people who have enjoyed the benefit of his professional skill regard him as a most competent, obliging, courteous and skillful physician. His popularity is fully attested by the liberal share of the work of the many able physicians in his field of labor.

Dr. Thompson was married November 28, 1877, at Maysville, to Kate Byrne, and they have an interesting group of six children: Agnes, Frank, Lewis, Nellie, Mason, Mary and Harry.

GEORGE DURELLE, Judge of the Court of Appeals from the Louisville District, son of George O. J. Durelle and Frances Mary Peirce, was born in Livingston County, New York, October 18, 1852.

His father was a native of New Hampshire and was educated in Bowdoin and Dartmouth Colleges. He graduated in medicine and surgery at Dartmouth in 1838 and practiced in Livingston County, New York, until his death, making a specialty of surgery, in which he was particularly skillful. His career was short but successful and promised to be far above the mediocre, and he had made a reputation for fine work in surgical cases when, in 1853, he died at the age of forty. He was an exceedingly kind man, of tender sympathies, of courteous demeanor, and made a host of friends both socially and in his profession. His ancestors were Huguenots who came to this country and settled in New England, where many of the name are found to-day.

Frances Mary Peirce Durelle (mother) was born in Livingston County, New York, in 1831; was educated in private schools in Rochester, New York, and is now a resident of Louisville. Her second husband was Professor S. B. Barton, at one time of Center College, and well known as a teacher in Danville and Louisville.

Shepard Peirce (grandfather) was the second white child born at Avon, New York. He was engaged in mercantile pursuits in that state, and was Justice of the Peace, Commissioner of Loans, and Postmaster of Livonia. He married Mary Cone Pitkin, a native of Connecticut, and a member of the Pitkin family, whose men were famous in law and in the ministry. In the direct line of ancestry in this family were William Pitkin, the founder, who was appointed by the King, Attorney-General of Connecticut, Chief Justice William Pitkin, Colonel Joseph Pitkin of the Crown Point Expedition, and Captain Richard Pitkin of the Revolutionary Army. Mary Lord, the wife of Colonel Joseph Pitkin, was a great-granddaughter of Governor John Haynes, the first Governor of Connecticut.

George Durelle's primary education was received from Professor Barton in Louisville and at Walnut Hill, Kentucky. He subsequently attended Pingry's School in Elizabeth, New Jersey, and graduated from the Hopkins Grammar School at New Haven, Connecticut—the oldest school except one in the United States. He was then fully prepared for college. He entered Yale in 1868, and continued his studies there until 1871. Returning to Louisville he was a teacher in the Sixth Ward public school for two years, and at the same time attended the Louisville Law School, from which he was graduated in 1874.

After practicing law for some time without an office associate he formed a partnership with Horace C. Brannin, which relation continued until 1882, when he was appointed Assistant United States District Attorney under President Arthur's administration and served four years. In 1886 he returned to the practice of law, and in 1889 was reappointed Assistant District Attorney under President Harrison's administration. After serving two years he resigned and resumed the general practice of law in the Civil Courts. He was frequently called on to act as Special Master of the United States Circuit Court in important and complicated railroad litigations.

In 1894 he was the leading counsel in the contested election case of Boyle vs. Toney, which resulted in favor of Judge Toney, but under such circumstances that he declined his seat on the Appellate bench; whereupon Major George B. Eastin was appointed to fill the vacancy until the November election, 1895. Mr. Durelle lost his case after a vigorous and well-managed contest, but his ardent labors against what he considered a great political wrong, brought him more conspicuously before the public than any former work he had done. His efforts in behalf of a professional brother and political friend were so generally appreciated that when he himself became a candidate for the seat which had been the subject of the contest, there was no one among the many Republican lawyers in the Fourth Appellate District who offered to contest the nomination with him, and he was nominated in the convention by acclamation.

Major Eastin was nominated by the Democrats, and Judge John G. Simrall was an independent candidate. The Democrats were confident of success, but Mr. Durelle received a plurality of two thousand five hundred and seventy-five votes, and a majority of over thirteen hundred over both opponents.

The new Judge left politics when he went to Frankfort to take his seat with Chief Justice Pryor, Judges Lewis, Guffy, Hazelrigg, Grace (since deceased) and Paynter; and after being duly installed he settled down to his new duties with industry and zeal, fortified by an extended knowledge of the law, and at once established himself in the confidence and good will of his associates and the members of the bar.

Mr. Durelle was married June 3, 1886, to Miss Louise Leib, daughter of the late Fred Leib of Louisville. She was educated in Miss Belle Peer's school, and attended the Warren Memorial Presbyterian Church, of which she was a member at the time of her death, November 23, 1895. She left two children: Frederic, born May 20, 1889, and Louise Marie, born November 13, 1895.

THOMAS C. DABNEY, deceased, of Cadiz, one of the most distinguished lawyers and jurists of Kentucky, son of Albert Gallatin Dabney and Ann Eliza Catlett, was born in Louisa County, Virginia, September 20, 1823, and died in Cadiz, Kentucky, November 12, 1886. He was educated under the able direction of Elder George P. Street, and after finishing his literary and scientific course at the age of eighteen, he took up the study of law, and soon afterwards came to Cadiz and was domiciled with the family of J. E. Thompson, who was then County and Circuit Clerk. Mr. Dabney became deputy clerk, at the same time pursuing his studies for the legal profession under the late Hon. C. D. Bradley, which having completed, he commenced to practice law in Cadiz in 1844.

While always deeply interested in politics, he never sought, nor would hold, a political office outside of the legal profession. He served for several terms as County Attorney; in 1852 was elected County Judge of Trigg County; in July, 1857, he was elected Judge of the Second Circuit Court District, which extended across the state at that time, embracing seven counties. His term expired in 1862, when, declining further election, he returned to the practice of law.

"Full forty years he walked hand in hand with law, the love of his youth, and with untiring perseverance and devotion he won a prominent and enviable place among her votaries. Envy and jealousy found no abiding place in his heart, but rejoicing in his brother's prosperity he gracefully yielded the palm to the victor, feeling as much pride in the clear judgment of the Court and in the energy and talent of the bar as he did shame in any act that would bring contempt upon the profession. Most truly did he ennoble a noble profession, ever striving to honor and exalt the adopted child of Blackstone, the legitimate offspring of Divinity. The dignity that characterized his every act and thought never forsook him 'e'en when his feet were slipping o'er the brink.' Vain and worse than useless are the eulogies of the dead, and unavailing indeed are clamorous praises of him whose life has been as a white tablet."

In his family circle Judge Dabney was kind, affectionate and unselfish to a fault. Wherever his name was known it was strongly fettered with piety, honor and fidelity on the one hand and modesty, purity and benevolence on the other. Chaste and delicate in his tastes he could not brook that which savored of coarseness or unrefinement. He was the proudest of men and yet the humblest, and so rare was the blending, so admirable the balancing that he was the esteemed friend of the prosperous and the ready counselor and help of the poor. Not even to his jealous and exacting profession—to which his heart was ever loyal—would he yield a moment of his hours of study and communion with the Book of Books. At the close of every day, and for hours, he would pore over and study the sacred history, which, like a golden beam of light, threaded his library, lending its hue to his favorite volumes. Such a life is written of no other man in this volume.

Judge Dabney was married March 7, 1848, to Susanna Rumsey, only child of the late James D. Rumsey of Hopkinsville, Kentucky, in which city she was born July 10, 1826. She died at her home in Cadiz, August 10, 1890. Her father, a native of Maryland, was a son of Dr. Edward Rumsey of Christian County, and they belonged to a family of gentlemen by inheritance. Possessed of the very first order of common sense, they supplemented their native talent with fine classical attainments, extensive reading and with such grace of manner that made any one of them a central figure in polite circles and as truly the valued guest of every cultivated household. It was in such an atmosphere that Mrs. Dabney was born and raised. She was carefully educated by her father and was as familiar with the dactyls of Homer as Longfellow was with the spondees of poor Dick Kirk. She continued her reading through life, and at her death had studied and understood more books than any other lady in the commonwealth.

Her great uncle, James Rumsey, and her own uncle, Edward Rumsey, were men of great ambition. To the former the credit is now universally conceded of discovering and adding the power of steam to the navigation of boats; and the latter, when quite a young man, was a representative in Congress from the Second District of Kentucky and was the intimate associate and peer of such men as Richard H. Menifee, Wise of Virginia, Ingersoll of Pennsylvania, and Prentiss of Mississippi. As a public speaker his points were as incisive as Wise, his rhetoric as rich and fertile as Sargent S. Prentiss, and his declamation as graceful as Menifee. In the early dawn of his brilliant career he was summoned home on account of the illness and death of his entire family of children, the loss of whom so humbled his spirit that he refused to return to his seat or appear again before a public audience. And he kept his word.

James Rumsey, the inventor mentioned above, possessed the delicate temperament of true genius—nervous, sensitive and refined. He died in London, England, of sudden heart failure, caused by intense personal excitement while lecturing on the application of steam power to navigation before the Royal Society.

"But the chief charm of this estimable lady (Mrs. Dabney) did not lie in the long line of her distinguished ancestry, her ripe scholarship, extensive reading, or finished culture, but in her native goodness as a woman, her kind and tender care as the mother of a large family, and the solicitude she manifested for the enjoyment and pleasure of a host of friends who were her almost constant companions and welcome guests."

The children of Thomas C. Dabney and Susanna Rumsey were: James R. Dabney, a graduate of Kentucky University, and late County Judge of Henderson County, died in Hopkinsville, September 23, 1895. Albert J. Dabney, lieutenant in the United States Navy, educated at Kentucky University and the Annapolis Naval College, Maryland, now living in Staunton, Virginia. His health having failed, he resigned his position in the United States Navy, and has since filled important chairs as teacher in colleges in Tennessee, Kentucky and in the military academy in Staunton. Cornelia, widow of J. R. Averitt, whose early death closed a prospective brilliant political career. Thomas C. Dabney died April 13, 1873, at the Kentucky University, Lexington. Annie S.; Minnie, wife of Judge Robert Crenshaw; E. F. Dabney, attorney at law of San Jose, California, a graduate of the Louisville (Ky.) Law School; Dr. A. S. Dabney, dentist of Paducah, graduate of the Baltimore Dental College. The Doctor, though a young man, is prominent in his profession, a bookworm and well-known genealogist; and Carrie Lee, wife of Edward Higgin of Denver, Colorado.

Judge Dabney's father, Albert Gallatin Dabney, was born in Louisa County, Virginia, in 1798; was a planter and owned many slaves; removed to Christian County, Kentucky, in the fall of 1830, with a family of four sons. While in Virginia he was a Major in the State Militia. He was a typical, old-time gentleman, and carried himself as he wore his title, with stately dignity.

Cornelius Dabney (grandfather) and his wife, who was a Miss Winston, lived in Louisa County, Virginia. He was a prosperous planter, a man of fine character and a worthy descendant of one of three brothers—Cornelius, John and Isaac—who fled from France upon the revocation of the Edict of Nantes. They wrote their names D'Aubigne, a name which is well known in France. The family crest was "Faithful and grateful." Judge Dabney's grandfather, Cornelius Dabney, was a descendant of Cornelius D'Aubigne from France, and he could trace his pedigree in an almost unbroken line to St. Bartholomew's historic eve of terror and persecution.

ROBERT CRENSHAW, leading lawyer and honored citizen of Cadiz, son of Robertson Crenshaw and Mary Frances Walden, was born in the precinct of Roaring Springs, Trigg County, Kentucky, June 4, 1847.

His father was born in Halifax County, Virginia, September, 1816, and came to Trigg County with his parents in 1819. He married Mary Frances Walden in 1839 and was a resident and farmer of Trigg County until the time of his death, which occurred February 12, 1853. He was a faithful member of the Christian Church, a Mason and an honored citizen.

Cornelius Crenshaw (grandfather) married Nancy Kent in Halifax County, Virginia, and came to Trigg County, Kentucky, in 1819. He was for many years a member of the United Baptist denomination, but afterwards associated himself with the Christian Church and was noted for his piety and good works. Before coming to Kentucky he had served in a Virginia company in the War of 1812, in which he was a commissioned officer stationed at Norfolk, Virginia.

Mary Frances Walden Crenshaw (mother) was a sister of Dr. J. C. Walden of Maysville, whose sketch and ancestry will be found in this volume.

Robert Crenshaw was raised by his uncle, Thomas Crenshaw, and educated under the teaching and direction of Professors A. J. Wyatt and G. P. Street. At the age of twenty he began the study of law under Judge Thomas C. Dabney. He commenced the practice of law in 1868. In 1872 he was elected County Attorney for a term of four years, during which time he also held the office of School Commissioner; and in 1884 was elected County Judge, and this office he filled during the whole term with great credit to himself and to the entire satisfaction of his constituents. On leaving the bench he resumed the practice of law, in which he has had a successful and brilliant career.

He has sometimes indulged in politics for the sake of his friends and the political weal, but has sought no favors outside of his legal profession. He has occasionally gratified a propensity for newspaper work by lending his aid to the local journals, and his writings have been much quoted.

In 1894 a vote was taken in Trigg County on the question whether whisky should be sold in the county, and Judge Crenshaw was selected as Chairman of the Executive Committee to canvass the county in the interest of the Prohibition party, which won the contest by over five hundred majority, an achievement of which he is very proud and for which he is greatly honored by the Christian people of his county. And this one incident is a fair index of the character of the man. He undertook a task which was by many considered unpopular and one in which few men could hope to succeed; but the magnitude of the undertaking nor the jeers of the enemies of temperance, nor the opposition of so-called business interests could not deter him from throwing the whole force and weight of his influence against a social wrong and in favor of the best interests of society.

Judge Crenshaw was married in 1877 to Minnie Dabney, daughter of Judge Thomas C. Dabney, the subject of the foregoing sketch, and it is hardly necessary to add that she is one of the most intelligent women of the state of Kentucky. She has made a name in literature and is a frequent contributor to literary and religious journals. Judge and Mrs. Crenshaw have a happy family of six children: Susanne Moore, E. Rumsey, Dabney H., Robert, John W. and Albert.

JOHN FRANKLIN HAGER, leading attorney-at-law of Ashland, son of Henry G. Hager, and grandson of Daniel Hager, Sr., was born in Floyd County, Kentucky, March 16, 1853. His mother died in 1856, and at the age of eleven years he went to Ashland and for two years attended the private school of J. B. Powell; was one year at school in Catlettsburg and another year at Masonic Academy, Louisa, Kentucky. In his boyhood, when not in school he was a knock-about hand on Big Sandy River steamers serving as cabin-boy, cook, watchman and "cub" pilot. At the age of fifteen he was employed by his uncle, S. P. Hager, a general merchant at Paintsville, and remained there for four years except a part of one year when he attended the public schools at Paris, Ill. At the age of nineteen he was appointed deputy clerk of the Magoffin Circuit Court, receiving one-third of the fees for his services, at the same time reading borrowed law books and qualified himself for examination for license, to practice law, which he obtained at West Liberty, November 13, 1873, being then under twenty-one years of age. He soon returned to Ashland and became a partner with John W. Hampton in the practice of law, succeeding as Hampton & Hager, the law firm of Ireland & Hampton, Mr. Ireland having been elected Judge of the Sixteenth Circuit. This partnership continued until 1880, when Mr. Hampton removed to Texas, since which time Mr. Hager has been engaged in a large practice alone at Ashland.

He served as Commissioner from Kentucky under appointment of Governor Buckner at the celebration of the Centennial of the Federal Constitution at Philadelphia in September, 1887; as Commissioner from Kentucky at the Centennial Exposition at Cincinnati in 1888; as Railroad Commissioner from May, 1888, to August, 1891, resigning the latter position several months before the expiration of his term. He was one of the Commissioners in charge of the State Treasury after the defalcation and flight of Treasurer J. W. Tate; was twice elected city attorney of Ashland, in 1878 and 1886, and with that exception has never been a candidate for or held an elective office. His law practice is worth many times the salary of any office within the gift of the people of the state.

Mr. Hager was married December 22, 1881, to Margaret Elizabeth Maupin and their family consists of three sons and two daughters, Gerald, Adele, Richard Buckner, Margaret Maupin and John F. Hager, Jr.

WILLIAM ELLIOTT, a leading tobacconist of Henderson, Kentucky, son of H. Clay and Elizabeth (Palmer) Elliott, was born in Daviess County, Kentucky, August 14, 1857. He was educated in the public schools of Henderson, and after leaving school he began the business of stemming tobacco and preparing it for the English market. In 1892 he built a large stemmery, which was burned May 1, 1895, with a loss of about $50,000. He subsequently bought the old Shelby property and equipped it thoroughly, in which he continued his business with only temporary interruption, and in which he has been remarkably successful. He is a man of great energy and push, of more than ordinary enterprise and of reliable business judgment.

He is interested in some of the leading business enterprises of the city, particularly the Farmers' Bank, a branch of the Farmers' Bank of Kentucky, at Frankfort, which has a capital of $360,000, the largest capital held by any bank in the state outside of the city of Louisville. Mr. Elliott is Vice-President of the Henderson branch of this strong financial institution. He has served six or eight years as trustee of the public schools, and has always taken a deep interest in the cause of education and in the moral and religious welfare of his city, being a member of the Methodist Episcopal Church and for fifteen years superintendent of the Sunday school. Mr. Elliott has performed well his part as a good citizen, voting according to the dictates of his conscience and using his influence in behalf of men and measures for the best interests of society.

He was married December 29, 1879, to Mary Nunn of Henderson; and the result of this union is a happy family of four children.

Mr. Elliott's father was a native of Nelson County, who removed to Daviess County after his marriage. His mother was a native of Washington County, Kentucky, and was a daughter of Robert Palmer, and granddaughter of the eminent jurist, Ben Hardin.

Dr. William Elliott (grandfather) is now living in New Haven, Nelson County, where he practiced medicine for many years, and is now ninety-seven years of age.

Robert Palmer (maternal grandfather) was a resident of Springfield, Washington County, Kentucky, and his mother was a daughter of Ben Hardin. (See Collins' History, p. 646.)

COLONEL THOMAS B. FORD, Circuit Clerk of the Franklin County Court, is a son of Harbin H. and Ann M. (Brooks) Ford, and was born in Owen County, Kentucky, February 7, 1841. He is descended from an old English family of early settlers in Virginia. He is a grandson of William Ford, who was born in Orange County, Virginia, and removed to Kentucky in 1816 and located on a farm near Lexington, where he died in 1820. Harbin H. Ford (father) was also a native of Orange County, Virginia, and removed to Kentucky in 1830, or about that time, locating in the vicinity of Lexington, where he made his home for several years, when he removed to Owen County and purchased real estate to the amount of about one thousand acres, and was at the time of his death one of the largest land owners in the county. He was an officer in the War of 1812, a member of the Baptist Church and a conscientious Christian gentleman. He died in Owen County. His wife, Ann Brooks, was of Irish origin, whose ancestors settled in this country about the time of the Revolution. She was born in Washington, D. C., in 1802, and died at Frankfort, Kentucky, in 1881. She was a devout Christian, a woman of strong character and was a communicant of the Baptist Church.

Colonel Thomas B. Ford lived with his parents on a farm in Owen County until in his fourteenth year, when he removed with his mother to Frankfort, where he attended Sayres Academy, a school in which many of the most eminent men in Kentucky were educated. Upon leaving this institution he read law and in 1862 was admitted to the bar. He practiced law most successfully for several years, and in 1874 was elected to the office of county attorney, which he held for four years. After the expiration of his term as county attorney, he was chosen superintendent of public schools, and in 1880 was re-elected to the same office. During his incumbency of this office the schools of Franklin County showed much improvement and the school fund of the county began to largely increase. In 1878 Colonel Ford was appointed clerk of the United States Court, which office he filled most capably and acceptably, continuously for a period of thirteen years, and which he resigned in 1891. In 1892 he was elected circuit clerk of Franklin County, which office he now holds. Colonel Ford has always taken an active interest in local and municipal affairs, and has been a member of the city council and served two terms as school trustee. He is a member of W. G. Simpson Lodge No. 472, F. & A. M., of Owen County, Dexter Lodge, K. of P., of Frankfort, and Frankfort Lodge No. 28, I. O. O. F. Colonel Ford and his sister still own the old homestead in Owen County. In 1881 he was united in marriage to Mamie Elliott, daughter of Benjamin T. Elliott of Frankfort, and they have one son, Elliott Ford. Not the least among Colonel Ford's accomplishments is his success in the field of literature. His talents in this line have been very versatile, as evidenced by his many well-known publications: "The Deadly

Blow," "The Governor's Daughter," "Norma Norton's Vow" and "The Perilous Plot;" and among his best known stories which have been published in "The Saturday Night" are "My Violin," a poem which has been much admired, as has also his opera, entitled "Lena," which was set to music by Professor Mauer; also his drama, "The Three Turks." Colonel Ford justly deserves the recognition he has received. He is at present the president of the Southern Literary Association, and is taking an active interest in the development of literature in the South.

McHENRY RHOADS, the efficient superintendent of the city schools of Frankfort, and one of the leading educators of the state, was born in Muhlenburg County, Kentucky, July 27, 1858. He grew up on a farm in his native county and in 1876 entered the West Kentucky College, and after a four years' course was graduated from that institution in 1880. After completing his studies, he became a teacher in the preparatory department and was subsequently assistant teacher in Natural Sciences in this college. At the end of three years he severed his connection with this institution and in 1883 was elected vice president of the Hartford College, where he remained eight years. During the last five years of his stay at Hartford he was editor and part owner of the Hartford Herald. In the fall of 1891 he was elected to his present position, superintendent of the city schools of Frankfort. Since he took charge the schools of the city have greatly improved and increased in attendance until it is now necessary to employ a corps of twenty-two teachers. In 1887 Mr. Rhoads married a Miss Ree Crawford, a daughter of Benjamin F. Crawford of Millwood, Grayson County, and they have two sons, Crawford Carlisle and Wayland.

McHenry Rhoads is a son of Absalom J. and Tabitha R. (Dennis) Rhoads. His father was born in Muhlenburg County in 1816. He was a prosperous farmer, a good citizen and a member of the Baptist Church. He died in his native county, February 21, 1888.

Solomon Rhoads (grandfather) was a native of Pennsylvania, who came to Kentucky and settled in Muhlenburg County long before that county was organized. He was a farmer and distiller, and married Rachel (Boone) Johnson, a third cousin of Daniel Boone. His death occurred in that county at the age of sixty years.

Henry Rhoads (great-grandfather) was born in Germany in 1737, and at the age of seventeen years he landed in this country, and became one of the earliest settlers in what is now Muhlenburg County. He was a member of the first legislature under the state government and named his county in honor of John Peter Muhlenburg. Henry Rhoads was a man of considerable prominence and influence, and was a soldier in the Revolutionary war.

Mrs. (Dennis) Rhoads (mother) was also a native of Muhlenburg County, where she lived until September 26, 1883, and died in the fifty-second year of her age. She was a daughter of Abraham Dennis, a native of South Carolina, who removed to Muhlenburg County when he was a young man, where he followed farming until the time of his death. His ancestors were from Ireland.

JOHN T. HODGE, a prominent and brilliant young attorney of Newport, Kentucky, was born near Florence, Kenton County, Kentucky, March 28, 1863. He is a son of Gen. George B. Hodge, a sketch of whose part in public affairs is appended.

John T. Hodge was educated in the public schools of Newport; read law with W. H. McCoy of Cincinnati; graduated from the Cincinnati Law School in 1887; was third in his class of one hundred and eighteen and received the degree of LL.B. He remained in the office of his preceptor until August, 1890, when he opened an office in Newport and was successfully engaged in practicing law until 1893, when he was appointed master commissioner, of which office he is the present incumbent.

Mr. Hodge is an active politician and a leader in the Democratic party, which has honored him with positions which demand the services of a man of good judgment and of great executive ability. He has twice been chairman of the Democratic county executive committee; was chairman of the Second legislative district committee for one term; is now chairman of the Newport Democratic committee; recently succeeded Hon. Harvey Myers as central committeeman; took a prominent part in the Democratic convention of 1895; was a Democratic candidate for elector in the presidential campaign of 1892, receiving thirty-five more votes than any other electoral candidate in his county, and in all of these positions has proved himself a man of great strength of character, a brilliant speaker and a leader of acknowledged ability.

Mr. Hodge was married April 4, 1891, to Virginia Lee Lovell, daughter of Howard L. Lovell of Covington. They are members of the Episcopal Church.

Mr. Hodge's father, Gen. George Baird Hodge, was born in Fleming County, April 8, 1828, and was educated at Maysville and in the Navy School at Annapolis, Maryland. He was midshipman in the United States navy in 1845; served as midshipman through the Mexican war; resigned in April, 1850; in 1853, at the age of twenty-five, he was the Whig candidate for Congress; made a brilliant, but unsuccessful campaign; then began the practice of law in Newport; was a member of the Kentucky house of representatives from 1859 to 1861 and was chairman of the committee on federal relations, when the celebrated resolution declaring the neutrality of Kentucky was passed, May 16, 1861; was candidate in 1860 for elector at large on the Breckinridge and Lane ticket; entered the Confederate army as a private soldier, September 23, 1861; was a member of the provisional government of Kentucky in 1861; member from Kentucky of the Confederate provisional congress, 1861-62; member of the first permanent Confederate congress, 1862; and when not attending the sessions of congress continued to serve in the army; was made captain and assistant adjutant-general of Gen. Breckinridge's division, 1862; promoted to major for distinguished gallantry at the battle of Shiloh, April, 1862; was made colonel, 1864, and brigadier general of cavalry the same year, and was in command of the military district of Mississippi and Louisiana at the close of the war, 1865.

Gen. Hodge resumed the practice of law in Newport in 1866; was candidate for presidential elector at large on the Greeley and Brown ticket in 1872, and received the highest vote cast, and was president of the electoral college which met in Frankfort, December 4, 1872. He was an able lawyer, a shrewd politician, a beautiful and forceful writer, a ready, eloquent speaker and was prominently mentioned as a candidate for governor in 1874, but at that time he removed to Longwood, Orange County, Florida, and made that his home until the time of his death in 1892.

His son, John T. Hodge, has inherited his talent in a remarkable degree and has laid the foundation for a brilliant career.

JOHN H. BARRET, a prominent business man and capitalist of Henderson, is a son of the late John H. Barret and Susan D. Rankin.

His father, for whom he was named, was born in Louisa County, Virginia, February 4, 1818; died in Henderson in 1890. He (father) received a good education in his native county, and followed the plow and endured the hardships and performed the rough labors incident to the life of a farmer's boy, but he was dutiful, obedient, energetic and thoughtful, and developed a sound judgment, exhibiting traits which qualified him for the higher responsibilities which he assumed later in life; and at the age of seventeen he left the parental roof in Virginia and joined his elder brother, Alexander Barret, who had gone to Henderson, Kentucky, about two years before. It was in December, 1835, that he accepted employment with his brother, who was then engaged in purchasing and stemming tobacco. He soon became a valuable assistant to his employer, and was with him about four years, when, having married Susan D. Rankin (December, 1839), he formed a co-partnership with his brother-in-law, James E. Rankin, and engaged in the sale of dry goods, which continued until 1852, when the firm dissolved by mutual consent, Mr. Barret having been tendered a partnership with his brother and former employer in the tobacco business. This business relation of the brothers continued until the death of Alexander B. Barret in 1861. The settlement of an estate of between three and four million dollars devolved upon the surviving partner as executor of his brother's will, and this he accomplished within five years; hundreds of legacies were paid off, accounts settled, books balanced and the estate divided without a jar, and this was considered "one of the most brilliant and successful financial and business achievements known to the business world."

The great stemming interest was carried on in the meantime by the surviving partner, John H. Barret, who eventually associated with him his sons, John H. and James R., and his son-in-law, James F. Rankin, the firm being known as John H. Barret & Co. For some years prior to his death (1890), the senior member of the firm took no active part in the details of the business of his firm, except by counsel and advice.

He was a leading spirit in the promotion and construction of the Evansville, Henderson & Nashville Railroad; the city authorities placed $300,000 worth of its bonds in Mr. Barret's hands as custodian, without security; he purchased the first locomotive for the road with his own money; was one of the organizers of the First National Bank; was mainly instrumental in establishing the woolen and cotton mills, in both of which he was a large stockholder; owned and cultivated hundreds of acres of land in Henderson County, large tracts in Hopkins and Breckinridge counties, and four thousand, eight hundred acres in Delta County, Texas, upon which he cultivated cotton and corn and was largely engaged in stock raising; had branch tobacco stemmeries in Uniontown and Owensboro; was a liberal supporter of the cause of religion, giving liberally to all denominations and all charitable organizations; was a Mason, but seldom attended his lodge; was no politician or office seeker, but was interested in the election of good men to office; a man of warm personal attachments and generous impulses, but not effusive, he was a good and true friend and a generous enemy. His death was a public calamity, and there was mourning in many households where his kindness had endeared him to the humble, and his exemplary life had commanded the love and respect of the whole community.

He was married December, 1839, to Susan D. Rankin, a woman of affectionate disposition, even temper, strong, good sense, active benevolence and earnest piety. Their three children, John H., James R. and Susan, were quite young, when their mother died in 1851. Mr. Barret was married again in 1852, to Mary Augusta Haddock of Smithland, Kentucky, and all of his four children by this marriage died in infancy. Upon the death of Mr. Barret in 1890, his sons, John H. and James R., and son-in-law, James E. Rankin, continued the business—in which they had been interested—under the old firm name of John H. Barret & Co., the subject of this sketch taking the place of his father as senior member of the firm.

Peter Straghan Barret, farmer, and his wife, Matilda (Wilson) Barret (grandparents of John H. Barret, Jr.) were natives of Louisa County, Virginia. John Barret, his paternal great-grandfather, and Henry Pendleton, his maternal great-grandfather, were born, lived and died in Virginia.

Susan D. Rankin Barret (mother) was a daughter of Dr. Adam Rankin, an eminent physician of Henderson, whose first wife was Elizabeth Speed, daughter of Captain James Speed and Mary Spencer. She was born in Virginia, February 7, 1774, came to Kentucky in 1782, and from that date until she was grown her life was spent amid the trials, dangers and privations incident to early Kentucky history. She was married to Dr. Adam Rankin, one of the pioneers of Henderson, to which place they went soon after their marriage, and his name is connected with the earliest events of that place. For many years he was prominent as a physician and public-spirited citizen, and no man stood higher in the estimation of his fellow men. The distinguished naturalist, Audubon, made his home with Dr. Rankin while he was sojourning in Henderson, and these two were personal friends.

An interesting sketch of the Speed family, of which Mr. Barret is a descendant, will be found elsewhere in this work.

John H. Barret, the principal subject of this sketch, attended the Henderson schools; was prepared for college in the celebrated school of B. B. Sayre at Frankfort, and graduated from the University of Virginia at Charlottesville in 1861. From that time he was associated in business with his father until the death of the latter in

1890, when he became senior member of the firm, as before stated.

The great tobacco stemmery was established about 1830 and has grown considerably during the sixty years of its existence. The present building covers an area of 230x60 feet, is four stories high, and its average annual output is 800 hogsheads, and this, together with the product of the branch houses, goes to the markets in the United Kingdom of Great Britain.

Mr. Barret is also president of the Henderson Woolen Mills, manufacturer of Kentucky jeans and jeans pants, a stockholder and director in the Henderson Cotton Mills; director in the Henderson National Bank, and the Ohio Valley Bank and Trust Company, and has interests in other enterprises of more or less magnitude. His business relations are virtually the same as were those of his father, and his reputation as a business man and citizen is, that of a worthy successor to his honored father.

Mr. Barret was married September 15, 1863, to Henrietta Offutt, a member of the distinguished family of that name of Shelby County. He has two children, Mary, wife of Dr. James W. Heddins of St. Joseph, Missouri, and Augusta, who is at home with her father, Mrs. Barret having died June 27, 1895.

DR. JAMES P. WILLIAMS, one of the leading dental surgeons of western Kentucky and prominent citizen of Henderson, was born in Winchester, Tennessee, January 18, 1865; son of James C. and Cynthia (Vaughan) Williams. His father was born in Virginia in 1821, and some years later removed with his family to Franklin County, Tennessee, where he became a farmer, and in 1846 married Cynthia Vaughan, and they had twelve children: Fulton, Indiana, Rufus, Martin, Marie, Jasper, Thomas, Mollie, Jennie, Jeremiah, Josiah and Cynthia. The father is still living in Tennessee, but the mother died in February, 1895.

Joshua Williams (grandfather) was a native of Jackson County, Alabama, who removed to Virginia and later to Tennessee.

Dr. James P. Williams, the subject of this sketch, received his education in Winchester, principally at the normal school, in which he received a very high rating in 1885. He then attended Vanderbilt University, and was graduated from the dental department in 1888.

He located in Owensboro, and was for six years associated with Dr. Armendt, a well-known dentist of that city, but removed to Henderson in 1884, where he has established himself in a lucrative business and in the confidence of the people, receiving a liberal share of their patronage. He is a member of the Cumberland Presbyterian Church and is active and enthusiastic in the work of the church.

GEORGE ALEXANDER LEWIS, editor and proprietor of the Roundabout of Frankfort, was born in that city, June 24, 1846, and is a son of George Wythe and Mary J. (Todd) Lewis. George W. Lewis was a native of Spottsylvania County, Virginia, and removed with his parents to Kentucky when fifteen years of age. He began life as a dry-goods clerk, but later became connected with the Frankfort Commonwealth in the capacity of bookkeeper and business manager, frequently contributing to the columns of his paper; in 1864 he removed to Lexington and, associated with his eldest son, J. B. Lewis, commenced the publication of the Nation and Unionist, of which he was editor. Although a Southern man by birth and education, he was a strong supporter of the Union during the Civil war, and his paper was the first in the state to advocate the re-election of Abraham Lincoln. Mr. Lewis was a man of strong convictions and firmness of character; he died July 19, 1865. He was a son of John and Jean Wood (Daniel) Lewis.

Mary J. (Todd) Lewis is an eminently pious woman, a constant worker in the Presbyterian Church, of which she became a member when she was a child. She was born and reared in Frankfort, where at the age of seventy-six she still resides. Her parents, George and Mary Ellis (Montague) Todd, were Virginians by birth and died when she was a child, and she was raised by an elder sister. Col. Zachary Lewis (great-grandfather) of Bel-Air, Spottsylvania County, Virginia, was an officer in the Colonial army during the French and Indian war, a messmate of

General Washington at Fort Cumberland, and was presented a sword by the latter, which is still in possession of the family. Col. Lewis afterward served in the Revolutionary army. His son John was an eminent educator in Virginia and Kentucky, and served as a captain of cavalry in Virginia during the War of 1812. From him such men as the late Governor and United States Senator John W. Stevenson, the eminent lawyer, Alexander Holladay of Virginia, Rev. Cadwallader Lewis, LL.D., and numerous others received the bulk of their education. His wife, Jean Wood Lewis, was a sister of Judge Peter V. Daniel of the Supreme Court of the United States.

George A. Lewis was educated in the best private schools of Frankfort, but left the school room early to begin the battle of life. In 1859 he was appointed a page in the house of representatives of the Kentucky legislature, which position he held during the sessions of 1859-60, '61-62, '63-64. During the session of 1861-62, one of his associates was Hon. W. O. Bradley, present governor of Kentucky, who served in a like capacity.

From 1853 Mr. Lewis has been a citizen of Frankfort, excepting one year spent in Lexington and a few months spent in Ohio County, where he had charge of the office of the Hartford Herald. For eighteen years he has been in business just across the street from where he was born. For twelve years he worked at the case as a compositor, but in June, 1878, established the Roundabout printing establishment, and from a small beginning of one boy and himself as the working force has built it up until now three papers, one daily and two weeklies, and a semi-monthly law magazine are issued from this plant. In July, 1880, he established the Kentucky Law Reporter, the only law magazine published in Kentucky. It has grown to be indispensable to every lawyer in full practice in the state.

Mr. Lewis was never in the war, but participated in two skirmishes with Morgan's raiders near Frankfort in June, 1864. He has served as commissioner of the Institution for Education of Feeble Minded Children, which he now holds by appointment by Governor Bradley. In November, 1893, he was elected member of the board of councilmen and served three months as president of that body. In March, 1892, Mr. Lewis made the race for the legislature to fill a vacancy, and with a normal Democratic majority of 800 to 1,000 he was only defeated by 222. He is one of the original incorporators of the Masonic Temple Company, and at present is a member of the board of directors; joined the Masonic order in 1870; has been a very active member, and for twelve years has served as master of Hiram lodge No. 4, one of the oldest lodges in the state; passed all the chairs in the lodge, Chapter, Council and Commandery. In 1891 was grand master of Grand Council of Kentucky, and at present is grand sword bearer of the Grand Commandery of the state; also past grand councilor of Kentucky Royal Templars of Temperance and past supreme herald of the United States in the same order.

Mr. Lewis was raised a Presbyterian, his father having for many years been presiding elder of that church. He is a Republican, casting his first ballot for General Grant.

February 17, 1874, he was married to Alice Giltner, daughter of Henry Giltner and Caroline (Cromwell) Giltner, and has no children.

He is the editor and publisher of the Frankfort Roundabout, a local and society paper, the oldest published in this city, also publisher of the Kentucky Law Reporter, and is one of the worthy citizens of Frankfort; industrious, against fraud and sham of all kinds, and is always found on the side of morality and justice.

JOHN WILLIAM GREENE of Owen County, circuit judge of the Fifteenth Judicial District of Kentucky, son of Jesse L. Greene and Caroline Cannon, was born in Grant County, Kentucky, August 8, 1842; was educated in the common schools of Owen, Grant and Kenton Counties and quit school at the age of twenty to enter the Confederate army; joined Company E, Fifth Regiment Kentucky Infantry in September, 1862, and served until the close of the war. He took part in many of the famous battles of that war, including Chickamauga, Missionary Ridge and every engagement of that campaign until the fall of Atlanta, and lost a limb in the battle of Jonesborough. He entered the army as a private, was elected second sergeant; promoted to orderly sergeant; elected second lieutenant and promoted to first lieutenant; and continued in service after losing a limb until the final surrender. He remained in Perry County, Alabama, and taught school for one term; returned to Owen County in the fall of 1865 and taught school; was elected sheriff of Owen County, August, 1866, and re-elected 1868; serving four years in all, and, having studied law previously, was admitted to the Owen County bar in 1871 and began the practice of his profession alone; became associated with William Lindsay in 1874, and was a member of the law firm of Greene & Lindsay for several years; was elected county judge in 1878 and served four years; was appointed member of the State Board of Equalization by Governor Buckner in 1889; was re-appointed and commissioned in 1891, but resigned and was elected to his present office as judge of the Circuit Court of the Fifteenth Judicial District in 1892. Considering the demands of a very extensive law practice when not on the bench, it is evident that Judge Greene has been a very busy man, and his neighbors say he was a brave and fearless soldier, a most efficient civil officer, a distinguished lawyer, an able and upright judge, and has made his own way in the world; starting amid humble surroundings, he has reached an enviable prominence in the legal profession and is highly esteemed by the members of the bar. He is a member of the Baptist Church and of the Odd Fellows fraternity. Having been frequently elected to office in Owen County, it is not necessary to add that he is a Democrat in good standing.

Judge Greene was married (first) in December, 1870, to Margaret M. Gaines, who was born in Henry County and died February 22, 1882. She was the mother of Frank C. Greene.

He was married (second) in October, 1884, to Mrs. Ada Williams, whose maiden name was Howard; a native of Gallatin County, whose first husband was Taylor Williams. There are three children by this last marital union: Maggie E., Anna May and John Howard Greene.

James L. Greene, father of Judge Greene, was born in Grant County, Kentucky, in 1819, and died August, 1893. He was educated in the schools of his native county, removed to Owen County in 1848, or about that time, and was principally engaged in farming, serving a time as a magistrate; was a member of the Missionary Baptist Church and a prominent Mason; was married in 1840 to Caroline Cannon, who was born in Grant County in 1819, and their children's names were: Emily C., John W. (subject), James S., Elijah L., R. C. Greene, Sallie, Mary, Owen Breckenridge, Willard, Jesse and Carrie.

Robert Greene (grandfather) was a native of Culpeper County, Virginia, and he and his brother William Greene came to Grant County, Kentucky; William was a teacher and Robert A. a pioneer farmer. He married Sallie Ford, a native of Kentucky; their children were: John F., William P., Jesse L. (father), James F., Elijah J. and Francis. Robert Greene died in Grant County in 1859.

John Greene (great-grandfather), a native of Virginia, came to Kentucky with his sons, William and Robert, and died in Grant County.

John Cannon (maternal grandfather) was born in Lexington, Kentucky, and was educated in the common schools of his day and removed to Grant County early in life and subsequently to Owen County, where he was a farmer and justice of the peace; was married about 1816 to Julia Wornon, who was born in Culpeper County, Virginia, and came to Kentucky with her parents. Their children were: Sallie, Caroline and William.

HARRY BLANTON BECK, Circuit Clerk of Owen County, Kentucky, son of David E. and Colie (Blanton) Beck, was born in Owen County, May 8, 1853.

He was educated in the schools of Owen County; left school when he was fifteen years of age and went to Montana Territory, where he was engaged in stock-raising for six years. After this he went to Dakota and became a miner. But when his step-father died in 1876 he returned to Kentucky and located in Bath County, where he engaged in a general merchandise business for four years. He then went to Owenton and engaged in merchandising until 1892, when he was elected to his present position as circuit clerk of Owen County. At the state convention in June, 1895, he was appointed a member of the State Democratic Central Committee from the Ashland District. He is an Odd Fellow and a Master Mason.

Mr. Beck was married May 8, 1878, to Annie Duncan of Carlisle, Nicholas County, Kentucky, daughter of C. H. B. Duncan of Louisville and Zilla (Carter) Duncan, a native of Nicholas County. Mrs. Beck was born in Paris, Kentucky, and educated in private schools at Frankfort, Kentucky. She was a member of the Christian Church. They had three children: Nannie Coleman, Ethel and Herndon Blanton (deceased). Mrs. Beck died January 26, 1888.

Dr. David E. Beck (father) was born in Wheeling, West Virginia, October, 1824, and was educated at Fairfield, Iowa. He graduated from a Philadelphia medical college, and began to practice medicine first at Fairfield, Iowa. In 1849 he left Iowa and settled in New Liberty, Kentucky, where he continued to practice his chosen profession until his death, May 13, 1858. He was a Democrat in politics and an Odd Fellow; married Colie Blanton in 1850. She was educated at New Liberty, Owen County, Kentucky, and was a member of the Missionary Baptist Church. They had four children: James, Harry B., Susan and a daughter who died in infancy.

James Beck (grandfather) was born in Ireland and immigrated to Wheeling, West Virginia. He had one son, John, by his first wife. His second wife was Sarah Evans, a native of Virginia, and by this marriage he had four children: William G., James Schriver, David Evans and Richard Simeon.

James Beck, Sr., died in Pennsylvania, and after the death of her husband Mrs. Beck kept a hotel in Wheeling, West Virginia, and Abraham Lincoln was for many years her boarder. She came to Kentucky when very old to end her days with her son. Here, of course, strong sentiment existed against Lincoln, and whenever such sentiments were expressed in the presence of Mrs. Beck she would indignantly defend her favorite boarder.

Henry Blanton (maternal grandfather) was a native of Kentucky, and for fifty years a merchant at New Liberty, Kentucky. Before the war he was a large slave owner. His brother, William Blanton, was a devout pioneer Baptist preacher.

Henry Blanton was originally a Whig and then a Democrat, and, like his brother in the ministry, a Baptist. He married (first) his cousin, Susan Blanton, a native of Virginia. His second wife was Mrs. Sarah Craig, nee Green, a native of Virginia, who was known far and wide for her strong religious convictions. By his first marriage he had five children: Bettie Ware, Susan Sneed, Dr. Carter, Margaret Coleman and Dr. William H. Blanton. Dr. Carter Blanton died at Hickman, Kentucky, while attending the yellow fever sufferers in 1878.

CHARLES LOUIS RAISON, JR., a resident of Newport and a prominent attorney-at-law, practicing in Cincinnati and also in Newport, was born in Greenup, Kentucky, October 29, 1849. He is a son of Charles Louis Raison and Amanda K. Corum, natives of Greenup County. His father was educated for the legal profession and was admitted to the bar, but having a preference for mercantile life, did not engage in the practice of law, but was for many years a successful merchant and prominent citizen of Greenup; but removed to Ashland, where he also engaged in mercantile pursuits, taking a lively interest in politics, and was elected county judge of Boyd County and was subsequently elected mayor of the city of Ashland. A Republican of strong convictions and a man of unusual force of character, he was a leader in his party and a man of affairs in the communities in which he lived. He was born in Greenup in 1823 and died in Ashland in 1887.

Mr. Raison's family history is one of unusual interest, showing his relation to the nobility of France for many centuries. His great-grandfather's name was Louis Modesta Raison de la Geneste, who married Lady Marie Thereza Langier. At his death his wife survived him with two children, Louis Raison de la Geneste (grandfather), and Lady Marie Thereza Clotilda Raison de la Geneste. His widow married Philip Ridore, a planter and owner of large estates in the Island of San Domingo. At the time of the insurrection of the negroes and massacre of the white inhabitants of the Island of San Domingo, Louis Raison de la Geneste (grandfather) was the owner of a large estate and many slaves. He and his sister escaped from the island and came to America. He came to Greenup County, Kentucky, where he lived and died. He married Avemathea Young, daughter of John Young, who was a native of Virginia, a man of large means, of high social standing and an officer in the Revolutionary war.

Lady Marie Louise Victoria Antoinette Raison de la Geneste, sister of Louis Modesta Raison de la Geneste, married Pierre Antoine Fontaine de Chaussenell, and they came to America and located in New Orleans, where they lived and died, and where many of their descendants now reside.

Louis Raison de la Geneste (grandfather) was an educated French nobleman, and the family is one of the oldest and strongest of the French nobility. The title is a matter of public record in France, and can be traced for many hundred years, showing that many of the ancestors were military men of renown. It has its coat-of-arms and crest and a history showing the title of the family for centuries. Notwithstanding this, Charles Louis Raison, the subject of this sketch, is thoroughly American. He never uses his title, preferring to be known simply as an American.

The parents of Amanda K. Corum (mother) came to Kentucky from North Carolina, in which state many of her relatives now reside. She is now living with her son in Newport.

Charles Louis Raison, following the example of his ancestors, was carefully and thoroughly educated under the helpful direction and assistance of his talented father, and after leaving school at the age of seventeen, was employed as bookkeeper for the Eastern Kentucky Railway Company in Greenup County, and was engaged in different capacities with various companies in the iron business in that section until 1873, and there began the study of law under D. K. Weis. He then took the law course in the University of Michigan, at Ann Arbor, and returning to Kentucky, was admitted to the bar in Carter County in 1875. He practiced in partnership with Hon. B. F. Bennett of Greenup until 1878, when he removed to Cincinnati and engaged in the practice of law in that city, taking up his residence, however, in Newport, preferring a home in his native state while doing business in the larger city across the river. His success was gratifying and encouraging from the start, and he soon found his proper place among the leading lawyers of the Ohio metropolis. In 1888 he formed a partnership with George H. Ahlering, the firm being known as Raison & Ahlering; and as they are residents of Newport, deeply interested in the welfare of that city, and prominent in all matters looking to its general growth and progress, they have an office in Newport as well as in Cincinnati, and receive a liberal share of the legal business of Campbell and adjacent counties.

Mr. Raison is a Republican, and while averse to holding office, being independent of the public crib, he takes the part of a good citizen in the selection of men and the adoption of measures looking to the improvement of the public service.

He was married in 1879 to Georgiana Wrightson, daughter of Hon. Thomas Wrightson, ex-state senator from Campbell County. They have two children living: Lizzie and Thomas Raison.

STANTON HUME THORPE, Clerk of the Madison Circuit Court, Richmond, son of Stanton Hume Thorpe and Sallie Wallace (Miller) Thorpe, was born on a farm in the eastern portion of Madison County, Kentucky, December 10, 1864.

His father was born in the same vicinity in 1832 and has been a resident of the county all his life, principally engaged in farming, and leading a quiet and unostentatious life; was assessor of the county for one term, but has not taken an active part in politics.

Thomas Thorpe (grandfather) was born, lived and died in Madison County, Kentucky, having reached the good old age of eighty-three years.

Zachariah Thorpe (great-grandfather) was one of the first settlers of Madison County, where he pre-empted land and became a prosperous farmer.

Sallie Wallace Miller Thorpe (mother) was born in Madison County, Kentucky, in 1837, and is now in her fifty-ninth year. Her father, Christopher J. Miller, was a native of the same county, was an industrious blacksmith and farmer of his native county. His father, Daniel Miller, was one of the very early settlers of that county.

Stanton Hume Thorpe, Jr., received his education in the public schools of the county, remaining on his father's farm until he was eighteen years of age, when he accepted a position as deputy circuit clerk in Richmond under his uncle, William H. Miller, and was thus employed for seven years. In 1892 he made the race for the clerkship and was elected clerk of the Circuit Court, of which he took charge January 1, 1893. He had performed the duties of the office for so many years that he was entirely familiar with every detail and fully qualified for his responsible position.

Mr. Thorpe is a modest young man of accommodating disposition, very popular with the members of the bar, efficient in the performance of his duties and enjoys the esteem of the people of his county, with whose interests he is fully identified. He is a member of the best society of Richmond, belongs to the fraternities of Masons and Odd Fellows, and is a consistent member of the Missionary Baptist Church.

He was married in August, 1886, to Henrietta R. Rayborn, daughter of Milton L. Rayborn of Madison County, and they have one son, Cecil Thorpe.

CHARLES H. ALEXANDER, D. D. S., leading dentist of Middlesborough, Kentucky, son of Cummins G. Alexander and M. Morrison, was born in Speedwell, Tennessee, August 15, 1863.

His father was born in Lebanon, Virginia, in 1829, and when a child went to Claiborne County, Tennessee, with his father; was a resident and farmer of that county until 1879, when he removed to Fincastle, Campbell County, Tennessee, where he is living at the present time. During the war between the sections, he sympathized with the South, but did not bear arms except as a member of the Home Guards, which was an important branch of the service in his section. Mr. Alexander has devoted his life to agricultural pursuits with commendable industry and excellent success. He is a man of fine traits of character, an exemplary Christian and a member of the Methodist Episcopal Church, South.

David Alexander (grandfather), a native of Ireland, came to this country with his father when five years of age; removed to Claiborne County, Tennessee, in the early '30's, where he was a farmer, and died in 1844. His father was a native of Ireland, who immigrated to Virginia in the early years of the present century.

Mary Morrison Alexander (mother) was a native of Hawkins County, Tennessee, and died in Claiborne County in that state in 1870. She was a member of the Methodist Episcopal Church, South, and was known and loved for her good works and many deeds of kindness.

Peter Morrison (maternal grandfather) was born and raised in Sullivan County, and was a tanner in Hawkins County, Tennessee.

Dr. Charles H. Alexander attended the county schools in Claiborne County. He was fifteen years of age when his father removed to Fincastle, where he attended the High School and afterwards finished his literary studies in Hiawassa College, near Sweetwater, Tennessee, always paying his own way. He was employed as a clerk in a Knoxville business house for two years before going to Nashville in 1886 to take a course in dentistry in State University of Tennessee, from which he was graduated in 1889.

He began his professional work as a traveling dentist, with headquarters at Jelico, Tennessee, in 1889, and remained there about a year, when he located permanently in Middlesborough, Kentucky, in December, 1889. He came to that city in the height of its prosperity, and did not desert it when reverses came. His confidence in the future of the city has not been misplaced, for the tide has turned and the city of Middlesborough offers greater and more substantial advantages for residence and business than ever before in its history. In 1896 Dr. Alexander took a postgraduate course in the American College of Dental Surgery in Chicago.

Dr. Alexander's preparation for the delicate work of his profession was very thorough and scientific. His work has been of the highest order, and of a character that commends him to the public. His patronage has come from the best people of the community, and he has established himself in the confidence of the entire neighboring public. It is no fulsome praise to say that Dr. Alexander is the most skillful and scientific dental surgeon in all that section of the country.

He stands well in polite circles, is a thirty-second degree Mason, a member of the Maccabees, a Knight of Pythias and a member of the Methodist Episcopal Church South.

JOHN D. COLLINS, M. D., a prominent physician of Covington, was born in Winchester, Clark County, Kentucky, July 11, 1823. His father, Dr. Orville Collins, was born in Clark County, near Winchester, in 1797, and was a resident and practicing physician of Winchester for fifty years, retiring some years prior to his death in 1880. He was an active member of the Christian Church, and during his latter years often preached the gospel. Being a man of strong convictions and great firmness of purpose, he was naturally a leader and a man of wide influence.

Dillard Collins (grandfather) was a native of Virginia, of Scotch-Irish parentage, who came to Kentucky and located in Clark County, within a mile of Winchester. He was colonel of a regiment in the War of 1812 and died when young.

Mary Christie Collins (mother) was born in Clark County, four miles from Winchester, in 1799, and died in 1859. She was a lady of unusual intelligence and refinement and was a beloved member of the Christian Church.

John Christie (grandfather) was a Virginian and an early settler and prosperous farmer of Clark County, a soldier in the War of 1812, after which he was known as Colonel Christie. Highly educated and exceedingly courteous in manner, he was a very popular man, in fact, a true Kentucky gentleman.

John D. Collins attended the schools of Winchester until twelve years of age, when he went to Hopkinsville and received a classical education in the seminary in that place. He read medicine with his father; graduated from the Missouri Medical College at St. Louis, March, 1845, and subsequently took a course in the Eclectic Medical Institute at Cincinnati, Ohio, graduating in 1853. He began the practice of medicine in 1845 at Madisonville and was one of the leading physicians in that section at the beginning of the Civil war, when he entered the Confederate army as a surgeon, and served in that capacity until the war was ended. In 1865 he located at Henderson and was engaged in the line of his profession in that city until 1881, when he removed to Covington and was for several years a general practitioner, but for the past several years has devoted his time and attention especially to the treatment of diseases of women. He is a member of the Kentucky State Medical Society; is prominent and active in the Christian Church, in which he is a communicant, and as a citizen enjoys the esteem of the best people of Newport.

Dr. Collins has been twice married; first in 1845 to Elvira Hatchett, daughter of Captain John A. Hatchett of Henderson. She died in 1866, leaving three daughters, two of whom are living: Lela, wife of J. D. Gunn of Tennessee, and Rosalie A. Collins, who is now and has been for twelve years past a teacher in the high school of Evansville, Indiana. He was married (second) in October, 1879, to Sallie McMillan of Mays Lick, Kentucky.

JOHN ROWAN ADAMS, Circuit Clerk of Oldham County, son of Allen Adams and Susan (Vance) Adams, was born in Oldham County, Kentucky, in 1848. He was educated in the common schools of the county and in Georgetown College. Leaving school in 1863, he taught for several years in Henry and Oldham Counties, and then engaged in farming and trading, selling his stock in the markets between Louisville and New York.

He was enterprising and successful as a trader; was elected sheriff of Oldham County in 1879 and re-elected in 1883. In 1886 he was elected county and circuit clerk, and discharged these offices so efficiently that he was re-elected in 1890. He is a Knight Templar in Masonry and a Knight of Honor, and was master of Lodges Nos. 156 and 47, F. & A. M., for twelve years.

Allen Adams (father) was born in Jefferson County, Kentucky, and educated in the common schools of that county. When Oldham County was formed in 1824 from parts of Jefferson, Shelby and Henry Counties the Adams farm was transferred to the new county, and there Mr. Adams engaged in general farming; was first a Whig and afterwards a Democrat in politics, and was a member of the Presbyterian Church. He married (first) Susan Vance, a native of Jefferson County, and she was the mother of four children, who survived her: Robert F., James A., John R., and Mary Agnes, wife of Dr. Alonzo Morrison, all of whom are living in Oldham County.

He married (second) Mrs. Thornton, nee Augusta Taliaferro, a native of Oldham County, and by this marriage there were five children: Mayo, Coleman C. and Richard (twins), Thornton and Sue.

Frank Adams (grandfather) was a native of Pennsylvania and came to Jefferson County, Kentucky, where he was a farmer.

Robert Vance (maternal grandfather) was born in Virginia and came to Jefferson County and married Nancy Adams.

OTIS SETH TENNEY, LL. D., one of the most accomplished and influential members of the Lexington bar, a practitioner in doubtful and intricate cases and thoroughly familiar with interstate and national laws, a native of New Hampshire, graduate of Norwich University, Northfield, Vermont, taking the degree of A. B. in 1845, A. M. in 1847, and LL. D. in 1889, has been a resident of the Blue Grass State since 1847, and has been practicing law in Lexington for ten years. His ancestry, taken from a volume devoted entirely to the genealogy, history and biographies of the Tenney family, is briefly given as follows:

Thomas Tenney, a member of the Reverend Ezekial Rogers' company from Yorkshire, England, arrived at Salem, Massachusetts, in 1638, and settled at Rowley, Massachusetts, in April, 1639. This Thomas Tenney was the great-great-great-great-great-grandfather of the subject of this sketch. Of his children, Deacon John Tenney (great-great-great-great-grandfather), born December 14, 1640, was the next descendant. He married (first) Mercy Parrat, born July 23, 1646; married (second) Susanna Woodbury, born February 16, 1648. Deacon John Tenney died April 13, 1722.

His son, Deacon Samuel Tenney (great-great-great-grandfather), was born November 20, 1667; married (first) Abigail Bailey, daughter of Deacon Joseph Bailey; married (second) Sarah Boynton, daughter of Captain Joseph Boynton and Sarah Swan Boynton; was a lieutenant in the Continental army; member of the Colonial Assembly in 1725, when, fifty years before the Declaration of Independence, he was one of thirty who voted against receiving the King's Charter, "a step more bold than that of the fifty-six signers of 1776." He died February 3, 1747, in his eighty-first year.

Joseph Tenney (great-great-grandfather) was born in Bradford (now Groveland), Massachusetts, March 16, 1698; married Abigail (Annie) Wood, daughter of John and Elizabeth Wood, February 14, 1722; members of the Congregational Church; removed to Norwich, Connecticut, in 1723, and afterwards to Woodbury, Connecticut, and died April 20, 1775.

John Tenney (great-grandfather) was born in Norwich, Connecticut, September 2, 1729; married Olive Armstrong, March 11, 1755; resided at Hanover, New Hampshire, where he arrived with an ox-team June, 1770. Mrs. Tenney died April 18, 1806, and John Tenney died February 19, 1810.

David Tenney (grandfather) was born in Norwich, Connecticut, May 15, 1759; married (first) Susanna Durkee, who was born November 7, 1765, and died February 11, 1788; married (second) April 9, 1789, Anna Jacobs, who was born August 23, 1765, and died May 8, 1813; married (third) Mrs. Priscilla (Smith) Dole. He was a soldier and pensioner of the Revolutionary War; died March 14, 1851. He raised thirteen children, ten of whom were living at his death, and at that time had eighty-nine descendants.

Captain Seth Tenney, father of Major O. S. Tenney, son of David and Anna Jacobs, was born in Hanover, New Hampshire, October 8, 1792; was married in Lyme, New Hampshire, December 31, 1818, to Esther Miller, who was born in Lyme, November 17, 1794, and died May 4, 1882. "Residence, Hanover; a farmer and Captain in

State Militia; served at Portsmouth, New Hampshire, in the War of 1812; died October 16, 1869." "He was a man and officer worthy of the name."

The children of Captain Seth Tenney and Esther Miller, his wife, were: Infant, born December 22, 1819, lived only a few days; Benjamin M., born June 14, 1821, died April 24, 1857; Otis Seth (subject), born December 4, 1822; Samuel Claflin, born February 27, 1825, farmer of London, Ohio; Esther Angeline, born December 12, 1826; Mary Marinda, born April 18, 1829, residence at Etna, New Hampshire; Charles Carroll, born November 22, 1831; David Culver, born December 28, 1834.

Major Otis Seth Tenney was born December 4, 1822, in Windsor County, Hanover Township, New Hampshire. His father was a Captain in the Continental Army during the War of the Revolution and carried a very handsome sword, which was brought to Kentucky by his son, from whom it was captured during the Civil War. Major Tenney received his education in the common schools of New England until the age of thirteen, then prepared for college at Norwich Institute, New Hampshire, and graduated at the Military University, at Norwich, in 1845.

After leaving college he began teaching a military school at Wilmington, Delaware, but removed to Kentucky shortly afterwards and established a school of the same kind at Mt. Sterling, at Old Fort Mason. In 1847 he commenced the study of law with Colonel Walter Chiles of Mt. Sterling, and in March, 1849, was admitted to the bar and began the practice of his profession in that place and continued without interruption until October, 1862, when he enlisted as a private in the Confederate army, but soon became Major of the Second Kentucky Cavalry, serving in that capacity until the close of the war when he returned to Kentucky and was paroled at Lexington.

Soon after his return from war he attempted to resume practice, but was not permitted to do so by the presiding judge, except by courtesy shown to a non-resident lawyer, it being decided that he was not a citizen according to the Expatriation Act passed by the Legislature in 1861-62. He appealed to the higher court at Frankfort and Judge Robertson rendered a decision (2 Duvall, Ky. Rep., p. 351) by which not only he but other ex-Confederate soldiers were allowed to practice at the bar. He continued his residence at Mt. Sterling, actively and successfully engaged in his profession, and in 1868 was a candidate for Circuit Judge of his district, and again in 1874, but was defeated by small majorities.

He removed to Lexington in 1882, and is now a distinguished member of the bar of that city, and is not only one of the first lawyers in Central Kentucky, but one of the most active and enterprising men in the community.

Major Tenney was married May 18, 1848, to Junia M. Warner, daughter of James Warner of Delaware, who is connected with some of the most distinguished families of the East. She was born September 29, 1820.

Their children, only two of whom are now living, were: Otis Seth, born February 20, 1849, died in infancy; Harriet H., born September 19, 1850, died July 25, 1854; Robert P., born December 2, 1852, died July 22, 1854; Lilian H., born July 17, 1855, married Joseph B. Russell of Cambridge, Massachusetts, May 20, 1880. Her husband is a brother of ex-Gov. W. E. Russell; Anna M., born April 6, 1857, married W. W. Hamilton of Mt. Sterling, February 5, 1878; Harriet H., died November 26, 1863.

JAMES GARRARD was born on the 14th of January, 1749, in the County of Stafford, in the (then) Colony of Virginia. At a very early period in the Revolutionary struggle, he engaged in the public service, and in the capacity of a militia officer, shared in the dangers and honors of that memorable war. While in service, he was called by the voice of his fellow-citizens to a seat in the Virginia Legislature, where he contributed, by his zeal and prudence, as much, or perhaps more than any other individual, to the passage of the famous act securing universal religious liberty.

He was an early emigrant to Kentucky, and was exposed to the perils and dangers incident to the settlement and occupation of the country. He was repeatedly called by the voice of his fellow-citizens to represent their interests in the Legislature of the state; and finally, by two successive elections, was elected to the chief magistracy of the commonwealth, a trust which, for eight years, he discharged with wisdom, prudence and vigor.

As a man, Governor Garrard had few equals; and in the various scenes and different stations of life, he acted with firmness, prudence and decision. At an early age, he embraced and professed the religion of Christ, giving it, through life, the preference over all sublunary things. In the private circle he was a man of great practical usefulness, and discharged with fidelity and tenderness the social and relative duties of husband, parent, neighbor and master. He died on the 19th of January, 1822, at his residence, Mount Lebanon, in Bourbon County, in the seventy-fourth year of his age.

COLONEL CURRAN POPE, son of Hon. Worden Pope, was born at Louisville, Ky.; graduated at West Point; promoted to brevet Second Lieutenant of Second United States Artillery, July, 1834, but resigned December, 1834; assistant engineer improvement of Kentucky and Cumberland Rivers, 1835; clerk of Jefferson County Court for seventeen years; Colonel Fifteenth Kentucky Regiment United States Infantry during Civil War; wounded at battle of Perryville, October 8, and died therefrom November 5, 1862.

COLONEL WM. B. ALLEN was born near Greensburg, Kentucky, May 19, 1803; educated in the celebrated schools of Rev. John How of Greensburg, and of Dr. Jas. Priestly of Nashville, Tennessee; taught school awhile; studied law with Samuel Brents, and began the practice before he was twenty-one; postmaster at Greensburg, 1823-28; Representative in Kentucky Legislature 1829, and made a speech in favor of a system of common schools; attorney Greensburg branch of Bank of the Commonwealth, 1829; an editor, 1834; clerk Greensburg branch of Bank of Kentucky, 1835-37, and cashier of same, 1837-57; master in chancery for Green County, 1843-45; resumed practice of law, 1858; compiled "The Kentucky Officer's Guide," 400 pp., 8 vo., 1859; county attorney, 1862-70; again master in chancery, 1866-70; was for many years Colonel Sixteenth Kentucky Militia; and for nearly fifty years has been one of the most active and prominent members and officers of the Masonic order in the state. But the crowning act of a long and useful life is his "History of Kentucky," issued November, 1872, 449 pp., 8 vo.

GOV. WILLIAM OWSLEY, born in Virginia in 1782, was the son of William Owsley and Catherine Bolin, whose sons were Samuel, Nudigate, William, who became Governor of Kentucky; Dr. Joel, Thomas and Major Jonathan. The daughters were Ann Middleton, Margaret Bayne, Mary Pearl, Patience and Chloe. Governor William Owsley became the most distinguished of this large family, and the fourteenth Governor of the commonwealth. He was one of those men who rose to distinction through energy and perseverance. His father was a man in moderate circumstances and of some political influence. Young Owsley was ambitious, energetic and industrious, and allowed no obstacle to deter him from accomplishing an object when once he made up his mind to that end. This energy and industry carried him from the humble position of a deputy surveyor to the Supreme Bench, and to the Chief Executive of the state. Judge Owsley was born in 1782, in Virginia. His father, also named William Owsley, emigrated to Kentucky in 1783, when his son was an infant but a year old. He settled in the vicinity of Crab Orchard, in Lincoln County, where he lived an honored citizen, and finally became High Sheriff of that county. Young William received a good education for the time, better than the majority of the youths. He taught school several terms, then became, under his father's administration, a Deputy Sheriff. It was in this latter position that he attracted the attention of Judge John Boyle, for many years a judge of the Court of Appeals of Kentucky, and its Chief Justice. Judge Boyle conceived a strong interest in the young man, and perceiving that there was something in him if properly developed, encouraged him to study law. He tendered him the use of his library, then one of the most extensive in the state, and the advantage of his own instruction. Young Owsley eagerly grasped the offer, and so studiously did he employ his time that he was admitted to the bar and commenced the practice of law in Garrard County. His success was assured from the start, and he soon attained to the highest rank as a lawyer. He became the warm, personal friend of Judge Boyle, and their friendship remained unbroken through life. Judge Owsley served several terms in the Legislature, in the Lower House in 1809-11 and '31, and in the Senate in 1832-34, where he distinguished himself as a young statesman of rare promise. In 1812, when then but thirty-one years of age, so highly was his legal ability regarded, that Governor Scott appointed him a Judge of the Court of Appeals. This position, however, he held but a short time, in consequence of the Legislature passing an act reducing the number of judges to three. Owsley being the youngest, both in age and appointment, resigned. But a vacancy occurring in 1813, he was appointed to that august tribunal by Governor Shelby. Judge Boyle had him appointed a Judge of the Court of Appeals some years before, and was now Chief Justice. The other member of the court was Benjamin Mills, a prominent member of the Bourbon County bar. Judge Owsley remained upon the bench until 1828, a longer period than any man in the state up to that time (except Judge Boyle) when he resigned and retired to private life. He finally removed to Frankfort, remaining there until 1843, when he purchased a fine farm in Boyle, upon which he located, giving up his law practice. In 1844 he was elected Governor of Kentucky on the Whig ticket over General William O. Butler, one of the most popular Democrats in the state, by 4,624 majority. As a Governor he devoted his best energies to a faithful discharge of the high and important duties of the office, and upon the expiration of the term he retired to his farm, where the remainder of his life was spent in peaceful retirement. He died in 1862, at the age of eighty years. "In personal appearance Governor Owsley was tall, slender and erect. In his private character he was irreproachable; in manner simple, though somewhat reserved. He held perfect command of his temper at all times, yet never failed to act with promptness and decision in times of emergency."

A member of the Owsley family, Harry Byran Owsley, has gathered together in book form the records of the Owsley family, in which a clear and unbroken record has been established, that "from facts and actual data" one is "enabled to look through the generations of the family back to the time of the Restoration, and, by inference, catch glimpses of its past, to a period much more remote."

THOMAS C. McCREERY, of Owensboro, was born in Kentucky, in 1817; was a student at Center College, Danville, Kentucky; studied law, but turned his attention to agricultural pursuits; was a candidate for presidential elector in 1852, and defeated; but in 1860 was elected, and voted for Breckinridge and Lane; was elected United States Senator February, 1868, as a Democrat, vice James Guthrie, resigned, and served until March 4, 1871, and again elected December 19, 1871, for six years from March 4, 1873 to 1879. He was an elegant, forcible and popular speaker.

REV. CARTER HELM JONES, pastor of McFerran Memorial Baptist Church, of Louisville, was born in Cakley, Nelson County, Virginia, November 30, 1861. His father, so well known to Baptists in general and to Southern people in particular, is Rev. J. William Jones, D. D., at present the chaplain of the University of Virginia, and is perhaps best known as the author of several comprehensive works on the lives of R. E. Lee, Jefferson Davis and others. On his mother's side Mr. Jones is a lineal descendant of Carter Baxton of Virginia, one of the signers of the Declaration of Independence, and otherwise his ancestry embraces many of the most noted names in the history of Virginia. The two institutions at which he studied with marked ability are Richmond College and the Southern Baptist Theological Seminary, at both of which he was fully graduated, being chosen at the former of these institutions as the valedictorian of the literary societies. He afterwards pursued special studies for a year under Prof. Noah K. Davis, at the University of Virginia. Though the general collegiate and the special theological training of Mr. Jones have been most thorough, we are persuaded that the influences which have contributed most powerfully to his usefulness and reputation are not to be sought for in the class room. It is our conviction that the two most powerful factors in a man's life are to be determined in answer to the questions: Who is he? And what were the influences that surrounded him in his early life? In answering these we believe that we shall arrive at the true source of Mr. Jones' power as a preacher and as a man. It has already been said that his family is an illustrious one, and to say that he is the son of his father may seem trite, but it furnishes a clue to the real estimation of his character. What was said concerning another member of the family by one of the faculty of the seminary might be in many other respects applied to him: "The son of your father could not but write well." We are convinced, too, that the apparently paradoxical union of sweetness and force to be found in both the man and his sermons is decidedly traceable, in a large measure, to the influence of his mother.

In answer to the second question we are brought to perceive the great moulding force of his life. The home of his father was the resort not only of Baptist ministers from every section of the country around, but of men whose names have become celebrated in the history of the South. Mr. Jones delights to tell of the times when a child he was brought into contact with such men as Lee, Davis and others. We have dwelt upon these things because of the conviction that it is absolutely inpossible to know a man or understand his power by simply inquiring what churches he has served or what stations he may have occupied. After leaving the University of Virginia, Mr. Jones accepted the pastorate of the First Baptist Church at Elizabeth, New Jersey, and it was there that his really remarkable career began. It was not long before he took a high position among the ministers, not simply of the state of his adoption, but of New York city and state as well, and the honors conferred upon him were distinguishing in the extreme. At one time he preached the sermon before the Baptist State Convention of New Jersey, at another, following O. P. Gifford and Wayland Hoyt, in an address before the Baptist Social Union of New York city. Before long, neighboring churches began to appreciate his abilities and the invitations he received to speak were numerous and complimentary. He, however, preferred to give his best efforts to his own church, which rapidly grew in numbers and efficiency under his preaching.

In 1889, in response to a unanimous call from the First Baptist Church of Knoxville, Tennessee, Mr. Jones removed to that city, and as a slight tribute to his work there, we copy the following from the Knoxville Tribune of April 30 of that year: "The story of Mr. Jones' career as the pastor of the First Baptist Church is a familiar one to the church going people of Knoxville. Since he accepted the pastorate there have been nearly four hundred and fifty names added to the church roll. Every Sunday the large and commodious First Church has been crowded with Baptists, numbers of other denominations and people of no denomination at all, who came there attracted by the power of his oratory and the sympathetic force of his appeal to the human heart. His departure from the city is a distinct loss to the community. He was and is an ideal citizen and one of practical benefit and a graceful ornament to any community. It is with profound regret that the citizens of Knoxville see him go." In 1891 Mr. Jones delivered the sermon before the Southern Baptist Convention at Birmingham, being the youngest man who ever enjoyed that distinction. As a lecturer he has attained considerable reputation, and his addresses on commencement occasions are particularly worthy of notice. In 1892 he preached the baccalaureate sermon at Lake Forest College, and in 1893 he delivered the address before the Y. M. C. A. of Washington and Lee University to one of the most cultured audiences ever assembled in Virginia, in a style entirely worthy of the brilliant occasion. Many of the seminary men will remember his stimulating address before the Broadus Literary Society recently. It is an overwhelming tribute to his popularity in Tennessee that a number of colleges asked him to deliver to them farewell addresses on leaving that state. As a preacher, he possesses unusual magnetism, a wealth of diction rarely equalled and a princely imagination. Perhaps the leading characteristic of his preaching is the stimulus which it imparts to his hearers. One who heard him for the first time recently remarked after service that she felt like she had been to church.

Mr. Jones preaches the Gospel; he is not obliged to resort to sensational subjects. Men instinctively raise their ideals and want to be better after hearing him. A gifted young lady speaking of his preaching recently said that she thought the remark made concerning Ruskin was applicable to him. A friend of Mr. Ruskin declared that whenever she was tempted to think that the meat was more than the life and the raiment more than the body, she read Ruskin. Mr. Jones' preaching elevates and inspires, and the knowledge of the man outside the pulpit serves to emphasize the best impressions he makes. We bespeak for him and wish him a future of ever-increasing usefulness, and we congratulate the McFerran Church and the people of Louisville on securing such a man.—Allyn K. Foster, M. D., in "Seminary Magazine," October, 1893.

JAMES CORBIN NORRIS, M. D., a distinguished and popular homeopathic physician of Augusta, was born September 26, 1859, and is the youngest of the nine children of Daniel and Rebecca (Pinkard) Norris. Daniel Norris was born in Mason County in 1825, and received his education, for the most part, in a high school in Germantown, which was at that time one of the best schools in Mason County. He is an intelligent and prosperous farmer of his native county and takes great delight in his home and is deeply interested in the success of his children. He is a leading member of the Christian Church and is greatly devoted to religious work in connection with that organization. He owned a number of slaves, to all of whom he gave their freedom during the war, in this following the generous example of his father, who freed a number of families of slaves about the time the Civil war began.

James Norris (grandfather), a native of Virginia, was one of the first settlers of Mason County, having landed at the mouth of Limestone more than one hundred years ago. He located at the head waters of the north fork of Licking river and cleared out a thicket in order to cultivate the land. He raised the first crop of tobacco that was ever grown in Mason County and became a prosperous farmer and one of the most exemplary citizens of the county. As above stated, he gave a large number of slaves their freedom at the beginning of the war, a conflict in which he took no part by word or deed. He was a very earnest and devoted member of the church, a faithful Christian and a most neighborly neighbor. His wife was Nancy McGraw, a member of an old family of Virginia, who died in 1866. Mr. Norris survived her until September, 1879, when he died and was buried by her side in the old Baptist Gilgal Church yard.

Dr. Norris' mother, Rebecca Pinkard Norris, was born in Bracken County in 1833. She was married to Mr. Norris in 1853 and died September 30, 1866, and is buried in the Christian Cemetery at Germantown.

Stanfield Corbin Pinkard (grandfather) was one of the most prominent business men of the county, having a large furniture manufactory and a tannery, besides doing an extensive business in buying and shipping tobacco. He was at one time very wealthy, but through security debts he was forced to give up a larger portion of his fortune. He was one of the most popular and best known men in his section of the state. He was a very generous supporter of the Christian Church, of which he was a faithful and consistent member. His wife was Rebecca Harman, a native of Germantown, who died in the month of April, 1880. Both Mr. and Mrs. Pinkard are buried in the Germantown Cemetery.

Dr. James C. Norris was educated in a select school in Augusta, and afterwards attended Bethany College in Virginia for two years, finishing his literary course in that institution in 1879. He taught a district school in Bracken County and then entered the Homeopathic Medical College at Cleveland, Ohio, and after taking a two years' course was graduated in 1884. He then served for two years in Huron Street Homeopathic Hospital as house surgeon, and in 1886 and 1887 he served as assistant physician in the Ohio penitentiary. He then went to Winchester, Kentucky, and practiced medicine in that place for three years and then returned to Augusta, where he has been quite successful and highly popular as a practicing physician. He is a member of the Ohio State Medical Society of Homeopathy and of the Kentucky State Society of Homeopathy, and a member of the city council of Augusta.

JOHN JORDAN CRITTENDEN, in honor of whom this county was named, was born in the county of Woodford, within a few miles of the town of Versailles, on the 10th of September, 1786. He is the son of John Crittenden, a Revolutionary officer, who emigrated to Kentucky soon after the conclusion of the war. He received as good an education as could be obtained in the Kentucky schools of that day, and completed his scholastic studies at Washington academy, in Virginia, and at the College of William and Mary, in the same state. On his return to Kentucky he became a student of law in the office of the honorable George M. Bibb, and under the care of that renowned jurist, he became thoroughly prepared for the practice of his profession. At that period the Green River country was the attractive field for the enterprise of the state, affording to the youth of Kentucky similar inducements to those that the west still continues to offer to the citizens of the older states. Mr. Crittenden commenced the practice of the law in Russellville, in the midst of a host of brilliant competitors. He went there unknown to fame—he left it with a fame as extended as the limits of this great nation. All the honors of his profession were soon his, and while his accurate and thorough knowledge of the law gained for him hosts of clients, his brilliant oratory filled the land with his praise, and the pride of that section of the state demanded that he should serve in the legislative assembly. He was accordingly elected to the Legislature from the county of Logan, in 1811; and that noble county conferred the same honor upon him in six consecutive elections. In 1817, and while a Representative from Logan, he was elected Speaker of the House of Representatives, having thus attained the highest distinction in the popular branch of the Legislature of his native state. That same honest pride which had impelled the Green River people to press him into public life, had spread throughout the state, and the people of Kentucky resolved to place him where the eyes of the nation might be upon him—confident that he would win honor for himself and advance the fame of those he represented. He was accordingly, in 1817, elected a Senator in the Congress of the United States, and although the youngest member of that body, no sooner had occasion presented, when it was meet for him to speak, than by the universal acclaim of the American people, he was hailed as among the foremost of our orators—as a fit colleague for Henry Clay himself—and as one who must take rank with our ablest statesmen. His private affairs requiring his unremitted attention, he withdrew from this theatre where he was winning golden opinions from all, to enter more vigorously upon the practice of his profession. In order that he might be enabled to do this in the most favorable manner, he removed to Frankfort, in 1819, at which place the Federal Court and Supreme Court of the state are held. But here, again, the same popular love and enthusiasm followed him, and he was compelled to yield a reluctant assent to the wishes of his friends, who desired him to serve them in the Legislature. He was elected from Franklin in 1825 —a period memorable in the history of Kentucky. In the Old and New Court controversy, no man occupied a more conspicuous point that Mr. Crittenden, and as the advocate of the laws and Constitution of Kentucky, and in the maintenance of a sound private and public faith, no man was more distinguished. He was three times elected to the Legislature from Franklin, and during one of the periods, he was again chosen speaker of the House of Representatives.

The troubles of that period having subsided, and the public service not requiring the sacrifice of his time and business, he again returned to private life, but was permitted a very short respite from the political arena; for, in 1835, he was once more sent to the Senate of the United States, and held the office by re-election until the coming in of the administration of President Harrison. By that patriot President he was appointed Attorney-General of the United States, and the appointment was hailed by men of all parties as the most appropriate that could have been made. The melancholy death of the President brought into power an administration that forfeited the respect of honorable minds. Mr. Crittenden left it, and resigned his office in a note which he sent to the President, that has been considered an admirable specimen of the manner in which a lofty mind can retire from place, when its possession cannot be held with self-respect.

He was elected to fill the vacancy occasioned by the resignation of Mr. Clay, and, at the next session of the Legislature, re-elected for the full term of six years, from March 4, 1843. In 1848 he resigned, having accepted the nomination of the Whig party to run for Governor of the state, to which office he was elected. He was appointed Attorney-General by President Fillmore in 1850, and retired with that administration. In 1853 he was again returned to the Senate, for the full term ending in 1861. He was elected to the House of Representatives in Congress in June, 1861, and was a member thereof at the time of his death, which occurred in Louisville, Kentucky, July 25, 1863.

Mr. Crittenden was, during the greater part of his life, a devoted friend of Mr. Clay; but it is known that there was an interruption in their friendship, caused by the participation of Mr. Crittenden in the nomination of General Taylor for President. Whatever may have been at one period the feelings of Mr. Clay towards his life-long friend, when they met afterwards, Mr. Clay advanced and said, cordially as of old, "Crittenden, how are you? I am glad to see you."

After the dissolution of the old Whig party, Mr. Crittenden became identified with the "Know-Nothing," or American, organization, which, however, had an ephemeral existence. Left, then, without a party, Mr. Crittenden yet uniformly opposed the measures of the Democracy.

But, conspicuous as was the whole of Mr. Crittenden's career, his latest efforts were his greatest. True to the conservative character of his nature, in his last term in the Senate he offered in that body a plan to adjust the difficulties between the North and South, known as the "Crittenden Propositions," which were discussed in the "Peace Convention" as well as in the Senate. He hoped, by this plan, to arrest the threatened secession of the Cotton States, and avert Civil War. He proposed to renew the Missouri line of 36 deg. 30 min.; to prohibit slavery north, and to permit it south of that line, as prescribed by the inhabitants thereof; to admit new states with or without slavery, as the constituents might provide; to prohibit Congress from abolishing slavery in the District of Columbia so long as it exists in Maryland or Virginia; and to pay for fugitive slaves rescued after arrest. These were the main provisions. He advocated them with characteristic earnestness, but his patriotic intentions were thwarted by their defeat.

Mr. Crittenden retired from the Senate in March, 1861, but he did not cease his efforts to avert a collision between the people of the two sections. He was the president of the "Border States Convention," held in Frankfort, Kentucky, in May, 1861, in which it was sought to mediate between the hostile parties. An address was issued, but the time for conciliation had past; indeed, the war had already begun, and Mr. Crittenden avowed himself in favor of maintaining the integrity of the Union at all hazards. He was elected to Congress from the "Ashland" District, and took his seat at the extra session in July, 1861, and frequently participated in the debates. He denounced the Confiscation Act, the Emancipation Proclamation, and the enlistment of negroes as soldiers, as obnoxious, dangerous, if not unconstitutional, measures; yet these, he admitted, were minor considerations as compared with the suppression of the rebellion.

The abolition of slavery, the destruction of the South, and the subjugation of the liberties of its people, attest the unblushing hypocrisy of these professions of the Radical party. Mr. Crittenden offered them in good faith, and the Union men of the border slave states accepted them in the same spirit; but the faith of the Northern war party was Punic faith. Their purpose was to keep it sacredly if they were beaten, but repudiate it if they were victorious. During that and the succeeding session, Mr. Crittenden labored assiduously to mitigate the horrors of the fratricidal war. His wise and patriotic counsels were disregarded, for each successive measure adopted only augmented the bitterness and widened the gulf that separated the two peoples. In his latest moments, Mr. Crittenden spoke of and deplored the disasters that had befallen the country.

Mr. Crittenden's intellect was of a superior order. By profession a lawyer, yet the political field was more congenial to him. Or perhaps it would be more correct to say that he entered political life so young that he naturally acquired a taste for the one, to the exclusion of the other. As an advocate, he stood almost without a rival at the bar; yet he was never a profound lawyer. He did not claim to be. He could have mastered any subject, but it would have been at the sacrifice of his political duties. He was a generous, magnanimous, and brave man—clear, comprehensive and decided in his convictions, and one who never shrank from the expression of them on any public question. His patriotism was never questioned by even the most bitter partisan enemy. Many of his countrymen entertained the hope that the highest office in the gift of the American people would be conferred upon him, but it was fated otherwise.

Mr. Crittenden was in two campaigns, in the War of 1812; as aid to General Ramsey in the expedition commanded by General Hopkins; and as aid to Governor Shelby, served with distinguished gallantry at the battle of the Thames.

JOHN SIMEON MULLICAN, sheriff of Daviess County, was born in Washington County, near Springfield, Kentucky, March 22, 1838, and is a son of John H. and Susan (Hayden) Mullican. His father was born near Emmittsburg, Maryland, and came to Kentucky with his father's family when he was very young, locating for a time in Washington County and removing to Nelson County in 1840, where he died in March, 1852. He was a most exemplary citizen, devoted to the work of the farmer and to the Catholic Church, having been converted to that faith after reaching his maturity. He deemed it a sacred duty to vote, but did not meddle with politics or aspire to office. He was largely interested in stock trading, but his chief pride was in his justly earned reputation as the best farmer in his county. His father, with whom he came to Kentucky from Maryland, was a native of Ireland. He was a farmer before and after coming to Kentucky, and owned a large tract of land in Washington County, where he built a very handsome residence.

Susan Hayden Mullican (mother) was born in Nelson County in 1795 and was a resident of her native county until her death in 1878.

Stanley Hayden (maternal grandfather) was a native of Virginia, where he married a Miss Hilton, also a Virginian, and subsequently removed to Nelson County, Kentucky. Mr. Hayden was a farmer and an excellent citizen; a member of the Catholic Church and a Democrat of the old school. The Haydens originally came from England.

John S. Mullican was two years old when his parents removed from Washington to Nelson County; was educated in St. Joseph College at Bardstown, completing his studies in 1858; sold dry goods for Quinn & Co. of Bardstown until 1861; went to Corinth and enlisted in Company E, Sixteenth Mississippi Regiment, C. S. A., under Capt. Hatch Murphy, and served in that regiment from June, 1861, till February, 1862, when he was transferred to the First Kentucky Regiment, commanded by Col. Thomas H. Taylor, now chief of police of Louisville, and was in the company commanded by Capt. Pat Thorp. His regiment was disbanded at the siege of Yorktown in March, 1863, and Private Mullican was honorably discharged on account of impaired health. During his career as a soldier he was in a number of fierce engagements, notably, the battles of Yorktown, Williamsburg, Chickahominy and several hot skirmishes near Richmond.

After spending six months in Bardstown, he removed to Daviess County and chose the independent life of a farmer, and his career as such was uneventful and unbroken until 1892, when he was elected sheriff of Daviess County for a term of two years. After completing this term, he was re-elected in 1894 for a term of three years under the new constitution, succeeding himself in January, 1895. In this official capacity Mr. Mullican has rendered faithful service, and by his very urbane, courteous and genial manner has added much to his popularity, and has established a name among the best citizens as an honorable citizen and capable official. Of course, he is a Democrat, and while he has been twice elected to an important and lucrative office by his party, he has never been a politician, his election having been due to his popularity as a citizen and an honest man, rather than to his party affiliations. He adheres to the religious faith of his parents, and is an influential member of the Catholic Church, and of the Young Men's Institute in connection with that church.

Mr. Mullican was married April 10, 1866, to Kate Stowers, daughter of A. H. Stowers of Daviess County. She was born in Daviess County in July, 1840, and after attending the common schools completed her education in Nazareth College, in Nelson County. They have eight children: James Stowers Mullican, married to Virgie Newman of Daviess County; John Vernon Mullican, married to Maggie Burnott of Daviess County; Bettie, Ollie and Oda (twins), Richard, Mamie and Addie.

DANIEL R. COLLIER, Adjutant General of Kentucky, one of the most widely known and popular Republicans of the state, was born in Garrard County, November 21, 1840. Besides having an ancestry to be proud of, Col. Collier has a record of his own with which his ancestors would be pleased if they were living. He took his first and last lessons in the common schools of Lancaster and was pretty well along when the great war broke out, and on the 23d of July, 1861, he enlisted in Company B, Third Regiment Kentucky Infantry; was elected second lieutenant and went into Camp Dick Robinson, near Lancaster, which was the first Federal recruiting post south of the Ohio river. The regiment was organized and commanded by Col. Thomas E. Bramlette, who was afterwards the war governor of Kentucky. By the resignation of Col. Bramlette and the promotion of Major McKee to the command of the regiment, Mr. Collier—who had served about a year as second lieutenant and had been promoted to captain of his company, on account of gallant services—was promoted to the rank of major. He held that rank about three months. Early in the morning of December 31, 1862, on the first day of the battle of Stone River, Col. McKee was killed while leading his regiment, and Major Collier assumed command. Gen. Haskell, in his report of the battle of Stone River, said: "In less than ten minutes after the fall of Col. McKee the gallant major, D. R. Collier, received two severe wounds, one in his leg and one in his breast, but nothing would induce him to leave the field." His commission as lieutenant colonel bore the date of that first day's battle at Stone River.

Col. Collier was in many hard-fought battles, including the siege of Corinth, Shiloh, Murfreesboro, McMinnville, Stewart's Creek, Perryville, and all the principal campaigns up to Stone River.

About five months after receiving the wounds mentioned, it being apparent that he would not again be able for active service, he resigned his commission and returned to his native county, engaging for a time in farming, stock-raising and in mercantile pursuits. He soon became a leader in Republican politics in his county and district, and one whom others were willing to follow. He wielded a strong influence among the voters of the Eighth Congressional District. President Harrison recognized the colonel's valuable services in the campaign of 1888, and in August, 1889, appointed him surveyor of customs and custodian of public property at Louisville, which offices he filled with signal ability until September, 1893.

He was a delegate to the Republican National Convention in 1892 which renominated Gen. Harrison, and not only cast his vote but controlled other votes for the popular president. During the gubernatorial campaign of 1894 he was one of Col. Bradley's most trusted lieutenants and willing workers, and when his friend and neighbor was inaugurated governor, on the same day he appointed Col. Collier adjutant general of Kentucky. And it was an appointment which gave general satisfaction throughout the state.

Col. Collier was married December 21, 1865, to Mary E. Hoskins, daughter of Col. W. A. Hoskins of Danville, who commanded the Twelfth Regiment Kentucky Infantry, and was a member of the Kentucky legislature in 1872. Mrs. Collier is a niece of Mrs. Dick Robinson, for whose husband Camp Dick Robinson was named as a compliment to his loyalty; also a niece of Mrs. James Ferris of Lancaster, who predicted thirty years ago that Col. Bradley would some day be governor of Kentucky. Col. and Mrs. Collier have three children; his eldest daughter, Roberta, is the wife of Robert L. Elkin of Garrard County, and has one child, Daniel Collier Elkin.

His son, William H. Collier, is in mercantile business at Lancaster, and Ida Frances Collier is at home.

Col. Collier is a member of the Christian Church, of the Masonic order, the Knights of Honor and, of course, a member in good standing of the Grand Army of the Republic.

Col. Collier's father, Alexander Collier, was a native of Garrard County, where he died in 1860. He received a good common school education and followed the occupation of a farmer most of his life; in politics a Democrat; in religious faith a Baptist.

Robert Collier (grandfather) was a Virginian, who married there and came to Garrard County, where he practiced medicine for many years. He was of Scotch-Irish extraction.

Rebecca Scott Collier (mother) was a native of Garrard County; received a good education in the schools of the county; was a devout member of the Baptist Church and a noble Christian woman; died in 1856.

Joseph Scott (maternal grandfather) was born in Virginia, of English parentage. After coming to Kentucky he first settled in Barren County, and subsequently removed to Garrard, where he was a farmer and an exemplary citizen.

GEORGE KELLY, M. D., a learned and able young physician of Lexington, son of a noted physician of Massachusetts, was born in Worcester, June 6, 1866. His father, Frank H. Kelly, M. D., fellow of the Massachusetts Medical Society, was born in New Hampton, September 9, 1827; after the district school he entered the academy in New Hampton, in which he studied the higher branches for three years; was employed in the dry goods store of James P. Simpson until 1846, when he left his native place and went to Boston. Remaining there several months, he went to Dover and read medicine with Dr. Bethnel Kirth, with whom he went to Cincinnati in 1847, where he attended a course of medical lectures; was afterwards associated with Dr. Aaron Ordway of Lawrence, Massachusetts, until 1851, when he removed to Worcester and located permanently, at once entering upon a most successful career in the practice of medicine, in which he continued for twenty-three years.

He was first president of the board of trustees of the Worcester City Hospital in 1870 and served in that capacity for thirteen years consecutively; joined the Massachusetts Medical Society in 1875 and delivered the annual address before the Worcester District Medical Society in 1880; was connected with city government in various capacities and at divers times, as member of the school board for two years, of the common council six years, of the board of aldermen and as mayor of Worcester in 1880 and 1881. During his administration as mayor the erection of the new building for the city hospital was commenced and a board of health was established. He was not only a very noted physician and elegant gentleman, but he was active as a citizen and bore his part manfully in his endeavors to advance the best interests of his city. He was the author of a book entitled, "Reminiscences of New Hampton," and also wrote a genealogical history of the Kelly and Simpson families, the Simpsons being related to his mother, who was a descendant of Thomas Simpson, the Revolutionary patriot. His mother was a daughter of Tristram and Ann Cram, whose ancestors were natives of Deerfield, New Hampshire.

Dr. Kelly was married (first) in Worcester, April 20, 1853, to Lucy Ellis Draper (mother), who was born at Dover, Massachusetts, September 3, 1828. She died in Worcester, May 22, 1873.

He was married (second) January 8, 1879, to Jennie P. Martin, with whom he lived until his death, which occurred October 25, 1891.

Dr. George Draper Kelly of Lexington was educated in the public schools of Worcester and at Phillips Academy at Exeter, New Hampshire, which institution he entered when fifteen years of age, graduating three years later. He then attended Harvard Medical School, from which he received his diploma in 1889; entered hospital service at the Massachusetts General Hospital in Boston, in which he received practical instruction, and after completing his medical studies he began the practice of medicine in his native city, where he remained about a year before locating in Lexington; was a member of the Society of Alumni of Harvard Medical School; of the Massachusetts Medical Society; of the Worcester County Medical Society, and attached to the staff of the Washburn Memorial Hospital.

On arriving in Lexington, he immediately began a promising career, unabashed by the presence of so many noted physicians, and he has met with great encouragement while doing his share of professional work in a distressingly healthy community. He joined the Kentucky State Medical Society and the Fayette County Medical Society in 1893, and is physician in charge of the Protestant Infirmary of Lexington.

MARMADUKE B. BOWDEN, Attorney-at-Law of Louisville, son of James H. Bowden and Nannie Morton, was born in Russelville, Kentucky, July 7, 1866, and educated at Bethel College. Poor health compelled him to leave school at nine years of age, but he returned to school when fourteen and remained for three years. He was greatly interested in geology and was engaged for one year in making a geological survey of Warren and Butler Counties. The display of Kentucky building stone at the Southern Exposition in 1883 was composed of specimens secured in part by Mr. Bowden for this purpose, and were polished at the Smithsonian Institution. They have since been exhibited as samples of the building stones of Kentucky, wherever Kentucky has been represented in an exposition. Mr. Bowden read law with his father and was admitted to the bar in July, 1885. In 1888 he served in the town council of Russellville, and in March, 1889, when not twenty-three years of age, was elected mayor of that town. He resigned in 1889 and removed to Louisville, where he has since been engaged in the practice of law. He was elected president of the Louisville Commercial Club, May 9, 1893, for a term of one year, and was re-elected for another year in 1895, and was elected colonel of the First Kentucky Regiment, Uniform Rank, Knights of Pythias, December 30, 1895.

It was partly due to Mr. Bowden's influence and energy that the G. A. R. encampment was brought to Louisville in 1895. He was at that time president of the Commercial Club, and directed all his efforts to that end, visiting different state encampments in the interest of Louisville, and presenting the Massachusetts, Illinois, Indiana and New York departments with Abraham Lincoln gavels. This, together with his eloquent orations, provoked a genuine enthusiasm and gained for him a national reputation. At the Indiana and Illinois encampments especially was his influence recognized, as strenuous efforts were making there to carry the encampment to St. Paul. But after Mr. Bowden's address the tide was turned in favor of Louisville. He also visited the Texas department and, in company with the Hon. E. J. McDermott, visited the Pennsylvania department, where Mr. McDermott was the orator.

Mr. Bowden was married February 14, 1888, to Lee Sandifer, daughter of Nicholas Sandifer, who was judge of the Garrard County Court for many years. She was born in Lancaster, Kentucky, and educated at Millersburg Female College.

James H. Bowden (father) was born in Morganfield, Union County, Kentucky, and attended school there until his thirteenth year; went to Louisville and worked for several years as a printer on the old Louisville Journal, earning enough money to enable him to attend school for a short term, after which he returned to Louisville and worked at printing at intervals until he completed his education. He studied law with the Hon. G. P. Edwards of Russellville and began to practice in Tompkinsville, Monroe County, Kentucky, October, 1855; remained there for eighteen months, and removed to Russellville, where he soon became eminent in his profession; was a member of the Kentucky legislature,

1875-6; was school commissioner of Logan County for a number of years, and in 1882 was elected judge of the Superior Court and was on the bench eight years, serving two terms. Since leaving the bench in 1890 he has practiced law in Russellville.

Judge Bowden married Miss Nannie Morton, May 14, 1857. She was born in 1843 and was the daughter of Marmaduke B. Morton (deceased), who was cashier of the Southern Bank of Kentucky, and after it went out of business, of the banking house of N. Long & Co., at Russellville. Their children are: Katie, who married Henry M. Caldwell; John S., died in 1876; Fannie, Marmaduke B., Elizabeth, Mary and Henry W.

John Bowden (grandfather) was born in Bristol, England, September 8, 1787. He emigrated to Baltimore in 1815, where he was an architect; he married (first) a Miss Tucker, also a native of England. There were two children by this marriage: John and Ann. He removed to Kentucky in 1819 and married (second) Lova Fauquier of Morganfield, Kentucky, and there were eight children by this marriage: Amelia; Rev. George F., killed while young by falling over a cliff; John, member of the Louisville Methodist Episcopal Conference, who was regarded as a man of fine ability, who died in 1846; Annie; Mary, married to Harry Duncan, and died in 1861; two of her sons are each commonwealth's attorneys in Missouri; Sarah, Thomas L., and James H. Bowden, father of Marmaduke B. Bowden of Louisville.

WILLIAM L. BROWN of London, judge of Laurel County Court, son of George P. Brown and Eveline McKee, was born in London, Kentucky, April 3, 1841, and was educated in the common schools, supplemented by a short term in Transylvania.

He was a clerk in his father's store, beginning at a very early age, and when only twelve years old began making trips for his father to South Carolina and Georgia with stock in which he was a dealer and trader. He kept this up, performing the duties of a man and transacting business for his father until about the beginning of the Civil war.

In 1860 he was elected lieutenant colonel of militia; during the war he was connected with the quartermaster's department and had charge of the post at Camp Pitman during 1864 and 1865. He was one of the original Republicans in his section of the state and was a delegate to the national convention in 1864 which nominated President Lincoln the second time, since which time he has taken a hand in every campaign, local, state and national, taking the stump in support of his party and throwing the weight of his influence against Democracy and in favor of Republican men and principles, and no man in Laurel County is more highly respected.

In 1876 he was admitted to the bar, having studied law previously under Judge Granville Pearl of London. Two years later he was elected county judge on a temperance platform, receiving more votes than both of the opposing candidates, Republican and Democratic. Previous to his term of service on the bench he was at different times deputy clerk of the County and Circuit Courts, deputy sheriff under different sheriffs, during which a party having been convicted of petty larceny and sentenced to receive "forty stripes save one," the deputy was forced to execute the order of the court. The culprit threatened to slay both the man who whipped him and the prosecuting witness. He made good his threat as to the witness, waylaying him, but was killed himself in a drunken row before he found an opportunity to slay the deputy sheriff.

He was elected county attorney and served his time in that office, doing efficient work for his county, and was a member of the committee in charge of the erection of the court house and superintended its construction. In 1894 he was nominated by the Republicans and again elected county judge, his present official position. Judge Brown has proven on more than one occasion that he is one of the most efficient officials the county has ever had, his career having been characterized by the most determined efforts to improve the condition of his county generally, while his voice has been heard on the side of law and order, and to his efforts in this direction more than to the influence or power of any other individual is due the present excellent reputation of Laurel County for good order, peace and quiet. Peerless in his opposition to disorder and in bringing law-breakers to justice, he has been the friend of education and progress. No man has done more in advocating the free school system, and he has always been found in the front ranks among the friends of higher education. The result of his labors in this direction are already apparent, but the foundation which has been slow and sure in building will tell more effectually upon future generations.

Judge Brown is a Christian man of strong spiritual impulses; a member of the Methodist Church and a lover of Christianity of whatever denomination or creed.

George P. Brown (father) was born in Garrard County, Kentucky, in 1813, and removed to Laurel County in 1840, where he died in 1868. He was a general merchant in London until after the Civil war; a man of good education and sound judgment; prominent in the affairs of his town and county; energetic and persevering in his efforts to advance the interests of society, and was particularly devoted to the cause of education. He served as school commissioner for several years and was largely instrumental in building the seminary, in which many of the young people of London have enjoyed the advantages of higher education.

He represented his county in the legislature in 1851 and could have had any office within the gift of the people of the county, simply for the asking.

Leroy Brown (grandfather), a native of Albemarle County, Virginia, came first to Garrard, and subsequently removed to Laurel County, where he was a farmer, returned to Garrard and died in 1863, having reached his eighty-eighth year.

He had eleven brothers, and several of them— he could not tell how many—fought for their country in the War of 1812, one of whom was governor of the colony of South Carolina. He claimed to be a cousin of General Robert E. Lee, his father having married a lady of that connection.

Eveline McKee (mother) was born in Knox, now Laurel County, in 1821, and though full of years is an active member of the Methodist Episcopal Church and a resident of London, where she is greatly loved for her many Christian graces.

William Houston McKee (grandfather), a native of Rockbridge County, Virginia, came to Laurel County in 1810, and died there at the age of eighty-six years. He was a farmer and a surveyor and a scholarly gentleman who left the impress of a noble life upon the community in which he lived.

John McKee (great-grandfather), a native of Dublin, Ireland, came to America and married a Miss Houston in Virginia, who was an aunt of General Samuel Houston of Texas.

CHARLES H. PRICE, a popular and successful lawyer of Middlesborough, was born in Kent, Portage County, Ohio, January 26, 1849.

His father, William B. Price, was born in Canada of American parents and was reared and educated in Ohio; removed to Jasper County, Indiana, in 1866, and died there June, 1895, in the seventy-third year of his age. During the earlier years of his business career he was a teacher and merchant, but for thirty years prior to his death he was engaged in farming pursuits. He enlisted in the One Hundred and Ninety-eighth Regiment Ohio Infantry, serving as orderly sergeant of his company; was postmaster at Solon, Cuyahoga County, Ohio, under President Lincoln's administration; was county commissioner of Jasper County, Indiana, and held other minor offices. He was a life-long Republican and was active and influential in his party. He was a member of the Methodist Church.

Captain William Price (grandfather), a native of Connecticut and of Irish parentage, removed to Ohio when he was a young man; founded the town of Kent in Portage County, and was engaged in the manufacture of silks. He was a captain of the old militia and a man of education and wide influence. He was killed by the falling of a mill-stone.

Susan M. Taylor Price (mother) is a native of Summit County, Ohio, and is now living in Jasper County, Indiana, in her sixty-ninth year. Her father was a native of Connecticut and for many years a farmer of Summit County, Ohio, where he died.

Charles H. Price spent his early years in the western reserve of Ohio, where his education began before his father removed to Indiana, and there he attended the common schools and Stockwell University. After leaving school he followed farming a while; studied law and was admitted to the Jasper County bar and began the practice of law in 1873; was elected clerk of the Circuit Court the same year, served two terms and at the expiration of his second term, in 1883, removed to Highmore, South Dakota, where he practiced law until 1890. While there he was city attorney, state's attorney, judge of the County Court and member of the convention which framed the present constitution of that state; was colonel on the staff of Governor L. K. Church, and a member of the commission that codified the laws of the territory; was defeated by the Republican candidates for circuit judge and the state senate, being the Democratic nominee for those offices, respectively. He also served his party as a member of the State Democratic Committee and as chairman of the County Committee.

In April, 1890, he came to Kentucky and located in Middlesborough, where he has become quite as prominent as a lawyer and citizen as he was in Dakota. He has, however, devoted his attention entirely to the practice of law, and, with characteristic modesty, has kept out of the way of men who have been Kentuckians longer, and has not sought political favors. The only offices he has held were those of special judge of the Circuit Court and member of the city school board. He has gained a lucrative practice in his new field and is recognized by bench and bar as one of the most able attorneys of Middlesborough and vicinity. He is a Knight Templar and Shriner in Masonry, a Knight of Pythias and an Odd Fellow, and is prominent in all of these orders.

Mr. Price was married in 1873 to Lizzie Jones, daughter of Jacob and Mary Jones of Jasper County, Indiana, and has two sons, Max T. and Don K. Price. Grace B. Price, a daughter, died in Indiana at the age of four years and four months.

CHARLES R. BROCK, Lawyer of London, Kentucky, son of Daniel R. Brock and Mary Lucas Brock, was born in Laurel County, Kentucky, May 9, 1865.

Daniel R. Brock was born in the same county in 1841, and is still a resident farmer in his native county, and is an active member of the Baptist Church, having been clerk of the Laurel River Baptist Association for many years. He married Mary Lucas, a native of the same county.

Ragan Brock (grandfather) was born in Union County, Tennessee, in the first year of the present century; came to Laurel County, Kentucky, in 1833, and was a farmer there until his death in 1876.

William Lucas (maternal grandfather) was a farmer and tanner in Laurel County, where he died in 1867.

Charles R. Brock had a varied experience in getting an education, and few young men have so persistently followed a purpose with ultimate success. A farmer's boy who was expected to perform a share of the labor of the farm and garden, his opportunity for schooling was limited, and his studies were practically confined to the common school curriculum until he was seventeen years of age, when he formed a determined purpose to secure for himself the advantages of a college education.

He attended Laurel Seminary at London and Union College at Barbourville, teaching and studying in alternate years until he was able to enter the Kentucky State College at Lexington, from which latter institution he was graduated in June, 1890, taking the degree of Bachelor of Science.

During the several years of his studies he taught at different times in the county schools, and in the London public schools of which he was principal for three terms, all the while pursuing and advancing himself in his college work.

After completing his college course he was an associate principal of Laurel Seminary for one year, and at the same time began the study of law. During the school year of 1891-92 he was teacher of mathematics and the German language in the Williamsburg Institute; and while there his spare moments were given to the study of his chosen profession under the practical guidance of Hon. R. D. Hill of Williamsburg, Kentucky. He was admitted to the bar in November, 1891, and after completing his term in the institute he entered into a partnership with his able preceptor.

After a very satisfactory practice for three years this partnership was dissolved by mutual consent in June, 1895, since which time Mr. Brook has been gaining a strong foothold, and by hard work and close application is now receiving a good share of the business of the courts in his native county. He is devoted to his profession and the pleasure of his office during the day is only surpassed when in the evening at home he and his lovely young wife enter upon literary and historical studies which they happily pursue together.

The details of a young man's ups and downs and his efforts to obtain an education are not of thrilling interest, but the example points a moral and may stimulate other lads to greater endeavor and lead them on to success. It also serves to show the character and pluck of this young man who is now upon the threshold of a successful career.

Charles R. Brock and Katherine Brown, daughter of Judge W. L. Brown of London, were married June 1, 1893. Mr. Brock is a member of the Baptist Church, and is now superintendent of the Sabbath School.

EDWARD J. HOWARD, City Attorney of Middlesborough, son of John A. Howard and Mary J. Keran, was born in Scotland County, Missouri, December 4, 1861.

His father, John A. Howard, was born in Clark County, Missouri, in 1836, and died in Leavenworth, Kansas, in 1892. He was a lawyer and a leading Republican politician; joined the Federal army as a private in the Twenty-first Regiment, Missouri Infantry, and was wounded in a skirmish in the Red River expedition, and this wound and the exposure incident to army life caused his death. He was in Leavenworth on business at the time of his death, having retained his home in Clark County, Missouri.

Thomas Flannery Howard (grandfather) was a native of Harlan County and removed to Clark County, Missouri, with his father about 1836, and died there. He was a farmer and a preacher in the Methodist Church.

John N. Howard (great-grandfather) was the first County Judge of Harlan County, Kentucky, and was a man of prominence and considerable means. He donated to the county the ground upon which the first court house was built, at Harlan C. H., the county-seat. He was a farmer and stock-raiser in that county and in Missouri, to which state he removed late in life and died there in old age.

Samuel Howard (great-great-grandfather) came from Virginia to Kentucky in 1795 and settled in what is now Harlan County. He was the ancestor of one branch of the Howard family in Kentucky. He was born in Buckingham County, Virginia, in 1762, and was a soldier in the Revolutionary War under General Washington, and was at Valley Forge, White Plains and Monmouth. He was present at the surrender of Cornwallis at Yorktown, and was one of the Revolutionary War pensioners in Kentucky. He died about 1840 in Harlan County. The Howards were originally from Scotland, whence they went to England hundreds of years ago, and thence to Virginia in a very early day.

Mary Keran Howard (mother) is a native of Scott County, Illinois, and is now a resident of Marceline, Linn County, Missouri. Her father, James S. Keran, was a native of Ohio; removed to Illinois and thence to Scotland County, Missouri, and finally to Tulare County, California, where he died, aged sixty-seven years. He was a farmer and minister in the Methodist Church. His parents were natives of Ireland.

Edward J. Howard was reared in Clark County, Missouri, and received a good education in the academy and public schools. After reading law for a time he came to Kentucky in 1888 and finished his course of reading at Harlan Court House, and was admitted to the bar in the same year and went to Middlesborough in 1889, where he located permanently in the practice of his profession. For three or four years he combined real estate operations with his law practice, but since 1893 has devoted his whole time to the law, and is now serving his second term as City Attorney of Middlesborough.

Mr. Howard has taken a lively interest in politics and was the Democratic nominee for Congress in the district in 1890. The regular Republican majority in the district is eleven thousand, and he reduced that majority to three thousand four hundred. This was a fair test of his popularity and is good evidence of his superiority as a campaigner. He is one of the leading lawyers of his city and section and has paved the way for a most brilliant and successful career. He is a member of the Missionary Baptist Church; is active in church work and a leading Knight of Pythias, being Vice-Chancellor of Lodge No. 83.

Mr. Howard was married in 1886 to Mary E. Long, daughter of William R. Long of Meredosia, Illinois, and has two sons living: Edward J. Howard, Jr., and George F. Howard.

DANIEL BOONE LOGAN, lawyer and citizen of Pineville, formerly of Morehead, where he led a company of citizens who suppressed the notorious Craig Toliver faction in Rowan County in 1887 (wherein he honored the memory of Kentucky's most distinguished pioneer, for whom he was named), was born in Carter County, Kentucky, April 23, 1858. He is a great-grandson of another pioneer, James Logan, who took no small part in the early trials of those who sought homes on "the dark and bloody ground;" so that he carries the blood of heroes in his veins while he bears the name of Daniel Boone, who was Kentucky's greatest citizen in his day.

Mr. Logan is a son of James Fleming Logan and Nancy McGlone Logan. His father, a native of Fleming County, removed to Carter County in 1853, where he was engaged in farming until the spring of 1869, when he removed to Greenup County and died December 5, 1869, aged fifty-two years. During the Civil War he was in the Federal army, serving in the Quartermaster's department.

Tobias Logan (grandfather) was born in Fleming County in 1796, and was a farmer there until 1853, when he also, with his son, James F. Logan, removed to Carter County, where he died in 1870, following his son to "that other country" within a few months after James F. Logan's death.

James Logan (great-grandfather) was born in North Carolina and came to Kentucky with his parents when he was a child, locating near Shelbyville. He subsequently took part in the Indian wars and was shot, scalped and left for dead at the battle of Blue Lick Springs, but he survived with the loss of his hair and an eye.

William Logan (great-great-grandfather) was a native of Scotland, who came to the United States and located in North Carolina, subsequently removing to Kentucky and settling near Shelbyville.

Nancy McGlone Logan (mother), now a resident of Rowan, was born in Greenup County, Kentucky. Her grandfather, Owen McGlone, was a native of Pennsylvania, and was one of the first settlers of Buffalo Fork of Tygart's Creek. His father was a native of Scotland and became a resident of Pennsylvania, where he and his wife died. His son Owen about 1800 settled on Buffalo Fork and died there about 1860. His widow reached the almost impossible age of one hundred and thirteen years, dying in 1885. His son, William Owen McGlone, was born in what was then Mason, but now Carter County, and resided there all his life. He was the father of Nancy McGlone Logan. He was a farmer and died in 1867. Daniel Boone Logan was reared in Carter County and received his education principally in the High Schools of Grayson, Bethel and Morehead. He was then engaged in teaching for a period of ten years in the counties of Rowan, Fleming, Carter and Bath, in the meantime pursuing his studies and endeavoring to advance himself in the profession into which he had drifted.

In 1885 he was appointed Master Commissioner of Rowan County, by Judge A. E. Cole, and while holding that office for two years he read law, and was admitted to the bar in 1886; practiced law in Morehead until 1890, when he came to Pineville, where he has since devoted his time to the practice of law in that section of the state.

It was while practicing law at Morehead, county-seat of Rowan, that he performed the most distinguished service for his state. The Rowan County feud between the followers of Craig Toliver and Cook Humphreys had become so disgraceful and serious that Mr. Logan went to see

Governor Knott to ask him to send the state troops into Rowan County to suppress the lawlessness of those factions. The Governor replied that he could not do this until the local authorities had exhausted their power; and, returning to his home, Mr. Logan organized a body of men to accomplish the arrest of those of the Toliver faction charged with the murder of his kinsmen, W. H. W. and J. B. Logan, and, together with the Sheriff of Rowan County, led them into Morehead, June 22d, 1887, for that purpose, with the result that is known to the world and has become a part of the history of the state. The whole history of the feud and its timely suppression under Mr. Logan's leadership has been written by the historians of the Filson Club, and the newspapers of the country gave full accounts from beginning to end, at the time of those stirring events.

Daniel Boone Logan was married in January, 1884, to Lizzie Evans, daughter of Captain Ben Evans, deceased, of Morehead. They have two daughters and one son: Gertrude, Virgie M. and Benjamin F. Logan.

Captain Evans, Mrs. Logan's father, was Captain of a company under General John H. Morgan in the Confederate army, and directly under Humphrey Marshall, and was killed at West Liberty. His place was taken by Judge Thomas F. Hargis, late Chief Justice of the Kentucky Court of Appeals, and now a resident of Louisville.

Mr. and Mrs. Logan are quite prominent in Pineville society, and he is a member of several benevolent orders, including the Masons and the Maccabees.

ROBERT HUGH TOMLINSON, a very able and successful lawyer of Lancaster, son of Joseph and Elizabeth M. (Jones) Tomlinson, was born in Garrard County, Kentucky, May 21, 1852.

His father was born in Newbern, North Carolina, in 1815; educated in Hendricks County, Indiana, to which place his parents removed when he was a child; came to Garrard County, Kentucky, when twenty-three years of age and was a farmer until recently, when he removed to Danville, where he is living in retirement: was a stanch Union man during the war; a Republican since and a man of strong convictions. He was reared a Quaker, but has been for many years a member of the Methodist Church.

William Tomlinson (grandfather) was a farmer near Newbern, North Carolina, where he lived and died. His father, William Tomlinson, was a native of Ireland, the date of whose coming to America is not recorded.

Elizabeth M. Jones Tomlinson (mother) was born in Garrard County, Kentucky, in 1826; married Joseph Tomlinson in 1842 in Hendricks County, Indiana; died in Boyle County, January, 1892, and is buried at Danville. She was a member of the Methodist Church and a most excellent woman.

Hugh L. Jones (grandfather) was born in Newbern, North Carolina; was engaged in steamboating; came to Kentucky and taught school in Garrard County, and married a Mrs. Taylor, whose maiden name was Judith Moss. He died in Garrard County in 1830. The maternal ancestors of Mr. Tomlinson were from England.

Robert H. Tomlinson was educated at Greencastle, Indiana, and in Transylvania University at Lexington, completing his studies in 1873; began the practice of law in Lancaster, August, 1874; was in partnership for a short time with William Robinson, and later with Judge George Denny until 1883, since which time he has attended a large practice without an office associate. He was City Attorney from 1880 to 1890; Chairman of the Democratic Committee for the same length of time; was appointed City Judge in 1881 to fill a vacancy; was elected to the legislature in 1889, and served as County Attorney from 1891 to 1894; is quite prominent in local and state politics, and has often been a delegate to State Democratic Conventions.

Mr. Tomlinson has a fine practice in the courts and is attorney for a number of corporations and building and loan associations, and was President of the Board of Trustees of Garrard Female College.

He is an active member of the Methodist Episcopal Church, in which he is a steward and trustee; is connected with a number of benevolent orders, including Masons, Odd Fellows, Maccabees, Knights of Honor and is Major of the First Regiment Uniform Rank of Knights of Pythias.

Mr. Tomlinson was married September 19, 1877, to Lou Marrs, daughter of Stephen and Margaret (Robson) Marrs, and a native of Anderson County. Her father was a grocer and died in October, 1888. Mrs. Tomlinson was educated in Franklin Institute and is an intelligent and accomplished lady.

The children of Robert H. and Lou (Marrs) Tomlinson are Margaret, Harry Denny, Annell and Robert Hugh.

REV. JOHN CLARKE YOUNG, D. D., a Presbyterian clergyman, and the most distinguished and successful of the presidents of Center College, at Danville, Kentucky, was born in Pennsylvania, August 12, 1803, and died at Danville, June 23, 1857, aged fifty-four. He spent three years in Columbia College, New York City, but graduated, at twenty, with the honors of his class, at Dickinson College, Carlisle, Pennsylvania; passed his theological course at Princeton Seminary; was pastor of the McChord Church, at Lexington, Kentucky, 1828-30; in 1830, when only twenty-seven, was made the president of one of the leading colleges of the West, Center College, which owed to him, until his death, much of its greatest glory and usefulness; it had six graduates in 1830, and forty-seven in 1857. He was twice, in 1832 and 1841, moderator of the synod of Kentucky, and in 1853 was moderator of the Presbyterian General Assembly (O. S.) His published writings were few; his forte was as a speaker or preacher; his power in the pulpit and in the church courts was remarkable.

REV. JOHN BRECKINRIDGE, D. D., was born at Cabell's Dale, in Fayette County, Kentucky, July 4, 1797, and died at the same place, August 4, 1841, aged forty-four. Some account has been given of his paternal ancestors, in the notice of his father and of his maternal, in that of his elder brother, Joseph Cabell Breckinridge. His education was conducted at the best schools in Kentucky, and at Princeton College, N. J., where he graduated, at twenty-one, with great distinction. While there he became a subject of divine grace, and determined to enter the ministry of the Presbyterian Church—against the earnest wishes of all his immediate family, not one of whom was at that time a professor of religion; they had destined him for the law. In 1822, just one year after he completed his theological course, he was chaplain of the Lower House of Congress; in 1823, settled in Lexington, Kentucky, as pastor of the McChord Church; was co-pastor, and then pastor, of the Second Presbyterian Church, Baltimore, 1826-31; at Philadelphia, as secretary and general agent of the Board of Education of the Presbyterian Church, 1831-36; a professor in the theological seminary at Princeton, New Jersey, 1836-38; secretary and general agent of the Board of Foreign Missions of the Presbyterian Church, 1838-40. At the period of his death, he was pastor-elect of the First Presbyterian Church, New Orleans, and also president-elect of Oglethorpe University, Georgia. He was a man of extraordinary gifts. With talents of a high order, pulpit eloquence rarely equalled in his generation, universally admired and beloved, it was no wonder that calls and invitations to churches, colleges and every sort of public employment suitable to a Christian minister, flowed in upon him and at times embarrassed him as to which it was his duty to accept.

REV. ROBERT JEFFERSON BRECKINRIDGE, D. D., LL.D., was born March 8, 1800, at Cabell's Dale, Fayette County, Kentucky, and died at Danville, Kentucky, December 27, 1871, aged nearly seventy-two. Of his paternal ancestors some account has been given in the notice of his father, and some account of his maternal ancestors in the sketch of his elder brother. He was educated at the best private schools in Kentucky, until sixteen; spent two years at Princeton College, New Jersey, one winter at Yale College, and graduated, at nineteen, at Union College, Schenectady, New York. In 1824 he commenced the practice of law at Lexington, and took an active part in politics; was elected in 1825, on the "Old Court" ticket, a representative from Fayette County in the Kentucky legislature, and was re-elected in 1826, '27 and '28. In 1829, after a long and dangerous illness, he joined the Presbyterian Church; soon after, was ordained a ruling elder; in 1831, was a commissioner to the General Assembly of the Presbyterian Church, which met at Cincinnati. He was licensed to preach the gospel in 1832; was pastor of the Second Presbyterian Church, in Baltimore, for thirteen years, 1832-45; president of Jefferson College, Canonsburg, Pennsylvania, 1845-47; pastor of the First Presbyterian Church, Lexington, Kentucky, 1847-53; professor of theology in Danville Theological Seminary, 1853-71.

While pastor at Lexington, Governor Owsley, in 1847, appointed him state superintendent of public instruction, and in 1851 the people elected him to the same position. He was selected for this office because of his great abilities and splendid executive talent, and did a noble work in reducing to a system the heretofore poorly digested common school laws, and infusing much of his own tireless spirit into the sluggish public sentiment of the day. While not the originator, he may not inaptly be styled the Father of the Common School System of Kentucky.

Few Kentuckians have enjoyed the reputation or exerted the influence of Dr. Breckinridge as a writer. The "Act and Testimony," in 1834, in the great controversy which resulted in a division of the Presbyterian Church, first gave him a national reputation. He was leading editor of several religious and general magazines and reviews; and author of a book of travels in Europe, in 1844, and of two able works on theology, in 1857 and 1859; and of numerous essays and public letters. He was among the mightiest controversialists of his generation.

WILLIAM NATHAN FOSTER, an able lawyer of Greensburg, Kentucky, son of John Standford Foster and Eliza Fulks, was born December 18, 1857, in Green County, Kentucky. He was educated in the country schools of Green County and in the academy at Canner, Hart County, Kentucky. After leaving school in July, 1881, he taught in the Green County District schools for three years; read law with Judge Towles of Greensburg; received license January, 1885, and began to practice in January, 1886, in partnership with his brother, Robert L. Foster, and this arrangement continued until the fall of 1886, when it was dissolved on account of his brother being elected county attorney. He is a Republican and a member of the Republican National League Club, and of the Baptist Church. He married, December 10, 1891, Miss Sallie C. Vaughn of Green County, daughter of W. N. Vaughn and Amanda Moore. She was educated at the Greensburg high school, graduating in 1883, and is a member of the Methodist Church. They have one child, Herman S., born June 25, 1895.

John S. Foster (father) was born in 1822 in Orange County, Virginia, and was educated in the county schools there. He came with his parents, in 1831, to Green (now Taylor) County. He was a farmer and originally a Henry Clay Whig, but in 1856 became a Republican, and was one of the four men in Green County who voted for Abraham Lincoln in 1860. He is a member of the Baptist Church; married Miss Eliza Fulks in February, 1845, and they celebrated their golden wedding in 1895.

J. S. Foster is a son of Josiah Foster and Biddie Mitchell of Orange County, Virginia. Josiah Foster was in the War of 1812. He was the son of Robert Foster, who came to America from Scotland in 1773; settled in Orange County, Virginia, and married Annie Monroe in 1778.

Mrs. Eliza Fulks Foster (mother) was a daughter of Nathan Fulks of Culpeper County, Virginia, and Fannie Richardson of Prince Edward County, Virginia. Eliza Foster was born September, 1822, and was educated in Virginia and Kentucky. She came to Kentucky with her parents in 1835, when they settled in Green County. She is still living on the farm, eight miles west of Greensburg, on Green river, and is a devout member of the Baptist Church. By her marriage with John S. Foster she had nine children, eight of whom are living: Josiah Foster, who joined the Federal army when sixteen years old, in October, 1862, and served until the close of the war, and now a farmer in Green County; James E. Foster, also a farmer in Green County; Mary E., wife of W. J. Sidebottom, a Green County farmer; Alice, wife of N. P. Gunun of Summerville, Kentucky; William Nathan, lawyer, Greensburg, Kentucky; Robert L. was three times elected county attorney, the youngest the state has ever had. He was considered one of the best lawyers of his age in Kentucky. He was born February 22, 1859; died April 20, 1895; Sallie, wife of S. T. Gorin; Fannie, wife of J. S. Mears, and John Marshall Foster, farmer of Green County.

Nathan Fulks (father of Mrs. Eliza Foster) was a son of Jackson Fulks of Ireland, who settled in Culpeper County, Virginia, when a young man; came to America in 1767, and married Dora Robertson in 1775.

FRANCIS MARION CAMPBELL of Springfield, clerk of the Circuit Court, son of George P. and Lucy (Martin) Campbell, was educated in the common schools of Washington County and in Texas, Kentucky, his last preceptor being James F. Rhinefort. After completing his education he was a teacher in the district schools in different parts of Kentucky for thirteen years, and at the expiration of that time he returned to his native county and engaged in farming.

In 1884 he was elected sheriff by the people of Washington County, and was re-elected in 1886, his term expiring in 1888. He then bought a half interest in the flouring mills in operation at Springfield, and held the position of secretary and treasurer of the mills until 1892, when he was elected to his present position as clerk of the Circuit Court. He is a director in the First National Bank of Springfield, and still retains his interest in the flouring mills, his eldest son giving his personal attention to that business. Mr. Campbell is a member of the Baptist Church, and in politics is a Democrat. He still owns the old Campbell homestead and cherishes a laudable sentiment in regard to its preservation.

Mr. Campbell was married in 1865 to Fannie Campbell, daughter of Nathaniel Campbell and Lucy Martin. Mrs. Fannie Campbell was born in Washington County in 1844, and educated in the public schools. She attended the Methodist Church, of which she was a devoted member at the time of her death, September 14, 1890. She is interred in the old family burying ground. Her eight children are all living: Arthur, Della, Lulie Bell, Myrtle, Robert Edgar, Theodora, Bessie and Pearl.

George P. Campbell (father), son of Nathaniel and Sallie (Pettit) Campbell, was born June 10, 1806; came from Ft. Wayne County, Virginia, in 1812, when only six years of age, and lived in Shelby County, Kentucky; was educated in the common schools of that county, and, after leaving school, engaged in farming and stock raising in Washington County. He was a member of the Baptist Church and his political affiliations were with the Democratic party.

He married, in 1830, Lucy Martin, daughter of Andrew and Susan Martin of Boyle County. She was born in Boyle County, Kentucky, in 1813 and educated in the public schools of that county, and was a member of the Baptist Church. They had nine children, six of whom are living: Micajah, deceased; Sarah, now Mrs. Elliott of Washington County; W. T. Campbell, farmer of Washington County; Francis Marion Campbell (subject); John C. Campbell of Bottsville, Washington County; Sue, deceased, who married John G. Howard; George Waller Campbell, a merchant of Willow Springs, Missouri—twelve miles from Kansas City; Lucy E., married the Rev. Purdom, pastor of the Bethlehem and Mackville Baptist Churches, and Samuel Campbell, postmaster and merchant of Jensonton, Washington County.

George P. Campbell (father) died September 24, 1886, and his wife died March 12, 1866. They are buried in the old family burial ground at the Campbell homestead.

REV. HENRY BIDLEMAN BASCOM, D. D., LL.D., a leading bishop of the Methodist Episcopal Church South, was born in Hancock, New York, May 27, 1796, and died at Louisville, Kentucky, September 8, 1850, aged fifty-four. His father emigrated to the West in 1812 and settled in or near Maysville, Kentucky; thence removed to Ohio, about five miles distant. The son assisted to support the family—at one time by driving a dray. He quit school at twelve, but read and studied in the spare moments from his work. At fifteen he began to exhort, soon after joining the Methodist Church; at seventeen was licensed to preach, first in southern Ohio; at eighteen, in West Virginia; at twenty and twenty-one, around Danville and Richmond, Kentucky; at twenty-two and twenty-three, in 1818-19, at Louisville, the first Methodist preacher ever stationed in that city. Henry Clay listened to his wonderful eloquence and had him elected chaplain of the house of representatives of congress, 1823-24. This extended his sphere of usefulness and gave him a national reputation. He preached to admiring thousands in the large cities.

He was president of Madison College, at Uniontown, Pennsylvania, 1827-28; agent of the American Colonization Society, 1829-30; professor in Augusta College, Kentucky, for ten years, 1831-41; president of Transylvania University, Lexington, Kentucky, 1842-48; the recognized leader in the convention of delegates from the annual conferences, held at Louisville in 1845, which resulted in the organizing of the Methodist Episcopal Church South; editor of the "Methodist Quarterly Review," 1846-50; prepared for publication, in 1849, a volume of his sermons, which met with great public favor; was elected a bishop, in 1850, and presided over the St. Louis conference, July, 1850—the only conference he lived to attend as bishop. On his return journey to his home at Lexington, Kentucky, he was too ill to proceed farther than Louisville, where he lingered for five weeks, until his death.

JUDGE JAMES HERVEY DORMAN, a leading and able lawyer of the bar of Owenton, son of Peter and Lucy (Kemper) Dorman, was born in Gallatin County, Kentucky, November 7, 1831. There was no school near that he could attend until he was twenty years of age. About that time, having earned some money, he entered Asbury (now De Pauw) University, Indiana and remained there for two years and then taught school for four years.

At the beginning of the war between the states, he entered the Confederate army. In 1862 he fought under General Lee in the Army of Northern Virginia, and at different times served under Generals Humphrey Marshall, John C. Breckenridge, Ransom, Longstreet, Morgan and Buckner. From the last named he obtained a furlough to celebrate his marriage with Miss Lizzie Gaines. He was a high private in the front ranks, but on one occasion he started from Lexington as captain of a company of seventy men, and when they reached Cumberland Gap they all deserted, declaring they had volunteered to fight in Kentucky and would not fight elsewhere. Judge Dorman then went on to Abingdon, Virginia, and enlisted as a private. He was in forty-two battles and was ten days at the siege of Knoxville, Tennessee, his entire service extending over a period of three and a half years. When the war closed all the money he had was twenty-five cents.

After returning home he taught school and resumed the study of law, reading at night, after school hours; and began to practice in Owenton in 1866, where he is still actively engaged and is one of the leading men of his profession.

From 1869 to 1874 he was in the state senate, and immediately after his term expired he was elected county judge, and held that office from 1874 to 1878, since which time he has acted as special circuit judge on several occasions, but has held no other office.

Judge Dorman was married March 16, 1864, to Lizzie Gaines, daughter of Col. Samuel Gaines, a Methodist minister. She is a native of Sullivan County, Tennessee, and was educated at a noted college in Asheville, North Carolina. They have four children living: William Gaines, Fannie, Letitia (deceased), Virginia Lee and James Hervey Dorman, Jr.

Judge Dorman is a man of many fine qualities. He is an active politician and a stanch Democratic adherent to principle, as his record abundantly proves. As a lawyer he stands second to none at the bar of Owenton, a bar famous for its legal celebrities. Judge and Mrs. Dorman are members of the Missionary Baptist Church.

Peter Dorman (father) was born in Accomac County, Virginia, September 3, 1803. He came to Kentucky at the age of eighteen and settled in Bourbon County, Kentucky, where he was educated in the primitive schools of that day.

When he was twenty-one years of age he moved to Gallatin County, Kentucky, and was a farmer in that county the remainder of his life and died January 3, 1873.

He married Lucy Kemper in 1830. She was born March 17, 1814. They had eleven children: James H., Fannie, Anna Eliza, John Wickliffe and Martin Luther (both John W. and Martin Luther were in the Confederate army), Elizabeth, Lucy, Emma, Henry, Peter and Atlanta.

Mathew Dorman (grandfather) was born in Accomac County, Virginia, of English ancestry. He came to Kentucky and died in Gallatin County. His wife was Atlanta Barnes of Accomac County, Virginia. They had nine children: Peter, Archie, Samuel, Lydia, Elizabeth, Lear, Silas, Jerubial and Mathew.

Mathew Dorman (great-grandfather) was a farmer of Accomac County, Virginia. He was in the Continental army, in Washington's command.

Jonathan Kemper (maternal grandfather) was born and educated in Fayette County, Kentucky. After residing there for many years, he moved to Owen County, where he died. They had nine children: Nathan, Robert Walker, Lucy, Alfred, Asa, Joshua, Elizabeth, Jonathan, Jr., and David.

Benjamin Kemper (great-grandfather) was born in Germany, and after his marriage there immigrated to Fayette County, Kentucky, where he engaged in farming.

EDWARD CROSSLAND, deceased, an eminent jurist and member of congress from Mayfield, Kentucky, son of Samuel and Elizabeth Harry Crossland, was born in Hickman County, Kentucky, June 30, 1827, and was educated in the common schools there. He farmed for a few years after leaving school, and was the first sheriff of Hickman County after the adoption of the constitution of 1850. He studied law with Col. Bowmar, and, being admitted to the bar, commenced to practice with Col. George W. Silvertooth and Col. W. D. Lannon. From 1857 to 1859 he represented Hickman and Fulton Counties in the Kentucky legislature. In 1861 he enlisted in the Confederate army, connecting himself with the First Kentucky Regiment, then under command of Col. Blanton Duncan and afterwards under Col. Thomas H. Taylor of Louisville. He was sworn into service in Virginia as captain of his company and served in that capacity one year, when he was promoted to the rank of major, and later to that of lieutenant colonel. Upon the disbandment of the regiment, he was assigned to duty as colonel of the Seventh Kentucky Infantry, then in Mississippi, and was in command of the Kentucky brigade with Forrests' Cavalry when the war closed. After the war he returned to the practice of law in the First Judicial District, his home being at Clinton, Hickman County. He was elected judge of the Common Pleas Court of his district in 1866, but resigned that office in 1871 and was elected to Congress from the First District, being re-elected and serving until 1875. When his congressional term expired he resumed the practice of law at Mayfield, Kentucky, and in all the courts of his judicial district. In 1880 he was elected circuit judge of his district and was on the bench until he died, September 11, 1881. He was a Mason, and it is needless to add that he was a Democrat.

Judge Crossland's wife, Mary Hess, daughter of Nelson I. Hess, was born in Trenton, Tennessee; was married to Judge Crossland in 1846, and is still living in Temple, Texas.

Nelson I. Hess, father of Mrs. Crossland, lived in Trenton, Gibson County, Tennessee, and was a physician and minister in the Cumberland Presbyterian Church. He married Adeline Northcutt and died in 1870. His mother was a sister of Joseph Hamilton Daviess of Mercer County, Kentucky.

The following is a public tribute to the memory of Judge Crossland:

The rapid resume of the civil and military positions held by Judge Crossland bear unquestionable testimony to the fact that he was deeply cherished in the affections of the people, and that his popularity was based upon their unbounded confidence in his ability and integrity. It was not the evanescent popularity of a day or a season, but that of a life-time; solid, impregnable. Nor was it undeserved. The people did not misunderstand or mistake him. "They loved him be-

JUDGE EDWARD CROSSLAND.

cause he first loved them." Every pulsation of his heart was in unison with their interests. He had a faculty of seeing things as the people saw them, and of feeling them as the people felt them. His thoughts and emotions came from the ready mould of his genius, glowing and commending their own worth to every one who listened to his words. In this respect he was a born orator. In the quickness of his perceptions and the rapidity with which his conclusions were reached he had few equals. His firm and deeply grounded principles of truth and honor and patriotism fortified him against the errors and vices of the mere political demagogue.

His affections were high and pure and generous, and chief among them was charity. In him charity of thought, word and deed was one enduring and overpowering enthusiasm.

As a soldier he was brave to recklessness of his own life, but the wounding or death of any of those under his command affected him to tears. In his death the district lost one of the purest and ablest of jurists.

He was always kind, brave, self-sacrificing and devoted. The soldier, the lawyer, the jurist, the statesman and the citizen, as well as the hero and patriot, is no more.

The Graves County bar adopted the following resolutions:

"That in the death of Judge Edward Crossland the people of the First Judicial District have been deprived of the services of an eminent and impartial judge; of a lawyer of extraordinary industry, fidelity and ability; sound in judgment and unblemished in integrity.

"That Graves County has sustained a calamity in being deprived of one of her ablest and most highly gifted citizens, who was kind, generous and hospitable and brave, with a heart alive to every noble and magnanimous impulse—whom the people of our own country delighted to honor." Signed by the Committee: W. N. Boaz, F. Metcalf, P. Lyles, and W. M. Smith.

Samuel Crossland (father) was born in South Carolina and came to Hickman County, Kentucky, in 1820. He married Elizabeth Harry in South Carolina and had two daughters: Elizabeth and Mary. He died in 1854 and is buried in Hickman County. His family is a very numerous one in South Carolina.

S. H. Crossland, son of Judge Crossland and Mary Hess, was born August 7, 1849, in Hickman County, Kentucky. He entered Washington and Lee University in 1867; he studied two years there and then read law in his father's office and attended the law department of the University of Louisville; was admitted to the bar in 1871 in Mayfield, and practiced in that judicial district; was elected county attorney in 1882 for one term; was elected commonwealth's attorney of the district in which he lived in 1886, then composed of eight, now only five counties. He went out of office in January, 1893, since which time he has been in the regular practice of his profession.

Mr. Crossland was married December 25, 1873, to Miss Mattie E. Smith, daughter of W. H. Smith of McCracken County, Kentucky. She died in December, 1895, and is buried in Mayfield, Kentucky. They had six children: Edward, Nannie, Lal., Caswell Bennett, Kathleen and Samuel. Mr. Crossland is one of the best criminal lawyers in his district, in fact, criminal law is his specialty, but he has a large general practice. He is greatly devoted to the memory of his distinguished father.

ROBERT M. JACKSON, Cashier of the First National Bank of London, eldest son of William H. Jackson and Maria McKee, was born in London, Kentucky, June 1, 1859. He received his general education in private schools in his native city, and graduated from the Lexington Commercial College, March 28, 1877.

He began his business career in the drug business with his father and brother, a firm which has done an extensive business from its beginning. November 9, 1885, he was appointed postmaster of London by President Cleveland and held that office nearly five years, and until his successor was appointed by President Harrison. It was conceded that he conducted the affairs of that office with fidelity and dispatch, devoting his whole time and most careful attention to its duties.

Upon the organization of the First National

Bank in December, 1888, he was elected vice president; and January 10, 1893, upon the retirement of R. C. Ford, he was elected cashier, since which time he has given his undivided attention to the affairs of the bank, with the result that it is now in a better condition than at any time in its history, and is one of the safest financial institutions in the interior of the state: It was in a large measure due to his ability and wise management that this bank was able to stem the financial storm that swept over the country in 1893, when many stronger institutions went down as a consequence of mistrust and doubt on the part of depositors.

He was appointed aide on the staff of Governor John Young Brown in 1891, but has never held, or been candidate for, any elective office. For four years past he has been chairman of the Eleventh Congressional District Democratic Committee, and in that capacity has done much efficient work for his party. He has done well for a man of his years and has bright prospects for the future. He is deeply interested in the welfare of London and Laurel County, is public spirited and enterprising, and ever ready to aid in the establishment of new companies and industries. He is quite prominent in Masonic circles, being high priest of the Royal Arch Chapter, and has taken the degrees of Knight Templar and the Mystic Shrine.

Mr. Jackson was married in 1880 to Alice Ewell, daughter of Hon. R. L. Ewell of London, a sketch of whose life and ancestry is given in this volume. They have one of the most attractive homes in London.

William H. Jackson (father) was born in Laurel County, Kentucky, in 1830, and has been a resident of London since 1856. He followed his trade as a blacksmith until 1868, since which time he has been engaged in the general mercantile and drug business. In 1867 he was elected jailer of the county and served one term, otherwise he has held no office.

Stephen M. Jackson (grandfather) was born, lived and died in Laurel County; was a modest, well-to-do farmer; a devout member of the Baptist Church, and a good citizen. He reached his seventy-fourth year and died in 1889.

John Jackson (great-grandfather), a native of England, came to the United States when a young man, with three brothers, and was among the first settlers of Madison County. He was a farmer and owned the ground upon which the city of Richmond now stands.

Maria McKee Jackson (mother) was born in Laurel County in 1841, and is now a resident of London. She and her husband are prominent members of the Methodist Episcopal Church. Her father, John V. L. McKee, a native of Virginia, of Irish parentage, became one of the earliest residents of Laurel County. He was a farmer and carpenter, and a highly esteemed citizen.

WILLIAM F. SCOTT, M. D., Superintendent of the Lexington Asylum for the Insane, son of Dr. John D. and Martha Ann (Farris) Scott, was born in Stanford, Kentucky, March 7, 1828.

His father, Dr. John D. Scott, was born in Garrard County, near Bryantsville, and removed to Stanford when a young man. He lived there and practiced medicine for many years. He was one of the most popular and successful physicians in all that section, and his practice enabled him to accumulate a large and valuable estate in land and slaves. Becoming independent, he retired from the practice of his profession and removed to Louisville, where he died at the age of sixty-five years. He was a Christian physician, a member of the Presbyterian Church, a man of great purity of character, a scholar and a true Kentucky gentleman.

His grandfather, John Scott, descended from an old Pennsylvania family, but was a native of Kentucky, and one of the pioneer farmers of Garrard County, before and after the admission of Kentucky to the union of the states. He was a man of advanced ideas, great personal influence, and accumulated great wealth.

Martha Ann Farris Scott (mother) was born near Walnut Flat, Lincoln County, early in the present century. She was a woman of unusual piety, a member of the Presbyterian Church, and was greatly esteemed for her intelligence and many personal graces.

William Farris (grandfather) was one of the

most noted breeders of race horses of his time, and accomplished a good work in the improvement of stock in his state, which was even at that time noted for fine horses. He was a very wealthy man. His wife (grandmother) was a Miss Owsley, cousin of Governor Owsley.

Dr. William F. Scott was educated in the high schools of Stanford and read medicine with Dr. Thomas Montgomery of that place, and with Dr. Reed of Hustonville. He graduated from the medical department of Transylvania University at Lexington in 1852, where he was a pupil of the celebrated Dr. Benjamin Dudley, and in the same year located in Somerset, Pulaski County, where he has since practiced his profession; has been a successful general practitioner and has the reputation of being one of the most skillful surgeons of southern Kentucky. By his faithfulness and kindness in the discharge of his duties, he has greatly endeared himself to every one throughout that section of country, and no man has more influence with the people of his community.

He has successfully performed all the difficult operations in surgery, including lithotomy, etc. In 1894, month of February, he performed an operation on Thomas Hurd, extracting a stone from the bladder weighing four ounces, one among the largest on record.

In 1862 he was appointed and commissioned surgeon in the Thirty-second Regiment Kentucky Volunteers, commanded by his brother-in-law, Col. Thomas Z. Morrow. He served with distinction as surgeon in the field for one year, and was post surgeon more or less throughout the war; was one of the charter members and stockholders and directors of the First National Bank of Somerset, organized in 1871; was president of the Board of Pension Examiners by appointment of President Benjamin Harrison, and has obeyed the call of his party in every case where his professional services have been required. He is an officer of the G. A. R. and a member of the Kentucky State and Pulaski Medical Societies.

Dr. Scott is progressive in his ideas, and notwithstanding his fidelity to the old school is ever ready to accept new and true principles which lead to advancement in medical science; is a constant student and a reader of medical and scientific literature, and is up to date in study and practice.

In 1860 Dr. Scott was married to Miss Margaret E. Bradley, an intelligent, accomplished young lady, daughter of Robert M. and Ellen Lotten Bradley. R. M. Bradley was one of the most noted land lawyers of Kentucky, and his wife one of the most excellent women of her time. Mrs. Scott is a sister of W. O. Bradley, governor of Kentucky. Dr. and Mrs. Scott have three sons living: Thomas M. Scott, who held a position in the revenue office under Col. Dan Collier; Ethelbert D. Scott, a lawyer of Lexington, and Dr. Samuel Scott, a young physician. Dr. Scott and his wife are members of the Baptist Church.

Dr. Scott has been a life-long Republican, and has rendered valuable service to the party in its earlier and later struggles for supremacy. In January, 1896, he was appointed by Governor Bradley superintendent of the Eastern Kentucky Asylum. The political aspect of his appointment was merely incidental, the doctor's qualifications for the office being paramount. His appointment has given general satisfaction, and he brings to his position ripe experience, devotion to duty, and is meeting the most sanguine expectations of his many friends and admirers.

JAMES GAYLE TODD, County Attorney of Owen County, son of Howard Todd and Willina Duvall, was born in Owen County, November 21, 1858. He was educated in the common schools in New Liberty and at Concord College. Upon leaving school at the age of sixteen, he engaged in farming and stock-raising, but began the study of law with Joseph Blackwell at New Liberty and was admitted to the bar in 1880; was in partnership with Joseph Blackwell there, but finally located at Owenton. In 1894 he was elected to his present position as county attorney of Owen County, on the Democratic ticket. Mr. Todd was married in 1884 to Kitty Kale of Owen County.

Howard Todd (father) was born in Scott County, Kentucky, in 1806, and was educated in the backwoods schools of that day, and was a trader and farmer in Owen County all his life. When fourteen years of age he was made deputy sheriff of Gallatin County, which then comprised the present counties of Carroll, Gallatin, Trimble and Owen. He served as deputy and sheriff altogether for fifteen years and was a delegate to the State Constitutional Convention from Owen County in 1849. Before the war he was an old line Whig and afterwards a Democrat. Mr. Todd was a hospitable Kentucky gentleman of the old school, a large land and slave owner, and, like most Kentuckians of that day, entered heartily into the spirit of the Masonic order.

Among the papers which he left is a receipt dated 1819, showing that John Gayle of Gallatin (now Owen) County had property listed at one thousand acres of land and a number of negroes. His total tax at that time was $5.40, showing the vast increase in taxation. Under the present rates his taxes would have been several hundred dollars.

Howard Todd married Willina Duvall, a native of Scott County, who was educated at Frankfort, and they had eight children: Lewis, Annette, Jennie, Pike, Bettie, Howard, Mattie and James Gayle.

Samuel Todd (grandfather) was born in Fredericksburg, Virginia; came to Scott County, Kentucky, in 1805, and thence to Owen County in 1807; was sheriff of Gallatin County, as is stated above, and was a member of the Missionary Baptist Church. He married Mary Willis, a native of Fredericksburg, Virginia.

John Duvall (maternal grandfather) was born in Maryland in 1784. He was a farmer by occupation and came to Scott County and became a very wealthy man; was a colonel in the War of 1812; served in the Kentucky legislature in 1827 and died in 1859. He married Jennie Branham, a native of Scott County, Kentucky. Their children were: Thomas, Howard, Alvin, Elizabeth, who married Dr. English; William P., who represented his district twice in the state senate and house of representatives; Burbridge, Edward, Annie, who married William G. Simpson; Martha, and John, Jr., who represented Owen County in the Kentucky house of representatives.

Judge Alvin Duvall, distinguished son of John and Jennie Branham Duvall, graduated with honors from Georgetown College; studied law under Governor James F. Robinson, and afterwards took a legal course in Transylvania University at Lexington; represented his county in the legislature in 1850; was appointed circuit judge in 1852; was judge of the Court of Appeals from 1856 to 1864, and in 1864 was again a candidate, when the military governor of Kentucky, Burbridge, caused his name to be stricken from the pollbooks three days before the election. General Burbridge then ordered his arrest on the ground that he was in sympathy with the Southern cause. To avoid the consequences of this high-handed usurpation of power, he fled to Canada, but after two months returned to Georgetown and resumed the practice of law; was appointed reporter of the Court of Appeals in 1866, and the two volumes of reports published by him have been highly commended. In May, 1866, he was nominated for clerk of the Court of Appeals and was elected by a majority of thirty-seven thousand, nine hundred and fifty-four votes over his Republican opponent. In 1868 he was elected president of the Farmers' Bank of Kentucky, which position he held until his death, in 1893.

EVAN EVANS SETTLE of Owenton, Kentucky, distinguished lawyer and politician, son of William H. and Harriet Evans Settle, was born in Frankfort, Kentucky, December 1, 1848.

His education was commenced at Frankfort under that distinguished educator, B. B. Sayre, and continued in the Louisville Male High School, from which he graduated in 1864, at the age of sixteen. He was first employed as a clerk in the provost marshal's office in Louisville in the winter of 1864-65, and upon returning to Frankfort was a clerk for one year in the auditor's office under W. T. Samuels. He went to Greenville, Mississippi, in 1866, and was a clerk there under W. A. Haycraft. In 1887 he returned to Kentucky and was employed in the United States District and Circuit Courts, of which A. J. Ballard was then clerk, and in 1868 went to Owen County and was for one year in the office of A. B. Roberts, County Court clerk. He studied law alone and has practiced in Owen

County since he obtained his license; was elected county attorney in 1878, re-elected in 1882 and again in 1886, but resigned that office in 1887, and was elected to the legislature by his party, and was re-elected in 1889; was a delegate to the St. Louis National Convention (Democratic) in 1888 and seconded the nomination of Governor Gray of Indiana for vice president. He was a candidate for the Democratic Congressional nomination in 1894 in the Seventh District against W. C. P. Breckenridge and W. C. Owens. In this memorable campaign there was a great deal of bad feeling and bitterness engendered between the candidates and their friends. Personal vituperation and abuse of each other was indulged in by the candidates and excitement ran very high. In striking contrast to the methods employed by the others to win the endorsement of their party was the dignified and high plane on which Mr. Settle conducted his campaign. He did not want to go to Congress on the issue of the private short-comings and misdoings of either of his opponents, and in accord with this positively refused to attack the moral character of either of them. He considered their public record only as a legitimate object of attack. This conduct won for him much commendation and many friends, but not quite enough votes, for in the unprecedented excitement of the campaign the other way seemed to be what the people wanted.

Mr. Settle married Lizzie R. Herndon, October 20, 1875. She was born and educated in Owen County. They have six children: Mary, Margaret, Evan E., Eunice, Horace H. and Harriet Clay.

Thomas P. Herndon, Mrs. Settle's father, was a soldier in the Mexican war and served in the Confederate army during the war between the states. His wife was Margaret Threlkeld of Owen County, Kentucky.

William H. Settle (father) was born in Franklin County, Kentucky, January 27, 1823, and was educated in the common schools there. He was a wholesale merchant and speculator in Frankfort and in Louisville, living in Frankfort until the beginning of the war, when he removed to Louisville, and invested largely in land at that place. Before the war he was an old line Whig and during the war was a Union man. He was a Democrat in politics and in religion a Presbyterian. He married Harriet D. Evans, who was born and educated in Frankfort. By this marriage there were five children: Evan E., Sallie, James H., Mattie and William.

Mr. Settle was married (second) October 23, 1861, to Mary W. McCraw, a native of Lynchburg, Virginia, and a daughter of Colonel Hill McCraw (well known in Louisville) and Nannie Elliott McCraw. The children of this marriage are William, Nannie, John, Joseph and Samuel. Mr. Settle died in 1886.

Joseph Settle (grandfather) was born in Franklin County, Kentucky. He was a millwright and gunsmith; married Sallie Sanders, daughter of Hugh Sanders, who came from Virginia and was a son of Nathaniel Sanders, a soldier of the Revolutionary war.

Evan Evans (maternal grandfather) was a contractor and builder, and was one of the architects who superintended the erection of the present state house at Frankfort. He was a native of Wales and came to this country in the early part of this century; settled first in Pennsylvania, where he married Mary Breese, also a native of Wales. They were Presbyterians. Their children were: John Evans, an eminent lawyer of Frankfort; James S. Evans, civil engineer and soldier in the Mexican war, and Humphrey Evans, who was also in the Mexican war and a major in the Confederate army, being in many important battles, in the Army of the Mississippi.

DAVID ROWLAND FRANCIS, ex-Governor of Missouri, was born October 1, 1850, in Richmond, Kentucky; educated in Richmond Academy and in the school taught by Rev. Robert Breck. In 1866 entered Washington University at St. Louis, graduated in 1870; engaged as shipping clerk for the firm of Rowland & Shryock for two years, then junior partner of said firm for two years. In 1878 established his own business, the D. R. Francis Commission Company, later engaged in the wholesale grain business, both enterprises being eminently successful, and his conduct of them entitling him, although young, to be called one of the ablest financiers in the city of St. Louis. He is a man of broad public spirit and endowed by nature with the qualities which stamp him as a leader of enterprises for the public weal. Is magnetic to an unusual degree and inspires the confidence of all with whom he is associated. He is identified with many corporations.

In 1883 was elected vice president of the Merchants' Exchange and elected president in 1884, in one of the most spirited contests ever held. He is vice president of the Mississippi Valley Trust Company and vice president of the Laclede Bank. In 1885 was nominated by the Democratic convention for mayor of St. Louis on the one hundred and eighty-fourth ballot. One of the issues of his campaign for the mayoralty was cheap gas, and it was largely due to his efforts after election that the rate for this necessity was reduced. He vetoed the Electric Elevated Railway bill on account of the small compensation received by the city for the franchise. During his administration $950,000 passed into the city treasury from the Missouri Pacific Railroad Company. In May, 1884, he was elected delegate-at-large from Missouri to the Democratic National Convention held in Chicago in June, and was one of the first politicians that recognized the adaptiveness of Grover Cleveland for the presidency. He gave Mr. Cleveland an ardent support. In 1888, August 22, he was nominated for governor of Missouri by the Democratic State Convention, and was elected in November of the same year—was inaugurated January 14, 1889. His administration was exceedingly popular. He displayed great executive ability in the management of it. It was characterized by wisdom and the spirit of legitimate progress.

Gov. Francis is a member of the Presbyterian Church and a Knight Templar. He was married January 21, 1876, to Miss Jane Perry, daughter of John D. Perry, and is the father of six manly boys: Perry, David Rowland, Charles Broaddus, Salton Turner, Thomas, Sidney Rowland.

He had two brothers, Thomas H. and Sidney Rowland, and two sisters, Hallie Francis Boyd and Mary Francis Ellerbe. Sidney Rowland Francis passed away December 4, 1893. He was a remarkable man, possessing many traits in common with Governor Francis. No man stood higher in the affection and esteem of the people of St. Louis. Although comparatively a young man, he had amassed a large fortune. Thomas H. Francis lives in St. Louis and has sterling business qualities. Hallie Francis, wife of William Boyd, passed away December 1, 1893, leaving three young daughters to mourn her irreparable loss. She was a woman of strong character, amiable and loving in her family relations, and in her religious convictions so devotedly and practically pious that she was a living epistle seen and known of men. Her husband, William G. Boyd, is a relative of Gov. Francis and associated with him in business. In 1894 he was elected president of the Merchants' Exchange, making the third of the immediate family who have held the position—David Pittman Rowland, an uncle, David Rowland Francis and William G. Boyd. Mr. Boyd has recently been elected vice president of the Mercantile Club.

Mary Francis Ellerbe, wife of the lawyer, Christopher P. Ellerbe, resides at Ferguson, Missouri, and in common with the other members of her family is endowed with mental qualities of a high order, and a distinctly attractive personality.

The father of Governor Francis was John Broaddus Francis. He was born in Madison County, January 21, 1819; educated in the same county; was deputy sheriff for three years and sheriff for four years of Madison County. Afterwards engaged in the mercantile business in Richmond. Later moved to Lincoln County and farmed; moved to Missouri in 1882, near St. Louis; died November 27, 1894, and was buried in Bellefontaine Cemetery at St. Louis. He was a Whig and a very enthusiastic politician, but loved his home so well that he did not care for office for himself. His zeal was in the interest of his party, and for the advancement of his friends. An upright, honorable gentleman of the old school, of stainless life and actuated by courteous, kindly impulses. The father of John Broaddus Francis was Thomas Francis, born in Henrico County, Virginia, in 1787; came to Kentucky when very young, and served in the War of 1812. His wife, Mary Broaddus, was the daughter of Edwin Broaddus, sixth in descent from the Edwin

Broaddus who came from Wales. He located on Silver Creek, Madison County, Kentucky; was the oldest magistrate in the county, and high sheriff; died in March, 1864. His wife died in 1862.

Thomas Francis, the grandfather of John Broaddus Francis, was born near Richmond, Virginia, at Bottomme Bridge; married Miss Bottomme.

The mother of Governor Francis, Eliza Caldwell Francis, was born in Richmond, Kentucky, February 27, 1830; educated at the school of the Rev. John Brown—the Madison County Female Seminary; was married December 5, 1849; is a devoted member of the Presbyterian Church. Her father, David Irvine Rowland, was born in Botetourt County, Virginia, November 12, 1802; came to Madison County in 1804; was a shoe manufacturer in Richmond, Kentucky, and a member of the Presbyterian Church. He was buried near Richmond. Her mother was Mehala Hogg Tyree, daughter of James Tyree and Mary Goddin of New Kent County, Virginia. She was born December 12, 1802; educated in Virginia, and married in Richmond, Kentucky; died April 20, 1868. Mrs. Francis' grandfather, Robert Rowland, married Francis Irvine, daughter of David Irvine and Jane Kyle. Both lived near Lynchburg, Virginia. Francis Irvine was the sister of William and Christopher Irvine, those incomparable men whose characters and services are indelibly impressed upon the history of Kentucky, and one of the ten Irvine sisters, who, imbued with the pioneer spirit of Scotch-Irish ancestry, at different times left their comfortable home in Virginia and journeyed on horseback through the wilderness to their adopted home in Kentucky, enduring all manner of hardships and exposed by day and by night to the attacks of savage foes, animal and human.

They intermarried with the prominent families of Kentucky, and in every instance were the ancestresses of influential and distinguished progeny. The influence of the descendants of David Irvine and Jane Kyle forms an interesting and instructive chapter in the history of Kentucky and sister states. The names of the ten pioneer Irvine women were: Mary Irvine Adams, Madalene Irvine Pittman, Amelia Irvine Hockaday, Elizabeth Irvine Talbott, Sallie Irvine Goggin, the celebrated Goggin family of Virginia; Margaret Irvine Pace, Jane Irvine Curle, Frances Irvine Rowland, Anna Irvine Goggin, Sophie Irvine Fox.

The last named was the mother of the late Judge Fontaine Talbot Fox of Danville, Kentucky. No words here can add to the fame of that revered and distinguished citizen. His memory is embalmed in the hearts of his associates on the bench and at the bar of Kentucky. Jane Irvine Curle was the ancestress of William Boyd, who married a sister of Governor Francis.

The Curles were men of broad public spirit. In the early days in Kentucky gave largely of their private means to enterprises for the public weal. Contributed $10,000 to secure the independence of Texas.

They were of English descent and owned an immense estate at Curles Neck, situated in a bend of James River, Virginia, noted as being the highest point on that river reached by the British during the Revolution, and was also just above the point to which McClellan retreated after his defeat near Richmond. Archibald Curle and Jane Irvine, his wife, the ancestors of William Boyd, were stanch Presbyterians. Mrs. Sophie Boyd, granddaughter of Archibald Curle and mother of William Boyd, is a widow and resides in Louisville, Kentucky. She is the mother of four sons who are successful business men, and two interesting daughters, Mrs. James Mahon and Mrs. Lily Stark. The ancestors of David Irvine were Scotch-Irish. From the time of Robert Bruce, when a part of the royal forests of Drum were awarded William de Irvine in consideration of valuable services, in every succeeding era of Scotch history we come upon honorable mention of the family. The military spirit dominated them. We read of their valor on many a hotly contested field. Captain Christopher Irvine commanded King James' Light Horse at the battle of Flodden. Alexander Irvine, twin brother of the ancestor of the Kentucky branch, closed the gates of Londonderry in the face of another King James and his flushed army, thereby securing civil and religious liberty to the British Empire.

"In view of the stupendous results of this intrepid action," says the Edinburg Review, "Alexander Irvine is justly entitled to be called, if not the greatest, certainly one of the greatest heroes the world has ever seen." In the American Revolution General William Irvine played a conspicuous part and many of his Irvine kinsmen served under him. In the early days in Kentucky the brothers, William and Christopher Irvine, and Christopher, the son of William, performed prodigies of service for the state.

In the war between the states, a number of the descendants of David Irvine were engaged, in rank from private up to general. It is to his mother, Eliza Caldwell Irvine Rowland, that Governor Francis owes his success in life. Mrs. Francis is a rare woman. As clearly as a signet makes an impression upon a sheet of white paper, she has impressed upon her children the intellectuality and strongly marked characteristics of a renowned ancestry. Governor Francis is a young man yet, and his friends predict for him still greater successes, and higher public responsibilities.

JAMES DAVID LANDRUM, physician, of Mayfield, son of James and Nancy Walden Landrum, was born in Barren County, Kentucky, October 1, 1822. He was educated in Christian County; studied medicine under Drs. Shelton, McKinney and Lindsay; also at Physio-Medical College, Cincinnati, entering there in 1848 and graduating in 1853. His first partner was Dr. L. D. Shelton in La Fayette, Christian County; later in Mayfield, from 1877 to 1892, he was associated with Dr. John L. Dismukes; was admitted to membership in the American Medical Association in 1859, and is a charter and life member of Graves County and West Kentucky Medical Societies, and is President of the Mayfield Medical Club (1896).

In 1850 Dr. Landrum was a first degree Mason and in 1864 was Grand Master of Grand Lodge of Kentucky, and in 1895 took the thirty-second degree, and is the oldest man in Kentucky, and it may be in the country, to take that degree. At the same time his son, William L. Landrum, and his grandson, W. T. Landrum, also became Masons of this high degree, the latter being the youngest to obtain that honor in the United States.

Dr. Landrum joined the Christian Church in 1839 and for the last twenty-five years has been an elder; is one of the three living charter members of that church in Mayfield. During the Civil War Dr. Landrum was contract surgeon with General Grant from March to September, 1862, when he resigned; was elected State Senator in 1863 as a Union man, and served until 1867. Since that time he has held no office and has practiced medicine in Mayfield, yet he is a great temperance worker, and an ardent Republican.

Dr. Landrum was married (first) in 1850 to Catherine Robbins, and she was the mother of five children, of whom are: William L., general agent for the Southern States of the Panly Jail Building and Manufacturing Company of St. Louis; Thomas J., of the firm of Bray & Landrum, clothing manufacturers of Louisville; and John W., secretary and general manager of Graves County Water and Electric Light Company.

Dr. Landrum's second marriage was to Mrs. Mary Virginia Fisher Anderson, widow of Captain Anderson of the Confederate army. She was educated at the school of Enos Campbell, Hopkinsville.

Dr. Landrum is essentially a leader, whether in professional, church or political affairs. For fifty-six years he has been an earnest, conscientious and untiring worker in his church. He has the love of his fellow-citizens, who recognize in him one of the highest types of American manhood.

James Landrum (father) was born in Amherst County, Virginia, and educated there; was a farmer in Virginia, and on coming to Barren County, Kentucky, in 1809, followed the same pursuit. From there he removed to Christian County, where he died in 1841. He was a member of the Primitive Baptist Church.

Thomas Landrum (grandfather) died at Amherst Court House, Virginia, at the age of ninety-six years. He was in the Revolutionary army, and his son James fought in the War of 1812. They belonged to the famous Scotch-Irish race.

Nancy Walden Landrum (mother) was born in

King William County, Virginia, and died in Graves County, Kentucky, in 1863, at the age of sixty-two years. She married James Landrum in 1814. She was a member of the Primitive Baptist Church. Her father, William Walden, was born in England and moved to King William County, Virginia, and subsequently to Kentucky, and was a wealthy farmer. He disinherited his daughter, Mrs. Landrum, because of her marriage. He married Nancy Anne Rhodes, of the famous aristocratic Rhodes family of Virginia.

DOCTOR NEWTON PORTER, M. D., a distinguished physician and Baptist minister of Eminence, son of Eli Porter and Martha Ball, was born in Henry County, Kentucky, January 17, 1816, and was reared in the same county. Dr. Porter being the seventh son, the old tradition probably induced his parents to christen him "Doctor," and that is his name as well as his title.

He attended the common schools of the neighborhood in which he lived until his fifteenth year, when, on account of his father's death and the necessity of his assistance in the support of the family, he was compelled to leave school. He then commenced to educate himself systematically, and before he was sixteen years of age began to teach school, and taught for sixteen years altogether in the vicinity in which he resided.

At one time he thought seriously of turning his attention to the profession of law, but was influenced and dissuaded from this course by friends who thought him better fitted for the medical profession. When twenty-three years of age, while engaged in teaching, he began the study of medicine under the instruction of Dr. N. Green of Carrollton. His method of study for twelve years was thorough and careful, and although he was compelled to practice on account of the importunities of friends, he would not allow himself to be considered fully equipped as a physician until he believed that he could conscientiously do so. Dr. Porter attended Georgetown College for a short time, but he is mainly self-educated.

He went to Louisville in 1847 and entered the Kentucky School of Medicine in 1850; graduated in 1851 with high honors, being chosen valedictorian of his class and selected for that honor by a unanimous vote, but he magnanimously requested that one of the students whom he especially admired be given the honor in place of himself, which request was granted. He began the practice of medicine in Eminence, Henry County, Kentucky, and was for many years the leading obstetrician of the state.

He was elected President of the State Medical Society in 1867, and delivered the address before that society at Danville, in April, 1868, and this address was published in the state reports. He was also for a number of years a member of the American Medical Association, but when he gave up the active practice of medicine in 1883, he withdrew from that society.

He joined the Baptist Church at the age of thirteen, and in 1841 was ordained minister of that denomination. From 1847 to 1848 he was pastor of the East Baptist Church at Louisville, and subsequently pastor at various times of the following churches: Fox Run Church at Eminence; Ballardsville Church in Oldham County; Hopewell Church in Henry County; Indian Fork Church in Shelby County; Christiansburg Church in Shelby County; the Baptist Church at Frankfort, and others at other places. During his long and active service for fifty-five years as a minister of the Baptist Church, he took part in the ordination of thirty-three ministers, aided in forming the constitution of six churches, preaching during that time on an average of once a week, and performed the marriage ceremony and the initial rites of church membership for hundreds of persons.

He is a man of the most remarkable energy, as is evidenced by the fact that while in the active service of the church he was also actively engaged in the practice of medicine. As a writer he is comprehensive and strong, his specialty being controversial religious themes. He is also a reviewer of marked ability, possessing the subtle acumen and logical discrimination that fits him for the work.

For a number of years he served as secretary of the Baptist ministers' state meeting; was President of the Board of Trustees of Eminence College for several years; President of the Eminence

Male and Female Seminary in 1862, till it ceased to be a school, and also President of the Board of Town Trustees at the same time. From 1867 to 1873 he was President of the Eminence and Shelby Turnpike Company, and at the same time a director in the Eminence Bank. He was Master of Eminence Lodge, Free and Accepted Masons, for about ten years; was clerk of the Sulphur Fork Baptist Association for nine years, and has been for fifteen years and is now moderator of the same; is also moderator of the Fox Run Baptist Church at Eminence and has been, for forty years, excepting intervals of a few years when absent; was surgeon for the Louisville and Nashville Railroad Company, between La Grange and Frankfort for several years and served in the United States army as Assistant Surgeon during the Civil War; not leaving his home but attending all detachments of the army, large and small, that located at Eminence, including the prisoners of war who were brought there.

Dr. Porter has always been a leader in any enterprise for the promotion of the welfare and best interests of the community in which he lives.

His has been a record of almost unparalleled usefulness, a long, stainless, honorable life, spent in the fear and love of God and in the service of his fellow men, and he is known and respected as he well deserves, as one of the bulwarks of Christianity of his day and generation.

He married (first) Mary E. A. Rees of Henry County, daughter of Thos. F. Rees, a native of Henry County. She died in January, 1852. By this marriage he had four children: Larmer, Joseph, Mary and Albert. He was married (second) in 1852 to Miss Keziah Scott, who is the mother of one child, Chitron Scott.

Eli Porter (father) was born in Culpeper County, Virginia, in 1772, and died on October 24, 1832. He emigrated to Kentucky, arriving in Henry County on Christmas Day, 1814. He was married in June, 1800, to Martha Ball, who was born in 1783 and died in August, 1833. There were fourteen children by this marriage, eleven of whom were sons.

Samuel Porter (grandfather) was born, lived and died in Culpeper County, Virginia. He was an old field school teacher. His father, great-grandfather of Doctor Newton Porter, was a native of Wales, and emigrated from Wales to Culpeper County, Virginia.

The Porters are connected with the most distinguished families of Kentucky. Henry Clay's mother was a first cousin of Eli Porter and ex-Governor Porter is also a near relative. The grandfather on the maternal side was John Ball, a native of England, who emigrated to Fauquier County, Virginia, and was a planter and known as "a Virginia gentleman." He served in the Revolutionary War as a Captain.

STANLEY MILWARD, Treasurer of the city of Lexington, was born in Fayette County, Kentucky, February 14, 1868, and is a son of W. R. Milward and Belle (Bright) Milward. He attended school at Lexington, made rapid progress and, when only twelve years of age, entered the State Agricultural and Mechanical College, taking the business course and graduating in 1885. He was first employed with the Chesapeake & Ohio Railroad Company in Lexington, but resigned to join his father who was engaged as funeral director and embalmer, in which business he is still engaged as those duties do not interfere with those of the important trust placed in his hands by the people.

That he is something of a politician is evidenced by the fact that in November, 1895, he was elected, as a Republican, Treasurer of the city of Lexington for a term of four years, over the popular Captain S. G. Sharp, who for twenty-eight consecutive years has held office, both state and municipal. In fact, Mr. Milward is the only Republican ever elected or appointed to that office in Lexington.

He was married October 16, 1889, to Miss Bessie Featherston, daughter of C. F. Featherston and Annie Beasley. They have two children: Annie, born 1892, and Margaret, born 1894.

Mr. Milward is quite a prominent man in various secret societies; belongs to Merrick Lodge, No. 31, I. O. O. F.; has filled all the chairs of the subordinate lodge and is now Grand Conductor of the Grand Lodge of the state, and Special Deputy Grand Master of the Twentieth District; also a member of Bethesda Encampment and Rebecca Lodge, I. O. O. F. He is very prominent in K. A. E. O. circles and was Charter Excellent Senator of Fayette No. 262, when it was organized at Lexington; has membership in the Improved Order of Red Men and A. O. U. W. and Maccabees; is very much interested in his lodge work and is naturally proud of the high offices he has held.

W. R. Milward (father) was born in Lexington, Kentucky, February 5, 1842, and is a son of Joseph Milward and Eliza Young. He enlisted in the Federal army in the fall of 1860 and was Colonel of the Twenty-first Kentucky Volunteer Infantry; served throughout the four years and after the close of that conflict returned to Lexington and engaged in the furniture and undertaking business with his brother, J. U. Milward. Mr. Milward is a member of the A. O. U. W. and R. of T.; is a Republican in politics and has always been active in the ranks and councils of that party in Lexington. He is a communicant of the Methodist Episcopal Church, and an interested worker in religious fields.

Arabella Bright Milward (mother) was born in Louisville, Kentucky, August 19, 1845, and is a daughter of Dr. John W. Bright, a very prominent physician of that city many years ago. Mrs. Milward is a thoroughly practical woman, a great reader and an able writer; is a member of the Methodist Episcopal Church; was married to W. R. Milward. April 10, 1867. They have four children: Stanley, W. R., Jr.; Anne Bell and John Bright.

WILLIAM HERNDON, a distinguished lawyer of Lancaster, son of Elijah and Ann (Crosthwaite) Herndon, was born January 10, 1843, in Irvine, Estill County, Kentucky, and was educated at a select school in Estill County; was a deputy clerk of the court under his father, studying law at the same time and was admitted to the bar in 1868. He entered the Union army in September, 1861, as a private in Company B, Eighth Regiment, Kentucky Infantry; was wounded at Dobyn's Ford or Ferry in 1862, and in January, 1863, was permanently disabled at Stone River and honorably discharged from service, having participated in other battles. After the war he attended school in Estill County and taught school there; was made postmaster at Irvine and served for several terms and was also employed in the Revenue Department, all of which positions he resigned.

In 1878 he resumed the practice of law in Lancaster with James H. Anderson, now of Louisville, with whom he was associated until 1889, since which time he has practiced without an office associate.

Captain Herndon was City Attorney from 1878 to 1880 and declined to qualify after re-election; was appointed in 1881 to serve as United States Commissioner, but resigned in 1884; elected Commonwealth Attorney of the Eighth Judicial District, composed of eight counties, in 1886, for a term of six years, and has been a delegate to all but one of the Republican State Conventions, since he began the practice of law at Lancaster. Both he and his wife are Presbyterians. He is a Mason, Knight of Pythias and a member of the Grand Army of the Republic. He is the leader of the bar at Lancaster and one of the most prominent Republicans of that district. A highly cultured man, he is socially one of the most popular citizens of Lancaster.

Captain Herndon married Helen Kinnaird, daughter of William H. Kinnaird of Lancaster, July 3, 1873. They have five children, four sons and one daughter: Horace, educated at Center College, Danville, Kentucky, and at Miami University, Oxford, Ohio; William Leslie, Ben D., Lewis and Annie Christian.

Elijah Herndon (father) was born in Winchester, Kentucky, January 8, 1812, and educated there; was a farmer in early life and was subsequently engaged in the mercantile business at Irvine for many years; was Sheriff of Estill County three terms, first under the constitution previous to 1850, and after that he held the office by election; was then clerk of the Estill Circuit Court. Mr. Herndon was a Baptist and was a leading Whig politician in his county, and, after the war, a leading Republican. He died from the result of sunstroke, November 7, 1876.

William Herndon (grandfather) was born in Charlotte County, Virginia; came to Winchester, Kentucky, in 1800; had been a planter in Virginia, but was not engaged in any business in Kentucky; married Katherine Winn. He and his wife both died in 1850. They had five children: John Patrick Henry, George, Elijah, Elizabeth and Sallie.

Jacob Herndon (great-grandfather) was a native of Charlotte County, Virginia, and was of Welsh extraction.

Ann Crosthwaite Herndon (mother) was born in Cynthiana, Kentucky, January 9, 1815, and was educated in Cynthiana and Paris, Kentucky. She died in Platt County, Missouri, while visiting a son, October 20, 1892, and is buried there.

JAMES DEE SIMPSON, secretary and treasurer of the Mayfield Woolen Mills, son of David M. and Susan J. (Hamilton) Simpson, was born in Humphrey County, Tennessee, February 15, 1856; was educated at Murray Institute, Murray, Kentucky, and Neophogen College, Cross Plains, Tennessee, and graduated in 1875 with the degree of A. B., finishing in 1877; then engaged in mercantile business at Farmington, Kentucky, with C. H. McDonald. The firm of Simpson & McDonald continued for about two years, when he sold his interest and removed to Mayfield and with Frank Bray and G. O. Duncan, engaged in the retail dry goods business for three years. In 1887 he bought a one-third interest in the Mayfield Woolen Mills, and, with the exception of two years, when he was in Arkansas, he has been with that company as secretary and treasurer since its organization.

He is a Democrat in politics, and in religion both he and his wife hold to the Universalist belief. He is a man of sterling business qualities, proving the advantage that accrues from culture and training in mercantile enterprises, as well as in professional life.

He was married October 2, 1878, to Fannie J. Cochran, daughter of J. C. Cochran of Farmington. Their only child, Clarence D., is sixteen years of age, and in the West Kentucky College at Mayfield. He is an athlete and lowered the world's record for his age last year for rapid cycling for all distances from one-twelfth of a mile to five miles.

David M. Simpson (father) was born in Ohio, March 17, 1812; when thirteen years of age he removed to Humphrey County, Tennessee, and became a planter in that county and removed to Graves County, Kentucky, in 1866 and lived there until 1879, when he removed to Clay County, Arkansas, and engaged in planting; was first a Whig and then a Democrat in politics, and in religion a Baptist. He is now living in Arkansas at the age of eighty-four years.

David Simpson (grandfather) was connected with the steamboat lines that plied between Cincinnati and New Orleans.

Susan J. Hamilton Simpson (mother) was the daughter of William and Mildred Hamilton. Her father was a descendant of Alexander Hamilton and was a building contractor and steamboat captain, with headquarters at Nashville, Tennessee. Susan J. Hamilton was born in Nashville, Tennessee, February 17, 1814; was educated in Nashville and married David Simpson in 1833. They had ten children, of whom six are now living. She was a member of the primitive Baptist Church, and died in Clay County, Arkansas, May 14, 1891, and is buried there.

HARVEY H. ROBERTS, a leading physician of Paris, son of John H. and Mary Johnson Roberts, was born in Walton, Boone County, Kentucky, July 26, 1865. He was educated at the Walton High School and at Georgetown College, and in 1886 took a course in a business college at Cincinnati, Ohio.

He began the study of medicine in the office of Dr. Bagby at Walton and continued under the instruction of that gentleman for four years. In 1887 he entered the Ohio Medical College, graduating in 1890; took a post-graduate course in 1893 at the "New York" Polyclinic, in general medicine and surgery and received private instruction in Cincinnati in hospital work under Doctors Ranserhoff, Dawson and other eminent physicians and surgeons.

After graduating in 1890 he located at Paris, engaging in the general practice of medicine and surgery; while in New York he made a specialty of diseases of the nose and throat and operative surgery; has written a number of articles for leading medical journals; is a member of the Kentucky Medical Association, the Mississippi Valley Medical Association, the Midland Kentucky Medical Association, the American Medical Association and the "Pan-American Congress," and is a subscriber to the principal medical journals of the country.

Dr. Roberts is a thoroughly wide-awake physician and spares no physical exertion nor medical research to entitle him to the front rank in his chosen profession.

He is deacon in the Christian Church, a Democrat in politics, an Odd Fellow and a Knight of Pythias.

He married Ella Graves of Georgetown, daughter of William and Susan (Smarr) Graves, November 12, 1890. They have one child, Hamilton, born May 14, 1895.

John H. Roberts (father) was born near Walton, Boone County, Kentucky, October 29, 1825, and was educated in the private schools in that county. He was engaged in farming and stock-raising all his life. He was a member of the Baptist Church, being especially active in establishing a church of that denomination at Walton, and was treasurer of the church from its organization until two years before his death, when he resigned on account of ill-health. He retired from farming in the latter years of his life and resided in Walton until his death in 1895. He married Mary Johnson, October 24, 1850, and three children were born to them: Columbus, born July 22, 1851; Harvey Hamilton, born July 26, 1865; and James Kirtley, born August 9, 1871. He was a stanch Democrat, but did not take any active part in politics. His wife, Mary J. Roberts, daughter of Hamilton Johnson, was born January 18, 1831.

Wm. Roberts (grandfather) was born in Jessamine County, Kentucky, in 1800; died July 20, 1877. He was a farmer and prominently connected with the business interest of his county. In religious convictions he was a "hard-shell" Baptist.

Phillip Roberts (great-grandfather) died at the age of eighty-four. He came from North Carolina to Kentucky, in the early pioneer days. He was in the War of 1812.

Sarah (Keene) Roberts (grandmother) was a daughter of Joseph Keene, Jr., born in 1797, and died October, 1865.

Joseph Keene, Sr. (great-great-grandfather), was prominently connected with the Revolutionary War and was over one hundred years of age at his death.

Hamilton Johnson (grandfather) was born June 16, 1799; died February 26, 1862; married Mary Tyndal October 17, 1822. He came to Kentucky from New Jersey in the early pioneer days. He was engaged in farming and trading in the general products of the country in those days.

Andrew Johnson (great-grandfather) was in the War of 1812, and died March 27, 1861, aged ninety-two years.

Mary (Tyndal) Johnson (grandmother) was born October 26, 1802; died September 21, 1880; was a daughter of John Tyndal.

John Tyndal (great-grandfather) was in the War of 1812; died June 18, 1861, aged ninety-three years.

HENRY ALBERT COTTELL, M. D., professor of physiology, histology and clinical diseases of the nervous system, in the medical department of the University of Louisville, editor of the American Practitioner and News, son of Charles Cottel and Phoebe Hanscom, was born in Calais, Maine, June 7, 1847.

His father is a native of Portsmouth, New Hampshire, from which place his family emigrated to the wilderness of Maine in February, 1813. He labored hard in youth; was self-educated, and came in middle life to be one of the best known men on the Saint Croix River. He was Justice of the Peace, and an extensive dealer in ship timber. In 1857 he removed to Illinois, where, after a brief residence in the towns of Warren and Rockford, he settled upon a farm in Will County, near Elwood. Here he still lives, hale, hearty, and in the enjoyment of all his faculties, at the age of eighty-seven.

He is a man of culture and of a wide scope of information, and is known as a contributor in prose and verse, to current literature. He has, however, never attempted anything ambitious, having preferred the hard but stable life of the farmer to the uncertain scramble for fame. In politics he was a Democrat in early life and cast his first presidential vote for Andrew Jackson. In 1856, however, he voted for Fremont, and has been a stanch Republican ever since. He is of a deeply religious nature, and has been a prominent member of the Methodist Episcopal Church for more than sixty years. He has always been a man of great energy and industry, doing thoroughly whatever he undertook to do.

Samuel Cottel (grandfather), a native of Portsmouth, New Hampshire, was for many years a resident of Maine, where he died at an advanced age. He was descended from a New York Dutch family, who spelled the name Kottel originally.

Phoebe Hanscom Cottel (mother), a native of Maine (Machias), was the daughter of Hiram Hanscom and Susan Weston (grandmother), who was a daughter of Hannah Weston (great-grandmother), who was a daughter of Captain Samuel Watts, an officer in the French and Indian War (1756-63), He fought at Crown Point, on Lake Champlain, under Winslow, and with General Wolfe at the siege of Quebec. He took part, with his son, Captain Samuel Watts, Jr., and son-in-law, Josiah Weston, in the capture of the British man-of-war Margaretta at the port of Machias, in June, 1775, and although advanced in years was the leading spirit in the celebrated achievement. Hannah Weston (his daughter) distinguished herself on this occasion by carrying a sack of ammunition weighing thirty pounds, from Jonesboro, through an unbroken forest, to Machias, a distance of sixteen miles. At this time she was sixteen years old and a bride. Her brother, Samuel Watts, shot and killed Captain Moore of the Margaretta. He was the first naval office killed in the war of the Revolution. Her husband, Josiah Weston, with her brother, Samuel Watts, received pensions for their services. Hannah Weston was the great-granddaughter of the celebrated Hannah Dustin, in whose memory a monument in the public square is one of the historic features of Haverhill, Massachusetts.

The first ten years of Henry A. Cottell's life were spent in Calais, Maine, when his father removed to Illinois, and the next ten years were spent on the farm and in the public schools of Rockford, Illinois, since which time, 1867, he has been a resident of Louisville. Coming to the city at the age of twenty years, fresh from the country, and unacquainted with city customs, he soon attracted attention as a musician of more than ordinary talent. He found employment in the music establishment of Louis Tripp, where he gained some knowledge of business, became acquainted with the best people in the city and made considerable advancement in music, in which he could give some of the professionals points; was employed as organist in one of the largest churches, of which George C. Lorimer was then pastor, while his services were in demand in musical societies and in public entertainments. But the fascinations of music and his pleasant associations with musical people and polite society did not change his purpose to study medicine, and in 1870 he matriculated in the medical department of the University of Louisville, from which he graduated in 1872.

His preceptor, Dr. J. M. Bodine, a distinguished anatomist, then as now professor of that chair and dean of the University, made Mr. Cottell his prosector in anatomy before the young man was graduated, and he has been regularly connected with the university ever since; first, as quiz-master in anatomy and physiology; from 1885 to 1892, as professor of chemistry and microscopy; in 1892, clinical diseases of the nervous system was added to his chair; and in 1895, upon the death of Professor Edward R. Palmer, he was transferred to the chair of physiology, his present position in the leading medical college in the city of Louisville.

In 1880 Dr. Cottell was called to the editorship of the Louisville Medical News, which, in 1895, was united with the American Practitioner and News, and since that time with Dr. David W. Yandell he has conducted that famous journal, under the name of the American Practitioner.

As a practitioner, Dr. Cottell has given especial attention to the nervous system, in which branch his success has been most gratifying. Of quiet disposition and modest demeanor, he has never sought notoriety or prominence, but in the profession and among the thousands of physicians who attribute their success largely to his helpful teaching he is known as one of the most talented educators in the medical profession.

Dr. Cottell was married in 1880 to Mary Van Buren Campbell, daughter of William Campbell and Fannie Minserrat Campbell of Baltimore, Md., now deceased. She was educated in the Nold Louisville Female Seminary, graduating with the first honors of her class. She is a vocalist of charming sweetness and power and a lady of highest culture and refinement. Their only child, James Ruffin Cottell, is a promising lad of six years. Dr. and Mrs. Cottell are members of Christ Church, the Episcopal Cathedral of Kentucky.

As a writer and speaker Dr. Cottell is well known to the profession. His editorials in the American Practitioner and News have high rank among medical essays, while his popular addresses delivered at the university commencements, viz.: Esthetics of Medicine, 1886; The Medical Millenium, 1895, and The Life and Character of Professor Edward Rush Palmer, 1896, are pronounced by competent judges to be oratorical and literary efforts of unusual merit.

JOHN LYNCH DISMUKES, prominent physician of Mayfield, son of Paul Dismukes and Sabina Bowman, was born near Nashville, Tennessee, December 20, 1830.

He received his literary and classical education at the University of North Carolina at Chapel Hill, graduating in 1852; and attended the medical department of the University of Pennsylvania, from which he graduated in 1856, and began the practice of medicine at Mayfield during the same year and soon became prominent in his profession.

He is a member of the American Medical Association; of the Tri-State Medical Association of Kentucky, Indiana and Illinois, and was elected its first vice president in 1876-77; of State Medical Association of Kentucky, and was its first vice-president in 1877; is a member of the Southern Kentucky Medical Association, of which he was president in 1874; and has contributed many articles on medical subjects to various journals throughout the country.

During the war he held the position of surgeon in charge of various hospitals in the Confederate army, especially field hospital surgeon of Pat Cleburne's Division of Hardee's Corps, and was wounded at Chickamauga and again at Franklin, Tennessee. He was one of the incorporators and directors of the Cairo, Tennessee River & Cumberland Gap Railroad. Dr. Dismukes is a Democrat in his political affiliations and a member of the Baptist Church.

In November, 1867, he married Imogen E. Taylor, daughter of Dr. James S. Taylor of Clinton, Louisiana. They have four children: Mamie Sabina, wife of H. H. Harris of Waco, Texas; James Taylor, dentist; Paul Isham, John L., Jr., educated at West Kentucky College, Mayfield, and later finished his literary studies at Clinton College; was at the University of Louisville for one year and graduated from the Kentucky School of Medicine, Louisville, June 21, 1894. He married Mary Landrum, daughter of Dr. William L. Landrum, December 18, 1895, and is now practicing medicine with his father in Mayfield.

Paul Dismukes (father) was born in Roanoke County, Virginia, in 1811; was educated at the academy near Clarksville, Tennessee, under Professor Thomas Terrill; was a planter in Davidson County, Tennessee; was a strong Southern sympathizer and had four sons in the Confederate army: Dr. John L. Dismukes, the subject of this sketch; Dr. Thomas Terrill Dismukes, also a surgeon; James Henry of the First Tennessee Regiment, died in hospital at White Sulphur Springs, Virginia, while in service; and Marcus L., who served under John Morgan and General Forrest. Mr. Dismukes was originally a member of the Presbyterian Church, but was baptized in his last illness by a minister of the Christian denomination. He died August 31, 1869, and is buried near Nashville, Tennessee.

Paul Dismukes (grandfather) was a planter in Virginia, but subsequently removed to Davidson County, Tennessee. He served in the Continental army during the Revolutionary War.

Paul Dismukes (great-grandfather) came from Wales to Virginia. There is a tradition that the family went from France, from a place called "Meaux," a suburb of Paris, to Wales, and that "De Meaux," as "Paul De Meaux," was finally changed to "Dismukes."

Sabina Bowman Dismukes (mother) was born in Charleston, South Carolina, in 1811 and received her education there. She married Paul Dismukes, January 18, 1829, and died September 30, 1844, and is buried near her husband in Davidson County, Tennessee, at the primitive Dismukes' plantation. The names of their children are: John L., Thomas T., Paul, James H., Marcus L., Esther Ann (deceased), Sarah, wife of Professor John McCready of the Sewanee University, Tennessee, formerly professor in Yale College; and Sabina Bowman Dismukes of Charleston.

John Lynch Bowman (maternal grandfather) changed his name to John Bowman Lynch in order to inherit the property under the old name, taking the name from his uncle, Thomas Lynch (and using the name of Lynch only), who was one of the signers of the Declaration of Independence, whose only son, Thomas Lynch, was lost at sea. John Bowman Lynch inherited the property. The estate is called Lynch Peach Tree Plantation and is in South Carolina near Georgetown. He studied medicine in the University of Pennsylvania, graduating in 1800, and while at college was considered very eccentric. He was a very wealthy man and kept a large home establishment. His wife was Ann Eliza Campbell of England. He died in 1866.

John Bowman (great-grandfather) married Miss Lynch, daughter of Thomas Lynch, signer of the Declaration of Independence for and from South Carolina.

FRANCIS THOMAS DURAND WALLACE, lawyer of Louisa, son of Thomas and Mary (Moore) Wallace, was born in Louisa, Lawrence County, Kentucky, March 26, 1850. His father traced his ancestry back to Sir William Wallace, the Scottish warrior and statesman, of whom was written the song: "Scots wha ha'e wi' Wallace bled."

Thomas Wallace (father) was born in Lafayette, Indiana, April 24, 1812. When he was but three years old his father removed to Clarke County, Ohio, where Thomas spent his boyhood days and received his education. He was a clerk in a store in Springfield, Ohio, for one year, and at the age of seventeen years came to Floyd County, Kentucky, where he was engaged as a cabinet maker for four years, and there married his first wife, Lizzie Everell, who died in 1839, soon after their marriage. In 1840 he removed to Louisa, and, his health having failed, he engaged in general trading and accumulated quite a handsome fortune. In politics he was a Whig, and during the Civil war, a Union sympathizer, but after the war he voted the Democratic ticket. He was very much interested in his business and cared little for politics, except from a general interest in the public weal. He was a Master Mason and a member of the Methodist Episcopal Church South. He was married (second) in 1841, to Mary Moore, and died in Louisa, July 29, 1871.

Thomas Wallace (great-grandfather) was a native of Virginia, where he was raised, educated and married. He came to Kentucky about 1795 and settled at Mays Lick, Mason County. Afterwards, about 1807, he removed to Clarke County, Ohio, where he purchased a large tract of land at a small price, and died there, March 13, 1813. He was said to be a very religious man, a member of the Presbyterian Church, which has been the religious faith of the family for centuries.

His wife's name was Ellen Ross, who belonged to a family of distinction in Scotland. Her parents were from the Shire of Ross, so called in honor of the Ross family. Some of her relatives are still living in Mason County, to which section they came from Virginia. The Ross and Wallace families were descendants of a people who were noted for their large frames and physical strength.

The children of Thomas and Ellen Ross Wallace were six sons and four daughters: John, William, Ross, James, Moses and Joseph (sons); Mary, Nancy, Deborah and Rachel (daughters). Mary died young; Nancy married James McClon of Madison, Indiana; Deborah married Preston Ross, her second cousin; both are now deceased; Rachel married John Ross, a brother of Deborah Ross' husband, and died young; John Wallace was a farmer and died on the farm given him by his father and was worth from $50,000 to $100,000; he married twice and had a large family by his first wife, but no issue by his second marriage. William Wallace was educated for the ministry before his father left Kentucky and was pastor of the Presbyterian Church at Paris until his death in 1816. He married a Miss Rankin of Lexington and they had four children, one of whom is the celebrated William Ross Wallace. The other three children were daughters: Ellen, Martha and Mary; the latter married John H. Harney, who was the editor of the Louisville Democrat; and she was the mother of William Wallace Harney, another distinguished poet, now of Florida.

Ross Wallace (grandfather) was a farmer and general trader. He married Elizabeth Neely in Bath County. His was an eventful life, an outline of which would require more than the limited space in this volume. The children were named William, Thomas (father), Deborah and Elvessie.

Elizabeth Neely Wallace (grandmother) was a widow when she married Ross Wallace, but was only seventeen years of age. Her first husband's name was Gibbs, a negro trader of Bourbon County, Kentucky (perhaps), who only lived about a year after their marriage and died by poison from his negroes on the Mississippi river, while on a trading tour. He left one child, Melissa Gibbs.

Mary Moore Wallace (mother) was born in Philadelphia, Pennsylvania, August 25, 1817. Her parents moved to (now West) Virginia in 1820, and she was educated in Marietta, Ohio, and at Barboursville, West Virginia. She married Thomas Wallace in 1841, whom she survives, and is now a resident of Louisa, in good health, and in the seventy-ninth year of her age.

Frederick Moore (maternal grandfather), a native of Holland, came to Philadelphia when he was a youth and was engaged in tanning there and later in merchandising. Following the War of 1812 he had a large stock of goods, and concluded that the only way to save himself from great loss was to remove to some point where he could trade his goods for furs and other produce of the country. So he came to Kentucky in 1816, or about that time, and settled near Cassville, Virginia, and there continued in business until 1871, when he removed to Louisa and died, May 23, 1873. His wife's maiden name was Pamelia Van Horn, a native of Philadelphia, who died in Louisa, Kentucky, August 1, 1881, at the advanced age of eighty-six years. Her parents were descendants of Hollanders.

Francis T. D. Wallace, the principal subject of this sketch, was educated in the schools of Louisa and at a commercial college in Portsmouth, Ohio; was associated with his father in general trading for a while, and in 1868, following the natural bent of his mind, he began the study of law in the office of Prichard & Harcher; was admitted to the bar of Louisa in November, 1870; opened his office in that place and began the practice of his profession under most favorable and encouraging auspices. In 1881 he was appointed local attorney for the Chattaroi, now the Ohio & Big Sandy Railroad Company, which position he held until 1892, when that company was merged into the Chesapeake & Ohio system, and Mr. Wallace was made assistant solicitor for that company with headquarters at Ashland.

Mr. Wallace began to take an active interest in politics when quite young, and one year after he was admitted to the practice of law, he was elected police judge of Louisa, and served in that capacity for a period of four years; was a member of the State Senate from 1885 to 1889 from the Thirty-second District, comprising the counties of Greenup, Boyd, Lawrence and Elliott, and in that body took rank as a wise, safe and conservative legislator, looking carefully after the interests of the people. During his term he introduced many measures for the material improvement of eastern Kentucky. Since the expiration of his term as Senator he has devoted his attention exclusively to his large and increasing law practice in Louisa.

In politics he is, and always has been, a Democrat; is a Shriner, Knight Templar, Royal Arch Mason and a member of the Knights of the Ancient Essenic Order.

Mr. Wallace was married September 16, 1872,

to Phoebe E. Wood, daughter of John Perry Wood and Lucy Alzina (Day) Wood. Mr. Wood was a general trader and stock dealer in New York. Mrs. Wallace was born in Hartford, Washington County, New York, September 7, 1852, and was educated at Fort Edward, New York.

ISAAC SHELBY, Kentucky's first state governor, was born on the 11th day of December, 1750, near to the North Mountain, a few miles from Hagerstown, in Maryland, where his father and grandfather settled after their arrival in America from Wales. In that early settlement of the country, which was annoyed during the period of his youth by Indian wars, he obtained only the elements of a plain English education; but, like his father, General Evan Shelby, born with a strong constitution, capable of bearing great privation and fatigue, he was brought up to the use of arms and the pursuit of game.

At the age of twenty-one he took up his residence in western Virginia, beyond the Alleghany mountains, having previously acquired a knowledge of surveying and of the duties of sheriff at Fredericktown. He was engaged, in his new residence, in the business of feeding and attending to herds of cattle in the extensive range which distinguished that section of the country. He was a lieutenant in the company of his father, the late General Evan Shelby, in the memorable battle fought the 10th of October, 1774, at the mouth of the Kanawha, at the close of which his father was the commanding officer, Colonels Lewis, Fleming and Field being killed or disabled. The result of this battle gave peace to the frontier, at the critical period of the colonies venturing into the eventful contest of the Revolution, and deterred the Indians from uniting with the British until 1776. This was, probably, the most severely contested conflict ever maintained with the Northwestern Indians; the action continued from sunrise to sunset, and the ground for half a mile along the Ohio was alternately occupied by each of the parties in the course of the day. So sanguinary was the contest that blood was found on each of the trees behind which the parties were posted. The Indians, under the celebrated chief, Cornstalk, abandoned the ground under cover of the night. Their loss, according to the official report, exceeded that of the Americans, the latter amounting to sixty-three killed and eighty wounded. This report was drawn up by Captain Russell, reputed to be the best scholar in camp, and the father of the late Colonel William Russell of Kentucky. The fortune of the day, as stated in Doddridge's Notes of Border War, was decided by a bold movement to the rear of the left wing of the Indians, led by Captain Evan Shelby, in which the subject of this memoir bore a conspicuous part.

The garrison at Kanawha was commanded by Captain Russell, and Lieutenant Shelby continued in it until the troops were disbanded, in July, 1775, by order of Governor Dunmore, who was apprehensive that the post might be held for the benefit of the rebel authorities. He proceeded immediately to Kentucky, and was employed as a surveyor under Henderson & Co.; who styled themselves proprietors of the country, and who had established a regular land office under their purchase from the Cherokees. He resided in the then wilderness of Kentucky for nearly twelve months, and being without bread or salt, his health was impaired, and he returned home.

In July, 1776, during his absence from home, he was appointed captain of a minute company by the committee of safety of Virginia. In the year 1777 he was appointed by Governor Henry a commissary of supplies for an extensive body of militia, posted at different garrisons to guard the frontier settlements, and for a treaty to be held at the Long Island of Holston river with the Cherokee tribe of Indians. These supplies could not have been obtained nearer than Staunton, Virginia, a distance of three hundred miles; but by the most indefatigable perseverance (one of the most conspicuous traits of his character) he accomplished it to the satisfaction of his country.

In 1778 he was engaged in the commissary department, providing supplies for the Continental army, and for an expedition, by way of Pittsburg, against the Northwestern Indians. In the early part of 1779 he was appointed by Governor Henry to furnish supplies for the campaign against the Chickamauga Indians, which he effected upon his own individual credit. In the spring of that year, he was elected a member of the Virginia legislature from Washington County and in the fall of that year was commissioned a major by Governor Jefferson in the escort of guards to the commissioners for extending the boundary line between that state and the state of North Carolina. By the extension of that line, his residence was found to be within the limits of the latter state, and shortly afterwards he was appointed by Governor Caswell a colonel of the new county of Sullivan, established in consequence of the additional territory acquired by the running of that line.

In the summer of 1780 Colonel Shelby was in Kentucky, locating and securing those lands, which he had five years previously marked out and improved for himself, when the intelligence of the surrender of Charleston and the loss of the army reached that country. He returned home in July of that year, determined to enter the service of his country and remain in it until her independence should be secured. He could not continue to be a cool spectator of a contest in which the dearest rights and interests of his country were involved. On his arrival in Sullivan, he found a requisition from General Charles McDowell, requesting him to furnish all the aid in his power to check the enemy, who had overrun the two southern states, and were on the borders of North Carolina. Colonel Shelby assembled the militia of his county, called upon them to volunteer their services for a short time on that interesting occasion, and marched in a few days with three hundred mounted riflemen across the Alleghany mountains.

In a short time after his arrival at McDowell's camp, near the Cherokee ford of Broad river, Colonel Shelby and Lieutenant-Colonels Sevier and Clarke—the latter a refugee from Georgia— were detached with six hundred men to surprise a post of the enemy in front, on the waters of Pacolet river. It was a strong fort, surrounded by abbatis, built in the Cherokee war, and commanded by that distinguished loyalist, Captain Patrick Moore, who surrendered the garrison, with one British sergeant-major, ninety-three loyalists, and two hundred and fifty stand of arms.

Major Ferguson of the British army, though a brigadier general in the royal militia and the most distinguished partisan officer in the British army, made many ineffectual efforts to surprise Col. Shelby. His advance, about six or seven hundred strong, came up with the American commander at Cedar Spring, and before Ferguson approached with his whole force, the Americans took two officers and fifty men prisoners, and safely effected their retreat. It was in the severest part of this action that Col. Shelby's attention was arrested by the heroic conduct of Col. Clarke. He often mentioned the circumstance of his ceasing in the midst of the battle, to look with astonishment and admiration at Clarke fighting.

The next important event was the battle fought at Musgrove's mill, on the south side of Enoree river, distant forty miles, with seven hundred men, led by Cols. Shelby, Clarke and Williams of South Carolina. This affair took place on the 19th of August, and is more particularly described in the sketch of Col. Shelby, inserted in the first volume of the "National Portrait Gallery," published in 1834, under the direction of the American Academy of Fine Arts. It has been introduced into the historical romance called "Horse-Shoe Robinson," and noticed also in McCall's History of Georgia, where the British loss is stated to be sixty-three killed and one hundred and sixty wounded and taken; the American loss, four killed and nine wounded; amongst the former, Capt. Inman; and amongst the latter, Col. Clarke and Capt. Clarke. Col. Innes, the British commander of the "Queen's American Regiment," from New York, was wounded, and all the British officers, except a subaltern, were killed or wounded; and Capt. Hawsey, a noted leader among the tories, was killed.

The Americans intended to be that evening before Ninety-Six—but at that moment an express from Gen. McDowell came up in great haste, with a short note from Gov. Caswell, dated on the battle-ground, apprising McDowell of the defeat of the American grand army under Gen. Gates, on the 16th, near Camden. Fortunately, Col. Shelby knew Caswell's handwriting, and by distributing the prisoners among the companies, so as to make one to every three men, who carried them, alternately, on horseback, the detachment moved directly towards the mountains. The Americans were saved by a long and rapid march that day and night, and until the evening of the next day, without halting to refresh. Col. Shelby, after seeing his party and prisoners out of danger, retreated to the western waters, and left the prisoners in charge of Clarke and Williams, to convey them to a place of safety in Virginia, for at that moment there was no corps of Americans south of that state. The brilliancy of this affair was obscured, as, indeed, were all the minor events of the previous war, by the deep gloom which overspread the public mind after the disastrous defeat of Gen. Gates.

Ferguson was so solicitous to recapture the prisoners, and to check these daring adventures of the mountaineers, that he made a strenuous effort, with his main body, to intercept them; but failing of his object, he took post at a place called Gilbert-town, from whence he sent the most threatening messages, by paroled prisoners, to the officers west of the mountains, proclaiming devastation to their country if they did not cease their opposition to the British government.

This was the most disastrous and critical period of the Revolutionary war, to the South. No one could see whence a force could be raised to check the enemy in their progress to subjugate this portion of the continent.

Cornwallis, with the main army, was posted at Charlottestown, in North Carolina, and Ferguson, with three thousand, at Gilbert-town; while many of the best friends of the American government, despairing of the freedom and independence of America, took protection under the British standard. At this gloomy moment, Col. Shelby proposed to Cols. Sevier and Campbell to raise a force from their several counties, march hastily through the mountains, and attack and surprise Ferguson in the night. Accordingly, they collected with their followers, about one thousand strong, on Doe run, in the spurs of the Alleghany, on the 25th of September, 1780, and the next day commenced their march, when it was discovered that three of Col. Sevier's men had deserted to the enemy. This disconcerted their first design, and induced them to turn to the left, gain his front, and act as events might suggest. They traveled through mountains almost inaccessible to horsemen. As soon as they entered the level country, they met with Col. Cleveland with three hundred men, and with Cols. Williams and Lacy, and other refugee officers, who had heard of Cleveland's advance, by which three hundred more were added to the force of the mountaineers. They now considered themselves to be sufficiently strong to encounter Ferguson; but being rather a confused mass, it was proposed by Col. Shelby, in a council of officers, and agreed to, that Col. Campbell of the Virginia regiment—an officer of enterprise, patriotism and good sense—should be appointed to the command. And having determined to pursue Ferguson with all practicable dispatch, two nights before the action they selected the best horses and rifles, and at the dawn of day commenced their march with nine hundred and ten expert marksmen. As Ferguson was their object, they would not be diverted from the main point by any collection of tories in the vicinity of their route. They pursued him for the last thirty-six hours without alighting from their horses to refresh but once, at the Cowpens, for an hour, although the day of the action was so extremely wet, that the men could only keep their guns dry by wrapping their bags, blankets and hunting shirts around their locks, which exposed their bodies to a heavy and incessant rain during the pursuit.

By the order of march and of battle, Col. Campbell's regiment formed the right, and Col. Shelby's regiment the left column, in the center; the right wing was composed of Sevier's regiment, and Maj. Winston's and McDowell's battalions, commanded by Sevier himself; the left wing was composed of Col. Cleveland's regiment, the followers of Cols. Williams, Lacy, Hawthorn and Hill, headed by Col. Cleveland in person. In this order the mountaineers pursued, until they found Ferguson, securely encamped on King's Mountain, which was about half a mile long, and from which he declared the evening before that "God Almighty could not drive him." On approaching the mountain, the two center columns deployed to the right and left, formed a front, and attacked the enemy, while the right and left wings were marching to surround him. In a few minutes the action became general and severe—continuing furiously for three-fourths of an hour; when the enemy, being driven from the east to the west end of the mountain, surrendered at discretion. Ferguson was killed, with three hundred and seventy-five of his officers and men, and seven hundred and thirty captured. The Americans had sixty killed and wounded; of the former, Col. Williams.

This glorious achievement occurred at the most gloomy period of the revolution, and was the first link in the great chain of events to the south, which established the independence of the United States. History has, heretofore, though improperly, ascribed this merit to the battle of the Cowpens, in January, 1781; but it belongs, justly, to the victory on King's Mountain, which turned the tide of war to the south, as the victory of Trenton, under Washington, and of Bennington, under Stark, did to the north. It was achieved by raw, undisciplined riflemen, without any authority from the government under which they lived—without pay, rations, ammunition, or even the expectance of reward, other than that which results from the noble ambition of advancing the liberty and welfare of their beloved country. It completely dispirited the tories, and so alarmed Cornwallis, who then lay only thirty miles north of King's Mountain with the main British army, that, on receiving information of Ferguson's total defeat and overthrow by the riflemen from the west, under Colonels Campbell, Shelby, Cleveland and Sevier, and that they were bearing down upon him, he ordered an immediate retreat—marched all night, in the utmost confusion—and retrograded as far back as Winnsborough, sixty or eighty miles, whence he did not attempt to advance until reinforced, three months after, by General Leslie, with two thousand men from the Chesapeake. In the meantime, the militia of North Carolina assembled in considerable force at New Providence, on the border of South Carolina, under General Davidson; and General Smallwood, with Morgan's light corps, and the Maryland line, advanced to the same point. General Gates, with the shattered remains of his army, collected at Hillsborough, also came up, as well as the new levies from Virginia, of one thousand men, under General Stevens. This force enabled General Greene, who assumed the command early in December, to hold Cornwallis in check.

The histories of the war at the south have never done justice to the sagacity and judgment of Col. Shelby upon another interesting occasion, just following the affair on King's Mountain. As soon as he had placed the prisoners beyond the reach of the enemy, he repaired to the headquarters of General Gates, and suggested to him the plan of detaching General Morgan towards the mountains. The details of this arrangement were submitted by him, and approved by Gates, and Greene had the good sense to adopt them, after he assumed the command. The result of his advice was exhibited in the splendid affair at the Cowpens, which added fresh laurels to the veteran brows of Morgan, Howard and Washington.

In the campaign of the fall of 1871, Colonel Shelby served under General Marion, a distinguished partisan officer, of the boldest enterprise. He was called down by General Greene to that lower country, with five hundred mounted riflemen from the western waters, in September, 1781, to aid the General in intercepting Cornwallis, at that time blockaded by the French fleet in the Chesapeake, and who, it was suspected, would endeavor to make good his retreat through North Carolina to Charleston; but, upon his lordship's surrender in Virginia, Colonel Shelby was attached to General Marion's command below, on the Santee, and was second in command of a strong detachment of dragoons, under Colonel Mayhem, ordered to carry a British post at Fairlawn, near Monk's Corner, eight or ten miles below the enemy's main army, under General Stuart. Information had been received by General Marion that five hundred Hessians at that post were in a state of mutiny, and would surrender to any considerable force that might appear before it. But the officer commanding the post having some apprehensions of their fidelity, had marched them off to Charleston, the day before Colonel Mayhem appeared before it. The post, however, was surrendered, with one hundred and fifty British prisoners. The British General at Ferguson's Swamp, nine miles in the rear, made great, though unavailing efforts to intercept Mayhem's party on their return with the prisoners to General Marion's encampment. Immediately after this excursion, the British commander retreated with his whole force to Charleston.

As the period for which the mounted volunteers had engaged to serve was about to expire, and no further active operations being contemplated, after the retreat of the enemy towards Charleston, Colonel Shelby obtained leave of absence from General Marion, to attend the assembly of North Carolina, of which he was a member, which would sit two hundred miles distant, about the first of December. Marion addressed a letter on the subject to General Greene, which Colonel Shelby was permitted to see, speaking in high terms of the conduct of the mountaineers, and assigning particular credit to Colonel Shelby for his conduct in the capture of the British post, as it surrendered to him after an ineffectual attempt by an officer of the dragoons.

In 1782, Colonel Shelby was elected a member of the North Carolina assembly, and was appointed one of the commissioners to settle the pre-emption claims upon the Cumberland River, and to lay off the lands allotted to the officers and soldiers of the North Carolina line, south of where Nashville now stands. He performed this service in the winter of 1782-3, and returned to Boonsborough, Kentucky, in April following, where he married Susanna, second daughter of Captain Nathaniel Hart, one of the first settlers of Kentucky, and one of the proprietors styled Henderson & Co., by their purchase of the country from the Cherokees.

After completing the organization of the government under the provisions of the constitution, by filling the various offices created by it, the earnest attention of the Governor was directed to the defense of the state against the Indian incursions, and the border war to which the people were exposed by their remote and unprotected position in the wilderness. General Washington's paternal regard to the same high object was manifested in the cautious and extensive arrangements which were made under the direction of General Wayne for a strong expedition against the northwestern Indians, who were stimulated and aided by the British and provincial forces occupying posts within our boundary. The confidence of Washington, as well as of the people of Kentucky, was reposed in the energy and patriotism of Governor Shelby. This was evinced in his almost unanimous elevation to the chief magistracy, as well as in the answer of the first Legislature to his message, and in a letter from General Knox, secretary of war, of July 12, 1792.

In the subsequent letter from the war department, the defensive operations for the protection of Kentucky were committed exclusively to his judgment and discretion, and whenever there was a prospect of acting offensively against the Indians of the northwest, the president made an appeal to his patriotism and that of the state, in furnishing mounted volunteers in aid of the regular force. His energy and the gallantry of Kentucky was signally displayed in the valuable succor rendered to General Wayne on the memorable 20th of August, 1794. His enlightened forecast, and the valor of Kentucky, presented on this occasion, as on the equally glorious 5th of October, 1813, the means of victory both in men and transportation, at a critical moment to the scene of action—to victories the most decisive in their results to any heretofore known in Indian warfare.

Whilst the people of Kentucky were interrupted in their business and prosperity by the attention necessary to the progress of the Indian War, they were annoyed by continued apprehensions of losing the navigation of the Mississippi, on which their commercial existence depended. In the midst of these difficulties, a new and unexpected occasion presented itself for the display of Governor Shelby's diplomatic sagacity. The complaints and remonstrances of the Spanish minister induced the general government to open a correspondence with Governor Shelby, for the purpose of suppressing an expedition, which was represented to be in contemplation, by La Chaise and other French agents, against the possessions of Spain on the Mississippi. Governor Shelby had no apprehensions that they would succeed in organizing the necessary force, and under this impression his reply to the department of state, October 5th, 1703, was forwarded, without considering that he had not authority under existing laws to interfere in preventing it. But the granting of commissions to General Clark and other influential individuals, and the actual attempt to carry the plans of French emissaries into effect, induced the Governor to examine the subject more thoroughly, and conceiving that he had no legal authority to interfere, he addressed a letter, January 13, 1794, to the secretary of state, expressing these doubts, and assuming an attitude, which, though professing the most devoted regard to the Union, had the effect of drawing from the general government a full development of the measures which had been pursued for securing the navigation of the Mississippi. These explanations by the department of state, and by the special commissioner, the eloquent Colonel James Innes, attorney-general of Virginia, who was deputed by General Washington to proceed to Kentucky to communicate with the Governor and Legislature, removed all ground of uneasiness, and created a tranquillity in the public mind which had not existed since the first settlement of the state.

At the close of his gubernatorial term, he returned to his farm in Lincoln, with renewed relish for the cares and enjoyments which its management necessarily created. He was as distinguished for the method and judgment and industry, which he displayed in agricultural pursuits, as he had exemplified in the more conspicuous duties of the general and the statesman. He was the model of an elevated citizen, whether at the plow, in the field, or in the cabinet.

He was repeatedly chosen an elector of president, and voted for Mr. Jefferson and Mr. Madison. He could not yield to the repeated solicitations of influential individuals in different parts of the state, requesting him to consent to be a candidate for the chief magistracy, until the exigencies of our national affairs had brought about a crisis which demanded the services of every patriot. In this contingency, he was elected, upon terms very gratifying to his feelings, a second time to the chief magistracy, at the commencement of the war, in 1812, with Great Britain.

Of his career at that eventful period, it would be impracticable, in the limits of this sketch, to present even an outline. His energy, associated with a recollection of his Revolutionary fame, aroused the patriotism of the state. In every direction he developed her resources, and aided in sending men and supplies to the support of the northwestern army under General Harrison. The legislature of Kentucky, in the winter of 1812-13, contemplating the necessity of some vigorous effort, in the course of that year, to regain the ground lost by the disasters at Detroit and at the River Raisin, passed a resolution authorizing and requesting the Governor to assume the personal direction of the troops of the state, whenever, in his judgment, such a step would be necessary. Under this authority, and at the solicitation of General Harrison, he invited his countrymen to meet him at Newport, and to accompany him to the scene of active, and, as he predicted, of decisive operations. Upon his own responsibility he authorized the troops to meet him with their horses. Four thousand men rallied to his standard in less than thirty days; and this volunteer force reached the shore of Lake Erie just in time to enable the commander-in-chief to profit by the splendid victory, achieved by the genius and heroism of Perry and his associates. It was a most interesting incident, which augured favorably of the issue of the campaign, that Governor Shelby should arrive at the camp of General Harrison precisely at the moment when Commodore Perry was disembarking his prisoners. The feelings of congratulation which were exchanged by the three heroes, at the tent of the General on the shore of Lake Erie, may be more readily conceived than described. The writer of this article had been previously dispatched by General Harrison to Commodore Perry, to ascertain the result of the naval battle, and, returning with Perry, was present at this interview.

In all the movements of the campaign, whether in council or execution, monuments of his valor and of his energetic character were erected by the gratitude of the commander-in-chief, of all his troops, and of the president of the nation, who spoke officially of his services with the veneration which belongs only to public benefactors. The Legislature of Kentucky and the Congress of the United States expressed their sense of his gallant conduct in resolutions which will transmit his name to posterity, "as a patriot without reproach and a soldier without ambition."

The vote of Congress assigning to him and to General Harrison each a gold medal, commemorative of the decisive victory on the Thames, was delayed one session in consequence of some prejudice prevailing in the public mind in relation to General Harrison. As soon as Governor Shelby was advised of this fact, he solicited his friends in Congress, through Mr. Clay, to permit no expression of thanks to him, unless associated with the name of General Harrison. This magnanimous conduct and the unqualified commendation which he gave of the career of General Harrison on that campaign, connected with a favorable report of a committee at the next session of Congress, instituted at the request of the General, of which Colonel R. M. Johnson was chairman, led to the immediate adoption of the original resolution.

Governor Shelby was unremitting in the aid which he extended to the operations of the general government during the war. He furnished troops to defend the country around Detroit, and dispatched an important reinforcement to General Jackson for the defense of New Orleans. His sagacity led him to send General Adair as Adjutant-General, with the rank of Brigadier-General, to meet the precise contingency, which actually occurred, of General Thomas being sick or disabled. The result of this measure was exhibited in the critical succor afforded by General Adair on the memorable 8th of January.

In the civil administration of the state, Governor Shelby's policy continued to establish and confirm the sound principles of his predecessors. Integrity, fidelity to the constitution, and capacity, were the qualifications which he required in public officers; and his recommendations to the Legislature enforced a strict regard to public economy and to the claims of public faith. In the fall of 1816, his term expired, and he retired again to the sweets of domestic life, in the prosecution of his favorite pursuit.

In March, 1817, he was elected by President Monroe to fill the department of war; but his advanced age, the details of the office, and his desire, in a period of peace, to remain in private life, induced him to decline an acceptance of it.

In 1818, he was commissioned by the President to act in conjunction with General Jackson in holding a treaty with the Chickasaw tribe of Indians, for the purchase of their lands west of the Tennessee River within the limits of Kentucky and Tennessee, and they obtained a cession of the territory to the United States, which unites the western population, and adds greatly to the defense of the country, in the event of future wars with the savages, or with any European power. This was his last public act.

In February, 1820, he was attacked with a paralytic affection, which disabled his right arm, and which was the occasion of his walking lame on the right leg. His mind continued unimpaired until his death, by apoplexy, on the 18th of July, 1826, in the seventy-sixth year of his age. He had been for many years a member of the Presbyterian Church; and in his latter days, was the chief instrument in erecting a house of worship upon his own land.

BENJAMIN F. BRIGGS, editor of the Mayfield Monitor, was born in Sumner County, Tennessee, August 27, 1848. He came to Graves County, Kentucky, with his father when quite young and clerked in his father's dry goods store until 1870. But he was not satisfied there and decided that the trade of printing would be more congenial to his taste, and he therefore learned printing under Mr. Warren, editor of "The Jackson Purchase." He was in the composing room of this paper for three years and was accredited with the greatest proficiency there.

In 1873 he established a weekly paper entitled "The Banner of Temperance," published in the interest of temperance, which scored an immediate success, and in 1875 founded "The Mayfield Monitor." This paper, under Mr. Briggs' excellent management, has reached a large and growing circulation, and wields a strong influence in the political, social and civil affairs of Graves County.

Mr. Briggs is a Democrat, and for three years was secretary of the Graves County Democratic Committee, supporting personally and through the columns of his paper, the platform and candidates of his party.

He is a man of fine literary attainments and wields a trenchant pen. He is a member of the Methodist Church, is a Knight of Pythias and a Knight of Honor.

Mr. Briggs was married April 26, 1883, to Mary Rives, daughter of John Rives. She was educated at Mayfield and is a most estimable and cultured woman. They have one child, Nell.

W. M. Briggs (father) was born in Bardstown, Kentucky, in 1814. He married Julia Watwood in 1839 and in 1840 he removed to Sumner County, Tennessee, and there engaged in mercantile business. He was a man of strong Southern sympathies and an old line Whig at first and afterwards a Democrat. He removed to Union County, Illinois, in 1861, where he died. His wife died in Gallatin, Tennessee, in 1854.

DAVID T. TOWLES, a leading criminal lawyer of Greensburg, son of George W. Towles and Fannie Mason, was born in Green County, Kentucky, June 6, 1830, and with the exception of one year at St. Mary's College, Marion County, he was educated in the common schools of Green County. After leaving school he taught in his native county for five years, studying law during that time. He secured his license to practice in 1853 and immediately began the practice of his chosen profession. He has made a specialty of criminal law, and since 1865 there has never been a murder case in his county that he has not been engaged in the defense. The first office that he held was that of assessor of Green County, to which he was elected in 1856 and held for a term of four years. In 1862 he was elected clerk of the County Court and held that office for twelve years and was county judge for eight years. He is now master commissioner of his circuit by appointment of Judge Patteson. Judge Towles is a Mason and was superintendent of the Methodist Sunday School for fifteen years. He was in the Mexican war and figured conspicuously in the historic battle of Buena Vista. For the space of seven months only he took part in the Civil war, ill health compelling him to resign his commission as captain of Company C, Thirteenth Kentucky Infantry, in the Federal army. In 1851 he married Martha A. Montgomery, daughter of David Montgomery and Tabitha Holland, both of Green County. Mrs. Towles was educated in the schools of her native county.

The Montgomery family originally came from Virginia. Her grandmother was scalped by the Indians and left by them for dead, but she was found by a party of immigrants on their way to settle in Kentucky and was taken care of by them.

Judge and Mrs. Towles had eight children, only three of whom are living: George W. Towles, a lawyer of Greensburg; Montgomery Towles, farmer of Green County, and Lena, widow of Luther L. Foster.

George W. Towles (father) was born in Culpeper County, Virginia, in 1793, and was the son of Joseph Towles and Martha Weatherall of Virginia. He married and came with his father to Kentucky in 1822 and settled in Green County. He received a common school education in Virginia and studied law there, receiving his license in Kentucky in 1830; begun the practice of his profession in Green County; was a Democrat and twice elected to the legislature from his county; was an earnest, consistent Christian and a member of the Baptist Church. He died in 1856. His wife was Fannie Mason, daughter of Enoch Mason of Culpeper County, Virginia, of the distinguished Virginia family of that name, one of whom was James M. Mason, United States Senator. Fannie Mason Towles was born in Virginia in 1800. She was a woman of remarkable strength of intellect and was known as a very devout member of the Baptist Church. She died in 1863 and is buried beside her husband at Summersville, Kentucky. Of their twelve children, only David T. Towles, the subject of this sketch, is now living.

George Washington Towles, son of Judge David T. Towles and Martha Montgomery, was born within six miles of Greensburg, September 25, 1860. He was educated in Greensburg and studied law in the office of his father and his father's law partner, Colonel Hudson; received his license in January, 1885, and for five years practiced his profession in Greensburg.

In 1887 he was elected city attorney; in 1890 he removed to Campbellsville to practice his profession, and in the same year was elected city attorney there. In the memorable race in Green County for county attorney George W. Towles made the race as a Democrat against his brother-in-law, Luther L. Foster, the Republican candidate, and was defeated by thirty-one votes, having made the best Democratic race in that county since the war. Upon his return to Greensburg he was made examiner of Green County.

He married Mary Chandler in December, 1885, daughter of Elzy Chandler and Lizzie Scott. Lizzie Scott Chandler was the daughter of a celebrated Baptist, John Scott. Mrs. Towles was born in Greensburg and educated there and in Louisville and Nashville, graduating at the latter place. They have three children: Frederick Mason, Elzy Chandler and David T. Towles.

JOHN M. HIGGINBOTHAM, President of the Citizen's Bank of Lancaster, son of William Higginbotham and Eleanor Roberts, was born in Garrard County, Kentucky, September 21, 1842. He was educated in the common schools of Garrard and Madison Counties and was a farmer in that county until the beginning of the war between the states, when he enlisted as a private in the Confederate army, serving throughout the war as a member of Capt. M. D. Logan's company in Third Kentucky Regiment of Cavalry, commanded by Col. R. M. Gano; after the regiment was captured on the Ohio raid he escaped and went back South and joined Gen. J. S. Williams' brigade in Gen. Jo Wheeler's division of cavalry. He participated in many a hotly contested battle, among them Chickamauga and Knoxville and those around Atlanta. In a skirmish near Lynchburg, Virginia, his finger was wounded so badly that it had to be amputated, and this was his only wound. He was also at the fight at Green River Bridge, where so many gallant young Kentuckians were killed —beardless youths most of them, fresh from the class room and the tender home circle. A handsome shaft now marks the spot where so many of his comrades fell on that eventful Fourth of July, 1863. After the war closed Mr. Higginbotham returned to Kentucky and again engaged in farming; was elected sheriff of Garrard County in 1878, although the county had previously been Republican, by a majority of one hundred and fifty votes. He served two terms in this office; he organized the Citizen's National Bank of Lancaster in 1882 and was made president, which position he now holds.

In 1885 he established a hardware business, and this he still manages in connection with two farms; one of which, situated about twelve miles from Lancaster, is the old Higginbotham farm. He has served as councilman of the city of Lancaster and has faithfully performed his duty as a citizen whenever called upon to do so.

November 24, 1886, he married Emma Palmer, daughter of John M. and Nancy Palmer. She was born in Garrard County and educated there. Mr. Higginbotham is an extremely popular man, honorable and conscientious in business, considerate and accommodating, courteous in his social relations and faithful in his religious duties in the Christian Church, of which he and his wife are members.

William Higginbotham (father) was born in Garrard County, January 1, 1812; was educated there and engaged in farming and was greatly interested in politics, as a Democrat. He was married in 1840 to Eleanor Roberts, daughter of James Roberts and Elizabeth Mitchell of Lincoln County. She was educated in the common schools and was a member of the Christian Church. They had ten children, six of whom are living: Alzira, wife of R. D. Ballard of Garrard County; Ellen, wife of Cunningham Stafford of St. Louis; Bettie, wife of F. M. Shumate of Boyle County; George T., farmer near Lexington, and Matilda, wife of Isaac Arnold of Guthrie, Oklahoma.

William Higginbotham died in April, 1880, and his wife died in November, 1888. They are buried in the old family burial ground in Garrard County.

Emmanuel Higginbotham (grandfather) was the descendant of one of the several brothers who came from Scotland to Amherst County, Virginia. From that place he emigrated to Kentucky in 1795, and settled in the eastern part of Garrard County on a farm. His wife's maiden name was Reid.

WILLIAM LOGAN was the eldest son of General Benjamin Logan, and was born at Harrodsburg on the 8th day of December, 1776. He was, probably, the fifth white child born in Kentucky. In 1799 he was a member of the convention which formed the present constitution of the state, being then only twenty-three years of age. His selection to this responsible office, so early in life, evinced the high opinion entertained of his character and talents by his fellow citizens. About the same time he commenced the practice of the law, and soon attained considerable eminence in his profession. He was frequently elected to represent his county in the legislature, and on several occasions was made speaker of the house of representatives. He was twice appointed a judge of the Court of Appeals, in which station he was noted for the propriety with which he discharged its various duties. In 1820 he was elected a Senator in the Congress of the United States. He resigned his seat in this body in 1820, for the purpose of becoming a candidate for governor of the state, but was not elected.

He died at his residence in Shelby County, on the 8th of August, 1822, in the forty-sixth year of his age. At the time of his decease he was generally looked to by the people of the state as the candidate for governor in 1824, and had he lived would no doubt have succeeded General Adair in that office.

WILLIAM WARFIELD of Lexington, one of the best known breeders of short-horn cattle in America, son of Benjamin Warfield and Sarah Caldwell, was born in Fayette County, Kentucky, at the old country home called "Grasmere," May 30, 1827.

Benjamin Warfield, his father, was born near Annapolis, Maryland, February 8, 1790, and was brought to Kentucky in the autumn of the same year, Elisha Warfield, his father, removing with his family to a farm near Bryant's Station, Fayette County.

The family originated in America with Richard Warfield, who, in 1637, emigrated from England and settled at Black Horse Inn, nine miles from Annapolis, Maryland. The family was a large and substantial one, owning a considerable body of real estate and taking an active part in local affairs.

Elisha Warfield, son of Benjamin, son of John, son of Richard Warfield (the immigrant) was active in advocating the resistance to Great Britain in 1774-6, and served on a committee of observation for Anne Arundell County. After his removal to Kentucky, he devoted himself to agricultural pursuits till his death in 1817.

Benjamin Warfield, the father of the subject of this sketch, graduated at Transylvania University and read law in Lexington and was there admitted to the bar. He then removed to Mount Sterling and began the practice of his profession. As soon as the war broke out in 1812, he volunteered, and on June 5th he was chosen First Lieutenant in Captain Samuel Williams' Company. In the next campaign he commanded a company in Colonel Richard M. Johnson's command, and was present at the battle of the Thames, where the Kentucky troops so brilliantly retrieved the defeat at the River Raisin. He was present in a number of engagements and was chosen by General William Henry Harrison for several special services, in one of which he was wounded by a ball in the thigh.

After the war he went to Cynthiana, where he practiced law till 1824. He also served in the Legislature during this period.

In 1824 he moved to Lexington and began the practice of the law in partnership with Robert Wickliffe, Esq., in which he was very successful till his retirement in 1831. From 1831 till his death, October 27, 1856, he devoted himself to his farm and the breeding of thoroughbred stock, in which he had long been interested.

The mother of William Warfield was Sarah Caldwell, who was born in Bourbon County, in 1799, and died in Fayette County in 1836. Her father, William Caldwell, was born in the Cumberland Valley, Pennsylvania, of Scotch-Irish parentage, was a soldier in the Revolution, serving in the Second Regiment of the Pennsylvania line, and lost an arm from a wound. Her mother was a Miss Sutherland.

William Warfield attended the school of Beverley Hicks so well known in "the old times," and afterward the public schools of Lexington. He graduated at Transylvania University in 1846, and several years after took two courses in the medical department, but never practiced medicine as a profession. He had early (1843) been entrusted by his father with the care of one of his farms, and became very much interested in the business. He especially fancied the short-horn cattle, and soon developed the herd which his father had begun as early as 1827. He was interested in a number of importations, and did a great deal to increase the knowledge of the breed in this country. No herd in America has so long and so interesting a history. The record of its victories in the show ring would fill a small volume. But it is as the basis of fifty years' scientific study of the theory and practice of breeding that the herd deserves most lasting fame. The results of this study have been embodied in a "History of Imported Short Horns" (1884), a volume of immense and accurate learning, unrivaled in the annals of the breed, and the "Theory and Practice of Cattle Breeding" (1888), a thorough discussion of the subject, which has met wide recognition both as a hand-book for the general reader and a text book in the agricultural colleges. Its sale in England has been a special indication of the writer's wide reputation. Besides these volumes Mr. Warfield has written a great deal for the "Breeders' Gazette," the "National Live Stock Journal," and the "London Live Stock Journal."

"Grasmere," the home of this herd, is one of the most beautiful farms of the Blue Grass region, and is about one mile from the city of Lexington. Since the burning of the house, some years ago, Mr. Warfield has made his home in Lexington. The herd to-day speaks eloquently for the skill of the accomplished breeder.

The Warfields were an old Whig stock and William Warfield was no exception to the rule. Mr. Lincoln asked him to accept a commission of Captain in the army in 1861 for the sake of the example, which he gladly did, although he was compelled on account of ill-health to resign in the winter of 1861-2. In politics he continues a Republican, and keeps up another family tradition in his devoted adherence to the Presbyterian Church.

He married December 21, 1848, Miss Mary Cabell Breckinridge, daughter of Rev. Robert J. Breckinridge, D. D., LL.D., and granddaughter of Attorney-General and Senator John Breckinridge, and of General Francis Preston. They have two living sons who, though still young men, have already made their mark. The elder son, Benjamin Breckinridge Warfield, D. D., LL.D. (born November 5, 1851), is now professor of Theology in Princeton (N. J.) Theological Seminary. He graduated with the highest honors at Princeton College, 1871, and Seminary, 1876. He also studied abroad in 1872-3, and at Leipsic, Germany, 1876-7. In 1878 he became professor of New Testament Literature in the Western Theological Seminary (Allegheny, Pa.), and in 1887, succeeded the celebrated Dr. A. A. Hodge in his present chair. He is the directing editor of the Presbyterian and Reformed Review, an able writer, fine linguist, and generally recognized as the leading theologian of the Presbyterian Church. The younger son, Ethelbert Dudley Warfield, LL.D. (born March 16, 1861), now president and professor of Political Science at Lafayette College, Easton, Pennsylvania, graduated at Princeton College (1882), studied at the University of Oxford, England, and in Germany (1882-3), and graduated at Columbia College (N. Y.) Law School (1885). He practiced law from 1885-8, when he became president of Miami University, Oxford, Ohio, whence he was called to Lafayette College in 1891. Mr. Warfield acknowledges the assistance of his sons in much of his literary work.

MARTIN J. BROWN, Attorney-at-Law of Newport, son of Frederick Brown and Margaret Miller Brown, was born in Warsaw, Ohio, May 30, 1860.

His father was a native of Germany, who came to Cincinnati, Ohio, in 1847 and made his home in that city until 1869, when he removed to Newport and died there in 1883, aged sixty-one years. He was a blacksmith by occupation and master of his trade, industrious and honorable in all his dealings. He was of the Catholic faith, and very faithful in his religious duties; was not much inclined to politics, but voted the Democratic ticket.

Margaret Miller Brown (mother), now living in Newport in her seventy-second year, was born near Baden, Germany. She is a member of the Catholic Church, and a woman of most excellent character.

Martin J. Brown was nine years of age when his parents removed to Newport. He was educated in a Catholic school at Delhi, Ohio; at St. Michael's in Cincinnati; at St. Vincent College in Westmoreland County, Pennsylvania, and finally at St. Xavier College, Cincinnati.

He studied law in the office of A. T. Root, who was then city attorney of Newport, and was admitted to the bar September 25, 1880, when he began the general practice of law, in which he now has a large clientele and a lucrative business. He has made a special study of law regulating corporations, and is special attorney for five or six organizations, building and loan associations, etc. He has devoted his time wholly to his large practice and has taken no active part in politics and has sought no office at the hands of the Democratic party, with which he affiliates.

Mr. Brown was married January 10, 1882, to Hattie Kearney, daughter of James Kearney, deceased, of Newport. She died in 1892, leaving a family of two sons and three daughters: Hattie, Mary, Lillian, George and Martin, Jr.

Mr. Brown adheres to the religious faith of his father and venerable mother.

WILLIAM HENRY GILTNER, Attorney-at-Law in the Columbia Building, Louisville, son of Professor William S. Giltner and Elizabeth (Raines) Giltner, was born in Eminence, Kentucky, January 23, 1870. He graduated from Eminence College in 1888, taking the degree of A. B., and the following year received the honorary degree of A. M.; spent two years in Harvard College, taking a special course in law, and received his certificate from that institution in 1890; studied law in Sedalia, Missouri, with H. T. Williams and was licensed to practice law in May, 1891; attended the lectures at the University of Michigan during the term of 1891-92, and graduated from that institution in June, 1892, and began the practice of his profession in Louisville in July of the same year. He was associated with Augustus E. Willson from October, 1892, until March, 1896, when he removed his office to the Columbia Building, making a specialty of real estate cases, wills, etc.

Mr. Giltner made no haste in entering his profession, but prepared himself most thoroughly for his work. He has made many acquaintances in the city, among whom he is exceedingly popular.

He is a Democrat from principle, but does not take an active part in politics and has no aspirations for office. He is a member of the Christian Church and of the Knights of the Ancient Essenic Order, of the Signet Club of Harvard and Kappa Signa Fraternity of Michigan University.

From the following sketch of his parents and their ancestry it will be seen that Mr. Giltner comes of excellent families.

William Spencer Giltner (father), ex-president of Eminence College, educator and Christian minister, son of John Giltner and Rosanna Sidner, was born in Bourbon County, Kentucky, May 18, 1827; was educated in Woodland Academy in Fayette County, and in Bethany College, West Virginia, from which he graduated in 1852, and was chosen valedictorian from a class of eighteen. After graduation he took charge of Sylvian Academy in Fayette County, and after that was principal of Tubman College in Paris—a school founded by Mrs. Emma Tubman of Augusta, Georgia; at the same time was pastor of the Christian Church at Paris, remaining there six years, and then removed to Eminence, August 6, 1858; took charge of the high school, which was chartered as Eminence College, in 1860, and had charge of that institution until 1893, when he was compelled to abandon active work on account of failing health. For thirty-six years he was the leading spirit in building up and fostering this institution of learning, where hundreds of men and women who are known in various spheres of life for their scholarly attainments and highly moral and religious character, have been educated and prepared for their life work. No man in Kentucky has performed a greater service for his state, and the college which he has established will be only one of his monuments, for Professor Giltner has accomplished a great work in the ministry and in building churches and procuring means to pay for them. He was the originator of the plans for building the Christian Churches in Eminence and Paris and other places, and solicited the funds to pay for their erection. He is a man of large scholarly attainments and of sincere religious convictions, self-sacrificing and earnest in his endeavors to promote the cause of education and untiring in his efforts to spread the gospel.

Professor Giltner was married in 1856 to Elizabeth Raines, daughter of Ayelette Raines; and they have six children: Anabel, now married to H. A. Brewer; Lizzie D., a skillful and accomplished musician, who completed her musical studies in Leipsic, Germany; Leigh Gordon Giltner of Eminence, Kentucky; Robert Raines, president Eminence Roller Mills Company; Frank Carleton and William Henry, a lawyer of Louisville.

Elizabeth Raines Giltner (mother) died June 8, 1894; was educated in private schools in Paris, and was a lady of rare culture and ability, who took an active part in her husband's work, penned many poems of merit, chiefly in memory of her departed friends, and wrote a number of plays, which were enacted by the school, always taking charge of the public entertainments of the college. She died June 8, 1894.

John Giltner, father of Professor W. S. Giltner, was born in Bourbon County, Kentucky, March 4, 1797, and died March 14, 1863. He was a member and an elder in the Christian Church, or the Church of the Reformation; was a friend and associate of Alexander Campbell, the founder of that church, and of Barton W. Stone and others who were prominent in the organization of that denomination in Kentucky.

Mr. John Giltner married Rosanna Sidner, and they had eight children: Martin, Archibald, Abram, William S., Mary Ann, Frances, Maggie and Henry Clay.

Abraham Giltner, grandfather of Professor Giltner, was a native of Bourbon County and lived in Bryant's Station when that fort was so frequently attacked by Indians. He married Katherine Lighter, a native of Bourbon County, daughter of Henry Lighter, who was a native of the same county.

John Giltner (great-grandfather) was a native of Maryland, who came to Bourbon County at the close of the Revolutionary War.

Bennett Giltner (great-great-grandfather) was a native of Amsterdam, Germany, and his father was John Giltner, one of three brothers who were of the body guard of King Frederick the Great. This John Giltner married Katherine Weber, daughter of a wealthy Amsterdam gentleman, who was so indignant because his daughter married a soldier that he disinherited her, but left the strange provision in his will that her portion of his property should be held in trust and allowed to accumulate for her children's children of the fifth generation, to whom it should be paid. This John Giltner, or Gildner, as the name was written in Germany, emigrated to New Amsterdam, where he lived, and his descendants settled in Pennsylvania, Ohio and Kentucky.

Mary Rosanna Sidner, Professor Giltner's mother, was born in Bourbon County, and her father and mother, Martin and Margaret Sidner, were natives of the same county, being members of Virginia families and pioneers of Kentucky.

Rev. Aylette Raines, Elizabeth Giltner's father, was one of the most distinguished preachers of the Christian Church. He was born in Spottsylvania County, Virginia, January 22, 1798, and died at Eminence College, September 7, 1881. His father, Jesse Raines, and his mother, Mary Dodd, were of English ancestry. On the occasion of the death of Rev. Aylette Raines, Rev. S. W. Crutcher preached a memorial sermon from the text: "Know ye not that there is a prince and a great man fallen in Israel this day?"

JUNE W. GAYLE, Sheriff of Owen County, son of James and Sallie (Green) Gayle, was born in Owen County, Kentucky, February 22, 1865. He received his education at Concord College in his native county and at Georgetown College. He left school at the age of sixteen and was appointed Deputy Sheriff and in 1892 was elected Sheriff.

He was married February 3, 1886, to Minnie Alexander, daughter of Phillip and Martha (Baker) Alexander. She was a native of Owen County, Kentucky, and was educated at Bellwood Seminary. They had two children: Mattie Belle and Lula, who died June 19, 1889. Mrs. Gayle died December 11, 1891.

James Gayle (father) was born in Owen County, Kentucky, June 28, 1825. He attended school until he was eighteen and then devoted himself to farming. He located at New Liberty, in 1865, and kept a hotel there for twenty-two years, when he retired from active business pursuits. He is a Democrat, a Mason and an Odd Fellow. He married Sallie Green in October, 1846. His wife was a native of Owen County and was educated in the schools of that county. They have nine living children: Lula, wife of Dr. Madison M. Riley, President of the Greenville Female Seminary, Greenville, Tennessee; Emma Eva, wife of Ben E. Garvey of New Liberty, Kentucky; D. Howard, Cashier of Citizens' Bank at New Liberty, Kentucky, who married Jennie Orr; Robert H., Secretary and Treasurer of the Daviess Coal Mining Company of Knoxville, Tennessee; June W.; Walter S., Cashier of the First State Bank of Monterey, who married Sarah Byrnes; Corrine, who married Charles M. Alexander, and died March 4, 1895; James Gayle, Jr., and Albert De Long Gayle. John Gayle (grandfather) was born in Caroline County, Virginia, November 26, 1777. He immigrated to Gallatin, now Owen County, Kentucky, in 1806.

He was a wealthy planter and large slave owner. He married Melinda Brassfield, a daughter of James Brassfield, a native of Woodford County, and they had ten children:

Elizabeth, John, Joanna, George, William, Sarah, Robert, James, Melinda and Thomas.

John Gayle (great-grandfather) was a native of Virginia, of Scotch-Irish ancestry. He owned plantations and slaves. He married Joanna Walden, who was also a native of Virginia.

Paschal Green (maternal grandfather) was born in Culpeper County, Virginia, in 1799, of English parents. He came with them to Gallatin County, Kentucky, in 1802. Twenty years later he went to New Liberty and engaged in merchandising. He was a Whig and a Mason of high rank, and he married Agnes Blanton, July 4, 1825. She was a native of Franklin County, Kentucky, and daughter of William Blanton and Eliza (Ware) Blanton.

John Green (maternal great-grandfather) was a native of Culpeper County, Virginia, a planter and slave owner. He married Anna Rhoderfer, who was born in the same county May 14, 1771.

JAMES W. SAYRE, Cashier of the Sayre Bank of Lexington, son of E. D. Sayre and Mary E. (Woodruff) Sayre, was born in Lexington, Kentucky. He was educated in private schools in Lexington and in the New York French Institute, from which he graduated in 1873. Returning to his home, he entered his father's bank as messenger and received a thorough training in the banking business, filling all of the intermediate positions from messenger up to his present office as cashier. So indefatigable has he been in the performance of his duties and in his attention to business, he has been absent from his post not more than six weeks altogether during the past seventeen years. He is a gentleman of broad culture and fine business ability; active in all public spirited enterprises, popular as a citizen, interested in the success of the Democratic party; is a thirty-second degree Scottish Rite Mason, Odd Fellow and Knight of Pythias; a member of the Presbyterian Church, and is a director in the Lexington Savings, Building & Loan Association, an organization that is conducted by some of the best business men of Lexington.

Mr. Sayre's wife is a daughter of H. L. Lovell of Covington, and was educated in the Sayre Institute at Lexington, and in the Southern Home School, Baltimore. They have two children, Willie Louise and Howell L. Sayre.

E. D. Sayre (father) was born in New Jersey in 1830, and came to Kentucky when he was a boy, and lived on a farm which is now a part of the site of Louisville. After receiving his education in the common schools, he was employed as a clerk in the foundry of Glover M. McDougall & Co., and after a time went to Lexington and began his remarkably successful and honorable career as a clerk in the bank of David A. Sayre. A more extended sketch of E. D. Sayre will be found in this work.

Mary E. Woodruff Sayre (mother) is a daughter of William Woodruff. Her mother died when Mrs. Sayre was an infant, and she was reared by her step-mother at Henderson and educated in that city. She is a devout member of the Presbyterian Church. The children of E. D. and Mary E. Sayre are E. D. Sayre, Jr., Sydney S. (Mrs. Carey), Mary L. (Mrs. Williams) and James W. Sayre.

JUDGE WILLIAM H. HOLT of Frankfort, Kentucky, was born November 29, 1842, in Bath County, Kentucky. His father, Joseph Holt, died in that county when his son was an infant. The maiden name of his mother was Miss Fanny Tyler. She is still living at Mt. Sterling, Kentucky, her name being now Mrs. Fanny Gossett, honored by all who know her, and yet in possession of all her faculties, although ninety-three years of age. Both lines of ancestry are English. The parents came to this state in their early married life from Connecticut.

Judge Holt received his early education at the common schools in his native county; afterward attended school at Twinsburg, Ohio; Fort Edward Institute, New York, and graduated at the Albany, New York, Law University in May, 1862, with the highest honors of his class. He was admitted to the bar May 5, 1862, and in June, 1863, began the practice of his profession at Mt. Sterling, Kentucky. Here he continued in active and lucrative practice until 1884, when he was elected a judge of the Court of Appeals of Kentucky. During all this time he avoided being a candidate for any office, although frequently urged to do so, but preferred to attend strictly to his practice, being the recognized leader of the bar in Eastern Kentucky. During the time he was an occasional newspaper writer and was Grand Master for one year of the Independent Order of Odd Fellows. While not aspiring to office, he took an active interest in politics, having always been a Republican. When a very young man he canvassed Eastern Kentucky for the thirteenth constitutional amendment, abolishing slavery; was twice a presidential elector; seconded the nomination of Hon. John Sherman at the Chicago convention in 1884 and has long been known as one of the Republican leaders in Kentucky. The district from which he was elected judge in August, 1884, was composed of over forty counties, and he enjoys the distinction of being the first and only Republican who has ever served his state as the chief justice of its highest court. Of undoubted integrity, untiring industry, fine intellect, eloquent in speech, he is known and recognized as one of the leading men of the state. Judge Holt is recognized throughout the state as one of the ablest all-round lawyers in Kentucky, and is on one side or the other of many of the most important cases that come before the courts of the commonwealth.

He was married October 19, 1864, to Miss Sarah Roberts, Gloucester County, New Jersey, who was of Quaker parentage. They have five children, the oldest, M. J. Holt, being a practicing lawyer in Oklahoma, and the oldest daughter being the wife of Hon. A. J. Carroll, late speaker of the Kentucky legislature.

SIMON BOLIVAR BUCKNER, ex-Governor of Kentucky, one of the leading statesmen of his state and section, was born in Hart County, Kentucky, April 1, 1823. He graduated at West Point in 1844, and as second lieutenant was assigned to the Second Regiment, United States Infantry, but was called to West Point the next year as professor of ethics, from which he requested to be relieved, that he might engage in the Mexican war, and this request being granted, he was with General Taylor in active service from the mouth of the Rio Grande to Saltillo. He landed at Vera Cruz with Worth's division in January, 1847, and in the siege there and at Cerro Gordo, at San Antonio and Cherubusco, at Molino del Rey and around the City of Mexico, he bore himself bravely and was brevetted first lieutenant and then captain for conspicuous gallantry. Returning from the Mexican war, he was appointed assistant instructor of infantry tactics in the United States Military Academy, and was thus employed from 1848 to 1855. He

JUDGE W. H. HOLT.

served in the regular army in the Indian country and elsewhere with a commission as captain. In 1860-61, as major-general, he was chief in command of the Kentucky State Guard, which command he resigned to enter the Confederate army. At Fort Donelson he was left in command after the escape of Generals Floyd and Pillow, and after vainly seeking an armistice, surrendered to General Grant with about twelve thousand prisoners, who were sent to Camp Morton and held six months for exchange.

General Buckner bore himself throughout that conflict with that distinction and ability of generalship which characterized him throughout his military career, and he determined to share the fortunes of his prisoner soldiers and was taken to Camp Morton, Indianapolis, from whence he and General Tilghman were soon after transferred to Fort Warren, near Boston, and there closely confined in a narrow prison, where they were denied all correspondence with family or friends. After five months of captivity he was exchanged at Richmond, Virginia, in August, 1862, when, promoted to the rank of major-general, he reported to General Bragg at Chattanooga. Subsequent to this his distinguished services at Mumfordsville, at Perryville, in charge of the defense at Mobile, at Chickamauga, in charge of the Southwest department of Mississippi, Alabama and Louisiana, and to the close of the war—during which time he was advanced to the high rank of lieutenant-general—all these enter too broadly with the general history of the war to be treated of in this volume.

His public career since the war, while he has been disposed to lead a quiet and retired life, has been one of which the people of Kentucky have been proud, and his election to the office of governor in 1887 was largely due to a desire on the part of the people to honor a man for whom they had the highest admiration, rather than from the usual political conditions which attend such elections. His administration of the affairs of the state was endorsed by men of all parties, and as, after the war, he had no truer, warmer friend than General Grant, to whom he surrendered in the early days of the Civil war, so he had no greater admirers in his own party than those who were of opposite political views. Naturally gifted with a high order of intellect, General Buckner has improved these with a thorough education in the highest institutions of learning in the country, and has largely improved his intervals of pleasure in his Hart County home with study and the perusal of the best literature of the day. Though modest in self-assertion before the public, he is held in high esteem by his friends, and is to-day one of the most conspicuous figures in the state of Kentucky.

MATTHEW M'KINNEY, a prominent journalist of Cadiz, son of Samuel and Charlotte Walker Rowlett McKinney, was born December 26, 1826, in Campbell (now Appomattox) County, Virginia. He attended school at Cadiz and Princeton, Kentucky; left school in 1848 and read law with Judge Collins D. Bradley, who was circuit judge of his district.

In 1852 he commenced to publish the "Kentucky Rifle" at Hopkinsville, which he continued to edit until 1854; was then engaged in farming in Trigg County for five years; from 1861 to 1864 was clerk of the County Court; was editor of the "Kentucky Yeoman" at Frankfort during the Tilden campaign, and in 1881 he began the publication of the "Telephone" in Cadiz; was a member of the Kentucky legislature from 1873 to 1875, and was elected county superintendent of schools in Trigg County in 1888.

Major McKinney was married August, 1855, to Jennie B. Watson, daughter of Thomas T. Watson, and they have three children: Mollie, wife of Judge Bingham; Charles, attorney-at-law, and Jennie.

Major McKinney and his family are members of the Methodist Episcopal Church.

Samuel McKinney (father) was born in Charlotte County, Virginia, and educated in the common schools; was a merchant and farmer of Halifax County, Virginia; came to Christian County, Kentucky, in 1832; removed to Trigg County in 1838, and was a merchant at Cadiz and Wallonia. He was a member of the Methodist Church and a very ardent Whig, although not an aggressive politician. He died in November,

1858, and is buried on his farm, four miles from Cadiz.

Charles McKinney (grandfather) married Miss Watkins, sister of Philip Watkins, whose son, William Watkins, is now on the plantation which has been in the Watkins family since granted them by the Crown of England for services rendered. The McKinney family originally came from England.

Charlotte W. Rowlett McKinney (mother) was born in Charlotte County, Virginia. She was married to Samuel McKinney in 1821, and died in 1873. She is buried near Cadiz; was a member of the Methodist Church and a woman of lovely Christian character.

Matthew Jewett Rowlett (maternal grandfather) married Miss Pettuss and lived and died in Halifax County, Virginia. The Rowletts also came to this country from England.

JOHN WILEY MATHEWS, Cashier of the Bank of New Castle and Secretary of the Henry County Trust Company, son of Caleb M. Mathews and Frances S. Edwards, was born in New Castle, Kentucky, November 20, 1843. He was educated principally in the Henry Male Seminary, under the special instruction of Rev. E. D. Isabel; left school when sixteen years of age and was employed as private tutor in his uncle's family, and in 1863, when twenty years of age, was appointed quartermaster at Camp Nelson, in the Union army, and was thus employed for two and a half years—until the close of the war; in 1866 he was a clerk in the Capital Hotel at Frankfort, and following this was superintendent of the Kentucky River Navigation Company, a position which he resigned in 1879, when he was appointed to his present position as cashier of the Bank of New Castle. He is also secretary of the Henry County Trust Company, and is interested in other financial and business enterprises of his city; was mayor of New Castle for several terms, being elected and re-elected by the people without his solicitation; projected and helped to organize the New Castle Cemetery Company; was chairman of the committee appointed by the Bankers' Association in connection with the revising committee of the constitutional convention (1891-92), which formulated the present banking laws of the state, and was thereby acknowledged one of the best informed bankers in Kentucky. He is, moreover, one of the substantial business men of New Castle. Mr. Mathews is a Democrat and is not afraid to say that he belongs to the sound money wing of that party, being able to give a reason for his convictions. He is a member of the Christian Church, of the Masonic order and of the historic Filson Club, and is active and useful in all of these.

Mr. Mathews was united in marriage, in 1865, with Yeba Hewitt, daughter of Judge Hewitt of Frankfort, and she has borne him thirteen children, ten of whom are living. The oldest was Mattie, deceased, wife of M. K. Weems of Quincy, Illinois, proprietor of the largest laundry in the West. (It was his great-grandfather who wrote the history of George Washington containing the first account of the story of the hatchet and the cherry tree.) The names of the other children of Mr. and Mrs. Mathews are Caleb M., Pryor, John, Joseph, George, Yeba, Lawrence D., Ruth E., Margaret G., Albert K., St. John, deceased, and Joanna, deceased.

Caleb M. Mathews (father) was born near Staunton, Virginia, and was educated with a view to the legal profession in the old Transylvania University, having previously enjoyed excellent advantages in private schools in Woodford and Jessamine Counties. He began the practice of law in Versailles and subsequently removed to New Castle, where he became known as one of the leading lawyers of that section, and continued in active practice there until the time of his death, which occurred in 1892. He was a prominent Mason, and was for many years a member of the Baptist Church. He married Frances S. Edwards and reared an illustrious family. His eldest daughter, Laura, was the wife of Dr. William B. Oldham of New Castle, now deceased; John W. (subject), and Dr. Joseph M., an eminent surgeon of Louisville, member of the faculty of the Kentucky Medical College, president of the State Board of Health, and author of a number of medical works.

Mrs. Mathews, nee Edwards, was the widow of

Hiram Beazley when she married Caleb M. Mathews, and had one daughter, Aphia, by her first marriage, who married Chief Justice Pryor of the Court of Appeals, and died January, 1895.

John Mathews (grandfather) was a native of Staunton, Virginia, and was only a small boy when he came to Kentucky with his parents. He was a wealthy farmer and owned large tracts of land in Woodford County. He married Sarah McDowell, daughter of Joseph McDowell, who was a brigadier-general on General Washington's staff, and a member of the Continental Congress. His father was also one of Washington's generals and a native of Virginia. The father of the elder General McDowell and the great-great-grandfather of John W. Mathews, was a native of Ireland, who came to this country and was the progenitor of the Virginia McDowells, and there is a tradition that one of his ancestors was a Gaelic king.

Wiley Edwards (maternal grandfather) was a native of Kentucky and a grandson of Robert Edwards, who made the ninety-nine years' lease of the Edwards estate, embracing valuable property in that city and including the site of Trinity Church. Mr. Mathews (subject) has in his possession a chest which that same Robert Edwards brought over from Wales when he came to America.

JOSEPH C. S. BLACKBURN, senior United States Senator from Kentucky, resident of Versailles, was born in Woodford County, Kentucky, October 1, 1838; educated at B. B. Sayre's school in Frankfort and at Center College, Danville, graduating from Center in 1857. He read law with George B. Kinkead at Lexington, was admitted to the bar in 1858 and practiced law until 1861, when he entered the Confederate army and served throughout the war; resumed practice in 1865; elected to the legislature in 1871, and again in 1873; was elected to the Forty-fourth Congress and re-elected, and was serving his fifth term in the Forty-eighth Congress when he was elected to the United States Senate in the Forty-ninth Congress, in which position he will remain until March 4, 1897, when, his successor not having been chosen, he will in all probability succeed himself. Senator Blackburn is one of the most conspicuous figures in American politics, and a leader of the free silver wing of the Democratic party. His extended experience in Congress and in politics has characterized him as a man of rare gifts and great power. He has few equals as a speaker; well informed, of instinctively quick perception, he is formidable in debate, whether in the deliberative assembly or before the people. His powers of elocution are exceptionally fine and his oratory is equalled by few men in public life. Of impulsive and ardent temper, behind a genial and chivalrous spirit, he is a general favorite with his friends, whose admiration rarely stops short of the wildest enthusiasm.

ANTHONY J. CARROLL, Attorney-at-Law and prominent politician of Louisville, was born at Buckners, Oldham County, Kentucky, September 2, 1864; attended the local schools and received valuable assistance from his talented mother in gaining the rudiments of his education, after which he attended Funk Academy, a collegiate school in La Grange, graduating in 1881. He then began his successful career in Louisville as a reporter for the Courier-Journal, serving as reporter and city editor until 1887, when he was transferred to the Evening Times, of which he was city editor until 1891, when he was elected to the legislature to represent the district comprising the Sixth and Seventh wards; continued his work in the Times office, with leave of absence during the sessions of the legislature of 1891-93; was re-elected in 1893 and nominated for speaker without opposition and by acclamation in the Democratic caucus and was elected speaker of the house, being the youngest man ever elected to that honor with a single exception, and being the first man ever elected or chosen in the caucus by acclamation in the history of the state. He was re-elected to that body in 1895, and had the Democrats controlled the house he would have been again chosen speaker without opposition, having received the Democratic caucus nomination without opposition. During his occupancy of the speaker's chair, there was never an appeal taken from his decisions or rulings, a fact that can not be stated of any other presiding officer in that body.

At the close of the session of 1894, having read law while in the newspaper office and in the legislature, he was admitted to the Louisville bar, and became associated in the practice of law with F. J. Hagan, and at once entered upon the profession which had been his choice for years. The universal acquaintance which he had made while engaged in newspaper work, and his wide popularity, having a friend in every acquaintance, enabled him to step into a lucrative practice at once.

His record as a legislator was pure and spotless, and his reputation for industry and integrity gave assurance of his honesty of purpose. Success had crowned his every effort, and this gave him a prestige and inspired confidence on the part of litigants. His services were sought and important cases placed in his hands, which older lawyers expected would have come to them, and his success in the legal profession was at once assured.

Mr. Carroll was married June 6, 1894, to Sarah F. Holt, daughter of ex-Chief Justice W. H. Holt of Frankfort.

Anthony Carroll, father of Anthony J. Carroll, was an extensive railroad contractor, who lived in Oldham County, where he purchased a tract of six hundred acres of land, upon which he made his home until his death in 1871, aged fifty-six years. He was a native of Ireland, where his father, Anthony Carroll, lived and died.

Elizabeth Collins Carroll (mother) was a native of Ireland and a highly educated and accomplished lady. She survived her husband, and died at her home in Oldham County in 1883, aged fifty-one years. Her father, Edward Collins, died on his native heath in Ireland.

JAMES H. HICKMAN, Mayor of Owensboro and one of the most influential citizens of that city, son of Dr. William A. and Burnette (Barbour) Hickman, was born in Bardstown, Kentucky, March 17, 1852. He was educated in St. Joseph College at Bardstown and in the University of Illinois; and, after completing his literary course, studied medicine and attended the medical department of the University of Louisville, from which he graduated in 1875. For five years following he was associated with his father in the practice of medicine, but abandoned his profession in 1880 to engage in the tobacco business with F. J. Clarke, under the firm name of Clarke & Hickman. This partnership continued until 1883, when Dr. Hickman was elected president of the Owensboro Wagon Company— one of the most successful manufacturing enterprises in that city—a position which he still retains. He is vice president of the First National Bank and has other investments and business interests, but has given especial attention to the management of the affairs of the Wagon Company.

After serving the public for several years as trustee of the School Board and as a member of the City Council, he was elected mayor of the city in 1890, and has been twice re-elected— in 1892 and 1894.

A man of superior business ability, of unswerving integrity, of genial, courteous demeanor, he is at once the exacting man of business and the generous friend of all who have dealings or intercourse with him. Nor is his popularity confined to party lines, for while he is a Democrat when it comes to a vote or a political contest, he knows no party in the discharge of his official duty, enjoying the confidence and respect of men of all parties.

He is a member of the principal benevolent orders, including Knights Templar, Knights of Pythias, Elks, Royal Arcanum and Knights of the Ancient Essenic Order, and is a member of the Methodist Episcopal Church.

Dr. Hickman was married October 1, 1877, to Adele H. Jackson, daughter of James S. and Sue (Hawes) Jackson. She was a native of Masonville, Daviess County, Kentucky. She died leaving three children, Virginia, Christopher and William.

Dr. William A. Hickman (father) was born in Shelbyville, Kentucky, October 26, 1816. He removed with his father to Sangamon County, Illinois, in 1833, where he remained four years, when he returned to Shelbyville and began the study of medicine.

In 1840 he entered the medical department of the University of Louisville, from which he graduated in 1842, and began the practice of medicine in Shelbyville. Finding, however, that his practice would probably conflict with his old friend and preceptor, Dr. G. W. Nuckols, he removed to Bardstown in 1840, where he was a leading physician for twenty-five years, when he turned over his lucrative practice to his brother, Dr. J. F. Hickman, and removed to Owensboro in 1865 and practiced medicine in that city and vicinity for another quarter of a century, when he went to Springfield, Illinois, to reside with his daughter, Mrs. James P. Radcliff. He practiced medicine there for a few years and then engaged in the drug business, in which he continued until his death, December 20, 1894.

Dr. Hickman was actively engaged in the practice of his profession for more than fifty years, and was a conspicuous figure in the communities in which he lived, a man of superior intellect, kind hearted and benevolent, with a good word for everyone, and his reputation as a physician was of the highest character.

He was the leading spirit in establishing the first railroad at Owensboro, and was the first president of the road. He was an active member of the Methodist Church for over sixty years, during which time he was an exemplary Christian gentleman.

Dr. W. A. Hickman was married (first) in 1844 at Bardstown to Burnette Barbour, daughter of William and Jane Barbour. She was born in Virginia in 1827, and died in Bardstown in 1853. Her parents having died when she was quite young, she made her home with her uncle, Ben Hardin of Bardstown. She was educated in Dr. Atkinson's school in Bardstown, and was a very highly accomplished member of the distinguished Barbour and Hardin families. Ben Hardin married Betsy Barbour, a sister of William Barbour.

William Hickman (grandfather) was born in Fredericksburg, Virginia, in 1790; removed to Sangamon County, Illinois, in 1833; then went to Springfield, Illinois, where he died in 1874. He married Mary E. Cardwell at Shelbyville, Kentucky, in 1813, and she died in Springfield, Illinois, in 1833. William Hickman was a merchant in Springfield and several times a member of the legislature. His father was a soldier in the Revolutionary war, and was present at the siege of Yorktown, and was one of the guards appointed by General Washington to take Cornwallis to Richmond.

MRS. LUCY DOWNS, the first white child born of American parents west of the Allegheny mountains, was a resident of Old Town, Greenup County, for over forty years. She was the daughter of Jeremiah and Lucy Virgin, born September 17, 1769, in what is now Fayette County, Pennsylvania, near Uniontown, which was then called Beesontown. She removed in 1790, with her parents and brother, Brice Virgin, to Limestone, now Maysville, Kentucky, and thence in 1792 to Cincinnati—where she was married September 20, 1800, under a marriage license issued by Gen. Arthur St. Clair, as governor of the territory of the United States northwest of the Ohio. In June, 1845, part of her regular family at Old Town were her daughter, granddaughter and great-granddaughter; she then distinctly remembered Gen. Washington's visit to her father's and a neighbor's in 1773 when surveying what was afterwards called Washington's Bottom.

WALTER O. BULLOCK, M. D., an eminent physician of Lexington, son of Samuel R. and Eliza Whitney Bullock, was born near Lexington, Kentucky, in 1842. His father died in 1849 and he was cared for by good and wise friends. He passed through the Sophomore class of the Transylvania University at Lexington and was then sent to the University of Virginia, where he remained until the beginning of the Civil war, when he enlisted in the Confederate service, and was with the army of the West until the close of the strife. He then began the study of medicine, entering first the University of Louisville, and from there going to Bellevue Medical College, New York City, where he graduated in 1869.

On his return home he was appointed demonstrator of anatomy in the Louisville Medical College and remained there for one year; practiced his profession from 1871 to 1875 in the state of Mississippi, and returning to Kentucky was appointed by Governor Blackburn superintendent of the Eastern Asylum for the Insane at Lexington, which position he held for three years. He has since been engaged in the active practice of his profession in Lexington. He is president of the Board of Medical Examiners, and surgeon for the Lexington Eastern Railroad.

Samuel R. Bullock (father), son of Waller and Maria B. Bullock, was born in Fayette County, Kentucky, August 1, 1817; graduated from Center College in 1838, and after completing his law course at the Transylvania University, began practice at Lexington. In 1845 he became a partner of J. C. Breckinridge and afterwards of James B. Beck. He was a brilliant lawyer and personally enjoyed the confidence of the community to an unusual degree, as was evidenced by his being made executor of many valuable estates. He died of cholera July 12, 1849. He married Eliza Whitney, who died in 1859.

The name Bullock has been a power in Fayette County for generations. The famous educator, Rev. Dr. Joseph Bullock, principal of Walnut Hills Academy, a celebrated female school located seven miles from Lexington, left his impress for good on the minds and characters of hundreds of Kentucky women and those of other states.

JOSEPH SAMUEL BOTTS, corporation lawyer of Lexington, son of H. C. Botts and Nannie Felix, was born in Woodford County, Kentucky, September 17, 1865. After the country schools, he attended W. L. Threlkeld's school in Lexington, and was in Georgetown College for five years, but was prevented from finishing his collegiate studies by illness. He then attended the law department of the University of Virginia and graduated with the honors of his class and with the degree of Bachelor of Laws; was elected judge of the moot court of the senior class, this honor being based upon the class and social standing and merit of the student and of the man. He was admitted to the bar in 1886 and at once began to give special attention to the legal business of corporations, in which he has been eminently successful, and is attorney for the following building and loan associations: The United States Savings and Loan Company of St. Paul; The United States Building and Loan Association of Louisville; Commercial Building and Trust of Louisville; Deposit Building and Loan Association of Lexington, and Fayette Building and Loan Association of Lexington, Kentucky, besides which he represents a number of the leading collection agencies throughout the country and many of the leading business firms of Lexington, including L. & G. Straus, Pearson & Clark, Williamson & Bro., Lindsey & Nugent and others. Mr. Botts is a thorough corporation, equity and commercial lawyer, in which line he has been eminently successful and has proven himself one of those useful factors which have been brought to the front by the advancement of the city of Lexington. He prosecutes his cases with good judgment and with vim and vigor, showing due respect to opposing parties, and his intense interest in every transaction inspires his clients with utmost confidence in his management and his fidelity.

H. C. Botts (father) was a son of Henry and Virginia Botts, and was born and educated in Montgomery County, Kentucky.

Nannie Felix Botts (mother), daughter of Joseph and Jane Shouse Felix, was born in Woodford County in 1839, and graduated from a female seminary in Versailles. She was a highly educated woman and an accomplished musician, having studied under Prof. De Roode and other eminent teachers. She married H. C. Botts in 1864 and died in Woodford County in 1865, leaving her only child, the subject of this sketch, to her mother, to whom he owes all of the qualities of his noble and useful manhood.

Jane Shouse Felix (grandmother and foster mother) was a daughter of Samuel Shouse and Katherine Perry. She died in 1894 and is buried beside her husband in the old family burial ground of her fathers.

Joseph Felix (grandfather) was born in 1808, and was a farmer in Woodford County, and also manufactured bagging and rope and had an extensive business with the South. He was a member of the Hillsboro Baptist Church; died in 1867, and is buried beside his wife, near Mortonsville. Their children are Elizabeth, wife of J. C. Hall; John I. Felix; William M. Felix; Cordelia, wife of C. T. Dale; Alice, wife of C. G. Skillman; Josiah Felix; Mary, wife of B. P. Carpenter; Emma, wife of L. J. Cleveland, and Nannie, deceased, who married H. C. Botts.

COL. CHARLES S. TODD, a soldier and diplomatist, son of Judge Thomas Todd of the United States Supreme Court, was born near Danville, Kentucky, January 22, 1791, and died at Baton Rouge, Louisiana, May 14, 1871, aged over eighty years. He was educated in the best schools of Kentucky; graduated at William and Mary College, Virginia, 1809; studied law with his father and attended the law lectures at Litchfield, Connecticut, under the celebrated Judges Gould and Rees, 1810; practiced law at Lexington, 1811-12; volunteered June, 1812, and was made acting quartermaster of the advance of the Northwestern army; was on Gen. William H. Harrison's staff, as division judge advocate of the Kentucky troops, December, 1812; bearer of instructions to Gen. Winchester, previous to the disastrous affair of the River Raisin; upon the recommendation of Gen. Harrison was appointed captain in the Seventeenth United States infantry, and soon after appointed aid to that commander, whose official report highly commended his important services in the campaign and particularly in the battle of the Thames; he subsequently acted as deputy inspector general of the Eighth Military District, then as adjutant general, and in March, 1815, was promoted inspector general, with rank of brevet colonel of cavalry. Gen. Harrison, in a letter subsequent to the war, to a member of President Madison's cabinet, expressed the opinion that "Col. Todd was equal in bravery and superior in intelligence to any officer of his rank in the army."

Upon the disbandment of the army in 1815, Col. Todd resumed the practice of law at Frankfort, and in 1816 married the youngest daughter of Gov. Shelby; was secretary of state under Gov. Madison, 1816; representative in the legislature from Franklin County, 1817 and 1818; charge d'affaires to Colombia, in South America, 1818-23; on his return, settled in Shelby County as a farmer; was a commissioner to the Presbyterian General Assembly in Philadelphia, 1837 and 1839, when the separation was effected, he sustaining the old school; was vice president of the Kentucky State Agricultural Society for several years, and delivered the annual address, 1839; in connection with Ben Drake, prepared sketches of Gen. Harrison, 1840, and became editor of the Cincinnati Republican, a Whig newspaper; accompanied Gen. Harrison to Washington, February, 1841, having been selected by him as United States minister to Vienna, but this appointment was prevented by the death of the president; in the summer of 1841 President Tyler appointed him to the mission of St. Petersburg, which he held until displaced by President Polk in the fall of 1845. At St. Petersburg, and during his visits to the interior of Russia and to the king of Sweden (Bernadotte, the only marshal of the great Napoleon who retained his crown), he was treated with most marked consideration.

GEN. THOMAS METCALFE, the tenth governor of Kentucky, was born in Fauquier County, Virginia, March 20, 1780. His mother was the Sally Metcalfe who was shot from her horse, on the 19th of January, 1781, by a British sentinel—whilst endeavoring to make her escape from the Elk Run neighborhood, in that county, where the American traitor, Gen. Benedict Arnold, with 1,800 British soldiers, was "exercising the most unheard of cruelty, indiscriminately on men, women and children, and committing wanton destruction of every kind of property." She recovered from her wound, and with her brave husband, a captain in the Revolutionary war, and "an acquaintance of George Washington," emigrated to Kentucky in 1785, and settled in Fayette, but removed in a few years to Nicholas County. They were poor and humble. in his early youth, young Metcalfe was sent to school only long enough to obtain a knowledge of the rudiments of an English education—sufficient, however, to inspire an ardent love for knowledge. At sixteen, he was apprenticed to an elder brother, a stone-mason. While learning his trade, his otherwise leisure hours were devoted to study and to books. What to other boys was labor and irksome, was to him relaxation and full of promise for the future. At nineteen his father died; and upon him fell a large portion of the burden—to him a cherished filial privilege—of caring for his mother and several children. As a mason he built, of stone, several court houses—at West Union, Adams County, Ohio; at Greensburg, Green County, Kentucky, in 1806 (still standing in 1873), and others, and laid the foundation of that at Paris, Bourbon County, which was burnt down May 8, 1872, but of which his uncle, John Metcalfe, built the superstructure. From his trade and his great earnestness afterwards as a public speaker, he received the sobriquet of the "Old Stone Hammer," by which he was familiarly and proudly known for forty-five years.

In 1809 he made his first public speech. A requisition had been made upon the state to vindicate the honor of the nation in the contemplated difficulties with old Spain. His own fire and enthusiasm were quickly communicated to the crowd, and volunteers flocked to his standard in numbers above his complement. He had twice before raised volunteers for contemplated service against Spain, and now for the third time was disappointed. He quietly doffed his military title and took up his stone-hammer. In 1812 he was elected to represent Nicholas County in the lower branch of the Kentucky legislature; and re-elected 1813, '14, '15, '16 and '17—in 1813, while absent as a soldier, receiving every vote in the county but thirteen. In the spring of 1813 he raised a company of volunteers, and at the battle of Fort Meigs was under Col. Boswell, on the left flank of the line on this side of the river, which defeated more than double its number of Indians; his intrepidity and gallantry secured the favorable notice of the commander-in-chief, Gen. William H. Harrison, afterwards president of the United States. In 1818 he was elected to congress, and re-elected four times; but during the last term, in 1828, he resigned to make the race for governor as the candidate of the National Republican (or Adams) party—being elected by 38,940 votes, to 38,231 for the able and popular Maj. William T. Berry, the Jackson candidate. The latter party elected John Breathitt lieutenant governor over Judge Joseph R. Underwood by 1,087 majority.

In February, 1827, Gen. Metcalfe was challenged to fight a duel by George McDuffie of South Carolina, for offensive language used in a newspaper article; he accepted and named rifles as the weapons at ninety feet. McDuffie, insisting on pistols, dropped the matter rather than fight with rifles.

Gov. Metcalfe served four years in the state senate from Nicholas and Bracken Counties, 1834-38; in 1840, and for some years, was president of the state board of internal improvement; and in 1848-49 filled by appointment of Gov. Helm the unexpired term of John J. Crittenden in the United States Senate. He died at his home at Forest Retreat of cholera, August 18, 1855, aged seventy-five years.

THOMAS HARRIS BARLOW, who was born August 5, 1789, in Nicholas County, Kentucky, and died June 22, 1865, in Cincinnati, Ohio, was the most ingenious and celebrated of Lexington inventors. His education was limited. He was a soldier of the War of 1812, in Colonel Richard M. Johnson's regiment. He built a steamboat at Augusta, Bracken County. After his removal to Lexington, he built, in the winter of 1826-7, a steam locomotive, with car attached, for two passengers, and with power to ascend an elevation of eighty feet to the mile. In May, 1827, it was opened to the public for exhibition, in a large room over Joseph Bruen's machine shop, where an oval track around the room was constructed, and the first "train" in western America put in motion. General Leslie Combs, Dr. Wm. S. Chipley and other old citizens are still living who took a ride at fifty cents a ticket. Samuel Robb purchased the novelty for travel—visiting Louisville, Nashville, Memphis and New Orleans, at which latter place it was burned while on exhibition. In 1827 he built another locomotive and sold it to a party who found it profitable to travel and exhibit it. In 1835 another locomotive—with two upright cylinders and lever beams, both engines attached to one axle, with crooks at right angles, and upright boilers—was built by Jos. Bruen, for the new railroad from Lexington to Frankfort, constructed of strap-iron rails spiked down to stone sills, which proved to be as unsubstantial as its advocates claimed it would be substantial.

In 1845, in the silversmith shop of his son, Milton Barlow, he made a small, rude planetarium, to illustrate the motion of the heavenly bodies in teaching his grandchildren. The idea grew as he studied and labored, and his son and Wm. J. Dalsem aided him in working out such combinations gearing as produced the minute fractional relative revolutions of the planets. After three years' patient labor, the first fine instrument was completed, and sold in 1849 to Girard College, Philadelphia. Other instruments were built during the next ten years, and after the exhibition of one at the World's Fair in New York, in 1851, sold for $2,000 each; two of the larger size to Congress for the Military Academy at West Point, N. Y., and the Naval Academy at Annapolis, Maryland, and one to the city of New Orleans—besides a number of smaller ones to colleges and public institutions. Thus has Kentucky the honor of presenting to the scientific world the only perfect instrument to show the motions of the solar system—the dates of all eclipses, of the transits of Mercury and Venus, and every other suggested problem during hundreds of years, that scientific men were curious to test it. It is one of the most exact and wonderful combinations of machinery ever made.

In 1840, Mr. Barlow had invented a rifled cannon, and made a model, but laid it aside. In 1855, encouraged by the liberality of Congress, in buying two of his planetariums, he obtained for his gun a patent, with the most comprehensive claims. Congress appropriated $3,000 for an experimental gun—which was cast at Knapp & Totten's great foundry in Pittsburgh, and taken to Lexington to be rifled and completed by the father and son. It weighed, finished, 6,900 pounds, was five and one-half inches bore, and twisted one turn in forty feet. It then was sent to the Washington navy yard to be tested, and developed greater accuracy and range than was expected. Although neglected for awhile by our own government, it attracted the attention of foreign ministers and agents, and is believed to have originated or suggested most of the rifled guns of Europe and the United States. Previous to this, Mr. Barlow invented an automatic nail and tack machine, which capitalists eagerly purchased. About 1861, a stroke of paralysis, from which he recovered but partially, cut short Mr. Barlow's usefulness as an inventor. His son Milton, on returning from the Confederate army in 1865, gathered up the fragments of $9,000 worth of planetariums built for educational institutions in the South—which could not reach them because of the Civil War, and which were broken to pieces or scattered by the malicious and destructive spirit of some Federal soldiers—and finished two in elegant style. One of these, by the liberality of the Kentucky Legislature, he was enabled to exhibit at the World's Exposition in Paris, France, in 1867—as Kentucky's contribution to that grand collection of the products of all civilized nations. It received the highest premium awarded to any illustrative apparatus.

STONEWALL J. DOUTHITT of New Castle, clerk of the Henry Circuit Court, son of Silas P. and Lucy (Clements) Douthitt, was born in Henry County, near Lockport, February 22, 1861. He was educated in the common schools and at the Central Normal School at Danville, Indiana. After leaving school at the age of twenty years, he was engaged in farming, and being of a very studious turn of mind and very fond of general reading, he intended to choose the profession of law for his occupation, but circumstances diverted him from this course.

He taught for a number of years in Henry County, and becoming interested in politics and being a Democrat, was elected clerk of the Circuit Court in 1887 and was re-elected in 1892. Mr. Douthitt was married in February, 1892, to Nannie Samuell, daughter of Richard P. Samuell and Annie (Smith) Samuell, who is a granddaughter of Abram Owen. She was born in Henry County and educated in the Henry County Male and Female College. They have one child:

Helen D., born August, 1892. They are members of the Baptist Church.

Silas P. Douthitt (father) was born in Henry County, September, 1828, and educated in the schools of the day. He was a farmer and extensive tobacco grower. He represented Henry County in the Kentucky legislature in 1875-6 and again in 1879 and 1880, having been elected as a Democrat.

He was married in 1850 to Lucy Clements, a native of Henry County, where she was educated. Their children were: Erasmus D., Fielding S., Rhelda, Stonewall J., Sidney T., Lula and Laura.

John Douthitt (grandfather), whose mother was a Helm, was born in Culpeper County, Virginia, in 1785 and died in 1868. He came to Henry County, Kentucky, with his father when he was twelve years of age, passing through the bluegrass region so as to settle near the Kentucky river in order to have access to easy transportation. During the War of 1812 he was appointed major of militia, but it was found unnecessary for him to engage actively. He married Theodosia Wilson, whose parents came from Virginia, and the children of this union were: James C., Thomas, Tapeley, Silas P., Harriet, Ann, Kate, Jane and Betsy.

Thomas Douthitt (great-grandfather) was a native of Virginia, and was in the War of the Revolution, coming to Kentucky after that time, as above stated.

John Clements (maternal grandfather) was born in Fleming County, Kentucky, about the year 1800; he was a member of the Baptist Church, a Democrat and a farmer; married Letitia Smoot.

Gustavus Adolphus Clements (maternal great-grandfather) was a native of South Carolina, who came to Kentucky in 1778 and was at Bryant's Station when Simon Girty raided that fort. He was one of the stanch-hearted old pioneers to whom those who came after and enjoy the fruits of their labor owe all honor and gratitude and kindly remembrance.

John Clements, a brother of Gustavus Adolphus Clements, was killed by the Indians at Blue Lick Springs.

JUDGE GEORGE ROBERTSON was born November 18, 1790, in Mercer County, Kentucky. His father, Alexander Robertson, who was born in Augusta County, Virginia, about a mile from Staunton, November 22, 1748, was the son of James Robertson—who, with his own father of the same name, emigrated about 1737 to America from the neighborhood of Coleraine, in the north of Ireland. They were a portion of the colony that settled on Burden's grant, in the then Trans-Allegheny wilderness of Virginia. Alexander Robertson was a near relative of William Robertson, the celebrated historian, whose nephew, John Henry, was the father of Patrick Henry.

On August 18, 1773, he was married to Margaret Robinson, at the residence of Col. John Howard (father of Gov. Benjamin Howard of Missouri) in Bedford County, Virginia. He was a man of strong mind, sterling moral qualities, and popular with his fellow citizens; was elected a member of the Virginia Federal Convention, at Richmond, June, 1788, and also elected a member of the Virginia legislature, the ensuing winter. With his family he emigrated to Kentucky, at Gordon's Station, December 24, 1779, during the hard winter. Near this spot, at Harlan's spring, the head of Cane Run, he built "the first fine house in Kentucky," and permanently located. In 1792, he was elected by the people the first sheriff of Mercer County. He died in 1802.

Margaret Robinson, the mother of George Robertson, was born April 13, 1755, on the Roanoke River, in what was then Fincastle, afterwards Bottetourt, and now Montgomery County, Va. She died at the residence of her son-in-law, ex-Governor Robert P. Letcher, in Frankfort, June 13, 1846, in her ninety-second year.

George Robertson, after attaining a good elementary education in the English branches, was sent, August, 1804, to Joshua Fry (then teaching on his farm five miles west of Danville, once owned and occupied by Colonel George Nicholas) to learn Latin, French and mathematics. From this he entered Transylvania, remaining until 1806; then spent four months in Rev. Samuel Finley's classical school at Lancaster, Kentucky, for six months more, being his assistant in teaching.

KENTUCKY BIOGRAPHIES.

In the spring of 1808 he went to Frankfort to study law under General Martin D. Hardin, but was disappointed; returned to Lancaster, and, under the direction of his brother-in-law, Samuel McKee, then a member of Congress, studied law until September, 1809, when Judges Boyle and Wallace granted him license to practice.

In November, 1809, when only a few days over nineteen years of age, he married Eleanor Bainbridge, who was less than sixteen, a daughter of Dr. Bainbridge, of Lancaster. The young couple set up for themselves in a small buckeye house with only two rooms, respecting which this remarkable coincidence of successive events is related with pride; Judge John Boyle had begun housekeeping in the same house, and while occupying it was elected to Congress, 1803-09; Samuel McKee began housekeeping in the same house, and succeeded Boyle in Congress, 1809-17; George Robertson commenced housekeeping in the same house, and succeeded Mr. McKee in Congress, 1817-21; Robert P. Letcher commenced housekeeping in the same house, and after an interval of two years succeeded Robertson in Congress, 1823-33. But for Robertson's resignation of the last term for which he was elected, 1821-23, there would have been no intermission. Thus, four young men in succession began housekeeping in this unpretentious buckeye log cottage, and represented that district in Congress for thirty years, with the single intermission of two years. In addition to this, two of them held the Chief Justiceship of Kentucky for over thirty-one years—Judge Boyle from March 20, 1810, to January 5, 1827 (seventeen years), and Judge Robertson from December 24, 1829, to April 7, 1843, and again from September, 1870, to September, 1871 (over fourteen years); and a third, Mr. Letcher, was Governor for four years, 1840-44. Nor were these all the honors most worthily conferred upon these four men.

After about two years, Mr. Robertson built up a fine practice, and in 1816, when only twenty-six, was elected to Congress against formidable opposition. He was twice re-elected without opposition; but did not serve out his last term, having resigned his seat in 1821. He soon acquired distinction in Congress; was Chairman of the Land Committee and a member of the Judiciary and Internal Improvement Committees; and drew and introduced the bill to establish a territorial government in Arkansas. To that bill John W. Taylor of New York offered an amendment interdicting slavery—which was elaborately discussed and produced great excitement. The restriction was carried by one vote; a re-consideration had, and the bill finally passed, divested of the restriction, by the casting vote of the speaker, Henry Clay.

In 1820, Mr. Robertson initiated—instead of the old system of disposing of the public lands on a credit, at a minimum of two dollars per acre—the present system requiring payment without credit, and reducing the minimum price to one dollar and twenty-five cents per acre, and the quantity that might be purchased to eighty acres; whereby any poor man who could command one hundred dollars might obtain a home. He advocated its adoption, although in opposition to most of the Western members led by Mr. Clay; the bill passed by a large majority. This measure has contributed more to the advancement and prosperity of the West than any ever adopted. Mr. Robertson's speech advocating its passage is published in his "Scrap Book."

In 1816, George Madison was elected Governor and Gabriel Slaughter Lieutenant-Governor of Kentucky for four years. Governor Madison died a few weeks after the election, and before he was inaugurated, and the Lieutenant-Governor was inaugurated as Governor. At the next session of the Legislature, December, 1816, a resolution passed the House of Representatives for a new election of Governor. This led to a popular excitement which, for more than a year, agitated the state almost to revolution. Mr. Robertson, in the summer of 1817, published, over the signature of "A Kentuckian," an argument against the "new election," in pamphlet form, which exercised a powerful influence in allaying excitement and settling the question against the new election.

He took an active part in the celebrated "relief" and "anti-relief," "Old Court" and "New Court" controversy in Kentucky. He was elected to the Legislature from Garrard County in 1822, and for several successive years, until that fearful contest was finally settled in 1826-7. He was elected Speaker of the House in 1823, but at the session of 1824 was beaten for Speaker by Robert J. Ward of Scott County. It was at this session that the act was passed to repeal the act organizing the Court of Appeals and to reorganize a Court of Appeals; it was hence known as the "reorganizing act." It was unconstitutional and revolutionary. After its passage, the anti-relief party was near disbanding. Mr. Robertson wrote, and by adroit management had entered upon the journal of the house, the protest against that act —which had the effect of uniting the "anti-relief" into an "Old Court" party. It was circulated far and wide, electrified the people, and became the text of the party. Through the influence of the principles enunciated and arguments promulgated in that document, the Constitution was in the end triumphantly vindicated and maintained. Mr. Robertson was re-elected speaker in 1825, '26 and '27. He was the author of the "Manifesto" of the majority in 1826-27, and delivered many public addresses during that contest; his letters and writings were powerfully effective, but the letters over the signature of "Plebeian" and published in the "Spirit of '76," were peculiarly efficient, and may yet be read with pleasure and instruction as masterly specimens of political essays.

Previous to the nomination, in 1828, of General Thomas Metcalfe, for Governor, the nomination was tendered to Mr. Robertson by a committee of the convention, but declined. Governor Metcalfe appointed him Secretary of State, the duties of which office he discharged for a short time. Judge Boyle having resigned his seat upon the appellate bench, and accepted the appointment of Judge of the United States District Court; Judges Owsley and Mills, after the termination of the contest in favor of the Old Court, resigned. George M. Bibb had been previously appointed Chief Justice. Judges Owsley and Mills were renominated by Governor Metcalfe, but rejected by the Senate. Mr. Robertson was nominated, December 24, 1828, and his nomination confirmed. He accepted, with the understanding that he might resign at the end of the year; at which time he was appointed Chief Justice. In 1843 he resigned this high trust, and returned to the bar and to a lucrative practice. In August, 1864, his name was placed upon the poll books as a candidate for Judge of the Appellate Court of the Second District. This was done only two or three days before the election, by friends who were alarmed at the open interference of the military, in threatening or ordering the arrest of candidates who were styled disloyal. In many parts of the district it was not known; yet he was elected by a large majority. An office tendered under such extraordinary circumstances could not be declined; and although then in his seventy-fifth year, he accepted it, discharging its onerous duties with diligence and ability until February 2, 1871, when he was stricken down, while actually presiding as Chief Justice, with paralysis— the result of too continuously overtasking, through a life of great labor, his splendid constitution. Although disabled from active duty, the bar indulged the hope of his ultimate restoration, and was unwilling for him to resign, especially during the summer vacation. But at the convening of the court in September, Judge Robertson, after, as Chief Justice of Kentucky, administering the oath of office to Governor Preston H. Leslie, immediately resigned—an act entirely voluntary on his part and then wholly unexpected. His short address at the time caused many in the large assembly attending the inauguration to shed tears.

Judge Robertson's death occurred at his home in Lexington, May 16, 1874, in his eighty-fourth year. Although prostrated by disease, and physically disabled, his mind was entirely unimpaired and his mental faculties wholly unobscured. He never sought office, but declined many that were tendered him. After his retirement from Congress, General Adair tendered him the offices, first of Attorney-General of Kentucky, and then of Judge of the Fayette Circuit; and as an inducement to his acceptance of the latter, the authorities tendered him a law professorship in Transylvania University. President Monroe offered him the appointment of Governor of Arkansas territory. In July, 1824, Hon. Richard Clough Anderson, Jr., then minister to Bogota, having expressed a desire to return home if Mr. Robertson would take his place, the mission to Colombia was tendered him, but declined, and Mr. Anderson determined to remain. In 1828, President Adams tendered him the mission to Peru, which was also declined. He four times declined seats in the Federal cabinet, of different grades, and twice a seat on the bench of the United States Supreme Court.

In 1848, and again, 1851-53, he represented his adopted county, Fayette, in the lower branch of the Kentucky Legislature.

In his long public life he was industrious, diligent and constant, performing as much labor as any man who ever held office in the state. His law lectures and political essays, some of which have been published in his "Scrap Book," Lexington, 1855, and his legal opinions as contained in the Kentucky Reports speak for themselves—evincing at once depth of thought, laborious research, accurate discrimination, and sound philosophy.

GEORGE W. ADAIR, a descendant of Governor Adair, a citizen of Maysville and the present county attorney of Mason County, was born in that county, and of which he has been a citizen all his life. For twenty years he has practiced law at the Maysville bar, which is one of the best in the state.

Isaac C. Adair (father) was a native of Virginia, but emigrated to Kentucky early in the present century. He wedded Sarah B. Conway, a daughter of Miles Conway, who was at one time judge of the Mason County Court.

Isaac C. Adair, the son of John Adair, died when his son George W. was only seven years of age. The latter was thrown entirely upon his own resources, and had the battle of life to fight unassisted. Mr. Adair is a Republican, and is the first man of the Republican persuasion to hold the office of county attorney in Mason County.

JOHN GORDON BURNETT HALL, County Judge of Hopkins County and resident of Madisonville, son of Dixon and Sallie (Henson) Hall, was born in Hopkins County, Kentucky, September 23, 1857. His father, Dixon Hall, was born in Hopkins County, Kentucky, April 29, 1811, and during the greater portion of his life was a farmer and merchant. He served several terms as justice of the peace, one term as deputy sheriff, and in 1878 was elected county judge, holding this office until 1882. In 1883, with his two remaining daughters and his son, Robert M. Hall, and family, he removed to Windom, McPherson County, Kansas, and engaged in mercantile business, but in 1892 he returned to Madisonville, where he remained with his son, John G. B., and his daughters until his death, September 29, 1894. He lived eighty-three years and three months. While he was modest and retiring in his disposition, his reputation for firmness and unyielding loyalty to his convictions was widely known and appreciated. This trait of his character was especially displayed while he was a county judge in his refusal to grant license for the sale of intoxicating liquors in any locality except upon proof of the necessity for such sale. This arrayed against him strong prejudices and continuous opposition of many, but drew to him friends equally as numerous and determined, cultivated a strong public sentiment against the liquor traffic and led to the adoption by a vote of the people of a strong prohibitory law, which continued in force throughout said county for ten years, and now prevails in a large portion thereof. He was a member of the Primitive Baptist Church and a conspicuous figure in the religious work of that denomination at Flat Creek.

Caleb Hall (grandfather) was born in central Kentucky, came to Hopkins County at an early day, took a prominent part in the organization of the county in 1806, the locating and laying out of the county seat, Madisonville, in 1807, and was bondsman for the first sheriff of said county. He died near 1860 and was about seventy-five years of age. His father came from Virginia.

Sallie Henson Hall (mother) was born in North Carolina, July 4, 1815, and was brought to Hopkins County, Kentucky, when quite a small babe by her father and family. They came in wagons over mountainous roads, and she was carried for great distances in the arms of her older sister,

Pollie Henson, who was then a young girl, and who died in 1894 at the age of ninety-one years. Sallie Henson was married to Dixon Hall December 19, 1832, and became the mother of ten children, the youngest of whom is the subject of this sketch. She was a faithful member of the Primitive Baptist Church, a kind and affectionate Christian lady, whom her friends loved and speak of in highest praise. She died September 6, 1873.

John G. B. Hall was educated in the schools of Madisonville, except a term in 1877 and 1878 in the Cumberland University at Lincoln, Illinois. After leaving school he read law with Polk Laffoon and William L. Gordon, a prominent legal firm of Madisonville, and was admitted to the bar in September, 1879; has devoted his best energies to the practice of his profession until the present time, and has the confidence of his people as a safe, painstaking and conscientious attorney. In 1884 he and C. C. Givens established the Hopkins County Gleaner, a weekly newspaper, which met with a phenomenal success, reaching a circulation of four thousand copies in fifteen months. He sold his interest to Mr. Givens, and in 1885 went to Kansas and located in Hugoton and assisted in the organization of Stevens County. He was elected first county attorney of the new county in 1886 and was re-elected in 1888. During his first term the county was divided into two factions, which grew very bitter towards each other and engaged in frequent battles. In one of these, which happened just over Stevens County line in "No Man's Land," south of Kansas, four of the Woodsdale faction were killed. The excitement and prejudice and desire for revenge were so great that the enforcement of law was impossible. Mr. Hall's friends were of the Hugoton faction, and although he tried to show favors to neither, his office was of such vital importance in the county seat contests and other county matters, a great effort was made to defeat him, but he was nominated on the first ballot over three opponents by the farmers' convention, there being no party lines, and was re-elected. In the following spring, 1889, after the Republicans had nominated their candidate for district judge of the district composed of twelve counties, the people who were dissatisfied held a People's convention, in which Mr. Hall received on first ballot a tie vote with the leading candidate, and within a few votes of a nomination, but was defeated on second ballot. In July of the same year he resigned his office of county attorney and returned to his native county in Kentucky, and resumed the practice of law. In November, 1894, he was elected county judge of Hopkins County, and in that respect, as well as in his devotion to the best interests of the community, he is following in the footsteps of his honored father, a faithful and upright judge. In politics he is a Democrat; in religion, he is a member and officer of the Christian Church.

NEWTON C. SHOUSE of New Castle, sheriff of Henry County, son of Dudley J. and Mary A. (Combs) Shouse, was born in Henry County, Kentucky, November 21, 1861.

His father was born in Woodford County, where he lived until 1840, when he removed to Henry County. For ten years of his early life he was engaged in teaching in the public schools of Woodford, Shelby and Henry Counties. For twenty-five years he was employed in the internal revenue department, performing duties in Henry and adjacent counties in the Fifth Collection District.

In 1890 he engaged in farming in Henry County, near Sulphur, where he has his home at present. He has been a very enthusiastic Republican since the war, and has taken an active and frequently a leading part in the affairs of his party in his bailiwick. He is a member of the Baptist Church and there is no truer, better man in Henry County than D. J. Shouse.

He was married April 22, 1845, to Mary A. Combs, and has eight children living: William T., Jennie V., James D., Nannie S., Thomas M., Ernest G., Sophronia and Newton C. Shouse. The father and mother of these children have entered upon the fifty-second year of married life.

Thomas Shouse (grandfather) was a native of Woodford County, Kentucky, where he was a farmer. He was a captain under General William Henry Harrison and fought in the battle of Tippecanoe, in which engagement he received a very severe wound. He was a good and true citizen, and a member of the Regular Baptist Church.

William W. Combs (maternal grandfather) was born in Henry County in 1801, and was a prominent farmer in that county. His wife's name was Mary Sanford, who was born in Henry County, Kentucky, in 1817.

Newton C. Shouse was educated in the public schools of Henry County, and in 1881 attended a commercial college in Louisville, graduating from the business department. From 1882 to 1884 he had charge of the registry department in the Louisville postoffice, since which time he has been successfully engaged in the leaf tobacco business in Louisville, and in Henry County. In 1894 he was elected sheriff of Henry County, being the first Republican ever elected to an office of that importance in that county. He has performed the duties of his office with fidelity and to the entire satisfaction of the citizens, by whom he is respected and trusted with implicit confidence.

Mr. Shouse is a member of the fraternities of Masons and Elks, and is a member of the Baptist Church, the church of his fathers.

He was married May 22, 1895, to Sallie C. Morris, daughter of David Morris, deceased, and Amanda (Ronner) Morris. Mrs. Shouse was educated at Fairmount College, Henry County.

DAVID CONGREVE LISLE, Postmaster of Winchester, Kentucky, son of Claiborne Lisle and Esther Hampton, was born in Clark County, six miles south of Winchester, June 1, 1854. He was educated in the common schools of the county and afterwards was a teacher in his native county for several years. He was the publisher and proprietor of the Clark County Democrat from 1883 to 1887, and while in the newspaper work was an active politician, and the columns of his paper were used to strongly advocate the principles of the Democratic party. In recognition of his services to his party, his brother, Congressman Lisle, secured for him the appointment as postmaster of Winchester in 1893.

He is a thorough and highly efficient business man, conscientious in the performance of his duties, and honorable in his dealings; a devoted husband and father, and very popular socially. His management of the postoffice has demonstrated the wisdom of his appointment and is appreciated by the public.

Mr. Lisle is a member of the Christian Church, an Odd Fellow and a Knight of Pythias. He was married April 26, 1886, to Mildred Winn, daughter of J. N. Winn and Mary Poston of Clark County. She was born December 17, 1865, and was educated in Daughter's College at Harrodsburg, Kentucky. They have three children living: Mary D., Nick Winn and Mildred.

Claiborne Lisle (father) was born in Clark County, July 22, 1820; was educated in the county schools, and was one of the original Democrats of the county. He is a prosperous farmer and a director and vice president of the Winchester Bank. His farm on which he has his residence is situated about seven miles from Winchester.

James Lisle (grandfather), a native of Clark County, was a son of John Lisle, who was one of the early settlers of Kentucky, he having located about a mile north of Boonesboro.

Esther Hampton Lisle (mother), daughter of George Hampton and Catherine Raut, was born in 1821 and died May 26, 1876. She was the mother of eleven children, of whom the following are living: David C. Lisle, James D. Lisle, Zipporah, wife of Henry Oliver of Arlen, Clark County; Thomas Lisle, and Minerva, wife of J. N. Hodgkin of Elkin, Clark County. Marcus C. Lisle, deceased, was elected to Congress in 1892, when he was only twenty-nine years of age, and died July 7, 1894, while discharging the duties of that office. He was born September 22, 1863, in Clark County, Kentucky, and after attending the common schools of the county took a two years' course at Kentucky University, Lexington, afterwards studying law at Columbia College, New York. After finishing the law course he practiced law at the Winchester bar, and was elected judge of the Clark County Court in August, 1889; resigning this office in 1893 to take his seat in Congress. July 27, 1887, he married Miss Lizzie B. Bean of Clark County, who died March 4, 1893, the day upon which he was to take his seat in Congress. They had one son, Claiborne Lisle, who was born September, 1889.

WILLIAM HENRY WADSWORTH.—

In the family Bible still owned and cherished by the descendants of the first-named, under date of 1632, the following memorandum is recorded:

"This day, Christopher and William Wadsworth came over in ye good ship Lion."

Of the antecedents of these two brothers, beyond the fact that they were of English birth and of the Puritan faith, were of excellent repute, and acquitted themselves as became true men, nothing is known to the writer. In this land they took root and put forth vigorous branches in the New England colonies; and if trees may be judged by the fruit they bear, it will be admitted that they must have come of good and sound stock. From Christopher descended Henry Wadsworth Longfellow, whose fame extends wherever the English language is read or spoken as the sweetest and greatest of American poets. William Wadsworth, the younger brother, was twice married, and was the father of ten children. The name of Joseph Wadsworth, a son of William by the second marriage, is inseparably associated with one of the earliest struggles of the colonies for the right of self-government, and will live in American history as that of the hero who preserved the charter of Connecticut by concealing it in the oak tree, which ever since has been known as "The Charter Oak." He had five children, the oldest of whom was a son named Joseph B. Wadsworth. This son had a son and namesake, who had eight children, the third of whom was a son named Timothy Wadsworth, who was the father of eleven children. Rhoda Wadsworth, the youngest child of Timothy, married Dr. Samuel B. Barlow, and was the mother of the late S. L. M. Barlow of New York City, so well known as an able lawyer, a successful financier, and a liberal patron of art and literature. The youngest son of Timothy was the late Adna A. Wadsworth, who was born in Hartford, Connecticut, on the 4th of May, 1795. He married in early life Mary Williams Ramsdell, daughter of Robert W. and Prudence Ramsdell of Hartford. Adna A. Wadsworth came to the West when a very young man, and located in Maysville, where he lived the rest of the days allotted to him in such a manner as to win the respect of all who knew him. Without the advantage of an academic or collegiate education, he was yet a man of intelligence and information, as well as one of strong natural sense. He did not accumulate riches, nor even an independence, but he left to his only son the more valuable inheritance of manliness, self reliance, courage, integrity and an honorable character. He was long the marshal of Maysville, and made an efficient and fearless officer. His wife died in 1824, at the age of twenty-three years, leaving a son, William Henry Wadsworth. He married a second time, but both his children by the second wife died in infancy.

William Henry Wadsworth, the subject of this sketch, was born in Maysville, Kentucky, on July 4, 1821. Upon the early death of his mother, the little boy found a home in the family of David Smith, who lived a short distance from Maysville, on the trace beaten in the prehistoric ages by the buffalo in their roamings from the prairies of central Ohio to the salt springs of Kentucky. It was while he lived at this place, the playmate of the young daughters of Mr. Smith, who admired his grace and brightness, and whom he never ceased to hold in kindly regard, that he was seized with the ambition, and revealed to them his purpose, to own the spot overlooking the beautiful river, which he finally purchased, and where the end of life came to him. To his remaining parent he was an object at once of affection and pride; appreciating the value of the opportunities which had been denied to himself, the elder Wadsworth made exertions to have his son well educated. The boy was sent to the best schools to be found in the locality in which he lived. At first to a country school on Tuckahoe Ridge, where he had as his playfellows and classmates the sons and daughters of the Virginian farmers who owned and occupied the lands for many miles around—then, as now, an uncommonly fine rural population. This was followed by several years of study at the Maysville Seminary, of which the late Jacob Rand and W. W. Richeson were the principals, and where he had as one of his schoolmates Ulysses S. Grant, whose home was then in Brown County, Ohio. His brilliant talents, his aptness in mastering all subjects with which he grappled, even at that early age, made a profound impression upon Gen. Grant, who, years after, in his headquarters at Millikin's Bend, spoke of him to the writer in terms of unstinted praise and the frankest admiration. The collegiate education of Mr. Wadsworth was obtained at the Augusta College, then in the height of its usefulness, with an able faculty and a large attendance of pupils. While of a playful temperament and fun-loving disposition, which remained with him through life, through the years of his boyhood and youth his assiduity in the acquisition of knowledge was remarkable. With a wonderfully retentive memory, quick perception, and great facility of acquisition and expression, he did not rely on these qualities, but was at once most painstaking and industrious—a thorough student. It was while attending college at Augusta that a bough was blown from a tree under which he was passing, and, falling upon him, broke his left shoulder and arm, inflicting the injury which left him crippled for life. After leaving college, at which he graduated with distinguished honor, he was for a time a clerk in the dry goods store of James Clarke, then a Maysville merchant, and thus earned the means necessary to enable him to prepare for the profession in which he was destined to shine with a light as steady as it was brilliant. His legal studies were prosecuted in the office of Thomas Y. Payne and Henry Waller, and under their instruction. The last named will be remembered as an accomplished gentleman and one of the ablest members of the Maysville bar of his time. Upon his admission to the bar, Mr. Wadsworth did not have to pass through the ordeal to which the young and untried lawyer is usually subjected—that of waiting through weary months, perhaps for years, for his first "case." Loved by his associates and by those of his own age, his industry, thoroughness and manliness had also attracted the attention and won the respect of the business community and of the farmers of a prosperous and wealthy county. Business came to him unsought, without resort to chicanery or doubtful methods, and without accepting cases which the higher class of lawyers prefer to avoid. Almost at a bound he gained the front rank in his profession in all northern Kentucky, and held it, if not without a peer, certainly with no superior, for nearly or quite half a century—no mean tribute to his worth when one calls over the list of able and brilliant men who were his associates or antagonists in many a stoutly contested battle in the courts.

In 1853 the Whigs of Lewis and Mason Counties tendered Mr. Wadsworth an unsought nomination as their candidate for the state senate, which he accepted, not without reluctance, and made his debut into the political arena in an able and thorough canvass of the Senatorial District. Such was his personal popularity, and so unmixed the esteem in which he was held by members of both parties, that the field was left free to him without opposition, and not only did he draw out the full strength of the Whigs, but the votes of a large number of Democrats also were recorded in his favor. At this time Mr. Wadsworth was a little more than thirty years of age. Those who were so fortunate as to hear him could not but remark that, if he had ever had any of the affectations of the "boy orator" or of the "young man eloquent" about him, he had certainly outgrown them. His speeches were earnest and animated, yet calm and dispassionate appeals to the reason and judgment of his auditors; clear cut, masterly arguments upon issues which strictly concerned them; free from all theatrical gesticulation and stage play, yet delivered with fervor and fire; without florid or exaggerated expression, and yet with a sustained beauty and purity of diction and sentiment running all through them from the beginning to the close which was unsurpassed. The term for which he was elected was for four years, extending over the sessions of 1853-4 and 1855-6. During these sessions he addressed the senate on a number of important questions, not only drawing crowded and enthusiastic audiences from the interested public, but never failing to carry his point and eliciting the most complimentary opinions from his associates.

Though he agreed with the leading principles of the American party, and actively co-operated with it in opposing the candidates and measures of the Democrats, Mr. Wadsworth never united with that organization. In common with many members of the bar in 1856, he favored the candidacy of E. C. Phister, who had been his classmate and townsman, and who, up to that time, had been a zealous Whig, for the circuit judgeship. But developments during the canvass forced upon many of the Whigs the conviction that the motives which had induced them to support Mr. Phister would be defeated by his election, and they insisted that Mr. Wadsworth should become a candidate in opposition. An election to the position would have been no advancement to Mr. Wadsworth, who was then in the enjoyment of a lucrative practice and in the full tide of a prosperous career. But he was not the man to hesitate when duty called or friends demanded personal sacrifices. He threw himself into the canvass with all his accustomed energy. Many Whigs were already committed to Phister, believing him to be one of them; Democrats, in the full persuasion that in the future he would co-operate with them, gave him their full strength; the combination was successful by a meagre majority. The announcement of his adhesion to the Democrats, which quickly followed the election of Judge Phister, fully vindicated the course of Mr. Wadsworth. During those years Mr. Wadsworth had been unremitting in the successful practice of his profession. In northern Kentucky he had no equal upon the hustings. His career as a legislator had been one of marked ability. In the canvass of 1860 the momentous issues involved stirred men's souls. Parties felt that it was a struggle for life, and they put forward their ablest men. It was at such a time that Mr. Wadsworth was chosen to form and lead the Union sentiment of the state as the candidate of the Bell-Everett party for elector from the state at large. The canvass he made in every district in Kentucky was conceded by all to have been one of exceptional power and brilliancy, arousing the Union men to the utmost enthusiasm and challenging the admiration of their most resolute opponents. John C. Breckinridge was defeated in Kentucky; the sentiment which kept Kentucky fast to her moorings within the Union and sent thousands of her sons into the Union army was crystallized during that canvass. It was felt and admitted that the result was in large measure due to the unanswerable arguments addressed to the good sense and judgment of the people by Mr. Wadsworth and the eloquent appeals by which he kindled and fanned into a flame their slumbering patriotism. The cause he had at heart triumphed through his efforts; but it was almost at the sacrifice of his own life; his physical endurance was unequal to the tax made upon it by his mental power; he retired from the canvass to be prostrated for weary months upon a bed of pain. Before he could leave his room one state after another had passed ordinances of secession, but Kentucky stood firm.

In May, 1861, the Union men of the Maysville district, assembled in convention at Grayson, without a dissenting voice, and without an intimation from him that he desired it, tendered him their nomination for Congress. His opponent in the race which ensued was John S. Williams, who had the prestige of a military career in the war with Mexico, had been a Whig member of the legislature, and to whom must be conceded power and skill in exciting passion and stimulating prejudice. This is not the place for a contrast of two men so utterly unlike. Col. Williams, after a few meetings with Mr. Wadsworth before immense audiences, with their passions at white heat, found that his interests required him to refuse further joint discussions. The majority in the district for Mr. Wadsworth was more than eight thousand; in his own county it was over fifteen hundred in a vote of twenty-five hundred; in Col. Williams' county the Union majority was large. The seed sown by Mr. Wadsworth the previous fall bore good and abundant fruit in the spring harvest. Mr. Wadsworth was re-elected in 1863 as a conservative Union man. He went to Washington desiring to give the administration a cordial support in every measure for the restoration of the Union and the maintenance of the constitution, and which tended to those ends. While to the end of the struggle, and in its every phase, he yielded to no man in devotion to the Union cause, he found himself unable to concur with the distinctive and announced policy of the President and of the majority in Congress on many measures which his judgment condemned as violations of good faith to the Union people in the Southern states, as calculated to prolong the war, to increase the bitterness of the strife, and to defeat the end in view as expressed in the Crittenden resolution. His dissent was frankly expressed and his opposition was openly made, his speeches while in Congress voicing the sentiments of the sincerest friends of the Union in the country and of thousands of the bravest soldiers who fought and died under its flag. While the war progressed he was in the field and under fire on a number of occasions under General Nelson, General Green Clay Smith, General Lew Wallace and others. His patriotism and devotion were tested and proved by the severest ordeals through which a man can pass.

The war over, Mr. Wadsworth, declining a re-election to Congress, returned to the practice of his profession. In 1868 he made a brilliant canvass of several of the Northern states in support of General Grant, and thereafter continued to act with the Republicans. He was offered and declined the mission to Austria. The commission was constituted to adjust the claims between this country and Mexico, and questions involving many millions were referred to that commission for adjudication. In cases in which the doors were open for so much fraud and perjury, General Grant was impressed with the fact that the honor of his administration not less than that of the United States, demanded that this government should be represented upon the commission by men of the very highest legal ability and of proved incorruptibility; by men whose personal characters would place their decisions above suspicion. His choice rested upon Mr. Wadsworth, to whose patriotism he made an earnest appeal that he would accept a place on the commission.

To this service and in the discharge of this great trust, Mr. Wadsworth devoted a number of the best years of his life, separated from home and family, performing arduous labor which sapped his strength, and at a salary far below the usual earnings of his practice. It was not a reward that was given to, but a sacrifice that was demanded of him. In very few instances were any of the questions arising in the adjudication of these claims referred to the umpire, Sir Edward Thornton, and in those instances they were invariably decided as Mr. Wadsworth had previously ruled.

In 1884 Mr. Wadsworth was a third time elected to Congress from the Maysville district, then largely Democratic, receiving the support of more than a thousand prominent Democrats of the district, some of whom had been Confederate soldiers, who desired in this public manner to express their appreciation of his worth, their confidence in his integrity, and their attachment to his person.

Mr. Wadsworth was of a delicate physical organization; it was as if his mental vigor and fire preyed upon his body. He was slender almost to the point of emaciation. His voice was clear, not strong; his articulation distinct, and pronunciation devoid of affectation. His manner was earnest, at times impetuous, almost to the point of vehemence. His diction was never florid, but was as simple as it was scholarly, chaste and elegant. His speech was never burdened with, nor his meaning obscured by, classical and poetical quotations, which, when used, were employed solely as the vehicles of demonstration. He never indulged in mere oratorical pyrotechnics; when his utterances were ornamented with metaphor, it served to give force and power to his argument. When roused by the magnitude of the issue, he could rise to a high flight of eloquence, but he was remarkable for the elegance of diction and the elevation of sentiment which was sustained throughout and which distinguished all his speeches. In this he more nearly resembled Mr. Crittenden than any other of our public men; but he was himself, and no imitator of another. The highest faculty of Mr. Wadsworth was his power of close, clear, incisive, vigorous, unanswerable reasoning. He was a good classical scholar and had made himself a proficient in several modern languages. A lover of polite literature, and a diligent reader of the best authors, his artistic taste was pleased and his lively fancy stimulated by the better class of poetry, of which he was a critical reader and excellent judge. Delighting in flowers, as he did in all things beautiful and lovely, he was an accomplished botanist. There are many who can testify that he was the embodiment of a noble and princely generosity, and there never was a truer nor a stancher friend. It need scarcely be added that he was utterly fearless.

Mr. Wadsworth was married to Miss Martha Morehead Wood, daughter of Charles Wood of Lewis County, and a member of a numerous and prominent family in northern Kentucky. They were the parents of seven children, of whom Adna A., William H., Charles, John G., S. B. Wadsworth and Mrs. Bessie Clarke are living. Mrs. Wadsworth died December 21, 1891. Her husband followed her on April 2, 1893. He was at the time general attorney for the Chesapeake & Ohio Railway Company in Kentucky, in which position he was succeeded by his son, law partner and namesake.

JAMES WILLIAM FERGUSON, late president of the Deposit Bank of Paris, was one of the most successful business men of Bourbon County. He was born in Winchester, Clark County, August 25, 1830; and is a son of Abram L. and Mary (Matson) Ferguson. His father was born in Fayette County, and his mother in Bourbon County. Abraham Ferguson (grandfather) was a native of Spottsylvania County, Virginia, who emigrated to Kentucky and became one of the pioneers of Fayette County, making his settlement in the eastern part of the county, near Childsburgh. The old Ferguson homestead, containing five hundred and thirty acres of land, is now owned by his grandson, William H. Ferguson. Abraham Ferguson was a very successful business man and became quite wealthy. He was one of the largest slave owners of his day. His father was a native of Scotland, and belonged to a prominent and influential family.

Abram L. Ferguson (father) was born in 1803. For many years he was engaged in mercantile pursuits in Winchester; and upon the death of his father in 1840, from inheritance and by purchase of the interests of other heirs, the old homestead came into his possession. He soon removed there, where he lived until his death in 1854. It then became the property of James W. and since of William H. Ferguson. Abram L. Ferguson married Mary Matson, and they had seven children, of whom two are now living: Robert M., a banker at Lexington and a wealthy real estate owner, and Mrs. Lucy Campbell, who resides in Berlin, Germany, for the purpose of educating her daughters in music. One of her daughters has the reputation of being one of the finest vocalists in Germany.

Noah Ferguson, deceased, a brother of James William Ferguson, resided for many years in Bourbon and Fayette Counties, and was a prominent farmer and horse breeder.

Thomas Matson (grandfather) was a Virginian, who joined one of the early tides of emigration to Kentucky and located on a farm about six miles southeast of Paris, near Bethlehem Church. He was prosperous as a farmer and a large slave owner. The Matsons are of distinguished English ancestry. Colonel Robert Matson of Missouri, an uncle of James W. Ferguson, was prominent in the late Civil war.

James W. Ferguson remained in Winchester until he was ten years of age, when, with his parents, he removed to the old homestead in Fayette County, in 1840. He received a good English education in the schools of his neighborhood, and continued to reside at home until 1856, when he wedded Martha Hume, a daughter of Captain William P. Hume of Bourbon County. He immediately removed to the latter county, purchasing a farm of two hundred and fifty-seven acres, five miles west of Paris, on the Hume and Bedford turnpike.

Captain Hume (father-in-law), who died in 1875, was one of the leading citizens of his county.

Eight children were born to Mr. and Mrs. Ferguson: William, deceased; Abram Lunsford, a farmer in Scott County; Maggie, wife of Thomas Waller of Cincinnati; Robert H., a farmer of the county; Lucy, wife of J. M. Hall of Bourbon County; Volney W., James W., Jr., also farmers, and Matilda, wife of James Thompson, farmer. Mr. Ferguson was most liberal with his children, giving each of them from four hundred to five hundred acres of bluegrass land, among the finest farms of the bluegrass region. He owned five thousand acres of land before it was divided among his children.

In 1889 he removed from the farm to Paris, having been elected president of the Deposit Bank of Paris in 1887. He was a director and one of the largest stockholders in the bank for thirty years, and for several years held the office of vice president. Bourbon County has one of the best agricultural associations in the state, and for six or eight years Mr. Ferguson was its president, always taking an active interest in the success of the Bourbon County exhibits at its fairs. This association has been in existence for over fifty-six years and is next to the Fayette County Association in importance, and for many years its county fair was the best in the state.

Mr. Ferguson was a deacon in the Christian Church. He had one of the finest homes in Paris. In the latter years of his life he gave his time in a business way to the management of the Deposit Bank, which is the oldest, with the exception of the Northern Bank, in the county, its capital being one hundred thousand dollars ($100,000), and its average deposits one hundred and eighty thousand dollars ($180,000).

FRANK P. KENYON, M. D., a leading physician of Middlesborough, was born in Plymouth, Michigan, March 1, 1853.

His father, Orrin Kenyon, was born in Wayne County, New York, and removed to Plymouth, Michigan, in 1828, when that section was little less than a wilderness; improved a farm and has been a resident and farmer there all his life, and is now approaching his ninetieth year. His father, Elisha Kenyon, was a native of Wayne County, New York; removed with his family to Michigan in 1828 and there died at the age of sixty-five.

Roxanna Fairman Kenyon, Dr. F. P. Kenyon's mother, was also a native of Wayne County, New York, and accompanied her father to the then far West, to which he had preceded her and prepared the way, returning for her. She there met her husband, and they were married, July, 1835, and celebrated their sixtieth wedding anniversary in 1895. She is now in her seventy-ninth year and in good health. Her father was a native of Massachusetts, who went to Plymouth, Michigan, and completed the ninety years of a very useful, but uneventful life.

Dr. Kenyon received an academic education in Ypsilanti, Michigan, and read medicine with Dr. T. A. McGraw, one of the most eminent surgeons of Detroit. He then attended the Detroit Medical College, from which he graduated in 1876. He supplemented his very thorough course in medicine by practice and study in the hospitals of Vienna and Berlin, and returning, located in Montague, Michigan, where he practiced successfully for eight years. His health failing there, he went to Fargo, North Dakota, and practiced for three years; but his health did not improve materially, and he was compelled to seek a milder climate, which he found in Knoxville, Tennessee, in the fall of 1888. He had only fairly established himself in that place when, in 1889, he was induced to seek a home in the Eldorado of Kentucky, and, with other Knoxville people, came to Middlesborough in the fall of 1889, when the boom was on, and finding a healthful climate and lucrative practice, he soon became a permanent and prominent citizen.

Thoroughly equipped for the duties of his profession by study and long experience, he was at once recognized as a skillful surgeon and excellent physician, and has enjoyed as large a practice as one could expect in a locality so conducive to health. He is one of the most scholarly and cultured gentlemen in the city, a man of influence in the community, and one of the most thoroughly accomplished physicians and surgeons in that section of the state.

He is a member of the American Medical Association, of the Kentucky Medical Society, and was the first president of the Middlesborough Medical Society. He is also a member of the Masonic order, Knights of Pythias and the Maccabees.

Dr. Kenyon was married in 1877 to Gertrude Shattuck, daughter of Nelson S. Shattuck of Reading, Michigan.

HUGH B. PHILLIPS, one of the most substantial business men of Owensboro, was born in Meade County, Kentucky, March 8, 1833.

He began business life as a commission and dry goods, grocer and produce merchant in Brandenburg in 1857 with Captain J. M. Phillips, remaining there until 1864, when he removed to Lebanon and engaged in general merchandising and commission business, in which his brother, James G. Phillips, joined him, forming the firm of Phillips & Bros.; was also a member of the firms of H. B. Phillips & Company, and J. G. Phillips & Company, merchants, in Columbia, Adair County; also of the firm of Hoskin, Bryant & Company, in Campbellsville, Taylor County; was interested in merchandising in Rockcastle with his brother (1881); was interested in mining at Livingston, Rockcastle County, at the same time; is a member of the firm of Phillip & Matthews at Owensboro, Kentucky, which is engaged in exporting tobacco to European markets, and is now a member of the firm of Phillips Brothers & McAtee, the largest wholesale and retail merchandising establishment of that city.

Mr. Phillips is a man of extraordinary executive ability, as may be inferred from the fact that he has made a success of every undertaking. Few men have larger or more diversified interests, and yet he has conducted them all, with the aid of his competent associates, in a manner that has proved him one of the finest business men in the state. He has traveled extensively in the United States and in Europe, Cuba and Canada, and although denied even an ordinary education in his younger days, he has gained by reading and observation a fund of information and a knowledge of affairs which few men possess.

Mr. Phillips was married (first) in 1862 to Lizzie Seymour, daughter of Austin Seymour; and she was the mother of six children: Annie, wife of John McChord; Rosa L., wife of W. H. Johnson; Julia, wife of John Polk; Minnie, married (first) Ray Edmunds, (second) Rev. Fred Hale; Hugh B., died October, 1890; Carrie, wife of O. W. Thomas of Lebanon, Kentucky; and Seymour.

Mr. Phillips was married (second) February 4, 1896, to Elizabeth H. Solomon of St. Louis, Missouri.

Thomas Phillips (father) was born in Washington County, Kentucky, in 1793, and died in Meade City, in 1847. He spent most of his life in farming; married Julia Maxwell, who was born near Lebanon, and died in Meade County in 1840. They were members of the Baptist Church and were noted for their religious convictions and good citizenship. They had nine children: Appoline, who married John Hall; Elizabeth, married Jabez Durham; Mary, married William Hendricks; Sarah, married J. S. Cox; Thomas; Captain Joseph M., now of Chicago; James G.; William D. and Hugh B. Phillips, the principal subject of this sketch.

Thomas Phillips (grandfather), a native of Virginia, of Scotch-Irish parentage, came to Washington County, Kentucky, and cleared a farm upon which he spent the remainder of his days. He was one of the pioneers of the state; settled on Hardin's Creek, Washington County, and the residence which he built over one hundred years ago is now in a good state of preservation, being first built of logs and since weatherboarded.

JOHN W. LEWIS, Member of Congress and distinguished lawyer of Springfield, son of William and Ann (Carlile) Lewis, was born in Green County, Kentucky, October 14, 1841. He graduated from Center College, Danville, Kentucky, in 1862, and in that same year began to study law at Greensburg, and was admitted to the bar in 1863. He remained in Greensburg until 1869, and then removed to Springfield, Kentucky, and formed a partnership with Hon. R. J. Browne. In 1867 he was the candidate of the third party in Green and Taylor Counties for representative in the state legislature, and in a strong Democratic district was defeated by only eighteen votes. The third party was composed of Union men in Kentucky who refused to join the Democratic ranks. In 1874 he was Republican candidate for commonwealth attorney of his district, and in 1876 was Republican candidate for Congress in the Fourth District, and again defeated. His presidential vote was cast for General McClellan in 1864, and in 1894 Mr. Lewis was elected to the Fifty-fourth Congress as a Republican.

Mr. Lewis is an able lawyer, indefatigable in the practice of his profession, and punctilious to the extreme in the honorable discharge of its responsibilities. He is a painstaking attorney, keenly alive to the interests of his clients, and the entire community has confidence in the efficiency of his legal methods. Mr. Lewis is a warm hearted man, devoted to his family and true to his friends. He is a man of fine conversational powers and of many prepossessing social qualities. Although an enthusiastic and uncompromising partisan, there is a vein of sentiment in his nature that enables him to recognize the better part of every man's nature, irrespective of politics and environment. No good thing in literature, either humorous or pathetic; no brilliant leadership in the field or in the House of Representatives, whether found in political comrade or in foe, is lost to Mr. Lewis through prejudice or narrow partisan conception. The following clipping from a leading paper in Kentucky will show the estimation in which he is held in his native state:

"There are but few Republicans in Kentucky whose names produce as pleasurable a sensation as that of John W. Lewis. Fighting the battles of the party, when it was apparently a hopeless minority, and when he was but a youth, he has grown in the esteem and affection of his countrymen, until the new party is a great party and John W. Lewis one of its trusted leaders. At all times, his word has been his bond, and it has never been forfeited. Political allies as well as opponents, alike, accord to him the courage of his convictions and that attribute of true manhood which could never, under any circumstances, do an unworthy act.

"His friends here who have known him through many years, would take his word, concerning any measure, however important, or regardless of what it might portend. If personal and moral courage added to intellectual ability of high order, and the qualities of an orator at once persuasive and convincing, be passports to a great place, then John W. Lewis possesses the qualifications to represent Kentucky in the United States Senate."

Mr. Lewis was married June 20, 1877, to Elizabeth Philips, daughter of James G. Philips, of Lebanon, and they have one child, a daughter. Wm. Lewis (father) was a native of Pittsylvania County, Virginia, and followed mercantile pursuits. He was a man of strong personality, with mental qualities of a high order and fine business ability. No man in the private walks of life ever stood deservedly higher.

He married Ann Carlile, daughter of Wm. Carlile of Green County. She is a most exemplary woman, kind, sympathetic, intelligent and a devoted Christian.

Her father, Wm. Carlile, was a farmer of Green County, energetic and prosperous, and a ruling elder in the Presbyterian Church (North), a very influential man in his county and church connection.

EDWARD BILTZ, Mayor of Newport, and a blacksmith and machinist doing business in Cincinnati, Ohio, was born in the latter city, June 10, 1848. His parents removed to Newport in the same year, and he has been a life-time resident of the city of which he is now the chief executive; was educated in the public schools; learned blacksmithing with his father, whose shop was in Cincinnati; when twenty-one years of age he bought his father's interest, and has continued the business of blacksmithing and manufacturing in that place with profitable results and increasing trade until the present time, employing a large force of skillful mechanics and doing a high class of work.

Mr. Biltz has been identified with the affairs of Newport for many years, having served as alderman prior to his election as mayor, and was a trustee of the waterworks for several years. He is a gentleman of excellent business qualifications and his standing in the community may be inferred from the honors that have been thrust upon him.

He was married in 1870 to Miss Sarah Miller, daughter of Peter Miller of Maysville, Kentucky, and they have five sons and one daughter living: Edward F., Charles H., George W., Lula May, Frederick B. and Howard M. Amy E. died in 1894 in her eighteenth year.

Mr. Biltz and his family are members of the Methodist Church South and he is a prominent Knight of Pythias and a member of the Royal Arcanum.

Charles Biltz (father), a native of Germany, came to the United States when he was six years' of age. His parents settled in Pennsylvania, and he remained with them until he was twenty years of age, when he went to Cincinnati and engaged in blacksmithing; removed to Newport in 1848, and is now retired from business in the seventy-second year of his age; a member of the Methodist Church and an honored and respected citizen.

Margaret Fable Biltz (mother) was a native of Germany and came to Cincinnati when a child; was educated there; married Mr. Charles Biltz in 1844, and died March, 1892. She was a member of the Methodist Episcopal Church and a woman of lovely Christian character.

GEORGE S. FULTON of Bardstown, able lawyer, distinguished citizen and state senator, son of Samuel S. Fulton and Margaret Anderson, is a native of Spencer County.

His father was born in Washington County, Pennsylvania, March 8, 1814, and was reared and educated in his native county, taking his collegiate course in Washington College. In his earlier years he was a teacher and gained considerable distinction as an educator. Coming to Kentucky in 1838, he taught in Jefferson County for two years, following which he removed to Spencer County in 1840, remaining there until 1848, when he returned to Jefferson County, and two years later removed to Nelson County and located on a farm near Bloomfield, where he made his home, and followed farming until his death, which occurred February 12, 1880.

Senator Fulton (grandfather) was a native of Washington County, Pennsylvania, and was a captain in the Revolutionary war.

Margaret Anderson Fulton (mother) was born in Lincoln County, Kentucky, October 16, 1816, and died in Nelson County, June 17, 1877. Her father, John Anderson, was one of the pioneers of Nelson County, and for a number of years a merchant in Bloomfield, where he died about 1826.

The children of Samuel S. and Margaret Anderson Fulton were Mary, wife of Bodine McClasky, who died May 2, 1896; George S., the subject of this sketch; Eugene, deceased; John A., formerly judge of the Nelson County Court, now chief deputy collector of internal revenue at Louisville; Samuel and W. A. Fulton of Florida.

George S. Fulton was born in Taylorsville, Spencer County, Kentucky, April 27, 1847. While he was quite young his father removed to his farm near Bloomfield and there the son "got his raisin'" and his primary education, incidentally gaining a practical knowledge of the science of farming. At the age of seventeen he entered Forest Home Academy in Jefferson County, in which school he finished his course in one year, for in this and in all of his school duties, he received valuable assistance from his father, who instructed him in the classics and higher mathematics; and in these he had anticipated the work in the academy, which enabled him to complete the course in much less time than is usually required by less favored pupils.

After quitting school he was engaged in teaching in Nelson County, and later had charge of the Covington Institute at Springfield for one year. He then (1868) began reading law, and in 1869 entered the law department of the University of Louisville, from which he graduated in 1872. He opened his office in Bardstown, May 9, 1873, and began a successful career, practicing in the courts of Nelson and adjacent counties, and to-day occupies a place of enviable prominence among the votaries of the law.

For twenty-three years or more he has labored with perseverance and untiring devotion, ever striving to uphold the dignity of his profession; enjoying a goodly share of the legal business of his section, walking uprightly, turning aside for no honors or emoluments other than the legitimate fruit of honest toil in the line of his profession. Of course, politics have interested him. Almost every good lawyer finds himself drawn into politics from circumstances or preference, if not from personal motives. But he has never been found scrambling for office. He may have found it necessary to run sometimes in order to keep out of office, and when he failed in 1892 and was elected to the state senate, it was no fault of his. The Fourteenth is one of the most important senatorial districts, and there was need of a good man, and he was captured by his friends, defeated for once in his life in his purpose to keep out of office, and having been chosen he obeyed the call.

He served on the Judiciary Committee and others in which a high order of legal ability was required, and throughout the deliberations of the two sessions in which he served his record is that of a white tablet neatly inscribed with deeds of honor. He took part in none of the questionable methods which characterized the session of 1896, save that he stood unalterably and unfalteringly by the nominee of his party, but counselled forbearance and honest effort for the promotion of the interests of the commonwealth.

Mr. Fulton was married October 8, 1874, to Kate R. Adams, daughter of Stephen G. Adams and Elizabeth Ray of Daviess County, and they have two sons, Eugene A. and Stephen G. Fulton. Mr. Fulton and his family are members of the Presbyterian Church, in which he has been a communicant since 1867.

JUDGE WILLIAM E. RUSSELL, an eminent lawyer of Lebanon, son of Andrew Russell and Elizabeth Echols, was born in Columbia, Kentucky, October 6, 1830, and was educated chiefly under the instruction of David Page, an eastern man who was employed as tutor in the Caldwell family.

Judge Russell also attended Hancock Academy, three miles from Columbia, conducted by W. H. Saunders, and when seventeen years of age, enlisted in the Mexican War, and was made Orderly Sergeant of the company in General John S. William's Regiment, in the same brigade with J. C. Breckinridge, and in General Scott's command. Upon the death of his Captain he was made Lieutenant and was for several months in command of the company. Peace being declared he returned to Columbia, June, 1848, and studied law under Isaac Caldwell; was admitted to the bar at the age of nineteen and immediately began to practice his profession. His first partnership was with Captain Edgar B. Gaither, who, with Theodore O'Hara, composed the famous poem, "The Muffled Drum's Sad Roll Has Beat," etc., and continued until Mr. Gaither died, and then, with Colonel Nathan Gaither until he removed to Harrodsburg. The Gaithers were cousins of the mother of Henry Watterson.

He was one of the Democrats, faithful and true, who opposed the Know-Nothing movement in 1854-5 and distinguished himself as one of the ablest speakers and most active men in opposition to that craze which swept the state like a cyclone and as quickly came to naught. In 1857 Mr. Russell was elected to represent his county in the Legislature and was one of the really representative men in that body. He continued in the practice of law in Columbia until 1867, when he removed to Lebanon, which has been his home and the central point of his professional career since that time.

In 1886 he was elected Circuit Judge by the people of the district composed of the counties of Mercer, Nelson, Washington, La Rue, Taylor and Marion. He made the race for Judge of the Appellate Court against Judge Joseph Lewis, and although he carried the city of Louisville by three thousand majority, was defeated. His standing on the bench is second to none and his fearless and determined advocacy of the principles he conceives to be for the good of the state make him a power in politics.

Judge Russell is one of the most prominent laymen in the Catholic Church, and, as his record in connection with that denomination abundantly proves, has been an earnest and enthusiastic member, giving his time and energies unstintedly to the work of the church. He has held the high and responsible offices successively of Supreme

Vice-President and Supreme President of the Catholic Knights of America, being elected to the latter office in 1883, and re-elected in 1885, and was sent as a delegate to New York in the interest of the order, showing the confidence reposed in his fidelity and executive ability. He declined a third term.

He was married November 14, 1854, to Susan Agnes Elder of Lebanon, daughter of Colonel Sylvester Elder and Elizabeth Dickens, a relative of Charles Dickens. Mrs. Russell was educated at Calvary Convent in Marion County and is a devout member of the Catholic Church. They have seven children: Sylvester; Fannie, wife of Colonel J. B. Watham of Lebanon; Henry, Emma, William Edwin, Jr., Lev. and Echols Russell.

Lev. Russell (son) was born in Lebanon, Kentucky, May 23, 1874. He attended St. Mary's College and read law with his distinguished father and his brother, Sylvester, and was licensed to practice in 1893. By hard work and close application to the duties of his profession he has obtained a splendid and varied knowledge of law and his friends predict for him a brilliant future. In manners he is as gentle and refined as a woman and his private character is an example of morality. His many good qualities have won for him golden opinions from all who know him.

Sylvester Russell, another son of Judge Russell, graduated from St. Mary's College in 1876 and began the practice of law in 1877. He represented Marion County in the Legislature of 1883-4; has been prominent in all the noted criminal cases in Marion County and adjoining counties since he entered upon the practice of law and has been connected with important litigation outside of the state. He obtained from a jury a verdict which was affirmed by a higher court for the largest damages ever obtained and affirmed in the state. Like most Kentuckians in the legal profession he is a ready debater and his wonderful reserve force based upon a genuinely profound knowledge of law, together with his indomitable spirit, elicit the admiration and confidence of the people. He was married July 17, 1878, to Lula Caldwell, who died. She was the mother of four children.

Andrew Russell (father of Judge W. E. Russell) was born of Scotch-Irish parentage in Lincoln County, Kentucky, in 1800, and was educated there. He owned a large farm in Adair County and employed the many negroes that belonged to his wife in cultivating the farm. He was married in 1823 to Elizabeth Echols of Virginia, who came when she was young to Adair County. She was a member of the Baptist Church and her husband belong to the Christian Church.

Andrew Russell came to Kentucky when the people lived in forts and, of course, endured all the hardships incident to pioneer life. Flora Russell, his cousin, and niece of General Logan Butler, the historian says, was tomahawked by the Indians.

In 1851 Andrew Russell went with his family to Dallas, Texas, and located there. At that time Dallas was very unhealthy and several of the children were taken ill and an elder brother and sister of Judge Russell died there in 1852 and are buried in Dallas.

The children of Andrew Russell and Elizabeth Echols were: Dr. Timolean, who died in Texas; Frances, deceased, who married Dr. Rice, and A. K. Russell and Bettie, first wife of Dr. John Clemens of Louisville, Kentucky, both of whom are dead, and Judge William E. Russell.

Three brothers came to Baltimore, Maryland, from Scotland; one went east and the other two went to Virginia, and one of these was Judge Russell's great-grandfather.

Colonel Sylvester Elder, father of Judge William E. Russell's wife, was the son of Joseph Elder of Baltimore, and his grandfather came from England with Lord Baltimore, and settled in Baltimore, Maryland. He was a cousin of Archbishop Elder of Cincinnati.

GUS W. RICHARDSON, farmer and politician of Guston, Meade County, and Deputy Collector of Internal Revenue, Fifth District of Kentucky, was born in Meade County, Kentucky, near Ekron, April 25, 1849. He was born and raised on a farm and has always been, and is, a farmer, and yet there have not been many months since he was nineteen years of age in which he has not performed official duty in one capacity or another. He was Deputy Sheriff for two years; was County Surveyor for four years; Magistrate four years, being elected in 1882; was elected to the Legislature in 1885; re-elected in 1887 and again in 1889, serving three terms in succession, an honor which had never been conferred on any former member, and he was only prevented from serving a fourth and perhaps other terms, by the sentiment in favor of rotation in office, and even this unwritten law was sustained by a meager majority of about 100 votes.

The most exciting race of his life was in the primaries of the Democratic party for the nomination for the State Senate in 1892, with Captain A. J. Gross, then Adjutant-General of Kentucky. It was the hottest contest Mr. Richardson ever had, and with the "machine" in favor of his opponent there were men who winked one eye when the vote was counted and the other man declared the nominee. In Meade County there were one thousand and eighty votes, and Mr. Richardson got all of them except one hundred and sixty-four, which is some evidence of the popularity of the man in his own county.

Mr. Richardson was appointed Deputy Collector of Internal Revenue in 1894, and placed in charge of the bonded accounts with distillers, one of the most important desks in the Collector's office at Louisville; and he is serving his country in that office at this writing, retaining his home and his farming interests in Meade County.

Mr. Richardson was married December 12, 1871, to Alice A. Thompson, daughter of J. H. Thompson and Elizabeth Wimp Thompson of Meade County. Their children are Julia T.; James Adrian, deceased; Orla Coburn; Gus Albert, and Anna Lucille.

Orla Coburn Richardson (father) was born March 13, 1807, in Whitehall, on Lake Champlain, New York, and came to Meade County, Kentucky, with his parents in 1809. He received only a limited education, but was a man of great natural ability and strength of character, and, like his son, was always a farmer and nearly always in office, as Magistrate, Sheriff and Representative in the legislature. He was a very popular man, and was particularly noted for his hospitality and charity. His house was always open to friend and stranger, and the ragged beggar was never turned away without some evidence of Mr. Richardson's kindness or generosity. He died June, 1882, having passed his seventy-sixth year.

He was twice married, first to Hannah Fulton of Meade County; and second, to the widow Roberts, nee Mary Shacklette, daughter of General Ben Shacklette. Mr. Richardson's children by his first marriage were David F., Mary, Orla D., Sarah, Hannah and Eliza; by his second marriage there were two children: Gus W., the subject of this sketch, and Julia, who was married November 5, 1868, to Benjamin S. Clarkson.

David M. Richardson (grandfather) was born in Vermont, September, 1765, and died in Meade County, September 15, 1832, in the sixty-seventh year of his age. He was a highly educated man; was a merchant in early life and, closing out business, he traded his small stock of goods for a tract of land in Meade County and removed to Kentucky in 1809.

Mary Shacklette (mother), who first married John Roberts, being left a widow with a farm and a large family, developed remarkable business ability and was a woman of more than ordinary accomplishments. As the wife of Orla Richardson and the mother of three sets of children, including stepchildren, she was loved and respected by all of them and she filled a large place in the social affairs of the neighborhood. She died in June, 1876.

General Ben Shacklette (grandfather) came to Meade County from Pennsylvania about 1800 and won his military title in one of the Indian wars. He was a successful farmer and was the first Sheriff of Meade County. He was born in Pennsylvania, but was of French origin.

ORVILLE MONROE WOOD, Mayor of Carrolton and the leading merchant in that city, son of William Wood and Mary S. Anderson, was born in Gallatin County, Kentucky, July 3, 1852.

His father, now a resident of Carroll County, is a native of Mercer County, Kentucky; removed to Gallatin County in 1845, and thence to Trimble County in 1859 and finally to his present home in Carroll County, in 1892. He has been actively engaged in farming nearly all his life; has been a member of the Baptist Church for over fifty years and has always enjoyed the respect and confidence of his neighbors.

David Wood (grandfather) a native of Virginia of English descent, spent most of the seventy-five years of his useful life in farming and was a resident of Carroll County for twenty years prior to his death. He was a devout member of the Baptist Church and was noted for his devotion to religious principles.

Mary S. Anderson Wood (mother), now residing with her husband in Carroll County, was born in Gallatin County in 1829. Her father, Richard Anderson, was a native of Virginia, who came to Kentucky when he was a young man and died in Carroll County in 1885, aged seventy-seven years. He was an intelligent farmer and like the Woods he and his house belonged to the Baptist Church. His son, Rev. James O. Anderson, who died a few years ago in Kansas City, was one of the most eminent divines in that denomination. The Andersons belonged to an old family of prominence of Virginia.

Orville M. Wood was reared and educated principally in Trimble County, remaining on his father's farm until 1879, when he engaged in mercantile business in Trimble County, continuing there, however, but one year when he removed to Prestonville, Carroll County, where he was engaged as a merchant until 1891, sold out and removed to Carrollton, and in 1891 formed a partnership with M. L. Downs under the firm name of Downs & Wood—in a general fire insurance agency. This firm was dissolved in November, 1891, when Mr. Wood purchased the store of W. L. Smith, who was the oldest merchant in the place, since which time he has given his attention to the business of this establishment, now the leading store of the kind in Carrollton.

In November, 1893, Mr. Wood was elected Mayor of the city for a term of four years and assumed the duties of that office in January, 1894. This election was a deserved compliment to Mr. Wood's ability and integrity as a business man rather than a political triumph, for he has not sought or cared for prominence in politics.

He is a prominent Mason and a Knight of Pythias, and has not forsaken the church of his father and mother and his grandfathers.

Mr. Wood was married February 3, 1873, to Esther J. Robinson, daughter of Samuel Robinson of Wetzel County, West Virginia, and has one son, named Gideon G. Wood.

HENRY L. MARTIN, President of the Citizens' Bank of Midway, was born in Woodford County, June 5, 1848, and is a son of Jesse and Margaret T. Martin.

He entered the Confederate army before he was fourteen years of age and was a daring scout in Morgan's command, and proved a brave soldier, who was entrusted with many important missions by the military authorities. His brilliant record as a soldier was the index to his successful business career and his political record is one of which to be proud.

He gained a national reputation as a representative of the Louisiana Bounty Bureau, securing the sugar bounties, and in that was instrumental in achieving one of the most pronounced legislative victories in the history of the country. The payment of the bounty meant the rehabilitation of the credit of the sugar producers, and enabled them to make another effort to recover from the results of former legislation. This bounty appropriation would have failed, notwithstanding the representatives in Congress who were friendly to the measure, if it had not been for the splendid supplemental work done by the Bounty Bureau, and the indefatigable individual efforts of such men as Henry L. Martin. A New Orleans paper in speaking of the work of the public-spirited citizens in this connection says:

"In according the praise in this connection it cannot be looked upon as invidious to say that Mr. Henry L. Martin is entitled to the highest praise for his splendid work in Washington. He made his first trip to that city in connection with the movement to secure the eight-tenths of a cent bounty appropriation, about December 15, 1894, and while he has returned to the city several times since he remained only a short time, and it

may be said that he has been on the ground watching the legislative battle ever since it began. And he has not been simply watching the contest, but has been taking a most active and potent part.

"To his efforts may be attributed directly the splendid work of Senator Blackburn, who so ably handled on the floor of the Senate the bounty amendment offered by the appropriations committee, and whose tact and parliamentary resources were such as to thwart the opposition of even such wily, able and experienced Senators as Gorman, Brice and Harris, and while Senator Blackburn was one of the champions in the fight for according equity and justice to the sugar producers, Mr. Martin was untiring in his labors with influential men in Congress, and his large acquaintance, pleasing address and forceful, concise and convincing manner of presenting the grounds upon which the appropriation for the payment of the bounty were based went a long way toward dispelling doubt and making converts."

Mr. Martin made his first political race in 1893 when he was elected to the Kentucky Senate by the Democrats of the Twenty-second District, embracing Woodford, Scott and Jessamine Counties. When the Legislature assembled he was appointed on some of the most important committees and was made Chairman of the Finance Committee—one of the most responsible in the Senate. His services in that body have shown a very high order of ability. Although the unfaltering personal friend of Senator Blackburn, he must not be set down as a free silver advocate.

Mr. Martin has a very extensive acquaintance in Kentucky and is well known in the South and throughout the country; and his reputation is that of a clear-headed business man of great mental activity, with a directness of purpose which insures success in his undertakings for himself and for his friends and the public. He is a gentleman of culture and literary tastes, and his home bears every evidence of elegance and refinement.

Mr. Martin was married (first) in 1871 to Katie Brooks of Scott County, who was the mother of four children, who survive. He was married (second) in 1886 to Lulie T. Stephenson, daughter of John T. Stephenson, of Maury County, Tennessee. She was educated in Columbia Institute, graduating in 1880 with the highest rank in her class.

Mr. Martin is the President of the Citizens' Bank at Midway, near which place he has a beautiful and attractive home and valuable farm, where he resides and where blooded horses are bred. He also owns a large stock farm near Columbia, Tennessee, and is engaged in the live stock business in New Orleans, being senior member of the firm of Martin, Thompson & Company. He is also largely interested in the David sugar plantation in St. James Parish, and has been very successful in all his commercial undertakings, as well as in his political aspirations and public services.

JAMES B. M'CREARY of Richmond, ex-governor of Kentucky and member of Congress since 1884, was born in Madison County, Kentucky, of pioneer ancestry. He graduated from Center College at the age of eighteen, studied law and graduated with the honors of a class of forty-seven in the Law College of the University of Tennessee in 1859, and began a lucrative law practice at Richmond; aided, in 1861, in recruiting the Eleventh Regiment, Kentucky Cavalry, for the Confederate army; was elected major, promoted to lieutenant-colonel, and served until the close of the war, serving with Morgan mainly, and with General Breckinridge latterly; was married June 12, 1867, to Kate Hughes of Fayette County; was delegate to the National Democratic Convention that nominated Seymour and Blair; elected to the legislature for three consecutive terms, 1869-71-73, and was speaker of the house during his second and third terms; was elected governor of the state in 1875 for a term of four years; and was elected to Congress in 1884, receiving a majority over his Republican opponent of 2,146 votes, and has been re-elected for each succeeding term. Gov. McCreary is remarkable for his wise and systematic methods of administration in both public and private affairs, and for the silent force of sagacious intelligence with which he has conducted the large and complex interests which have been under his charge for many years. Besides his law practice and much voluntary attention to current enterprise, he operates a large farm in Madison County and another in Alabama.

While speaker of the house, such was the justness and fairness of his decisions that not a single appeal was taken in four years. As governor his administration was orderly and successful, and yet without demonstration of effort. The most turbulent wars of factions in the mountains were suppressed when the local authorities were defied and powerless. Gov. McCreary adds to natural abilities of a very high order the advantages of a scientific and classical education. He is a lucid, forcible and attractive public speaker, of entertaining conversational powers and most winning and genial temper. Perhaps no man in Congress has more readily and diligently attended to the requests and wishes, not only of his district constituents, but of the entire state. Of handsome face and form and courteous bearing, his presence always attracts and pleases, while acquaintance improves the first impression. No public character of Kentucky has had a steadier outgrowth of reputation and advancement, and none has won more affectionate admiration or provoked fewer enemies. His future is promising, and should he remain in political life he is almost sure to follow the line of promotion open to him. (Smith's History of Kentucky.)

SPEED FAMILY, THE. It will be more convenient to present the members of this numerous family by giving the ancestry common to all and then a brief sketch of those who have been most prominent.

JOHN SPEED, English historian, geographer and antiquarian, was born at Farrington in the County of Cheshire, in the year 1552, in the time of Edward VI. This was sixty-eight years before the Mayflower brought the Pilgrims to Plymouth Rock. Walter Raleigh was born in the same year, and Shakespeare one year later.

His son, John Speed, was born in 1595; was a graduate of Oxford and an eminent physician, and was the author of a number of publications and a play which was acted in the theaters. He had two sons—John and Samuel; the latter was installed Canon of Christ Church, May 6, 1674, and was afterwards Vicar of Godalmin in Surrey County, where he died January 22, 1681. His brother John was born at Oxford, elected scholar at John's College in 1643, but was ejected for political reasons and afterwards restored. He took the degree of Doctor of Medicine in 1666 and practiced at Southampton as late as 1694. His son, James Speed, from whom all the Speeds in this country are descended, left Southampton, England, and settled in the eastern part of Virginia. He was born September 28, 1679, and came to America in 1695. He found his way to the County of Surrey on the south side of the James River, opposite the site of Williamsburg. He married Mary Pulley, September 6, 1711, and died March 15, 1719, aged thirty-nine years; she died June 3, 1733, aged forty. They had four sons: James, born June 16, 1712; John, born February 5, 1714; William T., born February 19, 1716, and Thomas Speed, born February 28, 1719. James and Thomas are lost sight of. John and William left records which show that they enjoyed such educational advantages as were common in those days, and are evidence that they had good training in their youth. Their parents had impressed upon their minds correct ideas and principles of virtue and morality and true ambition, which became an inheritance to them and their posterity.

John Speed, second son of James Speed and Mary Pulley, lived in Mecklenburg County, Virginia; married Mary Taylor, a widow whose maiden name was Mary Minstay, October 6, 1737. They lived together forty-five years; she died July 1, 1782; he died March 8, 1785. He was a man of large wealth and one of the most substantial citizens of Virginia; very prominent in the Episcopal Church, worshiped in a church built by him and known as "Speed's Church." Yet, in a letter to his son, Captain James Speed, who lived in Kentucky, he wrote of his approaching death; his health was impaired; "and, above all, I have a wounded spirit. I know I am going to leave this country, and where am I going? Not to Kentucky. God only knows; I do not. This is my grief."

John Speed and Mary (Minetry) Taylor had seven sons and four daughters: John, born April 3, 1738; James, born March 4, 1740; Henry, born March 28, 1742; Sarah, born February 14, 1743; Lewis, born January 25, 1745; Martha, born August 11, 1748; Joseph, born May 27, 1750; Lucy, born April 11, 1752; Mathias, born June 18, 1754; a son died in infancy and Mary died young.

Four of these brothers served in the Revolutionary War, and perhaps others: John, James, Lewis and Mathias certainly did. Lewis died of his wounds; James was shot through the body at the battle of Guilford C. H., North Carolina, March 15, 1781. He was never able to walk or stand erect afterwards, and in his old age he used a sled for going about. His son, Judge John Speed, writing in 1828, says: "I was born previous to the Revolution; my father was one of the patriots of that day who shed his blood for liberty and equal rights. In my youth I heard him and others of our fathers recount the oppression they resisted, the hardships, the privations they encountered and endured for their own, but more especially for our sake."

Captain James Speed, second son of John and Mary Taylor, married Mary Spencer December 10, 1767; and removed with his family to Kentucky in 1782, settling about four miles from Danville; and there lived, and died September 3, 1811.

His children were Thomas, born October 25, 1768; Mary, born June 8, 1770; John, born May 17, 1772; Elizabeth and James (twins), born February 7, 1774; Henry, born August 15, 1777; and Julia, who died in infancy.

Captain Speed was well educated; was a writer of some note and was one of the earlier judges of Kentucky. He owned slaves which he brought from Virginia, acquired large tracts of land and was involved in a number of land suits; he was a member of the Kentucky Conventions of May, 1785, and August, 1787; a member of the Political Club, and of the Society for the Promotion of Useful Knowledge, which were composed of the most enlightened men of the state. He was a candidate for delegate to the Constitutional Convention in 1792 and was defeated because he was an Emancipationist. His grandson, James Speed (Attorney-General United States), was beaten for the same office in 1849 for the same reason. From his letters to the Governor of Virginia and to members of his family it is seen that he was a man of great influence in public affairs and kindly affectionate to his family. An account of his children and their descendants says that Thomas was the ancestor of the Bardstown family; John was the ancestor of the Louisville family; Mary married William Smith of Madison County, and was the mother of Colonel John Speed Smith and grandmother of General Green Clay Smith, who died in 1895. Her daughter married Tom Fry and was the mother of General Speed S. Fry and his brothers and sisters. Elizabeth married Dr. Adam Rankin, whose descendants are in Henderson. James and Henry have no descendants living.

Major Thomas Speed, first son of Captain James Speed and Mary Spencer, was a resident of Kentucky from 1782 until his death in 1842. He was a representative in Congress and in the Legislature, and a Major of volunteers in the War of 1812. A sketch of his life would present a history of Kentucky through a most interesting period. He early displayed an aptness for learning and when still a youth was associated with men of mature years who were leaders in public affairs in the society at Danville called the Political Club, and must have possessed unusual and even extraordinary qualifications to be invited to join them at so early an age. He was made secretary of the club, and the records of that society were preserved through his care. His grandson, Thomas Speed, clerk of the United States Court of Louisville, has written a valuable book for the Filson Club, giving a full history of the Political Club. Major Speed was also secretary of the Kentucky Society for the Promotion of Useful Knowledge, an account of which is given in Collins' History. He was connected with the office of Colonel Christopher Greenup, clerk of the General Court, which he left in 1790 and engaged with his brother John in merchandising. They had stores in Danville and Bardstown. He was first married at Bardstown, December 11, 1796, to Susan Clayton Slaughter; and after her death he married Mary McElroy Allen, widow of Robert Allen. He was appointed clerk of the Bullitt and Nelson Circuit Courts. In 1817 he was elected to Congress and he made the trip on horseback by a route of eight hundred miles; was an omnivorous reader and an excellent writer, and frequently contributed to the National Intelligencer, published at Washington; was a friend and correspondent of Henry Clay. In 1821, 1822 and 1840 he was in the Kentucky Legislature. He was a refined, dignified and cultivated man, graceful and polished in manners, charming in conversation and pure and spotless in character. He died near Bardstown, February 20, 1842, and his wife died one year later.

Thomas Spencer Speed, oldest son of Major Thomas Speed, was born near Bardstown, August 30, 1814. In March, 1861, he removed to Daviess County; and ten years later returned to his native place and remained there until his death, March 16, 1892. He received an academic education at St. Joseph's College; sickness prevented his preparation for the ministry. He lived a retired life. He was an Emancipationist, and was glad when his own and other slaves were set free. His home was always open to his friends; was an elder in the Presbyterian Church, and his chief characteristic was his sincerity and devoted adherence to what he believed was right. A total abstainer, he would not use whisky even for medicine. He was fond of reading and was a great student of the Bible. He gave each of his children a good education, and was able to help them in their studies. He was married twice. First to Sarah Whitney Sparhawk, who was a native of New Hampshire, and a teacher in the Female Academy at Bardstown, of which Rev. Nathan L. Rice was principal. She died in 1842. The children of this marriage were: John James, died in childhood; William O., born September 8, 1839; and Thomas, born November 26, 1841. He was again married in 1846 to Margaret Hawkins at Crawfordsville, Indiana. There were five children of this second marriage: Spencer Hawkins, Austin Peay, Horace, Richard Canby and Louisa J. Speed.

THOMAS SPEED, son of Thomas S. Speed Bardstown, was born November 26, 1841. He was educated in Center and Hanover Colleges; joined the Union army in 1862 as a private; was made First Lieutenant and then Adjutant of the Twelfth Regiment, Kentucky Volunteer Infantry, and also served on brigade staff. The principal engagements he was in were the siege of Knoxville, Bean's Station, the various battles of the Atlanta Campaign, Columbia, Franklin, Nashville, taking Fort Anderson and Wilmington, North Carolina. After the war he studied law at the Michigan University and in the office of James Speed (Lincoln's Attorney-General), with whom he began to practice and was associated with him in law practice till the death of General Speed in 1887, after which he was in partnership with James Speed's son John, with whom he was associated until July 9, 1892, when he (Thomas Speed) was appointed clerk of the United States District and Circuit Courts at Louisville, an office which he has filled until the present time with marked ability. He is a writer of great force and clearness, and has written and compiled a volume entitled, "Records and Memorials of the Speed Family," from which the foregoing ancestry is taken in greatly abridged form. While this book was designed for the perusal of the numerous members of the Speed family, the ancestors of Thomas Speed were so prominent in state and national affairs, the memoirs are full of interesting facts and incidents in which every Kentuckian would be deeply interested. It is a volume of over two hundred pages, and is not in the book market.

He wrote an article on the battle of Franklin which was published by the Ohio Commandery of the Loyal Legion; also "The Wilderness Road," a Filson Club publication; and the "Political Club," published by the Filson Club, of which he is secretary. Mr. Speed is a valued contributor to the newspapers and periodicals upon political and historical subjects and his fund of information, with a ready command of pure English, enable him to write with ease and fluency, while his articles bear the stamp of truthfulness and reliability.

In his official capacity as clerk of the United

States Courts, he has the legal training and experience as a lawyer which are so essential to the understanding of his duties, and the keeping of the records of the courts is a kind of work for which he is qualified in an eminent degree. He has many of the chief characteristics of his illustrious ancestors, and is one of the present generation who have so faithfully sustained the good name of the Speed family.

Thomas Speed was married in 1870 to Lucy Madison Buckner; and they have two children: James Buckner, a graduate of Rose Polytechnic Institute, and a skilled electrical and mechanical engineer, now assistant superintendent of the Louisville Electric Light Company; and Mary Whitney.

Austin P. Speed, second son of Thomas S. Speed and Margaret Hawkins, was educated in Owensboro, studied civil engineering and assisted in locating the Louisville & Cincinnati Short Line Railroad, under the distinguished engineer, General St. John. He has been for many years in the coal business in Louisville, a member of the firm of Byrne & Speed; is a fine business man and is a director in several corporations in which he has investments, particularly the Ohio Valley Telephone Company. He married Georgia McCampbell of Louisville, daughter of William McCampbell, a well-known and prominent merchant of Louisville, and niece of the late J. H. McCampbell, secretary and treasurer of the J. M. & I. Railroad Company. They have one son, Goodwin Speed.

Dr. John J. Speed was the second son of Major Thomas Speed of Bardstown, born October 31, 1816; graduated from St. Joseph's College, Bardstown, and in medicine from Transylvania University in 1838. He first practiced medicine at Crawfordsville, Indiana. In 1846 he returned to Bardstown and practiced there until 1850 in connection with Dr. Alfred W. Hynes. In 1850 he moved to Louisville, where he resided until his death. He held a foremost position among the physicians of Louisville, having a thorough medical knowledge and great skill in practice. In 1874 he was elected president of the College of Physicians and Surgeons of Louisville. For a number of years he was professor in the Hospital College of Medicine, and for as many years was secretary of the State Board of Health. In 1861 he was appointed Postmaster of Louisville by President Lincoln, which office he held for eight years. He was a writer on medical subjects of considerable note. Many of his articles were published in the journals of the profession. He was a man of the highest personal character, frank and sincere in his nature, and of great culture and refinement.

He married Miriam Hawkins of Crawfordsville, Indiana. Their children were Rose Speed, deceased, and Louise Speed. The latter married Thomas Moore of Indianapolis, Indiana. Dr. Speed married (second) Miss Belle Tevis of Shelbyville, who is still surviving and lives in Louisville.

Judge John Speed of Louisville, son of Captain James Speed, was born May 17, 1772, and was ten years of age when he came to Kentucky with his father. He was the partner of his brother, Major Thomas Speed, in merchandising, and in the salt works at Shepherdsville. He bought a large tract of land near Louisville, on the Bardstown road, and built a large house, naming the place "Farmington;" reared a large family, all of whom partook of his sterling qualities. He dispensed that lavish hospitality for which "Farmington" is noted. Although a slaveholder, he was an emancipationist. He deplored the existence of slavery, but could not do otherwise than he did, and he treated his slaves humanely and made them comfortable and contented. He was a man of strong masculine characteristics, methodical and systematic in business; was Judge of the Quarter Sessions Court; was a volunteer Indian fighter in 1791; assisted in the equipment of troops and furnished supplies for the War of 1812; was a writer of great force for "The Focus," a paper published in Louisville. His first wife was Abby Lemaster, who died July, 1807. Two of her children, Mary and Eliza, survived her and lived unmarried to an advanced age. His second wife was Lucy Gilmer Fry. She was one of the large family of children of Joshua and Peachy Fry, and their marriage made an extensive kinship between the Speeds, Frys, Bullitts, Bells and others. The marriage occurred November 15,

1808. Judge John Speed died March 30, 1840. His wife survived him and died in Louisville, January 27, 1874. Their children were: Thomas, born September 15, 1809, died 1812; Lucy Fry, born February 26, 1811; James (Lincoln's Attorney-General), born March 11, 1812; Peachy Walker, born May 4, 1813; Joshua Fry, born November 14, 1814; William Pope, born April 26, 1816; Susan Fry, born September 30, 1817; Philip, born April 12, 1819; John Smith, born January 1, 1821; Martha Bell, born September 8, 1822; Ann Pope, born November 5, 1831, died 1838.

James Speed, Attorney-General under President Lincoln, son of Judge John Speed of "Farmington," was born at the homestead, five miles from Louisville, and was perhaps the most illustrious member of the Speed family, whose record of public service and excellent personal characteristics are well known and too voluminous for a brief sketch in a work like this. He served in the City Council, in both branches of the Legislature, and, as a leader and counsellor in the time of war, he advised the military officers in command in Kentucky, and his influence was very great upon the Union sentiment throughout the state. In 1864, he was appointed Attorney-General in President Lincoln's cabinet, serving until his resignation under Andrew Johnson in 1866. He presided over a convention of Southern Unionists in Philadelphia, which protested against the policy of Andrew Johnson; in 1868 he received the vote of the Kentucky delegation for Vice-President on the ticket with General Grant. After leaving the cabinet, he resumed the practice of law with Thomas Speed and continued in active work until his death in 1887.

He was married in 1841 to Jane Cochran, daughter of John Cochran of Louisville, sister of Garvin H. and Arch. Cochran, and her sister married Rev. John H. Heywood of Louisville. The children of James and Jane Cochran Speed were: John, Henry Pirtle, Charles, Breckenridge, James and Joshua.

JOHN SPEED, son of James Speed and Jane Cochran Speed, was born in Louisville in 1842. He was graduated at the Louisville High School and was a bank clerk, first in Louisville and later in Chicago, where he and his cousin, James B. Speed, worked together in the banking house of Badger & Company. The war coming on both the young men entered the Union service. John Speed enlisted as a private in the Ninth Kentucky Cavalry. His intelligence and capacity caused him to be promoted to Second Lieutenant in August, 1862. He served with his regiment under General Nelson against Kirby Smith in the Richmond (Kentucky) Campaign; was on General C. C. Gilbert's staff in the battle of Perryville; also served on General Nelson's staff and a short time on the staff of General Rosecrans. In May, 1863, he was made Captain and Assistant Adjutant-General and then served on Division Staff in the Army of the Cumberland. During the Atlanta campaign and march to the sea, he was on the staff of Major-General W. T. Ward, General Butterfield and others. In April, 1865, he was made paymaster with the rank of Major, but resigned June, 1865. His personal gallantry and valuable services were distinctly recognized by the commanding Generals in the West—Buell, Rosecrans and Sherman. After the war, whenever General Sherman would meet any of the Louisville family he would inquire, "How's John?"

Returning home Major John Speed went into business as dealer in plumbing and gas-fitters' supplies. This proving unprofitable, he gave it up, and entered the law practice with Thomas Speed, who is now clerk of the United States Courts, and was one of the most successful attorneys at the Louisville bar. After the appointment of Thomas Speed as clerk of the United States Courts, Major Speed formed a partnership with Judge James Speed Pirtle, but he retired from this firm and from practice in July, 1894, and removed to his farm in Spencer County. He was married in 1864 to Aurore Combe of Owensboro, Kentucky. They have two sons living: James and Shippen Speed; one son, John, died in infancy.

William P. Speed, son of Judge John Speed, grandson of Captain James Speed, and brother of Joshua F. and Attorney-General James Speed, was born at the Farmington homestead in Jefferson County. He married Margaret D. Phillips, an elder sister of the wife of his brother, J. Smith Speed. She died without children and he afterwards married Mary Ellen Shallcross, daughter of Captain John Shallcross, whose descendants constitute one of the leading families of Louisville. Of this marriage James B. Speed was born, a sketch of whom is given below. W. P. Speed removed to Booneville, Missouri, his wife having died, and was married there to Ardell Hutchinson, and they had two children: Austin P. and Laura. Mr. Speed made his home in Booneville until his death, June 28, 1863. He was a man of fine ability, having great natural quickness of intellect, and exceedingly bright and jovial in his temperament, and combined with this disposition he had a strong intelligent judgment. His early death prevented his coming to that greater prominence to which his talents would have inevitably carried him had his life been prolonged.

JAMES BRECKENRIDGE SPEED, one of the leading business men of Louisville, reputed to be the wealthiest man in the city, is the son of William P. Speed, late of Booneville, Missouri. He was educated in the schools of Louisville, and first engaged in business as a bank clerk in Louisville. He went to Chicago with his cousin, John Speed, and they were both employed as clerks in the banking house of Badger & Company. Both entered the Union service at the outbreak of the war, James B. Speed becoming Adjutant of the Twenty-seventh Regiment, Kentucky Volunteer Infantry, of which Charles D. Pennebaker was the first Colonel, and which was afterwards commanded by Colonel John H. Ward. He saw active service with his regiment in all the campaigns in the West, remaining with it until the spring of 1865. He then engaged in business in Louisville and his remarkable capacity for business was at once generally recognized. He progressed steadily until his standing to-day is such that it may be said he never had a superior in the city of Louisville. He is president of a number of large corporate enterprises, among which are the Louisville Cement Company, the Louisville Street Railway Company, and the Ohio Valley Telephone Company; and is director in various others, including banks, besides being the head of the firms of J. B. Speed & Company, dealers in cement, lime, salt, etc., and Byrne & Speed, dealers in coal. Any one of these enterprises would tax the powers of an ordinary man, but he has the capacity to take the active management of all of them with unerring judgment and unvarying success. In addition to these labors he attends not only to his own private estate, which is very large, but also attends to other estates entrusted to his care.

With a steady energy and a strong intellect he has built up enormous enterprises, given employment to thousands of persons, and everything in which he engages is solidly founded. He is entirely devoid of every semblance of ostentation and is generous with his means without a thought of publicity. With all his devotion to business he finds time to travel for health and pleasure in this country and abroad; is social in his nature and has a warm attachment for his friends and those allied to him by the ties of kinship.

He was married in 1867 to Cora Coffin, daughter of George W. Coffin, a wealthy citizen of Cincinnati, Ohio. Their children are Olive and William. Another child, Douglas Breckenridge, died in infancy.

Joshua Fry Speed, son of Judge John Speed, was born November 14, 1814. He was educated at St. Joseph's College, in Bardstown. After spending two years in the wholesale house of William H. Pope in Louisville, he went to Springfield, Illinois, where he spent seven years merchandising. At that place he became the friend and associate of Abraham Lincoln, Stephen A. Douglas, Colonel John Hardin, Colonel Baker, General Shields, Judge Gillespie, Nathaniel Pope and others. From his youth he regarded life with a businesslike seriousness, which led to great success. His acquaintance with Lincoln was very close, and when the latter became President Mr. Speed was his most trusted adviser. While in Illinois he took a lively interest in politics, and assisted in editing a paper. He returned to Kentucky in 1842 and married Fannie Henning, sister of James W. Henning of Louisville. Messrs. Henning & Speed became partners in the real estate business, and the partnership continued until Mr. Speed's death in 1882.

Mr. Speed's life was a very active one during the Civil War. He was the confidential adviser of President Lincoln concerning affairs in the West, and made frequent trips to Washington on matters of public interest. He was offered the position of Secretary of the Treasury by Mr. Lincoln, but he declined it.

The following words are from the pen of General John W. Finnell, Adjutant-General of Kentucky during the war:

"His position was peculiar. Without at any time an office, civil or military, he was the trusted confidant, adviser and counsellor of both the civil and military authorities of the state and nation all through the Rebellion. He was a man of few words, often painfully reticent; never in a hurry, never disconcerted. He seemed intuitively to know the right thing and the right time to do it. His compensation was found alone in the consciousness of duty performed. He uniformly declined to receive pay for any time or effort he was asked to give to the cause of his country."

From the close of the war until the end of his life he continued to live in Louisville, and was one of its most conspicuous citizens. He was engaged in many business enterprises, among others he was instrumental in building the Short Line Railroad.

Mr. Speed had no children. He died May 29, 1882, leaving a large estate. His widow, Mrs. Fannie Henning Speed, is still living in Louisville.

Major Philip Speed, son of Judge John Speed and Lucy Fry, was born at the old Farming homestead, April 12, 1819; married Emma Keats, daughter of George Keats, who was a brother of the poet, John Keats. He had a large family of bright and handsome children, and there was never a happier household; Mary Eliza married Enos S. Tuley. who was for nearly thirty years connected with the Louisville postoffice; George Keats Speed married Jennie Ewing, daughter of Dr. U. E. Ewing, a distinguished physician of Louisville, and died February 13, 1887; Peachy Austine (called Tiney) married Captain John F. Rogers of the United States army; Ella Keats (deceased) married T. B. Crutcher; John Gilmer Speed, now connected with Harper's Weekly and engaged in literary work for magazines, married Mary Craik Poindexter; Alice married Harry P. McDonald, an architect of Louisville; Fannie married M. J. O'Connor, an engineer, contractor and bridge builder; Florence, wife of Josiah McRoberts, patent lawyer of Washington, D. C.; and Thomas A. Speed, vice president of the Todd-Donigan Iron Company of Louisville, married Amelia Harrison.

J. Smith Speed, youngest son of Judge John Speed and Lucy Fry, was born February 21, 1821; was twice married, first to Elizabeth Williamson, who died without issue, and second to Susan Phillips. Their children were Elizabeth W., married Richard Jouett Menefee, son of the Kentucky orator and statesman, Richard H. Menefee; William P. of Chicago, married Belle Ellis of Bardstown; Joshua F., married Martha Nicholson of New York; Arch. C. of Chicago, married Mary Burns, and J. Smith Speed of Little Rock, Arkansas, married Mary Stewart Shallcross.

Martha B., daughter of Judge John Speed and Lucy Fry, married Thomas Adams, whose children were Kate, deceased; Lucy Ness, deceased; Gilmer S.; Bessie Innis, deceased, and James St. John.

Gilmer Speed Adams is a member of the firm of J. B. Speed & Company, a first class business man, agreeable and exceedingly popular, and a man of extensive information gained in reading and travel. His wife is a daughter of the late John M. Robinson, who was one of the most prominent wholesale merchants of Louisville.

LUKE P. BLACKBURN, Governor of Kentucky, 1879-83, was a son of Edwin M. Blackburn, and was born in Woodford County, June 16, 1816; graduated at Transylvania University, Lexington, and practiced in Lexington and Versailles, giving gratuitous services throughout the cholera scourge at Versailles in 1835; was a member of the Kentucky legislature in 1843; removed to Natchez, Mississippi, in 1846, to practice his profession; became famous for his devoted and generous services and sacrifices in the yellow fever epidemics of 1848 and 1854, in hygienic measures for the prevention and in the treatment of the disease; and made a national reputation for heroism and self-sacrifice in 1878, when he again volunteered his services and devoted his whole time to the sufferers from yellow fever at Hickman, Kentucky. His first wife, Ella G. Boswell, having died, he married in 1857 Julia M. Churchill of the distinguished family of that name in Kentucky. After taking a European trip he located in New Orleans, and there practiced medicine until interrupted by the Civil war, in which he took an active and important part for the South. By request of the governor-general of Canada, he visited Bermuda Islands for the relief of sufferers there, for which he received the grateful acknowledgments of the highest colonial authorities. In 1867 he retired to his plantation in Arkansas, but returned to Kentucky in 1873, and, as previously stated, rendered distinguished services in the yellow fever epidemic at Hickman in 1878. He never figured conspicuously in politics until 1879, when the grateful sentiment which existed in his state for his philanthropic labors in behalf of his fellow men made him governor of his native state, a reward for true heroism which the people had no cause to regret. He lived in retirement after serving his term, and died in Frankfort in 1887.

GEORGE B. BINGHAM of Cadiz, Judge of the Trigg County Court, son of Jabez and Virginia Daniel Bingham, was born in Trigg County, Kentucky, October 3, 1853. He was educated at Princeton College, Kentucky; attended the law department of the University of Louisville, and after leaving the law school in 1875 he went to Florida, and on returning to the state settled at Wallonia, Kentucky, his native place, where he engaged in the mercantile, farming and milling business. In 1890 he was elected county judge of Trigg and was re-elected in 1894. In 1891 he purchased a half interest in the "Telephone," a Democratic newspaper published at Cadiz and established fifteen years ago.

Judge Bingham is a Mason and a Democrat, and he and his wife are members of the Christian Church.

He is one of the foremost men in his community and deservedly enjoys the confidence and esteem of all the people.

He married Miss Mary W. McKinney, daughter of Major Mat McKinney, January 29, 1880, and they have two children, Edith and Jabez.

Jabez Bingham (father) was born in Athens, Ohio, February 27, 1827. He came to Trigg County, Kentucky, when sixteen years of age, and was educated in the common schools. He learned mill-wrighting and followed that trade for a few years, and finally settled at Wallonia, Trigg County, and engaged in farming, and was a magistrate of his district. In 1861 he raised a company of soldiers for the Confederate army, of which he was elected captain, and this company joined the Eighth Kentucky Regiment, under command of General Forrest. He was captured at Fort Donelson and some time after being exchanged was promoted to the rank of major of the Eighth Kentucky Cavalry, and served until the close of the war in that capacity.

When he returned to Trigg County after the war he became a builder and contractor and was extensively interested in farming. He held the rank of colonel in the Kentucky State Militia; was a member of the Methodist Church and a Mason of very high degree, and was especially interested in the work of that fraternity. In early life he was a Whig, but afterwards a Democrat. He was a man of strong convictions and had the courage of his convictions in a measure that distinguished him as a man of great strength of character.

In 1851 he married Virginia Daniel, and they had five children, only two of whom reached maturity, George B. and William Cranston.

In 1883 he was elected to the Kentucky legislature from Trigg County, and died a short time after the session adjourned, October 13, 1884.

Silas Bingham (grandfather), son of Silas and Irene (Rice) Bingham, was born in Vermont, on the southern shore of Lake Champlain, April 11, 1792. In 1796 his father settled in Athens, Ohio, and assisted in opening up the land secured by Wayne's treaty. He, together with the family of his brother and of his widowed sister and three other families, were the first settlers in that county. They suffered all the privations incident to pioneer life. Judge Bingham thus writes of those early days: "When venison was eaten for bread and bear meat for pork. The sugar maple yielded its sweets and wild berries were their only fruit. Lessons were learned from 'Long S' spellers and old English readers by the light of log fires in winter and by tallow dips in summer. This, too, after a hard day's toil shrubbing, plowing, hoeing and hunting for supplies for the larder. When the school master came it was esteemed a great privilege."

The wife of Silas Bingham, Sr., was a daughter of Major Rice of the Revolutionary army, and a granddaughter of Prof. Wheelock of Dartmouth College.

Silas Bingham, Jr., married Martha Cranston, whose father came to Ohio from Orange County, New York, in 1811. They had nine children: Royal, James, John, Jabez, Nira, Hannah, Irene, Martha and Ruth. Of this family only one son, John, and two daughters survive. Mrs. Bingham died in 1873.

The first of the sons who came to Kentucky was James, who settled in Union County, but removed to Trigg County in 1843, where he married a Miss Henry.

The first Bingham who came to the United States was an attache in the British naval service, who settled in Vermont.

Virginia Daniel (mother) was born in Trigg County. She was a member of the Methodist Church; died in 1867 and is buried at Wallonia. Her father, George Daniel, was born in North Carolina and came to Kentucky at an early age. He was high sheriff and a planter and trader in real estate. He accumulated a handsome estate, and was a leading citizen of the county.

HENRY MARTYN SKILLMAN, the oldest member of the medical profession now engaged in the active practice at Lexington, is the youngest child of Thomas T. and Elizabeth (Farrar) Skillman, and was born in the city of Lexington, Kentucky, September 4, 1824.

Thomas T. Skillman (father) was a native of New Jersey, born in 1786. Possessing only the rudiments of a common school education, but a thorough knowledge of the printing business, he came to Kentucky in 1809 with little capital, but with indomitable will, and a fixed determination to make a success of life. He located at once at Lexington, the seat of Transylvania University, and center of all the social, literary and political influence of the state. In 1813, he took to wife Elizabeth, daughter of Ebenezer Farrar. She was a lady of rare attainments, born in New Hampshire in 1786, and came with her parents to Lexington in 1789. Here she became a recognized leader among the women in every good work; was one of the founders of the Lexington Female Bible Society, and was for many years the president of the Lexington Female Benevolent Society. To her husband she was always an efficient co-worker, sharing with him all his trials, and sustaining him by her earnest co-operation in all his plans and aspirations. She survived her husband nearly thirty-nine years, dying in February, 1872, at the advanced age of eighty-one years, leaving to her descendants as a precious heritage the remembrance of her numerous Christian deeds and her many good works. The assistance of the leading clergymen of the day, prominent among whom was the Rev. John Poage Campbell, M. D., a man of distinguished ability, enabled Mr. Skillman, about the year 1813, to found the Evangelical Record and Western Review, a monthly magazine, having for its object the dissemination of sound evangelical truth, and the defense of the faith against every class of errorists. At a later date this magazine came under the editorial charge of Rev. John Breckinridge, the then gifted and brilliant young pastor of the McChord Church, and afterwards so well known throughout the country. In 1824 Mr. Skillman established the Western Luminary, the first religious newspaper in the West, and which continued to be published several years after the proprietor's death. He also founded in Lexington a publishing house larger than anything of the kind ever attempted in the Mississippi valley, from which was issued numerous standard religious works of permanent value, as well as tracts and pamphlets brought forth by the heated controversies of the day. It is appropriate to say that the name of Thomas T. Skillman on the title page of any book, tract or pamphlet as its publisher was sufficient evidence of its purity and fitness for the family circle. These various publications, through the agency of his brother, A. T. Skillman, long and favorably known as the leading book merchant of Lexington, were widely scattered throughout the state. It is worthy of mention in 1823 an edition of several thousand copies of the entire Bible, with the imprint of Thomas T. Skillman, publisher, printed from stereotype plates sent out from New York by the American Bible Society, were issued from his establishment in Lexington. This eminently good man and elder in the Presbyterian Church, and a frequent member of its highest courts, was suddenly stricken down by cholera June 9, 1833.

Henry Martyn Skillman was educated at the old Transylvania University, and, after leaving that institution, he spent several years with an older brother in acquiring a practical knowledge of drugs. In 1844 Dr. Skillman commenced the study of medicine under Drs. B. W. Dudley, J. M. Bush and E. L. Dudley, who were among the leading physicians and surgeons of their day. Dr. Skillman was graduated from the medical department of Transylvania University in 1847, and in the following year was made demonstrator of anatomy by his Alma Mater, and was thence transferred to the chair of physiology and pathological anatomy in the same institution. This latter position he held until, owing to the exigencies of the Civil war, and the destruction of their building by fire, this college was closed. During the war Dr. Skillman served two years as a contract surgeon for the government. In 1869 he served as president of the Kentucky State Medical Society; is a permanent member of the American Medical Association, and 1876 was a delegate to the International Medical Congress which met in Philadelphia. In 1889 was elected the first president of the Lexington and Fayette County Medical Society. Dr. Skillman has traveled quite extensively, visiting principal capitals of Europe, also Mexico and Cuba, which, with his natural social accomplishments, renders him a particularly agreeable and entertaining companion. Dr. Skillman is one of the most skillful, successful and accomplished physicians of Kentucky, and universally beloved.

Dr. Skillman's private practice and the many calls upon him by his professional associates in many of the surrounding counties sufficiently attest the high estimation in which he is held alike by the people and the medical fraternity.

MILTON ELLIOTT, a distinguished educator and Christian minister, president of West Kentucky College at Mayfield, son of William and Sarah Harris Elliott, was born in Estill County, Kentucky, April 22, 1837. He was educated at Irvine, Kentucky, under F. G. Gaylord, a distinguished educator of New York. Mr. Elliott assisted Professor Gaylord in the high school in Platte City, Missouri, from 1858 to 1859, and was afterwards placed in charge of the Kendrick Institute for Ladies and Gentlemen, at Monticello, Kentucky. This school building was destroyed by fire in July, 1870, and he then went to the College of the Bible at Kentucky University, where he remained until December, 1873. His health failing, he went to Estill Springs, and while recruiting his health taught and preached in his native county for eighteen months. In August, 1874, he founded at Kirksville, Madison County, the Elliott Institute, and taught there for nineteen years and preached every Sunday during that time in the Christian Church. In June, 1893, he accepted the presidency of Garrard College, Lancaster, Kentucky; and in September, 1895, became president of West Kentucky College at Mayfield and is still in charge of that institution of learning.

Professor Elliott is eminently successful as an educator. Although he has had control of West Kentucky College for so short a time, there is already a new impetus given to the work of the different departments. He is conscientious and painstaking in the extreme, and his natural aptitude for the work is aided by broad culture and ripe experience. His conduct of the college has given great satisfaction to its patrons. There are two hundred and seventy pupils enrolled and ten teachers employed. President Elliott is a Mason and ardent prohibitionist.

He married Juan Phillips of Monticello, Kentucky, daughter of Micajah Phillips, October 15, 1867. They have nine children: Minnie Le Grand, a music teacher in West Kentucky College; Henry H., first assistant of the high school of Paris, Missouri; William M., member of the senior class of the Kentucky School of Medicine; Milton, Jr., teacher in West Kentucky College; J. Nathan, a member of the senior class of West Kentucky College, who won the championship medal of the Declamatory League of Kentucky in May, 1894, and also the first prize in the Blue Grass Declamatory League in 1894; Florence S.; Mary E. and Julian Gaylord, who are in school, and Lucy Cecil, an infant.

William Elliott (father) was born in Madison County, Kentucky, July 3, 1807, and was educated there. He engaged in farming for a while in Kentucky; removed to Memphis, Missouri, in March, 1849, and died there September 5, 1849. He was a member of the Christian Church and a Whig in politics. He was a man of fine mind and of a kindly, sympathetic nature, but was earnest and firm in his convictions, and very conscientious in the discharge of duty.

He married Sarah Harris, February 21, 1828. She was born in Madison County, Kentucky, February 8, 1812. She was a devoted member of the Christian Church, in which faith she died, July, 1870. They had seven children: Milton, Nathan, Burgess, William H., Nancy B., married to Isaac B. Hon; Parmelia, married to Peter M. Hon, and Martha Jane, to Silas Campbell. Mr. Elliott's mother was married the second time to Pleasant M. Daniel, a man of sterling worth, whom Mr. Elliott loved as a father, and by this marriage there was one son, Pleasant Daniel, Jr.

Dawson Elliott (grandfather) was born in Virginia of English parents. He was a soldier in the War of 1812 and lived for sixty years in Madison County. He was a Whig in politics and held some county offices, although his principal occupation was farming. In religious views he held to the belief of the Christian Church. He was a pioneer member of the Christian Church. He married Parmelia Parrish, who died in 1866, he having died in 1860, and both of them are buried on the old homestead in Madison County.

Webber Harris (maternal grandfather) was born in Virginia of a family German by descent, and came in the early days of Kentucky history to Madison County. He was a farmer and amassed a handsome estate. His wife was Nancy Panley. He died March 7, 1865.

Mrs. Juan Elliott's mother was a Miss Jones, daughter of James Jones, who was a soldier in the War of 1812, and who afterwards represented his county in the legislature of Kentucky. His wife was Miss Mary Buster, whom he married in their native state, Virginia.

Mrs. Elliott's father, Micajah Phillips, was born in North Carolina, and when a boy emigrated with his parents, Cornelius and Rhoda Phillips, to Wayne County, Kentucky, where he spent the remainder of his life. As the schools of his county in his early life were very poor, his education was quite limited, but, having an ardent desire for knowledge, he became a man of unusual intelligence. He might truly be said to have been a self-educated man. He reared a large family, and died at the age of eighty-seven years.

GOVERNOR GEORGE MADISON was born in Virginia about the year 1763. His career was one of distinction in arms as well as the cabinet. He was one of the soldiers of the American Revolution. Before he was of age, whilst yet a boy, he threw himself in the ranks, and with a gallant bearing passed through the scenes of his country's first and great struggle for independence. He was also engaged in the battles which were fought by the early settlers of Kentucky with the Indians of the Northwestern territory. At the head of his company, Captain Madison was wounded at St. Clair's defeat in 1791; and he was again wounded in the attack upon the camp of Major John Adair by the Indians in 1792. Major Adair, in his report of that battle to Brigadier General Wilkinson, speaking of Captain Madison, whom he had ordered to take a party and gain the right flank of the enemy, says: "Madison's bravery and conduct need no comment; they are well known." This was his reputation in military life—to speak in favor of his courage was considered superfluous—all who saw him in the field, both men and officers, knew him to be brave—that knowledge came, as if by intuition, to all who beheld him—his looks, his words, his whole demeanor on the field, were emphatically those of a soldier. No hero ever shed his blood in the cause of his country more freely than George Madison; when called into her service, there seemed no limit to his patriotism, no bounds to his zeal in her behalf. It did in truth appear as if he considered himself—all he had, and all he could do—a free gift, a living sacrifice, to be offered up on the altar of his country.

JUDGE ELIJAH C. PHISTER was born in Maysville, Kentucky, October 8, 1822; a student of the Maysville Seminary; graduated at Augusta College, August, 1840; studied law at Philadelphia with Hon. John Sergeant, one of the ablest jurists and purest public men in the United States, and with Payne & Waller, leading practitioners of the Mason bar, and began the practice, June, 1844; was elected mayor of his native city, January, 1847, and re-elected January, 1848; circuit judge, 1856-62; representative in the Kentucky legislature, 1867-69, and re-elected, 1869-71, in which body he took a distinguished part; appointed by Gov. Leslie one of the commissioners to revise the statutes, 1872, but declined.

His profession, the idol of his early love, Judge Phister followed with an inflexibility of purpose which seldom fails to be awarded the very highest positions in the judiciary. He was suggested by gentlemen prominent in the profession as one of the ablest, firmest and purest of living judges. Later he served one or two terms in Congress before his death.

BENJAMIN W. PENICK, Cashier of the Greensburg Deposit Bank, son of Thomas Bailey Penick and Mary Ingram Penick, was born in Green County, June 3, 1841. He was educated principally in the schools of his county, and at Columbia High School and Georgetown College, graduating from the latter institution in 1860. He then returned to Green County and engaged in farming for a few years during the war, after which he studied law under General W. T. Ward, and, being admitted to practice at the bar, located in Greensburg and was elected circuit clerk in 1868 and was re-elected, serving in all for four consecutive terms of six years each. At one time he was employed in a responsible position with the Cumberland & Ohio Railroad Company.

Two years before leaving the clerk's office, in 1890, he was elected cashier of the Greensburg Deposit Bank by the board of directors of that institution, and for two years served in the double capacity of circuit clerk and cashier of the bank. He combines the business of banker and lawyer in a very unique manner. People come to his bank, make their deposits and receive legal advice from him in regard to their business enterprises. That he is considered as a man of ability and integrity is evidenced by the positions of trust he has held and still holds. His ability is measured by the success of the bank of which he is cashier, having in five years paid annually eight per cent. to stockholders, and accrued a surplus almost equal to that paid in capital stock.

Mr. Penick is a Democrat, a member of the Baptist Church, a Royal Arch Mason and an honorary member of the W. C. T. U.

He married (first) Bettie Brummal, daughter of Josiah and Mary Hundley Brummal. She was born in Green County in 1841 and was educated there and at the Shelbyville Academy. She was a Presbyterian, and died in that faith in 1872 and is buried at Motley Homestead, Green County. By this marriage he had four children: Brummal Penick of Green County; Mary Penick, wife of Dr. Archibald Stewart Lewis of Greensburg; William Clifton Penick of Green County, and Hundley Penick, his second son, deceased.

His second marriage was to Anna M. Hobson, daughter of General E. H. Hobson of Green County, whose sketch will be found in this work. She was educated at Danville, Kentucky, and is one of the pillars of the Presbyterian Church in Greensburg, Kentucky, and president of the Woman's Christian Temperance Union in that town; a woman remarkable for fixedness of purpose and adherence to her faith.

Thomas Bailey Penick (father) was the son of William Penick, who was a native of Virginia and settled in the southern portion of Green County, Kentucky, where Thomas B. Penick was born and educated. On completing his education he engaged in farming and stock-raising. He was a Whig and a deacon in the Baptist Church. About the year 1834 he married Mary Ingram, daughter of Benjamin and Elizabeth Ingram of Green County.

Elizabeth Ingram's mother was an Irvine. Benjamin Ingram's father was Garnett Ingram. Mary Ingram Penick was a member of the Baptist Church. She died in 1847, three years before the death of her husband, and they are buried side by side at the old Ingram homestead in Green County.

NIMROD INGRAM BUSTER, Vice President of the Mercer County National Bank, Harrodsburg, son of Charles Hayden and Marian Emerine (Ingram) Buster, was born in Wayne County, Kentucky, November 10, 1842; educated at Somerset and Monticello under Professors Burditt and Woolfolk; left school in 1861; was a Southern sympathizer, but did not go in the army on account of his father's feeble health; remained on the home farm until 1873, when he removed to a farm in Boyle County, where he is now engaged in stock-raising, making a specialty of breeding fine horses.

In 1889 he was elected director in the Mercer National Bank at Harrodsburg, and was elected vice president in 1891.

Nimrod Ingram Buster is deservedly a very popular man, commanding to an unusual degree the esteem and confidence of the communities with which he is identified; is strong in his friendships, and willing to go to any length for a friend, which is one of the marked characteristics of the Buster family. He is a Democrat in politics and belongs to the Knights of Honor.

Mr. Buster was married March 30, 1865, to Sallie Stephens Bobbitt, daughter of Alex. Bobbitt of Monticello. His wife was born and educated in Monticello. They have five children: Emma Theresa, educated at Daughter's College, Harrodsburg; John, educated at Kentucky University, Lexington; Sophronia, educated at Daughter's College; Nimrod, educated at Harrodsburg Academy, and Edward Everett, now in school at Harrodsburg.

Charles Hayden Buster (father), a native and farmer of Wayne County, Kentucky, was very much interested in politics for his friends, but not for himself, as he sought no office; was a member of the Christian Church and a Mason; died in 1867.

General Josiah Buster (grandfather), a native of Virginia, of English parentage, came to Wayne County, Kentucky, where he was a minister in the Christian Church. He was a farmer and tanner and a man of considerable property. He married a Miss Hayden.

Marian Emerine Ingram Buster (mother) was born in Wayne County, Kentucky; educated at St. Mary's Academy, an excellent school at Lebanon; was a member of the Christian Church, and died May, 1893.

Her father, Nimrod Ingram, was a native of Virginia, and was educated in that state. He married Nancy Cecil; came to Kentucky and was a farmer in Wayne County. The Ingrams and Busters are both of English descent.

GENERAL WILLIAM PRESTON, son of Maj. William Preston of the United States army and Caroline Hancock, daughter of Col. George Hancock of Botetourt County, Virginia (an officer of the Revolution and a member of Congress), was born October 16, 1816, near Louisville, Kentucky; received a classical education at St. Joseph's College, Bardstown, Kentucky, which was afterwards completed at New Haven, and at Harvard University, where he graduated, 1838; was admitted to the bar in Louisville; married Margaret Howard, daughter of Robert Wickliffe of Lexington, 1840; served as lieutenant-colonel of the Fourth Kentucky Infantry in the war with Mexico, 1846-47; was elected one of the three members from Jefferson County in the convention which formed the present constitution of Kentucky, 1849; took an active part in the debates of that body, especially against the anti-Catholic and "Native American" views advocated by Hon. Garret Davis; represented Jefferson County in the lower house of the legislature in 1850, and in the senate,

GOV. W. O. BRADLEY.

1851-53; was elector for the state at large in 1852; elected to Congress the same year to fill a vacancy, and re-elected, 1853-55; appointed envoy extraordinary and minister plenipotentiary to Spain by President Buchanan, 1858, but recalled at his own request in 1861; entered an energetic protest against the act of Spain in seizing, in violation of the "Monroe doctrine," the bay of Samana, with a view of re-establishing her monarchy over San Domingo—for which, and for his entire fidelity to his duty, he received the special thanks of William H. Seward, then United States secretary of state. He returned to the United States shortly after the first battle of Manassas, August, 1861, and urged the people of Kentucky to prompt and active resistance to the Lincoln administration. Finding the state already occupied by Federal troops, he left Kentucky and entered the Confederate army, serving until the battle of Shiloh upon the staff of Gen. Albert Sidney Johnston, who fell and expired in his arms, in the instant of a victorious assault upon the enemy.

Col. Preston was immediately transferred to the staff of Gen. Beauregard; in a week after the battle was commissioned brigadier-general, April, 1862; was at Corinth, Tupelo, guarded the line of the Tallahatchie, and aided in the defense of Vicksburg—the first siege of which was abandoned July 27, 1862, by Admirals Farragut and Porter and the Federal land forces; reached Kentucky in October, 1862, but too late to take part in the battle of Perryville; commanded the right of Gen. Breckinridge's division at Murfreesboro, and in the tremendous charge "into the jaws of death" across Stone river, in the face of two divisions and fifty-eight guns, when 1,700 men out of 7,000 fell; was transferred to the command of the troops in southwestern Virginia, in the spring of 1863; commanded a division at Chickamauga, September, 1863, in which—after the repulse by Gen. George H. Thomas of the Confederate attack of General Longstreet with Hood's division under McLaws, and the repulse of another attack by Hindman's division—Preston ordered Gracie's brigade to fix bayonets and renew the attack, and pressing after him his whole force with desperate enthusiasm, gained the whole of Missionary Ridge, and drove the Federals in one long confused mass headlong down the ridge and through every avenue of escape to Chattanooga. It was a grand victory, but at terrible cost—losing, out of 4,078 men, 14 officers and 184 men killed, 63 officers and 1,014 men wounded, and 61 missing, a total of 1,336, or one-third.

JOHN BOYLE, for more than sixteen years Chief Justice of Kentucky, was born of humble parentage, October 28, 1774, in Virginia, at a place called "Castle Woods," on Clinch River, in the then county of Botetourt, near Russell or Tazewell. His father emigrated, in the year 1779, to Whitley's Station in Kentucky, whence he afterwards moved to a small estate in the county of Garrard, where he spent the remainder of his days.

On the 3d of April, 1810, Judge Boyle was promoted to the Chief Justiceship, which he continued to hold until the 8th of November, 1826. The decisions of the Court, while he was upon the bench, are comprised in fifteen volumes of the State Reports, from 1st Bibb to 3d Monroe, and are marked with firmness and purity.

WILLIAM O'CONNELL BRADLEY, Governor of Kentucky, son of R. M. and Ellen Bradley, was born in Lancaster, Kentucky, March 18, 1847. He is of Irish ancestry, as his middle name indicates, his paternal great-grandmother being a relative of the Irish patriot and statesman, Daniel O'Connell. His parents were native Kentuckians, and his father, Robert M. Bradley, was one of the ablest lawyers in the state.

When Governor Bradley was quite young his parents moved to Somerset, where he lived until the breaking out of the war between the states. He then quit school and entered the Union army, first as a recruiting officer in Pulaski County, at the age of fifteen. He afterwards enlisted at Louisville as a private soldier, but remained in the service for a short time only.

He returned home and began the study of law and was prepared to practice before the legal age for admission to the bar. The Legislature, however, in recognition of his proficiency in the knowledge of law, passed an act authorizing any two of the circuit judges to grant him license to practice. This was a very unusual occurrence, the general law requiring th applicant to be twenty-one years of age. As soon as he obtained license, he entered upon the practice of his chosen profession, being associated with his father, who had returned to Lancaster.

In 1870, at the age of twenty-three, he made a brilliant race and was elected Prosecuting Attorney, and his service in that office was the stepping-stone to his success and great popularity. In 1872 he was nominated by the Louisville convention as presidential elector on the Grant and Wilson ticket in the Eighth Congressional District, and made a most brilliant canvass. At the age of twenty-five he was the Republican candidate for Congress in his district, and although he was not elected, he reduced the Democratic Congressional majority from over two thousand to six hundred and fifty votes. In the winter of 1875, at the age of twenty-nine years, he was nominated by his party in the Legislature for United States Senator, and received the unanimous vote of the Republican members of that body. In the fall of 1876 he again made the race as Republican nominee for Congress. He received nearly three thousand more votes than were ever polled before by any candidate of the Republican party in that district, but theDemocratic vote also being unusually large, he again failed of election.

He again made the race for Congress in 1882 and declined the empty honor of a nomination in 1884. He also declined the nomination for attorney-general in 1879; was a delegate to the national Republican convention at Chicago and seconded the nomination of General Grant; was a member of the National Republican Committee for Kentucky; was selected in 1884 by President Arthur to prosecute the Star Route thieves, but the attorney-general refused to allow a full and impartial trial and he retired from the case.

His campaigns of later years, and the part he has taken as candidate for governor in 1891, his speech in the national convention in 1892, his brilliant address in the Kentucky department of the World's Fair in Chicago in 1893, and above all his successful campaign as the Republican candidate for governor in 1895 are familiar to the people of his own state and to the whole country, no man having occupied a more prominent position in American politics in that time. In the late campaign he rendered the most signally brilliant and unprecedented service for his party by breaking the record of the great solid Democratic South, knit together, as it was supposed, in bonds of indissoluble union. This last phenomenal success of Governor Bradley has made for him a national reputation, and, in the opinion of many in the state and out of it, his present political possibilities are immense, having received the enthusiastic endorsement of the larger part of his party in the Republican State Convention for the nomination for President of the United States.

Governor Bradley is a man of fine legal ability and executive finesse. He is a fluent and attractive public speaker and possesses in an eminent degree that quality which is known as personal magnetism. Although he cannot be called a personally aggressive man, yet he has strong convictions upon what he conceives to be right and necessary and has the courage and independence to maintain his opinions.

He was married July 13, 1867, to Margaret Robertson Duncan, daughter of Dr. B. F. Duncan and a grand-niece of Chief Justice Robertson. She is a most intellectual and charming woman, fully qualified for her dignified position in the governor's mansion and in Frankfort society.

ROBERT M'AFEE BRADLEY, father of Governor William O. Bradley, was born in Madison County, Kentucky, March 27, 1808, and died in Lancaster, August 31, 1881. Of the great lawyers who were schooled and experienced in land legislation in the immediate history of Kentucky, none were more able or successful than Robert M. Bradley. So successful was he in his special work as land attorney that his opponents gave him the name of "land pirate."

In one of his many important land suits, forty witnesses were summoned by the defense and testified that the survey in question was made only ten years before. The only evidence Mr. Bradley introduced were blocks cut from the identified corner trees, showing the annulations since the marks were made. Standing before the jury with one of these blocks in his hand, and facing the court, he said: "I rely, not upon the testimony of man, the frail creature of the hour; influence, money or fear may corrupt him or warp his judgment. I offer the testimony of the Most High! Since these trees were marked by the surveyor's tomahawk, year by year, with His own immortal finger, He has drawn a line indicating the passing time. Tempest or sunshine, rain or storm, that invisible hand, with unerring certainty, recorded the fleeting years amid the stillness of the forest. No money can change, no power can warp the testimony. Not all the waters of the ocean can wipe it out. God placed it there, and there it must remain as long as those majestic trees lift their heads toward the skies. Here are the thirty lines drawn by the Divine hand! Which will you believe—the evidence of God or man?" The jury found a verdict for Mr. Bradley's client.

Mr. Bradley was never a candidate, and he had no desire for office, giving little care to matters outside of his profession, except his ardent advocacy in public and private of popular education. He was a man of very positive character, eloquent and majestic, and wielded a great power over a jury.

GEN. JOHN CABELL BRECKINRIDGE, only son of Joseph Cabell Breckinridge, a distinguished lawyer and politician, who, at twenty-nine, was twice speaker of the Kentucky house of representatives, and secretary of state for three years before his death at the early age of thirty-five, and grandson of John Breckinridge, who before his death at forty-five had twice been speaker of the Kentucky house of representatives, United States Senator, and attorney general of the United States in the cabinet of President Thomas Jefferson, was born in Lexington, Kentucky, January 15, 1821; graduated at Center College, Danville, September, 1839; adopted the profession of law; practiced for awhile at Burlington, Iowa, but returned to Lexington; was major of Third Regiment Kentucky Volunteers in the Mexican war, September, 1847-48; represented Fayette County in the legislature of Kentucky, 1849. This was his introduction into political life. He rose rapidly. In 1851 he was elected to the Federal Congress from the Ashland district after an exciting contest over Gen. Leslie Combs. The district was Whig, and Gen. Combs the devoted friend of Henry Clay. Breckinridge's chances were deemed hopeless; but his talent, his winning manners, together with his vigorous canvass, overcame all obstacles. He was triumphantly elected. He was re-elected in 1853, defeating ex-Gov. Robert P. Letcher, whom the opposition had put forward as their strongest man. The struggle in this canvass was even more protracted and violent than in the first race, but with precisely the same result. He retired from public life in 1855, having previously been tendered by President Pierce the mission to Spain, which he declined. In 1856 he was elected Vice President, in conjunction with Mr. Buchanan as President, and before the expiration of his term of service the Kentucky legislature elected him United States Senator, to succeed Mr. Crittenden for six years from March 4, 1861.

He announced his purpose of appealing to the sword, resigned his commission as United States Senator to the people of Kentucky, refusing to recognize a legislature overawed by bayonets, and called on the Kentuckians to make common cause with the South. He was appointed brigadier general, and at once placed by Gen. Albert Sidney Johnston in command of a brigade at Bowling Green. When the army fell back, Gen. Breckinridge's command formed part of the forces which made that wonderful retreat to Corinth, Mississippi. At Shiloh, in the critical charge where was lost the life of that great soldier, Albert Sidney Johnston, Gen. Breckinridge was there, animating his untried troops to deeds of daring and valor. Again he was called upon to cover the retreat of the army, a duty which was skillfully and efficiently executed. And the same service was repeated when the Confederates evacuated Corinth.

Breckinridge had now been promoted major

general, and commanded a division. In June, 1862, he was ordered to Vicksburg, and with his command successfully resisted the memorable bombardment of that important point, which was kept up during the month of July. The enemy, foiled in the attempt to capture Vicksburg, retired. Gen. Breckinridge was next ordered to take Baton Rouge, which was then occupied by the Federals. Although greatly outnumbered, he drove the enemy from his camps, which he destroyed and forced them to take shelter under cover of their gúnboats. The Confederate ram Arkansas was to co-operate in this attack, but the disaster which destroyed it rendered further operations by the land forces impracticable, and the Confederates retired unmolested.

On August 17, 1862, Gen. Breckinridge took possession of Port Hudson, and discovering its military strength, urged its defense as very important to the policy of holding the Mississippi river. Acting upon positive orders, Gen. Breckinridge, with his gallant Kentucky brigade (which followed his banner throughout the war) and some Tennessee troops, marched with alacrity to the succor of Gen. Bragg, who was then in Kentucky; but before reaching Cumberland Gap, a communication from Gen. Bragg announced his abandonment of Kentucky. At the battle of Murfreesboro, or Stone River, January 2 following, Gen. Breckinridge, by orders, led his division "into the jaws of death." He assailed an impregnable position of the enemy, losing 1,700 men out of less than 7,000. It was a fearful sacrifice, for which Breckinridge was in no measure responsible. Nevertheless, upon his command again devolved the arduous duty of covering the retreat of Bragg's broken army.

He continued with the Army of the Tennessee until May 25, 1863, when he was ordered to join Gen. Joseph Johnston in Mississippi. It was his command which gallantly repelled the assault of the enemy on Jackson, Mississippi, July 17, 1863. Shortly afterwards he again returned to Bragg's command, participated in the battle of Chickamauga, and commanded a corps at the battle of Missionary Ridge, which was fought November 25, 1863.

After consultation with the president, he was ordered to southwest Virginia, and assumed command March 3, 1864. While engaged in duty in his department, he was suddenly called upon by General Lee to march with all his available force to Staunton and the Shenandoah Valley to check the movement of Gen. Franz Sigel. On May 15th he attacked the general at New Market, and routed him, after a brilliant engagement. The Federal general was driven in full retreat to Winchester, but rendered pursuit impossible by burning the bridges in his rear. Gen. Lee sent Breckinridge a congratulatory dispatch, and an order to join him forthwith at Hanover Junction. The order was promptly obeyed, and Gen. Breckinridge's forces protected the rear of Lee's army and his line of communication when Sheridan made his great raid. He remained with Gen. Lee's army and bore a conspicuous part in the battle of Cold Harbor, fought June 2, 1864, when the Federal army was repulsed with fearful slaughter. Subsequently, in conjunction with Gen. Jubal Early, he foiled Gen. David Hunter in his attempt to capture Lynchburg, and pursued that officer into the mountains.

Gen. Breckinridge's troops were then incorporated with Gen. Early's, and he was placed in command of a corps. They next prepared for operations in Maryland, Virginia and the District of Columbia. On June 22 they took up the line of March. July 3, 1864, Breckinridge's command captured Martinsburg; July 5 the whole army crossed the Potomac at Shepherdstown; July 9 Breckinridge defeated and routed Gen. Lew Wallace at Monocacy, which left the way open to Washington. On the 11th the Confederates reached Silver Spring, only six miles from the Federal City, and within sight of the dome of the capitol. Skirmishing occurred the next day; but that night Gen. Early, for prudential reasons, ordered a retreat—re-crossing the Potomac at Edwards' Ferry on the night of the 13th. Gen. Breckinridge remained in the Valley, participating in the serious engagements there fought.

But a few days after the battle of Winchester he received orders from Richmond to return to southwest Virginia, which he did in time to repel the Federal forces which, under Gen. Stephen G.

Burbridge, were operating in that quarter. He continued in command of this department until February 4, 1865, when he was appointed Secretary of War, to succeed Hon. James A. Seddon, and was thus engaged to the close of the war.

After the fall of Richmond, and the collapse of the Confederacy he made his way to the Florida coast, whence he escaped in a small boat and reached Cuba in safety. He visited Canada and Europe, and returned to his home, at Lexington, Kentucky, a year or more afterward. Avoiding all political complications, he thenceforth devoted himself exclusively to his profession, and to business engagements as vice-president of the Elizabethtown, Lexington & Big Sandy Railroad. Like the great chieftain of the "Lost Cause," his course was singularly modest, retiring and prudent—deferential, in a marked degree, to that proscriptive policy of the party in power which deprived the nation, however unwisely, of the safe counsels of men of his stamp. Had a more liberal policy obtained, the eloquent voice of John C. Breckinridge would have been heard once more. But he died, all too soon, on Monday, May 17, 1875, aged fifty-four; shortly after a visit from Hon. Henry Wilson, then Vice-President of the United States—whose own near approach to the grave seemed to relax somewhat of the unforgivingness of his party friends toward the dying statesman and soldier.

GOVERNOR JAMES CLARK, the son of Robert and Susan Clark, was born in 1779, in Bedford County, Virginia. His father emigrated from Virginia to Kentucky at a very early period, and settled in Clark County, near the Kentucky River. The subject of this notice received the principal part of his education under Dr. Blythe, afterwards a professor in Transylvania University. He studied law with his brother, Christian Clark, a very distinguished lawyer of Virginia. When he had qualified himself to discharge the duties of his profession, he returned to Kentucky, and commenced the practice of the law in Winchester, in 1797.

He was several times elected a member of the State Legislature, in which body he soon attained a high and influential position. In 1810, he was appointed a judge of the Court of Appeals, and acted in that capacity for about two years. In 1812, he was elected to Congress, and served from the 4th of March, 1813, until March, 1816. In 1817 he received an appointment as Judge of the Circuit Court, for the judicial district in which he resided, which station he filled with great ability, and to the general satisfaction of the public, till the year 1824, when he resigned.

In 1825, he was elected to Congress to fill the vacancy occasioned by Mr. Clay's appointment as Secretary of State, and continued to represent the Fayette District in that body until 1831. In 1832, he was elected to the Senate of Kentucky, and was chosen speaker in the place of Mr. Morehead, who was then acting as Governor, in the place of Governor Breathitt, deceased. He was elected Governor of Kentucky in August, 1836, and died on the 27th of September, 1839, in his sixtieth year.

GOVERNOR CHRISTOPHER GREENUP was born about the year 1750, in the then colony of Virginia. When the American Revolution occurred, he was in the prime of youth. It was not in his nature to see his country engaged in such a struggle without engaging in it himself. He accordingly devoted his youth to her cause, and was one of the soldiers and heroes of that great conflict; and passed through its scenes of trial and hardship, acting well his part, and winning no small share of that honor which crowned the triumph of the American arms. In the bloody war which took place between the pioneers of the West and the Indian tribes, he also bore a part, and brought into active service against that formidable foe the skill which he had acquired during the Revolution. To the dangers of such a warfare he freely exposed his life, and risked, with a manly and brave heart, all its perils. After thus gaining for himself considerable distinction in arms, he settled in Kentucky, and on the 4th of March, 1783, was sworn in as an attorney-at-law in the old court for the district of Kentucky, established by an act of the Virginia legislature. On the 18th day of March, 1785, he was appointed the clerk of that court, which office he held during the existence of the court. In 1792 he was elected a member of Congress, and served as such until the year 1797. After this he filled the office of clerk of the senate of Kentucky to within a short time of his election as governor, which occurred in August, 1804. For four years he discharged the duties of this office with high honor and credit, both to himself and the state over which he presided. At the expiration of his gubernatorial term, he was elected to the legislature from the county of Franklin. In 1812 he acted as a justice of the peace for the same county. He served also many years as a director in the old Bank of Kentucky; and, after a long life of public service to his country, he died on the 27th of April, 1818, in the sixty-ninth year of his age.

WILLIAM PULASKI WALTON, Editor of the Interior Journal, Stanford, Kentucky, son of Thomas R. and Isabella Turner Walton, was born in Louisa County, Virginia, and educated partly in the common schools there, his studies being interrupted by the war between the states.

He remained at home during his father's absence in the Confederate army, but afterwards attended a college in Baltimore, Maryland.

He was deputy sheriff for two years, and deputy county clerk of Hanover County, Virginia, for some time. In 1871 he engaged in railroad enterprises, being a contractor on the Chesapeake & Ohio Railroad in Virginia and West Virginia, building a number of miles of that road; and was subsequently engaged in the same capacity with the Baltimore & Ohio and Cincinnati Southern Railroad, building in all about forty miles of road.

February 5, 1875, he bought the Interior Journal at Stanford, Kentucky. He has a peculiar and marked adaptiveness to newspaper work and has brought to his editorial chair a pen in touch with the finer sentiments of humanity that is the open sesame to the public confidence and general usefulness. As an editor, Mr. Walton is a modern Chevalier de Bayard, "sans peur et sans reproche," conscious of his own integrity and guided by a singly defined principle of action; he is uncompromising in his maintenance of what he conceives to be the right, feeling that the welfare of the masses depends upon the measure of the personal responsibility of the individual. His pen is a terror to evil-doers, and his generous and independent conceptions of true citizenship, irrespective of class or conditions, are encouragement to the right minded.

In his management of the Interior Journal he is the fin-de-siecle reporter, realizing that the newspaper is the mouth-piece of the people and that its function is to truthfully chronicle current events, the result of operative causes, by catching the fire of their passing and bringing humanity in touch with the hopes, ambitions, privileges and misfortunes of its kind. In consequence of Mr. Walton's methods, the Interior Journal is a most substantial and influential semi-weekly paper, and is the most widely circulated newspaper in the state outside, of course, of the larger cities.

Mr. Walton is especially strong in his friendships, will go to the same lengths for his friends that he would like to have them go for him, and for those who are fortunate enough to enjoy his friendship, his sympathy and unselfish personal interest are like a brother's. He is thoroughly in accord with the spirit of Masonry, and is a member of that order. In politics he is a Democrat, and of course a partisan; he feels too deeply not to advocate strongly, but he aims to be just and even generous in his estimates of men and of environments that largely determine action.

Mr. Walton has made money in the newspaper business where others would have failed, and has investments in other enterprises in and around Stanford; is the owner of the opera house and of other real property in that city; is interested in a Land Association in the eastern part of the state, and is a stockholder and director in several corporations.

He was married to Kate Huffman in September, 1875, who died May 6, 1892. In June, 1895, he was again married, his wife being Miss Mattie Owsley, daughter of Hon. John S. Owsley, Sr., of Lincoln County.

An eminent journalist of Louisville has paid the following tribute to the editor of the Interior Journal:

"Mr. Walton combines the dual faculties of a reporter and an editor in a stronger degree than any other man I know in Kentucky journalism. He and Emmett Logan, I should say, stand at the head. He has that nose for news which marks the true newspaper man, and when news has been collected he never hesitates to print it because it may not meet the approval of some magnate of his section. On the contrary, he gives it that prominence in his paper to which it may be entitled, and then writes an editorial comment upon it which usually reaches the very marrow of it. Walton is not learned in courtly phrases and his paper is not crowded with them. Yet he is a Virginia gentleman, and higher praise than this cannot be accorded. In all the years of his newspaper career it is doubtful if he ever wrote a sentence from mere wantonness. Yet he can be merciless when the cold letter of the law requires that he shall be so. If the circumstances demand the use of a bludgeon for the coarse offender, who would appreciate no other punishment, he has that bludgeon ready. If a rapier touch, keen, delicate and deadly, will better reach the vital point, there is in Kentucky journalism no defter hand than his. Utterly free from bombast or bravado, he is wholly without fear; gentle in thought and manner as the cavaliers of whose long line he proves so honorable a part; he is careless of danger and brooks no demand upon him for the suppression of the news, or the withholding of his honest opinions. As a conservator of the peace, a promoter of the best interest of society, the Stanford Interior Journal, under the management of Mr. Walton, has been equal to any twenty sheriffs in the counties about him; the superior of any regiment of state troops. Defying crime, whether in high or low places, and demanding that it meet its reward, he has made murder infamous and brought its direst punishment into fashion. No higher praise can be accorded this modest gentleman than to say that he is alike feared and respected by that class against whom his most earnest warfare has been waged.

"Walton is a partisan, as men of his temperament always are, but he is a very fair one. Ever ready and anxious to fight the battles of his party, he numbers among his friends many who hold opposing political opinions, and none among these can say that he ever sought or accepted an unfair advantage. He is a fair fighter and gives and takes his blows like the fearless gentleman that he is.

"His friendship is so warm, constant and devoted that I can find no words in which to describe it. It is enough to say that to those who have come within the charmed circle that encloses his intimates, he is a brother indeed and in fact."

Thomas R. Walton (father) was a son of William and Mary Warren Walton of English extraction, was born June 10, 1822, in Louisa, Virginia. George Walton, one of the signers of the Declaration of Independence, was a near relative of William Walton. Thomas R. Walton was educated in the common schools of Louisa, but removed when a young man to Hanover County, Virginia, and engaged in general farming and stock-raising. He was a Democrat and held a commission as captain in the Confederate army, but on account of delicate health, his service consisted principally in raising companies and drilling them in military tactics. In 1850 he married Isabella Lucetta Turner, daughter of William Turner, who was a steamboat owner on the Mississippi river. She was born in Vicksburg, Mississippi, September 17, 1825. She and her husband were members of the Methodist Church.

They had four children: Thomas R. of Florida; Mrs. I. N. Vaughan of Virginia; Edwin Claiborne of Stanford, and William Pulaski Walton. Thomas R. Walton died November 5, 1881, and his wife died April 17, 1877. They are buried side by side at the old homestead in Hanover County, Virginia.

CHARLES WILLIAM WHITE, Representative from Hardin County to the Kentucky Legislature, son of Benjamin F. and Jane (Pemberton) White, was born in Shelby County, Kentucky, September 27, 1857. He was educated in the common schools in Shelby County, and afterwards engaged in mercantile business. He is a Democrat of the most pronounced and uncompromising convictions; was elected to the Legislature from Hardin County, Kentucky, in 1892, and was re-elected in 1895. He has only resided in Hardin County six years and during that time has been chosen twice by the people of the county to represent them in the Legislature.

He was married on November 24, 1886, to Fannie Shaw, daughter of Judge J. R. Shaw. She was born February 28, 1871. Their only child, born September 11, 1887, is now attending the school at Elizabethtown. Mr. and Mrs. White are members of the Methodist Church.

Benjamin F. White (father) was born in Wheeling, West Virginia, February 15, 1804, and was educated there in the common schools. He was a stage contractor by occupation and a Democrat in politics. He came to Virginia when quite young, and during the latter part of his life he was proprietor of a hotel at Graefenberg, Kentucky. In his religious views he held to the belief of the Methodist denomination. Mr. White was a man of great social prominence and noted for his strong character.

Jane Pemberton White (mother), daughter of Richardson Pemberton and Sarah Hoell Pemberton, was born in Franklin County, June 15, 1836, and educated there. She was well known as "Aunt Jane White," and was noted for her sympathy, religion and hospitality. Her home was always a welcome haven for the Methodist preachers, to which denomination she belonged.

J. ALEXANDER IRELAND, M. D., of Louisville, son of William Ireland and Jane Stone, was born in Jefferson County, Kentucky, September 15, 1824. He received a good English education, with a fair knowledge of Latin and Greek; and at the age of seventeen began the study of medicine in the office of Dr. James F. Pendergrast in Jefferson County, and continued his medical studies under Doctors Bullitt and Cummins in Louisville; attended the lectures in the medical department of the University of Louisville in 1845-6, and, after continued study and careful preparation, attended a further course in the Kentucky School of Medicine, from which he graduated in 1851.

He began the practice of his profession in Louisville and remained in that city until 1854, when he removed to his farm in the county and practiced in that vicinity until 1864, at which time he was elected to the chair of Obstetrics and Gynaecology in the Kentucky School of Medicine. In order to fill this appointment he again became a resident of Louisville, and was professor in the Kentucky School of Medicine until that college was merged into the University of Louisville, and was then elected professor of Clinical Medicine in the university.

Upon the re-establishment of the Kentucky School of Medicine, he resumed his former chair in that institution, which he occupied until 1870, when he was elected to a similar chair in the Louisville Medical College, and has remained in connection with that college until the present time, having recently been elected Emeritus Professor of Obstetrics and Gynaecology, with full pay and no work! During his long connection with the Louisville Medical College, he served for a period of fourteen years as dean of the college, and while acting as professor in this institution he was elected to the chair of Gynaecology and Paedology in the Kentucky School of Medicine, with which he had been connected formerly, but declined the honor. From this it will be seen that of the forty-five years of Dr. Ireland's professional life, he has given a third of a century to the training of others in the science of medicine. But this constitutes only a small part of the labor performed in those years, for no one of the many distinguished men of the medical profession in Louisville has stood higher as a family physician, and his large general practice has been conducted with energy and industry and has been attended with a degree of success that has been as gratifying as it has been profitable, and would satisfy the ambition of any man.

Dr. Ireland's position in the medical societies of his times, his generous and able work in behalf of the local, state and national organizations of which he has been an enthusiastic member, has been generously recognized by the honors which have been conferred upon him from time to time, while his ability as a professor has been attested by the long service which he has rendered in the medical colleges, no less than three different institutions having sought his aid as teacher and professor in chairs of the highest importance.

In the earlier years of his medical career and prior to his active engagement in the practice of medicine, he was a preacher of the Gospel, having been licensed to preach (1848) in the Baptist Church; and while pursuing his studies and for several years after entering the medical profession, he was an ordained minister and the regularly installed pastor of several of the churches of his denomination, preaching in the Baptist Churches in Jefferson and Bullitt Counties and at Jeffersonville, Indiana. He is a life member of the General Association of Baptists and one of the most substantial, earnest and valuable men in that denomination.

His literary pursuits have been systematic and thorough and he has grown in the knowledge of men and affairs as he has grown in years; has contributed his share of work for the medical, religious and literary press, accomplishing all this in connection with and in addition to a very active practice of his vocation, in which, alone, he has been a very busy man.

Of very quiet and retiring disposition, with no attempt at personal display, his work, not yet finished, has been accomplished quietly and without the use of the ordinary and even legitimate means of advertising which are so frequently resorted to by ambitious men in the profession.

Foremost in the medical profession, prominent in the church with which he has been connected for near half a century, he has well nigh completed a life work upon which he may look back with pride and satisfaction and with the assurance that he is honored and loved by his associates in the institution in which he has labored longer than any other professor; affectionately remembered by his patients who have enjoyed his care as the gentle physician, and known and read of all men as the upright, Christian gentleman, whose example is worthy of imitation.

Dr. Ireland was married in 1848 to Sarah E. Cooper, daughter of Levin Cooper of Jefferson County, by whom he had one son, Dr. Henry Clay Ireland. He married (second) in 1859 to Susan M. Brown, daughter of Furtney Brown of Louisville, and by this marriage has one son, William F. Ireland.

Dr. Ireland's paternal grandparents were natives of Scotland, and his father, William Ireland, was a native of Kentucky, who followed agricultural and mechanical pursuits, and was one of the most substantial, upright and useful citizens of Jefferson County, where he lived until a short time before his death, when, his wife having died, he went to live with his son in De Witt, Ark., and died there in 1870.

Jane Stone Ireland (mother), whose parents were Virginians of English ancestry, was born in Nelson County, Kentucky. Dr. Ireland is the eldest of the four children of William and Jane (Stone) Ireland.

EDWIN PORTER THOMPSON, educator and author, eldest son of Lewis M. and Mary R. Thompson, was born near Center, Metcalfe County, Kentucky, May 6, 1834. He was left in his twelfth year to the care of a widowed mother, and consequently he was early disciplined in the school of self-reliance, a school that has graduated so many shining examples of American citizenship.

The bent of his mind was strongly intellectual, and inspired by laudable ambition and a genuine love for learning, he has step by step reached a high rank among the scholars of his native state. He was reared on a farm, but after he was nineteen years of age he was engaged in teaching principally until 1860, when he studied law; but the breaking out of the war between the states prevented his obtaining license at that time. His sympathies were entirely with the South in that fraternal struggle, and feeling that true manliness and patriotism called him where his feelings were so warmly enlisted, he entered the Confederate army and served until the end of the war in May, 1865. He was twice wounded; was a prisoner for five months, after the battle of Stone River; and after exchange he was promoted to a captaincy on the regimental staff, Sixth Kentucky Infantry.

He then engaged in farming; meanwhile and afterward writing the History of the First Kentucky Brigade and editing a magazine. But his most congenial occupation was that of teaching, and for many years he was president of Owen College, Harrisburg, Owen County, one of the most thorough in its various departments and one of the most ably conducted educational institutions in the state. He has made frequent contributions to periodical literature and is the author of an Academic Arithmetic, written before the war. The History of the Kentucky Brigade was a work of great labor, being one of the most complete and valuable among the records of the late war, and for its incident and sentiment peculiarly gratifying to the survivors of the famous historic body of Southern soldiers called "The Orphan Brigade."

In October, 1888, he was appointed by Governor Buckner to fill a vacancy in the office of state librarian; in March, 1890, was made private secretary to Governor Buckner, which place he filled during the remainder of Buckner's term; was elected superintendent of public instruction in August, 1891, which responsible position he filled for four years and four months, discharging the duties of the office with marked ability, and it may truly be said that no other man has done so much for the common schools of Kentucky. He is a genial, sociable gentleman, an engaging conversationalist, and impresses all who know him as possessing unusual qualities of head and heart. In his religious views he is a Baptist.

He married April 22, 1858, Marcella P. Thompson, a daughter of Nathan and Eliza (Stringer) Thompson.

Lewis Morgan Thompson (father) was born in Pittsylvania County, Virginia, and was brought to this state by his parents in 1815, when less than three years old.

His mother, Mary R. Thompson, was born and reared at Mt. Airy, the old family seat of her father, Waddy Thompson, in Metcalfe County. Her parents came from Pittsylvania County, Virginia, in 1809.

The following respecting Captain Thompson's present work is taken from the Louisville Times of January 27, 1896:

"The Hon. Ed Porter Thompson, ex-superintendent of public instruction, has long been collecting material for a work which will be a most important addition to the annals of Kentucky. Interest in the great struggle of 1861-65 seems rather to increase than diminish as the years go by, and the extraordinary part played by Kentuckians is a theme which should receive thoughtful investigation and be put to permanent record before the actors therein have all passed away.

"Capt. Thompson is as seduously engaged in this work on behalf of those who espoused the Southern cause as he was during his term of office in meeting every demand of that position. Though his admiration of these men amounts to enthusiasm, his work will not tend to provoke bitterness or keep alive any feeling of alienation consequent upon the different course adopted by Kentuckians of that period, but will be rather a contribution to the history of the state, by a man of broad and liberal views, which will increase the pride of the whole people in the renown which Kentucky has won upon the battlefields of the Republic. The civil (no less remarkable than the military) history of these men since the close of the war will receive special attention. The work will be in three volumes, denominated 'A History of Kentucky Soldiers in the Confederate Army,' the first of which will be the re-written history of the 'Orphan Brigade,' including Helm's cavalry regiment; the second, of the five infantry regiments whose gallant service has never been put to record, and the third will be devoted to the Kentucky cavalry."

COLONEL JOHN SMITH HURT, lawyer of Mount Sterling, Kentucky, son of Joshua and Elizabeth (Pebworth) Hurt, was born in Montgomery County, Kentucky, May 21, 1826. He was educated in the common schools of the county and at the academy in Mt. Sterling under Hugh B. Todd and William Raney. He left school at the age of eighteen and went to live with his uncle, Elder John Smith, at Owingsville, Kentucky, where he remained until 1846, and at the age of nineteen enlisted for the Mexican War in Captain Turpin's Company, Second Regiment Kentucky Volunteers—a splendid body of men commanded by Colonel McKee—and among numerous other engagements was at the battle of Buena Vista. Henry Clay, Jr., who was Lieu tenant-Colonel of this regiment, rode a white horse, and seeing that it attracted too much attention he brought it to Mr. Hurt to hold, but in the emergency of the terrible contest he remounted it and was killed soon after. Colonel Hurt returned to Owingsville after the war was over and studied law with Hon. Andrew Trumbo for two years and was admitted to the Owingsville bar. During the gold fever in 1849 he accompanied his brother Elisha to California and remained there two years, meeting with reasonable success. On his return to Owingsville in 1851 he was elected County Attorney and held that office two terms. He continued to practice law with fair success until 1861, when he immediately enlisted, and recruited a regiment at Olympian Springs for the Union army. This regiment was with General Nelson in the Big Sandy River expedition and in a number of small engagements and skirmishes. In June, 1862, he joined Buell's army near Mumfordsville and moved into Tennessee, where his regiment took part in the battle of Shiloh. Returning with Buell's army to Kentucky in the fall of 1862; he was in the battle of Perryville in October, 1862, and with General Buell followed Bragg into Tennessee after the battle of Perryville, but was detached from Buell in the winter of 1863 and returned to Kentucky and connected himself with Colonel Walker's regiment of cavalry. They had a slight skirmish with Colonel Cluke's regiment near Mt. Sterling and followed that leader as far as Owingsville when Cluke retired from the state.

Colonel Hurt was attached to Burnside's army in the summer of 1863 and was with him during his expeditions into East Tennessee. He commanded the Twenty-fourth Kentucky Volunteer Infantry at the siege of Knoxville, when it was besieged by Longstreet and was with General Sherman on his march from Chattanooga to Atlanta. He was in the battle of Resaca, where he commanded a brigade consisting of four regiments—the Twenty-fourth Kentucky, Sixty-third Indiana, One Hundred and Third Ohio and a Tennessee regiment—and of the eighteen hundred men in his command he lost five hundred and ninety-two. It was his brigade that captured the first line of works at Resaca. He was also engaged at the battle of Kenesaw Mountain near Atlanta and was in the battles around Atlanta, including the battle of Jonesboro, finally capturing the city.

Upon being mustered out in 1865 he returned to Owingsville and resumed the practice of law. He was a candidate for the Legislature on the conservative or Democratic ticket August, 1865, but was defeated—because of his advocacy of the repeal of the expatriation law depriving those who had been engaged on the Southern side during the war between the states, of citizenship—this together with his opposition to the posting of soldiers at the polls to prevent Colonel Hurt's friends from voting caused his defeat. In 1883 he was again nominated by the Democrats to represent the Ninth District and was again defeated, after which he retired from politics. He removed to Mt. Sterling in 1889, where he now resides and is engaged in a lucrative practice. He was engaged in the Rebecca Hamilton will case and in the criminal case of William N. Smoot, the Commonwealth vs. Adam Trimble, and for the Commonwealth vs. F. M. Ewing, executor of A. J. Ewing, which involved the sum of $44,000, together with other cases of importance. Col. Hurt has never married.

His father, Joshua Hurt, was born in Spartanburg District, South Carolina, in 1790. He first settled in Fayettesville, Tennessee, and fought under Jackson at the battle of New Orleans. He removed from Tennessee to Montgomery County, Kentucky, near Mt. Sterling, in 1820; to Sangamon County, Illinois, in 1830 or 1831, and was a member of Lincoln's company in the Black Hawk War. He was a member of the Christian Church and a devoted friend of Elder John Smith, his brother-in-law. He died in Illinois in 1831, and after his death his wife returned to her father's home in Kentucky.

He married twice, and the children by his first wife were: Berryman, Rebecca, Alfred, Moses, Elisha and John. He was married (second) in 1823 to Elizabeth Pebworth, and the children by this marriage were: William P., John S., James and Harvey G. Joshua Hurt voted for Jackson because he was a soldier under him, but he was always a Whig in politics.

Elizabeth Pebworth Hurt (mother) was born in Norfolk, Virginia, in 1802. She came when very young to Kentucky with her parents, who crossed the Allegheny Mountains in 1803 and settled in Montgomery County, Kentucky, three miles from Mt. Sterling, where her father purchased a small farm and where the descendants of his daughters still live. The name itself has no male representatives. Elizabeth Pebworth Hurt died in April, 1885. She was a member of the Christian Church.

Of the children of Joshua by his first marriage, first, Berryman, eldest son, was reared in Mt. Sterling, Kentucky, and was married three times. First, to a sister of Judge N. P. Reid; second, to Miss True of Fayette County; third, to Miss Berry of Bath County. In 1865 he moved to Sangamon County, Illinois, and died during a visit to Kentucky in 1888.

Second, Rebecca married a Mr. Pendleton, who was assassinated at Flemingsburg in 1835; third, Moses died in early manhood; fourth, Elisha grew up in Mt. Sterling and married Miss Belt of Flemingsburg, who died of cholera in 1833. He afterwards married Miss Lee of Mason County and they removed to Pike County, Illinois, and resided there until his death. He was a farmer, but in 1849 he crossed the plains with his half-brother, John S., and afterwards went into merchandising and accummulated quite a fortune. He returned to Pike County, Illinois, and was Captain and Quartermaster in General Grant's army at Fort Donelson and Shiloh, and was wounded at the latter place. He was the Sheriff of Pike County, Illinois, and held the office two terms. Fifth, John was born in Tennessee and reared in Montgomery County, Kentucky. He went to Texas in 1836, and served under General Sam Houston at the battle of San Jacinto. He returned to Illinois and afterwards was Captain of a company in Col. Baker's Regiment in the Mexican war. His company captured General Santa Ana's carriage after the General had escaped on one of the mules taken from the carriage. John Hurt went to California in 1850, and returned to Logan County, Illinois, and was Sheriff of that county one term. He married Miss McGraw of that county, and he died in 1856.

The children of Joshua Hurt and Elizabeth Pebworth (second wife) were: First, William P., who was born and attained manhood in Montgomery County; married Katherine Bruton of Montgomery County; removed to Greencastle, Indiana, in 1851; remained there one year and removed to Boone County, Missouri, and became first professor of mathematics in the Christian Female Seminary, Columbia, Missouri. He afterwards became its President and conducted the institution for about thirty years. He then returned to his farm in Boone County, Missouri, where he now resides.

Second, John S., the principal subject of this sketch; third, James Hurt, was born and reared in Montgomery County, and removed to Missouri when twenty-one years of age; married Miss M. McBride, daughter of Chief Justice McBride of Missouri. She died and he then married Julia Howard of Clay County, Missouri, and removed to Kansas City. He owned a ranch on Cimarron River in Colorado, accumulated a fortune and died in 1883. Fourth, Harvey, was born and reared in Montgomery County and married the widow Lee, whose maiden name was Mason. He was a successful farmer and owned a large farm three miles north of Mt. Sterling. He died in 1893. His widow and children survive.

Colonel Hurt's paternal grandfather moved from Virginia to South Carolina and his family were connected with the Methodist Church. Robert Pebworth (maternal grandfather) was a native of Norfolk, Virginia; and married Anna Mosley of that place. His family was of English descent, as were the Hurts.

The Hurt family has a splendid record as soldiers, citizens, lawyers, business men, educators, philanthropists and ministers of the Gospel. Wherever they have pitched their tents they have been known for their honor and sturdy citizenship.

WATTS PARKER, Judge of the Twenty-second Judicial District of Kentucky, was born February 23, 1848, in the village of Athens, ten miles east of Lexington, Kentucky. His early education was limited to the schools of the village and vicinity, and this education was discontinued before he was fifteen years old. At the age of seventeen he conceived the idea of becoming a physician, and to obtain means to enable him to attend medical lectures, he engaged in a small grocery business in his native village and read medicine until he was twenty, attending one course of medical lectures, during this period, at the Miami Medical College. At the age of twenty he abandoned the study of medicine, and at twenty-one engaged in a small mercantile business in Lexington, and there began the study of law. He soon returned to Athens, resumed business at that place, and there continued the study of law. In August, 1870, he was examined by Chief Justice Robertson for a license to practice law, and a license was granted by Judge Robertson and Judge Peters. Removing to Lexington in 1872, he began the practice of law, attended the Law School of Kentucky University in 1872 and '73 and received a diploma of that institution. In 1874 he was admitted to a partnership with J. R. Morton, and this partnership continued until the latter went upon the bench in 1883.

During this period the subject of this sketch served a term as city attorney, and was at one time a member of the School Board of Lexington. In 1884 he was appointed master commissioner of the Fayette Circuit Court, and this position he held until January 1, 1893. He was a commissioner of the Eastern Kentucky Lunatic Asylum for four years, and was president of the Central Bank from its organization until he assumed his duties as judge.

In November, 1892, he was elected judge of the district composed of the County of Fayette, with the county seat at Lexington, the term for which he was elected beginning January 1, 1893, and to continue five years.

He was married to Miss Bettie Burgin, March 7, 1878. Three children, Nellie Burgin, Mary Shepherd and Virginia, are the result of this union. In politics Judge Parker has always been a Democrat.

His parents were John E. Parker of Caroline and Rebecca Shepherd of Spottsylvania County, Virginia. They emigrated to Kentucky in 1832; his mother died in 1855; his father in 1881.

When a mere lad John E. Parker served as a soldier in a Virginia regiment in the War of 1812. He was a man of unusual energy, force of character and great courage. He was not prosperous in his business and died poor, but enjoyed the full confidence and respect of his fellow citizens. The subject of this sketch was thrown upon his own resources at an early age. He was named after his grandfather, Watts Parker, a native of Virginia and a soldier in the War of the Revolution.

GEORGE ALLISON HOLLAND, an able lawyer of Eminence, Kentucky, son of William Allison Holland and Eliza (Van Nuys) Holland, was born in Henry County, Kentucky, September 8, 1861. He was educated at Eminence College, graduating in 1880, and the next year entered the Louisville Law School, from which institution he graduated in 1882, and was admitted to the bar the same year. During this time he was a reporter for the Louisville Commercial and later was connected with the Courier-Journal in the same capacity.

In 1883 he went south and practiced law in Chattanooga until 1892 and while there was elected Alderman on the Democratic ticket. In 1889 he turned his attention to journalism and from 1889 to 1892 he was editor and proprietor of the Sunday Argus, a political organ published at Chattanooga.

Mr. Holland has always been greatly interested in politics, but too much engrossed in the legitimate practice of his profession to care for office. From 1892 to 1895 he traveled with his invalid wife through Mexico and the United States. He is a member of the Presbyterian Church and of the Masonic Fraternity and is a Knight of Pythias.

He was married in 1886 to Jean Neilson Gillespie of Chattanooga, daughter of Dr. Joseph and Penelope (Whiteside) Gillespie. She received her education at Vassar College and with her husband is a member of the Presbyterian Church. They have no children.

William A. Holland (father) was born March, 1825, in Edinburg, Indiana. He is a Mason and a member of the Christian Church. His wife is also a member of this denomination. Mr. Holland is a Democrat of the old school. In 1868 he established the "Constitutionalist" at Eminence, Kentucky, and is still owner and editor of that newspaper. It is probably the only paper of its age in the interior of the state that has never changed management since it was first established.

George B. Holland (grandfather) was the eldest son of John and Sarah Jones Holland. He was born at Wellsburg, Virginia, May 26, 1806, and married Rebecca French, who was born in Ohio, August 9, 1808. She was the daughter of Samuel and Elizabeth French, both of whom were natives of Pennsylvania.

John Holland (great-grandfather) was born in Baltimore, Maryland. His father was one of three brothers who came from England and settled respectively in Maryland, Virginia and South Carolina, from whom are descended the Hollands of those states. The celebrated author, Dr. J. G. Holland, belonged to the Virginia branch.

The Hollands were closely related to the Crouches. The Rev. Ben T. Crouch, a noted Methodist divine, revered and honored by the earlier Methodists in Kentucky, was a first cousin of Rev. George B. Holland. His brother, Dr. John W. Holland of Indianapolis, was noted for his scholarly attainments and professional skill.

Of Mr. Holland's mother's family an old record says: "The name of Van Nuys was taken from the name of a village in Holland. The Van denotes noble rank. Auk Jansen Van Nuys, commonly written in an old record Jans, whose ancestors' birthplace was Nuys, in Groutgen, Holland, and who came from Amsterdam, Holland, in 1651, to New Amsterdam, now New York, settled in Flat Brush in 1669. He was made magistrate in 1673 and in 1674 was a delegate from the Dutch towns to confer with Governor Colve. His first wife was Magdelene Pieterse, who was interred in the burial ground of the Dutch Reformed Church in Brooklyn (now Fulton Street), and from whom descended among others, upon whom no stain rested, Isaac Van Nuys, who married Vrouchie Quick, whose son, James Van Nuys, served in the War of 1812. He married Tiny Bois, daughter of Denina Bois and Anna Sebren. Their son, Dennis Bois Van Nuys, married Sally Ann Sams, and their daughter, Eliza Jane Van Nuys (mother) married William Allison Holland, father of George Allison Holland.

"Auk Jansen Van Nuys married (second) Elizabeth Jans, widow of Jacob Clausens.

"Of the Van Nuys family five were assassinated by the British during the Revolutionary War. Their names were: Margareta, Magdalena, Elizabeth, Maria and Jacobus, all children of Janache Ankurts Van Nuys.

"Maternal branch: Griffin Jones of Virginia, Welsh by descent, married a lady of Irish descent. From them was descended Joseph Kelly, who was Captain in the War of 1812, and in whose company William O. Butler, afterwards Major-General in the United States army, during the Mexican War, was orderly sergeant.

"Captain Joseph Kelly married Elizabeth Mallory, whose daughter, Parmelia Kelly, married James Sams of Virginia parentage. Their daughter, Sarah Ann Sams, married Dennis Bois Van Nuys and their daughter, Eliza Jane Van Nuys married William Allison Holland of English descent.

"On the Rhine is Castle Van Nuys, belonging to Count Van Nuys, who was of this same family."

The records of the paternal and maternal sides of Mr. Holland's family are very lengthy. On the maternal side is the history showing ancestors in the Revolutionary War and one uncle, John C. Van Nuys, in the Confederate army.

WILLIAM SCOTT BARBOUR, deceased, a distinguished attorney-at-law of Versailles, was a son of Philip D. and Fannie B. (Newman) Barbour of Jefferson County, Kentucky.

His father was a native of Orange County, Virginia, but was reared in Jefferson County, Kentucky, where he was one of the most progressive farmers of his time. He died in 1881, in the sixty-fourth year of his age. He was married (first) to a daughter of Caleb Dorsey of Jefferson County. She has two sons and one daughter: John D. Barbour, who has served two terms as Sheriff of

Jefferson County, and is a resident of Louisville; Dr. Philip C. S. Barbour, a resident of Louisville, a practicing physician and superintendent of the Louisville City Hospital; and Mary, deceased, who married J. William Newman. His second wife, Fannie B. Newman, is the mother of eight children: James P. Barbour, deceased, who was cashier of the Bank of Louisville; William Scott Barbour, deceased, subject of this sketch; Richard N. Barbour, general bookkeeper in the Fayette National Bank of Lexington; Sallie, deceased, who married Dr. Vansant of Mount Sterling; Maggie Pollock, wife of Dr. Willis H. Hobson of Harrods' Creek, Jefferson County; Sheridan Lee, recently married to Maud Hill of Paris; Edward R. and Fannie B., who are unmarried and reside in the old homestead in Jefferson County.

Philip C. S. Barbour (grandfather) was born in Orange County, Virginia, and came to Kentucky in 1819, locating near the line between Jefferson and Oldham Counties, where he spent the remainder of his days on his farm. His death occurred in 1861, at the age of seventy-two years. He was a prominent member of the Christian Church, as were his wife and nearly all of his children and his children's children. He married Margaret Pollock of Orange County, Virginia. Her ancestors were from Scotland and the Barbours are of Scotch-Irish descent.

Fannie B. Newman Barbour (mother) is a native of Orange County, Virginia. She still resides on the homestead near Louisville. Her father, James Newman, was a native of the same place. His home in Virginia is still known as Hilton, and is near the old home of President Adams, near Somerset, where he died. He was a very intelligent man; was educated for a profession and studied law, but preferred the independent life of the farmer and never practiced at the bar. He was a frequent contributor to the agricultural papers, and did much for the advancement of agriculture, in which he was deeply interested. His ancestors were English.

William Scott Barbour was born in Jefferson County, Kentucky, December 10, 1854, and received his education in the Lonsdale Academy in Madison County, Virginia, finishing at the University of Virginia. He taught school for some months after leaving school, and when eighteen years of age began the study of law under William R. Thompson of Louisville and finished his law course under ex-Governor Porter of Versailles, being admitted to the bar in March, 1877. He at once entered upon the practice of his chosen profession in Versailles and met with most flattering success. He was County Attorney for two terms, from 1882 to 1890, and was Master Commissioner of the Circuit Court from 1883 until the time of his death.

Mr. Barbour and Theresa Berryman, daughter of Edward N. Berryman of Woodford County, were married June 15, 1882.

He died at his home in Versailles, September, 1895, in the forty-first year of his age and in the prime of a busy and exemplary life.

LEONARD J. CRAWFORD, distinguished lawyer and leading Republican politician of Newport, son of Jacob H. Crawford and Mary Elizabeth Eckert, was born in Newport, Kentucky, April 29, 1860.

His father a native of Fleming County, removed to Newport when he was a young man and was a resident of that city at the time of his death. He was a pilot on steamers plying the Ohio River between Cincinnati and Pittsburgh, and was highly esteemed by his numerous acquaintances along the river and by all who knew him. Mary Elizabeth Crawford (mother) is a native of Campbell County, Kentucky, now residing near Newport, a devout Christian, member of the Methodist Episcopal Church, and a lady of the highest intelligence, education and refinement.

L. M. Eckert (maternal grandfather), a native of Campbell County and for many years a resident of Newport, retired from business and spent the latter years of his life on his farm in his native county. During his residence in Newport he was president of the City Council through several terms and was otherwise prominent as a leading and influential citizen. He was imposing in appearance, being six feet four inches in height and proportionately built; was very genial in his disposition and could tell a good story with great zest. He was a very strong and uncompromising

Republican; a member of the Methodist Church and died in the Christian faith in 1876, aged sixty-four years.

L. J. Crawford was educated in the Campbell County schools and in Hughes' High School in Cincinnati, from which he graduated in 1880; read law with Ben Butterworth and graduated from the Cincinnati Law School in 1882; located in Newport during the same year, where he has practiced law ever since, with the exception of one year's practice in Minneapolis, Minnesota. He has a large business of the most lucrative character, and is one of the best known attorneys in Kentucky; is very prominent in politics and a leader in the Republican party, not only in his city and county, but throughout the state; was the candidate of that party for Attorney-General in 1891; was presidential elector for the state at large in the campaign of 1892; was president of the Republican State League for three consecutive terms, 1892 to 1895, and delivered the address of welcome in behalf of the Kentucky Republicans at the National League Convention held in Louisville in 1893.

He is not only a lawyer and politician of widespread reputation, but a man of affairs and of means; director in the Newport National Bank and in the Covington Trust Company. He is a member of the Methodist Church, and in all of his relations to the legal profession, his political party, his business interests, the church and in society he is known and respected as a good and true citizen.

Mr. Crawford was married in 1883 to Ella J. Horner of Campbell County, and they have two sons: Leonard J. and Clay Crawford. As this goes to press he is conducting the defense of Scott Jackson in the celebrated case of the Commonwealth of Kentucky vs. Jackson in the Campbell Circuit Court at Newport.

BERRY LEWIS LITSEY, president of the First National Bank of Springfield, son of Uriah Litsey and Ellen Lewis, was born in Washington County, Kentucky, August 3, 1842.

Prominent among the early residents of Kentucky was Randolf Litsey, who came from Maryland and located near Springfield prior to the beginning of the present century. He was engaged in farming and later in the distillery business. He was born in 1770 and died in September, 1849. His wife, Mary Gregory, daughter of Richard Gregory, died in 1859.

Uriah Litsey, father of B. L. Litsey, was born October 15, 1813, and died in July, 1886. At the age of twenty-seven he purchased a farm on the Beech Fork, adjoining the farm on which stands the house where Thomas Lincoln and Nancy Hanks were married. He was married to Ellen J. Lewis, daughter of Berry and Mary Hays Lewis, October 7, 1841. Uriah Litsey was originally a Whig in politics, but after the dissolution of that party, identified himself with the Democrats. He was a member of the Presbyterian Church at Pleasant Grove.

Ellen Lewis Litsey (mother), now living in the family homestead near Pleasant Grove, is the mother of ten children, only one of whom, the eldest, is living. She is a devout member of the Presbyterian Church and a faithful Christian woman, who has seen much sorrow, but whose faith in a wise Providence is unshaken.

Berry Lewis Litsey was reared on a farm and attended the common schools at Pleasant Grove; also attending several sessions at the Taylorsville High School. Choosing agriculture, he purchased a farm in 1868 on the Beech Fork; was successful in farming and in 1878 purchased the farm on which he now lives near Pleasant Grove.

In August, 1890, he was elected Probate Judge of Washington County for a term of four years; was a delegate to the Democratic Convention in Chicago in 1892, representing the Fourth Congressional District, and has served his party and the public in various other capacities; was elected president of the First National Bank of Springfield in 1892; was elected by the people Judge of the Washington County Court in 1890 and held that office until January, 1895.

He is still engaged in farming near Pleasant Grove, having never lost interest in or failed to give attention to his farm, while serving in office or as president of the bank.

Judge Litsey was united in marriage February 3, 1870, with Catherine Hays, daughter of David R. Hays and Mary McMaken Hays of Pleasant

Grove neighborhood. She is a graduate of Nazareth College in Nelson County. Her parents were of Scotch-Irish extraction. The children of Judge Litsey and Catherine Hays are: Mary, wife of Jas. I. Martine of New York; Nellie Rebecca, Katie Bell and David R. Litsey, all of whom are at home except Mrs. Martine. Judge Litsey and his wife are members of the Presbyterian Church. He cast his first presidential vote for George B. McClellan.

JEFFERSON DAVIS PRYOR, M. D., of Mayfield, son of James Calvin and Emma Goodwin Pryor, was born July 5, 1861, in Graves County, Kentucky. He was educated in the Graves County schools and Clinton College, Hickman County; studied medicine at the University of Louisville, graduating in 1890; came to Mayfield and for three years was in partnership with Dr. Boyd; since then he has practiced medicine alone; is a member of the Graves County Medical Society and Southwest Kentucky Medical Society; a Democrat in politics and a member of the Missionary Baptist Church. He is also a Knight of Pythias, a Mason and Odd Fellow. He was married June 22, 1895, to Annie Watts, daughter of N. B. Watts of Mayfield, Kentucky. She was educated at Southwest Kentucky College, Mayfield, and is a member of the Christian Church. Dr. Pryor has a good practice, and is financially prosperous. He stands very high professionally and socially in Mayfield, takes great pride in his profession, and keeps well posted in the progress in medical science.

James Calvin Pryor (father), now a resident of Graves County, was born in Logan County, Kentucky, February 3, 1820; removed to Graves County when quite young; was educated there, and has been a farmer since reaching his majority. During the war he was not in the service, but was in sympathy with the South. His brother, Jack Pryor, was captain of a company in the Confederate army. James Calvin Pryor (father) is living on the homestead where he settled fifty-two years ago.

James Pryor (grandfather) was born in Logan County, Kentucky, and was one of the earliest settlers in Graves County, removing there in February, 1821, and his name appears among the first entries in the court records. He settled six miles east of Mayfield on Panther Creek, now known as Pryor's Precinct. He married a Miss Phelps. He loved the forests and was a great hunter in his younger days.

Jonathan Pryor (great-grandfather) settled at Pryorsburg, Graves County; owned many fine horses; was actively engaged in the improvement of land, opening roads, etc. He was a man of broad sympathies and was so recognized and sought by all who needed advice and assistance. The Pryors are Irish and belong to the same family as Judge Pryor of the Supreme Bench of Kentucky.

Emma Goodwin Pryor (mother) was born in Henry County, Tennessee, March 9, 1826, and removed with her father, Jesse Goodwin, to Graves County, where he was a farmer. His wife, Sukie Butler, was a woman of strong native intelligence, and her memory to the last was a veritable chronological table of events in Kentucky history. She was a member of the Primitive Baptist Church.

Mr. Goodwin (great-grandfather) was an Englishman, who served in the War of 1812.

LAWRENCE B. ANDERSON, General Insurance agent at Mayfield, son of Ervine Anderson and Eliza Lockridge, was born February 1, 1860, in Graves County, Kentucky; educated at the seminary in Mayfield, Kentucky, and taught school after graduating; was admitted to the bar in 1886, and elected County Judge in 1890, and since 1894 has been engaged in insurance work in Mayfield, Kentucky. He was married August 11, 1888, to Miss Daisy D. Bolinger, daughter of J. F. Bolinger, one of the leading men of Mayfield, and they have three children: Robert, John and Elizabeth. Mr. Anderson is a Democrat and a Knight of Pythias, and he and his wife are members of the Baptist Church.

He was indefatigable in the discharge of his duties while he held the office of County Judge; merited and won the esteem of his associates in the law and of the community at large.

Ervine Anderson (father) was born January 21, 1820, and was the first white child born in Graves after it was formed into a county; was educated in the common schools, and afterwards appointed deputy and circuit clerk—the two offices being together at that time—under his father. When twenty-two years of age he was appointed clerk of the County and Circuit Courts, and held that position until the war, being frequently elected. During the war he began to practice law, having studied under his father. With the change in the Constitution he was again elected county and circuit clerk; was a member of the Legislature from Graves County in 1871-2, and continued in the practice of law until his death, July 11, 1876. He was a Cumberland Presbyterian, a Mason, and a Democrat, being especially strong in his Southern sympathies. Before the war he was a very wealthy man, and after it had some fortune left. He had an abiding interest in the reputation and welfare of Graves County, and wielded a wonderful influence in the politics of the county.

John Anderson (father of Ervine Anderson) was born in what is now Albemarle County, North Carolina, and came to Kentucky after being educated in North Carolina. The purchase was not then incorporated into counties. He cleared up his farm, and in 1821, just as Graves County was formed, was elected clerk of the County and Circuit Courts, and held these offices until his death, in 1842. He studied law and practiced irregularly; was a man of great natural ability, and stood very high in the community. He was in the War of 1812; in politics a Whig. He married Rebecca Davenport in North Carolina. She died in 1866. The following is an extract from an old record made by John Anderson: "Emigrated from Caldwell County, Kentucky, to the district of country west of Tennessee River, and settled on Mayfield Creek in the woods, two and a half miles north of the present site of the town of Mayfield. We had to make our way through the woods from Tennessee River and were three days on the route, encamping in the woods of nights, and threading our way through the thicket by day. We arrived on the 27th of October, 1819, at our place of future residence, and pitched our camp. I built cabins and cleared land, and resided at that place until December, 1824, when the county of Graves having recently been organized, and myself appointed clerk of the County and Circuit Courts, I moved to the town of Mayfield, where I have resided ever since."

Eliza Lockridge (mother) was born in Graves County, Kentucky, May 8, 1829. She was married to Ervine Anderson October 15, 1844. She is a member of the Cumberland Presbyterian Church, and is now living in Mayfield. They had nine children, four sons and five daughters: Lawrence, John, married to Miss Martha Leach; Wiley, to Miss Annie Bray (now deceased); Annie, married Robert T. Albritton; Amelia, married Judge W. W. Robertson; Edith, married Stephen Carney; Emily, married J. R. Jamison; Albert, married Martha Grider, and Hester, married Gus G. Coulter.

Mrs. Anderson's father was Robert D. Lockridge, born in Lexington, Kentucky, November 5, 1805. He married Elizabeth Buchanan of Logan County in 1827. He was a physician, and died in Graves County in September, 1876. His father was also Robert Lockridge and owned a great part of the land that Lexington is built on, but sold it and went to Murray County, Tennessee, when his son Robert was a lad. He married a relative, Jane Lockridge. Robert (grandfather) married Miss Buchanan in Murray County, Tennessee. Eliza (mother) was the first white child born in Feliciana, Graves County, Kentucky. The Anderson name has been a power for good in that county for almost three-quarters of a century. The record of the father and grandfather of Judge Anderson is a priceless legacy to their children and grandchildren.

WILLIAM B. MOODY, an able young lawyer of New Castle and ex-County Attorney of Henry County, son of William Harvey and Virginia O'Bannon Moody, was born in Henry County, Kentucky, April 8, 1852. He was educated in the public schools of his native county and in the Baptist Seminary at Eminence, leaving the latter institution on account of poor health and taught in the public schools of Henry County for four years.

While teaching he read law, first with Judge Warren Montfort and then with Judge Barbour, who was at one time Judge of the Superior Court

KENTUCKY BIOGRAPHIES. 591

of Kentucky; was admitted to the bar in October, 1874, and began to practice at New Castle, June 1, 1875. From 1878 to 1886 he was County Attorney of Henry County; in 1880 began to edit and publish a Democratic paper, entitled "The Henry County Local."

He united with the Baptist Church when he was fourteen years of age, showing that his mind was early tinged with religious sentiment.

Mr. Moody was married December 25, 1876, to Carrie Belle Price, daughter of William B. and Anna (Ellis) Price, who was born in 1854 and educated at New Castle and Hillsboro, Ohio. They have one child, Anna Virginia.

William Harvey Moody (father) was a native of Henry County, Kentucky, and was educated in the schools of that county. In religion he was a Baptist, in politics a Democrat, by occupation a farmer; married Virginia O'Bannon, and they had five children: William B., George T., P. N., John E. and Emma, who married Dr. Rees. William H. Moody died in 1884.

His wife was educated at the Henry Female College at New Castle, and was a member of the Baptist Church. Her father, William O'Bannon, was a native of Virginia, and a pioneer of Kentucky.

Richard Moody (grandfather) came to Kentucky from Virginia, and married Lucy Woodsides. They were communicants of the Baptist Church.

HENRY SCOTT ROBINSON, a distinguished criminal lawyer of Campbellsville, son of John R. Robinson and Malvina (Scott) Robinson, was born in Campbellsville, Kentucky, June 6, 1861, and was educated in the schools of that place. He performed the duties of the farmer boy until he was nineteen years of age, and then read law with his father and Judge Montague; received his license in January, 1882, at Greensburg, Kentucky, and at once began the practice of law in Campbellsville; was elected county attorney of Taylor County in 1884 and re-elected in 1890, serving until January 1, 1895.

While discharging the duties of his office as county attorney with fidelity and industry, he was also engaged in the general practice of law, and has won distinction as a criminal lawyer of unusual ability, having been engaged in all murder trials of note in the district since his admission to the bar. He enjoys a large general practice, and is a man and a lawyer in whom the people have implicit confidence. His reputation is not merely local, but he is one of the best known of the younger attorneys in central Kentucky.

Mr. Robinson was united in marriage, August 26, 1883, with Hattie Taylor, daughter of Daniel G. Taylor and Lou Cowherd. She died September 25, 1889, leaving no children.

He was married (second) in October, 1892, to Minnie Sharp, daughter of William Sharp and Sue M. Pruitt; and they have one child (born September 21, 1893), Malvina, who is named for Mr. Robinson's mother.

John R. Robinson (father), son of Robert Robinson and Miss Rice (whose mother was a Puryear), was born in Taylor County, Kentucky, February 22, 1823. He worked on a farm until he was twenty-one, enjoying very little schooling, and then went to Campbellsville and was employed by his uncle, Pleasant Saunders, at eight dollars a month, in the tobacco business. Out of this small salary he saved money enough to enable him to attend school until he had acquired a fair education; read law with Judge E. L. Barbee of Campbellsville and soon after receiving his license to practice law was elected county attorney. He was the first magistrate in his district; was engaged in all of the important land cases, of which there were many in his earlier days, and was known all over the state as one of the ablest lawyers, not only in that particular line of business, but as a general practitioner of the highest ability. He is now well advanced in years and has retired from active practice; is a man of strong religious convictions, a member of the Cumberland Presbyterian Church and a highly esteemed citizen, in whom all who know him have the utmost confidence.

He was captain of Company E, Twenty-seventh Kentucky Volunteer Infantry, Union army, in the Civil war, having recruited the company himself; but, owing to the ill health of his wife, he resigned and returned home.

He married Malvina Scott of Greensburg, daughter of John Scott, who came to Louisville with his parents from Culpeper County, Virginia, when the present metropolis of the state had only a few shingle-roofed houses. He subsequently removed to Greensburg, which was then the larger city. His father, Randolph Scott, and his wife are buried a little south of Alcorn, where they settled and lived as pioneers and finally paid the debt of nature.

Malvina Scott 'Robinson (mother) was educated at Greensburg, and was a member of the Baptist Church. She was the mother of two children, the subject of this sketch and Malvina, who died August 23, 1864. Mrs. Robinson died June 30, 1864.

John R. Robinson was married (second) October 1, 1867, to Lydia Ann Barbee, daughter of John Barbee and Mary Ray, and a sister of Judge E. L. Barbee of Campbellsville. There were four children by this union: Nannie, wife of W. L. Young, master commissioner of the Taylor Circuit Court, also attorney-at-law and ex-school commissioner at Campbellsville; Bettie Robinson, the first woman who ever took the degree of A. B. at Georgetown College; Pleasant Saunders Robinson, engaged in the sawmilling and lumber business near Campbellsville, and Joe E. Robinson, a student in Center College.

The Robinson family is of Irish extraction, the progenitor having settled in Virginia on his arrival in this country before the Revolutionary war.

CHARLES W. SHORT, lawyer, editor, real estate dealer and judge of the Police Court of Pineville, son of Jonathan Short and Lucy Wing, was born in Greenville, Muhlenberg County, Kentucky, June 24, 1850. His father was a native of Muhlenberg (now McLean) County, and died in Greenville in 1883, aged sixty-one years. He was a merchant in Greenville during the greater part of his life, a member of the Presbyterian Church, and a most worthy and honored citizen.

David Short (grandfather) was born in Virginia in 1810, came to Kentucky and located in (now) McLean County, and was a farmer there until the time of his death in 1848. His father was a native of Germany and for many years a resident of Virginia.

Lucy Wing Short (mother), now residing in Greenville in her sixty-eighth year, was born in that city and has lived there all her life. She has been active as a member of the Presbyterian Church for many years, and is a woman of more than ordinary intelligence and of strong Christian faith.

Charles F. Wing (grandfather) was a native of New Bedford, Massachusetts, who came to Kentucky in the latter part of the eighteenth century, and upon the erection of Muhlenberg County in 1798 was made clerk of the Circuit and County Courts, which offices he held for many years; was circuit clerk until 1856, or a period of forty-eight years; was a captain in the War of 1812, serving in Canada under Gen. William Henry Harrison. He died in 1861, aged seventy-six years. He belonged to an old and respected family of Puritans in Massachusetts.

Charles W. Short was educated principally in the Greenville College, for boys, under the able teaching of Professor Hall, finishing his literary and scientific studies in the Kentucky State College in Lexington, following which he was deputy county clerk at Greenville for six years, reading law at the same time. In 1878 he was elected county superintendent of schools, holding that office for seven years, being three times elected. In January, 1885, he purchased the Muhlenberg Echo, a weekly Democratic newspaper, which he edited with ability for two years; sold the paper to W. H. Eaves and engaged in the tobacco business in Greenville in partnership with E. L. Younts; was in that business for three years, when, in 1890, he came to Pineville with the first boomers and engaged in the practice of law and dealing in real estate. In 1891 he was elected police judge, of which office he is the present incumbent, his term expiring in 1898. On the first of January, 1896, he organized the Cumberland Courier Publishing Company, and began the publication of a Republican weekly newspaper, of which he is the business manager.

Judge Short has been one of the most active, public spirited men of the new and flourishing city of Pineville, and with all of the duties of a large law practice, presiding in the City Court as occasion requires, looking after his real estate interests and fostering his newspaper enterprise, he is one of the busiest men in the mountain district of Kentucky. But he has the brains, with push, pluck and persistence, and will succeed in any undertaking.

He was married in 1871 to Sue Reno, daughter of J. E. Reno of Greenville, and has a family of seven children: Lizzie, Annie, Reno, Lucy, Mamie, Kate and Adeline. Judge Short and his family are members of the Methodist Church.

ISHAM MARION WILFORD, proprietor of the Wilford Mills, one of the substantial institutions of Mayfield, son of Robert Wilford and Ada Aliza Randolph, was born in Trigg County, Kentucky, July 20, 1832, and after his school days was a farmer in Graves County until 1881, when he purchased the Wilford Mills in Mayfield from his brother, N. Green Wilford, and in 1885 his son, Robert O., became interested with him in the milling business. Having devoted his life to the quiet and peaceful pursuits of the farmer and miller, he has not sought prominence or political preferment, though his Democracy has never been questioned. He has been more conspicuous in church matters than in politics, having been a life-long member of the Baptist Church and a faithful attendant upon its ordinances. He owns a large farm of valuable land in Graves County and is still interested in its cultivation. No man stands higher in the community, and he is known all over his section as a man of integrity, unswerving honesty and devotion to principle.

Mr. Wilford was married September 5, 1858, to Jincy Olivia Perry, daughter of O. H. Perry of Graves County. She died February 8, 1885, leaving six children, five daughters and one son: Robert Oliver, now in business with his father; Emma, widow of Henry Clay Gardner (who died March 25, 1896, leaving three children, Tracy, Agnes and Robert); Lula Green, wife of U. N. Graham of Mayfield; Rosa Lee, Bessie and May.

Mr. Wilford was married (second) to Mrs. Owen, nee Melton, November 18, 1887, and has one son by this marriage, Ben Wilford.

Robert Wilford (father) was born in North Carolina in 1810; was quite young when he came to Trigg County with his father, Isham Wilford, who died soon after coming to Kentucky; his mother married (second) William Armstrong. Robert became a trader and stockraiser, making frequent trips to the New Orleans market to sell his stock. He was married in 1831 to Ada Aliza Randolph, who was born in Trigg County in 1816. He died February 8, 1846, and she died on the same day of the same month in the following year. Their children were three sons and three daughters: Isham Marion, Nathaniel Green, James David (killed at the battle of Shiloh in the Confederate army), Robert Jasper, Eliza Jane and Mary Emeline, both deceased, and Melinda Frances, wife of Henry A. Rives.

The Wilfords are of Irish ancestry, but it is not known when the progenitor came to this country. Mr. Wilford's maternal grandfather, William Randolph, was a native of Virginia, who came to Trigg County early in the century and was a farmer, after clearing his land. He was twice married, his first wife being a Widow Cameron. His family consisted of two sons, David and Alexander, and three daughters. He died in Trigg County in 1847. He belonged to the distinguished Randolph family of old Virginia.

DANIEL BRECK, civil engineer of Louisville, son of Rev. Robert L. Breck, was born in Richmond, Kentucky, July 27, 1861, and graduated from Central University in 1880. He went to Leadville, Colorado, and spent some time in prospecting and hunting before taking a postgraduate course in the California University, concluding in 1883. He made a special study of civil engineering in both of these universities, and while in California built a sea wall at San Luis Obispo; assisted in the construction of a railroad from Port Harford, Cal., and also a railroad in Oregon; returned to Kentucky and accepted a prominent position in the engineering department of the Louisville & Nashville Railroad Company with headquarters in Louisville; promoted to roadmaster on the Short Line Division; from that to superintendent of the Owensboro Division, and is at present in the office of the president of the Louisville & Nashville Railroad Company at Louisville.

His father, Rev. Robert L. Breck, D. D., was born in Richmond, Kentucky, May 8, 1827, and after graduating from Center College at the age of seventeen years, he attended Princeton College, New Jersey, graduating from the theological seminary and has since received the degree of Doctor of Divinity from Princeton College.

He preached his first sermon in the old church on "Woodburn Farm" in Woodford County, since which time his name and work have been identified with the history of the Presbyterian Church and with Center College and Central University as one of the leading ministers in the church and as an educator of young men; was moderator of the General Assembly when the sectional division took place; took an active part in the historic events of those stirring times; was the prime mover in the organization of Central University and was its first chancellor, wielding a great influence and occupying a prominent place in ecclesiastical bodies and especially in the educational work of the church.

Daniel Breck is a grandson of Judge Daniel Breck, a member of Congress and judge of the Court of Appeals of Kentucky; a great-grandson of Major-General Green Clay of the War of 1812; also a great-grandson of General Levi Todd of the Indian Wars. His ancestors were intimately connected with the early history of Kentucky.

RODNEY HAGGARD, Judge of the Clark County Court, son of Augustine L. and Lou Ann Mullins Haggard, was born in Clark County, Kentucky, October 3, 1844, and educated in the common schools of the county and in the high school at Winchester.

At the age of seventeen he began teaching. When the war between the states broke out he dismissed his school and joined the Buckner Guards in Kirby Smith's command. He was a recruiting officer and raised a company, of which his uncle, Gordan C. Mullins, was elected captain and himself lieutenant. This was the first company raised for Chenault's regiment of John H. Morgan's command, and Judge Haggard was with this command until Gen. Morgan was captured in the Ohio raid, at which time he was in command of the remnant of the regiment, all his superior regimental officers having been killed, wounded or captured. He was then a prisoner on Johnson's Island until the close of the war. During his active service in the army he took part in a number of engagements, among which were the battles of Richmond, Kentucky; Hartsville, Tennessee; Green River Bridge, Mills Spring, West Liberty, Lebanon and a number of fights in Indiana and Ohio, and in fact was in all of the battles in which Morgan's command was engaged during his service with it, and was a gallant soldier.

After the war, not being twenty-one years of age, he resumed his work, studying and teaching school alternately until August, 1866, when he was elected sheriff of Clark County. This was the first regular election after the war, and the first at which he had ever voted; he was the youngest man who ever held that office in the state of Kentucky and the first to settle his accounts with the auditor for each year. In 1870 he was re-elected and began the study of law under Chief Justice James Sympson of Winchester and obtained license to practice his profession from the judge of the Court of Appeals; subsequently graduated from the Louisville Law School, was admitted to the bar in March, 1873, and has ever since his admission to the bar enjoyed a lucrative practice, being engaged upon one side or the other of all important cases in the county. In 1880 he was elected without opposition to the state senate from a district composed of Clark, Bourbon and Montgomery Counties, and served as senator for four years; made a splendid record as legislator, having introduced the act creating the State Board of Equalization, the act equalizing and extending exemptions, to require county attorneys to assist commonwealth attorneys in prosecutions in Circuit Courts and many other important measures, all of which still remain upon the statutes. He was elected county judge of the Clark County Court in 1893 to fill an unexpired term, and in 1894 was re-elected for the full term, and is now serving in that capacity. He has been the attorney for the Chesapeake & Ohio Railroad Company for fifteen years and attorney for the Kentucky Central Division of the Louisville & Nashville Railroad for twelve years. He is an able judge and an upright, trustworthy citizen and in whom the community places unbounded confidence. His natural qualities of sturdy, reliable manhood are enforced by the strong prestige of an honorable and honored ancestry. He has always been an active, unflinching Democrat, and his election has always been as the nominee of that party. He is a public speaker of much ability and his time and means have been freely given in the interest of his party.

He was married in February, 1868, to Mary E. Baldwin of Clark County, daughter of Lieutenant W. W. Baldwin, who was killed on the Confederate side in the disastrous fight at Green River Bridge, July 4, 1863. Her mother was Mary A. Eades Baldwin. They have seven living children: Leland, Frank Hunt, Annie Mildred, wife of J. W. McFarlin; Mary Rodney, John Henry, Rodney and Benjamin Wheeler.

Augustine Lewis Haggard (father), son of David T. Haggard of Albemarle County, Virginia, and Patsy Adams Haggard of Clark County, Kentucky, but originally from Virginia, was born in Clark County, June 3, 1820, and was educated in the common schools of that county.

He held successively the offices of justice of the peace, judge of the County Court, clerk of the Clark Circuit Court and master commissioner of the Clark Court of Common Pleas. He took a great interest in public affairs and was an active Whig until that party was merged into the Republican party, when he became a Democrat. He was a man of strong native ability and a philanthropist whose active benevolence was the outcome of religious principle, consequently he was very prominent in church work and his judgment much depended upon in church affairs, as well as in political circles. He divided his time between Winchester and his country home until he died, December 19, 1895, at his home six miles from Winchester. He is buried at Mt. Olive Cemetery on the Muddy Creek Turnpike Road, where three generations of the family are resting; himself and wife, his father, mother, grandfather and grandmother lie buried side by side. Nathaniel Haggard and wife, Elizabeth Craig Haggard, the great-great-grandfather and mother of Judge Rodney Haggard, are buried in a lot on the Boonesborough pike, two miles from Winchester and seven miles from Boonesboro.

John Haggard (great-grandfather), son of Nathaniel Haggard and Elizabeth Craig Haggard, was born in Albemarle County, Virginia, and married Mary Shepard.

Nathaniel Haggard (great-great-grandfather) came from Virginia to Kentucky when it was a wilderness and built a house two miles from the present site of Winchester, seven miles from Boonesboro. It is of hewn cherry logs and has portholes for defense in case of attacks from the Indians. That property and house have been in the possession of the male members of the family from pioneer days until the present time. All his ancestors have been Christian people and, like himself, members of the Baptist Church, and are of Scotch and English blood. Judge Haggard is now in the prime of life, full of mental and physical vigor, and has the promise of a bright future before him.

TYLER W. McATEE, one of the leading business men of Owensboro, son of Benjamin L. McAtee and Margaret Wilson, was born in Bardstown, Kentucky, November 19, 1849.

Benjamin L. McAtee (father) was born in Montgomery County, Maryland, February 14, 1799; removed to Nelson County, Kentucky, in 1812, and was educated in the Bardstown schools; became a stage line contractor and ran a line of stage coaches between Louisville and Nashville and between Louisville and Crab Orchard, known as the Easton & McAtee Stage Line. He sold his interest in these lines and retired to his farm, situated within a mile of Bardstown; went south to enlist in the Confederate army in 1861, but was compelled to return on account of feeble health, and died in 1862. He married Margaret Wilson in 1841, and they had four children: Benjamin L., Mary, Emily and Tyler. Mr. McAtee was a man of very generous disposition and used his large means liberally, dispensing hospitality lavishly and lending a helping hand whenever he could do a kind turn for a friend or neighbor. He is remembered as one of the most useful citizens—a representative man of his times. His father was a native of Scotland, who came to America about the beginning of the War of the Revolution and served in the Colonial army.

Tyler W. McAtee attended the common schools of Nelson County and Cecilian College in Hardin County, before entering the St. Louis University, from which he was graduated in June, 1870. He began his successful career as a clerk in the store of Spalding & Carlisle at Bardstown, where he remained for eleven years. In 1881 he formed a partnership with Phillips Bros. at Owensboro, the firm being known as Phillips Bros. & McAtee, which is now one of the leading business houses of that city. He is largely interested in other enterprises in Owensboro, being a director in the Bank of Commerce, secretary of the Owensboro Woolen Company and stockholder in the Owensboro Wagon Company; is a Knight Templar in Masonry; a member of the Southern Presbyterian Church, and a citizen of influence and good repute.

Mr. McAtee was married in 1878 to Sallie Rountree, daughter of R. H. Rountree. She was educated in Bellwood Seminary in Jefferson County, and is one of the most accomplished ladies in Owensboro society. They have three daughters: Margaret, Wickliffe and Elizabeth.

ALEXANDER JOHN ALEXANDER, son of Hon. Robert Alexander and nephew of the late Sir William Alexander of England, was born October 7, 1824, at Woodburn, his father's estate in Woodford County, Kentucky. He went to England and completed his education at Trinity College, Cambridge, and afterwards spent some little time in the routine of a counting house to prepare himself for practical business details before returning to America. In 1849 he returned to Kentucky and for a number of years—during the lifetime of his brother, Robert Aitcheson Alexander, then owner of the ancestral estate at Woodburn—he lived in Chicago, where he still has large financial interests. At the death of his brother he inherited the Woodburn estate and the great Airdrie estate of Scotland, the latter having passed by the Scottish law of entail to Sir William Alexander of England, and at Sir William's death, by the same law of entail, the estate came into the possession of Robert Aitcheson Alexander of Woodford County, Kentucky, the income from said estate amounting at one time to one hundred thousand dollars annually. The mineral products of Airdrie estate have been much reduced in late years, but they still yield a handsome annual income.

Mr. Alexander is an extensive breeder of race and trotting horses, and his private sales of blooded stock average yearly from seventy-five to a hundred thousand dollars, and yet he is in no sense a turf man, no entries on race courses ever being made by him personally or by proxy. He is a genuine lover of blooded stock, delighting in the occupation, and ambitious to keep up the well-merited fame of the Woodburn establishment.

The extensive blue grass acres at Woodburn, laid off in the artistic old English style in groups of trees here and there on the emerald sward and picturesquely beautiful in alternate light and shadow, have been for many years associated with many of the most famous names of Kentucky's blooded stock. Among the famous trotting and racing horses which have led lives of luxurious ease at Woodburn stock farm may be mentioned Lexington, purchased by Robert Aitcheson Alexander from Richard Ten Broeck for $15,000; Scythian, an imported famous English horse; Asteroid, King Alphonso, Australian, Glen Athol, Belmont, Woodford, Mambrino and Harold. In addition to the above mentioned famous racers and trotters and others which have since become known to fame was the stock of Southdown sheep, amounting often to eleven hundred head.

In 1873 the present owner of Woodburn, at a large stock sale in New York, paid $27,000 for the Tenth Duchess of Oneida, a calf of six months, and $19,000 for the Seventh Duchess of Oneida, a yearling. He has had extensive dealings with English stockraisers and in reality is one of the greatest stockbreeders of America, that factor being equally important with the agriculturist for the healthy physical and mental development of the masses.

Mr. Alexander is a man of culture, dignified

and courteous in manner, but without the slightest ostentation in life or character. He is unswervingly honorable in his business dealings, and his private life is absolutely stainless, his natural bent of morality being strengthened by strong religious principle. He is an elder in the Southern Presbyterian Church, and recently made a most munificent donation to the Theological Seminary at Louisville in connection with that body and intended as a memorial of a beloved and promising son, deceased. He is a man of delicate health, and it is to be regretted that a more vigorous constitution has not supported his broad, energetic spirit.

He was twice married; first to Lucy Humphries, daughter of David Humphries of Woodford County; and second to Miss Fullerton of Chillicothe. They have five living children.

Hon. Robert Alexander (father), second son of William Alexander and his wife, who was a Miss Aitcheson of Airdrie House, Scotland, was born in 1767 near Edinburgh, and educated at that place. He came to America and settled in Woodford County, Kentucky, before the state was admitted to the Union. After being educated at the University of Edinburgh and while young, he went to France, where he met Benjamin Franklin, and acted as his private secretary. He came to this country in 1785 (his father having preceded him), and in 1791 bought the estate of Woodburn in Woodford County, embracing twenty-seven hundred acres of the blue grass region, from the heirs of General Hugh Mercer, who had obtained it as a military grant from Virginia.

Hon. Robert Alexander was a man of broad, enterprising spirit, ready to serve his state in any capacity and deeply interested in its welfare and prosperity. He was a member of the Kentucky River Company, the first company chartered by the state for the improvement of rivers. When the first bank of Kentucky was chartered in 1807, he was made president of it, and also served in the board of directors. He was appointed to survey and fix the western boundary line between Kentucky and Tennessee lying between the Tennessee and Mississippi rivers; and found that those who had settled the eastern part of the line had made a miscalculation, thereby depriving Kentucky of valuable territory. In 1795 he was elected to the state senate, being re-elected and serving with distinction in that body. He was one of the most thoroughly educated men of his day, but entirely unostentatious and preferred a quiet home life.

He married the daughter of Daniel Weisiger of Frankfort. They had five children: Lucy, the wife of J. B. Waller of Chicago; Alexander John; Mary, wife of H. C. Deeds of London, England; William, died in childhood, and Robert Aitcheson, late proprietor of Woodburn Stock Farm. Hon. Robert Alexander died from injuries received in a fall at Frankfort in 1841.

William Alexander (grandfather) was a native of Edinburgh, Scotland, where many of his ancestors had lived, and where, in the seventeenth century, his father (the great-grandfather of A. J. Alexander) attained to the dignity of lord provost of that city. His first wife was Miss Aitcheson of Airdrie House, Scotland, and belonged to a family of considerable wealth and distinction in Lanark and Renfrew Shires in the west of Scotland. After her death he came to the United States and was married, the second time, to Miss Laport. He died in 1819 at the age of ninety on his son's estate of Woodburn in Woodford County. His eldest son, by his first marriage, Sir William Alexander, was a lawyer of very high standing and was elected to the bench as one of the barons of the Court of Exchequer, and knighted for distinguished services rendered the crown. He was never married.

RICHARD L. EWELL, a leading lawyer and Christian minister of London, son of Thomas M. Ewell and Miranda Fox, was born in Knox County, Kentucky, January 26, 1833. His father was born in the same county, where he married, and soon after the birth of the subject of this sketch went West to seek his fortune and was never heard from again.

Leighton Ewell (grandfather) was a native of Virginia, where he married and then came to Kentucky and joined the early settlers of Knox County; was sheriff of the county in 1830; removed to Ray County, Missouri, and died there in 1842, aged about sixty-five years. He was related to General Ewell of Virginia, a distinguished officer in the Civil war.

Miranda Fox Ewell (mother) was born in Knox County, Kentucky, April 30, 1816, and died in Laurel County, March 17, 1888. She was a member of the Baptist Church and was chiefly noted for her piety and goodness of heart.

Benjamin Fox (maternal grandfather) was born near Richmond, Virginia, and was stolen by the gypsies when a child and was never recovered or identified by his relatives. He was one of the earliest settlers of Knox County, where he lived until 1836, when he removed to Davis County, near Gallatin, Missouri, where he died in 1839, leaving a very valuable estate, considering the times and the peculiar experiences of his earlier years.

Richard L. Ewell attended school for a period of six months and fifteen days all told, but he was of a studious turn of mind, and with a thirst for knowledge he pursued his studies, reading by the traditional torch-light, and picked up a fair English education. Reared on a farm, he followed that occupation, which he understood better than any other, until the call for soldiers; and in October, 1861, he enlisted in the Union army, as a private in Company H, Twenty-fourth Regiment Kentucky Infantry, and served throughout the war, or until January 31, 1865, when he was mustered out of the service in Covington, having never lost a day from duty. In the later part of his service he was a Lieutenant, but for the most part he served in the ranks.

Returning to his home in Laurel County, he resumed farming, which he followed for one year; and in 1866 was elected clerk of the Circuit Court and in 1867 was elected County Clerk and performed the duties of both offices until 1874.

In the meantime he had read law and in September, 1874, he was admitted to the bar and made an argument in a murder case the same term in which he was sworn in as an attorney. And thus he began his career as an attorney-at-law—in the forty-first year of his age—in which he has been highly successful. His practice has steadily grown until he is one of the best known lawyers in Laurel and adjacent counties. He also has a valuable practice in the United States Courts and in the Kentucky Court of Appeals.

In 1890 Mr. Ewell was superintendent of the census in the Sixth Kentucky District. He is associated with his son-in-law, James D. Smith, in the practice of law, and they are largely interested in real estate transactions and are the owners of fifteen thousand acres of fine timber and coal lands in Kentucky.

Mr. Ewell has been a member of the Christian Church since 1859 and a preacher in that denomination, having preached the gospel at all times and in all places within his call, and in this work of love for the Christian religion he is as distinguished as he is as a lawyer. He has never used tobacco or taken a drink of whisky and is a strong advocate and example of temperance. In politics he has been an uncompromising Republican since the organization of that party.

Mr. Ewell was married, first, in 1853 to Burnetta Watkins, daughter of Luke W. Watkins of Missouri. She died March 1, 1865, leaving three sons and two daughters: America A., wife of James D. Smith, attorney-at-law of London (partner); Dr. Silas W. Ewell of Carroll County, Missouri; Alice, wife of Robert M. Jackson, cashier of the First National Bank of London; James A. Ewell, publisher and editor of two newspapers in Ritsville, Washington, and Richard R. Ewell, a farmer in Laurel County.

Mr. Ewell was married (second) May 1, 1866, to Julia A. Johnson, daughter of George W. Johnson of Laurel County, and has five children by this marriage; John H.; George W.; Robert L.; Logan M. and Pocahontas, wife of McCalla Fitzgerald, who is connected with the First National Bank of London.

HON. THOMAS F. PORTER, lawyer, was born in Richmond, Madison County, Kentucky, July 7, 1821. He received a thorough education at Richmond and in the schools of Bourbon County and at the age of nineteen entered the law department of Transylvania University, where he graduated in 1842, soon after locating in Versailles, Woodford County, to practice his chosen profession, and where he still resides. He early established a fine law practice and has been engaged in every important case occurring in his district almost from the very outset of his professional career. In 1853 he was elected by a large majority to represent his county in the Legislature. In 1857 he became the candidate of his party for the State Senate and although the Democracy had a minority in the district of six hundred votes and he was opposed in the race by the learned and popular Dr. Lewis Marshall, after a most exciting contest he was elected by a majority of thirty-nine votes. In the session of 1859 he was elected Speaker of the Senate to fill the place made vacant by the illness of Hon. Lynn Boyd, who had just been elected Lieutenant-Governor on the Democratic ticket. After the death of the Hon. Lynn Boyd, December 17, 1859, he at once honorably resigned the Speakership and on December 25 was unanimously elected as permanent Speaker of the Senate, presiding over that body with marked executive ability during the regular and many called sessions incident to the perilous times preceding the outbreak of the war between the states, and remaining ex-officio Lieutenant-Governor of the state until the adjournment of the Legislature sine die in 1861. He was nominated in the following April as a member of the projected famous Border State Convention and canvassed the eastern portion of the state in the interest of the project, but the purpose of the convention was not favorably received by the government, and the President of the United States having called on the Governor for troops the convention was considered impracticable and the nominees withdrew. He then became a candidate for re-election to the State Senate as the nominee of the Southern element in his district, but was defeated. About this time on account of his strongly avowed Southern sympathies he was compelled to leave the state and spent a few months in Nashville and New Orleans and although he returned and resumed the practice of his profession he was one of the most extreme and absolutely fearless advocates of the doctrine of states rights in the country. When Kentucky decided to remain in the Union, being unwilling to participate in a struggle against his state, he took no active part in the great contest, but underwent, as a friend to the South, many hardships and discourtesies incident to the stormy times of fraternal strife.

His career as President of the Senate was a signally honorable and brilliant one and the fairness and strict impartiality with which he discharged the duties of his office in the times that tried men's souls abundantly proved his catholicity of spirit, and his uncompromising adherence to principle as well as his thorough parliamentary finesse. At the close of his services as presiding officer of the Senate, in token of personal esteem and as indicative of the high value put upon his official record, he received from the Senate, through the hands of his old political adversary, General Rousseau, a beautiful and costly gift. The instances are worthy of note when a man for the general service of the state can successfully divorce himself from individual personal bias and rise above environment.

Mr. Porter has immense professional pride in the strict maintenance of the highest standard of the legal profession. He takes a warm personal interest in his clients and their cases, devoting to them his time and unstinted energies and conducting all his professional transactions on the highest principles of individual honorable responsibility. He appears to great advantage in a court room, is a lucid and forcible speaker, indulging in few fanciful flights and dealing directly with the points at issue, no crumb of evidence escaping his keen, logical observance and professional acumen. He is a singularly self-reliant man, his native pluck enforced by the substantial acquirements of a diversity of talent and his social qualities, his dignified ease of manner companionable, yet entirely removed from familiarity, make him equally as strong in society as in his profession.

Governor Porter has been twice married, first in 1846 to America McAfee. By this marriage he had one daughter, the wife of W. H. Craig, a merchant of Louisville, Kentucky. In 1848 he was again married to Susan V. Hancock, daughter of William Hancock of Woodford County. By this marriage there is living one child, the accomplished Jessamine Porter, who was a pupil of Emille Gramonte of New York.

Charles Porter (father) was a native of Virginia and emigrated with his parents to Kentucky early in the history of the state, living in Madison County until the subject of this sketch was thirteen years old, and then removing to a farm in Bourbon County. The history of the Porter family is this: Three brothers of this name who had followed the fortunes of the house of Campbell in the Highlands of Scotland came to this country in an early day, one of them settling in Pennsylvania, another in Virginia, and still another in Tennessee. From them are descended the Porters of their respective states, many of whom have been prominent in the affairs of the country.

JOHN L. CONN, a leading physician of Carrollton, son of Thomas Conn and Catherine Bradshaw, was born in Bardstown, Kentucky, October 8, 1859. His father was born in Jefferson County, and removed to Union County when he was a young man, and was a resident and farmer of that county until 1857, when he removed to Bardstown, where he lived the remainder of his days and died at the age of seventy years. His life was principally devoted to farming, but he was also engaged for a time in merchandising. He was for many years a member of the Christian Church, in which he was an active worker and a devout worshiper.

Jack Conn (grandfather), a native of Virginia, of Scotch-Irish descent, came to Jefferson County, Kentucky, when Louisville was a small village, and purchased land—as the records will show—which is now a part of the site of that city. He was a farmer and died there, aged seventy-eight years.

Catherine Bradshaw Conn (mother) was a native of Shelby County and died in 1885, aged sixty-five years. Her father, John Bradshaw, was a native of Bourbon County, of English ancestry; was a resident of Shelby County for many years, and died there.

Dr. Conn was reared in Bardstown, where he attended school, and finished his educational studies at a select school in Carrollton, under the teaching of Prof. J. T. English; read medicine with Dr. Prentice Meade of Carrollton and attended the Ohio Medical College at Cincinnati, from which he graduated in 1882; practiced medicine in Carrollton for about two years; removed to Anchorage, Jefferson County, and practiced in that vicinity until the winter of 1890, when he went to New York and attended the lectures at the Polyclinic College. Returning in the spring of 1892, he located in the city of Louisville, corner of Clay and Broadway; was engaged in the general practice of medicine in that city for one year, when, in 1892, he located permanently in Carrollton and formed a partnership with his preceptor, Dr. Prentice Meade. This pleasant and profitable relation was dissolved by the death of the senior partner in 1893, since which time Dr. Conn alone has been attending to the duties which formerly devolved upon the firm—having succeeded to the large practice of Dr. Meade, who was one of the most popular and efficient physicians in the city. Dr. Conn has met with most excellent success in his profession, and has established himself in the confidence of the people. He is quite active in politics and was chairman of the district convention which nominated Hon. Al Berry for congress; was elected a member of the school board in 1894, and is deeply interested in the cause of education, and in all matters pertaining to the advancement of his city and county.

EDWARD HENRY HOBSON, Senior Vice-Commander-in-Chief of the Grand Army of the Republic, railroad president, Republican politician and a leading citizen of Greensburg, is a son of Captain William and Lucy Kirtley Hobson and was born in Greensburg, Green County, Kentucky, July 11, 1825. He was given the advantages of a common school education at Greensburg and was for a short time in a school at Danville.

At the age of eighteen years he engaged in the mercantile business at Greensburg and looked after his father's interests on Green River. While engaged in these peaceful pursuits war was declared with Mexico and the young man, fired with inherited patriotic ardor, enlisted in Company A, Second Kentucky Infantry, and was elected Second Lieutenant of the company. In June, 1846, the regiment left Louisville on board the old steamer "Sultana" and was hurried on toward the scene of action. Soon after reaching Mexico Lieutenant Hobson's company was selected as escort for the supply train from Seralvo to General Taylor's army, then before the strong works at Monterey. This was a charge of great responsibility, showing the confidence placed in Mr. Hobson by his superior officers.

During the battle of Buena Vista his company was engaged in fighting along the line as heavy infantry and was four times detached as riflemen to repel the enemy's advances. At one time when detached from the main line, with sixty men Lieutenant Hobson was attacked by three hundred Mexican infantry. He defeated and pursued them until recalled by Colonel McKee for the final charge on the Mexican forces. In the night after the battle of the twenty-third, Lieutenant Hobson and his men bore in their arms the mangled remains of Colonels McKee and Clay to the camp on the battlefield. For his undaunted courage in this terrible engagement he was promoted to the rank of First Lieutenant. The regiment was in active service after the battle of Buena Vista until it returned to New Orleans, where it was mustered out of the service in June, 1847.

After his return from Mexico Mr. Hobson resumed his mercantile business. His bright military record, his fine business qualifications and personal integrity have obtained for him many positions of honor and trust. Like his father, he was and is an enthusiastic Mason, and held the position of Deputy Grand Master of the Masonic order for the state of Kentucky. He is a strong advocate of the common school system and for a long time was president of the Board of Trustees in Greensburg, and has always been deeply interested in the many industries and enterprises for the building up and development of the country.

When war for the suppression of the rebellion was declared he was president of the Branch Bank of Kentucky at Greensburg, having succeeded Mr. John Barret in that position. When the state was invaded by the Confederate forces under General Buckner in the fall of 1861, on the approach of the advance column, Mr. Hobson collected the bank funds—gold, silver and currency to the amount of $140,000, and, on horseback at night with five companions, carried the money to Lebanon, boarded a train and delivered the whole amount to Virgil McKnight, cashier of the Bank of Kentucky at Louisville. Mr. McKnight assured him that he was the only officer in all of the branch banks south of Louisville who had brought or sent him a dollar belonging to the bank.

When the war between the states seemed inevitable, Mr. Hobson was appointed by Simon Cameron, who was Secretary of War, Colonel of the Second Regiment Kentucky Infantry, and later on he recruited and was in command of the Thirteenth Kentucky Infantry, and assisted in organizing the Twenty-first and Twenty-seventh Infantry Regiments. His command was one of the first to move against the enemy at Shiloh; and for gallantry on that sanguinary field, April 7, 1862, he was promoted to the rank of Brigadier-General. As for other engagements, he was at the siege of Corinth and contributed largely to the success of the Union arms in that contest. At Perryville he commanded a special brigade and afterwards defeated the attempt to burn the railroad bridge at Munfordville during Morgan's first raid in Kentucky.

General Hobson was assigned to the command of the Southern Central Kentucky Division with headquarters at Munfordville, and while in command of this department had several engagements with Morgan and repulsed that famous cavalry leader at Marrowbone. From this place Gen. Hobson pursued Morgan a distance of nine hundred miles, being in the saddle twenty-one days with not over forty hours' rest, and overtook the raiders at Buffington Island, and broke them up, capturing, wounding and killing many of Morgan's command.

General Hobson also conducted a successful campaign against General Adam Johnson, completely annihilating his forces on the Cumberland River and breaking the Confederate control in Southwestern Kentucky. He was in the expedition to the Salt Works in Virginia and during this time his men lived on pawpaws, the General sharing their privations, a fact that endeared him greatly to his soldiers. The mountain campaign was a series of brilliant military tactics and strategic movements, and by the skillful handling of the troops he virtually saved the army. In this campaign the ability of General Hobson as a military commander was fully attested to the entire satisfaction of the government authorities, his troops and his superior officers.

General Hobson was twice wounded; in March, 1862, at Spring Hill, Tennessee, when drilling his regiment in the presence of General Buell and other Generals of the corps, his horse became unmanageable and fell backwards on him, fracturing one of the bones of his right leg; and still, with his injured leg swollen to twice its natural size, on the morning of April 6, when twenty miles from Shiloh, his men placed him on his horse and amid the wildest cheers he led them to their place in the line of battle, where they were engaged in the thickest of the second day's fighting at Shiloh. During this engagement General Hobson's horse was thrown under him and injured by the concussion of a bomb, but was not killed and the General remounted and rode him until the close of the battle. He closed his fighting in this battle by charging and capturing a six-gun battery and narrowly escaped from the successful exploit with his life, his clothing being cut and pierced by the enemy's bullets. His second wound was received during an encounter with Morgan at Kellass' Bridge, Kentucky, where he was shot in the elbow in consequence of which his left arm was paralyzed for several weeks. But he continued to perform cavalry service with his wounded arm resting in a sling. He has never recovered from the effects of this wound.

After the close of the war General Hobson returned to Greensburg and again engaged in mercantile pursuits. In 1869 President Grant appointed him Collector for the Fourth Kentucky Revenue District and he held this position for five years. He was a promoter of the Southern Division of the Cumberland & Ohio Railroad and succeeded in building the branch road from Greensburg to Lebanon, and is now president of that railroad company.

General Hobson was one of the organizers of the Republican party, and has been an acknowledged leader in state politics since the days when it was hardly safe for a Republican to express his sentiments in Kentucky.

He takes much interest in the affairs of the Grand Army of the Republic, and the year (1892-3) he was Commander of the Department of Kentucky—which position was given him unsolicited—was the most successful year for the Grand Army in Kentucky. At the Twenty-ninth Annual National Encampment of the Grand Army held in Louisville, September 8 to 13, 1895, General Hobson was elected Senior Vice-Commander-in-Chief. He belongs to the Union Veteran Legion and the Union Veterans' Union, also the Loyal Legion Commandery of Ohio; and wherever and whenever there is an organization or movement or demonstration in memory of the soldiers or the perpetuation of loyal sentiments he is with it heart and soul.

General Hobson was married October 12, 1847, to Kate Adair, daughter of Alexander and Elizabeth (Monroe) Adair. Her father was of Scotch-Irish descent and served as the first marshal of the territory of Florida. She was a niece of Governor Adair of Kentucky, and her mother was a sister of Judges T. B. and Benjamin Monroe. She was a native of Florida and was educated at Danville and Frankfort, Kentucky. She was a member of the Presbyterian Church, and died June 18, 1872. Their children were: William A. Hobson (deceased); Annie May Hobson, wife of B. W. Penick, of Greensburg; Atwood Monroe (lately deceased); John A., merchant at Greensburg; Edwena, at home, and Bettie K., wife of L. C. Alcorn of Greensburg.

Captain William Hobson (father) was born in Virginia, January, 1788. His mother died when he was very young, and his father being in indigent circumstances, he was taken charge of by his uncle, Jonathan Patterson, who removed to Green County, Kentucky, in 1796, bringing William with him, who was about seven years of age. He was apprenticed to Thomas R. Slaughter at Greensburg to learn the trade of harness and saddle making; and, having completed his term of apprenticeship, went to Danville and devoted himself for a few months exclusively to the common branches of an English education. Being then deprived of means to complete his schooling on account of the death of his uncle, he was compelled to leave school for the work-bench and went to Nashville, Tennessee, where he worked as journeyman saddler until he had accumulated some means and then returned to Greensburg and commenced business for himself, making his home there until his death.

He was an officer in the War of 1812, and served with distinction in General William Henry Harrison's campaign against the Indians on the Northwestern frontier. In times of peace, during many years he filled various town and county offices, and upon the establishment of an independent bank in Greensburg in 1818 he was elected one of the directors. For sixteen years, with only short intervals, he was director of the Branch Bank of Kentucky at Greensburg. For forty years he was a trustee of the town of Greensburg, and was generally president of the board, elected to the office without a dissenting vote. At the first election under the new Constitution (1850) Captain Hobson was almost unanimously elected Justice of the Peace, although there were four or five other candidates of high standing, and he held that office during life. He was a zealous Mason and treasurer of both chapter and council from their first organization in Greensburg; was also one of the trustees of New Athens Seminary for a number of years, and was, in short, almost indispensable to every enterprise in Greensburg that had for its object the promotion of the public weal. His record whether as a private citizen or public official was characterized by pure morality, strict integrity, disinterested benevolence, industrious habits and correct judgment. He died April 6, 1853, and in respect to his memory the Masonic fraternity at Greensburg erected a monument over his grave.

Lucy Kirtley Hobson (mother) was born November 8, 1793, and when she died was the oldest member of the Methodist Church in her section of the country. When a girl she came over the old Wilderness Road on horseback from Virginia to Kentucky. She was one of those pioneer women to whom the present generation owe so much of grateful remembrance.

Her parents, Thomas Kirtley and Judiath Lewis Kirtley, settled in Green County, Kentucky, where her father was a farmer and died in 1818. His wife died November 9, 1820, and both of them are interred in the old burial ground eight miles from Greensburg. Lucy Kirtley married Captain William Hobson, March 14, 1814, and had seven children, three of whom are living: A. G. Hobson, banker at Bowling Green; General E. H. Hobson and Luvenia M., who married Charles D. Allen. The other sons and daughters, now deceased, were Eliza, who married James D. Montley; James Thomas; Alonzo Thomas; Lucy Ann and W. J. Hobson.

Many facts of interest in the life of General Hobson are necessarily omitted from the foregoing sketch, particularly those concerning his military record, a complete outline of which would make a volume. But this will serve the main purpose of a work of this character, which is to place on record the names and character of men who have distinguished themselves in the service of their state and country, or have faithfully performed their duty in whatever station their lot may have been cast.

HENRY CLAY BOHON, cashier of the First National Bank of Harrodsburg, Mercer County, Kentucky, is the son of W. F. Bohon and Virginia Hutcherson Bohon; was born March 20, 1845, in Monticello, and was educated at the Kentucky University, when it was located at Harrodsburg. After leaving school in 1864 he entered business with his father and in March, 1873, took full control with Smith Hansford. The firm name was Bohon & Hansford, in Harrodsburg, until May, 1884. In that year he was elected cashier of the First National Bank, which position he now holds. This bank was organized twenty-three years ago, and is now running under an extended charter. Mr. Bohon was President of the Kentucky Sunday School Union for ten years; is now County President of the Kentucky Sunday School Union, and has been Superintendent of the Christian Church Sabbath School for fifteen years. He is an honorary member of the State Confederate Association, and is a man of pleasing address, and readily makes friends of all thrown in contact with him. While his industry and unswerving integrity merit the success he has achieved his many fine qualities of head and heart command the respect and esteem of the entire community.

Mr. Bohon married Miss Sallie Knight, daughter of Grant L. Knight of Jessamine County, Kentucky, December 15, 1869. She was born July 1, 1847; educated at St. Catherine, Marion County, Kentucky, at Daughter's College, Harrodsburg, and at Danville, Kentucky. They have five children: Mary, married Stephenson Haydon of Harrodsburg, now living at Lawrenceburg, Kentucky; Annie Belle, Nora and Nannie, who were educated at Daughter's College, and Henry Clay, Jr., now at Harrodsburg Academy.

W. F. Bohon (father) was born in Mercer County, Kentucky, October, 1812, and was educated in the schools of the county. He farmed for a while and was then in mercantile life for fifteen years. In 1857 came to Harrodsburg, and lived there until three years before his death, April 5, 1873; was a member of the Presbyterian Church, and a Democrat in politics. He married a descendant of the Owsley family of Kentucky, and was the father of seven children: Henry Clay; Dr. J. T. Bohon of Lincoln County; W. J. Bohon of Danville; George Bohon of Harrodsburg; R. S. Bohon of Decatur, Illinois; Elizabeth, wife of Linn W. Hudson; Mattie, wife of H. H. Peacock, Dallas, Texas. John Bohon (grandfather) lived in Mercer County, Kentucky.

GRANT GREEN, cashier of the Farmers' Bank of Kentucky, Frankfort, son of John Green and Martha Dixon, was born in Henderson County, Kentucky, February 3, 1826. His ancestors were from Fauquier County, Virginia, where the progenitor of the family in this country, coming from England, settled in 1717. His grandfather raised a large family of children, many of whom performed distinguished service for their country. All of the male members who were old enough to bear arms at the time joined the army and fought for American Independence.

Mr. Green's grandfather, Gabriel Green, came to Kentucky in 1815 and located in Henderson County, and was a Lieutenant in the Revolutionary army. His son, John Green (father), married Martha Dixon, daughter of Captain Henry Dixon, whose father was a Colonel in the Revolutionary war. She was eleven years old when her father came from Caswell County, North Carolina, to Henderson County, Kentucky. Their marriage was celebrated in 1820 and Mr. Green died in 1829, leaving four children to the care of his widow. He left no estate and it was a hard trial for the mother to provide properly for her children, but with almost superhuman effort, great endurance and self-denial, sacrificing every pleasure but that of caring for her children, she performed her task and brought her family to a position in the social and business world, of which she was justly proud. She educated them in the best schools of the day and brought them up to understand and appreciate the importance of industry and determined effort.

Grant Green, second son of this noble woman, began active life as a teacher in the school in which he had been a pupil, taking the place of teacher before his former classmates of his own age had finished their school days. In this he was very successful, and gave great satisfaction to pupils and patrons. His uncle, William Green, was Sheriff of the county in 1848, and he gave up teaching, reluctantly, to serve as deputy sheriff, which occupied him for two years; was then deputy clerk of the County and Circuit Courts and served until 1851, when he was nominated by the Democratic party for representative in the Legislature and elected. The sessions of that body were noted for the arduous labors, keen foresight and wisdom of the members. It was the second session following the adoption of the new constitution and the laws then existing had to be modified and changed and new laws enacted to conform to the Constitution. This Legislature was one of the ablest that ever met in Frankfort, performing its labors in a most satisfactory manner.

Mr. Green was appointed Assistant Secretary of State February 26, 1852, and afterward Secretary of State, by Governor Powell, who had defeated Archibald Dixon, the Whig candidate, and a cousin of Mr. Green. He served in that office until the expiration of Governor Powell's term of office, September 3, 1855. In the meantime he was a member of the Democratic State Central Committee, and in 1855 he was nominated for Superintendent of Public Instruction, but the entire Democratic ticket was defeated by the Know-Nothing party in that campaign, and Mr. Green returned to Henderson and began the practice of law with H. F. Turner; was elected County Judge in 1858; was elected State Auditor in 1859, and, resigning his seat on the bench, returned to Frankfort, January 1, 1860; and during the trying times of the war he managed the state finances with ability and giving universal satisfaction. The Legislative committee appointed at his request to examine his office at the close of his term made a very complimentary report of the management and condition of the office. He was defeated for a second term only through the interference of the Federal troops in the election (1864), and even then by a very small margin.

Returning to Henderson in 1864 he was engaged in the tobacco business for two years, when he associated himself with others in banking under the firm name of Green, Marshall & Co., and in May, 1868, was appointed cashier of the Farmers' Bank of Kentucky, at Frankfort, a position he has held for twenty-eight years, and in which he may continue as long as he lives or cares to give his attention to business. The stock of the Farmers' Bank was worth eighty-three cents on the dollar, when he took charge, and it was not long until it was worth its face value, and the bank is to-day one of the strongest in the state. This is the record, in brief, of one of the best men living in Kentucky to-day. It would be superfluous to add words of praise or comment upon a career that has been and is an open book. His life and his work have been largely in the service of the public, and he has performed every duty with fidelity, integrity and singleness of purpose, leaving no page in his history upon which he cannot look and point others to with pride and satisfaction.

Mr. Green was united in marriage February 28, 1855, with Kate S. Overton of Fayette County, Kentucky, a member of a distinguished family in Virginia, Kentucky and Tennessee. They have four children living: Henry Dixon, the oldest son, was drowned in the Ohio river at Henderson in 1867, at the age of ten years; Eliza Overton, the oldest daughter, married George B. Alexman of Greenville, Mississippi, and has one child, Grant Green Alexman; Grant Green, Jr., married Joe Gray of Woodford County, and they have four children; Dr. Walter O. Green, the third son, is a practicing physician in Louisville; Kate Overton, the second daughter, married William Raymond Worrall of New York; John Taylor, the fourth son, is pursuing his studies in Vanderbilt University, Nashville, Tennessee.

Martha Dixon Green (mother) was a daughter of Captain Henry Dixon, who was born in Caswell County, North Carolina, in 1777. He was a brother of Wynn Dixon, who was the father of Governor Archibald Dixon (see sketch of Dr. Archibald Dixon in this work). Captain Hal Dixon, as he was better known, came to Kentucky in 1808 and lived in Henderson County until 1853, when he removed to Union County, and died at Sulphur Springs in November, 1858. He was a remarkably large and muscular man, weighing ordinarily from 225 to 250 pounds; a man of indomitable will and absolutely without fear; very industrious and attentive to business; was for Jackson, against Clay and served one term in the legislature, but was not much inclined to politics. He married Mary Johnson of Virginia, who bore him twelve children, of whom the mother of Grant Green was the second child. The children of John Green and Martha Dixon were: Dr. Dixon Green (deceased), who married Miss Lambert of Arkansas, and second Miss Swift of Tennessee; Grant Green; John W. Green, who married Miss Randolph of Henderson County, and Mary Ann, deceased, who married Theodore Hall.

Henry Dixon, father of Captain Hal Dixon, was a Colonel in the Revolutionary War; was highly complimented for gallantry at the battle of Camden and died from wounds received in the battle of Eutaw Springs. Judge Schenk in his History of North Carolina, 1780-81, calls him "the Chevalier Bayard of the Revolutionary War," and compliments his action in the battle of Camden in these words: "Perhaps the most brilliant officer whose services enriched the annals of that memorable invasion was Major Hal Dixon, whose daring and impetuous course was so splendidly displayed among the scattered legions of Yates at Camden. He refused to fly when his comrades had been driven from the field and his devoted band had been left exposed to the bayonet charge on the front and flank. With a fine spirit, he faced his battalion to the charge from either side and fought as long as a cartridge was in his belt, then resorting to the bayonet himself, he cut his way through the attacking forces and made good his retreat."

HORACE W. TWISS, attorney for the Watts Steel and Iron Syndicate of Middlesboro, Kentucky, son of Quintin Twiss and Fannie Covey, was born in London, England, March 24, 1865, was reared in London and educated at Kings School in Canterbury; after leaving school he traveled in France and Germany for two years; returning to his home, studied law and was admitted to practice in London; became solicitor in 1890 and continued in the practice of law in his native city until 1892, when he came direct to Middlesborough, where millions of dollars of English money have been invested, and engaged in the practice of law in the new city. He is especially qualified for the legal work of the corporations doing business in and developing the great resources of Middlesborough and vicinity, and is employed especially as attorney for the Watts Steel and Iron Syndicate of Middlesborough. He has found other business in the practice of his profession and is now thoroughly established in his new home, the surroundings of which are in striking contrast with the scenes of his youth in the great city of London.

Before coming to America Mr. Twiss was married (1892) to Lilian Simms, daughter of Henry Simms of Bath, England, and they are members of the Episcopal Church of Middlesborough.

Quintin Twiss, father of Horace W. Twiss, a native of London, England, was employed in her majesty's treasury for thirty-five years, and is now retired and living in London, in the sixty-first year of his age. He is a devout member of the Church of England, as is his wife, who is also a native of London.

Horace Twiss (grandfather), also a native of London, was a distinguished barrister of the Queen's Council; was a member of Lord Beaconsfield's government, and came from a talented family. John Kemble was this grandfather's uncle, and Mrs. Siddons, the greatest actress England ever produced, was his aunt.

William Covey, the maternal grandfather of Horace W. Twiss, a native of Oxbridge, was a very prominent physician of London, where he died in 1888, aged seventy-five years.

This modest sketch of a scholarly gentleman of the highest legal attainments is intended to introduce Mr. Twiss to the people of Kentucky, with whom he has become identified in the development of the hidden resources of the mountains.

JOSEPH BARBOUR of New Castle, ex-Judge of the Superior Court of Kentucky, son of Joseph Barbour and Nancy Marshall Samuels, was born in Carroll County, Kentucky, in April, 1844, and educated at the Male High School, Paducah, Kentucky, and at Poughkeepsie, New York, but did not graduate from any literary institution. In 1866 he entered the Louisville Law School, from which he graduated in one year, and commenced the practice of law at New Castle, where he resided until 1886, when he was elected Judge of the Superior Court, never having previously aspired to office. He was re-elected in 1890 and was on the Superior bench until that court was abolished by the new Constitution, January, 1895. He then resumed the practice of law at New Castle, and is one of the leading lawyers in Kentucky. He is an active and a deeply interested politician, having been a delegate to many state conventions, and is a writer of great force and ability, wielding a ready and trenchant pen; was associated with J. D. Carroll in the compilation of the statutes of Kentucky, and is the author of Barbour's Digest of Kentucky Decisions, considered an authority by the bench and bar of the state. Mr. Barbour was married (first) in 1874 to Mary Webb, daughter of Hon. J. W,

Webb, a native of Henry County, and a prominent lawyer and politician. She was born and educated in New Castle. There were four children by this marriage: Levine, Webb, Nannie and Willie. In 1887 he was married (second) to Mrs. Sallie Chenault, whose maiden name was Webb, widow of Dr. Walker Chenault of Richmond, Kentucky.

Joseph Barbour (father) was a native of New York, but of Virginia ancestry. He was born in 1795 and educated in New York, and came to Carroll County, Kentucky, in 1840, where he had a contract to build the locks and dams on the Kentucky River. In the summer of 1844 he moved to Paducah, built large mills and was engaged in the milling business for a number of years. After that he was extensively engaged in farming in Marshall County. He was a man of broad public spirit and brought his remarkable energy to the furtherance of every public enterprise. He was a Whig in politics and also a strong secessionist, belonging to that old school of politicians denominated "fire-eaters" because of their extreme views. He died just at the beginning of the Civil War, April 8, 1861. He was married in 1842 to Nancy Marshall Samuels, whose grandfather was a nephew of Chief Justice Marshall.

JUDGE FONTAINE TALBOT FOX, late distinguished lawyer and jurist of Danville, Boyle County, Kentucky, son of William and Sophie Irvine Fox, was born January 28, 1803, near Richmond, Kentucky. He was educated at Nicholasville, at an academy taught by a Scotchman by the name of Reed, and studied law under Hon. Charles Cunningham. He was admitted to the bar in 1824 and commenced the practice of law at Somerset, but afterwards removed to Stanford, Lincoln County, Kentucky. In 1831 he was appointed by Governor Metcalfe to the office of Commonwealth Attorney for the Twelfth Judicial District. He was afterwards elected to this office by the people and held it many years, but after he gave it up he would never accept a case to prosecute any man. He was during his lifetime concerned in an immense amount of litigation extending over the entire state of Kentucky, and it is said of him that he probably made more money from the legitimate practice of law than any man of his time in the state. He lived lavishly, but did not accumulate a fortune because of his sympathetic, benevolent nature. In 1834 he ran for Congress as a Whig against Sherrod Williams, but was defeated because of the Whig vote being divided by Adam Beatty running as an independent. In 1836 he represented Pulaski County in the Legislature and Lincoln County in 1844. In 1855, having removed to Danville, Kentucky, he consented reluctantly to become the standard-bearer of his party—the Know-Nothings—in the Congressional contest, his opponent being the Hon. Albert Gallatin Talbot; but was again defeated. There was a bitter fight made against him by the Catholic and foreign element, and an immense amount of money used on the opposing side. There is a belief to this day in the district that he was rightfully entitled to the office.

In 1862 he was elected Circuit Judge of the Eighth Judicial District, which office he held until he resigned it in 1881. As an indication of his hold upon the people of his district, after he had resigned the office of Circuit Judge on account of age and feeble health, and when he was not a candidate for the office various county precincts voted for him solidly for Judge, declaring they would have no other.

Judge Fox was a man of incorruptible and exalted public and private character and possessed a personality as unique and clear cut as some masterpiece of art. He was never heard to utter an unkind word of any human being, choosing to be silent when he could not speak favorably, and with him friendship was a sentiment beautiful in its tenderness and phenomenal in its fidelity. As a citizen his heart and hand to a fault were responsive to every project for the public good. He was devoted to his family, often riding sixty-five and seventy miles on horseback over rough mountain roads in order to spend the Sabbath day with them and joining in the sports of his children with the zest of a boy. As a lawyer he had an exalted conception of the system of jurisprudence, recognizing its divine origin and prerogatives, and was faithful to the uttermost detail of its responsibility. He was called the widows' and orphans' friend, and the friend of the friendless, his heart of womanly tenderness bleeding or rejoicing over the misfortunes or welfare of his clients. As a jurist from a purely judicial standpoint, a cotemporary in the legal profession said, "That his judicial rulings, compared with the common run of judicial rulings, was like a clear stream of water running beside a muddy one."

In his personal responsibility as a jurist his character can best be summed up in his own words, when he delivered his decision in the famous Center College case of 1866: "My prejudices, my interests, my desires and my hopes are with the plaintiff, but my decision is a judgment in favor of the defendant."

As an orator he was magnetic and persuasive, and as a pleader at the bar, he possessed wonderful influence over a jury. In his social attributes, his conversational powers clear, epigrammatic, forcible, sparkling with wit and humor and anecdote and mellowed by sentiment, he was without a peer. In politics Judge Fox was originally an old-line Whig, but after the fusion of that party with the Republican he became an ardent Democrat.

In religion, he was a Presbyterian. He died April 7, 1887, and is buried at Danville, Kentucky. He married Eliza J. Hunton, daughter of Thomas and Ann Bell Hunton of Albemarle County, Virginia, where she was born November 21, 1809. Her father died soon after she came to Kentucky, leaving his widow in affluent circumstances.

Her three brothers were equally distinguished in the legal professions of Missouri and Louisiana.

Judge Logan Hunton was the author of the celebrated Allison letter that is accredited with the election of General Zachary Taylor, President of the United States. He declined a cabinet position under General Taylor, which was offered him in recognition of his services, and was made United States District Attorney for the state of Louisiana, a position more agreeable to himself and family. He amassed a large fortune.

Mrs. Fox is a woman of the old school, the type so rapidly passing off the stage of action. Womanly, home-loving, with great strength of mind and character dominated by religious principle, her influence for good is recognized and appreciated by all. She is a consistent member of the Presbyterian Church and was for many years president of the Ladies' Aid Society of her church. They had ten children who grew to maturity—the first, Thomas Fox, lawyer by profession, living at Danville. He was married, first, to Henrietta Clay Wilson, a widow and daughter of Judge Gist of Montgomery County, Kentucky. By this marriage he has two daughters: Eliza, now Mrs. John Rogers, living near Lexington, and Susan Fox, who resides at Danville. Mr. Fox was married, second, to Mary Moberly of Boyle County, Kentucky.

William McKee Fox (deceased), lawyer, represented Pulaski County in the Legislature for two terms and ran for the nomination of his party for Attorney-General of Kentucky, against Rodman, the incumbent. He also made a race for the Congressional nomination in 1878 and was defeated by a proxy vote. He was drowned in the Cumberland River. He was a man of brilliant mental parts with an all pervading personal magetism. It was said of him editorially in the Courier-Journal: "A typical Kentuckian, brave, impulsive, generous to a fault; genial, eloquent, ready, equally strong in society as in his profession, the man never lived with bigger heart or brighter intellect. He bent himself seriously to nothing that he did not illumine and wherever he appeared he was surrounded with a host of admiring associates."

Peter C. Fox (deceased), lawyer, was Major of Scott's Louisiana Cavalry on the side of the South during the war of the states. After the war he became a turf man and elevated his vocation—was extremely popular.

Judge Fontaine T. Fox, lawyer of Louisville, Kentucky, was elected to the Board of Aldermen in 1868; was Assistant City Attorney 1870-1873; appointed Vice-Chancellor by Governor McCreery in 1878. In 1886 he ran for Governor of Kentucky on the Prohibition ticket. He is the author of two works: "Fire Insurance Contracts," and "The Woman's Suffrage Movement in the United States." He has been pronounced by English and American critics as a writer of the purest English. He married Mary Barton, daughter of the late Professor Samuel Barton, who for many years was professor of mathematics at Center College, Danville. She died in October, 1894. He has five children.

Dr. Samuel Fox, a leading physician of Texas, has five children.

Felix G. Fox, attorney-at-law at Danville, Kentucky, a man of fine legal attainments.

Sophie Fox Sea (writer), author of a very popular story for children, a hymn that has obtained a national reputation and a number of short stories and poems of local celebrity. Mrs. Sea is the wife of Captain Andrew McBrayer Sea of the Confederate service, a commission merchant of Louisville, Kentucky, and a ruling elder in the First Presbyterian Church of that city. He is highly educated and springs from notable pioneer and Scotch-Irish ancestry. He inherited a handsome fortune from his father. John Oliver Fox (deceased) was a civil engineer. Charles C. Fox, City Attorney of Danville, and Master Commissioner of his district. He is a ruling elder in the First Presbyterian Church of his town and married Mollie Allen, daughter of Albert Allen of Fayette County, Kentucky, and niece of Madison Johnson. They have three daughters.

Annie Bell Fox Caldwell, wife of Jerry Caldwell of Danville, a descendant of the celebrated Clemens, Wickliffe and Caldwell families. He is a successful farmer, is president of the Farmers' National Bank of Danville and one of the ablest financiers in the state. They have five children.

William Fox (father) was born in Hanover County, Virginia, March 1, 1779. He clerked in company with Henry Clay in the office of his (Fox's) uncle, Peter Tinsley, of Hanover County, Virginia, and received from him a thorough training in penmanship and the practical branch of law. After he came to Kentucky with his parents he went to Pulaski County in company with Chief Justice Samuel McKee. They kept bachelor hall together for ten years, when McKee returned to Madison County. William Fox served as county and circuit clerks for forty-seven years. He was a man of rare qualities of mind and character and reverenced to an extraordinary degree by the people among whom he lived. He married (first) Sophie Irvine, daughter of David Irvine and Jane Kyle, and sister to the pioneers, William and Christopher Irvine. They had seven children. He married (second) Mary Irvine, daughter of Hail and Elizabeth Talbot of Luter Island, Missouri. William Fox died in Somerset, October 19, 1855. He had a large landed estate and many negroes.

Samuel Fox (grandfather) came to Kentucky from Hanover County, Virginia, about 1783. He settled in Madison County on the present site of Foxtown. He inherited a large estate under the old primogeniture law of succession. His wife was Rhoda Pickering, daughter of Richard and Lucy Pickering of Virginia. They lived together as man and wife for seventy-five years and had thirteen children. They were never known to have but one quarrel. He died in 1844; she died in 1841. They are buried at Fox's.

THOMAS JONES BIGSTAFF, a leading lawyer of Mt. Sterling, son of James M. and Mary (Jones) Bigstaff, was born in Bath County, December 11, 1862. He received his education at Georgetown College, from which he was graduated in 1884. Then for one year he attended Eastman's Business College at Poughkeepsie, New York, and was then a clerk in a bank for one year.

In 1886 he began the study of law with Judge B. J. Peters and with the law firm of Young, Mitchell & Young, and was admitted to the bar in 1887. About this time he was appointed attorney for the Traders' Deposit Bank at Mt. Sterling. In 1888 he formed a partnership with Edward C. O'Rear, the firm name being O'Rear & Bigstaff, of which he is still a member. They make corporate law a specialty and are attorneys for a number of turnpike companies, Eastern corporations and insurance companies.

Mr. Bigstaff is a member of the Board of Trustees of the city schools. In politics he is a Democrat and in religion a member of the Baptist Church.

He married in 1894 Alexine Benton, daughter of Hiram and Maria Crumb Benton. She was reared in Michigan and educated in Olivet and Albion Colleges, and graduated in the Chautauqua Course. They have one child, James M. Bigstaff, Jr.

James M. Bigstaff (father) was born in Bath County, Kentucky, May 20, 1842, and was educated at Owingsville and in the country schools. He left home at the age of fourteen to make his living; began as deputy in the circuit clerk's office at that age and served until he was nineteen, at which time he was engaged in general farming and stock-raising in Bath County; removed to Newport, Kentucky, in 1863; remained there a short time and then returned to Bath County and resumed farming, and in 1872 he removed to Mt. Sterling. His wife inherited eight hundred acres of land, which, by good business management and enterprise, Mr. Bigstaff has increased three-fold. He was president of the Exchange Bank for three years; resigned that position in 1884, organized the Traders' Deposit Bank and has been its president since its organization. He is a member of the Baptist Church and in politics a Democrat. He was married in 1862 to Mary E. Jones, a native of Bath County, Kentucky. She was educated at the Georgetown Seminary and is a member of the Baptist Church. Their children are: Thomas Jones, Sarah Fenton, Elizabeth Iles and Odd Samuel.

Odd Samuel Bigstaff (grandfather) was born in Bath County, Kentucky, and although almost self-educated, was a very highly cultured man and had a fine library, selected and purchased by himself. He was a physician and had a large practice extending from Bath County to the Ohio river. He was a thoroughly good and useful man, highly respected and beloved. He married Mrs. Fenton Arnold, widow first of John Arnold and then of David Arnold. Her maiden name was Fenton Bean, and she was born in Mason County and educated at Maysville. At the age of twenty-seven she had been three times married. She was truly a help-meet to Dr. Bigstaff; was companionable with him and assisted him greatly in his work; their children were: Sarah, who married John Hines; Richard, Benjamin, Samuel of Newport, Kentucky, and James M. Bigstaff. The Bigstaff family came to Kentucky from Culpeper County, Virginia. The original name in England was Bickerstaff, but those who came to America changed their name to Biggerstaff. Dr. Biggerstaff dropped the "ger" and wrote the name simply Bigstaff. The name Bickerstaff was discovered by chance. Mr. Bigstaff's father received an importation of cattle a few years ago from Bickerstaff Place, England. This name was traced and found to be the original name of this family. The coat-of-arms that was found consisted of a unicorn rampant. It is a tradition that one of the earliest ancestors was Jacob Staffe, who had several sons, one named Long, another Bicker, hence the name Longstaffe and Bickerstaffe.

Thomas T. Jones (maternal grandfather) was a native of Bath County and a farmer; was appointed colonel of the State Militia; married Elizabeth Boyd of Bath County, Kentucky, and their children were: James William, John Spencer and Mary Elizabeth.

John Jones (maternal great-grandfather) was a farmer owning several thousand acres of land in Bath County and as many hundred slaves. He was a turfman and was married three times. He was a very energetic and prosperous man.

PHILIP SLAUGHTER CAMPBELL, Fire Insurance Adjuster, of Louisville, Kentucky, son of Samuel and Martha Frances (Thompson) Campbell, was born in Middleburg, Loudoun County, Virginia, June 19, 1844, and removed with his father's family to Louisville in May, 1851, and here has since resided.

His father, Samuel Campbell, was the son of Patrick Campbell, who, with his brother Robert, came to this country from Scotland and, after they had served throughout the war in the American army during the Revolution, they settled—it is supposed—at Williamsport, Pennsylvania, where Samuel was born. When he was quite young both of his parents died, and he was raised by his uncle and aunt, and at about the age of twelve years, was taken to Winchester, Clark County, Virginia, where he grew to manhood. He died in Louisville, April 19, 1884, in his eighty-seventh year.

His mother, Martha Frances Campbell, was a

P. S. CAMPBELL.

daughter of William Mills Thompson and Catharine Wigginton (Boradus) Thompson of Culpeper County, Virginia, where both had been raised, as had their parents before them. She died in Louisville, June 21, 1869, in her fifty-seventh year. (Rev. John A. Boradus, deceased, of Louisville was a nephew of Catharine Wigginton Boradus Thompson above referred to.)

Philip S. Campbell—who was named for Rev. Philip Slaughter of Culpeper County, Virginia— received his education in the schools of Louisville. At the age of eighteen he began his business career in a retail drug store, and after two years changed to wholesale dry goods, which he followed for eight years, finally taking up fire insurance, March 1, 1871, by buying an interest in the business of W. H. Slaughter, the firm name being Slaughter & Campbell. This firm was afterwards changed to Lyman, Moore & Campbell, and then to Lyman & Campbell.

During his connection with the local fire insurance business, his firms represented some of the most prominent American and foreign companies and did a large and successful business for them. He engaged with Barbee & Castleman, managers Southern Department of the Royal Insurance Company, and London and Lancashire Fire Insurance Company, January 1, 1877, and traveled for them as special agent and adjuster for five years, afterwards being with J. H. M. Morris, manager of the Queen Insurance Company, for the same territory, and in 1891 he settled down to adjust fire losses in Louisville and vicinity only, in which undertaking he has been eminently successful. He is active, energetic and industrious, and has all of the qualities which combine to make what is known as a hustler. Popular, genial, polite and courteous in his dealings, he commands the respect of all with whom he is associated. Thoroughly posted in the laws and rules governing insurance, experienced in the peculiar complications which often arise in cases requiring proper adjustment of fire losses, he has established himself in the confidence of the prominent fire insurance companies of the country, who want fair dealings, prompt attention and intelligent handling of their business.

Philip S. Campbell was married October 4, 1870, to Elizabeth Milton, daughter of John Milton, deceased. Her father was born in Fayette County, Kentucky, and her mother, Louisa Ann Taylor, deceased, was born in Clark County, Virginia. John Milton was one of the most prominent business men in Louisville in his day, and at his death was cashier of the old Northern Bank of Kentucky, in that city, and both he and his wife were life-long prominent members of the Presbyterian Church. Mr. Campbell's parents were Episcopalians, his father having been an officer in that church for fifty years, although he was a Presbyterian before his marriage. His mother was an active worker in the church from early womanhood. P. S. Campbell and his wife are members of St. Paul's Episcopal Church, Louisville. They have one son living, Philip S. Campbell, Jr., who is employed as clerk in the insurance office of Barbee & Castleman. Their only daughter, Louise Milton Campbell, died July 17, 1894, in her twenty-third year. She had from early childhood been deeply interested in church work, and at the time of her death was teacher of a class of young ladies in the Sunday School of St. Paul's Church.

Mr. Campbell can trace his ancestry for several generations; on his mother's paternal side for about 300 years and on her maternal side about 200 years, to England and Scotland. On his father's side he cannot, with certainty, go beyond his grandfather, who was a soldier in the Revolutionary war. Col. Richard W. Thompson of Terre Haute, Indiana, is the only uncle Mr. Campbell has now living, and he is in his eighty-seventh year.

CHARLES WEEDEN WILSON, a brother of John R. and son of Samuel L. and Sarah (Ashby) Wilson, was born near Corydon, in Henderson County, Kentucky, February 12, 1848. He attended the district school in his neighborhood as opportunity offered and was a pupil in the State University at Lexington, when he was called home on account of his father's illness and took full charge of the farm and tobacco business as a partner of his father. After the death of the latter in 1876 Charles remained on the farm and took care of his mother until her death, after which he removed to Henderson, where he has continued successfully in the tobacco business and is one of the best known business men of Henderson.

His father, Samuel Long Wilson, was born in North Carolina in 1802, and came to Kentucky when thirteen years of age, and when he reached his manhood became a farmer in Henderson County. He was also extensively engaged in the handling of tobacco and built a large factory on his farm. ' His wife was Sallie Weeden Ashby, who was born in Fauquier County, Virginia, in 1813. They had ten children, seven of whom reached maturity. Mr. Wilson's father was a farmer and a tanner in North Carolina, who came to Kentucky in 1815 and was a farmer in Henderson County until the time of his death.

Robert Ashby (maternal grandfather), a native of Virginia, belonged to the renowned Ashby family in that state, who took such an active part in the late Civil war, and was closely related to the generals, Dick, Turner and John Ashby. Robert Ashby removed to Kentucky in the early days of the state, or possibly prior to its admission to the Union, having previously married Nancy Walton of Maryland, who was the daughter of a famous seafaring captain.

RAWLEIGH D. ARMSTRONG, Sheriff of Franklin County, was born in Bridgeport, Franklin County, Kentucky, November 29, 1849, and was reared on the farm on which he now resides and owns, receiving his education in the high school of Frankfort. After leaving school in 1877, he was appointed deputy sheriff under William Chinn and held that position for two years, when he engaged in farming and trading in live stock, in which business he has continued ever since. He has built up an extensive trade, and is now one of the representative farmers and traders of Franklin County. He has always been an active worker in the ranks of the Democratic party, and in 1892 he was elected sheriff of the county for a term of two years, at the expiration of which term (1894) he was re-elected without opposition, under the new constitution, for a term of three years. Mr. Armstrong was married (first) to Mary E. Hodges, daughter of Thomas Hodges of Franklin County. She died, leaving one son, who died in May, 1882, in the twenty-first year of his age. Mr. Armstrong's second wife was Mary Towles, daughter of Diamond Towles of Missouri, and she is the mother of two daughters and one son, who are now living: Mabel, Ruby and Rawleigh L. Armstrong.

Abel Armstrong, father of R. D. Armstrong, is a native of Woodford County, Kentucky, who removed to Franklin County with his parents when he was a small boy. He was reared on a farm and has always been engaged in agricultural pursuits. In politics he is a straight-out Democrat and has always taken a lively interest in the success of his party. He is still living on his farm near Frankfort, having passed his ninetieth year.

William Armstrong (grandfather) was a native of Culpeper County, Virginia, who came to Kentucky about the first year of the present century, and after living in Woodford County for some years, came to Franklin County, where he was engaged in farming until the time of his death, having reached a very old age. He married Sallie Wilson of Woodford County. R. D. Armstrong's great-grandfather, William Armstrong's father, was a native of Scotland and was of Scotch-Irish origin. He came to Virginia during the latter years of the eighteenth century.

Matilda Towles Armstrong (mother) was born in what is known as Clover Bottom, in 1832, and died in 1879 in the forty-second year of her age. She was a daughter of Rawleigh D. Towles, who was born in Culpeper County, Virginia. He came with his father to Woodford County, where he was engaged in general farming. The Towles family originally came from England, where they were highly connected.

COLONEL RICHARD M. JOHNSON, the third son of Colonel Robert Johnson of Scott County, was born in Kentucky in the autumn of 1781. The literary institutions of Kentucky were then in their infancy, and the facilities for thorough education exceedingly limited. Richard remained with his father until the age of fifteen, receiving only such instruction as the nature of circumstances would allow. At this age he left his father's house, intent upon advantages superior to those afforded in that vicinity, and entered a country school, where he acquired a knowledge of grammar, and the rudiments of the Latin language. Afterwards he entered Transylvania University, where, by unremitted industry, he made rapid progress in the acquisition of classic and scientific knowledge.

Upon quitting the university, he entered upon the study of law, under the guidance and instruction of that celebrated jurist and statesman, Colonel George Nicholas. On the decease of this gentleman, which took place a few weeks after his young student had entered his office, the subject of this biography placed himself under the instruction of Hon. James Brown, late a senator in Congress from Louisiana, and subsequently a minister from the United States to the court of France, but then a distinguished member of the Kentucky bar. With this eminent citizen he finished his preparatory studies, and at the early age of nineteen entered upon the arduous duties of his profession.

As a lawyer, he was eminently successful, and displayed the same active energy of mind and benevolence of heart which have since so eminently distinguished him in higher and more responsible stations. He despised injustice and oppression, and never omitted an occasion to render his services, without prospect of reward, where honest poverty or injured innocence was found struggling against the oppressions of wealth. The inability of a client to pay a fee never deterred him from attending sedulously to his cause, no matter how intricate and laborious were the services. By these means, even at so early an age, he secured to himself the just reward of his virtues, and the approbation and esteem of the public.

Scarcely had he been installed in the duties of his profession, before an opportunity was afforded for the development of that high and chivalrous patriotism which has since identified him with some of the noblest feats of American valor, and given his name to immortality. In 1802 the port of New Orleans, in violation of an existing treaty, was closed against the United States by the Spanish intendant. The occurrence gave rise to immense excitement throughout America, especially in the vallies of the Ohio and Mississippi, and a rupture between Spain and the United States, likely to end in war, was the consequence. Richard M. Johnson, then only in his twentieth year, with many other young men of his neighborhood, promptly volunteered his services to pass down the western waters and make a descent on New Orleans, in the event of war. In a few days, chiefly through his exertions, a large company was enrolled, and he was chosen to the command. The speedy adjustment of the dispute with Spain deprived him and the brave youths under his command of the opportunity of signalizing themselves and the state upon the field of battle.

Before he had reached the age of twenty-one, at which period the constitution of Kentucky fixes the eligibility of the citizen to a seat in the legislature, the citizens of Scott County elected him, by acclamation, to a seat in that body. As a member of the legislature, he acquitted himself with great credit, and to the entire satisfaction of his constituents. Having served two years in that station, at the age of twenty-four he was elected a representative in the Congress of the United States; and in October, 1807, being then just twenty-five, took his seat in that body.

He entered upon the theater of national politics at a period when party excitement ran high, and attached himself to the Republican party, more from a uniform and fixed devotion to the principles of democracy than from any purely selfish policy. He was immediately placed upon some of the most important committees, and at the second session of the term for which he was elected was appointed chairman of the committee of claims, at that time among the most important of the house committee.

In 1811 our relations with Great Britain were such as, in the opinion of many, to render an appeal to arms inevitable. Richard M. Johnson was among those who were convinced that no other alternative remained to the people of the United States; and accordingly, after supporting with great energy all the preparatory measures which the crisis demanded, in June, 1812, gave his vote for the declaration of war. This important measure was shortly afterward followed by an adjournment of Congress, when he hastened home, raised the standard of his country, and called around him many of the best citizens of his neighborhood, some of whom, schooled in the stormy period of the early settlement of the state, were veteran warriors, well suited for the service for which they were intended. With this battalion, composed of three companies, he hastened to the frontier, and when arrived at St. Mary's on the 13th of September, his force, by general order, was augmented by a battalion of mounted volunteers, and he elected to the command of the regiment thus formed. A portion of the regiment only, during that season, had any opportunity of an engagement; and this was a party of the mounted battalion, under Major Suggett, which, in communicating with Fort Wayne, besieged by a superior force, encountered an equal number of the enemy, whom it routed, killing an Indian chief of some distinction. After an active campaign of about ten months, Colonel Johnson returned home for the purpose of proceeding to Washington to re-enter Congress, having added to his reputation as a statesman that of an energetic and patriotic soldier.

In October, 1813, the decisive crisis in the operations of the Northwestern army arrived—the battle of the Thames, which led to a termination of hostilities in that quarter, was fought and won. The distinguished services of Colonel Johnson and his brave regiment in that sanguinary engagement have scarcely a parallel in the heroic annals of our country. The British and Indians, the former under the command of General Proctor, and the latter under that of Tecumseh, the celebrated Indian warrior, had taken an advantageous position, the British in line between the river Thames and a narrow swamp, and the Indians in ambush on their right, and west of the swamp, ready to fall upon the rear of Colonel Johnson, should he force a retreat of the British. Colonel Johnson, under the orders of the commander in chief, divided his regiment into two battalions, one under the command of his gallant brother James, and the other to be led by himself. Colonel Johnson with his battalion passed the swamp and attacked the Indians at the same moment that his brother James fell upon and routed the British regulars. The contest for a while between Colonel Johnson's battalion and the Indians was obstinate and bloody, the slaughter great, but success complete. The gallant colonel was in the very midst and thickest of the fight, inspiring by his presence and courage the utmost confidence of his brave followers, and though perforated with balls, his bridle arm shattered, and bleeding profusely, he continued to fight until he encountered and slew an Indian chief who formed the rallying point of the savages. This chief was supposed to be the famous Tecumseh himself, upon whose fall the Indians raised a yell and retreated. The heroic colonel, covered with wounds, twenty-five balls having been shot into him, his clothes and his horse, was borne from the battle ground, faint from exertion and loss of blood, and almost lifeless. Never was victory so complete or its achievement so glorious. Fifteen hundred Indians were engaged against the battalion of Colonel Johnson, and eight hundred British regulars against that of his brother. Both forces were completely routed, and an effectual end put to the war upon the northern frontier, distinguished as it had been by so many murderous cruelties upon the part of the savage allies of the British.

The war in that quarter now being ended, in a short time the army took up its march homeward; but Colonel Johnson being unable to continue with his regiment, was carried to Detroit, from whence after a short confinement he departed for home. After a distressing journey, during which he endured the most painful suffering, he reached his home in Kentucky early in November. In February, 1814, still unable to walk, he reached Washington city, and resumed his seat in Congress. Everywhere upon the route, and at the metropolis, he was met with the most enthusiastic and cordial greetings of a grateful people. Even his political opponents, deeply sensible of his sincerity, his patriotism and his valor, cordially united in doing honor to the man who had at so much sacrifice rendered such glorious service to the country. Congress, by joint resolution, made appropriate acknowledgment of his gallant deeds, and directed him to be presented with a suitable testimonial of his services.

He continued to serve his constituents in Congress until the year 1819, when he voluntarily retired, carrying with him the esteem of the whole nation. But his native state, of which he was justly the idol, would not suffer him to remain in retirement. The people of Scott County immediately returned him to the state legislature, and that body elected him to the United States Senate. An honor so exalted from a source so honored he could not resist; and accordingly, in December, 1819, he took his seat in the United States Senate, and after serving his term was unanimously re-elected, a circumstance which serves to show how well he preserved the confidence of the people of his native state, and how deeply he was enshrined in their affections.

His career as a legislator was scarcely less brilliant and useful than that in which he distinguished himself as a warrior. His speeches and reports are monuments of his wisdom and liberality as a statesman. The whole nation will bear evidence to his zeal and industry in support of all measures calculated to promote the end of free government—the happiness of the people. No man labored more indefatigably in behalf of private claimants than did Colonel Johnson; and so scrupulously faithful was he in the discharge of his duty towards all who applied for his services that he never failed while in Congress to attend to a single application that was made to him. The old soldiers of the Revolution, the invalids of the last war, and thousands of other persons all over the Union who had claims to urge upon the government had no truer friend in Congress than Colonel Johnson, as many of them now enjoying the bounty of the government through his instrumentality can bear most grateful testimony.

In 1836 he was made Vice President of the United States, and presided over the Senate with great dignity for the term of four years, at the expiration of which he retired to his farm in Scott County, Kentucky. The remainder of his life, with the exception of two terms in the state legislature, was assiduously devoted to improving his private fortunes, somewhat impaired by a too liberal hospitality and constant attention to public affairs. He was a member of the legislature at the time of his death, which occurred in Frankfort in 1850.

JOHN M. UNTHANK. After leaving school was a teacher of the common schools of this and Harland counties for eight or ten years, and was admitted to the bar in 1873, and has been engaged in the active practice of law here ever since. He represented Bell, Harland, Leslie and Perry counties in the Legislature in sessions of 1883 and 1884, and has served as special Circuit Judge of his circuit. Mr. Unthank was married February 4, 1859, to Miss Josephine, daughter of Alexander and Mary Moore of Bell County.

Mr. Unthank championed the first bill which became a law that prohibits the sale of whisky in his district and the law has never been repealed.

ALOYSIUS J. SPECKERT, one of the most successful young lawyers of Louisville, son of Col. Frank Speckert, was born in Aurora in 1867. His father, now prominent among the wealthy German citizens of Louisville, was born in Rhenish Bavaria, December 29, 1843, and came to this country, a poor orphan boy, in April, 1861; enlisted as a drummer boy at Aurora, Indiana, August 22, 1861, in the Thirty-second Indiana Volunteers, under Col. August Willich, and served with that fidelity and faithfulness which so distinguished the loyal German element in the war for the suppression of the Rebellion; returned to Aurora in 1865 and remained there until 1868, when he removed to Louisville and engaged in the retail grocery trade, and soon accumulated a handsome fortune. He was a member of the common council for ten years, in which he served the city faithfully. He has been a leader in a number of benevolent societies, serving as an officer in many of them; was captain of St. Martin's Commandery, Catholic Knights, for fifteen years, and was then elected lieutenant-colonel and later on was placed in command of the battalion, with the rank of colonel. Mr. Speckert was thrown upon his own resources at a very tender age, and has distinguished himself as a man of remarkable pluck and shrewd business tact.

A. J. Speckert was educated in the Louisville schools, and after reading law with Kohn & Barker, attended the University of Virginia; was admitted to the bar and again entered the office of his preceptors. Mr. Barker was elected city attorney, and that firm being dissolved, Mr. Aaron Kohn, David Baird and A. J. Speckert formed a law partnership in 1890, which was known as Kohn, Baird & Speckert. In 1893 he withdrew from that firm and was associated with Charles G. Richie, present judge of the County Court, owing to whose election in 1894 the firm of Speckert & Richie was dissolved, and Mr. Speckert became the head of the firm of Speckert, Kreiger & Bolderick.

Although still quite young, he has had large experience and has met with wonderful success as a lawyer; has managed his cases carefully, and is popular with the bar and the people. He is an eloquent speaker, and has made some powerful arguments in cases of the highest importance.

JOHN M. BROOKS, President and Resident Manager of the Middlesborough Town and Lands Company, son of Joseph A. Brooks and Margaret McMillan, was born near Knoxville, Tennessee, October 28, 1840. His father was born, lived and died in the same house, covering a period of seventy-eight years; was a farmer, a general in the State Militia, and an elder in the Presbyterian Church; a man of strong characteristics and of influence; a Christian gentleman and a distinguished citizen. His older brothers were in the Indian wars, and they all endured many privations incident to pioneer times.

Moses Brooks (grandfather), a native of Rockbridge County, Virginia, was a soldier in the Revolutionary war, in Campbell's Virginia Regiment, and at the close of that war removed to Abington, Virginia, and soon after settled in Tennessee, near Knoxville, where his son, Gen. Joseph A. Brooks, and his grandson, Captain John M. Brooks, were born.

John Brooks (great-grandfather), a native of the north of Ireland, of Scotch-Irish parentage, came to the United States and located first in Pennsylvania, next in Rockbridge County, Virginia, and finally in Washington County, Tennessee, when that was a part of North Carolina.

Margaret McMillan-Brooks (mother), now a resident of Knoxville, was born in Knox County, in 1808, and the history of her father and grandfather was almost identical with that of her husband's people.

John McMillan, grandfather of Capt. Brooks, was a farmer in Knox County, Tennessee, where he died in 1841.

Alexander McMillan (great-grandfather), a native of the north of Ireland, of Scotch-Irish descent, came over with John Brooks and was with them in their removals and neighbors in their homes. The McMillan family belonged to the most intelligent class of people in that part of Ireland, which was noted for educational advantages and the pure, moral and religious character of the citizens. They were Presbyterians of the strictest sect; and many of them who came to America were known as Reformed Presbyterians or Covenanters. Undoubtedly Captain Brook's ancestors on both sides of the house belonged to those old Scotch Covenanters, than whom no better people ever lived.

Captain Brooks had the usual experience of the farmer's son, working more than going to school. After the country schools, he attended the University of Tennessee in Knoxville, and before graduating enlisted as a private in the Confederate army, Company I, Second Tennessee Infantry, known as Asby's Regiment; was soon promoted to aide-de-camp, with the rank of captain, on Colonel Scott's staff—who was in command of a brigade—serving in that capacity during the war; was three times wounded and participated in many hard fought battles.

Following the close of the war, he was for several years engaged in the drug business in Knoxville; his store was destroyed by fire and he then engaged in the real estate and insurance business in that city until April, 1889, when he joined the stampede for Middlesborough; became interested in Middlesborough Town Company and in July was made president and resident manager of that company, which position he occupies to-day, the name of the company having been changed, however, to the Middlesborough Town and Lands Company. This corporate company has expended nearly five millions of dollars, English money, in developing the town, and Captain Brooks has had the entire management of the work, and the disbursement of the money. Further remarks as to his business ability or his integrity, honesty and faithfulness are unnecessary. He has accomplished a grand work, the history of which would make a volume.

Captain Brooks was married (first) in 1868 to Sopha Park, daughter of Rev. James Park, D. D., of the First Presbyterian Church, Knoxville. Mrs. Brooks died in 1886, leaving three sons and one daughter: James Park; Alma, wife of John Wasson of Fayette County, Kentucky; John M. and Robert C. Brooks.

Captain Brooks was married (second) in 1892 to Amelia McDowell, daughter of Joseph McDowell, formerly of Danville, now of Perryville, Kentucky. They are members of the Presbyterian Church.

GEORGE MOSBY DAVISON of Stanford, Judge of Lincoln County, was born in Stanford, Kentucky, March 23, 1855, and is the son of Edward M. Davison of Washington County, Virginia, and Martha (Vaughan) Davison of Lincoln County, Kentucky. Edward M. Davison was the son of Mosby Davison of Bedford County, Virginia, and Dorothy Tankersley of Caroline County, Virginia. Mosby Davison was the son of —— Davison and Sarah Mosby of Bedford County, Virginia. Dorothy Tankersley was the daughter of George Tankersley and Dorothy Roy of Caroline County, Virginia. George Tankersley was the son of George Tankersley, Sr., and Mary Long of King George County, Virginia, and George Tankersley, Sr., was the son of John Tankersley and Ann Beverly of King George County. The Beverlys, Mosbys, Longs, Tankersleys and Roys are ancient families of Virginia. The Tankersleys came from about Yorkshire, England, to Caroline County, Virginia, about the year 1715. (See Bishop Meade's History of Old Families of Virginia.)

Martha Vaughan Davison, mother of Judge Davison, is the daughter of Zachariah Vaughan of Culpeper County, Virginia, and Harriet Ball of Garrard County, Kentucky. Zachariah Vaughan was of Scotch-Irish extraction and the son of Joseph Vaughan and Elizabeth Weaver of Culpeper County, Virginia. Harriet Ball was the daughter of Rev. John Ball and Margaret Johnson of Garrard County, Kentucky. Margaret Johnson Ball was the daughter of Rev. Job Johnson and Sarah Mosby of Virginia. As to Revs. John Ball and Job Johnson see A. H. Redford's History of Early Methodism in Kentucky. Rev. Job Johnson and John Ball came from Rockingham or Buckingham County, Virginia, to Garrard County, Kentucky, about 1785.

Judge Davison was educated in the common schools and Stanford Academy, and in the private school of Prof. J. B. Myers, an eminent and successful educator; read law in the office of J. S. & R. W. Hocker and obtained license to practice April 26, 1880, and began practicing in January, 1881, at Stanford; was appointed to a position in the internal revenue service under the late Col. A. M. Swope of the Lexington District, which he filled till August, 1883, when he was transferred to the Seventh District under the late General W. J. Landrom, and resigned in October, 1885, and resumed the practice of law at Stanford. During his four years in the internal revenue service he filled many important and difficult assignments and gained the reputation of being a most efficient, valuable and painstaking officer; and was highly esteemed by his superior officers and the business public; in 1885 he again began the practice of law at Stanford; in June, 1886, he was unanimously selected chairman of the Lincoln County Republican Committee, which position he has continuously filled by unanimous elections. In September, 1886, he was appointed Master Commissioner of the Lincoln Circuit Court by Judge T. Z. Morrow, which position he held until March 5, 1893. At the August election, 1887, Judge Davison was elected to the Legislature from Lincoln County, as a Republican, defeating Dr. J. D. Pettus, the Democratic nominee, being the first Republican elected to the Legislature from Lincoln County; in the Legislature of 1887-

88 he was placed on important committees of the house, and was one of the Republican leaders of that session; in 1888 he was unanimously chosen as the Republican elector for the Eighth District and again in 1892, and in both of the Harrison campaigns. He was a valuable organizer and speaker in both the Eighth and Tenth Districts. Judge Davison was one of the charter members of the Republican League of Kentucky. In every campaign since 1883 he has been prominent in Republican politics. As an organizer he has no superior, perhaps, in the state, and his services are always in demand, though he is modest and unassuming and has never pushed himself to the front. In 1893 he declined the nomination for State Senator in this Republican District and again in 1894 he declined the nomination for Congress, preferring to give all of his time to his law practice, but the Republicans of Lincoln County in 1894 unanimously nominated him for County Judge. After a bitter contest he was elected over his clever and popular opponent, J. Walker Givins—the Democratic nominee—by a majority of one hundred and sixty, overcoming a Democratic majority of four hundred and receiving more votes than any person on either ticket. His popularity is fully attested by his election to the Legislature and County Judge in a county usually four hundred Democratic. Although Judge Davison has given much time and labor to politics in the past ten years, he has retained a fair law practice and has been engaged in many important cases.

JOHN R. SIMPSON, attorney for the Middlesborough Town and Land Company, and leading lawyer of that city, son of Judge William Simpson and Virginia Gilpin, was born in Glasgow, Kentucky, April 26, 1852. His father was born in Cannonsburg, Pennsylvania, in 1818; was educated in Jefferson College, Washington County, in that state; came to Kentucky in 1836; was engaged in teaching in Jefferson County near the present site of Lakeland Asylum for the Insane, for five years; was a writer in the office of the Clerk of the Court of Appeals for two years; was admitted to the bar and went to Burksville and practiced law until 1850, when he removed to Glasgow, and entering politics, was presidential elector in 1860 on the Bell and Everett ticket; was elected to the State Senate in 1863, and before completing his term of office was appointed in 1865 by Governor Bramlette to fill the unexpired term of Judge Joshua F. Bullitt, in the Court of Appeals. At the ensuing August election he was elected to succeed himself, and served as Chief Justice until his death, February 21, 1866.

George Simpson (grandfather) was a native of Scotland, and was a cabinetmaker in Washington County, Pennsylvania, where he died, having reached a good old age.

Virginia Gilpin (mother) was a native of King William County, Virginia; was married to William Simpson in 1848 and died in Glasgow in 1864, aged thirty-nine years. She and Judge Simpson were members of the Presbyterian Church and she especially was known for her piety and lovely Christian character.

John R. Simpson, left an orphan at an early age, was educated in Louisville; graduated from the law department of the University of Louisville in 1872 and practiced law in that city until 1876, when he removed to Columbia, Adair County, where he practiced his profession; was elected County Attorney in 1878, and after completing his term of office removed, in 1884, to Williamsburg, Whitley County, and was soon recognized as one of the leading lawyers of that section; was Democratic Elector in the presidential campaign of 1888; and in 1889 was employed by the companies then engaged in developing a section of country in and around Cumberland Gap, and especially in building the city of Middlesborough. He began at the very inception of this great enterprise, taking charge of the legal business of the capitalists who were interested in the development of the resources of the section, and before there was any town on the present site of Middlesborough; and while he has since become a resident of the city among the hills and has been engaged in the general practice of law there, he has continued in charge of the legal business of the original company, now changed to the Middlesborough Town and Lands Company, the K. C. & G. L. and Belt

Railroads and other companies and corporations that are identified with the city and its improvement.

In this stupendous enterprise he has found ample scope for his talent and ability as an attorney, and the work of his department performed under his direction has given great satisfaction to the various companies interested. These duties have been varied and in many instances difficult, requiring a high order of legal ability, and he has proven himself equal to the task.

Mr. Simpson was married in 1880 to Bettie Cravens, daughter of Timolean Cravens, a prominent attorney of Columbia, Kentucky. They have three sons and one daughter: William, John E., Reid J. and Mary V. Mr. Simpson is a Royal Arch and Scottish Rite Mason, is deacon in the Baptist Church and was Sunday school superintendent for eighteen years.

W. JACKSON HISSEM of Newport, attorney-at-law and State Senator from Campbell County, was born in Tyler County, West Virginia, March 12, 1863. He is a descendant of ancestry who were active soldiers of the Revolutionary War, and the War of 1812. He has some of the blood in his veins of the old Pennsylvania Dutch stock, from which state his grandparents moved in the beginning of this century to the wilds of West Virginia. When the subject of this sketch was seven years of age he moved with his parents to Campbell County, this state, where his father engaged actively in agricultural and mercantile pursuits. Young Hissem was of great service to his father, both behind the counter and upon the farm, where he worked with might and main during the spring, summer and autumn, attending the public school during the winter. He later attended a business college in Cincinnati, where he more firmly laid the foundation for a business career; engaged in mercantile business for himself, when he reached his majority; often served in local offices, where he was chosen by his fellow citizens.

In 1891 he was nominated by the Republicans to make the race for the Legislature; was elected and served during the Long Parliament, as that session is known. At the end of that session he was nominated by acclamation in the convention of his party for the State Senate, and elected, defeating an eminent lawyer and jurist. He was the youngest member of that body, and having drawn the short term, was re-elected in November, 1895, by the largest majority ever accorded a candidate in the county.

After a course of law covering a considerable period, Mr. Hissem was admitted to practice before the Court of Appeals in 1894, since which time he has practiced his profession at his home in Newport. He has never been defeated for any office to which he aspired. He has always been active in the councils of the Republican party.

He was married in 1887 to Nettie M. Pickens, daughter of Robert P. Pickens of Campbell County. They have two daughters as the fruit of that union: Leva, aged seven, and Ethel, aged five.

His father, Levi Hissem, was a native of Westmoreland County, Pennsylvania, and removed with his father to what is now Tyler County, West Virginia, when four years of age, and lived there until 1870, when he came to Campbell County. While in West Virginia he was a farmer and largely interested in the woolen, flour and lumber business. He was a Democrat prior to the Civil War, but since that time he has been an enthusiastic and consistent Republican. While deeply interested in political questions, he has never been a politician. His father, Jesse Hissem, was a native of Maryland, who removed to Westmoreland County, Pennsylvania; and lived there a number of years before locating in Tyler County, West Virginia. Before his death, in 1872, he removed to Meigs County, Ohio. His ancestors, as far as known, were Americans, having been among the first settlers in the United States. W. J. Hissem's great-grandfather was a soldier in the Revolutionary war.

Elizabeth Morgan Hissem (mother) was born in Virginia in 1820, and is living with her husband in Campbell County. They are members of the Methodist Church, and have been identified with the church work for over a half century.

Joseph Morgan (maternal grandfather) was born in Monongalia County (now) West Virginia, in 1792, and died in Tyler County, West Virginia, in 1884, aged ninety-two years. He was a soldier in the War of 1812, and was a relative of Morgan, the Indian fighter, mentioned in history. He was a farmer, a large dealer in cattle and a very successful business man.

HENRY KIRBY BOURNE, lawyer, of New Castle, Kentucky, son of Thomas J. Bourne and Sallie Pryor Beard, was born in Shelby County, Kentucky, September 2, 1862. He graduated from Center College, in Danville, Kentucky, in 1884, and from 1884 to 1886 taught Latin and Greek in the Henry Male and Female Academy. In 1886 he entered the law department of the University of Virginia, graduating in 1887, and immediately began the practice of law in Henry and adjoining counties.

He is also somewhat interested in farming. Mr. Bourne is a man of fine natural ability and was a close student, as his high standing at college will testify. He was valedictorian of his class at college and was class orator in the twenty-second of February exercises. He also won the Sophomore prizes in English literature and in Latin. Mr. Bourne is a Mason and a member of the Christian Church and his political affiliations are with the democracy.

Thomas J. Bourne (father) was born in Henry County, Kentucky, July 24, 1830, and after his education in the common schools became a farmer and stockraiser. He commenced flatboating in 1852, making thirteen trips to New Orleans between 1852 and 1858, carrying all kinds of produce, and at the same time shipping stock to the Southern markets.

In 1850 he removed to Carroll County, where he remained until 1861, when he returned to Shelby County, but in 1863 he again changed his location to Henry County, where he is now living. He is a Democrat in politics and a member of the Christian Church. He was married (first) in 1861 to Sally Pryor Beard, who was born in Lexington, Fayette County, Kentucky, June, 1834, and died December, 1870. She was educated in the private schools of Fayette County and was the mother of two children: Thomas Pryor, who was born July 9, 1866, and died May 21, 1878, and Henry K. Bourne, the subject of this sketch.

Mr. Bourne was married (second) to Bettie Beazley, who was born in Henry County in 1838. She was the daughter of Augustus and Sallie (Webb) Beazley. Mr. Bourne is of English ancestry. He is a Mason and a man of sterling qualities; a highly respected and prominent agriculturist.

Ben H. Bourne (grandfather) a native of Culpeper County, Virginia, came to Kentucky when very young with his parents; was a school teacher in early life, but afterwards was a farmer and was greatly interested in fine stock; removed from Henry to Carroll County in 1850; was a Whig in politics, and in religion a member of the Christian Church. He married, in 1828, Julia Waters, daughter of William Waters, and a native of Henry County, Kentucky. She died in Henry County in 1883. Ben H. Bourne died in Carroll County in 1852.

Joseph M. Beard (maternal grandfather) was born in Fayette County, Kentucky, and educated in Lexington; was a farmer by occupation; removed to Oldham County and engaged in farming and merchandising at Beards Station; was a Democrat and a Catholic; married Sally Foree, a native of Shelby County, Kentucky, daughter of William P. Foree and Elizabeth Major Foree. Their children are all deceased, except Dr. William F. Beard of Shelbyville, Dr. E. F. Beard of Shelby County, and Mrs. Thresa Gregory (Addie Beard) of Shelby County.

GEORGE B. EASTIN, Attorney-at-Law of Louisville, enjoys the distinction of representing the dignity of his profession in an unusual degree. His appointment by Governor Brown to fill a vacancy in the Court of Appeals, February 22, 1895, called forth expressions of approval from the members of the bar all over the state. The Louisville attorneys were especially hearty and sincere in their congratulations, for they knew the man and were able to judge of his fitness for the office to which he had been called, as if by inspiration. Gov. Brown could not have chosen a man of higher qualifications and it could not be said that there was in any sense a political significance in an appointment which had not been sought, and which would not have been made if the advice of politicians had been considered. Judge Eastin's friends were taken by surprise, if he was not himself, and the congratulations he received were of more value to him than the office. It was an honor which came as a recognition of true worth and ability, in one whose highest ambition had been to make a good name as a thorough gentleman in the practice of law, and having established himself in the estimation of bench, bar and public, he would have been content to remain; but the call to a higher place was accepted as a compliment to his dignified modesty and as a recognition of those qualities which count for little in a blustering electioneering campaign, but which make the capable lawyer and a faithful judge. His former teacher, Judge Muir, one of the senior members of the Louisville bar, expressed the sentiments of the professional brethren of Judge Eastin in these words: "This appointment gives me inexpressible pleasure. I have known Major Eastin ever since he was admitted to the bar. He was one of my pupils when I was a professor in the law department of the University of Louisville. He was a good student and had a fine legal mind. I predicted then what has since proved to be true, that he would attain eminence at the bar. He is a gentleman of courage and robust integrity and will prove himself an efficient and most admirable judge. In my opinion Gov. Brown has made an excellent selection." Judge Eastin filled the short term on the Appellate bench with honor to himself and the people whom he represented, showing that he was not only a man of a high order of intelligence, but possessed a legal mind that would adorn any court in the country. A few months of faithful service closed his official career, and he resumed his work at the bar in January, 1896, with the same quiet indifference to public recognition and honor that had characterized his professional career prior to his elevation to the bench.

Judge Eastin was a gallant soldier on the losing side in the war of the '60's, and came out of the strife, like a good many other young men, without means and out of a job. He served in Gen. Morgan's command as a captain, and the military title of major, by which he is familiarly known, was given him by courtesy. He found his way to Louisville, after the war, at the age of about twenty years, and in 1867 was graduated from the Louisville Law School; began the practice of his profession, and soon made his way to a position in the front rank of the Louisville bar, where his record is spotless, and where he is known as a man of sterling integrity. He married Fanny Castleman, a sister of Gen. John B. Castleman, with whom he is now traveling in Europe.

MARQUIS R. LOCKHART, Commonwealth Attorney of Campbell County and a leading member of the Newport bar, son of Sarah (Richardson) and Henry Lockhart, was born in Lexington, Kentucky, November 13, 1846.

His father, Henry Lockhart, was born in the northern part of Ireland and came to the United States with his parents when he was twelve years of age. They located on a farm in New York, and Henry remained there until he was of age, and then came to Lexington and engaged in stock trading, going South every year to sell horses and mules, which he bought in Kentucky. He owned a farm near Lexington, upon which he lived until 1861, and after the close of the Civil War he went to Paris and lived with his son until his death, which occurred in 1893, in the ninety-second year of his age. He was raised a Presbyterian, but connected himself with the Christian denomination after coming to Kentucky.

Sarah Richardson Lockhart (mother) was a native of Montgomery County; was a member of the Christian Church, and died at the age of sixty years. Her father, Marquis Richardson, was born in Clark County, Kentucky, but spent the most of his life on his farm in Montgomery County, six miles from Mt. Sterling, where he died, aged eighty years.

Marquis R. Lockhart attended the public schools in Lexington, the Kentucky University at Harrodsburg before the war, and was one year in the University of Lexington after the close of the war.

In May, 1862, he enlisted as a private soldier in the Confederate army, and served until his command was surrendered at Washington,

Georgia, in April, 1865. He was with General Basil Duke's regiment in Morgan's Indiana and Ohio raid; was wounded in the battle at Bull's Gap, East Tennessee, and saw some sharp fighting on many other occasions.

He was not quite twenty-one when he returned to Lexington, and attended the university one year to pick up some of the lost threads of his education. He then began civil life as an educator; taught in the public schools of Mt. Sterling for one year; turned aside for one year and acquired valuable experience as editor of the Mt. Sterling Sentinel; taught in the academy at Sharpsburg for one year; was principal of the Bethel Academy for Boys at Nicholasville for three years, and, in 1878, having read law while engaged in teaching, he was admitted to the bar and began the practice of his profession in Owingsville, Bath County. He remained there for two years and then removed to Covington, where he gained a large and lucrative practice, remaining in that city for six or seven years, and then removed to Newport, where he has given his best efforts to the requirements of his vocation and with most gratifying results to himself and his friends.

As a means of recreation, as well as for the advancements of the interests of the Democratic party, Mr. Lockhart has indulged to some extent in politics, and in 1892 his party rewarded his valuable services by electing him commonwealth attorney of Campbell County for a term of five years. He has had charge of this office since January, 1893.

Mr. Lockhart and Mattie Wilson, daughter of Harvey T. Wilson of Covington, were married in 1870. They have one son and two daughters: Henry, Riba and Sallie.

MILTON HARCOURT M'LEAN, lawyer of Covington, son of Martha A. (Rees) and Robert A. McLean, was born in Harrison County September 14, 1867. After attending school in Cynthiana and in Covington, he graduated with the highest honors from the Hillsboro, Ohio, College, in 1886. He was employed in one of the leading distilleries in Ohio for four years, occupying a responsible position, for which he was fitted by a thorough education. He then commenced the study of law in the Cincinnati Law School, in which he took the full course, graduating in 1891 with the second prize honor in a very large class. He opened an office and at once took a position among the brightest young men at the Covington bar; and by his industry and honesty of purpose, together with marked legal ability, he has acquired a practice of which an older lawyer might be proud.

Mr. McLean was married in 1891 to Anna Marie Bering of Highland County, Ohio, daughter of Major J. A. Bering of the Forty-eighth Ohio Volunteer Infantry, who served with great distinction during the Civil War. Major Bering has recently published an interesting history of his regiment in connection with a biographical sketch of himself, in which he has shown that he is a man of letters as well as a brave soldier.

Mr. McLean has an exceedingly interesting ancestry, being a relative of General George Washington, and a direct descendant of one of the best pioneer families of Kentucky.

His father, Robert A. McLean, was born in Harrison County, July 28, 1832, where for some years he was extensively engaged in the lumber and sawmilling business; but is now, and has been for many years, engaged in the distillery business in Covington. He is a member of all the leading secret orders, a member of the Methodist Church, and is a Democrat in politics.

Robert McLean (grandfather) was a native of Harrison County, and died there in 1860. He was sheriff of the county for many years. He married Cynthia Lewis, a native of Virginia.

Martha A. Rees McLean (mother) was born in Harrison County in 1838, and was married to R. A. McLean in 1856. Her father, Milton Rees, was a native of Kentucky and was a wealthy trader and farmer. His sons are following in his footsteps and are to-day among the largest traders in central Kentucky.

Mr. McLean's great-grandfather, Samuel Lewis, was one of the pioneers of Harrison County, where he bought a large tract of land. He came to Kentucky with others, including the McLeans, before the admission of the state to the Union. His daughter, Cynthia Lewis (grandmother) was related to General George Washington; her grandmother, Sarah Ball, and General Washington's mother, Mary Ball, were sisters. This record has been traced so accurately as to be beyond dispute, and the subject of this sketch manifests a pardonable pride in his noble ancestry, being a fourth cousin of the Father of his Country.

HON. ANDREW T. WOOD, lawyer, of Mt. Sterling, Kentucky, son of Henry S. and Flavilla Weaver, was born in Flemingsburg, Kentucky, November 18, 1834. He received his education in the common schools, and at the age of seventeen left school and drove a stage over the old line between Mt. Sterling and Maysville, and also from Mt. Sterling to Paris. He enlisted in the Union army, August 5, 1862, having previously been in the recruiting service for some time; was elected First Lieutenant Company A, First Regiment Kentucky Cavalry, and served in this company until it was mustered out of service. He was engaged in the fight at Triplett Bridge, with Scott's Cavalry, and also at Pine Grove in 1863, where there was a running fight for four days, until Scott was driven beyond the Cumberland and Tennessee Rivers. He also participated in many severe engagements in the eastern part of the state. He was mustered out with his regiment, September 1, 1863, and was then commissioned Major of the Seventy-first Regiment Kentucky Infantry, and served until the war was over.

In 1865 he began the study of law in Mt. Sterling with J. S. Dury, who died in 1867; completed his studies with Thomas Turner of that place; was admitted to the bar in January, 1873. He practiced at Mt. Sterling alone for a short time, and then formed a partnership with Thomas Turner. This continued until 1880, when he continued his practice alone for three years, and in 1883 became associated with B. F. Dury, and this partnership was dissolved in 1893, since which time he has practiced alone. He was City Attorney of Mt. Sterling from 1884 to 1886.

He was the Republican candidate for Congress in 1872, but was defeated, and at another time was a candidate for Judge of the Common Pleas Court, with a similar result. In 1891 he led the Republican party as its nominee for Governor of Kentucky, but, as he expected, was defeated by his Democratic opponent. Colonel Wood is a leading lawyer of Mt. Sterling; very active in Republican politics; a Mason of high degree and a member of the Methodist Episcopal Church.

He married Matilda Pickrell, a native of Henry County, daughter of Henry and Mary (Jackson) Pickrell, her mother being a cousin of Stonewall Jackson. Their children are: James H. Wood, John C. Wood, Railroad Commissioner of Kentucky; Currie F. Wood, William Hoffmann Wood and Henry S. S. Wood.

Henry S. S. Wood (father) was born in Virginia in 1806 and came to Flemingsburg with an uncle in 1812. He was educated in the schools of the county; was a farmer, and later was the owner of the Martha Mills, situated about five miles from Flemingsburg, and was accidentally killed the day Abraham Lincoln was elected President, in 1860. Mr. Wood was an ardent Henry Clay Whig, and a class leader in the Methodist Church. He married Flavilla Weaver, in July, 1828, and their children were: John, Matilda, Henry S., William H., Eliza, Mary and Thomas.

Thomas Wood (grandfather) was a native of Virginia, where he was a farmer, and died at the age of ninety-seven years. He married Mary Sweet, also a native of Virginia.

Thomas Weaver (maternal grandfather) was born in Virginia and came to Fleming County when a child. He was a farmer and died in 1815.

MICHAEL CASSIDY. Probably no person is more intimately connected with the early history of Fleming County than Michael Cassidy, who was born in Dublin, Ireland, October 22, 1755. While he and his brother Andrew were attending school their father sent them money by a relative to defray their expenses, and gave orders that it was not to be given to Mike, but to be placed in the hands of Andrew; at this Michael became offended and determined to leave home. He shipped as a cabin boy on a vessel called the Maryland Merchant; his brother followed him on board the ship and on his knees begged him to give up his rash intention, but all to no purpose, he had set his face toward the wonderful New World and from his course he was not to be turned.

He landed in America in 1767 and was apprenticed by the captain of the vessel to Robert Crayton of Baltimore, Maryland. He remained here until the breaking out of the Revolutionary War, when he enlisted and was present at the surrender of Cornwallis.

At the close of the war he emigrated to Kentucky and located at Strode's Station in Clark County; from there he moved to Fleming County and established what afterwards became noted as Cassidy's Station. From this time for ten years his life was one continual struggle with the blood-thirsty savages and the stubborn wilderness, endeavoring to hold his home and hearthstone.

His personal appearance was peculiar, being very low of stature, measuring only five feet three inches, and yet heavy enough to weigh one hundred and seventy pounds. There are many amusing stories connected with his "smallness." Upon one occasion his camp was surprised by the Indians, and his two companions, Bennett and Spor, were killed. Cassidy was overpowered and captured; his captors taking him for a boy turned him over to the smallest of their party to be butchered, but the victim did not propose to be led like a lamb to the slaughter, and so vigorous and persistent was the conflict that the other two Indians were compelled to assist in clubbing the boy. In falling his hand fell upon one of the Indian's knives, and rising to his feet he flourished it with such ferocity that the Indians gave back and Cassidy darted like a deer into the deep woods and made his escape. He carried to his grave the marks of this terrible conflict.

Upon another occasion, while a member of the Legislature, he was addressing the House, when the Chairman seeing his head just over the shoulders of those seated near him, cried out, "Is the gentleman from Fleming sitting or standing?" Tip-toeing to his greatest height, "Standing, sir," roars back Cassidy.

The grave of Stuart, the spy, who was killed by Cassidy, is still to be seen on the farm of William Robertson. This was to Cassidy the most regretful act of his life, although he was in no way to be blamed for it, and Stuart before he died completely exonerated him from all blame in the matter. Stuart, it seems, was employed by the whites, as a scout whose duty it was to keep them posted as to the movements of the Indians. To facilitate him in this he usually dressed in the guise of an Indian. It was understood among the whites that no gun was to be fired in hearing of the station except at a "redskin." One evening approaching the settlement he was tempted into shooting a large owl. Cassidy seized his gun and started in the direction of the firing. Stuart getting sight of him took refuge behind a low forked tree, and raising his head up between the forks to make himself known, was shot through the forehead by Cassidy.

Michael Cassidy was one of the most noted of the many brave pioneers and Indian fighters whose exploits gave to Kentucky the name of "the dark and bloody ground." More than thirty were his close and deadly conflicts with the savages—brave, resolute and watchful he was well fitted for his task and mission, and neither was the one left undone nor the other a failure.

Sitting to-day in perfect safety around our well-warmed hearthstones and groaning tables, riding in ease and pleasure over our McAdamized roads, or seated in the cosy car, we little realize or appreciate the hardships, dangers and privations of that sturdy band of men who made these things possible; it was a good idea that by these "sketches" they should once more stand before us in rugged honesty and undaunted courage.

Michael Cassidy seems to have enjoyed the confidence of the people of his community, having filled many positions of honor and trust. In 1797-98, before this county was formed, he represented Mason in the lower house of Kentucky representatives.

On the formation of Fleming County out of a part of Mason he became her first Senator in 1800-6. In 1808-9-17-20-22 we find him representing Fleming County in the lower house.

He was also one of the judges of the first court of quarter-sessions.

He married Mary Evans, daughter of Francis Evans, February 17, 1795. They had ten children, seven sons and three daughters, William Cassidy being the eldest and Samuel Evans Cassidy the youngest.

He died March 19, 1829, having been a member of the Presbyterian Church for thirty years and was buried at old Brick Union with the honors of war. In his coffin was laid away one of the most noted men connected with the history of Fleming County. His descendants are numerous and well known among the citizens of Fleming County.

SAMUEL SHAW, president of the German National Bank of Newport, was born in Campbell County, November 1, 1823. He is the son of Margaret (Moran) and Robert Shaw. His father was a Virginian, who married there and came to Campbell County, Kentucky, in the first year of the present century and purchased a large tract of land, which he cultivated until the time of his death, which occurred in 1827, at the age of forty-seven years.

John Shaw (grandfather) was of Irish birth, but he came to America when quite young and led the life of a farmer in Virginia, where he died.

Margaret Moran Shaw, mother of Samuel Shaw, was born in Virginia in 1772; was married to Robert Shaw in 1800; came to Campbell County the same year; died in 1856 at the age of eighty-four years. She was a devout member of the Baptist Church and a woman of fine intellectual attainments and great force of character.

Edward Moran (grandfather) was a native of Virginia, and a farmer. His father came to this country from Scotland and was also a Virginia farmer.

Samuel Shaw spent the days of his boyhood on his father's farm; receiving a good education in the common schools and in Parker's Seminary. After leaving school as a pupil he took the place of the schoolmaster and was engaged in the laudable occupation of teaching for several years. He then turned his attention to business as a grocer and flour merchant in Cincinnati, in which he was one of the most successful men of his day. He continued in the same line until 1882, when he sold out to his son-in-law, Chambers Phister, who has continued the business until the present time.

Mr. Shaw was elected to the Kentucky Legislature on the Republican ticket in 1880 and served two years, doing some very efficient work for his constituents.

In 1882, having disposed of his business in Cincinnati, Mr. Shaw was instrumental in organizing the German National Bank of Newport, and was made its president, which office he has held uninterruptedly since its organization. The bank has a capital of $100,000, and a regular surplus of $50,000, and carries individual profits amounting to $10,000. It is one of the most substantial banks in Kentucky, and its excellent standing is largely due to the wise and careful management of its president.

Mr. Shaw resides in the Highlands, where he owns a valuable farm to which he gives some attention. He was married in 1852 to Elizabeth Smith, daughter of Benjamin Smith of Campbell County. They have one son and five daughters: Ida, wife of Chambers Phister; Benjamin R.; Hannah, wife of L. K. Marty; Alice; Maggie, wife of W. P. Flanders, and Eva.

RICHARD GARNETT CALDWELL, vice-president and manager of the Paducah Building and Trust Company, is a son of James Shipp Caldwell and Arenca Wood Caldwell, and was born in Barren County, near Glasgow, Kentucky, September 18, 1849. His father was a native of Adair County, where he received his education in the common schools and subsequently removed to Barren County and was a farmer there until his death in 1885. During the war he took no active part in the struggle, but freely expressed his sympathy with the South. He was a very active member of the Christian Church, in which he was a devoted, faithful and consistent worker.

Beverly Caldwell (grandfather) was a Virginian by birth, who came to Kentucky early in the present century and located first in Green and afterwards in Adair County. He belonged to the old and respected Caldwell family of Virginia, whose ancestors came from Scotland and was related to John C. Calhoun. Mr. Caldwell married a Miss Hatcher of Virginia, who was the mother of James Shipp Caldwell (father).

Arenca Wood Caldwell (mother) was a native of Barren County, where she died in 1880. Her father, William Garnett, was a soldier in the Revolutionary War, and after the war was over he removed from Virginia to Barren County, where he became a large land-owner and a farmer on an·extensive scale, and was also a stock-trader. He married a Miss Willis of Virginia, and she was the mother of four children. The family was noted for its wealth and the large number of slaves which they owned before the war.

Richard Garnett Caldwell, received his education in the Barren County schools and in a private school in Glasgow, taught by a Mr. Lowell. He assisted his father on the farm for some years and was deputy sheriff of the county from 1867 to 1870; sold groceries in a retail house in Glasgow for one year and then went to Kemper County, Mississippi, and raised, bought and sold cotton and cane until 1880, when he returned to Kentucky and embarked in the drug business in Cave City; sold out his drug store in 1882 and for seven years following was general agent for harvesting machinery and spent most of the time traveling for his house. In 1889 he engaged in the real estate and building and loan business in Bowling Green, traveling a portion of the time in the interest of Louisville business firms, who were eager to secure his services.

His experience in building and loan matters in Bowling Green prepared him for the duties of his present position as manager of the Paducah Building and Trust Company, to which he came in 1893. During his residence in Paducah he has made an enviable reputation as a business man and public spirited citizen, having become identified with a number of enterprises of more or less magnitude; being vice-president of the Mercantile Collecting Agency and a director in the Paducah Fair Association. He is a Democratic voter, but is not deeply interested in politics. Like his father and mother he is a member of the Christian Church and he and his family are faithful attendants.

Mr. Caldwell was married December 16, 1873, to Fannie Davis, daughter of Ben Davis of Barren County. They have six children: Michael Garnett, Louisa, James Shipp, Duke Dickinson, William Ernest and Nellie.

INDEX.

Name	Page	Name	Page	Name	Page
Abbett, E. E.	20	Bell, C. S., Jr.	436	Bruce, John	395
Adams, Stanley	248	Beckette, O. F. L.	131	Brock, C. R.	490
Adams, Thos.	248	Beckett, A. L.	132	Brooks, L. H.	5
Adams, A. S.	301	Bennett, N. L.	237	Brooks, J. M.	616
Adams, J. W.	301	Berry, A. Y.	209	Brooks, Moses	616
Adams, David	301	Berry, J. M.	209	Boyle, John	573
Adams, Allen	475	Beyland, T. F.	290	Brossart, Rev. F.	127
Adams, J. R.	475	Bedford, S. W.	300	Bryan, Morgan	128
Adair, John	317	Bedford, T. W.	300	Bryan, Joseph	128
Adair, G. W.	543	Beck, J. B.	422	Bryan, Wm.	129
Adair, I. C.	543	Beck, H. B.	471	Browder, W. F.	134
*Aitkins, C. W.	397	Beck, D. E.	472	Browder, David	134
Aitkins, Geo.	397	Bibb, G. M.	287	Bronston, C. J.	151
*Allen, W. B.	478	Biggs, R. C.	144	Bronston, T. D.	151
Alexander, C. H.	474	Biggs, Wm.	144	Brent, W. D.	202
Alford, M. C.	171	Birge, T. C.	351	Brent, J. D.	202
Alexander, C. G.	474	Birge, W. C.	351	Bradford, T. S.	207
Alexander, A. J.	596	Bird, C. A.	420	Bradford, J. J.	207
Alexander, Robt.	597	Birney, J. G.	385	Breckinridge, Rev. John	494
Ament, S. P.	424	Biltz, Edward	553	Breckinridge, Rev. R. J.	494
Anderson, J. J.	72	Biltz, Chas.	554	Breckinridge, J. C.	576
Anderson, T. S.	404	Bingham, G. B.	567	Briggs, B. F.	522
Anderson, J. B.	404	Bingham, Jabez	567	Briggs, W. M.	523
Anderson, L. B.	589	Bigstaff, T. J.	609	Brock, C. R.	490
Anderson, Ervine	590	Bigstaff, J. M.	610	Bradley, W. O.	573
Arthur, W. E.	23	Blakey, G. D.	373	Bradley, R. M.	574
Arthur, Wm.	24	Blackwell, W. W.	217	Breck, Daniel	593
Armstrong, T. H.	177	Blackwell, P. A.	217	Breck, Rev. R. L.	593
Armstrong, J. W.	177	Blakey, G. D.	373	Bullitt, T. W.	1
Armstrong, R. D.	612	Blanton, J. I.	246	Bullitt, A. S.	1
Armstrong, Abel	612	Blanton, L. H.	246	Bullitt, Cuthbert	1
Arnsparger, Clifton	229	Black, J. D.	374	Bullitt, A. S.	315
Arnsparger, Stephen	229	Black, J. C.	374	Burke, Rev. E. A.	184
Asbury, H. B.	18	Blackburn, L. P.	566	Burns, J. M.	224
Aud, W. E.	234	Blackburn, J. C. S.	533	Burns, R. T.	224
Aud, H. T.	234	Bolling, Rev. W. T.	126	Burham, C. F.	235
Aull, W. T.	214	Bolling, W. T., Sr.	126	Burham, Thompson	235
Aull, Benj.	214	Boume, T. J.	620	Bueren, A. F.	247
		Boune, G. B.	620	Bueren, Francis	247
Ballard, James	14	Bowman, Wm.	248	Buell, D. C.	275
Barr, J. W.	37	Bowman, Benj.	248	Buford, H. M.	295
Barr, Wm.	37	Boone, Daniel	319	Buford, Henry	295
Baldeau, M.	145	Bowden, M. B.	487	Butler, W. O.	316
Bass, S. A.	158	Bowden, J. H.	487	Burton, R. A.	326
Bass, S. M.	158	Botts, J. S.	536	Burton, J. A.	326
Barbour, W. S.	586	Bohon, H. C.	603	Burchett, D. J.	358
Barbour, J. H.	173	Bohon, W. F.	604	Burchett, A.	358
Barbour, P. D.	586	Brown, C. M.	143	Buckner, F. W.	453
Barbour, N.	173	Brown, E. A.	143	Buckner, G. B.	453
Barbour, P. N.	288	Brown, L. B.	163	Buckner, S. B.	530
Barbour, Joseph	606	Brown, G. L.	162	Bullock, W. O.	535
Bates, W. E.	233	Brown, J. Y.	193	Bullock, S. B.	536
Bates, G. W.	233	Brown, T. D.	193	Buster, N. I.	572
Barker, H. S.	247	Brown, P. C.	238	Byron, W. A.	123
Barker, R. H.	247	Brown, T. L.	238	Byron, Andrew	123
Barnett, T. R.	268	Brown, G. N.	240	Byrne, W. A.	405
Baldwin, W. W.	409	Brown, E. H.	244	Byrne, James	405
Baldwin, Garrison	409	Brown, J. M.	245		
Barret, J. H.	467	Brown, M. J.	370	Caldwell, J. W.	81
Barret, P. S.	469	Brown, F.	370	Caldwell, S. B.	150
Barret, J. H., Sr.	467	Brown, W. L.	488	Caldwell, Austin	82
Barlow, T. H.	538	Brown, G. P.	488	Caldwell, Wm.	356
Bell, D. D.	120	Brown, M. J.	526	Caldwell, John	447
Bell, Henry	122	Bramlette, T. E.	284	Caldwell, Peter	356
Bell, J. F.	286	Breathitt, James	234	Caldwell, Richard G.	625
Bell, C. S., Sr.	431	Breathitt, John	346	Campbell, James	121
Bell, G. K.	435	Breathitt, J. W.	234	Campbell, James, Sr.	121
Bell, J. M.	436	Bruce, H. W.	394	Campbell, A. P.	246
Bell, W. S.	436	Bruce, Alexander	394	Campbell, A. P., Sr.	246

INDEX.

Name	Page	Name	Page	Name	Page
Campbell, J. P.	291	Dade, W. H.	372	Field, T. A.	92
Campbell, J. P., Sr.	291	Dade, H. F.	372	Field, John	92
Campbell, F. M.	496	Dallam, L. C.	3	Field, W. W.	222
Campbell, G. P.	496	Dallam, N. S.	3	Field, C. A.	222
Campbell, P. S.	610	Dandridge, Wm	139	Fithian, W.	107
Campbell, Samuel	610	Dandridge, W. F.	139	Fithian, Joseph	109
Casey, A. J.	256	Dalmazzo, W. J.	437	Fithian, Amos	109
Cabell, Wm.	137	Daughtery, F. E.	426	Forman, T. T.	188
Cason, W. S.	245	Daughtery, Daniel	426	Forman, Rev. E.	188
Caruth, A. G.	125	Davidson, E. M.	617	Fogle, J. E.	296
Cassell, J. L.	302	Davidson, G. M.	617	Fogle, McDowell	299
Cassell, T. J.	302	Davidson, J. H.	138	Fogle, R. H.	297
Cassell, Abram	302	Davis, W. J.	121	Ford, T. B.	465
Cassidy, Michael	623	Davis, Jonathan	121	Ford, H. H.	465
Carroll, Wm.	303	Davis, J. F.	232	Foster, J. S.	495
Carroll, Owen	303	Davis, R. D.	355	Foster, W. N.	495
Carroll, J. D.	377	Davis, E. P.	355	Fox, F. T.	607
Carroll, A. J.	377	Davis, Garret	385	Frantz, G. W.	90
Carroll, A. J.	533	Davis, Jefferson	336	Frantz, David	90
Carroll, Anthony	534	Day (Mrs.), M. B. R.	440	Fritz, J. S.	162
Carrick, J. C.	398	Desha, Joseph	389	Fritz, J. G.	162
Carrick, Robt.	398	Deane, G. M.	419	Frayser, T. H.	189
Carlisle, J. G.	399	Deane, S. M.	419	Frayser, Wm	190
Calhoun, C. C.	422	Dixon, Archibald	136	Fryer, L. P.	243
Calhoun, Rev. S.	423	Dixon, Wynn	137	Fryer, J. H.	243
Carothers, T. P.	453	Dismukes, J. L.	513	Francis, D. R.	503
Carothers, P. F.	453	Dismukes, Paul	513	Fultz, J. P., Jr	223
Chinn, Claude	242	Dora, F M	87	Fultz, J. P., Sr.	223
Chinn, J. G.	242	Dora, F.	87	Fulton, G. S.	554
Clark, James	577	Dora, J.	88	Fulton, S. S.	554
Clarke, J. B.	124	Dorman, J. H.	497		
Clarke, John	124	Dorman, Peter	497	Garrard, James	477
Clements, L.	195	Downs (Mrs.), L.	535	Gathright, J. T.	94
Clements, C. O.	196	Douthitt, S. J	539	Gathright, John	94
Clardy, J. D.	225	Douthitt, John	540	Galvin, J. W.	95
Clardy, J. C.	225	Drake, Daniel	274	Gayle, J. W.	528
Cleaver, W. W.	328	Duncan, H. T.	115	Gayle, James	529
Cleaver, David	328	Duncan, H. F.	291	Garr, C. R.	14
Cleaver, T. F.	331	Duncan, Rev. Wm.	291	Garr, B. L.	15
Clay, Henry	378	Durham, M. J.	4	German, L. W.	363
Clay, W. R.	421	Dunham, Benj.	5	German, E. S.	363
Clay, Samuel, Jr.	421	Dulaney, W. L.	306	Given, L. S.	92
Cox, George	85	Dulaney, Woodford	306	Giltner, W. H.	527
Cox, John	85	Durrett, R. T.	344	Giltner, W. S.	527
Cox, W. H.	187	Durbin, N. M.	360	Goodman, John	16
Cooper, Newton	215	Durbin, Daniel	360	Goodloe, W. C.	210
Cooper, Hugh	215	Durelle, George	460	Goodnight, I. H.	179
Coleman, R. S.	239			Graham, C. B.	8
Coleman, R. S., Sr.	239	Eastin, G. B.	620	Graham, C. E.	97
Coke, J. G.	260	Eagles, H. B.	292	Graham, Wm.	97
Collins, J. D.	475	Eagles, A. J.	292	Greifenkamp, Rev. B.	93
Collins, Lewis	276	Edwards, Ninian	314	Gray, A. J.	242
Collins, Orville	276	Elam, G. M.	180	Gray, Lynch	96
Corliss, J. W. R.	402	Ellis, W. T.	197	Gray, R. H.	242
Corliss, John	402	Elliott, Wm.	464	Gray, J. L.	96
Collier, D. R.	485	Elliott, Wm., Sr.	465	Graves, J. M.	266
Collier, Alexander	486	Elliott, Milton	569	Graves, W. W.	266
Cottell, H. A.	511	Elliott, Wm.	570	Grabfelder, B.	344
Cottell, Chas.	511	Evans, Silas	357	Greene, J. W.	470
Conn, J. L.	600	Evans, Silas, Sr.	357	Greene, Robt.	471
Conn, Thos.	600	Evans, D. L.	440	Green, Grant	604
Cowles, C. M.	124	Evans, G. D.	440	Griffith, J. T.	160
Compton, John, Sr.	305	Ewell, R. L.	597	Griffith, J.	160
Crabb, W. L.	304	Ewell, Leighton	597	Griffith, Wm.	161
Crabb, S. D.	304			Griffith, D. M.	161
Craddock, J. G.	407	Farley, Edwin	190	Grace, J. R.	172
Craddock, R. C.	407	Fant, W. S.	184	Greenup, C.	577
Crystal, E. L.	421	Fant, N.	184	Grundy, J. F.	268
Crystal, Geo.	421	Fallis, D. J.	391	Gould, I. P.	370
Crenshaw, Robt.	463	Fallis, George	391	Gould, I. P., Sr.	370
Crenshaw, R.	463	Felix, Rev. W. H.	91	Goetze, A. F.	368
Crittenden, J. J.	482	Felix, Joseph	91	Goetze, A.	368
Crossland, Edward	498	Feland, John	401	Guthrie, W. A.	93
Crossland, Samuel	499	Feland, Samuel	401	Guthrie, James	261
Crawford, L. J.	587	Feland, Thos	402	Guthrie, James	279
Crawford, J. H.	587	Ferguson, A. L.	550		
Curry, J. A.	83	Ferguson, J. W.	550	Hardin, Jno.	12
Curry, Wm.	83	Field, R. A.	16	Hardin, Martin	12
		Field, A.	16	Hardin, Ben	388
Dabney, C.	463	Field, Emmet	89	Hardin, M. D.	273
Dabney, T. C.	461	Field, Henry	89	Hardin, Henry	309

INDEX.

Name	Page	Name	Page	Name	Page
Haddan, J. B.	343	Hutchins, M. C.	201	Lancaster, John	376
Hall, W. C.	100	Hutchins, Benj.	201	Landrum, J. D.	506
Hall, J. G. B.	543	Hudson, Homer	258	Landrum, James	506
Hall, Thos.	100	Hutton, J. M.	342	Lee, Henry	276
Hall, Dixon	543	Hutton, James	342	Letcher, R. P.	285
Hanna, W. M.	100	Hurt, J. S.	582	Leigh, E. O.	300
Hanna, Thos.	100	Hurt, Joshua	583	Leigh, Rev. W. H.	300
Harrison, C. L.	101	Hynes, T.	33	Leslie, P. H.	318
Harrison, W. H.	101			Leathers, J. H.	371
Harris, Josiah	103	Ingram, W. H., Jr.	17	Leathers, Wm.	371
Harris, Josiah, Sr.	103	Ingram, W. H., Sr.	18	Lewis, G. A.	469
Hager, S. P.	155	Ingram, Wyatt	18	Lewis, G. W.	469
Hager, J. F.	466	Irvine, W. M.	75	Lewis, J. W.	552
Hager, Daniel	155	Irvine, Adam	75	Lewis, J. H.	157
Hailey, A. C.	179	Irvine, William	75	Lewis, John	157
Hailey, Carter	179	Irvine, David	76	Lincoln, Abraham	344
Hart, J. H.	194	Irvine, Caleb	134	Little, L. P.	429
Hart, Wm.	195	Ireland, J. A.	580	Little, D.	429
Hazelrigg, J. H.	196			Lillard, E. T.	457
Hazelrigg, D.	196	Jackson, W. L.	354	Lillard, Stephen	457
Hale, H. S.	267	Jackson, W. L., Sr.	354	Lindsay, James	345
Hale, Nicholas	267	Jackson, R. M.	499	Lindsay, Wm.	345
Hampton, M. F.	341	Jackson, W. H.	500	Lisle, D. C.	545
Hampton, Levi	341	Jarrett, C. F.	192	Lisle, M. C.	545
Hadden, J. B.	343	Jenkins, J. O.	106	Litsey, H. L.	588
Haygood, C. B.	369	Jenkins, John	106	Litsey, Uriah	588
Haggard, Rodney	594	Jeffrey, Alexander	351	Lloyd, H. T.	293
Haggard, A. L.	595	Jeffrey, John	351	Lloyd, Richard	293
Hetch, J. J.	19	Jeffrey, Rosa Vertner	352	Lockett, J. F.	117
Hewitt, Lafayette	108	Johnson, L. F.	265	Lockett, Rev. P. H.	117
Hewitt, Robt.	108	Johnson, Robt.	387	Lockhart, Henry	621
Henderson, L.	165	Johnson, W. P.	265	*Lockhart, M. R.	621
Hendrick, J. B.	258	Johnson, G. W.	388	Loomis, S. M.	118
Herold, M.	327	Johnson, Wm.	26?	Loomis, Rev. T. J.	118
Hegan, Francis	449	Johnson, R. M.	612	Loos, C. L.	147
Herndon, Elijah	509	Jolly, G. W.	309	Long, S. C.	262
Herndon, Wm.	509	Jolly, Nelson	309	Long, Gabriel	262
Hickman, Wm.	118	Jordon, Rev. J. D.	337	Logan, Rev. J. V.	455
Hickman, J. H.	534	Jones, J. P.	106	Logan, Alexander	455
Hickman, W. A.	534	Jones, Rev. C. H.	479	Logan, D. B.	492
Hissem, W. J.	619	Jones, Rev. J. W.	479	Logan, J. F.	492
Hill, Alexander	206			Logan, Wm.	525
Hill, A. D.	206	Karn, J. B.	114	Lyons, W. L.	226
Hill, T. M.	255	Kamleiter, Fred	115	Lyons, H. J.	226
Hill, Wm.	256	Kehoe, H. C.	168		
Hite, A. H.	343	Kehoe, James	168	*Matthews, C. M.	76
Hite, S. S.	343	Kelly, I. W.	307	Martin, Josephus	78
Hite, W. W.	403	Kelly, Griffin	307	Martin, Wm.	78
Hite, W. C.	403	Kelly, George	486	Mallory, J. H.	178
Hines, T. H.	417	Kelly, Joseph	308	Marshall, T. F.	271
Hines, W. W.	415	Kelly, F. H.	486	Marshall, Thos.	276
Higginbotham, J. M.	524	Kenton, Simon	277	Marshall, H.	280
Higginbotham, Wm.	524	Kenyon, F. P.	551	Marshall, T. A.	280
Holzhauser, G.	20	Kenyon, Orrin	551	Marshall, H.	280
Hobson, J. P.	104	Kimbough, H. W.	114	Marcellus, Cassius	276
Hobson, Joseph	104	King, Thos.	101	Marcellus, Cassius	276
Hobson, E. H.	600	King, Milton	103	Mathews, J. W.	532
Hobson, Wm.	602	King, C. L.	117	Mathews, C. M.	532
Hoge, C. E.	104	Kinner, S. G.	112	Martin, H. L.	558
Hoge, Rev. P. C.	104	Kinner, H. H.	112	Madison, George	570
Hodge, G. B.	467	Kimbley, J. F.	203	Merritt, G. W.	62
Hodge, J. T.	466	Kimbley, John	203	Merritt, Washington	62
Hodge, J. A.	169	Knott, W. T.	413	Meade, G. H.	416
Hodge, R.	169	Knott, J. P.	415	Meade, A. G.	416
Howard, H. C.	208	Kremer, H. L.	113	Metcalfe, Thos.	537
Howard, E. J.	491	Kremer, Chas.	113	Meddis, S. S.	74
Howard, Henry	208	Kraus, Wm.	318	Mitchell, O. M.	274
Howard, J. A.	491	Kraus, Philip	318	Mitchell, J. A.	174
Hopkins, J. C.	361			Mills, S. B.	181
Hopkins, J. C., Sr.	361	Lail, G. W.	119	Mills, W. P.	181
Hooe, J. C.	369	Lail, John	119	Milam, B. C.	252
Hooe, W. A.	369	Lawson, John	146	Milam, John	253
Houston, Sam.	163	Latham, Chas.	264	Minor, J. R.	310
Houston, Eli.	164	Latham, J. C.	264	Minor, E.	310
Holland, G. B.	586	Laird, B. F.	294	Milward, Stanley	508
Holland, G. A.	585	Laird, B. F., Sr.	295	Milward, W. R.	509
Holt, W. H.	530	Lang, W. C.	339	Monarch, M. V.	71
Hutchison, E. L.	14	Lang, Wm.	340	Morris, G. W.	129
Husband, L. D.	99	Lacy, A. T.	340	Moore, G. H.	264
Hughes, J. M.	102	Lacy, C. S.	340	Moody, W. B.	590
Hughes, Jesse	102	Lancaster, R. B.	376	Moody, W. H.	590

INDEX.

Moore, G. J.	264
Morehead, J. T.	285
Moorehead, C. S.	285
Moss, T. E.	48
Moore, J. H.	310
Moore, Lawson	310
Moore, E.	311
Moore, W. M.	338
Moore, Moses	339
Moore, W. G.	448
Moore, Wm.	448
Morton, M. B.	63
Morgan, J. H.	384
Muir, P. B.	10
Muir, Wm.	10
Mulligan, J. S.	484
Mulligan, J. H.	484
Murphy, A. G.	64
Myers, Harvey	73
Myers, Aaron	73
Myers, Harvey, Sr.	74
McLean, M. H.	622
McLean, Alney	313
McLean, R. A.	622
McHenry, J. H.	11
McHenry, B.	12
McClung, Rev. J. A.	274
McDonald, P.	26
McCane, J. A.	72
McCane, A.	72
McCane, J. A.	58
McCane, John	68
McCormick, Daniel	64
McKinney, G. J.	65
McBrayer, J. H.	69
McBrayer, A.	69
McArthur, J. M.	70
McArthur, Peter	70
McCorkle, W. H.	110
McCorkle, W. H., Sr.	110
McDowell, Samuel	140
McDowell, Ephraim	143
McDowell, W. A.	145
McDowell, Samuel	145
McDowell, H. C.	150
McConnell, J. H.	228
McConnell, Chas.	229
McNeill, Malcolm	236
McNeill, T. H.	238
McNeill, Rivers	243
McClain, Jackson	441
McClain, M. H.	441
McClain, Jackson	452
McClain, W. P.	454
McClain, James	454
McCreery, T. C.	479
McKinney, Matthew	551
McKinney, Samuel	531
McCreary, J. B.	559
McAtee, T. W.	595
McAtee, B. L.	595
Nagle, C. W.	215
Nagle, W. F.	215
Nelder, F. A.	57
Newman, J. P.	338
Newman, John	338
Netherland, W. N.	449
Norris, J. C.	481
Norris, Daniel	481
Nourse, Rev. W. L.	367
Nourse, Chas.	367
Oldham, J. Y.	76
Oldham, P. B.	76
O'Meara, J. P.	336
O'Meara, Thos.	336
Orendorf, Henry	133
Owsley, J. B.	400
Owsley, W. W.	400
Owsley, J. S.	439
Owsley, Samuel	439
Owsley, Wm.	478
Parker, Watts	584
Parker, J. E.	585
Parsons, Frank	53
Parsons, Rev. C. B.	51
Pattillo, Wm.	61
Patterson, J. K.	53
Pack, J. E.	252
Pack, John	253
Paynter, C. M.	334
Paynter, John	334
Parrish, J. H.	365
Parrish, I. N.	365
Pearson, L. D.	50
Pettit, T. S.	141
Pepper, J. E.	200
Pepper, Oscar	200
Pepper, Elijah	200
Penn, Shadrich	286
Pearce, C. B.	458
Pearce, Wm.	458
Pennick, T. B.	571
Pennick, B. W.	571
Pflanz, J. R.	410
Phelps, Zack	86
Phelps, J. S.	87
Phillips, J. F.	13
Phillips, H. B.	552
Phillips, Thos.	552
Phister, E. C.	571
Piper, S. A.	49
Pike, Samuel	116
Platts, G. E.	227
Poyntz, C. B.	2
Poyntz, S. B.	2
Powell, J. F.	192
Powell, T. W.	192
Powell, H. A.	199
Powell, H.	199
Poage, Wm.	227
Poage, H. C.	227
Pope, John	387
Pope, Curran	478
Porter, Rev. Newton	507
Porter, Eli	508
Porter, T. F.	598
Proctor, B. F.	152
Proctor, Benj.	152
Prouse, J. P.	190
Pretlow, Richard	57
Prentice, G. D.	287
Pratt, Rev. W. M.	353
Pratt, Samuel	353
Price, C. H.	489
Price, W. B.	489
Preston, Wm.	572
Pryor, J. D.	589
Pryor, J. C.	589
Ragdale, W. J.	333
Ragdale, W. E.	333
Rankins, W. J.	397
Rankins, B. H.	397
Raison, C. L., Sr.	472
Raison, C. L., Jr.	472
Rennie, Rev. Joseph	159
Reynolds, C. O.	263
Reynolds, O. A.	263
Reynolds, D. S.	450
Reynolds, Rev. Thos.	450
Reddick, J. T.	58
Reno, Lawson	335
Reno, L. R.	335
Rhoads, McHenry	466
Rhoads, A. J.	466
Richmond, Rev. J. M.	60
Rives, R. F.	205
Rives, Robt.	205
Riffe, J. M.	366
Riffe, Christopher	284
Riffe, H. R.	366
Richie, C. G.	329
Richie, H. C.	330
Rice, J. W.	335
Rice, J. M.	335
Richardson, R. C.	430
Richardson, S. Q.	430
Richardson, G. W.	556
Richardson, O. C.	557
Rodman, Thos.	44
Rodman, John	44
Rodman, James	299
Rowan, John	272
Roberts, H. H.	510
Roberts, J. H.	511
Rousseau, L. H.	283
Robertson, George	540
Robinson, H. S.	591
Robinson, J. R.	591
Rugless, L. B.	250
Rugless, Thos.	250
Russell, J. C.	269
Russell, J. W.	269
Russell, James	270
Russell, M. C.	366
Russell, Christopher	366
Russell, W. E.	555
Russell, Andrew	556
Sanford, L. M.	375
Sanford, Chas.	375
Sayre, J. W.	529
Sayre, E. D.	65
Sayre, David	67
Scott, J. W.	257
Scott, M. T.	257
Scott, Matthew	257
Scott, John	257
Scott, Chas.	386
Scott, W. F.	500
Scott, J. D.	500
Scott, M. K.	38
Schneider, J. W.	148
Schneider, Adam	148
Schroll, J. C.	182
Schorfield, C. B.	251
Schoolfield, G. T.	251
Schoolfield, G. T.	251
Settle, W. E.	268
Settle, E. E.	502
Settle, W. H.	503
Senour, W. E.	228
Senour, T. W.	228
Shouse, N. C.	544
Shouse, D. J.	544
Short, C. W.	592
Short, David	592
Shelby, Wm.	125
Sharp, S. G.	254
Sharp, Wm.	254
Shaw, Layfayette	216
Shaw, Samuel	625
Shaw, W. M.	216
Shelby, Thos.	126
Shelby, Isaac	516
Simrall, C. B.	21
Simrall, J. B.	332
Simrall, J. G.	66
Simrall, James	66
Sinickson, A.	110
Simpson, J. R.	618
Simpson, Wm.	618
Simon, J. T.	249
Simon, Francis	249
Simpson, J. D.	510
Simpson, D. M.	510
Simmons, W. L.	289
Simmons, J. E. H.	289
Skillman, H. M.	568
Skillman, T. T.	568

INDEX. 631

Name	Page	Name	Page	Name	Page
Smith, S. C.	39	Taliferro, W. A.	362	Walton, T. R.	578
Smith, A. W.	40	Taliferro, N.	362	Walton, W. P.	578
Smith, A. W.	46	Talbott, R. C.	411	Wallin, D. J.	406
Smith, James	46	Talbott, R. M.	412	Wallin, John	406
Smith, John	46	Terry, E. M.	41	Wallace, F. T. D.	514
Smith, W. M.	61	Terry, John	42	Wallace, Thos.	514
Smith, J. R. W.	111	Terry, W. M.	42	Warfield, Wm.	525
Smith, I. P.	111	Tenney, O. S.	476	Warfield, Benj.	525
Smith, J. S.	277	Tenney, Seth	476	Wadsworth, W. H.	546
Smyrl, Adam	77	Thompson, E. P.	581	Watkins, Joel	34
Sneed, S. K.	164	Thompson, Pinckney	80	Weir, James	230
Slaughter, G.	390	Thompson, P. B.	166	Weir, James, Sr.	230
Soaper, R. H.	97	Thompson, G. F.	459	Weaver, C. F.	330
Soaper, Wm.	98	Thomas, C. B.	212	Weaver, D. L.	330
Soaper, Thos.	98	Thomas, B. G.	213	Welch, J. C.	346
Southgate, F. H.	313	Thomasson, J. C.	314	Welch, T. R.	415
Southgate, James	313	Thomasson, J. V.	314	Wheeler, C. K.	33
Speed, James	284	Thorne, W. K.	437	Wheeler, James	34
Speed, John	560	Thorne, W. P.	437	Whitley, Wm.	273
Speed, Thos.	561	Thorne, John	438	White, C. W.	579
Spead, James.	561	Thorpe, S. H.	473	White, B. F.	580
Speed, T. S.	562	Tompkins, A. C.	176	Willis, G. L.	22
Speed, Thos.	562	Tompkins, W. W.	176	Willis, H. W.	22
Speed, I J.	563	Todd, G. D.	427	Withers, J. S.	27
Speed, James	564	Todd, H. I.	427	Withers, B.	27
Speed, John	564	Todd, J. G.	501	Williamson, J. A.	28
Speed, J. B.	565	Todd, Howard	501	Willis, J. C.	131
Speed, Philip	566	Todd, C. S.	537	Williams, G. W.	220
Speckert, A. J.	615	Towles, D. T.	523	Williams, Otho	220
Speckert, Frank	615	Towles, G. W.	523	Williams, T. D.	441
Stevenson, Rev. D.	25	Tomlinson, R. H.	493	Williams, Samuel	441
Stratton, J. A.	34	Tomlinson, Joseph	493	Williams, J. P.	469
Stratton, E. B.	34	Trimble, John	149	Wing, C. F.	275
Stratton, Wm.	35	Trimble, Robt.	149	Wilson, B. B.	347
Stirman, W. F.	35	Trimble, W. W.	149	Wilson, R. B.	347
Stirman, W. D.	35	Trimble, Robt.	270	Wilson, W. B.	359
Stirman, J. H.	38	Trimble, S. Y.	447	Wilson, W. H.	360
Stagg, James	84	Trimble, Rev. S. Y.	447	Wilson, E. K.	457
Stewart, James	315	Twiss, H. W.	606	Wilson, J. M.	457
Stewart, J. E.	315	Twiss, Quintis	606	Wilson, C. W.	611
Stewart, Ralph	315			Wilson, S. L.	612
Stewart, Robt.	153	Unthank, J. M.	615	Wickliffe, C. A.	389
Stewart, Rev. Robt.	153			Wood, O. M.	557
Stucky, T. H.	154	Vansant, R. H.	182	Wood, A. T.	623
Stucky, J. A.	155	Vansant, W. H.	182	Wood, David	558
Stucky, Harry	154	Vaught, Rev. J. O. A.	22	Wood, H. C.	283
Steele, D. W., Jr.	211	Venable, Nathaniel	79	Wood, H. S. S.	623
Steele, B. U.	447	Venable, T. S.	78	Worsham, A. J.	42
Striger, C. M.	219	Venable, S. L.	78	Worthington, E. L.	88
Striger, John	219	Veith, P. J.	387	Worsham, E. W.	43
Stine, D. H.	253	Violett, J. A.	328	Woodson, Urey	327
Stockton, Rev. Robt.	175	Violett, Leland	328	Wilford, I. M.	593
Stine, F. A.	253	Voss, John	402		
Steele, D. W., Jr.	211			Yager, Daniel	289
Sweeney, Rev. J. S.	45	Ward, A. H.	29	Yager, Arthur	289
Sweeney, Rev. G. E.	46	Ward, A.	29	Yeaman, Malcolm	23
Sweeney, Rev. Job	46	Wathen, C.	30	Young, F. O.	40
Sweeney, Moses	46	Wathen, B.	30	Young, R. B.	40
Sweeney, W. H.	408	Wathen, B. C.	30	Young, R.	40
Sweeney, Harvey	408	Wathen, H.	31	Young, A.	40
Sullivan, C. M.	332	Walker, E. D.	31	Young, B. H.	348
Sullivan, H. C.	332	Walker, J. D.	50	Young, Robt.	350
Swango, G. B.	185	Walker, Jacob	50	Young, John	350
Swigert, Phillip	259	Waller, B. L.	62	Young, S. A.	426
		Waller, F. F.	62	Young, Milton, Sr.	426
Taylor, Rev. W. C.	41	Watts, R. A.	170	Young, B. R.	427
Taylor, R. T.	41	Watts, Chas.	170	Young, Milton	443
Taylor, George	41	Warren, Joseph	217	Young, Rev. J. C.	494
Taylor, H. D.	55	Walton, Matthew	324	Yungblut, C. W.	350
Taylor, E. H., Jr.	392	Walton, J. H.	324	Yungblut, J. R.	350
Taylor, Zachary	393	Walton, M., Sr.	325		

INDEX
KENTUCKY BIOGRAPHIES

Prepared by
Eileene Sandlin
Ft. Worth, Tex.

Abbett, Anna G. 21
  Edward B. 21
  E. E. 20,21
  Harry 21
  Henry J. 20,21
  Jonathan 21
  Leon G. 21
  Mary J. F. (Gill) 20
  William 21
Abbott, James 335
  Josie 335
  Margaret 263
  Thomas Helm 453
Abell, John 377
  Mary Jane (Spaulding) 377
  Mary T. 377
Abercrombie, James 352
Adair, Alexander 602
  Elizabeth (Monroe) 602
  George W. 543
  Isaac C. 543
  John 296,317,318,543
  Kate 602
Adams, Adam S. 301,392
  Allen 475
  Ann 302
  Archibald 302
  Bessie Innie 566
  Caleb 301
  Charles 205
  Coleman C. 476
  David 301
  Ebenezer 301
  Elizabeth 302
  Elizabeth Sharp 301
  Frank 476
  Gilmer Speed 566
  James 302
  James A. 476
  Dr. James B. 361
  James L. 248
  James St. John 566
  Jane 301
  John Quincy 397
  John R. 476
  John Rowen 475,476
  John W. 301
  John Wood 302
  Joshua 301
  Kate 566
  Kate R. 555
  Lucy Ness 566
  Margaret 302
  Martha 302
  Martha E. 301
  Martha L. (Jordan) 248
  Dr. Martin 298
  Mary 302
  Mary Agnes 476
  Mary Irvine 505
  Mayo 476
  Nancy 476
  Precilla 301
  Rachel 251
  Rebecca 205
  Richard 476
  Robert 205
  Robert F. 476
  Sadie 301
  Stanley 248
  Stephen G. 555
  Sue 476
  Susan (Vance) 475
  Thomas 205,248,301,566

Adams, Thornton 476
  William 302
  William J. 301
Adamson, John 294
  Ruth 294
Addington, Lelia 299
Aitcheson, Miss 597
Aitkin Charles William 397, 398
  Dr. C. W. 15
  Daniel D. 398
  Emma 398
  Dr. George 397
  Jennie Browning 398
  Jennie Holiday (Duty) 397
  Maurice Duty 398
  Nathan Rice 398
  William 398
Akers, Miss 81
Albright, Mary 256
Albritton, Robert T. 590
Alcorn, L. C. 602
Alexander, Alexander John 596,597
  Charles H. 474
  Charles M. 529
  Col. 89
  Cummins G. 474
  David 474
  Lucy 597
  Martha (Baker) 529
  Mary 597
  Mary Morrison 474
  Minnie 529
  Phillip 529
  Rachel 206
  Robert 596,597
  Robert Aitcheson 596, 597
  William 596,597
  Sir William 597
Alexman, George B. 605
  Grant Green 605
Alford, Gov. 172
  Mitchell Cary 171
Allan, J. M. 182
Allen, Addie G. 267
  Albert 609
  Rev. Buford E. 267
  Charles D. 603
  Danah 195
  Elmira B. (Graves) 267
  John 326
  John R. 117
  Martha 413
  Mary McElroy 562
  Mary Sophia 195
  Miss...190
  Mollie 609
  Nancy D. 73
  Phil T. 194
  Robert 562
  William 340
  Col. Wm. B. 478
Alves, Annie 98
Ambler, John 276
Ament, Gabriel 424,425
  Samuel P. 424,425,426
Amos, Martha 365
Anderson, Albert 590
  Amelia 590
  Annie 590
  Augusta N. 61
  Capt....506

Anderson, Edith 590
  Elizabeth 135,589
  Elizabeth Blaine 368
  Emily 590
  Ervine 589,590
  Rev. Henry T. 167
  Hester 590
  John 404,554,589,590
  James B. 78,404
  James J. 72
  James O. 558
  Lawrence B. 589,590
  Lila P. 270
  Hon. Lucien 61
  Margaret 554
  Margaret Mills 171
  Martha 167
  Mary Ann 405
  Mary Ann Martin (Robertson) 404
  Mary (Robertson) 78
  Mary S. 557
  Mary Virginia Fisher 506
  Matilda Robertson 404
  Mildred 220
  Nancy D. 58
  Nancy Marshall 409
  Pattie Bransford 405
  Robert 589
  Richard 558
  Sallie Quicksall 78,404
  Hon. Simeon H. 171
  Susan Harris 405
  Thomas Sidney 404,405
  T. S. 79
  Walter 368
  W. George 270
  Wiley 590
  William 242
  William Kyle 404
  Worsham 409
Antle, John 35
Applegate, Elizabeth 39
Archer, Col. William B. 306
Argyle, Duke of 201
Armistead, Miss 169
Armour, Philip D. 201
Armstrong...77
  Abel 612
  Ada 177
  Amy Lee 177
  Caroline S. 178
  C. Q. 372
  Eliza Jane (Marshall) 177
  Eliza M. 178
  James 178
  James W. 177
  James Wesley 177,178
  Jane 178
  Jane Lee 178
  John 178
  Johnson 178
  Julia O. 178
  Kate 372
  Mabel 612
  Margaret 178
  Mary 178
  Mary Ann 178
  Matilda G. 178
  Matilda Towles 612
  Olive 476
  Percilla 302

Armstrong, Rawleigh D. 612
  Rawleigh L. 612
  Ruby 612
  Sarah Anne 178
  Thomas H. 177
  William 178,593,612
  William McKindree 178
Arnold, David 610
  Mrs. Fenton 610
  Isaac 524
  James 167
  John 265,610
  Sallie 265
Arnsparger, Christopher 230
  Clifton 229,230
  Fanny 230
  George 230
  James D. 230
  Lizzie 230
  Lucien Marion 230
  Martha 230
  Martha Todd 229
  Sobrina 230
  Stephen 229
  William S. 230
Arthur, Ann Eliza 238
  Gammel 24
  Ida Lee 252
  Jane 24
  John 24
  Margaret 24
  May 24
  Michael 24
  Nancy 24
  Sidney 24
  William 23,24
  William E. 23,24
Asbury, Carroll 363
  Henry Bascom 18
  Henry Bryan 19
  Jessie J. 19
  Mr....19
  Nina Mai 19
  Taylor 19
Ashburn, Judge...174
  Thomas 173
Ashby, Dick 612
  John 612
  Robert 612
  Sallie Weeden 612
  Turner 612
Atchison, Hamilton 129
  Julia 129
  Dr. Thomas 129
Atkinson, Mary 251
  T. J. 190
Aud, Atha Matilda 235
  Charles Z. 235
  Ellen 235
  George 235
  Guy G. 234
  Henry T. 234
  Hilliary T. 234,235
  Joseph B. 235
  Maggie 235
  Mary Joseph 234
  Mary Rock 234
  Regina 234
  Thomas C. 234
  Victoria 234
  William E. 234,235
Aull, Aquilla 214
  Benjamin 214
  Charlotte (McDaniel)214
  James 214
  James C. 215
  Leroy 215
  Maude L. 215
  William Thomas 214
  W. Jesse 215
Austin, Elizabeth 230
  James 94

Austin, John 94
Averitt, J. R. 463

Bacon, Ann F. 226
  Capt. Edmond 226
  Fielding 226
  Mary 312
Bailey, Abigail 476
  Joseph 476
Bain, William 92
Bainbridge, Dr....541
  Eleanor 541
  General Alpheus 53
  Elijah 341
  Kate I. 341
  T. A. 341
  Judge W. P. 45,222
Baldauf, Cora 145
  Ella Kahn 145
  Julius 145
  Leopold 145
  Levi 145
  Minnie 145
  Morris 145
  Nathan H. 145
Baldwin, Miss...3
  Anna E. 112
Ballard, Andrew Jackson 14
  Judge Bland 14,38,150
Baldwin, Garrison 409
  Henry 409
  Lucia 410
  Mary A. Eades 595
  Mary E. 595
  Mattie 410
  Nannie Marshall 410
  Robert Lee 410
  Sue B. 410
  William W., Jr. 409,410
  W. W. 595
Ball, Harriet 617
  John 508,617
  Margaret Johnson 617
  Martha 507,508
  Mary 623
  Mary A. 398
  Minnie 312
  Sarah 623
  Susannah 436
Ballard, James 14
  Pauline 13
  R. D. 524
  Susan Cox 14
Ballinger, Harriet 429
  Jane Logan 429
  Joseph 429
Band, Martha 183
Banion, Betsy 186
Bank, Caroline 427
  David 427
Banning...243
Barbee, E. L. 592
  John 592
  Lydia Ann 592
Barber, Ohio C. 201
Barbour, Capt...80
  Miss...388
  Ashburn Kennett 174
  Aubrey 183
  Betsy 535
  Burnette 535
  Daniel 173,174
  Edward R. 587
  Emiline (Houser) 174
  Fannie B. 587
  Fannie B. (Newman) 586, 587
  Dr. George Houser 174
  Hannah (Ashburn) 173
  Hervey 174
  James Hervey 173
  James P. 587

Barbour, Jane 535
  John D. 586
  Joseph 606,607
  Levine 607
  Maggie Pollock 587
  Mary 174,587
  Max Wilson 174
  Nannie 607
  Nathaniel 173
  Nathaniel J. 174
  Dr. Philip C. S. 587
  Philip D. 586
  Maj. Philip Norbourne 288
  Richard N. 587
  Sallie 587
  Sheridan Lee 587
  Sue 174
  Webb 607
  William 535
  William Scott 586,587
  Willie 607
  Wilson 174
Barclay, Eliza May 82
  Hugh 82
  Jane 307
  J. H. 178
  Matilda 412
  Sallie 175
  Sallie J. 82
  Samuel J. 175,307
  Thomas J. 82
  William 412
Bard, William 302
Barger, Sallie 297
Barker, Caroline M. (Sharp) 247
  Henry Stites 247
  Joseph 397
  Maxwell S. 247
  Richard H. 247
Barkley, Addie 41
  William L. 41
Barkstead, Susan 341
Barlow, Miss...399
  Fannie 150
  Frances (Cantrell) 150
  Helen 150
  James 150
  Kate 150
  Lawrence 150
  Martin 150
  Mary 150
  Milton 539
  Robert 150
  Dr. Samuel B. 546
  S. L. M. 546
  Thomas Harris 538,539
  William Pitt 150
Barner, Sarah 179
Barnes, Atlanta 498
Barnett, Sarah 305
  Judge Thomas R. 268
Barnhill, Rachel 114
Barr, Judge...38
  Mrs....38
  Anna W. 38
  Barbara 309
  Caroline H. 38
  Elise R. 38
  Hannah 364
  Jason Rogers 38
  John W. 37
  John W., Jr. 38
  Josephine P. 38
  Robert 364
  Susan R. 38
  William 37
Barret, Alexander 467
  Augusta 469
  James F. 468
  John H. 467,468,469
  Mary 469

Barret, Matilda (Wilson) 468
  Peter Straghan 468
  Susan 468
Barton, Mary 609
  Mattie B. 243
  Samuel 609
  S B. 460
  T. M. 243
Bartrim, James 367
  Sadie 367
Bascom, Rev. Henry Bidleman 496,497
Basher, Sallie 143
Bass, Almeta 158
  Bennett 158
  Cader 158
  Corilla 158
  Edwin Lucas 159
  Harmon 158
  Harriet 158
  Harrison 158
  Hearta 158
  Hetty 158
  Jones 158
  Julia 158
  Lucretia 158
  Mary (Chick) 158
  Mary Ellen 159
  Mary Frances 158
  Minnie Louise 159
  Nancy 158
  Oren 158
  Perlina 158
  Polly 158
  Russell Martin 159
  Scyon 158
  Scyon Ambler 158
  Scyon M. 158
  Solomon 158
  Thadeus 158
  Turner 158
Bates, Edward 233
  George W. 233,234
  Maria (Burgess) 233
  William Edward 233
  William Randall 233
Battaile, Mary 362
  Nicholas 362
Baufman, Kitty 203
Baxter, John G. 113
Baxton, Carter 479
Bayless, Dr. Benjamin 3
  Maria 3
Beach, Fannie 430
Bean, Fenton 610
  Lizzie B. 546
Beard, Addie 620
  Dr. E. F. 620
  Joseph M. 620
  Sallie Pryor 620
  Dr. William F. 620
Beardsley, Mrs...144
Beasley, Annie 508
Beauchamp, Nancy 88
Beazley, Aphia 533
  Augustus 620
  Bettie 620
  Frances (Edwards) 76
  Hiram 533
  Sallie (Webb) 620
Beck, Colie (Blanton) 471
  David E. 471
  David Evans 472
  Ethel 472
  Harry Blanton 471,472
  Herndon Blanton 472
  James 472
  James B. 14
  James Burnie 422,472
  James Schriver 472
  John 472
  Nannie Coleman 472

Beck, Richard Simeon 472
  Susan 472
  William G. 472
Becker, Mary C. 373
  Theodore 373
Beckette, Andrew L. 132
  Emily S. (Hatfield)132
  Hannah Lee 132
  James 132
  Oliver Francis Lee 131, 132
  Richard 132
Bedford, Capt...197
  Archibald 301
  Asa Kentucky Lewis 301
  Ella S. 300
  Hattie O. 300
  Henry W. 300
  Mildred (Houtchens)300
  Samuel W. 300,301
  Dr. Thompson Ware 300
  William K. 300
Bekkers, Father 128
Bell...84,108,174
  Mrs...237
  Adelaide Lancaster 436
  Arthur Hampton 436
  Charles Stewart 431,432, 433,434,435,436,437
  Clara D. D. 121
  D. D. 120,121,122
  Ellen Scott 433
  Emily Scott 436
  Flora Bunyan 436
  Frank Charles 436
  George Keatley 435
  George J. 431,433
  George Scott 120,122, 436
  Henry 120,122
  John Lambert 436
  John Moffatt 433,436
  Joshua F. 4
  Joshua Fry 286
  Lawrence E. 436
  Lewis Keith 437
  Louisa 367
  Margaret Elizabeth 437
  Nellie Munson 436
  Thomas 436
  Virginia Wickliffe 437
  Walter Stone 436
  William 431
  William Smith 436
  W. S., Jr. 436
Belt, Miss...584
Benedict...122
Benham, Henriette 288
  Joseph 288
Bennett, Caswell 173
  George W. 237
  Louisa (Perry) 237
  Norvall L. 237,238
  Waller 236
Bennington...125
Benton, Alexine 609
  Hiram 609
  Maria Crumb 609
Bering, Anna Marie 622
  J. A. 622
Bernheim, Bernard 456
  Isaac W. 456,457
Berry, Miss...584
  Dr. A. G. 209
  Allen G. 209
  Alvin F. 209
  Bailey D. 28
  Carrie E. 209
  Edgar Allen 209
  Henry 170
  Isaac 209,210
  James I. 336
  James Madison 209,210

Berry, James T. 70
  Jeremiah 336
  John B. 336
  Julia 336
  Lillian 209
  Louisa 170
  Luella 209
  Mary Laura 209
  Susan Hodge 170
  Virginia 336
  William A. 209
Berryman, Edward N. 587
  Theresa 587
Best, Margaret 164
  Sarah 164
  Thomas 164
Betts, Mary E. (Wilson) 39
Beverly, Ann 617
Beyer, Margaret 115
  Tobias 115
Beyland, Agnes 291
  Alice 291
  Beatrice 291
  Caroline (Meyer) 290
  Clifford 291
  D. G. 290
  Dorothy 291
  Ferdinand 290
  Walter 291
Bibb, Eliza H. 136
  George M. 136,287
  Richard 287
Bickerstaff...610
Bickett, Anthony 413
Bigger, Judge...49
Biggs, Lucy Davis 144
  G. N. 144
  Mary 415
  Dr. Romulus Culver 144, 145
  William 144
Bigstaff, Benjamin 610
  Elizabeth Iles 610
  James M. 609
  Mary (Jones) 609
  Odd Samuel 610
  Richard 610
  Samuel 610
  Sarah 610
  Sarah Fenton 610
  Thomas Jones 609,610
Bijur, Martin 10
Billingsby, John 179
Biltz, Amy E. 554
  Charles 554
  Charles H. 554
  Edward 553,554
  Edward F. 554
  Frederick B. 554
  George W. 554
  Howard M. 554
  Lula May 554
  Margaret Fable 554
Bingham, Judge...531
  Edith 567
  George B. 567,568
  Hannah 568
  Irene 568
  Irene (Rice) 567
  James 568
  Jabez 567,568
  John 568
  Martha 568
  Nira 568
  Royal 568
  Ruth 568
  Silas 567
  Silas, Jr. 568
  Virginia Daniel 567
  William Cranston 567
Bird, Albert 421
  Charles 421

Bird, Charles Albert 420,
      421
   Clarence 421
   George 421
   Nelson McKibben 421
Birge, Benjamin 351
   Ellen (Spellman) 351
   Ida 351
   Mary 351
   Nellie 351
   Thaddeus 351
   Thomas Crysostrom 351
   William 351
   William C. 351
Birkhead, Abraham 234
   Alice 234
   T. F. 196
Birney, Anna Reed 280
   James 280
   James G. 280,385
Bishop, C. H. 77
   Hannah 8
Biven, Mrs....421
Black, Judge...33
   Alexander 374
   Clarissa Jones 374
   Georgia C. 375
   Gertrude D. 375
   James D. 374,375
   John C. 374
   Pitzer D. 375
Blackburn, Church 263
   Edwin M. 566
   J. C. S. 14,67,111
   Joseph C. S. 533
   L. P. 67
   Luke P. 566,567
   Queenie Marshall 262
   Samuel Davis 262
Blackwell, Chapman 217
   Ernest 219
   Martha S. (Crymes) 217
   Paul A. 217
   Robert 217
   William W. 217,218,219
Blades, Samuel 124
Blaine, Alexander 368
   James G. 13,72,368
   Sarah Ann 368
Blair, Anna 376
   George A. 329
   Margaret 143
   Mary 421
   J. H. 143
   Samuel 421
   Samuel, Jr. 421
Blake, Lord Dudley 457
   Nancy 457
Blakemore, Lucy 395
   Thomas 395
Blakey, Ann Whitsitt 373
   Ann Hadin 373
   Churchill 373
   Churchill Haden 373,374
   Clayton B. 373
   George 373
   George Douglas 373
   George T. 374
   Hubert 373
   Lou 373
   Mary 373
   Nellie 373
   Theodore B. 373
   Thomas 373
   Thomas W. 373
Bland...126
Blankenbaker, Dorothea 15
Blanton, Agnes 529
   Bettie Ware 472
   Dr. Carter 472
   Colie 472
   Eliza (Ware) 529
   Elizabeth 246

Blanton, Elizabeth (Irvine)
      246
   Henry 472
   J. Irvine 246
   Joseph 246
   Lindsay H. 246
   Lindsay H, Jr. 246
   Margaret Coleman 472
   Mary Irvine 246
   Susan 472
   Susan Sneed 472
   William 472,529
   William H. 472
Blassinggame, Frances 362
Bledsoe, Col...389
   Benjamin 88
   Elizabeth 88
Bliss, William W. S. 139
Blume, Isaac 219
Bobbitt, Alex. 572
   Sallie Stephens 572
Boddie, Wiley P. 237
Bodine, Dr. J. M. 155
   Martha 400
Bodley, Temple 67
   William S. 67
Bohon, Annie Belle 604
   Elizabeth 604
   George 604
   Henry Clay 603,604
   John 604
   Dr. J. T. 604
   Mary 604
   Mattie 604
   Nannie 604
   Nora 604
   R. S. 604
   Virginia Hutcherson 603
   W. F. 603,604
   W. J. 604
Bois, Denina 586
   Tiny 586
Boker, Miss...305
Bolin, Catherine 440,478
   Mary 439
Bolinger, Daisy D. 589
   J. F. 589
Bolling, Ann E. 137
   Archibald 137
   Arthur 127
   Harriet Smith 127
   Helen Meade 127
   John P. 104
   Louise 127
   Margaret E. 127
   Mary Randolph 127
   Robert 137
   Robert E. 127
   Warner 127
   Warner T. 126,127
Bond, Rebecca E. 180
   William E. 180
Bonde, John H. 88
Bone, Dr. James P. 9
Boone, Daniel 45,114,119,
      128,138,165,319,320,
      321,322,323,324,466
   Jemima 321
   Leah 114
   Mary 128,129
   Rowan 131
   Squire 320
Boradus, Rev. John A. 611
Borders, Nora K. 333
Bosley, Margaret N. 423
   Nicholas G. 423
Bosnell, James 363
Boswell, Ella G. 567
Bottomme, Miss...505
Botts, H. C. 536,537
   Henry 536
   Joseph Samuel 536,537
   Virginia 536

Bourne, Ben H. 620
   Henry Kirby 620
   Thomas J. 620
   Thomas Pryor 620
Bowden, Amelia 488
   Ann 488
   Annie 488
   Elizabeth 488
   Fannie 488
   Rev. George F. 488
   Henry W. 488
   James H. 487,488
   John 488
   John S. 488
   Katie 488
   Marmaduke B. 487,488
   Mary 488
   Sarah 488
   Thomas L. 488
   Squire Turner 301
   Winefred M. 301
Bowman, Benjamin 248
   Ella N. 246
   George 248
   Jacob 246
   John 514
   John Lynch 514
   John P. 242
   Mary McElwee 249
   Nannie 312
   Philip 248
   Sabina 513
   Virginia 303
   Dr. William 248,249
Boyd, Sheriff...163
   A. 99
   Elizabeth 610
   Hallie Francis 504
   Sophie 505
   William 505
   William G. 504
Boyle...150,183
   John 573
   J. T. 171
   S. G. 116
Boynton, Joseph 476
   Sarah 476
   Sarah Swan 476
Braddock...140
Bradford, Eleanor 376
   Eliza Stuart 207
   Elizabeth 207,363
   John 195
   Dr. Jonathan Johnson
      207,208
   Dr. Joshua T. 208
   Louis Ewing 207
   Maria L. (Stuart)207
   Thomas Stuart 207
Bradley, Ellen 573
   Ellen Lotten 501
   Jerusha 201
   Lucy 252
   Margaret E. 501
   Robert M. 501,573
   Robert McAfee 574
   W. O. 102,167,501
   William O'Connell 573,
      574
Bradshaw, Catherine 600
   John 600
Bragg, Ann Blakemore 229
   Elizabeth 229
   Joseph 395
   Peter 395
   Thomas 395
   Walter L. 395
Braley, R. N. 184
Bramlette, Henry 169
   Martha 169
   Thomas E. 103,169,284
Branch, B. 237
   Juda 237

Brand...123
  George W. 116
  Lillie 116
Branham, Jennie 502
Bransford, Benjamin 190, 405
  John 190,405
  Judith 190
  Judith Amonette 405
  Martha Williamson 405
  Virginia Woodson 79
Brantley, Miss...158
Brassfield, James 529
  Melinda 529
Brawner, Isaac 203
  Mary 203
Braxton, Carter 140
Bray, Annie 590
Brazey, H. N. 190
Breathitt, Augustine Harvie 234
  Catherine A. 234
  Elizabeth S. 234
  Harry W. 234
  James 234
  John 346,347
  John W. 234
  Mary Caroline 234
  Peyton S. 234
  William 234,346
Breck, Daniel 593,594
  Rev. Robert L. 593,594
Breckenridge...24
  Fannie 183
  John C. 66,82,183,194
Breckinridge, John 137,494, 526,575
  John Cabell 575,576,577
  Joseph Cabell 494,575
  Mary Cabell 526
  Robert J. 526
  Robert Jefferson 494, 495
  W. C. P. 194
  William L. 153
Breese, Mary 503
Brent, Elizabeth Garvin 202
  John D. 202,203
  Joshua 202
  William D. 202,203
Brewer, Leah 84
  H. A. 528
Bridges, Elizabeth 406
  Hiram 406
  Mary 458
Briggs, Dr....84
  Benjamin F. 522,523
  Charles M. 286
  Nell 523
  W. M. 523
Bright, Jesse D. 49
  Dr. John W. 509
  Margaret 49
Brinkley, Charles 117
  Caroline 117
Briscoe, Stephen 413
Britting, Louis K. 100
  Minnie Bell 100
Britton, Colonel 46
  Margaret 46
Broaddus, Edwin 504,505
  Mary 504
Brock, Charles R. 490,491
  Daniel R. 490
  Mary Lucas 490
  Ragan 490
Brockman, Annie 205
  E. W. 115
  Frederick 115
Bronston, Charles Jacob 151,152
  Jacob 151

Bronston, Sallie A. 151
  Thomas S. 151
Brooke, George 276
Brooks...6,7
  Ada 7
  Alma 617
  Ann 465
  Charles G. 7
  Cyrus S. 7
  George A. 7
  James 300
  James Park 617
  John 7,616
  John M. 616,617
  Joseph A. 616
  Katie 559
  Lee H. 5,6
  Margaret McMillan 616
  Mary 370
  Moses 616
  Robert C. 617
  Rosella 7
  Samuel 370
Brossart, Very Rev. Ferdinand, B. G. 127,128
Brotherton, William A. 365
Browder, Bettie G. 134
  Caleb Ewing 135
  Charles 135
  David 134
  Edward M. 135
  Eugene Irvine 136
  Fannie Irvine 135
  Helen May 134
  James Thomas 134
  John 135
  John Caldwell 136
  Lucien McClure 136
  Marion Castner 136
  Richard 135
  Richard D. 135
  Robert 135
  Robert Irvine 134
  Wilbur F., Jr. 136
  Wilbur Fisk 135,135
  William C. 135
Brown, Albert E. 144
  Albert Young 163
  Alexander Lackey 241
  A. M. 104
  Amanda 447
  Angie R. 156
  Benjamin 240
  Benjamin Bernard 241
  Barbara Sunshine 163
  Cyrus Menander 143,144
  Colbert Cecil 241
  Edgar 241
  Eli H. 244
  Eli Houston 245
  Elizabeth 240,431
  Eliza Taylor 241
  Mrs. Emma 163
  Emma Frances 145
  Enoch A. 143
  Fannie 415
  Florence Huston 241
  Frances 241
  Frances H. Haney 240
  Frank. M. 239
  Frederick 370,526
  Furtney 581
  George 240,370,527
  George Llewellyn 163
  George N. 362
  George Newman 240,241
  George P. 488,489
  George W. 239
  Hattie 370,527
  Dr. Hawkins 40
  Henry 240
  Horace Stone 245
  Isabella 10

Brown, James 149,238,240
  James G. 239
  James Henry 241
  Mrs. Jessie M. 128
  John 240
  John McClarty 245
  John William 241
  John Young 137,172,193, 443
  Joseph 343
  Katherine 491
  Leroy 488
  Lew B. 163
  Lilian 370
  Lilliam 527
  Llewellyn Chauncey 163
  Lucy Murray 241
  Maggie 196
  Margaret Matilda 241
  Margaret Miller 526,527
  Martin, Jr. 527
  Martin J. 370,526,527
  Martin J., Jr. 370
  Mary 370,527
  Mary Quinn 241
  Mary (Rowland) 238
  Mary (Young) 193
  Maxfield 240
  Dr. M. D. 143
  Minerva (Murray) 245
  Nancy Frances 240
  Nannie 239
  Nannie McClintock 241
  Omar S. 143
  Paris C. 238
  Peter 10
  Richard 240
  Robert 240
  Robert J. 245
  Rose 377
  Sarah 240
  Sarah Elizabeth 241
  Sarah Ellen 245
  Susan M. 581
  Thomas 196,443,447
  Thomas C. 239
  Thomas D. 193
  Thomas L. 238
  Thomas Richard 241
  Thomas S. 156
  Washington Dorsey 245
  Sir William 240
  William L. 488,489
  W. L. 491
Browning, Ida J. 398
  William Reed 398
Brozeal, William 190
Bruce, Alexander 394,395, 397
  Amanda (Bragg) 394,395
  Eli M. 452
  Helm 396,397
  Horatio W. 394,395,396, 397
  John 395
  Lizzie Barbour 396,397
  Maria Preston Pope 397
  Mary 397
  Matilda L. 452
  Robert 458
Bruggman, Arnold 248
Brummal, Bettie 571
  Josiah 571
  Mary Hundley 571
Bruner, George W. 215
  Isabella (Head) 215
  Mary E. 215
Bruns, Frederick 403
Bruton, Katherine 584
Bryan, Abner 129
  Daniel 128,129
  Elenor 128
  Elijah 129

Bryan, Elizabeth 129
  Hannah 129
  James 128,129
  John 128,129
  Joseph 128,129
  Joseph H. 126
  Lewis 129
  Margaret 126
  Mary 128,129
  Morgan 128,129
  Phoebe 129
  Phoebe Elizabeth 303
  Rebecca 128
  Samuel 129
  Sarah 129
  Sarah (Pettit) 129
  Thomas 128,303
  William 119,128,129
Bryon, Ellen (Ryan) 123
Buchanan, Elizabeth 590
Buckner, Annie 454
  Annie Wooldridge 454
  Elliott 454
  Fannie 88
  Francis William 453,454
  Frank 454
  George B. 453
  Gordon W. 454
  Harry 454
  Joseph 454
  Lewis 454
  Lucy Madison 563
  Martha (Upshaw) 454
  Mattie Owsley 454
  Philip 88
  Robert 454
  Samuel Gordon 454
  S. R. 82
  Sherwood 454
  Simon Bolivar 530,531
  Susan 362,363
  Tabitha 88
  Thomas 454
  Upshaw 454
  William 362
  Dr. W. T. 233
Buell, Don Carlos 275
Bueren, Alexander F. 247, 248
  Catherine (Van Veen) 247,248
  Francis 247,248
  Godfrey 248
  Margarette 248
Buford, Abraham 296
  Bettie (Marshall) 295, 296
  Charles 296
  Henry 295
  Henry Marshall 295
  John 296
  Sallie Childs 292
  Temple 292
  Thomas 168
Bullitt, Alexander Scott 1,315
  Cuthbert 315 ,1
  Anna Priscilla Logan 2
  Benjamin 1
  John C. 2
  Joseph 1
  Mildred Ann Fry 2
  Sue 137
  Thomas W. 1,2
  William Christian 1
  W. J. 192
Bullock, Eliza Whitney 535
  Col. H. 119
  John M. 99
  Dr. Joseph 536
  Rev. Joseph J. 66
  Maria B. 536
  Mrs. Mary E. 99

Bullock, Samuel R. 535,536
  Waller 66,536
  Walter O. 535,536
  William F. 24
Bunyan, John 432
  Margaret 432
Burbridge, Stephen G. 141
  S. G. 183
Burchett, Addie 359
  Armstead 358
  Emma D. 359
  Drury 358,359
  Drury James 358,359
  Harlan Geiger 359
  John 359
  Mary 359
  Rebecca (Pigg) 358
Burdette, Annie M. 442
  Peyton 442
Burford, Elijah 369
  Miranda 302
Burgess, Edward 233
Burgin, Bettie 585
Burk, Miss...238
Burke, Annie 387
  Rev. Father Edmund A. 184
  Mrs. Fannie C. 225
  John 184
Burks, Carrie 176
  Henry H. 176
Burnam, A. R. 236
  Curtis F. 235,236
  Rev. Edmond H. 235
  E. Tutt 236
  James R. 236
  John 235
  John Field 235
  Lucinda Field 235
  Lucy 236
  Mary C. 236
  Robert Rodes 236
  Sallie 236
Burnham, S. H. 158
Burnam, Thomas 235,456
  Thompson 235,236
Burnett, Henry 4
  Muscoe 4
Burnott, Maggie 485
Burns, Bell Vivian 224
  Catherine 224
  Cora Lee 224
  Elizabeth 225
  Harrison G. 225
  James D. 225
  James Trimble 224
  Jeremiah 224,225
  John M. 224
  Keziah 225
  Lafayette 225
  Leonidas H. 224
  Maggie 224
  Mary 224,566
  Milton 224
  Minnie 224
  Nancy 225
  Robert 60
  Roland G. 224
  Rowland 225
  Rowland T. 224
  Sophia A. 224
  W. H. 224
  William 224
  William H. 225
Burress, Frances 342
Burriss, Amelia 250
  Mathew 250
Burton, Augusta Celesta 327
  Belle 327
  Eusebrie 327
  John A. 326
  Louisana (Chandler)326

Burton, Marion County 327
  Mary A. 326
  Richard G. 327
  Robert 326
  Robert Allen 326,327
  Robert Lee 327
  Susan 166
Bush, T. J. 116
Buster, Chrales Hayden 572
  Edward Everett 572
  Emma Theresa 572
  John 572
  Josiah 572
  Marian Emerine (Ingram) 572
  Mary 570
  Nimrod Ingram 572
  Sophronia 572
Bustow, Jasper 114
Butler, Miss...452
  Ben F. 103
  Logan 556
  Simon 278
  Sukie 589
  William O. 453
  William Orlando 316
Byar, Estella 19
Byers, Amanda 201
Byrd, Family 48
Byrne, James 405,406
  James, Sr. 406
  Kate 460
  Leo 406
  Margaret (Hughes) 405
  Martina 406
  Mary 406
  Walter 263
  William 406
  William A. 405,406
  Xavier 406
Byrnes, Sarah 529
Byron...124
  William Andrew 123

Cabell, Ann 137
  Eleanor 195
  Elizabeth 137
  Elizabeth Robertson 137
  John 137
  Joseph 137
  Mary 137
  Nicholas 137
  Robert 195
  William 137
Cagle, Charles 258
  Mary 258
Caldwell, Dr....151 -
  Mrs....92
  Addie 357
  Annie Bell 609
  Arenca Wood 625,626
  Austin 81,82
  Beverly 625
  Carrie C. 357
  David 81
  David C. 357
  Duke Dickinson 626
  Hamilton Peter 357
  Henry M. 488
  James Shipp 625,626
  Jeanette (Elder) 356
  Jerry 609
  John 81,447
  John L. 151
  John W. 82
  John William 81
  Louisa 626
  Louisa Harrison 81
  Lula 356
  Mary E. 151,357
  Matthew 151
  Michael Garnett 626
  Myr Morgan 151

Caldwell, Nellie 626
  Nettie A. 357
  Oliver 81
  Peter 356,357
  Pheba 302
  Richard Garnett 625,626
  Samuel B. 150
  Sarah 525
  S. B. 151
  William 356,525
  William Ernest 626
  Willie E. 357
Calhoun, Clarence Crittenden 422,423,424
  George 422,423
  John C. 151,422,626
  John R. 423
  Rev. Samuel 423
Callaway, Flanders 323
Cameron...593
Campbell...55
  Judge...34
  Alexander 45,143,147,154
  Alexander P. 246
  Ann Eliza 514
  Arthur 496
  Bessie 121,496
  C. A. 178
  Sir Colin 201
  Della 496
  Dr. Duncan R. 91
  Evan 201
  Fannie 496
  Fannie Minserrat 513
  Fay Ellis 247
  Fletcher Mills 247
  Francis Marion 496
  George P. 496
  George Waller 496
  James 121,201
  James, Jr. 121
  Jeanette 121
  John 45
  John C. 496
  John M. L. 148
  John P. 291
  John R. 336
  Louise Milton 611
  Lucy 550
  Lucy E. 496
  Lucy (Martin) 496
  Lulie Bell 496
  Mary 336
  Mary Boyd (Faulkner)291
  Matthew 201
  Micajah 496
  Martha Frances 610
  Martha Frances (Thompson) 610
  Mary Van Buren 513
  Myrtle 496
  Nathaniel 496
  Patrick 610
  Pearl 496
  Philip S., Jr. 611
  Philip Slaughter 610,611
  Robert 610
  Robert Edgar 496
  Sallie (Pettit) 496
  Samuel 496,610
  Sarah 496
  Silas 570
  Sue 496
  Talitha 45
  Theodora 496
  Wheeler 121
  William 513
  W. T. 496
Cannon, Caroline 470,471
  John 471
  Sallie 471
  William 471

Canterbury, America 316
  Ben Franklin 316
  Benjamin 316
  Elizabeth 316
  Flora 316
  Jackson 316
  Jeremiah 316
  Lawrence 316
  Milton 316
  Nancy 316
  Reuben 315
  Sarah 316
  Washington 316
Cantrell, Joseph 150
Cantrill...399
  Mary Helm 399
  John F. 399
Caperton, Hugh Gaston 261
  John 260
  John H. 261
  Julia 261
  Mary Eliza 261
Cardwell, John 265
  Mary E. 535
Carey, Sydney S. Sayre 530
Cargill, Duncan 42
Carico, Wilfred 196
Carlile, Ann 553
  William 553
Carlisle, John G. 14,168
  John Griffin 399,400
  William, Jr. 254
Carney, Stephen 590
Carothers, Caroline Thomas 453
  Elizabeth (Abbott) 453
  Mary Belle 453
  Patrick F. 453
  Robert Barr 453
  Robert L. 159
  Thomas Patrick 453
Carpenter, B. P. 537
Carr, William M. 40
Carrick, Alexander 398,399
  James C. 398,399
  Mary Helm (Cantrill)398
  Robert 398,399
Carroll, A. J. 530
  Anthony 534
  Anthony J. 377,533,534
  Benjamin 304
  Charles 203,377
  Eliza (Collins) 377
  Elizabeth Collins 534
  Dr. John 376
  John D. 376,377,378
  Louise 304
  Mary 303
  Owen 303,304
  Thomas 377
  William 303,304,377
Carson, Kit 192
  Thomas 152
Carter, Anne 82
  Anneta 159
  Ann Hill 140
  Caroline 376
  Charles 376
  James 305
  Margaret Letcher 5
  Robin 82
Cartmell, C. W. 410
  Elijah 129
  Mary 129
Caruth, Asher Graham 125
  Henry Clay 125
  Walter 125
Caruthers, John P. 237,238
Casey, A. J. 32
  Andrew Jackson 258
  A. W. 258
  Mary (Cagle) 258
  Walker 32,258

Casler, E. B. 42
Cason, Benjamin C. 245
  Edgar B. 246
  Hervey M. 246
  Nelson 245
  Rochiel Elker 245
  William S. 245
Cassell, Abram 302
  Albert 303
  Albert G. 303
  Benjamin F. 303
  Carrie 303
  Henry 302
  Herny B. 303
  James D. 303
  John B. 303
  John L. 302,303
  Joseph 303
  Lizzie 303
  Robert 303
  Susan 303
  Susan M. (Daniel)302
  Thomas B. 303
  Thomas J. 302
  Virginia 303
  William H. 303
Cassidy, Andrew 623
  Eliza 415
  Michael 623,624,625
  Samuel Evans 625
  William 625
Cassiday, James A. 368
  Mamie Lee 368
Castleman, Fanny 621
  John B. 172,621
Catlett, Ann Eliza 461
Cayce...205
  Fleming 225
Cecil, Nancy 572
  Sophia 240
  Thomas 240
Chambers, Dr. A. B. 21
  Nannie 21
Chandler, Elzy 524
  Lewis 203
  Lizzie Scott 524
  Mary 524
  Mollie Belle 203
  Richard 326
Chapeze, Benjamin 30,31
  Elizabeth 30
  Eulalie Fleget 30
  Dr. Henry 31
  Mary 30
  Susan 30
Chapman, Mary 415
Charde, Catherine 338
  Lawrence 338
Chastain, Eliza 108
  Rev. Louis 108
Chenault, Miss...33
  Courtland 197
  Pearl 358
  Dr. R. C. 358
  Mrs. Sallie (Webb) 607
  Dr. Walker 607
Chenowith, Mrs. Henry 1
Chick, Ambler 158
  Burril 158
  Davis 158
  John 158
  Judeth 158
  Mary 158
  Perlina 158
  Pettis 158
  Virginia 158
  William 158
Chinn, Barbara (Graves) 242
  Claude 242
  Dixey 242
  Edward 242
  Dr. Joseph G. 242

Chinn, Joseph W. 242
  Nannie 242
Christian...160
  William 1
Christie, Anna 84
  John 475
Christman, Josephine 224
Churchill...95
  A. H. 376
  Julia M. 567
  Malvina 376
Claiborne...166
Clardy, Benjamin 225
  Benjamin F. 225
  Elizabeth (Cayce) 225
  Fannie C. 226
  Fleming Cayce 226
  Henry H. 225
  James M. 225
  Dr. J. D. 194
  John C. 225
  John D. 225
  John F. 226
  Dr. Thomas F. 225
  William D. 225
Clark, Christian 577
  George 273
  George Rogers 33
  James 422,577
  John 106
  Mary A. 106
  Mrs. Onie J. 143
  Robert 577
  Susan 577
  V. C. 144
  W. T. 24
Clarke, Abner 124
  Bessie 550
  Bion, 124,125
  Clarence 125
  Cordelia 125
  Harry 125
  John 124
  John B. 125
  John Blades 124
  Katharine 125
  Mary (Blades) 124
  Robert 125
  Stephen 124
  William R. 124
Clarkson, Benjamin S. 557
Clausens, Jacob 586
Clay...301
  Anne 150
  Cassius Marcellus 276
  C. M., Jr. 194
  Elizabeth 395
  Green 276,594
  Henry 150,208
  Dr. Henry 421
  Henry 378,379,380,381,
    382,383,384,508
  Henry, Jr. 395
  Mrs. Henry 280
  John 421
  Keziah 224
  Littleberry Bedford 421
  Mary Belle 227
  Mary Rogers 421
  Rebecca (Cecil) 224
  Samuel 227
  Samuel, Jr. 421
  William 224
  William Rogers 421
Clayton, Lizzie B. 72
  P. H. 72
Cleaver, David 328
  David Irvin 329
  Esther 329
  George Hannibal 329
  Dr. J. F. 329
  Joanna (Grundy) 331
  Lucy Hemans 329

Cleaver, Lucy (Kirk) 328
  Thomas Foster 329,331
  Dr. William W. 331
  William Wells 328,329
  Willie Elizabeth 329
Cleland, Keturah 415
Clemons, Dr. John 556
Clements, Charles O. 196
  Gerald S. 196
  Gustavus Adolphus 540
  John 540
  Laura (Wagoner) 195
  La Vega 196
  Lucy 540
  Samuel A. 195,196
  William 196
Cleveland...198
  Annie 196
  Charles 197
  L. J. 537
Cobb, George Wadsworth 4
Cochran, Arch. 564
  Fannie J. 510
  Garvin H. 564
  Jane 564
  J. C. 510
  John 564
  Robert A. 169,188
Coffey, Alice 199
  C. R. 199
Coffin, Cora 565
  George W. 565
Coffman, M. 334
  Margaret 334
Coke, Elizabeth Blackburn
    262
  James Guthrie 260,262
  John Caperton 262
  Mary Elizabeth (Guthrie)
    260
  Richard 261
  Richard H. 262
  Richard Henry 260
Coldridge, Josiah 354
Coleman, Frances 240
  James H. 240
  Dr. John R. 240
  Mary 240
  Mary Gatlin 239
  Robert S. 239
  Thomas E. 240
  William H. 239
  Willie 59
Coley, Mary 127
Collier, Alexander 486
  Daniel R. 485,486
  Edward 62
  Ida Frances 486
  Rebecca Scott 486
  Robert 486
  Roberta 486
  Willam H. 486
Colling, George 178
Collins, Achilles 333
  Christpher 311
  Dillard 475
  Edward 534
  Eliza 377
  John D. 475
  Lela 475
  Lewis 276,277,439
  Mary Christie 475
  Dr. Orville 475
  Richard 276,439
  Rosalie A. 475
Colston, Rawleigh 276
Combs, John 309
  Leslie 171
  Mary A. 544
  William W. 545
Compton, Alexander 305
  Eleanor 305
  Elenor Williamson 305

Compton, Elizabeth 305
  John, Jr. 305
  John, Sr. 305
  Leonard Brisco 305
  Phillip Brisco 305
  Samuel 305
Condon, Mary 69
Conn, Catherine Bradshaw
    600
  Jack 600
  John L. 600
  Sallie 301
  Thomas 600
Conover, Mary 83
Conroy, Nora 168
Conway, Miles 543
  Sarah B. 543
  Sarah (Taliaferro) 393
Cook, Cora 99
  Cornelia 404
  Dr. John B.99
  John W. 99
  Mary E. 99
Coons, Mary E. 46
Cooper, Caroline (Rickerts)
    216
  Catherine (Rickerts)215
  Hugh 215,216
  John 216
  Levin 581
  Lucy 216
  Milton 216
  Newton 188,215,216
  Sarah E. 581
Copeland, Miss...415
Corby, Stella Elizabeth
    243
Corlis, Eva 402
  George 402
  John 402,407
  John William Respess
    402
  Maria (Rice) 402
  Mary A. 407
  Octavia 402
Corum, Amanda K. 472,473
Corwine, Rev. Richard 25
  Sarah 25
  Sarah Ann 25
Cosby, Miss...365
Cottel, Charles 511
  Phoebe Hanscom 512
  Samuel 512
  Henry Albert 511,512,
    513
  James Ruffin 513
Cotton, ...422
Coulter, Gus G. 590
Cousins, Johanna 406
Covey, Fannie 606
  William 606
Covington, Joseph 292
Cowell, Mary 85
Cowherd, Lou 591
Cowles, Charles M. 124
  Maria Ducker 124
  Ovid W. 124
Cowley, John 95
Cox, Ann Marie 85
  Edward 85
  Elizabeth R. (Newman)
    187
  Esther 85
  Frances 85
  Frederick 228
  George 85,86,187
  George Lissant 187
  Henry 85
  John 85
  J. S. 552
  Margaret 85
  Sallie Piety 14
  William H. 86

Cox, William Hopkinson 187, 188
Coyle, Clara 342
　Jane 342
　Stephen 342
Crabb, Alexander C. 305
　Alexander Compton 305
　Edward D. 304
　Elizabeth 305
　Elizabeth Compton 305
　Ellen 304
　Emily C. 304
　George 305
　James M. 304
　Jeremiah 304
　Jeremiah, Jr. 305
　John 305
　John P. 304
　Lindsey T. 306,438
　Nancy B. (Poston) 304
　Priscilla 305
　Priscilla Spigg 305
　Ralph 305
　Samuel 305
　Samuel Compton 305
　Stephen D. 304,305
　Stephen Drane 305
　Stephen T. 304
　Susan M. 304
　William L. 304
　William Owen 306
　W. L. 438
Craddock, Ann 407
　John Givens 407,408
　Richard Clough 407
Craig, Alice 3
　Rev. Joseph 267
　Mrs. Robert 12
　Sarah (Green) 472
　W. H. 599
Crain, James W. 15
　Sallie Rebecca 15
Cram, Ann 486
　Tristram 486
Cramp, Charles H. 201
Cranston, Martha 568
Cravens, Bettie 619
　Timolean 619
Crawford, Benjamin F. 466
　Clay 588
　Emma 301
　Jacob H. 587
　Leonard J. 587,588
　L. J. 77
　Mary Elizabeth 587
　Ree 466
　Rosa R. 60
　Thomas 60
Creel, Alexander H. 355
　Lucy (Neal) 355
Crenshaw, Albert 464
　Cornelius 463
　Dabney H. 464
　John W. 464
　Maggie 369
　Mary Frances Walden 463
　Robert 463,464
　Robertson 463
　E. Rumsey 464
　Susanne Moore 464
　Thomas 463
Crews, Ophenia (Rives) 205
Crittenden...68 ,137
　John 482
　John J. 38
　John Jordan 482,483,484
　W. L. 38
Crockett...266
　John W. 18
　Joseph 350
Cromwell...14
　Oliver 197
Crossland, Edward 121

Crossland, Elizabeth 499
　Elizabeth Harry 498
　Caswell Bennett 499
　Edward 498,499
　Kathleen 499
　Lal 499
　Mary 499
　Nannie 499
　Samuel 498,499
　S. H. 499
Crossley, Mary 249
Crouch, Rev. Ben T. 586
　David 267
Crow, John 51
　Warner 160
Crudup, John P. 238
Crump, Hattie 92
　Thomas J. 92
Crushew, R. C. 144
Crutcher, Elizabeth 33
　Sallie 33
　T. B. 566
　W. E. 222
　William 33
Crymes, Leonard 217
　Martha S. 217
Crystal, Ernest Linnwood 421,422
　George 421
　James E. 421
　Victoria (Deanne) 421
Culbertson, David 401
Cullom, Harriet 228
Culloney, Eliza 237
Culpepper, Elijah 200
　Sir John 200
Cummings, Eliza 239
　Margaret E. 239
　William 92,239
Cummins, Dr. David 154
　Moses 160
Cunnard, Catherine 21
Cunningham, Alexander 80
　Cleland T. 122
　Frances 122
　Mary 351
　William 351
Curd, John 262
　Spencer 262
Curle, Archibald 505
　Jane Irvine 505
Curlette, Jane 55
Curnutte, Reuben 112
Curry, Edwin Porter 85
　James A. 83,84
　James Howard 85
　Kate 84,85
　Katherine (Stagg) 83
　Mary 85
　Thomas Porter 85
　William 83
Curtis, Anna J. 363
　Nicholas 363
　Rebecca (Petticord) 363

Dabney, Albert Galatin 461, 463
　Albert J. 462
　Annie S. 463
　Dr. A. S. 148,463
　Carrie Lee 463
　Cornelia 463
　Cornelius 463
　E. F. 463
　Isaac 463
　James R. 462
　John 463
　Minnie 463,464
　Thomas C. 461,462,463
Dade, Albert Gallatin 372
　Henry Fitzhugh 372
　Jack 372
　Walter Holladay 372

Dailey, Henry, Jr. 14
Dale, C. T. 537
Dallam, "Pretty Betty Martim" 4
　Charles B. 4
　Charles Edward 4
　Clarence 4
　Edward Winston 4
　Elizabeth (Soaper) 3,4
　Frances Henry 4
　Francis Mathews 4
　James Lawrence 4
　Jane Marian 4
　L. C. 98
　Lucien Clay 344
　Maria 4
Dallard, Mary Elise 353
Dallam, Mary Frances 4
　Nathan Smith 3,4
　Richard 4
　Sarah (Hicks) 3,4
　Virginia Josephine 4
　William J. 3,4
Dalmazzo, James 437
　William J. 437
Dandridge, Adam Stephen 139
　Alexander Spottswood 139
　Dorothea 140
　Dorothea Spottswood 140
　Elise Winn 140
　John 139
　Martha 139
　Nathaniel West 139,140
　Philip Pendleton 139
　William F. 140
　William Fitzhugh 139
Daniel, ...135
　Charles 303
　Enos 303
　George 568
　John 303
　Peter 303
　Peter V. 470
　Pleasant, Jr. 570
　Pleasant M. 570
　Virginia 567,568
Daniels, Arjyra 331
Darnell...376
D'Aubigne, Cornelius 463
Daugherty, Charles H. 398
　Dr. Daniel 426
　Frank E. 426
　M. A. 426
　Sarah (Slevin) 426
Davenport, Rebecca 590
Davidson...139
　Catherine M. 138
　George 429
　James 138,429
　James T. 138
　John Hull 138
　Michael 429
　Sally Gilmore 345
　William 429
Davie, George M. 10
Daviess, Joseph Hamilton 276,498
　Mary 57
Daveiss, William 167
Davis, ...431
　Abel 331
　Amos 385
　Andrew J. Steele 233
　Basil Duke 122
　Ben 626
　Catherine 394
　Clarissa 122
　Cleland 122
　Daniel 122
　David 122
　Edith 122

Davis, Edwin 122
  Elias P. 355
  Elizabeth (Foster) 232
  Ethel Churchill 122
  Fannie 626
  Dr. F. A. W. 207
  Frances (Randall) 12
  Francis 122
  Garret 385,386
  George 365
  George T. 233
  George W. 145
  Henry 12
  James 121,232,440
  Jefferson 71,175,386, 387
  John 122,222
  John C. 233
  John F. 232
  Jonathan 121
  Joseph W. 28
  Kate 228
  Lewis N. 356
  Lizzie J. 233
  Lucy 144
  Martha 79
  Mary Stoddard 233
  Myrtilla Annie 356
  Myrtilla A. (Winn) 355
  Orrel M. 365
  Richard 355
  Richard D. 355,356
  Roscoe C. 356
  Samuel 167
  Sarah M. (Zimmerman)121
  Shipley 228
  Singleton 385
  Theophilus 232
  Warren Offutt 122
  William J. 121,122
  William J. S. 233
  William Kincaid 121
  William Leonard 167
  Worthington 167
Davison, Edward M. 617
  George H. 21
  George Mosby 617,618
  Martha (Vaughan) 617
  Mosby 617
Dawson, Lucy 305
Day, Florence 120
  Mary B. R. 270,440,441
  N. C. 120
  W. E. 440
Deakins, Alice Bell 328
  John T. 328
  Polly (Woodsides) 328
Deane, Allen 420
  Anna Belle 292,420
  Edward 420
  Guy M. 419,420
  Peter Francis 421
  Ruth Griffith 420
  Sallie Moorman 419
  Silas Mercer 419
  Somers 420
De Cantrill, Peter 399
DeCaux...187
Deeds, H. C. 597
de Irvine, William 505
Delano, Ira 165
  W. H. 165
de la Porte, Mademmoiselle Victoire 121
DeLime, Josephine 263
  Prof. Louis A. 263
De Meaux, Paul 514
Demonbreun, Mary 258
  Timothy 258
De Moville, Mary Magdalene 412
Denison, Daniel 421
  Elizabeth 421

Dennis, Abraham 466
Dent, Henry 53
  Minnie 53
Depew, Chauncey M. 201
Desha...118,149
  Joseph 389
Dewees, John Coburn 3
Deweese, Cornelius 265
  Florence 265
Dickens, Charles 556
  Elizabeth 556
Dickerson, Agnes Collins 439
  Anna 438
  Archibald 438
  Harriet (Dictum) 438
  Jefferson D. 439
  Richard A. 438
  R. T. 439
  Worth W. 439
Dictum, Richard 439
Diesel, Catherine 127
Dimmitt, Ezekiel 202
  Lydia Frances 202
Dingus, George 181
  Nancy 181
Dinwiddie...152
Ditto. Fannie 170
  Thomas 170
Dishman, Charles H. 170
  Charles Hunter 170
  Dorothy 170
  Susan Hodge 170
Dismukes, Esther Ann 514
  James H. 514
  James Henry 513
  James Taylor 513
  John L., Jr. 513
  John Lynch 513,514
  Mamie Sabina 513
  Marcus L. 513,514
  Paul 513,514
  Paul Isham 513
  Sabina Bowman 514
  Sarah 514
  Dr. Thomas 513
  Thomas T. 514
Dixon...454
  Archibald 118,136,137, 194,195,604,605
  Elizabeth Robertson Cabell 136
  Hal 605
  Henry 137,138
  Henry 604,605
  Henry C. 137
  Joseph C. 137
  Julia 137
  Maggie 137
  Martha 604
  Rebecca 194
  Rebecca Hart 137,138
  Susan Bell 137
  Wynn 137,605
Doak, Mary 179
Dodd, Mary 528
Doddridge, C. E. 178
Dodsworth, Mattie A. 238
  Robert 238
Dolan, Mary 191
Dole, Priscilla (Smith)476
Dongan, ...13
Doniphan, Joseph 124
Donnelly, Ann 184
Donoghue, Bridget 26
Donohoo, Lelia Campbell 189
Dora, Benjamin 88
  Elizabeth (Morris) 87, 88
  Ferdinand 87
  John 88
  Neppie Eugenia 88

Dora, Samantha Bell 88
  Thornton M. 87,88
  William 87,88
Dore...88
Dorman, Anna Eliza 498
  Archie 498
  Atlanta 498
  Elizabeth 498
  Emma 498
  Fannie 497,498
  Henry 498
  James H. 498
  James Hervey 497,498
  James Hervey, Jr. 497
  Jerubial 498
  John Wickliffe 498
  Lear 498
  Letitia 497
  Lucy 498
  Lucy (Kemper) 497
  Lydia 498
  Martin Luther 498
  Mathew 498
  Peter 497,498
  Samuel 498
  Silas 498
  Virginia Lee 497
  William Gaines 497
Dorsey, Caleb 586
  Elizabeth 193
  Nancy W. 245
  Noah 193
  Washington 245
Doswell, Elizabeth L. 36
  Thomas 36
Dougherty, Sally 377
Douglas...137
  Margaret 373
Douglass, Alexander 430
  Mary (Handley) 430
Douthitt, Ann 540
  Betsy 540
  Erasmus D. 540
  Fielding S. 540
  Harriet 540
  Helen D. 540
  James C. 540
  Jane 540
  John 540
  Kate 540
  Laura 540
  Lucy (Clements) 539
  Lula 540
  Rhelda 540
  Sidney T. 540
  Silas P. 539,540
  Stonewall J. 539,540
  Tapeley 540
  Thomas 540
Downing, Armistead 416
  John 416
  Robert 416
  Thomas 416
Downs, Lucy 535
Drake, Dr. Daniel 274,275
  Elizabeth 182
Draper, George Otis 117
  Lucy Ellis 486
Drennan, Martha 350
du Boeuf, Baron 121
Dudley, Alice 125
  Ambrose 353
  Dr. E. L. 257
  Patience 421
  Thomas 353,421
  William A. 116
Duhurst, John 51
  Mary Ann 51
Duke, Dr. Basil 276
  Basil W. 193
Dulaney, W. L. 158
  Eliza (Archer) 306
  Hiram W. 306

Dulaney, LeRoy 306
  Paul LeRoy 307
  William LeRoy 306
  Woodford 306,307
Dun, Walter A. 167
Dunbar, Frank F. 347
  George R. 347
  J. E. 26
Duncan, Annie 472
  Dr. B. F. 574
  C. H. B. 472
  Daniel 115,117
  Edmund 292
  Edward 117
  Eliza 117
  Eliza (Pike) 115
  Fanny 117
  Frances 10
  George Brand 116
  Harry 488
  Henry 291
  Henry Field 291,292
  Henry T. 115,116
  Henry T. Jr. 116,117
  Henry Timberlake 115
  Jane (Covington) 292
  Rev. Joseph 115,116
  Joseph Dillard 292
  Juliet (Mullins) 10
  Lilly 117
  Margaret 117
  Margaret Robertson 574
  Marion 10
  Mary Frances 4
  Nanny 117
  Raleigh 292
  William 291,292
  Zilla (Carter) 472
Dunlap, Sallie 95
  T. C. 95
Dunlop, Mrs. John T. 111
Dunn, George 104
  Mattie 104
du Pont, Francis G. 201
Durbin, Bessie 361
  Cassie 360
  Corilla Boracea 360
  Cullen 361
  Daniel 360,361
  Elizabeth 361
  Hosier 360
  John 361
  John Bonaparte 360
  Laura 361
  Mary 361
  Nancy 360
  Napoleon M. 360,361
Durelle, Frances Mary Peirce 460
  Frederic 461
  George 460,461
  George O. J. 460
  Louise Marie 461
Durham, Benjamin 4,5
  Benjamin J. 5
  Jabez 552
  James Wesley 5
  John 5
  Louis H. 5
  Margaret (Robinson) 4,5
  Milton Jamison 4
  Ora B. 5
  Robert M. 5
Durkee, Susanna 476
Durrett, John C. 87
  Reuben T. 344
Dustin, Hannah 512
Dutois...166
Duty, Jennie Holiday 398
  Littleton 398
Duvall, Alvin 502
  Annie 502
  Burbridge 502

Duvall, Edward 502
  Elizabeth 502
  Howard 502
  John 502
  John, Jr. 502
  Martha 502
  Robert 33
  Thomas 502
  William P. 502
  Willina 501,502
Dye, Cora B. 243
  John 243
  Mary 243
Dyer, Daisy Lee 426

Eagles, Albert James 292, 293
  Hawes B. 292
  Kate Coleman (Hawes) 292
  Marianne 293
  William 293
Eakins, John 118
Easterling, Nancy 181
Eastin, ...360
  Augustine 118
  George B. 620.621
  Zachariah 118
Earhart, Anna E. 319
Eatham, Hartwell 16
Eba, D. W. 403
  Jennie 403
Echols, Elizabeth 555,556
Eckert, L. M. 587
  Mary Elizabeth 587
  Thomas T. 201
Edmondson, Joseph 409
  Mary 408
  Wilson 409
Edmunds, Ray 552
Edrington, Rebecca 394
Edwards, Frances S. 532
  Ninian 314
  Obedience 298
  Robert 533
  Wiley 533
  W. S. 175
Elam, Charley M. 180
  George Milton 180
  George W. 181
  Harry B. 181
  James K. 181
  Martha 180,181
  Nancy C. 181
  Nancy (Dingus) 181
  Nimrod 181
  William 181
  William N. 180
Elder, Archbishop..556
  George 356
  Joseph 556
  Susan Agnes 556
  Sylvester 556
Elker, Samuel 245
Elkin, Daniel Collier 486
  Robert L. 486
Ellerbe, Christopher P. 504
  Mary Francis 504
Elliott, Benjamin T. 465
  Burgess 570
  Dawson 570
  Elizabeth 47
  Elizabeth (Palmer) 464
  Florence S. 570
  Hattie 454
  H. Clay 464
  Henry H. 570
  Mrs. Juan 570
  Julian Gaylord 570
  Lucy Cecil 570
  Mamie 465
  Martha Jane 570
  Mary E. 570
  Milton 569,570

Elliott, Minnie LeGrand 570
  J. Nathan 570
  Nancy B. 570
  Nathan 570
  Parmelia 570
  Sarah 496
  Sarah Harris 569
  William 47,464,465,569,570
  William H. 454,570
  William M. 570
Ellis...198
  Belle 566
  George 175
  Dr. J. W. 199
  Luther R. 199
  William T. 197,199
Elmaker, Horace 178
Elmore, Thomas 269
Embry, Bettie 182
Emison, Sallie M. 252
  William 252
Endera, Cora 103
  Henry 103
Enderlin, Mary M. 91
England, Thomas 297
  W. B. 297
English, Dr....502
  Elvira 32,33
  Emma 33
  Horace 33
  Robert 33
Erd, Frank I. 436
  Mary H. 436
Eubank,...206
Evans, Belam P. 358
  Ben 493
  David 440
  David L. 440
  D. L. 27
  Emaline (Davis) 440
  Evan 503
  Francis 624
  Green D. 440
  Harriet D. 503
  Hickman 358
  Humphrey 503
  James S. 503
  John 503
  Job 25
  Lizzie 493
  Mary 134,624
  Oliver P. 358
  Parmelia (Quisenberry) 357,358
  Peter 357
  Robert 149
  Sarah 25,472
  Silas 357,358
  Walter 440
Everell,.Lizzie 514
Everett...84,108,174
Everhart, Isaac 415
Ewell,...598
  Alice 500,598
  America A. 598
  George W. 598
  James A. 598
  John H. 598
  Leighton 597
  Logan M. 598
  Miranda Fox 598
  Pocahontas 598
  Richard L. 597,598
  Richard R. 598
  R. L. 500
  Robert L. 598
  Dr. Silas W. 598
  Thomas M. 597
Ewing, Jennie 566
  Sarah A. 251
  Thomas 251
  Dr. U. E. 566

Fackler, George 150
Fair, George C. 298
Fairfax, Lord 12,200
Fairleigh, James 31
  Mary 31
Fallis, Daniel James 391, 392
  George 391
  John T. 392
  Thomas 391
Fannin, J. L. 417
  Mary Edith 417
  Mary (Lock) 417
Fant, Atha 25
  Edwin L. 185
  James 184
  James M. 184
  Juliet 184,185
  Louise 184
  Lula 185
  Nelson 184,185
  Olive 185
  William Saunders 185
  William Slaughter 184, 185
Farley, Dora 192
  Edwin 190,191
  Edwin Phillip 192
  Herbert Warren 192
  Marie 192
  Mary (Dolan) 190
  Maud 192
  Michael 190
  Rosela Ilda 192
  William H. 192
Farra, B. F. 326
  Blanche 373
  Carrie 326
Farrar, Ebenezer 568
  Elizabeth 568
Farris, William 500
Farrow, Sue E. 188
Faulkner...135
  Charles James 291
  John K. 59
Fauquier, Lova 488
Featherston, Bessie 508
  C. F. 508
Fee, Elizabeth Bradford 363
  John 363
  Sallie 363
Feland, Andrew 401
  David 401
  James 401
  James H. 401
  John 190,401
  John, Jr. 401
  Joseph 401
  Logan 401
  Mary 401
  Nancy (Hamill) 401
  Samuel 401
  Thomas 401
  William 401
Felix, Alice 537
  Ann Bradford 92
  Cordelia 537
  Elizabeth 537
  Emma 537
  Jane Ann (Shouse) 536, 91
  Jennie 92
  John I. 537
  Joseph 536,537
  Josiah 91
  Josie 92
  Mary 92,537
  Mattie 92
  Nannie 536,537
  William H. 91,92
  William H., Jr. 92
  William M. 537
Ferguson, Miss...326

Ferguson, Abraham 550
  Abram L. 550
  Abram Lunsford 551
  James William 550,551
  Lucy 551
  Maggie 551
  Mary (Matson) 550
  Matilda 551
  Noah 550
  Robert H. 551
  Robert M. 550
  Volney W. 551
  William 551
  William H. 550
Ferris, Mrs. James 486
Ficklen, Mary 185
Fiddler, Lelia D. 335
Field...125,90
  Anderson 16
  Charles Anderson 222
  Cyrus 222
  Dorothea Crump 92
  Emmett 89
  Esther 16
  Henry 89
  James L. 92
  James M. 16
  James Thomas 92
  John 92,222,235,236
  John Smarr 223
  Lillian T. 223
  Lucinda 235
  Marie 16
  Mary Anderson 223
  Mary Ann (Eatham) 16
  Mary (Hicks) 92
  Mary (Young) 89
  Millie W. 223
  Nancy (Toleman) 222
  Reuben 53
  Richard 89
  Robert A. 16
  Robert Anderson 16
  Robert Arnold 16
  Timothy Alexander 92
  Vernon C. 16
  William H. 89
  William W. 222
Finley, Sarah 36
  William 400
Finnell, Robert 263
Fisher, Darwin E. 361
  John W. 361
  Mary L. 361
Fisk, John 203
  Robert B. 203
Fithian, Amos 109,110
  Dr. Frank 109
  Georgia 109
  Joel 107,109
  Joseph 109,110
  Nellie 109
  Philip Victor 109,110
  Sarah Dick (Sinickson) 107
  Sarah Sinickson 110
  W. 109
  Washington 107
  William 110
Fitzgerald, David 49
  Ellen 49
  McCalla 598
Fitzhugh...140
Flanders, W. P. 625
Fleckenstein, Dorothea 183
Fleming, Lewis 125
Flood...115
  John H. 77
  Mary S. 77
Flournoy, Thompson 158
Floyd, John 141
Flynn, Ann 27
Fogle, Annie 299

Fogle, Catherine 297
  Ebenezer 297
  D. Edgar 297
  Elizabeth A. 297
  Frances 297
  George Preston 297
  Isabelle 297
  James M. 297
  Jesse E. 296,297,298, 299
  Jesse Edwin 297,298
  Joel 297
  Lena J. 297
  Marietta 297
  Mary 297
  McDowell 296,297,298
  McDowell Addington 299
  Rachel J. 297
  Robert B. 297
  Robert H. 297
  Sallie Ann 297
  Sarah 297
  Sarah Hammet 298
  William McDowell 297
Foltz...223
Ford, Ann M. (Brooks) 465
  Elliott 465
  Harbin H. 465
  L. 77
  Sallie 471
  Sallie E. 449
  Thomas B. 465,466
  William 465
Fore, Peter 299
  William 299
Foree, Berry 375
  Elizabeth Major 620
  Sallie 375
  Sally 620
  William 44
  William P. 620
Forman, C. W. 188
  Ellen (Russell) 188
  Rev. Ezekiel 188
  M. Don 189
  Robert 188
  Samuel 188
  Thomas T. 188
Forrest, N. B. 192
Forshee...250
Fort...(widow) 62
Forwood, William H. 307
Foss, Dr. S. S. 182
Foster, Alice 496
  Eliza 495
  Fannie 496
  Herman S. 495
  James E. 495
  John 232
  John Marshall 496
  John Standford 495
  Josiah 495
  Luther L. 523,524
  Mary E. 495
  Mary S. 312
  Robert 495
  Robert L. 495,496
  Sallie 496
  William Nathan 495,496
Fowler, Birdie E. 291
  Edward 259
  Esther 259
  Gus 291
  J. 100
  Jacob 259
  Mintie 100
Fowles, Thomas 98
Fox, Benjamin 598
  Charles C. 609
  Eliza 608
  Felix G. 609
  Fontaine Talbot 505, 607,608,609

Fox, John Oliver 609
  Miranda 597
  Peter C. 608
  Samuel 609
  Sophie Irvine 505,607
  Susan 608
  Thomas 608
  William 607,609
  William McKee 608
Frame, Margaret 102
Francis, Broaddus 504
  Charles 504
  David 504
  David Rowland 503,504, 505,506
  Eliza Caldwell 505
  John Broaddus 504,505
  Perry 504
  Rowland 504
  Salton Turner 504
  Sidney Rowland 504
  Thomas 504,505
  Thomas H. 504
Franklin, Benjamin 32
  Sarah 459
Frantz, Christina Staebler 90
  David 90
  David W. 91
  Edwin A. 91
  Emma E. 91
  George W. 90
  George W., Jr. 91
  Harold W. 91
  Walter L. 91
Frayser, Benjamin 190
  Frederick Harris 190
  Giles Harris 190
  Judith Bransford 190
  Martha Bransford 190
  Mary 190
  Mary Susan 190
  Robert 190
  Susan M. 190
  Thomas H. 189,190
  Virginia 190
  William 189,190
Frazee, Joseph 325
Frazer, Harriet Morton 136
  Thomas A. 136
Frederick, Dr. A. S. 101
Fredin, Madame 25
Freeman, Lizzie 430
Freeze, G. P. 50
  Jennie 50
Frelinghuysen...84
French, Annie B. 106
  Elizabeth 586
  Rebecca 586
  Robert 54
  Samuel 586
  Stephen 106
  Y. N. 190
Frey, Martha (Campbell)336
  Mary 336
  William H. 336
Friend, Charles 184
  Luvina H. 184
Fritz, Cora Ruth 163
  Jane 163
  Jane F. Hord 162
  John G. 162
  John S. 162,163
  Solomon 162
Fry, John 286
  Joshua 231,286,563
  Lucy 566
  Lucy Gilmer 563
  Martha 286
  Peachy 563
  Speed S. 561
  Tom 561
Fryer, Frances A. 243

Fryer, John H. 243
  Louis P. 243
  L. P. 119
  Mabel L. 243
  Walter 243
Fulks, Eliza 495
  Jackson 496
  Nathan 495,496
Fuller, Esther 273
  Jacob 110
Fullerton, Miss...597
Fulton, ...554
  Eugene 554
  Eugene A. 555
  George S. 554,555
  Hannah 557
  John A. 554
  Mary 554
  Samuel 554
  Samuel S. 554
  Stephen G. 555
  W. A. 554
Fults, Benjamin Franklin 223
  Florence (Parker) 223
  John Parker, Jr. 223, 224
Fuqua, Perry 115
  Sallie 115

Gaar...15
Gaddy, George T. 29
Gaines, John P. 77
  Lizzie 497
  Margaret M. 471
  Samuel 497
Galbaugh, John 243
Gallup, G. W. 183
Galvin, Dr....96
  Catherine (Cowley) 95
  Dennis 95
  John W. 95
  Wallace 96
Gammel, Agnes 24
Ganaway, Polly 405
Gano, Camelia 263
  Stephen 263
Gant, Archibald 192
Gar, Andreas 15,16
  John 16
  John (Hans) 15
Gardiner, Thomas 214
Gardner, Agnes 593
  Henry Clay 593
  Robert 593
  Tracy 593
Garfield...94.185
Garland, Mary 455
  Dr. Richard 455
Garnett, A. Stella 78
  Dorcas (Ewalt) 78
  Fannie 339
  John P. 448
  Mary 167
  Thomas T. 339
  William 626
  William T. 78
Garr, Dr....15
  Andreas 16
  Andrew 15
  Benjamin Lewis 14,15
  Charles Crain 15
  Charles Russell 15
  Clyde Lewis 15
  Elizabeth Virginia 15
  Jacob 15
  John C. 16
  Kizia (Russell) 14
  Lorenz 15
  Mary Margaret 15
  Nathaniel L. 15
  Susan 15
Garrard, James 477,478

Garretson, Henry L. 448
Garvey, Ben E. 529
Garvin, Barbara (Maggard) 203
  Valentine 203
Gates, Horatio 133
  Sarah 413
Gathright, Eliza Austin 94
  John 94
  John T. 94,95
  Owen 94
Gatlin, Rev. Ephraim 239
Gattan, Sarah 65
Gay, Mrs. Lavinia 33
Gayle, Albert DeLong 529
  Corrine 529
  Elizabeth 529
  Emma Eva 529
  George 529
  Howard 529
  James 528,529
  James, Jr. 529
  Joanna 529
  John 502,529
  June W. 528,529
  Lula 529
  Mattie Belle 529
  Melinda 529
  Robert 529
  Robert H. 529
  Sallie (Green) 528,529
  Sarah 529
  Thomas 529
  Walter S. 529
  William 529
Gentry, Garland 254
George, Sallie 374
German, E. S. 363,364
  John 364
  Marguerite Elizabeth 365
  Philip 364
  Sarah J. (Westfall) 363, 364
  L. Wesley 363,364,365
Gibbs...515
  Lydia 415
  Melissa 515
  T. P. 415
Gibson, Berryman 200
  Hart 116
  James 200
  Jonathan 393
  Melinda E. 200
  Rachel 393
Gilbert, G. G. 163
Gildner, John 528
Gilkie, Miss...415
Gill, William 21
Gillespie, Jean Neilson 585
  Dr. Joseph 585
  Penelope (Whiteside)585
Gilliam, Dr. J. S. 170
Gillmore, Miss...238
Gilmore, James 110
  Mary F. 345
Gilmour, John 401
  Susan 36
Gilpin, Virginia 618
Giltner...197
  Abraham 528
  Abram 528
  Alice 470
  Anabel 528
  Archibald 528
  Bennett 528
  Caroline (Cromwell)470
  Elizabeth (Raines) 527, 528
  Frances 528
  Frank Carleton 528
  Henry 470
  Henry Clay 528

Giltner, John 527,528
  Leigh Gordon. 528
  Lizzie D. 528
  Maggie 528
  Martin 528
  Mary Ann 528
  Robert Raines 528
  William Henry 527,528
  William S. 527,528
  William Spencer 527
  W. S. 528
Gist...608
Given, Dixon 121
Givens...407
  Agnes 365
  Alexander 92
  David A. 92
  Elizabeth 365
  George 93,365
  Jane 365
  Joseph 365
  Lamme Steele 92
  L. S. 93
  Margaret Keller 93
  Sallie 365
  Samuel 365
  William 365
Glass, Mary Jane 87
  Virginia 264
  Zachariah 87
Glasscock, J. 119
Glaston, Ann 440
Glover, Phebe 206
Goddin, Mary 505
Goetze, A. F. 368,369
  August 368
  Earl 369
  Herman 368
  Sophia (Hartman) 368
Goggin, Anna Irvine 505
  Sallie Irvine 505
Gold, Jack 333
  Marion 333
Goldsborough...139
  Caroline 139
  Charles 139
  Nicholas 139
Goodall, Charles Parke 160
  Ellen Eugenia 160
Gooding...24
Goodloe, A. H. 211
  George 210
  John Kemp 37
  Robert 210
  William Cassius 135
  William Clinton 210
  W. O. 211
Goodman...17
  Henry M. 17
  Jane M. (Winter) 16
  John 16
Goodnight, Hoy 180
  Isaac 179
  Isaac Herschel 179
  Jacob 179
  Lucinda (Billingsby) 179
  Michael 179
Goodwin, Jesse 589
Gordon, Annie M. 61
  Isaac G. 61
  John 131
  John B. 171
  Samuel 454
  Sarah 454
Gorin, Marcellus C. 413
  S. T. 496
Gossett, Fanny 530
Gould, Dora A. (Martin) 370
  Isaac P. 370
Grabfelder, Emanuel 344
  Rena (Driefus) 344
  S. 344
Grace...173

Grace, George 172
  John R. 172
  Mary (Organ) 172
  William 172
Gragg, Elisha P. 22
Graham, Dr. 10
  Miss..13,309
  Alice (Parker) 9
  Charles E. 97
  Cyrus 8
  Cyrus B. 8,9
  Edwin R. 9
  Frances 9
  Harvey 8
  Jennie 9
  LeRoy 8,9
  Miriam J. 43
  Olive 9
  Rachel Ratliff 97
  Richard 8
  William 97
  U. N. 593
  Z. C. 97
Grahame, Hugh Methven 8
Granger, Delia 352
  John A. 352
Grant, Fred 46
  Joseph K. 87
Graves, Buford Allen 267
  Ella 511
  George Thomas 267
  James M. 266
  J. M. 266
  J. Maddison 267
  John 266
  Mary Elenora 267
  Polly C. (Graves) 266
  Richard Grant 266
  Susan (Smarr) 511
  Thomas 266
  William 511
  William W. 266
Gray, Mr. 96
  Andrew J. 242
  Catherine (Galbaugh) 242
  Cynthia 96
  James L. 96
  Joe 605
  John 243
  Lynch 96
  Mary Howlett 96
  Mary P. 233
  Mary Sephrona 96
  Patrick L. 96
  Richard H. 242,243
  Virgil 158
Green, Dixon 605
  Eliza Overton 605
  Gabriel 604
  Grant 604,605,606
  Grant, Jr. 605
  Henry Dixon 605
  John 529,604
  Judge John 231
  John Taylor 605
  John W. 605
  Kate Overton 605
  Martha Dixon 605
  Mary Ann 605
  Nathan 159
  Paschal 529
  Sallie 529
  Susan C. 231
  Walter O. 605
  William 604
Greene, Anna May 471
  Carrie 471
  Elijah J. 471
  Elijah L. 471
  Emily C. 471
  Francis 471
  Frank C. 471

Greene, Grant 197
  James F. 471
  James L. 471
  James S. 471
  Jesse 471
  Jesse L. 470,471
  John 471
  John F. 471
  John Howard 471
  John Wiliam 470,471
  Maggie E. 471
  Mary 471
  Nancy 199
  Nathaniel 193,199
  Owen Breckenridge 471
  R. C. 471
  Robert 471
  Robert A. 471
  Sallie 471
  Thaddeus 197
  Willard 471
  William 471
  William P. 471
Greenup, Christopher 577, 578
Gregory, Mary 588
  Richard 588
  Thresa 620
  Virginia A. 268
Greifenkamp, Bernard 93
Grider, Martha 590
Criff, Delia 345
  Samuel 345
Griffey, Lettitia 329
Griffin, Ray 338
Griffith, Ann 160
  Benjamin 160
  Carey 161
  Charles 160
  Charles Greenberry 160
  Clinton 162,231,420
  Daniel M. 160,161,162
  Eleanor 160
  Elizabeth 160
  Florence 162
  Greenberry 160
  Henry 160
  John H. 160
  John T. 352
  Joshua 161
  Joshua T. 160,162
  Katherine Howard 160
  Letitia 162
  Lucretia 160
  Lydia 160
  Margaret Calhoun 161
  Mary Ridgely 162
  Nicholas 160
  Orlando 160
  Philemon 160
  Remus 160
  Ridgely 161
  Rose 162
  Ruth 160.162
  Samuel 160
  Sarah 160
  Sophia 160
  Sue 420
  Todd 162
  Virginia 160,162
  Virginia Shelby 160
  William 160,161
  William Henry 161
Grimes, John 412
  Mary Hedges 412
  Sara 412
  William 412
Gross, Samuel 143
Grundy, Felix 268
  Felix B. 329
  Jane B. 415
  Joanna 329
Gunn, J. D. 475

Gunun, N. P. 496
Gutherie, J. J. 34
  Mary K. 34
Guthrey, Frankie 265
Guthrie...137
  Anderson 93
  Francis M. 93
  James 260,261,279
  Mary Elizabeth 260
  Nancy (Marcum) 93
  Samuel Richard 94
  William Alvis 93,94

Haddan, Blanche 343
  J. B. 343
  Margaret Brown 343
  Samuel 343
  Samuel D. 343
  Thomas 343
Haddock, Mary Augusta 468
Haden, Joseph 63
  Rebecca 63
Hagan, Catherine 376
Hager...134
  Adah 157
  Adele 464
  Amanda Burns 156
  Benjamin Franklin 156
  Daniel 155,156,464
  Daniel Marion 156
  Edgar 156,157
  Elizabeth 155
  Emily Elizabeth 156
  Frederick 156
  George 155
  Gerald 464
  Harry H. 156,157
  Hazel 157
  Henry 155
  Henry G. 464
  Henry George 156
  James M. 155
  John 155
  John F., Jr. 464
  John Franklin 464
  John Jackson 156
  John S. 156,157
  Jonathan 133
  Louisa 156
  Margaret Maupin 464
  Martha Ann 156
  Mary Elizabeth 157
  Mary Jane 156
  Paul V. 156
  Richard Buckner 464
  Samuel P. 155
  Mrs. Samuel P. 447
  Samuel Patton 156
  S. P. 464
  Violet (Porter) 155,156
  Violet Vertrees 156
  William 155
  William C. 156
  William James 156
Haggard, Annie Mildred 595
  Augustine L. 594,595
  Benjamin Wheeler 595
  David T. 595
  Elizabeth Craig 595
  Frank Hunt 595
  John 595
  John Henry 595
  Leland 595
  Lou Ann Mullins 594
  Mary Rodney 595
  Nathaniel 595
  Patsy Adams 595
  Rodney 594,595
Hailey, Alfred Carter 183
  Andis Buford 183,184
  Carter 183
  Curtis H. 184
  Elizabeth (Drury) 183

Hailey, John 183
  Mollie C. 184
  Stella 184
  William H. 184
Haldane, Sarah 291
Haldeman, W. N. 459
Hale, Mrs. 12
  Annie B. 268
  Fred 552
  Henry S. 267,268
  Henry S., Jr. 268
  Joseph Theodore 268
  Mary E. 268
  Nathan A. 268
  Nicholas 267
  Rhoda (Crouch) 267
  William Lindsey 268
Hall, Miss 193
  Mrs. 100
  Caleb 543
  Dixon 543,544
  J. B. 119
  J. C. 537
  J. M. 551
  John 552
  John Arnold 100
  John Gordon Burnett 543,544
  John W. 303
  Leslie Virgil 100
  Mary J. McCloud 100
  Mayme 119
  Olivia W. 153
  Robert M. 543
  Sallie E. 421
  Sallie (Henson) 543
  Theodore 605
Hallam, Theo F. 74
Hall, Thomas 100
  Walker C. 100
Hamill, John 401
  Nancy 401
Hamilton, Alexander 65,510
  Andrew 222
  Anna 342
  Elizabeth 50
  Elizabeth P. 65
  J. P. 178
  Mary W. 222
  Mildred 510
  Sarah 222
  Susan J. 510
  William 510
  W. W. 477
Hammer, Dr. 115
Hammet, Sarah 298
Hammond, Abby V. 68
  Ann 160
  John 160
  Nannie 238
  Ruth 160
Hampden, John 243
Hampton, Amelia 341
  Charles 157
  Esther 545
  George 545
  Gus Hornshell 342
  Harriet N. 436
  Henry 240,341
  Julia 341
  Levi 341
  Lizzie 157,341
  Mary 341
  Millard Filmore 341,342
  Sarah 240
  Wade 240
Hancock, Alice 348
  Caroline 572
  George 572
  Susan V. 599
  William 599
Handley, Alexander 415
  Rachel 36

Handley, Sallie 160
Haney, Henry 240
  Mattie B. 365
Hanford, Margaret 350
Hanley, A. C. 225
Hanna, Eliza 100
  James 100
  Jane 101
  Jane (King) 100
  John S. 100,101
  Margaret 100
  Margaret Smith 101
  Martha 100
  Samuel 100
  Thomas 100
  William M. 100,101
Hannah, Anna V. 182
  James W. 182
Hannum, Penelope 62
Hanscom, Hiram 512
  Phoebe 511
Harbison, Mr. 95
Hardin, Ben 30,388,390,396,465,535
  Benjamin 388,389
  Henry 309
  Jane Davis 12
  John 12,273,388,389
  John J. 273
  Martin 12
  Martin D. 11,273,388
  Mary (Waters) 12
  P. W. 194
  P. Wat. 31
  Rachel 309
  Sarah 12,388
Harding...352
Hardy, Frederick 196
  Winfred 196
Hargis, Thomas F. 169
Harman, Rebecca 481
Harms, G. R. 148
Harney, John H. 515
  William Wallace 515
Harper, Jesse 210
  Robert Goodloe 210
Harrahan, James J. 168
Harris, Cora 104
  Elizabeth 429
  Giles 405
  Hallie 104
  Henry C. 431
  H. H. 513
  John Claiborn 405
  Josiah 103,104
  Mahala 32
  Marie Louise 431
  Sallie 190
  Sallie Wiles King 103
  Sarah 570
  Summers Wurthum 104
  Susan Elizabeth 405
  Webber 570
  William O. 135
Harrison, Amelia 566
  Benjamin 30,82,137,431
  Mrs. Benjamin 258
  Carter 82
  Carter Henry 82
  Charles 82
  Charles Leonard 101
  Ellen 332
  George S. 414
  Hebe 11
  James O. 332
  Judith 311
  Julian 11
  Lydia 414
  Peyton 82
  Robert Carter 431
  Robert Peyton 82
  Sarah A. (Winwood)101
  William H. 101,102

Harrison, William Henry 13, 30,82,101,431
  Zephaniah 101
Harry, Elizabeth 499
Hart...126,384
  Charles F. 195
  David 138,195
  E. R. 39
  Garbriella Hawkins 194, 195
  Jane 413
  John Bradford 194,195
  John Hawkins 194,195
  Lucretia 384
  Myra Strother 441
  Nathaniel 138,195,520
  Susanna 520
  Susanna Rice 195
  Thomas 138,195
  Thomas J. 195
  William 195
Hartman, Sophia 368
  Valentine 368
Harvey, Capt...115
  Maria Hawkins 150
Hatcher, Miss 626
  Lucy 190,405
Hatchett, Elvira 475
  John A. 475
Hatfield, Adam 132
Hawes, Albert 293
  Ann 293
  Aylett 293
  Benjamin 293
  Clara 293
  Kate C. 293
  Kitty 293
  Richard 293
  Samuel 293
  Susan 293
Hawkins, ...7
  Margaret 562,563
  Miriam 563
  Strother J. 195
Hayden, Miss 572
  Lucy 310
  Mary 376
  Stanley 484
Haydon, Mattie 92
  Stephenson 604
  Thomas 92
Hayes, Pres. 258
  James, Jr. 40
  J. K. 40
  Lucy Webb 258
Haygood, Alma 370
  C. B. 369,370
  Clarence 370
  Dallas 370
  Plato 369
  Susan (Von Gundy) 369
  Walter 370
Haynes, D. O. 201
  Frank 96
  Gray 96
  James M. 96
  John 460
  Mary Frances 96
Hays, Catherine 400,588
  Charles 400
  David R. 588
  Martha 400
  Mary McMaken 588
Hazelrigg, Dillard 196
  Dyke L. 197
  Elizabeth (Greene) 196
  Elizabeth J. Greene 197
  Emily D. 197
  George 196
  Hattie A. 197
  James H. 196
  John 196
  May H. 197

Hazelton, Sophia 7
Headington, Zebulon 29
Heaverin, Nancy 72
Heddins, James W. 469
Hegan, Francis 449
Helm...540
  Ben. 397
  Ben Hardin 395
  James P. 397
  John L. 396
  Lizzie Barbour 396
  Lucinda Barbour 396
  Lucretia 23
Hemingray, J. C. 86
Hemmingray, Camilla 92
Henderson, Belle 229
  Bennett 350
  Duncan 403
  Elizabeth 341
  Elizabeth (Orendorf)310
  Isabella 403
  James 229
  Josephine 350
  Leonard 165
  Lucy 164
  Martha Rivers 237
  P. J. 310
  Richard 98,165
  Samuel 237
  Sarah Spangler 229
  Sue E. 310
  Susan 3
  Susan Fannie 98
Hendrick, J. Buford 260
  John Buford 259,260
  John R. 259
  Mary S. 260
  Mary (Swigert) 259
Hendricks, James 113
  William 552
Henning, Fannie 565
  James W. 565
Henry, Miss 568
  John 540
  Patrick 1,140,540
Henson, Pollie 544
  Sallie 544
Herbert, Andrew 327
  Caroline 327
Herbst, George 85
Herndon, Ann (Crosthwaite) 509,510
  Annie Christian 509
  Ben D. 509
  Elijah 509,510
  Elizabeth 510
  George 510
  Horace 509
  Jacob 510
  John Patrick Henry 510
  Lewis 509
  Lizzie R. 503
  Maggie 137
  Mary Lee 456
  Sallie 510
  Thomas P. 503
  William 509,510
  William Leslie 509
Herold, Andrew 327
  George 327
  Matthew 327
  Susan (Barwick) 327
  William 327
Herr, Alfred 343
  John 182,343
  John L. 344
  Ninette 344
  Susan 181
  Susan M. 162
Hess, John 371
  Mary 498,499
  Nelson I. 498
  Peter 371

Hetsch, Justus J. 19
Hevern, Mary 222
Hewett, Fayette 105
Hewitt,...532
  Eliza Chastain 108
  Fayette 108
  Fox 109
  John 108
  Robert 108
  Virgil 109
  Yeba 532
Heyman, D. I. 10
Heywood, John H. 564
Hickman, Burnette (Barbour) 534
  Christopher 534,
  James H. 534,535
  J. F. 535
  Paschal 118
  Virginia 534
  William 118,534,535
  William A. 534
Hicks, Mary Matilda 92
  Sara 4
  Sarah 4
Higgin, Edward 463
Higginbotham, Alzira 524
  Bettie 524
  Ellen 524
  Emmanuel 524
  George T. 524
  John M. 524,525
  Matilda 524
  William 524
Highton, Arthur 150
Hill, Alexander 206
  Alexander, Jr. 207
  Alfred David 206,207
  Alfred Dodd 96
  Anna 83
  A. P. 83
  Benjamin 206
  Cynthia 361
  Elijah 255
  Elizabeth (Nation)256
  Fay Fern 256
  George 166
  Helen Kimbley 207
  James 361
  James C. 105
  Jennie 255
  Mary Lee 207
  Maude 587
  Sally 166
  Theodore McDonald 255, 256
  William 256
Hills, B. F. 313
Hilton, Miss 484
Hinde, Miss 313
  Thomas 313
Hines, Miss 97
  John 610
  Sarah (Carson) 417
  Thomas H. 159
  Thomas Henry 417,418, 419
  Warren W. 417
Hirsh, Mary Elizabeth 364
Hissem, Elizabeth Morgan 619
  Ethel 619
  Jesse 619
  Leva 619
  Levi 619
  W. Jackson 619,620
Hitch, Archie 19
  Maria (Cramer) 19
  Tolitha B. 19
Hite, Abraham 403
  Alfred Herr 343,344
  Isaac 343
  Jacob 343

Hite, James P. 404
  Jennie (Herr) 343
  Joseph 403
  Lewis 403
  Mary Rose 403
  Samuel S. 343
  William Chambers 403
  William W. 403,404
  Yost (Jost) 403
Hitt, Sarah 25
Hobson, A. G. 603
  Alonzo Thomas 603
  Anna M. 571
  Annie May 602
  Arabella (Bolling) 104
  Atwood 104
  Atwood Monroe 602
  Bettie K. 602
  Caleb 104
  Charles N. 104
  Edward Henry 600,601, 602,603
  Edwena 602
  E. H. 571,603
  Eliza 603
  James Thomas 603
  John A. 602
  John P. 104
  Joseph 104
  Lucy Ann 603
  Lucy Kirtley 600,603
  Luvenia M. 603
  Mary B. 104
  Robert P. 104
  William 600,602,603
  William A. 602
  Willis E. 104
  Willis H. 587
  Willis W. 104
  W. J. 603
Hockaday, Amelia Irvine 505
Hodge, Antonia M. 170
  Edwin 169,170
  Eliza A. 170
  Emma 170
  George B. 466
  George Baird 467
  Henry 169
  John T. 466,467
  Joseph A. 169,170
  Lavinnia 169
  Mary 169
  Mary L. 170
  Nancy S. (Hughes) 169, 170
  Nellie 170
  Robert 169
  Thomas Ditto 170
  William A. 170
Hodges, Mary E. 612
  Thomas 612
Hodgkin, J. N. 545
Hoge, Charles E. 104,105
  Evelyne B. 106
  Hildred Merrill 106
  James 104,105
  Mary Kerr 106
  M. D. 160
  Percy Echols 106
  Peter C. 104
  Sarah (Keer) 105
  Stephen F. 106
Holbrook, E. 129
Holeman, N. M. 20
Holiday, Jennie 398
Holladay, Sallie Barrett 372
  Walter 372
Holland; Eliza (Van Nuys) 585
  George Allison 585,586
  George B. 586

Holland, George W. 586
  J. G. 586
  John 586
  Sarah Jones 586
  Tabitha 523
  William A. 585
  William Allison 585
Hollingsworth, Sarah 64
Hollis, B. O. 19
  Minnie 19
Holliway, N. M. 217
  Ruth Evelyn 217
Holloway, J. M. 133
  Louise 430
  Nannie S. 81
  William S. 81
Holmes, Eleanor 346
Holms, George B. 252
  Mary 252
Holt, J. M. 530
  Joseph 530
  Nellie Georg 254
  Sarah 534
  W. H. 534
  William 254
  William H. 530
Holzhauer, Clara 20
  Edna 20
  Gustavus 20
  Irma 20
  Louis P. 20
Hon, Isaac B. 570
  Peter M. 570
Hood...191
Hooe, John C. 369
  R. B. 369
  Sue B. (Burford) 369
  William Archer 369
Hoover, Miss 179
Hopkins, Edmond 161
  Elizabeth 361
  Elizabeth (Tabler) 361
  John 361
  John Calvin 361,362
  John Martin 361
  Martha 160,161
  Mary 137
  Monsie L. Martin 361
  Nellie 361
  Samuel 80,137
Hopkinson, Ann 85
Hord, William 162
Hornback, Miss 316
Hornbuckle, Richard 416
Horner, Ella J. 588
Hornshell, Katherine 342
  Washington 342
Horton, Annie 329
Hoskins, Alfred 425
  Mary E. 485
  Minnie Wilson 453
  W. A. 485
Houser...174
  Bertha 338
  Emaline 174
  Mathias 338
  Samuel T. 174
Houston, Miss 489
  David 164
  Eli M. 164
  Elizabeth 13
  Samuel 163,489
  Sarah Best 164
  William 164
  William Churchill 13
Houtchens, Mildred 300
  William E. 301
Howard...84
  Edward J. 491,492
  Edward J., Jr. 492
  George 208
  George F. 492
  Henry 208

Howard, Henry Clay 208
  John 124
  John A. 491
  John G. 496
  John N. 491
  Julia 584
  Katherine 160
  Margaret 572
  Mary 425
  Mary Keran 491
  Rachel 124
  Samuel 491
  Thomas 208
  Thomas Flannery 491
Howe...37
  Lord 110
  Nancy 37
  Sarah Ann 212
Howlett, John 96
Hoy, Ella 180
  Lucy Milliken 180
  Thomas J. 180
Hubbard, George 415
Hudgons, William 457
Hudnall, Anna 413
  Anna Maria 413
  Randolph 413
Hudson, Ann (Chance) 258
  Clifford 259
  Hendrick 258,260
  Henry 260
  Homer 258,259
  Ida Dell 259
  James 258
  John 258
  John Shelley 259
  Linn W. 604
Huffman, Kate 578
Hughes...245
  Andrew 406
  David W. 102
  James Madison 102
  Jesse 102
  Jessie 102
  Joseph 170
  Kate 559
  Lizzie 415
  Margaret 406
  Nancy S. 169
  Susie Wallace 152
  Thomas 406
  William 406
  William T. 152
Hull, Jacob 138
Hume, Eugenia 235
  Martha 550
  William P. 550
  William Stanton 235
Humes, Miss 238
Humphrey, Alexander P. 37,135
Humphries, David 597
  Lucy 597
Hunt...123
  Judge 67
  Carrie S. 452
  John W. 384
  Thomas H. 82
Hunter, Benjamin Franklin 182
  Jane 208
  W. G. 93
Hunton, Ann Bell 608
  Eliza J. 608
  Logan 608
  Thomas 608
Hurley, Henry 226
  Nancy 226
Hurt, Alfred 583
  Berryman 583,584
  Elisha 583,584
  Elizabeth (Pebworth) 582,583,584
  Harvey G. 583,584

Hurt, James 583,584
  John S. 583,584
  John Smith 582,583,584
  Joshua 582,583,584
  Moses 583,584
  Rebecca 583,584
  William P. 583,584
Husband...99
Husbands, Cook 100
  Dow 100
  Gip 99
  Harmon 99
  James B. 99
  James G. 99
  John 99
  Lorenzo D. 99
  Robert 99
  Sallie 100
  William 99
Huston, John B. 135
Hutchcraft, Lucinda 108
  Reubin 108
Hutchins, Benjamin 201
  Dimmitt C. 202
  Essie C. 202
  Eveline (Campbell) 201
  Marie 201
  Morris A. 201
  Morris C. 201,202
  Morris Campbell 201
  Samuel 201
Hutchinson, Ardell 565
  Edward L. 14
  Louisa (Bonneau) 14
  M. E. 14
Hutton, George 342
  James 342
  John 342
  John M. 342,343
  Luvenda (Jones) 342
Hynes, Abigail 33
  Andrew 33
Hyde, B. F. 337
Hynes, Elizabeth 33
  Hanah 33
  Nancy 33
  Polly 33
  Rachel 33
  Sallie 33
  Sally 33
  Thomas 32,33
  Thomas W. 33
  William 32
  William R. 33

Ichenhouser, Louis 145
Ingels, Joseph 119
  Mary Bruan 119
Ingram, Annie 18
  Benjamin 572
  Bushrod T. 18
  Elizabeth 572
  Emily 18
  Frank 18
  Garnett 572
  James 18
  Jane 18
  Kate (Milton) 17
  Louisa 18
  Loulou 18
  Marie L. 18
  Mary 572
  Matie F. 18
  J. Milton 18
  Nimrod 572
  William 18
  Wyatt 18
  Wyatt H.17,18
  Wyatt H., Jr. 17
Innes, Anne (Harris) 428
  Harry 428,429
  Maria K. 428
  Robert 429

Ireland, Henry Clay 581
  J. Alexander 580,581
  Jane Stone 581
  John Crit 438
  J. W. 438
  Mary K. 437
  William 580,581
  William F. 581
Irvine...572
  Dr....65
  Abner 246
  Adam 75
  Alexander 505,506
  Anne 145
  Bessie D. 75
  Caleb 134,135
  Caleb Ewing 135
  Christopher 76,505,506, 609
  David 75,505,506,609
  David C. 143
  David W. 76
  Elizabeth E. 134,135
  Elizabeth S. 75
  Elizabeth S. (Irvine)76
  Esther 415
  Francis 505
  Jane 505
  John 415
  Lee 327
  Margaret 415
  Mary 415,609
  Minerva (Stone) 75
  Robert Green 135
  Samuel 302
  Sophie 609
  Susanah Hart (McDowell) 75
  William 75,505,506,609
  William, Sr. 76
  William M. 75,76
Irving, Agnes 431

Jackson, Adele H. 534
  Andrew 27,146
  James S. 116,534
  John 500
  Maria McKee 500
  Mary J. 304
  Robert M. 499,500,598
  Sarah (Creel) 354
  Stephen M. 500
  Stonewall 111,159,623
  Sue (Hawes) 534
  William 304
  William H. 499,500
  William Lowther 354
  William O. 304
  W. L., Jr. 86
Jacobs, Anna 476
Jacob, Charles D. 87
  R. T. 13
James, King 200
  Mary 391
Jamison, J. R. 590
Jans, Elizabeth 586
Jarboe, Benjamin 235
  Edward 235
  Henry 235
  Ignatius 235
  Josephine 235
  Raymond 235
  Victoria 234,235
Jarnigan, Fannie 376
Jarrett, Charles F. 192
  Emily (Gant) 192
  G. W. 192
  James 192
Jefferson, Peter 431
  Thomas 41,205,226,431
Jeffrey, Alexander 14,35},352,353
  Alexander, Jr. 353

Jeffrey, Elizabeth (Mc-Connell) 351
  John 351,352
  Virginia A. 353
Jeffries, Marguerite 124
Jenkins, Grace 106
  Helen 106
  John 106
  Lemarian (Mann) 106
  J. Oliver 106
  Robert C. 106
  Ruth L. 106
  William 106
Jennings, Marian Smith 9
  Thomas 9
  William 9
Jeter, Willie R. 127
Jewett...194
Johnson...123
  Andrew 511
  A. S. 12
  Benjamin P. 266
  Cassandra F. 158
  Claude M. 352
  Drusilla 96
  Elexene P. 367
  Elizabeth 208
  Fannie 394
  Frank 184
  George W. 388,598
  Gertrude 303
  Hamilton 511
  I. P. 158
  James 387,388,614
  Job 617
  John T. 387,388
  Joseph 167
  Julia A. 598
  L. Frank 265,266
  Lizzie 409
  Madison 609
  Madison C. 135
  Margaret 617
  Mary 266,511,605
  Mary Elizabeth (Cardwell) 265
  Mary (Tyndal) 511
  Rachel (Boone) 466
  Richard M. 118,265,387, 388,409,612,613,614, 615
  Robert 612,387,388
  Rosa Vertner (Griffith) 352
  Thomas 120
  W. H. 552
  William 208,265,388
  William F. 266
  William P. 265
  William Stapleton 394
Johnston...83
  Albert Sidney 82,274
  Eliza 274
  James 65
  J. B. 20
  Josiah Stoddard 274
  Mrs. J. Stoddard 183
Jolly, Alcey 309
  George W. 309
  Gideon N. 309
  Horace 310
  Jesse 310
  John B. 309
  John L. 309
  Marian 310
  Nannie 309
  Nelson 309
  Percy 310
  Rachel (Hardin) 309
  Sarah 309
  Susie 310
  Thomas 309
  William Henry Harrison 309

Jones...107,570
  Addie 359
  Alvin A. 118
  Anna Amanda 107
  Anna Amanda Pogue 107
  Carter Helm 479,480,481
  Daniel D. 359
  Dolly 34
  Edward 106
  Elizabeth 409
  Evan 409
  Fannie Wells 107
  Griffin 586
  Harriet Milton 107
  Henry B. 110
  Hugh L. 493
  Isaac 374
  Jacob 490
  James 570
  James William 610
  John 610
  John Spencer 610
  Josie 230
  J. Paul 106,107
  J. William 479
  Lindsay 107
  Lizzie 490
  Lottie Culver 107
  Lula M. 369
  Margaret 342
  Mary 490
  Mary E. 610
  Mary Elizabeth 610
  Mary Louisa 107
  Minnie 118
  Moses 114
  Richard 342
  Robert William 107
  R. R. 17
  Sallie Flournoy 107
  Samuel 60
  Sarah Howell 107
  Thomas 369
  Thomas T. 610
  William 342
Jordan, Anne 311
  John D. 337
Julian, Ann M. 440
  Charles 440
  John 270

Kahn, Lena 145
Kain, Hannah 169
Kale, Kitty 501
Kalfus, Rosetta S. (Jones) 17
Kamleiter, Fred 115
  Henry 115
  John Frederick 115
  Katie 115
  Louisa 115
Kane, Thomas 133
Karn, Ann (Bustow) 114
  Christopher 114
  Eva 115
  Frederick 115
  Jasper Bustow 114
  Robert 115
  Rose 115
  Virgia 115
Kasson, Henry 7
Kaufman,,,14
Kauther, Amelia 20
Kavanaugh, Bishop 22
  George W. 103
Kaye, Amanda 87
  Amy 87
  John 87
Keagan, Mary F. 452
Kean, Franklin H. 456
Kearney, Hattie 370,527
  James 370,527
Keats, Emma 566

Keats, George 566
  John 566
Keen, Emma L. 94
  William 94
Keene, Joseph, Jr. 511
  Joseph, Sr. 511
Keenon, Uberto 253
Kehoe, Fannie Bruce 169
  Henry Charles 168,169
  James 168
  James N. 169
  J. Dexter 169
  Jennie 169
  Mark F. 169
  Mary 168
  Nora (Conroy) 168
  Pannell Bramlette 169
  Thomas 168
  William 168
Keith, Fanny 276
Kelly, Clinton W. 308
Keith, Luella 436
  Marvel Lewis 436
Keller, Abraham 93
  Margaret 76
Kellum, Mary M. 199
Kelly, Amy Jacobs 210
  Clinton Wayne 307
  Frank H. 486
  George 486,487
  George Draper 486
  Griffin 307,309
  Helen 307
  Isaac Newton 309
  Isaac Wesley 307,308
  Joseph 308,586
  Levian 309
  Mary 454
  Nancy 210
  Parmelia 586
  Rebecca 307
  Rebecca Jane 309
  Rebecca (Smith) 307
  Sallie Barbour 309
  Washington Irving 309
  William 210
Kelsey, Caroline 363
  Elizabeth 363
  Sallie Fee 363
  Sarah (Fee) 363
  William 363
Kemp...158
Kemper, Alfred 498
  Asa 498
  Benjamin 498
  David 498
  Elizabeth 498
Kemble, John 606
Kemper, Jonathan 498
  Jonathan, Jr. 498
  Joshua 498
  Lucy 498
  Nathan 498
  Robert Walker 498
Kennedy, James 54
  Janet 54
  Sarah 401
  Susan 34
  W. P. 42
Kenney, Sally Holliday 102
Kenny, Sarah 31
Kent, Nancy 463
Kenton, Simon 277,278,279
Kenyon, Elisha 551
  Frank P. 551,552
  Orrin 551
  Roxanna Fairman 551
Keran, James S. 491
  Mary J. 491
Kerper, George B. 149
Kerr, Harvey 197
  James 458
  John 148

Kerr, Nancy 457
  Rosetta E. 148
Keyser, Catherine Brinkley 224
Kilpatrick, George 307
Kimberland, Elizabeth 438
Kimbley, Frank E. 203
  Frank R. 204
  Hugh 204
  John 203
  John F. 203
Kimbrough, Daniel R. 114
  John M. 114
  Susan (Jones) 114
  William 114
  William W. 114
King...8
  Addie 117
  Alexander 117
  Anna 117
  Anna (McAfee) 100
  Charles L. 117
  C. L. 117
  Edward S. 117
  George W. 117
  Harbut 117
  Harbut A. 117
  Harvey 124
  James H. 117
  James T. 117
  Jane 100,101
  J. H. 117
  John M. 117
  Martha G. 117
  Mary 363
  Mary A. 117
  Maude 117
  Milton 103
  James C. 27
  Samuel 103
  Sarah I. 117
  Thomas 100,101
Kinkead, Joseph 37
  W. B. 116
Kinnaird, Helen 509
  William H. 509
Kinner, Ceres 113
  David 112
  H. H. 112
  Lute Bell 113
  Mary 113,343
  Mehala Curnutte 112
  Sallie 113
  S. G. 343
  Stephen Girard 112
Kinney, W. R. 168
Kirby, Elizabeth 29
  Maurice 118
Kirk, Annie (Horton) 329
  Ellen 303
  James 329
  Lucy 328,329
  Mary 415
Kirkpatrick, James 345
Kirtley, Judiath Lewis 603
  Lucy 603
  Thomas 603
Klein, John W. 91
Kneasbey, Lindley M. 67
Knight...62
  Grant L. 604
  Mollie 185
  Sallie 604
Knott, Abram 415
  Anna Maria 413
  Edward Whitfield 413
  Elizabeth 415
  Ellen 413
  Frances 413
  James Proctor 413,415
  Jane Hart 413
  Jennie Marion 414
  Joanna 413

Knott, Joseph McElroy 414
  Joseph Percy 413
  Kate Grundy 414
  Lloyd W. 413
  Margaret Marion 413
  Maria Irvine (McElroy) 413
  Mary 413,415
  Nancy 413,415
  J. Proctor 414
  Samuel 413
  Samuel Cleland 413
  Sarah 415
  Thomas Percy 413
  William 415
  William Sneed 414
  William T. 413,414,415
Knox, John 414
Krack, Etta Belle 114
  J. A. 114
Kraus, Louisa (Keyser) 318
  Philip 318
  William 318
Kremer...114
  Annie (Hendricks) 113
  Charles 113
  Henry L. 113
Kroger, B. H. 148
Kull, Catherine 147
Kyle, Jane 505,609

Lacey, A. T. 340,341
  Cecil Baker 341
  Charles Smith 340
  Mary Jane (Baker) 340
  Robert Dudley 340
Lackey, Alexander 362
  Elizabeth 362
  Mary (Morgan) 362
Lacky, Greenville 241
  Mary 241
Lady, Daniel 156
  Ida 156
Lafferty, W. T. 30
La Follette, David W. 111
Lail,...120
  Charles 119
  Charles E. 120
  George Shirley 120
  George W. 119
  Ina 120
  Jennie 120
  John 119
  Louisa 120
  Louisa (Ingels) 119
  Maud 120
  Rodney F. 120
  Wade Hampton 120
Lair, Helen H. 30
Laird, Bushrod Foley 294
  Charles 295
  Cordelia (Whitaker) 295
  Eugenea 295
  Martima 295
  Samuel B. 295
  Samuel Boden 295
Lamb, Rachel 310
  William 310
Lambert...605
Lancaster, A. B. 139
  Addie 436
  Ann 376
  Ann (Pottinger) 376
  Annie E. 377
  Benjamin 376
  Benjamin H. 377
  Catherine 376
  Ellen 376
  Henry 436
  James Madison 376
  John 376
  John A. 377
  Joseph B. 376

Lancaster, Joseph S. 377
  Magdalen 139
  Mary J. 377
  Mary T. 377
  M. P. 139
  Philip Henry 376
  Raphael 376
  Robert B., Jr. 377
  Robert Benjamin 376
  William 376
Landrum, James 506
  James David 506
  John W. 506
  Mary 513
  Nancy Walden 506
  Thomas 506
  Thomas J. 506
  William L. 506,513
  W. T. 506
Lane...24
Lang, Addie 340
  Archibald 340
  India 340
  James Maynard 340
  Martha Maynard 340
  Mollie 340
  Nellie 340
  Sarah 340
  Thomas 47
  Wallie Lee 340
  William 340
  William Crawley 339,340
Langhorn...352
Langier, Lady Marie Thereza 472
Lapham, J. S. 79
Laport...597
Laswell, Peter 438
Latham, Charles 264
  Charles M. 264
  John 264
  John C. 264
  Mary R. 264
  Nancy (Moorehead) 264
Laudeman, James H. 197
  Mattie 197
Lauder, Margaret 412
Lawrence...134,33
  Blanche 179
Lawson, Jack 146
  James 146
  John 146
  Katherine 242
  Robert 147
  Sarah 311
  Sarah (Travis) 146
Leach, Martha 590
Leachman, Mary A. 408
  Nannie 301
  Thomas 409
Leathers, Allen 372
  Annie 372
  Charles F. 372
  Elizabeth (Hess) 371
  John H. 371,372
  Stuart Robinson 372
  William 371
Lee...584
  Barton 251
  Calista 251
  Fitzhugh 176,372
  Hannah 132
  Harry (Light Horse) 138, 178
  Henry 140,276
  Joseph L. 36
  "Widow" (Mason) 584
  Matilda Ann 226
  Robert E. 104,132,140, 175,176,178,489
  Sarah 178
  William 132
Lefevre, Nancy 331

Le Grande, Jane (Michaux) 80
Leib, Fred 461
  Louise 461
Leigh, Edward O. 300
  Ferdinand 300
  James Walker 300
  Mary (Brooks) 300
  Robert W. 300
  William B. 300
  William H. 300
Lemaster, Abby 563
Leslie, Preston H. 318
Letcher, Ben 18
  Robert D. 18
  Robert P. 540,541
  R. P. 285
  Samuel M. 5
Lewis...355
  Ann (Carlile) 552
  Archibald Stewart 571
  Berry 588
  Charles Nelson 229
  C. N. 356
  Cynthia 622
  Douglas P. 208
  Eliza 158
  Elizabeth Porter 84
  Eliza Martz Reed 157
  Ellen 588
  Ellen J. 588
  Estill 290
  George Alexander 469,470
  George Wythe 469
  James 290
  J. B. 469
  Jean Wood 470,469
  J. I. 105
  John 157,469,470
  John W. 552,553
  Joseph 157
  Joseph H. 83,109,157
  L. A. (England) 356
  Lucy Bragg 229
  Mary 356
  Mary Hays 588
  Mary J. (Todd) 469
  Mildred 79
  Samuel 140,622
  Thomas 208
  Thomas P. 84
  William 552,553
  Zachary 469
Lighter, Henry 528
  Katherine 528
Lillard, Ephraim T. 457
  Rosanna (Hudgeons) 457
  Stephen 457
Lincoln, Mrs. 395
  President 395
  Abraham 174,201,344
Linde, Catharine 364
Lindsay, Andrew 345
  Andrew W. 345
  Bruce 345
  Charles 345
  James 345
  Marion 345
  Marion Semple 346
  Polly G. 345
  Sally D. 345
  Sally Gilmore 345
  William 345,346
Lingenfelder, Catherine 302
Linn, E. W. 402
  Mary Eleanor Kemper 402
  Medoria S. 144
  Octavia (Pearl) 402
Linthicum, Susan A. 170
  Rufus 170
Linton...35
Lisle, Claiborne 545,546

Lisle, David C. 545
  David Congreve 545,546
  Esther Hampton 545
  James 545
  James D. 545
  John 545
  Marcus 545
  Mary D. 545
  Mildred 545
  Minerva 545
  Nick Winn 545
  Thomas 545
  Ziporah 545
Litsey, Berry Lewis 588, 589
  David R. 589
  Ellen Lewis 588
  Katie Bell 589
  Mary 589
  Nellie Rebecca 589
  Randolf 588
  Uriah 588
Little Douglass 429
  George 429
  Lucius P. 429,430
  Robert 167
Livesay, Mary 199
Lloyd...139
  Elizabeth (Adamson) 293, 294
  Julia 294
  Richard 293,294
  H. Thomas 293,294
Lockett, Alvin 118
  Elmira (Eakins) 117,118
  Francis 118
  Hickman 118
  John Francis 117,118
  Marie 118
  Paschal H. 117
  Sarah 118
Lockhart, Henry 621,622
  Marquis R. 621,622
  Riba 622
  Sallie 622
  Sarah (Richardson) 621
Lockridge, Eliza 589,590
  Jane 590
  Robert D. 590
Loe, Magdalene 44
Logan, ...179
  Alexander 455
  Ben 367
  Benjamin 525,400
  Benjamin F. 493
  Mrs. (Carldwell) 376
  Caleb 2
  Catherine 400
  Daniel Boone 492,493
  Gertrude 493
  James 492
  James Fleming 492
  James Hervey 455
  James Venable 455,456
  James Venable, Jr. 456
  J. B. 493
  John 429
  Martha E. 456
  Mary McBrayer 456
  Mary Venable 455
  Nancy McGlone 492
  Polly 32
  Sandford V. M. 456
  Susan Maggoffin 456
  Tobias 492
  Virgie M. 493
  W. H. W. 493
  William 367,400,492,525
Long, Alexander 22
  Bessie 263
  Elizabeth (Curd) 262
  Gabriel 262
  John Slaughter 262

Long, Mary 263,617
  Mary E. 492
  Nelly 263
  Nimrod 262,263
  Spencer C. 262
  Stephen G. 263
  William R. 492
Longfellow, Henry Wadsworth 546
Longstaffe...610
Loomis, Harriet K. 118,119
  John W. 118
  Stephen M. 118,119
  Thomas J. 118
Loos, Mrs. 148
  Carrie D. 148
  Charles 148
  Charles Louis 147
  Emily K. 148
  Frederic V. 148
  Jacques G. 147
  Louisa L. 148
  Oberline T. 148
  Wilhelmina 148
  William J. 148
Lopez...38,39
Lord, Mary 460
Loudenback, Genevieve 169
Loughborough, Preston S. 89
Lovelace, Frances O. 99
Lovell, H. L. 529
  Howard L. 467
  Virginia Lee 467
Lowry, James 326
  Margaret 326
  Ruby 230
  Sobrina (Neal) 230
  William 230
Lucas, Mary 490
  Rebecca 315
  Rena 315
  William 490
Lumpkin, Martha 36
Lykens...316
Lynch...514
  Elizabeth A. 58
  John Bowman 514
  Lizzie 237
  Thomas 514
Lyne, George 20,165
  Selden 448
Lyons, Georgia 260
  Henry J. 226
  Jesse P. 260
  John 226
  Laura S. 227
  Luara Simmons 226
  Mary Rodgers 227
  Samuel Clay 227
  William L. 226
  William L., Jr. 227

McAfee, America 599
  Annie 101
McAllister, Charles 398
  Sallie Lyle 398
McArthur Alice 70
  Annie 70
  Charles 70
  Duncan 71
  Ida 70
  James Madison 70
  J. M. 252
  Mary 70
  Mary Michie 71
  Peter 70,71
  William H. 70
McAtee, Benjamin L. 595
  Elizabeth 596
  Emily 595
  Margaret 596
  Mary 595

McAtee, Tyler 595
  Tyler W. 595,596
  Wickliffe 596
McBeyer, Henrietta 312
  William H. 312
McBrayer, Alexander 69
  James A. 69
  John H. 69,70
  Martha E. S. 456
  Sandford 456
  Susan Wright 69
  William 69
McBride...584
  Miss 439
  M. 584
  William 265
McCambell, Agnes 345
McCampbell, Elizabeth 170
  Georgia 563
  J. H. 563
  Robert 170
  William 563
McCamy, David 302
McCane...73
  Harvey Clayton 72
  James A. 72
  James Allen 58
  Lewie Allen 72
  Nancy Anderson 72
  Nancy D. 58
  Samuel 72
  Thomas 58
McCann, Squire 69
  Ada 69
  James 69
  John 68
  W. E. 410
McChord, John 552
McClain, Annie 452
  Carrie (Hunt) 441,452
  Carrie Lucelia 441
  Elizabeth Hunt 453
  George 452
  Jackson 441,452,453
  James 452,454
  James Henry 452
  M. Hunt 441,452,453
  Virginia Cabell 454
  William 452,454
  William P. 454,455
McClanahan, Annie 311
  Elizabeth 193,199
  Thomas 193,199
  W. C, 77
McClarty ..245
  James 245
  Samuel 245
McClasky, Bodine 554
McCleland, Clarissa 63
  John 63
McClintock, George Bayless 241
  John D. 241
  John David 241
  Paul Brown 241
  Wallace Cecil 241
McClon, James 514
McCloud, Mary J. 100
McClung, John Alexander 274
  Mary 143,145
  William 274,276
McClure, Janet 429
  John 250
  Maggie T. 250
McColgan, William 415
McComb, Jessie 192
  Sudie 192
  Susan (Jeffries) 192
McConnell,...335
  Belle (Henderson) 228
  Charles 228,229
  Elizabeth 352
  James Henderson 228,229

McConnell, John McCutcheon 229
  Lucy Bragg 229
McCorkle, Alexander 110
  Charles E. 111
  E. W. 111
  Henry 111
  W. Howard 110
  John 110
  Samuel 110
  Walter E. 111
  W. Howard 111
  William H. 110
McCormack, Clarissa Harlow 63
McCormick, Ann 107
  Caleb 64
  Daniel 64
  Hannah 64
  James 64
  John 64
  John E. 60
  Joseph 64
  Laura Angeline 60
  Leah 64
  Leanna 64
  Louisa 63
  Martha 64
  Mary 64
  Nancy 64
  Sarah 64
  William 64
McCowan...358
McCoy, Mattie 413
McCracken, J. E. 148
McCraney, Hannah 350
McCraw, Hill 503
  Mary W. 503
  Nannie Elliott 503
McCready, John 514
  James B. 67,142,151,152, 559,560
McCreery, Thomas C. 142,479
McCue, (McHugh) Sarah 414
McCullough, Cynthia 350
  Robert 89
  S. D. 350
McCullum, Margaret 110
McDaniel, Abraham 214
  Henry 216
  Patsey 216
McDonald...27
  Flora 256
  Harry P. 566
  Jane 256
  Jennie 27
  John 26
  Margaret (Purcell) 26
  Patrick 26,27
  Patrick, Jr. 26
  R. B. 124
McDougal, John 205
McDowell, Amelia 617
  Bettie (Breck) 246
  Eliza H. 21
  Ephraim 76,77,140,143, 145
  H. C. 76
  Henry Clay 150
  James 77
  John 140
  Joseph 76,141,246,533, 617
  Lucien 15
  Sallie 246
  Samuel 140,141,143,145, 150
  Sarah 76,533
  Shelby 126
  Susanah Hart 76
  Wallace 76,143
  William Adair 145,150
  William C. 246

McDowell, William Wallace 126
McElroy, Abraham B. 329
  Anthony 90
  Archy 415
  Cecil Scott 415
  Eliza 415
  Esther 329
  George S. 414
  G. W..329
  Harriet Paulina 415
  Hugh 415
  Hugh Sneed 414
  James 414,415
  James Franklin 415
  John 415
  Keturah 415
  Lucy Ann 415
  Lydia 414
  Margaret 415
  Marion B. 414
  Mary (Buckner) 329
  Minnie 329
  Paul Irvine 415
  Philip E. 415
  Robert Lapsley 415
  Rosa 414
  Samuel 415
  Samuel Rice 415
  Sarah 415
  Sarah R. 413
  Sue 90,415
  William T. 415
McElwain, Ella 439,440
McElwee, Patrick 249
McEwin, Mary S. 266
  William 266
McFarland, Beatrice 206
  John S. 142
  Louisa 206
  Minerva 206
  Robert W. 206
McFarlin, J. W. 595
McGarvey, J. W. 155
  Nellie 155
McGlone, Owen 492
  William Owen 492
McGoffin...89
McGrath, Thomas 128
McGraw...584
  Nancy 481
McGready, Jane 18
  Joseph 18
McGuire, Iby 16
McHenry...13,14
  Barnabas 12
  Hannah (Davis) 11,12
  Henry D. 12
  John H. 12,13,31
  John Hardin 11,12
  L. S. 12
  Martin D. 12
  W. E. 12
  William H. 12
McKay, ...67
McKee, Eveline 488,489
  George 340
  Georgie 340
  John 489
  John V. L. 500
  John L. 103
  Maria 499
  Samuel 541
  William Houston 489
  William R. 167
McKendrick, J. S. 63
McKinley, Maggie 249
  William 249
McKinney...164
  Charles 531,532
  Charlotte Walker Rowlett 531,532
  Frances 311

McKinney, George J. 65
  Jennie 531
  Mary W. 567
  Mat 567
  Matthew 531,532
  Mollie 531
  Samuel 531,532
  Sarah Ann 64
McLean, Alney 313
  Martha A. (Rees) 622
  Milton Harcourt 622,623
  Robert 622
  Robert A. 622
McMichael, Robert 110
  Sarah B. 110
McMillan, Alexander 616
  Anna 412
  Elizabeth Frame 412
  James 412
  John 616
  Margaret 616
  Robert 412
  Sallie 475
  William 412
McMullen, Susan 185
McMurds, Andrew 350
  Elizabeth 350
McNamara, Anna 406
  George 406
McNeal, Elizabeth 326
McNeill, Alexander 237
  Alexander C. 238
  Amanda 237
  Angus 237
  Benjamin Franklin 238
  Catherine 237
  Cherrill 243
  Dorothy 236,237
  Dorothy Mesha 243
  Elizabeth 237
  Ellen Mesha 238
  Flora 238
  Harry 238
  Hector 236
  Henrietta 237
  Henry 236,237
  John 236
  John Pryor 237,238
  Malcolm 236,237,238, 243,244
  Malcolm Rivers 243
  Margaret 237
  Martha 237
  Pryor 237
  Rivers 238,243,244
  Thomas Henry 237,238,243, 244
  W. A. 238
McPherson, James B. 111
McReary, Mary J. 33
McRobert, Ann M. 40
McRoberts, Josiah 566

Mabry...205
Maccoun, Arabella 421
  James 421
Maccubbin, Elinor 160
  John 160
  Sarah 160
Macmillan, Robert 149
Madison...126,149,429
  Ambrose 392
  George 570,571
  James 392
Maes, C. P. 128
Magee, William 339
Magoffin...4,99
Mahon...39
  Mrs. James 505
Mahone...189
Major, A. H. 452
  John 375
  Martha 375

Major, S. I. M. 26
Mallory, Elizabeth 308,586
  John Helm 178
  Robert T. 178,179
  Sarah (Barner) 178
Manier, J. W. 439
Mann, Josiah J. 302
  Lemarian 106
Mansfield, George Washington 125
March...85
Marcum, Basil 93
Marion...196
Markley, Mary 113
Marrs, Lou 494
  Margaret (Robson) 494
  Stephen 494
Marsh...85
Marshall, John 2,149,296
  Miss 193,199
  Agatha M. 2
  Alexander K. 296
  Alexander Keith 276
  Alexander S. 2
  Charles 276,280
  Charlotte 276
  Edward C. 276
  Elizabeth 276
  Eliza J. 178
  Humphrey 276,280,281,282,283
  James 271
  James B. 2
  James Keith 296
  James M. 276
  Jane 276
  John 276,280
  John J. 280
  Judith 276
  Keith L. 2
  Louis 2,271,274,276
  Lucy 276
  Margaret 207
  Martin 178,363
  Mary Ann 276
  Myra L. 2
  Nancy 276
  Polly 276
  Susannah 276
  Thomas 276,296
  Thomas A. 280
  Thomas F. 276
  Thomas Francis 271,272
  William 2,276
  William C. 207
  W. J., Jr. 23
Martin, Alexander 240,241
  Alexander L. 362
  Andrew 496
  Elizabeth 4
  Elizabeth Sophia 241
  George Brown 241
  Henry L. 558,559
  Jennie P. 486
  Jesse 558
  John 293,370
  John P. 241,361
  Josephus 78
  Lucy 496
  Luther 133
  Margaret T. 558
  Mary F. (Whitehead) 78
  Mary W. 362
  Mildred 293
  Monsie L. 361
  Nettie 93
  Reed M. 93
  Susan 496
  William 78
  William H. 78
Martine, Jas. I. 589
Marty, L. K. 625
Mason, C. R. 105

Mason, Enoch 523
  Fannie 523
  H. P. 105,106
  James M. 523
  Lee Ann 412
  S. B. 105
Massie, Henry 167
Masterson, Edward 64
  Eleanor (Coleman) 64
  Leanna 64
Mathews, Albert K. 532
  Caleb M. 76,532,533
  George 532
  Joanna 532
  John 76,532,533
  John Wiley 532,533
  Joseph 532
  Joseph M. 532
  Joseph McDowell 77
  Laura 532
  Lawrence D. 532
  Margaret G. 532
  Mattie 532
  Pryor 532
  Ruth 532
  St. John 532
  Yeba 532
Matson, Mary 550
  Robert 550
  Thomas 550
Matthews, Mary 101
  William C. 101
Mattingly, T. A. 377
Mattox...168
  John W. 27
Maule, John 366
  Mary 366
Maupin, Margaret Elizabeth 464
Maxwell, James L. 231
  Julia 552
  Mary 251
  William 251
May, Sallie 57
Mayfield, Ann 61
Mayo, Cynthia F. 316
  Lewis 316
  Maria (Jones) 316
Mays, A. S. 415
  Matthew 172
Mead, Gretta 171
  W. W. 171
Meade, Albert Gallatin 416,417
  Anna 417
  Delbert Quigley 417
  Elizabeth (Hornbuckle) 416
  George Henry 416,417
  Luke Cullis 417
  Mary E. 417
  Pierce L. 417
  Richard 417
  William R. 417
Meades...126
Mears, J. S. 496
Medcalf, Rebecca 238
Meddis, Apphia Seaton 74
  George S. 74
  Godfrey 74
  Matthew 74
  Simpson S. 74
  Victor N. 74
Medley, Bishop 301
Meek, I. 178
Menefee, Jouett 566
  Richard H. 566
Meriwether, Edward 247
  Kate 247
Merritt, Allie 62
  Benjamin Leonard 62
  Charlotte 62
  Daniel 62

Merritt, Daniel Ross 62
  Eliza 62
  Fisher Harrison 62
  George Washington 62
  Henry Clay 62
  Leonard Ross 62
  Louisa Alice 62
  Lucy A. Waller 62
  Minnie Ross 62
  Montgomery 62
  Philander 62
  Richard 62
  Rosabella 62
  Rosa Lee 62
  Sory 62
  Vernon Washington 62
  Washington 62
  William J. 62
Merriwether, E. W. 178
Messinger, Daniel T. 312
  George 312
  Mary 312
  Nehemiah 312
  Samuel 312
Metcalfe...33,424
  John 538
  Mary 424
  Sally 537
  Thomas 537,538,542
Meyer, C. C. 41
  Ida 41
Michaux, Abram 80
  Bachbr 880
  James 80
  Jane 80
  John 80
  Paul 80
  Susanna 80
Micheaux, Elizabeth 79,80
  Nannie 79,80
Middleton, Mary 440
Mignot...351
Milam, Annie 253
  Benjamin C. 252,253
  Benjamin R. 253
  John 252,253
  John W. 253
  Moses 253
Miles...336
  Catherine 376
  Lyda 360
  Philip 376
Miller, Adam 449
  Amelia 162
  Bertha O'Donnell Cecil 48
  Carrie D. 17
  Christopher J. 474
  Daniel 474
  Esther 476
  Fannie E. 248
  George F. 229
  Griffith 162
  H. A. 162
  Henry 17
  James C. 48
  J. J. 116
  Len S. 248
  S. Malinda 439,440
  Margaret 370
  Mary J. (Hocker) 439
  Mary (Poe) 48
  Mattie B. 199
  Peter 554
  Sarah 554
  Thomas W. 439
  Virginia 162
  W. F. 199
  William H. 474
  W. M. 61
Milligan, Samuel 77
Mills, Arthur P. 182
  Eva 182

Mills, Jennie A. 247
  Mary E. (Moore) 181
  Roger Q. 247
  Samuel B. 181
  Susan M. 182
  William P. 181
  Worden S. 182
Milton, Elizabeth 611
  John 611
  Kate 18
  Liccie 131
Milward, Anne Bell 509
  Annie 508
  Arabella Bright 509
  Belle (Bright) 508
  John Bright 509
  Joseph 509
  J. U. 509
  Margaret 508
  Stanley 508,509
  W. R. 508,509
  W. R., Jr. 509
Minor...210
  Anna Clay 310
  Carrie Rule 310
  Emma Bertell 310
  Ephraim 310
  Ezekiel 310
  Florence Salle 310
  James Robert 310
  John B. 152
  John Lamb 310
  Mary Ware 310
  Nancy Lou 310
  Nancy (Sallee) 310
Minstay, Mary 560
Minuet, Peter 110
Mitchell, A. J. 96
  A. J., Jr. 96
  Biddie 495
  Elizabeth 524
  Elizabeth Ewing 135
  Elzy 174
  James 174
  James A. 174,175
  James P. 5
  Julius B. 176
  Katherine 176
  Louis A. 96
  Louise 176
  Martha 175
  Martha J. 5
  Martha Stockton 174,175
  Ormsby Macknight 274
  Robert 175
  Samuel B. 176
  William 175
Moberly, Mary 608
Moffat, John 431
  Sybella 432
Molsvarger, Caroline 417
  Pauline 417
Moody, AnnaVirginia 591
  Emma 591
  George T. 591
  John E. 591
  P. N. 591
  Richard 591
  Virginia O'Bannon 590
  W. D. 354
  William B. 590,591
  William H. 591
  William Harvey 590,591
Moore, Alexander 615
  Amanda 495
  Anna Miller 449
  Anneta 312
  Augustine 140
  Bacon Rochester 312
  Bernard 140
  Catherine (Fonda) 264
  Charles O. 311
  Christopher Collins 311

Moore, Daniel Lawson 312
  Dudley Bowman 312
  Elijah 311
  Ellen 29
  Enoch 16
  Frederick 515
  George 311
  George D. 265
  George H. 130
  George Henry 264,265
  George J. 264
  George S. 130
  Georgie 265
  Hugh Adams 449
  James 311
  James H. 310,311,312
  James Harrison 312
  Jane Murray (Rochester) 310
  Jennie 339
  Jesse 265
  Jessie Gano 449
  John Bowman 312
  John R. 23
  Jordan 206
  Joseph L. 311
  Josephine 615
  Julia Van Pradells 23
  Lawson 310,311
  Mary 514,615
  Mary Bacon 312
  Mary L. 339
  Mary (Magee) 339
  May Messinger 312
  Moses 339
  Percival 265
  Rebecca Ann 16
  Sally A. 206
  Sarah (Viser) 206
  Shirley 265
  Thomas 168,181,311,563
  Thomas R. 311
  Vincent 311
  Virginia 312
  Wallace 312
  William 124,311,448
  William G. 448,449
  William H. 312
  William M. 338,339
Moorman, Elizabeth 420
  James L. 420
  Jessie 366
  Sallie 420
  Silas Mercer 366
Monarch, Benita 72
  Daniel D. 72
  Ermine 72
  Henry Lamar 72
  Jessie 72
  M. V. 71,72
  Susan (Daviess) 71
  Thomas 71
Monin, Alice 46
Monroe...63
  Annie 495
  Benjamin 602
  Elizabeth 454
  James 426
  Nancy 425
  T. B. 602
Montgomery...176
  David 523
  Davis 167
  Elizabeth (Harper) Davis 167
  Martha 167
  Martha A. 523
  Mary 164
Montieth, Mary 201
Montley, James D. 603
Mosby, Sarah 617
Moses, Dr. 135
Mosley, Anna 584

Mosely, Aria 160,161
  Thomas 161
Moss...205,49
  Jesse Bright 49
  Josiah 42
  Judith Campbell Bullock 48
  Thomas E., Jr. 49
  Thomas Edward 48
  Thomas S. T. 48
Moran, Edward 625
Morehead...68
  Governor 12,448
  Charles S. 285,286
  James 448
  James T. 24,87,285
  Presley L. 448
Morgan...29,101,122,123,175
  Calvin C. 384
  Charlton 384
  Daniel 164,384
  David 12
  John 2
  John H. 158,193
  John Hunt 384
  Joseph 619
  Judith (Michaux) 80
  Myra 151
  Richard 384
  Thomas 384
Morlin, Louis M. 27
Morris, Gouverneur 201
  Albert 5
  Amos 201
  Amanda (Ronner) 545
  Anne 201
  Bishop 52
  B. S. 88
  Carrie 131
  David 545
  Dickison 88
  Elizabeth 16
  Elizabeth (Jones) 129
  George W. 129,130
  John 129
  John S. 131
  Robert 201
  Sallie C. 545
  Wallace W. 131
Morrison, Alonzo 476
  M. 474
  Peter 474
  R. J. 60
  W. 438
Morrow, G. H. 99
  Thomas Z. 501
Morse...48
Morton, Amanda Pocohontas 63
  Clarissa Louisa 64
  Clarissa M. 63
  Eleanor Beckwith 63
  Elizabeth 64
  Francis 64
  Francis Alexander 64
  George Richard 63
  Henry Prior 64
  James Hanna 64
  Jennie C. 123
  John 64
  John P. 122
  Joseph 64
  Joseph Jordan 64
  Joseph W. 63
  Joseph William 63
  Levi P. 201
  Marmaduke B. 64,488
  Marmaduke Beckwith 63
  Martha 64
  Martha L. 63
  Mary 64
  Mary Virginia 63

Morton, Nannie 487,488
  Overton Jordan 64
  Peter 63,64
  Peter Henry 63
  Rebecca 64
  Sarah 64
  Virginia 64
  William 82
  William I. 63,64
  William Jordan 63
Muir, ...10,11
  Belle 11
  Isabella 10
  Jasper 10
  Lilian 11
  Nellie 11
  Peter B. 10
  Sophronia 11
  Sydney S. 11
  Thomas R. 11
  Upton W. 10,11
  William 10
Mullican, Addie 485
  Bettie 485
  James Stowers 485
  John H. 484
  John Simeon 484,485
  John Vernon 485
  Mamie 485
  Oda 485
  Ollie 485
  Richard 485
  Susan (Hayden) 484
Mullins, Gordan C. 594
Muse, Martha 340
Munson, T. V. 433
  T. Volney 435
  William 433
  William Bell 433
Murphy, Abner 64,65
  Abner G. 65
  Abner Goff 64
  A. G. 15,64,65
  Basil 65
  Clara M. 65
  Eleanor 65
  Elias 65
  Elizabeth 64
  Elizabeth R. 65
  Emily S. 65
  George William 65
  Harriet 65
  Hiram 65
  Irwine S. 65
  Jane 65
  John 297
  Lydia 64
  Martha J. 297
  Mary 65
  Mary B. 65
  Rachel 65
  Robert 65
  Sallie 65
  Sarah 65
  Sarah Ann 64
  William 64,65
Murray...84
  John 245
  Minerva 245
Musselman, Jacob 249
Myers, Aaron 73
  Aurelia Bridgman 73
  B. F. 331
  Elizabeth 294
  Harvey 73
  Harvey, Jr. 74
  Jacob 33
  Louisa 154
  Thomas 294

Nagel, Catherine 215
  C. W. 148
  Charles W. 215

Nagel, Elfrida 215
  Herbert Lincoln 215
  William F. 215
Napier, Elizabeth 151
Nation, Elizabeth 256
  Joel 256
Neal, W. H. 59
Neely, Elizabeth 515
Neider, Adam 57
  Barbara 57
  Bertha Estelle 57
  Bonnie May 57
  F. A. 18
  Ferdinand Adam 57
  Maggie 57
Nelson, Mary 303
Nesbitt, Robert T. 413
Netherland, Maggie 449
  Robert H. 449
  William H. 449,450
Nevil, Anne 395
Newbold, Sallie 297
Newman, Ann 357
  Catherine 338
  Fannie B. 587
  James 587
  John 338,357
  John P. 338
  Oliver 338
  Samuel 338
  Stella 338
  Virgie 485
  J. William 587
  William H. 187
Nicholas, George 149
  John 303
Nicholson, Martha 566
Nisbet, James 19
  James, Sr. 19
Nooe, Bettie 457
  Lucy P. 457
  Nimrod 457
Norris, Daniel 481
  James 481
  James Corbin 481
  Rebecca 481
  William 243
Northcutt, Adeline 498
Northern...169
Norton, Brothers 150
Norwood...84
Nourse, Charles 367
  Charles E. 104
  Ella 104
  James 367
  Rosa Logan 367
  Wallace L. 367
Nunn...360
  Ella M. 192
  Mary 465
  Susanna 195
Nutting, Mamie 332
  J. P. 332

O'Bannon, Virginia 591
  William 591
O'Bryan, Elizabeth Ann 72
  William 72
O'Connell, Daniel 573
O'Conner, M. J. 566
O'Donnell, John 48
Offutt, Ella 200
  Henrietta 469
Ogden, Deborah 186
O'Hanlon, John 168
Oldham, Elizabeth 53
  Emily C. 53
  J. Harry 77
  John Y. 76,77
  Laura A. 76
  Presley B. 76
  William 53
  William B. 76,77,532

Oliver, Henry 545
O'Meara, Jere P. 336
  Mary 336
  Thomas 336
O'Neal, Frank 40
  J. T. 86
  Weden 119
Orendorf, Christian 133
  Henry 132,133,310
  Jesse 133
  Louisa Ormsby 133
  Marie Ormsby 133
  Mary Kane 133
  Mary Magdaline 133
  Mexico 133
  Stephen Ormsby 133
Ormsby, Mattie 133
  Stephen 133
Orr, Jennie 529
Overby, W. T. 50
Overton, Kate S. 605
  Waller 183
Owen, Abram 539
  Edward 306
  Edward P. 306
  Emma K. 109
  Grandison P. 306
  G. W. 109
  Mattie V. 306
  Mrs. (Melton) 593
  W. T. 12
Owsley...604,501
  Ann Middleton 478
  Chloe 478
  Ebswroth 400
  Emma McGee 439
  Harry 400
  Harry Bryan 479
  Isabella Pennington 400
  James M. 439,440
  J. B. 400
  Joel 478
  John 440
  John Bodine 400
  John S., Sr. 578
  John Samuel 439,440
  John Samuel, Jr. 400
  Jonathan 478
  Linda 439
  Maggie S. 439
  Margaret Bayne 478
  Martha Hays 400
  Mary 400
  Mary E. 439
  Mary Pearl 478
  Mattie 578
  Mattie H. 439
  Melinda Miller 439
  Michael 439
  Nudigate 478
  Patience 478
  Samuel 439,440,478
  Stephen Ephriam 400
  Thomas 400,440,478
  Thomas Miller 439
  Walter William 400
  William 171,400,439,
    440,478,479
Owsly, Almira 210
  William 210

Pabst, Fred 201
Pace, Carrie Hope 404
  Margaret Irvine 505
Pack, John E. 252
  Richard F. 252
  Sallie M. Emison 252
Page, William 178
Palmer...183
  Emma 524
  John M. 524
  Nancy 524
  Potter 46

Palmer, Robert 465
Panley, Nancy 570
Parish, John 59
Park, James 617
  Sopha 617
Parker, Alice 8,9
  Benjamin 8
  Charles 69
  D. S. 298
  John E. 585
  Mary E. 69
  Mary Howard Jenings 8,9
  Mary Shepherd 585
  Nellie Burgin 585
  Peter 8
  Peter P. 49
  Preston Piper 49
  Priscilla 102
  Samuel Alexander 49
  Thomas 102
  Virginia 585
  Watts 584,585
Parrat, Mercy 476
Parrish, Arthur Lee 365
  Belle 366
  Edward 366
  Edwin 365
  Elizabeth 365
  George 366
  George W. 365
  Guy 366
  Henry 366
  Hetty 366
  Isaac 365
  Isaac N. 365
  James H. 365,366
  James Howard 365
  Jane Givens 365
  Jessie 366
  John Otis 365
  Lester 365
  Lizzie Sue 365
  Lucien 365
  Maria Louise 366
  Marion 365
  Mary Martha 365
  Milton W. 365
  Moorman 366
  Nelson 365
  Nora 366
  Parmelia 570
  Rebecca 365
  Sallie 366
  Sarah Moorman 366
  Tennessee 366
  Walter Benjamin 365
  William E. 365
Parsons...52,53
  Charles Booth 51,53
  Edward Y. 53
  Eliza 24
  Emily 53
  Frank 53
  Sarah 24
  William 24
Patterson...54,55
  Alexander L. 55
  Andrew 53
  Andrew McFarland 55
  James Kennedy 53
  Janet 53
  Jeannie 55
  J. M. 19
  Jonathan 602
  Walter K. 55
  William 54
  William A. 55
  William Andrew 55
  William Kennedy 55
Pattillo, William 61
Paxton, Thomas Barbour 174
Payne...123
  E. P. 71

Payne, Lucy 429
Paynter, Charles A. 335
  C. L. 334
  C. M. 334,335
  John 334
  Norah L. 335
  Walker B. 335
Peacock, H. H. 604
Pearce, Charles Bridges
  458,459
  Charles D. 459
  Christian S. 459
  Hiram T. 459
  L. E. 459
  Samuel 458,459
  William 458,459
Pearson, Edward C. 51
  Emma L. 51
  George E. 51
  Kate 51
  Leila A. 51
  Lorenzo D. 50,51
  Lorenzo D., Jr. 51
  Peter 51
  Susan 51
Pebworth, Robert 584
Peers, Benjamin O. 277
  Mary Eleanor 277
  Valentine 277
Pegman, G. W. 178
Pegram, Sallie 135
Peirce, Frances Mary 460
  Shepard 460
Pelouze, R. F. 51
Pemberton, Richardson 580
  Sarah Howell 580
Pendleton...584
  Frances Samuellor 176
  Henry 176,468
  J. M. 153
  John E. 57
  Lila 153
  Mary 57
Penick, Benjamin W. 571,
  572
  Brummal 571
  B. W. 602
  Hundley 571
  Mary 571
  Mary Ingram 571
  Thomas Bailey 571,572
  William 571
  William Clifton 571
Penn, Shadrach, Jr. 286
  William 16
Pennington, Ephraim 401
  Isabella Ann 400
  Sabra 401
Pepper, Annette 200
  Elijah 200
  James E. 200
  Oscar 200
Perkins, Ben G. 448
  Ben T. 135
  Maria 448
  Sarah D. 36
  William N. 438
Perrin, Archibald 28
  Josephus 78
  Katherine Clopton 78
Perrine, Amanda 294
  Garrett 294
  Lucy 294
Perry, Charles 237
  Emily 209
  Henry 209
  Jane 504
  Jincy Olivia 593
  John D. 504
  Katherine 536
  Mary 158
  Mary Chambers 209
  O. H. 593

Peters...188
Petett, Nannie 242
  William B. 242
Pettit...142,143
  Duane 141
  Elizabeth 141
  Harry 129
  Harvey Blair 143
  Thomas S. 141
Pettuss...532
Pflanz, Grace 411
  John R. 410,411
  John Reinhard 410
  Mary F. Hollicher 410
  Stanley 411
  Virgie 411
  Willie 411
Phaland, John C. 158
Phelps...589
  Amy 87
  Caroline Shipp 87
  James S. 86,87
  John 87
  John H. 87
  Mary Glass 87
  Zack 86,87
Philips, Elizabeth 553
  James G. 553
Phillips, Abigail 13
  Abner 13
  Annie 552
  Appoline 552
  Asher 13
  Carrie 552
  Cornelius 570
  Elias 13
  Elizabeth 13,552,566
  Elizabeth Sue Simpson
  13
  Esther 13
  Frances 13
  Henry 167
  Hugh B. 552
  James G. 552
  J. G. 327
  J. M. 552
  John 13
  Jonathan 13
  Joseph 13
  Joseph Francis 13
  Joseph M. 552
  Josephine 13
  Juan 569
  Julia 552
  Juliette Eyre 61
  Louis W. R. 61
  Louise 414
  Margaret D. 564,565
  Mary 13,552
  Micajah 570
  Minnie 552
  Philip 13
  Rhoda 570
  Rosa L. 552
  Ruth 13
  Samuel 13
  Sarah 552
  Seymour 552
  Theophilus 13
  Thomas 552
  William 13
  William D. 552
Philpott, John S. 196
  Susan 196
Phister, Chambers 625
  Elijah C. 571
  Thomas R. 202
Pickens, Nettie M. 619
  Robert P. 619
Pickering, Lucy 609
  Rhoda 609
  Richard 609
Pickett, Agnes 439

Pickrell, Henry 623
  Mary 623
  Matilda 623
Pierce...136
  Franklin 1
  LaFayette 330
  Lulie 414
  Margaret 330
  Nannie 330
  William 414
Pieterse, Magdalene 586
Piety, Lady 14
  Lord 14
Pigg, James 358
Pike, Samuel 116
Pinkard, Lizzie 363
  Rebecca 363
  Stanfield 363
  Stanfield Corbin 481
Pinkerton, William 112
Piper, Annie E. 49
  Eliza A. 49
  Mollie Ryan 49
  Samuel 49
  Samuel Alexander 49
  Samuel Calvin 49
Pirtle, Henry 56
Pitkin, Joseph 460
  Mary Cone 460
  Richard 460
  William 460
Pittman, Madalene Irvine 505
Pitzer, Nettie 375
  Thomas J. 375
Plaster, Stephen 62
Platts, Charles Gilman 228
  David G. 227
  George E. 227
  Hannah Ann 227
Poage, Ann 392
  George 392
  Hugh Calvin 227
  January Paul 227
  John 392
  Judith Princess 227
  Maria 241
  Sarah E. 227
  Thomas Hoge 227
  William 227,241
Pocahontas 137
Poe, Family 48
Pogue, Anna Amanda 107
  Mary 306
  Sarah 335
  William 306,335
  William Lindsay 107
Poindexter, Mary Craik 566
Polk...300
  James K. 300
  John 552
Pollard, Elizabeth 205,206
  Isabella 205
  William H. 205
Pollitt, James 454
  Virginia 454
Pollock, Margaret 587
Poor...448
Pope, Albert A. 201
  Alfred T. 67
  Curran 478
  John 387
Porter...181
  Albert 508
  Anne 166
  Charles 599
  Chitron Scott 508
  Eli 507,508
  James 181
  Jessamine 599
  Joseph 508
  John M. 159
  John Marshall 447

Porter, Larmer 508
  Leona Brown 447
  Mary 508
  Nancy 167
  Newton 507,508
  Samuel 508
  Thomas F. 598,599,600
Poston, John 304
  Emily 305
  Mary 545
  Nancy 305
  Nancy B. 304
Potter, Belle 179
  P. J. 179
Pottinger, Ann 376
  Samuel 376
Powell, Adah Lee 200
  Allen 193
  Anna 199
  Anna B. 200
  Annie 193
  B. M. 199
  Burnett M. 200
  Caroline Butler 453
  Charles 453
  Cuthbert 137
  Della 193
  Edwin R. 193
  Elias L. 199
  Elizabeth 199
  Elizabeth Dorsey 192
  Eveline 193
  Fanny May 193
  Harbard A. 199
  Harbard Alexander 199
  H. A. 193
  Harrison 193,199
  Harrison A. 117
  Henry 193
  Ida 193
  James 199
  James Basil 193
  James F. 193
  James Frederick 192
  Jessie A. 200
  John A. 193
  John W. 193
  Lazerus 199
  Louisa 199
  Lucy 209
  Luke 209
  Maggie 193
  Martha Christina 200
  Mary 199
  Mary F. 193
  Melinda J. 200
  Nancy 199
  Nancy G. 199
  Olivia 193
  Olivia Nora 193
  Ozella 193
  Pattie 193
  Richard 193
  Ruby 193
  Ruth 193
  Sallie Sweetland 209
  Samuel H. 193
  Smith 199
  Susan B. 195
  Thomas Hart 200
  Thomas M. 193
  Thomas W. 192,193,199
  William S. 193
  Willoughby 193,199
Power, Marion 216
Powers...169
  David Pinckney 105
Poyntz...3
  Benjamin B. 2
  Charles B. 3
  Charles Baldwin 2
  Mary 2,3
  Samuel B. 2,3

Poyntz, William 3
Prague, Cassie 58
  Edward 58
  Mrs. Frank 58
  Sarah A. 58
Prather, Elizabeth 260
Pratt, Daniel D. 353
  David 354
  Nathaniel 354
  Sallie 354
  Samuel 353,354
  William M. 354
  William Moody 353,354
Prentice...123
  Clarence J. 288
  George Denison 287,288
  William Courtland 288
Prescott...15
Preston, Francis 526
  William 572,573
Prestridge, John W. 226
Pretlow...58
  Edna 57
  Richard 57,58
  Samuel 57
  Samuel D. 58
Prettyman...65
  Ida 259
Prewitt, Laura 155
  Levi 155
Price...280
  Anna 591
  Ann E. 437
  Carrie Belle 591
  Charles H. 489,490
  Don K. 490
  Grace B. 490
  Ignatius 437
  Isabella Downing 21
  John 21
  Josephine Downing 21
  Max T. 490
  Susan M. Taylor 489
  William 489
  William B. 489,591
Prichard, Samantha 132
  Wiley 132
Priest, J. A. 17,18
Prior, James 24
  Martha 63
Pritchard, K. F. 113
Procter, Agnes H. 152
  Benjamin 152
  Benjamin F. 152
  Thomas L. S. 152
Prowse, Charles 190
  Frank 190
  George O. 190
  John P. 190
  John P., Jr. 190
  Nonie 190
Pruitt, Sue M. 591
Pryor...376,533
  Dorothy 236
  Emma Goodwin 589
  Jack 589
  James 589
  James Calvin 589
  Jefferson Davis 589
  Jonathan 589
  Mary 376
Pulley, Mary 560
Purdom, ...496
Purdy, M. A. 97
  Margaret 97
  Milford 297
Pursell, Elizabeth 360
Puryear...591
Pyles, Alsie 186

Quarles, Roger 210
Quick, Vrouchie 586
Quicksall, Sallie 404

Quill, Barbara 57
Quinn, Susanna 80
Quisenberry, Jane 280

Radcliff, Mrs. James P. 535
Ragland, Mary 158
Ragsdale, Achilles 334
  Clark 334
  Douglas 334
  Elizabeth Mann 333
  Elizabeth Rogers 333
  Emily Foster 333
  Emily (Tillotson) 333
  Frances Hester 333
  Howell 334
  James 334
  James S. 333
  John H. 333
  Lucy 334
  Lucy Cooper 333
  Manfred 334
  Mary Rives 333
  Rebecca Hancock 333
  Roy 334
  Smith 333
  Thomas 334
  Will 334
  William E. 333
  William Edward 333, 334
  William J. 333
  William Jones 333
  William Jones, Sr. 333
Raines, Ayelette 528
  Elizabeth 528
  Jesse 528
Raison de la Geneste, Louis
  Modesta 472
Raison, Charles Louis 472
  Charles Louis, Jr. 472, 473
  Lizzie 473
  Louis Napoleon 212
  Thomas 473
Raison de la Geneste, Louis 472, 473
  Lady Louise Victoria Antoinette 473
  (Fontaine de Chaussenell Pierre Antoine 473)
  Lady Marie Thereza Clotilda 472
Raleigh, Matthew 292
  Ruth 292
Rammers...35
Ramsdell, Mary Williams 546
  Prudence 546
  Robert W. 546
Ramsey...80
Ramsay, Elizabeth 363
Ramsey, Nancy 412
Randall, Frances 12
Randolph...126, 605
  Ada Aliza 593
  Isham 82
  Jane 137, 431
  Susanna 82
  Susannah 431
  William 593
Raney, George P. 135
Rankin...515
  Dr. Adam 468, 561
  James E. 467, 468
  Susan D. 467, 468
Rankins, Blackstone H. 397
  Elizabeth (Barker) 397
  William 397
  William H. 397
Ranson, Frank B. 410
Rash, Agnes J. 19
  Benjamin Campbell 20
  Benjamin L. 19
  James R. 20

Rash, Otway W. 19, 20
  Stephen 19
Ratcliff, J. F. 359
Ratliff...358
  Alexander 97
Raut, Catherine 545
Rawlins, Elizabeth Triby 355
Ray, Elizabeth 413, 555
  Frances 413
  Joseph S. 158
  Mary 592
  Richard 413
  Samuel T. 415
Rayborn, Henrietta R. 474
  Milton L. 474
Rayne, Frances 413
Read, Susan E. 153
Reading, John 13
Reddick, Beulah 59
  Clifford 59
  James T. 58, 59
  James W. 58
  John A. 58
  Willie 59
Redman...214
  Father John 184
  Richard 214
Reed, Annie E. 233
  Belle 415
  Charles 169
  Elizabeth 88
  James 233
  John 88
  Lewis 157
  Matilda 88
  Nelson 443
  Theresa 443
  Thomas B. 280
Rees, Dr. 591
  Lucy B. 305
  Mary E. A. 508
  Milton 622
  Thos. F. 508
Reeve, John J. 137
Reichel, Anna S. 19
Reid...524
  N. P. 584
Remington...177
  Greenup 28
  Kittie 28
Reneker, Sora 88
  W. D. 88
Renick, Abram 196
  Sally 196
Rennie, Ella (Powell) 159
  Joseph 159
  Joseph R. 159
Reno, Amanda 336
  Campbell 336
  Cordelia 336
  J. E. 593
  Lawson 335, 336
  Lawson R. 335
  Mary 336
  Mary T. 335
  R___ T. 336
  Sue 593
  Virginia (Wrinn) Berry 336
  William 336
Renshaw...99
  Sarah 99
Respass, A. C. 410
Reynolds, Aaron 263
  Addie 264
  Admiral 450
  Catherine 263, 264
  Catherine Vernon 450
  Charles O. 263, 264
  Dudley S. 77
  Dudley S., Jr. 452
  Dudley Sharpe 450, 451,

Reynolds, Eli M. Bruce 452
  Elizabeth 452
  Frank 264
  Mary A. 452
  Mary (Nichols) 450
  Mollie 264
  Nathaniel 450
  O. A. 263, 264
  Sarah Freeman 450
  Tena 177
  Thomas 160, 450
  William 177, 178, 263, 264
Reynols, R. D. 43
Rhoads, Absalom. J. 466
  Crawford Carlisle 466
  Henry 466
  McHenry 466
  Solomon 466
  Tabitha R. 466
  Wayland 466
Rhoderfer, Anna 529
Rhodes, Nancy Anne 507
  Waitstill 402
Rhorer, Florence 43
Rice...556, 568, 591
  Ada 335
  Carrie Frances 335
  Daniel 195
  David 421
  Greenway 335
  Hudson M. 402
  Ida 229, 335
  James W. 335
  James William 335
  James William, Jr. 335
  John M. 229, 335
  John McConnell 335
  J. W. 229
  Solomon 263
  Susanna 195
Richards, Elizabeth 428
Richardson, Anna Lucille 557
  Charles 151
  David F. 557
  David M. 557
  Eliza 557
  Fannie 495
  Gus Albert 557
  Gus W. 556, 557
  Hannah 557
  James Adrian 557
  John Crowley 431
  Julia 557
  Julia T. 557
  Marquis 621
  Mary 557
  Mary H. 430, 431
  Orla Coburn 557
  Orla D. 557
  Robert Carter 430, 431
  Samuel Q. 430, 431
  Sarah 557
  T. G. 80
  William 431
Richie, Charles G. 329, 330
  H. C. 330
  Sophia Spurrier 330
  William H. 330
Richmond...61
  Ann (Dickey) 60
  John M. 60
  Margaret Craig 61
  Matthew 60
  William 60
  William Dickey 61
Rickerts, Catherine 216
  Ruliff 216
Riddle, Mary 432
Ridgeley, Elizabeth 160
  Johanah C. 114
  John 160
Ridgely, Katherine G. 160

Ridore, Philip 472
Ridpath, John Clark 32
Riffe, Christopher 284,368
  George Chilton 368
  Hugh Ray 367,368
  Hugh Ray, Jr. 368
  James M. 368
  John M. 367,368
  John M., Jr. 368
  Laura Cassiday 368
  Mary A. (Ray) 367
Rigdon, Stephen Douglas 88
  Thornton 88
  Thurman 88
Riley, Madison M. 529
  Thomas W. 10
Rind, Sarah 140
Rives, Catherine 205
  Charles Jefferson 205
  Florence Neal 206
  Franklin 206
  George Pollard 206
  Henry A. 593
  James 205
  Jennie 205
  John 523
  John Lewis 206
  Jordan Moore 206
  Mary 523
  Mary Belle 206
  Nancy 205
  Nebraska 205
  Noyal 205
  Polly 205
  Raymond 206
  Rebecca 205
  Robbie 205
  Robert 205
  Robert Henry 206
  Robert Franklin 205
  Sallie 205
  Stephen 205
  Susan 205
  Susan Cleveland 206
  Thomas 205
  William 205
  William Vincent 205
Rizer, Sophronia 10
Roach, Anna 85
  Edwin 85
Robards, George 166
  Nancy 166
  William 166
  W. O. 327
Robbins, Catherine 506
Roberts, Columbus 511
  Eleanor 524
  Hamilton 511
  Harvey H. 510,511
  Harvey Hamilton 511
  Henry 115
  James 524
  James Kirtley 511
  John 557
  John H. 510,511
  Mary Johnson 510
  Mary (Shacklette) 557
  Phillip 511
  Rose 115
  Sarah 530
  Sarah (Keene 511
  William 511
Robertson ...574
  Alexander 20,540
  Christopher 124
  Cordelia A. 124
  Elizabeth 124
  Donald 405
  Dora 496
  George 116,540,541,542, 543
  George H. 76
  Isaac 404

Robertson, James 540
  Sallie E. 20
  William 540
  W. W. 590
Robinson...13
  Barbara 209
  Bettie 592
  Celia 209
  Mrs. Dick 485
  Esther J. 558
  Henry Scott 591,592
  Jacob 5
  James 209,210
  Jmaes F. 126
  Joe E. 592
  John M. 566
  John R. 591,592
  Malvina 591,592
  Margaret 540
  Martha 350
  Nannie 592
  Pleasant Saunders 592
  Robert 591
  Samuel 558
  Stuart 130,350
Roche...79,80
  Susanna 80
Rochester, Ann 311
  Artemisia 311
  Elizabeth 310,311
  Esther 311
  Hannah 311
  Jane Murray 311
  John 311
  Nancy 311
  Nathaniel 311
  Nicholas 311
  Phillis 311
  Robert 311
  Sophia 311
  William 311
  William John 311
Rodes, Robert 269
  Shelly 269
Rodgers, Mrs. Charles G. 392
Rodman, David 442
  Hugh 44,299
  James 45,299
  J. L. 45
  John 44,45,299
  Mary 300
  Patsy Fore 299
  Patsy (Foree) 44
  Sarah T. 441
  Thomas 44,299,300
Roebling, John A. 171
Roemer, Mary V. 369
Rogers, ...163
  Elephalet 354
  George 157
  Jason 38
  John 354,421,450,608
  John F. 566
  Lewis 17
  Lillie P. 450
  Mary 163
  Nathaniel 354,421
  Sarah 157
  Susan 38
  William S. 421
Roland...224
Rollins, A. W. 236
  James S. 236
  Sarah H. 236
Rooter...178
Rose, A. 329
  Elizabeth Caroline 85
  Rebecca 302
Roseberry, Hiram M. 102
  Rebecca A. 102
Rosecrans...115,150
  W. S. 59

Ross, Ellen 514
  Mrs. George 352
  John 514
  Preston 514
Rothchild, Jettie 160,162
Roundtree, Samuel 21
  R. H. 596
  Sallie 596
Rousseau, Lovell H. 283
Rowan, John 272
  William 272
Rowe, Bessie R. 32
  J. Edwin 32
  Ella Walker 32
  Lulu E. 32
Rowland, David Irvine 505
  David Pittman 504
  Eliza Caldwell Irvine 506
  Frances Irvine 505
  Robert 505
  William 238
Rowlett, Matthew Jewett 532
Roy, Dorothy 617
Ruble, Mattie 414
Ruger...201
  Thomas J. 201
Rugless, Lindsay B. 250
  Socrates 251
  Thomas 250
Rumsey, Charles 231
  Edward 55,462
  James 55,231,462
  James D. 87,462
  Susanna 462
Runion...60
Rush...181
Russel, David A. 188
Russell...55
  A. K. 556
  Andrew 555,556
  Ann M. 269,270
  Bettie 556
  Christopher 366
  Christopher D. 367
  Echols 556
  Emma 556
  Fannie 556
  Flora 556
  Frances 556
  Henry 556
  James 270
  James B. 366
  John C. 269,270,441
  John W. 269,440
  Joseph 402
  Joseph B. 477
  Kizia 15
  Lev. 556
  Lila 270
  Milton C. 366
  Susanna Condie 402
  Sylvester 556
  Thomas M. 366
  Timeolean 556
  W. E. 477
  William E. 555,556
  William Edwin, Jr. 556
Ryan, David 59,60
  Helen Morrison 60
  James B. 59
  John 60
  Martha 59,60
  Solomon 60
  Thomas D. 59,60
  W. M. D. 178
Rymond, Nancy 350

Sacra, Marie L. 63
Sage, Elizabeth Norton 85
  Osmer 85
Sallee, Jacob 310

Sampson, Archibald 166
  Barbara 166
  Elizabeth Barbara 166
Sams, James 586
  Sally Ann 586
  Sarah Ann 586
Samuell, Annie 539
  Nannie 539
  Richard P. 539
Samuells, Robert Lee 309
Samuels, Nancy Marshall 606,607
Sanders, Hugh 503
  Nathaniel 503
  Sallie 503
Sandifer, Lee 487
  Nicholas 487
Sanford, Abram 376
  Berry Foree 375
  Charles 375,376
  Charles B. 375
  Daniel 375
  Daniel Lawrence 376
  Francis Symmes 376
  Hallie Hunter 376
  Harriet Hunter 378
  James Goslee 376
  John 58
  Lewis M. 378
  Lewis Major 376,375
  Lewis Major, Jr. 376
  Marie Humes 376
  Martha 375,376
  Mary 545
  Richard 375
  Robert Hunter 376
Sappington...360
Saunders,..45
  D. B. 80
  Maria 185
  Oliver 185
  Pleasant 591
  Samuel 185
  Susan E. 185
Savage, Emily 65
  Pleasant M. 65
Sayre...17,68
  B. B. 200
  David A. 66,67,530
  E. D. 121,529
  Ephraim D. 65,66
  Howell L. 529
  James C. 65
  James W. 529,530
  Mary E. 529,530
  Mary L. 530
  Sidney S. 121,530
  Willie Louise 529
Schaffer,...86
Schmidt, Susan 307
Schneider, Adam 148
  Catherine 148
  John Q. 148,149
Scholz, Charles 115
  Norman Frederick 115
Schoolfield, C. B. 251,252
  Edna Pearl 252
  Edward Raymond 252
  George Clarence 252
  George T. 251
  Isaac Bosman 251
  John Charles 252
  Mary 251
Schrader, Mary 155
Schroll, Dorothea 183
  Esther 183
  Henry Clay 183
  John C. 182
  John Randolph 183
  Laura 183
  Martin 183
  Mattie B. 183
  Thomas Benton 183
Scofield...201

Scott...250,258,39
  Anna 39
  Belle 39
  Charles 145,386
  Cornelius Suydam 257
  Elizabeth 39
  Ethelbert D. 501
  Etta 39
  Frank 39
  Harry 39
  Helen 432
  Henry Martyn Skillman 257
  Irene 39
  Isaac W. 257
  James 257
  John 38,257,432,500, 524,592
  John D. 500
  John M. 257
  John W. 256,257,258
  Joseph 257,486
  Joseph N. 257
  Keziah 508
  Lizzie 524
  Lucy W. 257
  Malvina 592
  Margaret 257
  Margaret Skillman 257
  Martha Ann 500
  Martha 38
  Mary 257
  Matthew T. 256,257
  Matthew Thompson 257
  M. K. 38
  Moses 257
  Randolph 592
  Richard 39
  Robert 257
  Ruebie 39
  Ruth 250
  Samuel 501
  Thomas M. 501
  Walter 39
  Sir Walter 432
  William 39
  William F. 500,501
  William T. 257
  Winfield 135,196
  Winnie 257,256
Sea, Andrew McBrayer 609
  Sophie Fox 609
Seaton, George 74
  John S. 181
Sebren, Anna 586
Seelbach, Charles 138
Seidelmann, Eva 15
Seltzer, Catherine 364
Semple, A. L. 11
Senour, Anna E. 228
  Bryant 228
  Tilman W. 228
  U. G. 228
  Wilford 228
  Wilford E. 228
Senteny, W. W. 303
Settle, Eunice 503
  Evan E. 168,269,503
  Evan Evans 502,503
  Harriet Clay 503
  Harriet Evans 502
  H. C. 269
  Horace H. 503
  James H. 503
  John 503
  Joseph 503
  Margaret 503
  Mary 503,268
  Mattie 503
  Nannie 503
  Sallie 503
  Samuel 503
  Simon 268

Settle, Thomas 269
  Warner Elmore 268,269
  William 503
  William H. 502,503
Seward, Mrs. Anneta 159
  W. C. 159
  William J. 159
Seymour, Austin 552
  Lizzie 552
Siddons...606
Sidebottom, W. J. 495
Sidner, Margaret 528
  Martin 528
  Rosanna 527,528
Sigel, ...115
Silverthorn, Hannah J. 397
  Isabella 397
  Samuel 397
Simmons, John E. H. 289
  Martha 289
  William 226
  William L. 289
  William Lyles 289
Simms, Henry 606
  Lilliam 606
Simon, Eliza 249
  Francis 249
  Jacob T. 249
  John 249
  Stella 250
Simonds, J. A. 138
Simpson...415
  Benjamin 13
  Clarence D. 510
  David 510
  David M. 510
  Esther 415
  George 618
  James Dee 510
  John E. 619
  John R. 618,619
  Mary 365
  Mary V. 619
  Pauline 13
  Reid J. 619
  Susan J. 510
  Thomas 486
  William 618,619
  William G. 502
Simrall...22,67
  Barrington 21
  Ellen 332
  Harrison 332
  James 66
  John 332
  John G. 66,332
  John W. G. 21
  Joseph B. 116,332
  Margaretta 332
  Mary Barton 21
  Nellie 67
  Sarah 332
  Sarah 66
Singleton, C. M. 427
  Hannah 99
  William 427
Sinickson, Andrew 107,110
  Sol. 110
  Thomas 110
Shachelford, Frances 298
  Gen. 144
Shacklette, Ben. 557
  Mary 557
Shallcross, John 565
  Mary Ellen 565
  Mary Stewart 566
Shaner, Piersol 102
  R. Ella 102
Shanklin, Agnes Virginia 49
  Ellen F. 49
  James Alexander 49
  S. A. 49

Sharp, Allenton B. 254
  Elizabeth 301,302
  Leslie 255
  Mary 254
  Maxwell 247
  Minnie 591
  Stephen 254
  Stephen G., Jr. 255
  Stephen Garland 254,255
  Virginia 255
  William 254,591
Shattuck, Exercise 402
  Gertrude 552
  Nelson S. 552
  William 402
Shaw, Alice 625
  Amanda Fitzallen 178
  Benjamin R. 625
  Eva 625
  Fannie 580
  Hannah 625
  Ida 625
  James 216
  James T. 79
  James Truman 78
  John 625
  John W. 227
  J. R. 580
  Lauretta 227
  Maggie 625
  Margaret 625
  Robert 216,625
  Samuel 625
  William McDonald 216
Sheffer, Sallie 117
Shelby...143,537,409
  Evan 125,516,517,518
  Florence 143
  Florence McDowell 126
  Isaac 76,125,126,162,
    516,517,518,519,520,
    521,522
  James 126
  Joseph Bryan 126
  "King Mountain" 141
  Sarah 143
  Thomas H. 143
  Thomas Hart 126
  Wallace McDowell 125,126
  William 409
Shelton, Commodore 412
  Melissa 417
  Nancy 412
Shepard, James B. 414
  Mary 595
Shepherd...242
  Adam 31
  Elizabeth 31
  Rebecca 585
Sheridan...198
Sherman...83
Sherrill, B. W. 63
  Dellah M. 61
  Lee 61
Sherwood, Maggie 57
Shine, M. T. 148
Shipp, Blannie 413
  Caroline 87
  Edwin T. 413
  Mattie 413
Shockley, Martha 253
  Thomas 253
Shoemaker, Louisa 96
  Price 96
Short, Adeline 593
  Annie 593
  Charles W. 592,593
  David 592
  Elizabeth 234
  Jonathan 592
  Kate 593
  Lizzie 593
  Lucy 593

Short, Lucy Wing 592
  Mamie 593
  Peyton 234
  Reno 593
  Sarah 210
Shouse, Dudley J. 544
  Ernst G. 544
  James D. 544
  Jane Ann 91
  Jennie V. 544
  Mary A. 544
  Nannie S. 544
  Newton C. 544,545
  Samuel 536
  Sophrina 544
  Thomas 544
  Thomas M. 544
  William T. 544
Shropshire, S. S. 178
Shultz, Christian 459
  Maria 459
Shumate, F. M. 524
Shuttleworth, Rachel 297
Skillman, Abraham T. 257
  A. T. 569
  C. G. 537
  Elizabeth B. 257
  Elizabeth 568
  Henry Martyn 568,569
  H. M. 257
  Thomas T. 568,569
Slack, Mary 28
Slaton...8
Slaughter, Gabriel 390,391
  R. C. 33
  Susan Clayton 562
  W. H. 611
Slevin, Sarah 426
Sloan...90
Small, Eliza H. 74
  George W. 74
Smarr, John H. 223
  Nannie E. 223
Smart, Benjamin P. 304
  Mary 304
  Robert J. 31
Smedley, John G. 102
Smith...299,100,40,47,48,
    112
  Abby H. Campbell 111
  A. H. 11
  Alexander 49
  Andrew 432
  Anna E. Baldwin 112
  Annie 40
  Anthony W. 40
  A. O. 375
  A. Wilkes 46,47,48
  Benjamin 625
  Bertha Evelyn Byrd 48
  Camilla 40
  Catherine 310
  Clara M. 291
  Cornelia 67
  E. B. 376
  Elizabeth 625
  Elliott Poe 48
  Emily Montford 40
  Endora 436
  Fannie M. 375
  Fountain 290
  Francis 437
  Green Clay 59,561
  Harriet 126
  Harriet L. Hunter 375
  Harry A. 61
  Henrietta A. 40
  Isaac 307
  Isaac P. 111
  James 46
  James D. 598
  James R. W. 111
  Jessie S. 40

Smith, John 46,101,184,
    307,583,584
  John Henry 40
  John M. 436
  John R. 309
  John Speed 277,561
  J. V. W. 51
  Kirby E. 171
  Lillian 40
  Lucien R. 61
  Lucinda 421
  Margaret 100
  Margaret Bunyan 432
  Margaret Dobbins 101
  Martha Cassandra 4
  Mary 301,47
  Mary J. 61
  Mattie E. 499
  Minerva A. 310
  M. V. 291
  Nannie T. 27
  O. M. 40
  Rebecca Jane 307
  Richard D. 310
  R. K. 124
  Robert 432
  Samuel C. 39,40
  Samuel R. 61
  S. C. 40
  Terry Pattillo 61
  Thomas P. 67
  Walter S. 40
  W. H. 499
  William 432,561
  William A. 40
  William M. 61
  Z. F. 171
Smoot, Letitia 540
Smyrl, Adam 77
  Gabriel 78
  Sarah Ann 78
Sneed, Kate Soaper 166
  Lucy Henderson 166
  Marianna Soaper 166
  Richard 164
  Stephen 164
  Stephen K. 164
  Stephen Kutesoff 164,
    166
  Susan Henderson 166
  William Soaper 166
Snell...173
Snodgrass...35
Snowdown...336
Soaper...99
  Elizabeth 3
  Henry 170
  Marianna 166
  Mary Lavinia 170
  R. H. 3
  Richard H. 98
  Richard Henderson 97
  Susan Cook 99
  Susan Fannie 97
  Susan Henderson 99,166
  Thomas 3,98,99
  William 3,97,98,166,170
Solomon, Elizabeth H. 552
Sorg, P. J. 50
Sory, Etta 62
  Thomas W. 62
Souard, Alfred 363
Soule, Bishop J. 52
Southall...205
Southerland, W. H. H. 300
Southgate, Addie 24
  Edward L. 313
  Emma 313
  Etha 24
  Eva S. 316
  Frank H. 313
  James 313
  Richard 313

Southgate, W. W. 24,316
Southwick, Charles 74
Spalding, Archbishop 376
  Bettie M. 42
  Daniel 42
  I. A. 443
  Leonard A. 376
  Lucy 443
Spangler, Ann 229
  Clinton 229
  Sarah 229
Sparhawk, Sarah Whitney 562
Sparks...352
Speaks, Martha 235
Spears, Nancy 212
  Polly 368
Speckert, Aloysius J. 615, 616
  Frank 615
Speed, Alice 566
  Ann Pope 564
  Arch. C. 566
  Austin P. 563,565
  Austin Peay 562
  Breckenridge 564
  Charles 564
  Douglas Breckenridge 565
  Eliza 563
  Elizabeth 468,561
  Elizabeth W. 566
  Ella Keats 566
  Emily 146
  Fannie 566
  Fannie Henning 566
  Florence 566
  George Keats 566
  Goodwin 563
  Henry 561
  Henry Pirtle 564
  Horace 562
  James 284,468,560,561, 562,563,564
  James B. 565
  James Breckenridge 565, 566
  James Buckner 563
  John 560,561,562,563, 564,565,566
  John Gilmer 566
  John J. 563
  John James 562
  John Smith 564
  Joseph 561
  Joshua 564
  Joshua F. 566
  Joshua Fry 564,565
  J. Smith 565,566
  Julia 561
  Laura 565
  Lewis 561
  Louisa J. 562
  Louise 563
  Lucy 561
  Lucy Fry 564
  Martha 561
  Martha B. 566
  Martha Bell 564
  Mary 561,563
  Mary Eliza 566
  Mary Whitney 563
  Mathias 561
  Olive 565
  Peachy Austine 566
  Peachy Walker 564
  Philip 564,566
  Richard Canby 562
  Rose 563
  Samuel 560
  Sarah 561
  Shippen 564
  Spencer Hawkins 562
  Susan Fry 564
  Thomas 560,561,562,563, 564
  Thomas A. 566
  Thomas S. 562
  Thomas Spencer 562
  William 565
  William O. 562
  William P. 564,565,566
  William Pope 564
  William T. 560
Spellman, Thomas 351
Spencer, Mary 468,561
Sperrier, Edward 330
Spottswood...139
  Alexander 140
  Dorothea 139
Spradling, J. H. 174
  Louise Barbour 174
Sproule, James 397
  Mary Ann 397
  Mary 397
Staebler, Jonathan 90
Staffe, Bicker 610
  Jacob 610
  Long 610
Stafford, Cunningham 524
  William 156
Stagg, Daniel 83
  James 84
  Simon 301
Stanley...158
  Josephine 416
  William 416
Stanton, Henry T. 23
  Ruth 23
Stark, Lily 505
Staton, John Edgar 402
  Octavia Jane 402
  R. E. 402
  William Linn 402
St. Claire,..13
Steel, Theophilis 175
  Aremetha R. 211
  Benjamin Ulen 447
Steele, Daniel 212
  Daniel W. 447
  Daniel Webster, Jr. 211
  Mrs. John 183
  W. J. 233
Steels, Mary 110
Steinberg, Nathan 51
Steinway, William 201
Stephenson, Eliza W. 439, 440
  George 439
  John T. 559
  Lulie T. 559
Stevens, ...409
  E. Sherman 19
Stevenson...26,109
  Daniel 25
  Evan 252
  John W. 24,73
  Laura 252
  Thomas 25
Stewart, America 315
  Forrest L. 316
  James 315
  James Elliott 315
  James Lewis 316
  John Wesley Mayo 316
  Mary 112
  Neva Sharon 316
  Ralph 315
  Warren Franklin Canterbury 316
Stine, Frederick A. 253
  Glorvina 253,254
  D. Harry 253,254
Stinson, Marcia A. 219
Stirman...37
  Fannie Conway 36
Stirman, Fredrick Victor 36
  James H. 36
  Joseph Scobee 36
  Middleton Goldsmith 36
  Rachel 35
  Wilbur F. 36
  Wilbur Fitzalan 35
  William Doswell 35
  William Wall 36
Stites, Henry J. 87
Stockdell, Ann 362
Stockton, Joseph B. 175
  Robert 175
Stone, Barton W. 45
  David 436
  Jane 580
  Laura 436
  Minerva 75,76
  William 76
Stood, Martha 128
Story...149
Stout...204
Stowers, A. H. 485
  Kate 485
Stratton, Elisha B. 34
  Frank L. 35
  John A. 34,35
  Mary Antle 35
  William 35
Street, Peter W. 40
  Susan J. 40
Stricker, Charles 70
  Mary J. 70
Striger, Catherine F. 219
  Charles M. 219
  John 219
  Mason 219
Strohmeier, Christina 402
Struby, Emma J. 163
Stuart, Alice W. 154
  Amelia 153
  Annie 153,154
  Benjamin 154
  David T. 153
  David Todd 153
  Florence 153
  Isabella 153
  James Peyton 208
  J. E. B. 111
  John 153
  Maggie 153
  Maria 208
  Mary 154
  Mary Lou 153
  Olivia 153
  Robert 153,154
  Susan Elizabeth 154
  Theodore 153
  Winchester 153
Stubbins, Sarah Ray 204
Stubblefield...340
Stublefield, A. B. 61
Stucky, Frederick 154
  Harry 154,155
  Harry Clark 155
  John McGarvey 155
  Joseph A. 154
  Joseph Addison 155
  Lillie E. 155
  Nellie McGarvey 155
  Sallie Kemp 155
  Sallie 154
  Thomas Hunt 154,155
  Virginia 154
  William Sweeney 155
Sullivan, Chattie Clifford 332
  Christian Mills 332
  Henry Christian 332,333
  Mollie 343
Sumter...122,155
Sutherland...525,42

Sutherland, J. W. 26
  May 207
  Susan 207
  William 207
Sutkamp, Julia 215
Sutterfield, Edward 60
Sutton, John A. 174
Suydam, Cornelius R. 257
  Jane Heyer 256
Swango,..187
  Abraham 185,186
  Caroline 185,186
  Charles S. 186
  Green Berry 185,186
  H. C. 186
  James H. 186
  John Morton 186
  Samuel 186
  Stephen 185
  William 186
Sweeney, Amanda 298
  Anna Eliza 298
  Charles 298
  Daniel 409
  Elizabeth 298,409
  Ella 409
  Emily J. 297,298
  Fannie 409
  G. E. 45
  George W. 45
  Gurin E. 45
  G. W. 298
  Harvey 408,409
  James 298
  Jesse G. 298
  J. J. 199
  Job 45
  Joel 298
  John S. 45
  John Steele 45
  Joseph A. 154
  Lizzie 409
  Marietta 298
  Mary 409
  Mary Edmondson 409
  Moses 45,409
  Sallie K. 154
  Sue 409
  Talitha 45
  W. G. 45
  William, Jr. 409
  William Henry 408,409
  William N. 297,298
  W. N. 199,298
  W. O. 155
  Zachariah T. 45
Sweet. Mary 623
Swift...605
  William 307
Swigert, Phillip 259,260
Swinford, Annie 27
  Charles L. 27
  John P. 27
  John Patterson 27
  McCauley C. 27
  Sallie 27
  Urban M. 27
  Virgil C. 27
  William 27
"Aunt Sylvia"...8

Tabb, Edward 410
  Letitia 410
  Martha A. 410
Tabler, William 361
Talbot, Elizabeth 609
  Hail 609
Talbott, De Moville 412
  Dorothy L. 413
  Edna Cecil 412
  Elizabeth Irvine 505
  Ethel Allen 412
  Gladys C. 413

Talbott, Robert C. 411,
  412,413
  Robert C., Jr. 412
  Samuel 412
  Samuel H. 412
  Sarah 366
  William F. 412
  William McMillan 413
Taliaferro, Anne 363
  Annie 362
  Anne Stockdell 363
  Elizabeth 362,363
  George Catlett 363
  Hay 363
  John 362,363
  John Champ 362
  Laura Augusta Caroline 363
  Lawrence 363
  Lizzie 363
  Lucy 362,363
  Lucy Mary 362
  Marshall 363
  Mary 363
  Mary King 363
  Mary Willis 363
  Matilda 178
  Matilda Ann 363
  Matilda B. 363
  Mattie 363
  Nicholas 362,363
  Nicholas C. 294,363
  William 362
  William A. 363
  William Alonzo 362,363
  William T. 363
Tankersley, Dorothy 617
  George 617
  John 617
Tarleton...110
Tarvin, James P. 100
Tate, Sarah 303
Taylor...126,108,167,174
  A. M. 90
  Ann Maddox 203
  Benjamin 393
  Caleb Jarvis 178
  Charles 393
  Charles H. 201
  Daniel G. 591
  Edmund 393
  Edmund Haynes, Jr. 392, 393,394
  Esther 41
  Fannie 57
  Frances 56,392,393
  George 41,393
  George Conway 393
  George Keith 276
  Hancock 393
  Harrison D. 55,56
  Harrison P. 57
  Hattie 591
  Henry Pirtle 57
  H. W. 90
  Imogen E. 513
  James 392,393
  James I. 41
  James S. 513
  Jessie 456
  John 57,393
  John Eastin 394
  Jonathan 393
  Jonathan Gibson 293
  Judith 493
  Leonard 65
  Louisa Ann 611
  Margaret 57
  Martha Thompson 393
  Mary 57,393,560
  Mary Ann 293
  Mary 561
  Matilda 404

Taylor, Mildred Martin 293
  Milton 56
  Nicholas 56
  P. Richard 452
  Rachel Gibson 393
  Randall 57
  Rebecca Edrington 394
  Reed 264
  Reuben 41,393
  Richard 393,394,405
  Richard, Jr. 393
  Robin 203
  Ruth 41
  Sallie 57
  Samuel M. 293
  Thomas 56,57
  Wesley 56
  William 393
  William Carson 41
  Zachary 139,393
Tebbetts, C. H. 84
  Elizabeth Porter 85
  James Curry 84,85
  Jonas M. 85
  Marian 85
  Mary Winlock 85
Tenney, Anna M. 477
  Benjamin M. 477
  Charles Carroll 477
Teaford, Daniel A. 345
Tenney, David 476
  David Culver 477
  Esther Angeline 477
  Harriet H. 477
  John 476
  Lilian H. 477
  Mary Marinda 477
  Otis Seth 476,477
  Robert P. 477
  Samuel 476
  Samuel Cliflin 477
  Seth 476
  Thomas 476
Terhune, Lettie 301
Terry, Bessie 42
  Charles 42
  Daniel 42
  Ella 125
  Emily 173
  Eugene M. 41,42
  Eugenia 42
  Florence 42
  Hattie 42
  John 41,42,125
  Mary Moss 41,42
  William 27
  William M. 42
Tevis...36,159
  Belle 563
  Julia A. 82
Thomas...65
  Barak G. 212,213
  B. F. 335
  Charles B. 212,213
  Elizabeth 65
  Leonard Taylor 65
  Lindsey 306
  Mary Ann 306
  Oswald 306
  O. W. 552
  Salina A. 212
  Sarah A. 212
  Sarah Ann 212,213
Thomasson, Henrietta 300
  John Clay 314,315
  Joseph M. 45,300
  Julius V. 314
  Mary W. 314
  Sarah E. 45
Thome, Amanda 208
  Arthur 208
Thompson, Agnes 460
  Alice A. 557

Thompson, Anne Porter 167
  Anthony 36
  A. P. 192
  Catherine Wiginton 611
  Charles 167
  Davis Montgomery 167
  Ed Porter 582
  Edwin Porter 581,582
  Eliza 582
  Elizabeth Barbara 167
  Elizabeth Wimp 557
  Emeline 409
  Frank 460
  Garnett 167
  George 166
  George Franklin 459,460
  Harry 460
  Hemia 305
  Henry 167
  James 36,409,551
  Jane 301,80
  J. H. 557
  John 166,167
  John B. 166,167
  John Burton 166
  Katherine 167
  Leonard 166
  Lewis 460
  Lewis M. 581
  Lewis Morgan 582
  Marcella P. 582
  Maria 167,443
  Martha 392
  Mary 460
  Mary R. 581,582
  Mason 460
  Mattie 167
  Nancy Porter 166
  Nathan 582
  Nellie 460
  Patsey 167
  Phil 167
  Phil B. 167
  Philip Burton 167,166
  Pinckney 80
  Richard W. 611
  Roger 166
  Sallie 167
  Sarah Tate 36
  Starling H. 81
  Stephen 443
  Susan Burton 167
  Volen 33
  Waddy 582
  William 80,166
  William B. 459
  William Irving 81
  William Mills 611
  William R. 33
Thorburn, James 159
Thorne, Agnes Pearl 438
  Andrew J. 438
  Ann 438
  J. J. 438
  John 438
  Levisa 438
  Mary Bernice 438
  Mary 438
  Mary K. 437
  Nancy 438
  Shelby T. 438
  William K. 438
  William Kimberland 437
  William P. 437,438,439
  William P., Jr. 438
Thornton, George W. 422
  Jane W. A. 422
  Mrs....476
Thorpe, Cecil 474
  Sallie Wallace 473
  Stanton Hume 473,474
  Thomas 473
  Zachariah 473

Threlkeld, Margaret 503
Thrift, Hester 311
Thum, W. W. 86
Thurman...142
  Allen G. 92
  Elizabeth 92
Tice, W. W. 61
Tiffany, Charles L. 201
Tilden...19
  Samuel J. 177
Tilghman...139
Tillman...88
Tillotson, Eleanor Rives 333
  Emily Ragsdale 333
  Sir John 333
  Joyce Wilkinson 333
  Mildred 333
  Nancy Yancey 333
  Rebecca Baynham 333
  Sarah Blane 333
Tinsley, Peter 609
Todd, Annette 502
  Ann Maria Starling 429
  Bettie 502
  Charles S. 162,537
  Charles Stewart 429
  Elizabeth Hanna 429
  Emily 395
  George 469
  George D. 427,428,429
  Hannah 153
  Harry I. 429
  Harry Innes 427,428,429
  Howard 501,502
  James Gayle 501,502
  James Madison 429
  James O. 230
  Jane 427,429
  Jennie 502
  John Harris 428,429
  Levi 594
  Lewis 502
  Madisonia 429
  Martha 230
  Mary Ellis 469
  Mattie 502
  Pike 502
  Richard 428
  Robert 317
  Samuel 502
  Thomas 428,537
  Virginia Shelby 161,162
  William 428
  William Johnston 429
Toleman, Nancy 222
Tomlinson, Annell 494
  Elizabeth M. 493
  Harry Denny 494
  Joseph 493
  L. 178
  Margaret 494
  Robert Hugh 493,494
  William 493
Tompkins...177
  Alexander C. 176
  Ben 210
  C. C. 157
  Frances Samuellor 176
  Frederick Windon 176
  Henry Pendleton 176
  John 176
  John N. 176
  Joseph B. 176
  William 71
  William W. 176
Tone, Laura A. 7
Toucray, Alexander 96
  Eleanor 96
  Sallis 96
Tousley, O. V. 111
Towles, David T. 523,524
  Diamond 612

Towles, Elzy Chandler 524
  Fannie Mason 523
  Frederick Mason 524
  George W. 523
  George Washington 523
  Joseph 523
  Lena 523
  Mary 612
  Montgomery 523
  Rawleigh D. 612
Trafton, Helen 452
Trent...13
Trible, Kittie 57
Trimble...412
  Allan 167
  Allen 77
  Bettie 448
  Carey A. 167
  Eliza Jane 167
  Eliza 149
  Grace 448
  James 150,362
  John 149,150,412
  Mary 448
  Mary E. Morehead 448
  Nellie 448
  Robert 149,150,270,271
  Selden Y. 447,448
  Sue 448
  William 149,448
  William W. 149,150
  W. W. 114
  Mrs. W. W. 150
Triplett, R. S., Jr. 231
True...584
Tuck...238
  Rebecca 238
Tucker...488
  J. G. 402
Tuley, Enos S. 566
Tunis, James Curry 85
  John Theodore, Jr. 85
  J. T. 84,85
Turner, Catherine 205
  Elizabeth 129
  Isabella Lucetta 579
  Oscar 99
  Stepphen 205
  Susan 205
  William 579
Twaddell, Isabella 421
Twiss, Horace 606
  Horace W. 606
  Quintin 606
Twyman, Buford 89
Tyler, ...112
  Charles R. 404
  Fanny 530
  Henry S. 87
Tyndal, John 511
  Mary 511
Tyree, James 505
  Mehala Hogg 505

Ulen, Annie E. 22
  Aremetha R. 212
  Benjamin 212
  C. S. 22
Underhill, William A. 405
Unthank, John M. 615
Upshaw, Martha 453
Usher, Charles 215
Utz, Bertha Hanke 149

Valandingham, Elizabeth 203
Vananarsdall, Sallie 301
Vanarsdale, George 301
Vance...62
  Robert 476
  Susan 476
Van Cleave, A. C. 409
Vanderbilt, William H. 105
Van Hook, Frances 421

Van Hook, Lawrence 421
Van Horn, Pamelia 515
Vanice, Cornelius 302
Van Nuys, Auk Jansen 586
  Dennis Bois 586
  Elizabeth 586
  Eliza Jane 586
  Isaac 586
  Jacobus 586
  James 586
  Janache Ankurts 586
  John C. 586
  Magdalena 586
  Margareta 586
  Maria 586
Van Sant, Dr. 150
Vansant, Dr. 587
Vansant, Harold Henderson 182
  Louvisa Hunter 182
  Mexie 182
  R. H. 131,132
  Rufus Humphrey 182
  William H. 182
Varble, Mamie 35
  Pink 35
Vaughan, Cynthia 469
  Mrs. I. N. 579
  Joseph 617
  Zachariah 617
Vaughn, Rebecca 205
  Sallie C. 495
  Susan 205
  W. N. 495
Vaught, Andrew 22
  Anna Louise 22
  Ann L. 22
  Kate H. 22
  Mattie M. 22
  Osgood Andrew 22
  Sarah H. 22
  S. K. 22
  Stephen K. 22
  William P. 22
Veith, Carl 387
  Catherine 387
  Frederick 387
  Helen 387
  Phil J. 387
Venable, Abraham 79
  Cantey McDowell 4
  Elizabeth Mary 79,177
  Elizabeth Thompkins 79
  Goodridge Wilson 79
  James 455
  James Anderson 78
  Joseph 79
  Martha 79
  Mary Ann 79
  Matilda Tyler 79
  Nathaniel 79
  Nathaniel Benjamin 79
  Madam Pattie 79
  Samuel Lewis 79,177
  Thomas S. 79,404
  Thomas Samuel 78,79
  Virginia 177
  Virginia Woodson 78
Vertner, Daniel 352
Vinson, G. R. 359
Violett, James A. 328
  Leland 328
  Luther Francis 328
  Mary Hill 328
  Polly 328
  Walter 328
Virgin, Brice 535
  Jeremiah 535
  Lucy 535
Von Grundy, Christian 369
Voorhees, Dan W. 168
Vose, Christina 402
  Christina Strohmeier 403

Vose, Clarence Eba 403
  John 402,403
  John Raymond 403
  William Wentworth 403

Wade, Elizabeth 36
Wadsworth, A. A. 169
  Adna A. 546,550
  Charles 550
  Christopher 546
  John G. 550
  Joseph 546
  Joseph B. 546
  Rhoda 546
  S. B. 550
  Timothy 546
  W. H. 202
  William 546
  William H. 550
  William Henry 546,547, 548,549,550
Wagoner, Harry 195
Walden, J. C. 463
  Joanna 529
  Mary Frances 463
  William 507
Walker...328
  Clara 293
  E. Dudley 258
  Elijah Dudley 31,32
  Elvira English 32
  G. W. 178
  Henry 70
  Jacob 50
  John 50
  John D. 50
  J. R. 69
  Lida 32,258
  Lizzie Crutcher 32
  Lulu Dix 32
  Mahala 31
  Mahala Logan 32
  Melissa Hamilton 50
  Nathan Harris 32
  Patsey 245
  Peachey 231
  Richard Logan 31,32
  Robert Dudley 32
  Sallie Ann 32
  Thomas 2,286
  William 32
  William L. D. 32
WallBannister 36
  Boyd 36
  Rachel Anne 36
Wallace, Abigail 131
  Caroline 131
  Deborah 514,515
  Elizabeth Neely 515
  Ellen 515
  Ellen Ross 514
  Elvessie 515
  Francis T. D. 515
  Francis Thomas Durand 514,515,516
  James 131,514
  John 514,515
  Joseph 514
  Martha 515
  Mary 514,515
  Mary (Moore) 515,514
  Moses 514
  Nancy 514
  Priscilla 367
  Rachel 514
  Ross 514,515
  Thomas 514,515
  William 205,514,515
  William Ross 515
Waller, Benjamin 62
  Benjamin Leonard 62
  Ben F. 63
  Cora 62

Waller, Eliza 62
  Frank F. 62,63
  George 62
  Harold M. 63
  J. B. 597
  Joseph K. 63
  Lucille 63
  Lucy A. 62
  Mary E. Sherrill 63
  Nannie 62
  Otis S. 63
  Sallie 62
  Thomas 551
  William H. 62
  Wilson 62
  Zachary Taylor 62
Wallin, Corlis 407
  David Jackson 406,407
  John 406
  William Bridges 407
Walters, Addie 417
  Alfred 363
  George 363
  Isaac 363
  John L. 363
Walton, Clara Belle 326
  Edwin Claiborne 579
  George 325,579
  Isabella Turner 578
  John H. 324
  Mary Warren 579
  Matt 172
  Matthew 324,325,326
  Nancy 612
  Susan Isabelle 324,325
  Thomas R. 578,579
  William 579
  William Pulaski 579
  W. P. 439
Ward...123,30
  Andrew 29
  Andrew Harrison 29
  Artemus 29
  Ashley F. 30
  Bertie M. 30
  Catherine 30
  Elizabeth 29
  Ellen 417
  Harry R. 30
  John Q. 27
  John Quincy 189
  Junius 67
  Mollie M. 29
  Paul S. 30
  William 29
Ware, Davidella 301
  Elizabeth 30
  James 301
  Kernan 301
  Sallie 301
  Thompson 301
Warfield, Benjamin 525
  Benjamin Breckinridge 526
  Elisha 525
  Ethelbert Dudley 526
  John 525
  Richard 525
  William 525,526
Warford, William 185
Warner, James 477
  Junia M. 477
Warren, Joseph 271
Washington, Gen. 422,429
  George 140,186,622,623
  George Steptoe 429
  William Augustine 140
Wasson, John 617
Waterfield, William 6
Waters, Julia 620
  William 620
Watham, J. B. 556
Wathen...336,30

Wathen, Benedict 30
  Chapeze 30,31
  Eulalie 31
  Jane Murray 31
  Richard 30
Watkins...205,532
  C. C. 13
  Elizabeth 34
  E. S. 162
  Gurnetta 598
  H. C. 162
  Joel 34
  Luke W. 598
  Philip 532
  Rose Yandell 162
  Samuel 34
  Shelton 162
  Sue R. 162
  Virginia 162
  William 532
Watson, Anne 37
  Jennie B. 531
  John 37
  Martha Ann 302
  Mary 452
  Miranda 302
  Thomas T. 531
  Wesley 302
Watts, ...409
  Annie 589
  C. B. 18
  Charles 170
  David 170
  Elizabeth 170
  Julia B. 171
  Margaret Mills Anderson 171
  N. B. 589
  Philip H. 170
  Robert A. 170,171
  Robert A., Jr. 171
  Samuel 512
Watwood, Julia 523
Waugh, James E. 438
Wayne...13,132
Weatherall, Martha 523
Weaver, Charles F. 330,331
  Daniel L. 330,331
  Elizabeth 331,617
  Flavilla 623
  Harry Marion 331
  Hattie A. 331
  Henry W. 331
  Jerrie Arjyra 331
  Jonathan 330
  Jonathan R. 331
  Maggie Rose 331
  Thomas 623
Webb, Isaac 257
  Isaac N. 308
  James 258
  J. W. 606,607
  Levian 308
  Mary 606
  Thermuthis Hannah 308
  Winnie 257
Webber, Catherine A. 234
Weber, Katherine 528
Weems, M. K. 532
Weil, Meyer 191
Weir, Anna Belle 231
  Anna 230,231
  David 231
  James 230,231
  John E. 231
  Levi C. 201
  Nora 231
  Paul 231
  Susan 231
Weisiger, Daniel 597
Weisinger, Harry 11
Welch, Alexander 416
  Amanda 416

Welch, Elizabeth 401
  John 415,416
  John C. 346,416
  John M. 401
  Lizzie 415,416
  Mary F. 401
  Nancy 111
  Nathaniel 416
  Thomas R. 415,416
Wellington, Duke of 85
Wellman, Ceres 113
  Jeremiah 113
  Zerelda 113
Wells, Carrie 75
  Edward 357
  Francis 190
  H. B. 75
  Mary 357
West, Ann 440
  Elizabeth 25
  John 139
  Martha C. 238
  Thomas 25
  Unity 139
Westfall, Simeon 364
Weston, Hannah 512
  Josiah 512
  Susan 512
Wheat, Mary 49
  Zack 103
Wheeler, Charles K. 34
  Charles Kennedy 33
  Elizabeth 33,34
  James 33,34,121
  Margaret E. B. 40
  Mary 34
  Mary K. 121
Wheelock, Prof. 568
Whipp, C. M. 298
Whitaker, William 295
  William, Jr. 295
White, Benjamin F. 579,580
  Charles William 579,580
  H. E. 256
  Helen 412
  Henry Kirk 412
  Jane 579,580
  Julius 183
  Margaret 412
  Mary Isaphine 256
  Mary P. 184
  Rhoda 185
  Robert 412
  W. P. 17
Whitehead, John 78
  Lazarus 199
  Mary 199
  Mary F. 78
  Nimrod 78
Whitley, William 273
Whitney, Eliza 536
Whitsett...135
  Margaret 373
Whittis, Eliza 331
Wickham...104
Wickliff...123
Wickliffe...68
  Charles 389
  Charles Anderson 390
  Lydia 389
  Mike 116
  Robert 389,572
Widrig, T. A. 148
Wiles...103
  Sallie 103
Wilford, Alexander 593
  Ben 593
  Bessie 593
  David 593
  Eliza Jane 593
  Emma 593
  N. Green 593
  Isham 593

Wilford, Isham Marion 593
  James David 593
  Lula Green 593
  Mary Emeline 593
  May 593
  Melinda Frances 593
  Nathaniel Green 593
  Robert 593
  Robert Jasper 593
  Robert O. 593
  Robert Oliver 593
  Rosa Lee 593
Wilhoite, Christina 15
Wilkes, Ida L. 411
  Perry 411
Wilkinson,...13,201
Williams, Ada 471
  Anna 239
  Cynthia 469
  Cynthia 469
  E. T. 148
  Frances 239
  Fulton 469
  G. A. 96
  George 222
  George Washington 220, 221
  Hamilton W. 222
  Hugh Anderson 222
  Indiana 469
  Ione 222
  James C. 469
  James H. 443
  James P. 469
  James Russell 222
  Jasper 469
  Jennie 469
  Jeremiah 469
  John H. 239
  John M. 443
  John S. 111,186
  Joshua 469
  Josiah 469
  J. R. 443
  Lizzie 442
  Margaret 412
  Marie 469
  Martin 469
  Mary 132
  Mary G. 65
  Mary L. Sayre 530
  Mildred 222,220
  Mollie 469
  Nannie 442,443
  Otho 220
  R. D. 138
  Rives 40
  Rufus 469
  Ruth 222
  Samuel 441
  Samuel W. 443
  Sarah T. Rodman 441
  Taylor 471
  Theophilus 222
  Thomas 469
  Thomas D. 441,442,443
  Thomas H. 441
  William 222
Williamson...29
  Elizabeth 566
  John A. 28
  Lawrence 29
  Samuel 28
Willis...626
  Albert S. 35
  George Lee 22
  Henry 22
  Jackson S. 22
  James Emmons 131
  John C. 131
  Mary 502
  Mary Ellen Gordon 131
  Mary J. 22

Willoughby, Julia 45
Wills, Bettie B. 136
  John M. 136
  Sarah A. 225
Wilson...24
  Agnes 439
  Aquilla 360
  Archibald 171
  Benjamin B. 347,348
  Benjamin Dunbar 348
  Charles A. 163
  Charles Weeden 611,612
  Dorothy 62
  Earl 360
  Elizabeth M. 347
  Emma 193
  Ethelbert Reed 348
  Eugene K. 457,458
  George 415
  George H. 348
  Grace 360
  Hansford 360
  Harvey T. 622
  Henrietta Clay 608
  Horace H. 348
  James 111,193,347,415,
    439,458
  James J. 347
  James M. 458
  John C. 360
  John M. 457
  John R. 611
  John T. 187
  L. B. 360
  Lucy 439
  Margaret 595
  Mary 235
  Mary J. 360
  Mattie 622
  Miles 360
  Nancy Kerr 458
  Nathaniel 235
  Reuben B. 347
  Sallie 612
  Samuel Long 612
  Sarah 611
  S. C. 117
  Theodosia 540
  Virginia 111
  Walker H. 360
  W. B. 360
  Wes B. 359,360
Windsor, Emily C. 204
Wing, Charles F. 55,275,
  592
  Edward Rumsey 55
  Lucelia W. 55
  Lucy 592
Winn, Douglass I. 355
  J. N. 545
  Katherine 510
  Mary B. 140
  Mildred 545
  Robert 140
Winslow...20
Winstead, A. S. 43
Winston...463
  David Y. 261
  Elizabeth 261
  Jennie 261
Winter, George 141
  Jane M. 17
  Susan 294
Wintersmith, ...103
Winthrop...13
Winwood, Benjamin 101
Wise...132
  John S. 135
Withers, Benjamin 27
  Eliza 28
  Eliza Perrin 28
  Elizabeth 28
  James S. 27,28

Withers, Robert 27
  Rodney S. 28
  William A. 27
  William T. 27
Withrow, Isaac 415
Wolfe...133
Wolverton, S. 62
Wood...301
  Abigail 476
  Andrew T. 623
  Charles 550
  Currie F. 623
  David 558
  Dolly 188
  Eliza 623
  Elizabeth 302,476
  Gideon G. 558
  Henry C. 283
  Henry S. 623
  Henry S. S. 623
  Hunter 160
  James H. 623
  John 476,623
  John C. 623
  John Perry 516
  Lucy Alzina 526
  Martha Morehead 550
  Mary 623
  Mary S. Anderson 558
  Matilda 623
  Orville Monroe 557,558
  Phoebe E. 516
  Thomas 623
  William 557
  William H. 623
  William Hoffmann 623
Woodbury, Susanna 476
Woodruff...141
  Mary E. 66
  William 530
Woods, Archibald 210
  Avey 210
  Susan 210
Woodsides, Lucy 591
Woodson, Judith 80
  Lanbourn 80
  Richard 79,80
  Urey 327,328
Wooldridge, Kate 454
Wooley...123
Woolsey, Edward J. 150
Worley, Rebecca 203
Wormald, James 85
Wornon, Julia 471
Worrall, William Raymond
  605
Worsham, A. J. 43
  Andrew Jackson 42
  Arch D. 43
  D. C. 43
  Edwin 170
  Elijah W. 42,43
  E. W. 43
  George A. 43
  Hodge 170
  John C. 43
  L. 170
  Ludson 43,170
  Mariam 42
  Mariam J. 43
  Mary Lavinia 170
  Milton R. 43
  Virginia Rhorer 43
Worthington...89
  Edward Leslie 88
  Madison 88
  Samuel 88
  Thomas T. 88
Wright, Hamilton 92
  John 69,430
  Katherine 430
  Martha 430
Wrightson, Georgiana 473

Wrightson, Thomas 473
Wrinn, Paul 336
Wurtham, Charles L. 104
Wykoff...299

Yager, Arthur 289,290
  Daniel 289
  Diana 289,290
  Frank J. 289
  Rodes Estill 290
Yard, Edward 13
Yates...304
Yeaman, Caldwell 23
  George H. 12,23
  Harvey 23,165
  James M. 23
  John H. 23
  John Rochester 23
  Julia 23
  Lelia 23
  Malcolm 23
  Malcolm H. 23
  Marion V. P. 23
  Mary Lucretia 23
  Stephen Minor 23
  William Pope 23
Young...333
  Alice 443
  Ambrose 40
  Andrew 350
  Archibald 350
  Avemathea 473
  Bryan R. 427,443
  Bennett H. 87,348,349,
    350
  Clotilda 350
  Colby 242
  Eliza 509
  Eliza J. 186
  Elizabeth 443
  Frank O. 40,41
  George 163
  Hannah Ann 350
  Henry 89
  Hugh 186
  Jack Spalding 443
  Jane 40
  John 350,427,443,473
  John Clarke 494
  Joseph 350
  Lizzie 167
  Mamie 443
  Maria Thompson 427
  Martha 350
  Mary Haddan 350
  Milton 426,443,444,445,
    446,447
  Nancy Elizabeth 350
  Richard 40,305
  Richard B. 40
  Robert 350
  S. A. 195
  Stephen A. 426,427
  Sue Spalding 443
  Tabitha 350
  Thomas 350
  W. L. 592
Yungblut, Anna 350,351
  Charles Walter 350,351
  John R . 350

Zimmerman, Ellen 294
  Eugene 295
  Solomon 294

#

www.ingramcontent.com/pod-product-compliance
Lightning Source LLC
Chambersburg PA
CBHW020629300426
44112CB00007B/64